PSYCHOLOGY
of Exceptional
Children
and Youth

CONTRIBUTING AUTHORS

Nettie Bartel, Ph.D., *Temple University*

Lynn Kay Brown, Ph.D., *University of Michigan*

William M. Cruickshank, Ph.D., *University of Michigan*

Jon Eisenson, Ph.D., *San Francisco State University*

Samuel L. Guskin, Ph.D., *Indiana University*

Peter Knoblock, Ph.D., *Syracuse University*

Lawrence J. Lewandowski, Ph.D., *Michigan Department of Mental Health*

Berthold Lowenfeld, Ph.D., *Emeritus, California School for the Blind*

T. Ernest Newland, Ph.D., *Emeritus, University of Illinois*

Joseph Newman, Ph.D., *University of Pittsburgh*

James L. Paul, Ed.D., *University of North Carolina*

Helen Rusalem, Ed.D., *Learning Capacities Research Project*

Herbert Rusalem, Ed.D., *Learning Capacities Research Project*

Derek A. Sanders, Ph.D., *State University of New York at Buffalo*

Franklin C. Shontz, Ph.D., *University of Kansas*

E. Paul Torrance, Ph.D., *University of Georgia*

FOURTH EDITION

PSYCHOLOGY
of Exceptional Children and Youth

edited by
William M. Cruickshank
University of Michigan

prentice-hall inc., englewood cliffs, n.j. 07632

Library of Congress Cataloging in Publication Data

CRUICKSHANK, WILLIAM M   ED.
    Psychology of exceptional children and youth.

    Includes indexes.
      1. Exceptional children—Psychology.   I. Title.
[DNLM: 1. Child, Exceptional.   2. Handicapped.
3. Adolescent psychology.   4. Child psychology.
WS105.5.H2 P974]
BF723.E9C78 1980   155.4'5   79-15560
ISBN 0-13-733808-2

Printed in the United States of America

10 9 8 7 6 5 4 3 2 1

Editorial/production supervision
  and interior design by Joyce Turner
Cover design by Saiki/Sprung Designs
Manufacturing buyer: John Hall

Prentice-Hall International, Inc., *London*
Prentice-Hall of Australia Pty. Limited, *Sydney*
Prentice-Hall of Canada, Ltd., *Toronto*
Prentice-Hall of India Private Limited, *New Delhi*
Prentice-Hall of Japan, Inc., *Tokyo*
Prentice-Hall of Southeast Asia Pte. Ltd., *Singapore*
Whitehall Books Limited, *Wellington, New Zealand*

CONTENTS

PREFACE

Since 1920, the combined effect of several important influences has brought exceptional children and youth to the attention of professional people and society in general in a very dramatic way. World Wars I and II, with their universal military conscription, subjected almost the entire male population of the United States to complete physical, psychological, and psychiatric examinations, and directed public attention to the large percentage of men who, due to physical disability, mental retardation, illiteracy, or psychiatric disorders, were rejected as unfit to assume this major responsibility of citizenship. The Korean conflict and the distasteful Vietnam war, together with the results of the two World Wars, have created a widespread interest in, and concern about, the general problems of rehabilitation.

The first edition of this book appeared in 1955. In it was a statement by the Editor-Author emphasizing the validity of assigning physically handicapped children to the regular grades for their educational experiences. This statement was one of the early motivations that culminated, in the late 1960s, in concepts of normalization, both by deinstitutionalizing and mainstreaming. In this fourth edition, Drs. Herbert and Helen Rusalem evaluate carefully the psychological aspects of different special education environments, and their evaluation appears here for the first time in any text in the field.

Medicine and allied sciences have progressed markedly since the twenties. Psychological inquiries and research have added much to our understanding of the role of handicaps in the lives of children, their parents, and society in general. Medical and clinical pharmacological inquiries have contributed greatly to the control of epilepsy, to an understanding of cardiac disturbances, and to basic information regarding congenital disorders. True congenital deformities, many developmental disabilities, perceptual processing deficits, and many other problems still pose unanswered questions to the professions. Nevertheless, through the radio microscope, the "brain scan," evoked-response EEG techniques, and through some better developments in psychological measurement, our knowledge, treatment, care, and understanding of the disabled person is improving.

Since 1955, much has happened in the United States and elsewhere in the interest of exceptional children and youth. The Congress of the United States has provided grants for research and study that have stimulated the total growth of the field. Some, although in no way enough, leadership personnel have been trained in major universities and colleges through such funds, and these people are taking their places in positions of responsibility throughout the country. The United States Department of Health, Education, and Welfare, through many of its agencies, has brought new life and direction to its programs in the several states through direct grants, research service, and study. Chief among these agencies that affect education directly or indirectly are the Office of Child Development, the Office of Developmental Disabilities, the Bureau for the Education of the Handicapped, the Maternal and Child Health Service, The National Institutes of Health, The National Institute of Mental Health, and the Vocational Rehabilitation Administration.

As government investment in programs for the handicapped has increased, that of private foundations—long the primary support of these efforts—has decreased. Private foundations must again assume their major share of this effort, for there is much yet to be done. The Executive branch of the government has been active at the highest levels. The Panel on Mental Retardation initiated by order of President Kennedy was continued by succeeding presidents as the President's Committee on Mental Retardation. The President's Committee on the Employment of the Handicapped has served to focus national attention on its primary responsibility. Added to this list is the recent President's Committee on Mental Health, created by President Carter, a further evidence of national concern for those with various types of physical, mental, or emotional variance.

Although much remains to be investigated concerning the psychological growth and development of exceptional children and youth, psychological understanding has grown sufficiently exact to warrant a single publication dealing with this problem. This volume, prepared by psychologists and by those with a broad background in psychology as well as in their primary professional discipline, is devoted solely to the psychological considerations of the influence of deviation upon normative growth and development of children and young people. The phrase "exceptional child and youth" means those who, by reason of a physical or intellectual variance, are considered unique among their peers. Thus, chapters that deal with the psychology of the intellectually superior pupil are included along with those dealing with inferior intellectual ability. Chapters that deal with all the major groups of physically disabled children are, of course, also included.

A companion volume, the *Education of Exceptional Children and Youth* has been published since the first edition of the *Psychology of Exceptional Children and Youth* appeared in 1955. These two volumes together have been recognized for more than two decades as providing a remarkable background for the total field of psychology and education of exceptional children and youth.

The editor and the contributing authors have long stated that the field of the psychology of the exceptional is too complicated and diverse to be treated adequately by a single author. We believe that no one author can be so uniformly authorative on all facets of this broad field as to be able to treat each one with experience, personal investigation, and deep understanding. The strength of this book, as of its companion volume in the field of education, continues to lie in part in the fact that each chapter has been prepared by one or more authorities in a given field.

As in the previous revisions of this work, attempts have been made to strengthen the book even more. The editor has always sought to secure as contributing authors the leaders in the various fields. Of the sixteen authors, six are new to the writing group. All the remaining chapters have been vigorously revised, and several have been completely rewritten.

Dr. Franklin C. Shontz brings a broad perspective to Chapter 1, providing a treatment of several theories regarding the impact of disability on growth and development. Dr. Derek A. Sanders has written a new chapter on the psychological problems of those with impaired hearing. Drs. Herbert and Helen Rusalem have added a new element to the book, one in response to the changing place of the handicapped in the school society. Dr. Lynn Kay Brown has taken a new look at the relationship between psychology and mental retardation.

Dr. Berthold Lowenfeld continues to present an expanded treatment of the psychology of the blind and visually impaired. The greater amount of space accorded to his chapter reflects not only the fact that Dr. Lowenfeld is one of the world's great authorities in the field, but also that such a discussion does not adequately exist elsewhere.

Since 1971, when the third edition of *Psychology of Exceptional Children and Youth* appeared, much has happened in the field. Mainstreaming, for good or for bad, is with us. We have seen the movement toward noncategorical approaches wax and wane, as realities of disability and their impact on learning and adjustment became obvious to those who moved too rapidly. Research has continued slowly to provide new insights. Concepts of interdisciplinary research and practice which involves psychologists, have slowly progressed but not sufficiently to answer the problems to be solved. A new category, learning disabilities, is upon us in all its glorious state of confusion, and will be with us until logic, reason, and historical accuracy assume a proper role. A new group of categories, developmental disabilities, has appeared, and now has both professional and political implications and manifestations. Suffice it to say that the current and continuing critical attitude toward this professional field can only result in a significant understanding in the future. The contributing authors of this edition commend their chapters to the serious student of psychology and education in the expectancy that many will be motivated to further study, research, and professional careers that will contribute to new understandings of exceptional children and youth.

William M. Cruickshank
Ann Arbor, Michigan
Winter, 1979

PART ONE

Foundation Concepts

Four significant chapters are included in this first part, Foundation Concepts. Here the reader will find ideas which undergird the whole of the psychology of exceptional children and youth.

Theories of the psychology of disability, carefully analyzed in relationship to the major psychological theories of human adjustment, comprise the first chapter, by Franklin C. Shontz. Here the reader will find a discussion of the psychoanalytic theory, the client-centered phenomenological concepts of Rogers, the behaviorist theories epitomized in Skinner's work, the ecological psychology of Barker and his associates, and other important concepts that have directed the thinking of psychologists. Shontz discusses each fully and points out its relationship to the field of disability.

The sociological foundations of disability are discussed in Chapter 2. Nettie R. Bartel and Samuel L. Guskin, two authors who have dealt extensively with the field of educational sociology, bring this thinking to the field of disability and make applications which serve to further clarify its complexities.

In Chapter 3 the reader will find a discussion by T. Ernest Newland pertaining to "the major assumptions that underlie psychological testing." Here also are discussed the issues and problems that are raised by these assumptions insofar as child variance is concerned.

Since 1960 there has been a significant movement, mostly on the basis of theory and with little or no consequential research as a base, to normalize the education of exceptional children and youth through the integration of these pupils into the regular educational programs of the schools. The special class, the special school, the regular class, resource rooms, and other learning environments are discussed in Chapter 4, with particular attention to their psychological implications for the exceptional learner. Drs. Helen and Herbert Rusalem bring to this topic a wealth of experience, and add significantly to this volume.

Chapter 4 will not receive universal applause in spite of its excellent coverage. The unfortunate book which propelled education into the concept of "mainstreaming" is delicately not discussed or mentioned by the authors. This is to their credit. The concept of "structure" which is more and more being considered as fundamental to both educational environment and instruction on the other hand might have been stressed in greater force. Likewise the growing backlash from parents and from many educators regarding mainstreaming, which the sudden imposition of P.L. 94-142 and its minimal national planning caused, must be reason for concern for any who plan for the education of all children. Paul and his associates (1978) suggest that nearly two years of preplanning involving the total community should antedate the initiation of mainstreaming of any sort. How much time, we must ask ourselves, was provided by the national leadership to solid community planning in the situation we face now? Costs and dollars are also important. The issue of the costs of the IEP (Individualized Educational Program) or, as in the state of Michigan, the EPPC (the Educational Planning and Placement Committee), have not been recognized at either the national or local levels as a significant barrier to appropriate educational or environmental planning. The costs of these issues alone are sufficient to bring the house down and to bring the hopes of P.L. 94-142 to a complete standstill. Chapter 4 by the Rusalems is an important chapter, for it produces the basis for argument, dialogue, and opinion, each or all of which could strengthen the weaknesses of the present public law in behalf of the consumer and his or her family.

The discussions in Part One, of psychological theory, sociological concepts, measurement and assessment, and environmental considerations provide four significant strands that will run through all the remaining chapters of this book, each of which should be read in light of these discussions.

W.M.C.

1 Theories about the Adjustment to Having a Disability

Franklin C. Shontz

Ph. D., Professor of Psychology and Director of Rehabilitation Psychology, University of Kansas.

Physical disabilities have both personal and social implications. The personal implications appear in two forms: as the *effects* that disabilities impose and as the *reactions* of individuals with disabilities to those effects. The social implications are apparent in the actions, attitudes, and policies of society toward people with handicaps. The personal implications are the primary concern of this chapter, and the social effects are discussed when particular theories treat them as a major influence on personal adjustment.

A disability's personal *effects* are its immediate consequences upon sensory, motor, or cognitive functioning. For example, two effects of arthritis are limitations of movement and pain in the joints. *Reactions* consist of the thoughts and actions a person employs to manage the problems in living that the disability precipitates. For example, refusal to acknowledge the gradual onset of deafness or blindness is a *reaction* to sensory loss, not a direct *effect* of tissue damage.

LEVELS OF DISABILITY CONSEQUENCES

The difference between effects and reactions may be better appreciated by distinguishing among four overlapping levels of conse-quences of disability. The first level consists of effects that can be explained without reference to higher-level influences. This level may be exemplified by the perceptual problem of a person with damage to the left side of the brain, who can respond to stimuli in the left visual field but not in the right visual field (right *homonymous hemianopsia*). This effect is *direct,* because only one type of intermediate process affects the influence of damage to the optic pathways on behavior: homonymous hemianopsia can be explained in neurological terms alone.

A person with left cerebral damage may also speak in an unintelligible jargon. This too is an effect of disability; it is a type of aphasia. In aphasia the relationship between disability and effect is *instrumental;* damage to the central nervous system interferes with a complex network of learned relationships (language). In addition to being the direct result of tissue damage, instrumental effects are responsive to higher-level reactions, such as changes in mood. Aphasia may be more severe on some occasions (for example, when the patient feels discouraged) than on others.

A person with cerebral damage who is angry about his or her condition provides an example of the third level of consequences. Anger is an *emotional reaction* of the whole person. Though influenced by neural or glandular states, anger is best understood in psychological terms as an expression of frustration at the loss, discomfort, and threat imposed by disability.

Finally, at the fourth level, patients who become excessively dependent on others also exhibit reactions to disability. However, these reactions are still more inclusive, global, or *molar,* than reactions at the third level. Reactions at this fourth level involve the whole personality; they are not responses to physical disorder but to an entire context of disability, culture, personal history, and current social values. They are highly individual, and the type or severity of physical disability plays no more than a contributory role in causing them to have the character they do (Shontz, 1977).

The theories described in this chapter concern molar (fourth-level) and emotional (third-level) reactions. The direct (first-level) effects of disability are matters for medicine or physiology, while the instrumental (second-level) effects are the focus of other rehabilitation specialties such as physical therapy, occupational therapy, and speech pathology.

HISTORICAL TRENDS

Traditionally, psychologists in rehabilitation have attempted to solve problems of emotional response and adjustment that were interfering with their clients' progress. Psychologists were first asked to assist in managing clients who seemed to be unmotivated or had become management problems. Psychologists brought to bear on these problems the theories and techniques that were popular at the time (Shontz, 1978).

Psychoanalysis

During the 1940s and 1950s, most theories of personality focused upon internal, mental, or emotional forces, especially those that act unconsciously. Consequently, psychological problems associated with disabilities were described in terms derived from the study of functional neuroses or psychoses (see, for example, Michael-Smith, 1962). The causes of maladjustment (castration anxiety, unresolved Oedipal conflicts, etc.) and the cure for it (intensive individual psychotherapy) were expected to be the same for conditions brought on by physical disability as for conditions of mental origin.

In time, many who worked with persons having disabilities found that, although their clients had suffered traumas which seemed sufficient to cause a variety of mental illnesses, neurosis was no more prominent among persons with disabilities than among those without disabilities. More importantly, psychoanalytic treatment was expensive and impractical in terms of time required and availability of qualified therapists.

Client-Centered Theory and Innovations in Counseling Techniques

In the 1950s some psychological theories began emphasizing conscious, self-directed processes. Among the theorists at the forefront of this development were Carl Rogers and Gordon Allport. Carl Rogers developed client-centered counseling, a type of psychotherapy specifically designed for short-term application. This type of counseling fit more conveniently into rehabilitation schedules, which are typically crowded and of limited duration. Furthermore, client-centered counselors did not require medical training, did not charge prohibitive fees, and were readily available because they were trained in comparatively high numbers. In addition, group therapy techniques, like those devised by Jacob L. Moreno, promised to make counseling six or eight times as effective by the simple expedient of treating that many persons at once.

Environmental Determinism

The 1960s and 1970s saw an acceleration of the tendency to externalize the causes of problems of adjustment. This trend was stimulated in part by social psychology, which emphasized that environmental conditions as well as personal characteristics enter into the causation of behavior.

Also important was the increasing popularity of behaviorism, which maintained that response probability (behavior) is altered by recurrent environmental conditions (contingent reinforcements). A particular form of behavioristic technology, operant behaviorism, seemed to promise a form of push-button control over behavior that was most attractive to a society just entering the space age.

Finally, ecological psychology, especially as developed by Roger Barker and his colleagues (Barker, 1963; 1965; 1968; Barker & Gump, 1964; Barker and H. F. Wright, 1951; 1955), pressed the argument that most behavior is caused by environmental forces. The development of ecological psychology paralleled a growing recognition that problems of adjustment in people with handicaps can often be ascribed to environmental factors, like architectural barriers or denial of rights of social and civil participation (Vineberg & Willems, 1971; Willems, 1971; B. A. Wright, 1972; 1973).

The Third Force

Counterbalancing the trend toward externalizing the causes of behavior have been the existentialistic and humanistic approaches, the so-called third-force psychologies. Some of these approaches take a pessimistic stand by stressing the hopelessness of the human condition. However, most have an optimistic outlook: they claim that psychological growth can bring about the spontaneous emergence of unsuspected satisfactions. Interest in third-force theories continues to develop, though their impact on rehabilitation practice has not yet been felt.

Which Trend Is Right?

This chapter contains both negative and positive biases. Negatively, it assumes that

no single theory of personality is universally or eternally correct. Positively, it assumes that different theories are equally valid under different circumstances. Though there is no complete theory of personality, many are partially or circumstantially valid. As the following statement from 1859 shows, that is not a new idea: "Progress, for the most part, only substitutes one partial and incomplete truth for another; the new fragment of truth being more wanted, more adapted to the needs of the time, than that which it displaces" (John Stuart Mill, *On Liberty*. Quoted in *Contemporary Psychology*, 1976, *21*, p. 588).

Theories respond to the needs of people. To the extent that emerging theories successfully solve the problems to which they are addressed, people's needs change. Then, old theories, which once seemed revolutionary, are displaced—not because they are wrong, but because they become outdated as new problems emerge, demanding new viewpoints and new solutions.

THEORY, IN AND OUT OF THE LABORATORY

The theories described in this chapter are not the sort that a laboratory scientist uses in designing controlled experiments, such as in studying memory for nonsense syllables. The theories discussed in this chapter are more ambitious. They explain the psychological reactions of whole persons. A theory that begins in the laboratory carries with it an aura of precision and validity. But precision diminishes as the possibility of controlling conditions decreases. In settings like rehabilitation agencies, precision is currently unachievable, for no one can manipulate or measure all the forces that influence behavior in such complex settings.

Status of Theories of Reactions to Physical Disabilities

Partly because they concern complex, uncontrollable events, theories about psychological reactions to having a physical disability are not highly sophisticated. Another reason for their lack of sophistication is their recency. Serious consideration was not given to the study of the psychological aspects of physical disability until the late 1940s. Since then, rehabilitation has expanded, but interest in developing comprehensive theories has not grown commensurately. At best, a dozen scholarly books have appeared on the subject of reactions to disability, and of these no more than half have exerted major influences on psychology or rehabilitation.

Another difficulty is that theorization is often rejected in favor of proposals for practical solutions to immediate problems. The director of a rehabilitation institution recently explained why staff members refused to attend training seminars and lectures: besides feeling that they were too busy with administrative duties, the staff felt that the speakers talked too much about theory. The staff wanted only to learn new treatment techniques that would make their work more efficient; nothing else could draw their interest.

If this were an isolated incident, it would scarcely deserve mention; but such is not the case. At conventions of the American Psychological Association, attendance at how-to-do-it workshops is always much larger than at sessions where research reports and theoretical papers are presented. Enthusiasm for operant behaviorism, biofeedback, and meditative techniques reflects the interest of professionals in finding immediate solutions to problems that resist solution by more conventional means. When B. F. Skinner invented operant techniques, he rejected theorizing as a matter of principle. In his early work, he insisted that operant methods, which he believed were all that psychology required, were purely descriptive and non-theoretical (Evans, 1968; Hall, 1967; Skinner, 1950). Skinner's views anticipated, and perhaps helped shape, attitudes that have reached full development in recent years.

The Uses of Theories

A contrasting view is presented in the following statement of William O. Douglas, who was writing not about psychology, but about the education of lawyers:

> The body of "knowledge" pounded into the heads of law students does not survive long after Bar examinations are passed. Law, like engineering, changes fast. The so-called "practical" facts soon become obsolete. The only knowledge of permanent value—in law as elsewhere—is theoretical knowledge. Theoretical knowledge, critical judgment, and the discipline of learning are the only enduring aspects of legal education which make the individual readily adaptable to changing situations and problems (1974, p. 169).

No one has expressed the same idea more succinctly than the famous psychologist Kurt Lewin, who said, "There is nothing so practical as a good theory" (Marrow, 1969, p. viii).

Implicit in the Douglas and Lewin statements is the premise that, without theory, practice cannot function effectively or improve. If history is any guide, we may anticipate that currently fashionable techniques will not succeed as completely as their advocates now hope. New problems will arise and theories will be needed to stimulate the invention of new techniques. But even if currently popular techniques prove successful, a sound theoretical foundation must eventually be provided to explain their operation.

Characteristics of Good Theories

Meyerson (1971, pp. 1–74) listed six characteristics of good theories. His list is especially useful because it stresses features that make a theory valuable in complex situations like those that determine reactions to physical disability. The following discussion is derived from and elaborates upon Meyerson's list:

1. A good theoretical explanation is a generalization; yet it does not lose its validity when applied to individuals. Explanations derived from group averages in massed data are limited because few individuals are average. An ideal generalization applies to all persons and accounts for apparent exceptions without violating the assumptions of the theory.

2. A good theory describes the greatest amount of data in the fewest terms. That is, it makes the fewest assumptions, defines the fewest concepts, and postulates the fewest mechanisms necessary for explaining behavior. Essentially, this requirement overcomes the tendency to confuse labels with explanations.

3. A good explanation stresses *functional relationships* rather than mere associations. For example, a good theory does not rest with the assertion that disability *A* is accompanied by trait *a* while disability *B* is accompanied by trait *b*. Such statements describe only associations. A good explanation reveals *why* and *how* particular effects arise from particular causes. This requires defining and tying together concepts, constructs, or intervening variables of a type that can be applied to many different situations. Examples of such intervening variables are ego strength, contingencies of reinforcement, coping strategies, and differentiation of the life space.

4. A good explanation facilitates making decisions. No theory is useful if it leads only to the conclusion that nothing can be done or that what ought to be done is unfeasible (e.g., cure all patients, overthrow the government, or provide everyone with long-term, intensive psychotherapy). To be good, a theory must stimulate the development of practical plans of action.

5. Good explanations are dynamic (as opposed to static), genotypic (as opposed to phenotypic), and oriented toward the contemporaneous situation (as opposed to dwelling on the past). A static explanation merely describes a state or an observed correlation; a dynamic explanation describes forces that generate observed states or correlations. To do this, a good explanation gets below superficial appearances (phenotypes) and seeks out underlying causes (genotypes). Furthermore, a good explanation concentrates on what is happening now rather than upon what happened in the distant past. Without denying the possible importance of past events, a good explanation concentrates on the present problem related to them and on what can be done about the problem in its current form.

6. Finally, a good explanation stimulates research. In applied settings, it might suggest new approaches to care, the effectiveness of which could be evaluated by objective means. The broadest implication to this statement is that good theories do not provide final answers; often their most valuable contribution is to acknowledge ignorance by raising researchable questions.

Implicit and Informal Theories

Many theories about reactions to disability are implicit or informal. An *implicit* theory is no more than a prejudice; though not openly expressed, it influences expectations and decisions. For example, people often erroneously assume that certain disabilities are so distressing that anyone who has them must be psychologically disturbed. Someone who is blind is expected either to live in perpetual depression or to possess super-normal adaptation powers that make acceptance of the condition possible. This type of implicit theory is often hidden behind attitudes of exaggerated pity or statements that lavish praise on blind persons for such relatively commonplace achievements as graduating from college or traveling unattended.

An *informal* theory makes public statements but does not show how they are derived; it does not express itself in language that permits it to be tested and it does not suggest procedures for measuring the variables it describes. Often, the only difference between an implicit and an informal theory about reactions to disability is whether statements are made openly about the relationship between disability and behavior. That difference, however, is not trivial: an explicit assertion, however foolish, can be tested; implicit theories work their effects in the dark.

The following statement, which summarizes many common beliefs, qualifies as an informal theory about psychological reactions to physical disability:

> Problems of psychological adjustment differ markedly depending on the type and severity of handicap, the age of onset of the condition, the ways in which the handicap impinges on the individual's productive or vocational life, the extent of disablement, and the reaction of those close to the handicapped person. Counseling is extremely helpful to handicapped persons.

The statement includes what might be called common-sense assertions; they seem reasonable, though in fact there is little systematic evidence to support them. In fact, in many cases physical damage is severe but psychological maladjustment does not appear. Similarly, many persons with minor physical disorders develop problems of adjustment far out of proportion to their body state. Like adults, some children with disabilities adapt well, some adapt poorly. Finally, though counseling may be helpful in specific cases, the statement gives the impression that everyone with a disability should have it. In fact, most persons with disabilities get along perfectly well without professional psychological intervention.

The preceding comments are not meant to imply that factors such as those mentioned in the statement never influence individuals. What is at issue is whether factors like these deserve to be presented as behavior-determining variables in a formal theory of psychological response to disability.

Stereotypy. A serious problem with implicit and informal theories is that they foster stereotyped thinking. Examples of stereotypy are beliefs that certain illnesses are brought on by specific personality conflicts, or that certain types of personality are caused by specific physical conditions. These beliefs continue to influence clinical and rehabilitation practices, even though

available evidence provides no firm support for them (Shontz, 1970; 1971).

Resistance to change. Another problem with informal or implicit theories is that they are not subject to modification by experience. Prejudices about physical disability are as unreasonable as prejudices about any other aspect of human behavior. Acceptance of theories of this type is more an act of faith than a conviction derived from systematically collected evidence.

Vagueness. Even the few formal theories that explain body-behavior relations often use language that suggest a higher level of sophistication than they actually possess. For example, it sounds impressive to say that a patient suffers a disturbance of the *body image.* But, if a curious newcomer were to search the scientific literature for a clear definition of the term *body image* he would find none (Shontz, 1969; 1974). Finally, vague theories often substitute labels for understanding. Failure to define concepts blocks inquiry and stifles the criticism that is needed to stimulate research and to provoke refinement of ideas.

To acknowledge this vagueness in theories about the psychological aspects of disability is not to imply that they lack value. In a field where little is known, any theory has value—if it is explicit. A theory provides a common language for describing important phenomena, discussing relations among them and proposing explanations of them. With careful thought and hard work, even a crude theory can be made more useful and precise.

THEORIES BASED ON THE DIRECT STUDY OF REACTIONS TO DISABILITY

Few conventional theories of personality have been developed from direct observation of persons with physical disabilities. By *conventional theories of personality* we mean those typically covered in modern surveys (for example, Hall & Lindzey, 1973;

Corsini, 1977). Among these theories are: psychoanalysis and its derivatives (such as ego psychology); behaviorism of the types espoused by John Dollard, Neal Miller, B. F. Skinner, and Albert Bandura; C. G. Jung's analytic theory; Harry Stack Sullivan's interpersonal theory; factor theories, as developed by Raymond B. Cattell and H. J. Eysenck; personology, as represented by Henry A. Murray, Gordon Allport, and Robert W. White; the existentialistic views of theorists like Rollo May; and the growth-oriented theories of Carl R. Rogers and Abraham H. Maslow. Even humanistic psychology, the "third force" of the late twentieth century, has not examined problems associated with physical disablement.

Occasionally, persons with physical illnesses or disabilities have been studied to exemplify or elaborate particular theoretical points. For example, Janis (1958) used observations of a single patient to provide a psychoanalytic study of reactions to illness and surgery. But rarely have observations of persons with disabilities provided the data base upon which a significant theory has been built or against which one has been validated.

Adler's Theory

Because of his early concern for problems arising from "organ inferiority," Alfred Adler is sometimes cited as a theorist who studied physical disability. However, the idea of organ inferiority never provided a foundation for a full-fledged psychology of disability, and Adler's interests turned to other matters (Ansbacher & Ansbacher, 1956). Adler's theory has also been interpreted as implying that physical disability is a source of feelings of inferiority. These feelings either become overwhelming or they stimulate psychological developments of the opposite type, a reaction called *compensation*. It was once believed that compensation (making up for inferiority in one sphere by becoming superior in another) is the goal of good rehabilitative practice. However,

this idea so seriously oversimplifies the actual situation that it has lost its influence. It is mentioned here only as a matter of historical interest.

Goldstein's Organismic Theory

One exception to the tendency to ignore persons with physical disabilities is Kurt Goldstein's *organismic* theory (Goldstein, 1939; 1940; 1942), which was developed from the study of individuals who had suffered damage to the brain. Current authorities rarely cite Goldstein as one who contributed a theory of psychological reactions to disability, but his influence is evident in the views of those who have applied field-theoretical principles to the problem. These include Roger G. Barker, Tamara Dembo, Lee Meyerson, and Beatrice A. Wright, whose ideas are summarized later in this chapter. Goldstein's influence also appears in the thinking of Carl Rogers and Abraham Maslow, both of whom stress growth and self-actualization, though not specifically as responses to disability.

Goldstein's theory emphasizes the unity of the organism (holistic integrity). His theory expresses faith in the organism's propensity to grow and develop effectively (actualize itself) when free of external or internal interference. Goldstein maintained that the organization of a whole often overrides the meanings of the parts that comprise it. This doctrine may be illustrated by Wright's (1968) description of how an undesirable fact may be constructively accepted into the self-concept. Wright maintained that if the situational context is encouraging, acknowledgment of undesired personal characteristics can strengthen a person's self-concept. In the language of organismic theory, this is like saying that the whole (an overall context that supports self-worth) can exert such a dominant influence over a part (a bit of information about oneself) that the part, though potentially disruptive in isolation, reinforces rather than diminishes the whole.

A major contribution of Goldstein is his distinction between *abstract attitude* and *concrete behavior*. Abstract attitude is a flexible and differentiated way of assimilating experiences, which facilitates integrating each into a more complexly organized whole. It enhances self-actualization because it increases personal complexity and wholeness. When applied to the effects of disability, the abstract attitude enables the person to see continuities rather than disparities between the past and the future, and to find new solutions to the problems that disability imposes.

By contrast, concrete behavior treats each thought or event as unique, specific, and isolated. Concrete behavior cannot produce growth because it does not enhance integration or produce more complexly organized structures. Yet, even concrete behavior serves the whole organism, for it prevents threatening experiences from destroying complex structures. For example, a person who denies a disability is not trying to *avoid* an unpleasant reality, but is trying to *preserve* personal integrity by holding at bay an acknowledgment that would destroy the entire self-concept. Psychoanalytic theory regards denial as a defense; organismic theory regards it as a coping mechanism that treats the denied condition concretely (as if it were specific, isolated, and unrelated to the rest of the self).

Other theorists have tended to treat Goldstein's theory as if it applied only to functions affected by brain damage; but Goldstein proposed it as a general theory of personality. Its value is evident in the extent to which it has influenced the thinking of others, many of whom do not recognize the degree to which they are in its debt.

APPLICATIONS OF OTHER CONVENTIONAL THEORIES

As has been shown, most conventional theories were not derived from the study of persons with disabilities, and therefore offer little assistance in explaining reactions to physical disability. Considerable adjustment, elaboration, and extension has usually been necessary before these theories could be applied to the problem. If theoretical extension goes far enough to produce radically new ideas, a revised theory may emerge and stand by itself. (This happened, for example, to psychosomatic theory: in its early form it owed a great deal to Freudian psychoanalysis; its most radical versions still do; yet psychosomatics today stands as an independent specialty that has generated theoretical ideas of its own.) The following sections direct attention to instances in which a well-known theory has been borrowed without gross modification and has been applied to disability.

Psychoanalysis

Personality types. Despite a decline in the dominance of Freudian psychoanalytic theory, it remains an important source of explanations of reactions to physical illness and disability. One way of using it has been to apply its well-known typologies to medical or rehabilitative patients. In the following list, the *first three character types* are presumed to stem from problems at early stages of psychosexual development; the *other four* represent subsequently adopted defenses against impulses from earlier stages (Kahana & Bibring, 1964, pp. 108–123). Though psychiatric labels are applied to the types, they represent normal reactions to physical illness.

1. *Oral.* These people are characterized by feelings of helplessness and dependency, and by excessive demands for attention. They react to sickness or disability as opportunities to regress to a secure, infantile state. They equate food, medicine, and care with love, and neglect with abandonment.

2. *Compulsive.* These people are made anxious by any hint of loss of control. They are rigid and opinionated, and they demand that everything be done exactly in the manner pre-

scribed. Though obstinate, they are often hard workers. They admire efficient, clean care, which compensates for their own internal hesitancy, doubt, and indecisiveness.

3. *Hysterical.* These people rely on being attractive and impressive. Consequently, they are dramatic, flighty, emotionally expressive, often charming and seductive. They interpret illness or disability as threats to their attractiveness or potency, so they constantly bid for attention, admiration, or sympathy. In fact, they may overdo it to such a degree that they are suspected of malingering (faking an illness). Unlike the compulsive type, the hysterical person feels relatively little need to know medical details about his or her physical condition.

4. *Masochistic.* This person is long suffering and self-sacrificing, sometimes presenting elaborate public displays of moans, groans, and complaining. Masochists want love and care, but they expect to receive it only in return for their own misery. Providing sympathy for such patients usually does not help. They need to see recovery as another task or burden to be borne for the sake of others.

5. *Paranoid.* Patients of this type feel persecuted and oppressed, and find fault with everything and everyone. They are guarded, querulous, and defensive, likely to retaliate in righteous indignation against presumed insults or offenses. Such people are difficult to deal with. They should be listened to, but not given sympathy. They should be asked for tolerance, and their attention should be directed at final goals, with the idea that these goals will be worth the injustices that must be endured in the current situation.

6. *Narcissistic.* This patient feels powerful and all-important. Such persons are smug, vain, even arrogant or grandiose. They insist on having "only the best," and are quick to find fault with and lose confidence in those who care for them. However, beneath their bravado they fear that they are not appreciated and will not be competently cared for. Their demands are attempts to assure themselves that these fears are unjustified.

7. *Schizoid.* This type is aloof, reserved, remote, and apparently uninvolved in what is going on. Such persons are noncompetitive; often they are unsocial. They are also likely to be

a bit eccentric, perhaps involved in religious or dietary fads. Generally speaking, it is not wise to attempt to "break through" to such persons. It is best simply to give them competent and sympathetic care and otherwise leave them alone.

Kahana and Bibring described these seven types in the context of their appearance in general medical settings. However, the types are so general that they may be expected to appear in reaction to long-term as well as acute conditions. Psychoanalytic theory presumes that basic personality structure is laid down early in life, and that all reactions to stress are shaped by and flow through that structure without altering its basic design.

Defense mechanisms. Psychoanalytic theory is also known for its concept of defense mechanisms. These, too, have been used to explain reactions to illness and disability. Although the following summarization was derived from a discussion of the problems of hospitalized adolescents (Hofmann, Becker, & Gabriel, 1976, pp. 56–65), the mechanisms are available to all persons with disabilities.

The patient who uses the defense of *intellectualization* represses the emotional impact of his or her condition and consciously engages in rational concern about its factual aspects. Generally, intellectualization by patients is favored by staff and produces cooperative behavior on the part of the patient, as long as repressive forces remain intact.

Rationalization is described by Hofmann, Becker, and Gabriel as being similar to intellectualization; but the patient who rationalizes is less concerned about learning facts and more inclined to adopt a fatalistic attitude of passive acceptance. A better term for this mechanism might be *acquiescence* because it does not produce coping or generate realistic understanding on the part of the patient.

Regression implies the return of the patient to a state of childhood dependency. Regression is normal in the early stages of illness or injury, and it can be helpful when the patient is required to be passive and dependent in order to gain maximum benefit from care. However, it must be given up during convalescence.

Reaction formation is a compensatory, or counterphobic, device by which a patient substitutes positive actions and beliefs for lost skills or beliefs that are too frightening to face. For example, a person may react against the fear of doing something new by convincing himself and others that he is eager to try it. In mild form, reaction formation is useful for fostering mastery and substitution of goals.

Patients may also respond to their feelings of guilt, despair, or disgust by *projecting* them onto others. To control the feeling that they have been responsible for their own illnesses, they may accuse the doctors or nurses of incompetence or cruelty. Projection is at the heart of many liability suits and malpractice actions.

When concern over one's personal condition is transferred to an emotionally more distant matter (for example, the welfare of other patients), the result is *displacement*. Displacement is often a useful coping mechanism.

Acting out occurs when a patient converts energy from anxiety into action and engages in provocative, aggressive, or rebellious behaviors that create management problems on the ward.

Withdrawal is an attempt to manage stress by retreating into oneself. It may follow outbursts of rage or periods of depression, and may manifest itself in sullenness, passive compliance, or apparent apathy. Temporary withdrawal is helpful; however, when prolonged, withdrawal is maladaptive.

Denial constitutes refusal to admit the reality of one's physical state, despite clear evidence of its existence. Many authorities regard denial as maladaptive in all its manifestations. A subsequent section of this chapter, on crisis theory, presents a view which sees denial as a necessary and recurring stage in adaptation.

Behaviorism

Behavioristic techniques, particularly those that concentrate on operant or instrumental (as opposed to respondent) acts, are more concerned with producing behavior than with explaining current or past events. Consequently, behavioristic technology has recently stepped into rehabilitation and medical settings, promising to solve problems that have resisted solution and to increase the efficiency of service by instituting programs of behavior control (Fordyce, 1971; Ince, 1976; Michael, 1970).

Strictly speaking, behaviorism has not produced an explanation of reactions to physical disability, although some efforts have been made to relate behavioristic principles and rehabilitation practices to problems of adjustment to disability (Asken, 1976). In its extreme form, behaviorism conceives of the person not as an active agent, responsible for his or her own choices and actions, but as a passive respondent, an emitter of behaviors which are in principle infinitely modifiable by environmental conditions. Less extreme forms of behaviorism recognize the importance of internal psychological processes and treat the client as a coparticipant in treatment (Mahoney, 1974; 1977). However, the full impact of these forms of behaviorism on rehabilitation practices is yet to be felt.

To extreme behaviorists, the matter of primary importance is for the behavior the patient produces to be appropriate to the goals of treatment. These goals are (1) to decrease undesirable behavior, and (2) to produce and maintain new, desirable behavior.

A behavioristic explanation for depression following the onset of disability is that the loss of reinforcements, typically experienced by recently disabled persons, is responded to as if it were a punishment. (A *punishment* is an event that reduces the probability of emitting acts that were taking place at the time the event occurred.) Denial of a disability is explained as a type of avoidance behavior used to escape punishment. Aggression, too, may occur in response to the loss of reinforcers.

Rehabilitation may extinguish undesirable behaviors such as depression, denial, or aggression by not reinforcing (rewarding) them or, if necessary, by punishing them. It may also provide positive reinforcements to guide (or shape) emergent behavior in desired ways. The following recommendations provide a more detailed picture of how behaviorism might approach problems in rehabilitation.

a. Use therapists as social reinforcers by training them to deliver reinforcements (praise, smiles, etc.) at appropriate times and to withhold them otherwise.

b. Give clients specific tasks rather than generalized instructions. It is better to tell patients exactly when to do things than to tell them in a nonspecific way to "be more cooperative."

c. Make the responsiveness of the staff contingent upon productive, cooperative client behavior.

d. Adjust the administration of reinforcements systematically so that clients must show steady progress to receive them.

e. Interrupt unproductive activities on the client's part and substitute appropriate activities for them.

f. Provide concrete and specific evidence of success and improvement.

g. Use punishment in response to aggression only as a last resort. When possible, extinguish aggression by non-response.

h. Work with families by teaching them how to use reinforcement to increase productive behavior from the client and, especially, how to withhold reinforcement for behavior that does not reflect progress.

i. Adopt the principle that motivation is determined by contingencies of reinforcement, not by internal states of clients.

j. Always assume that if a specific training program is unsuccessful, the cause is a defect in the program, not in the client. In a suitably arranged environment, desired effects must occur without fail.

The work of Fordyce, Fowler, Lehmann, De Lateur, Sand, and Trieschmann (1973) illustrates how behavior theory may be used to develop treatment techiques. These authors define pain as a set of behavioral acts, or operants. *Operants* are behaviors that can be brought under control of their consequences; the frequency of their occurrence can be increased or decreased by the environment. Just as pain behavior may be treated as an operant, pain-free or "well" behavior may be increased through selective reinforcement.

Fordyce and his associates selected thirty-six patients who suffered from pain that had failed to respond to surgical or conservative medical treatment. These patients all agreed to participate in a special program that was carried out in a comprehensive rehabilitation center and which required at least four weeks of inpatient care. The histories of most patients suggested that they had typically received positive reinforcements for pain behavior.

Specific pain behaviors were identified for each patient. Among the most frequent were: taking medication, moaning, gasping, verbally complaining of pain, and producing identifiable gestural or facial expressions. Efforts were made to extinguish these behaviors, either by withholding reinforcements or by breaking the consistency of the relationship between reinforcements and the behavior. An example of the latter technique is to change from delivering pain-relieving medication on a flexible schedule (when needed by the patient) to delivering it on a fixed interval schedule (such as every four hours), irrespective of the patient's need.

Specific "well" behaviors were also identified. These consisted of performing prescribed exercises in physical therapy, performing demanding tasks in occupational therapy, walking laps of a measured course, and spending time on a work assignment. The reinforcers used for encouraging well behaviors were rest and attention. Rest periods were provided *before* patients reached their maximum tolerance levels on activities, so that they would be reinforced for success rather than for fatigue, discomfort, or pain. Performance quotas were gradually increased so that reinforcement became contingent upon improvement.

The data showed a significant decrease in amounts of medication taken, and significant increases in distances walked, activity units performed, and number of hours per week spent sitting, standing, or walking. Verbally, patients reported some reduction in distress after treatment. However, they still claimed to be experiencing pain.

These findings raise the question of whether the manipulation of observable behavior alters the actual experience of pain. However, because behaviorism is not a science of inner experiences, this question is hypothetical. Behaviorists often point out that subjective states can only be measured by verbal reports, which are notoriously inaccurate. On the one hand, the patients' experiences may have remained the same, but some may have minimized reports of its intensity after treatment (perhaps out of gratitude for the help they received, or because of extinction of verbal pain behavior). On the other hand, experiences of pain may have diminished, but the patients may have tried to be consistent with themselves and reported more pain than they actually had.

A related question is whether the pain reported by these patients was psychological rather than physical. If such were the case, a critic might argue that the program did not affect real (physical) pain; it only changed mental pain. The behaviorist could argue that the results still show that at least this component of pain can be controlled by environmental manipulations. Furthermore, the results seem to cast doubt on those explanations of psychological pain that imply that the only cure is to restructure the personality. Apparently, pain behavior can be reduced by manipulation of the environment alone.

This research lacked comparison groups of similar patients who were exposed to all the conditions except behavior modification, or of similar patients who were exposed to no treatment. Also, it did not include patients who were given other forms of therapy for as many hours as the experimental subjects were exposed to environmental manipulations. Consequently, the study did not prove that the results were due to operant conditioning alone. However, the study does provide a model of how operant techniques can be applied to modify behavior related to physical disability.

SPECIALIZED DEVELOPMENTS FROM CONVENTIONAL THEORIES

Specificity Theories

A *specificity theory* attributes specific personality patterns to specific physical conditions. Perhaps the most ubiquitous theory about reactions to disability is that each form of atypical physique is associated with its own personality type.

Psychosomatics. The psychosomatic version of specificity theory says that each type of illness or disability results, at least in part, from a particular type of personality conflict. Examples of this version are found in the work of Alexander, French, and Pollack (1968, pp. 11–16).

Rheumatoid arthritis in females is said to result from a "masculine protest," stemming from parental restriction of muscular expression. Arthritic women are said to have histories of being tomboys and to have tendencies as adults to dominate others. They have difficulty controlling their intense muscle eroticism; this produces a continuous flow of aggressive impulses toward the extremities. In men, arthritis is explained as a result of using muscle eroticism to defend against feminine identification.

Neurodermatitis is said to stem in part from a craving for physical closeness, from conflict over exhibitionism, from masochism, and from skin eroticism in which scratching serves as a substitute for masturbation.

Duodenal peptic ulcers are thought to stem from conflicts between conscious strivings for independence and unconscious dependency needs. In psychoanalytical terms, the person with this type of ulcer is an overcompensated oral character.

Psychosomatic theory was formulated to explain physical reactions to psychological problems. However, most modern psychosomatic theorists claim to have adopted a *holistic* philosophy. They recognize the integrity of the organism, the unity of mind and body, and the impossibility of making simple cause-effect statements about the relationship between personality and physical illness or disability (Lipowski, 1970; 1974a; 1974b).

Somatopsychological relations. The somatopsychological version of specificity theory asserts that each physical disability produces particular kinds of experiences (such as sensory deprivation or phantom limbs) which cause people who have that form of disability to develop the same type of personality. The following statements are drawn from a description of psychological practices in rehabilitation (Ince, 1974, pp. 458–461):

Amputations may produce fear of loss of social acceptance, loss of self-regard, depression, inability to control tension, resentment and general emotional reactions, anxiety, impulsivity, poor stress tolerance, shame, guilt, self-pity, worry over family affairs, paranoid reactions, phobic reactions, indifference, isolation, pessimism, phantom pain, or lack of realism with respect to the importance of the disability.

Cerebral palsy may be associated with intellectual retardation, depression, anger, negativism, immaturity, variability of motivation, impairment of self-concept, dependency, excessive fantasy, strong needs for affection, unrealistic planning, or paranoid thinking.

Spinal cord injuries tend to be associated with anxiety, dependency, depression, guilt, despair, hostility, suspiciousness, negativism, unrealistic thought and planning, or lack of acceptance of the condition on the part of the patient.

Three questions. Any complete specificity theory must be prepared to answer three basic questions. Each question has three parts. The first part asks whether persons with disabilities are distinctive; the second asks, "if so, how?" and the third asks, "why?"

The first question is: Do the personalities of people with disabilities or handicaps differ from the personalities of people without disabilities or handicaps? If so, how do they differ and why do the differences display the features they do?

The second question is: Do the personalities of people with one type of disability or handicap differ from the personalities of people with other forms of disability or handicap? If so, how do they differ, and why do these differences display the features they do?

The third question is: Do the personalities of people with the same disability differ from each other? If so, how do they differ and why do the differences display the features they do?

Research to determine the personality characteristics of persons with disabilities is hampered by problems of theorization and procedure. Only a few hints about the complexity of these problems can be provided here. For one thing, the terms "disability" and "handicap" have no universal meanings. Although these terms seem to refer to conditions of the body, several authorities cogently maintain that disabilities and handicaps are not things or conditions; they are social judgments. Are people with an endomorphic (rounded, soft) physiques disabled? Or are they disabled only if they want to become ballet dancers? Is diabetes a disability when it is controlled by diet, or does it only become a disability when it interferes with daily activities? Is a young violinist who loses an arm more or less disabled physically than an aged person who suffers the same loss while being well cared for in a nursing home?

Difficulties also arise in measuring degrees of disability. It may seem obvious that people whose spinal cords have been severed have the same disability. Yet, slight differences in the level of transection may have profound functional implications. Someone who retains genital sexual functioning does not have the same physical disability as someone who loses it. Conversely, conditions that differ physically may be virtually identical in their psychological implications. The subjective impact of intensive medical care, physical immobility, and isolation are much the same whether a patient suffers accidental damage to the spinal cord or the aftereffects of orthopedic surgery.

On the psychological side of the picture, currently available psychological measures are usually inappropriate. Standard tests of personality, such as the Rorschach and the Minnesota Multiphasic Personality Inventory, are unsatisfactory because they were developed for use in psychiatric settings. They are either insensitive to personality changes due to disabilities or they distort the meaning of the changes they detect.

Tests designed for specific investigations may be sensitive to the problems of persons with a particular disability who live in a particular setting, but these tests usually cannot be used under other conditions. For example, a scale may be designed to measure amputees' acceptance of their prostheses. But that test probably cannot be used to compare these patients with people who suffer from rheumatoid arthritis, though that condition can be as crippling as amputation.

Paradoxically, failure to solve methodological problems serves to keep specificity theories alive. When a study fails to reveal personality differences between groups, or when the differences it reveals are small, an investigator can argue that larger differences would appear if the measures were more reliable, valid, or relevant. Unfortunately, investigators do not correct such deficiencies and repeat their studies; weak findings thereby retain an aura of respectability be-

cause they have not been subjected to critical re-evaluation.

Specificity theories do not maintain that all persons with the same disability have identical personalities. Actually, specificity theories may recognize individual differences among persons with similar conditions. As one author recently put it, "Not all patients with a particular disability exhibit all of the difficulties included within each group . . . *Each patient is an individual, differing from all other individuals, regardless of the commonality of a medical diagnosis*" (Ince, 1974, p. 458; italics in original).

Centralization and Decentralization

Psychosomatic theory has become so closely identified with psychoanalysis and the specificity hypothesis that other explanatory possibilities are easily overlooked. One intriguing alternative is Bakan's (1968) theory of disease, pain, and sacrifice. This theory integrates several ideas into a coherent explanation of illness and, by implication, of disability and handicap as well.

A major source of inspiration for this theory was Selye's (1956; 1973) observation that disease is not an outside agent that attacks the body, but is produced by the organism itself as it copes with threat. Other important sources were Freud's concepts of personality defense and the wish for death (1950; 1961).

Just as Selye described the physiological opposition between inflammatory and anti-inflammatory reactions, and as Freud described the psychological opposition between Eros (life-preserving) and Thanatos (life-destroying) tendencies, Bakan distinguished between *telic centralization* and *telic decentralization*. These processes are organismic: they operate both physiologically and psychologically.

Telic (purposeful) centralization assures that, in an integrated organism, subsystems are subordinated to a single, unifying, and overriding determinant. On a social level, telic centralization may be exemplified by a well-trained surgical team, in which everyone's behavior is directed toward a common goal. The living human being displays centralized functioning constantly; effective biopsychological organization depends upon it.

Telic decentralization has the opposite effect of inducing subsystems within the organism to function independently. In the surgical team example, each specialist has an area of competence which is not infringed upon by the others and is preserved as a unique responsibility and possession; the team includes an anesthetist so that the others will be free to concentrate on their own tasks. In the human body, specific organs perform unique services and are physiologically protected from undue influence by other body processes.

Centralization and decentralization are opposite tendencies, and either would destroy the organism if unchecked by the other. Centralization would homogenize the organism and render its parts ineffective. Decentralization would produce anarchy and disorganization, preventing coordinated activities. Effective organismic functioning results from a synthesis in which subsystems communicate with each other and engage in mutually supportive interaction (Shontz, 1975, p. 125). Breakdown of the synthesis of centralizing and decentralizing processes is equivalent to disease, disability, or handicap, and the resultant experience is that of becoming ill or crippled. Typically, breakdown results from the failure of centralizing (integrating) tendencies to retain control over behavior. The person feels victimized by decentralizing forces that are beyond control by effort of will.

Six Principles
of Individual Adaptation

Also derived from holistic theories are six general principles presented by Shontz (1975, pp. 191–198) as aids to understanding patients with physical illnesses or disabilities.

Multiple causality. In everyday life, most actions have more than one cause. To understand a person, therefore, means to reject the idea that all actions can be traced to single causal agents, traits, or skills, and to appreciate the contributions of all relevant causes to behavior.

Integration. The person always attempts to function as an integrated whole. All determinants of behavior constitute a unified system or field of relationships. The system often has properties that are more important than single determinants considered separately. For example, a patient's resolve to succeed in rehabilitation may become an overarching consideration that governs and organizes everything he does.

Interpreted reality. Many problems in rehabilitation are traceable to failure on the part of professionals to realize that all persons respond to their own interpretations of reality. When interpretations of the professional and the client agree, communication flows smoothly; when they do not, effectiveness breaks down.

Contemporaneity. Behavior is determined by forces actually present in the situation at the current moment. Although the current situation incorporates elements that reflect the past and anticipate the future, these affect behavior only if they are actually present contemporaneously with behavior. This principle is best understood in relation to the one that follows.

Construing the past; anticipating the future. People look backward to the past and forward to the future. Furthermore, they act and think in ways that maximize construed integration of past, present, and anticipated future experiences. This principle also applies when a person changes, for even a decision to change is made in relation to a past state of affairs and projects itself to some anticipated future.

Unity of organism and environment. This principle is radical but not new (Angyal, 1941). It asserts that a person is not an entity within an envelope of skin, but a complex of organism-environment relationships. What happens to these relationships is the most important determinant of well-being. For example, death is not frightening because it ends biological existence, but because it means loss of ties that have been built over years of development and have made life worth living.

Body Image

The concept of body image was developed into a theory of personality by Paul Schilder (1950), whose approach was influenced by psychoanalysis. A body image is a mental representation of the self as an organic entity. It differentiates out of sensory experience during the first few months and years of life. In normal development, one's physical body becomes the locus of self-identity. Once that happens, the body image serves as the base to which later self-related experiences are referred. For example, a spanking is normally regarded as punishment to the whole child, not just to the target of the slap.

The best known modern exponent of body-image theory is Seymour Fisher (1970; Fisher & Cleveland, 1965; 1968). According to Fisher, experiences from various body regions become associated with specific traits during development. For example, Fisher maintained that in men, sensations in the lower back tend to become associated with traits of the "anal character" as described in classical psychoanalytic theory (Fisher, 1970).

Fisher and Cleveland (1968) developed the idea that the body image delineates a boundary that separates self from environment. Using responses to inkblots, they developed scores purported to measure the extent to which the body-image boundary either is firm and serves as a "barrier" or is vulnerable to environmental "penetration."

Although a natural course of theoretical development would be to extend body-image theory to the explanation of psychological reactions to physical disability, this step has not been taken. The results of the few at-tempts to relate barrier and penetration scores to reactions to disability have been inconsistent and equivocal.

The general term *body-image disturbance* is frequently used to explain why a patient has difficulty adjusting to a disabling condition. But usage of this sort is not precise; the term is applied to problems that are too diverse to be covered by a single heading. A survey of meanings that have been assigned to the term *body image* was undertaken by Shontz (1974). None was found to explain adequately the relationship between body image and physical disability.

Theories of Grief and Mourning

The use of theories of grief and mourning to explain reactions to illness and disability has its roots in the tendency to assume that reactions to such conditions are the same as those that occur following the death of a loved one (Wright, 1960). The foundation for this type of theorizing was the idea that grief is an illness or disease (Lindemann, 1944). This proposal provided a "mental pathology" as a psychological counterpoise to the body pathology that defines a physical illness or disability.

Theories about grief and bereavement are broad because grief may be occasioned by the actual or anticipated loss of anything valuable. The loss may be physical, social, or mental; anything that produces the feeling that a positively valued part of oneself has been or soon will be irretrievably lost can instigate grief.

Grief and crisis. Theories about grief typically assume that one course of recovery is much the same as another, regardless of what activates grief. Another section of this chapter describes a theory of crisis and growth which also postulates a sequence of stages of adaptation. Indeed, theories about crisis and those about grief have much in common; many occasions that produce a sense of loss also qualify as crises.

The most important distinction between

theories of crisis and those of grief is that theories of grief cease to apply when the pathological symptoms have run their course, whereas crisis theory may treat resolution as a process of growth, not recovery. Therefore, crisis theory more readily accommodates to the possibility that adaptation brings a new stage of development at a higher level of maturity than that which existed previously.

Grief and bereavement. The type of grief that first attracted interest was that arising from bereavement, the loss of a loved person through death, and this is still a subject of major interest (Parkes, 1972). It is apparent that physical illness, disability, and the threat of death may also create losses of sufficient importance to trigger grief. Grief and mourning have also been reported in reaction to loss of sexual functioning (Orfirer, 1970; Romm, 1970), to sensory loss (Altshuler, 1970), to losses of external organs, to disfigurement, and to chronic illnesses in general (Blacher, 1970). *Loss and Grief* was made the title of a book on psychological aspects of medical care (Schoenberg, Carr, Peretz, & Kutscher, 1970); a later volume, dealing with the psychological aspects of care of patients with terminal illnesses, was entitled *Anticipatory Grief* (Schoenberg, Carr, Kutscher, Peretz, & Goldberg, 1974).

Death of a loved person. Parkes (1972) drew an analogy between grief and a physical wound. Grief disturbs functioning, and a person who grieves is treated like someone who is sick: the sufferer is allowed to miss work; others make decisions for the bereaved; they talk in hushed tones while in the person's presence; and so forth. Like a physical wound, grief heals by itself unless complications set in.

Grief reactions pass through a succession of "clinical" stages, which blend into and replace one another. The first stage is numbness, characterized by a sense of loss of reality and by depersonalization. This is followed by pining, a series of attempts to restore contact with the lost person. During pining the bereaved mentally goes over past relations with the lost person, often in a ruminative or obsessive way. The loved one returns in images and dreams, while thoughts, memories, and false hopes minimize the impact of the loss. Pining is interpreted as an attempt to restore emotional ties with the dead person through reunion. One extreme form of attempt is suicide: joining the loved person in death.

Pining normally gives way to depression, in which the loss is perceived as a punishment for the bereaved. The punishment is regarded as unjust, so depression alternates with anger; it is accompanied by irritability, bitterness, and often by feelings of being physically unwell. The bereaved searches for someone to accuse or blame—the self, God, the doctors, or the dead person.

In the final analysis, depression results from the feeling that part of the self has been taken away. Grief is the experience of this damage to the self. One way to achieve relief is to restore attributes of the lost person through psychological identification. The bereaved person may try to become like the deceased or to find another person (a child, perhaps) to replace the deceased.

Two complications that may occur during recovery are prolongation and delay. Prolongation may be caused by the desire to continue the dependency on, sympathy from, and control over others, which are privileges that society allows bereaved persons. This is called secondary gain.

Delay may be due to denial of the loss (for example, by holding on to the belief that reports of death are erroneous). Or, it may be due to self-imposed suppression, or "stifling," applied in the belief that loss of emotional control is a sign of weakness or mental illness. Delay is likely to be paid for by more intense suffering when the truth is finally accepted.

Grief is never a steady state; suffering tends to come in waves. Recovery occurs as a series of "turning points," each preceded by suffering and followed by relief. Essentially, grief is explained by assuming that all persons resist change and are reluctant to give up possessions, people, status, and expectations (Parkes, 1972).

Family reactions. Grief may be stimulated by the loss of a family member, in which case the entire family is caught up with the process of adjustment. The same is true in cases of disability, where the entire family is often involved in the process of adaptation. This chapter, however, stresses personal reactions; family influences are considered as the need arises, but are not the focus of attention.

Anticipation of death. Theorists who stress the loss and threat of disablement usually feel that the ultimate loss (hence the ultimate disability) is the loss of life, and the ultimate threat is the threat of death. Moreover, some disabilities are progressive and terminate in death. Much may therefore be learned by examining current thinking about death and dying. The translation of these thoughts into terms relevant to disability is straightforward.

Becker (1973; 1975) explained the quandary of modern humanity as a product of its institutionalized denial of death. Fundamental to Becker's thinking is the assumption that every individual tries to become self-sufficient by asserting his or her superiority to death. This assertion may take a variety of forms, such as believing in the immortality of the soul or working to create an enduring scientific theory. Whatever form it takes, it is both necessary and illusory. Every human being senses that the intolerable reality of death lies in wait.

Paradoxically, to live normally demands neurosis; for repression, self-deceit, and denial of reality, all of which are neurotic, have come to be regarded as normal in a world that is built on the illusion that death can somehow be conquered or escaped. In this hopeless situation, evil is unavoidable; it is a necessary consequence of attempts to triumph over death. The assertion of self-

hood requires an accumulation of power: power to master nature, to control fate, to manipulate others, and to accumulate life for oneself. The assertion may take place vicariously, by identifying with some inspirational cause or by killing others, as if sacrifice satisfies death and keeps it away a while longer.

Becker's views constitute a philosophy rather than a psychological theory; but they have important theoretical implications. They seem to explain why many people avoid contact with those who have physical disabilities and why most people are poorly prepared to adjust to disability when it occurs to them. Physical disability is a *memento mori* that everyone avoids if possible.

Becker's approach also makes a point that is commonly ignored by conventional psychological theories. It is that, in the final analysis, each individual is responsible for finding a personal solution to the problems of life; the environment cannot be blamed for failure to do so. Finding a solution is a creative enterprise and, if well executed, it may produce a degree of genuine personal or cultural enhancement and growth (Campbell, 1970).

Terminal illness. More directly applicable to understanding reactions to disability is the study of persons with terminal illnesses. This subject is currently attracting a great deal of attention, and its study has already yielded insights into the human condition.

Weisman (1972) noted the tendency for people to feel that death, decay, disease, and destruction (which certainly include disability) are all associated with personal degradation and damnation. Other common beliefs, all misconceptions, are that death is horrible and must be avoided at all costs, that only a crazy person would want to die, and that the natural response to thoughts about death is denial. A terminal patient's calmness is often wrongly taken as evidence that the patient does not know or is refusing to believe what is happening. Along with others (most notably, Kübler-Ross, 1969), Weisman observed that calm acceptance of death is perfectly possible and that denial is by no means a necessary or desirable reaction to the prospect of dying (pp. 28–30).

Weisman made several other points that are worth keeping in mind when considering any theory that seems to assume that specific physical disabilities symbolize the anathema of death. One of the most important points is that the misery associated with terminal illness is not evoked by the prospect of death, but by the prospect of prolonging a meaningless existence. What matters to the patient is not avoiding death, but maintaining "significant survival." Continued biological life is only one condition that must be fulfilled to maintain significant survival. The others are the maintenance of freedom of choice (competence) and the retention of self-respect (responsibility) (p. 57). Physical pain is a source of *primary suffering* and should be controlled, but *secondary suffering* is also vitally important; it stems, not from physical sources, but from demoralization (pp. 132–136).

Another important point is that denial occurs less frequently than most people think (pp. 56–78). Furthermore, when it occurs, the reasons for its activation are usually psychosocial, not existential. In other words, denial is fostered by the environment, particularly by people whose actions imply that acceptance of death is inappropriate, even when one is dying.

While people often attribute denial to patients when it does not exist, at least one form of subtle denial may exist and go undetected. This is *third-order* denial, in which the patient may seem hopeful and courageous, but only because he or she has rejected the probability of personal extinction. The surface behaviors associated with this form of denial are so socially desirable that their real cause may go unquestioned.

Second-order denial is somewhat more evident since it consists of false inferences about extensions and implications of an ill-

ness, as when a patient who is paralyzed believes that exercise alone will bring about complete return of normal functioning. *First-order* denial is obvious because it consists of a flat refusal to accept even the basic facts of one's condition. Weisman observed that the giving up of denial is not usually accompanied by panic, as one might expect, but by reactivation of the past and by an attempt to make sense of the condition in the context of the person's whole life experience.

Modern culture fosters denial: the clergy deny death by concentrating on the afterlife; morticians deny death by referring to it as sleep; the military assures its soldiers that heroic remembrance is an honorable way of achieving personal survival; physicians encourage dying patients to believe there is hope for a cure. Under such conditions, it is easier for a patient to conform by denying than to insist on the right to face reality.

Finally, neither denial nor adaptation takes place at a specific time; both evolve in stages. Weisman called the stages of denial acceptance, repudiation, replacement, and reorientation (p. 61). *Acceptance* implies a preliminary recognition of the reality of the situation. *Repudiation* means rejecting that portion of reality that is unacceptable. *Replacement* means finding a new interpretation that is less threatening. *Reorientation* means reorganizing life around the changed circumstances under which it must be lived. The psychosocial stages of adaptation to death, Weisman called: *denial and postponement; mitigation and displacement;* and *counter-control and cessation* (pp. 102–121).

Kübler-Ross (1969) described five stages in adaptation to terminal illness: denial; anger or resentment; bargaining ("If I get well, I promise to live a better life,"); depression; and acceptance or resolution. The fact that these stages do not agree in name with those listed by other authorities is less important than the fact that the authorities agree that stages occur, that adjustment takes place over time, and that it does not run a smooth course.

SPECIFIC DISABILITIES AS LOSSES OR THREATS

A classical example of the theory of loss adapted to explain reactions to physical disability is Schoenberg and Carr's (1970) discussion of reactions to losses of external organs, such as occur in amputation, mastectomy, and disfigurement. This discussion is based on the assumption that the loss of a body part is equivalent to the death of that part and of all other objects or activities it symbolizes. For example, loss of a woman's breast represents not just the loss of a physical entity, but the loss of femininity and all that it implies.

The loss of a body part may also be psychologically equivalent to the death of a loved person. In consequence, grief, depression, and anxiety are universal responses to body-part loss. Reactions are further complicated by the fact that loss may reactivate responses to earlier, similar experiences. Additionally, the contemporaneous attitudes and actions of others (such as family members) determine responses in specific cases.

Following amputation, phantom-limb sensations normally occur. But if they are persistent, are denied, or are painful, it may be because they are serving defensive purposes, such as to delay anxiety or provide a socially acceptable retreat from burdens and responsibilities. In disfiguring conditions, anxiety stems from fear of rejection by people who are important in the person's life. Adjustment requires the development of a new body image, or mental picture of the physical self.

Altshuler (1970) applied the theory of loss to sensory disorders, particularly to blindness and deafness. He notes that disability can represent punishment and that personal reaction is amplified by the symbolic significance of the eyes and ears, which can

represent such psychosexually important regions as the mouth, anus, or genitals. According to Altshuler, disturbance in reaction to sudden blindness is normal; in fact, the absence of disturbance in such an instance justifies an ominous prognosis.

Many authorities stress the difference between persons who are congenitally blind and those who became blind adventitiously, but there is still some question about whether these differences are reflected at molar levels of adjustment. Similar uncertainties surround the effects of sudden versus lifelong deafness. Altshuler apparently agrees with Myklebust (1960) that congenital absence of an important sensory pathway virtually assures faulty personality growth. Of the congenitally blind, Altshuler says that they may develop tortuously toward a normal adjustment under optimal circumstances; but presumably, the highest levels of personal growth are not accessible to them because of their primary sensory disadvantage.

Blacher (1970) postulated that loss of health in chronic illness is reacted to as are all experiences of loss, namely by mourning, grief, and denial. The age at onset of a disabling condition is important because reactions differ depending upon the stage of development at which they occur. As do most theories that regard illness as loss, this one assumes that the effects of childhood illness can only interfere with personality growth. Similarly, the theory assumes that illness in adulthood does not stimulate the development of a new, higher level of maturity, but provokes regression, a return to infantile modes of behavior.

Change

Kelly (1955; 1968) advocated the idea that people do not respond directly to reality, but to their own ideas about it (personal constructs). Generally, these constructs form a coherent system of beliefs which more or less successfully guide behavior. So fundamental are these beliefs that, when reality comes into conflict with a personal construct that resists change, the person does not change the construct, but attempts to alter reality—if necessary, at the cost of considerable effort, distortion, and suffering. For example, a powerful belief that someone is your enemy will make you do things to provoke that person so that, even if he was not your enemy before, he becomes one as a result of these provocations.

Kelly had little to say about physical disability. However, Marris (1974, pp. 1–22) began with a set of propositions that are strikingly similar to Kelly's, and from these he developed a comprehensive theory about loss and change. Although Marris's theory also ignored reactions to disability, the relevance of its concepts is easily demonstrated.

The basic proposition of Marris's theory is twofold. First, it asserts that life is manageable only to the extent that current experiences can be integrated into conceptual structures, which are built from past experiences and provide guides for expectations about the future. That is where the relevance of Kelly's theory comes in. Second, the theory maintains that adaptive beings (individuals or societies) are conservative. They are intolerant of ambiguous events, and resist altering their conceptual structures; they assimilate new experiences into these structures, if possible, and avoid contact with or recognition of new experiences that cannot be assimilated. To grasp the significance of these ideas, we need only substitute the term *disabilities* for the phrase *new experiences* in the preceding sentence.

Some changes do not disrupt continuity; they merely replace one content with another, as when a man finds that he will have to wear a brown suit instead of a blue one, and either serves his purpose equally well. Other changes produce growth by expanding past experience without contradicting it. Skills learned in rehabilitation that enhance functional potential exemplify this type of

change. Still other changes represent losses. They produce discontinuities that may stimulate the development of inventive solutions to problems, if they are sufficiently challenging, or despair and grief if they are unmanageable.

Mourning is the process by which the afflicted person becomes reconciled to loss (pp. 29–32; 84–103). In accordance with the principle of conservatism, the person attempts to retain continuity with the past, despite the necessity to face the future. The purpose of mourning is not to find a substitute for what has been lost, but to discover meaning in the loss that occurred.

Though Marris did not devise names for the stages of adaptation to loss, he cited (p. 29) three stages mentioned by Bowlby (1961), similar to stages described by others:

1. Focusing on the lost person, function, or object and attempting to recover it.
2. Disorganization; pain and despair; giving up.
3. Reorganization, incorporating the image of the lost object and new objects as well.

Marris held that modern society tends to reject mourning and deny the need for it. One reason for this is that people are increasingly tending to avoid intense commitments; mourning, therefore, may not occur because, since nothing is too important, little of importance can ever be lost. This view is rooted in and supported by Protestant doctrines of individualism.

Another reason for rejecting mourning is that modern society tries to provide substitutes for all things. Different brands of cars and appliances perform the same operations equally well. If a thing breaks, wears out, or is lost, one merely goes to the store and buys another. People, too, are made to seem interchangeable. (Doubtless, attempts to develop artificial organs are motivated, at least in part, by the well-meaning desire to provide equally good substitutes for lost body parts.)

However, the logic of substitution as a

cure or preventative for grief is false: no substitute can satisfy the sufferer. The sufferer's commitment to the first object must be maintained, and new developments must be continuous with that commitment. Thus, if a person experiences a loss of a leg, it is unreasonable to expect grief to be absent just because that person receives a prosthesis free of charge.

This theory represents an improvement over theories which assert that grief is an illness. However, even this theory does not account for the fact that people often emerge from grief more mature than they were before loss occurred. That deficit is taken care of in the next theory.

Crisis and Growth

A natural consequence of believing that disability inevitably constitutes threat is to assume that the only possible consequences of such conditions are negative; that is, distressing, disturbing, and tending to produce maladjustment. However, a few theorists taking their inspiration from Maslow (1970) have maintained that successful adjustment does not imply merely overcoming depression and accepting loss; it produces positive psychological growth.

Fink (1967, pp. 592–597) developed this idea in the context of a theory of adaptation to crises. A crisis is a turning point in life that demands the reorganization of an individual's psychological structure. Whether an event becomes a crisis depends on the extent and permanence of reorganization required to cope with it. A physical disability constitutes a crisis if it disrupts many of a person's important activities.

Adaptation to crisis takes place in stages. The first is *shock* or *realization;* it occurs when the person initially apprehends the extent of disruption the crisis has produced. In the second stage, *defensive retreat,* or denial, restores the sense of safety and security that is needed to make endurance of the situation possible. A degree of denial is not merely convenient or useful; it is necessary. Denial becomes maladaptive only if it interferes with ultimate growth. *Acknowledgment,* the third stage, is actually a cyclical sequence of substages in which realization alternates with defensive retreat; defensive retreat is given up bit by bit, and reorganization of the psychological structure takes place incrementally, accommodating to the altered total situation.

At the time of the initial impact of crisis, disturbance is profound and intense. As the stages progress, however, the extent of personal involvement and the frequency of cyclical readjustments diminish until equilibrium is attained. Apparently, a similar course of adaptation, with decreasing intensity of fluctuating readjustments, occurs in the equilibration that takes place when a population is attacked by a new destructive parasite (McNeill, 1976, pp. 58–59).

If a true crisis occurs, all stages must be passed through. During some of these, the sufferer may appear to be mentally ill. For example, in severe crises, realization often produces emotional reactions that might be classified by an outsider as depressive. Defensive retreat may produce withdrawal, repression, or misperception of reality, which could seem nearly psychotic to someone not in the sufferer's position. Even during acknowledgment, some reactions may be similar to cyclical or episodic psychopathology. Yet, no stage is intrinsically pathological. Maladaptation occurs only when the person fails to progress through the stages at a reasonable rate.

The cycle of acknowledgment-retreat-acknowledgment-retreat recurs many times before adaptation is complete. When it is complete, however, the level of psychological development the person achieves exceeds that which existed before the crisis.

Fink's theory has been modified by Shontz

(1965; 1973; 1975), but not in its two basic assumptions: first, that normal adaptation is a developmental sequence; and second, that success produces growth and increased psychological maturity.

SOCIOCULTURAL PERSPECTIVES

Though no one doubts that illness and disability are objective conditions, some of the most important aspects of illness and disability are social. The sociological approach to illness was developed mainly by Parsons (1951; 1972), who described the "sick role": a set of expectations that society applies to persons who qualify.

According to this theory, illness is an institutionalized role type. The sick role is appropriate for persons whom society regards as having undergone a "generalized disturbance of the capacity of the individual for normally expected task or role-performance, which is not specific to his commitments to any particular task, role collectivity, norm, or value" (1972, p. 117). The incapacity must be one for which the sufferer cannot be held responsible; that is, the individual must be unable to overcome the incapacity by an act of decision making or will. Outside therapeutic help is therefore presumed to be needed to restore the person to health.

Once given the right to be sick, the person is granted exemption from normal obligations. The exemption is not a privilege but an obligation. Once someone has been labeled sick, that person must act like someone who is sick regardless of wishes to remain normally active. Other obligations of the sick role are to seek competent help and to cooperate in getting well. The sick role is temporary, and attempts to prolong it meet with counter pressures to conform.

The concept of the sick role has been developed into elaborate analyses of the ways in which society treats the problems of illness. For example, Parsons (1972) pointed out that it is distinctively American to believe that dependency threatens recovery and must be overcome by insisting that the patient work hard to get well. In the Soviet Union, sick-role status is more difficult to obtain, but patients are typically encouraged to relax and enjoy being cared for once their illnesses have been acknowledged.

Because its units of analysis are whole cultures, sick-role theory has been criticized for being too general to explain individual behavior (Twaddle, 1972). Here, the term *culture* includes not only nationality but factors such as social class, ethnicity, age, and sex (insofar as stereotyped behaviors are associated with each).

The concept of "illness behavior" has been developed (Mechanic, 1962; 1972) to refer more specifically to individuals' responses. For example, a patient may use illness as a way of solving personal problems or reacting to stress. In the extreme, a person may find that illness not only permits withdrawal from difficult social obligations but affords definite advantages, such as the opportunity to make claims on others, and provides an honorable excuse for failure. Although this theory stresses the multiplicity of behavior-determining processes in individual cases, its socio-cultural basis is revealed in the comment that "In the final analysis, illness and social disability are socially defined" (Mechanic, 1972, p. 136).

Generally, theorists regard the sick role and illness behavior either as helpful or, at worst, as benign in their effects. However, a few authorities feel that the power placed into the hands of physicians has been misused to such an extent that medical practice now does more harm than good (Illich, 1976). Whether or not such radical views are correct, they point out the fact that the incidence of disability is affected by the state of the medical arts. Obviously, many medical advances have created disabilities by keeping people alive who would otherwise have died. Cases in point are patients with spinal cord injuries, who are now protected from diseases that were once fatal.

But medical advances have other effects, which are less obvious and which increase the incidence of disabilities. Medical treatment sometimes fails, or has side effects that leave patients disabled (such as the results of thalidomide use or of anoxia in incubators). Even successful treatment may indirectly increase the apparent incidence of illness and disability, by defining certain conditions as being disabling that had never been so defined before. For example, orthodontic techniques have so changed American standards of facial beauty over the years that today a much higher proportion of children with crooked teeth are regarded as handicapped and as requiring "treatment."

Not the least important changes have taken place simply because diagnostic and case-finding techniques are so refined that nearly everyone is exposed to the scrutiny of professionals who are empowered to label people as sick or disabled. Mental retardation has become prominent in part because tests have become available to measure it, and society sees to it that these tests are administered to almost everyone.

SOCIAL-PSYCHOLOGICAL THEORIES OF REACTIONS TO DISABILITY

Field Theory

Meyerson (1963a; 1963b; 1971) undertook the task of integrating sociological insights (such as those cited in the preceding section) with psychological concepts, to achieve a new way of explaining reactions to disability. The basic premise of the resulting theory is that "disability is not an objective *thing in a person,* but a social value judgment" (1963b, p. 11; italics in original).

"Handicaps" are socially imposed limitations placed on persons who may or may not be sufficiently different from others to be regarded as atypical. A simple example of a handicapping but normal physical state is being too short to become a policeman or enter the armed services. In these situations, it is more correct to say that the handicap is in the rules than in the person who fails to qualify. By the same token, when a person who is blind has difficulty crossing a street with heavy traffic, the difficulty does not exist because the person is blind, but because safe crossings are not provided. According to this analysis, the blind person is handicapped by society, not by lack of vision.

It is consistent with Meyerson's view to note that a body condition that differs markedly from the norm is more appropriately called an "atypical physique" than a "disability." The word *disability* suggests that the condition itself is handicapping. The term *atypical physique* attributes no loss or gain to the condition; it stresses only that the condition differs from what society regards as normal, average, or necessary. In some instances, atypical physique may be a mark of distinction rather than a handicap. Meyerson cites instances (such as the once-popular practice in China of binding a girl's feet to keep them from growing to normal size) where disabling conditions are looked upon as signs of aristocratic upbringing (1963b, pp. 8–19).

Whether typical or atypical, physique serves several important functions. As a social stimulus, it arouses expectations in others and provides criteria for assigning people to social roles. As a stimulus to oneself, it influences self-perception directly, through comparison with past body states or personal ideals, and indirectly, through perception of the reactions of others (1963b, pp. 15–16).

Up to this point, Meyerson's theory provides insights into the nature of disabilities and handicaps, and it stresses the importance of physique as a stimulus of special significance. However, for completeness it needs to relate social pressures to individual reactions. Meyerson accomplished this by identifying a three-step process in which each later step can occur only if those before it take place. The steps are:

1. The person recognizes that he or she lacks a tool that is required by the culture in which the person lives.
2. Others perceive this lack and devalue the person for it.
3. The person accepts the judgment of being less worthy, and engages in self-devaluation (1963b, p. 17).

If culture did not require the tool, self-devaluation would not take place (no culture requires all its members to hear sounds of 20,000 cycles per second). Also, if the lack were not perceived by others, or if they did not devalue the person for it, self-devaluation would not take place. Most important is the assertion that even when devaluation by others occurs, self-devaluation follows only if the individual accepts the judgment of being unworthy. If that judgment is rejected, personal devaluation (which is psychological maladjustment) does not occur.

This theory does not discuss the medical type or severity of disability, because the theory is firmly based on the premise that *variations in physique alone do not cause psychological maladjustment.* Emotional handicaps are caused by reactions to the mediating influences of social forces (1963b, p. 17).

New and overlapping situations. To further integrate the socio-cultural and personal frames of reference, Meyerson borrowed descriptive tools from Lewin's field-theoretical approach (Lewin, 1936). He also extended the theorizing of Barker and his associates (Barker, Wright, Meyerson, & Gonick, 1953) by applying Lewin's concepts of *new* and *overlapping* psychological situations to the analysis of the psychological aspects of handicap. In these expressions, the term *situation* refers to the entire field of psychologically relevant forces operating on an individual at a given time.

A new situation contains regions the person has never entered before (1963b, pp. 33–42). For example, persons with disabilities, who are unfamiliar with life outside rehabilitation agencies or away from their homes, face many new psychological situations when they begin to function in the world at large. A new situation may be an exciting challenge to someone who is prepared to meet it and is confident of success. However, new situations can cause trouble for the unprepared person who does not know the paths to goals. Such a person is both attracted to the situation by the apparent benefits it provides and repelled from it by fears of what might happen on the way to goals. New situations are typically unstable, and vacillation occurs as the person tries to discover how best to proceed. If a new situation persists too long and if the person cannot perceive progress toward worthwhile goals, it is likely to produce anger, despair, and maladjustment. Meyerson recommended that, in the interest of good psychological adjustment, newness in the lives of persons with disabilities be minimized.

An *overlapping* situation is one in which two or more sets of behavior-determining forces operate simultaneously. Typically, overlap occurs among social roles (1963b, pp. 42–51). It does not always produce discomfort; the roles of father, worker, husband, and adult male overlap, but are usually not too incompatible to coexist in the same person.

In situations where disability makes a difference, the roles of being disabled and of being nondisabled are incompatible. They may be *antagonistic,* in that adopting one role rules out adopting the other. A person who tries to conceal a disability encounters antagonism of roles, for one cannot act like a disabled and a nondisabled person at the same time.

Incompatible roles may also be *exclusive,* which means that even if a person refuses to adopt one role, he or she may still be rejected from another which seems more desirable. This would occur if a child who cannot hear refuses to accept the identity of being deaf but is still prevented by other children from engaging in "normal" activities.

Strategies of adjustment. Meyerson outlined three strategies that persons with disabilities may use to deal with antagonistic or exclusive overlap (1963a, pp. 144–168). Although he described these originally in the context of a discussion of reactions to impaired hearing, he also described them in a later discussion of reactions to all forms of disability (Meyerson, 1974). The first strategy

is essentially withdrawal from the world of the nondisabled: the person stays within the restricted but apparently safe role of the disabled person (area A in Figure 1–1). This strategy provides a clear definition of the self, and may be useful to individuals who have ample contacts with others who have disabilities, or to persons who find identification with their conditions advantageous in such work as promoting civil rights or rehabilitation legislation.

The strategy of withdrawal has two disadvantages. One is that it may cut its user off from valuable contacts. A blind person who associates only with other blind people is as deficient in social contacts as a sighted person who avoids everyone with a disability. The other disadvantage is that with-

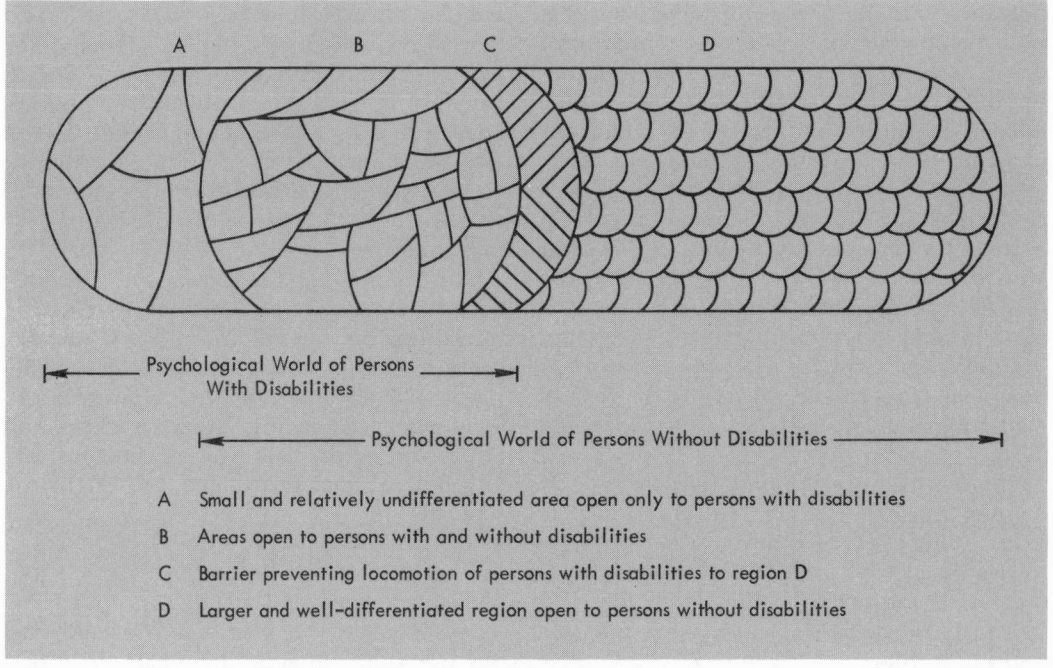

FIGURE 1–1.   Comparison of the psychological worlds of persons with and without disabilities. (Reprinted by permission of Prentice-Hall, Inc. Adapted from Meyerson, 1963b, p. 44.)

drawn people may become egocentric, over-valuing their own problems, developing hypersensitivity to others, and becoming unable to make plans that take into account the needs of others, especially of persons without disabilities.

The second strategy of adjustment is the opposite of the first. It consists of rejecting the world of disability and aspiring to live only in the regions of nondisability (area D in Figure 1–1). Often the result is that the person is placed in antagonistic, overlapping situations. This adjustment pattern tends to be more common among the adventitiously disabled—people whose disabilities were acquired relatively late in life. It is often an "as if" adjustment (Wright, 1960) in which the person pretends that the disability either does not exist or has little effect on his or her life.

The advantage of this strategy is that it promises to expose the person to a larger, better-differentiated world. However, its disadvantages are manifold. For one thing, it exposes the person with the disability, who by definition lacks a socially required tool of adjustment, to situations that are for that reason certain to be difficult, awkward, and ambiguous. Obviously, people who adopt this strategy must develop skill, energy, and tolerance for frustration to overcome the obstacles that will surely be placed before them (area C in Figure 1–1).

Another disadvantage of this strategy is that it encourages extreme reactions of overcompensation or denial. In overcompensation, the individual concentrating on achieving exceptional goals sacrifices many limited but perhaps necessary gratifications in an attempt to gain great but perhaps inaccessible ones. In denial, the person sacrifices the accurate perception of reality and engages in self-deception, which can only impede adjustment in the long run. Finally, the person who uses this pattern of adjustment, but does not engage in denial, is certain to be exposed to devaluation. If the person with the disability accepts the values of

the nondisabled, a lowering of perceived self-worth, depression, and despair are sure to follow.

The third strategy of adjustment involves compromise. The person enters the world of the nondisabled, but only to the extent possible. This individual strives to live on the "common ground" that is accessible to people with and people without disabilities (area B in Figure 1–1). For example, a homebound person might sustain active contact and participation in the world of the nondisabled by using the telephone and typewriter to conduct a business.

This seems an ideal strategy, for it promotes self-awareness and coping without requiring withdrawal, denial, or overcompensation. However, this form of adjustment still exposes the person who adopts it to the injustices of society and to others' devaluations. For the adventitiously disabled, it imposes constant consciousness of what has been lost (the part of the life space that can no longer be entered); yet it does not offer the apparent safety of retreat into self-deception or the promise of overcompensated victory. For the congenitally disabled, it imposes constant pressure to enter new, dangerous situations, while threatening to take away what security there is in living in a restricted but manageable world. In short, this form of adjustment has all the disadvantages and advantages of every compromise: in its efforts to achieve balance, it may yield mediocrity, and at a price the person may find too high to pay.

Though Meyerson does not stress the point, there is no logical reason why an individual must be fully committed to one pattern of adjustment. Someone who is blind may live mostly by the third strategy, but become fully identified with others who are blind when participating in organized activities to aid the blind. The same person may adopt the second strategy when applying for a job, by insisting that he is as able to function as well as someone with no disability and that his blindness must be disregarded by the employer who makes the hiring decision.

Meyerson concludes by pointing out that society should not impose conditions that require people with disabilities to be maladjusted, then berate them for their maladjustment. This view, that society causes maladjustment, evolves into the argument that all problems of the disabled stem from the environment; hence their solutions are to be sought, not in psychological theories, but in environmental changes. That argument is taken up in a subsequent section (1963b, pp. 47–49).

Perspectives: Outsiders and Insiders

Of all the contributions to general theory that derive from studying persons with physical disabilities, few provide more provocative insights than the proposal by Dembo (1970) of a distinction between the psychology of observers (outsiders) and the psychology of sufferers (insiders). Dembo introduced this idea in an attempt to explain why so little psychological research is applicable to rehabilitation. Her explanation was that conventional psychology differs so greatly from the psychology of sufferers that it is a contradiction to speak of "utilizing" knowledge gained by traditional means to relieve suffering in extra-laboratory situations.

Most professionals are taught only the psychology of the outside observer, for that is traditional psychology. Traditional psychology and the psychology of the insider differ in many ways: in their *definitions of problems;* their *perceptions of the locus of problems;* their attitudes toward *subjectivity* and *values;* their *temporal perspectives;* the sizes of the *units of measurement and conceptualization* they employ; and their *decision-making criteria.*

In traditional psychology, the *definition of a problem* is constructed in terms of its theoretical relevance; a problem is considered to be solved only when it is integrated into a formal theoretical framework.

However, in the psychology of people who suffer, a problem is a personal trouble that needs to be alleviated; it is regarded as solved only when a remedy has been found; relief, not explanation, is the goal.

Outsiders and insiders also differ in the apparent *locus of the problems* they wish to solve. Traditional scientists regard problems as existing "out there" in the realm of theory or empirical fact. Sufferers' problems are personal and immediate.

Traditional psychology distrusts *subjectivity;* it regards verbal reports as undependable and inaccurate. The sufferer maintains that subjective experience is the only valid criterion of truth, for who but sufferers can know when their problems have been solved?

Classical science also has a traditional attitude toward *values;* it regards itself as value-free. Young scientists are taught to remain emotionally aloof from their subject. Of course, anyone observing an argument between scientists who have drawn opposing conclusions can see that scientists are not free of emotional involvements in their work. Both outsiders and insiders have values; only the character of the values differs.

Traditional psychology takes pride in its long-range *temporal perspective;* it seeks truth that will last forever. The scientist is willing to tolerate delay if the end result is knowledge that will be eternally valid. By contrast, sufferers have no wish to wait; they cannot afford to; the remedy they need is needed now.

If psychology were constructed from the point of view of sufferers, it would use more restricted *units of measurement and conceptualization.* The traditional scientist tends to think abstractly, in quantitative language and in terms of long-range probabilities and population means. By contrast, sufferers think in terms of concrete problems and individual cases.

The values of traditional science are consistent with the belief that the best way to improve patient care is to devise a test that permits rejecting patients for whom there is little hope for success. In this way, resources would not be wasted because treatment would be supplied to those for whom the probability of improvement is greatest. Among sufferers, a different set of *decision-making criteria* are appropriate. Especially where serious illness and disability are involved, insiders insist that care be given to everyone, even in the face of apparent incapacity to benefit.

People with handicaps understand all too well the tendency of outsiders to underestimate the potentialities of persons with disabilities. Too many "exceptions" have occurred in their experience, and too few outsiders understand that even a very small change may have immense functional implications. An excellent example of misunderstanding is described in Spar's (1973) observation that the restoration of only 5 percent of vision does not seem worthwhile to ophthalmologists accustomed to treating people with normal vision. But to a person who is legally deaf and blind, a 5 percent improvement in visual capacity can mean the difference between being able and unable to travel.

Diller (1971) argued that, in rehabilitation, patients who seem to have the poorest chances for success need the care most; therefore, it is they who should receive most attention, not the people who need the care least. Clearly, this is an insider's view; it contradicts outsiders' assumptions about the most effective way of using treatment resources.

Dembo's ideas do not merely provide another theory about contrasting ways of perceiving the same reality; they point to the existence of two different, in most ways contradictory, sciences of psychology. This answers one question: why is so much conventional psychological research irrelevant to extra-laboratory problems? but it raises another: how can the two psychologies be reconciled?

Dembo (1969) stresses that traditional psychologists must start taking the needs, wishes, opinions, and knowledge of sufferers into account. Persons with disabilities must participate in the selection of problems for research and must suggest ways of improving methodology. These proposals sound one-sided, with outsiders making all the concessions. But because the situation is currently so unbalanced in favor of conventional approaches, traditionalists will, of necessity, be required to yield, if equilibrium is to be achieved.

In addition to emphasizing the differing perspectives of outsiders and insiders, Dembo made important contributions in stressing the role of values in adjustment, the significance of relations between professional and client, and those between nondisabled persons and persons with disabilities. Many of these ideas are incorporated into Wright's social-personal theory (1960), which is described in a subsequent section.

Professional-client relations. Leviton (1971; 1973) compared the expressed viewpoints of patients (insiders) and care-givers (outsiders) in a rehabilitation setting. These were solicited in interviews of forty-five professionals and forty-five recipients of services. Though only some of the findings can be summarized here, these are sufficient to illustrate the main issues.

Quantitatively, differences between expressed opinions of clients and professionals were not great. Roughly 70 percent of both groups said that clients should participate in decision making (1973, pp. 10–28). About 80 percent of both groups agreed that professionals should become more emotionally involved (develop closeness, warmth, friendliness) with clients (1973, pp. 28–39). About 60 percent of both groups agreed that independence should be promoted (1973, pp. 50–57) and that a degree of risk is permissible (as opposed to a constant policy of safety first) in rehabilitation (1973, pp. 57–61).

However, professionals supported a realistic (as opposed to a "hopeful") approach to the future more strongly than did the clients. Among clients, the need for hope was most strongly expressed by those who needed help most. Also, clients advocated much more strongly the policy of giving equal consideration to patients who have little chance of being improved (1973, pp. 40–45).

This study did not examine actual practices; thus it did not establish whether clients actually participate in decision making or whether professionals do, in fact, become emotionally involved with their clients or take risks in rehabilitation. But it did show that there is verbal agreement on these issues. The data are encouraging to the extent that this agreement represents congruence of basic philosophy, that the results are capable of being translated into action, and that they can be generalized to other agencies.

The disagreements suggest areas where more understanding is needed. Generally, clients felt that treatment should be given to all who need it, sometimes to the extent of giving more treatment to clients with the poorest prospects (1973, pp. 45–50). Clients also saw hope as a desired incentive: to them, hope was not a matter of establishing a schedule for achieving goals; it meant holding a generally positive outlook. Clients tended to think of "reality" (which professionals regard as good) as having negative emotional significance because it represents what one cannot do; it is opposed to hope (1973, pp. 40–45).

Setting effects. Theories that stress the inadequacy of the viewpoint of the outsider can be used to explain reactions to disability in environmental terms. Such theories stress the point that when difficulties arise, they are due to the insensitivity of the social environment to the needs of the sufferer.

Rehabilitation experienced a pronounced growth of consumer movements beginning in the 1960s (Brieland, 1970). These movements contained a strong component of "anti–guinea-pigism" and stressed the superiority of "self-help" to the delivery of services by "outsiders." Brieland pointed out that, in the contemporary world, the medi-

cal hospital provides a poor model for rehabilitation. Rehabilitation must be a joint effort between professional and client, and should be facilitative rather than curative or therapeutic.

Brieland did not maintain, as would others (Meyerson, 1963, 1971; Roth & Eddy, 1967; Shontz, 1967), that long-term maladjustment in persons with disabilities is usually due to environmental pressures. However, Brieland's recommendations were consistent with the trend to attribute problems in rehabilitation, not to psychological disturbances of patients, but to the setting in which they are treated.

Several authorities have commented unfavorably on the traditional role of psychologists in rehabilitation (Asch, 1970; Conroe, 1974; Hanson, 1974). These authorities argue that traditional professional roles are of no help to clients; they may even be harmful, if they place the psychologist into the same "outsider" status as others on the treatment team.

Among the changes these authors recommend is the abolition of formal office appointments, in favor of informal contacts with clients in the treatment setting itself. More important is the suggestion that the psychologist serve as the client's advocate, who makes sure that the client's views are taken into account by the rest of the staff. This approach rejects the traditional counseling model, which defines the psychologist as a professional who helps clients because they are incapable of solving problems on their own. If society is to provide settings that do not promote poor adjustments, rehabilitation must stop being a one-way relationship in which aid is delivered to helpless sufferers by omniscient and omnipotent professionals. It must become a community which engages the cooperative efforts of client, family, and staff in ways that allow each to contribute to the solution of the problems that disability engenders.

Theories advocating environmental change. Carried to its extreme, the argument that problems of adjustment are caused by the environment can be taken to mean that there is no psychology of disability. For, if persons with handicaps are helpless in the face of external pressures, then it is more important to improve environmental conditions than patients' mental states.

Arguments like these originally became popular because they promised to free people with disabilities from being treated as victims of their own emotions. However, the same arguments may justify making persons with disabilities into victims of their environments. Operant behaviorism provides an example of how this might be achieved. It derives from a rationale that could bring the client back under the thumb of outsiders, who construct environments that enhance desirable and reduce undesirable acts, according to outsiders' own definitions of those terms.

The theorist, who says that there is no special psychology of disability, typically has more humanistic goals. Having seen persons with disabilities being victimized by stereotypes and denigrated by devaluing pity, the theorist wishes to reassert the dignity of these persons by demolishing oversimplified assertions about their inner states. The following examples are drawn from the literature on blindness, but the arguments apply to all disabling conditions.

Monbeck (1973) maintained that stereotyped thinking causes the pity that is lavished on persons who are blind to be out of proportion to the limitations that blindness imposes. The stereotypes that most require change are those that lead people to fear and feel excessively sorry for the blind. Among these are the false beliefs that blind people are helpless; that they all desire desperately to see again; and that the blind are psychologically different from the sighted, either inferior or superior (through compensation, or through the development of special "gifts," senses, or mental powers).

The eyes have powerful symbolic meanings. They are associated with light, consciousness, fertility, and magical or spiritual potency. Loss of vision has equally powerful meanings, for it is associated with darkness, which symbolizes chaos, gloom, evil, death, ignorance, and the unconscious. When sighted people encounter a person who is blind, they respond to these symbolic meanings rather than to the individual. They are unable to regard someone who is blind as being merely a person without vision, though that would be the rational thing to do.

Because sighted people react irrationally, a blind person cannot expect them to be changed by appeals to reason. However, someone who is blind need not therefore become a victim. When a person who is blind develops the capacity to detect irrational behavior in others and to refuse to grant such behavior validity, that person has taken an important step toward adjustment to blindness.

Instead of placing the causes of problems inside people who are blind, Monbeck's argument attributes them to the prejudices of people who are not blind. Thus, by shifting from the outsider's viewpoint to the insider's, this theory implies that, while there is no "special psychology" of blind people, there is a special psychology of sighted people who deal with the blind. The theory avoids implying that the blind are helpless. Quite the contrary, it says that once they recognize the source of their problems they can refuse to respond in expected ways and can assert their rights to being treated appropriately.

In another analysis of the same subject, Kirtley (1975) began by identifying the stereotypes that sighted people hold about blindness, and commented on the revulsion that sighted people typically feel when in contact with the blind. Like Monbeck, Kirtley concluded that these attitudes are universal and timeless; they are practically innate. However, instead of developing the idea that the problems of the blind originate in the attitudes of the sighted, Kirtley took another tack. He stressed the fact that blind persons are characterized by no personality pattern which differentiates them either from the sighted or from people with other disabilities. Furthermore, he found no basis for distinguishing psychologically between the congenitally blind and persons who were blinded adventitiously. The problem of adjustment to blindness is one of resolving a conflict of identity, not of adjusting to loss of vision. Consequently, there is nothing unique to blindness to cause problems different from those that arise whenever any identity conflict must be resolved for any reason.

On the basis of extensive reviews of research attempting to relate physical illnesses and disabilities to personality, Shontz (1970; 1971, pp. 42–60; 1977, pp. 318–322) also found no solid evidence that different personality types are closely associated with different forms of illnesses and disabilities, or that type or severity of body disorder has any direct effect on quality of overall psychological adjustment. Thus, Shontz confirmed and broadened Kirtley's assertions about the inadequacies of the specificity hypothesis in this field of investigation.

Shontz agreed that there can be no "special" theory of reactions to physical disability. However, he felt that systematic study of persons with physical disabilities is nonetheless justified. Their life situations make accessible for scrutiny psychological processes that could never be produced in controlled experiments. Furthermore, no better population can be found for the study of psychological growth, particularly in the case of those persons for whom adaptation comes to a successful conclusion. Shontz's argument is that the study of persons with disabilities is valuable because it provides insights that have implications for everyone.

Social-Personal Theory

Eclecticism. One way to attempt to bring together clinical and research evidence regarding reactions to disability is to select and combine from several theoretical sources those concepts and ideas that seem most valid. The work of Siller represents this strategy most clearly. His approach is psychosocial (1967b), and his research on the measurement of attitudes toward persons with disabilities has gained well-deserved recognition (Siller, Chipman, Ferguson, & Vann, 1967; Siller, Ferguson, Vann, & Holland, 1967). Siller maintains that "a full understanding of the dynamics underlying a reaction to the disabled requires recognition of intrapsychic, experiential, and social factors" (1976a, p. 71). To gain this understanding, his theory relies on concepts drawn from psychoanalysis (examples: ego, id, projection), sociology (deviance), social psychology (attitudes), and integrative theories, such as the one discussed in the next section.

As a theoretical approach, eclecticism has its merits (Allport, 1964); however, in this instance at least, simplicity is not one of them. Although Siller's views are comprehensive, they cannot be summarized concisely because they do not exist in the form of a few fundamental and systematically inter-related principles.

An integrative approach. Wright's (1960) comprehensive theory of psychological reactions to disability also has a social-personal orientation; it sees reactions to disability as integrated responses to social-environmental pressures on the one hand and to personal processes on the other.

Wright's ideas developed from an intensive investigation of persons with physical disabilities, conducted just after World War II (Dembo, Leviton, & Wright, 1956) and from her work with another group of scholars and investigators, headed initially by Roger G. Barker—who published the first comprehensive survey and critique of psychological research on physical disability and developed the concept of *somatopsychology* (Barker, Wright, & Gonick, 1946; Barker, Wright, Meyerson, & Gonick, 1953; Wright, 1959).

The latter group adopted a Lewinian field-theoretical approach, and their views had a social-psychological orientation. After they published their initial works, their ideas were elaborated on by both Meyerson and Wright. Meyerson (whose theory is described elsewhere in this chapter) later became more behavioristic, favoring the use of operant conditioning in rehabilitation practice, while employing constructs about inner psychological states in speculative, theoretical, or didactic discussions.

Wright's theory remained social-psychological, placing greater emphasis on "internal" constructs: feelings, values, and the self-concept. It stressed relations between persons with disabilities and persons who were able-bodied, and proposed that the severity of handicap could be increased or diminished by environmental conditions. The theory tended to be eclectic, incorporating findings and ideas from research and theories of many kinds, and it has stood the test of time because it is comprehensive and resilient. It continues to provide satisfying insights to people who are experienced in working with the disabled, and it is intuitively appealing to people who are not.

Status considerations: "As if" behavior. Wright's analysis begins with a consideration of the status positions of people with disabilities. In general, this status is described as being similar to that of other underprivileged minority groups. However, the situation is somewhat more difficult for the disabled because persons with physical disabilities do not share a common or distinctive heritage with each other; therefore, it is harder for them to develop shared goals and pride in group identity.

Because of the threat of being placed into inferior social positions, and because of society's pressure to idolize normal standards of physical functioning and appearance, people with disabilities may prefer to resist being identified as such. A disability is often taken as *prima facie* evidence of personal as well as social inferiority; someone with a disability may therefore react by trying to deceive himself and others into thinking that the disability does not exist ("as if" behavior). This creates difficulties because such deceit arouses guilt and prevents acceptance of one's identity: "as if" behavior

can be carried out only by a person who remains vigilant lest he reveal his disability (Wright, 1960, pp. 13–56).

Wright's theory recognizes that not all social reactions to persons with disabilities are repressive or denigrating. In some respects, society places them in a salutary status position (1960, pp. 57–85). For example, society often acknowledges that people with disabilities may display positive, even admirable, personality characteristics and may have gained depth of understanding as a result of having suffered.

"As if" behavior, and other devices (such as overcompensation) that are designed to evade prejudices, become less necessary if the person accepts the disability as nondevaluating and establishes a sufficiently strong sense of personal identity and self-worth. Much of this theory is therefore devoted to delineating the conditions under which self-worth develops.

Coping versus succumbing. Central to understanding the attitudes and adjustment to disablement is the proposition that the perceived nature of a misfortune is influenced by two vastly different frameworks or orientations (Wright 1960, pp. 59–70; 1975). On the one hand, the succumbing framework highlights the negative impact of having a disability. It emphasizes what the person cannot do, what is denied to the person, what beats the person down. The possibility of living with a disability on satisfactory terms is minimized or ignored. On the other hand, the coping framework orients the person to scan problems in search of solutions and satisfactions. People with disabilities are viewed as being able to take an active role in meeting life's problems. Their assets are valued irrespective of their standing against some norm; what each person can do is appreciated. Both person and environment are seen as sources for constructive change.

The conceptualization of the coping and succumbing frameworks has been applied to fund-raising and health-care campaigns. It has also been applied to understanding reactions to disability-related objects or activities (Wright, 1967; 1974). For example, viewed in a succumbing way, a wheelchair is an unattractive symbol of incapacity; viewed in a coping framework, the same wheelchair is an admirably designed vehicle that opens up opportunities to people who have difficulty walking.

Expectation discrepancy. Another key concept is expectation discrepancy, a state in which an observed fact fails to coincide with what had been anticipated (Wright, 1960, pp. 70–78). The person, whether outsider or insider, then feels a need to explain why the discrepancy took place; at this point, important changes in adaptation can occur. For example, if a person with a disability performs more competently than was thought possible, the way is open for revision of conceptions of the seriousness of the physical condition and of the plight of the person who has it.

The outcomes of resolution in expectation discrepancies are not always favorable. Viewed in a succumbing framework, a better-than-expected performance could be interpreted as a matter of luck; or its value could be discounted as not amounting to much (walking six steps is not "really walking"). The concept of expectation discrepancy helps explain why the presentation of information alone is not always effective in altering attitudes and beliefs.

Devaluation; spread; the requirement of mourning. In Wright's theory (as in Barker's, Dembo's, and Meyerson's), an important concept in explaining adverse psychological reactions is *devaluation of the person.* Inferior social status, along with emphasis upon the succumbing aspects of disability, work their effects on the individual by expressing or implying that all persons with disabilities are diminished in total worth (Wright, 1960, pp. 131–132). The tendency to respond to loss of a specific body part or function by lessening the value of the whole person is called *spread* (Wright, 1960, pp. 118–128).

For a person with a disability, spread may occur in response to the *requirement of mourning;* this is a set of forces that makes someone who has experienced a loss feel that guilt, shame, and suffering are necessary and appropriate responses to his or her condition (Wright, 1960, pp. 242–243). These forces may operate on both the social and the individual levels; the extent to which they function within the individual is determined by the degree to which the person has incorporated social judgments into his or her own self-concept.

Social implications. As is evident, this theory is consistent with the proposition that personal adjustment to disability can be expected to show improvement commensurate with society's acknowledgment that persons with disabilities have the same rights, and should have the same opportunities, as everyone else. A good example of this proposition is the recommendation by Wright that persons in rehabilitation not be treated in a subsidiary role, but be admitted to treatment teams as co-managers of their own programs.

The theory can also be called upon to support the formation of self-help groups of persons with disabilities. Obviously, such groups provide a means for individuals to share concerns and strengthen each other by jointly asserting their legitimate demands. If the theory is correct, the resulting benefits will not merely affect social attitudes; they will improve the personal adjustments of many who have disabilities, and they will make physical disability less traumatic for those who encounter it for the first time. Differentiating personal characteristics from conditions in the environment that aid or hinder adjustment has also been stressed and examined as a problem of causal attribution (Wright, 1975).

Values. Along with recognition of the importance of social and environmental variables, a central theme in this theory is its stress on values and value changes. The theory postulates two important value gradients: the *status-value* gradient, which is essentially socially or culturally determined, and the *self-connection* gradient, which reflects how crucial a particular object or characteristic is to a person's self-concept. Something that is high on one gradient may not be high on the other. High status value is associated with being a country-and-western music star; but that achievement is high on the self-connection gradient only for persons who desire it. As a rule, integrity and attractiveness of the personal body are high on both gradients. Consequently, when disability occurs, the loss is usually accompanied by loss in self-esteem, until the person is able to interpret the meaning of the disability within a revised system of values.

Four value changes conducive to accepting a disability as non-devaluating have been distinguished (Wright, 1960, pp. 108–137; 1967):

1. *Enlarging the scope of values:* widening one's personal perspective to include positive interests beyond the disability and the self.
2. *Subordinating physique:* allowing values other than physique to assume greater potency.
3. *Containing disability effects:* preventing disability-related limitations from spreading to nondisability-connected areas of life.
4. *Upholding asset evaluation:* placing the emphasis upon what the individual can do in relation to situational (rather than normative) standards; allowing the person to make use of his abilities without being discredited or shamed by unwarranted comparisons or status judgments.

Developmental considerations. In dealing with developmental problems associated with disability, this theory stresses the importance of separating knowledge about the succumbing aspects of disability from the core of the child's self-concept. The best way to achieve this is to have those who love the child help him become aware of the negative aspects of disability within a coping framework. A context of interpersonal acceptance allows the child to experience that he or she

is loved in spite of the disability, and to establish a core of self-esteem that is sufficiently strong to endure the rejection that children with disabilities often encounter.

Adolescence may pose especially difficult problems. It is a time during which physique assumes particular importance, even for children without disabilities. Physical functions affected by a disability are therefore likely to seem especially significant during this period, for they will be evaluated in a context of generally heightened body awareness.

Another reason for difficulty is that the adolescent with a physical disability must endure at least two kinds of overlapping situations. The first is the overlap between adulthood expectations and childhood expectations; this type of overlap is a common concern for all adolescents. The second is the overlap between expectations that the young person act and think like someone with a physical disability and expectations that he or she act and think like someone with a typical physique. These types of overlap tend to exacerbate each other, and resolution of either can be more difficult than is the case when disability is not present to complicate the process. Problems of adjustment can also be expected when disability prolongs an adolescent's period of economic dependence, postpones marriage, or interferes with emotional separation from parents.

People with disabilities often report that adolescence is a trying time, especially with respect to sexual adjustment. But blame for these problems cannot be placed on disability alone, for adolescence is equally trying for many adolescents who do not have disabilities. Many factors enter into the creation and resolution of problems of adjustment in adolescence; physical deviation is only one of these factors, and often it is not the most important (Wright, 1960; pp. 179–207).

Interpersonal relations and self esteem. Wright's theory does not propose a specific psychology of disability. It rejects the idea that particular body conditions are associated with particular personality types. It also rejects the notion that degree or severity of disability is correlated in any systematic way with level of maladjustment. It regards physical disability as a potential source of problems; but it sees positive valuing processes, the encouragement of hope, and an emphasis on coping potentialities as powerful forces for counteracting or mitigating these problems.

The theory's major focus is on the use of interpersonal relations to strengthen self-esteem: "Inner strength and self-respect grow in a relationship in which the person feels that he has an important role in planning his life and that what he says and what he feels are regarded as important" (Wright, 1960, p. 346). This statement contains the most important features of social-personal theory. First, it identifies positive adjustment in terms of intrapersonal characteristics (inner strength and self-respect). Second, it stresses the interpersonal environment, as a determinant of the extent to which positive inner adjustment can take place. Finally, it emphasizes values, by attributing growth of positive adjustment to conditions that foster feelings of personal worth.

SUMMARY AND CONCLUSION

The consequences of disability appear at four overlapping levels of causal complexity. Direct effects contain the fewest intermediate processes between physical state and behavioral response. Instrumental effects influence intermediate processes, affect more complex learned adaptive behaviors, and are sensitive to higher-level consequences. Emotional reactions are still more general, because they occur at the level of feelings rather than that of specific acts or skills. Molar reactions are most inclusive; they are individualized and reflect the overall meaning of disability in the whole life situation of the person.

This chapter described theories about reactions at the highest levels. These theories have followed the same course of historical development as other theories in psychology. None has proved to be wholly correct, but all contribute valuable insights. A tendency exists to dispense with theorizing, in favor of direct problem-solving approaches. However, theories serve essential purposes when properly constructed and understood.

A good theory is both generalizable and applicable to individuals. It describes relevant phenomena in the fewest possible terms. It stresses relationships rather than mere associations. It facilitates practical decision making. It is dynamic, genotypic, and oriented to contemporaneous events and forces. It stimulates research by asking important questions and suggesting new courses of action.

Because they are recent and difficult to test, most theories about molar reactions to physical disability are either implicit or informal. Sometimes they foster stereotyped thinking, and often they are resistant to change.

Conventional theories of personality pay little attention to problems of adjustment to disability. Adler's concept of organ inferiority has not proven useful, although the related notion of compensation once exerted a powerful influence on rehabilitation practices. Goldstein's holistic approach profoundly affected other theorists whose views later became important in psychology and rehabilitation.

Psychoanalytic personality types and defense mechanisms have been used to explain reactions to illness and disability. Six types of patients identified by this theory are: oral, compulsive, hysterical, masochistic, paranoid, narcissistic, and schizoid. The defense mechanisms that have been identified as relevant are: intellectualization, rationalization (or resignation), regression, reaction formation, projection, displacement, withdrawal, and denial.

Behavioristic theories focus less on providing explanations than on devising techniques for making people with disabilities behave in desirable ways. Consequently, behaviorism stresses the need to control the environment, especially the provision of reinforcers, to assure that patients' responses are appropriate to the goals of rehabilitation.

Specificity theory is the doctrine that specific physical illnesses or disabilities are associated with particular molar adaptive reactions. Psychosomatics stresses the importance of personality problems in causing physical illnesses. Somatopsychology sees illness and disability as raising important problems that both the individual and the wider society must face. Both approaches have tended to develop holistic views, which de-emphasize the distinction between the psychosomatic and the somatopsychological directions of causation.

Bakan's theory of telic centralization and decentralization integrates research on stress with psychoanalysis and the holistic approach. Shontz's six principles of individual adaptation represent an effort to express the essentials of holism. The principles are: multiple causality; integration; interpreted reality; contemporaneity; construal of the past and anticipation of the future; and unity of organism and environment.

The concept of body image provides a base upon which many have attempted to build unified theories of personality. However, the meanings assigned to the term *body image* are too varied to support optimism that this development will occur.

Theories of grief and mourning provide explanations of reactions to physical illness and disability. One group of theories maintains that grief is an illness that occurs in response to the loss of something important to the self-concept. Reactions to loss occur in stages: first comes numbness; then pining; then depression and anger. Recovery from grief is automatic, like the healing of a wound, provided that complications do not occur.

Some points of view are based on the idea that death, being the ultimate loss, is the focal point around which all psychological adjustment is organized. However, there is disagreement about the meaning of death. On the one hand, it is described as the source of ultimate and overwhelming terror. On the other hand, studies of the dying show that the prospect of death need not be horrifying and that death is often well-accepted if the patient is not demoralized by social forces. Adaptation to death takes place in stages, which Weisman identified as: denial and postponement; mitigation and displacement; and counter-control and cessation. Kübler-Ross identified them as denial, anger, bargaining, depression, and acceptance.

Theories that deal with change and crisis resolution have broader applicability than theories of grief and loss. The former make the point that mere replacement of a lost object or function is not enough; adaptation is a search for meaning, not for substitutes.

One form of crisis theory identifies three basic stages in adaptation: realization, defensive retreat, and acknowledgment. The last two stages recur in cycles and eventually produce a psychological structure that is better differentiated and more mature than the one that existed before the crisis.

A number of theories take a socio-cultural perspective. They identify illness and disability, not as physical states, but as deviations from social norms. The concept of the *sick role* recognizes that society provides special status for people whom it regards as being ill or disabled. The concept of *illness behavior* explains reactions to illness in more individualistic terms while still placing stress on cultural conditioning.

Field-theoretical approaches integrate social and individual factors into a comprehensive explanation of reactions to disability. They usually accept the axiom that disabilities are social judgments. Meyerson's theory emphasizes that maladjustment occurs only when a person accepts devaluation imposed by others. This theory reveals the special dangers associated with new and overlapping psychological situations. It identifies three basic strategies of adjustment to disability: identification with the world of disability; identification with the world of the nondisabled; and compromise. Each may be appropriate for different types of persons or circumstances.

Dembo proposed that differences between the viewpoints of outsiders (professionals or scientists) and insiders (sufferers) produce two essentially different sets of psychological principles. The value systems associated with these principles are often so contradictory that they prevent one system from adequately utilizing knowledge gained in the other. Dembo maintained that conventional psychology will contribute meaningfully to rehabilitation only when it becomes willing to incorporate and adapt to the views and needs of sufferers.

Because outsiders seem to have all the power, it is easy to develop an approach that blames all problems on the environment. Most extreme are theories that, in effect, accuse persons without disabilities of distortion of reality in their perceptions of people with disabilities. Less extreme views assert that the psychological problems of persons with disabilities are the same as the problems everyone experiences in establishing personal identity. Adjustment is only made more difficult for persons with atypical physiques by the insensitivity of the environment to their special requirements.

The most comprehensive theory is social-personal theory. Although this theory recognizes the social origin of many problems, it also emphasizes internal factors such as feelings, values, and self-regard. Siller's theory represents an eclectic approach. Wright's theory includes considerations of social status, of forces that stress the coping or succumbing aspects of disability, of social and personal expectancies and expectation discrepancies, of reactions to loss and devaluation, and of the role that personal values play in adjustment. This theory is comprehensive, flexible, and intuitively appealing. Most important, it satisfies many of the criteria of a good theory of molar reactions to physical disability.

REFERENCES

ALEXANDER, F., FRENCH, T. M., & POLLOCK, G. H. *Psychosomatic specificity, Vol. 1: Experimental study and results.* Chicago: University of Chicago Press, 1968.

ALLPORT, G. A. The fruits of eclecticism—bitter or sweet. *Acta Psychologica*, 1964, 23, 27–44.

ALTSHULER, K. Z. Reaction to and management of sensory loss: Blindness and deafness. In B. Schoenberg, A. C. Carr, D. Peretz, & A. H. Kutscher (Eds.). *Loss and grief: Psychological management in medical practice.* New York: Columbia University Press, 1970, pp. 140–155.

ANGYAL, A. *Foundations for a science of personality.* New York: Commonwealth Fund, 1941.

ANSBACHER, H. L., & ANSBACHER, R. R. *The individual psychology of Alfred Adler: A systematic presentation of selections from his writings.* New York: Basic Books, 1956.

ASCH, M. J. The psychologist in the spinal cord injury center. *Psychological Aspects of Disability,* 1970, 17, 79–82.

ASKEN, M. J. Behavioral techniques and orthopedic disability: A review. *Rehabilitation Psychology,* 1976, 23, 41–64.

BAKAN, D. *Disease, pain and sacrifice: Toward a psychology of suffering.* Chicago: University of Chicago Press, 1968.

BARKER, R. G. (Ed.). *The stream of behavior.* New York: Appleton-Century-Crofts, 1963.

————. Explorations of ecological psychology. *American Psychologist*, 1965, *20*, 1–14.

————. *Ecological psychology*. Stanford: Stanford University Press, 1968.

BARKER, R. G., & GUMP, P. V. *Big school, small school*. Stanford: Stanford University Press, 1964.

BARKER, R. G., & WRIGHT, H. F. *One boy's day*. New York: Harper & Row, 1951.

————. *Midwest and its children*. New York: Harper & Row, 1955.

BARKER, R. G., WRIGHT, B. A., & GONICK, M. R. *Adjustment to physical handicap and illness: A survey of the social psychology of physique and disability*. New York: Social Science Research Council, Bulletin 55, 1946.

BARKER, R. G., WRIGHT, B. A., MEYERSON, L., & GONICK, M. R. *Adjustment to physical handicap and illness: A survey of the social psychology of physique and disability* (rev. ed.). New York: Social Science Research Council, Bulletin 55 (rev.), 1953.

BECKER, E. *The denial of death*. New York: The Free Press, Macmillan Publishing Co., 1973.

————. *Escape from evil*. New York: The Free Press, Macmillan Publishing Co., 1975.

BLACHER, R. S. Reaction to chronic illness. In B. Schoenberg, A. C. Carr, D. Peretz, & A. H. Kutscher (Eds.). *Loss and grief: Psychological management in medical practice*. New York: Columbia University Press, 1970, pp. 189–198.

BOWLBY, J. Process of mourning. *International Journal of Psychoanalysis*, 1961, *42*, 319–320.

BRIELAND, D. Rehabilitation psychologists: Roles and functions. In W. S. Neff (Ed.). *Rehabilitation psychology*. Washington, D.C.: American Psychological Association, 1970, pp. 265–286.

CAMPBELL, J. *The masks of God: Creative mythology*. New York: The Viking Press, 1970.

CONROE, R. M. The psycho-ecological approach: A new model for psychologists functioning on spinal cord injury service. *Rehabilitation Psychology*, 1974, *21*, 34–38.

CORSINI, R. J. (Ed.). *Current personality theories*. Itasca, Ill.: F. E. Peacock, Publishers, 1977.

DEMBO, T. Rehabilitation psychology and its immediate future: A problem of utilization of psychological knowledge. *Rehabilitation Literature*, 1969, *16*, 63–72.

————. The utilization of psychological knowledge in rehabilitation. *Welfare Review*, 1970, *8* (4), 1–7.

DEMBO, T., LEVITON, G. L., & WRIGHT, B. A. Adjustment to misfortune—A problem of social-psychological rehabilitation. *Artificial Limbs*, 1956, *3*, 4–62.

DILLER, L. Cognitive and motor aspects of handicapping conditions in the neurologically impaired. In W. S. Neff (Ed). *Rehabilitation Psychology*. Washington, D.C.: American Psychological Association, 1971, pp. 1–32.

DOUGLAS, W. O. *Go east young man: The early years*. New York: Random House, 1974.

EVANS, R. E. *B. F. Skinner, the man and his ideas*. New York: Dutton, 1968.

FINK, S. L. Crisis and motivation: A theoretical model. *Archives of Physical Medicine and Rehabilitation*, 1967, *48*, 592–597.

FISHER, S. *Body experience in fantasy and behavior*. New York: Appleton-Century-Crofts, 1970.

FISHER, S. & CLEVELAND, S. E. Personality, perception, and body image boundary. In S. Wapner & H. Werner (Eds.). *The body percept*. New York: Random House, 1965, pp. 48–67.

————. *Body image and personality* (2nd ed.). New York: Dover Publications, 1968.

FORDYCE, W. E. Behavioral methods in rehabilitation. In W. S. Neff (Ed.). *Rehabilitation Psychology*. Washington, D.C.: American Psychological Association, 1971, pp. 74–108.

FORDYCE, W. E., FOWLER, R. S., JR., LEHMANN, J. F., DE LATEUR, B. J., SAND, P. L., & TRIESCHMANN, R. B. Operant conditioning in the treatment of chronic pain. *Archives of Physical Medicine and Rehabilitation*, 1973, *54*, 399–408.

FREUD, S. *Beyond the pleasure principle* (trans. by J. Strachey). New York: Liveright, 1950.

———. *The ego and the id* (trans. by J. Strachey). New York: Norton, 1961.

GOLDSTEIN, K. *The organism: A holistic approach to biology derived from pathological data in men*. New York: American Book Co., 1939.

———. *Human nature in the light of psychopathology*. Cambridge, Mass: Harvard University Press, 1940.

———. *After-effects of brain injuries in war*. New York: Grune & Stratton, 1942.

HALL, C. S., & LINDZEY, G. *Theories of personality* (2nd ed.). New York: John Wiley & Sons, 1973.

HALL, M. H. An interview with "Mr. Behaviorist," B. F. Skinner. *Psychology Today*, 1967, *1* (5), 65–70.

HANSON, R. W. The psycho-ecological approach to spinal cord injury rehabilitation: A behaviorist perspective. *Rehabilitation Psychology*, 1974, *21*, 39–43.

HOFMANN, A. D., BECKER, R. D., & GABRIEL, H. P. *The hospitalized adolescent: A guide to managing the ill and injured youth*. New York: Free Press, Macmillan Co., 1976.

ILLICH, I. *Medical nemesis: The expropriation of health*. New York: Pantheon Books, Random House, 1976.

INCE, L. P. *The rehabilitation medicine services*. Springfield, Ill: Charles C Thomas, 1974.

———. *Behavior modification in rehabilitation*. Springfield, Ill: Charles C Thomas, 1976.

JANIS, I. *Psychological stress*. New York: John Wiley & Sons, Inc., 1958.

KAHANA, R. J., & BIBRING, G. L. Personality types in medical management. In N. E. Zinberg (Ed.). *Psychiatry and medical practice in a general hospital*. New York: International Universities Press, 1964, pp. 108–123.

KELLY, G. A. *The psychology of personal constructs, Vol. 1 & 2*. New York: Norton, 1955.

———. Man's construction of his alternatives. In G. Lindzey (Ed.). *The assessment of human motives*. New York: Rinehart, 1968.

KIRTLEY, D. D. *The psychology of blindness*. Chicago: Nelson-Hall, 1975.

KÜBLER-ROSS, E. *On death and dying*. New York: Macmillan, 1969.

LEVITON, G. L. Professional-client relations in a rehabilitation hospital setting. In W. S. Neff (Ed.). *Rehabilitation Psychology*. Washington, D.C.: American Psychological Association, 1971, pp. 215–247.

———. Professional and client viewpoints on rehabilitation issues. *Rehabilitation Psychology*, 1973, *20*, 1–80.

LEWIN, K. W. *Principles of topological psychology*. New York: McGraw-Hill Book Co., Inc., 1936.

LINDEMANN, E. Symptomatology and management of acute grief. *American Journal of Psychiatry*, 1944, *101*, 141–146.

LIPOWSKI, Z. J. New perspectives in psychosomatic medicine. *Canadian Psychiatric Association Journal*, 1970, *15*, 515–525.

———. Introduction: Current trends in psychosomatic medicine. *International Journal of Psychiatry in Medicine*, 1974, *5*, 303–308. (a)

———. Physical illness and psychopathology. *International Journal of Psychiatry in Medicine*, 1974, *5*, 483–497. (b)

MAHONEY, M. J. *Cognition and behavior modification*. Cambridge, Mass.: Ballinger, 1974.

———. Reflections on the cognitive-learning trend in psychotherapy. *American Psychologist*, 1977, *32*, 5–13.

MARRIS, P. *Loss and change*. New York: Random House, 1974.

MARROW, A. J. *The practical theorist: The life and work of Kurt Lewin*. New York: Basic Books, 1969.

MASLOW, A. H. *Motivation and personality* (2nd ed.). New York: Harper & Row, 1970.

McNEILL, W. H. *Plagues and peoples*. Garden City, N.Y.: Anchor Press, Doubleday, 1976.

MECHANIC, D. The concept of illness behavior. *Journal of Chronic Diseases*, 1962, *15*, 189–194.

———. Response factors in illness: The study of illness behavior. In E. G. Jaco (ed.). *Patients, physicians, and illness* (2nd ed.). New York: The Free Press, Macmillan Co., 1972, pp. 128–140.

MEYERSON, L. A psychology of impaired hearing. In W. M. Cruickshank (Ed.). *Psychology of exceptional children and youth* (2nd ed.). Englewood Cliffs, N.J.: Prentice-Hall, 1963, pp. 118–191. *(a)*

———. Somatopsychology of physical disability. In W. M. Cruickshank (Ed.). *Psychology of exceptional children and youth* (2nd ed.). Englewood Cliffs, N.J.: Prentice-Hall, 1963, pp. 1–52. *(b)*

———. Somatopsychology of physical disability. In W. M. Cruickshank (Ed.). *Psychology of exceptional children and youth* (3rd ed.). Englewood Cliffs, N.J.: Prentice-Hall, 1971, pp. 1–74.

MICHAEL, J. L. Rehabilitation. In C. Neuringer & J. L. Michael (Eds.). *Behavior modification in clinical psychology.* New York: Appleton-Century-Crofts, 1970, pp. 52–85.

MICHAL-SMITH, H. Psychological factors in the therapist-patient relationship in the rehabilitation process. *Rehabilitation Literature,* 1962, *23,* 66–69, 95.

MONBECK, M. E. *The meaning of blindness: Attitudes toward blindness and blind people.* Bloomington, Indiana: Indiana University Press, 1973.

MYKLEBUST, H. R. *The psychology of deafness: Sensory deprivation, learning, and adjustment.* New York: Grune & Stratton, 1960.

ORFIRER, A. P. Loss of sexual function in the male. In B. Schoenberg, A. C. Carr, D. Peretz, & A. H. Kutscher (Eds.). *Loss and grief: Psychological management in medical practice.* New York: Columbia University Press, 1970, pp. 156–177.

PARKES, C. M. *Bereavement: Studies of grief in adult life.* New York: International Universities Press, 1972.

PARSONS, T. *The social system.* New York: The Free Press, 1951.

———. Definitions of health and illness in the light of American values and social structure. In E. G. Jaco (Ed.). *Patients, physicians, and illness* (2nd ed.). New York: The Free Press, Macmillan, 1972, pp. 107–127.

ROMM, M. E. Loss of sexual function in the female. In B. Schoenberg, A. C. Carr, D. Peretz, & A. H. Kutscher (Eds.). *Loss and grief: Psychological management in medical practice.* New York: Columbia University Press, 1970, pp. 178–188.

ROTH, J. A., & EDDY, E. M. *Rehabilitation for the unwanted.* New York: Atherton Press, 1967.

SCHILDER, P. *The image and appearance of the human body.* New York: International Universities Press, 1950.

SCHOENBERG, B., & CARR, A. C. Loss of external organs: Limb amputation, mastectomy, and disfiguration. In B. Schoenberg, A. C. Carr, D. Peretz, & A. H. Kutscher (Eds.). *Loss and grief: Psychological management in medical practice.* New York: Columbia University Press, 1970, pp. 119–131.

SCHOENBERG, B., CARR, A. C., PERETZ, D., & KUTSCHER, A. H. (Eds.). *Loss and grief: Psychological management in medical practice.* New York: Columbia University Press, 1970.

SCHOENBERG, B., CARR, A. C., KUTSCHER, A. H., PERETZ, D., & GOLDBERG, I. (Eds.). *Anticipatory grief.* New York: Columbia University Press, 1974.

SELYE, H. *The stress of life.* New York: McGraw-Hill, 1956.

———. The evolution of the stress concept. *American Scientist,* 1973, *61,* 692–699.

SHONTZ, F. C. Reactions to crisis. *Volta Review,* 1965, *67,* 364–370.

———. Behavior settings may affect rehab. client. *Rehabilitation Record,* 1967, *8* (2), 37–40.

———. *Perceptual and cognitive aspects of body experience.* New York: Academic Press, 1969.

———. Physical disability and personality: Theory and recent research. *Rehabilitation Psychology,* 1970, *17,* 51–69.

———. Physical disability and personality. In W. S. Neff (Ed.). *Rehabilitation Psychology.* Washington, D.C.: American Psychological Association, 1971, pp. 33–73.

————. Severe chronic illness. In J. F. Garrett & E. S. Levine (Eds.). *Rehabilitation practices with the physically disabled.* New York: Columbia University Press, 1973, pp. 119–148.

————. Body image and its disorders. *International Journal of Psychiatry in Medicine,* 1974, *5,* 461–472.

————. *The psychological aspects of physical illness and disability.* New York: Macmillan, 1975.

————. Handicap, physical: Psychological aspects. In B. B. Wolman (Ed.). *International Encyclopedia of Psychiatry, Psychology, Psychoanalysis, and Neurology* (vol 5). Boston, Mass.: Van Nostrand Reinhold (Aesculopius Publishers), 1977, pp. 318–322.

————. Psychological adjustment to physical disability: Trends in theories. *Archives of Physical Medicine and Rehabilitation,* 1978, *59,* 251–254.

SILLER, J. Attitudes toward disability. In H. Rusalem & D. Malikin (Eds.). *Contemporary vocational rehabilitation.* New York: New York University Press, 1976, pp. 67–80. *(a)*

————. Psychosocial aspects of physical disability. In J. Meislin (Ed.). *Rehabilitation medicine and psychiatry.* Springfield, Ill.: Charles C Thomas Publisher, 1976. *(b)*

SILLER, J., CHIPMAN, A., FERGUSON, L. T., & VANN, D. H. Attitudes of the nondisabled toward the physically disabled. *Studies in Reactions to Disability: XI.* New York: School of Education, New York University, 1967.

SILLER, J., FERGUSON, L. T., VANN, D. H., & HOLLAND, B. Structure of attitudes toward the physically disabled. *Studies in Reactions to Disability: XII.* New York: School of Education, New York University, 1967.

SKINNER, B. F. Are theories of learning necessary? *Psychological Review,* 1950, *57,* 193–216.

SPAR, H. J. The deaf-blind. In J. F. Garrett & E. S. Levine (Eds.). *Rehabilitation practices with the physically disabled.* New York: Columbia University Press, 1973, pp. 497–524.

TWADDLE, A. C. The concepts of the sick role and illness behavior. *Advances in Psychosomatic Medicine,* 1972, *8,* 162–179.

VERNON, M. Early profound deafness. In J. F. Garrett & E. S. Levine (Eds.). *Rehabilitation practices with the physically disabled.* New York: Columbia University Press, 1973, pp. 461–496.

VINEBERG, S. E., & WILLEMS, E. P. Observation and analysis of patient behavior in the rehabilitation hospital. *Archives of Physical Medicine and Rehabilitation,* 1971, *52,* 8–14.

WEISMAN, A. D. *On dying and denying: A psychiatric study of terminality.* New York: Behavioral Publications, Inc., 1972.

WILLEMS, E. P. T. The interface of the hospital environment and patient behavior. *Archives of Physical Medicine and Rehabilitation,* 1971, *53,* 115–122.

WRIGHT, B. A. (Ed.). *Psychology and rehabilitation.* Washington, D.C.: American Psychological Association, 1959.

WRIGHT, B. A. *Physical disability—A psychological approach.* New York: Harper & Row, 1960.

————. Issues in overcoming emotional barriers to adjustment in the handicapped. *Rehabilitation Counseling Bulletin,* 1967, *11,* 53–59.

————. Strengthening the self-concept. In J. F. Magary, L. F. Buscaglia, & B. Light (Eds.). *Sixth annual distinguished lectures in special education and rehabilitation.* Los Angeles: University of Southern California, School of Education, 1968, pp. 24–38.

————. Value-laden beliefs and principles for rehabilitation psychology. *Rehabilitation Psychology,* 1972, *19,* 38–45.

————. Changes in attitudes toward people with handicaps. *Rehabilitation Literature,* 1973, *34,* 354–368.

————. An analysis of attitudes—Dynamics and effects. *New Outlook for the Blind,* 1974, *67,* 108–118.

————. Social-psychological leads to enhance rehabilitation effectiveness. *Rehabilitation Counseling Bulletin,* 1975, *18,* 214–223.

2 A Handicap as a Social Phenomenon

Nettie R. Bartel

Ph.D., Professor of Special Education, College of Education, Temple University.

Samuel L. Guskin

Ph.D., Professor of Education, Department of Special Education, School of Education, Indiana University.

In the fields of special education and rehabilitation it is generally assumed that one is dealing with disabled or handicapped individuals; that is, persons who have certain intrinsically unhealthy or undesirable characteristics which has been or may be diagnosed by a physician or psychologist and which require a distinctive treatment procedure. In this chapter we take the position that what is distinctive about and common to all handicapped individuals is not so much their own characteristics as it is the characteristic response of others to them. A handicapped person is someone whom others think is incompetent or unattractive; someone whom others want to help or protect or avoid. Physicians, psychologists, educators, and rehabilitation experts merely rationalize and institutionalize the layman's pity and antipathy. That is, professionals create terminology, organizations, and treatment patterns which foster and stabilize the distinctive status relationship between handicapped persons and others.

The fields of special education and rehabilitation exist not only because many children have certain distinctive physical and behavioral characteristics, but because *our society chooses* to treat such children differentially, because other people define them as creating a problem, and because social agencies, particularly the schools, choose to create special arrangements for dealing with them. In this chapter we shall draw out the implications of this definition of the exceptional child and adult in terms of social response rather than individual characteristics. In doing so we shall find that the traditional categories of exceptionality vary considerably in their appropriateness and that further categories such as racial or ethnic minorities fit these social definitions as well as do conventional categories such as mental retardation and orthopedic disability.

We are not the first to take this approach, and we shall draw heavily on other sociological and social-psychological writings in the area, especially Barker and Wright (1952), Freidson (1965), Goffman (1963), Guskin (1963, 1977), Mercer (1973), Scheff (1966, 1974), and Szasz (1961, 1970). Probably Freidson's social definition of handicap is closest to our own. He states (p. 72): "What is a handicap in social terms? It is an imputation of difference from others; more particularly, imputation of an *undesirable* difference. By definition, then, a person said to be handicapped is so defined because he deviates from what he himself or others believe to be normal or appropriate."

It has probably always been recognized that disabilities have social consequences. Among the points mentioned in popular and professional lore are that nondisabled persons behave differently toward the disabled, that the disabled feel uncomfortable in normal social situations, that frustration and feelings of inadequacy stemming from limited competence lead to inappropriate social behavior, that the sensory, motor, or intellectual limitations themselves make normal social interchange difficult. Educational and rehabilitation agencies have usually included the reduction of social inadequacies and social problems as major goals of their activities. Perhaps the major weakness in our understanding has been the nature and consequences of our own professional activities. We have largely operated or been trained in medical settings with the result that we see our role as diagnosing and treating the illness of the individual. We tend to see social adjustment problems as a function of problems within the individual, and we are so enamoured with our diagnostic skills that we see the client's acceptance of our diagnosis as the major prerequisite for his "recovery" or adjustment.

This approach is analogous to that of a physician diagnosing the symptoms of a patient in an attempt to discover his "real" condition—is the patient suffering from an iron deficiency or a malfunctioning thyroid? Similarly, the psychologist pores over responses to the Rorschach or the Stanford-Binet in attempts to decide whether the subject is, or is not, a sociopathic personality with or without schizoid features; whether the individual is a low educable retarded person or really a high trainable individual; whether his IQ is 51 or 48. In each case a social consequence follows the diagnosis. Thus, depending on the diagnosis of the physician or psychologist, the subject may be placed in a community hospital, a convalescent home, a mental-health clinic, an institution for the mentally ill or mentally retarded, or a school or class for the educable or trainable retarded person—in each case, with others of his kind. The assumption is that some individuals *are* mentally ill, mentally retarded, physically disabled, or delinquent, and that a society is simply acknowledging the presence of preexisting, objective characteristics when it labels them as such and groups them according to their own kind.

This position has been defended in the literature by such writers as Gibbs (1972), Gove (1970, 1974, 1975), Fabrega and Manning (1972), Smith (1975), and Gordon (1975). In general, these writers have sought to establish that persons ultimately labeled as deviant have intrinsic, in some cases genetic, predispositions to that particular form of deviance; that their objective behaviors or appearance distinguish them from non-labeled groups; that many persons voluntarily seek out a deviant label; that labels are not irreversible; that persons with many resources are as likely, or more likely to be labeled than persons with few resources; and that there are many positive consequences of being labeled (such as special treatment or compensation).

The theoretical and empirical literature on this subject is far from conclusive, and it is likely that the debate over labeling will continue for some time. It is likely, given the complexity of the phenomena being investigated, that no one perspective will adequately account for the various forms of deviance in the society, or even for all instances of any one form. For example, Guskin (1977), in evaluating the labeling perspective's usefulness in understanding social processes in mental retardation, states that the perspective seems most useful with the mildly retarded, as opposed to the more severely involved. Further, according to Guskin, the labeling perspective appears to account quite well for the social system within the school, but less well when one looks at the society as a whole.

The societal perspective does facilitate the examination of a number of questions that are frequently disregarded in discussions of the education of handicapped children. In what social or educational circumstances are children likely to be labeled different, disabled, or deviant? What are the processes through which deviant social identities are acquired? How will the child and his parents, peers, or teachers react to the social redefinition? What changes in group membership and group interactions are likely to ensue?

The purpose of this chapter is to reorient thinking about disabled persons, to shift from a focus on the problems of the disabled individual to a focus on the disabling reactions of other persons and society as a whole. The thesis of this chapter is basically that society creates and exacerbates a handicap by identifying and labeling a "condition" and by responding or treating differentially persons so labeled. The hope of this argument is that by identifying society and social response as the source of handicapped behavior we can develop some effective methods of reducing the degree of handicap.

SOCIETY AS A CREATOR OF HANDICAP

Let us assume that you now have no diagnosed disability. Is it possible that without changing your personal, physical, or social characteristics directly you can become a handicapped person? What would be required for society to define you as handicapped? Some attribute of yours would have to be reacted to as seriously unattractive or incompetent to the extent that others would want to avoid you or protect you. Consider the following possibility: You're white and you take a summer job in a camp for poor children, having answered an advertisement and applied by mail. You know a substantial proportion of the children will be black. When you arrive at the orientation session for counselors and children, you find that all the children and all the remaining counselors are black. They are surprised to find a white member on their staff. The counselors are not only black but are highly involved in asserting the value of blackness, "soul," and so forth. You have eight weeks ahead of you in this environment. Isn't your "whiteness" going to be a physical disfigurement or disability in this setting? Given the norms of this black group, everyone is courteous, but careful not to be seen as your friend or your date. You are faced with a difficult adjustment problem—you can't pass. Perhaps you can minimize your white social characteristics and be sure not to be seen as attempting to assert the appropriateness of your own standards or appearance. But regardless of your strategy, it is impossible for you to have normal social relationships in this setting. You must do the best you can, recognizing that all will see you as different and as less adequate in a critical characteristic. The essence of being handicapped is present. A social group defines standards that an individual cannot meet and then treats him as unacceptable or of lower status for failing to meet these standards.

This exercise must surely convince you that you can be handicapped, without changing your own characteristics, merely by a change in society's reaction to you. Furthermore, what initially starts out as an evaluation by *others* that you have lesser status, attractiveness, or competence quickly presents *you* with problems of self-esteem, social adjustment, and emotional tension which may in fact lead to less competent behavior on your part. By reversing the racial properties in the illustration, you can also see that being black must surely be a handicap in a white society, which may help explain why blacks often may avoid the strain of integration to seek out the comfort of homogeneous black subgroups. This influence of others' expectation about one's self upon one's own self-evaluation and behavior will be discussed at some length later.

In a more formal way, society creates deviants by selecting certain attributes or norms and calling them desirable. Individuals who fail to conform to these attributes or norms are then considered deviant and treated accordingly. The processes underlying this phenomenon are considered in the following section.

SOCIAL CATEGORIZATION

Although human beings are presumed to differ on a great number of traits, attributes, behaviors, and beliefs, classifications are ordinarily made according to only a few of these. Thus, individuals are commonly thought of as belonging to similar groups according to skin color, for example, but not according to the color of eyes or hair. Similarly, individuals are sorted (in schools) according to intellectual ability, but often not according to perceptual or motor ability.

In some instances school children have been (and still are) grouped on the basis of attributes that are completely irrelevant to school achievement, or grouped in ways that clearly attenuate their academic performance. The most conspicuous example of this occurrence is in the grouping of school children on the basis of skin color (Coleman et al., 1966). Again, orthopedically handicapped children are frequently excluded from school, but not necessarily because they are unable to benefit from classroom instruction.

In other areas of life classification, patterns of various public and private institutions of the society reveal inconsistencies. To cite an example from a professional field, Phillips and his associates (1975) note that typical psychiatric classification schemes have little to do with observable behavior in real life situations and typically carry no implications for the treatment that the client should undergo. The classification of individuals as delinquent varies greatly from state to state and within the same state as to what behaviors shall determine such a status. An informal type of classification operates in the belief among many employers that high school dropouts are necessarily incompetent workers. Actually, these employers' refusals to hire dropouts probably are more the result of custom than of any rational belief that skills learned in the later years of high school make the individual a more competent waitress, truck driver, gasoline station attendant, or whatever. Perhaps the best-known inconsistency in classification practices in this country is the fact that an individual 18 to 21 years old is considered a juvenile as far as drinking alcoholic beverages (in most states) is concerned, but is considered an adult as far as vulnerability to the draft in wartime is concerned.

These examples are meant to illustrate that much of the everyday categorizing and classifying of people is not highly rational, consistent, relevant, or useful. Even if we are willing to posit that some kind of innately given "urge to classify" (Menninger, Mayman, & Preger, 1963) is characteristic of *Homo sapiens,* we are still left with the question of who gets classified and into what kind of group.

Dexter (1958; 1964) has been more specifically concerned with the antecedents of classification patterns in this country. In particular, he has raised the question of why intellectual deviance rather than other forms of deviance (for example, awkwardness) forms the basis upon which individuals are categorized. Dexter suggests that the practice of classifying persons as mildly retarded is an outgrowth of the ideology of (1) the "Protestant ethic," with its emphasis upon achievement as a justification of one's righteousness, and (2) the French Revolutionary notion of equality, with its concern not only that the *opportunity* be equal but that the obligation to take advantage of the opportunity be equal. Dexter further contends that these twin ideologies led to compulsory education in America; consequently, a requirement for initiation into adult social status has become a "demonstration of formal skill in coordinating meaning"—that is, in reading, writing and arithmetic. He postulates that some mentally retarded persons become social problems only because of this requirement and not because of any inherent biological attribute. If this is true, much of the cost and trouble of retardation in our society is due to the socially prescribed role of the retarded rather than to any actual deficit in intelligence.

It may be that it is quite appropriate for the school to "discover" a child's intellectual deviance. Festinger (1954) suggests that a group is likely to be differentiated on the basis of some ability that is relevant and important to it. In the school, intellectual ability is of great relevance and importance; consequently, the school population is likely to be sorted according to intellectual criteria. We could hypothesize that when the school is made particularly aware of intellectual performance, or when its level of intellectual capability is made suspect, it would tend to redefine and sharpen the boundary where normalcy in intelligence ends and where deviance begins—or, to quote Dentler and Erikson (1959), "locate its position in social space by defining its symbolic boundaries" (p. 106).

Wright (1960) has some suggestions as to why certain traits of individuals rather than others tend to be used by particular groups as the basis of differentiating the deviant from the nondeviant. She suggests that there are at least two aspects of a particular trait that help determine its importance: (1) *Self-connection gradient* refers to the degree to which traits are seen as more or less related to the central "core" of the individual himself. For example, the size of a person's feet is not seen as closely related to the "real" person, and we do not ordinarily categorize people on the sizes of their feet. On the other hand, such traits as skin color or ethnic origin are seen by many people as integral to what kind of a person an individual "really" is. Wright suggests that traits described by the verb "to be" are more closely connected to self than those described by the verb "to have." Thus we speak of an individual as *being* intelligent or retarded, but as *having* brown or blond hair. (2) *Status value gradient* refers to the degree that certain attributes are more highly prized in our society than are other attributes. For example, the ability to achieve (intelligence) has high status value in our culture; therefore, persons lacking in this ability will be perceived as deficient in a part of the "self." Athletic ability is also highly prized in this society (witness the size of the salaries paid to professional athletes). Consequently, individuals who exhibit physical disabilities that interfere with their motor functioning are likely to be classified unfavorably.

LABELING, DEFINING, AND RECOGNIZING HANDICAPS

We have suggested how society creates handicaps through defining standards that others cannot meet and through creating distinctive modes of treatment for those who fail to come up to the arbitrary standards of a group. Society and social groups have a much more efficient way of handicapping an individual or group. Without clearly evaluating the extent to which an individual or group meets their own standards, a person may be rapidly identified as distinctively incompetent or unattractive merely by having a label placed upon him; for example, the labels "mentally retarded" or "mentally ill." There are few who feel that such labels are acceptable for themselves: Edgerton (1967) shows that among forty-eight subjects leaving an institution for the mentally retarded, he was unable to find one who accepted the definition of himself as retarded. It is obvious why this is the case. The labels "mentally retarded" or "mentally ill" immediately set into operation a series of value judgments about the individual, perhaps a series of important consequences for social interactions, even legal intervention, and a major change in life circumstances.

The application of the label "mentally ill" is so significant for the individual and his associates that there is often an extensive period of negotiation, in "non-developed" as well as modern western societies, before such labels are accepted as legitimate. A study by Edgerton (1969) of the recognition of mental illness in certain East African groups illustrates how a large proportion of those labeled "mentally ill" are labeled as such because the label is functional for the individual, his clan, or some other group. In one instance, a clan was able to avoid retribution for a murderer who was labeled "psychotic." In another case, an individual who was diagnosed as being mentally ill was rediagnosed as being only temporarily disturbed—in response to pressure from the members of his family, who had high personal involvement in the future professional success of the child. In our own society, we see similar negotiations in the case of murderers whose attorneys are attempting to keep them from facing the death penalty, or in the case of spouses attempting to rid themselves of unhappy marriages. A more common situation involves placing the label "mentally retarded" on a child within the public schools, where teacher, psychologist, principal, and parents may become involved in the negotiations (which the parents usually lose). A study by Hersh (1969) suggests there may be at least an unconscious conspiracy between teacher and psychologist to define a child as "incompetent." In Hersh's investigation, examiners were given biased referrals from teachers, indicating the teacher's estimate of the child's competence. Unknown to the testers, the referrals were assigned at random to children. On an individual intelligence test, examiners obtained lower IQ scores for those children with negative referrals than they did for

comparable children on whom they had received favorable referrals. In a more typical public school situation, the psychologist may know that a teacher and principal desperately want to remove a child from his regular class, and the only place for him to go is a "special class for the mentally retarded," for which the child must obtain an IQ of 70 or less to qualify. It seems unlikely that under these conditions the psychologist will expend effort in motivating the child or will give him the benefit of the doubt.

The negotiation of an appropriate label for a child who is having academic or behavior difficulties, not surprisingly, results in quite different outcomes depending on a number of factors, including social class and race. Franks (1971), in a study of eleven Missouri school districts that provided services for both mentally retarded and learning disabled children, reported that the percentage of black children in the classes for the mentally retarded was 34.21 percent, while in the classes for the learning disabled it was only 3.22 percent.

As one would expect, data such as these have been used extensively in a number of court challenges to existing practices in school systems throughout the country. In fact, a number of educators have become disenchanted with labels of any kind. Why then, is labeling so prevalent? We have already suggested its efficiency: If a person has been provided with the label, he does not need to go through the full evaluation process with each individual he meets. The major advantage of this is to protect the observer from a serious error based on inadequate information. The problem with the control that labels have over our behavior is that most labels either are not based on valid information or lead to invalid treatment assumptions. The label "mentally retarded," for example, may be assigned to a child on the basis of his performance on an intelligence test given in a language that he is only beginning to learn. The label "emotionally disturbed" may be the result of the teacher's inability to cope with an overactive child. The treatment for the "retarded" child may be placement in a class where the teacher avoids teaching academic subject matter, thus further retarding his academic growth. For the "disturbed" child, treatment may consist of placing him with a group of aggressive children equally unacceptable to their teachers, and also termed "disturbed," who may teach him more unacceptable behavior. Notice how the treatment may only compound the problem and foster greater incompetence or unacceptable behavior in the child.

The potential advantage of the labeling process can be seen in those cases where the label prevents mistreatment of a person who would otherwise be assumed to be capable of more acceptable behavior. Knowing a person is deaf prevents us from treating him as being insulting when he doesn't respond to our requests. Being forewarned that a child is retarded will enable us to be wary of interpreting failure on a task as intentional uncooperativeness. Nevertheless, even an appropriate-seeming interpretation of a label can have unfortunate effects. As we have suggested above, children legitimately labeled retarded or disturbed are frequently placed in an environment with other children of similar diagnosis. This treatment appears self-defeating when one considers that their problem might in fact derive from having lived in an emotionally, socially, or intellectually inadequate environment. In fact, an influential theory on the etiology of delinquent behaviors suggests that this undesirable behavior is the result of excess association with persons exhibiting the behavior (Sutherland & Cressey, 1960). If children learn from their peers—and most persons agree that they do—then placing deviant children with others of their own kind is disastrous, for they will simply learn more delinquent, disturbing, or retarded behavior. The normal classroom and community environment might be a much more positive place for them.

The greatest problem of labels is their tendency to become overgeneralized. Instead of thinking of a child who has intellectual limitations or emotional problems, we think of a "mentally retarded child" or an "emotionally disturbed child." Wright (1960) has called this generalizing of the defect to the whole person a "spread effect." Persons expect that a child so labeled will differ from others in many respects aside from the specifically diagnosed disability.

One example of the tendency to set low expectations for groups designated as "handicapped" has been noted by Avery (1971). In this study, teachers who were accustomed to working with sighted children, but were now working with visually handicapped youngsters, were found to be satisfied with minimal achievement from their blind students. The combination of the label "visually handicapped" with such observable behaviors as lack of assertiveness apparently led these teachers to expect, and to be satisfied with, academic incompetence on the part of their pupils.

SOCIAL ROLES AND EXPECTATIONS

We have seen how labels can have varied consequences for the way persons are perceived by others. However, the importance of these consequences is limited by the extent to which such perceptions lead to differences in behavior. Those labels that refer to specific positions in our society, such as occupations, not only lead to perceptions of likely personal characteristics but also to perceptions regarding likely and desired behaviors to be shown by members of this category (Hughes, 1945). Such perceptions are often called "role expectations," that is, expectations of behavior to be found in particular roles. Teachers are expected to do different things than secretaries; parents are expected to do different things than children; husbands to behave differently than wives. Are disabled persons expected to do things differently than nondisabled persons?

"Expectation" has two meanings—the

belief that something is likely to happen, and the desire or demand or obligation that a particular thing happen. Both meanings are relevant in the processes through which one individual comes to view another as deviant, and in the viewer's subsequent attitudes toward the deviant. Goffman (1963) has pointed out that the anticipation in meeting a stranger has a component of expecting that he will possess certain attributes —a sound, whole body, functioning sensory abilities, normal intellectual ability, and so on. However, people do not merely anticipate that this will be the case; they transform their anticipations into "normative expectations, into righteously presented demands" (p. 2).

If people see a person with dark glasses and a white cane, they are more careful in how they walk near him, and may offer him help in crossing a street. He may accept, despite a lack of need, because he has found that people respond more pleasantly when he lets them lead him than when he refuses their offer. His family and friends may assume that he will never be self-supporting and never marry, and his attempts at courtship and independence may be rebuffed by others who can't see his competencies; only his disability. In such an instance, the social group has defined the role of "blind person" as one similar to that of a child, and the result may be childlike role behavior; that is, withdrawal into a comfortable dependency on his parents and friends.

The existence and implications of the blind-person role have been studied by Scott (1969). Scott points out that many activities termed rehabilitative are in fact socialization procedures by which the person with impaired vision is inducted into the blind-person role. Thus Scott argues that there is nothing intrinsic to blindness that causes blind people to be docile, helpless, or dependent. "Blindness is a social role that people must learn to play. Blind men are made."

When the assumption of dependence leads to dependent behavior, we are observing an instance of what has been called a "self-fulfilling prophecy." Rosenthal has written much and carried out many studies on this topic. In his earlier studies Rosenthal (1966) found that the results of psychological experiments were influenced by the experimenter's beliefs. For example, if the experimenter was told he was working with bright rats, the rats earned better learning scores than if the experimenter had been told he was studying dull rats. Rosenthal felt that the results of these studies had considerable applicability to educational problems; that teachers who believed that they had good students would get better work from the same students than if they expected poor performance.

In one well-publicized study, Rosenthal and Jacobson (1968) found that school children designated at random as "potential bloomers" by an experimenter gained more on tests of intelligence over the course of a year than children not so designated. Unfortunately, the study has several weaknesses in experimental methodology and reporting (see, for example, Thorndike, 1968). Nevertheless, the interest it aroused has led to further work on the "self-fulfilling prophecy."

Rosenthal and Jacobson proposed that the effect they found might have resulted from unconscious cues about the child's competence, which were conveyed from the teacher to the child through the teacher's facial expression, gesture, tone of voice, and so forth. The child's feelings of competence might then have led him to try harder and do better. An alternative interpretation is that teacher expectancy is most likely to influence pupil behavior when the expectation results in very overt changes in the pattern of teaching. Thus, a teacher may put a first-grade child into a higher or lower reading group, based on tests or on knowledge of the child's family; how quickly the child learns to read may then be determined by his reading group's rate of exposure to new reading material.

Guskin (1978) has suggested that it is helpful to organize alternative explanations about the "expectancy effect" in terms of a sequential causal formulation. The most simple explanation would be a direct-line relationship between the expectancy (on the part of the teacher) and the achievement (on the part of the child). Alternately, if one visualizes the expectancy effect becoming operational in a sequential fashion, it becomes possible to separate out the various aspects of the phenomenon for investigation. The sequence is that of a label (for example, "slow learner") leading to an expectancy on the part of someone (perhaps a teacher) to react in a certain way to the child in question (such as by presenting easier material) —which in turn leads to different behavior on the part of the labeled child (he learns less)—which in turn leads to poorer achievement—which causes the original label to be reinforced and the cycle of interaction to be maintained.

Beez (1968) investigated this kind of phenomenon in a controlled teaching situation. Each of sixty summer-school graduate students was asked to tutor a 5-year-old Head Start child randomly characterized on a contrived psychological report as having either high or low learning potential. Those tutors who were given reports that indicated a high expectancy for their pupils presented more words for their pupils to learn. The learning achievement of the pupils reflected the tutors' expectancies, with the high group averaging about six words, the low group averaging about three. In short, what the teacher believed as a consequence of the prior report influenced the number of words he or she presented—which, in turn, influenced the number of words learned by the pupil. Pupil response thus supported the teacher's initial belief about the pupil, though in reality it was directly a result of teacher behavior, not pupil competence.

Observations showed that fewer words were presented and learned when the teacher's expectancy of pupil ability was low, and that this came about because the teacher spent more time explaining and re-peating words. Further analysis showed that differences in learning could be accounted for by teacher expectancy, but not by teacher experience or pupil competence. The study also found that tutors rated the two groups of children differently—in accord with expectancies—on ratings of competence, task performance, future school success, and other measures.

The dramatic findings of this study—that critical differences in teaching pattern and resultant learning can be dependent upon the expectancies for pupils held by teachers —seem to have enormous implications for the education and treatment of the physically and mentally disabled. The handicapped may have less chance of becoming normal because they are felt to need special teaching; that is, teaching at a lower level of competence. What seems to be critical here is whether the assumption is made that the person has potential for intellectual (or motor or social) development, or whether it is assumed that he can make little progress. A parallel belief of the teacher or rehabilitation worker is that he can have an impact on the learning or adjustment of the pupil or client.

The expectancy studies we have presented examine reactions to information about a person, rather than cues from the person. One could build expectancies from interaction with the person, rather than seeking information about the person from other sources. The empathy or individual-sensitivity orientation often found in the helping professions emphasizes the need for accurate perception of the characteristics and feelings of the individual with whom one is working. Much research has investigated the possibility that one could identify persons who are particularly accurate in perceiving others, and that these persons would be particularly effective in dealing with others. Unfortunately, these hypotheses have not been supported. Accuracy in judging one person is largely unrelated to accuracy in judging other persons; accuracy in judging one kind of behavior is largely unrelated to accuracy in judging other kinds of behavior. Much of whatever accuracy does exist in judging others is the result of accurate stereotypes. That is, a judge can more accurately size up an individual if he has an accurate perception of what people in general are like; he can more accurately evaluate a specific 8-year-old if he knows what 8-year-olds in general are like. Very little accuracy is added by the degree to which the judge individualizes his evaluation (Cline, 1964). In other words, the understanding that a perceiver has of persons in a particular position or place in society, is his best clue to understanding individuals. This fits very well with the importance that role expectations have for behavior.

ROLE EXPECTATIONS, SELF-CONCEPT, AND BEHAVIOR

It has been shown that expectancies held by others may influence role performance. The general phenomenon is not difficult to understand. When speaking to a young child, an adult talks differently than when speaking to another adult. When an adult talks to an adolescent whom he thinks is childlike, he will speak differently than to an adolescent he thinks is adultlike. The result of talking at a lower level may be to arouse a lower-level response. If you ask a simple question, you are likely to get a simple answer. This expectancy effect is then mediated by the behavioral changes in the person holding the expectations, and may not require that the actor (the person for whom expectations are held) be aware of the expectations. The Beez and Carter studies illustrated this: the preschool children were probably not aware of what tutors' expectancies were. The children tried equally to learn the material they were presented; but tutors' expectancies led to different presentation rates.

In contrast to this behaviorally mediated effect is the kind of mediation proposed by Rosenthal and Jacobson (1968), in which the teacher unconsciously and subtly communicates a positive or negative evaluation of the child to him. This then leads the child to see himself as relatively adequate or inadequate. His own self-estimate then influences his behavior. If he thinks he can cope with something difficult, he will attempt it. If he thinks he is incompetent, he gives up. There is considerable evidence that children who achieve more poorly in school see themselves as less academically competent than their peers (Brookover *et al.*, 1965). However, it is difficult to demonstrate that low self-evaluation leads to low performance. (It is more obvious that poor performance leads to recognition of relatively low ability.) The most dramatic way of demonstrating the influence of self-perception on performance is to try to influence self-perception and to note its effects on behavior. Few studies have shown this effect. One interesting investigation by Brookover and his colleagues (1965) involved training parents to improve their children's self-evaluation regarding academic ability. The training program resulted in improved academic performance on the part of their children. However, this effect did not carry over to the next academic year. Furthermore, similar training programs with teachers and other personnel failed to modify children's achievement. It appears, then, that the most effective way to modify children's self-evaluation is to improve their performance. But the reverse effect, getting self-evaluation to influence performance, is more difficult to institute.

The self-evaluation referred to above is a direct estimate by the child of how well he does in school. Another kind of self-concept that might mediate between others' expectations and a child's behavior is locus of control, which was examined earlier as it influenced teachers' behavior. The child's feeling that what he does really makes a difference is related to how well he performs in school. Generally, as he gets older and more competent, he comes to feel more internally controlled (Bialer, 1961). The degree of internal control is related, however, to the child's ability and achievement in school: the lower the ability and achievement, the more external the control. Those groups that perform more poorly in school are as a group more external (Battle & Rotter, 1963; Bartel, 1968; Coleman *et al.*, 1966). As a result of failure in school or poor opportunities outside of school to influence their environment, these children feel less potent. Again, the most likely way to increase a person's feeling of potency is probably to demonstrate that one can have some impact in obtaining rewards from the environment.

Lipp *et al.* (1968) attempted to measure the way in which internally controlled and externally controlled physically disabled subjects performed on a perceptual task measuring defensiveness about disability. Contrary to their hypothesis, Lipp and his associates found that externally controlled subjects were less denying of their disability than were internally controlled subjects. This finding is consistent with the logic expressed by Bialer (1961, p. 317) when he states that externally controlled subjects are not likely to have, or are incapable of having, feelings of inferiority, because they do not see themselves as responsible for their failures. Thus, it is interesting to note the possibility, in the case of handicapped persons, that the externally controlled individuals may manifest satisfactory adjustments, feeling that their condition is due to luck, fate, chance, or the will of God. On the other hand, the internally controlled handicapped person, who by definition believes that his success or failure in the world is a result of his own doing, may feel guilt-ridden and blame-worthy.

Though there is little evidence that disabled persons have lower general self-evaluation than others, it seems reasonable to expect that disabled persons have particular areas in which they feel impotent or incompetent. These may be based on realistic limitations. As Wright (1960) has indicated, the problem is to prevent the spread of this effect to the rest of the self-concept.

Two possible mediators for expectancy effects have been discussed: changes in the behavior of others, and changes in self-evaluation. A third method is the societal institutionalization of expectancies; that is, the creation of formal procedures for handling persons for whom special expectancies exist. A child is placed in a special class for the physically or mentally handicapped; an adult is sent to a residential "school"; rehabilitation agencies are charged with responsibility for specific tasks. In these cases, the disabled person is treated differently from others as a result of formal rules, regulations, and laws—and not merely because other individuals who interact with him hold special expectations for him. The effects of treatment arrangements for the disabled will be discussed later in this chapter.

PLAYING THE DISABLED ROLE

The discussion thus far has focused on the individual as a relatively passive receiver of others' expectations. An alternative view sees the individual as actively seeking a satisfying role by matching those expectations that fit the desired role and by violating those expectations associated with distasteful roles. This way of viewing the disabled role may be seen in the work of Braginsky, Braginsky, and Ring (1969) in the area of mental illness.

Braginsky *et al.* (1969) claim that mentally ill persons are largely like other people and that their distinctive behavior results from the special situation in which they are placed. Thus they feel that chronically mentally ill persons in institutions are there because they want to be there, and that they treat the residential hospital much as other people would treat a resort hotel, as a place of leisure which enables them to avoid the stresses of daily living. To demonstrate the self-motivated aspect of the behavior of such patients, these investigators noted what happened when they told one group of patients they were about to be interviewed to determine whether they should leave the hospital, and told a comparable group that the purpose of the interview was to determine if they should be placed in a "locked ward." The first group acted much sicker in the interview, described more serious symptoms to the interviewer, and in general described themselves less favorably than did the patients in the second group. Thus, the long-term institutionalized mental patient can make himself look healthy to prevent being thrown into an unpleasant locked ward, or he can appear disturbed to prevent being put back into the nonhospital community— where he does not have the skill to cope with the demands of living.

This analysis may be appropriate for other handicapped persons as well. Handicapped persons may make themselves appear more or less competent and attractive to maximize their personal satisfaction. An extreme, and obvious, case would be beggars who simulate or emphasize handicaps to arouse pity and collect money, as in Brecht's *Threepenny Opera*. In the play, Mr. Peachum is a businessman who provides the training and equipment to enable poor persons to simulate helpless, pitiful, handicapped persons. One can move from this extreme to the fund-raising campaigns of some agencies for the handicapped, which have been criticized for portraying overly dependent persons (Wright, 1960). Another illustration might be a blind person who carries a cane, not for mobility reasons, but to be sure that others recognize his disability and make allowances for it. In contrast, another blind person who has serious difficulty getting around may avoid use of guide dogs or canes and put himself through an extremely difficult and dangerous training process to master simulation of normal mobility patterns.

The child who has been having school difficulty and has been referred for testing for special class placement (and is perhaps about to be classified as mentally retarded by the schools) may pass or fail the psychological (IQ) examination depending on his awareness of the purposes of the testing and his motivation to remain in the regular class. Similarly, a child who is retested by the schools after placement may modify his performance to match his desire to remain in, or leave, the special class. Thus, a child who has been in special classes for three years may perform well if he thinks there is some danger of being placed in a class for the more severely retarded children, and may perform poorly if he anticipates that he might be thrown back into a regular class. In fact, such performance discrepancies might be used as an objective criterion for child satisfaction with special classes.

In summary, many behaviors that we think of as intrinsic characteristics of mentally ill, mentally retarded, or physically handicapped persons may be attributed to their desire to match role expectations associated with more satisfactory outcomes and to violate expectations associated with unsatisfactory outcomes.

PERSONAL MANAGEMENT OF STIGMA

The individual's problems in management of his life circumstances within a "treatment" setting are very different from those out in the "real world," where the disability may open the person to devaluation by others.

In a penetrating analysis, Goffman (1963) has examined the question of personal management of a stigma. Goffman sees the problem as one that is common to the human situation: at one time or another, the most normal individual finds himself in a social situation in which some little failing or trait becomes salient, threatening relationships with shame or embarrassment. Thus there are situations in which it is a disadvantage to be black or white, Jew or Gentile, rich or poor, intellectual or retardate. From Goffman's point of view, then, those who are visibly stigmatized form one end of a continuum, frequently or constantly finding themselves in situations where an attribute must be actively managed. At the other end of the continuum are the "normal," who only occasionally need to manage unfavorable information about themselves.

The degree of visibility of a handicap affects the degree to which an individual needs to be concerned with stigma management. This factor is involved in the distinction that Goffman makes between the *discredited* and the *discreditable*. Individuals with highly visible blemishes, such as disfiguring scars or amputations, are discredited; they rarely, if ever, are able to pass successfully, because the stigma is immediately evident to others. The major problem faced by this group of individuals is that of tension management—how to minimize the obtrusive and disruptive effects of the attribute.

Discreditable individuals, on the other hand, are those whose disabilities are less visible and more easily concealed; for example, epileptic or mentally ill individuals. The prime concern of this group is that of information control—when, where, and to whom to reveal what. Whereas the discredited concentrate on covering or minimizing the effects of their disability on others, the discreditable exert effort in the precarious task of passing—trying to conceal those bits of personal information that might identify them as different. Both represent attempts to approximate normalcy, probably because of the great social rewards that inhere in being considered normal.

Whether the possessor of a given attribute will expose his trait, try to cover it, or pass depends on the value assigned to the deviant trait by the society in which he finds himself, of course, and also on the values that the individual himself attributes to the trait.

Special situations arise when the values of the individual and those of the larger group in which he finds himself do not coincide. This situation may arise from a need of the group to feel that its value system is not being challenged. For example, if intellectual competence or physical prowess are valued by members of the group, it follows that

individuals deficient in these areas are expected to feel inferior, guilty, and blameworthy. This kind of expectation is articulated by the friend of an individual recently blinded: "You're a blind man now, you'll be expected to act like one. . . . People will be firmly convinced that you consider yourself a tragedy. They'll be disconcerted and even shocked to discover that you don't" (Chevigny, 1946; cited in Wright, 1960, p. 15). Similarly, whites are frequently taken aback by blacks who confidently assert that "black is beautiful," when for years whites had tried to believe that "they (Negroes) were to be sub-human–quasi-humans who not only preferred slavery but felt it best for them" (Grier & Cobbs, 1968, p. 32). The "nice" black was the one who had made a virtue of identification with the aggressor (whites) and had adopted an ingratiating and compliant manner, implying his own inferiority (Grier & Cobbs, 1968, p. 66).

One factor that all forms of physical and mental disability have in common is that their presence is disturbing to others with whom the individual possessing the characteristic interacts. Goffman describes this disturbance as arising out of a discrepancy between a virtual social identity and an actual social identity—between the expectation that an individual will be whole, normal, and unblemished and the observation that he is in fact deformed, defective, or blemished (1963, pp. 2–3). The expectation becomes a righteously presented demand that the individual should approximate an ideal of what is normal, conforming, or good. By definition, the individual who fails to do so is considered not quite human.

There is some experimental evidence bearing on others' reactions to the disabled. Kleck (1968) has carried out a series of experimental studies on reactions to a person with a simulated leg amputation. In one investigation, in which the "amputee" was an interviewer, it was found that there was greater physiological arousal (GSR) when interacting with the amputee than when interacting with a nondisabled interviewer: shorter answers were given to questions from the amputee than from the nondisabled; and the person interviewed expressed more frequent conformity to the interviewer's beliefs when the interviewer was an amputee. The results suggest greater anxiety or tension and less naturalness when interacting with a disabled person.

In a similar study, Kleck filmed the behavior of the subject being interviewed and' had him rate the interviewer. Kleck found more favorable impressions of the disabled interviewer than of the nondisabled, less movement in the presence of the disabled, and less variation in focus of visual attention. As in the earlier study, opinions were distorted in the direction of that of the amputee. These findings also imply less freedom or more tension when interacting with the disabled.

In a third study, the nondisabled person was asked to train two other persons in origami (Oriental paper folding) after being trained himself. One of the persons he trained was an "amputee" (both were confederates of the experimenter). The training sessions were monitored by a hidden television camera. Kleck measured the distance between the trainer and his student and found that the average interaction distance was less when interacting with the "normal" than the "disabled" person. However, this effect occurred only in the first teaching session, not the second. Similarly, a difference in impressions occurred only after the first and not the second session. The difference favored the amputee. Finally, disabled learners in both sessions were rated as more interested and motivated in the learning task. As in the first two investigations, verbal statements by the nondisabled seemed to be biased in favor of the disabled, but nonverbal measures suggested less comfort with the disabled. The third study adds the suggestive finding that some of the differences wear off after a period of time.

A series of studies by Jones (1968) ex-amined the influence of the presence of a simulated "blind" person on the performance of other persons on a learning task. Although there was no observable influence on the learning task, subjects *said* their performance was impaired as a result of interaction with the blind person. This effect seems likely to appear in desegregation situations, where white teachers and students may complain about the harm done to the teaching and learning process. Similarly, teachers may complain that the presence of a retarded child reduces teaching efficiency, though this has not yet been demonstrated. Persons do experience tension while in such situations; this may lead them to think their performance is impaired when in fact it is not.

Farina and his associates have conducted a related series of investigations. Farina and Ring (1965) examined the influence of interaction with a presumed mentally ill person, on performance on a cooperative game. Both persons were naïve subjects. Alternately, one, the other, or both (or neither) were privately informed that the other was mentally ill. It was found that perceiving the co-worker as mentally ill enhanced performance. However, when the co-worker was perceived as mentally ill, subjects preferred to work alone; they also tended to blame the mentally ill partner for inadequacies in their joint performance. The results make it clear that discomfort may accompany improved performance under certain conditions.

There is evidence that individuals vary in their levels of discomfort with different handicapped or deviant groups. In a study with counsellor trainees, Riggs (1974) found that trainees expressed greater discomfort when working with ex-mental patients than with "culturally deprived" blacks, but felt that the latter group had a better prognosis for successful employment than the former. Although the Farina and Riggs studies relied on verbal reports of subjects to indicate their discomfort in working with the handicapped, a more recent study (Marinelli, 1974) found such verbal reports to be supported by physiological data. That is, subjects interacting with facially disfigured persons exhibited a higher heart rate than when working with non-disfigured persons.

In a study designed to assess the relative impact of two possible sources of difference —physical handicap and race, Katz (1976) measured the behavior of white elementary pupils interacting in a laboratory setting with white and black adult females. In one-half of the situations, the adult was seated in a wheelchair, simulating a physical handicap; in the other half of the situations, she moved around freely in a normal manner. On the three criteria—physical distancing, imitation, and helping behavior—the subjects showed no differences whether the adult, black or white, was in a wheelchair or not. With the white adult, however, as compared to the black adult, significant differences, showing less social distance, were found. The study is of interest since it shows that children's perception of (physical) handicap in an adult is a less powerful factor in influencing their behavior than is their perception of the race of the interactor.

These investigations were carried out in laboratory settings, which enabled control and measurement but raise questions about how well we can generalize to more typical situations. Schoggin (1965) reported an investigation in which observations were obtained in natural settings. Patterns of reactions of parents and teachers to physically handicapped children and to the nondisabled were found to be very similar. The children in this study were, however, only mildly disabled and were attending regular classes.

PARENTAL RESPONSE TO DISABILITY

Probably the most widely discussed reactions to disability are the responses of family members. The distinctive impact of a handicapped child on family relations most likely begins at the point of the parents' definition or labeling of a child as handicapped (Farber, 1968, p. 153). In the case of children who exhibit obvious disabilities at the time of birth, a major revision is required in the parents' expectancy that the infant will be normal. Many parents find an unfavorable diagnosis of their child unacceptable, and spend time and resources seeking a physician or an agency which will yield a diagnosis that is more amenable to their beliefs (Wolfensberger, 1967). One would expect that in cases where the observable stimulus properties of the child were relatively incongruous (as in the case of a physically normal-looking child with greatly impaired motor or intellectual development) the parent might be even more reluctant to relinquish beliefs of normalcy than if the stimulus properties of the child were congruous and unambiguous, as in the case of the variety of physical stigmata associated with Down's syndrome (Tallman, 1965).

Where prior beliefs regarding a child's essential normalcy are well entrenched (through verification over a period of years), as with an older child adventitiously brain-damaged or suffering from Wilson's disease, parents' belief systems would have to undergo drastic changes to accommodate the changed characteristics of the child. One would expect from studies of selective perception and attitude change that rather convincing evidence would be needed to bring about belief changes (Bruner, 1951).

Once a member of a family is defined as "different," changes are made in the way the remaining members of the family interact with him, with each other, and with the community (Farber, 1968, pp. 152–176). Several investigations have examined the extent of change in family life due to the presence of a child who is defined as handicapped. Some of the effects of a handicapped child on the mother are common to different kinds of disabilities; others are more specific. Klebanoff (1959) reported that mothers of brain-injured, retarded children and mothers of schizophrenic children were similar in child-rearing attitudes and that these attitudes were different from those of mothers of normal children. On the other hand, Cummings, Bayley, and Rie (1966) found differences in evidence of maternal stress in comparisons among the mothers of mentally retarded, chronically ill, and neurotic children. These results may suggest the existence of a general change in attitude of mothers who learn there is something "wrong" or "different" about their child, plus additional effects that are dependent upon the unique nature of the child's disability and the management and personal adjustment problems it creates.

Although studies have been done on the extent to which college students and others make distinctions between various types of exceptionality (Guskin, 1963), there is little known about the extent to which parents of exceptional children distinguish their children from those with other forms of deviance. This question is an important one because the degree to which the parent believes his child is like or unlike another type of exceptionality may influence the way he interacts with his child and the behavior that he elicits from the child. Thus the parent of a hyperactive brain-impaired child may reinforce infantile, incompetent behavior if he believes his child is similar to mentally retarded children. On the other hand, if he believes brain injury is akin to emotional disturbance, he may tolerate outbursts of uncontrolled temper, but not immature behavior. The degree to which parents identify their child with specific types of deviance is also likely to affect decisions regarding whether and where to institutionalize, the prognosis for school and employment success, the possibility of a "cure," and so on.

Parents' perception of a disability may or may not resemble that of professionals. There is a wide variation in the extent to which parents accept the diagnostic label that professionals deem appropriate for their child. From the researcher's point of view,

this is an especially difficult question to work with, because those parents who reject the negative evaluation of their child (as emotionally disturbed, mentally retarded, or brain-injured, for example) are generally not available for research purposes: Either (1) they do not bring their child to the attention of professional agencies; or (2) if they do bring their child to a child-guidance clinic, psychologist, or the like, and refuse to accept the proffered diagnosis, they are not likely to remain available for further study. Families (or teachers or employers) who are able to successfully cope with the unusual individual to the extent that he is able to pass as normal should be intensively studied: their coping strategies might provide clues to formal treatment and rehabilitation agencies on how to successfully integrate these individuals into the larger society. At present, most of the research information on the families of the exceptional has been gleaned from families that have not been successful in avoiding the formal classifying of their child as deviant; that is, most of the studies have been done with families who bring their children (or have them brought) to psychiatrists, family or child clinics, and courts, or with families that belong to such organizations as the National Association for Retarded Citizens. In one sense we have been studying only those families that have been unable to induct their children into normal roles, either as a result of the severity of the child's disability or the inadequacy of the family's coping strategies.

An interesting situation presents itself in cases in which children are professionally diagnosed and categorized as exceptional without the consent of the parents. Such a situation exists in most American public schools, where, due to compulsory education laws, a captive population is present. Routine administrations of intelligence tests effectively stratify children into normal and subnormal groups. This classification procedure has important implications for the child: Changes are made in the type of curriculum to which he will be exposed, the kind of classmates he will have, the type of vocation he will be trained for, and the type of diploma he will receive when he graduates. How does the parent react to this? The question is an intriguing one, since most of the children classified as mildly retarded have no salient distinguishing characteristics, and most have been considered normal by their parents to that point (Meyerowitz, 1967).

The evidence available (Meyerowitz, 1967; Olshansky & Schonfield, 1965) indicates that most parents in this situation do not accept the professional diagnosis which is imposed by the schools, but persist in expressing their beliefs in the child's normalcy.

FORMAL MANAGEMENT OF DEVIANCE

All social systems, whether the family, peer group, school, or society at large, develop machinery for the detecting and processing of individuals who are considered different in characteristics important to the group. The identification and management of deviants occurs both formally and informally. Detection and processing of deviance may be as informal and uncomplicated as a parent discovering his child engaging in forbidden sexual activity, spanking him, and sending him to bed without supper (or a teacher having a child stand in the corner for hitting another child). However, of greater interest here are the formal agencies in a society that are established for the sole purpose of identifying and controlling individuals who are considered in need of such control. Depending on whether one is interested in behavioral, physical, or mental deviance, these agencies might include: the police force, courts, and prisons; rehabilitation workers and hospitals; or systematic procedures in the public schools for testing children's intelligence and placing them appropriately in special classes, schools, or institutions.

Freidson (1965), in his elucidation of the functions of rehabilitation agencies, notes that they carry on four major activities: (1) they specify what personal attributes shall be called handicaps; (2) they identify the population that meets the specifications; (3) they attempt to gain access to the target population; and (4) they attempt to modify the behavior of the target population to conform more closely to what the institutions believe are its potentialities.

The specification of one attribute rather than another as a manifestation of difference is not frequently considered to be an aspect of social control. However, several interesting observations can be made if one takes seriously the possibility that the labeling of a particular characteristic as a handicap itself constitutes a first step in the management of deviance.

It has been documented that the incidence of a variety of deviant behaviors and characteristics varies with such factors as social class and ethnic background. Many possible interpretations may be suggested for this phenomenon. First, there may be systematic differences in the rate at which lower-class, as compared with middle-class, individuals do in fact violate rules that are commonly accepted by both groups. A second alternative exists in the possibility that selective recording of deviation occurs; for example, individuals with high incomes are more likely to be able to afford a psychiatrist than are low-income individuals. Although psychiatrists may thus see more high-income patients, we cannot, therefore, argue that high-income individuals have a higher rate of mental illness than do low-income people. Similarly the recording of criminal behavior is usually the function of police departments. If there are systematic biases in the attitude of the police toward certain groups, or if systematic political pressure is brought to bear on police to clean up crime in certain neighborhoods, official records will show variations in crime rate that have very little to do with the actual rate of crime.

Another possibility is that the rules are made by groups of individuals who do not adequately represent the social norms of all social classes. Thus middle-class city councils may pass laws against hustling—laws that legitimately represent the interests of the middle-class residents but not those of the lower-class residents (Reiss, 1961). In this kind of situation, the hustling rate of the middle-class group means something quite different from the rate of the lower-class group. One group is violating a commonly held and supported norm; the other group may be violating a norm that is perceived as neither valid nor appropriate. A fourth possibility is that a rule is made by one group explicitly or implicitly for the purpose of controlling the behavior of another group. Thus stringent laws may be developed for the purpose of limiting vagrancy, when it is well known that this behavior is engaged in by persons who are disproportionately of lower socioeconomic status. On the other hand, price fixing or tax evasion through loopholes in the laws (behavior typically more characteristic of the middle class) may be regulated only loosely and be enforced even more loosely. A fifth possible interpretation of varying indexes of incidence of deviance is that the regulations apply equally to all groups, but that sanctions are brought to bear disproportionately against one group as opposed to another. An example of this practice is illustrated by the studies of Cohen and Short (1961). It was reported that middle-class boys do not get as far in the legal process when they are apprehended for delinquent acts as do boys from slum areas; that is, proportionately fewer middle-class boys get taken to the police station, get booked at the station, have a hearing before a judge, are convicted, and are sentenced. The "drop-out" rate of middle-class boys along the route of legal processing is so high that sentencing and commitment to a corrective institution involves mostly lower-class boys. Similarly, Garfinkel (1949) reported that the punishment rates of whites and blacks who are believed to have committed

homicide vary greatly. The point is that practically nothing can be said regarding the actual comparative behavior of low- and middle-class groups, whites and blacks, if only conviction rates are looked at.

Similar interpretations are tenable as explanations of higher or lower rates of exceptionality for one or another ethnic or social-class group. Consider the following fact: a disproportionately large number of children in classes for the educable mentally retarded are lower class and/or black (Dunn, 1968, p. 6). How is this phenomenon to be explained? The following alternative explanations present themselves: (1) proportionately more blacks than whites are mentally retarded; (2) present tests are appropriate measures of the intelligence of white children but not of black children; (3) white legislators and school officials are aware of the fact that black children do more poorly than white children on conventional IQ tests; they have therefore decided that IQ testing presents a convenient, presumably valid, "scientific" procedure for separating middle-class children from lower-class blacks and whites; (4) equal proportions of black and white children are mentally retarded; but due to differential referrals by classroom teachers, differential reactions to the testing situation by pupils, and differences in urgency for placement of blacks and whites on waiting lists, black children are more likely to end up in special classes for the mentally retarded.

Mercer (1965; 1973) has presented data which directs itself at explaining these issues. The study began as a basic research epidemiology·in the city of Riverside, California. Among the findings were that school-age children were overrepresented in numbers labeled "mentally retarded" by one or more social agency or organization. (These findings were consistent with that of the "Six-hour retarded child" described by the President's Committee on Mental Retardation, 1970.) Further, it was found that persons in the lower socioeconomic categories were greatly overrepresented and those from the higher socioeconomic statuses were underrepresented. In addition, Caucasians were underlabeled: only about 60 percent as many as one would expect, based on their proportion of the population, were labeled. Blacks were overrepresented by about 50 percent, and Mexican-Americans were overrepresented by about 300 percent. The underrepresentation of Caucasians and the over-representations of Mexican-Americans held true even when socioeconomic status was controlled for. The disproportionate ethnic representations was found particularly among children labeled by the public schools, as opposed to those labeled by medical or other agencies.

Mercer (1965, 1973) also studied the processes through which children in the public school get labeled as "mentally retarded." Her data indicate that the ethnic disproportionality is not found at the initial referral time, but becomes evident at the point that IQ testing takes place. Mercer concludes that the use of a uni-dimensional IQ test is a major element of a procedure whose outcome is "institutional racism," and that such tests should be used only as one aspect of a multicultural pluralistic assessment package that looks at community adaptive behavior as well as IQ.

The above interpretations of the identification and sorting processes engaged in by just one institution—the public schools—are not meant to be exhaustive. But they are illustrative of the way institutions are created for and exist for the maintenance of a particular social system—in this instance, a social system that is interested in the maintenance of a stratification pattern that allocates most of its resources to the people at the top and very little to people at the bottom (Farber, 1968). It is not coincidental that the social system that is being maintained represents powerful factions of the social structure. Thus, Becker (1963) states:

Differences in the ability to make rules and apply them to other people are essentially power differentials (either legal or extralegal).

Those groups whose social position gives them weapons and power are best able to enforce their rules. Distinctions of age, sex, ethnicity, and class are all related to differences in power, which accounts for differences in the degree to which groups so distinguished can make rules for others. . . . Enforcement is selective, and selective differentially among different kinds of people, at different times, and in different situations (pp. 17–18, 133).

Once a deviant is detected, what procedures are engaged in by others to rehabilitate or treat him? Societal notions about how certain deviants should be treated have varied from time to time and from place to place. Although there are cases where deviates are exalted and other cases where they are integrated into society, almost all forms of treatment have involved some variation of segregation (Freidson, 1965, p. 76). The degree of segregation may range from seeing a psychiatrist, parole officer, or itinerant speech therapist once a week to drastic, permanent separation; that is, extermination. Historically, this last procedure has been used to rid societies of individuals who represented differentness on a variety of criteria. Among the Wogeo, a New Guinea tribe, deformed infants are buried alive (Wright, 1960, p. 254); during the Middle Ages, among Europeans, countless individuals were burned at the stake because they were believed to be witches; in more recent times, and among presumably civilized people, millions of Jews were put to death within one decade. All of these actions, and many others, have been justified at one time or another as essential for protecting the tribe from evil spirits, keeping the society "pure," or providing a "solution" to a national "problem."

Extermination as a solution to social problems is also implicit in such practices as sterilization. Although sterilization as a form of social control has been losing popularity in recent years, genetic and eugenic thinking have had a recent revival (Gottesman, 1968; Jensen, 1969; Reed & Reed, 1965). Certainly, birth control is being widely suggested as a solution to both national and international social problems.

At present our most common forms of segregation are our prisons for the behaviorally different; special schools and residence centers for those with impaired sight and hearing; mental institutions for the emotionally different; residential institutions and public school special classes for the intellectually different; rehabilitation centers and hospitals for the physically different; and ghettos for the ethnically and racially different. Most of these settings are typically justified because of some presumed habilitative or rehabilitative function that is supposed to be occurring. In fact, however, no defensible data have yet been published that indicate that these arrangements are effective in facilitating the inmates' return to and adjustment within the larger society (Braginsky *et al.,* 1969; Dentler, 1967; Edgerton, 1967; Goffman, 1961; Plaut & Kaplan, 1956; Roth & Eddy, 1967; Tappan, 1951).

The different types of segregation vary in the degree to which they are able to exert control over individuals. Thus Goffman (1961), in his discussion of asylums, states:

> When we review the different institutions in our Western society, we find that some are encompassing to a degree discontinuously greater than the ones next in line. Their encompassing or total character is symbolized by the barrier to social intercourse with the outside and to departure that is often built right into the physical plant, such as locked doors, high walls, barbed wire, cliffs, water, forests or moors; these establishments I am calling total institutions (p. 4).

Roth and Eddy (1967) conclude from their study of a rehabilitation hospital that total institutions serve social control functions by becoming the chief depositories for unwanted members of a society. The relevant characteristic that the inmates of the institution have in common then, is not some physical, mental, or behavioral trait (these

only determine what *kind* of institutional placement they are technically eligible for), but the fact that all of them are unwanted members of society.

> Our society has many homes for unwanted people. In addition to our custodial homes, . . . we have numerous mental hospitals, institutions for the retarded, nursing homes, old-age homes, training schools for delinquents, and so on. The specific kind of institution a person "qualifies" for is often arbitrary. . . . Such institutions all perform much the same function, and we suspect that the choice of which institution the patient goes to is often an accident of the person or agency he happens to fall into the hands of. . . . To the patient who is stuck in such an institution, it often makes little difference which one he ends up in, except that the facilities and personnel at one may be somewhat more tolerable than those at another (Roth & Eddy, 1967, pp. 198–199).

Whatever the kind of total institution, society offers some organizational rationale for its existence. As Roth and Eddy put it (p. 199), "Although institutions for the unwanted all do much the same thing, they have differing 'excuses' for their existence, and these excuses make some difference in how they operate."

The handling of many human needs by the bureaucratic organization of blocks of people fits in closely with the function which the total institution serves—the effective disposition of the unwanted.

The official rationale for the existence of the institution varies with the real or imputed characteristics of the clients to be taken care of—in particular, whether or not the inmate's condition is seen as being caused by volitional acts of the individual. In cases where the responsibility for the condition is seen as residing within the individual, as in certain conceptions of criminality, management consists of some form of punishment; in cases where no motivation toward deviance is seen in the individual, as in the case of the blind, treatment tends to be couched in "caretaker" or permissive terms (Freidson, 1965, p. 76). Nevertheless, the question of causality is not easily resolved, even within each form of exceptionality. This appears to be particularly so when competing conceptual models regarding the nature of the exceptionality are contrasted. Thus, if a disease or illness model is used to explain the occurrence of delinquency, quite different assumptions are made concerning the causality of the condition, as compared to the assumptions made when a nonmedical model is employed. The "sick" boy is not responsible for his condition—it is contracted from a contaminating environment; the "bad" boy is responsible for his condition—he is making the wrong decisions and thus messing up his life. In the former case, treatment will emphasize a therapeutic, "healthy" environment; in the latter, treatment will be rationalized in terms of getting the individual to change his mind about how he is going to behave, through punishment of the "bad" behavior and/or encouragement of "good" behavior.

Within the United States, the official rationale for the existence of institutions has undergone changes from time to time (Davies, 1959). These changes have been accompanied by concomitant variations in clientele being served. For example, the emphasis on institutional care for the retarded shifted from a rehabilitative thrust to a custodial orientation when the nature of the population considered to be in need of this particular form of control changed from the mildly retarded to the more severely retarded. It became necessary to reformulate the raison d'être of the institution.

Institutionalization remains a popular social response to exceptionality in the United States, although there are systematic differences in the extent to which the various religious and ethnic groups use this form of social control with members of their own group. Saenger (1957) reports that Jewish families are more likely to institutionalize a severely retarded child than are Protestant

and Catholic families; Catholics are most likely to care for the child in his home. Plaut and Kaplan (1956), in their study of Hutterite communities, found that these groups rarely, if ever, institutionalize their members.

In the last few years, the American philosophy and practice of institutionalization has undergone dramatic changes. Concomitant with a number of court decisions (for example, *Wyatt v. Stickney,* 1972), past institutional practices have been severely criticized and sweeping changes have been called for in the name of "normalization." One key proponent of the normalization principle, Wolfensberger, puts it this way: "On programmatic, ideological, and fiscal grounds, the present institutional system is essentially unsalvageable. Indeed . . . it is the duty of every institution's superintendent to do all he can to phase out his institution, and to encourage the new residential and service model" (Wolfensberger, 1971, p. 36).

The thrust of the normalization principle is that handicapped persons should live as "normal" lives as possible (as close as possible to how the non-handicapped live) in terms of housing arrangements, freedom to come and go as they please, freedom to take risks, to have "normal" sexual and reproductive lives, and to be involved in all decisions concerning themselves. Operationally, the greatest impact of the normalization principle thus far on American institutions has been in plans for phasing out large institutions and the corresponding development of small hostel-like facilities based in the communities.

As is usually the case with major changes in social policy, the normalization trend is not based on empirical data showing greater effectiveness or efficiency of the changes proposed by its advocates (See, for example, Edgerton *et al.,* 1975). Rather, it reflects and is reflected by the current *Zeitgeist,* which emphasizes civil rights of individuals, is anti-institutional (especially antigovernmental institutions), and is deeply committed to the democratic, the individualistic, and the humanitarian.

The normalization ideology has also found expression in public policy toward those handicapped individuals who would not ordinarily be institutionalized, particularly in the educational arrangements made for this group. Although the literature already contained expressions of the unacceptability of the non-normalizing, segregated arrangements made for the handicapped (Dunn, 1968; Bartel & Guskin, 1970), it was not until the historic *PARC vs. Pennsylvania* (1972) that the uncompromising *right to education* of the handicapped was clearly established, and that the priority for non-segregated educational treatment was clearly codified. Subsequently, through both litigative and legislative actions, the doctrine of *least restrictive alternative* has emerged. Broadly speaking, this doctrine is similar to the normalization principle in that it stipulates that the preferred setting for the handicapped is with the non-handicapped, in as typical a physical environment as can accommodate the individuals involved. Educationally, this has meant a demise in the popularity of self-contained segregated schools, residences, and classrooms, and a search for workable alternative arrangements in which handicapped, especially mildly handicapped, youngsters are educated with their non-handicapped peers for a portion or all of their educational experiences. The implementation of the *least restrictive alternative* in education has become known, in part, as "mainstreaming"; the child is placed in the "mainstream" of education, as opposed to some separate setting.

The desirability of mainstreaming has been mandated in the recent (1975) federal legislation, Education of All Handicapped Children Act, PL 94–142. Because of the substantial funds this legislation will make to the states, and because a state plan favoring the least restrictive alternative is made a criterion for state eligibility for funding, it can be expected that enormous strides will be made in the next few years toward the goal of educating handicapped pupils in as "normal" an educational setting as possible.

It is interesting to note here, again, that the far-reaching changes in public policy toward the education of the handicapped have not come about as the result of research studies showing the superiority of mainstreaming over the conventional self-contained classes. This is somewhat surprising, since the literature contains no paucity of research on the topic. In fact, cluttered as the literature is with studies comparing the performance and adjustment of special-class and regular-class retardates, one could hope for definitive answers to these questions. Unfortunately, most of the studies are vulnerable to devastating criticisms of methodology, as pointed out by a number of reviewers (Gardner, 1966; Guskin & Spicker, 1968; Kirk, 1964; Spicker & Bartel, 1968). Most of the methodological criticisms directed at the earlier studies were circumvented by Goldstein, Moss and Jordan (1965). These investigators randomly assigned beginning first-grade children, IQs of 50 to 85, to either regular classes or newly created special classes, thus avoiding biased sampling and the problem of the effects of previous academic failure on school performance. A special curriculum was implemented, the special-class teachers were specially trained and supervised, and measures were developed to assess social and functional skills as well as academic achievement. Essentially, the results of this careful four-year study confirm the findings of the earlier studies: Educable mentally retarded children in special classes perform no better and no worse than EMRs in the regular grades.

Investigations comparing the social and emotional adjustment of regular and special-class children have to a large extent employed measures of undemonstrated validity or reliability; in addition, many of the studies were subject to serious sampling bias. The best designed of the investigations—two substudies of the Goldstein, Moss, and Jordan (1965) study—were conducted by Meyerowitz (Goldstein *et al.,* 1965; Meyerowitz, 1962). These two studies of personal and social adjustment found special-class retarded children more likely to subscribe to self-derogatory statements and to interact less with neighborhood peers than children left in the regular grades. One can only conclude that the superiority of special-class retardates' personal and social adjustment remains to be demonstrated (Gardner, 1966; Guskin & Spicker, 1968; Spicker & Bartel, 1968).

Similarly, comparisons of the postschool adjustment of special-class and regular-class retarded pupils (Carriker, 1957; Peck, 1964) fail to present convincing evidence that special-class placement results in clearcut, overall long-term benefits in terms of social and vocational adjustment.

The major finding that can be gleaned from the assortment of inschool and postschool studies just referred to is that attaching the label of mental retardation to an individual and segregating him in a special class with other individuals of similar evaluation has yet to be shown to result in unique social, educational, or vocational advantages for that individual. If singling out individuals as deviant (that is, placing them in special classes) is to be justified as of benefit to the individual, it must be justified in terms of positive, favorable evidence rather than on the basis of a lack of negative, unfavorable evidence. Society, of course, may be forced to recognize (or admit) that its goal is not individual benefit of the handicapped but comfort or protection of others.

It is noteworthy that most EMR children pass as normal throughout their lives except during the school years, during which the availability and presumed appropriateness of intelligence tests provides a convenient "scientific" basis for identifying intellectual deviants and subjecting them to special treatment. The high prevalence rate of identified retarded pupils in the chronological age (CA) 8–15 range has been noted by Gruenberg (1964) and Farber (1968) in their reviews of epidemiological studies. Although Gruenberg cites the finding of increased prevalence during the school years and a decline thereafter as "the most important single finding of these surveys" and that "the phenomenon cries out for investigation," no such investigation has, to date, been reported. It is our opinion that this finding is more related to the schools' remarkable propensity for labeling children as retarded than to a propensity for children to become retarded during their school years and again unretarded after they drop out of school.

Related to this observation are the findings of two studies (Meyerowitz, 1967; Olshansky & Schonfield, 1965). Both of these studies reported that most parents of mildly retarded children rated their child as normal or above in intelligence when asked to evaluate his mental status. One conclusion that may be drawn from these studies is that the criteria employed by the schools to relegate an individual to the status of EMR are irrelevant to or ignored by that group of most significant others—the individuals' families. According to Olshansky, Schonfield, and Sternfeld (1962) "the majority of the (so-called) mentally retarded children are able to meet most of life's changing expectations except those of the schools as currently structured" (p. 61).

SOCIETAL REDUCTION OF HANDICAPPING

If society can be held responsible for creating handicap, it should be possible for society to reverse the process and reduce handicap. One implication of much we have written here is that handicapping could be reduced by minimizing the segregation of disabled or otherwise different individuals. A second implied suggestion is elimination of diagnostic procedures that cannot be demonstrated to result in successful treatment attempts. A third implication is that reduction of handicapping might occur by totally avoiding treatment whenever the effectiveness of the treatment cannot be demonstrated. The suggested elimination of ineffective diagnostic and treatment procedures is based on our assumption that diagnosis and treatment may sharply reduce the likelihood of progression through a normal life career. A related implication is that if treatment is necessary and useful, the more invisible the service the more likely its reduction of the social condition known as "handicap."

Much else we have discussed has implied that labeling and "handicapping" serve important functions for society, and thus that society will resist reduction of this process. Dentler and Erikson (1959) imply in their discussion of deviance that improving the status of the handicapped within a group may reduce the effectiveness with which the group can motivate others to meet norms. Thus it seems that it would be easier to convince social groups to keep deviant members in their midst than it would be to convince them not to differentially label and treat them within the group. Most importantly, it is necessary that in suggesting realistic change we consider the needs actually served by social treatment patterns, rather than the humane rationale publicly presented.

SUMMARY

A handicap is a social condition, a condition created by society. A person's bodily or behavioral condition becomes a handicap only to the extent that society, other people, or the person himself define his condition as distinctive and undesirable. This definition consists of verbal labeling, distinctive interpersonal reactions, and/or special treatment techniques, all of which imply unattractiveness, incompetence, or both. The result of this social definition is to create distinctive environments and behaviors, which sequentially remove the person further and further from normal life patterns and, in time, convince all concerned that the person truly is handicapped. Because most persons sense the serious social consequences of being different, they exert great effort to avoid being seen as different by those whom they value. When they are known to be different, they exert great effort to cover their differentness —that is, to remove it from the focus of negative attention. These attempts to pass and cover, along with the substantial creations of society to cope with those who are different, provide extensive evidence for the need to examine handicaps as social conditions. Finally, this approach suggests directions for prevention and treatment of handicap— directions that are antithetical to the current approaches of our educational and rehabilitation agencies.

REFERENCES

ASCH, S. E. Forming impressions of personality. *Journal of Abnormal and Social Psychology,* 1946, *41,* 258–290.

AVERY, C. D. A psychologist looks at the issue of public versus residential school placement for the blind. In R. L. Jones (Ed.), *Problems and*

Issues in the Education of Exceptional Children. Boston: Houghton Mifflin, 1971.

BARKER, R. G., & WRIGHT, B. A. The social psychology of adjustment to physical disability. In J. R. Garrent (Ed.), *Psychological aspects of physical disability.* Rehabilitation Service series No. 210. Washington, D.C.: Federal Security Agency, Office of Vocational Rehabilitation, 1952, pp. 18–22.

BARTEL, N. R. Locus of control and achievement in middle-class and lower-class children. Unpublished doctoral dissertation. Indiana University, 1968.

BARTEL, N. R., & GUSKIN, S. L. A handicap as a social phenomenon. In W. M. Cruickshank (Ed.), *Psychology of Exceptional Children and Youth* (3rd ed.). Englewood Cliffs, N.J.: Prentice-Hall, 1970, pp. 75–114.

BATTLE, E. S., & ROTTER, J. B. Children's feelings of personal control as related to social class and ethnic group. *Journal of Personality,* 1963, *31,* 482–490.

BECKER, H. S. *Outsiders: Studies in the sociology of deviance.* New York: The Free Press, 1953.

BEEZ, W. V. Influence of biased psychological reports on teacher behavior and pupil performance. *Proceedings of the 75th APA Annual Convention.* Washington, D.C.: American Psychological Association, 1968, pp. 605–606.

BIALER, I. Conceptualization of success and failure in mentally retarded and normal children. *Journal of Personality,* 1961, *29,* 303–320.

BRAGINSKY, B. M., BRAGINSKY, D. D., & RING, K. *Methods of madness: The mental hospital as a last resort.* New York: Holt, Rinehart & Winston, Inc., 1969.

BROOKOVER,, et al. Self-concept of ability and school achievement II. U.S. Office of Education Cooperative Research Project, No. 1636, Lansing: Michigan State University, 1965. (ERIC ED003294)

BRUNER, J. S. Personality dynamics and the process of perceiving. In R. P. Blake & G. V. Ramsey (Eds.), *Perception—an approach to personality.* New York: The Ronald Press Company, 1951, pp. 121–127.

CARRIKER, W. J. A comparison of post-school adjustment of regular and special class retarded individuals served in Lincoln and Omaha. U.S. Office of Education Cooperative Research Project, No. 146, 1957.

CLARK, S. M., & FARBER, B. The handicapped child in the family: A literature survey. In B. V. Sheets & F. Barber (Eds.), *The handicapped child in the family.* New York: United Cerebral Palsy Research & Educational Foundation.

CLINE, W. B. Interpersonal perception. In B. A. Maher (Ed.), *Progress in experimental personality research,* Vol. 1. New York: Academic Press, Inc., 1964, pp. 221–284.

COHEN, A. K. *Deviance and control.* Englewood Cliffs, N.J.: Prentice-Hall, Inc., 1966.

COHEN, A., & SHORT, J. F. Juvenile delinquency. In R. K. Merton & R. A. Nisbet (Eds.), *Contemporary social problems.* New York: Harcourt, Brace & World, Inc., 1961, pp. 77–126.

COLEMAN, J. S., et al. *Equality of educational opportunity.* Washington, D.C.: U.S. Department of Health, Education, and Welfare, 1966.

CUMMINGS, S. T., BAYLEY, H. C., & RIE, H. E. Effects of the child's deficiency on the mother: A study of mothers of mentally retarded, chronically ill, and neurotic children. *American Journal of Orthopsychiatry,* 1966, *36,* 595–609.

DAVIES, S. P. *The mentally retarded in society.* New York: Columbia University Press, 1959.

DENTLER, R. A. *Major American social problems.* Chicago: Rand McNally & Co., 1967.

DENTLER, R. A., & ERIKSON, K. T. The functions of deviance in groups. *Social Problems,* 1959, *7,* 98–107.

DEXTER, L. A. A social theory of mental deficiency. *American Journal of Mental Deficiency,* 1958, *62,* 920–928.

————. On the politics and sociology of stupidity in our society. In H. S. Becker (Ed.), *The other side: Perspectives on deviance.* New York: The Free Press, 1964, pp. 37–49.

DUNN, L. M. Special Education for the mildly retarded—Is much of it justifiable? *Exceptional Children,* 1968, *35,* 5–22.

EDGERTON, R. B. *The cloak of competence: Stigma in the lives of the mentally retarded.* Berkeley: University of California Press, 1967.

————. On the "recognition" of mental illness. In S. C. Plog & R. B. Edgerton (Eds.), *Changing perspectives in mental illness.* New York: Holt, Rinehart & Winston, Inc., 1969.

EDGERTON, R. B., Eyman, R. K., & SILVERSTEIN, A. B. Mental retardation system. In N. Hobbs (Ed.), *Issues in the Classification of children,* Vol. 2. San Francisco: Jossey-Bass, 1975, pp. 62–87.

FABREGA, H., JR., & MANNING, P. K. Disease, illness and deviant careers. In R. A. Scott & J. D. Douglas (Eds.), *Theoretical perspectives on deviance.* New York: Basic Books, 1972, pp. 93–116.

FARBER, B. Effects of a severely mentally retarded child on family integration. *Monographs of the Society for Research in Child development,* serial No. 71, 1959, *24* (2) .

————. *Mental retardation: Its social context and social consequences.* Boston: Houghton Mifflin Company, 1968.

FARBER, B., JENNE, W. C., & TOIGO, R. Family crisis and the decision to institutionalize the retarded child. *CEC Research Monograph,* series A, 1960 (1) .

FARINA, A., & RING, K. The influence of perceived mental illness on interpersonal relations. *Journal of Abnormal Psychology,* 1965, *70,* 47–51.

FESTINGER, L. A theory of social comparison processes. *Human Relations,* 1954, *7,* 117–140.

FRANKS, D. J. Ethnic and social status characteristics of children in EMR and LD classes. *Exceptional Children,* 1971, *37,* 537–538.

FREIDSON, E. Disability as social deviance. In M. B. Sussman (Ed.), *Sociology and rehabilitation.* Washington, D.C.: American Sociological Association, 1965, pp. 71–99.

GARDNER, W. I. Social and emotional adjustment of mildly retarded children and adolescents: Critical review. *Exceptional Children,* 1966, *33,* 97–105.

GARFINKEL, H. Research notes on inter- and intra-racial homicides. *Social Forces,* 1949, *27,* 369–381.

GERTH, H., & MILLS, C. W. *Character and social structure.* New York: Harcourt, Brace & World, Inc., 1953.

GIBBS, J. P. Issues in defining deviant behavior. In R. A. Scott & J. D. Douglas (Eds.), *Theoretical perspectives on deviance.* New York: Basic Books, 1972.

GOFFMAN, E. *Asylums: Essays on the social situation of mental patients and other inmates.* Chicago: Aldine Publishing Company, 1961.

————. *Stigma: Notes on the management of spoiled identity.* Englewood Cliffs, N.J.: Prentice-Hall, Inc., 1963.

GOLDSTEIN, H., MOSS, J. W., & JORDAN, L. J. The efficacy of special class training on the development of mentally retarded children. U.S. Office of Education Cooperative Research Project, No. 619. Urbana: University of Illinois, 1965.

GOTTESMAN, I. I. Biogenetics of race and class. In M. Deutch, I. Katz, & A. R. Jensen (Eds.), *Social class, race, and psychological development.* New York: Holt, Rinehart & Winston, Inc., 1968, pp. 11–51.

GOVE, W. R. Societal reaction as an explanation of mental illness: An Evaluation. *American Sociological Review,* 1970, *35,* 873–884.

————. Individual resources and mental hospitalization: A comparison and evaluation of the societal reaction and psychiatric perspectives. American Sociological Review, 1974, *39,* 86–100.

————. Labeling and mental illness: A critique. In W. R. Gove (Ed.), *The Labeling of deviance: Evaluating a perspective.* New York: Wiley, 1975, pp. 35–81.

GRIER, W. H., & COBBS, P. M. *Black rage.* New York: Basic Books, Inc., 1968.

GRUENBERG, E. M. Epidemiology. In H. A. Stevens & R. Heber (Eds.), *Mental Retardation: A review of research.* Chicago: University of Chicago Press, 1964, pp. 259–306.

GUSKIN, S. L. The influence of labeling upon the perception of subnormality in mentally defective children. *American Journal of Mental Deficiency;* 1962, *67,* 402–406.

————. Dimensions of judged similarity among

deviant types. *American Journal of Mental Deficiency,* 1963, *86,* 218–224.

———. Theoretical and empirical strategies for the study of the labeling of mentally retarded persons. Paper presented at the Tenth Annual Gotlinburg Conference on Research in Mental Retardation, Gotlinburg, Tennessee, March 11, 1977.

———. Theoretical and empirical strategies for the study of the labeling of mentally retarded persons. In N. Ellis (Ed.), *International Review of Research in Mental Retardation.* New York: Academic Press, 1978.

GUSKIN, S. L., & SPICKER, H. H. Educational research in mental retardation. In N. R. Ellis (Ed.), *International review of research in mental retardation,* Vol. 3. New York: Academic Press, Inc., 1968, pp. 217–278.

HERSH, J. B. Influence of biased referral reports in a clinical testing situation. Unpublished manuscript, Indiana University, 1969.

HUGHES, E. C. Dilemmas and contradictions in status. *American Journal of Sociology,* 1945, *50,* 353–359.

JAFFE, J. Attitudes of adolescents toward persons with disabilities. Paper presented at the meeting of the American Psychological Association, New York, 1965.

JENSEN, A. R. How much can we boost IQ and scholastic achievement? *Harvard Educational Review,* 1969, *39,* 1–123.

JONES, R. L. Cognitive functioning in the presence of the disabled. Paper presented at the meeting of the American Psychological Association, San Francisco, 1968.

KATZ, P. A. White children's attitudes toward blacks and the physically handicapped: A developmental study. *Journal of Educational Psychology,* 1976, *68,* 20–24.

KELLEY, H. H., *et al.* Some implications of social psychological theory for research on the handicapped. In L. H. Lofquist (Ed.), *Psychological research and rehabilitation.* Washington, D.C.: American Psychological Association, 1960, pp. 172–204.

KIRK, S. A. Research in education. In H. A.

Stevens & R. Heber (Eds.). *Mental retardation: A review of research.* Chicago: University of Chicago Press, 1964, pp. 57–99.

KLEBANOFF, L. Parental attitudes of mothers of schizophrenics, brain-injured and retarded, and normal children. *American Journal of Orthopsychiatry,* 1959, *29,* 445–454.

KLECK, R. E. Stigma conditions as elicitors of behavior in face-to-face interaction. Paper presented at the meeting of the American Psychological Association, San Francisco, 1968.

LIPP, L., *et al.* Denial of disability and internal control of reinforcement: A study using a perceptual defense paradigm. *Journal of Consulting and Clinical Psychology,* 1968, *32,* 72–75.

MARINELLI, R. P. State anxiety in interactions with visibly disabled persons. *Rehabilitation Counseling Bulletin,* 1974, *18,* 72–77.

MENNINGER, K., MAYMAN, M., & PREGER, P. The urge to classify. In K. Menninger (Ed.), *The vital balance.* New York: The Viking Press, Inc., 1963, pp. 9–34.

MERCER, J. Understanding career patterns of persons labeled as mentally retarded. *Social Problems,* 1965, *13,* 18–34.

———. *Labeling the retarded.* Berkeley: University of California Press, 1973.

MEYEROWITZ, J. H. Self-derogations in young retardates and special class placement. *Child Development,* 1962, *33,* 443–451.

———. Parental awareness of retardation. *American Journal of Mental Deficiency,* 1967, *71,* 637–643.

MILLER, H. *Rich man poor man.* Signet Book. The New American Library of World Literature, Inc., New York, 1965.

MILLER, H., & STERNFELD, L. Mentally retarded or culturally different? *Training School Bulletin,* 1962, *59,* 18–21.

OLSHANSKY, S., & SCHONFIELD, J. Parental perceptions of the mental status of graduates of special classes. *Mental Retardation,* 1965, *3,* 16–20.

OLSHANSKY, S., SCHONFIELD, J., & STERNFELD, L. Mentally retarded or culturally different? *Training School Bulletin,* 1962, *59,* 18–21.

PECK, J. R. Success of young adult male retardates. U.S. Office of Education Cooperative Research Project. No. 1533. Austin: University of Texas, 1964.

Pennsylvania Association for Retarded Children (PARC) vs. Commonwealth of Pennsylvania, 343 F. Supp. 279 (E.D. PA 1972).

PETERSON, G. F. Factors related to the attitudes of nonretarded children toward their educable mentally retarded peers. *American Journal of Mental Deficiency,* 1975, *79,* 412–416.

PHILLIPS, L., DRAGUNS, J. G., & BARTLETT, D. P. Classification of behavior disorders. In N. Hobbs (Ed.), *Issues in the classification of children,* Volume I. San Francisco: Jossey-Bass, 1975, pp. 26–55.

PLAUT, T. F. A., & KAPLAN, B. *Personality in a communal society: An analysis of the mental health of the Hutterites.* Lawrence: University of Kansas, 1956, pp. 50–55.

President's Committee on Mental Retardation. *The six-hour retarded child.* Washington, D.C.: U.S. Government Printing Office, 1970.

REED, E. W., & REED, S. C. *Mental retardation: A family study.* Philadelphia: W. B. Saunders Company, 1965.

REISS, A. J., JR. The social integration of queers and peers. *Social Problems,* 1961, *9,* 102–120.

RIGGS, R. C. Attitudes of counsellor trainees toward three client groups. *Rehabilitation Counseling Bulletin,* 1974, *18,* 78–82.

ROSENTHAL, R. *Experimenter effects in behavioral research.* New York: Appleton-Century-Crofts, 1966.

ROSENTHAL, R., & JACOBSON, L. *Pygmalion in the classroom: Teacher expectation and pupils' intellectual development.* New York: Holt, Rinehart & Winston, Inc., 1968. (a)

———. Teacher expectations for the disadvantaged. *Scientific American,* 1968, *218* (4), 19–23. (b)

ROTH, J. A., & EDDY, E. M. *Rehabilitation of the unwanted.* New York: Atherton Press, Inc., 1967.

ROTTER, J. B. Generalized expectancies for internal versus external control of reinforcement. *Psychological Monographs.* 1966, *80* (1, whole No. 609).

SAENGER, G. The adjustment of severely retarded adults in the community. A report to the New York State Interdepartmental Health Resources Board. Albany, New York, 1957.

SCHEFF, T. J. *Being mentally ill: A sociological theory.* Chicago: Aldine Publishing Company, 1966.

———. The labeling theory of mental illness. *American Sociological Review,* 1974, *39,* 444–452.

SCHOGGIN, P. Observed behavior of mothers and teachers toward children with physical disabilities in natural situations. Paper presented at the meeting of the American Psychological Association, New York, 1965.

SCOTT, R. A. *The making of blind men.* New York: Russell Sage Foundation, 1969.

SMITH, R. T. Societal reaction and physical disability: Contrasting perspectives. In W. R. Gove (Ed.), *The labeling of deviance: Evaluating a perspective.* New York: Wiley, 1975, pp. 147–156.

SPICKER, H. H., & BARTEL, N. R. The mentally retarded. In G. O. Johnson & H. Blank (Eds.), *Exceptional children research review.* Washington, D.C.: Council for Exceptional Children, 1968, pp. 39–109.

SUTHERLAND, E. H., & CRESSEY, D. R. *Principles of criminology* (6th ed.). Chicago: Lippincott, 1960.

SZASZ, T. *The myth of mental illness: Foundations of a theory of personal conduct.* New York: Hoeber-Harper, 1961.

———. *The manufacture of madness: A comparative study of the inquisition and the mental health movement.* New York: Harper & Row, 1970.

TALLMAN, I. Spousal role differentiation and socialization of severely retarded children. *Journal of Marriage and the Family,* 1965, *27,* 37–42.

TAPPAN, P. W. Objectives and methods in correction. In P. W. Tappan (Ed.), *Contempo-*

rary correction. New York: McGraw-Hill Book Company, 1951.

THORNDIKE, R. L. Review. *American Educational Research Journal,* 1968, *5,* 708–711.

Time Magazine, 1969, March 14, p. 74.

TUMIN, M. M. *Social stratification: the forms and functions of inequality.* Englewood Cliffs, N.J.: Prentice-Hall, Inc., 1967.

WELLER, L., *et al.* Social variables in the perception and acceptance of retardation. *American Journal of Mental Deficiency,* 1974, *79,* 274–278.

WOLFENSBERGER, W. Counseling the parents of the retarded. In A. A. Baumeister (Ed.),

Mental retardation: Appraisal, education, and rehabilitation. Chicago: Aldine Publishing Company, 1967.

———. Will there always be an institution? II. The impact of new service models. *Mental Retardation,* 1971, *9,* 31–38.

WRIGHT, B. A. *Physical disability: A psychological approach.* New York: Harper & Row, Publishers, 1960.

Wyatt vs. *Stickney,* 344 F. Supp. 387 (N.D. Ala. 1972).

ZIMBARDO, P. G. A Pirandellian Prison. *New York Times Magazine,* April 9, 1973, pp. 38–60.

3 Psychological Assessment of Exceptional Children and Youth

T. Ernest Newland

Ph.D., *Professor Emeritus of Educational Psychology; former Director, School Psychology Program, University of Illinois, Urbana.*

"Everything depends, not upon the figures, but upon the analysis; not upon the precise instruments, but upon the right questions."

—Hugo Munsterburg, 1892
address to the American
Psychological Association

"For psychology, every measurement is only a means to qualitative analysis."

—Author unknown

The purposes of this chapter are to review briefly the major assumptions that underlie psychological testing and to indicate major measurement problems regarding these assumptions with respect to exceptional children and youth. Results actually obtained in testing in the different areas of exceptionality will be presented only for the purpose of illustrating assessment problems in this field, since the major psychological findings are incorporated in the chapters on the several kinds of exceptionality. Only a few of the hundreds of devices and techniques will be mentioned—solely to illustrate the problems or attempts at solution of some of the problems which are indicated.

Our discussion of examination procedures and problems will be pointed toward the accomplishment of a maximally meaningful psychological assessment of exceptional children and youth, made even more important now with the enactment of Public Law 94–142—the Education for All Handicapped Children Act. Yet, to attain this, we would need the contributions of a full and competent staff. Case studies, social studies, the reports of medical diagnostic and treatment specialists, and full educational histories would be required, and we should need to "staff" such children in the light of all such information before we could expect to have complete bases for sound and complete psychological assessments of the children. This is beyond the scope of this chapter. We shall limit our concern to problems involved in the obtaining and integrating of information within a psychological or psychoeducational framework. Further, we shall confine ourselves to a consideration of the nature of the content of psychological reports rather than to the reports themselves.

If this chapter identifies more problems than it settles, it is in part a result of the status of examination procedures in this field and in part a result of the author's desire to have this kind of educational impact upon the student.

The words *testing* and *assessing* mean definitely different activities. The term *testing* will be used to denote the exposure of a client to any given device, whether group or individual, essentially for the purpose of obtaining a quantitative characterization of one or more traits of that client. *Assessing*, on the other hand, includes not only this quantitative depiction of the client, but also the qualitative and integrated characterization of the client as a dynamic, ongoing, total organism functioning in a social setting. Without resorting to an illustrative full-length report of the assessment of a child, the following excerpted statements from clinical reports may suggest more clearly the contrast between qualitative and quantitative characterizations:

(a) He was 5 feet 4 inches tall [quantitative], but he didn't really stand up straight while he was being measured [qualitative].

(b) She earned an IQ of 67 on this test [quantitative], but she didn't seem to apply herself in the examination situation [qualitative].

(c) It is interesting to note that he consistently named differences but did not name similarities [qualitative], even though he did fail this part of the test [quantitative].

(d) Her constantly asking the examiner if her responses were correct and her frequent biting of her fingernails during the examination session suggested feelings of insecurity [qualitative]. This behavior, and some others like it, make me wonder if the IQ of 83 which she got on the Binet [quantitative] gives us a true picture of her rate of mental development.

There tends to be relatively less of the qualitative aspect in testing than there is of the quantitative aspect in assessing. Even though much of the following discussion will deal with the testing approach, the greater significance of the use of the assessment approach will, it is hoped, become apparent.

Even though this book is concerned with exceptional children and youth up to the age of 21, most of the discussion and the research cited will pertain to exceptional children from the high-school level downward. The term *exceptional children*, as used in this chapter, will signify either this more limited age range or a specific part of it.

It is particularly important in this chapter to bear in mind that the terminology used to denote different kinds of exceptional children is confusing. In the first place, the term *physically impaired* will be used here to refer to a group of exceptionalities—the orthopedic, the sensorily impaired, the physically delicate, the brain-injured, the epileptic, and the like. The brain-injured will include both the cerebral-palsied and those who have, or are believed to have, higher-level neural impairment not reflected in motor dysfunction. The deaf will be regarded as a part of the acoustically impaired, just as the blind will be regarded as falling in the category of the visually impaired. The term *mentally retarded* will be used, in a limited sense, to refer to those exceptional children whose intellectual retardation is not so severe as to warrant their falling in the range of mental deficiency nor so slight as to warrant their being regarded as "slow learners." The mentally retarded, then, will be thought of as having intelligence quotients roughly comparable to 1960 (L–M) Stanford-Binet IQs falling in a range from about 50 to about 75 or 80.* The mentally superior and gifted will be regarded as those with Stanford-Binet IQs of 125 and above.

In the second place, it certainly is not safe to assume that the different types of exceptionalities are "pure" types. A child with a speech impairment, for instance, also may have a hearing loss, or some higher central

---

* Hereafter, any unqualified reference to intelligence quotients or mental ages will be in terms of the 1960 Binet. If either has been ascertained by any other test, the name of that test will be used—as Otis IQ, PMA mental age, or WISC verbal test age.

nervous system involvement, or he may be socially and emotionally maladjusted. A visually impaired child may be mentally superior, or he may have a speech impairment, or he may also be brain-injured. However, our discussion will be restricted intentionally either to such "simple" types of exceptionality or to types of exceptionality in which the designated conditions are regarded as the *primary,* but not the sole, bases upon which the educational and social needs of such children are being met or are being studied. The psychological examination and assessment of children of any multiple-exception type involve a compounding of the problems peculiar to each of the involved areas of exceptionality, as in cases such as the mentally superior, severely involved athetoid; the deaf-blind; the blind cerebral-palsied; or the speech-impaired emotionally maladjusted.

ASSUMPTIONS UNDERLYING PSYCHOLOGICAL TESTING

In considering the following assumptions, it is quite likely that the student will think most often in terms of the measurement of the intelligence of a child. The assumptions, however, also underlie the processes of ascertaining such things as the nature of the child's emotionality, his educational achievement, his vocational aptitudes, his motor skills, his height, his weight, or even his temperature.

In this connection let us use the word *testing* to mean the process of using any device (test, inventory, scale, thermometer) in the examination of an individual. More explicitly, *testing is the controlled observation of the behavior of an individual to whom stimuli of known characteristics are applied in a known manner*. It would follow, then, that if the same stimulus (from the observer's point of view) were applied in the same manner (from the observer's point of view), the differences in the responses of the individuals so stimulated would be a function of differences within the individuals. The following assumptions inhere in this process:

1. It is assumed that *the observer is adequately prepared* and skilled in the procedures of getting the subject to respond effectively (rapport), of applying the stimuli (test or test items), of recording the responses of the subject, and of evaluating (scoring) those responses according to the instructions for the standardized use of the device. In the majority of cases, the standardized procedures are adhered to rigidly. Later we shall consider certain studied departures from these procedures in connection with the examination of certain kinds of exceptional children.

2. It is assumed that *the sampling of behavior* in the test situation *is both adequate in amount and representative in area*. The safest way to judge a basket of strawberries would be to examine each strawberry and then base one's judgment on the total sample. But people don't do that. Some look only at the top, and others tip up the basket and look at a few more. In the area of human behavior, we can't sample all of it, but by acceptable statistical methods we can determine how small a sample we can safely take. Similarly, we can't sample every different area of behavior, but we can and do sample those that, statistically, have been found to yield adequate reliability and validity.

3. It is assumed that *the subjects* being tested *have been exposed to comparable,* but not necessarily identical, *acculturation*. Even if the language problem is ignored, a personality test or inventory or a vocational aptitude test developed for use in the United States could well be of little or no value if used in Thailand or on the Zulus. Certain other tests are nearly as inappropriate' when used on certain types of the physically disabled whose worlds have been seriously circumscribed—as, for instance, Berko (1953) pointed out in connection with the cerebral palsied. Less often, but equally important, certain children may give evidence of having been "hothoused," given rather intensive cultural training consciously or unconsciously, by adults who, quite understandably, want their children to do well.

4. It is assumed that *error will be present* in the measurement of human behavior. Error is

present in any measurement, whether it be in the distance to Jupiter, the weight on the bathroom scales, the length of a table, or in vocational aptitude, intelligence, or emotional adjustment. Statistical procedures enable us both to ascertain the magnitude of error in any given kind of measurement and to allow for that error in connection with any given measurement. We do not think of a child as having earned an absolute or infallible IQ on any given test, but as having an IQ on that test falling between a point some 5, 10, or more points above the obtained one and another point some 5, 10 or more points below it.

5. It is assumed that only *present behavior is observed.* Behavior on any given test is as of that particular time on that particular test. It is a sample within a relatively long period of time. It must be remembered that a child is observed as reacting in this way (or these ways) to this stimulation (test) at the time and under the conditions of this test. But this condition does not make futile or meaningless the process of testing or examining because of the next assumption, plus certain kinds of statistical insurance that has been or can be taken out with respect to the validity of the behavior sampled.

6. It is assumed that *future behavior* of the child *is inferred.* The statement "Every diagnosis is a prognosis" illustrates the close association between the process of measuring present behavior and the act of using the results of that measurement in endeavoring to predict how the subject will act, regarding the particular areas of behavior observed, at some later time. The man is significantly overweight now; therefore he will be a less desirable insurance risk. The woman just passed her driver's examination; therefore, the state issues her a permit for future driving. The child does very well on an intelligence test, and someone says he should be good college material. Another child does quite poorly in an examination situation and is therefore regarded as unlikely to respond effectively in future learning situations. Or, even, a child who actually has performed ineffectively in an examination situation is judged (inferred) to be actually capable of profiting from a treatment or training program, because certain conditions are believed to have impaired or distorted his present performance.

This two-step process of measuring and inferring is both reasonable and dangerous. On the one hand, it is the only thing we can do. A child performs normally in the first and second grades. That is to say, he is promoted to the next higher grade in the average amount of time. Therefore we make the guess that he will perform normally in the next higher grade, assuming no intervening distraction. Similarly, he answers correctly the same number of test items as did the average third grader; therefore, we *assume* that he is likely, in other related situations, to behave the way other third graders have behaved. On the other hand, such predictions have three important sources of potential error. Predictions may be faultily based either upon too limited a sample of behavior or upon a sample of behavior that bears no sound relationship to the predicted behavior. A fifteen-minute test involving the manipulation of some blocks can well provide a precarious basis upon which to predict that a child can acquire verbal symbols and use them meaningfully. Even a good sample of behavior which would serve satisfactorily for predicting behavior within the next year or so can lose much of its value for the prediction of behavior five to ten years later. It must be remembered, too, that these predictions are not statements of certainty; they are actually probability statements, made in the sense of "the chances are."

Measurement in the areas of intelligence and emotionality quite commonly involves an additional inferring process. In the case of school learning retention, some kind of achievement often is measured, and then an inference is drawn concerning the capacity that made such achievement possible. In projective testing, for instance, we see inferences drawn with respect to basic personality structures from what often appear to the clinically untrained to be irrelevant behavior samples.

Thus we see that inferences are drawn from a present sample of behavior both with respect to what later behavior will be and with respect to what caused the behavior that was observed in the process of examination or measurement. It is particularly important to recognize that the results obtained in testing or assessing are used as the basis for inferences which have varying degrees of predictive strength. This realization especially is necessary in dealing with exceptional children because they are, by the varying natures and complexities of their exceptionalities, the ones for whom many of our testing devices and procedures may be at least in part inappropriate.

VARIABILITY AMONG TESTS

Only very slowly are those who deal in the school setting with the results of tests of "intelligence" coming to recognize the necessity of differentiating among those devices. Perhaps even slower is their realization of the extreme importance of clearly denoting the specific measures obtained by means of these devices. Let us examine the importance of such precise communication with respect to "average" children and youth; the major implications of this with respect to the exceptional will become apparent repeatedly.

In order to simplify our consideration, we shall assume that normal, adequate, and otherwise satisfactory conditions existed in all the testings that are discussed. One further clarification is needed as regards the connotation of the term *IQ* as used in this portion of the chapter. Not infrequently—as in the question, Is the IQ constant?—one discovers that the person posing the question may use the IQ to denote, in some global fashion, the child's biologically determined potential for learning, a characteristic minimally reflecting the effects of any environmental influence upon it. Others may use the IQ to denote not only this basic capacity of the organism but also the extent to which it may have been modified by the child's rearing and culture, whether in a nurturant manner, in a nonnurturant manner, or in a detrimental way. In this second sense the IQ is used to denote what may well be regarded

as the child's "effective intelligence." However, in addition to this ambiguity—as between just basic, native, biological potential, and potential-as-realized-and-operating—the IQ may denote simply some kind of score by which the child's performance on some test of "intelligence" is characterized. For our purpose in this section, we shall use IQ in this third sense—a score earned on some test of learning aptitude. As we shall see, this will improve our communication *somewhat;* but even this has come to contain disconcerting ambiguity.

In the 1920s, the early days of school group-intelligence testing, when a group was said to have an average group test IQ of 121, or when any given child was referred to as having an IQ of 85 on some group test, the idea being conveyed was reasonably clear to those communicating. In most communities, a class so characterized would have been a fairly "bright" class: the child was possibly a "slow learner." *As of that time,* when teachers thus described or compared their classes or children, different teachers talked in terms of pretty much the same characteristic. This was due primarily to the fact that the group tests then in use were so similar in content. The behaviors sampled by the group tests of that time tended to be much the same from test to test. (The individual tests of those days, many of them the forerunners of most of our present "performance" tests, sampled considerably more diverse forms of behavior.)

Subsequently, the predominantly verbal group tests came increasingly to be infused with or replaceable by tests that involved less reading and/or less use of verbal response by those taking them. Interspersed among items like "Boy is to girl as man is to (1) house (2) animal (3) woman (4) business," there were items such as " ⋈ is to ⬚ as ☐○ is to (1) ⊙ (2) ⫏ (3) ◘ (4) ☖ ." The child reacting to both of these types of items was called upon to do the same *kind* of thing, but in the first case, he employed words whose meanings he had learned; in the second, he did not need to use words to perform successfully. Then there developed complete tests, such as the Cattell Culture-Fair Tests, that employed no verbal content. Later came the kind of group test of "intelligence" which is more common now—that having one section of verbal items and another section of nonverbal, or "nonlanguage" items.

As a result, present group tests of learning aptitude have become much more heterogeneous: some depend upon sampling only what has been learned by means of fundamental psychological processes; some involve a sampling not only of what has been learned but also of the processes that have been involved in that learning; and some sample predominantly, or (hopefully) solely, the processes that are essential to school learning. The scores (IQs) earned by means of these different kinds of behavior samplings are, therefore, no longer as likely to connote the relatively homogeneous sampling of earlier group tests. As a result, it has become even more necessary to qualify the obtained score by the name of the test, such as Kuhlmann-Anderson IQ, Otis Gamma IQ, or Cattell Culture-Fair IQ. This kind of specification is additionally necessary by virtue of variations among tests in their validity, adequacy of standardization, and other respects. For similar reasons, it is necessary to identify clearly the individual test by means of which an IQ has been obtained.

If intelligence tests—or, better, tests of learning aptitude—are to be used to make a sampling of behavior, on the basis of which some predictions as to likely ease of learning in school are to be made, and if the major kind of learning to be predicted is symbol acquisition, the devices used to measure that aptitude should yield reasonably consistent results. Disconcertingly often, educators find this not to be the case, as illustrated by five different average IQs obtained on 284 different twelfth-grade students tested within a single semester: 96.4, 103.7, 105.5, 114.2, and 118.2. One of the tests used was entirely nonverbal; another, a mixture of verbal and non-

verbal; and a third, the heavily verbal Primary Mental Abilities Test. Equally extreme variations have been found on first-grade children when they have been given even well-standardized group tests of "intelligence" or "mental maturity."

As further illustrative of the necessity of understanding the natures of different devices and being able to recognize the different things they "say" about children, there are (unpublished) data obtained by this author in the process of seeking to obtain meaningful measures of the learning potentials of some children of Mexican-American migrant workers in an Illinois summer-school program. Under his supervision, the children were given the Peabody Picture Vocabulary Test (PPVT), the seventh edition of the Kuhlmann-Anderson (group) test (K-A), and the Cattell Culture Fair (group) Test (CCFT). Forty-eight children (33 boys, 15 girls; 6–0 to 10–0 years old) took all three tests. The median IQ on the PPVT was 70.5 ("mentally retarded"?); on the K-A, 87.88; and on the CCFT, 94.75. To the uninformed, these figures could be disconcerting or dangerous, depending upon the inferences drawn from them. To those who are psychologically grounded, instead of psychometrically "hooked," they convey much valid information—as will be seen later.

Chronologically paralleling this confusing state of affairs as regards group tests has been that of individual intelligence testing. Even as the Binet and early adaptations of it were coming into use, "performance" tests were being developed and used, many of them having been used in World War I testing. Appearing at first as separate tests were the Seguin Form Board and its adaptations, the Witmer Cylinder, a myriad of form board tests from the Wallin Peg Bords to the more complicated Dearborn and Lincoln Hollow Square tests, picture and figure completion tests, the Kohs Color Cube Test, and maze tests. They then were incorporated, either as they were or in modified form, into batteries such as the Pintner-Patterson, the Grace

Arthur, the Merrill-Palmer, and the Cattell scales. Because these were individual tests, they were used only clinically. It was out of such a background that the performance part of the Wechsler-Bellevue came into being and was thus included in the Wechsler Intelligence Scale for Children. The fact that children's scores on such nonverbal tests contributed a much less adequate basis for predicting their verbal learning behavior than did their performance on verbal tests was early established, although that fact now appears to be largely overlooked.

The semi-relevance of what has just been said about this group of performance tests to what was said earlier about nonverbal group-testing attempts must be considered most critically. There is the danger (as shown by uses to which the results of such testing have been put, particularly with respect to certain kinds of impaired children) of assuming implicitly that because the item "⋈ is to ⊠ as . . ." is a nonverbal kind of item and because, say, a figure completion item such as the Feature Profile also is a nonverbal kind of item, they both sample the same kind of psychological process and, therefore, are likely to have the same or similar predictive value with respect to the child's primary chore in school—that of symbol acquisition. That such an assumption is not warranted is shown by the low correlations, long a matter of record, between the two kinds of performance and with educational achievement.

At least some of the confusion regarding results of widely differing tests—all purporting to measure learning aptitude—would seem to be capable of resolution by thinking about such tests in terms of factors that appear to be related to the extent to which scores earned on them increase with age. On the average, scores on the Raven Progressive Matrices, for instance, increase discriminatingly until the age of 12 or 13. At the other extreme, increases in scores on the Concept Mastery Test (CMT) can occur up to the age of 50. "Maturity" on the Binet is reached from 13 to 15 years. Adult performance on the Wechsler increases until 20 to 30 years. Miller Analogies scores may "peak" somewhat after that, but significantly below the CMT. (See Bayley, 1955; Bayley & Oden, 1955; Guertin *et al.*, 1962.) In part these differences may be the result of the way in which these tests have been standardized. But, for our purposes here, another psychologically important variable, which may well be thought of as a continuum, seems to parallel the range from the Matrices to the CMT. If we examine the kinds of behavior sampled by the devices mentioned, we note that neither the administration of nor the responding to the matrices necessitates the use of verbal behavior. Given, for instance, a box with three Xs and a blank space in it occupied by a ? to be replaced with one of the following: $\bigcirc$, $\triangle$, $-$, X, $\bigcirc$, the subject quickly and easily can point to the X in the series as belonging in the box with the three other Xs. However, if we take an imaginary item to represent those in tests "peaking" later, we find a behavior sampling of this sort: "mortarboard:commencement::bikini:—— (1) dancing (2) swimming (3) preaching (4) drawing." Here, the meaning of the pattern — : — :: — : — long since has been learned, thus causing the difficulty of the item to inhere in the meanings of the words in order to satisfy the relationship called for in the proportion. It is suggested, then, that the continuum from Matrices-type tests to CMT-type tests can be paralleled by a continuum ranging from sampling learning potential in terms of *psychological processes fundamental to learning* to the sampling of learning potential essentially in terms of the *products of learning*.

THE MEANING OF NORMS

Individual test performances take on social meaning when they are thrown into perspective by means of norms. Measurements that are recorded have to be compared in order to give them meaning. For instance, we say Mary is 51 inches tall—a fact that, in and of itself, is meaningless. It takes on meaning when we are able to say that Mary is taller than her twin brother or is as tall as the average 8- to 9-year-old girl or is taller than 80 percent of her fellow 7-year-olds. Knowing how average 7-year-olds, average 8-year-olds, and average 9-year-olds learn, we have a somewhat fuller understanding of Jim's probable ease of learning when we know his mental age to be 7 years 6 months. This was made possible by the fact that the person standardizing the test that was used on Jim had ascertained how a *typical* population at each age level in question had performed on that test. It is of particular importance here to note that a studiously typical population is sought for the standardization of the bulk of the measuring devices used. Mechanically using such devices on certain types of exceptional children, therefore, may be completely without justification. To make modifications of such devices by using only parts of the original standardized device, to modify slightly the material or procedure for even parts of the original standardized device, or to try to combine usable parts of differently standardized devices—each necessitates the carrying out of sound research to show that such tamperings do not invalidate the process of comparing the findings with the original norms. It must be recognized that statistically buttressed short forms of the Binet and the Wechslers, and even some of the "quickie" tests, have been identified or developed more for the purpose of psychometric convenience and gross quantitative discrimination in screening rather than for the purpose of yielding psychoeducationally meaningful qualitative information.

Obviously, the significance attached to this varies with the kind of exceptional child being examined. If the child is exceptional *only* by virtue of some deviation in learning aptitude, devices standardized to measure this kind of behavior are applicable as standardized. On the other hand, tests involving speech to any significant extent would yield ambiguous results if used on children with serious motor involvements affecting speech. Certain manipulation tests, used in a standardized, timed manner on certain kinds of motor-impaired children, would yield completely misleading results. When tests that include a considerable sample of acculturation are used on children who have not had a broadly "normal" exposure to that culture, it is inevitable that questions will be raised as to the validity of the results obtained.

Mainly in areas of exceptionality other than those of the intellectual deviant, there is a very real question as to the extent to which the test performances of the severely orthopedically impaired, or the sensorily impaired, or of those with marked speech impairments, or even of those who are emotionally maladjusted, should be depicted in terms of scores that have been obtained in the normal standardizations and uses of the device. If only devices standardized on a random sampling of a normal population are used on the exceptional, still excluding from our consideration the intellectual deviant, should the performances of the exceptional be stated in terms of the normal? If so, the exceptional stands to suffer by such a comparison because many of the conditions that constitute exceptionality are recognized clinically as conditions that tend to impair rather than enhance an individual's performance. If, on the other hand, devices are standardized on only the specific populations of, for instance, the physically impaired, there remains a problem of giving a meaningful social perspective to the performances of such persons on such devices. If, further, normally standardized devices are modified or "adapted" to the conditions of the exceptional, the meaning of the results so obtained, when compared with the norms for the original unmodified or unadapted device, becomes at best ambiguous.

In one sense, the last three sentences in the above paragraph may be regarded as overstatements. Take, for instance, a bead-stringing task for which there are age norms. Assume that an athetotic 10-year-old takes the test and, in the prescribed amount of test time, is able to string only as many beads as the average 5-year-old. It still may be socially worthwhile to know the level of the 10-year-old's functioning in this skill, even though the test was not standardized on children with a motor involvement such as his. Whether the test was "fair" to this child depends upon the inferences that someone may draw with respect to his performance. In fact, logically, no test is "unfair"; only the user of a test can be "unfair," and his inferences may be unwarranted.

Assuming the appropriateness of norms for the different types of exceptionality, how should the performance of a given exceptional child on a particular device be characterized or interpreted? Should this child be described as being in the bottom 1 percent of the general population on a given trait, or should he be regarded as doing very well in view of the conditions operating in his case? On the one hand, his scholastic standing may be far below the grade level at which some persons might expect him to be working. On the other hand, he may be doing as well as he is capable of doing. The mental retardate, for instance, may be succeeding in school as well as can be expected on the basis of his mental capacity, but he still may be doing so poorly that he cannot be expected to succeed as a clerk in a small grocery, where he would be required to make out slips, read invoices to check incoming goods, or even read names and addresses when making deliveries. The problem here is not an out-and-out either/or choice; it is, rather, one of deciding which to use when. For purposes of educational planning and motivation, we consider the child's performance in terms of *his* potential. For purposes of vocational planning, and for certain research purposes, however, his status must

be conceived of in terms of his skills, or lack of them, in comparison with comparable skills of others. The assumption of a constant frame of reference, or a failure to distinguish clearly between different frames of reference, often causes considerable confusion in the assessment of exceptional children and youth.

The establishment and use of local, regional, and national norms, advocated by many, can present problems with respect to the interpretation of children's test performances. Community A or Region A, whose children's average performance falls below the average on national norms, becomes "average"; by the same token, the average performance which falls above the average on national norms becomes "average." In both of these types of conditions, internal differences among sub-populations remain, but they are perceived from different frames of reference. In view of the fact that such a large percentage of our population is so highly mobile, the communication value of locally normed test information on children must be seriously examined. A child's test information which is perceived in terms of District A's local norms may be thought of in District B in terms of its own local norms or in terms of national norms, which may be perceptibly different from those of District A. Local norms can be delusional. In one school district, for instance, the average reading comprehension performance of its fourth graders was at the low-third-grade (national) level, which, through local norming, became the "norm" for its fourth graders. As a result, children subsequently scoring at the low-third-grade level on such testing were considered "normal." Even though nationally normed learning aptitude testing was done annually in this district, the results of such testing were not used to suggest the pupils' reading expectancy levels; so, this kind of "normality" was quite comforting to the school staff. In evaluating the children's test performances, the psychologist would do well to understand clearly, in the cases of youngsters coming into his district from another, whether whatever data accompanying him are in terms of local, regional, or national norms, and, if he is working in a district having local norms, to make it a point to understand the child's performances not only in terms of such norms but also in terms of national norms.

We have seen thus far that (1) when any client is tested or assessed, he is, in effect, being observed under conditions that are controlled as much as possible; (2) certain concepts and assumptions are involved in any testing or assessing, whether the client be average or exceptional; (3) special problems are encountered in testing or assessing the exceptional—whether it be attempted on the exceptional by the mechanical use of a device developed for and standardized upon the nonexceptional, or whether it be attempted by means of a device standardized upon a given kind of exceptional children, or whether one tries to take the shortcut of "adapting" conventional devices for use with the exceptional; and (4) that while these problems vary somewhat from one kind of exceptionality to another, the problems are common to various areas of measurement. Certainly, the more one is sensitive to the problems that have been indicated, the more one is hesitant to accept uncritically IQs reported on various kinds of the physically impaired, especially when there lurk in the background implicit assumptions that IQs (or other quantifications) are comparable in a one-to-one relationship from one device to another, or from one impaired group to another, or from one impaired group to a non-impaired group.

As has been indicated, practically all the devices that have been used in trying to ascertain the psychological picture of the physically impaired have been developed on essentially normal populations. This is understandable in view of the fact that, in most cases, such devices were the only ones available and because it was desired to depict or describe the impaired in terms of the nonimpaired population with whom they had to live and compete. Take, for instance, the reporting of mental, or even achievement, test results on the deaf in terms of how they performed on devices that had been standardized on essentially nondeaf subjects. Consider, likewise, the dangers of this type of characterization of the performances of the severely orthopedically disabled. However, no research evidence has been presented which demonstrates that the basic assumption regarding exposure to comparable acculturation has been satisfied.

TEST ADAPTATIONS

The point has been made that any test must be thought of as a controlled pattern of stimuli which is presented to a client in a uniform manner in order that the client's responses to those stimuli can be recorded and measured. Whether or not the original standardized pattern of items can be altered without lowering the validity of the total performance is an important question since, in examining children who are emotionally disturbed or even seriously ill at ease in the examination situation, some psychologists prefer to start their testing with performance or nonverbal items rather than with the verbal items with which the test was started when it was standardized. That such an approach tends more quickly to establish rapport with such subjects is generally accepted among clinicians. Fortunately, some research (Frandsen, McCullough, & Stone, 1950) on the effects of so altering the stimulus pattern of the 1937 Binet indicates that the validity of the total test response is not impaired by this particular type of modification of the test procedure.

It is a not infrequent practice among those making psychological examinations of the motor-impaired to make other adaptations of tests to their clients by omitting certain items on which the examiner feels certain the client cannot perform. Certain vocabulary items are omitted if speech is severely impaired, and manipulation and drawing items are omitted if the client's hands are severely involved. This departure from the standardized stimulus concept of a test both involves a decrease in the sample of the client's behavior and, when "corrections" are made for the whole test on the basis of the parts of the test which were used, usually implies that each item in the test has equivalent measurement value.

Table 3–1 depicts the problem in a considerably oversimplified form. Let us assume that in the test in question ten kinds or "areas" of behavior are sampled, such as vocabulary, comprehension, maze tracing, picture identification, identification of similarities, and so on. Let us assume, also, that four 9-year-olds are examined by means of this device. Child 1 is examined in all ten areas and earns an IQ of 150, which becomes part of the basis upon which he may be characterized as mentally superior. Child 2, tested in the same ten areas, performs in a manner that suggests that he may be a candidate for a class for the mentally retarded. Child 3, who has a gross speech impairment, is examined in only eight of the ten areas, and he earns an IQ on that test of 65, numerically comparable to the one earned by Child 2. In like manner, Child 4, a manually impaired child, is examined by the same test,

which has been adapted to his condition and he is found to have an IQ numerically comparable to those of Child 2 and Child 3. We are justified in assuming psychological comparability among these total test performances only insofar as it has been shown by research that behavior samplings in each of the areas III, IV, VI, and VII are of equal psychological value among themselves and also as related to the other areas of behavior sampled. In spite of the fact that it is yet to be shown by research that these conditions have been met, numerous studies have been published in the field of the exceptional, purporting to show comparisons among exceptionalities, between certain exceptionalities and the nonimpaired, and within certain areas of exceptionality. Such studies have included test adaptations grossly lacking in psychological or statistical justification.

Although this problem is more clearly recognizable in connection with attempts to measure learning aptitude, it exists in a slightly modified form with respect to attempts to measure emotional adjustment, vocational aptitudes, and educational achievement. Whereas it is present in such attempts at measurement with the acoustically impaired and the speech-impaired, it is more commonly, and perhaps more dangerously, encountered with the cerebral-palsied.

Illustrative of ambiguous, if not mislead-

TABLE 3–1
HYPOTHETICAL TEST BEHAVIOR SAMPLING
OF FOUR CHILDREN

"Areas" of Behavior Sampled in the Total Test

Child	I	II	III	IV	V	VI	VII	VIII	IX	X	IQ
1	x	x	x	x	x	x	x	x	x	x	150
2	x	x	x	x	x	x	x	x	x	x	65
3	x	x	x		x	x		x	x	x	65
4	x	x		x	x		x	x	x	x	65

TABLE 3–2
AMBIGUOUS IQ DATA

IQ	Percent	Age	Percent
Below 25	7	1–5 years	40
25–50	16	6–10	31
51–70	15	11–15	20
71–80	13	Over 15	9
81–90	17		
91–110	18	Speech	
111–130	4	Poor	61
131–150	0.3	Fair	28
Undetermined	10	Good	11

ing, data presented about the cerebral-palsied are the IQ data given in table 3–2. On the basis of these data, Bond (1953) stated that 40 percent of his 300 cases "must be classed as aments."

From a psychological point of view, one immediately asks questions such as these about such data: By means of what test or tests were these IQs obtained? Because the IQs were all thrown together in the same tabulation, is it not assumed that these IQs have both numerical and psychological comparability? Were the tests adapted to the subjects? If so, do the results from such adaptations have numerical and psychological comparability? In view of the fact that 40 percent of these cerebral-palsied clients were less than 6 years of age, how psychologically meaningful are such IQs? Because we know that the younger the child the greater the size of error in the psychological measurement of him, how much additional possible distortion resulted due to the crippled condition of these children? Since 61 percent were reported as having "poor" (presumably including "no") speech, to what extent are these data further clouded by that factor? What skill did this psychologist possess that enabled him to determine IQs in all but 10 percent of his 300 cerebral-palsied clients, 40 percent of whom were under 6 years of age and 61 percent of whom had poor speech? No small amount of curiosity would be evidenced as to the extent to which these intelligence quotient data would be affected by hearing impairments in these subjects. Questions such as these can well be raised with respect to a number of other reports on the intelligence quotients of the cerebral-palsied and certain other orthopedically impaired children.

When one turns to the severely acoustically impaired—particularly those born with this impairment or having it from an early age*—some of the same questions arise, and new ones occur due to the fact that the psychological conditions attending this latter group differ significantly from those attending, say, those cerebral-palsied who have normal hearing acuity. We shall confine our consideration here to problems attending the attempts at the measurement of learning aptitudes but recognize that measurement of emotional adjustment, vocational aptitude, and educational achievement involves certain directly comparable problems. We have difficulty, for instance, in believing that our basic assumption concerning the general

* For convenience, hereafter called the "deaf."

comparability of the acculturation of such impaired subjects has been satisfied, particularly if devices developed for use with the nonimpaired have been used on them and the results stated in terms of a normal population. For a long time, devices standardized on a hearing population were administered to deaf children and youth and their performances characterized in terms of mental ages or IQs derived from data on children with normal hearing. That the deaf did significantly less well on these devices than the hearing was clearly evident. But did this fact indicate that the basic capacities of the deaf were as low as the test results suggested? Because at least most of the devices which were used sampled heavily in the verbal and conceptual areas, particularly regarding hearing subjects, one very properly can raise the question: Was the acculturation of the deaf enough like that of the hearing (on whom the devices were standardized) to warrant the use of the same device on the two groups? Because so many mental measuring devices measure achievement (from which capacity to achieve is inferred), had the deaf the same opportunities to achieve (acquire percepts and form concepts) as did the nondeaf standardizing population?

This fact was early recognized and led to two lines of endeavor. Reasoning from the assumption that basic learning aptitude is likely to be "normally" distributed within a large population (such as the deaf) unless there are factors known to be operating to impair or distort it (as contrasted with affecting the *manifestation* of that learning aptitude), and that the average of that distribution should be not much, if at all, below the average of a comparable hearing population, ways were sought to obtain a "truer" picture of the basic mental capacities of the deaf. Because devices used were predominantly verbal, it seemed reasonable to get at the basic learning capacity of the deaf in a nonverbal manner. This seems like a wonderful idea, and it would be if we could be certain that the kinds of nonverbal behavior

sampled provided as good a predictive basis (of subsequent school learning) as did the verbal behavior samplings. However, most measures of nonverbal behavior developed on a hearing population do not provide as good a basis for predicting success in school learning as do measures of verbal behavior. In the case of the deaf, the use of hearing-standardized nonverbal tests was found to be more effective in indicating school learning than was the use of hearing-standardized verbal tests. Steps were taken next to improve upon this admittedly makeshift situation by developing nonverbal tests that could be used with the deaf and standardizing these materials on the deaf. A roughly parallel developmental history has existed with respect to the areas of the cerebral-palsied and the blind. First, existing devices were employed, with little if any modification from their original form; certain parts of the devices were then omitted and/or substitutes were made; then either wholly new devices were made or planned, or administration procedures and norms were developed for the particular exceptionality.*

Making adaptations in the individual ex-

* Regarding the initial basic assumption (concerning the normality of learning potential distribution) as equally plausible with respect to the deaf and the blind may seem, at first blush, defensible. However, the author questions its validity with respect to at least those who have been born deaf. He suspects that in persons born deaf the major psychological process underlying all learning—the innate predisposition of the organism to generalize—does not receive as much reinforcement, both intentional and incidental, as is true in the case of individuals without such acoustic impairment. As a result, it is believed, this process which originally may have had a potential of "normal" operation, well may come to function at something lower than its original potential due to lack of stimulation. This concept of reduced effective stimulation logically is part of a picture of deprived acculturation, a special case of faulty acculturation as that term is used in this chapter. The possible fruitfulness of this concept with respect to other kinds of exceptional children also should be explored. See, for instance, Newland (1960).

amination of exceptional children may consist, then, in those adaptations that are made in the testing procedures and in those that involve modifications of the device or devices used. Adapting testing procedures where the content of the device employed remains intact—although possibly presented in a modified order—is essentially a matter of employing psychological tactics in the testing situation. Here, the examiner may read the standardized test items to blind subjects; may allow a child to use a typewriter in giving his responses if he has a major speech or handwriting problem; may observe the eye movements of the subject as he identifies parts of a test item (where other children might write or point with their fingers in responding); might start with motor items rather than with verbal items in the case of a child whose problem involves the communication area; or might even rearrange some Binet items into WISC form if research warranted taking such liberties with the material. Here the primary objective is to obtain as psychologically meaningful responses as possible from the child to the total content of the test employed.

Adaptations that involve modifications of devices, either by the omission of a few of the kinds of behavior samplings or by selecting only certain parts of tests or scales, constitute something quite different. As was indicated earlier, this is done sometimes with no regard for the major psychological and statistical problems involved. Adaptations such as these are made for two reasons. Perhaps more commonly, the examiner employs only those parts of the device for which he can communicate the directions and to which he believes the child is capable of responding. The extreme of this is seen in the case of the use of "performance," nonverbal tests with the acoustically impaired. Attempts have been made to describe adaptations of a number of tests for use with the cerebral-palsied, as reported by Sievers & Norman (1953), Allen & Collins (1955, 1958), and Katz (1956, 1958). In some instances, only some of the tests that make up a Wechsler or Binet may be utilized, because of insufficient time to administer the entire device or because the examiner believes, for one reason or another, that certain tests, or items, cannot be employed. Usually, arithmetically neat extrapolation procedures (sometimes of questionable psychological validity and limited in statistical justification) are specified for use in estimating what the "whole" behavior sample would have yielded. Generally, however, the communication problem is the major determinant of such adaptations, particularly in the cases of disabled subjects.

On the other hand, the psychologist may decide that he wants to study a child with respect to certain kinds of psychological functionings. He then employs only those parts of tests that he knows, or believes, involve the kind of behavior in which he is interested. He may, for instance, be particularly interested in the child's conceptualization behavior, or in the child's memory span, or in the child's fund of general information, or how he functions arithmetically, or how he learns in the clinic situation, and the like. Three conditions must be satisfied if the psychologist is going to use test materials in this manner. He must know the parts played by different kinds of behavior in the learning process. He must have evidence that the tests which he uses to obtain such behavior samples throw valid light upon such facets of learning. And he must have a normative background in terms of which he can interpret the results of his sampling. He must understand, for example, the difference in conceptualization behavior between a child who says that a bus and a railroad car are alike because they both have wheels and a child who says that they are alike because they are means of transportation. And he needs to know at what ages children are likely to respond in each of these two manners.

This type of clinical evaluation of children with cerebral defects is well described by Taylor (1959). By means of a variety of tests, for which she provides rationale, directions, and normative data, she samples behavior in terms of perception, reasoning, and learning—paying somewhat more attention to how the child functions than to the rate of development in these areas. Clinically, the procedures she describes have potential value with respect to children with learning disabilities.

The decisions as to whether and how test adaptations should be made must therefore be based, first, upon the assumptions initially made regarding the distribution of the trait being studied in the particular kind of exceptional subject. Is an essentially normal distribution of learning aptitude assumed as in the case of the visually impaired, the socioemotionally maladjusted, the orthopedically disabled, or of the total population in terms of which the mentally retarded and the mentally superior are described? Are test adaptations (or selections) made for the usually unstated purpose of causing the deviant to be perceived as less deviant than he really is (for school learning), as in the use of somewhat higher nonverbal performance scores in place of the predictively more meaningful verbal scores? The psychologist must make his basic assumptions explicit, and is obligated to try to help the educator understand them and interpret test results in terms of them.

Other adaptations are necessary for certain of the exceptional. One kind of such adaptation involves the modification of methods of evoking the desired kinds of responses. These adaptations of the administration of the test are made only for the purpose of improving communication between the examiner and the examined, and every effort must be exerted to do nothing that will alter the psychological nature of the behavior being sampled. Imagine, for instance, a card that had printed on it, in randomly related positions, pictures of a cat, a tree, a bat (mammal), a tricycle, a flower, an elephant, and a house. Suppose that a speech-impaired child is shown a picture of a mouse and is asked, "Show me all here (on the large card) like that (the mouse)." The child can, by pointing, give the examiner a psychologically meaningful indication as to whether he functions at a low conceptual level (selecting the cat because of the commonality of the whiskers), or go so far as to include the bat (as one kind of animal), indicating a high level of conceptualization. However, to use a picture of a person as a means of helping a deaf individual understand that he is to "draw a person" would help him to get the idea of what he is to do, but would limit or invalidate the psychological intent of the test.

Another concept to be kept in mind in making test adaptations for any markedly deviant child, or group of deviant children, is that psychologically meaningful indications of learning potential can be differentially ascertained in terms of evidence bearing upon the psychological operations involved in his learning and in terms of evidence as to the extent to which he has learned. (This will be developed more fully later in the chapter.)

The matter of adapting tests for use with the exceptional must be evaluated in terms of the whole range of points developed in this section. Particular areas of exceptionality present their unique demands, and the nature of the adaptations will need to vary also according to the area of psychological measurement—whether it be learning aptitude, academic achievement, socioemotional adjustment, or vocational aptitude.

MEASUREMENT APPROACHES AND PROBLEMS

We have considered at some length certain assumptions basic to and difficulties inherent in attempts to examine the exceptional. On the basis of these, the student should be able to determine for himself certain possible uses of specific devices and procedures.

The number of devices that have been well developed for the purpose of sampling different kinds of human behavior runs frustratingly into the hundreds. Other less well-standardized and validated devices that have been used, many of which might add significantly to our understanding of human behavior if they were provided with scientifically acceptable bases, increase the total amazingly. To consider each of the best and most promising of these, with respect to particular types of exceptionality, would lead us into a mass of detail that would be interesting but, in large part, highly transitory. It will better serve our purpose here to consider only illustrative attempts at measurement of certain types of behavior in certain of the areas of exceptionality. Some of these attempts have been made, others are being initiated, and some need to be undertaken.

Psychologically, we strive continuously to think in terms of the "whole individual" reacting in varying situations. However, measurement in this molar sense has not been accomplished. What we have to do is, consciously, artificially, to deal, one at a time, with certain facets of the individual, and then to reconstitute the individual into a dynamically meaningful whole. For our purpose, we shall concern ourselves with representative measurement approaches and problems in specific areas: limited aspects of physical condition, intellectual potential, socioemotional adjustment, educational achievement, and vocational aptitude.

As we consider these facets of different kinds of exceptional children and youth, we recognize that some evidences of some of these areas overlap to varying extents with certain evidences of others. A child needs a certain amount of intellectual capital and educational achievement in order to comprehend and react meaningfully to an inventory on social adjustment or to certain tests of vocational interest. Even if the items in such devices are read to him, he must be able to understand and remember what is read if his responses are to have even elementary validity. In spite of this, the areas can be regarded as partially and (if competent research has been done on the devices used) identifiably discrete. Bear in mind, too, that we shall refer to the exceptionalities as though they were single rather than multiple exceptionalities.

The Physical Area

During the early years of an individual's life, inferences concerning intellectual growth are based essentially upon evidences of physical growth and development. This is understandable because the nervous system must grow for muscles to function and for cognitive behavior to occur. When certain muscles are seen to function, this is taken as evidence that certain neural growth has occurred. When normal stimulation does not evoke a given motor response, it is inferred that neural growth has not occurred, due either to lack of time for such growth or to the presence of some pathological condition. If the nature of a variety of motor responses of an 18-month-old infant is comparable to the nature of those of only a 9-month-old, then one is usually highly suspicious of mental retardation or of some contributing pathology, or of both. (One does not generalize wisely on a single sample of behavior!) As a result, the physical developmental picture serves as a major basis on which inferences are drawn concerning mental development.

Two "packaged" approaches illustrate the involvement of motor information in the overall assessment of young children. Their having been standardized upon preschool-aged children makes them potentially helpful with respect to the mentally retarded of school age. The well-standardized Bayley Scales of Infant Development (1969), for children 2 to 30 months old, incorporate a Mental Scale, a Motor Scale, and an Infant Development Record—the last tapping adaptive and interpersonal behaviors. The

Denver Developmental Screening Test (Frankenburg & Dodds, 1970), reflecting a pediatric rather than a psychological parentage, and normed for children 2 to 6 years of age, samples four areas: gross motor, fine-motor adaptive, language, and personal-social. The systematic description of the motor performances (and functions) of children of whatever type of exceptionality has value, even when their behavior is compared with that of nonexceptional children, since in doing so, the *range* of any child's behaviors may be more suggestive than the fact that he has deviated from the "normal" in any of them. Assets thus tend more quickly to be capitalized upon, and liabilities often may suggest remedial or corrective steps to be taken.

In interpreting behavior samples of this sort, one must remember that the manifestations of some mild neuropathological conditions may not appear until later. Illustrative of this is the case of a child who, at the age of 18 months, was very thoroughly and apparently competently examined, both neurologically and psychologically, in a clinic of high repute. The official report of that clinic, undoubtedly justified at that time, contained not even a suspicion of any neurological involvement. When the writer saw the child, at the age of 5, there were motor and sensory responses that suggested some neural involvement. Subsequent examination of the child by a competent medical authority confirmed the suspicion of mild athetoid involvement with an accompanying moderate hearing loss.

The problem of characterizing the motor levels of children handicapped by neuromuscular disorders has been attacked by Johnson, Zuck, and Wingate (1951). Drawing upon Gesell's 1947 developmental data and preparing situations and devices which call for more complex behaviors, they have constructed an individual test by which they endeavor to ascribe motor ages to such impaired children. Standardized originally on "normal" children, for whom the original data unfortunately are not available, norms are established for functioning both with upper extremities and with lower extremities. The children can be examined both with and without braces, thus making possible a determination of the benefits of bracing and the effects of other corrective work.

Illustrative of a different basis for the study of the motor competencies of children, youth, and adults with neuromuscular involvements are the check lists prepared by Brown (1950; 1951) and others. Her Daily Activity Record provides a means for checking 100 routine behaviors—including speech, dressing, undressing, eating, locomotion, rising, and sitting down—and for recording progress in learning such physical activities. The Brown-Bogert Pre-Vocational Motor Skill Inventory (1951) is intended for use with "any person of any age who has one or more extremities free for motor skills." One hundred activities are listed in this device, also, but they differ from the essentially self-care activities of the Daily Activity Record by including behaviors such as fixing a plug on an electric cord, extracting a nail, packing groceries in a carton, and putting a key in a padlock. Although the time allowances for both these devices, and the age placements of the items in the latter inventory, still may require more rigid statistical validation, the instruments and their underlying rationale have much to commend them. Distefano, Ellis, and Sloan (1958) have made some evaluations of overall motor coordination, especially with the mentally retarded, by means of the Oseretsky test.

If we disregard the psychogenic aspects of speech impairment and instead deal with it essentially as a motor function, the problem of identifying the behaviors that constitute speech impairment is facilitated by the many check lists, sets of pictures, and other stimuli for evoking speech behavior, which are in the armamentarium of the speech correctionist.

Although it is not within the proper domain of the psychologist to make diagnoses regarding the presence or absence of brain damage, he often can detect behavioral cues on the basis of which to invite consideration by the neurologist. Sometimes his suspicions are aroused by digit, letter, or figure reversal, or rotations, and—on some projective tests—by certain bizarre or stereotyped perceptual behavior (Piotrowski, 1940). Such hunches tend to be dangerous when they are expressed by the neophyte; they are not 100 percent certain with experts, as voiced by Doll (1947) and Wittenborn (1949). Illustrative of psychologists' validated attempts to ascertain the presence of brain injury are the Graham-Kendall Memory-for-Designs Test, Benton's Visual Retention Test, the work of Reitan, and others. The extent to which these approaches can validly be used with the deaf and blind is yet to be demonstrated.

The measurement of auditory and visual efficiency will not be discussed here, since those procedures and problems are discussed in the chapters on the acoustically and the visually impaired. Suffice it to point out here that certain problems in these areas parallel those in the area of measuring learning potential. In all three areas, for instance, there is first the need for gross and reasonably effective screening, as a result of which children so screened out undergo more intensive and extensive individual examination by more highly trained persons. Audiometric and vision screening procedures vary in validity just as group learning aptitude tests do. Further, just as a child of normal or above-average mental capacity may not do well on a group learning-aptitude test because of emotionality or a number of other factors, just so, for instance, a child may "fail" in a group testing situation because of wax in his ears, a cold, or other causes.

Helpful to some extent in the total psychological assessment of exceptional children and youth are the evaluated measurements of their different gross structural features. Clinicians vary in the amount of attention they give to such aspects as body type, head girth, cephalic index, changes in chest size with inspiration and expiration, and stage of development of the wrist bones. Height and weight norms, interpreted in the light of the nature of the child's parental stock and health history, can be helpful in understanding and characterizing these aspects of the child. Martin's (1955) carefully obtained data on the heights and weights of children and youth, ages 5 through 20, have been augmented by the 1977 NCHS Growth Curves, prepared by Hamill, for children from birth through 18 years of age. Recording and studying the physical developmental history of children, by teachers and parents in checking gross growth and by pediatricians in working correctively on growth problems, are facilitated by the Wetzel Grid technique (Wetzel, 1948), increasingly being included in baby record books and being adapted for depicting educational and intellectual growth. Based upon the fact that children tend to have their own physical growth rates, successive plottings of height-weight status can reveal departures from the children's channels—which, in turn, are taken to be indicative of some disturbance of growth patterns due to physical or emotional factors.

The physical behavior pattern of a child may be distorted not only by neuromuscular and structural anomalies and physiological dysfunctions, but also, with at least equal prevalence, by excessively solicitous and inhibiting parental care. Unless one is clinically highly perceptive of traces of cues in such cases, the degree of physical involvement is likely to be regarded as considerably greater than it actually is. In such instances, the orthopedist, the neurologist, or the pediatrician can give the psychologist some valuable cues, and often the psychologist can find behavior potentialities of much value to the medical specialists.

The Area of Intelligence

The earlier discussion of assumptions and problems of measurement in general, and the illustrations presented to show how easily the results of attempts at measurement of learning aptitude in particular can be contaminated, are of particular import with respect to the problem of ascertaining the learning capacity of all types of exceptional children.

General problems. As this discussion has progressed, the reader has probably become concerned about the seeming confusion of the measurement of "intelligence" as a total, all inclusive something with the measurement of aptitude for school learning. More precisely, we are concerned here with the *learning aptitude(s)* of children—their susceptibility to, or ease of, school academic learning, which is dominantly symbolic (essentially verbal) in nature. This must be recognized as different from the "intelligence" of adults, which suggests potential general adaptability (Wechsler, 1975). It must be recognized that the Binet was developed with respect to children's learning potential, whereas the Wechsler Adult Intelligence Scale was developed to suggest potential for the general adaptability of adults, and analogical adaptations of it were made for use with children.

It is hoped, also, that the reader has become concerned with allusions to "basic" learning capacity and illustrations of measured learning capacity. An understanding of these terms will contribute much to a comprehension of the significant measurement problems of the exceptional, to a sound basis for critical evaluation of the studies reported in this field, and to an adequate background in light of which to perceive the strengths and weaknesses of current and future attempts at measurement in this area.

Granted that it would be psychologically convenient to be able to measure an overall, all-inclusive intelligence either within a given area of exceptionality or among all areas, the bulk of the efforts has been, and probably will continue to be, directed toward the measurement of those aspects, or kinds, of intelligence which are most directly related to the learning of a certain kind of behavior that seems to play a major part both in just living with people and, more specifically, in learning in school situations.

Because the provision of school learning situations constitutes the bulk of society's organized efforts in the interests of children, the measurement of the "intelligence" or "mental capacity" of these children becomes largely, if not essentially, the measurement of learning aptitude geared primarily to school situations but also to many nonschool situations.

As of this orientation, *children's learning aptitude is regarded as the potential of the organism to acquire symbols, to retain those symbols, and to communicate meaningfully by means of those symbols.* This "educator's definition" includes much more than vocabulary acquisition. Symbols may be spoken or written. They may be verbalized or nonverbalized. Symbols represent both objects and relationships between objects. Symbols —whatever their nature (gestures, figures such as "?," "$\sqrt{}$," and "Σ," pictures, or words) —are essential to oral and written communication: they express both percepts and concepts; they are the elements by means of which thought is conveyed and comprehended. The child, for instance, may rub his stomach as a nonverbalized means of communicating the idea that he is hungry, that he likes something, or that he has a stomach ache. He may say, "John is taller than Sue," using the symbol "taller" for the relationship between two persons. He may cringe, in a completely unverbalized manner, at a frown because this facial "symbol" in another portends a threatening relationship between another and himself. Having acquired symbols, he uses them in "intelligence" tests, in personality inventories, in vocational aptitude tests (either verbal or nonverbal), in educational achievement tests, or in projective devices. In light of this, then, the measurement of this aspect of intelligence becomes the measurement of the child's susceptibility to acquire symbols.

Lest this perception of intelligence be regarded as rejective of or insensitive to Guilford's "Structure of Intellect" (1967), it should be observed that the initial orientation here is intentionally molar, in contrast to his highly differentiated (and integrated) conceptualization. In a sense, the view presented here can be perceived as including all of his "contents," primarily with regard to his "semantic" category.

"Creative" behavior, the educator's extrapolated implication of Guilford's psychological construct of "divergent thinking," has been the focus of much educational literature. A failure to apply a social-contribution criterion in differentiating between divergent thinking and creativity has underlain research seeking evidence of creativity in the mentally retarded, as illustrated in Tisdall's 1962 study. (If divergent thinking equals creativity, it would appear to follow logically that any error response is a "creative" response.) Creative production by different kinds of exceptional children and youth is yet to be validly researched, and undoubtedly needs to be nurtured. Some of the testing efforts in this area could have relevance and promise. The Wallach and Kogan (1965) analysis of the creativity-intelligence distinction warrants careful study. At least the bulk of this behavior will be symbolic in nature.

The second terminological problem here arises with respect to our belief, or evidence, as to how close we come to the measurement of this susceptibility to symbol acquisition. When test performance is minimally contaminated by such conditions as emotional overlay, sensory impairment, motor involvement, or abnormal acculturation ("hothousing" or gross deprivation), we regard such test behavior as very strongly indicative of basic capacity. To the extent that test performance is clouded by any of these conditions, we get results that do not accurately reflect that *basic* capacity. The term *basic capacity,* or *basic intelligence,* is used here to denote more nearly the biologically inherent learning-potential of an organism. We continually hope that the behavior which reflects it is as little culturally contaminated as possible, but have the constantly lingering suspicion that it is at least a little distorted in that regard.

The likelihood of test performances validly reflecting the basic capacities of children varies with the population of which those children are a part. If they were a group randomly selected out of a large heterogeneous public school population, basic capacities would be likely to be fairly accurately reflected in significantly more than half of those in such a group. If the children were among a random selection of those brought into a psychological clinic for examination, the basic capacities would be reasonably clearly suggested in only a small minority of them. Again (and this is most important for us here), if the children were all exceptional, it would be highly unlikely that basic capacities would be reasonably clearly reflected in more than a very small percentage of the group. For reasons that have been suggested in this chapter and that have been presented in the other chapters of this book, the test performances of a very large percentage of exceptional children tend to be clouded by these conditions of emotional overlay, sensory impairment, motor involvement, and abnormal acculturation. Whereas such likely contaminations are recognized in the area of tested educational achievement and are suspected in the areas of emotionality and vocational aptitudes, they are particularly significant psychologically in the area of mental capacity measurement, both because of the higher frequency of attempts at measurement in this area and because of the cruciality of attempts at such measurement.

It appears desirable, then, to distinguish clearly between *basic* capacity and *manifest* capacity. We shall use the term *manifest capacity* to denote that performance level which is immediately and most easily apparent in the test situation, the interpretation of which is unaffected by any qualitative explanations. It is the test indication of what the client did—how he scored according to standardized procedure of test administration. It involves no guessing by the examiner as to how much better or worse the client really is. It is the unmitigated performance at the time of testing. It is reasonably safe to assume that by far the major percentage of published reports of the learning aptitude of various types of exceptional children are reports of this manifest capacity. To the extent that readers of such reports assume that these manifest capacities are synonymous with the basic capacities of these children—to that extent, may harm be done these children by means of distorted educational and social planning for them.

Because it is the manifest capacity which is indicated by the gross performance on the test, it should be noted that the basic capacity is inferred by the clinician. To the uninitiated, this inferring process may seem quite nebulous and the result of such inferring as only a wild guess. To the person who has worked clinically, rather than mechanically psychometrically, with children, this process is psychologically sound and real, and the results of it are supportable estimates. In some instances, basic capacity is taken to be indicated more by certain parts of certain tests (vocabulary versus memory span, for instance); in other instances, the clinician's inference as to basic capacity stems from the quality of performance rather than from the quantity of performance in the examining situation. This is admittedly a subjective process, but the subjectivity occurs within a trained clinician's frame of reference rather than within the frame of reference of a psychologically untrained person. The chances for and magnitude of error in such "measurement" of this basic capacity are clearly greater in such estimation by properly trained persons than is the case in the standardized use of psychological devices in ascertaining evidence of manifest capacity. But the clinician believes that a more meaningful psychological indication of the child's real potential is thereby communicated.

An illustration or two may help clarify the matter. An emotionally disturbed 10-year-old boy earned a 1960 Binet mental age of 8 years and 6 months under competent examination (his manifest capacity). However, it was apparent to the examiner that the boy's basic capacity was greater than the one reflected in the examination situation. In fact, it was estimated that the boy's real potential would be nearer that of an average 10- or 10½-year-old if the boy could be helped in his emotional adjustment. After the boy was put for a year in a therapeutic situation, which, in the judgment of the clinical staff, had been partially successful, he earned a Binet IQ of 105. This was still believed to be somewhat below his "true" rate of intellectual development. A 7-year-old cerebral-palsied girl was examined by a psychometrist by means of parts of the Binet and parts of several performance scales. The results were reported in terms of intelligence quotients, and the girl was recommended for placement in a program for the trainable because her performance (manifest capacity) appeared to indicate that she was considerably lower than a Binet IQ of 50 would suggest. Yet, on reexamination by a psychologist, there were qualitative indications that she was functioning then, with allowances made for the motor handicap, at a 5- or 6-year level (her basic capacity). The results of a year's trial in a treatment center and special class for the cerebral-palsied supported the findings of the psychologist rather than those of the psychometrist.

It should not be assumed from the foregoing that only the basic capacity is psychologically and socially significant. Knowing the manifest capacity of a child, one is helped to know his "effective intelligence"— the level at which one can expect the child to function *at that time*. Having some idea of the basic capacity of that same child, if the two be different, one can know what to expect of that child, if and when the extenuating conditions or factors have been changed or if the child is helped to learn methods of compensating, in whole or in part, for them.

It should be emphasized that such disparities between manifest and basic capacities do not always exist. In a few cases, they are large; in some, little, if any, disparity exists. The likelihood of such disparities in the case of the exceptional is greater than in the case of the nonexceptional. As a rule, basic capacity tends to be greater than manifest capacity, although clinics are not without instances of children "testing beyond themselves." The frequency and size of error tend to be greater in the case of group devices than in the case of devices competently individually administered. Certain group devices have greater chances for error than others, even when they are competently administered and scored. The age of the child tested is also a factor to be considered. A comparable situation exists with respect to the various individual tests and scales. For reasons of this kind alone, it will be seen why no small number of published studies presenting the IQs of impaired children, or even of studies on reportedly nonimpaired children, have been confusing and actually misleading to the uninformed. As has been suggested, the very fact that some children are exceptional should make us at once highly critical of the results obtained on such children by merely conventional approaches to the measurement of their mental capacities. This in no way vitiates conventional usage of devices to ascertain the learning aptitude of not less than three-fourths of the totality of our school-age children, under the assumptions that have been stated; it suggests only that an intelligent caution be exercised with respect to the undertaking of this task in the cases of at least those 15 to 20 percent of our preschool and school-age children and youth who constitute the exceptional group. Healthy skepticism is rightly maintained at all times with respect to all test results; it is only more so with respect to the exceptional.

It is essential to emphasize, then, especially regarding group tests, that low test scores always are much more suspect than are high scores. The chances of error being present in an obtained low score are much greater than in high scores. A low score that is "untrue," or is not accurately indicative of the basic capacity of a child, still has psychological significance because it is of value to know that the child scored "artificially" low and to know that there are, or can be, times when he can or will stumble. The wise psychologist always assumes—and tries to make it clear to others that they too should assume —that the scores that children earn in his examinations of them suggest *minimal* expectations which should be held for them.

Good group intelligence tests have their major value (still short of perfection) as screening devices, for the initial identification of the mentally superior; they have decreased screening value (but are still practical) with respect to the mentally retarded; and they are of still less screening value in reflecting verbal learning capacity as we go from the socially and emotionally maladjusted to the speech-impaired, the sensorily impaired, the seriously involved orthopedically impaired, and the disadvantaged. In the case of the orthopedically impaired, the tests have high practical screening value, provided the children on whom they are used have no interfering motor impairments and no major cultural impoverishment. With respect to some children with cerebral-palsied conditions, and certain others who are known to be brain-damaged, the possible effect of conceptual dysfunctions needs also to be considered.

The need for more definitive depiction of the learning capacities of exceptional children, and for reduction in the error of such measurement, necessitates individual examination of them. In such an individual examination approach, greater adaptation of the procedure is possible in terms of the characteristics of the child. Rapport is established in the face-to-face situation, whereas indifference or fright may exist under group testing. The child who, for purely physical reasons, is enabled under individual examination procedures to take his time, or to react only to situations that have been selected so as not to prejudice the sampling of his behavior, is not cut short by time limits and is not forced to enter into or avoid completely (fail) a variety of test situations that were found to have meaning with respect to the nonimpaired. Less culturally contaminated behavior samplings can be made by means of certain individual procedures in the case of the child who presents a history of marked cultural deprivation as a result of sustained physical confinement, whereas most conventional group devices may involve a heavy sampling of behaviors that are completely irrelevant to such a child's psychological history.

DIFFERENTIATIONS WITHIN LEARNING APTITUDE

There is a manner of perceiving and understanding children's learning aptitude test results which helps in the differentiation between what were earlier referred to as *manifest capacity* (gross performance reflected in conventional test scores) and *basic capacity* (a clinically-inferred potential which may be different from the raw performance). "Intelligence" and learning aptitude tests for children can profitably be examined in terms of the extent to which they sample the psychological processes that make learning possible and the extent to which they sample behavior according to what has been learned, or in terms of *process* (Ps) and *product* (Pt). Regarded in the light of this orientation, manifest capacity usually reflects a child's status (score) as a result of his performance on some unspecified mix of Ps and Pt behavior samplings. Such a score is not entirely without value in suggesting his academic potentiality, but should be in-

creasingly questioned as his physical condition and/or acculturation are not typical. Basic capacity, on the other hand, is best inferred when proper consideration is given to his performance on Ps samplings* (Newland, 1972, 1977).

A few examples of test items or of prototypes will help make clear the important differentiation between the two kinds of behavior sampling. Most easily recognized are items dominantly sampling Pt: "Show me your nose," "Show me the picture of an umbrella." "Name the days of the week." "How many eggs are there in a dozen?" "What is missing?" (The stimulus is a picture of a numbered playing card with one of the spots missing.) "How many legs does a centipede have?" "How far is it from New York City to Los Angeles?" and the like. Certain tests—for instance, the Peabody Picture Vocabulary Test and the Information subtests of the Wechslers—dominantly sample Pt.

Samplings of Ps are highly varied. The child is confronted, for example, with cards on which the following may be printed: a triangle, a circle, and a triangle; or a green circle, a red circle, and a green circle; or a triangle, a circle, a square, and a pentagon; or pictures of a hoe, a rake, a spade, and a tricycle; or (if the words are known to the child and if he can read), the word series, "child, man, dog, woman." (For average 11-year-olds, where the item falls on the Binet, the item, "In what way are a snake, a cow, and a sparrow alike?" is a Ps-dominant item; for average 6-year-olds, it would be a Pt-dominant item.) On the Ps-dominant item where the child is confronted with a group

---

* Interestingly related to this conceptualization, which was arrived at clinically, is Cattell's (1965) positing, on the basis of the results obtained by factor analysis, fluid general abilities, similar to but not identical with Ps, and crystallized general abilities, similar to but not identical with Pt. Ps is relatable to Guilford's (1967) "operations"; Pt is relatable to his "products."

of pictures representing a boy, a girl, a man, a house, and a woman, he is asked to indicate the one that does not belong, or is different. Illustrative tests that predominantly sample Ps are the Raven's Matrices, the Columbia Mental Maturity Scale, at least the early portion of the Leiter International Scale, and the Cattell Culture Fair (group) Test.

Individual tests such as the Binet and the Wechslers are made up of a mixture of Ps samplings and Pt samplings. Some group tests have separate sections which sample Ps and Pt. The Kuhlmann-Anderson group test is made up of a mixture of Ps and Pt sampling items; the amount of Ps sampling strongly dominating the tests for children up to the third grade level and the relative amount of Pt sampling increasing in the tests for the older children.* Thus, it must be clearly recognized not only that different tests of learning aptitude "say" different things about school children, but also that different parts of the same test may "say" quite different things psychologically.

Graphically shown in Figure 3–1 is what is involved in a Ps-Pt perception of children's tested learning aptitude in regard to at least educational achievement. "Intelligence" tests make behavior samplings that consist of varying mixtures of Ps and Pt. (Probably no sampling is purely Ps or purely Pt.) On the basis of the subject's performance on any pool of items, inferences are drawn regarding his capacity to achieve in school learning. The more the sampling is dominated by Ps, the shorter the inferential gap is; the more the sampling is dominated by Pt, the longer the inferential gap is.

The following important generalizations regarding the nature of and the relationship between Ps and Pt are of particular signifi-

* The phenomenon of IQs decreasing with the increasing ages of school children very well may be a function of the test contents' shifting from predominantly Ps sampling at the lower age levels to predominantly Pt sampling at the higher age levels. This is especially likely to be true with regard to the disadvantaged or deviant populations.

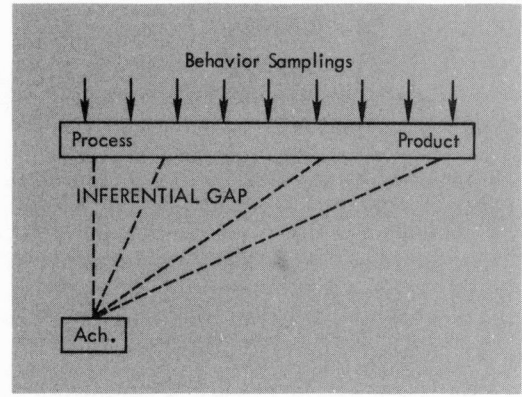

FIGURE 3–1. "Intelligence" Test

cance with respect to the understanding and ascertainment of the learning aptitudes of exceptional children and youth, whether by means of individual or of group tests. Certain of these generalizations clearly emerge from quantitative and clinical evidence on Ps and Pt; others are considered opinions based upon that background.

1. Children learn initially, and not just in school, because the psychological operations necessary for that learning (Ps) are present and ready to function. What they learn (Pt) is at first a result of the operation of Ps, but a combination of Ps and Pt makes possible subsequent learning. With increasing age, Pt plays an increasingly important role; this helps account for the pervasive measurement of achievement (Pt) from which the capacity to learn so long has been inferred.

2. Behavior samplings in terms of Pt tend to "peak" much later than do those of Ps, as illustrated by the CMT *vis-à-vis* the matrices-like tests (Cattell, 1965).

3. Pt is much more reflective of the acculturation of the individual than is Ps. However, Ps still is susceptible to nurturance. The extent to which nurturance is beneficial to Ps depends basically upon the neural development of the child.

4. While at least certain Ps functionings are ready to operate *ab initio* in the child and

others may appear as his neural development progresses, and even though the incidental stimulation and demands of everyday living evoke functionings of Ps, Ps can "wither on the vine" due to lack of appropriate stimulation. This is clearly apparent in the case of young deaf children and of other psychologically disadvantaged children. That nurturance is productive has been shown not only in the case of deaf children (Rudio, 1972) but also in clinical work with a variety of exceptional children, especially the mentally retarded and some children with learning disabilities.

5. Whether an item, or a group of items making the same kind of psychological demand, should be regarded as dominantly sampling Ps or Pt depends upon the age, or developmental, level and the acculturation of the child.

6. The decision as to whether Ps or Pt is being dominantly sampled, primarily in the cases of individual children or even of a seemingly culturally homogeneous group of children, rests fundamentally upon the clinical judgment of the examiner.

7. Proper differentiation between Ps and Pt in the learning aptitude test results of the 15 to 25 percent of children in whom this is most crucial can be both socially and educationally productive. The data presented on page 111 on the Mexican-American children illustrate this. The findings of Strein and Ysseldyke (1974) regarding disadvantaged and advantaged children in Pennsylvania also clearly suggest this.

8. The learning aptitudes of children must not be perceived only in terms of Ps or only in terms of Pt. Even before the child enters school, his learning is contributed to by both Ps and Pt. Just what "mix" is best for any child depends in part upon his present condition and in part upon the nature of the learning demands he experiences. A school program that involves solely or primarily rote learning makes little demand upon Ps.

9. There are six kinds of manifestations of the operation of Ps that are easily discerned: (1) the identification of differences ("Which one is different?"); (2) the identification of identities ("Which one is just like this?");

(3) the identification of similarities ("Which one is most like this?"); (4) the extension of progressions ("Which one comes next?"); (5) the completion of proportions (the "A:B::C:?" kind of item); and (6) the completion of patterns (figures, matrices, pictures). The psychological functioning involved in these manifestations of Ps are describable in terms of Spearman's education of relationships and education of correlates. The kinds of stimuli used in test items involving these manifestations of Ps should be thought of in terms of Guilford's "contents"—figural, symbolic, and semantic. However, when the latter two are involved, it must be known or strongly presumed that the child, or children, being tested by means of them knows (Pt) what the test elements are. Sampling Ps requires that the child discover and use relationships among known elements rather than that he name, describe, or otherwise demonstrate his knowledge *per se* about the elements. There very well may be other more complex, higher cognitive levels of functioning, but these manifestations of Ps appear to be the most fundamental ones.

10. Tests differ in the extent to which they sample psychoeducationally relevant behaviors. The Binet makes more such samples than do the Wechslers. Guilford (1967, p. 472) has observed the involvement of twenty-eight of his components of the Structure of Intellect in the Stanford-Binet L-M and eleven of them in the WAIS—most of these in the cognitive area. Some group tests include separate Pt-dominant samplings—the verbal or language section, and Ps-dominant samplings—the "non-language" or "non-verbal" section.

11. It must be recognized that many tests serve a psychometric function, in that they discriminate quantitatively among known groups, and that some tests lend themselves to yielding psychoeducationally qualitative information. It is to the latter end that this differentiation between Ps-dominant behavior sampling and Pt-dominant behavior sampling is advanced.

Such a consideration of the nature of the behaviors sampled by different kinds of "intelligence" tests should result in much less confusion regarding the varied scores that children earn. In view of the fact that such different conditions are reflected by children's scores on samples of such differing natures, the combining of such scores must be regarded as arithmetically rewarding rather than psychologically informative.

Performance Depiction

The way in which an exceptional child's performances in test situations may be represented varies with the social and clinical factors attending those examinations. Most frequently, characterizations of these performances have tended to be in terms of intelligence quotients. Less frequently, mental ages, test ages, centile, stanine, and standard-score designations have been used. Still less frequently in the past, though increasingly now in most clinics, these performances have been characterized in broader, less definitive terms. Intelligence quotients indicate only *rates* of mental development. The "deviation quotients" of the Wechsler scales and of the 1960 (L-M) Stanford-Binet can be taken roughly to indicate relative rates of development, but differ in certain respects from their forerunner, the computed intelligence quotient—which was obtained by dividing an obtained mental age by the chronological age and multiplying the result by 100. All such quotients, however, have primarily administrative value. Educationally, they have somewhat more value at the time a child normally enters school, have very limited value between that point and the high school level, and acquire more value from the high school age on up. Mental ages or test ages, however, have primarily educational value, because they indicate *levels* of mental development and thereby can be suggestive of the levels at which the children might be expected to work in school.

The use of the term "test age"—always, of course, preceded by the name of the capacity test on which it was earned—has much merit. It is not nearly so broadly connotative as

"mental age," especially in the cases of those who are concerned with intelligence as contrasted with learning aptitude; and it can serve in reminding its user to keep raising the basic question as to just what relationship it has to the school learning demands made upon the child. Centile and standard-score characterizations have less educational value below the high-school level. Some rightly regard all such specific designations as unwarranted with respect to certain of the more physically impaired and use such characterizations as "roughly the potential level of an average 9-year-old," or "educable," "trainable," and "subtrainable." The majority of our considerations in this chapter are in terms of *level* characterizations.

The depiction of a child's performance serves two purposes. On the one hand, it can indicate how the child has performed with respect to some kind of group. (He scored below the average of his age mates, at or near that average, or above that average. If he scored at the 15th centile, he did less well than 85 percent of his age mates.) This sort of characterization of his performance, in light of a social frame of reference, has value for certain occasions. Many educators and too many parents perceive a child's performance in such a manner, too often stopping there.

On the other hand, coming increasingly into use is the practice of perceiving a child's performance in terms of his own profile, which involves different kinds of performance. While it is true that such characterizations necessitate the use of social norms (He performed on Test A much like a 5-year-old, but he scored like an average 7-year-old on Test B and like a 3-year-old on Test C.), the primary focus of concern is how the child himself did rather than whether he was much better or worse than other children his age, or much better or worse than some child in his class or neighborhood. Thus the child's achievement levels in different subject-matter areas (or skills) can be perceived with respect to his own learning-aptitude level. Whether the child is bright, average, or dull, this manner of depicting his performance can be helpful not only to the teacher but also to the child's parents and to the child himself.* Such individual profiling is being used increasingly with respect to children with learning disabilities, with the peaks suggesting areas of relative strengths and the valleys indicating possible areas for remedial or corrective action.

Special Problem Areas

We shall consider, mainly, representative examples of individual examination approaches that have been tried, adapted, and developed for certain of the exceptionalities. Some of these devices and approaches will be seen to be employable with more than one kind of exceptional child; some will be usable with only one kind.

*The cerebral-palsied.*** Children who have neuromuscular involvements present difficult assessment problems. The picture is considerably more complicated with respect to those who are cerebral palsied. Although this section deals with problems pertaining only to this group, it will be apparent that many of these exist in the cases of children with orthopedic involvements.

The greatest liberties in endeavoring to adapt individual examinations have been taken with respect to the cerebral-palsied. The greater the physical involvement of such children, the greater has been the need either to make such adaptations or to develop ex-

---

* A form helpful to this end and showing illustrative data on a gifted child can be found in *The Gifted in Socioeducational Perspective* (Newland, 1976, pp. 87–89).

** The term "cerebral palsy" is used in the sense of the definition: "Any abnormal alteration of movement or motor function arising from defect, injury, or disease of the nervous tissue within the cranial cavity."

amination procedures appropriate to the demands of this type of exceptionality. In fact, in the absence of individual devices suitable for use with the cerebral-palsied, a "cafeteria" approach generally has been used. Depending upon the condition of the particular child, certain items from one scale are used in connection with other items lifted from other scales, on the assumption that all such items, taken together, psychologically rather than additively, would give at least a general idea of the mental level at which the child was functioning or could function. In the hands of the psychologically less well prepared, this procedure can be dangerous, particularly if the assumption is made that such items from different devices, and often sampling quite different kinds of behavior, are comparable on a one-to-one basis. However, when such items are selected with a view to the sampling of consciously presumed or known types of psychological functioning, and when the examiner has an adequate background of preparation and experience with normal children, reasonably meaningful qualitative and quantitative approximations of the intellectual potential of such a child can be obtained, as nicely exemplified by Taylor (1959).

Obviously, a definitive IQ characterization of the cerebral-palsied child by the former procedure is based upon assumptions that still need to be supported by research, and hence may be misleading. Some rough ideas of the rates of mental development of these children by these procedures can be inferred, but a pinpointing by IQs is a psychometrist's and statistician's dream rather than a psychological reality. Again, IQ characterization can be of some value to the administrator, but the indication of the level(s) of the child's intellectual functioning(s) is the crucial datum for the teacher, therapist, and parent.

The measurement of the learning capacities of the cerebral-palsied, early discussed by Bice (1948) and Haeussermann (1952), presents problems that are considerably more challenging than is the case with other types of exceptionality. Test results obtained in the process of identifying the mentally superior and the mentally retarded are comparatively easy to verify in terms of social and educational criteria. In the cases of children with other impairing conditions, except *perhaps* those with aphasia and epilepsy, there is reason to assume that organic pathology per se plays little or no part in the actual lowering of the basic learning capacities of such groups. When we come to the cerebral-palsied, however, our realization that the condition results from brain-centered nervous system pathology and our still relatively great ignorance of the extent to which basic learning capacity is thus impaired combine to provide us with extremely ambiguous criteria on which to evaluate results obtained from existing measuring devices or on which to standardize new devices suited to the unique perceptual and communication needs of this group. Some psychological research reveals a limited picture of their perceptualization processes, and these can contribute to, or even be a part of, faulty conceptualization. With our definition of basic learning capacity, such conceptualization impairment would appear to be grounds on which to reasonably suspect some basic retardation; the question is, how much?

The need, therefore, for the development of devices and procedures that can be used with the cerebral-palsied is at once apparent. The problem here is not so much with those who are only mildly involved, since, with moderate caution, available approaches can be used. The major difficulties exist with respect to the examination of those of moderate and severe neuromuscular involvement. In such cases, communication is a problem, both regarding the use of verbal responses by the subjects and, in some cases, regarding the sensory impairment of such cerebral-palsied children. In some instances, where these children are physically unable to speak, they also are unable to point. In such cases, the examiner may have to rely upon the child's eye movements (Taibl, 1951) and, if nystagmus renders this avenue of communication doubtful, even upon the facial expression of the child. In addition to the problem of communication, there are those of the meaninglessness of rigid time limits; the highly varying and often grossly distorted cultural backgrounds; the possibility of the confusion of figure and ground in at least the visual field; the wide age range; the possible relatively higher fatigability; the possible interference of more and greater emotional factors, such an excessive dependence on the parents; and conditioning against clinical settings. Add to all these problems the fact that the term "cerebral palsy" has come to include a variety of conditions that might materially complicate the psychological picture, and it will be seen how difficult the proper intellectual evaluation of these children actually is. The fact that this group is numerically smaller, for instance, than the blind group (regarding as blind those with a Snellen rating of 20/200 and worse in the better eye after maximal correction) also adds to the difficulty of soundly standardizing a test or a test battery on this population.

Because some of the difficulties attending the intellectual evaluation of the cerebral-palsied are in common with those encountered with other types of exceptional children, it is understandable that attempts would be made to develop devices that could be used with other kinds of children as well. Illustrative of one attempt of this sort was the Columbia Mental Maturity Scale (Blum, Burgemeister, & Lorge, 1951), which was developed for individual use with children in the mental-age range from 3 to at least 10 years. This device, revised in 1971 and heavily tapping Ps, may be administered either conventionally or by pantomime.

From the time of the early Binets, young

subjects have been asked to point out parts of a pictured doll, to give the verbal symbols for pictured objects, and to use words in describing pictures. That there would appear complete tests based upon vocabulary (symbol acquisition, in the terminology of this chapter) should be quite understandable, since measures of this kind of achievement would be highly predictive of further, similar achievement. Some of the group intelligence tests of the 1920s were entirely vocabulary tests, and vocabulary per se constituted a significant portion of the total behavior sampling of many others. Among individual intelligence tests the 1929 Van Alstyne Picture Vocabulary Test, revised in 1960, antedated the Ammons Full-Range Picture Vocabulary Test and Dunn's Peabody Picture Vocabulary Test. The Van Alstyne Test is limited to the mental age range of 2 through 7 years, the Ammons Test has norms ranging from kindergarten through the twelfth grade, and the Peabody Test has normative data for levels from 1 year 9 months to 18 years. Each of these devices involves confronting the subject with cards, each bearing pictures about which the subject is asked questions and to which the subject can point in giving his responses. For exceptional children and youth who have gross difficulty in speaking, these tests help meet the communication problem; but it must be remembered that tests such as these sample recognition behavior, rather than recall and verbal production as in the vocabulary test of the Binets and Wechslers. In any of these tests involving cards with pictures, differences among scores for preschool and for school children have quite different connotations, since they so fully sample *product,* in contrast with the Columbia Mental Maturity test which heavily samples *process.* Regarding the test performances of this kind of youngster especially in terms of process is a must. (The girl referred to on page 94 was so evaluated.)

Less culturally contaminated are the Raven Progressive Matrices,* which consist of geometrical designs among which relationships must be ascertained in order that the subject can select, from a multiple-choice situation, that design which will complete correctly the whole pattern, or matrix. Tracht and Taibl have used the 1938 matrices with the cerebral-palsied. The psychometric results obtained by means of this device (some suggesting less mental retardation among the cerebral-palsied than has been generally reported) do not concern us particularly here, since they, too, need to be evaluated in terms of the concepts developed thus far in the chapter. That it predominantly taps Ps gives it psychological appeal. Its adaptability, especially with respect to means of communication by the one using it and by the one taking it, makes it clinically desirable. However, some of its users have felt some dissatisfaction with the adequacy of its standardization, even on British subjects. With well-established American norms, and with research showing that the figure-ground idiosyncrasies of the cerebral-palsied are not clouding the picture, this device could well be found to have much value in psychometric work with this kind of exceptional child, especially since it so dominantly samples Ps. Regardless of the extent to which Taibl's psychometric data may be found to be valid, the pains to which he went in ascertaining and establishing a psychologically sound means of communication with the cerebral-palsied children can well serve as a

* There are three series of these matrices. The 1938 series consists of five sets of twelve items each, the items arranged in a presumed order of difficulty and the sets increasing, overlappingly, in difficulty. The 1947 series, intended for children from 5 through 11 years of age, consists of the first two sets of the 1938 items plus an interposed set, with colors used in all three sets. The 1962 revision, the Advanced Progressive Matrices, Sets I and II, consists of twelve and thirty-six plates, respectively, and provides more "ceiling" than did the earlier series. The normative data are British. Court (1972, 1974) has compiled research bibliographies on the Matrices.

goal for those who would examine such children.

Not completely unrewarding and unpromising, but as yet nondefinitive, exploratory attempts have been made to adapt other devices for use with the cerebral-palsied. These have consisted of: taking extant test items and setting them up in a multiple-choice form in which the child can point to his answer to the question; "blowing up" items, such as the Porteus Mazes, which the child may normally attempt or in which the child may direct the examiner how to proceed; the examiner's offering test item responses with respect to which the child indicates the correctness or incorrectness of the examiner's statements. It should be recognized that Porteus made no claim that his mazes measured "intelligence" in the sense used here (Porteus, 1965). They are more appropriately included in Wechsler's measurement of general adaptability.

It is well to keep in mind that the learning capability of cerebral-palsied children, and other children with at least major orthopedic involvements, is (perhaps much more so than in the cases of other exceptional children) only partly a function of their basic capacities. Of at least equal importance are the nature and strength of the child's motivation. The cerebral-palsied child who communicates by hitting his chest or leg to indicate "yes" or "no," and the one who uses a typewriter as a means of communication, and the one who turns pages by means of a rubber-tipped stick, and countless ingenious others, all give evidence of learning and, therefore, can be presumed to have significant capacities to learn. But of at least equal importance is the fact that they have a *drive* to do that learning.* The different

combinations of drive and intelligence in such children present different kinds of challenges to the clinician. Consider, for example, the following kinds of children:

1. The child who has a strong drive and high capability presents the simplest clinical challenge because he is so highly responsive.
2. The child who has a strong drive and low learning aptitude presents less of a challenge to the clinician because there is a good basis for communication, although the parents of such a child often mistake effort or perseverance for learning potential and achievement.
3. The child who has a weak drive and low learning aptitude usually is reasonably quickly and clearly identified as such, but the clinician needs, nevertheless, to make additional efforts to check the intellectual aspects very carefully, especially in terms of Ps, lest he be misled by the behavior sampled.
4. The child who has a weak drive and high potential is most likely to be faultily diagnosed, since communication has badly broken down.

Teachers and therapists who work with such physically involved children benefit little from evaluations that throw light only upon learning capacity.

The brain-injured. The importance of the effectiveness of communication to and from the exceptional demands constant consideration in the assessment process. Is the input, the stimulus, properly controlled and delivered so that we have reasonable assurance that the subject "receives" it? Is the output, the subject's response, received by the examiner in such a manner that it can be scored or evaluated? On the basis of the responses evoked, inferences are drawn regarding the capacity of the individual to perform in certain ways—in this case with respect to how he is likely to learn. It is necessary, now, to give a bit more considera-

---

* For our purpose here, a child is regarded as having a "strong drive" to the extent that he appears to be outgoing in his relationships with his environment (people, objects, and conditions), if he is inquisitive and curious, if he "bores in," if he is active. Aggressive behavior is regarded psychologically as

more of an asset than a liability. The significance of a "strong drive" is tempered but not lost if it is compensatory in nature.

tion to what may happen between input and output. That which is, or occurs, between stimulus reception and response manifestation—aptly denoted by some as "the black box"—is regarded here as the "mediational process." The examiner must unremittingly remember that input and output are (or can be) *observed* and that what happens in between these is *inferred*.

The term *mediational process* is taken here to denote either or both the neural structure between sensory and motor structures and the way in which that intervening neural structure operates. In the case of the cerebral-palsied, the problem is relatively simplified by virtue of the fact that aberrations in their gross behavior are attributed to neuropathology in the motor area of the brain. Aberrations in perceptual and cognitive behavior would suggest neuropathology in more than the motor area.

According to this definition, when there is known or validly inferred pathology in this intervening neural structure, we may properly speak of brain damage. The neuronal deficiency of the familial mental retardate tends not to be regarded as a kind of brain damage. But when extragenetic conditions arrest or otherwise impair the normal growth, development, and functioning of this intervening neural tissue, the term *brain damage* has been used to denote the condition. This structural aspect of the mediational process is not, per se, the proper concern of the educator, nor of most psychologists (excepting those concerned with neurophysiology).* However, when this intervening neural structure functions in certain ways, the learning of the individuals in school and social situations may be impaired. The psychologist observes behavior that appears unusual, and he tries to find out if it

* See, for instance, the provocative review of research on the effects of inadequate nutrition on neuronal development in animals and infants by Eichenwald and Frey (1969).

is related to known or inferred difference in the intervening structure. He then infers that the different behavior he has observed is caused by the presumed or established difference in the neural structure. The results of his inferential procedure, about what there "is" between the stimulus and response, can be clouded by the fact that at least most of the different behaviors that have been reasonably validly attributed to some kind of brain damage also have been equally validly attributed to learning, usually accompanied by a large emotional component. The question as to whether there really is a brain syndrome has been raised by Pond (1960). The psychological assessment of the exceptional in terms of brain damage, a disturbingly oversimplified and a distressingly heterogeneous category, must be made with a full sensitivity to the numbers and kinds of facts and inferences that are involved, as well as with a proper regard for the law of probability (emotional factors are more probable than neural factors) and the law of parsimony.

Ever since the 1930s when Werner and Strauss differentiated between the endogenous and the exogenous, the reports of psychologists and the literature of psychology and education have teemed with references to and reports of research on the "brain-injured." With the increasing sensitivity to and growing literature on this group, there has been an attending proliferation of relevant and semirelevant terminology—in fact, to a point where one authority in the field has noted that some forty different such terms have been used denoting or relating to such a condition. Understandably, certain learning problems were found to be related to, or even attributable to, brain injury. Out of this background, "learning disabilities" has become an area of increasing concern. Unfortunately, sufficiently definitive differential diagnostic information is not adequate to make at all clear the extent to which the two categories of children who are brain-injured and children who have learning disabilities overlap.*

Generally, research on such differential diagnosis has been more frustrating than fruitful. Only very limited illustrative research is referred to here; the spectrum can be sampled in the works of Benton (1955), Reitan (1958), Rowley (1961), Hunt (1961), Lessing (1961), Scheerer (1961), and Cruickshank (1966). Herbert, in reviewing the concept and testing of brain damage in children, observes: "If a child was found to be suffering from some learning disability or perceptual abnormality, such a finding would be more useful than the label 'brain damage'" (1964, p. 211). Kirk, McCarthy, and Kirk's 1971 revised Illinois Test of Psycholinguistic Abilities and Frostig's tests and training materials are illustrative of a number of attempts along the lines suggested by Herbert.

It should be borne constantly in mind that only inferences are being drawn about what takes place (or exists) in the mediational process. It is hoped that some programmatic research on bona fide brain-injured children (somehow sharply defined as to kinds and extents of involvement) will be undertaken in terms of some systematic theory of intelligence, such as Guilford's operations in cognition, memory, divergent thinking (a rich field here!), convergent thinking, and evaluation.

One of the continuing questions that bothers the person who tries to make a psychological assessment of the brain-injured concerns the extent to which the aberrations which he finds in his behavior samplings can validly be attributed to the neural damage

---

* Those who regard the mediational aspects of this problem area simplistically would do well to explore the matter further. Leads such as these would be found enlightening: the 1975 Rourke article in the *American Psychologist;* Reitan's 1974 statement on cerebral dysfunction in children; and Luria's aptly titled book, *The Working Brain* (1973).

per se and to what extent they may be as plausibly, and more simply, attributed to some other condition. Nudd (1957), for instance, compared the free responses of brain-injured children and those of non-brain-injured children to pictures depicting social interaction, and found that non-brain-injured children gave more of the kind of response usually expected of the brain-injured. Some of her evidence suggested that emotional rather than neurological factors might be playing the larger determining role.

The deaf. The psychological problems associated with attempts at the measurement of the learning aptitude of the deaf are of particular significance. Here the problems of cultural deprivation and emotional overlay continue to demand recognition. But more important and fundamental factors enter the picture. Whereas in the case of the cerebral-palsied a major problem is the means and clarity of communication by the child to the examiner, in the case of the deaf a major problem is the communication of the examiner to the child. Of at least equal psychological significance is the fact that the conceptualizations, if not actually the conceptualization process, of the deaf may well be grossly impaired. The deaf child not only receives fewer stimuli on which to conceptualize, but also runs a greater risk of perceiving those stimuli in manners other than those intended by the examiner. Whether or not this impairs the conceptualization process is not the concern of the chapter; the fact that conceptualizations are impaired is relevant, since normal or average acculturation consists of the acquisition of enough conceptualizations for ordinary communication. The significance of this is at once apparent with respect to the possibility of measuring the learning potential of the deaf. Such measurement aims at getting evidence of either the capacity of the individual to conceptualize on presumably novel stimuli, or the extent to which conceptualization has occurred (achievement), from which the capacity to do so is inferred. As the ease and adequacy of communication increase, both conceptually and auditorially, the unique measurement difficulties tend to disappear, and we approach only the normal problems of measuring basic learning capacity.

As is apparent in the chapter on the acoustically impaired, the deaf do not constitute a homogeneous group, whether defined in terms of hearing acuity or in terms of adequacy of communication, or some combination of both. Our line of reasoning concerning these is at once seen as more plausible with respect to those born with the hearing losses indicated in our definition, or acquiring them early as a result of conditions other than, say, scarlet fever, meningitis, and athetosis. In such cases, the part played by neural pathology raises still further complicating questions.

Intentionally omitted from specific mention here are the numerous studies of the performances of the acoustically impaired on tests originally developed for use with the nonimpaired, attempts at standardization on this group of such devices, and studies of the correlations between tests highly varied in purpose. These can be investigated more fruitfully by the interested student in the summaries in Pintner, Eisenson, and Stanton (1941) and in original form in the *Volta Review,* in the *American Annals of the Deaf,* and in *Exceptional Children.*

The Pintner Non-Language Mental Tests constituted the first and most extensive approach made to the group-intelligence testing of the deaf by one who comprehended the complexities of the problem. The difficulties of communicating, even in the necessarily small group situations, and the highly varied structurings of the different psychological and physical characteristics of deaf children helped materially to shift interest to individual examination of the deaf. Illustrative of attempts to develop devices specifically for the individual examination of deaf children are the Ontario School Ability Examination, which appeared in

1936, and the Hiskey-Nebraska Test of Learning Aptitude, which became available in 1941 and was revised in 1966. Both of these devices were standardized on and for deaf subjects. The Ontario was standardized on an age range of 5 through 22, whereas the norms for the Nebraska are for children between the ages of 4 and 10 inclusive, although one-year extrapolations are provided at both extremes. Without attempting to delineate the strong points and weaknesses of these tests, it is interesting to observe how they both illustrate a common step in adapting and developing measuring devices for the impaired.

In order to sharpen the consideration of getting evidence of the learning capability of deaf children, note the representative kinds of behavior sampling in the Hiskey-Nebraska test as shown in the listing below.

Memory for colored sticks

Bead stringing (copying and remembering)

Pictorial association

Block building (from pictures)

Memory for digits (subject reproduces one to five digits, presented visually, and then hidden)

Completion of drawings

Pictorial identification

Paper folding

Visual attention span (one to six pictures, briefly exposed, to be identified among fifteen possibilities)

Puzzle blocks (cubes, variously cut up, to be reassembled)

Pictorial analogies (pictured equivalents of the type: "Man:House::Bird:?")

As stressed earlier, the thoughtful examiner needs always to be asking himself, What is the nature of the relationship between the kinds of behavior samplings he is making and the school learning demands which the child will be facing? Contributive to the answer to this question is the more specific question: Just what psychological demand(s) does each item make upon the child? This type of querying has been sharpened further by seeking to answer the questions: Is this test item predominantly tapping the psychological operations by means of which the child does his learning (Ps)? Is this test item predominantly sampling what the child has learned (Pt)? Examine the kinds of Hiskey samplings in light of questions such as these and in terms of the varied kinds of goals of the learning of deaf children.* Certainly some amount and kind of learning aptitude must underlie both achieving in the conventional academic areas and acquiring receptive and expressive communication skills of whatever nature—signing, speech reading, and so forth. But it well may be possible that the two (or more) kinds of learning to be predicted should be regarded as different criteria against which measures of learning aptitude need to be validated separately.

Here, again, we see the evidences of the cafeteria approach (which was mentioned with respect to examination procedures employed on the cerebral-palsied) with, however, the manner of communication altered in view of the impaired hearing acuity. Here, though, the items selected in the cafeteria have been assembled and abetted by others statistically into what the author believes to be an effective device for the indication of the learning potential. This is one step slightly in advance of the present status of testing the cerebral-palsied. This step, it will be noted, is predicated upon the

* It will be noted that "memory" is considerably sampled—both explicitly and implicitly. Memory, or, better, "remembering," plays an ephemeral role in all school learning, and its importance depends upon the nature of the learning demands made upon the child. It is important to differentiate among different kinds of remembering behavior—rote-immediate, rote-delayed, meaningful-immediate, and meaningful-delayed. In the latter two kinds, precise reproduction of the stimulus usually is replaced by a paraphrased, or equivalency, rendering of the stimulus. Memory is not regarded here as Ps, but Ps is involved in the latter two kinds of remembering.

assumption that the types of behavior sampled by the Binet, and others from which the items were adapted or upon which they were modeled, are psychologically crucial in the measurement, either directly or indirectly, of basic learning capacity. In fact, this kind of test construction dominantly characterizes the numerous "school readiness" tests, many of them individual. In large part, items were selected for tests because the test maker liked them and/or because they had been found to discriminate well and correlate well with school learning behavior. Evidence that some theory of intelligence supports the item selection process is seldom found.

As a matter of seeming necessity, and in spite of the long-known fact that, generally, "performance" type behavior samplings are of lower predictive value of book-learning capability than are those of a verbal nature, the non-verbal portions of the Wechslers are quite widely used with the deaf. Opinions, yet to be supported systematically by meaningful data, are generally favorable to such partial uses of the Wechslers, just as they were with respect to the desirability of the earlier performance tests over verbal tests. The Arthur Adaptation of the Leiter International Performance Scale, although not specifically developed for use with the deaf, has been used on them. Leiter results on deaf children have been reported by Birch and Birch (1951), with interesting and ambiguous disparities found between them and those obtained on the Arthur Performance Scale and on the early Nebraska. A few are trying the Progressive Matrices on the deaf and are entertaining the suspicion that this device will be found to be still more rewarding. On the basis of the responses of 1,400 hearing and 1,054 deaf subjects, all between the ages of 3 and 16, a revision of the Snijders-Doman Non-Verbal Intelligence Scale has been made. It involves a variety of behavior sampling—block design, picture completion, picture arrangement, visual memory, drawing and copying of designs, and sorting of objects and cards. The scale is structured in terms of "psychological viewpoints": form, combination, abstraction, and memory.

Considerable work in the area of individual learning aptitude testing of the deaf is still needed before the situation can be reasonably stabilized. Particularly germane with respect to testing in this area of exceptionality is the general question of what kind of behavior sample can provide the best basis for predicting the school learning of those so tested. The tendency has been for workers in this area to take those parts of tests which most easily can be communicated to the deaf, and then to seek to identify that pattern of such tests which either discriminated between successive year levels or which yielded positive correlations with the amounts learned, or both. The sizes of such correlations leave much to be desired. This approach has tended to result in almost exclusive use of performance-type tests —long known to yield results that correlate poorly with the results of schooling, at least in the case of the hearing. The convenience in the use of such performance tests plus the chance of evoking higher scoring responses on such tests (this latter being a boon at times to many working with the mentally retarded as well) have tended to impede the development of a pattern of behavior sampling that might be significantly more predictive of the deaf's acquisition and use of symbols. Many of these tests appear to sample *process* more heavily than *product*. Here the problem would appear to lie, however, in the possibility that secondary psychological processes are being sampled rather than those processes more fundamental to the symbolic learning of the deaf. On the basis of the process-product concept developed earlier, one would assume that the kinds of behavior sampling involved in the Columbia, Leiter, and the Raven Matrices should be more fruitful, particularly with the young deaf.

It must be remembered that learning ca-

pacity tests are given for the purpose of getting indications of how well children will learn in school. The learning product of the public schools, with the nonimpaired children, is still a great deal more clear-cut and generally agreed upon than is the learning product of the deaf, where the picture is tremendously clouded by a confusion of goals such as "learning speech-reading, language, speech, and school subjects," "learning in a sign-dominated world," "learning in a speech-reading-dominated world," "learning to adjust," and the like. The ambiguity of any one of these and use of different ones in different studies make for an elusive predictive target against which to validate any test of the learning aptitude of the deaf.

The blind. With the blind, as with the other kinds of physically impaired, the a priori assumption has been made that their learning potential, whether basic or manifest, is made up of the same component parts that are present and operative to the same extent as in the case of the nonimpaired. This is probably a much more convenient point at which to start than if we were to assume the psychological naïveté of, say, Binet when he first undertook the task of identifying those kinds of behavior that served as indicators of learning capacity, or if we were to start back at the point where many performance tests were made in the hope that some of them would have predictive value for at least something. Our success in discovering those kinds of behavior that in combination are reasonably predictive of the learning behavior of children who are predominantly nonimpaired, while helpfully suggestive in attacking this problem for the impaired, must be regarded as potentially restrictive of our perception of all the psychological factors operating in the case of the impaired. Because of perceptual or conceptual impairment or distortion and because of the unique communication problems of the various impaired groups, certain behavior samples that are important with respect to the nonimpaired may be of much less or of no significance with respect to the impaired, and vice versa. For a thoroughly adequate approach to this area of measurement, we need a factor analysis, within each handicap area, of a wide variety of both old and new test approaches in order to ascertain for the different kinds of impaired what the primary mental abilities are and to ascertain the relative part that each such ability plays. Until we know that the primary mental ability pictures for all the kinds of impaired are the same as those for the nonimpaired, we must accept only provisionally the majority of our current testing approaches in this area.

This is not to imply that what has been done in the area of the total and severely visually impaired is without value. Research evidence that has been accumulated, from the early 1920s, by Samuel P. Hayes, his early co-workers, and his students, on the improvement of mental test scores with chronological age, on the relative stability of the intelligence quotients of blind children, and on the correlations between intelligence test performance and educational achievement indicates quite the contrary. The question remains whether or not the adaptations of the Binets and the Wechslers, significant as they have been, represent a psychologically adequate sampling of the behavior of the blind and the severely visually impaired.

Viewing this area, as we did that of the cerebral-palsied and the deaf, we again see that unique problems arise with respect to communication, perception, and conceptualization. Communication is much more nearly normal than in the former areas: when it is impaired, it is essentially as a result of perceptual and conceptual distortions. "White as the driven snow," "blood red," and "sneeringly" mean something quite different to the blind than they mean to the physically impaired who can see, since to the blind they may well mean "cold-wet-slippery," "warm-wet," and a particular voice quality or word sequence. Perceptual

restrictions of this sort, with the attending conceptual impoverishment, have a direct bearing upon our assumptions of comparable acculturation. Test items that are known to involve this kind of contamination are, fortunately, identifiable and replaceable. Whereas no small part of the blind child's communication with his world is through the senses of touch and kinesthesis, we have yet to ascertain statistically the part that these as well as other senses play in his learning behavior. These avenues are only slightly tapped and little explored in present intelligence test procedures.

C. J. Davis, at Perkins, has had under way the standardization of an adaptation of the 1960 Binet for the blind. The standardization of this author's Blind Learning Aptitude Test (BLAT) on 961 educationally blind residential and day-school children, aged 6 through 16, in twelve states was completed in 1969.* Aimed at sampling behavior in terms of Spearman's g factor, the BLAT is a highly reliable individual, nonverbal test, the items of which are solved by cutaneous-kinesthetic exploration involving no braille-reading ability. Although the nature and the extent of its contribution to the assessment of the learning potential of blind children is yet to be firmly established by research, it is known to discriminate better in the 6-to-12-year age range, and, because it so heavily taps *process,* it should have particular value in the cases of the younger children entering educational programs from highly divergent backgrounds of acculturation. Hecht (1965) found that BLAT scores in combination with Hayes-Binet and WISC Verbal scores yielded higher correlations with measured educational achievement than did any of them singly, the BLAT-Hayes-Binet combination being higher; this was found to be the case also in three schools in the South. While results on BLAT correlate

---

* BLAT, distributed by the author, presently is used in thirty-one states and in eleven foreign countries.

satisfactorily highly with those on the Hayes-Binet and on the WISC-Verbal, its results correlate higher than those of the other two tests with measured educational achievement.*

In the physical exploration of their total environment, the blind are markedly less mobile than the deaf. In the psychologically crucial years of infancy and early childhood, their physical dependency has tended to approach that of the severely orthopedically impaired. This often contributes to the impairment of the communication process in the examination situation. The sampling of the behavior of any dependent child is always a real problem for the clinician; it is considerably more so in the case of the blind. It must constantly be kept in mind that, first, it is difficult to get certain behavior samples from such children and, second, there is the ever-present question of the extent to which the sample that is obtained has been psychologically contaminated by a long, impoverishing, constricting relationship with adults. A further problem, perhaps a psychological corollate of the above, that often affects communication between the psychological examiner and the blind is the occasional presence of "blindisms," those socially irrelevant and often bizarre motor behavior patterns (twisting, squirming, gesticulating, posturing) that are often misleading to the lay person and distracting to the clinician, especially if he has had limited experience with the blind.

With respect to this area, too, we need to raise questions on the validity and implications of this generalization: To the extent that blindness is independent of an inheritable defective syndrome, and to the extent that blindness is independent of neural pa-

thology directly involving the higher mental processes—to such an extent, we should expect a distribution of basic learning capacity similar to that of the total (normal) population. Note that this has been suggested with respect to only *basic* capacity and not to manifest capacity, since we already have considered some of the major factors that can contribute to considerable disparity between the two.

As has been indicated with respect to the deaf, the accuracy of the measurement of learning capacity is reflected in the degree to which such measurements agree with the amounts learned. Certain learnings of the blind are quite different from those of the nonimpaired, though probably less so than those of the deaf, and the presence of emotional problems often impairs the efficiency of the learning process, particularly in the cases of the adventitiously blind. But assessment of the learning potential of the blind encompasses more than just evaluating them with respect to their capacity for academic learning. As the blind are coming increasingly to be allowed or expected to commingle with the sighted in schools and to move independently in the community, an added facet of their learning requires increasing attention. With the increasing use of the braille writer, still another kind of learning is involved. The potentials of the blind for spatial and fine motor learning also need to be ascertained, with due attention paid to the facilitating or inhibiting effects of emotionality in such learnings.

The disadvantaged. In general terms, any child whose acculturation is negatively deviant in some socially important aspect from that of the generality of the population is, at least so far as that aspect is concerned, disadvantaged with respect to the generality of the population. Psychoeducationally speaking, any child whose social and/or psychological milieu mitigates against his being enabled to capitalize adequately upon his potentials is disadvantaged.

It has been unfortunate that, from a psy-

---

* Interestingly, some retest scores on BLAT tended to be higher than the initial scores, suggesting that the initial testing may have been nurturant to, or "awakening" of, the Ps manifestations which it taps. Whether the initial or retest scores differ in predictive value is yet to be ascertained.

choeducational point of view, disadvantaged children have been regarded as those whose ethnic or racial backgrounds have been atypical or deviant. Some have quite properly perceived them in terms of a larger overriding frame of reference—as those children reared in, coming out of, and tending to continue to live in socioeconomically limited conditions. Fundamentally, disadvantagedness inheres in the failure to provide nurturant conditions appropriate to the child. Probably at least 20 percent of our general school population should be regarded as disadvantaged.

If these statements be accepted, it logically follows that many, if not most, of our exceptional children should be regarded as disadvantaged. The period of increasing social, educational, and psychological concern for the deviant minority, from roughly 1945 to 1965, was antedated by Witmer's work at the turn of the century when he introduced the term "clinical psychology" to denote intensive work with individual children who were having trouble learning, and by Pintner's stressing in the 1920s that the gifted were the most retarded children in the schools, although he did not characterize them as disadvantaged. To the distressingly deviant acculturation already pointed out with respect to the deaf, the blind, and other "back room" physically impaired children, can be added the kind of situation represented by the difficulty of Spanish-speaking children with the PPVT, because of the absence of gerunds in their language, and that of the quite bright school entrant whose gross inadequacy in the quantitative area resulted from his having been reared in a highly verbal, nonquantitative college professor's home.

The concepts and procedures appropriate to assessing the exceptional are directly relevant to the assessment of those disadvantaged who are not exceptional. The learning aptitudes of the disadvantaged in particular must be carefully differentially perceived in terms of Ps and Pt. In all likelihood, the disparity between Ps and Pt is greatest in the disadvantaged. In the case of the learning aptitude of the Illinois children of Mexican-American migrant workers, cited earlier, they scored distractingly below average in Pt (PPVT) but quite a bit more like average in Ps. Most interestingly, some 10 percent of these children earned IQs on the K-A and on the CCFT which would suggest that they could be regarded as candidates for education as gifted children. The more specific data are shown in Table 3–3.

TABLE 3–3

INTELLIGENCE QUOTIENTS EARNED BY CHILDREN
OF MEXICAN-AMERICAN MIGRANT WORKERS

33 boys–15 girls

	PPVT		K–A		CCFT	
	Boys	Girls	Boys	Girls	Boys	Girls
Highest	175	106	130	114	158	154
Q_3	81	89	96	107	111	111
Median	73	65	86	92	91	103
Q_1	69	58	83	81	82	83
Lowest	23	31	67	78	64	64

During the standardization of the BLAT (predominantly tapping Ps), the means of the black children fell typically one standard deviation below those of the white children on the Hayes-Binet and on the WISC-Verbal tests; but, for all the twelve states involved, the BLAT averages, across ages, of the black children were only slightly below those of the white children. The 1974 Strein-Ysseldyke finding (page 98) further illustrates this type of situation.*

Thinking in terms of the disadvantaged, it would be well to review the generalizations about Ps and Pt presented on pages 97–98, particularly Numbers 4, 5, and 8. Although a full consideration must be given to the role that Ps plays especially in the early learning of the disadvantaged, the contributive value of Pt must not be overlooked, as Anastasi (1967) points out so well. In terms of one kind of reality, the disadvantaged have to do their learning in school situations where a certain amount of Pt is at least helpful, if not necessary. But the teacher who has a child who presents a Pt-dominant picture of a first grader needs to know, and be able to act in the light of, the fact that he has the basic potential (Ps) of a third grader in order to be able to confront him with legitimate (for him) learning possibilities.

Attempts to adapt tests developed and standardized in this country for use with non-English-speaking children, as superficially appropriate as this appears, can result in distracting contamination, even from a psychometric standpoint. To translate "um-brella" into "paraguas" or "sombrilla" may be suitable for some Spanish-speaking children, but for the child newly arrived from Colombia it very well may not be meaningful, since umbrellas were not a part of his culture. Test content and/or directions translated into quite acceptable Castilian Spanish may not be comprehensible to Mexican-American children who have been reared in a Spanish *patois,* and vice versa. Culture appropriateness becomes increasingly a matter of concern as one goes from figural to symbolic to semantic in test content. Even when there are culturally appropriate equivalencies to use in the translation, care must be taken that the new word is of the same difficulty level in the other culture as it is in ours; changing the difficulty level of a word can make the item easier or more difficult in the translation than it was in the original, thus altering the demand of the item. (A parallel exists, of course, when test adaptations are made for use with minority groups in our own country.)

Constructing tests for use with minority groups in this country calls for sound psychological grounding on the part of the constructor. The now-defunct, formally published Davis-Ealls test, developed in protest against the Binet because Binet results correlated so highly with socioeconomic level, involved the use of pictures in the test booklet and the examiner's asking the children questions about the pictures. But the questions made such psychological demands on the children that the resulting correlations were as high or higher than the ones which prompted the whole futile effort. At least certain tests developed specifically for use with blacks (and on which they score higher than do the whites) have been more born of protest than based upon psychological theory, or even sound psychometrics. Their sampling of highly esoteric Pt in the black culture invalidates the thoroughly legitimate purpose of reflecting their basic learning potentials—which can be done by means of Ps-dominant sampling.

* An interesting and potentially highly significant condition is found in the educational achievement test results of the high school and college level deaf. Their educational retardation is least in word recognition and in arithmetic computation (where rote learning is more heavily involved) and greatest in reading comprehension and in arithmetic reasoning (where Ps is involved to a greater degree). It seems highly probable that this condition exists because Ps was not sufficiently nurtured during their early development—that this is the underlying nature of their disadvantagedness.

Some disadvantaged and exceptional children either come from backgrounds in which the motivational tempo is markedly slow or have learned that it seems futile to apply themselves in the test situation as assiduously as is the case with most children. It is worthwhile, if not necessary, to find out not only how such children perform when they have all the time they need, but also how they perform under timed conditions. To this end, it is well to note what the child did within the prescribed time and also find out what he does when he is allowed to complete the test at his own pace. (On group tests, the examiner can unobtrusively note, or make a mark on the test, where the child was working when the time expired; on an individual test, or item, the examiner can make such a note in his record.) The scores shown in Table 3–3 reflect performances under conventionally timed conditions, but "untimed" scores also were obtained. (Interestingly, the boys scored higher under untimed conditions than did the girls.) When the individual performances of these children were discussed with their teachers, both the test data and the teacher's observations revealed that, illustratively, one boy in particular did much better when allowed to proceed at his own pace than when he was supposed "to keep up with the class." Under the conventional time limit, a cerebral-palsied girl earned a scaled score of 3 on the Wechsler Digit-Symbol test, but a score of 11 when she was allowed to complete the test in her own laborious way. She had been "diagnosed" as "mentally retarded" by a psychometrist; a psychologist, also evaluating her performance in terms of Ps and Pt, rightly believed that her total test performance clearly suggested that she was a bit above average in her basic potential.

Summary. As we consider the whole area of intellectual measurement of the exceptional, we see that the problems related to it, particularly with respect to those who are seriously impaired, are numerous and complicated. The professional and scientific literature on exceptional children teems with reports of results obtained by administering intelligence tests to these children. To the psychologically untrained, the reported results may well seem hopelessly confusing. Some data are taken to indicate improvement of basic intelligence; some, to indicate the uselessness of the tests by which the results were obtained; some, to indicate the relative brightness of different types of exceptional children. The differences between IQs obtained at successive times on the same populations, or between children with different kinds of problems, or between different kinds of tests on the same groups of children, have caused some to jump almost blindly to conclusions on the nature of the social promise of some groups of children, or of some specific children; to enthuse hastily concerning the merits of given methods of treatment, education, or medication; or, even, to solve dilemmas by arbitrarily, and with no small amount of psychological blindness, taking the highest of a number of scores or performances as valid. It is no wonder that so many psychologically less well oriented educators have decided to avoid these apparent contradictions and confusions by refusing to use even well-standardized tests, or that they have protected their teachers and children by salting away in their files such seemingly errant data.

If, hypothetically, only one person were to have used only one measuring device, variations or differences still would have existed for the reasons we have considered thus far. But different people used different devices intended to measure different aspects of the potential of different children at different times and under differing conditions. Even had the proper persons used the proper devices on the proper subjects, normal errors of measurement would have been disconcerting to the uninitiated. The presence of the highly varied and major psychological problems in the examination of different types of exceptional children, especially the physically impaired, serves to complicate the picture to such an extent that one is surprised at the relative consistency of such results as reported by Street (1942), for instance, rather than dismayed at seeming discrepancies. Three understanding and protective attitudes will help:

1. We need to entertain a persistent and healthy concern and to employ every legitimate checking procedure we know in the cases of all children who make test scores that suggest mental retardation.

2. So long as we recognize that our examination procedures, with their inherent assumptions, shed immediate, quantitative light on what the operating levels of the children are at the times of the use of those procedures (their manifest capacities), and so long as we, or some others, draw careful inferences from those examination results as to what the basic capacities are, we shall be safeguarding the interests of those children, their parents, their teachers, their therapists, and society.

3. Conventionally obtained scores always should be regarded as minimal evidence.

The Socioemotional Area

The designation of this area is intentionally broad because it is the bias here that, whatever the emotional picture of the individual may be, it is the impact of that emotionality upon interpersonal relationships that is of major importance. This is not to deny the value of studying the social development or status, or the emotional development or status, per se, in order to obtain a psychologically sound picture of an individual; it is, rather, to emphasize the interrelatedness of these aspects of behavior in that individual. Whenever we consider these subareas separately, it will be with the constant realization that they have been only artificially isolated for the sake of descriptive convenience.

In fact, it is difficult, if not impossible, to consider the social behavior of a child without introducing factors or conditions that, in themselves, are not social but are really physical, intellectual, or emotional.

Regarding the child socially, we can think of a child's ability to get around in his environment. (Does he play in different parts of the house, at times away from his adults? Does he play with children in the block? Does he go to the store for his mother? Does he participate in social group activity such as clubs, games, and so forth? Does he date?) Or we can think in terms of his physical growth and development (Can he crawl, walk, or run?), or in terms of his being able to communicate with those in his environment (speech, sensory adequacy, conceptual development). We can think in terms of his having sufficient mental maturity to enable him to go about the neighborhood with reasonable caution; or to enable him to remember what he went to the store for, or how to get to and from the store; or to enable him to understand or count when he plays games. Or, we can think in terms of whether he is sufficiently outgoing to enjoy being with, and to be accepted by, his peers.

Take, for instance, the item, "Cares for self at table," which appears at the IX-X level of Doll's Vineland Social Maturity Scale. The extent to which a child can do this adequately can be determined by a number of factors, singly or in combination, as in the case of any of the following 9-year-olds: a child, of average intelligence, having a highly overprotective or exacting mother; or a blind child; or a manually involved cerebral-palsied child. The scale is a highly useful device with which to quantify social competence, but its author and wary users of it are well aware that it reflects also "limitations imposed by intelligence level, emotional attitudes, social conditioning, disposition, and the like." They also fully recognize that scores earned on it must "be interpreted with due regard for special limiting circumstances," which include physically disabling conditions.* The difficulty of con-

* This type of device has been used for goal-setting purposes by following this line of reasoning: Granting that the various behaviors which are to be

ceiving of social development and/or maturation as a completely discrete behavioral entity has resulted in the development of very few devices purporting to measure it, and helps account for the larger number that forthrightly purport to measure socioemotional development or adjustment.

The social frame of reference. The determination of overall social status (in terms of social distance from the group, or from members of the group) by means of a sociometric approach has been attempted with a number of the types of exceptional children, as illustrated in the studies by Force (1954) and Soldwedel (1957). This seemingly innocuous and plausible method of asking children to name those of their classmates whom they like as leaders, playmates, friends, neighbors, and the like (to mention only the positive nominations), then recording frequency of nomination, and plotting the interrelationships indicated by the nominations, has raised disturbing questions as to the validity (Is actual social status thus identified?), the permanence (How evanescent is the status identified?), and the generality (Is overall social status truly represented by high frequency of nomination as a seat neighbor, for instance?) of the data so obtained. The fact that this and other sociometric approaches—such as the "guess who" technique that was first used by Hartshorne and May (1929)—must be used only on those children who either can read or can comprehend the statements that are presented orally to them tends to limit their valid use insofar as young children or mentally impaired children are concerned.

---

checked on such a scale represent competency expectancies for the different age levels, to what extent can children not yet having the competencies normally expected at or near their age levels be helped or trained to do such things for themselves. Such a use can be made also with Doll's Pre-School Attainment Record (1966), which has social components among its 118 behavior samplings of eight aspects of behavior regarded as essential preconditions to learning.

Most attempts to ascertain "social adjustment," "socioemotional adjustment," or "emotional adjustment," whether so named or only implied, by means of rating scales, check lists, and inventories have been for the purpose of finding out whether or not the kind of exceptionality under study differs from the normal group, or whether or not a specific exceptional child is "normal." Reports of the extent to which the sensorily impaired, the orthopedically impaired, and the intellectual deviants have problems, or are "maladjusted," have appeared with considerable frequency in the literature of this field. With respect to these, the student may feel obliged to raise questions such as the following concerning the meaning of such findings: Generally, are the norms, on the basis of which any such comparative observations are made, psychologically meaningful with respect to the kind of exceptional children on whom the device was used? Certain personality inventories and check lists may be used quite appropriately with mentally superior children of given ages, but how appropriate are they when used on mentally retarded children who cannot comprehend effectively enough to respond meaningfully, or on some physically impaired children whose backgrounds and experiences have been distorted in the sense of their not having had certain opportunities to respond in situations sampled by means of the devices? The reading of the items to children of either of these impaired groups not only does not avoid these difficulties, but also introduces at least two others—auditory memory span and auditory comprehension. Often overlooked in the uses of generally standardized devices involving the child's responding, either directly or indirectly, concerning himself are the nature and extent of conceptualization present in the child so responding. In one kind of examination setting, it is definitely psychologically meaningful for a child to respond to the word "spells" either as a verb or as a noun; but to assume, as is the case in the normative uses of these devices, that all children will respond solely in terms of only one meaning can lead to at least ambiguous results. Consider the difference in the underlying meaning attached to the same "yes" answer to the question, "Do you prefer a play to a dance?" when that reply is given by a youth with no orthopedic or other physical involvements and when it is given by a paraplegic. Both could receive the same score, but each would have different psychological meaning.

The use of rating scales, the results of which are evaluated in terms of norms, involves some of these same problems. In these, the behaviors tend to be more objectively described in order to facilitate the use of such devices. However, the term *withdrawing* can have one meaning when checked for a physically impaired child in a nonimpaired group, and quite another for a nonimpaired child in the same group. Further, unless the behavior is quite specifically described, such a term can be interpreted variously by different raters. In fact, a very real question remains concerning the extent to which the one doing the rating of a child projects himself into the ratings, thus producing a picture that is a mixture of what some of the child's behavior may be and of how the rater feels about, or perceives, that behavior. The distortion of "true" pictures, obtained by such inventories, check lists, and rating scales, or by the subject's so describing himself, or by having another describe him is a factor that always has to be taken into consideration; but, with judicious use and cautious interpretation, such evaluations can be of some value. Fortunately, there is an increasing use of check lists by means of which the presence of actually-observed behavior is indicated by the observer ("At least once a week he has 'talked back' when corrected.") over the use of devices which require the observer to infer the presence or absence of behavior. ("He resents authority.")

One attempt to get around the verbal aspects of self-reporting on social adjustment is Jay's *A Book About Me* (1952), intended for use with kindergarten and first-grade children. With this device the child is confronted with a variety of pictured situations under headings such as "My Mother," "My Daddy," "My House," "Things We Have at Our House," "Things I Do at Home," "Things I Can Do All by Myself," "People I Know, See, and Like," and "Which I'd Rather Do"—all situations in which he is to identify himself. Pictured under "Things I Am Afraid Of," for instance, are a fire, a child being spanked, a storm, a snake, a policeman, a doctor, a father scolding a child, a larger boy shaking his fist at a smaller one, an oncoming car at a street intersection, a child going into a dark room, a bulldog, bugs, flies, and a spider. Although this has been intended primarily for the average early school child, it and other possible approaches patterned after it should be of much value if used individually with different exceptional children.

The individual frame of reference. The approaches illustrated thus far are intended primarily to throw light on the adjustment of individuals to groups or on how individuals representing the groups react to other members in that group. The emphasis was on the social frame of reference within which the individual is operating. In addition to this necessary and useful conception of the problem of adjustment, it is very helpful to find out, if possible, the dynamic emotional structure with which the individual reacts to the members of his group and in terms of which his social peers react to him. The emphasis here is upon such aspects of the individual as his perceptions of himself, his needs, drives, and emotional tensions.

The responses of any person to any stimulus at any time are psychologically colored, often unconsciously, by the way he feels at the time and by his background of emotional and intellectual experiences. No small amount of research has been done to tease out and identify emotional manifestations involved in, or constituting parts of, performances on capacity achievement and aptitude-measuring instruments. Enthusiasms having varying amounts of validity have been expressed, for instance, with respect to learning-aptitude test responses wherein a child consistently goes the longer way in child-to-school mazes, or wherein a child completely ignores (rejects) his immediate environment in the word-naming item, or wherein digit memory span is at variance with other test behavior. Starting at least with the early work of Binet and the users of free-association tests, many psychologists have endeavored to devise test stimuli which, without appearing to the subject to do so, would evoke responses that would throw greater light on the emotionality of subjects. The assumption here is that the nature of his responses to such stimuli will be more a function of the subject's emotionality than of the stimuli themselves. In current terminology, the subject "projects" himself into the stimuli in terms of his own needs, tensions, and emotional outlook on life, and the devices are called projective tests. Only representative of a voluminous literature in this area are: Frank (1948), Goodenough (1949), Ames *et al.* (1952, 1959), Abt and Bellak (1959), Ledwith (1959), Rabin and Haworth (1960), and Mursten (1965).

The apparent plausibility and the seeming lack of threat to the subject being so examined have contributed heavily to the development of some 200 of these devices on the basis of varying kinds and qualities of research. A child may model an innocuous chunk of clay into a person, a chair, a cube, a ball, a snake, or some other object or animal. He may complete the sentence, "What I want is . . ." by adding "to go home," "to be an aviator," "to get even with Harry," or a number of other possibilities. He may draw lines more away from himself than toward himself. He may fill in solidly a geometric figure, or only a part of it, or he may attach drawings to it. He may draw a house with smoke coming out of the chimney, or with many or few openings, using a whole

page for his drawing or using only a very small portion of it. In all these and other projective test stimuli situations, there is at least reduced likelihood of his feeling personally threatened by his being asked, or allowed, to do these things, and he is not likely to be aware that he is throwing some light on his emotional adjustment—a thing about which he may not feel able to talk and for which he may not have the verbalizations or concepts with which to talk.

With the blind, verbal and other ambiguous sound stimuli have been used, and they have been provided with objects and materials which they can manipulate in unstructured situations. Special sets of ambiguous pictures involving discernibly physically disabled individuals have been employed with the orthopedically disabled. Solomon and Starr (1968) have developed the School Apperception Method, using a series of ambiguously pictured school situations.

The potential clinical values of using such tests with the exceptional appear to be great even though most of the tests are regarded by many as not well validated in a predictive or normative sense. The importance of the emotional adjustment of the various kinds of exceptional children and youth, especially the impaired, with respect to their education, their social adjustment and their vocational placement and adjustment, is only beginning to be recognized. That each area of exceptionality would be explored, at least in part, by this time by means of at least one kind of projective approach is understandable. Thus far, children who were mentally retarded, blind, and nonsensorily physically impaired have been studied the most by projective approaches.

Our concern here is with the problems attending the use of projective approaches as a part of the total examination or psychological assessment process, rather than with the enumeration of the types used or with the study of the results reported. It is interesting to observe that, in general, the initial use of projective methods of getting at the nature of the emotionality, or of the emotional adjustment, of individuals has followed much the same basic pattern as characterized the initial use of tests of mental capacity. In both, a very few were well standardized before they were generally used, but a large number of devices have sprung up mushroomlike. Just as certain responses to tests of learning aptitude were regarded as throwing some light upon the emotionality of those taking them, just so have some responses to projective devices been interpreted as throwing light upon the mental capacity of the subjects. In both cases, many inadequately trained persons made use of the devices, gaining a false sense of competency and dealing with their response data with an unwarranted sense of the definitiveness and implications of the behavior so elicited.

Attending the use of projective approaches are essentially the same assumptions and the same problems as in the use of mental capacity measures. Behavior is sampled. A general comparability of background, both experiential and developmental, is assumed. Responses are taken as *indicative* of emotional conditions rather than being taken as the condition they indicate, and thus these behavior samples are taken as the bases for inferences. There is error in such measurement due to sizes and natures of samplings and to the possible variability within the individual from time to time. The validation problem is, perhaps, greater in the projective area due to the difficulty in setting up acceptable criteria and to the greater possible impact of subjectivity on the scoring and analysis of the subject's responses.

To these disturbing but not necessarily invalidating difficulties or problems which are present in the use of such approaches on the nonexceptional, we must add also those that are involved in working with the exceptional. Here, too, are the problems of communication and conceptualization. We can't present the ambiguous sound stimuli of one device to the deaf, but we can use it with certain other types of exceptionality. If for projective purposes we present bas-relief outlines of a house to blind subjects, to what extent and in what ways can we safely compare their responses with those of sighted subjects? Deviant experiential backgrounds, perhaps even further limited by mental retardation, may render useless pictorial or incomplete-sentence projective materials. The verbal responses to certain projective stimuli may be impaired or distorted due to limited conceptualization; such responses may well have a significance that renders them noncomparable with those of nonimpaired subjects.

In spite of all these problems that figure importantly in the use of projective devices and procedures on the exceptional, important additional information can be obtained by this type of approach. This is true, however, only under these conditions, which are not unique to this area:

1. The devices must be used by persons who are competent in their uses and well oriented in the personality dynamics in the light of which inferences are drawn concerning emotionality, and in the assumptions underlying psychological measurement.

2. The devices must have validity that has been established with respect to the type or types of exceptionality on which they are used. Implied or expressed assumptions of such validity, however plausible they may seem, must be based on sound research.

3. The devices must be such as to permit clear communication *to* the exceptional child or youth, to permit unambiguous and adequate communication *from* the subject, and must not presume the use of concepts, verbalized or otherwise, which, for any physical, social, or intellectual reason, are not reasonably likely to be in the repertoire of the subject. At best, the responses or patterns of response elicited can serve as a basis for hunches which the examiner must validate in terms of the child's behavioral history. And the examiner must be

ever alert to the possibility that his interpretations may be as much, or more, a function of his own dispositions as of the subject's dynamic structure.

The socioemotional adjustment of any child, not just the exceptional, must be ascertained and perceived in terms of two seemingly disparate frames of reference. In the light of the general adjustment of children of his own age, and perhaps of his own cultural milieu, it is important to know if he is maladjusted, or dysfunctional. This is part of the reality in which his significant others will have to help him to get along. If he is dysfunctional, it is essential that his behavior be understood in terms of his own development, perceptions, and history—from an individual frame of reference. Only thus can he be helped to do the learning and relearning that may be necessary for him to approximate the social norm to the extent that his total condition warrants. For each child, there has to be an accommodation between the social norm (taking care that this does not constitute blind regimentation) and a behavior pattern that retains the essence of individuality, taking care that this not be construed to mean rampant, irresponsible, or antisocial egotism. Total psychological assessment, not just an awareness of scores on tests, inventories, and rating scales, is essential to this end.

Commonality of acculturation. We have emphasized, with respect to both the intelligence and socioemotional areas, the effect of the impact of grossly deviant backgrounds upon the responses of exceptional children and youth to devices in these areas. To understand the significance of this acculturation problem, two questions need to be answered: (1) How much can a child's background differ from those of other children and still be within the normal range? (2) When does a child's response become bizarre —completely at odds with the normality of the responses upon which the test is statisti-

cally or clinically standardized—and therefore have some special significance? To some, these questions are regarded as so unanswerable that they view the use of standardized examination procedures with thorough apprehension. This extremist position of throwing the baby out with the bath does not seem warranted, even though specific categorical answers may not be given to the questions. Rough limits within which the answers can be sought can, however, be indicated.

Environmental backgrounds can be thought of as ranging from psychologically impossible, absolutely identical environments of two or more persons through some that are quite similar, through some others that are roughly similar, to highly dissimilar, and on out on the continuum to the completely unique background for each person. No test is standardized for general use on an unattainable identity of backgrounds. Nor are any tests standardized on the logical impossibility of unique personal backgrounds. The use of "unselected" populations for standardization purposes, even on the basis of prior selections such as deaf children, blind children, cerebral-palsied children, or even mentally retarded or gifted children, carries with it the recognition of the presence of an admittedly wide variety of normally different yet roughly common backgrounds. Here, also, normality is a range and not a point on our continuum, but the range does not include the extremes of gross cultural deprivation we have mentioned. Put more specifically, our cerebral-palsied, for instance, come from homes that vary considerably in emotional atmosphere, cultural level and opportunity, presence and kind of siblings, amount and kind of orthopedic attention, educational facilities, and the like. But a few children (and these occur also in other areas of exceptionality) come from backgrounds that are even more different, and will have had even more limited opportunity to come into contact with magazines, television, radios, and interpersonal and interobject contacts. Hence, they will have lacked in both the stimulation value and in the experiential value that normally, though still in widely varied manners, would have been present in the lives of their more fortunate peers. In the cases of exceptional children, then, it is not the response alone of the child who has been so deprived, but rather the response-as-having-come-out-of-his-background. Again, once a device is selected by the clinician as appropriate to a child of a given type of exceptionality, it can be used rather forthrightly on a major percentage of his group (hence, such testing tends to have an overall value). But great care must constantly be exercised with certain other children of this type of exceptionality regarding the nature of their responses in the light of their backgrounds.

The Area of Educational Achievement

In considering the problems of measurement in this area, we concern ourselves more with the *what* of the individual than with the *why* and *how*. Here, the primary concern in examining the individual is to find out what he has learned, what he can do educationally. Regardless of his limitation or his superiority, he reads at some particular grade level, and that is the place at which the educator must start work with him in reading. Such educational levels are the points from which the educators try to bring him up to those indicated by capacity tests and in the light of the facilitating or hampering effects of his emotionality and exceptionality. Measurements in the areas of learning capacity and socioemotional adjustment contribute to the total picture of the individual by helping us understand how he was able to achieve as much as he did, or why he wasn't able to achieve any more than he did.

This contrast between the purpose and the nature of the results of measurement in this area and those of the areas considered

earlier is of value primarily in showing the reasons why some of the assumptions made with respect to measurement of learning capacity and emotional adjustment do not apply here. We try to measure educational achievements in order to find out what they are; we do not draw inferences on the basis of them as to how well adjusted a child is socially or emotionally (although we may well want to find out if his emotional condition is or has been such as to impair the effectiveness of his learning). Regarding the results of measured educational achievement, we do not have the manifest performance–basic-capacity gap problem that we have with respect to measured learning capacity. Nor do we have in this area, quite as much as in the measured emotional adjustment, the tendency to generalize with respect to more global behavior. As in other measurement areas, we accept, understand, and allow for, both statistically and clinically, the presence of our errors of measurement, because we are working with a normally varying individual and because we have to use a sampling approach in our measurement. Similarly, we use the depictions of educational performance, whether they be in terms of educational grade status or stanines, as having meaning, not only in terms of the performances of the population on which the achievement tests were standardized, but also—and this too often is not done —in terms of how the child performed in the light of his measured learning aptitude. As has been stressed, it is important to consider his educational achievement, not only in terms of a social frame of reference, but also in terms of his own picture.

Insofar as most of the types of exceptionality are concerned, we recognize the appropriateness of the use of such norms in understanding the particular child. But in some cases, we purposely depart from certain standardized test administration procedures and, at times, from certain of the content. In the case of an emotionally disturbed child, or of a motor-involved child, we may give the test under normal, timed conditions, but have him mark how far he got at the designated time limits. We may then let him proceed with the tests as far as he can, in the hope of getting fuller understanding of his total educational output. Spelling tests, usually administered orally, may have to be adapted into multiple choice, synonym, or some other method of presentation. Special consideration must be given to test items involving either sound words (the crowing of a rooster, the screeching of a car's brakes, and the like) or color and certain object-depiction words in the cases of deaf or blind children who may encounter them in standardized tests or word lists. These alterations have to be kept in mind in trying to interpret the test performances of such children in the light of the norms which are provided. Some have endeavored to regard any such limited performances as percentages of what the total might have been, and then have characterized the child's "true" educational performance in terms of this "corrected" total. So long as the results so obtained are regarded as even coarser approximations than are obtained in the normal use of such devices, this method can have some value.

The conceptualization-communication problem exists in this area, too, but with impacts that differ somewhat from the situation in the two previous areas of measurement. Achievement test approaches have been modified by the use of large-type achievement tests for children who are partially sighted, by the development of achievement tests in braille for those who are blind, by the motor impaired's use of the typewriter, by use of objective test items in the place of handwritten responses for children with certain motor disabilities, and by the reading of test items to children with other kinds of disabilities, thus facilitating communication both to and from these kinds of children. Regarding the conceptualization aspect of our examination problem, it takes on a different significance in this area of measurement, since our interest here is in

ascertaining whether or not the conceptualizations being tested have been acquired by the children as a means both of communication and of acquiring other concepts. Here the conceptualizations are the products being measured, rather than the means by which one tries to get a picture of learning capacity or emotional adjustment.

At times there may be merit in endeavoring to find out the average educational test performances of epileptic, cerebral-palsied, blind, or deaf children of different ages (ignoring any false implications as to any homogeneity of such age groups). From the standpoint of stimulating research on the learning processes of, especially, the sensorily impaired, there may well be some value in knowing, for instance, that the educational achievements of the deaf tend with frustrating consistency to run below those of their chronological peers. This type of information by itself is of limited value; but when it is thrown into relationship with their learning potentials, it takes on added and truly provocative meaning. By using the timed-untimed procedure, potentially helpful information thus can be obtained regarding the child's manner of working: He may be disposed to be just deliberate; he may be reflecting the tempo of his home or social peer culture; he may have been "turned off" by his educational experiences; or he may dash rejectingly or just haphazardly through the items.

But with exceptional children and youth in particular, we are obligated to deal with and think in terms of *individual* performances. In the area of educational measurement, the key problem is the consideration of the amount of achievement in the light of the individuals' capacity to achieve. In terms of their ages or grades, the mentally superior tend to do exceptionally well, in one sense, on such achievement tests, and the mentally retarded tend to do poorly. But these performances take on entirely different meanings when we view them in light of the learning potentials out of which they come.

It is then that we see clearly that the mentally retarded tend to work up to their capacities and that the mentally superior are the more educationally retarded. Allowing for all of the errors that we know exist in our measurements of the exceptional, it is still beneficial and desirable to evaluate each individual's educational achievements in terms of his capacity to achieve. For the psychologist, teacher, and parent, the consideration of his performance in each of the different parts of an achievement test, with respect to his capacity to achieve, is of much more value than any "battery median" or average, although the latter by itself may have information value for a school administrator, as may "class medians" or averages.

The evaluation of the educational achievement of exceptional children and youth not only inherits some problems that plague efforts to this end with respect to all children, but it also involves problems unique to this area. Because the area of reading is so important, only it will be used to illustrate a more general point. In his study of 410 published reports of correlations between measures of academic achievement and "intelligence," over the period from 1925 to 1965, it is understandable that Twaranovica (1973) found the majority to be in the area of reading; but it is distracting that the term *reading* denoted to the many authors everything from a completely gross and undifferentiated (and undefined) meaning of the term to aspects as specific as phonetics. The Wide Range Achievement Test is used extensively with exceptional children, purporting to yield measures of "reading" and of "arithmetic." Yet its measure of "reading" reflects only the simplest form of word recognition, and its measure of "arithmetic" is only of computation. These are the simplest and least socially significant outcomes of school learning, falling far short of the more crucial functions of comprehension and reasoning; they are also the kinds of learning in which gains in scores are most easily obtained—probably one reason why this test is so widely used.

The matter of educational achievement in exceptional children can be quite complex, as illustrated in the following instance. A 9-year-old boy sitting in the third grade (regarded as one-year retarded in terms of conventional age-grade standards) was referred for examination by his teacher because "he just couldn't read." Certain facts were revealed: (1) He recognized only the simplest of words, and these only in isolation. He neither read short sentences nor gave evidence of comprehending them. (2) Valid psychological examination revealed a learning capability roughly comparable to that of an average 7-year-old. This was ascertained primarily in terms of process. (3) He had started school at the conventional first-grade age of 6, when he probably had the "book learning" capability of an average 4-year-old. (4) His teacher was not qualified to "teach" even average first graders; he was a former school janitor who was recognized as being able to get along with young children and therefore able to "keep the class in order." (5) The boy had a hearing loss in each ear of 30–40 decibels. (6) He had been promoted in order to keep him with his "peers."

To anyone who has worked with elementary school children, the outcome of this concatenation of conditions is all too clear. An effort was made to help his third-grade teacher by developing the following points: (1) She would need to be sensitive to the boy's hearing loss; some suggestions were made regarding this. (2) The boy would need to be worked with initially at the reading readiness level, from which he should be able to progress reasonably rapidly (other factors being favorable) to a primary level of competence. In thus working with him, she would need to recognize the probability of his having been negatively conditioned against such (or any?) learning by his prior frustrations in having been expected to learn as well as children generally are expected to learn. (3) Assuming these efforts to be productive, her near future expectations for him should be in terms of those for second graders. (4) He should be re-evaluated in a year or so, especially but not exclusively in order to see if higher expectations for him could be warranted.

Readiness tests, most of them in the area of, or heavily oriented to, the area of reading, can be a source of much information that can be helpful in getting a fuller understanding of educational achievement or nonachievement. While they have been with us since the early 1930s, they have proliferated with the increasing concern for pupils with learning disabilities. They can be particularly helpful in facilitating the exploration of more channels of input and more manners of output. Certain parts of many tests, such as the Detroit Test of Learning Aptitude and the Illinois Test of Psycholinguistic Abilities, can be quite helpful in this regard.

Criterion referenced testing. According to Glaser and Nitko (1971), the essence of a criterion referenced test is that it be "deliberately constructed so as to yield measurements that are directly interpretable in terms of specific performance standards." This wording is particularly germane to the measurement of educational achievement and adjustment. Some enthusiasts have expressed impatience or dissatisfaction with what long had been done in testing in a rather conventional sense because such testing was perceived as not being criterion referenced. Other advocates promulgating the concept have sought to render a much-needed service in trying to cause the practice of testing to be perceived as potentially more broadly contributive than had been the case. It is well to bear in mind that very few tests have been standardized without their creators having had some purpose in mind—without some criterion (well or poorly stated) in terms of which they were believed to be capable of yielding results that had some bearing upon achievement or potential for achievement (the implicit or explicit criterion). Thus, the essence of criterion referenced testing has been with us for a long time. The extension and broadening of behavior sampling and criteria have emerged more slowly. (Some actually appeared in

social studies in the early 1930s, but their time had not yet come.)

However, the behaviors that have been measured, say in the area of educational achievement, have been so lumpy or gross or have been so limited in individual and/or social relevance that other facets needed also to be measured. For instance, tested knowledge in social studies bore less than desired relevance to certain important social behavioral outcomes. Further, the manner in which the measures have been obtained, perceived, and used has not been as educationally or socially productive as it could be. For instance, a measurement on a youngster was taken to be indicative of how he performed as compared with the average of his age or grade group, rather than as revealing how he was doing in terms of his own developmental picture. The frame of reference was social rather than individual.

Three things characterize the reform suggested by the advocates of criterion referenced testing: (1) the identification of additional socially and developmentally relevant behaviors that were to be described predictively—the criteria; (2) the development of tests or procedures to measure with respect to these criteria; and (3) the perception and use of the results of such testing in terms of the child's developmental picture—a point that has been stressed in this chapter. It is possible that the relatively recent upsurge of emphasis on criterion referenced testing has in it a protest against the emergence of tests for which the criteria had been poorly or inadequately defined. Obviously, the assessment of exceptional children and youth must be done with a full sensitivity to the information yielded by criterion referenced testing—whether of the "old" type or of emerging ones, as in the area of "creativity."

Summary. A relatively simplified assessment of educational achievement requires sensitivity to and action in the light of three important dyadic conditions: (1) recognition of the child's performance in terms of norms, and the reflecting of his achievements in terms of his own condition; (2) recognition of his molar achievements (reading, arithmetic, and the like) and also of the sharper psychoeducationally meaningful differentiation of these into their component parts (auditory and visual word recognition, reading comprehension, arithmetic concepts and reasoning, arithmetic computation, etc.); and (3) constant evaluation of the relationships between Ps and Pt to the school tasks confronting the child. The use of the psychoeducational profile chart, suggested on page 100, can be highly facilitative in this.

The Area of Aptitude Measurement

In the preceding paragraphs we considered the outcomes of such educational measurement primarily as direct evidence on status. The child was found to read at third-grade level, could perform simple arithmetic operations at a fifth-grade level, or had language-usage competence similar to that of an average fourth-grader. This contrasted with the purposes of measurement in the two preceding areas which, to varying degrees, were to ascertain *the basis for* further work with the exceptional child or youth—his susceptibility to learning in school and, perhaps, certain aspects of his promise under therapy. In a manner largely similar to the orientation in physical and educational status measurement, measurement of aptitudes is largely the ascertainment of the amounts of particular skills and interests that can function as they are, and partly measurement of susceptibilities to further training toward given job competencies.

The term *aptitude* is taken here to refer to certain of those habits (including attitudes), sensory acuities, and muscular coordinations of an individual that are known to predispose him to acceptably efficient performance in a given type of activity. Unless specifically indicated otherwise, this activity is regarded as either vocational or prevocational in nature. This predisposition may be "embryonic" and relatively simple, as in the case of certain speed of movement tests; or it may be heavily structured and involved, as in the case of the use of pliers or other tools in an object assembly test of considerable complexity. Intelligence has been dealt with in this chapter as learning aptitude or susceptibility to learning. Reading-readiness tests are intended to measure a certain kind of aptitude for, or susceptibility to, learning to read. Emotional adjustment can affect general aptitude as in the case of an "unstable" person, or it can be a factor in determining whether an individual would do well in a given kind of work, as in the case of an "outgoing" person, or as in the case of a person who would feel more secure in the laboratory or among bookshelves. A "motor age" of an individual who is crippled may well have an important bearing on whether he can be expected to work at a drill press, or on a watch repair job, or as a keeper of a tool cage in a large plant. In like manner, whether a person can read or compute (educational achievement) can have particular significance with respect to a wide variety of occupations. All of these areas of potentiality and skills have a bearing upon, and can well be a large part of, the basis for vocational placement, as can sensory acuity, yet there remain certain other behavior samplings that research has shown to be relevant to success in certain occupations. It is in the sense of these areas of behavior that we shall consider the measurement of aptitude.

Behavior sampling in this area has been essentially of two kinds: attempts to ascertain the nature of the interests of the individual, insofar as they are known to be relevant to certain occupations, and attempts to ascertain the nature of sensory acuities and muscular coordinations that are known to be or are regarded as playing important parts in the performance of given tasks. The inference gap, to which we have referred in other areas of measurement, is greater with respect to the measurement of interests than in the case of measurement of sensory acuities or motor skills. But the reasoning is straightforward and the limitations are reasonably apparent. If the interests and preferences of, say, successful architects can be found to be significantly different from those, say, of successful computing machine operators or real estate salesmen, then, depending to some extent on the age of the individual, if a person's interests and preferences most closely resemble those of architects, such a person has at least that much in his favor if he desires to become an architect. If a person just does not have fine motor coordinations and, perhaps, good visual memory, he might well have difficulty in succeeding at watch repairing.*

In each of the other areas, measurement in only one of them has little, if any, value. Just so does aptitude measurement alone have limited value. Interests have value in suggesting aptitudes but must be supported by certain amounts of intelligence, certain kinds of emotionality, mobility and other motor competencies, and educational skills. Similarly, errors are present in our behavior samplings, and we need research assurance that the behavior sampled has adequate predictive value with respect to given occupations or occupational areas. Rapport and good motivation are needed in the examination, just as in any other area.

Because our primary concern here is with

---

* Intentionally omitted here is the consideration of the usual gamut of aptitude tests. Devices such as the Detroit Mechanical Aptitude Test are heavily loaded with samplings of knowledge about things mechanical—whether, for instance, the subject knows a pipe wrench from a claw hammer. In a sense, one who is better informed regarding an area of activity has a better aptitude for it. In the case of tests of musical aptitude, behavior is sampled in terms of aspects such as tonal discrimination, tempo discrimination, memory for each, and the like. Graphic artistic aptitude tends to be tested in terms of appreciation. Certain recently publicized tests of "creative writing ability" depend so heavily upon verbal factors already identified in most intelligence testing that their unique contribution as tests of creative writing aptitude is by no means clearly established.

direct evidence of the compatibility of present interests and preferences with given established occupational areas and also with the present susceptibility of the individual to training to a competency level in a given occupation, or family of occupations, it is understandable that few tests need to be developed specially for the exceptional. As a result only a few aptitude measuring devices have been developed specifically for the exceptional, and the major effort has been in improving the means of communication with respect to existing devices. This has resulted in more work with the blind person than with other exceptionalities. The relative instability of interests in the younger age groups and the attending delay in specific vocational guidance have understandably narrowed to the upper end of the age scale of our group the approaches to the measurement of their aptitudes. However, in the case of the mentally retarded, it is apparent that at least certain of the measurement approaches present unique problems in the area of concept adequacy on their part and the resulting communication efficacy of the devices which might be used. The most promising area of exploration with respect to this problem might well be the development and use of pictorial approaches involving the use of pictures to be checked in addition to the pictures of tools, machines, gear movements, and belt or rope routings over pulleys.

Some early work along this line was done by Weingarten (1958), and Geist (1959) developed a picture interest inventory for use with adults. Parnicky, Kahn, and Burnett (1968) have developed the Vocational Interest and Sophistication Assessment sets of pictures on the basis of the interests expressed by 3,000 male and female retarded youths and adults. The San Francisco Vocational Competency Scale (1968), usable with retardates, has become available. The Minnesota Vocational Interest Inventory (1965), for use with ninth-graders and up, limits its verbal sampling to skilled and semiskilled levels. Vocational interest and aptitude scores earned by those below the high school level must be viewed with great caution.

The placement tests used in civil service, other public employment, and industry usually are rather specialized forms of aptitude tests. Generally, they are intended to reflect the individual's adequacy for more specific kinds of employment (clerk, typist, policeman) rather than larger areas of employment as suggested, for instance, by the Kuder General Interest Survey. If we exclude from our consideration those occupations for which certain of the orthopedically disabled and certain of the sensorily restricted cannot be considered, there are many occupations, or levels of occupation, for which many of the remaining exceptional will need to have their aptitudes ascertained. Such occupations will range from those making very little verbal demand (construction work and the like) to those the verbal demands of which are very heavy (from certain clerical work to copy writing, or the gifted's involvement in, for instance, law). For certain kinds of employment, beginners must have specified kinds and amounts of information (Pt); for others, beginners need not have such information, but must be known to possess the basic capacity which will enable them to acquire that information on either pre-job or on-the-job training (Ps). Especially for disadvantaged youth seeking employment of the latter nature, Ps-dominant testing would do much both to enhance their chances of employment and to reduce criticism of "unfair" testing practices. This presumes, of course, that such tests have been properly validated for such use—that they adequately predict for the type of employment with respect to which they are used.

It is well to keep in mind that in this area, too, we are dealing in terms of probabilities. We are still in the realm of "the chances are. . . ." Further, we are safer in our guesses or estimates when we recognize that we use the results of some of our measures of vocational interest mostly to suggest the unde-

sirability of a given occupation or group of occupations. Given the results of one or more vocational interest inventories on a youth, our statement to him might well run in this fashion:

> More than your responses or scores on these devices is needed to help you make a decision about what you might consider as a kind of life work. However, as far as the results of these devices alone are concerned, the chances are about seven out of ten that _____ might be a good type of work for you to consider favorably, but the chances are eight or so out of ten that _____ would be a good area to avoid. Of course, this doesn't mean that you are sure to succeed in the work (or area) for which you scored well. You have to have also the appropriate skills, special aptitudes, basic capacity, and, especially, a strong motivation for that kind of work.

THE ASSESSMENT PROCESS

Analysis

Regardless of the kind of exceptionality the individual possesses and regardless of the age of the exceptional individual, the sampling of various areas of behavior must be carried out for the purpose of throwing light upon specifiable and psychologically significant aspects of the individual. In contrast to a testing approach that results from giving *a* test to get *a* score, there is the more important need to study the individual in terms of certain psychological constructs, or from certain psychological frames of reference that bear clearly upon the situation with respect to which the individual is being studied. A very significant approach of this sort is the one described by Taylor (1959), mentioned earlier. A somewhat different structuring of the clinician's task is presented in the next few paragraphs. The assessment process will be considered in terms of obtaining behavior samples that will enlighten the clinician regarding the subject's conceptualization behavior, his interpersonal relationships, his communication, his energy level, and the validity of information obtained about the subject from others. This will be done by stating only a few questions that illustrate what the clinician must be asking himself about the client as he works with him.

Conceptualization. What is his present level and quality of conceptualization? In view of the subject's history, what reasonable implications can be drawn regarding the client's subsequent conceptualization—his rate and ultimate level of growth in this area? What has been the nature of the subject's acculturation? Has he had a normal exposure? Or has he been reared in an impoverished or culturally sterile environment? Or has he been hothoused? If the child shows the effects of such hothousing, what are the implications of the results of such activity with respect to the child's capacity to benefit from it? How does he learn in the clinic situation?

Interpersonal relationships. How does the subject relate to the clinician? How has he related to others in his environment? Is he "outgoing"? If so, is this behavior of good quality? Does it have a compensatory basis? Is it soundly compensatory, or is it overcompensatory? Is he "withdrawing"? Is this behavior really a manifestation of good quality self-sufficiency? Or is it the result of his having learned to retire to situations that must be, for him, less threatening? Is he quite distractible? Is this a function of his basic insecurity or other emotional tension? Or is it better attributable to low mentality? Or to hearing loss? How does he respond to motivation in the clinic situation? Does he become interested in the test situation, or is he concerned primarily with pleasing you? Is he excessively concerned with meeting time limits, or does he excessively seek approbation? Is he aggressive in the clinic situation? If so, is he justified in being so? Have the significant adults in his world taken him so often to clinics for examination and treatment that he resents being with you in an-

other one? Or has he become resigned to it? How much residual psychological integrity has he?

Communication. How well is he receiving? Does he, possibly due to a hearing loss, give evidence of misinterpretation of words he hears? Is his asking for repetition of directions due to hearing loss, emotional need, or short attention span? Are any of his posturings or the closeness with which he watches you suggestive of any possible hearing loss? Is inattentiveness due to hearing loss, legitimate fatigue, or some other condition? Does he see well what is shown him? Are there any posturings or other physical adjustments that may be compensatory for poor vision? Are there any cutaneous-kinesthetic anomalies affecting his reception of stimuli? Are there any anomalies in the motor area? May they be due to inadequate maturation? To neural impairment? To emotional tension? Is motor anomaly limited to eye movement, speech, locomotion, manipulation, breathing, or common to two or more? (Questions regarding the mediation aspect of the communication process—what happens after the stimulus is received and before the response is made—will not be raised here specifically, since much that has been said [and asked] in regard to conceptualization and in regard to Taylor's procedures applies here.)

Energy level. Is the vigor of his response appropriate to the demands of the situation? Does he overreact? If so, is this a healthy, animal energy? Does it have a plausible emotional basis, as in certain overcompensatory behavior? If below the demands of the situation, may it have resulted from repressive treatment? From a debilitated physical condition? From understandable fatigue? From medication? From his rejection of the clinical situation?

Nature of information. To what extent is your clinical evaluation of the subject based primarily upon what you have actually observed? To what extent are you dealing with your own inferences as though they were observed behavior? To what extent is the developmental and social background information that you obtained from someone else a careful report of specific behavior, or to what extent does it consist of ambiguous, inferred generalities, such as "nervous," "stubborn," "withdrawn," and the like? Has your information about the subject come from a hyper-critical or excitable or basically insecure person? To what extent has your background information on the child come from an adult who is excessively ambitious for (or rejecting of) the child? Or has it come from a person of low psychological perceptive acuity?

These are only some of the many questions the psychologist always asks himself as he seeks to acquire an understanding of any individual—exceptional or otherwise—in order to try to make a psychologically sound assessment of him. It is apparent that, to do so, he cannot be "test-bound." But, in doing so, he needs:

1. To have a normative background in terms of which he can decide that a given child's conceptualization is that of, say, an average 10-year-old, or decide that the child is insecure, or that he has good psychological integrity. To be able to do this, he needs to have acquired much experience in terms of which he has valid expectancies for average nine-month-old infants, seven-year-olds, ten- and fifteen-year-olds. He needs to know the various ways in which children handle their feelings of insecurity. He must be able to differentiate between psychological integrity, or ego strength, and psychological façade.

2. To have a knowledge of what behaviors *may not* suggest, as well as of what they *may* suggest. The child hastily diagnosed as a "mirror writer" may after all be only a youngster, like one with whom the writer worked, who "saw her sister write this way and get a lot of attention," and similarly wanted attention. Or perhaps the child reported as "shifty eyed" and untrustworthy is actually nystagmic. Or, the child reported as "clumsy" may be a developmental problem; or he may be fearful of running and going up and down stairs be-

cause his crossed eyes render him deficient in depth perception; or he may be "clumsy" because he is muscularly tense as an integral part of an emotional problem; or, least likely, he may have some central nervous system impairment. Or, the situation may be something like the case of the child who had shown "uncontrollable behavior" at various times over a period of three years, and who was found to have an infection of the ear that became severe at times and "drove the child wild."

3. To understand the nature of the child's motivation, especially the extents to which it is extrinsic and intrinsic. To say resignedly that a child "won't apply himself" and thus to place on him the responsibility for not performing appropriately is only to expose one's ignorance as to how children become motivated to perform. The child who does things only to satisfy significant others in his environments learns to function only at the lower level of extrinsic motivation. Only by wisely capitalizing upon such motivation and by making certain that the child experiences success in what he is doing can he come slowly to learn to be intrinsically motivated. He comes to like to do things, to do them on his own, because he has succeeded in them.

4. To have a sound understanding of and a deep feeling for the legitimacy of differentness. While the clinician must have an understanding of the normal, in terms of which he can understand deviants, he is constantly aware, perhaps more fully than most parents and teachers, that in the psychological sense a norm is only a statistical statement, an average, for some defined group. To him such a norm need not be something to be attained by a given youngster, because it may be unreasonably high for one child or restrictingly low for another. The exceptional child has a "right to be different" and to expect the school and society both to understand his difference and to capitalize upon it.

5. To have a full comprehension of and sustained sensitivity to the parts played by social factors in children's milieus. Economic limitations, adequacy, or abundance can affect observable behavior. The child may be responding to the aspirations of or neglect by his family, or to

the implicit or explicit demands of his own social group—in school or out of school. He may be expected by his family, or even by his teachers, to perform at a level higher than his basic capacity and skill competencies indicate as appropriate for him. He may be functioning at a lower-than-possible level because that is how his family operates, or how his social peers perform, or even how he is enabled to function in the school setting. As important as the school may be in a child's life, it is only a part of his total social living and learning, and much of his learning has taken place before he enters upon formal schooling.

6. To be sensitive constantly to the importance of the interaction of the many facets of behavior that he necessarily explores in isolation.

Synthesis

Let us imagine a piece of cloth that has been woven out of a variety of colored threads. An intricate design is woven into this piece of cloth. Because of the nature of some of the dyes, parts of some of the exposed threads have faded and other parts have been soiled, so that the color you see in them is quite different from that you would find if you turned the cloth over or if you pulled those threads out of their sheltered positions within that pattern. Some of the cloth is well worn, meaning that some of these threads are thinner, even a bit shaggy, in spots. Perhaps, by some fluke in the patterning and weaving process, some particularly strong or well-dyed thread figures only to a very minor extent in what one sees on looking at the whole piece of cloth. One could look at the whole piece of cloth and make certain meaningful observations to the effect that it is soiled, faded, thin, worn, in need of replacing, usable for certain things, and so on. These are socially appropriate evaluations of this piece of cloth, given the implied frames of reference for them.

Certain persons, because of their particular functions in society—such as the weaver, the dyer, and the patternmaker—may well decide to describe (an elementary kind of evaluation) the pattern in terms of the number of threads per inch, the percentage of color to a square inch, the use of straight-line or curved-line elements in the pattern, the tensile strength of the threads used, the chemical analysis of the dyes used, or any one of a number of other facets of this piece of cloth. Each of these will have a social value within its frame of reference. Given enough samples of each of these separate elements, socially meaningful (but not meaningful insofar as this one piece of cloth is concerned) generalizations could be made concerning such thread strengths, stability of such patterns, permanency of such dyes, and so on. But none of these studies of single aspects of this piece of cloth can be taken to represent the cloth; "clothwise," such single evaluations or descriptions are meaningless.

The analogy with the examination of the individual—particularly if he is exceptional —need not be labored. The layman or novice tends to make gross evaluations, all of them psychologically valuable and some of them valid regarding the person so evaluated. But the psychologist, aspiring to the objectivity of the scientist, is faced with the two problems of science. He must analyze the whole individual into parts or functions in order that he can get clearer and more objective pictures of those functions. Then, if society is to benefit from his intensive studies of these elements, he must try to reassemble those functions into the whole individual, emphasizing certain of those functions for some purposes, and emphasizing others for other purposes, but at all times concerning himself with the whole individual. This synthesizing process gives psychological meaning to the studies of the artificially isolated functions, enhancing some, limiting others. The psychological tester tends to stop with or describe the individual primarily in terms of his work at the analysis stage. If the psychologist would *assess* the individual, he would go through the analysis stage making as many controlled observations as he deems necessary in order to synthesize his findings into a psychologically meaningful picture of the total functioning dynamic individual. This is not simply an additive process. A person's health may be somewhat below average and his intelligence may seem less than average; yet, the strength and nature of his motivation may well be such that he performs on a job considerably better than either of the first two characteristics would lead one to expect.

This need for synthesis holds where any sound psychological evaluation of an individual is undertaken. It is often difficult to achieve when working with the nonexceptional. It is doubly necessary and much more difficult in connection with the exceptional, since misleading or obscuring conditions so often enter their behavioral pictures. This difficulty often is compounded by the fact that, because of a dearth of appropriately well prepared persons, less well qualified individuals endeavor to make assumptions and use procedures that may have more validity in a nonexceptional frame of reference.

The interrelating of the varieties of information obtained in the assessment process must be accomplished with as full a comprehension and understanding as possible of the *total* social picture in which the exceptional child or youth has been, is, and probably will be functioning.

Although it was necessary for convenience of discussion and description to concern ourselves with aspects or functions of the exceptional as though they were pure, isolated identities, the interrelatedness of these five areas of measurement repeatedly became apparent. The paradox of the psychological absurdity of dealing with functions one at a time and the scientific impossibility of meaningfully concerning ourselves with an undifferentiated total called an individual constitutes a continuum within which the psychologist must always operate.

The point was made, in the discussion of learning aptitude, that the psychologist had to use an almost intuitive approach, but that in doing so he had a fairly meaningful set of reference points as a result of having been well grounded in his preparation and experience with less involved children. As a result of the important part played by such background, we encounter the point of view that effective measurement in markedly atypical cases is much more a matter of the person making the evaluation than it is of the particular device used. Even though reasonably adequate psychological pictures of the disabled can thus be obtained, the kind of data so obtained is often recognizably inadequate for rigid statistical analysis. In other words, the determination of the mental level or rate of mental development in such cases tends more to be an art than a science. This being the case within a given area of measurement, the synthesizing of these areas of measurement tends even more to be a matter of art. Calling either of these processes something less than scientific need not cause us to reject them as useless and completely meaningless. The need for rigorous research on the validity of these important and necessary processes is unmistakably apparent.

SUMMARY

The concepts and assumptions fundamental to all measurement underlie the examination and assessment of the exceptional. We sample behavior and assume, with varying degrees of confidence, that our samples give us adequate cues as to the totality of learning-proneness, emotionality, achievement, or aptitudes. For a number of reasons—but especially since the organism we are observing under controlled conditions is a growing and adapting one, and, since we have to resort to samples of its behavior, we are bound to have errors in our measurements. At times the behavior we observe has to serve as a basis for inferring a capacity for further similar behavior, as in the case of the measurement of mental capacity. Both the performance under observation and the inferred basic capacity to perform are of psychological importance. The consideration of this performance in terms of *process* (Ps) and of *product* (Pt) is particularly crucial in the case of the exceptional, with the inferential gap increasing as the behavior sampling shifts from Ps to Pt. At other times there is less, if any, need for such inference, since it is the degree of skill in evidence at the time of observation (testing) that is of primary social value, as in the case of educational achievement or certain vocational aptitudes.

Certain of our assumptions and problems are common to all the areas of the psychological evaluation of the exceptional. Even though measurement error is known or knowable, it is at times not recognized. But it can be reduced. Pervading the processes of psychologically evaluating the exceptional are problems pertaining to the nature and status of their conceptualization processes and problems involved in communication. The first of these necessitates the careful consideration both of the verbalized content employed in the behavior sampling process and of the evaluations made of the responses given in the examination situations. This latter bears also upon the means of communicating, by the exceptional child or youth, with the examiner, and also makes special demands regarding the sensory avenues employed in getting through to him. The communication problem appears to have received more attention than the conceptualization problem.

Fundamentally, the enactment of P.L. 94-142, unfortunately limited to "handicapped" children, makes no new assessment demands. For many, it spells out more fully what sound assessment should entail; for a few, it is feared it may accelerate the concoction of ill-conceived practices of limited validity.

The examination of exceptional children and youth is, by the very nature of their being exceptional, an exacting and difficult task requiring the services of highly skilled and qualified persons. The presence of motor and sensory impairment and of major emotional involvements, singly or in combination, materially complicates the process. The psychological assessment of these children and youth, the necessary synthesizing of the results of physical, intellectual, socioemotional, achievement, and aptitude measurements, is even more difficult. Although sound research is badly needed to show us how to make these processes more scientific and less a matter of art, their results can still play a significant part in our understanding of, and educational and social planning for, the exceptional.

REFERENCES

ABT, L. E., & BELLAK, L. *Projective psychology: Clinical approaches to the total personality.* New York: Grove Press, Inc., 1959.

ALLEN, R. M., & COLLINS, M. G. Suggestions for the adaptive administration of intelligence tests for those with cerebral palsy. *Cerebral Palsy Review*, 1955, *16*, 11–14, 25; and 1958, *19*, 6–7.

AMES, L. B. *et al. Adolescent Rorschach responses.* New York: Harper & Row, Publishers, 1959.

———, LEARNED, L., METRAUX, R. W., & WALKER, R. N. *Child Rorschach responses.* New York: Paul B. Hoeber, Inc., 1952. The exceptional children reported on include emotionally maladjusted delinquents, mentally superior, endogenous and exogenous defectives, enuretic children, children with extremes in reading skills, and those with tics.

AMMONS, R. B., & AMMONS, H. S. *Full Range Picture Vocabulary Test.* Missoula, Mont.: Psychological Test Specialists, 1948.

ANASTASI, A. Psychology, psychologists, and psychological testing. *American Psychologist,* 1967, *22,* 297–306.

ARTHUR, G. *The Arthur Adaptatation of the Leiter International Performance Scale* (Manual). Beverly Hills, Calif: Western Psychological Services; or Chicago: C. H. Stoelting Co., 1952.

BAYLEY, N. *The Bayley Scales of Infant Development.* New York: The Psychological Corporation, Inc. 1969.

————. On the growth of intelligence. *American Psychologist,* 1955, *10,* 805–818.

————, and ODEN, M. H. The maintenance of intellectual ability in gifted adults. *Journal of Gerontology,* 1955, *10,* 91–107.

BENTON, A. L. *The Revised Visual Retention Test: Clinical and experimental applications.* New York: The Psychological Corporation, Inc., 1955.

BERKO, M. J. Some factors in the mental evaluation of cerebral palsied children. *Cerebral Palsy Review,* 1953, *14,* 6, 11, 15.

BICE, H. V. Psychological examination of the cerebral palsied. *Journal of Exceptional Children,* 1948, *14,* 163–168.

BIRCH, J. R., & BIRCH, J. W. The Leiter International Performance Scale as an aid in the psychological study of the deaf. *American Annals of the Deaf,* 1951, *96,* 502–511.

————. Predicting school achievement in young deaf children. *American Annals of the Deaf,* 1956, *101,* 348–352.

BLUM, L. H., BURGEMEISTER, B. B., & LORGE, I. The Mental Maturity Scale for the Motor Handicapped. *School and Society,* 1951, *73,* 232–233.

————. *Columbia Mental Maturity Scale* (revised). New York: Harcourt Brace Jovanovich, 1972.

BOND, N. B. Cerebral palsy profile in Mississippi. *Exceptional Children,* 1953, *20,* 98–99.

BROWN, M. E. Daily activity inventories of cerebral palsied children in experimental classes. *Physical Therapy Review,* 1950, *50,* 415–421. (*a*)

————. Daily activity inventory and progress record for those with atypical movement. *American Journal of Occupational Therapy,* 1950, *4,* 195–204, 261–272; and 1951, *5,* 23–29, 38. (*b*)

————. Pre-vocational Motor Skill Inventory. *American Journal of Occupational Therapy,* 1953, *7,* 153–163, 188.

CATTELL, R. B. Theory of fluid and crystallized intelligence: A critical experiment. *Journal of Educational Psychology,* 1965, *54,* 1–22.

————. Are I.Q. tests intelligent? *Psychology Today,* 1968, *1,* 56–62.

COURT, J. H. *Researcher's Bibliography for Raven's Progressive Matrices and Mill Hill Vocabulary Scales.* Bedford Park, S. Australia: Flanders University, January, 1972. (There are two supplements: June, 1972, and January, 1974.)

CRUICKSHANK, W. M. (Ed.) *The teacher of brain-injured children.* Syracuse: Syracuse University Press, 1966. See especially Part III, Cognitive, perceptual, and motor competencies, pp. 137–221.

Detroit Tests of Learning Aptitude. Indianapolis, Ind.: Merrill Co., Inc., 1968.

DISTEFANO, M. K., JR., ELLIS, N. R., & SLOAN, W. Motor proficiency in mental defectives. *Perceptual and Motor Skills,* 1958, *8,* 231–234.

DOLL, E. A. Psychometric pitfalls in clinical practice. *Journal of Consulting Psychology,* 1947, *11,* 12–20.

————. *Measurement of social competence.* Minneapolis: Educational Test Bureau, 1953.

————. *Vineland Social Maturity Scale.* Circle Pines, Minn.: American Guidance Service, Inc., 1965.

————. *Preschool Attainment Record.* Circle Pines, Minn.: American Guidance Service, Inc., 1966.

DUNN, L. M. *Peabody Picture Vocabulary Test.* Nashville: American Guidance Service, 1965.

EICHENWALD, H. F., & FREY, P. C. Nutrition and learning. *Science,* 1969, *163,* 644–648.

FORCE, D. *A comparison of physically handicapped children and normal children in the same elementary school classes with reference to social status and self-perceived status.* Doctoral dissertation, University of Minnesota, 1954.

FRANDSEN, A. N., MCCULLOUGH, B. R., & STONE, D. R. Serial versus consecutive order administration of the Stanford-Binet Intelligence Scales. *Journal of Consulting Psychology,* 1950, *14,* 316–320.

FRANK, L. K. *Projective methods.* Springfield, Ill.: Charles C Thomas, 1948.

FRANKENBURG, W. K., & DODDS, J. B. *Denver Developmental Screening Test.* Denver, Colo.: Ladoca Project and Publishing Foundation, Inc., 1970.

FROSTIG, M., & HORNE, D. *The Frostig Program for the Development of Visual Perception.* Los Angeles: Follett Publishing Company, 1964.

GEIST, H. *The Geist Picture Interest Inventory.* Missoula, Mont.: Psychological Test Specialists, 1959.

GESELL, A., & AMATRUDA, C. S. *Developmental Diagnosis* (3rd ed., edited by H. Knoblock & B. Pasamanik). New York: Harper, 1974.

GLASER, R., & NITKO, A. J. Measurement in learning and instruction. In R. L. Thorndike (Ed.), *Educational Measurement* (2nd ed.). Washington, D.C.: American Council on Education, 1971, pp. 652–670.

GOODENOUGH, F. L. The appraisal of child personality. *Psychological Review,* 1949, *56,* 123–131.

GRAHAM, F. K., & KENDALL, B. S. *Memory-for-Designs Test:* Revised general manual. *Perceptual and Motor Skills,* Monograph Supplement No. 2, 1960, *11,* 147–148.

GUERTIN, W. H., RABIN, A. I., FRANK, G. H., & LADD, C. E. Research with the Wechsler Intelligence Scale for adults. *Psychological Bulletin,* 1962, *59,* 1–26.

GUILFORD, J. P. *The nature of human intelligence.* New York: McGraw-Hill, 1967.

HAEUSSERMANN, E. Evaluating the developmental level of cerebral palsied pre-school children. *Journal of Genetic Psychology,* 1952 (first half), *80,* 3–23.

HAMILL, P. V. V. NCHS Growth Curves for Children, Birth to 18 Years, U.S. Hyattsville, Md.: U.S. Department of Health, Education, and Welfare, Public Health Service, National Center for Health Statistics. Series 11, Number *165,* November, 1977.

HARTSHORNE, H., & MAY, M. A. *Studies in service and self-control.* New York: Macmillan, 1929.

HECHT, P. J., & NEWLAND, T. E. Learning potential and learning achievement of educationally blind third-graders in a residential school. *The International Journal for the Education of the Blind,* 1965, *15,* 1–6.

HERBERT, M. The concept and testing of brain-damaged children. *Journal of Child Psychology and Psychiatry,* 1964, *5,* 197–216.

HISKEY, M. S. *Hiskey-Nebraska Test of Learning Aptitude.* Lincoln, Neb.: Union College Press, 1966.

HUNT, B. M. Differential responses of mentally retarded children on the Leiter Scale. *Exceptional Children,* 1961, *28,* 99–102.

JAY, E. S. *A book about me.* Chicago: Science Research Associates, Inc., 1952.

JOHNSON, M. K., ZUCK, F. N., & WINGATE, K. The Motor-Age Test: Measurement of motor handicaps in children with neuromuscular disorders such as cerebral palsy. *Journal of Bone and Joint Surgery,* 1951, *33A,* 698–707.

KATZ, E. A method of selecting Stanford-Binet Intelligence Scale test items for evaluating the mental abilities of children severely handicapped by cerebral palsy. *Cerebral Palsy Review,* 1956, *1,* 13–17.

———. The "Pointing Modification" of the revised Stanford-Binet Intelligence Scales, Forms L and M, Years II through VI: A report of research in progress. *American Journal of Mental Deficiency,* 1958, *62,* 698–707.

KIRK, S. A., McCARTHY, J. J., & KIRK, W. D. *Illinois Test of Psycholinguistic Abilities.* Urbana, Ill.: University of Illinois, 1971.

Kuder General Interest Inventory. Chicago: Science Research Associates, 1970.

LEDWITH, N. H. *Rorschach responses of elementary school children.* Pittsburgh: University of Pittsburgh Press, 1959.

LESSING, E. E. A note on the significance of discrepancies between the Goodenough and Binet I.Q. scores. *Journal of Consulting Psychology,* 1961, *25,* 456–457.

LURIA, A. R. *The Working Brain.* London: The Penguin Books, Ltd., 1973.

MARTIN, W. E. *Children's Body Measurements.* Washington, D.C.: U.S. Government Printing Office, U.S. Office of Education Special Publication No. 5, 1955.

Minnesota Vocational Interest Inventory, New York: The Psychological Corporation, Inc., 1965.

MURSTEN, B. I. *Handbook of Projective Techniques.* New York: Basic Books Inc., Publishers, 1965.

NEWLAND, T. E. Language development of the mentally retarded child. In N. E. Wood (Ed.), Language development and language disorders: A compendium of lectures. *Monographs of the Society for Research in Child Development,* serial No. 77, 1960, *25,* 71–87.

————. Prediction and evaluation of academic learning by blind children: 1—Problems and procedures in prediction and 2—Problems and procedures in evaluation. *The International Journal for the Education of the Blind,* 1964, *14,* 1–7; and *14,* 42–51.

————. *The Blind Learning Aptitude Test.* Report, USOE Grant No. OEG-3-6-061928-1558. Urbana, Ill.: University of Illinois, 1969.

————. Assumptions underlying psychological testing. *Journal of School Psychology,* 1973, *11* (4), 316–322.

————. *The Gifted in Socioeducational Perspective.* Englewood Cliffs, N.J.: Prentice-Hall, Inc., 1976.

————. Tested "intelligence" in children. *School Psychology Monograph.* 1977, *3* (2), 1–44.

NUDD, E. M. *Perceptions of pictured social interaction by brain-injured and non-brain-injured children of normal intelligence.* Unpublished doctoral dissertation. University of Illinois, 1957.

PARNICKY, J. J., KAHN, H., & BURNETT, A. D. *Standardization of the Vocational and Sophistication Assessment (VISA): A Reading-Free Test for Retardates.* Bordentown, N.J.: E. R. Johnstone Training and Research Center, 1968.

PINTNER, R., EISENSON, J., & STANTON, M. *The psychology of the physically handicapped.* New York: Appleton-Century-Crofts, 1941.

PIOTROWSKI, Z. Positive and negative Rorschach organic reactions. *Rorschach Research Exchange,* 1940, *4,* 147–151.

POND, D. Is there a syndrome of "brain damage" in children? *Cerebral Palsy Review,* 1960, *4,* 296–297.

PORTEUS, S. D. *Porteus Maze Test: Fifty Years' Application.* Palo Alto, Calif.: Pacific Books, 1965.

RABIN, A. I., & HAWORTH, M. H. (Eds.). *Projective techniques with children.* New York: Grune & Stratton, Inc., 1960.

RAVEN, J. C. Raven Progressive Matrices. Cambridge, England: H. K. Lewis & Co., Ltd., 1938, 1947, 1956, 1962. Distributed in this country by The Psychological Corporation, Inc., New York, and by Western Psychological Services, Beverly Hills, California.

REITAN, R. M. Qualitative versus quantitative mental changes following brain-damage. *Journal of Psychology,* 1958, *46,* 339–346.

————. Psychological effects of cerebral lesions in children of early school age. In R. M. Reitan & L. A. Davison (Eds.), *Clinical Neuropsychology: Current Status and Applications.* Washington, D.C.: Winston, 1974.

ROURKE, B. P. Brain-behavior relationships in children with learning disabilities. *American Psychologist,* 1975, *30* (9), 911–920.

ROWLEY, V. N. Analysis of the WISC performances of brain damaged and emotionally disturbed children. *Journal of Consulting Psychology*, 1961, *25,* 553.

RUDIO, J. L. *Nurturing concept attainment with hearing impaired children.* Doctoral dissertation, University of Illinois, 1972.

San Francisco Vocational Competency Scale. New York: The Psychological Corporation, Inc., 1968.

SATTLER, J. M. *Assessment of Children's Intelligence.* Philadelphia: Saunders, 1974.

SCHERER, I. W. The prediction of academic achievement in brain injured children. *Exceptional Children*, 1961, *28,* 103–106.

SIEVERS, D. J., & NORMAN, R. D. Some suggestive results in psychometric testing of the cerebral palsied with Gesell, Binet, and Wechsler Scales. *Journal of Genetic Psychology*, 1953, *82,* 69–90.

SNIJDERS, J. T., & SNIJDERS-DOMAN, N. *Non-verbal intelligence tests for deaf and hearing subjects.* Groningen, Holland: J. B. Wolters, 1959.

SOKAL, MICHAEL M. APA's first publication. *American Psychologist*, 1973, *28,* 277–292.

SOLDWEDEL, B., & TERRIL, I. Sociometric aspects of physically handicapped and non-handicapped children in the same elementary school. *Exceptional Children*, 1957, *23,* 371–372.

SOLOMON, I. L., & STARR, B. D. *School apperception method.* New York: Springer Publishing Co., Inc., 1968.

STREET, R. F. I.Q. changes of exceptional children. *Journal of Consulting Psychology*, 1942, *6,* 243–246.

STREIN, W., & YSSELDYKE, J. E. Process- and product-dominant testing of disadvantaged and nondisadvantaged children. *Exceptional Children*, 1974, *40,* 451–452.

TAIBL, R. M. *An investigation of Raven's Progressive Matrices as a test for the psychological evaluation of cerebral palsied children.* Doctoral dissertation, University of Nebraska, 1951.

TAYLOR, E. M. *Psychological appraisal of children with cerebral defects.* Cambridge, Mass.: Harvard University Press, 1959.

TISDALL, W. J. *The efficacy of a special class program in the productive thinking abilities of educable mentally handicapped children.* Doctoral dissertation, University of Illinois, 1962.

TRACHT, V. S. Preliminary findings on testing the cerebral palsied with Raven's Progressive Matrices. *Journal of Exceptional Children,* 1948, *15,* 77–79, 89.

TWARANOVICA, J. A. *A study of reported relationships between intelligence and school achievement as measured by standardized tests.* Doctoral dissertation, University of Illinois, 1973.

VAN ALSTYNE, D. *Van Alstyne Picture Vocabulary Test.* New York: Harcourt Brace Jovanovich, Inc., 1960.

WALLACH, M. A., & KOGAN, N. *Modes of Thinking in Young Children: A Study of the Creativity-Intelligence Distinction.* New York: Holt, Rinehart & Winston, 1965.

WECHSLER, D. Intelligence defined and undefined. *American Psychologist,* 1975, *30,* 135–139.

WEINGARTEN, K. P. *Picture Interest Inventory.* Los Angeles: California Test Bureau, 1958.

WEPMAN, J. M., & WEINER, P. S. *Standardization and validation of a diagnostic test battery for language impaired children.* Chicago: University of Chicago Press, 1967.

WERNER, H., & STRAUSS, A. Types of visuomotor activity in their relation to low and high performance ages. *Proceedings of the Association on Mental Deficiency*, 1939, *44,* 163–168.

WETZEL, N. C. *The treatment of growth failure in children.* Cleveland: National Education Association Service, 1948.

WITTENBORN, J. R., & SARASON, S. B. Exceptions to certain Rorschach criteria of pathology. *Journal of Consulting Psychology*, 1949, *13,* 21–27.

4　Psychological Aspects of Special Education Environments

Herbert Rusalem and Helen Rusalem

Ed.D., and Ed.D., Co-Directors, Learning Capacities Research Project, Sun City, Arizona.

The process of designing, prescribing, and implementing educational environments for exceptional students is a desirable procedure in special education. Almost without exception, special educators develop settings that foster optimum growth, incorporating educational components that, hopefully, are beneficial for the development of each handicapped child. This concern is more than episodic because decisions about school or class settings for exceptional students are made, not only when a school placement is under consideration, but also, on a day-to-day, almost hour-to-hour, basis as the instruction of each child proceeds. In some instances, educational environments are chosen on an intuitive basis; but increasingly, educators, parents, and students are searching for a body of expertise in this area that will reduce trial and error and eventuate in a more targeted selection of educational ecologies that are congruent with a child's needs. In recognition of this need, both general and special educators have devoted time and resources to the task of exploring the psychological implications of various special education settings, hoping thereby to add precision to placement and program decisions.

SOME GENERAL EDUCATION BACKGROUND

Experiments in psychology and education continue to confirm, in both animal and human situations, that enriched environments foster growth, and conversely, that impoverished environments produce retardation (Krech *et al.*, 1960, 1962, 1966; Sherman, 1933; Sherman & Key, 1932). The critical role of environment in shaping human behavior and performance is further underscored by studies of fraternal and identical twins reared in different environments, and comparisons of the status of children removed from one setting and placed in another. Although the various studies differ in detail and in their interpretation of findings, there is a consensus about certain main points (Lefrancois, 1973):

1. It is possible to alter behavior by altering the environment.
2. Isolation and deprivation have deleterious effects upon children.
3. Institutional environments often are perceived as actual or potential causes of decrements in children's performance.

4. Some of the damaging effects of early experiences in an unfortunate or limited environment can be reversed.

5. Reversal of the effects of deleterious life circumstances usually occurs more expeditiously and more fully during the earlier years of life.

6. Although heredity also is a vital influence on development, the emphasis in education tends to be on environment because environment can be controlled more definitively by educational intervention than can genetic factors.

In the realm of educational practice, it has been demonstrated that learning is influenced by such environmental variables as class size, previous experience, and students' interests and achievements (Walberg & Ahlgren, 1970). As defined by Walberg (1971), environment is "a stimulus aside from instruction that predicts learning." In this context, various environmental factors have been found to have an impact upon learning, including differences in curriculum structure, formality, difficulty, and pace (Anderson, 1971), class size (smaller classes were perceived in this study as being more cohesive and difficult—Anderson & Walberg, 1972), grade level, with high school sophomore and junior level classes being perceived by students as being less desirable milieus than elementary and middle-school levels (Walberg, House, & Steele, 1973), and teacher personality (Walberg, 1968).

Anderson and Walberg (1974) concluded that the relationship between environmental factors and learning is not merely one between a physical setting and an individual's performance. On the contrary, the student's perceptions of the environment (often varying in some respects from the perceptions of educators) can markedly influence student performance. To date, most of the general education attempts to control educational ecological variables have focused upon planned physical or psychological modifications in the school or class setting rather than upon efforts to alter students' perceptions of the environments in which they are expected to learn.

The concept of physical space and its management adds still another dimension to the study of learning environments. For example, Montessori (1964) suggested that rigid physical classroom arrangements result in the acquisition of barren and meaningless knowledge rather than in real intellectual and affective growth. Similarly, Rolf (1961) noted that larger classrooms tend to give teachers more job satisfaction, and, by implication, should result in better teaching and, hopefully, better learning. In spatial terms, learning seems to be influenced by such ecological variables as the position of children's seats in relation to classroom windows (Harmon, 1945), the layout of classroom furniture (Sommer, 1969), the position of a student's seat in the class seating plan (Sommer, 1969), and the general ecosystem of the school (Barker & Gump, 1964).

Although data concerning the relationship between student performance and environmental features are abundant, the state of the art of research in this area still leaves much to be desired. Thus, although a relationship between physical space and learning seems clear enough, little information is available that links specific spatial interventions to specific changes in student behavior. As a consequence, Sommer (1969) concluded that, as a group, teachers tend to be insensitive to the psychological implications of environmental interventions and that they do not use environmental "treatments" as effectively as they might in fostering student development.

Since teachers and fellow students constitute important elements in the learning environment, it is important to consider the impact of other persons upon the learning of an exceptional child (for example, in a mainstreaming situation) and the stimulus value of the exceptional child himself in determining the impact of the learning milieu upon him. Although studies of this interpersonal variable are few in number in both general and special education, it is well recognized that such factors must be taken into account in designing environments for the exceptional child.

This brief survey suggests that general educators are concerned with the same types of environmental variables as special educators. In the context of this chapter, the general education experience may be useful in pointing out selected special education directions, including:

1. Special educators are rightfully concerned with the learning ecology of the exceptional student.
2. Physical features in the learning environment are likely to influence the school behavior and performance of exceptional students. Cruickshank makes much of this point in his approach to the education of children with learning disabilities (1977).
3. Although evidence is less certain in this area, interpersonal environmental variables seem to shape many of the responses of exceptional children.
4. Current findings suggest that ecological approaches to the education of the exceptional student merit fuller consideration.
5. Insofar as specific recommendations for the placement and instruction of exceptional students are concerned, the general educational literature offers only generalities rather than definitive guidelines.

Accordingly, an attempt will be made in the sections that follow to examine aspects of the special-education literature dealing with the effects of various environments on the learning and behavior of atypical children, in the hope that such a discussion will help special educators to cope with the environmental components of their work more effectively.

SOME CURRENT CONCERNS RELATING TO SPECIAL EDUCATION ENVIRONMENTS

A recent development in special education has been the opening of new initiatives in the selection of an environment in which an exceptional child should be educated. Historically, highly specialized educational settings dominated the available options. Recently, much larger proportions of exceptional children in all disability areas assumed participatory roles in regular class environments. In this mainstreaming process, it was noted that successful integration did not occur automatically. On the contrary, certain controllable conditions were found to be important facilitators of regular class participation. Favorable consequences tended to occur more frequently when the receiving general teacher was "right" for the child (Davis, 1970; Simches, 1970). Furthermore, it was noted that immediate integration is not always possible and that careful pacing and preparation often are necessary to insure the proper assimilation of the special child in the regular classroom (Smith, 1973, Paul et al., 1978). At the same time, it was observed that the negative labeling of "exceptional student" could be more readily eliminated in an integrated class environment, as contrasted to previous efforts confined largely to changing the label (Rosenthal & Jacobsen, 1968). In the course of this movement, specialists in the field extended their efforts to the out-of-school environment. For example, Reynolds (1975) called for the conduct of diagnostic and treatment procedures in the context of the child's normal environment so as to reduce excessive regulation and dehumanizing institutionalization.

Although the idea of freeing the exceptional child from segregative environments swept special education with the impact of a tornado, other voices cautioned against possible excesses that might ensue from indiscriminate mainstreaming, suggesting that further empirical testing of all special education interventions was needed before an unconditional commitment to any of them could be made (Nelson & Schmidt, 1971). In a similar vein, Gordon (1970) observed that human flexibility requires educators to subordinate their commitment to any educational environment to the human needs of the individual concerned. Concurrently, Rusalem and Rusalem (1971) advocated the establishment of proving grounds to test the presumed advantages and disadvantages of various educational provisions for exceptional children. Similarly, Elser (1959) had noted earlier that additional data are needed concerning the degree of acceptance felt by exceptional children in integrated environments and the implications of such data for special education programs.

A current expression of educational caution was articulated by Heller (1972), who called into question some basic special education assumptions about school environments, noting that unanswered questions about special-education interventions still prevail, including:

1. Are special-education classes instructionally inferior?
2. Are special-education teachers poorly trained?
3. Can regular-class teachers be helped to become more accepting of special educators' prescriptions?
4. Is academic performance more important than social performance in the education of exceptional children?
5. Can the existing general-education system be adapted to accommodate the mainstreamed exceptional child?

The current emphasis upon mainstreaming has roots in both philosophical and research concepts. Philosophically, it was felt that segregated education is inconsistent with the democratic ideal and is repugnant to the belief that the severely handicapped child is in many respects "normal" and will be functioning for most of his life in a "normal" world. From a research point of view, reviews of efficacy studies suggested that academically and socially, exceptional children often gain substantial benefits from participation in an integrated class program. Unfortunately, many of these efficacy studies have deficiencies in research design, implementation, and interpretation, and their findings are not universally accepted as conclusive

support for mainstreaming. Furthermore, the special and general education classes that served as the settings for these studies were not always representative of effective instructional conditions. One can only conjecture at this point what the findings might have been if the special-education programs and teachers in these researches had been consistently excellent. Nonetheless, special education is taking forceful action toward greater integration, leaving to subsequent study the matter of unequivocal supportive evidence.

THE ROLE OF ENVIRONMENT IN SPECIAL EDUCATION

Segregated special education environments are viewed today with much less confidence than they once were, in part because of the findings of studies of the post-school experiences of special-education graduates. In one study (Stanfield, 1973), it was concluded that substantial proportions of moderately retarded children did not readily become integrated into the post-school community. In fact, some 40 percent of these subjects never left their homes to go anywhere unchaperoned, and only 4 percent had friends in the community whom they could visit. In vocational terms, Ladson (1976) concluded that a vast majority of handicapped students who complete secondary-level programs are not ready to enter meaningful and rewarding employment. Such findings fostered skepticism about traditional special education settings and encouraged explorations into the values and limitations of alternate educational environments for the exceptional child.

Although it is widely believed that the regular class environment is almost invariably superior to that of the special class for certain groups of exceptional children, unanimity on this point has not yet been achieved. Some specialists suggest that the regular class usually is a favorable milieu for certain disability groups (Goldstein, Moss, & Jordan, 1965). Indeed, as early as the 1930s, some investigators reported clear advantages for the regular class setting (Bennett, 1932; Pertsch, 1936), a conclusion supported by the findings of subsequent observers (Cassidy and Stanton, 1959; Vacc, 1972). Less enthusiasm for the regular class environment has been expressed by specialists who suggest that integrated education is not necessarily the most favorable of all educational environments for many special children (Kaplan, 1967). More frequently, the position is taken that definitive evidence supporting one or another of these environments is still fragmentary and that additional data are needed upon which to reach reasoned conclusions (Watson, 1975; Wynne *et al.,* 1975). Paul and his associates have much to say on this point (1978).

Traditionally, there has been a tendency for special educators to take strong positions in support of one or another educational environment. Underlying this process has been the premise that one instructional setting can be devised which meets the needs of a large proportion of exceptional students. Flowing out of this premise are the two overarching questions to which this chapter addresses itself:

1. Is there adequate support in research, experience, and/or philosophy to justify an all-or-none approach?
2. Does the available evidence delineate the impact of various learning environments on exceptional children?

Educational Placement in Various Environments

Educational placement is a day-to-day arena in which special educators, general educators, parents, and others play out an important aspect of the drama of instructional environments. When decisions are made concerning the placement of a child, the practical aspects of developing and using educational environments come into focus, and reality takes the center stage. Although a wide variety of placement procedures are used in special education, there is general agreement that a comprehensive diagnosis of the learning and social attributes of the child is necessary or that data should be derived from many sources to form the basis for a placement decision. Ordinarily, a multidisciplinary team approach is favored, since it has been observed that various disciplines (administrators, diagnosticians, regular teachers, and special teachers) differ in their perspectives and points of emphasis, each contributing its own insights (Hannaford, 1975; Wood, 1968). It is recognized that interdisciplinary teamwork often necessitates compromises and that some outcomes may only approximate the ideal program for a child. However, despite its limitations, the interdisciplinary team is thought to offer a superior avenue for selecting educational environments for the exceptional child. In this regard, it is generally recommended that parents (as team members) be given a significant role in the decision-making process.

Placement teams differ in many respects, but in making placement decisions, almost all take into account such factors as family structure, intellectual functioning, the nature of the disability, the community, the child's cultural background, the student's earlier educational and social experience, and in-school behavior (Hannaford, 1975; Heber, 1959; Kaufman, 1975; Mullen & Itkin, 1961; Rowitz & Lei, 1975; Rubin *et al.,* 1973; Swift & Spivak, 1969). A number of suggestions have been offered for selecting a suitable environment for an exceptional student. First and foremost is the admonition that all of the environments from which a choice is to be made should meet equally high educational standards (Lippman & Goldberg, 1973), and that all should be susceptible to adaptation when necessary to meet individual need (Mosley & Spicker, 1975).

Throughout the literature there is expressed a mounting appreciation of the crucial role played by the school environment in the development of the exceptional child and a growing realization that every educational placement has vital implications for the student's subsequent experience. This emerging awareness seems closely related to the general trend in American education toward a more complete understanding of the special role of educational environments in the lives of all children. Indeed, general education can offer relevant guidelines derived from educational programming for the disadvantaged. For example, the following educational provisions have been found to be helpful:

1. an atmosphere of hope and expectation (Lee & Schroder, 1969)
2. reasonably spacious physical quarters (Norland, 1974)
3. teacher encouragement of personal autonomy (Kuzma & Stern, 1972)
4. student interaction with children from a broad variety of backgrounds (Pumphrey et al., 1970)
5. cultivation of feelings of self-worth, confidence, trust, and creativity (Kodman, 1970)
6. early intervention (Kuzma & Stern, 1972)

In general, observers feel that an educational environment can be structured that can maximize the growth of minority group children and, by implication, exceptional children as well. At our current stage of development, the environmental aspects that have received the most attention tend to be those that common sense suggests would be closely related to child development. Although data about these environmental variables lack precision and sophistication, they can be quite meaningful in special education. The fact that they are not receiving adequate emphasis in the education of the exceptional suggests that there is an educational lag in this field.

DIMENSIONS OF EDUCATIONAL ENVIRONMENTS FOR SPECIAL CHILDREN

Certain aspects of special education environments have attracted greater attention than others. Among these are those outlined below.

Degree of Segregation in the Educational Setting

Special educational environments extend from marked separation of special children from the educational mainstream to ongoing assimilation into regular school activities (Kinkaide, 1975). The perceived advantages of the latter range all the way from conserving public funds (Santiesteven, 1975) to fostering optimum child development. Of course, there are those who are less certain about the efficacy of mainstreaming (Shattuck, 1946).

Origin and Availability of Supportive Services

Traditionally, supportive assistance to the special child and the family, such as psychosocial, recreational, family counseling, and vocational development services were made an integral part of the special environment in the belief that general school and community resources could not, or would not, deliver such services to severely handicapped children. Increasingly, the values of such services in strengthening mainstreaming efforts are being underscored (Kinkaide, 1975).

Architectural Barriers

It is widely held that all physical barriers to full access to education for atypical children should be removed. In this connection, the emphasis is on eliminating environmental deterrents that extend beyond the most common barriers (such as stairs, unsuitable bathrooms, uneven floors, and inaccessible water fountains). For example, Birch and Johnson (1975) suggested that the amount of space available to the child can have an impact upon learning and behavior.

Instructional Procedures

In keeping with recommended individualization of instruction for the exceptional student, a wide variety of teaching methods is available for use in special and general education environments that can facilitate a child's learning and development. For example, behavior modification techniques (Gallagher & Heim, 1974) and programmed materials (Bland, 1976) have been introduced into special education environments with generally favorable effects upon selected children.

Parental Participation

Special educators universally agree that parents constitute a major variable in special educational environments. In addition to serving as cooperators with, and comanagers of, school programs, the parents of an exceptional child can have important inputs into special education environments through assisting in behavior-modification activities, tutoring, preparing materials, organizing community support for the special education program, and assisting teachers on field trips (Karnes & Zehrbach, 1972). Parents who participate directly in special education environments can contribute to the psychological climate of the classroom through providing gratifying and growth-stimulating relationships to exceptional children of other families. (See Paul *et al.*, 1978.)

Teacher-Consultants

Special education specialists may be assigned to work with the mainstreamed child and/or the regular classroom teacher to supplement existing educational environmental provisions. This specialist functions through direct one-to-one service to the child, consultation with the classroom teacher, preparation of special materials and procedures, and advising supervisors, administrators, and other school personnel. These teacher-consultant services also may flow out of a resource room in which exceptional children spend part of each school day. However it may be delivered, the service constitutes a major element in the exceptional child's educational environment, extending,

enriching, and adapting it to meet individual needs. As suggested by Adelman (1972), teacher-consultants are thought to effectively reduce the need of the child for even more specialized and isolated educational settings.

Sensory Stimulation

Studies of sensory deprivation suggest that planned sensory stimulation in an educational environment affects child growth and development. For example, among children who are limited by deafness, blindness, and severe orthopedic restrictions, unless "nattural" sensory stimulation can be augmented, retardation may occur in one or more areas of child growth. Accordingly, special educational environmental designs have been created for children with such losses (Morris, 1974). In practice, enriched sensory stimulation or reduction can be equally applicable on an individual basis for children with learning, emotional, and intellectual problems, and, for that matter, other children as well.

Life Skills

Educational environments may be restricted by the life skills of individual exceptional children. Thus, a low level of toilet training, self-feeding, or mobility may restrict some children to institutional or home settings, contraindicating full participation in a regular school program. In such instances an educational environment that trains the child in life skills may become an essential component in service to certain severely disabled students (Reynolds, 1962).

Special Equipment and Devices

Selected tools used in educating exceptional children (Braille books, hearing aids, ramps, therapy equipment, educational TV, and special audio devices) often become vital features of the special education environment, both in terms of structuring the physical milieu and creating a special psychosocial climate for the child. Thus, the use of Braille materials in a regular classroom may require certain types of desk space and, because of the absence of two-dimensional pictures, may make the child's learning experience different from that of other children. The meaning of special services in an educational environment for the child, the teacher, and the social group has received relatively little research attention, and consequently, generalizations about their impact cannot be made with confidence.

Early Intervention

Early special-education intervention in the lives of exceptional children has been advocated for many years. Accordingly, strong efforts now are being made to identify special children during infancy, if possible, and to make family and early childhood education provisions for exceptional children in all sections of the United States. Selected and early intervention programs are being supported by federal and state funds, making it possible for larger numbers of disabled young children to receive early "treatment." In general, early childhood education therapies and training are becoming increasingly sophisticated as these programs mature. Indeed, certain environmental features of special education settings (itinerant teachers, special education consultants, learning centers, supportive social work, and stepped-up parent involvement) are being introduced into both general and special early childhood education (O'Brien, 1975).

Special Educators as Environmental Variables

Special educators tend to perceive themselves differentially both in positive and negative terms from other educators. In positive terms, special teachers tend to regard themselves as better trained, more capable of offering individualized instruction, and more sensitive to individual needs. Negatively, they may see themselves as being disadvantaged in the educational establishment, with a lower social status and with unwarranted professional restrictions being imposed upon them by administrators and general teachers (Jones, 1966). To the degree that these self-perceptions and peer attitudes do, indeed, exist among special educators, they constitute an important influence on educational environment. In practice, any professional difference that may be sensed by special educators becomes an environmental component that can shape student learning and development.

Peers

Fellow students, both disabled and nondisabled, form an essential variable in the educational environment of an exceptional child. Although peer influence has received extensive consideration in the field, little research is available that definitively establishes its impact upon handicapped youngsters. It has been suggested that peer interactions can be critical in the mainstreaming process and that efforts (still not extensively spelled out or tested) should be made to maximize the support that exceptional students received from such interpersonal contacts. For example, the involvement of nondisabled students in a tutoring role in special education (Irving, 1975) produced equivocal results over the short term, with only some of the handicapped students revealing measurable personality and behavior improvement. For the present, findings concerning the part played by fellow students in the educational environment of special children are too fragmentary to warrant generalization.

Work Components

Special education secondary-level environments sometimes contain work components in the form of work-study programs, remunerative employment on community job sites, prevocational and vocational training, participation in sheltered workshop activities, and structured career education, among others. Reports suggest that a vocationally oriented environment adds a compelling reality to the school experience and promotes educational motivation, social maturity, and employment readiness.

Instructional Procedures

Teaching methods constitute an important component in the educational environment of exceptional children. For example, an open classroom approach was found to facilitate teacher acceptance of children's deviant behavior, resulting in fewer referrals for special class service and more student-initiated activity (Bartel, 1972; Craig & Holman, 1973). Among the other educational procedures that have had reported environmental impact upon special children are behavior modification, language enrichment, and intensive mental health treatment (Kopchick, 1975; Rubin, 1962). Although some comparative effects of selected instructional approaches have been reported, the literature is less clear about possible criteria for prescribing a targeted instructional procedure for an individual exceptional child at any point in the child's development. Therefore, it may be said that at this time, we know more about reported group consequences of certain teaching methods used with defined samples of special children than we do about how to choose and implement this educational ecological variable to maximize an individual student's learning.

The environmental variables discussed above constitute only an illustrative list. Although study and experience suggest that these variables (as well as others) are important in shaping the educational environment of exceptional children, our knowledge about them tends to be descriptive rather than prescriptive. For the most part, defini-

tive guidelines generally are not available for everyday classroom use for an individual exceptional child. Through hunch and intuition, effective special educators probably will continue to orchestrate individually, such environmental features successfully. However, for them and especially for less intuitive special educators, a more systematic approach to the selection and use of educational environments continues to be a first-order need.

PSYCHOLOGICAL IMPLICATIONS OF VARIOUS SPECIAL EDUCATION ENVIRONMENTS

Special educators usually recognize that various school environmental options can have both favorable and unfavorable implications for exceptional individuals in the class group. Currently, educational environments of various types have their advocates and opponents. In some instances, the values perceived by one group as inherent in a particular environmental option are viewed negatively by another group. It is difficult to bring about a resolution of these educational environmental controversies because the limited evidence now at hand often refers to a limited population, classroom situation, or school setting. Consequently, the claims noted below for one or another educational environment are primarily conclusions arrived at through personal feeling and one's personal educational philosophy. Rarely does a special educator who is committed ideologically to a particular environment perceive the educational potential of that alternative in the same terms as a colleague who has serious ideological doubts about that option. Like most professionals, therefore, special educators tend to perceive existing data in a manner that is consistent with their prevailing frame of reference. For this reason, the present-day claims made for or against various educational settings should be accepted with caution, if at all.

Even in this context however, more general statements can be made about the psychological implications of various special education settings:

1. With certain exceptions (particularly in regard to severely disabled children) less segregated settings are considered by most special educators to be more favorable for child growth and development than more segregated ones.
2. With certain exceptions, educational arrangements that retain the child in his family and community are considered to be psychologically more conducive to child growth and development than those which sever a child from his roots.
3. With certain exceptions, educational environments that "normalize" the child through encouraging common experiences and interactions with others in the larger society are considered to be more desirable than environments that divert the child from the "mainstream."
4. Even as special educators make provisions for the integration of the child into family and community life, they are conscious of the concomitant need of many exceptional individuals for intensive special services that may necessitate participation in a special environment.

In effect, special environments that remove the child to some extent from the ongoing educational process in his community generally are favored only when less special environments are insufficient to meet a child's significant needs. Thus, all things being equal, less special educational setting is preferred to a more special one. In real life, however, all things are rarely equal and judgments have to be made in the light of available resources and the practical pressures of administering educational programs. Judgments about what is an optimum educational environment are often tempered by practical realities and human fallibility. The discussion that follows presents some of the psychological attributes of a variety of educational environments which have been dis-

cussed in the literature by psychologists and educators who have had occasion to observe them. In considering them, the reader should be aware of the fact that each is strongly influenced by prevailing educational and social conditions.

The Residential Program

Almost always considered an environment to be prescribed after all other alternatives have been rejected, the residential school alternative requires the child to spend most or all of his time in an institutional environment apart from his family and home community. Hopefully, the benefits derived by the child in the residential environment one day will enable him to return to a less segregated and isolated educational setting. But this is not assured because the severity of the child's problems may be so limiting and/or the readiness of families and communities to accept them may be so minimal that early return to integrated education can be doubtful.

Some psychologically relevant benefits that have been attributed to the residential setting are:

a. Favorable social acceptance even when physical, intellectual, emotional, and social atypicalities are extreme (Jorgensen & Glad, 1968).
b. Continued preparation for entry into community living (Jorgensen & Glad, 1968). In practice, some residential institutions offer programs specifically designed to accelerate child readiness for community resettlement (Connor, 1976).
c. Opportunities for highly specialized and expensive therapies, treatments, and interventions (such as those that may be required by deaf-blind, autistic, or trainable mentally retarded children). Whenever an otherwise unobtainable adapted environment is needed to sustain or improve the functioning level of the child, a residential setting may be indicated. In such instances, it is felt that the residential school may be more capable of devising and

delivering the more highly specialized around-the-clock services needed by certain severely disabled children (Sinclair & Clark, 1973).

d. Protection from physical, social, or psychological damage that might occur to a severely disabled child in a less sheltered environment (Jorgenson & Glad, 1968). Community living can demand a degree of psychological adaptability, physical resilience, and frustration tolerance that exceeds the capacities of a severely handicapped child. Continued exposure to mounting stress resulting from an incongruence between the child and the community environment can eventuate in an exacerbation of the individual's problems to such a degree that entry into a more protected environment may be indicated.

e. Enhancement of the self-concept. In having an opportunity to interact with others who may be even more limited than he is in certain respects, the exceptional child may gain reassurance about his own competence in the context of "shared misfortune" (Devereux, 1956).

f. Because of their specialized nature, residential programs may be able to see greater potential in the severely disabled student. When viewed against a backdrop of "normalcy" by educators who are accustomed to working with children in the "average" range, the exceptional individual may, indeed, be considered to have relatively low potential. In a residential program, on the contrary, the point of reference is exceptionality, and thus, the seriously limited person may be viewed in a rubric governed by entirely different norms (Dolan, 1972).

g. Response to modest vocational potential. It is claimed by some that students with very limited career potential are likely to have this potential explored and developed more fully in the specialized residential environment than in the community milieu (Anderson and Stevens, 1969). Specialized vocational equipment and personnel, on-campus work-training sites, special prevocational training centers, and the extensive job-related resources of residential settings may make it a preferred vocational development site for selected severely disabled students.

h. Specialized instructional programs. Some spe-

cial educators hold that the residential program is better equipped to provide certain specialized instructional procedures, such as behavior modification, multi-modal learning, training in self-monitoring of behavior, orientation and mobility instruction, acquisition of self-help and daily living skills, motor training, and learning to live in a structured social unit (Wilson, 1974).

i. Time resources. Through working with the severely disabled child 24 hours a day, under controlled conditions, a residential program may be able to allot student time more efficiently to various educational and social activities without being "locked" into the dimensions of a typical 9 AM to 3 PM school day, the constraints of school bus schedules, or the arbitrary demands of a family for a child's time. Since the education of a multihandicapped exceptional child can be highly time-consuming for staff and students alike, a program that organizes educational activities over a 24-hour daily time span may be more conducive in some cases to child growth than one that functions within 4- to 6-hour time blocks five days a week (Johnson & Tuttle, 1971).

j. Structured diversified curriculum. Some educators claim that intensive well-structured specialized curricula needed by some exceptional children can be developed more readily in a residential setting. Beyond paralleling community-based learning experiences, residential programs can extend into life skills, socialization, and vocational training areas without family and community distractions. For example, some residential environments for multi-handicapped children can offer prevocational and vocational training with less concern for unrealistic parental expectations and biases (Corker, 1974).

k. Individualization. A residential environment is thought by some to be especially favorable for individualizing instructional programming for the exceptional child (Millman & Davis, 1974). An argument in support of this position is the tendency for residential schools to have relatively low pupil-staff ratios theoretically enabling students to receive more faculty attention day in and day out (Johnson & Tuttle, 1971).

Therapeutic Aspects
of Supervised Group Living

The fuller control of the child exercised by the residential school is reputed to be helpful in planning and implementing comprehensive, therapeutically oriented programs for the severely disabled. Beyond the possibilities for structuring complex "therapies," residential group living provides social learning opportunities not available in other educational environments (Dowling, 1975; Maier, 1975).

Since residential school programs have been assessed over decades, criticisms and defenses of them abound in the literature. In considering the negatives, it is advisable to view them in the context of a particular student population. In some instances, a valid criticism of residential schools relative to one student group may be far less persuasive when applied to a quite different student group. For example, the perceived weaknesses of a residential school program for serving educable mentally retarded students may not be weaknesses at all when the referent group is deaf-blind or profoundly retarded. Since a list of the reported shortcomings of residential programs could extend over many pages, only a sample of them will be noted below for illustrative purposes:

a. Residential programs segregate the child from the environment in which he may be required to function later in life, thus excluding him from day-to-day training in a real-life context (Guarino & Sage, 1973).

b. Residential schools can become convenient receptacles or warehouses for severely disabled persons who are rejected by their families and communities despite the fact that a community educational placement would be far more desirable (Guarino & Sage, 1973).

c. The reality of the institution is not the reality of the mainstream. Thus, exceptional children in residential programs learn how to function in an artificial and unreal setting, which may have limited relevance for postschool adjustment. This criticism often is especially pertinent in vocational activities.

d. In a residential setting, the handicapped child may fail to acquire a realistic picture of how others in the mainstream will perceive him and react to him (Mayadas, 1975). For example, in the limited confines of a residential school, the student may learn to view himself as being musically talented. Yet, using the norms and expectation of mainstreamed children, a reasonable observer may consider such talents to be modest, indeed.

e. Many residential school environments are so highly regimented that it is difficult for the exceptional child to develop personal autonomy and self-direction. Yet, a far higher level of initiative, decision-making, and self-care may be critical for the student's subsequent participation in the community (Mayadas, 1975).

f. Some residential school environments can be so stultifying and stimulus-poor that they prevent the severely handicapped child from developing intellectual curiosity, a broad behavioral repertoire, and acceptable levels of social sensitivity.

Discussions about residential programs for exceptional children can be emotional in tone, and many voices raised against them. All too often, opponents and advocates of residential settings seem to be functioning in different orbits. Yet, when the student population under discussion is more precisely defined, the contending parties tend to resolve some of their differences. On occasion, the controversy about residential programs seems to swirl around a general anathema to any type of residential education for anyone. Such a position may evolve out of the past shortcomings of residential settings as much as from their present attributes. Yet, if consideration is given to very seriously limited children and highly deprived family and community environments, few, if any, special educators would advocate the total elimination of all residential school programs for all exceptional children. However infrequent the need for residential education may be, it is important for that option to be available for students who can benefit from it.

Special Day Schools

Day schools for handicapped children provide a specialized daytime school environment for the exceptional child while concurrently retaining him in his home and community. In this manner, such schools offer home and community living plus some advantages of a residential educational setting, including a custom-designed environment, a skilled, self-contained staff, flexibility in curriculum design and programming, fuller control over educational variables, focus upon the special problems that characterize a disability configuration, and acceptance of the child and his problems under a custom-made educational shelter. Concurrently, the child receives the benefits of home and community living (Olshin, 1971; Waldman, 1972; Weinstein, 1969). Despite their perceived value, day schools have not been widely studied in psychological terms. It may be reasonably supposed that educational segregation during the school day in a special school carries with it some danger of stigmatization and impaired self-concept. Despite this, however, when a child's disabilities are so severe that education cannot proceed successfully on regular school premises, a day school program may, in fact, constitute a preferred educational setting. This seems especially true when normalization of out-of-school social community and the family experiences can be arranged even though the child may have to be separated from his community school program.

The Special Class

Once considered the shining hope for improved educational services for handicapped children (at least when compared with more segregative educational arrangements), the special class is now viewed with greater skepticism. Not only is the "self-contained" special class that isolates the child from the school mainstream coming into question, but so also is its offspring that integrates the atypical child into certain selected regular school activities such as music, art, and assembly programs. The reexamination of the special class goes beyond the philosophical principle that unless absolutely necessary, such classes are inconsistent with the American ideal of educational pluralism. In conducting reviews of mainstreaming reports, some special educators have concluded that, both academically and socially, special classes achieve no more than regular classes. Indeed, in some cases they may put the atypical child at a developmental disadvantage (Johnson, 1962). In this regard, it should be kept in mind that many of the available studies have methodological and statistical deficiencies.

On the positive side, it has been argued that the unique environment of a special class facilitates the matching of learners' needs with appropriate educational interventions without disengaging children from regular school and community. Thus, smaller class groups, specially trained teachers, custom-designed and adapted equipment, and more sophisticated individualized teaching methods that presumably characterize the special class are thought to generate improved academic and social progress among exceptional children (Adelman, 1971). Despite this exception, consistent evidence is lacking that the special class does, indeed, result in marked improvement for many children (Johnson, 1962). Along with these reports of inconsistent outcomes for the special class, there has been an undercurrent of concern as to whether the added costs of this environment are justified by the reported degree of student progress.

Concurrently, there has been uncertainty about the validity of some student gains attributed to the special class. Thus, in reviewing the comparative efficacy of the special and regular class settings for exceptional students, special educators often arrive at very limited generalizations because the studies upon which they attempt to base their conclusions have serious weaknesses (Johnson, 1962; Kirk, 1964). As Kirk notes, most special education program evaluation studies are short-term in nature and thus fail to take into account the possible longitudinal effects of regular and special class attendance. Even at best, efficacy measures can be fraught with error (Schultz et al., 1971), because it is difficult to know whether the outcomes reported really are a function of the regular and special class settings investigated or of extraneous factors in the situation. Furthermore, the instruments and techniques used by the researcher can be imperfect, or as Kirk suggested, short-term observations may reveal limited outcomes.

For these and related reasons, reported findings comparing regular and special classes for exceptional children sometimes can seem contradictory or inconsistent. Accordingly, the reader should be thoughtful about accepting claims of superiority for one or another educational alternative and should weigh the evidence offered in support of these claims very carefully. Some of these claims are presented below.

Evaluations of Preschool Mainstreaming

Program evaluations conducted on preschool classes tend to support nonsegregated "Head Start" types of early childhood experiences for handicapped children (Haring et al., 1969; McKinney & Krueger, 1974). In such a setting, not only do young exceptional children appear to make short-term behavioral gains, but these gains tend to persist in subsequent school performance. Furthermore, these findings are not limited to more "intact" youngsters since even severely disabled young children are reported to have

benefited from participating in integrated Head Start–type preschool programs (Klein, 1975).

Academic Achievement

In the area of reading, Goldstein et al. (1965) reported that educable mentally retarded children assigned to regular classes achieved significantly higher scores in reading than comparable students in a special class. However, two years after the termination of this program, the exceptional children in the special class tended to "catch up" in reading performance with those in the regular class. Bennett (1932), in an early efficacy study, found that mentally retarded children placed in a regular class performed at higher levels of academic achievement than those placed in special classes. Additionally, it was reported that the difference favoring participation in regular classes persisted even after extended periods of time. Similar comparisons of academic achievement favoring the regular class have been reported by other authors (Pertsch, 1936; Thurstone, 1959). However, some studies of this type are more equivocal in their findings or actually favor the child in the special class (Glavin et al., 1971; Hewett et al., 1969; Moore, 1973). It is difficult to know if the positive and negative findings are really contradictory, or if the special conditions prevailing in each study account for the differences. For example, Moore (1973) used highly successful teachers of students with extreme learning problems in his special-class condition and attained results that favor the special over the regular class. In view of these research problems (Cassidy & Stanton, 1959) the tentative generalization can be made that special education classes do not necessarily produce improved performance when compared to regular classes (Baller, 1936). However, even this statement can be made only cautiously about exceptional children in general, since some disability groups (such as educable mentally retarded students) have been studied more intensively than other groups.

Social Acceptance

Some educators hold that academic achievement is related to the degree of affection and attention that children receive (Zigler, 1966). Thus, in considering educational environments for the exceptional, attention has been paid to the level of acceptance attained by the atypical child in the school milieu. Johnson (1950) concluded that the special-class environment was more accepting of the mentally retarded child than was the general class, especially in regard to the seriously limited child. On the other hand, Thurstone (1960) reported greater social acceptance of exceptional students enrolled in regular classes, while Gottlieb and Davis (1973) found virtually no difference. These divergent results suggest that few conclusions can be reached at this time about the values and limitations of special and regular classes in fostering social acceptance.

In the social area, special educators wonder about the implications of disability labels for the self-concept and acceptability level of the exceptional student. However, the negative aspects of labeling are not necessarily limited to students enrolled in special classes. For example, Edgerton and Sabagh (1962) concluded that the effects of the labeling process is, in many instances, determined not only by the label but by the evaluation of that label by the exceptional child and those around him. A further caution is suggested by Goldstein (1963), who indicated that labeling can be as common in a regular as in a special class; for instance, when children call the atypical individual derogatory names. By and large, the reports of personality and behavioral outcomes of various educational environments show few consistent trends when special and regular classes are compared. Thus, Pertsch (1936) found that on personality measures, retarded boys achieved higher performance levels in regular classes than in special classes but that retarded girls did not. On the other hand, Cassidy and Stanton (1959) reported higher teacher ratings of the adjustment of exceptional students in regular than in special classes.

Vocational Adjustment

It has been argued that the more extensive vocational resources available in some special class situations (as compared to regular classes) promote improved occupational adjustment among handicapped students. Although there is support for this position in relation to fostering employment readiness and subsequent entry into work (Dinger, 1961), most of the studies of vocational adjustment and career development of exceptional students have been fragmentary, at best. In fact, relatively little is known about the prevocational and vocational training potentials of various special and general education environments. As a result, the hypothesized vocational superiority for exceptional students in special, as contrasted to regular, classes is yet to be tested in effective organized studies.

The process of comparing the outcomes of regular and special class placements has been made more complicated by the fact that different procedures may be used in different systems to effectuate class placements. For example, extensive dependence upon cognitive factors in arriving at placement decisions has been challenged by educators such as MacMillan (1971), who advocates more extensive consideration of social and emotional factors in making placement decisions, even when some form of special cognitive remediation is clearly indicated. Zigler and Butterfield (1968) suggest that motivational factors should be given greater weight in the process. Furthermore, Snapp and Woolfolk (1971) indicate that cultural differences often play an excessively prominent role in assigning a child to a special class. In actuality, it is advocated that academic, sociological, linguistic, and self-care factors should be taken into account in qualifying a child for special education environments, rather than disability factors alone or test scores alone. When labels or other "extraneous" elements are given undue weight in the assignment process, inappropriate placements become more frequent. These "misplacements" can and do muddy the findings of studies concerning exceptional children's academic and social performance in various educational environments. A final aspect of the special class that merits discussion is the fact that since it offers an alternative to a residential school or a regular class placement, it forces educators to evaluate children and to make informed placement decisions. Theoretically, if all exceptional children were placed only in residential or regular class environments, an extensive evaluation of the student would be less necessary. However, because the special class exists as a third alternative, a more comprehensive assessment of the child is required and finer judgments need to be made (Englehardt, 1970).

The Resource Room

The resource room is an intermediate option between the special class and the regular class, designed to reap their advantages and avoid their pitfalls. As an "in-between" alternative, which assists the student to cope with regular class conditions, the resource room has been reputed to have the following psychological attributes:

General Advantages. It has been claimed that the resource room generates greater academic, social, and emotional growth among mildly and moderately handicapped children than does the special class (Walker, 1974). More specifically, evidence has been presented showing that exceptional children perform better in reading when in combined resource and regular classroom environments than in special classrooms, and at a reason-

able cost (Sabatino, 1972). In a somewhat broader view of this educational alternative, Vallett (1970) sees the resource room as suitable, not only for exceptional students enrolled in regular classes, but also as a learning center for exceptional children enrolled in special classes. In terms of academic skills and knowledge, it has been reported that the word-reading and vocabulary competencies of mildly to moderately handicapped children were improved by participation in resource room activities (Walker, 1974). At the very least, there appear to be few, if any, indications that the resource room results in negative academic outcomes.

Social Development By reducing social isolation and stigma, the resource room is reputed to contribute to the social development of the exceptional child (Sabatino, 1972). Control exercised over the time spent by the student in the regular and the resource class environments enables the resource teachers to engineer a gradual reintegration of the child into the school mainstream, moving the student along at a pace that is in accordance with the readiness of both the exceptional student and the receiving regular class (Creswell, 1973). This reintegration process is fostered by cross-categorical student groupings that bypass disability labels and focus on children's abilities and needs (Hammill, 1972). In general, it is claimed that, at least among educable mentally retarded students, fewer social problems develop in the resource room than in the special class.

The Teacher Variable. Increasingly, resource room teachers are reaching out in ever-widening circles to impact regular classes and school services, as advocates of the exceptional child and as guides of co-teachers with regular class educators (Jenkins & Mayhall, 1976). This has led to a concept of a resource from "without walls" through which regular class teachers are helped to cope more effectively with the problems of exceptionality encountered in the mainstreaming process (McDonnell,

1974). From this perspective, the resource teacher conducts a psychologically meaningful support system for the general educator in such areas as instructional assistance, lesson preparation, shared educational responsibility, and acquisition and use of specialized educational resources. These assists tend to improve regular teacher morale and expedite the acceptance of exceptional children into the mainstream (Reger & Koppmann, 1971; Snapp, 1972). Indeed, the possible psychological influence of the resource room teacher upon other educators is considered to be so strong that some observers suggest that this relationship can well be the key to the long-term reintegration of many exceptional children (Glavin, 1973).

Regular Class Environment with Supportive Services

Many exceptional students who are enrolled in regular classes require continuing supplemental supportive services. In response to this need, special educators have offered a wide range of interdisciplinary interventions that vary so widely from one school system to another that it is difficult to generalize about their psychological impact on exceptional students in general. However, it is now well accepted that these supports make it possible for some exceptional students to function in the integrated classroom, even if the precise contribution of each of these services is not yet fully understood. Currently, as Siegal (1969) indicates, mainstreaming confronts students and educators with such problems as negative self-concept, anxiety, experience deprivation, attentional difficulties, organizational and administrative limitations, poor program coordination, and deficits in the child's abstract thinking, social behavior, and perceptual skills. Many of these problems cannot be readily solved in the regular classroom without assistance from a panoply of specialized disciplines that enrich the child's regular class program. Although firm

outcome data are not available, it is widely held that selected interdisciplinary supports in the regular classroom yield psychoeducational benefits for the exceptional child, including those discussed below.

Acceptability of the Exceptional Child. Greater social acceptability seems attainable in the regular class when supportive services are offered (Iano *et al.*, 1974; Kennedy & Bruininks, 1974), especially when the exceptional child is placed in a regular class group whose intellectual level is comparable to his own (Baldwin, 1958; Johnson & Kirk, 1950; Jordan, 1959), particularly if the exceptional child is congenial and relatively free from disturbing personality and behavior characteristics (Jones *et al.*, 1972). If, on the other hand, existing conditions in the regular class are unsupported by special services, slower progress seems to be made toward the acceptance of the exceptional child into the regular-class social structure expected (Justman & Maskowitz, 1957).

Participation of the Regular Class Teacher. A number of strategies have been devised to help regular class teachers to become more effective educators of the exceptional child who is placed in the regular school environment. These include: having the exceptional child replace a troublesome child who is reassigned elsewhere (Byrnes, 1976); using older, more capable students as peer tutors for the handicapped child (Byrnes, 1976); providing inservice training and consultation to regular class teachers (Byrnes, 1976); having the regular class and the special teacher engage in team teaching (Fallis, 1976); training regular teachers to do precision teaching (Haring, 1971); structuring a "helper" rather than a "crisis" role for the supporting teacher (Morse, 1976); and providing the general educator with ready access to such special services as consultants, tutors, and reading, speech, and language specialists (Coleman *et al.*, 1975).

Student Behavior. Although there is some evidence that regular and special class environments do not produce differential behavioral effects (Swift & Spivak, 1969), some special educators contend that the regular class fosters more mature and acceptable student behavior among exceptional children. For example, Budoff and Gottlieb (1974) observed that mainstreamed educable mentally retarded students tended to become more internally controlled and reflective in a regular class environment. Similarly, Blum (1971) reported that mainstreamed exceptional children tended to adapt to a regular class milieu subsequent to initial adjustment problems. This positive effect became especially evident when special children were instructed in the use of behavior-modification techniques for altering the behavior of peers toward them. Improved behavioral functioning also was noted by Taylor and Soloway (1971) in the context of a learning center developed for them. This center experience not only accelerated the movement of exceptional students toward reintegration, but at the same time it was useful for other students at the school, lessening the hazards of segregation and labeling.

Impact on Nondisabled Peers. Data are scanty concerning the impact of the mainstreamed exceptional student on his nondisabled peers. In one study, Grosenick (1970) reported that no negative effects were observed on the other children in the regular class environment over the short term. If anything, the participation of atypical children tended to exert a positive influence on the nondisabled children. Similarly, Csapo (1972) found no negative consequences on "normal" students who were assigned to function as peer models for exceptional youngsters. Indeed, among the emotionally disturbed children studied, the intergroup interactions helped exceptional children to acquire more appropriate behaviors and facilitated handicapped student adaption to the mainstream environment.

In most instances, participation in regular classes seems associated with more favorable development for all concerned. In this process, regular classroom teacher function-ing is a key variable in determining the success of the mainstreaming effort. Some regular teachers are not professionally or psychologically prepared to serve exceptional children effectively in their rooms. In order to promote teacher acceptance and effectiveness, special educators have used a variety of strategies that seem to work. However, very little is known about effective means for dealing with administrator attitudes and leadership, the degree of community support for mainstreaming, the position taken by teachers' associations and unions, the impact of parent groups, and the types of supports available to the regular class teacher. Favorable reports concerning mainstreaming for exceptional children are so numerous that one might readily conclude that properly designed and implemented regular classroom programs for carefully selected students usually achieve their objectives.

The Hospital Class. Classes conducted in a medical environment for hospitalized children constitute a special residential education situation. Imbedded in a predominantly medical or psychiatric setting, hospital-based classes cope with a variety of special instructional problems, including the higher priority ordinarily assigned to medical and psychiatric, as compared to educational, procedures, the limited or inappropriate space assigned to the educational program, the physical and emotional discomfort that may be experienced by the child in the unfamiliar institutional environment, the limited time available for instruction in a child's crowded therapeutic schedule, and the difficulty that some hospital personnel have in accepting and working with educational interventions in a therapeutic milieu. Despite the problems, many hospital classes seem to yield important gains for certain exceptional children.

Rusalem (unpublished) studied the academic and social gains made by exceptional children during a two-month stay on an orthopedic service of a general hospital located in the inner city. In this setting, exceptional children who earlier had experienced academic and social deprivation in conjunction with their participation in community school programs made accelerated progress in the hospital class. Important contributing factors seemed to be the individualized instruction offered in the hospital class and the children's relationships with nurturing hospital teachers and teacher aides. For this group, at least, the hospital class was an enriching educational experience that produced dramatic elevations in intelligence and reading-test scores and improved interpersonal relationships with both adults and peers in the medical milieu. Follow-up studies conducted six months after the termination of each child's hospitalization revealed that members of the group initially transferred their new, more positive perceptions of the educational process into their respective community schools. However, the continuing limitations of their home and school environments gradually eroded the attitudinal and academic gains that had been made in the hospital, and within six months their original school problems were reactivated. A similar follow-up of "graduates" of a hospital-based educational program reported by Briggs (1973) suggested that a large proportion of formerly hospitalized physically limited children were functioning successfully in the unsheltered community subsequent to hospitalization.

Observations of children who were hospitalized for emotional problems indicate that the introduction of selected environmental variables into a hospital class can have a positive influence on exceptional children, including: behavior modification (Kravetz & Forness, 1971); the prescription of psychiatric drugs (Yang *et al.,* 1973); ample and appropriate physical space for educational purposes (Rieger, 1972); and constructive attitudes on the part of hospital personnel and peers toward the student and his educational experience (Rieger, 1972). In working with autistic youngsters, Treffert *et al.* (1973) found that toilet-trained children

with later autistic speech symptoms that developed by 5 years of age, tended to function more effectively in a hospital class situation, than similar students did without these attributes. In another study, it was found that hospitalized emotionally disabled young children benefited from daytime participation in a community nursery school program, although transportation to and from the hospital did constitute a management problem (Rieger & Leiken, 1969).

Since recommendations for the hospitalization usually originate with physical or mental health-care personnel, educators tend to play a minor role, if any, in the hospitalization decision-making process. Whatever the reasons may be for hospitalizing a child, most observers agree that, even if the hospitalization is brief, it is to the child's advantage to have a school experience in conjunction with his hospital treatment. In addition to becoming an integral part of treatment, an educational component is considered to have value in normalizing the child's experience and providing linkages to community education facilities that will be vital to the child in the posthospitalization community environment. In some respects (most demonstrably with exceptional children who have suffered deprivation in the community setting), hospital-based educational services can improve a child's attitude toward education and accelerate his educational and social growth. As noted by Kravetz and Forness (1971) and Rusalem (unpublished), additional studies are needed to test innovative means for generalizing these in-hospital gains to the school, community, and family environment when the time comes for the child to reenter the less restricted posthospital world.

Home Instruction. Assignment to home instruction environment once was made by medical prescriptions based upon a physician's judgment of a child's presumed inability to manage one or more significant physical or emotional aspects of the school milieu due to serious illness or disability, lack of transportation, safety factors, or behavior problems. As school-based special-education programs became more sophisticated, as transportation facilities improved, and as public resolve strengthened to provide group educational experiences and a barrier-free school environment to as many handicapped children as possible, the proportion of physically limited children on home instruction began to decline. Concurrently, increasingly troublesome questions were being raised about the necessity and desirability of home teaching for emotionally and behaviorally handicapped children. In time, professional workers and parents began to understand that education services provided at home are not only costly, but psychologically disadvantageous for many children. In interviews conducted with a sample of children on home instruction, Rusalem (unpublished) found that students served in a home environment felt that the experience had impaired their social development and had aroused within them feelings of isolation and loneliness. This effect occurred even among homebound children who were keeping pace academically with comparable students in community-based classes for handicapped students.

Some children with severe physical limitations and/or severe emotional limitations are placed on home instruction on spurious grounds. In actuality, even today, some homebound students could function adequately in class situations if suitable adaptions were made in out-of-home educational environments. Rusalem (unpublished) found that the assignment of a child to home instruction is not only a function of a child's physical and emotional status, but also of the readiness of a school district to arrange an adequate educational environment for him. Thus, types of handicapped children in one district who are placed on home instruction fit readily into school programs in another district. In such instances, the difference may be transportation, essential supportive services, barrier-free schools, or individualized

instruction. In this regard, Lyons and Powers (1963) concluded that a comprehensive assessment of the child and the educational options actually or potentially available to him should be conducted prior to exempting a student from school-based instruction. All too often a child's behavior problems can become the overriding basis for assigning him to home instruction, rather than an assay of his needs, capacities, and opportunities.

In positive terms, a home instruction may be used as a "therapeutic intervention" as well as an educational site of "last resort." In such a therapeutic framework, the home instruction program offers individualized activities and services that prepare the child for the earliest possible return to the community school, weaning him away from the home and fostering gradual readaptation to the school environment (Lyons & Powers, 1963). Since prolonged participation in home instruction is considered to have negative psychological consequences for a student, the "returning child" may bring certain problem behaviors back to school with him. In such cases, it may be necessary to provide continuing supervision and support to the re-entering child until he gives evidence of his growing ability to cope with the school environment.

In response to the belief that unnecessary assignments may be made to home instruction because of inadequacies in the school, the family, or the community, special educators have worked as intensively with the physical and human ecology of the child as with the child himself. Thus, for more than twenty-five years, the Federation of the Handicapped in New York City, in cooperation with the New York City Board of Education, provided group experiences at a center-city rehabilitation facility for physically and emotionally limited teenagers on home instruction (Willson, 1962). Through the federation program, many of these students began to view themselves as community members and in their routine out-of-home activities began educating their families, the school system, and their communities about their ability to function successfully in community-based facilities. For other severely handicapped "homebound" children (such as the deaf-blind) arrangements have been made for the children and their parents to have joint community seminar and workshop experiences so that possibilities for out-of-home education could be explored under favorable circumstances. An approach of this type helps parents of multihandicapped children to become more effective teachers of their own young children in the home setting and to function as more efficient members of the habilitation team. The outcomes of this approach were so positive in one study that some of the parents brought non-disabled siblings of the handicapped child to the program so they, too, could learn to be of greater service to the "homebound" youngster (Wiehn, 1970).

The limited evidence concerning home instruction suggests, from an educational perspective, that the home environment creates crucial social problems for the "homebound" child and is perceived by educators, children, and, in some cases, parents to be a less desirable educational alternative for many children. Accordingly, unless mandated by incontrovertible medical or psychiatric realities, home instruction should be avoided lest the child suffer enduring and perhaps irreversible negative psychological consequences. Findings concerning the academic outcomes of home instruction are still being developed, but the current emphasis on reducing cognitive isolation suggests that, at the very least, a school-based environment provides a broader spectrum of educational opportunities, experiences, and options for the child, and by inference, constitutes a more promising educational environment for most special children.

Exclusion from a Formal Educational Environment. The educational exclusion of any exceptional child is universally de-

plored. Indeed, such a denial of service is thought to have catastrophic consequences and, thus, is generally considered to be an unacceptable alternative. As part of the human rights movement, special child advocacy efforts currently are focused on insuring access to education for all, even when the drain upon financial and human resources is heavy.

To this end of extending educational opportunities for severely handicapped children, the diagnostic or assessment class has emerged as one approach that merits consideration. Designed primarily for multi-handicapped and severely disabled children whose placement constitutes a challenge, the diagnostic or assessment class attempts to identify previously undiagnosed or partially diagnosed capacities and potentialities and, through initial interventions, starts the child on the road to realizing possibilities within him. Wherever possible, this environment prepares the youngster for subsequent entry into other appropriate special-education programs (Escovar, 1976; Kennedy, 1969).

Although outcome data regarding the effects of assessment classes are still sparse, the general impression is that they can improve educational placement decisions through actually engaging in early phases of a tentative "treatment" program and through using ongoing "treatment" as a diagnostic tool. In the course of this, the assessment class can have a psychological impact on parents who feel despair and despondency about the exclusion of their children from one or more educational environments. Through participation in diagnostic classes, some parents begin to see previously unrecognized possibilities in their children and their communities. If nothing else, diagnostic classes convey to parents and children a measure of school interest and concern and a sense of hope in relation to the child's educational possibilities. Thus, although definitive data about their efficacy are still lacking, assessment classes appear to offer a promising approach to children who do not readily conform to a school's qualification system.

Special Living-Educational Arrangements. Retention of an exceptional student in a family or a foster home may be unfeasible or contraindicated, particularly during the adolescent and young-adult period, although Dickerson's report would prove otherwise (1978). In an effort to avoid custom institutionalization, special educators may turn to a hostel-type of living and education arrangement for members of this group. In this environment, a small group of severely handicapped individuals share the same living quarters and participate in a program designed expressly for them. Environments of this type have been used with wheelchair-bound adults (Lufburrow, 1975); severely retarded individuals (Sanders, 1969); and the visually impaired (Hatlen, 1975), among others. These facilities often conducted in homes, apartments, or special buildings, almost always offer special-educational services for their residents. Although specialized curricula for these groups have been slow in developing, "hostel" programs usually include instruction and practice in daily living skills, mobility, social and recreational skills, and vocational readiness; in some instances, sheltered workshop activities are built into the total program. Generally, hostel environments are not merely shelters for the "unwanted," but habilitation centers that provide new and more meaningful learning opportunities for severely disabled individuals. As may be expected, this educational alternative has stirred some controversy among special educators because of its segregative aspects and the negative attitudes of some community members to having such facilities in their neighborhoods. Reports emanating from these programs tend to suggest that favorable outcomes occur with some frequency in serving seriously limited individuals who cannot otherwise fit into community education and employment. In time, as additional hostel facilities are opened in a growing number of communities throughout the United States and as more formal evaluations of them are conducted, a greater volume of data concerning their impact upon the disabled individual, the family, and the community will become available. At that time, an assessment of their psychological impact upon exceptional individuals will become more possible.

Special Camping and Recreation Programs. Although a nationwide trend seems evident toward widening the enrollment of exceptional children in existing camps and recreational facilities for nondisabled children, it is generally conceded that a need will continue for specialized facilities of this type for selected severely handicapped youngsters. Special camping and recreational program elements for handicapped children often include: behavior modification, group "therapy," therapeutic contracts, individualized programming, avoidance of standardized measures and norms (Stroudenmire & Comola, 1973), and adapted physical facilities and equipment (Rickard *et al.,* 1975). Such programs almost invariably report that they engender growth in exceptional children who cannot be served adequately in more general camping and recreational situations.

Although attitudes toward these facilities are generally favorable, relatively little is known about which recreation and camping environments are most effective with which disability groups and which programs' components and emphases most readily yield specified psychological outcomes.

Work-Study Programs. A remunerative work-study component in special-education programs for disabled teenagers is reputed to add reality, immediacy, and relevance to the total school environment. Although work-study arrangements vary from one school system to another, most are reported to foster improved student retention, better performance in some academic areas, especially those related to the work experience, enhanced preparation for subsequent entry into community jobs, and a higher level of realism about the world of work.

In one study (Chaffin & Spellman, 1971) student gains associated with a work-study experience included better performance on postschool jobs, a lower school drop-out rate, and higher earnings after leaving school. The authors of this study concluded that a work-study program enhances student employability for students with vocational limitations. Work-study programs emerge from the concept that remunerative work is an important component in the educational experience of handicapped adolescents. However, until recently, this concept was put to the test principally with educable mentally retarded students. Program outcomes for other disability groups are still being evaluated, but favorable reports are likely to be presented in the years ahead.

Special Classes at Clinics and Treatment Centers. Clinics and day-treatment centers for the health and mental-health care of children often provide special education services on their premises as part of their comprehensive multidisciplinary treatment programs. In these terms, such facilities have some of the attributes of both outpatient therapeutic programs and special day schools for the handicapped. In some instances, these clinical programs serve severely handicapped children who are not considered ready to participate in community-based special education programs. Through providing multidisciplinary treatment of the child and the family, and through coordination of "in-house" and community resources, such clinic- or center-based programs seek to cope with relatively complex and difficult problems. A measure of their contribution lies in the probability that many of these children would otherwise be excluded from most specialized programs for exceptional children because of the severity of their problems.

Despite the seriousness of the physical, intellectual, and emotional conditions dealt with in these programs, even modest outcomes can be significant. For instance, Berko (1972) reported that 25 percent of the very limited children served in her sample subsequently were placed successfully in less segregated educational environments. In a diagnostic teaching clinic for deaf children, Osborne *et al.* (1971) observed that a clinic service enabled teachers to understand the child more fully and to deal with the child's multiple problems more effectively. In a hospital-based program offering a day class for learning-disabled children, Yang *et al.* (1973) noted a degree of progress among those served. In view of the fact that the children served by specialized clinics and centers have failed elsewhere, the reported gains made seem promising.

Boarding Homes. Boarding homes customarily provide exceptional children with a relatively short-term residence with a "foster" family, hopefully in conjunction with required supportive services. Such homes serve an especially useful purpose when a family interpersonal crisis, or a parental absence leaves the child stripped of the customary supports at home. Under these circumstances, the foster family is asked to augment the child's education experience by providing professionally supervised home training and instruction. Relatively few reports of boarding home educational outcomes with exceptional children appear in the special education literature, and consequently, little is known about the environmental impact of this option. Generally, however, it has been noted that boarding homes can provide a respite for parents from the day-to-day management of their atypical youngsters, or vice versa. Increasingly, boarding homes are assuming habilitative as well as child-care functions. Thus, while the exceptional child is in the boarding home, attempts are made by boarding home, school, and community personnel to work with both the child and family toward an early return to the family home (Berkam,

1975). We know so little about such programs that there is a real need for program demonstrations and evaluation studies designed to explore the potentialities, values, and limitations of boarding-home arrangements and to provide guidelines for the use by educators of this resource for exceptional children who have been put at risk by troubled family situations.

Other Educational Environments. Exceptional individuals also are served in a variety of other educationally related environments, most of which have been evaluated only superficially, if at all. For example, centers for handicapped college students, established with support from the U.S. Office of Education, are breaking new ground in helping colleges and universities to create more functional environments for seriously impaired college-level students. Although definitive findings have yet to emerge from these new programs, observations indicate that they are having a positive impact upon the learning and social conditions provided by many colleges for exceptional students. In contrast to England and the European continent, which have a tradition of segregated college education for the severely disabled comparable to that of Gallaudet University in the United States (Lowe, 1973), the focal American effort has been centered almost completely upon mainstreaming (Akamu, 1971).

Among others, the educational environment of private vocational schools can offer instructional flexibility and adaptation that rival or surpass public vocational training programs (Belitsky, 1969). Sheltered workshops have gone well beyond the typical physical sensory and intellectual disabilities, with some opening their doors to narcotics addicts, severely mentally retarded, and seriously emotionally disabled adolescents. Chapple (1973) reported that a workshop environment was useful in serving violent acting-out "psychopaths and sociopaths" and narcotics addicts in a combined therapy and rehabilitation regimen. During the first three months of service in this setting, positive changes were observed in the participants, and after six months, these gains were even more firmly established. Other, even less-explored special environments merit stepped-up evaluative efforts, including self-help groups, "encounter" situations for the handicapped, mental-health centers serving severely disabled children, services with a religious orientation, programs conducted by parent groups, total communication environments (Kopchick, 1975), open classrooms (Bartel, 1972; Craig & Holman, 1973); learning centers (O'Brien, 1975; Sontag, 1976); peer models (Irving, 1975); highly controlled classrooms (Rutter & Bartuk, 1973); experimental physical environments (Morris, 1974); teaching machines (Bland, 1976); service in a research context (Dantona, 1976); radio programs (Baine, 1975); and reduced stimulation (Fassler & Bryant, 1971). So little has been reported about these alternative environments that they can be merely listed at this time as relatively untested alternatives.

KNOWN AND UNKNOWN ASPECTS OF SPECIAL EDUCATION ENVIRONMENTS

The literature concerning special-education environments indicates that some conclusions can now be reached about them. Among these are:

1. A prescription for an educational environment is a vital component in the educational plan developed for any exceptional child.

2. Special educators have been quite creative in developing a broad range of alternative learning environments for atypical students from which selections may be made for an individual youngster.

3. The outcomes of child experiences in these environments that have been reported in the literature tend to be favorable.

4. At this time, attempts to generalize from limited local feasibility studies to other educational settings should be undertaken with great caution.

5. Most of the special educational environments devised for the exceptional child still await the initiation of more systematic evaluation procedures.

6. In some instances, therefore, it is difficult to know whether the reported outcomes in a particular special education environment are a function of the environmental intervention employed or the school and community conditions in which such projects are imbedded.

7. Coping with an array of partially tested educational environments and instructional components, special educators currently have access to few guides to assist them in the selection and management of an optimum environment for each child.

8. The tendency, therefore, for special educators is to function in this area with limited research and limited tools.

The last conclusion leaves many vital questions unanswered. Some of these questions are:

1. In selecting an educational environment for the exceptional child, are special educators able to predict probable success and failure of each environmental option with sufficient precision to warrant parent and administrator confidence in such judgments?

2. How can special educators improve their predictive competency, and consequently, achieve greater success in matching individual children and educational environments?

3. To what extent may the results derived in one school system concerning the use of a particular environment be generalized to other school systems?

4. Should special educators trust their instincts and "gut reactions" more than the limited currently available reports of demonstrations and studies in making placement decisions?

5. How can the field of special education organize itself to accelerate the process of answering these and other critical questions about the suitability of alternative educational environments for an exceptional child?

CONCLUSIONS

All too many exceptional children have been placed in educational environments through being assigned to arbitrary disability categories. Crude groupings of this kind have troubled special educators because they feel deeply committed to principles of individual differences and individualization of instruction. As a group, they do not trust labeling procedures and service prescriptions keyed to these labels. Unfortunately, this sensitivity to individual differences has not prevented special educators from seeking educational solutions through research studies and demonstrations that yield group data. Nor have they been sufficiently reluctant to apply group findings to an individual case, even when the similarity between that case and the study group is open to doubt. While functioning as advocates for individualized treatment of handicapped children, some special teachers continue to search for *the* reading system, *the* instructional materials, and, in our area of interest, *the* environment that will fit a defined group of handicapped youngsters. Since a commitment to individualization and a quest for group solutions are incompatible, strains have developed within the field. Such strains become increasingly evident as group data about educational environments such as those reviewed fail to provide adequate service guidelines that consistently place each exceptional child in that environment which will produce optimum growth at each stage of development.

The route taken by special education to establish a number of alternative environments (residential, special class, and mainstream settings, for example) and then to slot children into these options with the hope of achieving a "best fit" seems to violate the individualization principle. Although such a procedure may be acceptable in terms of cost, administrative convenience, instructional compromise, or ease of teacher intervention, it focuses on presumed comparabilities among exceptional children that may not exist in reality. In practice, the labeling of environments can be as pernicious as the labeling of children. Indeed, gross errors are almost inevitable when broadly grouped children who are very different from each other are placed in broadly grouped educational environments in which the "fit" is highly approximate. Furthermore, the findings emerging from group studies are generally probabilistic. That is, the results can be more accurately applied to some children in the middle of the distribution and less accurately to the "exceptional." Many of the psychosocial problems of handicapped children derive from just such a condition—the "laying upon" them of group generalizations that are not necessarily applicable to them. While criticizing employers and lay persons for stereotyping exceptional individuals, educators and researchers themselves seem to feel few compunctions about relating the identified central tendency of a group to an exceptional child who, by definition, is atypical, and therefore a "deviant" from the norm.

The foregoing is by way of suggesting that the available data, derived as they usually are from group observations and analyses, tend to have limited value for serving a severely disabled child whose differences from other children are substantial, even within the same disability category. Concurrently, educational environments also are individual in nature. For example, in applying the label "special class" to a particular environment, special educators often conceal or overlook extensive variations in the attributes of that class of environment. Merely lumping such classes together because they share a few characteristics is as much a violation of individual differences as when we arbitrarily categorize, for instructional purposes, a group of exceptional students as visually impaired or cerebral palsied. Educators who are really committed to concepts of individual differences are likely to have real doubts about taking the group-data

route in their search for improved procedures for structuring and prescribing educational environments for handicapped children. In operational terms, group findings that have not yet provided a useful instructional base for an exceptional child are equally deficient in devising an educational setting for that child.

Future developments in making special education more congruent with individual differences will depend on the ability of special educators to break out of the group-assignment mold and move on to other perspectives which offer greater promise for fulfilling the individualization ideal. One such approach may be an individualized analysis of the unique instructional needs of each exceptional child and the development of that unique instructional environment that will best satisfy individual needs. In this framework, no two instructional environments for any two exceptional children would be identical, and the classification of environments by such names as "special class," "regular class," or "residential school" would become unnecessary. Only those educational-environment components required by a student would be incorporated in his special-education program, and if some of these components do not currently exist in a school system, they would be created expressly for his purposes.

Such an approach is still so uncommon that little has been written about it. However, some steps leading toward it have been taken by Rusalem and Rusalem (unpublished) in their Learning Capacities Research Project. This project was founded on the premise that the differences in needs, styles, and capacities among severely disabled children are so critical that attempts to match a finite repertoire of learning environments with individuals can no longer be presumed to fulfill our mission. Discarding the practice of "slotting" students into a relatively small number of mass-produced educational environments, these investigators developed child-evaluation techniques that define more precisely the educational settings needed by an individual exceptional child, and have demonstrated in four states that existing facilities for secondary-level students can house an infinity of educational environments. Without reference to "prepackaged" settings (e.g., a special class or a residential school), the Learning Capacities approach focuses upon answering the question: What are the attributes of that educational environment that will meet the unique needs of *this* child more effectively than any other?

In the course of serving more than 3,000 individuals since 1974, the Learning Capacities Research Project staff has not yet recommended two identical prescribed learning environments for any two individuals. This is a consequence of working with the environmental variable on an individualized level, conceding nothing to administrative convenience or exigency or to practitioner tendencies to classify human beings into arbitrary dehumanized groupings. Once the Learning Capacities team (including the parent, the child, the Learning Capacities specialist, and significant others) has defined a child's optimum environment for learning, the Project and the educational facility work together to construct and implement such an environment for *one* child. This is not always easy, since educators may articulate a stronger verbal commitment to individual differences than they are prepared to accept in daily practice. Furthermore, some educators may be ready to compromise too freely with practical problems of time, money, teacher motivation, and administrative burdens.

Throughout its life, the Learning Capacities Research Project has been demonstrating day-in and day-out that it is possible to individualize learning and habilitation secondary-level environments (in terms of setting, child strategies, and instructional procedures) within the reality limits of school and agency programs. The most costly of all educational interventions are those that fail children, not those that make greater demands on school systems and communities. By this criterion, the results of the project efforts have been promising. Hundreds of severely disabled students who were experiencing failure in educational programs have been "fitted" with project help into more suitable educational environments and have moved on to higher levels of academic, social, and vocational functioning.

In a learning-capacities framework in which environmental categories are eliminated in favor of individually prescribed educational environments, school facilities become increasingly consonant with each child's style and capacities. Furthermore, educational settings do not compete with one another for community approval. Instead of functioning as advocates for one or another educational environment, special educators in a learning-capacities framework become advocates of the child's individual ecological needs, regardless of whatever label someone cares to put on it. As an alternative to a category-centered approach that makes arbitrary placements of youngsters into preexisting, rigid educational structures, the Learning Capacities Project is exploring the practicality of actually doing what special education says it is doing. The outcomes of the project suggest that it is as practical to program learning environments for exceptional children as it is to conduct an assembly line for them. As a by-product of this effort, we no longer have to choose up sides in advocating this environment or that for groups of exceptional children. Replacing such a competitive outlook is one which promotes a creative process of formulating unique environments for unique children, each of which can be tested in terms of how effectively it assists the student to realize his potential.

REFERENCES

ADELMAN, H. S. Remedial classroom instruction revisited. *The Journal of Special Education*, 1971, *5* (4) , 311–322.

———. The resource concept: Bigger than a room. *The Journal of Special Education*, 1972, *6* (4) , 361–367.

AKAMU, T. Facilities and services for handicapped students at college in Hawaii. *Rehabilitation Literature*, 1971, *36* (5) , 134–138.

ANDERSON, G. J. Effects of course content and teacher sex on the social climate of learning. *American Educational Research Journal*, 1971, *8* (4) , 649–663.

———, & WALBERG, H. J. Class size and social environment of learning: A Mixed Replication and Extension. *Alberta Journal of Educational Research*, 1972, *8* (4) , 227–286.

———. Learning environments. In *Evaluating educational performance; A source book of methods, instruments, and examples*, H. J. WALBERG, (Ed.) . Berkeley, Cal., McGutchan Pub. Corp., 1974.

ANDERSON, R. M., & STEVENS, G. D. Practices and problems in educating deaf retarded children in residential schools. *Exceptional Children*, 1969, *35* (9) , 687–694.

BAINE, D. FM Radio transmitters in "in situ" behavioral management. *Mental Retardation Bulletin*, 1975, *3* (1) , 156–159.

BALDWIN, W. K. The social position of mentally handicapped children in the regular classes in the public school. *Exceptional Children*, 1958, *25* (2) , 106–108, 112.

BALLER, W. R. Study of the present social status of a group of adults who, when they were in elementary school, were classified as mentally deficient. *Genetic Psychology Monographs*, *18* (3) , 1936.

BARKER, R. G., & GUMP, P. *Big school, small school*. Palo Alto, Cal.: Stanford University Press, 1964.

BARTEL, N. R. *The Philadelphia open classroom project*. Washington, D.C., Bureau for the Education of the Handicapped, Technical Report No. 242, 1972.

BEHRENS, R. F., & BERKOWITZ, A. J. Public education for trainable mentally retarded persons. *Journal for Special Educators of the Mentally Retarded*, 1973, *10* (1) , 21–26, 28.

BELITSKY, A. H. *Private Vocational Schools and Their Students: Limited Objectives, Unlimited Opportunities*. Cambridge, Mass.: Schenkman Pub. Co., 1969.

BENNETT, A. *A comparative study of subnormal children in the elementary grades*. New York: Bureau of Publications, Teachers College, 1932.

BERKAM, W. Boarding homes: A resource for handicapped children and schools. *Bureau Memorandum*, 1975, *16* (4) , 22–24.

BERKO, F. G. An effort to teach the multiply handicapped child. In *Professional preparation for educators of crippled children*, F. Connor, J. Wald, & M. Cohen (Eds.) , New York: Teachers College Press, 1972

BIRCH, J., & JOHNSON, K. *Designing schools and schooling for the handicapped*. Springfield, Ill.: Charles C Thomas, 1975.

BLAND, E. Learning resource services for the handicapped. *Exceptional Children*, 1976, *43* (3) , 161–163.

BLUM, E. Fitting in. *Teaching Exceptional Children*, 1971, *3* (4) , 172–180.

BRIELAND, D. A followup study of orthopedically handicapped high school graduates. *Exceptional Children*, 1967, *33* (8) , 555–564.

BRIGGS, J. W. The development of a multi-discipline centre for the treatment and education of physically handicapped children. *Special Education in Canada*, 1973, *7* (4) , 19–25.

BUDOFF, M., & GOTTLIEB, J. A comparison of EMR children in special classes with EMR children who have been re-integrated into regular classes. *Studies in Learning Potential,* 1974, *3* (4), 62–68.

BYRNES, M. Positive attitudes: A must for special programs in public schools. *Teaching Exceptional Children,* 1976, *8* (2), 82–84.

CASSIDY, V., & STANTON, J. An investigation of factors in the differences between children in special and regular classes in Ohio. Columbus, Ohio: Ohio State University Press, 1959.

CHAFFIN, J. D., SPELLMAN, C. R., REGAN, C. E., & DAVISON, R. Two followup studies of former educable mentally retarded students from the Kansas work-study project. *Exceptional Children,* 1971, *37* (10), 733–738.

CHAPPLE, E. Rehabilitation of character disturbed adolescents through productive participation. *Rehabilitation Record,* 1973, *14* (5), 1–7.

COLEMAN, P., EGGLESTON, K., COLLINS, J., HOLLOWAY, B., & REIDER, S. A severely hearing impaired child in the mainstream. *Teaching Exceptional Children,* 1975, *8* (1), 6–9.

CONNOR, L. Mainstreaming a special school. *Teaching Exceptional Children,* 1976, *8* (2), 76–80.

CORKER, D. The development of a vocational program in a residential school for the visually handicapped. *The New Outlook for the Blind,* 1974, *68* (1), 25–28.

CRAIG, H., & HOLMAN, G. The open classroom in a school for the deaf. *American Annals of the Deaf,* 1973, *118* (6), 675–685.

CRESWELL, D. Integration is a two-way street. *Education in Canada,* 1973, *13* (3), 4–7.

CRUICKSHANK, W. *Learning Disabilities in Home, School and Community.* Syracuse: Syracuse University Press, 1977.

CSAPO, M. Peer models reserve the "One bad apple spoils the barrell" theory. *Teaching Exceptional Children,* 1972, *5* (1), 20–24.

DANTONA, R. Services for deaf-blind children. *Exceptional Children,* 1976, *43* (3), 172–174.

DAVIS, F. R. Demand-degradable teacher standards: Expediency and professional Thantos." *Mental Retardation,* 1970, *8,* 37–40.

DEVEREUX, G. *Therapeutic education.* New York: Harper Bros., 1956.

DICKERSON, M. V. *Our Four Boys.* Syracuse: Syracuse University Press, 1978.

DINGER, J. Post-school adjustment of former educable retarded pupils. *Exceptional Children,* 1961, *27,* 353–360.

DOLAN, W. The first ten months of the rubella living-unit. *The New Outlook for the Blind,* 1972, *66* (1), 9–14.

DOWLING, S. Treatment in cottage programs for children with severe developmental disturbances. *Child Welfare,* 1975, *54* (6), 395–405.

EDGERTON, R. B., & SABAGH, G. From mortification to aggrandizement: Changing self-conceptions in the career of the mentally retarded. *Psychiatry,* 1962, *25,* 263–272.

ELSER, R. The social position of hearing handicapped children in the regular grades. *Exceptional Children,* 1959, *25,* 305–309.

ENGLEHARDT, G. M. Increasing the efficacy of special class placement for the socially maladjusted. *The Journal of Special Education,* 1970, *4* (4), 441–444.

ESCOVAR, P. L. Another chance for learning— The assessment class. *Teaching Exceptional Children,* 1976, *9* (1), 2–3.

FALLIS, J. R. The key to integrated learning for children who are hearing impaired. *Volta Review,* 1975, *77* (6), 363–367.

FASSLER, J., & BRYANT, N. D. Disturbed children under reduced auditory input: A pilot study. *Exceptional Children,* 1971, *38* (3), 197–204.

FORCE, D. Social status of physically handicapped children. *Exceptional Children,* 1956, *23,* 132–134.

GALLAGHER, P., & HEIM, R. The classroom application of behavior modification principles for multiply handicapped blind students. *The New Outlook for the Blind,* 1974, *68* (10), 447–453.

GLAVIN, J. Followup behavioral research in resource rooms. *Exceptional Children,* 1973, *40* (3), 211–212.

GLAVIN, J., QUAY, H., & WERRY, J. Behavioral and academic gains of conduct problem children in different classroom settings. *Exceptional Children,* 1971, *37* (6) , 441–446.

GOLDSTEIN, H. Issues in the education of the educably mentally retarded. *Mental Retardation,* 1963, *1,* 10–12, 52–53.

GOLDSTEIN, H., MOSS, J., & JORDAN, L. *The efficacy of special class training on the development of mentally retarded children.* Urbana, Ill.: University of Illinois, 1965.

GORDON, E. *Building a socially supportive environment.* New York: Columbia University Press, 1970.

GOTTLIEB, J., & DAVIS, J. Social acceptance of EMR children during overt behavioral interactions. *American Journal of Mental Deficiency,* 1973, *78* (2) , 141–143.

GRAYSON, J. A playground of musical sculpture. *Music Educators Journal,* 1972, *58* (8) , 50–54.

GROSENICK, J. Assessing the integration of exceptional children into regular classes. *Teaching Exceptional Children,* 1970, *2* (3) , 113–119.

———. Integration of exceptional children into regular classes: Research and procedures. *Focus on Exceptional Children,* 1971, *3* (5) , 1–8.

GUARINO, L., & SAGE, D. The private residential program: A response to L. Zneimer. *Exceptional Children,* 1973, *39* (7) , 567–568.

HAMILTON, A. Teaching handicapped children and their parents. *American Education,* 1973, *9* (8) , 22–26.

HAMMILL, D. The resource-room model in special education. *The Journal of Special Education,* 1972, *6* (4) , 349–354.

HANNAFORD, A. Criteria for special class placement of the mentally retarded; Multidisciplinary comparison. *Mental Retardation,* 1975, *13* (4) , 7–10.

HARING, N., HAYDEN, A., & NOLEN, P. Accelerating appropriate behaviors of children in a Head Start program. *Exceptional Children,* 1969, *35* (10) , 773–784.

HARMON, D. B. Lighting and child development. *Illuminating Engineers,* 1945, *40,* 190–228.

HATLEN, P., LeDUC, P., & CANTER, P. The blind adolescent life skills center. *The New Outlook for the Blind,* 1975, *69* (3) , 109–115.

HEBER, R. A manual of terminology and classification in mental retardation. *American Journal of Mental Deficiency Monograph,* 1959.

HELLER, H. The resource room: A mere change or real opportunity for the handicapped? *The Journal of Special Education,* 1972, *6* (4) , 369–375.

HEWETT, F., TAYLOR, F., & ARTUSO, A. The Santa Monica project: Evaluation of an engineered classroom design with emotionally disturbed children. *Exceptional Children,* 1969, *35* (7) , 523–529.

IANO, R., AYERS, A., HELLER, H., McGETTIGAN, J., & WALKER, V. Sociometric status of retarded children in an integrative program. *Exceptional Children,* 1974, *40* (4) , 267–271.

IRVING, J. Friends unlimited: Adolescents as helping resources. *Children Today,* 1975, *4* (4) , 14–17.

JENKINS, J., & MAYHALL, W. Development and evaluation of a resource teacher program. *Exceptional Children,* 1976, *43* (1) , 21–29.

JENKINS, J., MAYHALL, W., PESCHKA, C., & JENKINS, L. Comparing small group and tutorial instruction in resource rooms. *Exceptional Children,* 1974, *40* (4) , 245–251.

JOHNSON, G. A study of the social position of mentally handicapped children in the regular grades. *American Journal of Mental Deficiency,* 1950, *55,* 60–89.

———. Special education for the mentally handicapped: A paradox. *Exceptional Children,* 1962, *29* (2) , 62–69.

———, & KIRK, S. Are mentally handicapped children segregated in the regular grades? *Journal of Exceptional Children,* 1950, *17,* 65–68.

JOHNSON, G., & TUTTLE, D. Education and habilitation of multiply handicapped blind youth. *The New Outlook for the Blind,* 1971, *65* (2) , 56–61.

JONES, R., & GOTTFRIED, N. The prestige of special education teaching. *Exceptional Children,* 1966, *32,* 465–468.

JONES, R., LAVINE, K., & SHELL, J. Blind children integrated in classrooms with sighted children: A sociometric study. *The New Outlook for the Blind,* 1972, *66* (3) , 75–80.

JORDAN, A. Personal-social traits of mentally handicapped children. In *An evaluation of educating mentally handicapped children in special classes and regular classes,* T. Thurstone (Ed.) . Chapel Hill, N.C.: University of North Carolina, 1959.

JORGENSON, O., & GLAD, T. Adolescent psychiatry in a private Danish institution. *Journal of Learning Disabilities,* 1968, *1,* 30–41.

JUSTMAN, J., & MASKOWITZ, L. *The integration of deaf children in a hearing class.* New York: Bureau of Education Research, City of New York Board of Education, 1957.

KAPLAN, H. Looking at schools from inside the hospital. *Exceptional Children,* 1967, *43* (1) , 43–44.

KARNES, M., & ZEHRBACH, R. Flexibility in getting parents involved in the school. *Teaching Exceptional Children,* 1972, *5* (1) , 6–18.

KAUFMAN, M. Mainstreaming: Toward an explication of the construct. *Focus on Exceptional Children,* 1975, 7 (3) , 1–11.

KENNEDY, E. Diagnostic preschool for atypical children. *Exceptional Children,* 1969, *36* (3) , 193–199.

KENNEDY, P., & BRUININKS, R. Social status of hearing impaired children in regular classrooms. *Exceptional Children,* 1974, *40* (5) . 336–342.

KINKAIDE, P. Normalization and the handicapped. *Mental Retardation Bulletin,* 1975, *3* (1) , 128–132.

KIRK, S. Research in education. In *Mental retardation: A review of research,* H. Stevens & R. Heber (Eds.). Chicago: University of Chicago Press, 1964.

KLEIN, J. Mainstreaming the preschooler. *Young Children,* 1975, *30* (5) , 317–26.

KODMAN, F. Effects of preschool enrichment on intellectual performance of Appalachian children. *Exceptional Children,* 1970, *36* (7) , 503–507.

KOPCHICK, G. A total communication environment in an institution. *Mental Retardation,* 1975, *13* (3) , 22–23.

KRAVETZ, R., & FORNESS, S. The special classroom as a desensitization setting. *Exceptional Children,* 1971, *37* (5) , 389–392.

KRECH, D., ROSENZWEIG, M., & BENNETT, E. Effects of environmental complexity and training on brain chemistry. *Journal of Comparative and Physiological Psychology,* 1960, *53,* 509–519.

————. Environmental impoverishment, social isolation, and changes in brain chemistry and anatomy. *Physiology and Behavior,* 1966, *1,* 99–104.

————. Relationships Between Brain Chemistry and Problem-Solving Among Rats in Enriched and Impoverished Environments. *Journal of Comparative and Physiological Psychology,* 1962, *55,* 801–807.

KUZMA, K., & STERN, C. The effects of three preschool programs on development of autonomy in Mexican-American and Negro children. *The Journal of Special Education.* 1972, *6* (3) , 197–205.

LADSON, M. Regional education programs for handicapped persons. *Exceptional Children,* 1976, *43* (3) , 160–161.

LEE, R., & SCHRODER, H. Effects of outward bound training on urban youth, *Journal of Special Education,* 1969, *3* (2) , 187–205.

LEFRANÇOIS, G. *Of children: An introduction to child development.* Belmont, Calif.: Wadsworth Publishing Co., 1973.

LIPPMAN, L., & GOLDBERG, I. *Right to education.* New York: Teachers College Press, 1973.

LOWE, P. Two years at Hereward College (England) . *Special Education,* 1973, *62* (3) , 12–14.

LUFBURROW, W. A new independent hall. *Journal of Rehabilitation,* 1975, *41* (3) , 18–20, 36.

LYONS, D., & POWERS, V. Follow-up study of elementary school children exempted from Los Angeles city schools during 1960–61. *Exceptional Children,* 1963, *30* (4) , 155–162.

MacMillan, D. An examination of developmental assumptions underlying special classes for educable retardates. *California Journal for Instructional Improvement,* 1969, *12,* 165–173.

————. Special education for the mildly retarded: Servant or savant. *Focus on Exceptional Children,* 1971, *2* (9) , 1–11.

Maier, H. Learning to learn and living to live in residential treatment. *Child Welfare,* 1975, *54* (6) , 406–420.

Mayadas, N. Houseparents' expectations: A crucial variable in the performance of blind institutionalized children. *The New Outlook for the Blind,* 1975, *69* (1) , 77–83.

McDonnell, J. *Impact of Title VI program in the State of Oregon.* Salem, Oregon: Oregon State Department of Education, 1974.

McKenna, J. Special education holds new vistas for children. *Special Education in Canada,* 1975, *49* (3) , 4–5, 22.

McKinney, J., & Krueger, M. *Models for educating learning disabled* (MELD) . Washington, D.C.: Bureau of Health, Education and Welfare, 1974.

Miley, B. An integrated resource model. *Pointer.* 1973, *18* (2) , 149–157.

Millman, H., & Davis, J. Assessing behavioral change: A reliability study of the Devereux Child Behavior Rating. *Devereux Forum,* 1974, *10* (1) , 6–12.

Montessori, M. *Spontaneous activity in education.* Cambridge, Mass., Robert Bentley, Inc., 1964.

Moore, W. *A study of the extreme learning problem program in Oregon.* Salem, Oregon: Oregon State Department of Education, 1973.

Morris, R. A play environment for blind children: Design and evaluation. *The New Outlook for the Blind,* 1974, *68* (9) , 408–414.

Morse, W. The helping teacher/crisis teacher concept. *Focus on Exceptional Children,* 1976, *8* (4) , 1–10.

Mosley, W., & Spicker, H. Mainstreaming for the educationally deprived. *Theory into Practice,* 1975, *14* (2) , 73–81.

Mullen, F., & Itkin, W. *Achievement and adjustment of educable mentally retarded children in special classes and in regular classes.* Chicago: Board of Education, 1961.

Nelson, C., & Schmidt, L. The question of the efficacy of special classes. *Exceptional Children,* 1971, *37* (5) , 381–383.

Norland, E. Active children fail to thrive in a cramped environment. *Research in Norway,* 1974, 30–38.

O'Brien, R. Early childhood services for visually impaired children. *The New Outlook for the Blind,* 1975, *69* (5) , 201–206.

Ohrtman, W. One more instant solution coming up. *The Journal of Special Education,* 1972, *6* (4) , 377–381.

Olshin, G. Model centers for preschool handicapped children. *Exceptional Children,* 1971, *37* (9) , 665–669.

Osborne, K., Bellefleur, P., & Bevan, R. An experimental diagnostic teaching clinic for multiply handicapped deaf children. *Exceptional Children,* 1971, *37* (5) , 387–389.

Paul, J., Turnbull, A., & Cruickshank, W. *Mainstreaming: A Practical Guide.* Syracuse: Syracuse University Press, 1978.

Pertsch, C. *A comparative study of the progress of sub-normal pupils in the grades and special classes.* Unpublished Doctoral Dissertation, Teachers College, Columbia University, 1936.

Pumphrey, M., Goodman, M., Kidd, J., & Peters, E. Participation of retarded children in regular recreational activities at a community center. *Exceptional Children,* 1970, *36* (6) , 453–458.

Reger, R., & Koppmann, M. The child-oriented resource room. *Exceptional Children,* 1971, *37* (6) , 460–462.

Reynolds, M. The responsibility of the school for trainable retarded children. *Exceptional Children,* 1962, *29* (1) , 53–56.

Reynolds, M. More process than is due. *Theory Into Practice,* 1975, *14* (2) , 61–68.

Rickard, H., Serum, C., Forehand, R., & Lattal, K. Problem solving attitudes of children in a recreation camp and in a therapeutic camp. *Child Care Quarterly,* 1975, *4* (2), 101–107.

RIEGER, N. Changing concepts in treating children in a state hospital. *International Journal of Child Psychotherapy,* 1972, *1* (4), 89–114.

RIEGER, N., & LEIKEN, S. Hospital preschool for the emotionally disturbed. *Mental Hygiene,* 1969, *53* (2), 196–199.

ROLF, H. *Observable Differences in Space: Use of Learning Situations in Small and Large Classrooms.* Berkeley, Cal.: Unpublished Doctoral Dissertation, University of Cal., 1961.

ROSENTHAL, R., & JACOBSEN, L. *Pygmalion in the classroom.* New York: Holt, Rinehart, & Winston, 1968.

ROTBERG, J. Punishment in the classroom. *Education and Training of the Mentally Retarded,* 1973, *8* (2), 118–122.

ROWITZ, L., & LEI, T. Differentials in characteristics between city and suburban admissions to a state clinic for retarded children. *American Journal of Mental Deficiency,* 1975, *80* (2), 167–171.

RUBIN, E. Special education in a psychiatric hospital. *Exceptional Children,* 1962, *29* (4), 184–190.

RUBIN, R., KRUS, P., & BALOW, B. Factors in special class placement. *Exceptional Children,* 1973, *39* (7), 525–532.

RUSALEM, H., & RUSALEM, H. Implementing innovative special education ideas. *Exceptional Children,* 1971, *37* (5), 384–386.

RUTTER, M., & BARTUK, L. Special educational treatment of autistic children: A comparative study II; Follow-up findings and implications for services. *Journal of Child Psychology and Psychiatry,* 1973, *14* (4), 24–70.

SABATINO, D. Resource rooms: The renaissance in special education. *The Journal of Special Education,* 1972, *6* (4), 335–347.

———. Revolution: Viva resource rooms. *The Journal of Special Education,* 1972, *6* (4), 389–395.

SANDERS, J. A. Pilot course in lifemanship for severely retarded youth. *Exceptional Children,* 1969, *35* (9), 747–748.

SANTIESTEVEN, H. *Out of their beds and into the streets.* Washington, D.C.: American Federation of State, County, and Municipal Employees, 1975.

SCHULTZ, E., HIRSHOREN, A., MANTON, A., & HENDERSON, R. Special education for the emotionally disturbed. *Exceptional Children,* 1971, *38* (4), 313–319.

SHATTUCK, M. Segregation versus non-segregation of exceptional children. *Exceptional Children,* 1946, *12,* 235–240.

SHERMAN, M. *Hollow folk.* New York: Crowell, 1933.

SHERMAN, M., & KEY, C. The intelligence of isolated mountain children. *Child Development,* 1932, *3,* 279–290.

SIEGEL, E. *Special education in the regular classroom.* New York: John Day, 1969.

SIMCHES, RAPHAEL, F. The inside outsiders. *Exceptional Children,* September 1970, *37* (1), 5–16.

SINCLAIR, I., & CLARK, R. Acting-out behavior and its significance for the residential treatment of delinquents. *Journal of Child Psychiatry,* 1973, *14* (4), 283–291.

SMITH, A. *Mainstreaming: Idea and actuality.* Albany, New York: New York State Education Department, 1973.

SNAPP, M. Resource classrooms or resource personnel? *The Journal of Special Education,* 1972, *6* (4), 383–387.

SNAPP, M., & WOOLFOLK, A. *An examination of children in special education between 1957–1970.* Austin, Texas: Unpublished, 1971.

SOMMER, R. *Personal space.* Englewood Cliffs, N.J.: Prentice-Hall, 1969.

SONTAG, B. (Ed.). Specific learning disabilities program. *Exceptional Children,* November 1976, *43* (3), 157–159.

STROUDENMIRE, J., & COMOLA, J. Evaluating Camp Climb-up: A two-week therapeutic camp for exceptional children. *Exceptional Children,* 1973, *39* (7), 573–574.

St. Paul Technical Vocational School. *Vocational training for the deaf in a normally hearing environment.* Springfield, Va.: National Technical Information Service, undated.

STANFIELD, J. Graduation: What happens to the retarded child when he grows up? *Exceptional Children,* 1973, *39* (7) , 548–552.

SWIFT, M., & SPIVAK, G. Achievement related classroom behavior of secondary school normal and disturbed students. *Exceptional Children,* 1969, *35* (9) , 677–686.

TAYLOR, F., & SOLOWAY, M. The Madison School plan: A functional model for merging the regular and special classrooms. In *Instructional Alternatives for Exceptional Children,* E. DENO (Ed.) . Arlington, Va.: The Council for Exceptional Children, 1971.

No author. Survey of Radio Systems for Hearing Impaired Children. *Teacher of the Deaf,* 1975, *73,* 155–159.

THURSTONE, T. An evaluation of educating mentally handicapped children in special classes and regular classes. Chapel Hill, N.C.: University of North Carolina, School of Education, 1960.

TREFFERT, D., McANDREW, J., & DREIFURST, P. An inpatient treatment program and outcome for 57 autistic and schizophrenic children. *Journal of Autism and Childhood Schizophrenia,* 1973, *3* (2) , 138–153.

VACC, N. A study of emotionally disturbed children in regular and special classes. *Exceptional Children,* 1968, *35* (3) , 197–206.

———. Long-term effects of special class interventions for emotionally disturbed children. *Exceptional Children,* 1972, *39* (1) , 15–23.

VALETT, R. The learning resource room for exceptional children. *Exceptional Children,* 1970, *36* (7) , 527–530.

WALBERG, H. (Ed.) . *Evaluating educational performance: A source book of methods, instruments, and examples.* Berkeley, Cal.: McGutchen Pub. Corp., 1974.

———. Teacher personality and classroom climate. *Psychology in the Schools,* 1968, *5,* 163–169.

———. Models for optimizing and individualizing school learning. *Interchange,* 1971, *3,* 15–27.

———, & AHLGREN, A. Predictors of the social environment of learning. *American Educational Research Journal,* 1970, *7,* 414–419.

WALBERG, H., & ANDERSON, G. Prospectives of the achieving urban class. *Journal of Educational Psychology,* 1972, *63* (4) , 381–385.

WALBERG, H., HOUSE, E., & STEELE, J. Grade level, cognition and affect: A cross-section of classroom perceptions. *Journal of Educational Psychology,* 1973, *64,* 142–146.

WALDMAN, M. Psychotherapy and learning therapy in a special school. *Journal of Learning Disabilities,* 1972, *5* (3) , 165–169.

WALKER, V. The efficacy of the resource room for educating retarded children. *Exceptional Children,* 1974, *50* (4) , 288–289.

WATSON, M. *Mainstreaming: The educable mentally retarded.* Washington, D.C.: National Education Association, 1975.

WEINBERG, R., & WOOD, F. (Eds.) . *Observations of pupils and teachers in mainstream and special education settings: Alternative strategies.* Reston, Va.: Council for Exceptional Children, 1975.

WEINSTEIN, L. Project Re-Ed schools for emotionally disturbed children: Effectiveness as viewed by referring agencies, parents, and teachers. *Exceptional Children,* 1969, *35* (9) , 703–711.

WIEHN, VIRGINIA. An early childhood education program for deaf-blind children. *The New Outlook for the Blind,* December 1970, *64* (10) , 313–315.

WILLSON, E. Group therapy experience with eight physically disabled homebound students in a prevocational project. *Exceptional Children,* 1962, *29* (4) , 164–169.

WILSON, D. Teaching multiply handicapped blind persons in a state hospital. *The New Outlook for the Blind,* 1974, *68* (8) , 337–343.

WOOD, F. The educator's role in team planning of therapeutic educational placement for children with adjustment and learning problems. *Exceptional Children,* 1968, *34* (5) , 337–344.

WYNNE, S., ULFELDER, L., & DAKOF, G. Mainstreaming and early childhood education for handicapped children: Review and implications for research. Washington, D.C.: Department of Health, Education and Welfare, 1975.

YANG, D., FISCH, M., & LAMM, S. Rehabilitation of learning disabled children in a hospital class using psycho-active drugs. *Journal of Learning Disabilities*, 1973, *6* (7) , 486–491.

ZIGLER, E. Research on personality structure in the retardate. In *International Review of Research in Mental Retardation*, E. Ellis (Ed) , Vol. I. New York: Academic Press, 1966.

———, & BUTTERFIELD, E. Motivational aspects of changes in IQ test performance of culturally deprived nursery school children. *Child Development*, 1968, *39*, 1–14.

PART TWO

Psychological Components of Language and Sensory Disorders

During the past few years there has been a tremendous emphasis on the "noncategorical" aspects of exceptionality. The concept is a good one and one which we had voiced long before it became a widely accepted mode of educational operation. The issue in noncategorical special education, for example, is not the concept itself, but the meaningless manner in which it is carried out in schools. The fact of the matter is that there is such a disability as blindness; the deaf youth does exist as a person to be challenged by educational opportunities; the child with a cleft palate, or with an organic problem resulting in malfunctional speech, is still a person of our times. These children and youth have needs that must be met, psychologically and educationally.

The *concept of noncategorical* was initially intended to mean that a child would be evaluated carefully, and that an educational program would be devised to meet the unique psychoeducational characteristics that were demonstrated. Children then would be grouped for educational purposes on the basis of common psychoeducational needs, rather than on the basis of historical medical categories. In truth, this approach to noncategorical education has never been practiced. Teachers have not been taught how to teach from this point of view; psychologists have not been taught how to evaluate pupils and to examine, both quantitatively and qualitatively, and report their findings in a way that is fully usable by educators. Education and psychology together could be dynamic forces in the lives of children and youth if they were carried out in this manner. But even under the best of circumstances, the fact of a disability remains.

Regardless of what point of view one holds, categorical or noncategorical, a psychoeducational program must be based on individuals and all of their characteristics. This includes the disability.

171

Psychology of Exceptional Children and Youth takes a categorical approach in Part Two and in the chapters that follow. This is not done to defy current thought, but to provide for the reader basic knowledge about selected disabilities so that thorough understanding can be brought to the youths who have them and a better psychological understanding of their needs will then be forthcoming.

Jon Eisenson, long associated with this book, continues to provide a thorough treatment of the nature, the causes, and the methods used to alleviate speech and language disorders as hurdles to successful adjustment. Derek A. Sanders, a new author on this writing team, approaches in a fresh and vibrant manner the adjustment problems of children and youth who have hearing losses. Finally, Berthold Lowenfeld, long respected for his leadership in the area of the blind—as a psychologist, researcher, and administrator—continues to provide a definitive presentation on the psychological problems of the visually impaired.

The categorical approaches that these and other contributing authors take in this volume, and in its companion volume, *Education of Exceptional Children and Youth,* should make the noncategorical educational practice a more certain and viable reality.

W.M.C.

5 Speech Defects: Nature, Causes, and Psychological Concomitants

Jon Eisenson

Ph.D., Professor Emeritus of Hearing and Speech
Science, School of Medicine, Stanford University; Distinguished
Professor of Special Education and Director of The Scottish Rite
Institute for Childhood Aphasia, San Francisco State University.

Speech may be defined as a mode of communication that employs oral and/or visual symbols according to the rules and conventions of a linguistic code. Speech disorders, therefore, may be considered as defects or imperfections in oral or visual production (words or signs), even though the encoded verbal or equivalent visual sign formulation is presumably intact. Language disturbances refer to deficiencies in decoding (comprehension) or defects or impairments of formulation (encoding).

The implication of this division between speech and language disorders may be expressed in the generalized statement that speech defects comprise "noise" that, according to nature and degree of severity, interferes with the reception and interpretation (decoding) of the message. We may, however, take the position that speech necessarily involves language; that speech is not solely a manner of producing a code, but requires a symbol (linguistic) code. Language defects, therefore, may be subsumed under speech defects. We shall, in this chapter, limit our discussions to "legal children"—those who are ordinarily considered to be members, or at least eligible for membership, in our school-age population. Such children are 5 to 21 years of age.*

Speech Defects: Listener and Speaker

From the point of view of the listener, any child who speaks so that he distracts attention from what he is trying to say (the message) to how he is saying it (manner of production) may be considered to have defective speech. We assume, of course, that the age of the child is properly considered.†

The amount of distraction and, therefore, the degree and significance of the defect may vary. Objectively, a child's speech is significantly defective when the amount of distraction is sufficient to make it difficult to

* Realistically we should lower our minimum age to 3 years. In many communities children who are identified as having language (communication) problems or other problems that may impair educability are entitled to special schooling as early as age 3, and in a few states even much earlier.

† We will use the terms *speaker* and *listener* even though the speaker may be using signs and the listener is in fact a viewer.

communicate readily with a normal listener. Normal listeners are persons whose hearing, visual perceptive abilities, intelligence, expectations, and motivations make it possible for them to wish to and be able to understand what a speaker is attempting to communicate.

Defective speech has another aspect—a subjective one. From this viewpoint speech may be considered defective if the speaker is unduly self-conscious or apprehensive about objectively small deviations. Any speech deviation is a defect when it looms large enough in the speaker's mind so that it becomes a factor that contributes to difficulties in social, educational, and vocational adjustments.

Specifically, speech may be considered defective if it is characterized by one or more of the following:

1. It is not readily audible.*
2. It is not readily intelligible.*
3. It is vocally unpleasant.
4. It is visibly unpleasant.
5. It is labored in production or lacking in conventional rhythm and stress.
6. It is linguistically deficient.
7. It is inappropriate to the individual (content or manner of production) in terms of age, sex, and physical development.
8. The speaker responds to his or her own speech as if one or more of the above were present.

Types of Speech Defects

Speech defects are frequently divided into four major types:

1. Defects of articulation (sound production)
2. Defects of phonation (voice production)
3. Defects of fluency (stuttering and cluttering)

* The reader may draw parallels between an oral/aural system and a manual (visual-visual) system. I believe that the characteristics of a predominantly oral-aural linguistic system hold for one that is predominantly visual.

4. Language dysfunctions (delayed speech and aphasia).

For practical purposes, a second type of classification may be considered. This classification is based on categories of speech-defective individuals rather than on speech defects. For example, a cerebral-palsied child may show defects of language delay, voice, and articulation. Most children with cleft palates have defects of articulation as well as of voice. With this in mind, the following classification should be found useful:

1. Defects of articulation, including omissions, distortions, or substitutions of speech sounds
2. Defects of voice, including those of quality, loudness, pitch, variety, or adequate duration
3. Stuttering (stammering)
4. Cluttering
5. Delayed language development, including developmental aphasia
6. Cleft-palate speech
7. Cerebral-palsied speech
8. Impairments of previously developed language functions (aphasic involvements)
9. Speech defects associated with defective hearing.

INCIDENCE OF SPEECH DEFECTS

The incidence of speech defects is an approximation based in part on where the data were collected. A more subjective aspect derives from who made the judgments as to whether a sample of speech should be considered significantly deviant or defective. Still another aspect might determine both incidence and classification. Dialectical differences are expressed in pronunciations, vocabulary usage, and syntax. We need to be mindful not to confuse such differences with speech defects. We need also to be on guard that differences that superficially may appear to be sound omissions, for example, a final /s/ or /t/ or /d/, may not in fact be omissions of syntactic markers. A child may not produce a final /s/ because of failure to understand or use

TABLE 5-1
PROJECTIONS OF CHILDREN WITH SPEECH DEFECTS IN THE UNITED STATES—BASED ON AN ESTIMATE OF A POPULATION OF 225,000,000

Type of Speech Problem	Ages 5–21 years		All Ages	
	Percent	Number	Percent	Number
Functional Articulatory	3.0	1,500,000	3.0	6,000,000
Stuttering	.7	350,000	.7	1,400,000
Voice	.2	100,000	.2	400,000
Cleft Palate Speech	.1	50,000	.1	200,000
Cerebral Palsy Speech	.2	100,000	.2	400,000
Retarded Speech Development	.3	150,000	.3	600,000
Impaired Hearing (with Speech Defect)	.5	250,000	.5	1,000,000
Total	5.0	2,500,000	5.0	10,000,000

SOURCE: National Institute for Neurological Diseases and Stroke Monograph No. 10, U.S. Department of Health, Education, and Welfare National Institutes of Health, 1969, p. 18.

plural forms. Similarly, a final /t/ or /d/ may be omitted because a child does not understand the use of these sounds to mark past tense.

With these reservations in mind, we will present estimates of the incidence of speech and language defects in the school-age population of the United States.

Based on a review of the literature on estimates of defective speech in the school-age population, Perkins (1977) arrives at a compromise total estimate figure of 12,500,000. However, Perkins admits, "This compromise based on a population of 200,000,000 is gross at best and should be taken none too seriously" (p. 4). If we accept the general assumption that the present overall population in the United States has a larger increase in the number of adults and a proportionately smaller number of school-age persons, our figures would need to be revised. In the not too distant future we should be able to get new and more accurate estimates (better ap-

proximations). As of now, we will go along with an approximation of 5 percent.

Sex Distribution

Milisen (1971, p. 249), on the basis of several survey studies on the incidence and sex distribution of speech defects among grade-school children, found a general consensus that at all age levels there are more males than females in the identified population of children with defective speech (p. 249). Nothing in the more recent literature supports any basis for a change of that conclusion.

In regard to type of speech or language defect, we find a high proportion of males to females in each category. The proportionate sex difference is smallest for so-called functional articulatory defects and highest for stuttering, where there is a ratio of 3–4 males to each female (Andrews & Harris 1964, p. 161; Eisenson and Ogilvie, 1977, p. 336). Speech or language disorders with organic etiologies also have a higher representation of males than females. In general we may conclude that there is a higher incidence of speech defects among boys than among girls in the school-age population.

Some "defects" of speech that are included in the broad categories of language delay and articulation may be manifestations of slight maturational differences between the sexes and expressions of individual differences in maturation. Thus Perkins (1977) observes:

> We can conclude from studies of maturation that a child has a greater probability of outgrowing an articulatory defect before the fourth grade than after. What age does not reveal are those children who will not improve spontaneously (p. 258).

Unfortunately, although we have many published tests to assess proficiency for articulation, we are not burdened with many instruments that can reliably predict or prognosticate the children who are likely to "outgrow" their deviant (from an adult point of view) articulations from those who may need help and early intervention. One such instrument is the Van Riper and Erickson (1969) *Predicative Screening Test of Articulation* (PSTA). Van Riper (1978) considers this test to be "an instrument which, when applied to first grade children with articulation errors, seems able to predict fairly well those children who will 'outgrow' their misarticulations by the time they enter the third grade" (p. 171).*

SPEECH AS A DEVELOPMENTAL PROCESS

We need to appreciate that children are not miniature adults in their acquisitions (comprehension and production) of speech. *Child*

* For a review of tests of articulation see C. Van Riper, *Speech Correction* (6th ed.). Englewood Cliffs, N.J.: Prentice-Hall, 1978, pp. 166–171.

Language is not a miniaturized version of adult language (See Table 5–2.). Yet, somehow, by age 5 almost all normal children speak in a manner that resembles more closely that of the older speakers in their environment than of their own efforts in their first year as speakers.

The vast majority of children develop the proficiencies needed for speech over a period of time beginning in some instances as early as 8 or 9 months of age and extending, usually, through ages 7 and 8. In regard to vocabulary, there is no ceiling age either for the comprehension or production of lexical items. If we view speech as consisting of a processing of the sound system (articulate-phonemic component), the lexical system (vocabulary), and the grammatical system (syntax), we can make several statements related to these components. Articulatory proficiency is normally reached about age 7. That is, most children indicate by the way they speak that they have mastered the sound (phonological) system, the identifiable phonemes and phonemic combinations of their language. Van Riper (1978, pp. 105–108; Eisenson & Ogilvie, 1977, pp. 151–153; Winitz, 1969, p. 76).

Vocabulary growth, as we have indicated, has no ceiling age. Productive vocabulary, the vocabulary of use, appears to show a faster rate of growth between ages 3 and 5 than between 6 and 8 (Templin, 1957, pp. 114–116). Grammar (syntax), at least in regard to the most frequent and conventional forms, is usually well established by age 5. However, the use of complex forms (for example, combinations of passive, negative, and interrogative and subordinate structures) are achievements that continue beyond age 8, certainly up to age 10 (Chomsky, 1969).**

** Carol Chomsky found considerable variability related to age in regard to children's ability to understand constructions that involve such words as *ask* and *tell*; e.g., "Ask John to leave," and "Tell John to leave." Other constructions that show differences in comprehension and errors in production include

Personally, we believe that syntactic development, especially in relationship to semantics for both the comprehension and production of meaning, continues for at least 5 years beyond age 10. The relationship between semantic development—the mastery of the semantic system—and the components of language are reviewed by Dale (1972, 146–157).

CAUSES OF DEFECTIVE SPEECH

We must never lose sight of the truism that a speech defect is the defect of a *person*. Thus, what may constitute a primary cause of a defect for one individual may have little or no etiological significance for another. Some children with minor organic anomalies of the articulatory mechanism, such as malocclusions, may have unmistakable articulatory defects. Others, with measurably greater anomalies, may have entirely adequate ar-

---

words such as *want* and *expect*; e.g., "I want to leave," and "I expect to leave." Some children in the 5 to 10 years age range used the *ask* and *tell* synonymously. Testing indicated that they did not understand the difference. Similar observations were made for *want* and *expect*. In general, Carol Chomsky found an increase in the comprehension and appropriate use of the terms in these constructions that correlated with age. At age 10, most children were proficient in their comprehension and use of these constructions. However, a few 10-year-olds did worse than some 5-year-old children.

Contrary to the commonly held view that a child has mastered the structures of his native language by the time he reaches the age of 6, we find that active syntactic acquisition is taking place up to the age of 9 and perhaps even beyond. . . . By tracing the child's orderly progress in the acquisition of a segment of his language, we are able to observe, for a set of related structures, considerable variation in rate of acquisition in different children together with a common, shared order of acquisition. Quite simply, although we cannot say just when a child will acquire the structures in question, we can offer reliable judgment about the relative order in which he will acquire them. (Chomsky, 1969, p. 121).

ticulation. Some children regress in speech proficiency when new siblings are brought into the family. Other children take the arrival of new brothers and sisters in apparently easy stride. Even stutterers, who as a group are fairly predictable as to what factors will increase or decrease the severity of their stuttering, vary extensively when considered as individuals. The causes of speech defects that we shall consider refer to the various groups of children with disorders of speech when they are studied as groups. In the final analysis the only certain way of knowing why a given child has a speech defect, and what this defect may mean, is to study the child's dynamics, and reactions to his or her speech. The implications of diagnoses and a philosophy for the management of the child with defective speech related to diagnosis is considered in detail by Darley and Spriestersbach (1978, chap. 1) and by Van Riper (1978, chap. 2).

Organic Causes

Some speech defects are clearly organic in origin. The articulatory and vocal difficulties of the child with a cleft palate can, at least initially, be attributed directly to the type and severity of the cleft. Hearing impairment, if it begins early and is relatively severe, may directly account for defects in articulation and voice. Malocclusions and dental irregularities, if severe, may be responsible for some degree and some types of defective articulation, though such physical deviations, as indicated earlier, do not make it inevitable that a given child will have faulty articulation. Cerebral-palsy conditions that involve the speech mechanism are directly responsible for defective speech. Implications for language acquisition in the cerebral-palsied are related to brain damage associated with aphasic involvements, and problems that may be associated with hearing and listening impairment. Beyond this, there are more general implications related to mental retardation for some cerebral-palsied children. Congenital (developmental)

TABLE 5–2

DEVELOPMENTAL SCHEDULE FOR NORMAL LANGUAGE ACQUISITION*

Developmental Stages	Birth Cry	Babbling	Lalling	Echolalia
I *Prelingual Developmental Stages*	Undifferentiated—birth to 3 weeks. Differentiated—beyond 3 weeks. Cooing—beginning with 8 weeks —"squealing, gurgling sounds, vowel-like in character, sustained for 15 to 20 seconds." Responds to human sounds by smiling and possibly by cooing. By 20 weeks vowel-like production is modified by consonant-like sounds with labial fricatives. The infant is a universalist in his sound making.	By or before 6 months, cooing changes to babbling, which resembles one-syllable utterances. Neither the vowels nor the consonants have fixed recurrences; most frequent utterances resemble ma, mu, da, di.	By 8 months, reduplication (sound repetition) becomes frequent; intonation patterns are discernible in utterances; "utterances can signal emphasis and emotion."	By 9 to 10 months, sound play and apparent imitation of sound patterns of the environment. Responses-differential adjustments to utterances of speakers in environment may show clear indication of comprehension of several single words or utterances.

II *Word Identification and Identification Language*
By 12 months, increase in sound and identification imitation (replication); definite indications of understanding; may say "mama," "dada"; may be able to play (obey simple commands) such as "Show me your eyes . . . nose." May utter words such as "mama," "dada," "doll," to identify events.

III *True Speech*
By 15 to 18 months the child uses words to bring about events (anticipatory language); vocabulary may range from three to fifty words. Some words are used as demands or commands rather than as labels.

IV *Syntactic Speech—24 months*
Words are combined into two-word phrases; many are combinations not directly taught.

V *Communicative Intent*
By 30 months, communicative intent is clear because the child will show frustration if not understood; most rapid increase in vocabulary to date, and proportionately for rest of life.

VI *Syntactic Competence*
By 3 years, has mastered much of the grammar (syntax) of the language of the environment.

VII *Individuolect*
By 4 years, child shows considerable mastery of the grammar used by members of his or her environment. The child also begins to express himself or herself in own "rhetorical" style.

* The "developmental" schedule for normal language acquisition is based on Lenneberg's observations for the first three years (1967, pp. 128–130). Lenneberg is not, however, responsible for any of the interpretations.

aphasia is, by definition, language delay associated with central nervous system dysfunction and related underlying perceptual impairments (Eisenson, 1972). Cluttering, according to Weiss (1964, p. 1) is "the verbal manifestation of central language imbalance" and is based on hereditary predisposition.

Functional Causes

Many children with apparently normal speech mechanisms nevertheless have defects of articulation and/or voice. In some instances, imitation of an older sibling, a playmate, or an adult may account for the defect. Children learn to articulate, vocalize, and use language "by ear." If what they hear is faulty, and if they have no cause to be negatively inclined to what they hear, they will learn to speak in a faulty manner. In an important sense, speech faults that are based on imitative patterns may indicate normal adaptative behavior. If the influential and respected members of a child's environment speak in a given way, the child, having no basis to determine that such speech is not appropriate, should be expected to imitate what he or she hears, *unless he or she is negatively inclined either to the individuals or to the general environment.*

It may well be that some so-called functional articulatory cases may in fact be expressions of slowly developing neurological systems and so of poor control of the organs of articulation (developmental oral dyspraxia). In other instances, as already suggested, articulatory omissions may actually be expressions of delayed language, and specifically of slowness in the acquisition of syntactic markers for plurals, possessives, and verb-tense endings.

Psychogenic Causes and Correlates

Several studies during the period 1940–1965 have supplied data that support the impression that many defects of speech are basically psychogenic. When the defects are found in children, their origin, when not organic or imitative (learned by imitation of a model with whom the child identifies) are presumed to be psychogenic. Frequently the assumption is that the defect—whatever it may be—arises out of the children's reaction to their environment and particularly to their parents. It is not at all surprising that some investigators have interpreted their findings to indicate that the primary maladjustments exist in the parents of the speech-defective children. Wood (1946), for example, found that on the whole a group of fifty speech-defective children showed better adjustment than the parents. Despite this, about half of the children to whom the Thematic Apperception Test was administered revealed dynamisms that suggested frustration, withdrawing tendencies, and a sense of lack of affection. Only three of the twenty-five children to whom the TAT was administered manifested no preponderance of unfavorable dynamisms. Maladjustments of the parents were determined on the basis of the findings of the Bernreuter Personality Inventory and the California Test of Personality. Both mothers and fathers tended to have poor adjustment scores. Eighty-six percent of the children had one or both parents who were below the 35th percentile in self-adjustment; 64 percent had one or both parents who were below the 35th percentile in social adjustments. The mothers, as a group, were significantly totally less well adjusted than the fathers. A specific significant finding was that the social standards of the mothers were very high in comparison with other adjustment scores.*

When this is viewed in relation to the emotional instability of the maternal group, it appears probable that the speech-defective

* We may raise the question at this point whether more recent findings, as reviewed in a survey study by Bloch and Goodstein (1971) are a result of better assessment instruments, improved procedures for evaluating the results of findings, or a combination of both.

children had imposed upon them a set of very high standards in an atmosphere of habitual emotional outbursts on the part of the parents.

In general, Wood concludes:

. . . on the basis of this study that functional articulatory defects of children are definitely and significantly associated with maladjustment and undesirable traits on the part of the parents, and that such factors are usually maternally centered.

The findings on stutterers are varied and not altogether consistent. Parents often are considered to be "different" and to have traits with serious implications for their children. Johnson (1967, p. 17) observes that "As a rule, in the beginning it is the mother who is a key member of the problem." However, in regard to stutterers themselves, after surveying the literature on maladjustments of stutterers, Johnson (1967) concludes:

It does seem incontrovertible that in some cases the experience of stuttering produces a certain amount of personality maladjustment and, in addition to this, there appears to be no ground for assuming that among people who stutter there would not be the same proportion as of the general population who have the customary kinds and grades of personality maladjustments. By and large, stutterers are people who stutter (p. 261).

We may question the apparent indictment of the parents of stutterers and the assertion that, despite the influence of their parents, the children who become stutterers are essentially normal persons except that they stutter.

Van Riper (1973, pp. 418–420) devotes the concluding section of his book *The Treatment of Stuttering* to the subject of parent counseling. It is logical to assume therefore that parental attitudes are associated with the abnormal speech of their children and that these attitudes need modification more so than for parents of children without

speech problems. The array of parental attitudes and the varying needs for counseling are described by Van Riper (1973, p. 418). Some parents are certain that the stuttering is merely a temporary aberration of development, that the child is sure to outgrow it eventually. Others view it as a bad habit like thumb sucking, to be broken as quickly as possible. When one of the parents or other members of the family possess it, the disorder may be viewed as a family curse to be endured or contained. Some see it as a social disgrace, a future occupational disability or merely as an irritating nuisance to communication. Many parents come to us with a profound sense of guilt, believing that somehow they have caused the child's difficulties and are directly responsible for their continuance. We also find a wide variety of anxiety and hostility reactions of various degrees of intensity.

We may compare Van Riper's clinical observations with those of Andrews and Harris based on a long-term study in England. Andrews and Harris found two trends among the mothers of stutterers based on findings of a school survey in Newcastle-upon-Tyne. One group, coming from the lower socioeconomic class, included a significant portion who

showed an inability to manage themselves, their homes or their husbands, not so much on account of neuroticism as through some degree of inadequacy of intellect and personality. In the upper social groups, however, there were able neurotic mothers who, fitting Johnson's description, appeared to have made excessive demands on their children (Andrews & Harris, 1964, p. 161).

Travis (1971, pp. 1009–1033) has some very strong opinions about the dynamics between stutterers and their parents that he considers to be a key to the speech behavior of children and to be germinal to their stuttering. Stuttering is a special case of the universal conflict between closeness and distance, involvement and autonomy, intimacy and autism. His experiments in closeness have been too painful to stand and he has suffered a reaction of self-banishment. He has settled for a minimum relatedness, which does not include free talking about his thoughts and feelings. Rightly or wrongly he has interpreted the responses of another as adversive (Travis, 1971, pp. 1010). Further, Travis believes that when a child is convinced that his parents are convinced that he is just stuttering, then a certain relief follows in the stuttering. The stuttering is misleading the diagnostician and successfully serving the purpose of obscuring, if not entirely covering, the really dreaded preoccupations with speaking the truth. Really stuttering is a manifestation of a fear to speak the truth to oneself or about oneself to another. It occurs most frequently in those families that place a high premium upon the truth and then punish its verbalization. To the extent that a child can be self-conscious comfortably, he will not stutter (Travis, 1971, p. 1014).

It is important to appreciate that Travis is presenting his views of stutterers and their parents from his position as a psychoanalytically oriented clinician.

Perkins (1977, p. 223) makes several discerning and objective observations about stuttering and personality. These observations include the following:

> All efforts to demonstrate unique personality characteristics in the stutterer that distinguish him from the non-stutterer have come to nought. . . . Dissonance between the clinician and the researcher is great when it comes to their cognition about the personalities of stutterers. . . . Clinicians who work psychotherapeutically remain convinced that they are observing evidence of personality conflicts, yet researchers have been unable to substantiate it.

Bloch and Goodstein (1971), after reviewing a series of investigations published during the period between the mid 1950s and 1968, concluded:

In general, there continues to be little evidence that the stuttering child has a particular pattern of personality or is severely maladjusted. Greater anxiety in interpersonal relationships, with attendant symptoms of oversensitivity and shyness, has been noted in stutterers; but, considering the premium placed on early and effective verbal communication in our culture, it is unclear whether these findings result from etiological or from expected consequential factors in stuttering. Thus far, research on the stuttering child remains largely descriptive, with some investigators reporting a positive relationship between stuttering and adjustment. External criteria—for example, school achievement and social relationships—have not been correlated with these findings. In particular, the effect of stuttering upon the child's self-perceptions, his peer relationships, and his choice of activities and interests have not been closely examined as factors relevant to therapeutic planning (pp. 306–307).

However, Bloch and Goodstein note:

> There is some evidence to support the conclusion that stutterers' parents, while not maladjusted themselves, do tend to play a role in the development of stuttering, primarily through attitudes of criticalness and overprotection which may be implicitly conveyed to the child (p. 310).

After their review of studies involving possible personality differences among adult stutterers, Bloch and Goodstein conclude:

> In summary, the most general conclusion to be drawn from the studies of adult stutterers is that while stutterers appear to exhibit some differences in personality from normal speakers, there is little evidence to support the contention that they are neurotic or severely maladjusted. Although there is evidence that adult stutterers are somewhat more anxious, somewhat less self-confident, and somewhat more socially withdrawn than nonstutterers, there is additional evidence that efforts to differentiate stutterers from nonstutterers in terms of a particular syndrome of maladjustive traits have proved unfruitful (p. 310).

Beech and Fransella, in an earlier writing (1968), come to much the same conclusions as Bloch and Goodstein. Beech and Fransella surveyed the literature on personality aspects of stuttering from the turn of the century to the mid 1960s. Their conclusions include the following (pp. 124–125):

1. There is no persuasive evidence to support an assumption that stutterers are of a particular personality type or share a group of personality traits that differentiate them from nonstutterers.

2. Though the evidence about the self concept of stutterers is conflicting, there is some indication to suggest that they are not quite ready or willing to accept themselves as they are. Further, individual stutterers may view other stutterers as having certain personality traits that they do not attribute to themselves.

3. There is some indication that stutterers do have a higher anxiety level than non-stutterers. There may also be differences in anxiety level between certain subgroups of stutterers.

4. There is a lack of unequivocal evidence that as a group stutterers are either more neurotic or more maladjusted than non-stutterers.

5. As a final critical note, Beech and Fransella observe:

Studies investigating the personality of stutterers are characterized by interpretations that are at variance with the statistical findings; contamination effects resulting from the person who conducts the experiment also being the one who scores the projective tests or assesses outcome of treatment; lack of adequate control groups; inappropriate or inadequate statistical treatment. There has also been hardly any attempt to take into account that female stutterers may not have similar personality traits to male stutterers or that they may be more neurotic.

INTELLIGENCE, EDUCATIONAL ACHIEVEMENT, AND SPEECH DEFECTS

At this time we will consider the overall relationship between intelligence, educational achievement, and defective speech. Later we will present more detailed considerations for groups according to major classifications of speech and language impairments.

The studies we shall consider will be divided into three categories:

1. The relationship of speech defects to intelligence in children of school age as a whole
2. Intelligence of speech-defective children with physical handicaps
3. The incidence of speech defects among children known to be of below-average intelligence

Intelligence

The findings of Carrell in one of the older studies are generally supported by more recent observations. Carrell (1936) analyzed a school population of 1,174 children. He found that the speech-defective children, taken as a group, were lower in average intelligence than the general population. Curtis (1967) makes the general observation that "Speech imperfections are more frequent among children of low intelligence than among those who are average or above in mental capacity" (p. 132).

In their survey on the classification and incidence of speech defects, Eisenson and Ogilvie (1977, chap. 1) present several studies that report a higher incidence of impaired speech among children in the below-average range of intelligence. Irwin and Marge (1972) note that ". . . intelligence certainly plays a role, not only in the rate of acquisition, but at early stages in the quality and quantity of linguistic performance" (p. 79).

Later we will present the results of several studies on the prevalence of speech and language defects among children who are identified as mentally retarded. For the present we will note that onset of speech, acquisition of syntax, and articulatory proficiency are all delayed among the severely mentally retarded. Further, but with occasional exception, the degree of delay and severity of defect are positively related to the extent of retardation. Often the most obvious defect appears to be one of a lack of articulatory proficiency. Thus we find the following observation in the NINDS Monograph on *Human Communication and Its Disorders* (1969):

> There is also evidence indicating that on a statistical frequency basis development of normal articulation is related to general intellectual development. That is, children for whom the classification of mental retardation is appropriate show a substantially higher incidence of defective articulation than do children of normal intelligence. However, there are many instances of functional articulatory problems which seem completely unexplainable on such a basis (p. 169).

We need to be mindful that many types of speech disorders have articulatory problems as an obvious defect. Cerebral-palsied and cleft-palate children have problems of articulation as part of syndromes of impairments related to their underlying cause.

Among physically handicapped children with speech defects, the cerebral-palsied show a higher proportion of those mentally below average than does the total population. Most objective findings, even when allowances are made for the nature of the motor disabilities, indicate that disproportionately large number of cerebral-palsied children are also mentally retarded. Wolfe (1950), for example, found that 26 percent of the subjects of his study were so limited in intelligence that they had to be considered uneducable. Survey studies by Bice and Cruickshank (1955) support this finding.

Muller-Gerhard (1972) found that multiply handicapped preschool children—those who were cerebral palsied and had associated visual and hearing handicaps in addition to speech impairments—had IQs of 55 or lower, based on the nonverbal items of the Merrill-Palmer Inventory.

For a detailed consideration of cerebral-palsy speech syndromes see Mysak (1971, pp. 673–694); Van Riper (1978, pp. 389–392); Eisenson and Ogilvie (1977, chap. 16); and Perkins (1977, pp. 134–139).

Sometimes the condition of cerebral palsy is not readily apparent, especially in its implications for speech. Jones (1975) observes: "Abnormalities in oral pharyngeal function can be early clues to general neurological abnormality . . . and can be predictive of future impairment in the area of speech" (pp. 404–405).

We have made similar observation about children who, despite their understanding of speech, cannot speak intelligibly. We consider these children to have oral (verbal) dysprax (Eisenson, 1972, chap. 10).

The Mentally Deficient

The consistent finding of studies of speech defects among mentally deficient children is that the incidence of defects is considerably higher than it is among the population as a whole. The chief cause of language delay for onset as well as slow development, is mental retardation. Generally, the degree of retardation is positively related to the amount, delay, and severity (quantitative and qualitative) of language and speech impairments. Matthews (1971), based on a survey of the literature on the relationship of mental retardation to speech defects, says: ". . . the data permit us to conclude that the incidence of speech defects in populations of mentally retarded is high—considerably higher than in the general population" (p. 805).

Lillywhite and Bradley (1969, p. 11) report that in a survey of the educable mentally retarded in Portland, Oregon, 12 percent were found to have speech or language defects.

Whether the differences in speech and language between mildly to moderately mentally retarded children and normal children are essentially quantitative or qualitative has become a subject of recent speculation. Discussions along this line may be found in the chapters by Cromer and Menyuk in an edited volume by Schiefelbusch and Lloyd (1975). For detailed considerations of the language of the mentally retarded, we recommend Schiefelbusch (1972).

Educational Achievement

The consensus of evidence shows that children with defective speech (including students on a college level) are somewhat retarded in school progress as compared with children with normal speech. The amount of retardation would, of course, be much greater if we were to include those speech-defective children who are also mentally deficient and who must therefore either attend special schools or be institutionalized as uneducable. Surveys, such as those of Carrell (1936), upon which the general conclusion of slight educational retardation is drawn, are concerned with children in regular schools and so exclude the severely mentally deficient and other special groups who are more greatly retarded.

Children accurately identified as dyslexic are usually delayed in onset of speech and in language acquisition. Van Riper (1972, p. 177) observes as a clinician that, "Failures in school subjects, especially in reading, may be a direct consequence of defective articulation." Our own impression is that both the reading and articulation difficulties are more likely to be related to an underlying slowness in language acquisition.

Insofar as reading is concerned, if it is taught on the basis of auditory perception and associations with visual perception, then reading and speech failures are inevitably correlated. This is the position of Eames (1950). In more extreme form, we see the reading failures of dyslexic children. For a review of this literature, see Chase (1972) and Powers (1971, pp. 863–866).

Myklebust (1975) sums up the consensus of observations on dyslexia in relationship to oral language as well as written language:

That dyslexia is a complex condition, however, is apparent because of the evidence that many of these children also have deficiencies in spoken language. They might fall 2 to 3 years below average in facility with the spoken word. Moreover, they are severely limited in use of the written word; they write fewer sentences, less words per sentence, and are inferior in use of syntax. Factor analysis and intercorrelation studies show that dyslexics vary from the normal in various cognitive processes; they are less able to relate the auditory and visual facets of letters, syllables, and words. In addition, and perhaps of considerable consequence, they are deficient in ability to integrate meanings, although interneurosensory processing was achieved (p. 426).

For a scholarly, multiauthored treatment of the relationship of reading, language, and learning we recommend the special issue of the *Harvard Educational Review,* Vol. 47, No. 3, August 1977.

Some other possible causal relationships between speech and reading problems can be explained along the following lines. Defects of articulation may cause errors of pronunciation and so cause errors in the interpretation of the written word. It is also possible, especially in insecure children, that the child's awareness and concern over his defective speech may reduce his ability to concentrate on and so to comprehend what he is reading. A third factor is that faulty speech, especially faulty articulation and stuttering, may disturb the rate and rhythm of reading, interfere with proper phrasing, and therefore with the comprehension of the written symbol. A fourth possibility is that a child, aware of his speech deficiency, may become negatively inclined to all forms of oral expression. The attitude may be generalized to silent reading and so may indirectly influence an area of achievement that the child might otherwise enjoy and in which normal proficiency might otherwise be expected.

The likelihood that reading disability might be the cause of defective speech, except possibly for stuttering, is remote and small. For most children, articulatory proficiency is attained for a large majority of speech sounds before formal training in reading ordinarily begins. This is especially true in schools that have a flexible program in the teaching of reading and do not begin formal teaching until reading readiness is clearly demonstrated. In regard to stuttering, the possibility exists that small children who have difficulty with oral reading may generalize this difficulty to include oral recitations and possibly conversational speech. We have treated several stutterers who date the onset of their stuttering to unhappy incidents associated with oral reading in classroom situations.

PHYSICAL DEFECTS

Most speech-defective children are physically normal. At least their defects of speech cannot be directly attributed to the existence of a specific physical disability. Nevertheless, the incidence of physical anomalies among children with speech defects is considerably higher than in the school-age population at large. On the basis of the NINDS report (1969, p. 18) the figure is approximately 350,000, or 16 percent of the speech-defective population.* Chief among these are cleft palate, cerebral palsy, and hearing impairments. Deformities and growths of the larynx or pharynx, and neurological impairments affecting the control of the vocal bands, soft palate, or muscles of the throat may be the cause of vocal defects. These conditions, however, occur relatively infrequently in children. Enlarged adenoids is a much more common cause of voice disturbance. In addition, there are minor organic anomalies such as dental malocclusions and high palatal arch, which are found to occur more frequently among speech-defective children than in the population at large.

Of late, considerable interest has been shown by orthodontists and speech pathologists in oral irregularities and articulatory defects associated with "tongue-thrust" swal-

low. Many children who habitually protrude their tongues between their teeth in the act of swallowing also demonstrate extreme tension in the mouth-enclosing musculature. The forward thrust of the tongue tends to produce oral malocclusion characterized by anteriorly displaced incisors. In a study of a population of children between 6 and 18 years of age, which included 668 with tongue-thrust swallow, 230 of the group were found to have sibilant distortion (Fletcher, Casteel, & Bradley, 1961). This incidence is considerably larger than would be expected by chance and significantly larger than the incidence of sibilant distortion among the children in the study whose normal swallowing habits were free of tongue-thrust. Hanson (1976) reviews the literature on tongue-thrust and suggests criteria for when specific therapy is advisable.

It is likely that residuals of infant neuropathologies have continued influence in the form of retarded speech development or in defective articulation. Although it is not always possible to demonstrate this relationship, the impression of many speech pathologists, including the present writer, is that it exists among many young children with retarded or distorted speech. Jones (1975, pp. 404–405) supports this position.

An early supporting study along this line was made by Eustis (1947). He reports that 48 percent of individuals over 6 years of age (of a family tree covering four generations), in addition to specific speech and reading disabilities, showed one or more of the conditions: left-handedness, ambidexterity, and body clumsiness. Eustis believes that these conditions suggest a syndrome, hereditary in origin, which is characterized by a slow rate of neuromuscular maturation and probably implies retarded myelination of the motor and association nerve tracts. "It is suggested that this inherited tendency to delayed neuromuscular maturation is the single factor from which all the various aspects of the syndrome may develop."

Surveys of organic anomalies associated

---

* This figure would be considerably higher if we included clutterers and at least some of the children with retarded speech development.

with articulatory defects may be found in Van Riper (1978, pp. 167–169), Irwin (1975, pp. 515–524), and Perkins (1977, chaps. 5–8).

Motor Development and Motor Abilities

Although it is frequently not possible to find evidence of specific neurological deficit,* or of motor involvement, as an etiological associate for most children with defective speech, there is a fair amount of evidence to indicate that the general picture of the development of motor abilities is less favorable for the defective in speech than for the population at large (Berry and Eisenson, 1956, p. 12).

SENSORY IMPAIRMENTS

If we approach this matter from the point of view of handicapped children with specific sensory impairments, such as the hard-of-hearing, the deaf, and the blind, we will find a larger incidence of speech defects than we would in the population at large. If we exclude these special populations with significant hearing and visual losses, we will find a lack of unanimity in the results of studies related to sensory impairments among speech-handicapped children. Most of the studies concern children with articulatory defects. Most, also, are concerned with some aspect of auditory functioning.

Van Riper (1978, pp. 164–166) considers hearing loss (acuity of hearing), poor auditory memory span, and difficulties in phonetic discrimination to be causes of defective articulation. He prescribes specific exercises

* We recognize that children with minimal brain damage and associated motor dysfunctions often have speech problems. Further, we are aware that children as well as adults may have oral apraxia that may be associated with other motoric problems. LaPointe (1975, pp. 496–498) reviews some of the literature on oral apraxia and its implications for speech.

to improve auditory memory span and phonetic discrimination.

After a review of some of the literature on the relationship between auditory discrimination and articulatory proficiency, Perkins (1977) concludes: "Clearly, auditory discrimination and articulation are connected, but available evidence does not yet prove which causes which" (p. 261). Our own impression is that children do understand a considerable amount of oral language before they begin to speak, and that generally, comprehension exceeds production. Certainly most children show awareness that *pasghetti* is not *spaghetti* before they can produce the food in proper syllable sequence. Further, we believe that the present tests of auditory discrimination are simpler than the complex task of listening to (hearing, perceiving, and processing) speech. So, tentatively, we take the position that our answer as to the relationship of auditory discrimination to speech is not at hand, because we have no procedures for testing what is involved in the discriminatory judgments *and* sequencing of a flow of speech at the normal rate of utterance.

Some of the apparent inconsistencies in findings, especially where discrimination for nonspeech events is concerned (for example, musical pitch, pure tones, and so forth) may be appreciated by the position that the speech code (speech mode) is perceived and processed differently and in different parts of the cerebral cortex than nonspeech sounds. Liberman *et al.* (1967) state:

> The conclusion that there is a speech mode, and that it is characterized by processes different from those underlying the perception of other sounds, is strengthened by recent indications that speech and nonspeech sounds are processed primarily in different hemispheres of the brain.

Thus, an individual may have difficulty in phonemic (speech events) discrimination and processing and yet have no difficulty in the appreciation of musical events or of mechanical or animal noises. The possibility to us that there may really be no such impairment as "functional articulatory defects" is a real one.

Infantile Speech

Menyuk (1964), from another point of view, argues against the notion of *infantile speech* as constituting a category of delayed or defective articulation. Menyuk studied the grammatical production of children with so-called infantile speech and age peer children (age range 3 years to 5 years 10 months; mean IQ of the infantile speech group 125.7 compared with 126.4 for the normal speakers as measured by the Ammons, 1958, Full Range Picture Vocabulary Test). The relatively high IQ of the infantile speech group is of special importance in the light of the conclusion that:

> The term infantile seemed to be a misnomer since at no age level did the grammatical production of a child with deviant speech match or closely match that of a child with normal speech. The children with deviant speech, in the terms of the model of grammar used for analysis, formulated their sentences with the more general rules whereas children with normal speech used increasingly differentiating structures as they matured.

In a later article, Menyuk (1975) presents her views on the quantitative versus qualitative positions as explanations for delayed language. Again she emphasizes that children who are seriously delayed in language development generally show delays in all aspects of language—semantic, syntactic, morphological, and phonological. This position is supported by a study by Morehead and Ingram (1973) in which language sampling was used as a procedure for assessing the speech productions of children who were severely delayed in language development.

We will return to our considerations of children with delayed or disordered language later in this chapter.

Impaired Hearing

We accept as a truism that hearing for speech—the ability to make semantic sense out of a flow of speech sounds—involves considerably more than the ability to detect the presence of an auditory signal. Hearing (listening), as we have indicated, involves the related functions of receiving, perceiving (discriminating and sequencing), and assigning meaning to the received signals. Of course, if the signals are not received because of possible deficiencies of the hearing mechanism, other functions and processes cannot normally take place. The relationship between impairments of hearing, language acquisition, and psychological implications are considered by Derek Sanders in Chapter 6 of this text ("Psychological Implications of Hearing Impairment") and so will not be considered in this chapter.

PERSONALITY ASPECTS AND ADJUSTMENT PROBLEMS

Are speech-defective persons, and particularly speech-defective children, likely to be more maladjusted than children who are free of speech defects? Do some speech-defective persons have aspects of personality that our culture tends to consider undesirable? These are questions we raise and anticipate that we will not and probably cannot answer adequately.

In this section we shall consider studies and points of view on the speech-defective population as a whole and primarily on those with so-called functional disorders. Some of the studies and points of view have already been considered in our discussion of the psychogenic basis of defective speech.

Speech Defectives as a Group

Van Riper (1978, pp. 22–23) is especially impressed with the speech-defective's tendency to employ either aggressive or withdrawal behavior reactions to the penalty behavior of his associates. Hostility and anxiety seem to be the key behavioral traits of speech defectives. These arise as a result of the penalties our culture places on disordered speech.

Johnson (1967) summarizes the effects of speech disorders on personality to highlight their circular influence.

> The psychology of the handicapped is basically the psychology of frustration. The handicap of impaired speech is no exception to this general rule. In fact, there is hardly anything more frustrating, in ways that matter deeply, than something that constantly interferes with our relationship to other people. . . .
> The relationship between speech and personality is . . . a two-way affair. They affect each other. And the effect is not only circular, but also cumulative . . . speech characteristics, once created, tend to affect the personality in ways that insure their further development (pp. 74–75).

Bryngelson (1971) devotes an entire chapter to the relationship of speech and personality. He observes (p. 175): that "psychologists and speech pathologists do deal specifically with neurotics" (p. 175). Particularly, in regard to stutterers, Bryngelson says, "I urge you to be cognizant of the need for emotional hygiene in the treatment of the stutterer" (p. 182).

Powers (1971) sums up her impression on studies of emotional factors and adjustment problems associated with speech disorders and particularly with functional articulation defects. She says:

> Both theoretical and clinical discussions in the writing of speech pathology are replete with confident statements about the paramount importance of emotional and personality factors in the etiology and treatment of speech disorders, including functional articulatory disorders. Research, however, has barely nibbled around the edges. There is little to show of an objective nature, and that little is inconclusive (p. 870).

Perkins (1977, pp. 213–229) reviews the literature on the relationship of speech to personality as developmental correlates with emphasis on Freudian psychoanalytic theory. Perkins also reviews the literature of studies dealing with personal adjustments of speakers with articulation, voice problems, stuttering, and psychoses. He concludes that "although speech disorders cannot be attributed with confidence to specific types of psychopathology, still, speech problems do appear among all the major groups of personality and emotional disturbances (p. 227).

The review of the literature by Bloch and Goodstein (1971) on functional speech disorders for the period 1958–1968 yielded few conclusive findings. So, we are left with strong clinical impressions that all too often are not supported by experimental data. Bloch and Goodstein conclude:

> In spite of steady research efforts to differentiate speech-disordered and normal-speaking persons, the results have continued to be inconsistent and there is no evidence that either the parents or the speech-defective individuals themselves are severely maladjusted or have an identifiable personality pattern. The sources of some inconsistencies have been clarified through the use of within-groups variables, the simultaneous comparison of several speech-defective groups, and the use of several personality measures in a single study. The criteria for subject selection, however, remain unclear, the reliability and validity of the assessment techniques are questionable, and sample size remains small (p. 311).

This, we believe, continues to be the situation as of this writing. As clinicians, we entertain the impression that persons with disorders of speech considered as a total population are not as well adjusted as are persons without disorders of speech. (Individual exceptions are, of course, numerous for both populations.) This is so for so-called functional disorders and more so for persons whose disorders are on the basis of brain damage or a peripheral organ anomaly. We join Bloch and Goodstein and others in wishing that studies employing assessment instruments for the measurement of personality factors and adjustment would permit of equally strong impressions.

In the discussions that follow we will have occasion to review studies and their findings related to personality, adjustment, and intellectual status, for identified groups with speech and/or language impairments.

TYPES OF SPEECH AND LANGUAGE IMPAIRMENTS: CORRELATED FACTORS

Retarded Language Development

Definition: The child with delayed or retarded language is one whose competence (comprehension) and/or performance (production) is significantly below what we expect on the basis of age, sex, and intelligence. Ordinarily, it is performance or production rather than competence that is used as a measure of achievement. Conventionally, aspects of performance include articulatory proficiency, vocabulary size and sentence production (length and syntactical or grammatical complexity and "correctness").*

The discussion that soon follows excludes those children who have any recognized organic or intellectual impairment that may directly account for the language delay, both ·in onset and development. We will emphasize the point, however, that severe mental deficiency is the most frequent cause of delayed language development.

Later we will present a chart that highlights some of the features of the different "types" of children who are significantly retarded in language development. Before considering some of the causes of presumably

nonorganic language delay, we will review the usual course of development and the environmental circumstances that usually accompany normal language acquisition.

Normal Language Acquisition: Developmental Highlights

In the interest of brevity, we will present our view of normal language acquisition in a series of statements that may appear to be more generalized than we intend. Perhaps each statement should be preceded with the reservation clause, "Other things being equal, which all too often they may not be."

1. It is normal for children to speak by 15 months of age. By 30 months they should be speaking so that well-intentioned strangers should be able to understand most of what they say.
   a. By 24 months, most children include some conventional grammatical features in their utterances.
   b. By 36 months most children, use a majority of the rules (syntax) of their language.
2. Language acquisition is a creative achievement. To be a speaker of a language means that on the basis of a limited number of rules and a limited vocabulary, an individual ultimately will understand a potentially infinite number of utterances and will be able to produce in turn a potentially infinite number of statements.**
3. By 30 months of age, if a child shows no evidence of either the comprehension or production of language, there is cause for concern that the child is language delayed or will show disorder in language development.
4. Only the most severe environmental deprivation or an organic anomaly will prevent the onset of language by 30 months or, at the outset, by 36 months. Usually, certain developmental and environmental conditions prevail

---

* For a discussion of the relationship between competence (comprehension or understanding) and performance, see Lenneberg (1967, pp. 284–292), Dale (1972, pp. 36–38) or Cazden (1972, p. 3).

** Slobin (1973, p. 175) states that in order for a child to construct a grammar of his/her language, he/she must have two basic cognitive capacities: (1) To "cognize" the physical and social events that are encoded in language, and (2) To process, organize, and store linguistic information.

if the child is to comprehend and produce language.

a. The child has hearing adequate to receive speech signals.
b. The child has an intact and developmentally proficient central nervous system that permits the reception, perception, and processing of speech signals at the rate at which they are normally produced.
c. The child hears enough speech from one or more human beings with whom he or she can identify and relate in a positive way so as to accept speaking as a mode of behavior.*

Table 5–3 highlights a normal child's speech acquisition stages and the usually correlated motor achievements.

Delayed Language: Quantitative or Qualitative?

Menyuk (1975) asked a fundamental question in an essay, "Children with Language Problems." Her question is, "What's the problem?" One position that is fairly widely held is that children who are significantly delayed in language acquisition are basically slower but essentially similar to normal children. On this assumption, added time and increased stimulation should bring the delayed-speech child up to potential. This, however, does not imply that were time not a factor, that in time the retarded-language child would more and more approximate the achievement level of the normal child, that is, not if the retarded-language child was also significantly mentally retarded. Differences in size of vocabulary, degree of abstraction, and sentence complexity would continue to differentiate mentally retarded from normal children.

If, however, the language acquisition processes are different, and overall differences

between children with retarded language development were basically qualitative, then our assumption would dictate different remedial approaches. Menyuk believes that, though quantitative differences are evident, the essential differences are qualitative. She suggests the need for research to identify the differences and to develop programs when the crucial differences are identified.

Essentially the same position is held by Carrow-Woolfolk (1975). She says: "Clinical observation and studies of individual children have led this author to a belief that language-disordered children are different from, rather than slower than, the nonlanguage-disordered child" (p. 431). Carrow-Woolfolk points to differences in the use of the verb to be, in omission errors, grammatical markers, and lexical items as critical distinctions between children who are delayed and "disordered" in language acquisition and those who are normal. Rhetorically, we believe, Carrow-Woolfolk asks: "Are the language-disordered child's semantic intentions developed out of proportion to his capacity to translate these to grammatic relations and modulations?"

Carrow-Woolfolk (pp. 432–435) outlines her theory of child language disorders and differential approaches based upon kinds of children who are delayed and/or disordered in language acquisition. For an "opposing" position, one that argues that the differences between children who are significantly delayed in language and normal children is essentially quantitative, see Morehead and Ingram (1973).

Our own position is that the quantitative-qualitative issue is more determined by the bias of the investigator than by the achievements of the child. When quantity becomes significant, the effect is qualitative. A thorough language assessment, if there is language to assess, should tell us where a particular child is, what the child knows and can produce, and where the child needs to be moved from where he or she is. If this position is taken, it would not make too

---

* An excellent yet brief treatment of the problems and issues in describing and evaluating the early language acquisitions of children may be found in Bloom and Lahey (1978, chaps. 2 and 3).

TABLE 5–3
HIGHLIGHTS OF NORMAL SPEECH AND MOTOR DEVELOPMENTAL STAGES*

Approximate Age Range	Language Acquisition Features	Usual Motor Achievements
Pre–Verbal Stages		
Birth to 4 weeks	Cries whenever uncomfortable, with little apparent difference in crying according to the specific cause but with variations according to type of cause—e.g., pain, hunger.	Cries or sleeps; most physical (motor) behavior involves the entire body.
4 to 16 weeks	Coos and makes "laughing" sounds; vocal play includes vowels and some consonant sounds involving tongue and lip activity; may engage in vocal "dialogue" with mother or another speaker.	Shows awareness and need for human sounds; turns head in the direction of the source of the sound. Usually is able to support head when lying in a prone position. By end of this period, infant is likely to "discover and inspect" his or her hand.
20–24 weeks	Vocalizes when comfortable. Cooing and considerable babbling with consonants that modify the identifiable vowel and vowel-like cooing; makes some nasal sounds (m, n) and some lip sounds including lip vibrations suggesting a "Bronx cheer."	Can sit up with support. Arm and leg movements show better control. May be able to pick up a cube.
6–7 months	Sound productions now include self-imitation (lalling). Many of the sound productions resemble one-syllable utterances that may include *ma, da, di, do*.	Can sit without props; if necessary uses hands for support; increased proficiency in picking up objects; can reach with either hand; smiles at own image.
8–9 months	Considerable self-imitative sound play; is also likely to imitate (echo) syllables and words he or she hears.	Can stand up, holding on to an object for support; can grasp a small object with thumb in apposition to index finger; can pull a string to secure an object.
Verbal Stages		
10–11 months	Repeats words he or she hears with increased proficiency. Responds appropriately to many word cues for familiar things and "happenings." The precocious child may have several words in production vocabulary used as labels for things.	Indicates understanding of many verbal directions by appropriate behavior; cooperates in games; can pull self up to a standing position; may take a side step while holding on to a fixed object.
12 months	Still likely to be echolalic, but so proficiently that child sounds as if he or she has quite a lot to say; first labeling (identification) words for most children. Increased responses to verbal stimuli.	May stand without support; may walk if held by one hand; some children may take first steps alone. Most will "walk" on hands and feet.

TABLE 5–3 (Cont.)

Approximate Age Range	Language Acquisition Features	Usual Motor Achievements
By 18 months	Increases word inventory possibly from 3 to 50 or more words; vocalizations reveal intonational (melody) pattern of adult speakers. May begin to use two-word utterances.	Walks without support; runs; can manage cubes well enough to build a two-block tower; may begin to show hand preference. Can throw a ball and turn pages of a book.
24–30 months	Understands hundreds of words and sentences. Speaking vocabulary increases beyond 50 words, many of which are used as commands. Increased use of two-word utterances. May use intonation for yes/no questions.	Walks comfortably. With opportunity, can walk up or down stairs usually setting both feet on each step before going to next step.
30–36 months	Marked increase in vocabulary growth (proportionately greater than at any other point throughout childhood). Utterances include syntactical features used by adults. Utterance (sentence) length increases from 3 to 5 or more words. Uses *wh* question forms in usual order of *where, who, what, why, how, when*. Understands most of what is said by a "reasonable" adult. Articulation improving and most utterances are intelligible to "reasonable" older listeners. Some "infantile" sounds may persist such was *w* for *r* or *l*.	Can balance on one foot. Can jump. Hand and finger coordination adequate for building a tower with as many as six blocks.
36–48 months	Speaking vocabulary may be in excess of 1,000 words. Syntax closely approximates that of older speakers in environment. Child can say whatever he or she needs to make wants, thoughts, and intentions clear. Except for voice, the child's speech is much like the key members of his or her environment.	Hand preference usually well established. Can run proficiently. Can walk stairs with alternating steps.
48 months plus	Articulation under good control except, possibly, for *s, r, l, th*. Syntax almost completely like that of adults. Nevertheless, child has own personal speech style using favorite words and ways of "turning a phrase."	Can hop on one foot, usually on side of preferred hand. Can throw a ball at or to an intended receiver. Can ride a tricycle and walk a straight line.

* Adapted from table in Lenneberg, E. (1967, pp. 128–130). *Biological Foundations of Language.*

much difference for the child whether the clinician views the delays or disorders as quantitative or qualitative.

Language Delay: Parental Influences

In our earlier discussion of the psychogenic causes of defective speech, reference was made to several studies concerned with the parents of speech-defective children. These studies tended to indicate that parents, and especially the mothers, of young speech-defective children were more maladjusted than control-group parents. Among the undesirable traits and attitudes found to exist to a greater degree among the test-group parents were increased neurotic tendency, lower self- and social-adjustment, greater overall emotional instability, rigidity, perfectionism, overprotectiveness, and restrictiveness. In addition many of the mothers were found to have unrealistically high expectations of what constitutes appropriate language performance for their children. Often we find that mothers of children with delayed speech are overprotective, rigid, highly critical, and restrictive in their demands upon their children. It is possible, therefore, that when a child who is physically and intellectually normal fails to develop speech, the basis of the retardation may be in the child's reaction to the parents' maladjustments. The speech delay may often be both a reaction to the psychological environment and a manifestation of the child's own maladjustment.

Kleffner (1973) makes a clinical observation about children who are significantly delayed in language development:

Communication among members of the family in the presence of the child will lack those verbal modifications which would acknowledge his presence and the possibility of his participation—they will talk as if the child is not there. The child may accommodate to his lack of language by increasing his disregard of the speech of others and by decreasing his attempts to talk (p. 11).

Along the same lines, Chess and Rosenberg (1974, p. 101), writing as psychiatrists making clinical judgments say: "In the cognitively normal child with speech usage below age there may be a tendency to inhibit speech in situations where rebuff or misunderstanding are anticipated" (p. 101).

Rejection. Much of the attitude of the parents considered in the studies previously cited probably constitutes an unconscious rejection of the children. Children who sense such rejection and who cannot identify with parents, and especially with the mother, are likely to be delayed in speech development. Mowrer (1960, pp. 79–86) points out that a child must first identify himself with a parent with respect to speaking behavior before he or she begins to wish to speak. The child must, of course, be physically and intellectually mature and ready before the identification will motivate true speech. The rejected child either makes no such initial identification or may lose the identification once rejection is sensed.

Parental rejection that takes the form of continuous disapproval and criticism, of speech as well as of other forms of behavior, may cause the child to stop talking or reduce the amount of talking. When the rejection takes the form of indifference, the ordinary rewards that strengthen speech behavior and that stimulate renewed efforts at speaking are absent. Speech, then, may continue on an infantile level.

Goldfarb (1961), discussing the schizophrenic child, observes:

The speech model presented by a pathologically perplexed parent may be diminished in phonatory and rhythmic range. Further, in the face of unstructured emotional communication by this kind of parent, the child responds with confusion and unawareness of what is expected of him, so that he never achieves the complicated techniques required for connotative expression (p. 200).

Ruesch (1957) in his discussion of autistic, withdrawn, or outright schizophrenic children and their disturbances in communication or their failure to develop conventional communicative skills, also considers the parents' own behavior to be the fundamental cause.

> The parents' unresponsiveness in non-verbal terms prevents the child in the early years of life from learning how to relate through *movement and action*. The absence of early appropriate and gratifying communication through action, gesture, and object leaves traces (p. 133).

Some of the traces are in inadequate speech both for the expression of affect and for developing normal relationships through conventional communicative behavior.

Negativism. When the rejection takes the form of excessive criticism, the child may demonstrate that rejection is a two-way mechanism. The child may begin by rejecting the parents. If so, the child may also negate speech, through which he or she became aware of the parental criticism and disapproval. Such a child may occasionally become overtly unresponsive to human sounds and manifest a conscious awareness only of mechanical or animal noises. The child may either fail to develop speech or, if he or she had begun to use speech, regress to a preverbal stage of speech development.

The intelligent child who is severely retarded in speech has a deficient tool for making adjustments to his environment. As the child grows older, without adequate means for expression and communication, he or she must frequently deny his or her own developing needs and so entertains frustration. If the child does not engage in self-denial, he or she invites frustration by having no proficient means to communicate wishes or to elicit responses for their satisfaction.

We believe that negative familial influences and, more generally, a negative environment, are more likely to influence the development of speech than speech onset. The nature and content of what the child may say and the circumstances for talking are likely to be influenced by negative features in the child's speech environment, and so by negativism toward speaking.

Behavioral Traits Accompanying Delayed Language

It is, of course, not possible to make any direct inquiry or study through adjustment inventories of what is disturbing the child with delayed speech. Conclusions must be drawn from observations of the child's environment, from personality studies of the child's parents, and from direct observation of the child's behavior. Conclusions and implications have been drawn relative to the influence of parental maladjustment on the child. Observations will now be made of the behavior of the child—of what the child does in the company of other children. For the most part, these will be limited to direct observations of the child with delayed speech in a play situation in a speech clinic. The author has been in charge of such clinics since 1946 and has had delayed-speech groups under the immediate supervision of a psychologist and one or more speech clinicians since that time. The groups have varied in size from four to nine children.

Most idiopathic delayed-speech children resort to direct means to make their wants known or to impress their feelings upon others. These direct means may include literally forcing another child, or an adult, to enter into a situation and striking out at an undirected object or person. Frequently, the object or person struck at may be one very recently brought into the situation created by the child. The striking out may probably be considered the child's way of responding to something or somebody that does not readily understand why it was wanted and what role it was expected to assume.

Some children with delayed speech isolate themselves, as far as the physical situation permits, from others in the room. They will spend periods of up to an hour or more "playing" with a single toy object or just sitting off to one side apparently doing nothing. One boy of five spent his first four months in the clinic sitting high up, silent and alone, on the top of a four-foot jungle gym.

Some delayed-speech children appear to enjoy close physical contact with older persons and with inanimate objects. They may be seen to rub their bodies along the walls as they move from place to place. They rub their faces against their toys. Occasionally and very impulsively, they will grab hold of another child, or a clinician, and cling with great force for a moment before releasing the person. Apparently, there is a need for sensuous contact, which the child obtains from accepting unsuspecting individuals or objects.

Emotional lability characterizes the behavior of many delayed-speech children. They act with impulsiveness and excessiveness, at least when compared with most normally speaking children. They yell and cry quickly and more loudly, break toys, knock down block houses, fling objects around, tear papers, throw pencils, chalk, and crayons, and in general keep things flying about them.

All the characteristics just considered do not set the child with delayed speech off from other children. As a group, the behaviors of delayed-speech children differ in degree and not in kind from normally speaking children. Their mechanisms of adjustment or maladjustment are like those of other children, except that they are less expertly used. Some delayed-speech children are even well-behaved and appear to have made an adjustment to not speaking. Some reveal no factors in their case histories that can explain why they do not speak. Most, fortunately, learn to speak after a while and improve in their adjustment patterns as speech is developed.

Chess and Rosenberg (1974) found that 99 of 139 children with disorders of speech had behavior problems. Of the total number, 81 were identified as having delayed onset or development of speech.

General considerations of delayed speech and language development may be found in Carrow-Woolfolk (1975, pp. 429–436); Brown (1967); Eisenson and Ogilvie (1977, chap. 9); Kleffner (1973); Renfrew and Murphy (1964), Van Riper (1978, chaps. 4 & 5); and Wood (1964). Pronovost, Wakstein, and Wakstein (1966) have an excellent research report on the speech behavior and language comprehension of a group of autistic children.

Congenital (Developmental) Aphasia and Language Retardation

Despite opposition to the use of the terms *congenital* and *developmental aphasia,* they have become part of the professional literature on severe language retardation in children, and so will be used in this discussion.* We take the position that congenital or developmental aphasia (dyslogia) is an identifiable syndrome that must be separately considered among the organic causes of severe language retardation. Perhaps what sets it off most from other kinds of language retardation is that onset as well as development are seriously delayed.

When we make the diagnosis of congenital aphasia, we are obligated first to make certain that the child so designated is not severely mentally retarded, is not suffering from severe hearing impairment, and is not one who is primarily autistic or schizophrenic. On the positive side a diagnosis of congenital aphasia implies a need to establish, directly or on the basis of perceptual dysfunctions, that the child has a central nervous system pathology before language can be normally established or else to

* Objections and reservations about the use of these terms may be found in Carrow-Woolfolk (1975, p. 429) and Kleffner (1973, p. 13).

demonstrate that the child has atypical CNS functioning on a maturational (congenital) basis. We believe that congenital aphasia is a relatively infrequent cause of language retardation, but it is, nevertheless, a cause that cannot be argued away semantically. Congenital aphasia is not a diagnosis arrived at by default. The term is *not,* from our point of view, synonymous with idiopathic language delay. In the broadest sense the developmentally aphasic child is one with central nervous system impairment (dysfunction) and severe language delay.

Differential diagnostic features of developmental aphasia (dyslogia). Eisenson (1972, chap. 4) amplifies the concept of developmental aphasia and suggests the use of *dyslogia* as a synonymous term. Differential features include the following:

1. Perceptual dysfunction in one or more sensory modalities, but not in all modalities.
2. Auditory dysfunction over and above what would ordinarily be implied on the basis of conventionally determined hearing loss. Such dysfunctions include difficulty in speech sound (phonemic) discrimination and phonemic sequencing.
3. Sequencing difficulties that are especially pronounced for auditory speech events but that may also be present for visual events.
4. Intellectual inefficiency over and above any objectively determined intellectual limitation. The aphasic child needs optimal conditions, an absence of "noise" to perform at or close to intellectual potential.
5. In regard to verbal ability, impairment may be "complete" or virtually so for both the comprehension and production of language. Often children who begin to acquire language continue to use single words or two-word utterances when their age peers are able to employ conventional grammatical sentences. In general, we may characterize the productive language of the less severely developmentally aphasic children as lacking in conventional syntax and having a marked negative deviation from the language norms of their age peers in regard to size of vocabulary (compe-

tence and production), length of utterance, and complexity of syntactic formulations.

The underlying perceptual disturbance we believe is primarily for auditory-speech events. This dysfunction we consider to be related initially to defective storage capacity for speech sounds and to a defective capacity for the discrimination and sequencing of sounds in contextual utterance, especially when the child is required to process speech signals at a rate at which such signals are normally produced by most speakers. (See Eisenson, 1972, chap. 2, and Eisenson & Ingram, 1972, for detailed explanations of perceptual functions and dysfunctions related to developmental aphasia.)

Developmental background: aphasic development and the aphasic child. Children who fail to develop language or are significantly retarded in some aspect of language development because of congenital cerebral pathology or pathology with onset before true speech is normally achieved (by the end of the second year) are frequently found to be *out-of-phase* in their general sensory, motor, and perceptual development. In regard to these functions they are literally dys-phasic or a-phasic in that they do not follow anticipated patterns in the development of their sensory-motor skills and the behavior that is associated with such skills. Their sequential development is more highly individualized than our norms lead us to expect. Developmental manifestations that normally go together—that correlate and are in phase for normal children—show a lack of such correlation or phasing in children with known brain damage. Dreifuss (1975) notes:

The study of children who demonstrate undue delay in the development of speech frequently also show a delay in the development of hemispheric dominance as expressed in handedness. Many of these children show evidence on neurological examination of bilateral hemisphere disturbance. . . . It is concluded that for non-development of cerebral dominance, as judged when speech and handedness do not develop, bilateral cerebral disease is frequently present, although this might be slight as evidenced by neurological examination (p. 385).

Clinicians are often confronted with assessing nonverbal children for whom brain damage of atypical cerebral maturation cannot be clearly demonstrated by either clinical history or neurological diagnosis. We consider the diagnosis of congenital aphasia to be in order if the developmental history and psychological evaluation show the predominant features of the child with established brain damage. In a very important sense the psychological findings, especially in regard to perceptual functioning—those that may well be regarded as the "extended neurological"—are the essential determinants.*

As a final note on differential diagnosis (see Table 5–4), we wish to reemphasize that the clinician needs to be certain that severe mental retardation and/or hearing deficiency is not singly, or in combination, basic to the language delay. We need to be mindful that some clinicians consider such children to be schizophrenic. It might be of some comfort to appreciate that the term *childhood schizophrenia* is really an omnibus designation that in several important respects overlaps our criteria for congenital aphasia. Goldfarb acknowledges this in describing the setting of his research on childhood schizophrenia. Says Goldfarb (1961) "The staff was impressed with the great variation among the children in the single diagnostic category 'childhood schizophrenia.' The children differed markedly with respect to symptoms, defenses, and general level of ego develop-

* Our thinking is based on the assumption that the potential for speech is a human species specific function. Failure, therefore, to achieve this potential in the absence of deafness, severe mental retardation, or early childhood psychosis constitutes an implied indictment of the central nervous system as a mechanism for language acquisition.

ment. They also differed in responsiveness to treatment" (p. 7). We should like to consider the possibility that some children were not responsive to treatment because they were misdiagnosed as schizophrenic rather than appropriately diagnosed as congenitally aphasic (dyslogic) children.

For additional views of developmental aphasia see Eisenson and Ogilvie (1977, chap. 16) and Myklebust (1971, chaps. 46 & 47). For therapeutic approaches see Eisenson (1972, chaps. 5–10).

THE RIDDLE OF STUTTERING*

The Problem(s) and a Definition

The literature on stuttering, both professional and lay, is long, vast, and inconclusive as to theories of origin and therapy of choice. Any person with a bias can, by selective reading, find support for a position as to cause, concomitants, or treatment. Perhaps the greatest weaknesses in our study of stuttering, or of stutterers, is the premise or assumption that what we regard as stuttering is indeed a single symptom or symptom complex that therefore should have a single cause. Logically, of course, there should also be one therapeutic approach more efficacious than all others. Experience, however, suggests that this is not so. Stutterers have or have not improved by exposure to varieties of treatment including oral surgery, cauterization, castigation, psychoanalysis, various forms of psychotherapy including behavior modification, conditioning, and desensitization. Some stutterers have improved by direct attention to their symptoms and others by obeying suggestions if not direction to ignore their symptoms. Some insist that they literally "gave up" stuttering by their own determination. The catalog of positions is long,

* We shall use the term *stuttering* as essentially synonymous with *stammering*.

TABLE 5–4

IMPORTANT POINTS FOR DIFFERENTIAL DIAGNOSIS OF SPEECH AND LANGUAGE DISORDERS

Diagnosis	Medical History	Developmental History	Symptomatology	Management	Prognosis
Peripheral Deafness (Severe Hearing Impairment)	In majority of cases family history of infectious disease	Normal milestones; normal vocalization during prelingual stages. Abnormal persistence of babble and complete absence of words.	Normal affect; gestures only but usually eager to communicate; plays constructively and with concentration; no reaction to any but very loud sounds.	Establish diagnosis by audiogram; hearing aid; special training in visual (manual) and/or total method (manual plus oral).	Written language fairly good but not up to age expectation. Oral communication usually poor (may be entirely absent) but depends on age of onset, degree of deafness, and instructional method.
Mental Retardation	May include signs and symptoms of central nervous system disease or familial history of retardation.	Slow but steady if without neurological impairment; motor development sometimes better than cognitive.	Comprehension slightly ahead of speech production. Language is consistent with that of a younger child and usually free from bizarre stereotypes. Understanding, vocabulary, syntax delayed and usually correlated with amount of retardation.	May benefit from direct language training emphasizing vocabulary and syntactic (grammatical) constructions.	Good if IQ is 50 or above by chronological age seven. Lower IQ children may learn a considerable amount of functional language.

Congenital Inarticulation (Cluttering)	Perinatal stress with cranial nerve signs after birth. Family (paternal) history of similar disorder; dyslexia common.	Relatively normal milestones, except for development of vocalization, may be awkward and slow in development of laterality and manual dexterity.	Usually normally intelligent with normal affect and good motivation for communication; certain consonants consistently omitted or distorted; voice and intonation pattern intact. In severe cases no intelligible speech at all but in all cases understanding of language appears to be normal.	Preschool child: prevention or correction of secondary mental health problems in patient and parents. School child: assure proper instruction in reading and writing. Speech correction in 2nd or 3rd grade.	Depends on severity of defect but some spontaneous improvement in nearly all cases. Except for severest defects, disorder is outgrown or decreases in severity by early teens. Reading and writing problems may persist.
Early childhood (Acquired) Aphasia	Trauma, cerebral vascular accidents, infections involving brain.	Usually within normal limits.	Under 4 years: short period of complete loss of language followed by rapid reacquisition. After 4 years: well-formed constructions but apraxia, word-finding difficulty, inappropriate utterances, confusion, jargon, telegraphic style may persist.	After first 6 months of spontaneous recovery, speech rehabilitation often helps to encourage patient and restore self-confidence. If learning difficulties are associated with aphasia, academic help should precede other forms of therapy.	Dependent upon age at cerebral insult: recovery is usually complete in children under 10 with the recovery period lasting 3–6 months or less in preschoolers and up to a year in older children. In teenagers residuals become increasingly likely with advancing age. In the young adult symptoms present a year after injury may become chronic.

TABLE 5–4 (Cont.)

Diagnosis	Medical History	Developmental History	Symptomatology	Management	Prognosis
Childhood Psychosis	Typically, noncontributory.	Normal for motor milestones. Progress is irregular with surprise advances or regressions; socialization defective.	Usually mutism with occasional indications that comprehension of language has been acquired but motivation to speak is lacking; sometimes language is well developed but bizarre in its use; normal communication process either not established or interrupted.	Treatment often restricted to psychiatric aspects of disorder. Amplification of sound is contraindicated.	Except for primary autism, potentially good for speech and language but subordinate to prognosis of primary psychiatric disease.*

SOURCE: Adapted from Lenneberg, E. H. Language disorders in children. In *Language and learning: Investigations and interpretations.* Harvard Educational Review Reprint Series No. 7, 1972, pp. 170–171.

* We view primary autism as an expression of developmental differences in children. These differences, we believe to be associated with an atypical maturation "schedule" of the cerebral mechanisms or of pathology of these mechanisms. The results are idiosyncratic perceptions and cognitions that are expressed in peculiarities of language ranging from almost complete absence to persistent echolalia, and egocentric (nonsocialized) verbal usage. According to our own "prejudices" primary autism may well be considered as a subcategory of developmental (congenital) aphasia.

and sometimes "through every passion raging." Each position has claimants and can cite cases for success. Probably because each may be selectively right, we have found no widely accepted theory as to the origin of stuttering; neither have we wide acceptance that perhaps the word ought to take the plural form "stutterings" so that causes for what may be related disorders, and treatments relative to the disorders, may be found.

In their introduction to the Andrews and Harris monograph (1964), Court and Roth state that, based on techniques of covarying clusters of features, the analysis conducted in this study

> . . . showed in effect that there were three relatively separate forms of stutter. They differed in respect of such features as social class origin, intelligence, personality of the mother, quality of family life, early or late onset of stutter and the presence of other intellectual and emotional disabilities. . . . The utilization of tentative groupings of this kind can also help to ensure that patients submitted to further investigation will be subdivided into relatively homogeneous groups. In this manner, enquiry, whether concerned with the definition of causes or the evaluation of treatment, might be enabled to lead to more clear and fruitful results.

This is a position that we heartily endorse.

Before proceeding further in our discussion, we shall pause for a practical or operational definition, acknowledging that even a definition reveals bias. We shall accept Van Riper's (1978) to the effect that *"Stuttering occurs when the flow of speech is interrupted abnormally by repetitions or prolongations of a sound or a syllable or posture, or by avoidance and struggle reactions"* (p. 257). Van Riper, in emphasizing abnormal interruptions, distinguishes stuttering from normal hesitation phenomena and normal disfluencies. We should also note both the similarities and differences between stutter-

ing and cluttering (see our discussion on cluttering). Several other definitions may be found in Eisenson (1975).

In this work (Eisenson, 1975), six authorities present their viewpoints as to the essential cause or causes of stuttering, and their therapeutic approaches to stutterers. The present author, who is also the editor of and a contributor to the work, believes that the viewpoints on stuttering in this monograph and in general can be classified into three major but not altogether discrete groups along the following lines:

1. The stutterer has difficulty in speaking—he blocks, hesitates, repeats, grimaces, and so forth—because of an unconscious (repressed) need to do so. The stutterer is essentially a neurotic individual who expresses his neuroticism in part through his deviant speech.

2. Stuttering constitutes a breakdown or failure in functioning of the complex of neuromuscular, linguistic, and intellectual activity required for communicative speaking. This breakdown may occur temporarily for any speaker, but it is likely to be relatively chronic for those who are either emotionally or constitutionally predisposed to such impairment.

3. Stuttering is a learned form of speech behavior characterized by "anticipatory struggle." It thus becomes an avoidance reaction that is associated with a fear of hesitation in speech or otherwise of speaking in a manner the individual has learned to regard as stuttering.

We shall not, in our discussion, seek to support or to refute any of these theoretic positions. Instead we shall evaluate further some of the recent literature as it touches upon the psychological implications of being a stutterer. We shall be especially concerned with studies that seek to discover: (1) how the psychological environment of stutterers is different from that of normally speaking children and (2) how the adolescent and young adult stutterers differ psychologically from adolescents and young adults who do not stutter. How do nonstutterers view and respond to stutterers?*

Environmental Influences of Young Stutterers

Johnson, an eminent student of stuttering and stutterers, argued emphatically that stutterers are essentially normal children. He held (1967) that stuttering arises as a result of an interaction between a listener and a speaker—"that is, of the speaking child, and those others, chiefly the child's authority figures, his parents primarily, who listened and reacted evaluatively to his speech" (p. 239). Presumably, the authority figure or figures misevaluated the child's normal disfluencies as stuttering so that

> In due course, evidently by virtue of the disruptive perceptual and evaluative reactions to his own speech behavior, the problem came to involve disturbances of speech, in an overt expressive sense. It seems necessary to conclude, therefore, that the listener does more than the speaker to set in motion the interactions to the creation of the stuttering problem (1959, pp. 261–262).

Johnson therefore, directed our attention to an environment that includes authority figures who misevaluate the speech of the child and, by virtue of this misevaluation, create a problem in the child. However, we may ask what is there about this child that influences him to accept misevaluations and so leads him to become a stutterer? The underlying implication is that the parents have excessively and unrealistically high expectations that the child attempts but fails to meet. We may also ask why the implications of the interactions and unrealistic expectations are

* In our earlier discussion we presented the results of some survey studies on psychological aspects and parental attitudes about the speech-defective population as a whole. Some of these studies were specific to stuttering.

so much more severe for boys than they are for girls.

Reviews of the literature relative to home environments and parental pressures permit conclusions that vary with individual studies. Studies that tend to support the view that either or both parents are unrealistic in their expectations, overdemanding, or perfectionistic include those of Moncur (1952), Bloodstein, Jaeger and Tureen (1952), Darley (1955), Wyatt (1969), Johnson (1959) and Goldman and Shames (1964). Studies that failed to find any significant differences in the attitudes or expectations of parents of stutterers compared with parents of nonstutterers include those of Andrews and Harris (1964), Berlin (1960), and Seligman (1966). Reviews of the literature on environmental factors in stuttering may be found in Van Riper (1971, pp. 276–277), Bloch and Goodstein (1971), Perkins (1977, pp. 316–317), and Bloodstein (1975, pp. 42–50).

Though experimental studies may not be conclusive, impressions of clinicians often leave little room for doubt. Stutterers as well as their families are described in no uncertain terms in keeping, we believe, with the perceptual prejudice of the clinician. Thus Travis (1971) attributes both the origin of stuttering and its generalization to parental influence. Says Travis: "The interpersonal pattern between child and parent that flowered the stuttering originally trained the stutterer to prefer his stuttering relationship with other people as well (p. 1010). Further, Travis describes stutterers as being laden with guilt because of "unspeakable feelings" they entertain. The stutterer, observes Travis, "has an obscure and growing sense of being profoundly in the wrong, though for no discernible reason. May he avoid if possible the feeling that his very existence is an effrontery to his parents and even to others. Finally, may he avoid the feeling that just to be alive is both a fault and his own fault" (p. 1010).

Glauber, speaking as a psychoanalyst with a Freudian orientation, held that stuttering was a uniquely total family disorder that results in an oral-fixation neurosis in the stutterer. So, Glauber asserted (1958):

I have been impressed that regularly the oral-narcissistic fixation in the stutterer flows from the partial resolution of the primary identity with the mother. Furthermore, the meanings of this fixation may be found in the primitive struggles, aims, and self-images inherent in this symbiosis. For this reason it is essential to understand the personality of the mother of the stutterer and the rather unique mother-child relationship. The father's role is also significant, but becomes so at a later stage in the life of the child. These facts may be restated thus: the father is actually important in the maintenance of the neurosis as the mother is in its precipitation. Because of the observations, about to be elaborated, it is neither banal nor superfluous to state that the stutterer's disorder—at least the young stutterer's—is uniquely a total family disorder. Needless to say, this fact is of paramount importance in the therapy of the child stutterer (p. 97).

Glauber believed that the stutterer and the mother "are extremely attuned to the anxieties of each other" (p. 98). Glauber's profile of the stutterer's family includes the following (pp. 101–105):

The mother is a "stutterer" in personality, as the father is much more frequently and overtly in his speech. . . . The mother . . . has a poorly differentiated sense of self. She is part child, part tomboy, part wife-husband . . . . We would diagnose her as a narcissistic character with hysterical and compulsive features. . . . [The father of the stutterer is described as] a passive-dependent type. . . . Among the chief characteristics of the stutterer are inhibitions and passivity (pp. 101–105).

Somewhat more kindly, Wyatt (1969, chap. 6) also attributes the beginning of stuttering to a child-parent (mother) anxiety relationship. According to Wyatt, if the mother-child relationship is disturbed when the child is in the grammatical-acquisition stage of speech, further language learning

may be delayed. Another possibility is that the child may regress to an earlier stage of language acquisition. Disturbances may also be expressed in initial symptoms of stuttering. Feelings of anxiety and anger may bring about a change in how the child perceives his or her mother and so further complicate the already impaired mother-child relationship. Unless the relationship is improved, the ultimate result may be the development of chronic anxiety, depression, and the use of defensive mechanisms on the part of the stutterer, as well as evidence of advanced (chronic) stuttering.

It may be of some interest to learn how persons other than parents and clinicians view stutterers. Woods and Williams (1976) investigated how nonstutterers viewed stutterers, and whether there were stereotypes or preconceptions about personality aspects of stutterers, particularly about stutterers being anxious persons. Woods and Williams employed a semantic-differential procedure that required subjects to rate a concept or trait on a bipolar scale. Woods and Williams found that their data suggest "that many people expect a stutterer to be different from a nonstutterer in certain undesirable ways." Nonstutterers do have stereotyped expectations about stutterers. Interestingly, the traits attributed to boys and men were remarkably similar. Among the common assumed traits are anxiety, shyness, lack of self-confidence, and tendency to social withdrawal.

We may again return to some basic questions for which we have no answers. Why do stutterers seem to present a personality picture to others that, except for anxiety, they seem not to have of themselves? Is there indeed a stuttering personality that evokes an intuitive response but that is not subject to objective identification or assessment? Do stutterers have "undefinable" traits that are not captured by personality inventories?

Perhaps we have no firm answers to these questions because we somehow assume that stutterers are a homogeneous group, and so we expect them to have behavioral traits that as individuals they may or may not have, or may have in varying degrees. It might be more fruitful to look for differences among stutterers than to assume that stuttering—however variously defined—makes for a special population. Perhaps if we seek possible relationships between the supposed etiology or onset of stuttering and the manner, occasions, and use made by the speakers of their stuttering we might enhance the likelihood of obtaining more useful data and pertinent conclusions than we presently have.

Although not particularly concerned with personality aspects of stutterers, clinical theorists such as Brutten and Shoemaker (1967) and Wolpe (1958) take the position that, however learned, stuttering is basically maladaptive behavior that needs to be unlearned. Wolpe tends to emphasize anxiety features in the stutterer, and his therapy is directed, by techniques of reciprocal inhibition, to reduce the anxieties associated with speaking and so to reduce or eliminate stuttering. Essentially the same approaches are recommended by Brutten and Shoemaker.

In a later writing, Brutten (1975, chap. 3) emphasizes the need to deal with and modify the variety of behaviors associated with stuttering. So, Brutten observes: "What stuttering is and what can be done to bring about its modification are inexorably tied together" (page 201). Brutten criticizes most therapeutic procedures because "the behavioral characteristics of stuttering moments are not specified. They are not made explicit even though the component behaviors are neither constant from instant to instant nor from speaker to speaker" (page 201). If Brutten is correct, his position may explain why results of investigators yield such highly variable data and permit of so many different conclusions.

Constitutional (Organic) Factors in Stutterers

Are we likely to find more consistent differences in constitutional predispositions if

not of specific organic factors when we compare stutterers with nonstutterers? In this area, too, the search has been long and the results hardly conclusive. Yet we believe that recent procedures and improved techniques, as well as more sophisticated insights as to what to look for, may be providing answers that suggest that many if not most stutterers are constitutionally different from their nonstuttering peers.

Van Riper (1971, pp. 340–344) presents the results of a cross-cultural survey of studies for the period 1913–1966 on hereditary factors in stuttering. Except for one questionnaire study the data clearly pointed to a hereditary, and so presumably a constitutional, factor in stuttering. From our point of view, some of the findings of the Van Riper survey permit the following conclusions.

1. In every population study there were more male than female stutterers. The ratios ranged from 2 to 1, to 5 to 1, males to females, with a 4 to 1 ratio about the median.
2. There were more stutterers in families of the stutterers in the study than in families of nonstutterers.*
3. Among twins there was a higher incidence of stuttering than in single-born children.
4. As a total population, stutterers had a higher incidence of delayed onset and development of speech than children regarded as normally fluent.

* Two recent investigations are particularly significant on the inherited constitutional predisposition for stuttering. Record, Kidd, and Kidd (1976) examined the incidence of stuttering within families of stutterers. "Data reveal a significant familial concentration, an increased incidence rate among relatives of stutterers, with a significant difference between male and female relatives." Howie (1976) studied possible genetic factors by measuring intrapar similarity in disfluency among forty-two pairs of twins, each pair including at least one stutterer. She found the concordance for stuttering to be higher (59 percent) in identical twins than in fraternal same-sex twins (15 percent). Howie concluded that genetic factors are clearly involved in the etiology of stuttering. However, because there is less than 100 percent concordance in identical twins, environmental influences are also important.

Dichotic Listening. Most studies employing dichotic listening* indicate that the differences in the perception (processing) of auditory signals, speech and nonspeech, that hold for adult nonstutterers do not hold for stutterers. Specifically, right-handed nonstutterers show a right-ear preference (left-cerebral dominance) for speech signals and a left-ear preference (right-cerebral dominance) for nonspeech events. The findings on stutterers are more variable than on normally fluent speakers. Studies on dichotic listening are reviewed by Eisenson (1975, pp. 413–414). Van Riper (1971, pp. 358–359) reviews several studies on auditory laterality. Other studies on cerebral dominance and organic differences are reviewed by Van Riper (1971, pp. 351–360).

An exception to the general finding on auditory laterality is reported by Slorach and Noehr (1973). However, children rather than adults were the subjects of this study. These investigators observed that certain groups of stutterers did show special (atypical) patterns of lateralization, but they did not suggest this to be a general finding.

Delayed Auditory Feedback (DAF)

In his discussion and review of the literature on disturbed (delayed) auditory feedback, Van Riper (1971) observes:

* In the "classical" dichotic listening procedure competing signals of the same type are simultaneously sent to the two ears. These signals may be of speech (digits, alphabet letters, syllables, or words) or of nonverbal auditory events (musical tones or other balanced nonspeech signals). The subject is required to report what each ear hears. Thus the accuracy of the "reporting ear" is determined. The difference in accuracy between the "reporting ears" is considered to be an indicator of ear preference. On the accepted assumption that the contralateral hemisphere is the primary processor of the signals, cerebral dominance or a lack of cerebral dominance is established.

For a review of dichotic listening and other studies related to cerebral dominance for speech see Kimura (1975), and Krashen (1975). *Brain and Language,* vol. *1*, no. 4, 1974, is entirely devoted to the subject of cerebral dominance.

The research is still incomplete but what we have shows the fluency breaks similar to stuttering can be produced in normal speakers by altering the auditory feedback of their speech output. Furthermore, a marked reduction in stuttering can often be achieved by the same process (pp. 382–383).

On the basis of his observation, with which we concur, Van Riper inferred "the possible existence of a perceptual disability in stuttering, probably organic in nature."

Just why a delay in auditory feedback should produce disruption in speech that at least overtly sounds like stuttering, and the same delay increases fluency (decreases stuttering manifestations) in most stutterers, is not clear. We believe that at least for certain stutterers—and perhaps for most—the slight difference in reaction and auditory monitoring time may permit these speakers to overcome or compensate for innate neurophysiological differences that distinguish them from nonstutterers. Timmons and Boudreau (1972, pp. 476–484) take such a position. In their research review article, Timmons and Boudreau present a hypothesis that stresses that there are both internal and external feedback disruptions due to physiological characteristics of individuals. They also propose that anxiety and its concomitant physiological factors act as catalysts to feedback disruptions.

Although we can only conjecture about the phenomenon of DAF, it is being used as a therapeutic procedure. The effect is not only to reduce stuttering behavior but usually also to slow down the speech output of stutterers. Our own conjecture is that the DAF permits stutterers the additional moment of time they need to integrate motor-kinesthetic feedback with auditory feedback so that in monitoring their speech they can decide whether the sounds and the movements feel "right." Slowing utterance, a usual outcome of DAF training, may provide the same needed moment of time. Thus stutterers—or at least many if not most stutterers—can overcome the implications of the differences of their neurological mechanisms.

Electroencephalographic Studies (EEG)

Studies of electrical recordings of brain waves of stutterers have been going on since the early 1930s. Comparisons of studies are likely to be misleading because recent procedures as well as knowledge in the reading of EEG recordings are considerably more sophisticated today than they were during the period of the early studies. Sayles (1971) found abnormal or borderline EEGs in almost half (48 percent) of a population of twenty-three male stutterers as compared with 12 percent in twenty-five male nonstutterers. Van Riper (1971, pp. 347–351) reviewed EEG studies performed over a 35-year period in the United States and abroad. Abnormalities of EEG recordings were found in fourteen experiments, while in eight studies no significant abnormalities were found. In summarizing the studies Van Riper (1971) says:

> Our impression, . . . is that a rather strong case can be made for the presence of atypical EEGs in a larger number of stutterers than would be expected by chance and that young stutterers are more likely to show them than older ones. It also seems tenable that their significance for stuttering may lie in their interference with the bilateral gating of the afferent and afferent nervous impulses required for smooth motoric speech. What produces these abnormal EEGs is less clear, but they may imply some sort of neurological damage or malfunctioning (p. 351).

Although the riddle of stuttering has not been solved, we agree with Van Riper that the implications of a neurological difference between many stutterers and nonstuttering peers has become increasingly strong during the past two decades.

Intelligence

Stutterers may be found in speakers throughout the measurable range of intelligence. We know stutterers who are in the intellectually superior range and many who are well within the normal range of intelligence. However, stuttering, or speech behavior that in overt features resembles stuttering, seems to be more prevalent among the severely retarded than in the middle and upper levels. Among the mongoloid (Down's syndrome), the incidence of stuttering is much higher than in the population at large. Gottsleben (1955) reported stuttering among 33 percent of institutionalized mongoloid residents as compared with 14 percent among institutionalized retardate persons who were not mongoloids. Even among the latter retardate patients, the incidence of stuttering is remarkably high.

Van Riper (1971, 42–45) reviews other studies among the retarded in whom stuttering and/or cluttering is reported with considerably higher incidence than in the population at large. To be fair, characteristics or features of stuttering are not always described in the studies. However, the burden of evidence seems to be clear, and it only adds to the enigma. Van Riper (1971) asks some discerning questions that may shed light on the enigma.

> Why if stuttering is basically learned behavior, do we find such a high prevalence in children who find learning most difficult? . . . Mongoloid children show organicity in many ways. Is their high prevalence of stuttering a reflection of neurological deficits which make the sequential timing of speech movements unusually difficult? . . .
>
> The incidence of all types of speech defects is very high among the mentally retarded. It might be merely that the temporal dimension of speech is affected equally with those of articulation, voice, or symbolization (pp. 42–43).

Sheehan takes exception to the findings of Van Riper and others, relative to the prevalence of stuttering among the mentally retarded. On the basis of his own studies and those of his collaborators involving surveys of institutionalized retarded residents, Sheehan (1970) concludes: "Assertions that stuttering appears more frequently among the retarded, or relates to either end of the distribution of intelligence, appear totally unfounded" (p. 119).

We are at a loss to explain Sheehan's findings relative to the retarded because they are exceptional. His findings and conclusion relative to other areas in the distribution of intelligence are in keeping with earlier findings by Darley (1955). Sheehan believes that stutterers do not differ from nonstutterers in regard to their incidence in dimensions of intellect. Specifically, says Sheehan (1970), "Stuttering is not related to the lower end of the scale any more than it can be shown to be related to the upper end" (p. 150).

School Achievement

Differences between stutterers and nonstutterers in regard to school achievement may be related to factors of intelligence and/or underachievement related to factors other than intelligence. If we accept the consensus of findings that stutterers have a higher prevalence at the lower end of the intelligence distribution, we should also expect correlated lower-school achievement. We find support in this expectation in a survey study by Schindler (1955, pp. 348–357) of 20,000 Iowa school children. Schindler found that the stutterers showed a mean school-grade retardation of about one-half school year for nonstutterers. On the basis of standardized tests in grades three to five, Schindler found "possibly significant" retardation only in basic language skills at the elementary level and basic arithmetic skills at the advanced level. In regard to oral reading skills, based on Gray's Oral Reading Test (grades two to six) results indicated an average retardation of approximately one year.

Andrews and Harris found a negative small difference for stutterers compared with nonstutterers in their survey study in England. On the basis of the Schonnell Reading Tests, Andrews and Harris (1964) concluded

that "stutterers tend to have no particular difficulty with tests of reading beyond that which would be expected from the differences in distribution of intelligence between the two groups" (p. 100).

On higher school levels, the relationship between stuttering and achievement becomes even more inconclusive. A process of self-selection may tend to reduce the number of marginal achievers, and the same process may increase the prevalence of persons in the higher intelligence range. We could find no evidence to support any direct relation between stuttering and school achievement beyond the elementary school grades.

CLUTTERING

We shall discuss *cluttering* at this point in our treatment of speech and language disorders because of its apparent resemblance to stuttering, and because we accept the position of Weiss that cluttering is a disorder with an "organic flavor," which "might be only one aspect of a generalized disorder of all channels of communication" (1964, p. 5).* Weiss points out that by an "organic flavor" he means that though there are no clear neurologic symptoms, "they run parallel to symptoms caused by an organic disease but have no concomitant signs of organicity" (p. 7).

Symptoms of cluttering include repetition of monosyllabic words or of the first syllable of polysyllabic words, poor formulation of utterance associated with excessive speed of articulation, slurring (telescoping) as rate of utterance increases, and what appears to be a compulsion for rapid utterance, or at least a rate of utterance too rapid for the clutterers' ability as speakers. Weiss also notes that the "clutterer's inability to find the words he needs in sufficient time to main-

---

* The monograph by Deso Weiss on cluttering includes a historical review of the problem and theories as to etiology and treatment.

tain a smooth flow of speech causes him to prolong vowels, most often at the ends of words. . . . This is in effect a stalling device during which he searches for the next word" (p. 23). Weiss believes that: "Because the clutterer is inept at finding the necessary words to express his ideas, his speech is studded with clichés and repetition of words and phrases" (p. 24).

Articulation is generally imprecise. Vocal monotony becomes pronounced when speech becomes rapid. Often the total utterances become unintelligible.

Weiss argues that the clutterer has a poorly integrated thought process and generalizes that "the clutterer's haphazard and tentative thinking in preparation for speech reflects his general approach to all undertakings. This is the basic characteristic of cluttering and hence one of the prime targets of therapy" (p. 36).

Background History of Clutterers

The case histories of many clutterers suggest that retarded language development is both an individual and familial trait. Weiss (1964, p. 51) reports a higher than expected incidence of speech disorders, including cluttering on the paternal side, in the family. Although some psychiatrists view cluttering as a neurotic manifestation, the prevailing point of view is that it is probably organic in origin. Luchsinger and Landolt (1951), cited by Weiss, report an incidence of almost 100 percent of positive electroencephalographic findings. DeHirsch (1961) regards cluttering as a manifestation of a lack of maturation of the central nervous system. Arnold (1960) considers cluttering to be an expression of poor auditory perception, which he designates as *perceptual dysgnosia*.

Perkins (1977) considers *cluttering*, or *tachyphemia*, to be useful terms for identifying problems of rate and rhythm which are associated with symptoms of general language disability. Perkins observes: "To the extent that it includes problems of fluency

it overlaps stuttering. Clutterers can do what stutterers do—struggle with dysfluency—but additionally, clutterers tumble erratically through speech, blurring intelligibility as they go" (p. 325).

Related Symptoms

Cluttering is viewed by Arnold (1960) and by Weiss (1964, p. 7) as a disorder of *central language imbalance*. According to Weiss, this imbalance includes such features as delayed language onset, delayed language development, dyslalias, reading and writing difficulties, disorders of rhythm and musicality, and, as general characteristics, disorderliness and restlessness.

Clinical Impression and Prognosis

The clinical impression of the cluttering child is that he is "rather loosely put together." He is awkward in his movements and is often ambinondextrous and generally imprecise, if not patently "sloppy" in his productions. Weiss reports (1964) that the clutterer is

. . . deficient in his sense of harmony in language functions and must exert extra effort if he wishes to speak, read, and write acceptably. . . . Cluttering (Central Language Imbalance), then, we consider to be a basic constitutional characteristic of an individual's general disposition (p. 10).

A differential diagnostic and therapeutic observation is made by Weiss (1964, p. 69) in distinguishing cluttering from stammering (stuttering). Whereas the stammerer tends to do worse as he attends to his speaking, the clutterer tends to improve. The clutterer speaks more poorly when relaxed; the stammerer tends to speak better. Other differential characteristics are summarized by Weiss (1964, chap. 4), which, if we accept his notions, clearly differentiate stammering from cluttering and suggest, as well, the differential nature for therapy.

TABLE 5-5
SOME SIMILARITIES AND DIFFERENCES BETWEEN
CLUTTERERS AND STUTTERERS

	Clutterers	Stutterers
Familial history	May be present, especially on the male side; may have clutterers or stutterers as relatives	May be present, much more often in males than females
Onset and acquisition of speech	Often delayed	May occasionally be delayed, but not as often or as long as for clutterers
Likelihood of awareness	Probably unaware	Often aware, sometimes to level of anxiety
Responses to own speech	Indifferent	Apprehensive, anxious
Likely result of		
a) speaking after instruction to be careful	Improve	Increase of stuttering behavior
b) interruption and reminder to slow down	Improve	Anxious, tense blocked speech
Speaking when aware of importance of situation	Usually improve	Usually worse
Speaking when relaxed, at ease	Worse	Improve
Reading new material	Better at outset; deteriorates as reading progresses	Worse
Reading familiar material	Worse	Improve

Table 5-5 highlights some essential similarities and differences between clutterers and stutterers.

CLEFT PALATE

The problems of the cleft-palate child are related to the cosmetic aspects, problems directly involved with speech, and problems related to temporary or chronic hearing loss. Speech difficulties per se are, of course, directly related to the nature and extent of the palatal cleft and/or the lip and dental anomalies. Excessive nasality is a common voice characteristic where palatal cleft or palatal insufficiency is involved. Velar control may also be affected because of neuro-muscular impairment Morris (1975, p. 528) Van Riper (1978, pp. 359–363).

Varying degrees of hearing loss are relatively common. Pannbacker (1969), in a survey study of 103 subjects ranging in age from 3 to 41 years, found that subjects with cleft lip only and congenital palatal insufficiency were not found to have "socially significant audiological defects." Cleft-palate cases, with or without cleft lip, were found to have the same frequency of hearing loss. Approximately two-thirds of the cases had hearing loss of 15 decibels or more in either ear. Perkins (1977, p. 197) and Estes and Morris (1970, p. 769), and Heller, Hochberg, and Milano (1975, p. 775), report that hearing loss occurs more frequently in persons with cleft palate than in the general population.

Linguistic Proficiency

Problems of voice and articulation have long been recognized as common in the cleft-palate population. Recent findings indicate that there are also deficiencies in linguistic proficiency, at least in the school-age range.

Smith and McWilliams (1968) reviewed and reported the results of several studies on the general linguistic proficiency of cleft-palate children. They also investigated the linguistic abilities of a group of cleft-palate children (eighty-six males and fifty females) ranging in age from 3 to 11 years. The Illinois Test of Psycholinguistic Abilities was used to assess language competence and performance. Their data reveal that "cleft-palate subjects manifest a general language depression with particular weakness in vocal expression, gestural output, and visual memory. Moreover, in the samples studied, there was a tendency for language weaknesses to become more marked as age increased" (p. 248).

Moll (1968), after reviewing the literature, concludes:

> It appears that individuals with cleft lips and cleft palates are retarded in some degree in language development. This retardation seems to exist on almost every dimension measured in the various studies: these children exhibit less verbal output and a more simple language structure than children without clefts. . . . It must be emphasized that the conclusions about retarded language development refer to cleft-palate subjects on the average; obviously not all children exhibit retardation in language skills (p. 110).

Morris (1975, p. 528) comes essentially to the same conclusion: "At the very least, it seems wise to emphasize the importance of language stimulation in clinical management programs for all children with clefts" (p. 528).

Intelligence

The consensus of findings indicates that cleft-palate children as a special population score somewhat lower on tests of intelligence than do their age peers. This is particularly so on verbal test items.

Based on his own study and a review of the literature, Goodstein (1968) concludes: "The findings . . . suggest a generally mild to moderate degree of intellectual impairment, with the distribution of IQ for the group of children with cleft palate displaced to the lower end of the distribution" (pp. 209–212). The differences we should note are generally more pronounced in the verbal than in the performance areas. Though the mean IQ ranged from 94 to 99, we reemphasize that a given child with cleft palate can be found anywhere on the intelligence range, including genius.

Estes and Morris (1970) came to essentially the same conclusion after their review of the literature. The data of their own study involving a population of 466 children with orofacial clefts permitted them to conclude: "The cleft-palate children obtained higher WISC Performance Scale IQs than WISC Verbal Scale IQs indicating an apparent deficit in skills related to verbal activities as compared to those skills related to performance activities" (p. 765).

Psychosocial Implications

Perkins (1977) sums up his impressions of the psychosocial effects of cleft palate with a discerning observation:

> Clinicians are often of the opinion that persons who have suffered the unfortunate accident of being born with cleft lip or palate must also suffer severe social and psychological consequences. This opinion seems so obviously and logically justified that failure of the research evidence to support it is startling. . . . Of course, the reason why no more frequent or severe psychosocial problems have shown up may be because the tests that have been used are too insensitive or are not measuring important variables. That the clinical opinion would seem to have some justification is seen in the depressed language output of cleft-palate persons (pp. 197–198).

For detailed considerations of various aspects of problems related to cleft palate, see Eisenson and Ogilvie (1977, chap. 15), Perkins (1977, chap. 8), Spriestersbach (1973), Van Riper (1978, pp. 358–362), and Westlake and Rutherford (1966).

OTHER GROUPS

The personality aspects and, more generally, the psychology of the hard-of-hearing, the deaf, and the cerebral-palsied will not be considered in this chapter. Some aspects of the problems of these groups of speech-defective children with sensory and motor disabilities were taken up in our overview of types of speech-defective persons. These groups are considered in detail by recognized authorities elsewhere in this text.

We have paid no special and separate attention to the vocally defective child, except as vocal defects are associated with organic disorders. The reason for this is that, except for clinical case studies, there is a paucity of available literature of objective psychological studies of the vocally defective child. However, the subject is treated in texts and monographs such as Boone (1977), Eisenson and Ogilvie (1977, chap. 12), Greene (1972), Johnson (1967, chap. 4), Perkins (1977, chap. 13), and Van Riper (1978, chap. 7).

SUMMARY

In most respects, the defective in speech differ in degree but not in kind from the normally speaking population. Taken as a group, the differences are not great. On an individual basis the difference may be great, small, not discernible, or nonexistent. Taken as a group, speech-defectives are somewhat retarded intellectually and educationally. They have somewhat more difficulty in their adjustment efforts than do the normally speaking. In individual instances, it is not clear whether these adjustment problems are caused by the defect in speech or whether the speech defect is but one additional manifestation of the somewhat maladjusted personality.

Objective studies relating to the personality pictures and adjustment problems have, for the most part, been undertaken with adolescents and adults. Some attempts to do as much for children have been reported. On the whole, the differences appear to increase as the children grow older. The adolescent and adult speech-defectives appear to have considerably more problems in adjustment than do the children. This observation, however, may really mean that our measuring devices for adjustment differences are better when applied to older speech-defectives than they are when applied to children. It may also suggest that older children who maintain their defective speech experience frustration and develop other reaction patterns that our culture considers to be maladaptive.

There is considerable evidence that clinical impressions as to behavioral manifestations and adjustment problems of persons with defective speech are at variance with the results of studies employing standardized tests and inventories. We may conclude either that persons with defective speech are test-wise or/and that the aspects of personality and adjustment have not been identified or somehow fail to assess what may be critical in the reactions of and to this special population.

REFERENCES

ANDREWS, G., & HARRIS, H. *The syndrome of stuttering*. London: The Spastics Society and William Heinemann, Ltd. 1964.

ARNOLD, G. E. Studies in tachyphemia: signs and symptoms. *Logos*, 1960, *3*, 25–45. (*a*)

ARNOLD, G. E. Studies in tachyphemia. *Logos*, 1960, *3*, 82–95. (*b*)

*ARTLEY, A. S. A study of certain factors presumed to be associated with reading and speech difficulties. *Journal of Speech and Hearing Disorders*, 1948, *13*, 351–360.

BEECH, H. R., & FRANSELLA, F. *Research and experiment in stuttering*. London: Pergamon Press, 1968.

BERLIN, C. I. Parents' diagnoses of stuttering. *Journal of Speech and Hearing Research*, 1960, *3*, 372–379.

BERRY, M. F., & EISENSON, J. *Speech disorders*. Englewood Cliffs, N.J.: Prentice-Hall, 1956.

BICE, H., & CRUICKSHANK, W. M. Evaluation of intelligence. In W. M. Cruickshank and C. M. Raus (Eds.), *Cerebral Palsy*. Syracuse, N.Y.: Syracuse University Press, 1955, chap. 3.

BLOCH, E. L., & GOODSTEIN, L. D. Functional speech disorders and personality: a decade of research. *Journal of Speech and Hearing Disorders*, 1971, *36*, 295–314.

BLOODSTEIN, O. Stuttering as tension and fragmentation. In J. Eisenson (Ed.), *Stuttering: a second symposium*. New York: Harper & Row, 1975, pp. 1–95.

————, JAEGER, W., & TUREEN, J. A study of the diagnosis of stuttering by parents of stutterers and non-stutterers. *Journal of Speech and Hearing Disorders*, 1952, *17*, 308–315.

BLOOM, L., & LAHEY, M. *Language development and language disorders*. New York: John Wiley, 1978.

*BLUEMEL, C. S. *The riddle of stuttering*. Danville, Illinois: Interstate Publishing Co., 1957.

BOONE, D. *The voice and voice therapy* (2nd ed.). Englewood Cliffs, N.J.: Prentice-Hall, 1977.

Brain and language, 1974, *1* (4). (This issue is entirely devoted to dichotic listening studies).

BROWN, S. In W. JOHNSON & D. MOELLER (Eds.), *Speech handicapped school children*. New York: Harper & Row, 1967, chap. 6.

BRUTTEN, G. J. Stuttering topography: Assessment and behavior change strategies. In J. Eisenson (Ed.), *Stuttering: a second symposium*. New York: Harper & Row, 1975, pp. 199–262.

BRUTTEN, G. J., & SHOEMAKER, P. J. *The modification of stuttering*. Englewood Cliffs, N.J.: Prentice-Hall, Inc., 1967.

BRYNGELSON, B. Speech and personality. In L. E. Travis (Ed.), *Handbook of speech pathology and audiology*. Englewood Cliffs, N.J.: Prentice-Hall, 1971, pp. 175–182.

CARRELL, J. A. A comparative study of speech-defective children. *Archives of Speech*, 1936, *1*, 179–203.

CARROW-WOOLFOLK, E. Disordered language and its management. In E. L. Eagles (Ed.), *Human communication and its disorders*. New York: Raven Press, 1975, pp. 429–436.

CAZDEN, C. B. *Child language and education*. New York: Holt, Rinehart & Winston, 1972.

CHASE, R. A. Neurological aspects of language disorders in children. In J. V. Irwin & M. Marge (Eds.), *Principles of childhood language disabilities*. Englewood Cliffs, N.J.: Prentice-Hall, 1972, pp. 99–135.

* Although no direct references may have been made to the items with asterisks, they are included because they are of historical or contemporary significance in the areas of speech or hearing disorders.

CHESS, S., & ROSENBERG, M. Clinical differentiations among children with initial language complaints. *Journal of Autism and Childhood Schizophrenia, 4,* 1974, 99–109.

CHOMSKY, C. *The acquisition of syntax in children from 5 to 10.* Cambridge, Mass.: M.I.T. Press, 1969.

*CLEMENTS, S. D. *Minimal brain dysfunction in children.* NINDB Monograph No. 3, U.S. Department of Health, Education and Welfare, Washington, D.C.: Government Printing Office, 1966.

*CRITCHLEY, M. Aphasiological nomenclature and definitions. *Cortex,* 1967, *1* (3), 3–25.

*CRUICKSHANK, W. M., BENTZEN, F. A., RATZEBURG, F. H., & TANNHAUSER, M. T. *A teaching method for brain injured and hyperactive children.* Syracuse, N.Y.: Syracuse University Press, 1961.

CURTIS, J. Disorders of articulation. In W. Johnson & D. Moeller (Eds.), *Speech handicapped school children.* New York: Harper & Row, 1967.

DALE, P. S. *Language development.* Hinsdale, Illinois: The Dryden Press, 1972.

DARLEY, F. L. The development of parental attitudes and adjustments to the development of stuttering. In W. Johnson (Ed.), *Stuttering in children and adults.* Minneapolis: University of Minnesota Press, 1955.

DARLEY, F. L., & SPRIESTERSBACH, D. C. *Diagnostic methods in speech pathology* (2nd ed.). New York: Harper & Row, 1978.

*DAVIS, H., & SILVERMAN, S. R. *Hearing and deafness* (rev. ed.). New York: Holt, Rinehart & Winston, 1970.

DEHIRSCH, K. Studies in tachyphemia, IV: Diagnosis of developmental language disorders, *Logos,* 1961, 3–9.

DREIFUSS, F. E. The pathology of central communicative disorders in children. In E. L. Eagles (Ed.), *Human communication and its disorders,* vol. 3. New York: Raven Press, 1975, pp. 383–392.

EAMES, T. H. The relationship of reading and speech difficulties. *Journal of Educational Psychology,* 1950, *41,* 51–55.

EISENSON, J. (Ed.), *Stuttering: a symposium.* New York: Harper & Row, 1958.

———. *Aphasia in Children.* New York: Harper & Row, 1972.

———. (Ed.), *Stuttering: A second symposium.* New York: Harper & Row, 1975.

———, & INGRAM, D. Childhood aphasia: An updated concept based on recent research. *Acta Symbolica,* 1972, *3,* 108–116.

EISENSON, J., & OGILVIE, M. *Speech correction in the schools* (4th ed.). New York: The Macmillan Co., 1977.

ESTES, R. E., & MORRIS, H. L. Relationship among intelligence, speech proficiency, and hearing sensitivity in children with cleft palates. *Cleft Palate Journal,* 1970, *7,* 763–773.

EUSTIS, R. S. The primary origin of the specific language disabilities. *Journal of Pediatrics,* 1947, *31,* 448–455.

FLETCHER, S. G., CASTEEL, R. L., & BRADLEY, D. P. Tongue-thrust swallow, speech articulation and age. *Journal of Speech and Hearing Disorders,* 1961, *26,* 201–208.

*FURTH, H. G. *Thinking without language.* New York: The Free Press, 1966.

*FURTH, H. G. On the nature of language from the perspective of research with profoundly deaf children. In D. Aaronson & R. W. Rieber (Eds.), *Developmental psycholinguistics and communicative disorders.* Annals of the New York Academy of Sciences, 1975, *263,* pp. 70–75.

*GIBSON, E. J., & LEVIN, H. *The psychology of reading.* Cambridge, Mass.: M.I.T. Press, 1975.

GLAUBER, I. P. The psychonalysis of stuttering. In J. Eisenson (Ed.), *Stuttering: A symposium.* New York: Harper & Row, 1958.

GOLDFARB, W. *Childhood schizophrenia.* Cambridge, Mass.: Harvard University Press, 1961.

GOLDMAN, R., & SHAMES, G. A study of goal-setting behaviors of parents of stutterers and parents of non-stutterers. *Journal of Speech and Hearing Disorders,* 1964, *29,* 192–194.

GOODSTEIN, L. D. Psychological aspects of cleft palate. In D. C. Spriestersbach & D. Sherman (Eds.), Cleft Palate and Communication. New York: Academic Press, 1968.

GOTTSLEBEN, R. H. The incidence of stuttering in a group of mongoloids. The Training School Bulletin, 1955, 51, 209–218.

GREENE, M. C. L. Disorders of voice. Indianapolis: Bobbs-Merrill, 1972.

GREGORY, H. H. Learning theory and stuttering therapy. Evanston, Illinois: Northwestern University Press, 1968.

HANSON, M. L. Tongue thrust: a point of view. Journal of Speech and Hearing Disorders, 1976, 41, 172–184.

HELLER, J. C., HOCHBERG, I, & MILANO, G. Audiological and otological evaluation of cleft palate children. Cleft Palate Journal, 1975, 7, 774–783.

*HIRSH, I. J. Temporal aspects of hearing. In E. L. Eagles (Ed.), Human communication and its disorders, vol. 3. New York: Raven Press, 1975, pp. 157–162.

HOWIE, P. M. The role of genetic factors in stuttering. Abstract of report to the 1976 Convention of the American Speech and Hearing Association, 18, 1976, 9, p. 656.

Human communication and its disorders. National Institute of Neurological Diseases and Stroke Monograph No. 10. U.S. Department of Health, Education and Welfare, Public Health Services, National Institutes of Health, Washington, D.C.: Government Printing Office, 1969.

IRWIN, J. V. Normal articulatory function: Detection, diagnosis, and management of abnormal articulatory function. In E. L. Eagles (Ed.), Human communication and its disorders, vol. 3. New York: Raven Press, 1975.

——, & MARGE, M. (Eds.). Principles of childhood language disabilities. Englewood Cliffs, N.J.: Prentice-Hall, 1972.

JOHNSON, W. Stuttering. In W. JOHNSON and D. MOELLER (Eds.), Speech handicapped school children (3rd ed.). New York: Harper & Row, 1967.

——. The onset of stuttering. Minneapolis: University of Minnesota Press, 1959.

JONES, M. H. Habilitative management of communicative disorders in young children. In E. L. Eagles (Ed.), Human communication and its disorders. New York: Raven Press, 1975, pp. 403–420.

KIMURA, D. Cerebral dominance for speech. In E. L. EAGLES (Ed.), Human communication and its disorders. New York: Raven Press, 1975, pp. 365–372.

KIRK, S. A., McCARTHY, J. J., & KIRK, W. D. The Illinois test of psycholinguistic abilities (rev. ed.). Urbana: University of Illinois Press, 1968.

KLEFFNER, F. R. Language disorders in children. Indianapolis: Bobbs-Merrill Co., 1973.

KRASHEN, S. D. The development of cerebral dominance and language learning: More new evidence. In D. P. Dato (Ed.), Developmental psycholinguistics: Theory and application, Georgetown University Round Table in Language and Linguistics. Washington, D.C.: Georgetown University Press, 1975, pp. 179–192.

LAPOINTE, L. L. Neurological abnormalities affecting speech. In E. L. Eagles (Ed.), Human communication and its disorders, vol. 3. New York: Raven Press, 1975, pp. 493–499.

*LENNEBERG, E. H. Biological foundations of language. New York: John Wiley, 1967. 1967.

*——. Language disorders in children. Language and learning; investigations and interpretations. Harvard Educational Review Reprint Series, No. 7, 1972, 170–171.

LIBERMAN, A. M., COOPER, F. S., SHANKWEILER, D. P., & STUDDERT-KENNEDY, M. Perception of the speech mode. Psychological Review, 1967, 74 (6), 431–461.

LILLYWHITE, H., & BRADLEY, D. Communication problems in mental retardation. New York: Harper & Row, 1969.

LUCHSINGER, R., & LANDOLT, H. H. EEG investigations in stammering and cluttering. Folia

Phoniatrica, 1951, *3* (cited by Weiss, 1964, 48–49).

LUPER, H. L., & MOLDER, R. L. *Stuttering therapy for children.* Englewood Cliffs, N.J.: Prentice-Hall, Inc., 1964.

MATTHEWS, J. Communication disorders of the mentally retarded. In L. E. Travis (Ed.), *Handbook of speech pathology and audiology.* Englewood Cliffs, N.J.: Prentice-Hall, 1971, pp. 801–818.

MENYUK, P. Comparison of grammar of children with functionally deviant speech. *Journal of Speech and Hearing Research,* 1964, *7* (2), 109–121.

————. Children with language problems: What's the problem? In D. P. Dato (Ed.), *Developmental psycholinguistics: Theory and application.* Georgetown University Round Table on Language and Linguistics. Washington, D.C.: Georgetown University Press, 1975, pp. 129–144.

MILISEN, R. The incidence of speech disorders. In L. E. Travis (Ed.), *Handbook of speech pathology and audiology.* Englewood Cliffs, N.J.: Prentice-Hall, 1971.

MOLL, K. L. Speech characteristics of individuals with cleft lip and cleft palate. In D. C. Spriestersbach & D. Sherman (Eds.), *Cleft palate and communication.* New York: Academic Press, 1968.

MONCUR, J. P. Parental domination in stuttering. *Journal of Speech and Hearing Disorders,* 1952, *17,* 155–164.

MOREHEAD, D., & INGRAM, D. The development of base syntax in normal and linguistically deviant children. *Journal of Speech and Hearing Research,* 1973, *3,* 330–352.

MORRIS, H. L. Evaluation of management regimes for cleft palate. In E. L. Eagles (Ed.), *Human communication and its disorders,* vol. 3. New York: Raven Press, 1975, pp. 525–535.

MOWRER, O. H. *Learning theory and the symbolic process.* New York: John Wiley, 1960, 79–86.

MOWRER, O. H. Speech development of the young child: The autism theory of speech development and some clinical applications. *Journal of Speech and Hearing Disorders,* 1952, *17,* 263–268.

MULLER-GERHARD, N. Results of psychological examinations with speech tests in pre-school children with hearing and speech disorders. *Folia Phoniatrica,* 1972, *24,* 214–221. (English Summary).

MURPHY, A. T., & Fitzsimons, R. M. *Stuttering and personality dynamics.* New York: The Ronald Press Company, 1960, chap. 6.

MYKLEBUST, H. R. Learning disabilities and minimal brain dysfunctions in children. In E. L. Eagles (Ed.), *Human communication and its disorders,* vol. 3. New York: Raven Press, 1975, pp. 421–428.

————. Childhood Aphasia: An Evolving Concept, and Childhood Aphasia: Identification Diagnosis, Remediation. In L. E. Travis (Ed.), *Handbook of speech pathology and audiology.* Englewood Cliffs, N.J.: Prentice-Hall, 1971, chapters 46 and 47.

MYSAK, E. D. Cerebral palsy speech syndromes. In L. E. Travis (Ed.), *Handbook of speech pathology and audiology.* Englewood Cliffs, N.J.: Prentice-Hall, 1971, pp. 673–694.

*NEWBY, H. A. *Audiology* (4th ed.). Englewood Cliffs, N.J.: Prentice-Hall, 1979.

*NORTHERN, J., & DOWNS, M. P. *Hearing in Children.* Baltimore: Williams & Wilkins, 1974.

*OLERON, P. A study of the intelligence of the deaf. *American Annals of the Deaf,* 1950, 179–195.

PANNBACKER, M. Hearing loss and cleft palate. *Cleft Palate Journal,* 1969, *6,* 50–56.

PECKARSKY, A. *Maternal attitudes towards children with psychogenically delayed speech.* Unpublished doctoral dissertation. New York University, School of Education, 1952.

PERKINS, W. H. *Speech pathology* (2nd ed.). Saint Louis: C. V. Mosby, 1977.

POWERS, D. J., & QUIGLEY, S. P. Deaf children's acquisition of the passive voice. *Journal of Speech and Hearing Research,* 1973, *16,* 5–11.

POWERS, M. H. "Functional Disorders of Articulation: Symptomatology and Etiology." In L. E. Travis (Ed.), *Handbook of speech pathology and audiology*. Englewood Cliffs, N.J.: Prentice-Hall, 1971, chap. 33.

PRONOVOST, W., WAKSTEIN, M. P., & WAKSTEIN, D. J. The speech behavior and language comprehension of autistic children. A report of Research to the National Institute of Mental Health, Public Health Service, 1966.

RECORDS, M. A., KIDD, K. K., & KIDD, J. K. Stuttering among relatives of stutterers. Abstract of report to 1976 Convention of the American Speech and Hearing Association. ASHA. 1976, *18*, 9, p. 656.

RENFREW, C., & MURPHY, K. *The child who does not talk*. London: William Heinemann, Ltd., 1964.

ROTTER, J. B. A study of motor integration of stutterers and non-stutterers. In W. Johnson (Ed.), *Stuttering in children and adults*. Minneapolis: University of Minnesota Press, 1955.

RUESCH, J. *Disturbed communication*. New York: W. W. Norton & Co., Inc., 1957.

SAYLES, D. G. Cortical excitability, perseveration, and stuttering. *Journal of Speech and Hearing Research*, 1971, *14*, 462–474.

SCHIEFELBUSCH, R. L. *Language of the mentally retarded*. Baltimore: University Park Press, 1972.

SCHIEFELBUSCH, R. L., & LLOYD, L. E. (Eds.), *Language perspectives: Acquisition, retardation, and intervention*. Baltimore: University Park Press, 1975.

SCHINDLER, M. D. A study of educational adjustments of stuttering and non-stuttering children. In W. Johnson (Ed.), *Stuttering in children and adults*. Minneapolis: University of Minnesota Press, 1955, pp. 348–357.

SELIGMAN, J. The personality, attitudes, and behavior of parents of children who stutter: An annotated bibliography. *Journal of Ontario Speech and Hearing Association*, 1966, *2*, 35–106.

SHEEHAN, J. G. *Stuttering: Research and therapy*. New York: Harper & Row, 1970.

*SILVERMAN, S. R. The education of deaf children. In L. E. Travis (Ed.), *Handbook of speech pathology and audiology*. Englewood Cliffs, N.J.: Prentice-Hall, 1971, pp. 399–430, 431–438.

SLOBIN, D. I. Development of Grammar in C. A. Ferguson & D. I. Slobin (Eds.), *Studies of child language development*. New York: Holt, Rinehart & Winston, 1973.

SLORACH, N., & NOEHR, B. Dichotic listening in stuttering and dyslalic children. *Cortex*, 1973, *9*, 295–300.

SMITH, J. O. Speech and language of the retarded. *The Training School Bulletin*, 1962, *58* (4), 111–124.

SMITH, R. M., & McWILLIAMS, B. J. Psycholinguistic abilities of children with clefts. *Cleft Palate Journal*, 1968, *5*, 238–249.

SPRIESTERSBACH, D. C. *Psychosocial aspects of the "cleft palate problem,"* Vols. I and II. Iowa City: University of Iowa Press, 1973.

TEMPLIN, M. *Certain language skills in children: Institute of child welfare monograph series*. Minneapolis: University of Minnesota Press, 1957.

TIMMONS, B. A., & BOUDREAU, J. P. Auditory feedback as a major factor in stuttering. *Journal of Speech and Hearing Disorders*, 1972, *37*, 476–484.

TRAVIS, L. E. The unspeakable feelings of people with special reference to stuttering. In L. E. Travis (Ed.), *Handbook of speech pathology and audiology*. Englewood Cliffs, N.J.: Prentice-Hall, 1971, pp. 1009–1033.

VAN RIPER, C. *The nature of stuttering*. Englewood Cliffs, N.J.: Prentice-Hall, Inc., 1971.

———. *The treatment of stuttering*. Englewood Cliffs, N.J.: Prentice-Hall, Inc., 1973.

———. *Speech correction*. Englewood Cliffs, N.J.: Prentice-Hall., Inc., (5th ed.) 1972; (6th ed.) 1978.

———, & ERICKSON, R. A. A predictive screening of articulation. *Journal of Speech and Hearing Disorders*, 1969, *34*, 214–219.

VAN RIPER, C., & IRWIN, J. V. *Voice and articulation*. Englewood Cliffs, N.J.: Prentice-Hall, Inc., 1958.

WEISS, D. A. *Cluttering.* Englewood Cliffs, N.J.: Prentice-Hall, Inc., 1964.

*WEST, R. W., & ANSBERRY, M. *The rehabilitation of speech* (4th ed.), New York: Harper & Row, 1968.

WESTLAKE, H., & RUTHERFORD, D. R. *Cleft palate.* Englewood Cliffs, N.J.: Prentice-Hall, Inc., 1966.

*WILSON, J. J., RAPIN, I., WILSON, B. C., & VAN DENBURG, F. V. Neuropsychologic function of children with severe hearing impairment. *Journal of Speech and Hearing Research,* 1975, *18,* 634–652.

WINITZ, H. *Articulatory acquisition and behavior.* Englewood Cliffs, N.J.: Prentice-Hall, Inc., 1969.

WOLFE, W. G. A comprehensive evaluation of fifty cases of cerebral palsy. *Journal of Speech and Hearing Disorders,* 1950, *15,* 234–251.

WOLPE, J. *Psychotherapy by reciprocal inhibition.* Stanford, California: Stanford University Press, 1958.

WOOD, K. S. Parental maladjustment and functional articulatory defects in children. *Journal of Speech Disorders,* 1946, *11,* 255–275.

WOOD, N. *Delayed speech and language development.* Englewood Cliffs, N.J.: Prentice-Hall, Inc., 1964.

WOODS, C. L., & WILLIAMS, P. Traits attributed to stuttering and normally fluent males. *Journal of Speech and Hearing Research,* 1976, *19,* 267–278.

WYATT, G. L. *Language learning and communication disorders in children.* New York: The Free Press, 1969.

6 Psychological Implications of Hearing Impairment

Derek A. Sanders

Ph.D., Professor of Communicative Disorders, Faculty of Social Science, Department of Communicative Disorders and Sciences, State University of New York at Buffalo

Apprehension is one of the most common reactions of a person who, for the first time, enters a sound-isolated room for a hearing test. This concern arises not from any fear of the test itself, but from the apparent deadness of the room which, while not eliminating sound completely, reduces it to abnormally low levels. Departure from the room upon completion of the test is frequently accompanied by a sigh of relief and a comment such as, "I wouldn't like to have to stay in there too long." Students who could well isolate themselves in these sound rooms to study in peace choose not to do so, protesting that it is too quiet to allow them to concentrate.

These observations illustrate the very basic contribution that hearing makes to our sense of well-being. Despite the frequent pleas for quiet, it is the selective reduction or elimination of undesired sounds that is sought, not the elimination of sound itself. The constant monitoring of the ever-changing sound patterns of the environment represents a major factor in the maintenance of a sense of well-being and security.

Hearing impairment, to varying degrees, shuts off the child or youth from environ-mental sounds that constitute an integral part of the events occurring around him. Added to this deprivation of auditory awareness are the effects that hearing deficiency has upon the ability to communicate freely and effectively with family, peers, and other persons. This may constitute a major hindrance to successful educational, occupational, and social acceptance into a hearing society.

It is not surprising, therefore, that the impact of a hearing impairment on a child or youth is all-pervasive. It extends far beyond the immediately apparent impairment of communication. Its ramifications may be seen in all aspects of development and social adaptation. To some degree, the hearing impairment will influence the child's ability to interact with others, to share ideas and feelings, to learn as others do, and to discover his own self. The hearing-impaired child will share with other handicapped children, the problems arising from the stigma of being different. However, the communication difficulties experienced by hearing-impaired individuals not only compound the problem, but also greatly complicate the task of surmounting it.

It is the purpose of this chapter to examine how a hearing impairment in a child or young person affects the development and maintenance of psychological integrity. To do so, it will be necessary first to consider the role that hearing plays in the well-being of a person with normal auditory function.

NORMAL HEARING—ITS ROLE IN PSYCHOSOCIAL ADJUSTMENT

Of the five senses man possesses, hearing and vision are the most sophisticated. They comprise "distance" senses, in contrast to the "near" senses of touch, taste, and smell. Like all sensory modalities, the auditory system provides the organism with information about change occurring in its environment. The sensory end-organ of hearing (organ of Corti), represents an interface, or boundary, between the world and the nervous system. This system will come to know about that world in terms of its own sensitivities. It is important to recognize that the world cannot be taken into the system. To know the world necessitates that the system record information *about* what is happening in its environment. It does this by sensing how it has been changed by changes occurring in the medium to which it is sensitive. Piaget (1951; see also Piaget & Inhelder, 1966) emphasizes that the child initially "knows" his world strictly in concrete sensory-motor terms. Only later is the relationship to the physical event expanded to incorporate a representational function that is independent of the sensory-motor involvement. Thus a person's perceptions of the world are constrained by the sensitivity of the sensory organs themselves. Until language develops, an individual can only become aware of things that affect him sensorily.

There is reason to assume that we *perceive* in terms of how we process what we *receive* (Sanders, 1977). Processing is determined by the fidelity of the sensory end-organs, in this case the organ of hearing.

Thus, any impairment in a sensory system results in a reduction of the capacity of the child or young person to be influenced by objects and occurrences that would normally stimulate him. If the impairment is not total, a distortion of the information concerning what happened will occur, because less than the total stimulus pattern will be detected.

It is reasonable to assume, therefore, that since the hearing-impaired child or youth receives a distorted pattern of auditory information, his auditory-perceptual experiences will differ from those of a normal-hearing person (Altshuler, 1976). Important to a sensitive appreciation of the difficulties experienced by hearing impaired persons is an awareness that the hearing impairment modifies the perceptual world. The problem is not simply one involving a reduction of sensitivity to sound; it concerns the whole process of structuring an awareness and understanding of things, events, people, and even the self. The hearing-impaired child must develop his perceptions using an auditory system which distorts or even eliminates information that the normal developing child uses to build his understanding of the world. For this reason, it is helpful to consider briefly the role that normal hearing plays in facilitating adaptation to the changing environment.

Man's relationship to his surroundings, including the people in it, is transactional. That is to say, behavior arises from an interplay between the person and his environment. It is the pattern of this relationship which is modified by any handicapping condition. The sensory modalities serve the function of intermediaries between a person and the physical world of people, things, and events. They monitor the world, bringing the brain a continuous flow of information about constantly occurring changes in the person/environment relationship. The normal auditory system plays a critical role in this monitoring process. It responds to the sound patterns generated by events. A direct relationship exists between a sound and its source, since each source gives rise to a characteristic pattern of sound vibrations. This permits us to differentiate among the sound patterns of a vacuum cleaner, a jet engine, footsteps, or a person speaking. Thus, sound serves an important referential function. The auditory characteristics of things and people are as integral a component of them as are the visual, tactile (touch), gustatory (taste), or olfactory (smell) attributes. It is not that hearing creates a world of sound, but that it provides access to the acoustic properties of the physical environment that is already there.

Levels of Auditory Awareness

The level of auditory awareness of the changing environment ranges from reflexive function, as evidenced by an eyeblink response or a flinch evoked by a sharp loud noise, to the very careful listening behavior exhibited by a physician using a stethoscope. It is known that the normal auditory system is functioning physiologically before birth (Johansson, Wedenberg, & Westin, 1964), so that the infant is never without stimulation. Even during sleep, auditory monitoring of the environment continues at a level that serves an arousal function. During the awake state, changes in the general pattern of background acoustic activity automatically activate more conscious levels of perception whenever they exceed preset levels of acceptance. This ever-present preconscious level of background stimulation provides a relationship with the environment which serves as the foundation for conscious auditory awareness. It also provides a foundation for the emotional stability of the hearing individual, creating a necessary sense of the maintenance of an ongoing contact with the environment (Sanders, 1975; Ramsdell, 1970).

Beyond this preconscious level of sound, hearing makes available information about specific events. Infants soon learn to make use of the referential value of sound, attributing meanings to different sound patterns. In this way, the child learns to predict what is happening from what he hears. This perceived relationship between what is heard and what is occurring allows sound to serve a very important alerting function. Hearing, therefore, plays a role in protecting an individual by alerting him to an impending danger. Moreover, since the sound reaching each ear is slightly different (in loudness, time of arrival, and phase), a sound source can be localized quickly, further facilitating appropriate action. This alerting orientation function is not, however, restricted to protection. It also alerts the person to the many everyday events monitored by hearing, such as the telephone, the striking clock, machinery, the end-of-class bell, or his name being called in assembly. Being involved with the world necessitates constant monitoring of events and appropriate adaptive behavior. Thus our auditory system constantly scans the auditory environment, recording all auditory events within its sensitivity range. However, it brings to the conscious awareness of the child only those stimuli associated with events that are relevant to his immediate needs of interest, or those that are strong enough or novel enough to override these present criteria for attention. In this way, hearing permits the child or adult to remain an active participant in the events of his environment and therefore in society.

It is the socialization of man which has resulted in the highest form of auditory perception. Sound, and, therefore, hearing, serves as the most important tool for the interaction of people. Man is influenced, and influences others, primarily through the use of spoken language. It is this ultimate level of auditory perception which expands his perceptual environment to a limitless degree. It is true that the basis for this form of human interaction, verbal language, is not confined to sound transmission; it may be written or signed, using any of several formal systems of visually encoded symbols. Nevertheless, it is spoken language which provides the most efficient and effective system of human interaction, both between individuals and within groups. Speech links together the cognitive-linguistic systems of all parties.

The development of the comprehension and use of spoken language in the child permits learning to occur in a manner that is unequalled by any other system. It not only permits the sophisticated discovery and definition of the environment, but also plays an important role in the child's development of a concept of self and self-worth.

MAJOR FACTORS AFFECTING THE IMPACT OF A HEARING IMPAIRMENT ON A CHILD

The effect of an impairment of hearing, whether it be congenital or acquired, is to prevent or disrupt the normal pattern of interaction between the individual and the world. This occurs because damage to the organ of hearing impairs its ability to record accurately the pattern of the sound wave. The reduced efficiency of the organ of hearing means that some, most, or all of the energy that makes up the sound wave is not recorded by the system.

Type of Hearing Impairment

The type of hearing impairment suffered by most children who need long-term special help in adapting to the demands of the environment is called *sensorineural*. The problem lies in the process of internalizing into the auditory neural pathways the components of the complex sound wave. This occurs at the sensory end-organ with its associated auditory nerve. Sensorineural hearing impairment accounts for almost all congenital hearing disorders. It may also occur at or after birth, as a result of illness or injury which damages the organ of hear-

ing. Unlike most types of the more common *conductive* hearing impairment, in which the organ of hearing is intact, sensorineural hearing impairment is irreversible. A conduction or transmission deficiency more or less reduces all component vibrations fairly evenly. Sensorineural deficits, however, usually reduce sensitivity to some frequency vibrations more than others. A variety of patterns of sensorineural hearing impairment can be observed, but generally the sensitivity to middle and high frequencies is most seriously affected. The uneven character of the loss or reduction of sensitivity adds frequency distortion to the problem of loudness reduction. As a result, even when sound is made loud enough for the child with sensorineural impairment, it is distorted, often to the point of being barely recognizable. By contrast, restoration of loudness to a child with a conductive deafness overcomes the problem almost completely, since the amplified sound energy reaching the organ of hearing is internalized normally.

Although the great bulk of children who need and receive special help in overcoming the handicap of hearing impairment are those with sensorineural deficits, the effects of untreated conductive hearing problems must not be minimized. A conductive hearing deficiency is frequently a potential threat to the general health of the child, since it is often caused by disease of the middle ear. For this reason alone, medical or audiological consultation is imperative for any child suspected of not hearing adequately. One of the characteristics of conductive hearing difficulties is their tendency to fluctuate markedly as the infection subsides and then reoccurs. Thus, the child experiences significant variations in his ability to hear. This is reflected in noticeable changes in his behavior. He tends to be responsive when he hears well, but fails to pay attention, or misinterprets what has been said during those periods when his hearing is poor. He may understand easily when noise levels cause the speaker to raise his voice to overcome the effect of the noise. For the child who has a conductive hearing deficit, this may provide the increased intensity necessary to bring speech within his range of hearing.

Severity of Hearing Impairment

The severity of a hearing deficit refers to the extent of the loss of sensitivity to sound; it reflects how much more intense sound has to be to approximate useful levels of loudness. Normal ranges of sensitivity to sound permit a person to understand speech when it is not more than a whisper, but also to tolerate high noise levels. The functional (useable) range of hearing in man is bounded at the lower limit by the threshold of sound detection, and at the upper limit by discomfort and pain. Speech must be raised above the detection level to be useful for comprehension by hearing alone, without the aid of visual cues. For a comfortable level of conversational speech the intensity must be 100,000 times greater than that needed just to follow the gist of what is said. The result of sensitivity reduction is a narrowing of the area of useable hearing. As the amount of hearing deficit increases, the effect upon the child's ability to relate to his auditory environment becomes more severe. This is particularly true in terms of the ability to understand and use spoken language. Children with mild to moderate hearing deficits will acquire many language competencies naturally, though most of them will need help with more advanced skills. When the hearing deficiency is severe or profound, special intervention programs will be necessary to ensure maximum oral language development.

Severity of hearing impairment is still used as a criterion for classifying children in terms of the type of behavior they will exhibit and the needs they will have. For example, the Annual Survey of Hearing Impaired Children and Youth (1973) classifies

as *deaf,* children with hearing deficits of greater than 85 dB (International Standards Organization) in the better ear. Those children with lesser hearing deficits are classified as *hearing impaired.* The emphasis has fortunately moved progressively away from classification by audiogram toward classification by behavior. However, even this method has very dangerous implications for how a child is treated and, therefore, how he adjusts. This topic will be considered in greater depth in a later discussion. Meanwhile, it is important to recognize that the relationship between the severity of the hearing impairment and the resultant behavior of the child is by no means an absolute one. A wide variety of factors influence his adaptive behavior and achievement. When children are classified by severity of hearing impairment, the expectations for each individual child are derived from observation of the average performance of children who have previously been thus classified. The application of valid and reliable statistical data across groups of children with matching characteristics is justifiable. Predictions concerning the performance of an individual child, however, cannot and should not be made from group data. To do so is to expect too much of some, and far too little of others. Furthermore, the performance of the group is in no small part a measure of the effectiveness of the teaching and intervention procedures. It must be assumed that new methods utilizing new technology may well produce remarkably higher levels of performance. To fail to make this assumption will result in the self-fulfilling prophecy that the children in a given category can only be expected to achieve a predetermined level of performance. That this will be so is ensured by teaching to those expectancies (Ross & Calvert, 1973).

For the purposes of this chapter, the term *hearing impaired* will be used to describe all children with significant levels of hearing deficit from mild to profound. Qualifying terms such as *mild, moderate, severe,* and *profound* serve to indicate the amount of deficit without categorizing the child as functionally deaf or hearing impaired. In this way, it remains clear that no *a priori* assumptions concerning performance and adjustment potentials can be made on the basis of the audiometric information alone.

Pattern of Hearing Impairment

Hearing deficit results from a reduction of sensitivity to sòund energy. Each sound source distributes the multiple energy vibrations in a particular arrangement across the frequency range. The resultant sound-wave pattern, peculiar to its source, becomes referential to that source. Speech also consists of complex energy arrangements which refer to the manner in which the sound wave was produced. The various speech wave patterns, articulated according to the rules of the language, comprise a coded representation of the speaker's linguistic intent. The fidelity of the pattern is, therefore, extremely important in the process of learning to understand and use spoken language and, to a lesser degree, to the continued use of the language already learned.

Sensorineural hearing impairment, in most instances, not only reduces sensitivity to sound energy, but does so in a nonlinear or uneven manner across the normal frequency range. This not only results in a reduction in the loudness of speech and other sounds, but, even more important, it adds a distortion factor by disrupting the relationship between the parts of the complex pattern. This relationship is crucial to the ease and correctness of perception of speech. The pattern of hearing deficit that results from the uneven reduction of loudness is as important as any overall measure of sensitivity. From an understanding of the acoustic structure of different speech sounds it is possible to gain some appreciation of the confusion which a hearing-impaired child experiences when he hears speech. Children's perceptions of speech and en-

vironmental sounds will vary markedly in terms of the severity and pattern of hearing deficit. As a direct result, they will experience various degrees of difficulty in learning to make sense out of the auditory information broadcast by objects, events, and people in their environment. Since sound, particularly speech, plays such an important role in the life of man, difficulty in its reception and interpretation must be expected to be reflected in the developing child's manner of coping with the many demands placed upon him. A direct relationship cannot be said to exist between the severity and pattern of hearing impairment and the child's difficulty in adapting to his world. Nevertheless, it is fair to say that the greater the severity of the hearing deficit, particularly when the speech frequencies are affected, the greater will be the probability of adjustment problems the child will encounter unless help is given early in life.

The Audiogram

The information concerning the severity of the hearing deficit can be conveniently displayed on a chart called an audiogram (Figure 6–1). This chart plots the extent of the deficit at points across the range of frequencies known to be present in speech. The frequencies are indicated on the horizontal scale; the severity of the hearing deficiency is indicated on the vertical scale. The latter is shown as a comparison between the amount of acoustic energy necessary for an average person with normal hearing to first detect sound (0 dB), and the amount needed by the person with deficient hearing. Average normal hearing is represented by the zero level; however, the normal hearing range extends to 20 dB above average threshold (0 dB).

The decibel is a unit which, on a logarithmic scale, represents the ratio between two quantities or amounts, in other words, how much greater B is with reference to A. When a logarithmic scale is used, the com-

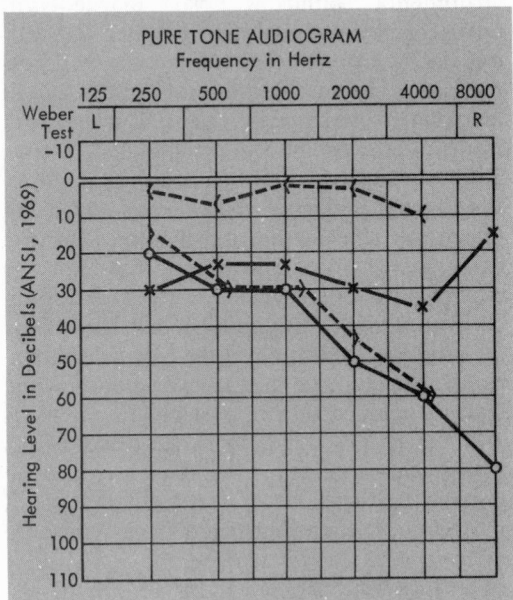

FIGURE 6–1. Pure Tone Audiogram

figuration. The configuration may be described to convey how the severity of the impairment is distributed across the frequency range. Thus, an audiogram may indicate the impairment to be a *moderate high frequency impairment,* a *moderate, flat deficit,* or a *mild, relatively flat hearing deficiency.* A number of occuring patterns may be described in this way.

The audiogram also depicts the subject's hearing sensitivity when, instead of using air-conduction sound via the eardrum and conducting bones (ossicles) of the middle ear, bone-conducted sound is sent to the cochlea by a vibrator placed on the mastoid bone behind the ear. Bone-conduction thresholds are plotted as brackets, pointing right (>) for the right ear and left (<) for the left ear (Fig. 6–1). Bone-conduction testing bypasses the components of the air-conduction pathway (eardrum and ossicles). If the thresholds it produces are superior to those obtained by air-conduction testing, the component represented by the difference between air and bone conduction can be said to be due to a transmission problem (conductive component). The remainder of the deficiency is sensorineural.

Effect of the Hearing Impairment Upon Speech Perception

Since speech sounds comprise a complex interaction of vibrations, their energy is distributed across the frequency range in a pattern characteristic of each particular sound in a particular phonetic context. The pattern and severity of a hearing impairment will determine which components of any given speech sound are available to the listener. As more components are weakened or eliminated, the effect on speech discrimination, and therefore on speech intelligibility, will increase. The distorting effect of different patterns of hearing impairment will differ. Some children will have residual hearing only for low tones. They may respond promptly to sound by virtue of their

parison is expressed in terms of the number of times the first quantity must be multiplied by itself to produce the second quantity. Hearing deficit expressed in decibels is, therefore, a measure of the ratio between the energy (sound pressure) necessary to permit sound detection by a person with normal hearing, and the energy level needed by a person with reduced hearing to perform the same task. Each decibel level indicates how many times greater the sound is when compared to the reference sound pressure to which 0 dB is related.

The audiogram indicates thresholds for single frequency sounds called *puretones,* which are generated by a hearing test instrument called an audiometer. Right-ear thresholds at each discrete frequency tested are indicated by circles; left-ear thresholds, by crosses. The thresholds in decibels *sensation level* (that is, above audiometric zero reference level) are linked together to produce an audiometric pattern, curve, or con-

ability to hear the low-frequency components, but will be quite unable to distinguish between sound sources. Speech, for these children, will be heard as no more than inflectional patterns of the low-frequency components of voice. Other patterns of residual hearing will permit many of the middle-frequency components to be heard, but speech will be lacking in clarity. Comprehension, in this case, will vary depending on such factors as familiarity with the language structure, topic of conversation, quality of listening conditions, and a number of other variables.

As a result, a child with a hearing impairment that distorts speech is likely to exhibit inadequate communication behavior. His responses to speech tend to be erratic, leading to misunderstanding of the problem and mislabeling of the child. Failure by those who relate with the child to understand the perceptual world that underlies his adaptive behavior creates even greater problems for him. Only when the teacher or support personnel have insight into the child's problem, can appropriate behavioral strategies be developed which will facilitate problem solving. To assist the teacher in achieving this goal, the audiologist will provide information about the child's ability to perceive speech.

The speech audiometric data will vary depending upon the child's language competence. For children with fair language development, speech discrimination ability will be stated as the percentage of correctly identified single-syllable words. The word lists usually used were standardized on adults. Each list contains speech sounds in proportion to their incidence in normal conversation. For this reason they are referred to as *phonetically balanced words* (abbreviated PB words or simply PBs). With younger children, or those whose recognition is more limited, a phonetically balanced kindergarten word list is used (PBKs). Variations of this list may be developed by the audiologist to ensure that the words fall

within the individual child's recognition vocabulary. The usual test procedure requires the child to repeat the word spoken by the tester at a comfortable loudness level fed to the child through headphones. Each ear is tested separately. A simpler procedure involves a multiple choice, closed-set response task. Each test word is visually depicted together with three or more other pictures. The names of the items or events are acoustically fairly similar. The child is asked to point to the object or event named. A standardized test used for this purpose is the Word Intelligibility Picture Identification Test (WIPI) (Ross & Lerman, 1971).

The effect of hearing impairment cannot, however, be measured simply in terms of identification of spoken words. There is some question about the relationship between speech intelligibility and speech comprehension (Blesser, 1974; Sanders, 1977), at least in normal-hearing subjects. This relationship in the person with a congenital hearing impairment must be even more suspect. The reason for this is that the ability to perceive speech is so heavily influenced by knowledge of the rules governing language structure. The more familiar a child is with the rules of the language, the less dependent he will be upon the speech signal. With normal hearing and language competency, an adult needs less than 50 percent of the acoustic signal to comprehend spoken language. This assumes that he is familiar with the concepts involved. Few hearing-impaired children have such linguistic competency. Their ability to tolerate a distorted speech signal is, therefore, low. Thus, the highly important contribution that a preconscious knowledge of linguistic structure has on the perception of speech has direct relevance to the problems confronting the child with hearing impairment. One of the most critical factors affecting language acquisition in the hearing-impaired child, and, therefore, his subsequent adaptation and adjustment patterns, is the age at which hearing impairment occurs.

Age of Onset of Hearing Impairment

It has already been stressed that the roots of the child's social adjustment lie in his effectiveness in communication. While it can be argued convincingly that language is not a prerequisite to thought (Furth, 1966), language, of some form, is prerequisite to communication. The form most universally used is spoken language, which is acquired normally through constant exposure to it from birth. It is clear that the infant develops increasing sophistication in the use of hearing as he grows and is exposed for longer waking periods to the spoken language of his culture.

It appears, however, that the infant is responsive to auditory stimulation from the very early age of only a few weeks, or perhaps even from birth. Evidence is accumulating to show that even within the first few weeks of life infants respond selectively to sound, including speech sounds, with a surprising degree of sophistication (see Morse, 1977; Eimas, 1975a). Eisenburg (1970) demonstrated differential emotional responses in babies to sounds of different frequencies (pitches). High-frequency sounds tended to cause distress while low-frequency tones soothed the infant. Several researchers (Morse, 1972; Eimas, 1975; Eilers & Minifie, 1975) have demonstrated that babies can make discriminations between speech sounds even when they are as similar as /p/ and /b/ or /t/ and /d/.

An even more important finding is that, from birth, the infant not only responds selectively in a passive manner to sounds, but actively relates to auditory events in order to exert control over them. For example, in a study by Butterfield (1968), one-day-old infants were given a pacifier which, when sucked, activated a tape recorder to play music. These newborn infants consistently demonstrated extended bursts of sucking, correlated with reinforcement by the music. This was a clear behavioral response

with the purpose of exerting control of the sound stimulus.

Evidence of this nature emphasizes that auditory perceptual function in humans has become so sophisticated that man seems to have incorporated a great deal of basic auditory behavior into his genetic makeup. The acquisition of verbal language seems, therefore, to be a process which the auditory system is ready to begin very soon after birth. Much of the capacity to decipher and acquire the rules of spoken language from information in the acoutsic signal may be innate (Chomsky, 1966). Certainly, hearing is not a prerequisite to the babbling stage of speech. Northern and Downs (1974) have observed that the vocalizations of deaf infants up to 5 or 6 months of age differ in no way from those of their hearing peers. Nevertheless, beyond the initial stage, the activation and shaping of linguistic behavior occurs as a result of environmental exposure to spoken language. The child must hear speech to learn verbal language in a normal manner, and he must hear it constantly in context, for a considerable period of time. Furthermore, it has been argued that there exist optimal periods in a child's early life when language can most easily be learned (McNeill, 1966; Lenneberg, 1967).

A congenital hearing impairment deprives a child of the necessary exposure to language during the critical early years. Language acquisition, as a result, becomes an increasingly laborious process as the age at which intervention is first begun increases. The maximum potential for language achievement also decreases as intervention is delayed. It is believed that temporary sensory deprivation in children produces deprivation of the central processes critical to perception. The effect is believed to persist even when normal sensory function is restored. Elliott and Ambruster (1967), in a study of the effects of delayed diagnosis and treatment of deafness in children, found results to support the hypothesis that hearing-impaired children who are not iden-tified at an early age and who are not provided sound amplification or placed in an appropri-ate educational setting may experience a spe-cial type of sensory deprivation, the effects of which are only partly reversible (p. 223).

These authors go on to state that in many instances subsequent stimulation in small classes and the efforts of highly supportive and conscientious parents failed to compen-sate for the effects of early deprivation.

The age at which deafness occurs, and equally important, the age at which diag-nosis is made and intervention procedures are begun, will have a crucial effect upon the child's subsequent pattern of cognitive development, communication, academic achievement, and social adaptation. The critical factor appears to be whether or not the hearing deficit occurs before the acquisi-tion of verbal language, or at least before language learning processes have been ac-tivated. It is usual, therefore, when con-sidering the impact of hearing impairment upon child development patterns, to dif-ferentiate between two groups of children: those who can be classified as prelingually hearing impaired, and those whose deficit occurred postlingually. This differentiation will be used in subsequent discussion of ad-justment of children with impaired hearing.

Age of Diagnosis and Intervention

The age of onset of hearing impairment as a factor influencing the adaptive behavior of hearing-impaired children cannot be di-vorced from the age at which the problem is diagnosed and intervention procedures are begun. The severity and pattern of hearing impairment sets limits upon how much of speech and environmental sound a child will hear. However, the ultimate achievements of the child will be determined by a variety of factors, not the least of which is the de-gree to which the hearing deficit can be compensated for. The habilitation of con-genitally hearing-impaired children has as

its primary goal the implementation of strategies aimed at developing in the child patterns of learning, communication, and psychosocial adjustment. These strategies are designed to minimize the potentially harm-ful effects of the hearing deficit. It is first and foremost a preventative process, and secondarily an ameliorative process.

Early diagnosis is crucial to maximal re-sults from intervention, since it permits the management of the influences in the child's environment, most particularly parent-child interaction, to maximize normal develop-ment patterns. The early fitting of an ap-propriate hearing aid, the provision of coun-sel and support for the child's parents in their struggle to understand and cope with the implications of having a hearing-im-paired child, the shaping of the child's environment, and his parent's behavior to effect a rich cognitive/linguistic learning climate, are a few of the many intervention procedures which will be effective when ap-plied to the very young child. The psychol-ogy of hearing impairment applies, there-fore, as much to the psychology of family adjustment as it does to the adjustment which will be made by the child.

PARENTAL REACTION TO THE DIAGNOSIS OF HEARING IMPAIRMENT

The Dangers of Generalization

The serious effects that often arise from reacting to the classifying label given to a child have been stressed by Ross and Calvert (1973). The same effect occurs when state-ments, valid when applied to a large group, are applied to an individual or his family. It is all too easy, in writing and reading about handicapped persons, to assume that what is stated applies to every member of the group. No greater disservice can be done to the handicapped individual than to de-prive him of that individuality by assigning him a stereotype personality with its stereotype behavior. No professional person can be excused for the depersonalization of disabled people in this manner. It is the responsibility of the helper to discover the personality of the disabled individual, not to tell him what it is.

This important observation must continuously be borne in mind when reacting to the subsequent information and discussion in this chapter. The broad generalizations made by this author and by others quoted is justified only in terms of observations drawn from large numbers of subjects. The feelings and reactions described are known to be common, but not inevitable. The purpose of the information presented is to help the reader to understand and to sympathise with persons who experience problems. In no instance should the assumption be made that a person either will feel or react according to these group data. Each person is an individual, and must be treated as such.

The emphasis is on the word *may,* not on the word *will.* It is the reader's responsibility to filter what has been written through this cautionary prelude to subsequent discussion.

Normal Expectancies

To understand the experiences which many parents undergo when they discover that their child is handicapped, it is necessary to reflect on the adjustments which a couple begin to make once they become aware of the pregnancy. The need for these adjustments is accentuated at the time of the birth.

The birth of a normal child, particularly the first, often gives rise to a period of some considerable stress. The event changes the very nature of the couple's relationship, and calls for a reassessment of each partner's own self-concept. This necessitates "a continuous mutual and reciprocal set of adjustments" (Worby, 1971). During the pregnancy, the couple explore the idea of parenthood in a far more concrete manner than is possible before the pregnancy. At the same time, expectations begin to be developed concerning what the child will be like, and what its future will hold. These two processes, the adjustment to a parental concept of self and the development of expectancies concerning the child-to-be, play an important role in the subsequent emotional reactions of the parents. Even when the child is not the first in the family, the process is repeated, though generally to a somewhat lesser degree. The anticipations of what the child will be like are derived from perceptions of the actual and desired self, and from perceptions of important others, including parents, husband or wife, brothers and sisters, and earlier children. These perceptions are also influenced by what the culture considers essential in the perfect child (Solnit & Stark, 1961). The child represents, therefore, a potential fulfillment of the parents' unrealized aspirations. This anticipation constitutes an essential component of parenthood. It plays a more dominant role for the mother than the father, because of the mother's function in childbearing (Ross, 1964). Mother and child are intimately related from conception. She assumes responsibility for the nurture of her child, and has to face and deal with her doubts concerning her potential adequacy for the task of motherhood. Later, she may blame herself for any defects the child may have.

The father's role differs. He is provider in another sense. The father's image of his child-to-be is more likely to emphasize hopes for the future than the present. He contemplates the things he and his child will do together, the pride he will feel in his offspring's achievements. For the father, the testing of these hopes is deferred. He will not have to face with the same immediacy, the implications of his child's being hearing impaired or otherwise less than perfect (Boles, 1959). Most fathers have limited contact with their young infant. The child is often asleep when the father leaves for work and ready for bed when he returns. The weekends thus provide the only extended period of father-child contact. It should be noted, however, that in a study that included an investigation of the extent of the participation of the fathers of disabled children in early childcare practices, fathers were found to be quite active (Barsch, 1968). The best image of the husband's helpfulness during the feeding and diapering period was presented by the mothers with deaf children and those whose infants were blind. The general finding reported by Barsch was that both parents acted cooperatively in child rearing during infancy period.

Parents in Western cultures are encouraged to have children, but as Zuk (1962) and Kvaraceus and Hayes (1969) have pointed out, this expectation is predicated upon the assumption that the children will be normal and capable of making a desired contribution to a society that is highly competitive in nature. Society's attitude toward those who are unable to make the expected contribution, or who are not believed to be capable of doing so, has been ambivalent at best. Furthermore, relatives (particularly grandparents, who are only once removed from parentage) as well as friends confer praise on the parents when the child conforms to their image of desirability. In such expectations lie many of the problems which must be confronted by the parents when they learn that their child is hearing impaired.

Confrontation with this reality does not usually occur within the first 6 months of their child's life. Hearing impairment is a physical deficiency which in most cases is revealed only by deviations in developmental response to sound. While the condition is commonly congenital, it is not visible at birth; nor are its effects apparent to the untrained observer until months, or sometimes even years, later. It has already been pointed out that even children with little or no residual hearing babble in a manner which is undistinguishable from that of hearing children. Moreover, it has been demon-

strated that the severely hearing impaired child increases vocal output just as a normal child as a result of the visual reinforcement arising from people speaking to him (Northern & Downs, 1974). Thus, during this period, the parents' emotional ties to their apparently normal infant grow in a normal manner.

Normal Parent-Child Interaction

The role of parenthood is a learned one. The image of parenthood, as has been stated, is derived from the knowledge and perception of one's own parents and from the observation of societal expectancies. However, the greatest learning occurs when a couple become parents themselves. This is particularly true for the mother. One of the important influences in her adjustment to her new role is the influence of the appearance and behavior of her child (Gordeuk, 1976). The early developmental behavior of the hearing-impaired child does not deviate significantly from that of his hearing peers. Thus, the parent-child interaction patterns, predicated upon the perceived normality of the infant, evolve naturally. The relationship is based upon a growing definition by the mother of her role as a parent, and her increasing confidence in her ability to accommodate the demands that arise from that role. In this sense, the psychological implications of hearing impairment do not become operative until after the parents have stabilized their new family relationships, until after the mother has been reassured falsely of the wholeness of her child. The empathy of both parents increases rapidly during these early months, together with their confidence in their own ability to appreciate and respond effectively to the needs of the child. MacKeith (1973) stresses that parents learn to love their child, that love is not present *ab initio* (p. 69), but grows during the early weeks.

This normal relationship between the parents and their as-yet-undiagnosed hearing-impaired child continues, in most instances, well into the second half of the child's first year of development, even when the hearing impairment is severe. When there is considerable residual hearing for low-tone components of speech, the normal parent-child relationship may extend through the second year before serious doubts about the child's ability to communicate begin to grow primarily in the mother's mind. The importance of the normality of this early parent-child interaction makes the subsequent diagnosis of abnormality even harder to accommodate than when it is made soon after birth.

Suspicions, Diagnosis, and Reactions

The most alert parents, particularly those who have an older, normal-hearing child, may begin to have vague concerns about a baby when the babbling decreases without the anticipated progress into the normal use of the jargon that represents a mimicking of adult speech patterns. Parents may also observe a reduction in the child's responsiveness to their communications. Something seems to be wrong. Sometimes these suspicions that all is not well with the child do not occur until much later. Suspicions always result in anxiety.

Frequently, the mother may be unable to communicate her anxiety, partly because she does not yet have a concrete idea of what it is that causes her concern. When she does express her anxiety to other family members, she is often met with assurances that she is worrying unnecessarily (Malkin, Freeman, & Hastings, 1976), that some children take longer than others to begin to talk—an observation which is not incorrect. The anxiety grows, however, as the child conforms less and less to normal expectancies. At some point, the mother consults her pediatrician or family physician. Unfortunately, the evidence shows that in the majority of the instances this fails to lead to rapid identifica-

tion of the problem. In from 25 percent (Sarlin & Altshuler, 1970) to 54 percent (Malkin, *et al.,* 1976) of the cases, the possibility of hearing impairment is rejected by the physician. The parent is once more reassured that nothing is wrong (Rainer, Altshuler, and Kallmann, 1969).

This delay in diagnosis of hearing impairment, which ranges from $8\frac{1}{2}$ to 25 months depending on the severity of the impairment (Malkin *et al.,* 1976), extends the period of insecurity and growing anxiety experienced by the mother. It frequently disrupts the normal pattern of interaction and the developing triadic relationship of mother, father, and child (Worby, 1971). By the time the parents are able to obtain a definitive assessment of the child's behavior, it is not uncommon for a high level of anxiety to exist.

When a diagnosis of hearing handicap is made, most frequently in terms of "deafness"—a word that has enormous negative emotional impact, the parents frequently experience a major trauma. Up to this time, the parent-child relationship has been established on normal expectations. It has been based upon the mother's sense of confidence in her role, on her self-image as a successful parent of a normal infant. A diagnosis of hearing impairment, with the associated implications of physical handicap and imperfection, is likely to shatter this relationship. The trauma and associated grief have been described as highly similar to that experienced by parents when their child dies. An understanding of this reaction constitutes an essential component in a knowledge of the psychology of hearing impairment in children.

Much has been written on the topic of parental reaction to the realization that their child is less than perfect (Gordeuk, 1976; MacKeith, 1973; Kvaraceus & Hayes, 1969; Ross, 1964). The effects may be viewed in terms of the impact on the mother's image of herself, on her image of her child, and on her ability to relate to her child on the basis of expectancies arising from awareness and knowledge of developmental behavior. To a lesser extent, the father faces the same problems. The result is a disruption of the preparatory and adaptive process of parenthood, which prevents further normal development of the role (Gordeuk, 1976).

The seriousness of this effect cannot be too strongly stated. Gasson (1966) considers the impact of unresolved, adverse family reaction to be so harmful as to constitute a greater threat to the child's development than does the disability itself. Worby (1971), in considering the role of parents in relation to the normal child, states: "Besides getting a sense of the world through his parents, the child's emerging sense of self is highly dependent upon how his parents see him." As a result of the diagnosis, parents almost always experience depression (Altshuler, 1976; 1974). They no longer have the same child. The normal child for whom they had such hopes, and to whom they had learned to relate with confidence and pride, has been replaced by a child who represents the unknown (Altshuler 1974).

Subsequent adaptive behavior seems to follow a common pattern characterized by three stages (Gordeuk, 1976; Solnit & Stark, 1961).

1. *Shock and disbelief,* frequently resulting in denial of the problem. Unable to accept the reality, the mother often may seek to repudiate the diagnosis through attempts to normalize the child in her own perceptions (Kapke, 1970). This is a period of intense disappointment accompanied by reexperience of the hopes and dreams she held for her normal child.
2. *Awareness of the reality of the loss of the normality of her child,* and a balancing of this by a gradual realization of the implications of the diagnosis in objective terms. Solnit and Stark (1961) emphasize that during this period the mother is learning to cope with the reality of the defective child and the equally real loss of her desired child.
3. *Mourning of the lost child,* which gradually

resolves the grief. The loss is acknowledged, and the emptiness of the child's future is acutely felt. During this stage, the parents begin to be capable of developing a relationship with their handicapped child. Yet, they are faced with the fact that the child represents a constant reminder of their lost aspirations. Altshuler describes this.

> The parental dilemma is how to love a child who represents such a reminder. Anger is evoked by the insolubility of the problem and the presence of the handicap; and anger, threatening to spill over at the child, in turn elicits and enhances guilt about responsibility for the handicap (1974, p. 369).

It is of considerable interest to note that severely hearing-impaired parents whose children are born with the same handicap appear to react differently to the diagnosis. Schlesinger (1969) states:

> Deaf parents of deaf children appear to expect the diagnosis and to accept it at a much earlier age. (They) cope with the crisis of diagnosis more easily and quickly while their hearing counterparts prolong and intensify it. Even following the diagnosis, deaf parents appear to be more comfortable with their deaf children, admit to fewer eating and toilet training problems, and permit earlier independence and autonomy. Once the initial diagnosis is made, deaf parents are less likely to seek confirmatory diagnosis or a miraculous cure.

It appears, therefore, that once the initial shock has been adjusted to, the major psychological problem confronted by the parents of most hearing impaired children is that of filling the void left by the loss of their earlier child-image. They must develop a whole new set of expectancies appropriate to their new child. They must learn to feel close to a child that is strange (Altshuler, 1976). Sensitive, realistic counsel by a person who is aware of the processes of adjustment and skilled in relating to people is, regrettably, too often not available. Parents frequently must go through the tortuous adjustment period alone, despite the fact that data indicate that families with a handicapped child are vulnerable to breakdown, and that mothers and siblings appear to be in most jeopardy (Connor, Rusalem, & Cruickshank, 1971).

Appropriate early intervention designed to minimize the effects of hearing impairment in childhood has made great advances in helping parents to deal with the major practical issues of management of their children's developmental needs. In so doing, they contribute much to minimizing the psychological impact of hearing impairment. This, to a major extent, arises from the effect of the deficit upon the development of normal patterns of communicative interaction between the child and his parents, and later between the child, his peers, and important adults. These patterns of adjustment are established during the early preschool years.

ADJUSTMENT IN THE PRESCHOOL YEARS

It will be the purpose of the remainder of the chapter to examine the difficulties commonly experienced by the hearing-impaired child or young person as he progresses through the preschool and school years. In accord with the previous emphasis on these problems as being family-centered in nature, consideration will be given to the adjustments to be achieved by the child as a member of the family unit.

As a result of difficulty in separating the psychologically significant effects of the disability from normal patterns of adjustment demanded by this handicapping condition, considerable misunderstanding of individual and family behavior often occurs (Cruickshank, 1948). Cruickshank emphasizes the need to be aware of two types of psychological adjustment problems encountered by the disabled child. These are: (1) those which might be expected to occur as a part of the

process of normal development. These problems arise from the effort to expand the self while maintaining the integrity of the self-concept already established; and (2) those problems arising specifically from the interference in the achievement of desired goals by the effect of the disability itself. It has been pointed out that these two types of problems are closely interwoven (Connor, Rusalem, & Cruickshank, 1971). However, it is essential to avoid a concept of the adjustment mechanisms of individuals and families which attributes all deviant behavior to the disability itself. Such an attitude deprives the disabled person and his family of the essential normality of their behavior. It exacerbates the impact of the stigma that must be dealt with.

Instead of concentrating upon the labeling of behavior as "characteristic of a parent with a hearing-impaired child," or "typical of the deaf," it is necessary to focus upon the rationale for such behavior. The assumption may be made that all behavior represents an attempt to deal with a situation, to resolve a problem within the individual's perceived alternatives. The individual's adjustment patterns, thus, must be viewed as normal for the problem *as he perceives it*. Lack of appropriate understanding of the nature of the problem leads to the development of inappropriate expectancies, with the resulting ineffective behavior.

Parental Concerns

Parents of the very young hearing-impaired child may at first pursue a variety of solutions to the problem of their infant. Many of these are recognized by the professional as being doomed to be nonproductive. Sensitive counseling directed at helping the parents to come to know the true nature of the problem they confront, together with experiences arising from their own search for a solution, in most cases leads to a growing acceptance of the child and an increasing awareness of alternative approaches to their difficulties. For this reason, effective management of the adjustment needs of the preschool hearing-impaired child is parent-centered rather than child-centered. The parents, in gradually becoming knowledgeable of the nature of their child's disability, develop the capacity to approach problems cognitively, making possible the difficult undertaking of "realigning mental operations with an undesirable, inescapable situation" (Gordeuk, 1976, p. 64). They learn to understand and accept their intense negative feelings, and begin to want to work with preschool guidance specialists to formulate new expectancies and new strategies for problem solving. At this point, the availability of factual information about hearing impairment and the limitations it places upon certain systems of communication and learning is essential. An awareness of the resources and methods available to maximize the child's ability to surmount these limitations will help to assure a comfortable parent-child relationship and to preserve "the nutrient matrix in which healthy development can flourish" (Altshuler, 1976, p. 116).

Parent-Child Interaction

The primary goal during the preschool years of the hearing-handicapped child is to reestablish the natural parent-child relationship essential to normal psychological development. Initially, the mother's perceptions of her child are in terms of her own inadequacies. However, once she begins to feel more comfortable with her now-identified disabled infant, this anxiety begins to give way to a more outwardly directed concern for social acceptance of the child (Mercer, 1970). At this time the mother needs practical guidance and support in the task of developing new, positive, but realistic expectancies. It is understandable that she may again have serious doubts about whether she can learn to be a "good" mother, this time to a hearing impaired child. Supportive help, involvement in prac-

tical management issues, and the normal potential of the child for growth and development, given appropriate stimulation and learning conditions—all serve to help parents regain self-confidence. Within the limits of their situation, parents are usually anxious to commit themselves to do all they can to help their child. However, they will need considerable support, for much will be demanded of them.

The most acute source of stress for both the parents and the child lies in the difficulty they will have in communication. Schlesinger (1969) describes this problem as "traumatic." The difficulties, along with frustration and anxiety, begin even before the age at which verbal interaction would normally occur. It has already been stressed that infant behavior is responsive to auditory feedback within a few weeks of birth. The probably innate responsiveness to the human voice, mentioned earlier, allows the child with normal hearing to maintain a sense of well-being through the awareness of mother's voice. Later, this referential use of sound will be extended to include other sounds made by mother as she pursues her activities within reach of the baby's hearing. Thus, the child is helped to stabilize his perception of his environment. The parent-focused environmental monitoring lays the foundation for communication. The mother expects growing anticipatory behavior in her child, and rewards it by her natural responses.

Deprivation or limitation of hearing prevents or impairs this normal process. The result is that the child is limited in his comprehension of his environment and in his development of appropriate adaptive behavior (Kennedy, 1973). The normally developing patterns of parent-child interaction are disturbed. The situation is usually further aggravated by the awareness of the mother that her infant cannot hear her. Lacking knowledge and experience in relating to hearing-impaired children, the parent feels inadequate in handling the child. The inclination not to talk as much, or at all, to the infant who cannot hear, is common. The parents may also feel that they must speak with exaggerated articulation, or unusual slowness. The situation becomes a far greater source of anxiety when the child reaches the age at which the parent expects to be able to control his behavior and stimulate his learning through the normal channel of verbal communication.

Language Delay and Resultant Adjustment Difficulties

Language development, both its comprehension and use by a normal child, appears to be such a natural process that parents give little thought to the all-pervading role it plays in the child's interaction with his environment and the people in it. There is evidence to show that an innate reciprocal relationship exists between the speech of an adult and the patterns of an infant's bodily movements, even in newborn babies. Furthermore, it is believed that this probably represents the mechanism by which the foundations of spoken language are laid. Condon and Sander (1973) have shown that as early as the first day of life, the newborn moves his whole body in precise and sustained patterns that are synchronized with the articulatory structure of adult speech.

The mother-child bond appears to be dependent from the very beginning on hearing and on spoken language. Later, the parent uses speech to define the child's experiences, to guide him in knowing his world, to protect him from potential dangers, to help him cope with his frustrations, anger, fear, and terrors. Spoken language is used to localize the source of pain or discomfort, and to soothe hurt bodies and feelings. Thus, the continued development and definition of this parent-child bond is also heavily dependent on speech communication. As language competency grows, the child's participation in this interpersonal interaction becomes increasingly active. The inter-

change serves growing cognitive and emotional needs, facilitating the process of parent-child separation. The ties of the parent, initially physical in nature, can be extended through the use of spoken language. Through definition, description, warnings, and even threats, the parent uses language to instill a model of parent values and judgments concerning what is safe and socially acceptable behavior. The child internalizes the parent image and is able to recreate verbally the language content of instructions and warnings. Church (1963) has described the very different nature of the thought processes of the prelingual and postlingual child. It is no longer believed that thought is not possible without language (Furth, 1966), but the development of a sophisticated system of symbolic representation changes the processes by which thought and memory occur.

A congenital hearing deficiency disrupts or prevents this whole process of language and communication development. Its effects reach into every aspect of the child's intellectual and social growth and, in most instances, will place a heavy strain on the elements of normal psychological growth and on the developing parent-child relationship.

The anxiety and frustration experienced by a mother will be related to her ability to anticipate her child's needs. The increasing complexity of those needs demands a coding system of equal sophistication in order to identify them. At the same time, the mother needs to be able to use language to modify and control her child's behavior. A language system is essential for dealing with the elements of time and place outside the immediate context, in the "not-here-not-now" situation. Without verbal language, the mother's relationship to the child remains bound to situational cues, pointing and gesturing, and her ability to pre-guess the child's needs. In Meadow's words, "Those who do not have language are restricted by the tyranny of both time and space" (1976, p. 71). It is not possible to modify behavior of a severely hearing-impaired child through persuasion, or to distract him quickly in a situation of immediate threat, such as reaching for the handle of a pan of hot water. When the non-speaking child cries, it is often almost impossible to discover the cause of the behavior, or to help him to absorb and cope with the event when it is known.

The frustration and sense of helplessness, the anger and resultant guilt that this worsening situation creates becomes, for many parents, an almost intolerable burden. The situation is a serious one, for, deprived or limited in their means of communication, the very nature of their relationship is at stake.

The situation described represents one encountered by many parents who have a hearing-impaired baby. It does not apply to all families. What must be stressed is that the difficulties of parent-child interaction and of child-management practices, which all parents experience, are enormously complicated by any limitations placed upon the ability of parent and child to interact through a system of symbolic communication. The extent to which this occurs is a function of a range of factors, including those discussed earlier. In addition to the natural variability of potential abilities and manifest behavior of hearing-impaired infants, the resilience of each family will differ. Some cope remarkably well from the time the diagnosis is made; others need every possible means of support to retain their viability.

Language Intervention

It has been emphasized that language difficulties lie at the root of the problems directly related to the impairment of hearing. The effects of the resultant parent-child communication difficulty have been discussed. It seems obvious, therefore, that a lowering of parent frustration and anxiety might be expected to accrue merely from the knowledge that a systematic approach to remediation of this major problem has begun. For many parents whose children have been shown to have mild or moderate hearing impairments, this assumption proves true. Those parents whose children are believed to have only small amounts of useable residual hearing are seldom so fortunate. This group of parents, instead of finding relief through unequivocal guidance in dealing with the task of stimulating language growth in the child, often find their confusion and anxieties multiplied (Rhodes, 1972). They discover that they are caught up in a most unfortunate and unpleasant conflict between two widely differing views of how to teach language to severely hearing-impaired children. The debate is over the question of whether these children should be taught "orally" or by a method commonly referred to as "total communication" (Simmons-Martin, 1976).

Oral Method

The oral method is more accurately described as auditory/visual/oral. Teaching depends exclusively upon the child's ability to make maximal use of his limited residual hearing, augmented by the recognition of the visible cues to speech ('speech reading" or "lip reading"). The recoding of auditory information into tactile cues using a vibratory keyboard may further aid in the development of the ability to comprehend spoken language. Speech production is taught utilizing the same sensory inputs (Ling, 1976; Calvert & Silverman, 1975). There are a number of refinements to the pure auditory approach to oralism (Krug, 1968; Hart, 1964; Groht, 1958), but essentially they are all based upon the conviction that both language and speech can be taught this way and that academic content information can be learned through spoken and written language.

Even within the oral school, schisms exist.

One concerns the issue of whether all sensory modalities should be used in teaching speech and language (Sanders, 1971), or whether teaching should be confined primarily to the use of the auditory modality (Stewart, Pollack & Downs, 1964; Pollack, 1970; Rupp, 1971).

Total Communication Method

The advocates of this method adhere to the philosophy that every possible means of communicating with the severely hearing-impaired child should be exploited. The primary emphasis is on the development of cognitive and linguistic skills, rather than on speech communication. Total communication, therefore, may include, along with spoken language, the use of finger spelling and any of several systems of sign language. It is not within the scope of this chapter to consider the various manual-sign systems currently in use. Excellent reviews are available (Quigley, 1966; Wilbur, 1976; Northern & Downs, 1974).

The total-communication approach has become widely accepted and is used in teaching both preschool and school-age children. A review of studies offered in support of this approach has been provided by Nix (1975). A somewhat more philosophical treatment of the topic can be found in Garretson's discussion (1976). However, strong opposition has been voiced to the method by supporters of the auditory/oral approach. Oralists believe that only by placing heavy demands upon the use of residual hearing at an early age will the auditory system become organized to extract meaning from speech. Many oralists object that despite claims to the contrary, total communication in practice is not total. They argue that the approach simply disguises the teacher's emphasis upon the use of manual communication (Moffatt, 1972; Lloyd, 1973).

At the present time it is hard to resolve the conflict between these two schools of thought. Cogent arguments can be made in support of both approaches. However, relatively little is known about the nature of the auditory process involved in learning to understand and use speech. Even less is known about the effect of stimulating two sensory systems simultaneously, particularly when different patterns of linguistic information are used. What is clear is that the issue should not be approached in the political terms of proving one method to be correct, or even superior. To do so is to make the a priori assumption that all children will learn best by one method. The task must be to determine the criteria for selecting a method most appropriate for a given child. How is an early decision to be made that a child does or does not have the potential to learn, to understand, and to speak intelligibly? How can it be determined whether a child will or will not have the capacity to acquire cognitive, linguistic, and academic knowledge through the use of spoken language? Even if the information becomes available, and the political decisiveness is resolved, there remain considerable logistical problems in making available both systems in all communities.

The concern here is not to provide a careful review of systems of teaching very severely hearing-impaired children. The purpose of the foregoing discussion is to indicate the turmoil that parents frequently encounter when, of necessity, they come face to face with the theoretical and political debates that rage over teaching methods. This occurs at the same time when frustration arising from acute communication problems with their child are at a peak. Thus, instead of finding relief, the parents are faced with even more complex problems which only add to tension and anxiety. The enrollment of the parent and child in a preschool program that uses one or the other method may not eliminate the anxiety (Rhodes, 1972). The parents continue to wonder whether the training their child is receiving is the most appropriate. This is particularly true in situations where the parents were not involved in the discussion concerning which method would be used, or where only one method is available. Parents meet other parents whose children are being taught by the alternative method. Since both parents have usually become politicized by the advocates of the two opposing schools of thought, each raises serious questions and even doubts in the other's mind. Parents are also exposed to conflicting arguments concerning methods of teaching, in various paraprofessional journals and even in popular magazines (Kenny, 1962). Having doubts concerning whether the best choice has been made for their child is a worrying experience for any parent. If a child's oral-communication skills are not developing as rapidly as expected, concern and frustration will be high. On the other hand, the fact that the child uses sign language but seems not to attempt to speak, presents similar doubts.

Communication and Child-Management Patterns

It is clear that the communication between the parents and their severely hearing-impaired child is extremely limited during the important early developmental years. As Meadow points out, these are the years "when parents and children would ordinarily have the most constant and exclusive contact with each other" (1976, p. 2). Piaget has stressed that:

> Until a definite form of language is acquired, interpersonal relations are limited to the imitation of corporal and other external gestures and to a global affective relationship without differentiated communication. With language, by contrast, the inner life can be communicated. In fact, thought becomes conscious to the degree to which the child is able to communicate it (1967, p. 19).

Rainer (1969) believes that the barriers of communication, which disrupt interpersonal relationships, have a cumulative effect upon the child's emotional and social devel-

opment. The effects of the communication breakdown can be seen in the manner in which the parents are forced to relate to the management of their child. The physical control, which in the normal hearing child is gradually replaced by verbal control, must be retained as the basis of the management of the child with little language. Problems can be dealt with only as they occur. The parent must use a minute-by-minute management model since it is not possible to caution the child verbally. Punishment is resorted to more frequently as a training method, and is of necessity more physical; all too frequently, the child does not understand why he was punished. The parent realizes this, often regrets the action he was forced to take, and experiences guilt for administering what is felt to be an unavoidable but unfair form of punishment. On many occasions, the parents must demand obedience without the ability to communicate the reason for the demand. "Because I say so," in too many instances must suffice. Without the explanation to indicate what it is in his behavior that is unacceptable, without an understanding of the appropriateness of behavior (for example, why he is punished for something when out with mother, but not punished for the same behavior at home), social contextual rules cannot be acquired. In other words, the parents cannot teach the child the contingencies for punishment and reward.

An equally frustrating management situation arises from the problem of communicating past or future events. As has been explained, if past experience cannot be reconstructed verbally, the parent has great difficulty in cautioning a child about the implications of anticipated behavior. For the same reason, great difficulty will be encountered in communicating to a child why a particular demand cannot be satisfied immediately or, perhaps, at all. The frustrated child, deprived of the justification for the rejection of his demand, unable to communicate his anger verbally, is very likely to throw a temper tantrum. The parent reacts to this either by punishment, which is often against his own better judgment, or by succumbing to the demand, also recognized as an inadequate solution.

> The deaf child does not learn easily to control his demands for immediate gratification by learning that sometimes he can expect to be given something at a later time (Meadow, 1976, p. 4).

The difficulty of controlling the behavior of the hearing-impaired child with little verbal language results in a pattern of parent management which fosters dependency in the child (Malkin, et al., 1976). It is simply easier to do things for the child than to try to explain and teach how they should be done. Dependency in the deaf child fosters self-helplessness; the child comes to believe that his own actions will not influence or relate to the outcome of events and experiences, that he is not capable of being effective in a need situation (Hooker, 1976; Dweck, 1976; Parke, 1976). This has considerable implications for the child's developing self-esteem. The dependency of early childhood, particularly in a child-management model which reinforces it, may have cumulative effects. Just as complex skills are based upon the acquisition of simpler prerequisite abilities, so the ability to assume responsibility for more important aspects of one's life is dependent upon having competently handled, simpler responsibilities. The cumulative effects of this are illustrated by Meadow (1976), who cautions professionals against working with the parents of the adolescent or young adult who is deaf, rather than encouraging older children to begin to assume responsibility for their own lives.

The important point of this discussion is that the limited communication skills which young, severely hearing-impaired children demonstrate represent a major problem in terms of child management. The difficulties

the parents have in understanding the child's needs, in modifying his behavior, and in encouraging independence, together with the child's inability to react to frustration in acceptable ways, frequently result in childhood behavioral disorders (Altshuler, 1974).

Parents do the best they can to cope. The success that families have in handling stress will vary as a function of the richness of the personalities of the family members. The richer the personality, the more variety the individual's repertoire of responses and ways of adapting (Robinson, 1970). Great understanding is required on the part of those who work to minimize family stress arising from having a child with a hearing impairment. Primarily required is the noncritical acceptance of family reactions. Parents should not be blamed for their inability to cope, for these are the families most in need of professional support. The adjustment of the family members to the child's disability is of primary importance, since their attitudes will play a major role in the development of the child's self-image (Meadow, 1976; Worby, 1971).

Preschool Development and Problems

The child's early development is almost exclusively dependent upon the interaction of innate determinants, with the influences exerted by his immediate family (Gesell & Armatruda, 1945). Essential to the healthy psychological adjustment of a child is the development of satisfactory relationships with his parents.

> Without proper relationships, there is no doubt that the growing child may have no outlet for his impulsive needs and restlessness. He may, therefore, behave destructively, have temper tantrums and, in a vicious circle of parental interaction, may further alienate the parents. The important process of learning how to adjust to parents, with its trials and tribulations, its rewards and punishments and finally its internalized set of psychological

rules, is necessary for the development of a social sense and feeling for others. If this broad educational process is shut out by reason of isolation at home, the child may grow up with severe difficulties in this area. The development of conscience and of the ability to handle power and the formation of proper self-identification are also direct consequences of the relationship to the family and depends upon communication (Rainer & Altshuler, 1973, p. 154).

Thus, adjustment of a child with a hearing impairment will be influenced greatly by the degree of adjustment that the family makes to the reality of his disability and their attitudes toward it (Sussman, 1970). The child comes to know himself as a person in terms of how others respond to him—most particularly his family, and later his playmates, teachers, and other significant adults with whom he comes into contact. The child whose parents are able to come to terms with the hearing handicap, who accept it as an integral part of him, will experience positive feedback. His disability will be dealt with in a practical manner, with little emotion. This child will tend to develop a self-image that is not significantly affected by the hearing impairment. If, however, the parents have been unable to resolve their negative feelings, experience feelings of shame or embarrassment, or have not developed a feeling of closeness with their "different" child, the child will be aware of the absence of true positive emotion and behavior, and most likely will experience negative cues. These negative or positive projective feelings will constitute the raw material from which the self-image must be developed.

The older preschool child, for example, is very sensitive to parental attitudes to the hearing aid he must wear. He learns whether it is considered a stigma, or whether it is simply an aid to hearing. He observes his parents' reactions to his poor speech intelligibility in the presence of others, the fact that he gestures to make himself understood,

or that he asks questions loudly in quiet places. In many ways, the child learns that he is acceptable as a child, but he may also learn that in many ways he is unacceptable as a child with a hearing impairment. Since deafness is not a visible handicap, the parents and the child are faced with the dilemma of whether to conceal the stigma, and thus deny the true self, with the ever-present risk of disclosure, or to reveal it and accept the anticipated negative reaction. The problems of the discredited and the discreditable are complex, and cannot be discussed here. An excellent treatment of this aspect of stigma has been provided by Goffman (1963).

The problems involved in developing a positive self-regard in the hearing world increase as the child moves beyond the protective world of the family. As the child grows beyond the age at which hearing children become highly verbal, his differentness becomes increasingly noticeable. His attempts to communicate, or his failure to try, identify him as not normal. The number of stress situations which he and his parents encounter increase. Involvement in a preschool program for hearing children, or participation in an integrated hearing/hearing-impaired preschool as part of a special program brings the child into continuous contact with the demands and expectancies of the hearing world.

For the child with a very severe hearing deficit, nursery school placement represents the beginning of the conflict over the method of teaching language. He may experience the side effects of parental concerns originating from reluctant participation in a program which uses total communication because no alternative exists, or from increasing frustration as the child fails to do well in an auditory/oral program. A child inappropriately placed in an oral program will not learn to communicate acceptably well with the teacher or his peers in class. The effectiveness of communication among severely hearing-impaired children, in general, has been shown to be poor (Hoemann, 1972). However, it should be noted that, in a study of preschool programs for hearing-impaired children, which represented different communication methods, the children used sign language to communicate with each other regardless of the type of communication system to which the school was committed (Tervoort & Verbeck, 1967; Moores, McIntyre, & Weiss, 1972; Moores, Weiss, & Goodwin, 1974). Thus, children in an oral program may develop feelings of guilt about using manual communication with their peers. This arises from the fact that often they are chastised for its use by orally committed teachers or parents.

Control of Child Behavior

One of the major problems faced by the parents of any disabled child arises from the concern which they experience in administering discipline. Unlike his hearing peer, the hearing-impaired child cannot plead his case. His gesticulations and facial grimaces, made in an attempt to explain the situation, frequently are misinterpreted by parents or other authority figures as an aggressive reaction to punishment. This problem is one that persists as long as the communication gap does (Rodda, 1974). As a result of the communication difficulties and of inappropriate parent management strategies, hearing-impaired children often experience an exaggeration of the behavioral difficulties that characterize the development of a normal-hearing child (Vernon, 1969). Altshuler (1974) has emphasized that such behavioral problems are as much problems of the family as they are of the child. Given his immaturity, the child is limited in the ways in which he can react to stress. It is not uncommon for the child to convert the stress from conflict and frustration into such symptoms as irritability, aggression, temper tantrums, or eating and sleeping problems. In some instances, the symptom may arise from a problem directly related to the effect of the hearing deficit. For example, the refusal to go to sleep without a light on, or

insistence on having a parent present in the room, is not unreasonable for a child whose contact with the world around him is lost once his eyes are closed or the physical presence of the parent is removed. However, Altshuler stresses that the relationship between the behavioral symptoms and the underlying cause is rarely direct. He states that, "the entire repertoire may be brought into effect by a wide gamut of tension-evoking circumstances" (1976, p. 32). Parents of hearing-impaired children are as well equipped to deal with these problems as parents of normal children. It is understandable, however, that the total demands placed upon them by all factors in their lives, together with the particular problems of learning to help their handicapped child, may prove to be beyond their personal resources for coping. The reaction of parents to this overload situation may be to become overprotective, requiring little disciplined behavior in the child, succumbing to temper tantrums, yielding to demands, and rearranging the family relationships to accommodate the child's difficult behavior. Often when this happens, there is increasing friction among family members. The father and mother may disagree on how to handle the child's behavior. The child may come to serve as a scapegoat for other problems facing the parents.

A more common pattern of handling problems arising from communication difficulties is for the parents to adopt an autocratic relationship to the child. Since explanations for expectancies and demands cannot be given, the child is required to do things because the parent demands that they be done. Much of the time, the parent simply does for the child what he should be capable of doing for himself. It takes enormous amounts of time, patience, and often inconvenience to foster self-reliance in a normal preschool child. Schlesinger and Meadow (1971) have shown that the mothers of hearing-impaired children exerted far more direct control over their child's behavior than mothers of hearing children. The mothers studied allowed the child less freedom of action, were less flexible in responding to the child's needs and behavior, and gave less positive feedback or encouragement. It must be remembered that these are simply mothers who have hearing-impaired children; they are not a special breed of mother. Many of the parents have other normal-hearing children. Thus, their way of handling the child must be seen as the reaction of a normal parent to an abnormal situation. The parent is not abnormal; only the task is.

In summary of this section, it is stressed, therefore, that a hearing impairment in a young child will result in special demands being placed on all members of the family. The extent and severity of those demands will depend primarily on the degree to which they impede the development of the normal communication bond between child and parent. A number of factors will contribute to this; however, generally speaking, the more severe the hearing deficit, the greater the amount of family adjustment that will be called for. Since the communication gap is minimized when the parents themselves are severely hearing impaired, the adjustment problems of hearing-impaired children in these families are likely to be less.

ADJUSTMENT IN THE EDUCATIONAL YEARS

Preschool Education

Structured education for the normal child begins with kindergarten or first grade at age 5 or 6 years. If structured education is the criterion for identifying the beginning of the school years, then it is necessary to recognize that for the hearing-impaired child this may begin as young as $2\frac{1}{2}$ years of age. Kennedy (1973) has contrasted the nature of the preschool experience of the hearing child with that of his hearing-impaired counterpart. For the normal child, preschool education is aimed at the development of social skill, cooperative play, imagination, and creativity. It is usually a loosely structured learning which these children must achieve to compensate for the reduction in amount of casual learning (which the hearing child acquires through verbal interactions), and this leaves little time for play as a major learning process. Kennedy points out that the preschool education of hearing-impaired children concentrates on the development of specific behaviors; auditory and visual communication training, speech therapy, structured language development and cognitive growth. The process is habilitative in orientation rather than being aimed at fostering independent explorative learning. The goal is to provide the child with the skills necessary for survival, skills which the normal-hearing child acquires naturally, leaving time in preschool for the use of those skills in exploring his world. The whole philosophy of the preschool education of hearing-impaired children is embodied in the term *preschool training*, which is often used to identify this process. Kennedy says:

> The child is therefore expected to conform, to attend, and to function in a structured situation at a much younger age than normal children. Much of the teaching at this level is in training the child to match. The children learn to imitate the positions of the articulators for speech, to imitate the teacher's actions in response to a visual stimulus, to imitate fingerspelling, to imitate writing and the reinforcement is given for the closest match. The children are so trained to match that initiative is effectively discouraged (1973, p. 26).

Lane (1976) has stated that hearing-impaired children become educationally retarded in part because they are deprived of experience in problem solving:

> Parents and teachers of hearing impaired children think for them, anticipate and avoid errors, and prevent the child from learning through trial and error. The justification is that there is so little time to learn so much— and the deaf child grows up without the

experience he needs to attack new problems without the fear of making mistakes (1976, p. 105).

Given these autocratic environmental experiences at home and in school, it is to be expected that the hearing-impaired child will be more dependent upon others than will a hearing child. He will show less initiative and will develop fewer self-help skills. Studies have been conducted using the Vineland Scale of Social Maturity to assess the maturity of hearing-impaired children in comparison with their hearing peers. The results showed the hearing-impaired child to be deficient in self-help skills (Meadow, 1975). It is important to note, however, that a discrepancy was shown to exist between what the child was capable of and what he normally did for himself (Meadow, 1976). Meadow points out that this suggests that parents generalize from the child's difficulties on a limited range of performance tasks, to a much wider range of tasks which should not be affected by his disability. It is this tendency to assume inability that fosters learned helplessness and a poor self-image, since social development and self-identity are intimately linked (Meadow, 1976). Once again, however, the evidence suggests that the degree to which effective parent-child communication has been established is a crucial factor. In a study of the maturity, independence, and responsibility of students in a residential school for the deaf, the subjects were divided into two groups. One group had deaf parents; the parents of the students in the other group had normal hearing. Teacher ratings on all three traits were consistently higher for the students of deaf parents (Schlesinger & Meadow, 1972).

Grade School Adjustment

MacKeith (1973) points out that parents experience a number of crisis periods when feelings about their handicapped child intensify. One of these is the crisis surrounding the question of whether or not their child will attend a normal public school. Thus, in addition to having to deal with the question of the method by which the child will be educated, parents must also face the issue of where the child will go to school. A wide range of educational models exist for hearing-impaired children. Some localities provide several alternatives for the child; others offer little choice. The situation concerning the availability of educational alternatives is expected to improve as Public Law 94-142 is enforced. This law stipulates that a handicapped child may be placed in special or separate classes only when normal classroom placement with full supplementary aides and services will not adequately meet his learning needs. Even so, parents will always face the stress arising from the decision-making process concerning the setting in which their child will be educated.

Residential Placement

For most parents this represents the type of educational placement that is fraught with the greatest anxiety. An attempt is often made by the parents to assuage the guilt arising from a feeling of responsibility for having given birth to a handicapped child. Overprotection of the child is one of the atoning behaviors shown by many parents in this situation. To have to contemplate parting with the child at the tender age of 4 or 5, to send him away to a residential school for his education, often constitutes an anguishing situation for parents. Residential placement in these circumstances simply heightens the guilt, since it adds evidence easily interpreted by the relatives and friends as rejection. These feelings are often reinforced by comments from well-meaning friends who, while they may acknowledge the necessity for the placement, express the opinion that they could never themselves muster the courage to face the separation. Unless adequate counsel is provided, many parents consider a residential school for the deaf to be evidence of the extent of their failure to produce a normal child. Society still assigns a stigma to segregated facilities for handicapped persons. The very fact of segregation attests to the nonnormality of those who are not acceptable in the mainstream of society. Images are still evoked by the words "deaf and dumb," which remain engraved in the masonry of some schools.

Residential placement also holds for the parents a real threat to family ties. This is not an irrational feeling. The housemother comes to serve in a surrogate parent capacity for the young child, while parent contact is severely limited. The parental anxieties are exacerbated when the child comes home for weekends. At school teachers develop a high level of ability in understanding "deaf speech," and even oral teachers learn to understand the manual language used by their pupils. As was mentioned earlier, severely hearing-impaired children communicate among themselves using manual language; this is understandable since they have difficulty in comprehending normal speech and find the poorer speech of their peers even more difficult to interpret. Thus, when the child comes home the parents find considerable difficulty in communicating with him. Furthermore, the child lacks the facility of interacting with his siblings or children in the neighborhood.

Fear That the Child's Differences Will Be Intensified

Parents assume correctly that a segregated environment will foster in the child a personal and social identity that is different from that of his hearing peers. Even at a preschool level, differences in personal relationships have been shown to exist between severely hearing-impaired and hearing youngsters (Herder, 1948; Darbyshire, 1977). Later, the separateness of the residential population tends to increase, even to the

extent of having a Deaf Miss Teenage America contest. The severely hearing-impaired individual educated exclusively in a residential setting lacks exposure to the thought patterns and social behaviors of the hearing world. He becomes part of a subculture, which makes integration into a hearing world upon graduation difficult for reasons which, by that time, extend well beyond the basic communication difficulty (Kennedy, 1973; Greenberg, 1970).

The parents may not be aware of the specific effects of segregated education. But in a society where the concept of the neighborhood school is so highly valued, residential education of their child is, understandably, not considered desirable.

Day School or Special Class Placement

The apprehension is somewhat less if placement in a school for the deaf is made on a day-attendance basis. The cultural and linguistic influences remain strong, but are reduced by the continued influence of the family on the child living at home. A similar situation occurs when the child is educated in separate classes for hearing-impaired children, often found in public school systems. These have the added attraction to parents of being housed in a normal school. The population of hearing-impaired children in any given unit is relatively small compared to that of a school for the deaf; thus the parents feel that the child is identified with the normal school rather than with the special class that would immediately identify his differentness.

Most special class programs profess their goal to be the integration of hearing-impaired children into the normal classroom. The extent to which real integration occurs varies enormously from school to school. In many settings, it involves little more than token integration in such subjects as gym and art. The fact remains that there is a high degree of segregation. As for the day school for the deaf, in most instances the child must be bused out of the community—another fact which identifies his differentness.

Parents expecting the normalization of their child's education through placement in a special class in a normal school may experience concern, disappointment, and anger if this fails to occur. Their hopes may be further dashed if the child develops no friendships with the normal-hearing children in school. This is likely to be the case, for he has little contact with them in school and does not return with them to the same neighborhood. Friendships within his own neighborhood also will be harder to make and maintain, since these are usually school related.

Normal School Placement

This represents the ideal for any parent. A child's physical presence in a normal classroom for hearing children signifies to them his normality; it is an indication that the effect of the disability is minimal. As a result of legislation and changing philosophies concerning the education of handicapped children, more and more will be placed in the mainstream of the normal educational system. However, even the normal school placement of their hearing-impaired child does not alleviate all stress. The parents of the handicapped child may continue to experience high levels of anxiety concerning the child's academic performance; they may worry about the teacher's ability to understand and accommodate their child's special needs, and they may be concerned about his acceptance by his hearing peers. So many factors determine a child's potential for success in a normal classroom that it is unwise to make specific statements. Northcott (1973) has identified five of the major requirements for success: (1) active utilization of residual hearing; (2) full-time hearing aid use if prescribed; (3) social, academic, cognitive, and aural-oral skills within the normal range of behaviors; (4) competence in understanding and exchanging ideas with others by use of speech, reading, and writing; and (5) self-direction in completing tasks in hand.

The important point is that the personal pride of the parents is invested in the child's success; thus their concern may be high.

Adjustment and Achievement

It is not the concern of this chapter to consider the intellectual, linguistic, and academic performance of hearing-impaired children. This information has been reviewed elsewhere (Avery, 1975). However, a brief summary of these three major areas of development is of relevance, since they have implications for the attitudes of others toward hearing-impaired children and youth, and ultimately for the young person's concept of himself.

Intellectual Capabilities

Considerable research efforts have gone into the study of the effects of language retardation on the intellectual development of the hearing-impaired child. For many years it was firmly believed that language was a prerequisite to thought and, therefore, that cognitive development was subsumed under language (Templin, 1950; Myklebust & Brutten, 1953; Oleron, 1953). This theoretical view has greatly influenced the manner in which severely hearing-impaired children have been taught. The paramount concern of teachers was naturally the teaching of language.

> The effort to give them some degree of speech and a command of language makes a continual demand on the teacher, almost to the exclusion of all else (Denmark & Eldridge, 1969, p. 261).

Piaget (1951) challenged the view that cognitive development is dependent upon linguistic development. He argued to the contrary, that cognition arises from experience with the environment, that it develops naturally, and in fact forms the basis for the subsequent development of structured language.

Furth (1961, 1966, 1973) has applied Piaget's theory to the psychology of severe hearing impairment. He accepts the view that cognitive capacity develops independently of exposure to spoken language. Furth is of the opinion that the role of spoken language in intellectual performance tasks is restricted to the enhancement of the subject's efficiency in solving certain types of problems. He demonstrated that severely hearing-impaired children do not differ from their hearing peers in their performance on conceptual learning tasks that are not reduced in difficulty by specific language experience. However, when the conceptual task could be reduced in complexity through the use of specific language, hearing children, by virtue of higher levels of language competence, demonstrated higher scores than their matched hearing-impaired peers (Furth, 1961). In another study, Furth (1971) again showed that on a range of tasks assessing rule learning, use of logical symbols, memory, and perception, the language handicap of severely hearing-impaired children did not impair their performance in relation to the scores obtained by hearing children. Furth reasoned, therefore, that the depressed cognitive performance evidenced by hearing-impaired children derives more from general experience deprivation than from language retardation or innate difference.

> The basic development and structure of the intelligence of the deaf in comparison with the hearing is remarkably unaffected by the absence of verbal language. One can reasonably assume that the major area in which the deaf appear to be different from the hearing is in variables related to personality, motivation, and values. If substantial differences are found, they will be likely due to experimental and social factors of home, school and the deaf community (Furth, 1966, p. 227).

The emerging view of the intelligence of hearing-impaired children, spearheaded by Furth, is that in perception, learning, cognition and memory processes these children do not differ significantly from their hearing peers. Like them, they tend to define their experience by classifying the world into conceptual categories. These categories are then used as the basis for linguistic organization and for storage and recall of information (Hoemann & Ullman, 1976). However, Furth (1971) and Hoeman and Ullman (1976) have cautioned against premature sweeping generalizations based upon limited evidence. These authors conclude that, despite some convincing research findings, it still remains difficult to ascertain conclusively whether the reduced performance of hearing-impaired subjects has its origin in innately different intellectual or cognitive development, or arises from factors unrelated to what is being measured.

Hearing-impaired children and their parents have in the past had to face the widespread opinion that severe hearing impairment from infancy resulted in depressed cognitive abilities. This general opinion exerted considerable influence in limiting the expectancies held for hearing-impaired students. Poor performance too frequently has been accepted as commensurate with their attributed inferior cognitive abilities. This becomes part of the total image of the hearing-impaired population, and those who are so classified are treated accordingly.

> Thus we have too much acceptance of lower standards of performance, too low aspirations for deaf children compared to their normal peers. This insidious situation fosters and nurtures the paternalism which so frequently enmeshes deaf people as they seek to participate in and direct their own destinies (Switzer & Williams, 1967).

If the accumulated evidence convincingly shows that there is essentially no difference between the intellectual and cognitive potentials of severely hearing-impaired and normal children, our concept of the nature of this handicap will have to change. A change in professional attitudes will be positively reflected in the parents' image of their child and, because attitudes affect behavior, in the teacher-child and parent-child relationships, and ultimately in the self-image of the child himself.

Academic Pressures and Adjustment

The extent to which the hearing-impaired child will approximate normal levels of academic achievement will be influenced by numerous factors. The influence of the variables discussed earlier in this chapter with regard to the impact of early hearing impairment are likely to be reflected upwards into the school years. These factors are augmented by a number of educational variables arising from the type and appropriateness of the educational placement of the child, the extent of the support services available to him, and all the usual variables that affect the educational success of any normal-hearing child. The majority of the studies of academic performance of hearing-impaired children have reported on those with severe or profound hearing deficits. Lane (1976) has reviewed the trend in results over the period 1921–1975. She refers to a summary made by McClure (1966) of the results of several educational studies. These studies showed that graduates from schools for the deaf achieved grade-level performances ranging from 3.1 to 12.8 with a median grade of 7.9, while nongraduates of high school age ranged in grade-placement levels from 0.9 to 10.5, with a median grade of 4.7. The terminal reading grade for graduating students was below third-grade level (Lane & Baker, 1974). There appears to be a high level of agreement among subsequent studies, the results of which do not differ significantly from those reviewed by McClure (1966). Lane summarizes her discussion of academic achievements of severely hearing-impaired children over the past fifty-four years:

In summary, there has been some slight improvement in educational achievement of the deaf, but the educational retardation is still one of the greatest barriers to academic and vocational success of the deaf (1976, p. 101).

Some authors have placed much of the blame for this educational retardation on the institutionalization of children. Integrating the child into public school classes, even on a part-time basis, is currently advocated as a solution to this problem. In some instances, this proves effective. However, it also creates the potential for stress. The severely hearing-impaired child educated in part or totally with his hearing peers frequently has difficulty in keeping up. For example, at age 12 few of these children can read at better than third-grade level. When this is the case, the child becomes increasingly aware of his inferior academic performance. He also realizes that his communication skills are not adequate for the increasing sophistication of academic and social interaction. This growing awareness of inferior school performance may threaten his self-image, causing him to define himself as a failure.

These comments appear to be generally justified. However, in accord with the caution urged earlier, it is again stressed that such results are not inevitable. Given careful selection of students and appropriate support programs, success is possible (Matter, 1976).

Children with less than severe hearing impairment are being mainstreamed into normal classes in increasing numbers. Normal communication skills in public schools are prerequisite to good academic performance. This is evidenced by the concern expressed over hearing children who read poorly. Hearing impairment usually results in a reduction in the level of verbal language and communication skills, particularly reading. Therefore, unless special help is provided to these children, many, perhaps most, will fail to achieve normal levels of academic performance. Awareness of their failure, once again, tends to result in self-debasement and loss of motivation.

The concern here is not with the academic

performance itself, but with the effect that it can have on the child's image of himself. In order to expand the self, in order to face the risks associated with self-discovery, a high level of reward is necessary. Repeated experiences of failure and defeat result in a shrinkage of child/environment relationships until a level is reached at which some sense of stability can be achieved. Frequent failure will result in avoidance of challenge and withdrawal from demanding situations. Even if the academic performance is successful, social integration may not be satisfactory. A child needs to find acceptance by his peers; he needs a group of friends with whom he can share experiences. Poor communication skills and difficulty in following the subtle language cues of the teenage subculture can mean rejection by the group. Social integration, therefore, represents an area of potential stress for the hearing-impaired child. By virtue of his placement in a normal school, he may find himself unaware of the social expectancies, or he may be unable to meet them because of poor communication skills.

It must be stressed, once again, that what is being described here is the type of difficulties that occur when the demands of a normal school placement exceed a child's capacity to adapt adequately. These problems are by no means inevitable; many quite severely hearing-impaired students are functioning acceptably and even exceptionally in regular school placements. In some cases the child's own resources, despite impairment of hearing, permit him to cope with the demands made upon him, with only little modification of the educational environment. In other cases a child succeeds because of intensive support services. However, it must be emphasized that unless these children's needs are met, poor academic progress and poor social adaptation may defeat the whole purpose of the normal placement. Thus "mainstreaming" is in itself neither good nor bad; it is either appropriate or inappropriate for a particular child. The decision as to its potential value and hazard must be reached

very carefully after consideration of all influential factors likely to be relevant for a given child.

The situation naturally becomes more problematic during the teenage years, which for all children are noted for the stresses that arise from the rapid period of maturation from child to adult. For the hearing-impaired child this period is frequently more difficult than for an average-hearing child. The teenage period emphasizes the importance of heeding Cruickshank's (1948) appeal to separate normal developmental problems arising from the expansion of self-concept from those specific to the disability. The hearing-impaired teenager will experience the same self-doubts, the same need to test and reject authority, the same need to be reassured of his acceptability by his peers, and the same reassurance of his potential worth to society as do his hearing friends. In addition to these normal anxieties, he has to cope with the overlapping implications of his disability. The hearing-impaired teenager, like his hearing friends, must face the realities of a highly competitive employment market. Each student, at some point, must assess his own abilities and achievements and compare them to the expectancies of the careers in which he may be interested. Again, as will many hearing students, the hearing-impaired teenager will have to come to terms with the fact that his chance of success in certain fields is limited. He must not only face the odds which the hearing student encounters, but, in many instances, must take into account less than advanced language and communication skills, and perhaps a poorer academic performance than his intelligence justifies. In addition, his impaired hearing will disqualify him from careers in which good hearing is a requirement.

The career choice difficulties are no different from those encountered by hearing students who also have assets and limitations and who also must face keen competition for desired careers. Nothing is impossible if a student is able to fulfill the requirements for a particular career. Some hearing-impaired students realize outstanding achievements against seemingly impossible odds. However, as is true for hearing persons, these are the exceptions rather than the rule.

It is to be expected that, as support services in public schools, community colleges, technical institutes, and universities are increased, and as opportunities improve, the expectancies for these students will increase, as will their own horizons and achievements. It remains a fact, meanwhile, that many hearing-impaired students and their families are concerned over their future viability in the competitive market. They are concerned about limited career opportunities and about being underutilized by society. They experience concern over what their future in the adult world will be.

Social Adjustment

Some aspects of the social and emotional development of hearing-impaired children and youth have already been considered in this chapter. It is intended in this section to do no more than provide a profile of characteristics that have been identified among children with hearing impairment. The profile, which may be constructed from personality tests conducted with severely hearing-impaired children and youth over many years, includes characteristics of egocentricity, rigidity, immaturity, impulsiveness. Only one study (Vegely, 1971) indicated the subjects tested as having normal personality characteristics. Rodda (1974) indicated that in three states alone (Ohio, Indiana, Kentucky), with a known deaf population of 16,000, a minimum of 1,930 deaf persons will experience behavioral problems of a severity warranting some type of special help. Rodda states that if the range were to include mild to severe problems, the number would increase by a factor of 4, which would represent half of the deaf population involved. However, these findings must be interpreted carefully. They may reflect only the limitations arising from the effects of the sensory deficit upon interpersonal interaction, rather than being rooted in psychological maladjustment. It is not intended to minimize the seriousness of the adjustment problems and needs of hearing-impaired children and youth, but rather to modify the view a helper takes of them. Altshuler says, "It is nothing short of miraculous that the majority of deaf children develop to be normal neurotics like the rest of us" (1974, p. 370). It is suggested that the overwhelming characteristic of hearing-impaired children and young adults is the normal way in which they react to their disability, the problems it generates, and the stigma it carries. They react as a hearing person would react if placed in the same stressful situation. Goffman (1963) has detailed the shared reactions evidenced by people with a variety of different types of physical and social stigma. Freedman and Doob (1968) even demonstrated, in a controlled study, that the same behavioral reactions exhibited by stigmatized persons are readily evoked in normal subjects if they are led to believe that they are "different." Reivich and Rothrock (1972) reported the results of an analytic study of the behavior problems of children and adolescents in a school for the deaf. The authors observed that "the factor structure of problem behavior in the present population of deaf school children was more similar to than different from, the other populations that have been studied" (1974, p. 101). Thus, the behaviors encountered in children with impaired hearing do not differ significantly from those found among hearing children. A hearing impairment creates a different perceptual reference (Altshuler, 1976, p. 118). When this is taken into consideration, the observed behavior becomes understandable, even reasonable, with those terms of reference. Meadow (1976), for example, explains how the impulsiveness shown by children who are deaf is not difficult to understand when we recognize that the child is unable to base his actions on "careful, coherent, advanced planning" which allows for postponement of immediate gratification in favor of long-term gains. Such planning requires that the child have a clear perception of time, a concept closely bound to linguistic definition.

Similarly, as was discussed earlier, socialization is heavily dependent upon communication. The process of individualization, referred to by Altshuler (1974), involves the differentiation of self from others and the realization of the relationship of one's behavior to the behavior of others. Language is essential to the achievement of individualization (Meadow, 1976); without it, it is difficult to acquire an appreciation of how others feel. The hearing-impaired child, lacking an appreciation of emotions, tends to behave in an apparently egocentric manner.

Earlier in this chapter, the dependency behavior often seen in hearing-impaired children was discussed. It was explained that the pressures on parents make it necessary for them to set up a highly structured home environment for the child in order to get things done. This structure is similarly built into preschool training programs for hearing-impaired children. With this knowledge in mind, it is not surprising that the characteristic of rigidity has been attributed to many hearing-impaired children. They are trained in a rule-bound system, and tend to generalize the rule for lack of understanding of the premise upon which it is based.

When communication difficulty disrupts normal parent-child relationships, when a child becomes aware of rejection by parents and/or peers, it is almost inevitable that he will incorporate the resulting feelings into his self-image. The experiences he has at school will further contribute to his concept of self-worth. Unless he is able to relate successfully to the teacher and the other students, the child will become increasingly isolated and will almost certainly judge himself to be unworthy of the respect of others. When progressive academic failure is added

to social failure, it is to be expected that social and emotional difficulties will occur.

In a study mentioned earlier (Schlesinger & Meadow, 1972), children of deaf parents were rated superior in maturity, responsibility, and independence to deaf children of hearing parents. Those same deaf children of deaf parents also scored significantly higher on a self-image test than did the students of hearing parents. The difference in self-image between the groups was strongly evidenced by the young children, but decreased as the ages of the groups compared increased. The lowest self-image scores were obtained by children whose parents had high levels of educational achievement, a finding that Meadow interpreted to mean that higher parental expectancies, when not attainable, may result in negative self-concepts (Meadow 1976). Rainer, Altshuler and Kallmann (1969) have also observed that the adjustment of a child with hearing impairment is generally better if at least one member of his family suffers from the same disability.

The psychological and social adaptation of hearing-impaired children appears, therefore, to constitute a more difficult task than for their hearing peers. The basis of the problems encountered lies in the poor communication skills possessed by these children. Difficulty in learning the nature of the social demands made, poor levels of success in relating to hearing persons, and poor academic attainments will contribute to a lowered self-image and to behavioral adjustment problems. Yet, these effects are not caused by the hearing impairment, they arise from the perceptions the child develops of himself and his disability.

In general, personality maladjustment is more common among physically disabled persons than among physically normal persons, there is no causal connection between the handicap and the maladjustment. It is the individual's attitudes, not merely the disability itself, that are the primary determinants of his mode and level of adjustment (Coleman, 1964).

REFERENCES

ALTSHULER, K. Z. The social and psychological development of the deaf child: Problems, their treatment and prevention. *Social and Psychological Development,* Aug., 1974, 365–376.

———. Psychiatry and problems of deafness. In *Psychology of deafness for rehab. counselors.* Baltimore: University Park Press, 1976.

AVERY, C. B. The education of children with impaired hearing. In W. M. Cruickshank & G. O. Johnson, (Eds.). *Education of exceptional children and youth.* Englewood Cliffs, N.J.: Prentice-Hall, Inc., 1975.

BARSCH, R. H. *The parent of the handicapped child: The study of child rearing practices.* Springfield, Ill.: Charles C Thomas, 1968.

BLESSER, B. Discussion: Aiding speech reception of hearing impaired listener. In *Sensory Capabilities of Hearing Impaired Children,* R. Stark (Ed.). Baltimore: University Park Press, 1974.

BOLES, G. Personality factors in mothers of cerebral palsied children. *Genetic Psychology Monograph,* 1959, *59,* 159–218.

BORNSTEIN, H., WOODWARD, J., & TULLY, N. Language and communication. In *Psychology of deafness for rehabilitative counselors,* B. Bolton (Ed.). Baltimore: University Park Press, 1976, pp. 19–41.

BUTTERFIELD, E. C. An extended version of modification of sucking with auditory feedback. Working paper no. 43. *Bureau of Child Research Laboratory Children's Rehabilitation Unit.* University of Kansas Medical Center, 1968.

CALVERT, D. R., & SILVERMAN, S. R. *Speech and deafness: A text for learning and teaching.* Washington, D.C.: A. G. Bell Association for the Deaf, 1975.

CHOMSKY, N. *Aspects of the theory of syntax.* Cambridge, Mass.: The M.I.T. Press, 1966.

CHURCH, J. *Language and the discovery of reality.* New York: Random House, Inc., 1963.

COLEMAN, J. C. *Abnormal psychology and modern life.* Glenview, Ill.: Scott, Foresman & Company, 1964.

CONDON, W. S., & SANDER, L. W. Neonate movement is synchronized with adult speech. *Science,* 1973, *183,* 99–101.

CONNOR, F. P., RUSALEM, H., & CRUICKSHANK, W. M. Psychological considerations with crippled children. In W. M. Cruickshank (Ed.), *Psychology of exceptional children and youth* (3rd ed.). Englewood Cliffs, N.J.: Prentice-Hall, Inc., 1971.

CRUICKSHANK, W. M. The impact of physical disability on social adjustment. *Journal of Social Issues,* 1948, *4,* 78–83.

DARBYSHIRE, E. O. Play patterns in young children with impaired hearing, *The Volta Review,* 1977, *79,* 1:19–26.

DENMARK, J. C., & ELDRIDGE, R. W. Psychiatric services for the deaf. *The Lancet,* 1969, Aug. 2.

DENNIS, W. *Children of the creche.* Century Psychology Series. Englewood Cliffs, N.J.: Prentice-Hall, Inc., 1973.

DWECK, C. S. Children's interpretation of evaluative feedback: The effect of social cues on learned helplessness. *Merrill Palmer Quarterly,* 1976, *22,* 2, 105–110.

EILERS, R., & MINIFIE, F. Fricative discrimination in early infancy. *Journal of Speech and Hearing Research,* 1975, *18,* 158–167.

EIMAS, P. D. Developmental Studies of Speech Perception. In *Infant perception,* Vol. II, L. B. Cohen & P. Salapatek (Eds.). New York: Academic Press, 1975, pp. 193–231. (a)

———. Auditory and phonetic coding of the cues for speech. Discrimination of the r-1 by young infants. *Perception and Phychophysics,* 1975, *18,* 341–347. (*b*)

EISENBERG, R. The development of hearing in man: An assessment of current status. *ASHA,* 1970, *12,* 119–123.

ELLIOTT, L. L., & ARMBRUSTER, V. B. Some possible effects of the delay of early treatment of deafness. *Journal of Speech and Hearing Research,* 1967, *10,* 209–224.

ERIKSON, E. H., 1950 in Kennedy, A.E.C., 1973. The effects of deafness on personality, *Journal of Rehabilitation of the Deaf,* 1973, *6,* 22–23.

FREEDMAN, J. L., & DOOB, A. N. *Deviancy: The psychology of being different.* New York: Academic Press, 1968.

FURTH, H. G. The influence of language on the development of concept formation in deaf children. *Journal of Abnormal and Social Psychology,* 1961, *63,* 2, 386–389.

——. Linguistic deficiency and thinking: Research with deaf subjects 1964–69. *Psychology Bulletin,* 1971, *76,* 58–72.

——. *Thinking without language: Psychological implications of deafness.* New York: Free Press, 1966.

——. *Deafness and learning: A psychosocial approach.* Belmont, California: Wadsworth, 1973.

GARRETSON, M. D. Total communication. *The Volta Review,* 1976, *78,* 4, 88–95.

GASSON, W. Psychopathological environmental reaction to congenital defect. *Journal of Mental and Nervous Disease,* 1966, *142,* 453–459.

GENTILE, A. Annual survey of hearing impaired children and youth. Washington, D.C.: Office of Demographic Studies, 1973.

GESELL, A., & ARMATRUDA, C. *The Embryology of Behavior.* New York: Harper, 1945.

GOFFMAN, E. *Stigma: Notes on the management of a spoiled identity.* Englewood Cliffs, N.J.: A Spectrum Book, Prentice-Hall, Inc., 1963.

GORDEUK, A. Motherhood and a less than perfect child: A literary review. *Maternal-Child Nursing Journal,* 1976, *5,* 57–68.

GREENBERG, J. *In this sign.* New York: Holt, Rinehart & Winston, 1970.

GROHT, M. A. *Natural language for deaf children.* Washington, D.C.: Gallaudet College Press, 1958.

HART, B. O. A Child Centered Language Program. *Report of the Proceedings of the International Congress of the Education of the Deaf and of the 41st Meeting of the Convention of American Instructors of the Deaf.* U.S. Government Printing Office: Gallaudet College, Washington, D.C., 1964, pp. 504–514.

HENNESSEY, J. Hospitalized toddler's responses to mother's tape recordings during brief separations. *Maternal-Child Nursing Journal,* 1976, *5,* 69.

HERDER, G. M. Adjustment problems of the deaf child. *Nervous Child,* 1948, *7,* 38–44.

HOEMANN, H. W. The development of communication skills in deaf and hearing children. *Child Development,* 1972, *43,* 990–1008.

——, & ULLMAN, D. G. Intellectual Development. In *Psychology of Deafness for Rehabilitation Counselors.* Baltimore: University Park Press, 1976, chapter 3.

HOOKER, C. Learned Helplessness. *Social Work,* 1976, *21,* 194–198.

JOHANSSON, B., WEDENBERG, E., & WESTIN, B. Measurement of tone response by the human fetus. *Acta Otolaryngologica,* 1964, *57,* 188–192. Stockholm.

KAPKE, K. A. Spina Bifida: Mother-child relationship. *Nursing Forum,* 1970, *9,* 310–320.

KENNEDY, A. E. The effects of deafness on personality: A discussion based on the theoretical model of Erik Erikson's eight stages of man. *Journal of Rehabilitation of the Deaf,* 1973, *6,* 22–33.

KENNY, V. A better way to teach deaf children. *Harper's Magazine,* March, 1962, 61–65.

KRUG, R. *Teaching Syntax to Young Deaf Children.* Boulder: Edumat Assoc., 1968.

KVARACEUS, W. C., & HAYES, N. E. *Is Your Child Handicapped?* Boston: Porter Sargent, 1969.

LANE, H. S. Academic achievement. In *Psychology of deafness for rehabilitation counselors,* B. Bolton, (Ed.). Baltimore, Md.: University Park Press, 1976, pp. 97–107.

———, & BAKER, D. Reading achievements of the deaf: Another look. *The Volta Review,* 1974, *76,* 279–291.

LENNEBERG, E. H. *Biological Foundations of Language.* New York: John Wiley & Sons, 1967.

LING, D. The hearing impaired pre-schooler: A family responsibility. *Hearing and Speech News,* 1971, *39,* 5, 8–13.

———. *Speech and the hearing impaired child: Theory and practice.* Washington, D.C.: The Alexander Graham Bell Association for the Deaf, 1976.

LLOYD, L. Mental retardation and hearing impairment. In PRWAD *Deafness Annual,* vol. 3, A. G. Norris (Ed.). Washington, D.C.: Professional Rehabilitation Workers with the Adult Deaf, 1973.

MACKEITH, R. Parental reactions and responses to a handicapped child. In *Brain and Intelligence,* F. Richardson (Ed.). Hyattsville, Md.: National Educational Consultants, 1973, pp. 131–138.

MALKIN, S. F., FREEMAN, R. D., & HASTINGS, J. D. Psychosocial problems of deaf children and their families: A comparative study. *Audiology and Hearing Education,* 1976, *2,* 3, 21–29.

MATTER, G. In the current with only one oar. In *Mainstream Education for Hearing Impaired Children and Youth,* G. Nix (Ed.). New York: Grune & Stratton, 1976, pp. 157–168.

McCLURE, W. Current problems and trends in the education of the deaf. *Deaf American,* 1966, *18,* 8–14.

McNEILL, D. The capacity for language acquisition. *The Volta Review,* 1966, *68,* 17–33.

MEADOW, K. P. The development of deaf children. In *Review of child development research,* vol. V. E. M. Hetherington, J. W. Hugen, R. Kron & A. H. Stein (Eds.). Chicago: University of Chicago Press, 1975, pp. 439–506.

———. Personality and social development of deaf persons. In B. Bolton (Ed.), *Psychology of deafness for rehabilitation counselors.* Baltimore: University Park Press, 1976.

———. Personality and social development of deaf persons. *Journal of Rehabilitation of the Deaf,* Jan., 1976, *9,* 3.

MERCER, R. T. *Responses of five multigravidae to the event of the birth of an infant with a defect.* Doctoral dissertation, University of Pittsburgh. Cited in A. Gordeuk, Motherhood and a less than perfect child—A literary review. *Maternal Child Nursing Journal,* 1970, *5,* 57–68.

MOFFATT, S. *Helping the child who cannot hear.* New York: The Public Affairs Committee. Public Affairs Pamphlet No. 479, 1972.

MOORES, D., McINTYRE, C., & WEISS, K. Evaluation of programs for hearing impaired children. Report of 1971–1972, Research Report 39, Minneapolis: University of Minn., 1972. 1972.

MOORES, D. F., WEISS, K. L., & GOODWIN, M. W. 1974 Evaluation of programs for hearing impaired children: Report of 1973–1974. Research Development and Demonstration Center in Education of Handicapped Children. Research Report 81, Minneapolis: University of Minn., 1974.

MORSE, P. A. The discrimination of speech and non-speech stimuli in early infancy, *Journal of Exceptional Child Psychology,* 1972, *14,* 477–492.

———. Infant speech perception. In D. A. Sanders, *Auditory perception of speech, An introduction to principles and problems.* Englewood Cliffs, N.J.: Prentice-Hall, Inc., 1977.

MYKLEBUST, H. R., & BRUTTON, M. A. A study of the visual perception of deaf children. *Acta Oto-laryngologica* (Stockholm), 1953, suppl. 105.

NIX, G. W. Total communication: A review of studies offered in its support. *The Volta Review,* 1975, *77,* 8, 470–494.

NORTHCOTT, W. Introduction. In *The hearing impaired child in a regular classroom,* W. Northcott (Ed.). Washington, D.C.: A. G. Bell Association for the Deaf, 1973, pp. 1–10.

NORTHERN, J., & DOWNS, M. *Hearing in children.* Baltimore: Williams & Wilkins Company, 1974.

OLERON, P. Conceptual thinking of the deaf. *American Annals of Deaf,* 1953, *98,* pp. 304–310.

———. The development of an auditory function. *Otolaryngologica Clinics of North America Symposium on Congenital Deafness,* 1971, *4,* 319–335.

PARKE, R. D. Social cues, social control and ecological validity. *Merrill Palmer Quarterly,* 1976, *22,* 2, 111–123.

PIAGET, J. *Play dreams and imitation in childhood.* New York: Norton, 1951.

———. *Six psychological studies.* New York: Random House, 1967.

———, & INHELDER, B. *La psychologie de l'enfant.* Collection "Que suis-je." No. 369. Paris: Presses Universitaires de France, 1966.

POLLACK, D. *Educational audiology for the limited hearing infant.* Springfield, Ill.: Charles C Thomas, 1970.

POLLACK, M. C. Special applications of amplification. In *Amplification for the hearing impaired,* M. C. Pollack (Ed.). New York: Grune & Stratton, 1975.

QUIGLEY, S. P. Language acquisition. *The Volta Review,* 1966, *68,* 68–83.

RAINER, J. D. Psychiatric services for the deaf: Some unmet needs. *Journal of Rehabilitation of the Deaf,* July, 1969, *3,* 1.

———, & ALTSHULER, K. Z. New directions in psychiatry for deaf people, *Deafness Annual,* 1973, *3,* 147–157.

———, & KALLMANN, F. J. *Family and mental health problems in a deaf population* (2nd ed.). Springfield, Ill.: Charles C Thomas, 1969.

RAMSDELL, D. A. The psychology of the hard-of-hearing and deafened adult. In *Hearing and Deafness* (3rd ed.), H. Davis & S. R. Silverman, (Eds.). New York: Holt, Rinehart & Winston, 1970, p. 438.

REISEN, A. H. The development of visual perception in man and chimpanzee. *Science,* 1947, *106,* 107–108.

———. Effects of stimulus deprivation on the development and atrophy of the visual sensory system. *American Journal of Orthopsychiatry,* 1960, *30,* 23–36.

REIVICH, S. R., & ROTHROCK, I. A. Behavior problems of deaf children and adolescents: A factor-analytic study. *Journal of Speech and Hearing Research,* 1972, *15,* 1, 93–104.

RHODES, M. J. From a parent's point of view. *The Deaf American,* 1972.

ROBINSON, M. Family reaction to stress. *Medical Social Work,* 1970, *22,* 191–199.

RODDA, M. Behavioral disorders in deaf clients. *Journal of Rehabilitation of the Deaf,* 1974, 1–13.

ROSS, A. O. *The exceptional child in the family.* New York: Grune & Stratton. 1964, Chapter 11, pp. 51–70.

ROSS, M., & CALVERT, D. The semantics of deafness. In *The Hearing impaired child in a regular classroom,* W. Northcott (Ed.). Washington, D.C.: The Alexander Graham Bell Association for the Deaf, 1973, pp. 13–17.

———, & LERMAN, J. *Word intelligibility by picture identification.* Pittsburgh: Stanwix House, Inc., 1971.

RUPP, R. R. An approach to the communicative needs of the very young hearing impaired child. *Journal of the Academy of Rehabilitative Audiology,* 1971, *4,* 11–12.

SANDERS, D. A. *Aural Rehabilitation.* Englewood Cliffs, N.J.: Prentice-Hall, Inc., 1971.

———. Hearing aid orientation and counseling. In *Amplification for the Hearing Impaired,* Michael C. Pollack (Ed.). New York: Grune & Stratton, 1975.

————. *Auditory perception of speech. An introduction to principles and problems.* Englewood Cliffs, N.J.: Prentice-Hall, Inc., 1977.

SARLIN, M. B., & ALTSHULER, K. Z. *Expanded Mental Care for the Deaf,* New York: New York State Psychiatric Institute, 1970.

————. Group psychotherapy with deaf adolescents in a school setting. *International Journal of Group Psychotherapy,* 1968, *18,* 337.

SCHLESINGER, H. S. The deaf pre-schooler and his many faces. In *International Seminar of the Vocational Rehabilitation of Deaf Persons,* L. Lloyd (Ed.). Washington, D.C.: U.S. Department of Health, Education and Welfare, 1969.

————, & MEADOW, K. P. *Deafness and mental health: A developmental approach.* San Francisco: Langley Porter Neuropsychiatric Institute, 1971.

————. *Sound and sign: Childhood deafness and mental health.* Berkeley: University of California Press, 1972.

SIMMONS-MARTIN, A. The central institute for the deaf demonstration home program. In G. W. Nix (Ed.), *Mainstream education for hearing impaired children and youth.* New York: Grune & Stratton, 1976, pp. 217–226.

SOLNIT, A. J., & STARK, M. H. Mourning and the birth of a defective child. *Psychoanalytic Study of the Child,* 1961, *16,* 523–537.

STEWART, E. L., POLLACK, D., & DOWNS, M. P. A unisensory program for the limited hearing child. *ASHA,* 1964, *6,* 151–154.

SUSSMAN, A. The comprehensive counseling needs of deaf persons. *Hearing and Speech News,* Sept./Oct., 1970, 12–13, 24.

SWITZER, M. E., & WILLIAMS, B. R. Live problems of deaf people. *Archives of Environmental Health,* 1967, *15,* 249–256.

TEMPLIN, M. C. *The development of reasoning in children with normal and defective hearing.* Minneapolis: University of Minnesota Press, 1950.

TERVOORT, B., & VERBECK, A. Analysis of communicative structure patterns in deaf children. V.R.A. Project RD- 467, 6445 (Z. N. O. Onderzoek NR: 585-15). Groningen, The Netherlands, 1967.

VEGELY, A. B. Performance of hearing impaired children on a non-verbal personality test. *American Annals of the Deaf,* 1971, *116,* 427–434.

VERNON, M. Sociological and psychological factors associated with hearing loss. *Journal of Speech and Hearing Disorders,* 1969, *12,* 541–563.

WIESEL, T. N., & HUBEL, D. H. Extent of recovery from the effects of visual deprivation in kittens. *Journal of Neurophysiology,* 1965, *28,* 1060–1072.

WILBUR, R. B. The linguistics of manual languages and manual systems. In *Communication Assessment and Intervention Strategies,* L. Lloyd (Ed.). Baltimore: University Park Press, 1976.

WORBY, C. M. The family life cycle: An orienting concept for the family practice specialist. *Journal of Medical Education,* 1971, *46* (3), 198–203.

ZUK, G. The cultural dilemma and spiritual crisis of the family with a handicapped child. *Exceptional Children,* 1962, *28,* 405–408.

7 Psychological Problems of Children with Severely Impaired Vision

Berthold Lowenfeld

Ph.D., Superintendent Emeritus, California School for the Blind.

Impairment of vision causes many practical as well as theoretical problems. The psychological aspects of these problems will be treated here under three headings: Cognitive Functions, Mobility, and Personality and Social Factors. In general it can be said that blindness creates problems *sui generis* only in the area of cognitive functions and mobility. The congenitally and totally blind child experiences the world around him by sensory functions that the seeing child does not employ for this purpose, and he builds up his knowledge of the object world in ways that are essentially different from those of seeing children. As a result, it appears to be as impossible for the seeing to imagine the world of the blind as it is for the blind really to understand the experience of the seeing. In achieving mobility, the blind also make use of sensory means rarely if ever employed by the seeing. The personality and social effects of blindness, however, are similar to those caused by other conditions that either handicap the individual or set him apart in one way or another from the normal, the majority, the customary, or the better-organized. A blind child may develop feelings of insecurity because of negative parental attitudes, due to his blindness, just as other children may develop them for the same or different reasons. Thus social and emotional effects of blindness are nonspecific, although they may be characteristic as reactions to blindness or to environmental influences caused by it.

For reasons of presentation, the three factors are treated separately. In reality such separation does not exist. Cognitive functions and mobility have their strong emotional and social implications, whereas emotional and social factors may intensely influence cognitive functions and mobility.

Some problems caused by blindness have received much attention and investigation, but others have fared less well. The comparatively small number of blind children, with the resulting wide scatter in age, intelligence, socioeconomic background, and geographic location, has retarded research. It makes research based on large groups or on matched groups rather difficult and often impractical. Although the past decades have, largely as a result of governmental support, produced more research than ever before, the literature on the psychological effects of blindness in children is still quite limited;

in many areas, experiences, observations, and theoretical presentations continue to be the only contributions available. A basic tenet for those concerned with psychological practices has been stated by Raskin (1962, p. 341):

All essential psychological practices can be carried out with persons with visual defects. This includes psychological appraisal from infancy to adulthood, the evaluation of intelligence, aptitude, achievement, adjustment and personality organization, and the procedures of counseling and psychotherapy.

Psychological problems of blindness received early attention in the eighteenth century with the question of how a successfully operated on, congenitally blind person would react to his first optical impressions. The philosophers Locke, Berkeley, and, later, Diderot theorized considerably about sensory problems of the blind. During the early period of scientific psychology, William James, Wilhelm Wundt, and others discussed in their standard works problems of the blind, particularly their spatial perception. The first systematic study dealing with psychological problems of blindness as such also dates back to the experimental laboratory of Wundt, where Theodor Heller conducted investigations that he reported in his *Studienzur Blinden-Psychologie* (1895). Psychological research in the field of the blind has dealt mainly with problems of sensory experiences of the blind as compared with those of the seeing, with the ability to perceive obstacles, and with the measurement of intelligence, a field in which Samuel P. Hayes made the outstanding contribution. In 1933 Thomas D. Cutsforth's *The Blind in School and Society* was published as the first major work dealing with personality problems of the blind. Since then, the emotional and social implications of blindness have received increasing attention.

A unique contribution was made by Helga Lende when in 1940 the American Foundation for the Blind published her *Books about the Blind: A Bibliographical Guide to Literature Relating to the Blind,* of which a new revised edition came out in 1953. It was not until 1976 that a continuation of this work appeared: *Blindness, Visual Impairment, Deaf-Blindness: Annotated Listing of the Literature, 1953–1975,* compiled by Mary K. Bauman. This publication goes beyond Lende's book by providing a cross-referencing analytical subject index and by assuring its continuity through the publication of a semiannual listing of current literature.

DEFINITION, DEGREES, AND CAUSES OF VISUAL IMPAIRMENT

There are mainly three ways in which pathological conditions in the eye may result in impaired vision. The visual acuity may be reduced, the field of vision may be limited or defective, and color vision may be imperfect. Extrinsic, or external, muscle imbalances may also produce visual impairment, as for instance in amblyopia ex anopsia, a dimming of vision resulting from disuse of the eye due to strabismus.

Visual acuity is measured by the use of the Snellen Chart and expressed in the form of a fraction. A visual acuity of 20/200 means that the eye can see at the distance of 20 feet what a normal eye can see at 200 feet, or in other words, an object that a normal eye can see 200 feet away must be brought to within 20 feet in order to be discerned by the eye with a visual acuity of 20/200. In this pseudo-fraction the "numerator" and the "denominator" may be changed. In visual acuities better than 20/200, the denominator is usually changed, as for instance in 20/70; in visual acuities below 20/200, the numerator is usually changed, as for instance in 5/200. This is proper enough since such low acuities are actually measured at distances less than 20 feet.

The *field of vision* may be affected in two ways: an eye may have central vision with the peripheral field restricted to a certain angle, or the eye may have a scotoma, a spot without vision—which, if in the center of the field of vision, may cause loss of central vision. Restrictions in the field of vision are mapped out with the perimeter, an instrument that indicates the field limitations in the various directions on a chart.

Color vision is determined by the discrimination of the three qualities of color: hue, saturation, and brightness. In the rare case of total color blindness, all colors are seen as shades of black, gray, and white. Most color blindness is partial, wherein the person has difficulty in distinguishing between certain colors, usually reds and greens. Color blindness by itself, though a visual impairment, is generally not regarded as coming within the scope of visual handicaps. However, some eye conditions that reduce vision also result in total or partial color blindness.

According to the most widely accepted definition of blindness, a person is considered blind if he has "central visual acuity of 20/200 or less in the better eye, with correcting glasses, or central visual acuity of more than 20/200 if there is a field defect in which the peripheral field has contracted to such an extent that the widest diameter of visual field subtends an angular distance no greater than 20 degrees" (Hurlin, 1962, p. 8). Under this definition, all the following individuals are considered "blind": those who are totally blind; those who have light perception (ability to distinguish darkness and light), or light projection (ability to indicate the source of light); those who can distinguish hand movements in front of their eyes; who have form or object perception; who have "traveling vision"; and those whose vision can be measured with the Snellen Chart up to and including 20/200. This definition does not take into consideration the important factor of near vision or reading vision, or any defects within the

peripheral field that do not result in a contraction of the field itself but block out certain areas.

During an era in which ophthalmologists were cautious about the use of the eyes, particularly for reading, the definition of blindness given above was a fairly adequate tool in determining educational placement of children. Although a few decades ago the use of the eyes was considered harmful for many types of visual handicaps, ophthalmologists recommend now that visually handicapped children use their sight without any special restrictions. The eyes are visual receptors, and just as a camera does not suffer from use, neither do the eyes. This change of approach made the previously defined demarcations of visual acuity far less meaningful. Many children with visual acuities considerably below 20/200 are able to read print, large type or even regular size, if they can bring it close to their eyes or use magnifying glasses, as they are now encouraged to do. Also, modern technology and optics provide a variety of instruments for reading and related activities that can be used to great advantage by children with low vision. A "functional" definition of blindness is sought that will realistically determine which children should be considered visually handicapped. Barraga (1976) proposes the following educational definition: "A visually handicapped child is one whose visual impairment interferes with his optimal learning and achievement, unless adaptations are made in the methods of presenting learning experiences, the nature of the materials used, and/or in the learning environment" (p. 16). She also suggests that among visually handicapped children, those who are blind, have low vision, or are visually limited should be distinguished.

The cause of blindness often has psychological implications for the individual. Whether blindness is inherited or acquired through accident or disease may, for instance, be an important factor in explaining an individual's reaction toward his parents.

Hatfield (1975), of the National Society for the Prevention of Blindness, presented the most recent national data on blindness in school-age children. They are derived from a representative sample of 3,885 students (19.2 percent of the 20,216 students, 5 to 19 years of age, enrolled in 1968–1969 in U.S. public school classes as well as in the residential schools for the blind, and registered with the American Printing House for the Blind). On the basis of this number of legally blind students, and on the estimated total elementary and secondary school enrollment of about 51 million, Hatfield arrived at a blindness rate for school-age children of 39.3 per 100,000 students enrolled, or 1 in 2,500.

Almost one-third of the students were without useful vision (being totally blind, or having only light perception or light projection). Another one-third had vision ranging from motion/form perception to less than 20/200; and the remaining one-third had 20/200, the upper Snellen measurement limit for those classified as legally blind.

Table 7–1 presents the distribution of causes of visual impairment, according to Hatfield (p. 10). It shows that in 1968–1969 the largest known cause of blindness among school children was still retrolental fibroplasia (RLF). RLF accounted for 23.8 percent (5.8 percent in whom excessive oxygen use was established and 18 percent where use of oxygen is unknown). RLF is an eye disease that since 1942 (but mainly between 1949 and 1954) caused blindness almost exclusively in prematurely born babies. After intensive and painstaking medical research,

TABLE 7–1
PERCENTAGE DISTRIBUTION OF BLIND
SCHOOL CHILDREN BY ETIOLOGY

		Percentage
Infectious diseases		2.8
Rubella	1.3	
Toxoplasmosis	0.7	
Other	0.7	
Injuries and Poisonings		7.9
Excessive Oxygen (RLF)	5.8	
Other	2.1	
Neoplasms		3.7
General diseases		1.4
Central nervous system	0.9	
Other	0.5	
Prenatal influence		49.9
Hereditary	41.5	
Other congenital	8.3	
Unknown to science		0.8
Not reported		33.6
RLF (use of oxygen unknown)	18.0	
Other	15.6	

Adapted from Hatfield, E. M., Why are they blind? *Sight-Saving Review*, 1975, p. 10.

it was found in 1954 that the major cause of this condition was the administration of high concentrations of oxygen over prolonged periods of time to prematurely born infants. Since 1954 the application of oxygen in incubators has been carefully controlled, and RLF is practically eliminated. In the peak years of this disease, some states reported that almost 80 percent of their blind preschool children were blind as a result of it. It has been estimated that RLF caused blindness in more than 10,000 babies who have now reached adulthood.

The statistics of students enrolled in 1968–1969 do not reflect the effects of the maternal rubella epidemic in the United States in 1963–1964, which caused about 30,000 stillbirths and spontaneous abortions; and an almost equal number of children, as a result of it, were born with multiple handicaps and survived. Among them were thousands of children with blindness and such additional impairments as mental retardation, deafness, cerebral palsy, orthopedic disorders, epilepsy, and cardiac disease. In 1976 these children constituted a considerable part of the enrollment in public school special-education classes and, especially, in residential schools. Fortunately, a rubella vaccine has become available and it is now possible to prevent maternal infection by immunizing children against rubella.

Assuming that retrolental fibroplasia and maternal rubella will be reasonably controlled, the trend in the relative increase of multihandicapped children will still continue—because prenatal causes, not only affecting the eyes but producing additional abnormalities, are on the increase, while causes that affect only the eyes (infectious diseases, accidents) have decreased.

The large percentage of blindness shown in Table 7–1 as *prenatal influence* and *unknown to science* (50.7 percent) proves that our medical knowledge of causes of blindness is still far from satisfactory.

According to the annual report of the American Printing House for the Blind, in 1976 there were 26,958 legally blind children on its registry, of whom 19,596 (73 percent) were attending public school facilities for blind children and 7,362 (27 percent) were in residential schools. A full description of educational provisions for visually handicapped children is given by Taylor (1973).

AGE AT ONSET OF BLINDNESS

Visually handicapped individuals may have been born with a visual impairment or may have lost their sight completely or partially at any time during their lives. The extreme case of blindness is one in which the person is totally blind from birth. According to observations made by Toth (1930) and others, individuals who have lost their sight before about 5 years of age do not retain any useful visual imagery. Schlaegel (1953) confirmed this, stating that visual imagery tends to disappear if vision was lost before the age between 5 and 7 years. He also found that subjects with the poorest vision had the least number of visual responses. Various studies on dreams of the blind, reported by Blank (1958, p. 160), confirm that the critical period for retaining visual imagery in dreams is the age between 5 and 7 years. This "is also the period of cerebral structural maturation, the completion of early childhood ego development, and the beginning of latency." Therefore, children who lost their sight completely during the early years of their lives must also be regarded as extreme cases. If children have some sight, they observe visually and also visualize in their memory. Those who lose their sight completely or partially after 5 years of age may retain a more or less active visual frame of reference. They may, for instance, observe an object by touch and form a visual idea of it based on their past visual experiences. Of course, their visual observation is limited according to the degree of sight retained.

On the basis of this discussion, we must distinguish the following gradations of visual impairment so far as influence on sensory and memory activities is concerned:

1. Total blindness, congenital or acquired before the age of 5 years
2. Total blindness, acquired after 5 years of age
3. Partial blindness, congenital
4. Partial blindness, acquired
5. Partial sight, congenital
6. Partial sight, acquired

Of these six categories, the first four come within the definition of blindness, and children who belong to these four groups are considered blind, for educational purposes. Those who belong to the fifth and sixth groups are partially seeing children.

Hatfield's report (1975, p. 9) shows that 51.4 percent of the students in her study were born blind and 25.2 percent became blind in the first year of life. There were 31.2 percent with no useful vision; 29.7 percent with vision from 5/200 to 20/200; and 32.6 percent with 20/200 visual acuity.

It has been pointed out that a visual-acuity test is in most cases used as the indication of a person's degree of sight. Such a test, however, does not always give a true indication of the individual person's "visual efficiency." Many experienced observers have noted that some children with very low vision make much better use of vision than others who have a higher visual acuity. Such factors as general intelligence and environmental influences are assumed to be influential. Viktor Lowenfeld (1957, p. 462) considers inclination toward the visual type or the haptic type the most important factor determining whether the remaining sight is an asset or an irritation for the individual. Barker, Wright, Meyerson, and Gonick (1953) also call attention to this fact: "It is the adequacy of each individual's vision for the particular tasks of his life that is crucial for a somatopsychological definition of blindness, rather than the optically measured visual acuity" (p. 271).

In the following discussions it must be kept in mind that the effects of blindness are fully operative only in those children who have no sight and no workable visual imagery. For all others, adaptations and modifications in kind as well as in degree will have to be made according to the extent of their visual handicap.

COGNITIVE FUNCTIONS

Experiencing the Object World

Children who are blind or have lost their sight early in life must rely upon their remaining senses for gaining knowledge of the world around them. In attempintg to determine the importance of the remaining senses for the blind child's development, it is necessary to understand the basic functions of hearing and touch as cognitive means. Hearing gives certain clues in regard to distance and direction of the object, provided the object makes any sound. It does not convey any concrete ideas of objects as such. A blind person may, for instance, walk under a tree and hear the wind blow through the leaves. His past associations and experiences may enable him to interpret what he hears so that he can say whether the tree has leaves, needles, or is barren, whether the leaves are dry or fresh, how far away from the ground they are, and how thick the foliage is. His olfactory impressions may permit him to say whether the tree is in bloom or even what kind of tree it is. But all these clues will not give the blind person any idea of the shape and size of the leaves, the formation of the branches and trunk of the tree, and of its general appearance. Knowledge of the spatial qualities of objects can only be gained by touch observations in which kinesthetic sensations take part. The importance of hearing is in the area of verbal communication, in locomotion, and in general as an indicator of audible clues.

Lacking sight, actual knowledge of the

object world can be gained only by touch experiences. Lowenfeld (1950, p. 91) points out that tactual space perception of the blind is different from the visual space perception of the seeing. The main reason for the difference is to be found in the fact that tactual perception requires direct contact with the object to be observed. As a consequence, blind people can observe only those things that are accessible to them. The sun, the moon, the clouds, the horizon, and the sky are inaccessible, and can be explained to blind people only by the use of analogies from other sensory fields. This method must also be used in explaining to blind people such visual phenomena as shadows, perspective, and reflection of light. Many objects are too large to be observed by touch; for instance, a mountain or a large building. Other objects are too small and cannot be observed by touch with any degree of accuracy; for instance, flies or ants. Of course, microscopic observations can only be made visually. Fragile or delicate objects like butterflies, certain flowers or parts of flowers, snowflakes, or a spider's web also cannot be observed tactually. Objects in motion, live objects, and objects in certain conditions such as burning, boiling, or cooking cannot be observed by touch because they either change their shapes or positions or because direct contact with them would be dangerous. Liquids do not have shapes of their own, and are often difficult to observe by touch when kept in containers. This is also the case with mercury in narrow glass tubes, as used in thermometers and various gauges.

Many of these restrictions in observation hold true, not only for the blind person who has never seen, but also for the person who becomes blind later in life. Although he may have a very clear idea of the visual appearance of these objects, he cannot actually observe the object itself. He may, for instance, know what a thermometer looks like, but cannot read the temperature it indicates. If it is understood that visual observation permits perception of a situation as a whole,

and of the objects within the situation according to size, shape, distance, position, and color, it must also be recognized that tactual observations have their own characteristics and advantages. Touch perceptions relate, with the restrictions already discussed, to the size, shape, and position of objects. In addition, they also give such experiences as surface quality (roughness, smoothness, evenness), temperature, and weight. These qualities cannot be gained by visual observations, although seeing people may secure them if they bring their touch organs into play. The average person is inclined to neglect tactual observations almost completely because of the dominance of sight over all other senses. For instance, most seeing people are completely satisfied by looking at a sculpture without giving themselves the stimulating experience of observing it by touch. Another most important advantage of touch, as compared with vision, is that it does not depend upon light. Also, it is often easier to explore with the fingers rather than to get into a position where sight could be applied. Often, tactual observation is the only observation that can be made, as in some medical examinations.

There is a further important difference between sight and touch so far as activity of these senses is concerned. When a person is awake, his eyes are almost continuously open to stimulation coming from the outside world. This is different for touch activities. The hands as touch organs must be actively applied for the purpose of observation. Also, when they are applied, the horizon of touch extends only to the limited area of the outstretched hands. Observations beyond that limit can only be made if the person moves toward or follows the object to be observed. It is true that the exposed areas of the skin are open to stimulation by air currents and temperature, but this in no way compares with the perceptual activity of sight.

Hearing enables a blind person to gain information through verbal communication and to keep in contact with his social and physical environment. However, in respect to the latter, his efficiency is curtailed. People may stop talking or may not talk at all, so that he is unaware of their presence. Persons may move away or enter a room without being heard. It may not always be obvious to the blind person whether a comment is being directed to him or to someone else. Many things do not give any sound; others may sound only under certain conditions, such as leaves when the wind is blowing. Continuous sound such as that of rain may drown out all other audible clues; and snow deadens sounds that may indicate changes in the environment. All these factors contribute to more chances for being less adequate in meeting the demands of the situation. Therefore, it can be assumed that they increase a blind person's nervous tension and insecurity.

With the exception of taste, which permits touch observations because the tongue and the mouth envelop or at least touch the object, the other senses relate only sensory clues indicating the presence, location, or nature of certain objects. In passing by a garden, for instance, one can smell if there are certain trees or plants around, provided the wind does not blow in the opposite direction. As one walks on the street, such places as a drugstore, a shoestore, or a food market can be ascertained by their specific odors. Also, the exposed skin surface reacts to changes in air current and in temperature, which may give a blind person clues concerning the spatial characteristics of his surroundings. Walking along the walls of buildings feels entirely different from walking along a garden fence, along shrubs, or in open space.

Space and Form Perception

The process by which space perception is attained by touch has been the subject of considerable research. Heller (1895) and Steinberg (1920) agree that the touch sense

is the only original spatial sense of those who were born blind. Heller distinguished two types of tactual perception by the hands. Enveloping touch is that in which small objects are enfolded by letting either one or both hands observe the object. This type of tactual perception he called "synthetic touch" because the form of the object is perceived as a whole, more or less simultaneously. In observing an apple, for instance, children will gain an idea of the shape of the fruit by enfolding it in their hands. This enveloping touch is applied not only to smaller objects but also to larger ones when only parts of them are subjected to closer observation. The other type of tactual perception is applied to large objects that extend beyond the limited scope of one or both hands, as in the observation of a chair. Here the moving hands follow the shape of the object and, if it is a very large one, the whole body may actively participate in the process. This method has been called "analytic touch" because it consists of successive impressions gained by observing parts of the object. These successive impressions, however, cannot remain isolated, but must result in a unified "touch idea" of the object. Without such unification, blind people would not have any workable concept of larger objects or of their environment.

German psychologists considered this phenomenon of unification to be the central problem of blindness, and various explanations have been given for it. Steinberg (1920, p. 139) assumes, as a result of experimentation in which Gestalt psychological principles were applied, that there is a mental process of "expansion of tactual space." Heller (1895, p. 68) believes that there is a contraction of tactual space in which large objects are reduced by a special mental act until a simultaneous idea of the total object is achieved. Another theory postulates the perseveration of the earlier perceptions until they combine with the later ones into a spatial and temporal continuum, a spatial Gestalt. Senden (1960; published in German,

1932) reviews the reports and studies of others concerned with the problem of the perception of space and shape in congenitally blind persons who recovered their sight after eye surgery. He comes to the conclusion that tactual perceptions do not result in awareness of space. The congenitally blind person creates temporal schemata and verbal concepts that are "a surrogate for the spatial awareness he lacks." Others disagree with this point of view, including those who discuss in an appendix to his book the significance of Senden's work for related disciplines. Studies by Juurmaa (1973), who also gave a detailed review of past work on the phenomenon of spatial conceptualization without vision, and studies by Revesz (1950), Rosencranz and Suslick (1976), and many others have not given us a convincing explanation of either the nature or the development of spatial concepts without vision.

Whatever the explanation may be, the fact that blind individuals are able to reproduce all kinds of objects, small and large, in modeling and handwork, and that they can recognize objects on the basis of previous observations, is evidence that they must be able to unify separate perceptions into one total concept of the object.

All tactual observations of the fingers, hands, arms, or other parts of the body have a kinesthetic component, because muscle sensations are involved in these movements. For example, in observing a chair with both hands, the touch movements of the two hands and arms may proceed in different directions and with changing distances between them. Therefore, the actual spatial experience is made up, not only by the touch contacts with the object, but also by the variety of muscular sensations accompanying the touch movements.

Tactual perception results not only in spatial experiences but in a number of other touch sensations. The surface of the skin has specialized nerve endings, which are the receptors for pressure, pain, warmth, and cold. Sensitive spots for these sensations are dispersed over various areas of the body in varying density. Experiments reported by Hayes (1941, pp. 16–48) have shown that blind individuals have no better discrimination in regard to cutaneous sensitivities than do seeing persons.

Color Ideas

Space and form can be perceived through sight as well as by touch. Color perception, however, is a function of the retina, and no other organ can take it over. When the retina is destroyed, when it cannot be affected by light stimulation, when the stimuli received by the retina are not carried back to the interbrain and the cortex, or when the visual areas of the brain are destroyed, total blindness occurs and color vision is absent.

Therefore, persons who have been born blind or have lost their sight so early that they do not have any visual memory do not have any real ideas of color. Because they live in a world that makes constant use of color observations and color references, they build up substitutive ideas for color on the basis of verbal, sensory, and emotional associations. They hear people talk, for example, about the blue sky; as a result, all or some of the different sensations and emotions caused by fine weather may build up as a substitutive idea for the color blue, in this case a pleasant one. On the other hand, the commonly unpleasant connotation that this color carries in the proverbial "blue Monday" may give the word *blue* a different emotional character. Because such color associations vary from individual to individual, and also from time to time, the substitutive color ideas are not constant. Blind children learn the common color associations such as blue sky, red blood, white snow, and green grass because they are a part of their socially needed vocabulary. However, because they cannot experience color, their attention should be directed toward aspects of situations and objects that can be experienced by them, in order to avoid purely verbal preoccupation. Excessive and unrealistic use of color words by blind individuals is not rare; in many cases, it can be regarded as a compensatory mechanism.

Colored audition, which is a form of synesthesia, plays an important role in the ideational life of many persons who have lost their sight during childhood or later on. In this phenomenon, color sensations are closely attached to auditory sensations, and may appear regularly in response to certain auditory stimulations. These secondary sensations of color are called photisms. Photisms may be attached to a variety of experiences and ideas. Wheeler and Cutsforth have published research on this problem and examined the function of synesthesia in learning (1921), in the development of meaning (1922) and concepts (1925), and in other thought processes. Voss (1930), in his extensive study of color-hearing of the blind, enumerates photisms attached to timbre of tones and sounds, especially of various musical instruments: varying pitch of tones of an instrument; single tones within a scale; major and minor scales; voices of persons; vowels and consonants; various emotions; numbers; days; months; geographical names, particularly those of cities and countries; names of the notes of the scale; and so on. These photisms, once present in an individual, are quite inflexible, although they vary from person to person. Of course, only persons who have seen colors can experience colored audition, because imagination cannot create anything that was not experienced previously by the senses.

Sensory Acuteness

The assumption that the loss of one sense is compensated for by a more or less automatic improvement in the acuity of the other senses is one of long standing and perseverance. Three explanations might be considered for this. The wish to have nature act according to justice, and thereby relieve one of feelings of guilt or the responsibility to help, ascribes to other minorities similar facilities. Secondly, the fact that blind individuals may learn to use their senses better than those who can rely upon sight gives some actual support to this assumption. Finally, there is a widespread tendency to consider anything the blind can do as admirable and superior, which only disguises a tendency to consider them inferior.

It is not surprising that experiments to determine the differences in sensory acuteness of the blind and the seeing were performed to a considerable extent around the turn of the century, when experimental psychology began to be practiced in many laboratories, particularly under Wilhelm Wundt in Germany and William James in the United States. Hayes (1941, pp. 16–48) reviewed in detail the various studies that tested the comparative abilities of the blind and the seeing to distinguish the direction of sound, to determine the distance of sounds, and to discriminate the intensity of sounds. Hayes also reviewed studies of acuteness of smell, taste, and touch; discrimination of lifted weights, of passive and active pressure, and of tactual space; sensitiveness to changes in temperature; and acuteness of the vibratory sense, particularly in the deaf-blind. Fisher (1964) investigated the capability of spatial localization in blind and sighted subjects. His experiments gave no support to the two hypotheses (1) that the acuity of hearing is improved in the blind and (2) that they develop an extra sense of some kind. Auditory discrimination ability of visually handicapped children was again investigated by Hare, Hammill, and Crandell (1970). No significant differences were found between the usually handicapped and the sighted children of similar mental and chronological ages. The authors believe that lack of training in auditory perceptual skills from early childhood on may well account for differences between visually impaired and sighted children in certain abstract and conceptual skills that were found in other studies (Axelrod, 1959; Rubin, 1964; Worchel, 1951).

There is no experimental research available on pain sensitivity, on the sense of balance, or on the organic sense. Hayes (1941, pp. 63–80) investigated the memory of blind children—rote memory, recall, and logical memory—and found no superiority in this field either. He concludes: "In memory, as in sensation, compensation is not a gift but the reward of persistent effort" (p. 79). Therefore, any higher efficiency of the blind in interpreting the sensory data perceived must be the result of attention, practice, adaptation, and increased use of the remaining faculties.

Almost twenty years later, Axelrod (1959) examined the effects of blindness on two levels of sensory functioning: a basic tactile level where light-touch sensitivity and two-point acuity of three finger tips were tested; and a "higher level" where sense data received through the haptic and auditory modalities were utilized. He did not find any generalized rise of sensory acuity in the early-blind group; on the contrary, they did significantly less well than sighted subjects on the "higher level" complex-task performance. These results stress the importance of early visual learning for later problem solving. Axelrod adds:

brain damage associated with, or consequent to, blindness of early onset cannot be ruled out as a factor" but continues: "The difference between early-blind and sighted groups on the complex tasks were, though statistically significant, nonetheless small; they should not be regarded as evidence of gross impairment of intellective processes (p. 73).

A great deal of hypothesizing was required to bring some coherence to the interpretation of the data of this study. This indicates that the last word on the problem of "sensory compensation" may not yet have been spoken. There may be processes in operation that so far have eluded experimentation.

There are only a few studies on the widely assumed superior abilities of the blind in music. Seashore and Ling (1918) and Merry (1931) found no superiority in the blind. Pitman (1965) reviewed a few other publica-

tions in which blind persons' musical capacities were examined. He concluded: "The studies mentioned, although by no means conclusive, would seem to suggest that in music the blind are of generally average ability by reference to norms available for the sighted" (p. 64). In his own investigation, the musical ability of 90 blind children was assessed by the Wing Test of Musical Intelligence and compared with a control sample of 130 sighted children. The blind children tested higher than the sighted ones, but their superiority showed up in those subtests where perception was of particular importance. This superiority he ascribed to the blind children's concentration on aural communication, and he concluded "that fundamentally the blind are no better at music than the sighted" (p. 77).

The belief that blind people have a superior ability to interpret human voices also belongs in this category. It is unquestionably true—and we know it from various autobiographical and other reports—that some blind persons can remember and recognize many voices even after a long lapse of time. They also develop through continuous practice the ability to discern in voices certain moods, emotions, attitudes, and such traits as sincerity, tact, friendliness, and their opposites. On the other hand, it often happens that blind individuals rely too much upon the voice as an indicator of a person's character, and either accept or reject the person on that ground alone. In this respect they are not different from seeing persons who form impressions on the basis of pleasant or unpleasant appearances. Cantril and Allport (1935) conducted some experiments in which blind and seeing subjects were asked to judge from voices vocation, age, interests, and such features of personality as introversion and extroversion. They found, contrary to the popular belief, that the blind are less accurate in their judgments than the seeing. They explained this by the fact that the blind have fewer opportunities to observe and to study personality and also have no visual assistance in correcting their errors in judgment. These experiments have been made with a small number of persons and can only be considered as preliminary. The problem of interpretation of voices and its influence on the blind is one that should receive further attention. Regardless of the objective validity or invalidity of the judgment which blind people form in listening to voices, it is a fact that they are strongly influenced by them and find in the variety of timbres and modulations a source of enriching social experiences.

Intelligence and Concept Development

Samuel P. Hayes has, since 1918, reported on his studies in connection with the standardization of intelligence tests for blind children. In his *Contributions to a Psychology of Blindness* (1941), Hayes collected his writings dealing with various psychological problems of blindness and with the intelligence and academic achievements of blind children who were then largely attending residential schools for the blind. He found that they had a mean IQ of slightly above 93; that congenitally and adventitiously blind children did not differ in intelligence, though their "mental constitution" may well be essentially different; that many blind children "blossom out" under the favorable conditions of a good residential school, particularly if their home environment was inferior; and that the Hayes-Binet Scale is far from satisfactory with younger and older children (1942, pp. 225–226).

Since Hayes made the latter statement, the verbal parts of the Wechsler scales have become widely used in testing the visually handicapped. Hayes (1950) recommended their use and reported consistent high correlations between the Interim Hayes-Binet Intelligence Tests for the Blind and the Wechsler Bellevue Scale. In an item analysis of the latter, he showed its value in use with blind students.

A thorough investigation of the performance of blind and sighted children on the WISC was undertaken by Tillman (1967), who used in his studies 110 educationally blind and an equal number of sighted children, matched for age and sex. In order to determine how appropriate the items of the WISC are for blind children, he evaluated their performance in terms of item difficulty curves, t-tests, and subtest reliabilities. He found "that blind children score about the same as normal children on Arithmetic, Information and Vocabulary, but did less well on Comprehension and Similarities" (p. 73). The application of factor analyses led him to a number of educationally important conclusions regarding the ability structure of blind as compared with sighted groups: (1) blind children retain experiences as facts equally well as normal children, but these experiences are less integrated and tend to stand alone; (2) blind children tend to approach abstract conceptualization problems from a concrete and functional level, and consequently lag behind the sighted children; (3) for blind children Vocabulary appears to be only word-definition whereas it has much more than a word-naming function for sighted children; and (4) the blind are quite comparable to the sighted in numerical ability.

In a further exploration of the comparability of WISC profiles of blind and sighted groups, Tillman and Osborne (1969) confirmed that blind children do less well on Similarities and better on Digit Span. The results "suggest that specific differences between blind and sighted groups are to be found in conceptual development and in short-term memory" (p. 4).

Some of these findings were confirmed by Smits and Mommers (1976), but their factor analysis revealed that, except for Digit Span, the factor patterns of the subtests were less scattered for the blind than for the seeing. They ascribe this lesser specificity of the subtests for the blind to their greater dependence on verbal information.

The concept formation of blind children

in the field of scientific and technical phenomena was thoroughly investigated by Boldt (1966; 1969). He distinguished, according to the results of his studies of 103 visually handicapped children, ten different modes of theory formation on three different levels, "leading from the naïve subjective relationship with phenomena, through a pragmatic oriented quasi-objective relationship, to an understanding of the environment as totally disassociated objects" (p. 7). In this "process of progressive disassociation of subject and object," blindness and near-blindness has a retarding influence.

Zweibelson and Barg (1967) investigated concept formation as one aspect of language development. They rated children's responses in the Similarities and Vocabulary subtests of the WISC according to whether they were concrete (a specific characteristic of the object is considered to be the content), functional, or abstract (summing up all essential characteristics of the object) definitions. The blind children functioned primarily on a concrete and functional-conceptual level, using abstract concepts to a far lesser degree than their sighted peers. The authors recommend, therefore, that blind children be supplied with concrete experiences, both with objects and situations, and that a multisensory approach as well as training in reasoning tasks be used according to the child's needs and level of development.

These results are in line with Rubin's (1964) valuable study on abstract functioning in the adult blind. Rubin found that adult congenitally blind subjects did less well on abstraction tests than did sighted or adventitiously blind groups. He also stressed the importance of the age at onset of blindness for abstract functioning and for tests involving this ability. Studies to be reported on later (under the heading Orientation and Locomotion) also point out the importance of vision for the ability to visualize in performing spatial tasks.

Juurmaa (1967) raised many interesting and important questions—some similar to those investigated by Tillman and others—which deserve to be topics of research. However, his study has a number of faults; he applied refined statistical analyses to inexact data, which were collected from inadequate samples under adverse and insufficiently controlled testing conditions. He used many tests that were only cursorily described, appear difficult to quantify, and are not replicable. Similar and other methodological objections were raised by Tillman, Bashaw, and Bradley (1969).

Witkin, Birnbaum, Lomonaco, Lehr, and Herman (1968) gave a special battery of perceptual and problem-solving tests, and clay models of the human figure, to twenty-five congenitally totally blind boys and girls and twenty-eight sighted boys and girls. They wanted to test the hypothesis that "lack of vision is likely to hamper development of articulation and to foster dependence on others" and that, therefore, "congenitally blind children may be expected to show less differentiated cognitive functioning than their sighted peers" (p. 767). The study confirmed that blind children are more global in cognition than the sighted, who are more articulate (that is, more analytical and structuring). Blindness slows the pace of the usual progression in cognitive development from the global to the articulated. On the other hand, the blind children were superior to the sighted in tasks requiring sustained auditory attention, and about equivalent in verbal-comprehension ability. Differences in the kind of experiences they had while growing up explain the superiority in auditory attention and the lag in development of articulation.

Differences in the kind of experiences blind children have were the topic of an investigation by Kephart, Kephart, and Schwarz (1974). "The manner in which the blind children are processing personal and environmental information appears to result in fragmented and distorted understandings of simple straightforward concepts" (p. 427). The authors call for more research that will enable blind children to learn to process information gained from total sensory experiences.

Gottesman (1971) compared congenitally blind children, sighted, and sighted blindfolded children in their object-recognition abilities. In another study (1973), he gave these groups two identical balls and changed the shape of one of them to test for conservation of weight and volume. He later summed up the significant findings of both studies as follows:

(1) Vision and visual imagery were not necessary for the performance of Piagetian tasks of haptic perception and conservation development. Touch and tactile imagery may explain the ability of the group of blind children to respond successfully. (2) The sequential development of age and stage were found to be appropriate to both groups. (3) Vision was not necessary in responding to actual tasks, as noted in the success of the sighted blindfolded group. On the task of conservation, this group performed more accurately than did the other groups (Gottesman, 1976, p. 99).

Higgins (1973) conducted a carefully arranged study of Inhelder's and Piaget's theories with congenitally blind children. The results indicated:

Contrary to expectations, the blind subjects of this study did not display a developmental lag that could be attributed to a delay in the formation of intellectual structures. Their apparent shortcomings were found to originate in the limitations of tactile perception. . . . The condition of total congenital blindness *per se* is not sufficient to produce a delay in the formation of the intellectual structures underlying classification (p. 40).

The phrase "contrary to expectations" above refers to such previously mentioned studies as those of Axelrod (1959), Tillman (1967), Zweibelson and Barg (1967), Witkin *et al.* (1968), and also to some studies that are based on Piagetian theories and have found blind children lagging in fundamental cognitive activities: in conservation of substance, weight, and volume (Miller, 1969); in the ability to recognize conservation of substance (Tobin, 1972); in conservation of weight (Brekke, Williams, & Tait, 1974); and in attainment of classification and seriation concepts (Friedman & Pasnak, 1973).

Finally, Swallow (1976), in a survey of current literature under Piagetian viewpoints, concluded:

The need for direct, concrete experience for blind children is of paramount importance. Direct physical experiences with the real object, total sensory and conceptual involvement with concrete objects, appropriate verbal interaction with other children and adults will help to give blind children a knowledge of the realities around them (p. 280).

In view of the increased interest in applying Piagetian theories to visually handicapped children, the following statement by Piaget appears to be highly relevant:

Blind infants have the great disadvantage of not being able to make the same coordinations in space that normal children are capable of during the first year or two, so that the development of sensory-motor intelligence and the coordination of actions at this level are seriously impeded in blind children. For this reason, we find that there are even greater delays in their development at the level of representational thinking and that language is not sufficient to compensate for the deficiency in the coordination of actions. The delay is made up ultimately, of course, but it is significant and much more considerable than the delay in the development of logic in deaf and dumb children (1970, pp. 46–47).

Newland (1961; 1964) recognized the need for a test of learning aptitude developed specifically for and standardized upon the blind. He suggested an approach in which those psychological processes that make achievement possible are assessed. His Blind Learning Aptitude Test (1961), BLAT, uses a variety of embossed geometric figures of increasing complexity in order to determine the ability of children to distinguish tactually some of the figures that do not belong in a given group (see chapter 3). The BLAT is an individual, nonverbal, untimed test (taking 20 to 45 minutes) for functionally blind children. It was standardized on 961 residential and day-school children, and is most meaningful in the 6-to-12 year age range. It is a highly reliable instrument that correlates better with measured educational achievement than do the Hayes-Binet and the verbal WISC (Hecht & Newland, 1965).

Wattron (1956) reported a successful attempt to use adapted Kohs-type blocks that have smooth and rough sides, instead of the white and red colors. The Ohwaki-Kohs test is a modified version of the Kòhs Block-Design Test, which substitutes different types of fabric for the colors used by Kohs. Ohwaki, Tanno, Ohwaki, *et al.* (1960) reported significant correlations between its scores and school achievement for Japanese blind children. Suinn, Dauterman, and Shapiro (1966) used the Ohwaki-Kohs test at Stanford University and found it useful with blind adults, though their experience indicated the need for a modification of the test materials. The use of a number of other performance tests has been reported (Dauterman, Shapiro, & Suinn, 1967), but none has been satisfactorily explored or standardized to make it practically applicable, particularly so far as its use with blind children is concerned.

Davis (1962) reported that he and his associates at the Perkins School for the Blind were nearing completion of an adaptation of the 1960 Standford Revision of the Binet-Simon Scales,

in which a definite effort has been made to substitute items calling for the use of tactual perception and organization as substitutes for those items in the original test calling for visual perception and organization. . . . so that a single meaningful test will result (pp. 50–51).

Though no detailed account of this Perkins-Binet test has yet been published, Davis (1970) reported that the tentative form of the test was administered to 2,187 subjects; as a result, Form N for subjects with no useful vision and Form U for those with usable vision were established. Coveny (1972) confirmed the Perkins-Binet's reliability and validity, and considers it a valuable clinical instrument providing educational data not available from using verbal tests like the Hayes-Binet or the WISC.

According to recent studies, there are two causes of blindness that appear to have definite effects on the intelligence of children affected by them: retinoblastoma and bilateral congenital anophthalmos. Williams (1968)—a British psychologist who devised the Williams Intelligence Test for Children with Defective Vision (1956), widely used abroad—reports on a study of fifty children whose blindness was caused by retinoblastoma, a malignant tumor of the eye, originating from immature retina cells. Retinoblastoma may be present at birth, or the tumors are discovered before the child is 6 years of age. There is a hereditary factor involved in the disease, and there is no sex linkage. Retinoblastoma is a rare disease, and experienced observers have noted that practically all children whose blindness is caused by it show superior intelligence. Williams compared the IQ scores of fifty retinoblastoma cases with seventy-four non-retinoblastoma subjects who were blind but had no additional handicaps. The retinoblastoma group had a mean IQ (on the Williams Intelligence Test Scale) of 119.72 as compared with the control group's mean IQ of 102.81. The difference was highly significant. The IQ range of the retinoblastoma group was from 101 to 146, with 78 percent of the children scoring above 110. No definite explanation for this phenomenon can be given. Williams's findings were confirmed by Levitt, Rosenbaum, Willerman, and Levitt (1972); by Thurrell and Josephson (1966); and by Chase (1970), who also pointed out that retinoblastoma is a genetic defect and that its study may help in clarifying the genetic contribution to intellectual development.

Congenital anophthalmos, a lack of eye-structure formation in which part of the embryonic structure of the brain fails to develop, is also a rare cause of blindness. In most, but not all, cases it results in developmental retardation and is associated with additional handicaps, according to a study by Bachelis (1967). A majority of the cases in the study had subnormal IQs, many of them requiring custodial care, though there were some who showed superior intelligence and good adjustment. There was a high incidence of associated handicaps, as was expected because congenital anophthalmos is due to a generalized genetic disturbance. The author recommends early comprehensive diagnostic evaluations in order to identify and treat any possible additional handicaps.

There has been a rekindling of interest in psychological evaluation, caused by the dissatisfaction with past testing and by the educational and psychological needs of multi-handicapped blind children. But this time, what is sought is not a measure of intelligence, such as IQ, but rather a more global indication of the child's current capacity and his potential for future growth. This, rather than formal testing, is what assessment is designed to provide, often using prolonged, intensive, and informal observation by trained personnel. This may require temporary placement of the child in a diagnostic center or in an assessment group or class (Escovar, 1976). The October, 1975 issues of the *New Outlook for the Blind* and of *Education of the Visually Handicapped* are devoted to the topic Assessment of the Visually Handicapped and contain much valuable information.

Achievement Test Results

The first report on the use of an achievement test with the blind was published in 1918 by Hayes, who used a reading test with blind pupils. In 1927, Maxfield published her *Adaptation of Educational Tests for Use with Blind Pupils,* in which she gave directions for the administration of parts of the Stanford Achievement Tests and the Gray Oral Reading Check Tests. Since then, many achievement tests have been used and adapted for use with the blind, such as the Metropolitan Achievement Tests, the Sones-Harry High School Achievement Test, and the Myers-Ruch High School Progress Test. The Stanford Achievement Tests in their various forms have been used most widely in schools for the blind. The 1973 edition of this test promises, according to Morris (1974), to be the most useful to date. The College Entrance Examination Board also offers its tests in braille for those blind students who plan to enter college. Hayes (1941, p. 155) found two basic changes necessary in adapting achievement tests for use with blind pupils: (1) greater detail in preliminary instructions, and (2) an increase of three times the time allowance given for seeing pupils. This ratio was indicated as desirable in a study by Caldwell (1932).

Nolan (1962) questioned this "somewhat arbitrary ratio" as established by Hayes in 1937. He mentioned particularly that braille Grade 1½ has been replaced by braille Grade 2 and that the ratio between braille and print reading may not be "the same at all grade levels and for all forms of material commonly presented in achievement tests (p. 494). Lowenfeld, Abel, and Hatlen (1969) investigated the braille reading rate and found that on the fourth-grade level, blind children need about twice as much reading time as seeing children; on the eighth-grade level, about one and one-half to twice as much time. They concluded: "As a result of the present study, revision of the time allowance to about twice the time as compared with seeing children seems to be indicated" (p. 29).

Although blind pupils show, grade by grade, about the same achievement as seeing pupils, Hayes pointed out (1941) that "blind children average at least two years older than seeing children in the same grades, so comparisons by age, either chronological or mental, demonstrate their retardation" (p. 216). Lowenfeld (1945) confirmed this and considered various factors responsible for this age-grade retardation, such as environmental influences resulting in lack of opportunities for observations, slower acquisition of knowledge as a result of blindness, and slower braille reading. Lowenfeld (1955) indicated that more recent data might "show a change due to the increased use of aural sources of information, such as the Talking Book and the radio, and to the greater integration of blind children with seeing children" (p. 231). Lowenfeld, Abel, and Hatlen (1969) found indeed a considerable narrowing of the age-grade differences between blind and seeing students.

There are very few reports available that deal with the use of achievement tests with visually impaired children. Trismen (1967) undertook an equating study of parts of the Sequential Tests of Educational Progress (STEP) to relate scores on the braille forms to existing norms. The social studies, science, and mathematics tests were given to about 270 visually handicapped students registered as braille readers in twenty-nine residential schools. He came to the conclusion "that, in general, the blind equating samples used in this study are roughly comparable in achievement level to the national norms samples, when tested under untimed conditions with instruments which have been specially adapted for their use" (p. 423).

The Verbal Scale of the Wechsler Adult Intelligence Scale and the Haptic Intelligence Scale for Adult Blind (Shurrager & Shurrager, 1964) were used by Streitfeld and Avery (1968) with thirty-one residential school students, age 16 to 19 years. They found that both tests were equally good in predicting academic achievement for totally blind students; but for the partially sighted, the WAIS was better in predicting academic

success. They recommended further research using the Haptic Intelligence Scale for a variety of purposes. The use of an abbreviated Haptic Intelligence Scale was suggested by Avery and Streitfeld (1969).

Cundick, Crandell, and Hendrix (1974) examined the problems involved in group testing of blind persons, such as presentation of test items and recording of answers. They recommend the use of prerecorded cassette tapes and of a tactual answer board.

Bauman (1973a) added a new interest inventory to the three most widely in use with the visually handicapped—the Kuder Preference Record, the California Occupational Interest Inventory, and the Strong Vocational Interest Blank. The new PRG Interest Inventory for the Blind is entirely based on jobs, hobbies, and interests of blind people; it does not involve confusing comparison systems; it is easy to administer (by tape recording, and with a non-braille mechanical answer system); and it works well with adults and teen-agers.

The most valuable source of information on tests and testing techniques for use with blind pupils and adults is *A Manual for the Psychological Examination of the Adult Blind* (Bauman & Hayes, 1951), which also includes information concerning special considerations of a blind client's history and sources for securing testing material. Bauman (1973b) and Scholl and Schnur (1976) updated and enlarged this manual.

The Use of Touch in Cognition

If blind children are to gain experiences comparable in reality value to those of seeing children, they must acquire them through touch observations. Such experiences are particularly essential during the elementary grades when children form the basic concepts of their environment. Objects or situations can either be observed in reality or as models. If an object is too large, the model will represent it in a contracted form; if an object is too small, the model will show it enlarged and most likely also reinforced. A model is only a substitute for the real experience and is always in some way incomplete or distorted. For example, if animals are represented in stuffed form, they may be true to size, shape, and surface quality, but do not give the feeling of warmth, life, and motion that one gets when observing the animal alive. If only a model of the animal is used, size and texture are given up, the motion is "frozen," and the only quality preserved for observation is shape. These shortcomings are, in one or the other combination, true for all teaching models. It is therefore necessary for teachers to take great care that their pupils will not form misconceptions about certain qualities of the object presented, particularly in regard to its actual size.

Mandola (1968) calls attention to the fact that the use of models involves perceptual problems which have not been explored, and that the wide use of models by teachers of the blind rests on the assumption that tactual aids make the abstract concrete; this has neither been proven nor systematically investigated, and there is certainly need for research in the area. However, with the precautions already voiced and those subsequently given, the use of models appears to be pragmatically justified until proof to the contrary is provided. It has been found successful with countless blind children by generations of experienced teachers in this country and abroad.

Although there is almost no research available on the psychological and educational problems of touch observation as such, a few comments based on experience are offered here. The ability to observe by touch and to manipulate develops with the child. The cutaneous senses, prehensory and grasping abilities, kinesthetic sensations, time experiences, and, last but not least, coordination and intelligent interpretation, are brought into action according to the child's developmental level. The younger the child is, the simpler must be the experiences from

which he can gain. At first he will be limited in observing, as well as in verbalizing, his experiences. But by practice he will acquire the ability to observe better, to differentiate objects according to size, weight, shape, material, surface, temperature, and to give verbal reports of his observations.

Simultaneousness is characteristic of visual observation, whereas successiveness is characteristic of touch observation. Every part of the object must be covered by or brought under the touching hand, often not only once but frequently, so that both the large forms and the finer details can be observed. In addition to this individual need for more time, there is a group factor that must be considered. Many children can, at the same time, look at an object, whereas only one child can observe it by touch. If touch observation is limited to the hours of instruction only, it will either consume too much time or the individual child will be confined to only a cursory inspection of the object. For this reason, material for observation should be left in the classroom so that the pupils can continue their observation during their free time. The teacher may call the attention of the pupils to certain characteristic features and let them proceed on their own with the actual observation—either in preparation or in a follow-up of the instruction period. In this directed but unsupervised observation, totally blind children and those with partial or normal sight gain mutually from their experiences.

The fact that blind children must, in their acquisition of actual object knowledge, rely on the touch senses puts them at a serious disadvantage in experiencing objects and situations in their totality. For seeing children, sight is the unifying agent that enables the individual in a short time to observe situations in toto and to combine part experiences into wholes. Sight also serves as an organizer of discrete experiences, and facilitates the reduction of form varieties to simpler patterns or schemata. The blind child gains many impressions by the use of his senses: he may hear or smell something; he may feel air currents or temperature changes; and he may have actual touch contact with the object or situation or with parts of them. But all these experiences are discrete and unorganized, and remain so unless guided observation or teaching lends organization and structure to them. Teaching by the unit method has, therefore, a special purpose in the blind child's education. It gives him those unifying experiences that he often cannot gain because of his lack of sight.

The young blind child forms his own concepts of his environment as he grows into it. These concepts, incomplete and distorted as they may be, suffice for his purposes and satisfy the child's restricted curiosity. A desire to know more about things, to know them in reality and fully, must often be awakened and encouraged in blind children. The preschool years should stimulate such inquisitiveness in the young blind child; but often this is suppressed by an ill-conceived "touch taboo." Then, the more difficult task of reestablishing this desire for exploration is left to the teacher.

In the process of his observations, the child does not react with one sense but with his total sensory equipment; he hears, smells, and, if given opportunity, tastes. Hearing and smelling have, in common with sight, the characteristic that they need not be applied but are continuously open to stimulation; the sense of taste, like touch, functions only when its organ comes into direct contact with the object to be tasted. Thus, children will hear and smell while they are awake, although their observations need to become conscious ones in order to be of real value.

Children, and also adults, may listen to the twitter of birds again and again without noticing the great variety of bird sounds—it is just twitter to them. Once their attention is called to the specific song of, say, the robin, and this recognition is sufficiently implanted, they will not fail to recognize it. In walking through a wood, one may smell a peculiar

odor that can be traced to rotting wood. Once this connection between the odor and its source is firmly established, the child will know how to make use of it as a clue to the presence of rotting wood or other material in the same condition. Thus, besides recognition, "implanting" and "establishing" are necessary processes before an experience can become of value for future use. The concept of "passive" and "active" knowledge, as elaborated in the field of creative growth by Viktor Lowenfeld (1957, p. 110), is a most useful one in this connection. The methods by which education succeeds in transforming passive into active knowledge are the same for seeing and blind children, and include motivation, insight, exercise, activity, repetition, and various forms of reinforcement. Which of these will be used in a given situation with the individual child or with a group of children is a decision that must be left to the teacher.

Confirmation of the need of congenitally totally blind children for concrete experiences with objects and situations, and for unifying structuring experiences (elaborated on above, and more closely explained by Lowenfeld, 1950) comes from a variety of studies, such as those by DeMott (1972), Harley (1963), Nagera and Colonna (1965), Omwake and Solnit (1961), Rubin (1964), Swallow (1976), Zweibelson and Barg (1967), and others. Bauman (1946) stated that studies of test results

> . . . point very strongly to the desirability of including in the education of blind children far more contact with practical materials of possible vocational value, such as tools. The inability of some blind individuals to deal with this type of material suggests lack of previous contact with it rather than lack of fundamental ability to comprehend it (p. 153).

Normally, a child acquires his knowledge of tools by observing when anyone in the family does some work in which tools are used, or when he can watch a workman performing his job. Where the seeing child can watch from a distance, the blind child must have direct contact with the object to be observed; this is his greatest obstacle to the casual acquisition of knowledge and experience. It implies that blind children must be given special opportunities for observation in order to make their environment real to them. This will help them avoid falling into a pattern of unreality that so often interferes with their later adjustment to the requirements of life.

Deutsch (1940) investigated the effect of lack of sight on the sense of reality in the person born blind. He gave twenty-eight blind pupils a box containing seven wooden blocks of various shapes, which the subjects were asked to name and arrange in the order of preference. They were asked to enumerate the forms of the blocks from memory, and it was also observed how they reacted to removal of one or more of the blocks while they were playing with them. Deutsch noticed that the curiosity of the person born blind was more quickly satisfied than that of the seeing, that some subjects were inhibited about feeling the figures, and that observation of loss of some blocks resulted in a striking readiness to give up reality and escape into fantasy.

The ability of blind children to recognize by touch simple embossed pictures has been studied and reported on by Merry and Merry (1933). On the basis of a series of experiments, they reached the following conclusions:

It seems unwise to expend any considerable amount of time teaching blind children how to recognize tactually pictures of three-dimensional objects. If, however, the needs of the child demand instruction upon the identification of simple figures in two dimensions, time for such work seems justified. . . . It may be of value to make use of embossed designs of a bi-dimensional type in the education of blind children, but it is very doubtful if embossed pictures of tri-dimensional objects, wherein

perspective is involved, possess any real meaning for children without sight, even after systematic instruction (p. 163).

The idea of using embossed pictures in the education of blind children is an old and often tried one. In addition to the experiments just discussed, the accumulated experiences of teachers of the blind also prove that embossed pictures of three-dimensional objects are of no practical value. Usually they are made by using three-dimensional dots or lines or raised surfaces for the purpose of making tangible two-dimensional outlines of objects as perceived by vision. Thus, perceptual qualities of vision, such as perspective, base line, light and shadow, and distinctness are applied to the sense of touch, which does not function according to them. To be concrete, the embossed outline of a dog gives the shape of this animal as it is seen. The hands, observing a real dog, or a part of it, by touch, move in three dimensions and embrace the object or parts of it in an act of three-dimensional perception. They do not follow the visually perceived outline of the object. In an embossed drawing, the dog's four legs are represented in one plane, whereas to the sense of touch they are actually at the "four corners" of the dog's body, as a blind child expressed it. The embossed outline, therefore, constitutes not a representation but a symbol of the object, which becomes meaningful only by added verbal interpretation and explanation. Of course, the situation becomes far more involved if different objects of varying size and positions requiring perspective drawings are presented.

The Merrys' conclusions indicate that the use of embossed material in the teaching of geometry, geography, and other subjects should be successful and, also, that embossed pictures of essentially two-dimensional objects, such as a wheel, a hand, or a pair of scissors, can be recognized.

Two problems in presenting tactile materials for the use of blind students have been dealt with in separate studies. Schiff and Isikow (1966) examined how tactual information—in the form of histograms varying in bar length, regularity, tactile quality (height, textures), and combinations of these (redundancy)—is accurately interpreted by legally blind high school students. All variables, except for tactile quality and redundancy, had significant effects on response time and error scores, with some qualifications for the latter. Time and error measures were found to be relatively independent from each other. The authors discuss theoretical and practical implications of their findings.

Morris and Nolan (1963) used sixty braille-reading students in order to determine: (1) minimum outer dimensions for seven discrete areal symbols, such as squares consisting of lines of dots, of straight lines, of slanted lines; and (2) whether differences exist according to the grade placement of the students. Their experiments established minimum outer dimensions for the tactual symbols, and also revealed grade-level inequities in the ability to identify correctly areal symbols as they diminished in size.

The effects of size and complexity on tactual discrimination were examined by Berla (1972). Large figures were discriminated as accurately as small ones, but the former required more time than the latter. Also, as complexity increased, discrimination took longer. Inappropriate finger movements were considered to be mainly responsible for poor performance.

The whole field of tactual representation of spatial and visual symbols that play such an important role in nonvisual communication is in urgent need of expanded research.

Considerable research is going on in the field of electrical stimulation of the skin. This means of communication is being explored in connection with reading devices to make print accessible to the blind, and in connection with guidance devices to improve mobility of the blind (Foulke, 1963).

Creative Activities

Viktor Lowenfeld (1939, 1957) has studied extensively the creative activities of blind and partially seeing children, and the psychological factors involved. He distinguished two different modes of perception: haptic and visual. The haptic mode is based on immediate bodily experiences and is primarily concerned with the tactual space around the individual. The visual mode is concerned with his environment and with the visual integration of it. Lowenfeld found that the amount of sight is not a determining factor in the person's inclination toward one or the other type. A haptically minded individual might be disturbed by his remaining sight, while a visually minded individual would be greatly aided by it. Creative activity, which permits the individual child to express himself according to his mode of functioning, is an important means of adjustment. By releasing emotional tension and rigidity, it can help to overcome feelings of inferiority and isolaton from the environment. The author exemplifies his findings with numerous illustrations that show the importance of his distinction as derived from visually handicapped children for the general field of art education. His observations concerning the tactual-kinesthetic perception of space show that the blind are capable of achieving simultaneous spatial images through an act of integration of successively perceived tactual impressions. He also concluded that, in modeling by the blind, objects receive their proportion by the value they have for the individual in a given situation. Thus the perspective of the blind in modeling is a perspective of value. So far as creative activities of blind children are concerned, he warned of the danger of imposition of visual characteristics by the teacher, and stressed "that the most primitive creative work born in the mind of a blind person and produced with his own hands is of greater value than the most effective imitation" (1957, p. 446).

Verbalism and Speech

The congenitally and totally blind child cannot be aided in his learning of speech by imitation—which plays a great role in the development of seeing children. He can only learn from what he hears and from occasional touch observation. Therefore, his progress in speech development may be slower than that of seeing children. But it is not only the speech development, but also the acquisition of word concepts that is affected by blindness. Cutsforth (1932) refers to this as "verbal unreality," because the blind child may learn to name many things without having any real experience or idea of them. He investigated this tendency toward verbal-mindedness, and his experiments showed a strong tendency of the blind children participating in this study to employ visual concepts, when other sensory concepts were just as available and would have been much more meaningful and familiar in experience. Naturally, a large number of wrong visual responses was found. Cutsforth believes this indicates that the pupils preferred risking a doubtful visual response rather than giving their own experiences.

Nolan (1960) repeated Cutsforth's experiment and found that significantly fewer visual responses were made by his group of blind children. He concluded "that 'verbal unreality' is not a significant problem for the group studied." He also reported that responses to four of the stimulus words were available for 1,000 sighted children. In a comparison of these with the ones obtained in his study, the responses of the blind children closely resembled those of normally seeing children. Though Nolan's data do not give any reasons for this change, one can assume that modern methods used in the education of present-day blind children may have something to do with it and that Cutsforth's findings, reinforced by the observations of others, are in part responsible for the change.

The relationship of verbalism to age, intelligence, experience, and personal adjustment among blind children was explored by Harley (1963). Forty children, from 7 to 14 years of age, who were blind or had only light perception, were given three tasks: a pretested list of words from the Gates Reading Vocabulary for the Primary Grades, to obtain definition of the words; identification of the items representing these words, to obtain verbalism scores; and the Tuddenham Reputation Test, to obtain adjustment scores. Verbalism was assumed to exist when a child gave an acceptable definition of a word but could not accurately identify the object by some sensory means. Visually oriented verbalism was assumed to exist when a child employed words referring to color or brightness in defining the name of a given object. The results showed that there is a relationship between verbalism and the three personal variables of chronological age, intelligence, and experience, as predicted. No such correlations were found between personal adjustment (the fourth personal variable) and verbalism, and between visually oriented verbalism and the four personal variables. Verbalisms were higher in the areas of food, farm, and nature than in the areas of home, clothing, and community. The results of this study emphasize "that blind children need a unique program in order to help them learn simple concepts that sighted children have developed through incidental learning" (p. 53).

The concept of verbalism has come under theoretical scrutiny in an article by Dokecki (1966). He argues from the psycholinguistic point of view that word-produced meaning (verbalism) is no less meaningful to the blind individual than word-thing relationships are. Although educators have followed the notion that "verbalism is meaningless and must lead to loose thinking" (p. 527), he contends that there is no proof that this is actually the case. Also, it has not been shown that verbalism results in poor academic performance or poor adjustment. Dokecki differentiates between verbalism as determined by Cutsforth—he considers this a "controlled association method"—and the way in which Harley used it in his study where he asked for identification of the object by sensory means. Only Harley's "visually oriented verbalism" corresponds to the Cutsforth and Nolan definition. Dokecki concentrates his disapproval on Cutsforth's evaluation of the effects of nonsensory-based language in the blind. However, he is implicitly critical of educators of blind children who practice concreteness in teaching as a countermeasure against verbalism and its effects, even though this has been practiced since educational methods for blind children were developed.

In an adaptation of Harley's (1963) procedures, and with some additional experiments, DeMott (1972) wanted "to demonstrate the degree to which concrete words having visual connotations share similar meanings for individuals differing in visual experience" (p. 1). There were no significant differences between the blind, the severely visually impaired, and the normally sighted subjects; this confirmed Dokecki's contention. "The blind youngster, just as the sighted, learns many words and their meanings through context and by their use within the language. The criticism that blind youngsters use many words which, to them, are meaningless, is contradicted by the present study" (DeMott, p. 8). Consequently, DeMott warns that to "bias the blind or visually impaired youngster toward discontinued use of those words which denote visual experience would be tantamount to experiential deprivation." He recommends that "experience and familiarity with many objects in a variety of settings should be pursued for its contribution to intellectual development and not as a substitute for language" (p. 80).

Maxfield (1936) published a preliminary study of the spoken language of eight preschool blind children, based on the verbatim report of observations. Although she re-

garded her work more as a methodological study, it contains some interesting results. Among the older children, 40 to 50 percent of the responses (about twice the percentage then found in seeing children) were concerned with things. Blind children asked more questions and gave fewer commands than seeing children. Their responses also were more frequently incomplete and emotionally toned. Blind children used proper names of persons more frequently than did seeing children. Maxfield considers some of these differences indications of the blind child's need for gaining security.

Tillman and Williams (1968) compared thirty-five blind residential school children with thirty-five sighted children in two tasks —word association and word usage. They found that word association results show "that both groups are at the same developmental level, that the sequence of acquisition is similar, that is, first nouns and adjectives, later verbs and adverbs, and that rate of acquisition is about the same. However, with reference to word usage, interpretation of results is less clear (p. 40).

Stinchfield (1933) discussed speech disorders among blind children and found, in a survey, that about half of the children showed some speech defects, ranging from mild oral inaccuracies and letter substitution to lateral lisping, sigmatism (a form of stammering with imperfect pronunciation of the "s" sounds), and severe oral inaccuracies. She recognized that in blind children such speech defects are usually remedial and that the prognosis is much better than in the case of deaf children. The development of speech disorders in blind children is due to the fact that the congenitally blind child must learn speech without being able to learn by visual imitation the formation of speech sounds and the accompanying bodily movements and gestures. He depends solely on the acoustic imitation and production of speech. Stinchfield found more dyslalia (speech defects of organic or functional origin, dependent upon malformation or imperfect innervation of the tongue, soft palate, or other organs of articulation) than any other type of speech defect. In a speech survey of 220 children in a residential school, she found letter substitution, lisping, and stuttering the most frequently occurring speech defects besides unspecified mild oral inaccuracies.

Various authors have suggested psychological causes for speech defects among the blind, such as infantilism, egocentricity, emotional gratification, feelings of inferiority, and overcompensation; but no study has actually demonstrated for blind children the connection between speech defects and any particular psychological reaction pattern.

Brieland (1950) summarized observations of various authors on differences of speech in blind and seeing children as follows:

> (1) The blind show less vocal variety. (2) Lack of modulation is more critical among the blind. (3) The blind tend to talk louder than the sighted. (4) The blind speak at a slower rate. (5) Less effective use of gesture and bodily action is typical of the blind. (6) The blind use less lip movement in articulation of sounds (p. 99).

Berry and Eisenson (1942) considered monotony and lack of appropriate modulation to be characteristic voice defects of the blind. Cutsforth (1951, pp. 103–120) discussed voice and speech and their relationship with personality development. He mentions particularly lack of stimulation, faulty sound analysis, synesthetic imagery, and faulty projection as causes of speech defects. The last-mentioned he considers the most common one, and he calls the use of a loud voice without specific directional projection the "broadcasting voice of the blind."

Brieland (1950) compared the ratings on speech performances of eighty-four matched pairs of blind and sighted pupils 12 to 18 years old. The ratings indicate that there were no significant differences in general vocal effectiveness or in vocal variety; the blind were judged significantly superior in pitch modulation, whereas the sighted were fa-

vored in ratings of bodily action and in degree of lip movement. He concluded that his findings "failed to show the inferiority in the use of the voice which the literature on speech of the blind would lead one to expect" (pp. 102–103). The superiority in pitch modulation may result from a greater reliance of the blind upon verbal means of expression, whereas the superiority in bodily action of the seeing is due to the influence of the visible components of social communication. He suspects that observers become unduly sensitive to small defects in the blind, and thus tend to judge them more unfavorably than they would judge seeing persons.

A survey by Rowe (1958) arrived at conclusions that even favor the blind. She screened 148 school-age blind children for speech defects and took tape recordings that were independently judged by two speech therapists. Her findings indicate that the percentage of speech defects found was low when compared with general estimates. She ascribes these favorable results to good preschool counseling services, to the fact that in the surveyed group no cases with major secondary handicaps were included, and to the good schooling which these children received. The methodology of this study, however, is open to serious questioning.

Two studies attempted to clarify the different incidence findings of past studies. Both used as their population only children in residential schools for the blind. Miner (1963) found 33.8 percent to have some sort of speech deviation, four to five times higher than the incidence in public schools. Articulation problems were found to be the largest category and were present in 25 percent. No differences were found between boys and girls or between braille and partially seeing students. There was only one stutterer among all the children, and he was a partially seeing child. Weinberg (1964), however, found that stuttering in blind children is within the range of incidence for the general population. LeZak and Starbuck (1964) found that 49.8 percent showed some speech disorders, with 36.9 percent falling into the articulation category. The authors of both studies recommend that residential schools provide speech therapy programs adapted to the needs of the students.

Practically all incidence data on speech deviations of blind children are derived from surveys of residential school populations and cannot be considered as representative of blind children in general. A comprehensive study of speech problems among blind children is long overdue.

Touch Reading

The psychological processes involved in reading are complex, and not less so if the reading organs are the fingers rather than the eyes. Blind children learn to read and write braille, which is a system of embossed dots to be read by the fingers. The full braille sign consists of six embossed dots, two vertical rows of three, of a size that can be covered simultaneously by the pulp of a finger. Braille Grade One is written in full spelling; Braille Grade Two makes use of contractions representing letter combinations, syllables, or words.

Early research on touch reading has largely centered on the mechanics of the reading process. Bürklen (1932) published his important experimental study on touch reading in German in 1917 (translated into English in 1932). He agrees with Heller (1895) that the vertical arrangement of six dots (2×3) is the best possible one for touch reading. The readability of the various letters of the alphabet is not determined by the number of dots, but by their characteristic formation. He found that all fingers could be used in touch reading, but that the first and second fingers of both hands are the preferred ones. The index fingers of both hands are predominantly used as reading fingers. There are different touch motions employed in reading: the up-and-down motion and the horizontal motion. Good

readers move their fingers horizontally with a minimum of up-and-down motions; less skilled readers interrupt their horizontal movement by frequent up-and-down motions, which may also form loops. Bürklen also recognized that the touch motions are connected with different pressure of the fingers. Good readers exert slight and uniform pressure, whereas poor readers employ strong and variable pressure. There is little decrease of touch sensitivity even after hours of touch reading, which is also not particularly fatiguing. Touch reading is three to four times as slow as visual reading. Reading of words and sentences is done by a unifying perception of word pictures, similar to visual reading. Only with difficult or unknown words is a dissection of the word picture necessary. Reading with both hands is fastest, but the left hand alone reads somewhat better than the right hand.

Concerning alternatives to the six-dots arrangement, it should be inserted here that a more recent study by Foulke and Warm (1967) indicated that a 4×4 matrix is of "maximum efficiency with respect to the encoding and decoding of information" (p. 186).

Maxfield (1928) wrote the first book dealing with methods of teaching braille reading. She agrees largely with Bürklen, except that American experiences have demonstrated that one-handed readers who use the right hand are more efficient than those who use the left. She underlines the importance of relaxation and correct posture in reading, and recommends that children should be trained to read silently without lip movement or inner speech. She observed that many of the best readers read ahead on a lower line with the left hand before the right hand has finished the preceding line, and recommends that this be encouraged if children show any inclination toward it. She also recommended the word method of teaching braille reading and the early teaching of contracted braille.

Holland and Eatman (1933) made moving-picture records of the finger movements, which revealed, among other facts, the importance of the amount of time spent in making return sweeps—between 6 and 7 percent of the total reading time, with good readers spending less time than poor readers. Also, good readers make fewer regressive movements than poor readers, whose performance is in general less uniform. Holland (1934) also studied the speed and pressure factors in reading braille, and confirmed Bürklen's findings (1932). He observed that pressure varies within a given line, with less variation in the case of fast readers. Fertsch (1947) also used a moving-picture camera in studying hand dominance. She explains the discrepancies in past findings by the differences in performance of good and poor readers. Readers whose both hands are equally effective in perceiving braille read faster, and among them are fewer poor readers than among those who use either the right hand or the left hand dominantly. Those with the right hand dominant perform better than those with the left hand dominant. Good readers read a substantial amount of material with the hands functioning independently, of which the right hand reads about twice as much as the left hand. Poor readers read very little material with the hands independently, since they keep right and left fingers close together.

In another study, Fertsch (1946) found silent braille reading considerably faster than oral braille reading. Independence in the functioning of the hands is characteristic of good readers in making return sweeps as well as in regressive movements. She also found that reading habits become established by about the time a pupil has reached the third grade, and do not change noticeably with increase in reading experience.

Horbach (1951) published a study in which he reports observations and experiments on touch reading. He concludes that these experiments give full confirmation to his initial assumption that the processes of tactile and visual reading are the same, not only in their final results, but also in the progress of the reading act. Differences found, particularly in the rate of reading, are only of a gradual nature. Thus he confirmed many of the assumptions of Bürklen's early study.

Lowenfeld, Abel, and Hatlen (1969) presented the results of a braille-reading study that was undertaken with the support of the U.S. Office of Education. It describes the status of braille reading instruction in 1965 in local and residential schools in the United States, and reports the results of tests and observations that were derived from a sample of 200 students, 50 each on the fourth- and eighth-grade levels in local and in residential school classes for the blind. The book also includes a review of research on braille reading, a chapter dealing with special problems in braille reading, and other information concerning the history of braille and such topics as readiness for learning to read and the teacher's role in the reading program.

The survey of the status of braille-reading instruction, representing replies of 520 teachers, revealed a considerable uniformity of methods, with only two areas of substantial differences: two-thirds of the teachers used the word or sentence method; one-third began braille reading instruction with the braille alphabet, and shifted to the word method when the children had learned enough letters to permit this; no uniformity was revealed in the use of fingers encouraged by teachers in braille reading instruction. There were no significant differences between methods of teaching braille reading in local schools and in residential schools.

In connection with the application of the reading part of the Sequential Test of Educational Progress and the Paragraph Meaning part of the Stanford Achievement Test, data on personal characteristics of the students and on their reading behavior were secured. Only 11.5 percent of the 200 students in the study had any measurable visual acuity, with a maximum of 5/200 (Snellen measurement), the optimum vision allowed for participants in the study. Of the fourth graders, 54 percent, and of the eighth graders, 70 percent were blind as a result of RLF. The study required that participating students have no marked additional handicaps. In contrast to past studies, it was found that the differences in age between blind students and their seeing peers were not more than 1.2 years on the fourth-grade level and only two to three months on the eighth-grade level. IQs of fourth graders were about normal, and those of eighth graders above normal, as compared with seeing students. Reading comprehension was at least equal to seeing norms. Reading rate was about twice that of seeing readers for fourth-grade students and even less than that for those in the eighth grade. On the basis of these results, it was recommended that reading time allowance for blind students should be reduced (from the then practiced two and one-half to three times) to only twice that allowed for seeing students. It should be noted that rapid braille reading instruction (Crandell & Wallace, 1974; McBride, 1974) promises even higher reading rate attainments.

Among the other findings of this study are the following: blind children in local schools were at least equal in reading rate and comprehension to those in residential schools; students with high reading comprehension belong to the group of fast readers, and those with low reading comprehension to that of slow readers; specific hand-use or finger-use did not correlate significantly with reading rate scores or with reading comprehension scores. There were trends to have a slightly better chance to be efficient braille readers for those who read with both hands as compared with those who use only one hand and, particularly for reading rate, for those who use more fingers than the index fingers. The study confirmed results of previous studies concerning other aspects of braille reading, such a regressive movements, rubbing letters, losing the place in reading, and silent speech movements, which are all characteristic of

less efficient braille readers. So far as hand-use and finger-use is concerned, the study indicated that there is no justification for considering any specific ones as a prerequisite for being an efficient braille reader. Therefore, teachers should not insist on a specific hand- or finger-use to the exclusion of what an individual student prefers.

Nolan and Morris (1965) developed and validated a Roughness Discrimination Test as a reading readiness test for young blind children. The test consists of a set of sixty-nine cards upon each of which four pieces of sandpaper are mounted. Three of these pieces are alike, and one is rougher than the others. The child must find the piece of sandpaper that feels different from the others. The test shows good predictive validity for success in braille reading and also correlates significantly with reading time and reading error scores of second-grade braille reading students.

The problem of how blind children (and adults, for that matter) who cover with their reading fingers only one or a few letters at a time, combine these letters into whole words and sentences has been widely discussed. It is assumed that the word or short sentence when read in braille becomes (similar to visual reading) a whole, a gestalt; only as such is it meaningful to the reader. Felden (1955) distinguished four different gestalt formations in the reading process: the acoustical gestalt—the sound of the word; the acoustic-motoric gestalt—the word as it is spoken; the optic gestalt—the meaningful whole word; and the vibratory gestalt—which becomes of great importance with deaf and deaf-blind children. Whereas the acoustic and the acoustic-motoric gestalt formations are the same for seeing and blind children, the optic gestalt becomes a tactile for the blind. Felden stresses that this is not a simple equation, but that tactile gestalt formation in the touch-reading process of the blind is in need of scientific research and clarification.

Nolan (1966) and Henderson (1966) discussed some of their research which, they contend, provides some indication that, in braille reading, it is not the whole-word shape but the individual braille character that is the perceptual unit in word recognition. Nolan found: "When we compare the time necessary to recognize a word with the sum of the times required to recognize the characters it contains, we generally find that the word recognition time is longer. This is, of course, opposite to findings for regular print reading" (p. 12). Henderson concluded that "increasing the rate of identification of isolated braille characters was accompanied by a significant increase in the rate and accuracy of the total reading process" (p. 10). This was also the result of a study by Umsted (1972). On the other hand, Crandell and Wallace (1974) found "that rather high speeds of braille reading, without loss of comprehension, can be attained through a relatively short period of training" (p. 18); they suggest that this requires a modification of the single-cell perceptual theory.

This proposition, that it is not the whole word but the single braille cell that is the perceptual unit in braille reading, was further elaborated in *Perceptual Factors in Braille Word Recognition,* by Nolan and Kederis (1969). In it they report nine research studies with such topics as: legibility of single-cell braille characters; influence of dot numbers and dot position on word recognition; influence of braille contractions on word recognition; and effect of character-recognition training on braille reading.

Among the studies that notice and confirm a similarity between braille reading and visual reading is that of Pick, Thomas, and Pick (1966). They presented to twenty-six braille readers two types of pseudo-words, one type pronounceable and the other type unpronounceable, and measured the speed with which the two types were read. Most subjects spent more time reading the unpronounceable than the pronounceable pseudo-words. The authors concluded that this indicates that braille print readers, just as sighted print readers, use grapheme-phoneme correspondences as grouping principles in the perception of braille.

In his research on *Visual Reading and Braille Reading* (1974), Kusajima concluded that "in tactile reading, comprehension occurs through appreciation of whole word and whole sentence configurations (not through the integration of individual letters) and through the cognitive linking of sentence meanings" (p. 58). Hampshire (1975), in reviewing research on tactile and visual reading, concludes that it is

> reasonable to assume, therefore, that the observed differences in print and braille reading are not fundamental and must be more a function of the compatibility between the stimulus and sense channel used, these being the only areas of real departure between the two modes of reading (p. 150).

The many similarities noted by educators and researchers between braille reading and print reading, the success of the whole word and sentence method with blind children, and the fact that many efficient braille readers read ahead with the left hand before finishing the line with the right hand, must together be regarded as at least tentative proof that tactile reading, similar to visual reading, is a process of recognition of meaningful wholes.

Some studies that investigated problems of tactile reading used children who are described as "blind" or "legally blind." Because many of these children can read braille or print by the use of their sight, and may have to read it letter by letter, the results of these studies cannot be considered valid, even if the children were blindfolded.

The whole area of touch reading poses many problems as yet unsolved and some not yet investigated. Readability of letters and contractions, the mental processes involved in touch reading, reading readiness and its indications, development of reading skills and its components, methods of teaching touch reading to adults; all are problems that need further investigation. For any research on the processes of touch reading, only subjects who cannot and do not apply sight for reading should be used; otherwise, visual-reading habits may carry over into touch reading and invalidate the results.

An interesting study dealing with a problem, which in the past has received scant, if any, attention, was undertaken by Barraga (1964). It was the purpose of this study to test the hypotheses that low-vision children could achieve an increase in visual discrimination by a short period of experimental teaching in visual discrimination, and that their near-vision acuity would be significantly increased by such training. Ten pairs of blind children with low vision (6/200 or less), who also met other specific criteria, were matched on the ability to make visual discriminations of reading readiness items of the Visual Discrimination Test. This test was specifically designed for the study and showed good validity and reliability. Over a 2-month period, the experimental group received approximately 30 hours of intensive and individualized teaching geared to improve the functional use of their low vision. All members of the experimental group showed significant enhancement of their Visual Discrimination Test scores. There was also a significant difference between the experimental and control groups.

The hypothesis, that recorded near-vision acuity of experimental subjects would increase, was not supported by the results. Nor was there any difference in visual acuity between the experimental and control groups. However, visual word recognition and reading ability were considerably increased for some experimental subjects.

The author states:

The data of this experiment strongly suggest that blind children with remaining vision could improve their visual efficiency to the degree that they would be able to use their low vision more effectively for educational pur-

poses if a planned sequence of visual stimulation were available to them in their early school years (p. 71).

The Visual Discrimination Test as used in the experiment, a lesson-plan sequence, and forty-four daily lesson plans for a visual stimulation program are given in detail (Barraga, 1964).

The results of this study have, indeed, far-reaching implications for low-vision children. Further experiments should be conducted with legally blind children who have better vision than 6/200 and with partially seeing children in order to determine whether their visual discrimination can also be improved by planned visual stimulation lessons.

The Visual Efficiency Scale (Barraga, 1970), a revision of the before-mentioned Visual Discrimination Test, consists of forty-eight visual discrimination items in four subtests. Its reliability and validity were confirmed by three studies (Harley & Spollen, 1973; 1974; Harley, Spollen & Long, 1973). Barraga (1973) discusses the utilization of sensory-perceptual abilities and gives a clear account of each system, its receptive capabilities, the information it conveys, and its significance in concept development and learning.

Touch reading is slow, and this slowness has been made responsible for either retarding blind children in their educational progress or demanding of them a much greater expenditure of time for their studies. The fact that only a limited amount of reading matter is available in braille or in recorded form also exerts its influence, because much material must still be read aloud to blind students. In an early study, Lowenfeld (1945) compared rates and comprehension of braille and Talking Book reading, the latter with and without sound illustrations. He found that story-telling material was equally well comprehended by braille and by Talking Book reading, but comprehension of textbook material was better by braille than by Talking Book reading. He recommended, therefore, the use of Talking Books for supplementary reading on all grade levels and particularly with slow learners, whereas textbooks should preferably be studied in braille. Because Talking Books are normally read at a rate of 180 to 200 words per minute, many blind readers whose braille reading rate is low can cover more reading matter by using Talking Books or other recorded or taped material.

A further speeding up of recorded reading was suggested by Enc and Stolurow (1960), who conducted experiments to determine whether "time compression" as developed by Fairbanks, Gutman, and Miron (1957) would result in more efficient reading. It was found that over the range of 160 to 233 words per minute, faster rates were more efficient than slower ones. Foulke (1967), Kederis, Nolan, and Morris (1967), and others have further studied the use and effect of time-compressed recorded speech.

Foulke, Amster, Nolan, and Bixler (1962) also studied the influence of word rate on comprehension, and pointed out that "those losses in comprehension that were statistically significant were not all educationally important, especially when the time saved in presenting the material was considered" (p. 141).

Hartlage (1963) compared listening comprehension of the blind and the sighted and concluded: "With the variables of age, intelligence, and sex controlled, sightedness vs. blindness was not found to be a significant variable in listening comprehension" (p. 5). Thus, studies on listening comprehension conducted with the blind and those conducted with the seeing apply equally to both groups, although it must be recognized that reading by listening is far more important for blind students than it is for the seeing.

A useful and detailed review of the literature on listening and research that deals with it is provided by Daugherty (1974), who also lists twenty-five problems for research in this area.

MOBILITY

For those who are totally blind or who have only light perception, the task of getting about is one of the most difficult to perform. No comprehensive research on the psychological factors involved in mobility is available. Work on the perception of obstacles, which occupied European scientists around the turn of the century, received particular attention in Cornell University studies published from 1944 on. Obstacle perception, however, is only one factor of importance in the ability to get about. It received more intensive scientific attention only because the blind seemed to possess an ability that the seeing appeared not to have; namely, the ability to avoid obstacles without having bodily contact with them. This fact had been recognized by Diderot in 1749, when his "Letter on the Blind for the Use of Those Who See" was published.

Obstacle Perception

Bürklen (1924) and Hayes (1935) reported extensively on the anecdotal and autobiographical material as well as on the first scientific attempts to investigate the hypothetical obstacle sense. Hayes provided a summary of theories to explain the obstacle sense, covering the research up to 1935. He distinguished four different types of theories explaining the obstacle sense: (1) a heightened response of some sense organ, known or unknown—in this category belong the pressure theories, the auditory theories, and the temperature theories; (2) perceptual interpretation of cues from one or more sense organs, such as a combination of pressure, sound, and temperature changes; (3) an indirect and complicated response to sensory cues; and (4) occult explanations that assume magnetic or electrical phenomena, vibrations of the ether or of some other hypothetical substance, or vestigial organs in the skin (paroptic vision), and give other subconscious or miraculous explanations.

Dolanski (1930) conducted extensive experiments with forty-two subjects in which he moved (without noise and without production of air currents) small disks toward the subject seated in a chair. The disks were moved either in "frontal approach" or in "lateral approach" toward the subject's face or one of his ears. The distance at which disks of a given size were detected was always greater with the lateral approach than with the frontal approach. He used a variety of materials for the disks, but the material of the disks did not affect the results. Dolanski experimented with his subjects in four conditions: with their faces uncovered; with thick paper flaps affixed to the sides of the head in perpendicular direction and in front of the ears; with a cardboard mask covering the face; and with ears plugged with cotton. His results indicated that audition is responsible for obstacle perception. In the second series, no obstacles were detected on the frontal approach, which made audition impossible, whereas the lateral approach permitting audition showed the same positive results as the first series, where the face was left uncovered. No obstacles were detected in the fourth series, in which audition was eliminated. In the third series, when a cardboard mask covered the face, the disks were discovered as well with as without the mask, which indicated that pressure and temperature cannot be responsible factors.

The most extensive research on the perception of obstacles by the blind was undertaken by a team of psychologists at Cornell University and continued elsewhere. In the first of these studies, Supa, Cotzin, and Dallenbach (1944) used blind and blindfolded subjects who were placed at various distances in front of either a wall or a portable masonite board approximately four feet square with its lower edge two feet above the floor. In walking toward the obstacle, they were asked to indicate their "first perception" of it and then to approach it as closely as possible without touching it—the "final appraisal." In the four main experiments,

various controls, similar in effect to those used by Dolanski (1930), were introduced in order to reduce or eliminate certain sensory cues. Two different receptors of sensation were considered: (1) the exposed areas of the skin, and (2) the ears. The stimuli acting on each of those receptors could be either (a) air currents and air waves that are outside the auditory range, arousing only cutaneous sensation, or (b) sound waves that could be heard and that also might arouse cutaneous sensation in the ear or on the exposed areas of the skin. In the first main experiment, the exposed areas of the skin were covered; in the second, the ears were plugged and shielded from all stimulation. In the third experiment the exposed areas of the skin were left open to air and sound waves, as in the second, but all stimuli that might have reached the ears were drowned by means of a sound screen—a constant, continuously sounding tone of moderate intensity, conducted by wires to a set of headphones worn over the ears of the subject. In the fourth experiment the stimuli were reduced to sound waves, and their action was limited to the ears. This was achieved by placing the subject in a soundproof room with high-fidelity headphones through which he could listen to the sounds of the experimenter who, carrying a microphone, walked in another room toward the obstacle. The latter arrangement was criticized by Jerome and Proshansky (1950) because "electrical transmission systems usually respond to sounds in a manner that differs from the ear's response in a number of important ways. Those differences that are probably most relevant to the present problem are amplitude and directional response" (p. 467). The results of the experiments of this study led to the following conclusions:

1. Stimulation of the face and other exposed areas of the skin by "air-" and sound waves is neither a *necessary* nor a *sufficient* condition of the perception of obstacles by our Subjects.
2. Stimulation of the skin by reflected breath is

neither a *necessary* condition nor, as far as "facial pressure" is concerned, a *sufficient* condition for the "final appraisals" by our Subjects.

3. The pressure theory of the "obstacle sense," insofar as it applies to the face and other exposed areas of the skin, is untenable.

4. Aural stimulation is both a *necessary* and a *sufficient* condition for the perception of obstacles by our Subjects (p. 182–183).

Further experiments were conducted to clarify some remaining questions. Worchel and Dallenbach (1947) determined with deaf-blind subjects that audition, not cutaneous stimulation, was the aural mechanism responsible for obstacle perception. Cotzin and Dallenbach (1950) established that changes in pitch were necessary and sufficient conditions, and were considered to be a result of the Doppler effect (the phenomenon in which the pitch of a sound rises when the source of the sound approaches the listener). At normal walking speed, high frequencies of about 10,000 cycles and more are necessary, while those of about 8,000 and below are insufficient. McCarthy and Worchel (1954) demonstrated with a blind bicycle rider that speed does not impair object perception; this supports the Doppler-shift theory. Ammons, Worchel, and Dallenbach (1953) repeated the Cornell experiments outdoors and confirmed that auditory cues were the most reliable, accurate, and universal ones. Worchel, Mauney, and Andrew (1950) examined the distribution of obstacle-perception ability and found that seven out of thirty-four subjects did not possess it. Worchel and Mauney (1951) established with these seven failures that a systematic course in object perception may assist the blind and shorten their usual trial-and-error learning. Rouse and Worchel (1955) confirmed that blind subjects, like blindfolded seeing ones, have a veering tendency, mostly to the right, which is consistent for the same individual and is not increased by removal of auditory or facial tactile cues.

Cratty, Peterson, Harris, and Schoner (1968) have conducted basic investigations on perceptual-motor behavior, some of them with reference to blind children. An analysis of their data revealed the following details: in the absence of auditory clues, it is predictable that a blind individual will veer about 36 degrees of angular rotation per 100 feet of forward progress; the blind are more sensitive to decline than to incline, or to left-right tilt in their walking surfaces; congenitally blind adolescents are more sensitive to gradients, and veer less than do the older adventitiously blinded; the longer an individual has been blind the less he will tend to veer and the more accurately he can detect gradients; tactually inspecting bent wires, indicating the amount and direction of an individual's veering, can significantly reduce his veering tendency; a blind individual using the presently advocated cane techniques can successfully detect the curvature of a curb if it has a radius of at least 5 feet. These and other of their findings have important implications for mobility training. Cratty *et al.* (1968) and Harris (1967) found that blind individuals with high anxiety walked slower and veered about twice as much as relaxed blind subjects did.

At the Cleveland Society for the Blind, Norton (1960) used binaural tape recordings of various sounds and of active travel conditions to train normal hearing to greater usefulness. A manual has been published describing the project and the training procedures.

In search for a guidance device, the Haskins' Laboratories examined the problem of the obstacle sense. Jerome and Proshansky (1950) found certain deficiencies in the experiments conducted in the past. They used four blind subjects in their own experiments. In a "differentiation test," the blind person's ability to differentiate between the presence and absence of objects in his immediate environment was examined. It showed that they all possessed an obstacle sense operating with various degrees of accuracy at different distances. With the increase of distance between the subject and the test object, a regular decrease in obstacle perception occurred, but marked individual differences were noted. The subsequent "avoidance test" was designed to test the more complicated task of avoiding obstacles while attempting to circulate among them either with or without aural obstruction. Real obstacles and symbolic obstacles were used and rotated on an obstacle course through which the subject had to make his way without contacting any of the objects. There was a reliable difference between scores on real and symbolic obstacles when no sensory obstruction was used. Also, on real objects, the difference between aural obstruction and no obstruction was reliable. However, the differences between errors on real and symbolic objects were negligible with aural obstruction. These data indicate that the avoidance of obstacles depends upon aural sensations. The authors conclude:

. . . because these studies were carried out in a sheltered area from which air currents and abrupt temperature changes were almost completely eliminated, the results must be interpreted as indicating that, when other sources of information have been excluded, the blind person is capable of avoiding obstacles on the basis of aural cues alone (p. 473).

The study reported further on testing procedures for the evaluation of obstacle-avoidance devices.

Griffin (1958) reviewed the literature on orientation and made challenging suggestions for future research in this field. He asks whether we can learn from bats, and recommends that we first study "the language of audible echoes" and explore "what kinds of sound field will produce the most information and the most readily recognized echoes." He recommends research to determine the type of sounds that are most effective in echolocation—as for instance, the frequency-modulated pulses used by certain types of bats. "Any human adaptation of echolocation would necessarily require that the blind man generate clearly audible sounds, probably a series of clicks" (p. 320). Blind people, he believes, will not want to make themselves conspicuous unless they can secure real independence in mobility by it. He warns of continuing hasty attempts to construct portable guidance devices, and recommends instead a more patient program of basic research.

Although it is recognized that obstacle perception as such is only one factor influencing a person's mobility, the other factors have received little attention and almost no scientific investigation. There is, for instance, no study available that would show the effects of the restriction in mobility on the personality formation of the blind or on his relations to others on whom he must frequently depend in order to get about.

It is obvious that blind individuals are from infancy restricted in their ability to expose themselves to experiences, as compared with nonhandicapped individuals. Because blindness imposes limitations in the perceptual area, this added restriction due to limited mobility calls for special instructional methods if it is to be compensated for at least partially. Lowenfeld (1950, pp. 94–96) discussed the effects of this restriction and noted that differences in mobility show themselves already among young blind children. Some hardly dare to step out into unfamiliar grounds, and hesitate even in familiar surroundings, whereas others show a surprising facility in getting about. While the blind child is very young, he leaves his environment only when accompanied by others. When he gets older and must adjust to living in the world at large, his restriction in mobility becomes a factor of major importance. If he has not been encouraged to develop his ability to move about and has not achieved a reasonable degree of independence in it, his whole success may be jeopardized. He may, in the extreme case, not only take help for granted, but may develop a generalized expectancy of help characteristic of regression. He may also develop a resentment against his dependency and project this resentment toward the seeing society as a whole. Educators of the blind are familiar with these reactions, although they have not been the subject of systematic studies.

Many have recognized that the task of getting about, results in increased nervous strain for the blind person. Cutsforth (1951) also stressed the unavoidable injury to the ego of the blind person as a result of his position of dependency in locomotion:

> Since the blind live in a world of the seeing, it is necessary to procure visual aid and information. Whether this be volunteered or solicited, it represents a curtailment of self-expression and is registered emotionally as such. Thus, the act of asking a stranger the name of an approaching street car is an admission of inferiority for which there must be compensation. And the thoughtful, kind-hearted guide through a traffic jam must be pleasantly thanked for his assistance—society demands it —while the emotions demand that he be cursed or struck down with the cane (p. 73).

Orientation and Locomotion

Lowenfeld (1950, pp. 94–96) has pointed out that mobility has two components: mental orientation and physical locomotion. Mental orientation has been defined as the "ability of an individual to recognize his surroundings and their temporal or spatial relations to himself" (Warren, 1934, p. 189), and locomation as "the movement of an organism from place to place by means of its organic mechanism" (p. 154). Both functions are necessary for mobility, but are of a different nature. In the task of orientation, the blind person must keep in his mind a "mental map" and relate himself to it while he is moving toward his intended destination. If he is experienced, he will rely upon various clues coming to him from his environment; for instance, the audible traffic

signal at a certain corner, the change in ground level at a certain point, the air current indicating open space, and of course all kinds of odor sensations. He also will make use of his "muscular memory," which Villey (1930) described as follows:

> It is by it that, without counting the steps and without looking at them, we know that we have reached the top of our staircase. Our legs have registered, in a way, the number of contractions they had to make. Not only can this muscular memory retain very well the height of a staircase, but also the dimensions of a room and the distance between two walls. It instigates the blind man to repeat, with perfect regularity, the movements that have become habitual to him (p. 126).

He also employs his time sense in tracing his position on the mental map. The more familiar he becomes with his route, the more mechanically he recognizes his surroundings and his own relation to them. But in order to move about safely and in a goal-directed way, the blind person must also be able to follow a safe path and to avoid harmful obstacles. In doing this he makes use of all his senses. His sense of hearing is constantly active in observing all kinds of sounds, including echoes; he interprets odors in relation to their various sources; he notices changes of temperature and air currents and what they indicate; his feet follow the surface of the ground and notice changes in it; he observes distances, not by counting steps but in terms of time, movement, and sound. Thus any observation he can make and any clue he can obtain is interpreted for the purpose of locomotion as well as orientation. Obstacle perception as such also has its important place, although it cannot be employed effectively in many situations; for example, in moving in crowded or noisy places, or under unfavorable weather conditions, when rain and winds drown out or snow deadens the necessary perceptions. Psathas (1976) made a similar distinction by describing and analyzing orientation and navigation as parts of mobility.

In the task of getting about, blind persons have always relied upon human assistance. They also have made use of the cane and, lately, of dog guides. Human assistance can take over both factors of mobility, locomotion as well as orientation. The cane, which functions as a lengthening touch organ or feeler, indicates to the blind person, if skillfully used, an obstacle-free spot where he may put his foot. The dog guide indicates an obstacle-free space into which the blind person may safely move. Both cane and dog guide leave the task of orientation to their user.

Educators and rehabilitation personnel are giving increased attention to mobility training as an essential part of a blind individual's adjustment. Training in mobility under all kinds of conditions and in the use of the cane are included in many school and rehabilitation programs. Although no experimental evidence of the superiority of any method of cane travel is available, practical usage has confirmed the superiority of the Hoover (1950) technique of cane travel, which was developed in the rehabilitation program for war-blinded servicemen. According to this technique, the cane is used in a pendulumlike scanning motion to make certain that the place where the foot will be moving is free of obstacles. A white cane, longer than the usual cane—it should reach to the breastbone of the user—is required. Techniques to meet various situational demands have been worked out, and training in the use of the cane proceeds according to a set course of study (Suterko, 1973).

Mobility-training specialists stress the importance of early childhood experiences in this area. Hapeman (1967) discussed a framework of needed basic concepts, which, though closely dependent upon each other, can be divided into three main classes: (1) concepts needed for understanding the true nature of the environment (body-image, nature of objects, nature of fixed, movable, and moving objects, nature of terrain, nature of sounds and odors); (2) concepts needed for achieving and maintaining orientation (path of moving objects, positions of objects in space, directions, sound localization); and (3) concepts needed for efficient mobility (distance and time, following a sequence of fixed objects, turning, detouring, moving with and against moving objects). He stressed the importance of concrete learning and that, though exactness of many of the concepts is not necessary, awareness of them is important.

A number of articles have appeared that describe and discuss mobility training from preschool through school age (Ball, 1964; Cratty, 1969; Curriculum Guide, 1966; Eichorn & Vigaroso, 1967; Hartong, 1968; Johnson & Gilson, 1967; Schulz, 1972; and Wilson, 1967).

Lord (1969) reported on the development of scales for the measurement of orientation and mobility of young blind children, and Harley, Merbler, and Wood (1975) developed the Peabody Mobility Scale to measure orientation and mobility in multihandicapped blind children. The importance of posture for mobility, as a cause for as well as an effect of its success, was thoroughly discussed by Siegel (1966).

Finestone, Lukoff, and Whiteman (1960) included a chapter, "Aspects of the Travel Adjustment of Blind Persons," in a study dealing with the demand for dog guides. Their findings indicate that "human guide users represent minimal travel performance, cane travelers achieve a midway position well above human guide users, while dog guide users are in turn markedly above both groups" (p. 13).

Worchel (1951) investigated space perception and orientation of the blind in three experiments, for which he used thirty-three totally blind students and a matched group of sighted students. In the first experiment, he wanted to determine the role of visualization in tactual form perception. He used simple geometrical blocks and found that in reproductions by drawing, and in verbal descriptions, sighted subjects were significantly better than the blind, and accidentally blinded subjects were significantly better than the congenitally blind. He interprets this as indicating that touch alone is not as efficient in the perception of tactual forms as is touch aided by visual images. However, in the test on form recognition, in which the subjects had to select among four blocks one that was similar in shape to the stimulus block, the blind and sighted did equally well. In this test, visualization was not required. The author indicates that the tests were done with simple forms and that more complicated ones may show different results. Similar experiments by Ewart and Carp (1963) confirm Worchel's findings that visual imagery is not a critical factor in the form recognition of various shapes of blocks. The second experiment of Worchel's study required the imaginal construction of a total form after parts of the form had been perceived by touch. The results indicated again that "the use of visual imagery is of definite aid to the sighted and to the accidentally blinded in imaginally manipulating tactual perceptions" (p. 20). It is interesting to note that the ellipse and circle were easiest recognized after tactual perception of parts of them, whereas the semicircle was most difficult. The third experiment is the one dealing directly with the problem of spatial orientation and with the role of visualization in it. The subjects were led along two sides of eight different-sized, right isosceles triangles and asked to return without guidance via the hypotenuse to the starting point; or they were led along the hypotenuse path and asked to return without guidance along the two legs of the triangle. The experiments were made in an open area, where auditory cues gave no undue advantage to the blind. The sighted subjects were significantly superior to the blind, and there was no difference between the accidentally and the congenitally blinded. Introspective reports given by some of the subjects indicated that the blind and the sighted used time in estimating distances. The sighted used visual imagery in determining direction. The study demonstrates the importance of visual imagery in orientation and confirms that, besides auditory cues, time assists the blind in distance orientation.

Worchel's findings that, in the performances that he tested, the sighted were superior to the accidentally blind and the congenitally blind, were confirmed by Drever (1955) in experiments using spatial tests. His findings also suggest the existence of certain basic skills built up through the early years, and that later learning has little effect.

A Tactual Performance Test involving a modification of a Seguin Formboard was used with blind and sighted children in a study by Eaves and Klonoff (1970). No differences were found between the two groups, though within the group of blind children, those with guiding vision acted more like the sighted than did the totally blind ones.

Spatial and nonspatial reasoning ability of blind and sighted children was investigated by Hartlage (1976). The two groups performed similarly on nonspatial questions, but blind children's performance on all spatial questions was inferior at every age level to that of the seeing. This confirmed conclusions of earlier studies by Hunter (1964) and Hartlage (1969) that vision is crucial in the development of spatial ability.

Cratty and Sams (1968) started their study on the body-image of blind children with the assumption "that to help a blind child grasp some of the simpler concepts of his spatial world, one must first help him find out about the space nearest him and, indeed, to find out about himself" (p. 2). A body-image survey form was administered to ninety-one children at the Frances Blend School for the Blind, in Los Angeles. The children were asked to identify planes of the body (such as front, back, and so forth) and body parts. They were also scored for making accurate movements of the body, discrimination between left-right dimensions of the body, and between the left and right of the tester and of objects. Based on mean scores of responses, the order of difficulties from easiest to most difficult was: body parts, body movements, body planes, laterality, and directionality. Intercorrelations, comparisons of scores of subgroups, of scores by age, and other statistical details were supplied. The authors discussed the educational implications of their findings and developed a training sequence for the spatial education of blind children—which they consider essential, particularly for mobility instruction.

In a book with pragmatic and operational orientation, which also includes theoretical guidelines, Cratty (1971) discussed with thorough documentation the development and educational management of body image, manual abilities, spatial orientation, muscle control and motor coordination, sound utilization, cognitive mapping, and mobility training of blind children from birth through adolescence. He considers sequential perceptual and motor education in the early months of life a precondition for later development of spatial awareness and for mobility. He outlines in detail, and with illustrations, a program for this purpose, and points out areas where research is needed.

Geographic orientation in the blind was the topic of a study in which McReynolds cooperated with Worchel (1954). In their geographic orientation tests, the congenitally blind did as well as the accidentally blind; the degree of blindness, etiology, age at blindness, age, IQ, and sex were not significant factors in geographic orientation. They conclude that "visual imagery does not seem necessary to geographic orientation."

Garry and Ascarelli (1960) conducted training experiments in orientation and spatial organization with a group of congenitally blind "good" and "poor" performers. They reported positive effects of training in these skills, though the trained "poor" performers did not achieve the level of the untrained "good" performers.

Maze tests have been used to determine learning ability and evaluate intelligence. Studies by Koch and Ufkess (1926), Knotts and Miles (1929), and Merry and Merry (1934) showed: that the stylus maze is more difficult for the blind than for the seeing, whereas the high-relief finger maze is less difficult for both groups; that the ability to learn the maze correlated higher with mental age than with chronological age; and that the finger maze is a valuable supplement in testing the intelligence of blind children. There is no agreement concerning the superior or inferior maze-learning ability of the blind as compared with the seeing. Duncan (1934) found that past visual experience influenced success in maze learning more than did the actual degree of sight present, and also that those who had perfect vision for at least a year seemed to be the most successful ones in learning the maze. She also observed that fifteen of the blind group of fifty-nine failed to draw square corners in reproducing the maze, and that the greatest degree of vision among these fifteen was "finger perception." Only two of the thirty sighted subjects failed to draw square corners. This observation tends to support the Worchel findings concerning the difficulty of directional orientation without visualization.

MacFarland (1952) was interested in observing in a maze-learning situation the methods used by blind subjects who were visually oriented. He found that tactual methods had more lasting effect than visual orientation, that motivation affected the degree of learning, and that blind persons seemed more motivated than the others. The method of solution used by blind persons was different from that of the other groups:

They worked slowly and carefully in the first trials, exploring every part of the maze; then they began to eliminate errors systematically. It was apparent that this group employed an attack based at least in part on "visualization" (ultimate construction of a mental image of the entire board) plus kinesthetic memory (p. 262).

This ability to construct a mental image of an object or situation as a result of successive observations of parts of it seems to be a decisive factor. Its importance was also stressed by Viktor Lowenfeld (1939, pp. 115–124) in his research on the drawings of partially blind children and on the modeling of the blind and the deaf-blind.

Two important distinctions were added by a study on maze learning by Berg and Worchel (1956). To the visual and tactual-kinesthetic factors, they added verbalization as an aid in maze learning, and also concluded that different mazes call for the use of different sensory processes. They used a multiple U maze, which was held to be a motor and visual maze, and a unidirectional X maze, which was held to require verbalization for its mastery. The subjects were twenty-eight totally blind, twenty-eight deaf, and twenty-eight normal children, matched on the basis of age, sex, IQ, and age at the onset of the sensory loss. On the U maze they found the normals and blind equal, and each surpassing the deaf, suggesting that verbalization plays a significant role in the mastery of this kind of maze. On the X maze, normals performed better than the blind, and they in turn better than the deaf. This is interpreted as indicating that although verbalization is important, visualization is also an aid in the learning of this kind of maze.

PERSONALITY AND SOCIAL FACTORS

Personality is the psychophysical organization of the individual as modified by his life experiences. This includes hereditary as well as environmental factors. The child who is congenitally blind experiences the world in his own way, which is different from that of most other children, and must also cope with special difficulties in getting about. His personality is affected by these differences, and it can be assumed that, by reason of his handicap, he is more likely to be under nervous strain and to harbor feelings of insecurity and frustration. But before discussing the findings concerning the effects of blindness on the individual, another source of possible conflicts must be considered; that is, the attitudes toward blindness and the blind.

The Influence of Environmental Attitudes

The attitudes of the public toward the blind have been discussed in many articles, and practically all authors of books dealing with the blind felt called upon to make some statements about this topic. Barker *et al.* (1953) reviewed publications on attitudes toward the blind and found that "there is almost universal agreement among the blind and those who work with them that blind persons are commonly perceived to be helpless and dependent and are frequently placed in underprivileged social situations" (p. 276).

Lowenfeld (1975), in his book *The Changing Status of the Blind: From Separation to Integration,* considers the attitudes of the public toward the blind, along with economic factors, and the agency system, as the three forces that are unfavorable to the integration of the blind into society. Monbeck (1973) devotes a large part of his book *The Meaning of Blindness* to attitudes toward blindness and blind people in the past and at present, to attitude changes, and to their psychosocial origins. He traces these attitudes to folklore, fairy tales, and myths, and describes in detail fifteen ideas about the blind that are basic to common attitudes.

Rusalem (1950) supplied one of the first experimental studies on this problem. A questionnaire answered by graduate students in a social psychology class showed on the whole favorable responses that did not support the negative attitudes generally assumed to be operative toward the blind. Rusalem comments that "these attitudes are highly complex and may never be explained in terms of a single simple hypothesis" (p. 287).

Chevigny and Braverman (1950) discussed

at length the attitudes of the public toward the blind, and of those in work with the blind. They call attention to the fact that the blind are a minority group, and while the content of the set of ideas about the blind may be different from that entertained about other minorities, the manner of operation is the same. They examine the underlying reasons for the particular attitudes toward blindness and the blind in psychoanalytic terms, and attempt to give an explanation of the adjustment and reorganization process required in meeting those ideas about blindness that form the constant in the social environment.

Attitudes Toward Blindness (1951) contains three papers representing various fields of learning. The first deals with the problem from the point of view of the psychiatrist (Schauer); the second considers the cultural-sociological aspects (Himes); and the third presents the approach of the clinical psychologist (Braverman).

The minority status of the blind and other attitudinal problems toward blindness were explored in two important studies. Gowman (1957) examined the sociological position of the war blind in American social structure, and Lukoff and Whiteman (1961) published a preliminary report of their experimental research on attitudes toward blindness. The latter research, as with many others, was supported by a grant from the Federal Office of Vocational Rehabilitation. Because both studies, though dealing with problems of the adult blind, have in some parts implications for the status of blind youth, their pertinent results will be reviewed here.

Gowman (1957, pp. 64–96) reports on a questionnaire study exploring attitudes of high school seniors toward blindness. When asked to rank five potential injuries as to their impact upon themselves and their prospective mate, four-fifths of them placed blindness for themselves in the first position. There is greater variability concerning the mate, but blindness is still considered the most difficult disability to accept. Middle-

class males were the only ones who assigned blindness to the second position as far as its impact on their mate is concerned. Lower-class subjects showed a tendency to react to blindness by focusing on assumed limitations and by stereotypical conceptions. Middle-class subjects related more to the visually disabled because of an apparent sophistication and middle-class humanitarian values.

Lukoff and Whiteman (1961) investigated the attitudes of sighted persons toward blindness by questioning three major groups: graduate social-work students, undergraduate college students, and a group of middle- and low-income housing inhabitants. Their findings confirm the importance of environmental attitudes for the kind of adaptation the blind person makes to his handicap. Family members and sighted friends of the blind person are most likely to influence his attitudes of independence. Their findings suggest four relatively independent components of sighted people's perception of the blind: (1) the degree to which sighted persons perceive blindness as personally frustrating; (2) the conception of blindness as distinct from attitudes toward blind people; (3) readiness to interact with blind people; and (4) differences in the degree of feelings among the sighted in thinking about or interacting with blind people. The question of how blind people perceive the sighted was examined by an analysis of data derived from a sample of 500 blind individuals in New York State. A majority of them believe that sighted people have little understanding of the blind, that they are surprised if a blind person can do something, that they consider blind people braver than the average sighted, and that most sighted people pity the blind. Members of the blind sample also tended to agree that they expect favored treatment in regard to pensions and job opportunities. Their interaction with sighted people is characterized by a pattern of submissiveness.

The authors summarize the reciprocal perceptions of the blind and sighted groups as follows: blind people's perception of the sighted is realistic in considering them naïve, lacking understanding of blind people, and overly pitying—all of which they are; it is unrealistic to ascribe to the sighted both negative and positive stereotyping attitudes—which they do not have, since almost half of them contended that blind people are capable of doing just about everything without help.

Attitudes have cognitive as well as affective dimensions, as Siller, Ferguson, Vann, and Holland (1967) and Lukoff (1972) have pointed out. The cognitive component of attitudes is more amenable to influences than is the affective: "There is a substantial cognitive component wherein negative orientations toward the blind are attributable to lack of information or experience with blind persons who are independent, and therefore rooted in rather readily modified perspectives" (Lukoff, 1972, p. 10).

Parents are the most important persons in the social environment of the child, and their attitudes profoundly affect his life. Parents' attitudes also reflect in some way, those of the general public of which the parents are a part. Sommers (1944) has made a thorough study of "some of the factors conditioning the behavior and the personality of the adolescent blind" and has attempted "to find out whether there exists a relationship between parental attitudes and actions and the blind child's behavior pattern and attitude toward his handicap" (p. 1). She obtained her results by three different methods: (1) the California Test of Personality was administered to 143 adolescent blind; (2) a questionnaire especially designed for blind children was answered by 120 of the adolescent blind subjects, and another questionnaire by 72 of the parents of these subjects; and (3) controlled interviews were conducted with 50 blind subjects and their parents.

So far as the California Test of Personality is concerned, Sommers concluded that it, like other personality tests designed for the seeing, does not adequately measure the personal and social adjustment of this group. Barker et al. (1953, p. 282) agreed with Sommers in questioning the general validity of personality inventories in research with the blind. The life situations of the blind differ greatly from those of the groups used in standardizing the inventories, and also many items in such inventories are of "different interpretive significance" for persons with normal sight and for those who are blind. They suggested detailed item analysis of personality inventories that may lead to hypotheses for further investigation.

The questionnaires revealed a wide variety of attitudes and feelings among the visually handicapped. They indicated that emotional disturbances and maladjustments result more frequently from the conditions and social attitudes of the blind person's environment than from the sensory handicap itself. The lack of uniformity in the reactions also disproves any assumption that blindness by itself can be the dominant cause of behavior deviations. The blind children were most aware of their handicap in such social situations as when people refer to their handicap or feel sorry for them or try to help too much; at sports and games requiring sight; when going to or eating at a strange place; when crossing streets, traveling, or window-shopping. The question "What do you feel one misses most by being unable to see?" brought replies clustering around the following activities: sports, games, car driving, traveling; enjoyment of sights of nature; facial expressions; movies, exhibitions, reading material; independence; normal home life, social life in general. More blind than seeing children indicated that they worried. Three times as many blind as seeing children worried about their own future and the future of the world (finding a job, financial insecurity, and the like). But schoolwork, tests, and teachers were the main worries of both blind and seeing children.

The interviews with the parents disclosed that:

Persistent feelings of frustration on the part of the parent seemed to arise from a sense of unfulfillment resulting from the fact that the birth of a child with a handicap as apparent as blindness failed to meet the concept of the kind of child which the mother had expected; while the contradiction between maternal devotion and an irrepressible sense of repulsion caused by the blindness seemed to create feelings of irreconcilable conflict (p. 102).

The case studies indicated four different reasons why parents manifest conflicts in their relationship with their handicapped child: (1) blindness is considered a symbol of punishment, and parents look upon their blind child as a visitation of divine disapproval; (2) fear of being suspected of having a social disease; (3) feelings of guilt due to transgression of the moral or social code or to negligence; resentment of the state of pregnancy, attempted abortion, marital discord, and the like may be the reasons for these feelings; (4) blindness in a child is considered a personal disgrace to the parents.

The ways in which the parents reacted to the handicap of their children fell into five fairly distinct categories: acceptance of the child and his handicap, denial reaction, overprotectiveness, disguised rejection, and overt rejection.

Sommers stressed that sharp lines of demarcation cannot be drawn and that some overlapping of attitudes is to be expected. Acceptance of the child and denial reaction are considered positive attitudes because they permit the child to grow, to develop, and to participate. Overprotection and disguised and overt rejection are negative attitudes that interfere with or stunt the child's growth.

Important for the general formation of attitudes toward a blind child is the following statement by Sommers:

The meaning the child's handicap held for his parents, especially his mother, the intensity of her emotional reactions, and the kind of adjustment she was able to make seemed to depend largely on the psychological makeup of the individual parent, her marital relationships, and her own personal and social adjustments to life (p. 105).

It is interesting to note that Sommers' five types of parental attitudes resemble very closely those that Kanner (1972) distinguishes as operative for children in general: acceptance, perfectionism, nonrejecting overprotection, rejection, overt hostility, and neglect. The category of perfectionism closely resembles Sommers' denial reaction.

The adjustive behavior of the blind adolescents studied by Sommers was closely related to the parental reactions, and showed the following six patterns: wholesome compensatory reactions, hypercompensatory reactions, denial reactions, defensive reactions, withdrawal reactions, and nonadjustive behavior reactions.

Sommers considers only the last-mentioned behavior as strictly nonadjustive. So far as the individual is concerned, the other reactions reduce emotional tension and assist him to adjust to his environment, although they may not always be approved socially. Even withdrawal assists the individual in making some kind of adjustment to his disability. Although in general one particular adjustment mechanism is predominant, in some instances several modes of adjustment were used.

Sommers also studies the relationship between the child's adjustment and parental attitudes, as rated by a series of twelve evaluation scales covering the physical, cultural, and emotional environment of the home, the parental attitudes toward the child, and the child's attitude and reactions. The statistical data presented by Sommers only complement her qualitative findings and insightful analysis.

Sommers warns against directly attacking a specific personality maladjustment in a handicapped child, because this means merely to battle against the symptoms and not to attack the underlying trouble. According to the findings of her study,

The answer to the problem of how to effect a more satisfactory development in the personality of handicapped children would seem to lie in building up in the parents of these children wholesome attitudes toward the handicap, as well as in the education and guidance of the child himself (p. 105).

In this she finds herself in agreement with others who have studied the emotional problems of physically handicapped children.

Meyerson (1953) pointed out that the Sommers study, though most valuable, has certain weaknesses, particularly in its lack of statistical support. He points to the urgent need for additional research along similar lines. Cowen *et al.* (1961) carried forward our research efforts in this area. This volume will be discussed later because its main emphasis is on personality adjustment, though it deals in some parts with parental attitudes.

The motor performance of visually handicapped children was studied by Buell (1950), who compared scores of the blind, of the visually handicapped, and of the seeing in such activities as track and field, the Iowa Brace Test, running, jumping, and throwing. He found that overprotective attitudes of parents influence performance in track and field events and in a stunt-type test in a significant way. Neglected children were found to perform normally in motor acts. He concluded that "as far as motor performance is concerned, parental neglect is to be preferred to overprotection." Therefore, "one cannot overemphasize the harm done to visually handicapped children by overprotective parents" (p. 59).

Although considerable research has been done on the attitudes of parents toward their visually handicapped children, the important problem of attitudes of professional workers toward the blind has received only scant attention. Blank (1954) discussed from a psychoanalytic point of view the unconscious conflicts about blindness that may interfere with the professional worker's ef-

forts in helping blind individuals. Among these conflicts are overidentification, subjective "blind spots" about blindness, unconscious sadistic trends, and erotic countertransference reactions. He recommends making psychoanalytic consultation available to case workers, teachers, and supervisory personnel, but warns against considering psychoanalysis a panacea.

There are a few studies available that deal with attitudes toward visually handicapped children as expressed in, for instance, prestige of and preference for teaching them, acceptance, and social distance. Jones and Gottfried (1966) studied the prestige attributed to teachers of exceptional children. Their findings indicate that teachers of the blind receive top ranking by practicing teachers and teachers of the mentally retarded, and high ranking by college students. In general, special education teaching carries higher prestige than regular class teaching.

In another study (Murphy, 1960), rating scales were administered to 309 teachers, special educators, principals, and other teaching personnel. They were asked to rank eight groups of exceptional children according to their preference for teaching them and according to how much they knew about them. The visually handicapped were ranked as least preferred for teaching (except for the delinquents) and also as those about whom the participants considered themselves least informed. However, special educators tended to rank the visually handicapped in a more favorable position. This result is interpreted as a moderate indication that favorable attitudes toward teaching a group are associated with knowledge about the group. Rusalem (1962) pointed out that the results of this study need to be considered with caution, because its participants were confronted with a forced-choice situation in which ranking distance was constant. Also, attitudes toward a specific group are not necessarily expressed by this ranking in which the teacher may indicate what he presumes to be the difficulties in working with this group. For instance, braille may be regarded as extremely difficult, and this may induce the teacher to assign a low-preference rank to the visually handicapped.

High school and college students considered blindness the worst handicap they could have (Siller, Chipman, Ferguson, and Vann, 1967), and college faculty members also judged that blindness presented the worst handicap for college students (Newman, 1976).

The question whether contact with blind persons plays a role in the formation of attitudes held toward them by sighted individuals has been inconclusively answered by past studies, according to Bateman (1964). In her own experiments, conducted by giving a questionnaire to students in an introductory college course in special education, she found that personal contact with blind individuals does not appear to affect the attitudes of sighted adults, that information-giving techniques improve expressed adult attitudes toward blind persons, and that one hour "identification with the familiar" (using cartoons in which blind children's abilities are positively related to the subject matter of the cartoon) was as effective in reducing negative attitudes as were six traditional lecture-discussion hours plus textbook material. Bateman recognized that expressed opinions may not actually be indicative of attitudes toward blindness and that her study did not examine how durable the changes produced were. Also, college students are not necessarily representative of the general public. Therefore, further studies are needed in this area.

In another study (Wyder, Wilson, and Frumkin, 1967) the hypothesis that the amount of positive knowledge an individual possesses about blindness is directly related to the positiveness of his attitudes toward blindness was tested by administering the Wright-Remmers Handicap Problems Inventory to sixty-four teachers. This inventory is a checklist of 280 items dealing with the impact of disability on personal, family, social, and vocational adjustments. Only in the area of family adjustment did the positively informed group of teachers perceive the blind as significantly less handicapped than did the uninformed group of teachers. There were no significant differences in the perceptions of personal, social, and vocational adjustments by the two groups. The Handicap Problems Inventory used 100 disabled persons as its normative group. These handicapped people viewed blindness significantly more positively than did the nondisabled teachers in this study, regardless of the amount of positive information about blindness which they possessed.

Bateman (1962) also investigated sighted children's perception of the abilities of blind children. She found that subjects who had known blind children appraised blind children's abilities more positively, and increasingly so with the number of blind children known; positiveness of appraisal increased with grade levels, particularly in grades three through six; and urban children were more positive in their appraisals than rural children.

The acceptability of twelve groups of exceptional persons and nonexceptional persons by high school students was examined by Jones, Gottfried, and Owens (1966) in terms of scaled social distance in seven interpersonal situations. The average and gifted are ranked as the most acceptable groups in most of the situations, while the severely mentally retarded are placed at the opposite end of the acceptance continuum of the distance scale. The blind rank, in general, in the lower or middle section of the acceptance continuum, depending upon the interpersonal situation.

In a sociometric study, Jones, Lavine, and Shell (1972) investigated the question of acceptance of blind children by their sighted peers in the classroom, and the sociometric characteristics of those sighted children who showed a high degree of acceptance of their blind classmates. Blind children tended to fall below the median (were less acceptable) on most items, though "stars" as well as rejectees were found among them. In the main, those sighted children who accepted the blind favorably tended themselves to be below median, or were isolates.

Steinzor published three articles dealing with attitudes toward visually handicapped children and toward blindness. In the study "School Peers of Visually Handicapped Children" (1966a), she reported the results of interviews with 108 boys and girls after they completed four sets of stories dealing with various interpersonal relations in which either sighted or blind individuals were involved. On the elementary school level, lowest attitudes of cooperation and highest attitudes of rejection were found with those classmates who were in classes with blind children for the first time. Attitudes improved as children had more classroom experiences with blind children. Most positive attitudes were found in those sighted children who had been with blind children before and who were presently in other classes. The author interprets this as a reaction of "shock at first encounter" and favorable attitudes *post factum*. In junior high school, attitudes of cooperation toward blind students were positive and highest for those who attended classes with the blind. Attitudes of independence (respect for another person's needs without entering into cooperative activities) diminished under influence of contact and turned into attitudes of cooperation. The author concludes: "According to these results, therefore, one can recommend, without reservation the full participation of visually handicapped adolescents in schools for the sighted" (1966a, p. 314).

Eaglestein (1975), in reporting the acceptance of nine high school students by their regular classmates in public school, agrees with this positive evaluation of regular school placement. However, he found some evidence that, although the students were socially well accepted, the longer they were in the school the lower their social status became, leading to a certain degree of rejection. This is contrary to the findings of Bateman (1962) and Steinzor (1966a).

In the article on attitudes of visually handicapped children toward their blindness, Steinzor (1966b) reported results of interviews with eight "normal" blind children in elementary school and with six in junior high school. The elementary pupils put strong emphasis on visual residues in terms of functions they can perform, with complete blindness having the connotation of a most negative stereotype; they wanted to find a common ground between themselves and the sighted, particularly in learning and in doing things; and their wishes and aspirations for the future were normal, though they did not always show an awareness of positions that could not be held by visually handicapped people. The junior high school students showed this awareness and also a "feeling of living in two separate worlds divided by a gap that could not be closed no matter how much good will one might have" (p. 310). They also felt that the sighted held attitudes of superiority, and expressed the wish for respect and equality, though they recognized the need for interpretation of the sighted world to them. Most of these students, in contrast to those on the elementary level, mentioned the wish to have sight. The author concluded:

> The ability to recognize their handicaps and to accept them, their aspirations to find a place in a world based on sight, their ability to identify themselves as persons rather than as blind, and the strength not to gloss over differences between sightedness and blindness seemed to be the main theme expressed by this group of young handicapped people. Their awareness of being blind was paralleled by their recognition of the necessity of adjusting to the sighted, their standards and their ways (p. 311).

Steinzor (1967) also published an article dealing with siblings of visually handicapped children. This exploratory study deals with siblings of visually handicapped children with complicated conditions; therefore, it cannot be considered indicative of sibling reactions to "normal" blind children. Such a study is badly needed and should have high priority on any research program involving attitudes toward blind children.

One final point should be made concerning attitudes toward the blind—they are changing. Himes (1958) pointed this out and discussed some indications of this change, such as the growth of a new social consciousness, the change in agency programs, the emphasis on rehabilitation, and the impact of the actively oriented war blind. He states: "Viewed in broad perspective, change appears as a tendency to melt down and remould the traditional stereotypes of the blind" (p. 334). The effects of continued and improved research also help in promoting this change.

Effects on Personality

A contribution unique in its kind and in its influence was made by Cutsforth (1951) with his book *The Blind in School and Society,* which was originally published in 1933. Cutsforth's own insight into the problems of blindness, his training as a clinical psychologist, his knowledge of the literature concerning the blind, his interviews with blind children, and his case studies make the book a most valuable source of information about the psychological effects of blindness. Many research studies were written later which only confirmed what Cutsforth had stated, although he was often unable to provide adequate scientific proof of his assumptions. Some of his assumptions did not or will not stand up under scientific scrutiny, due, in part, to the fact that under the influence of his own writings, conditions have changed so that they no longer support his suppositions. Cutsforth discussed the importance of the home environment for the preschool blind child, the problems

that blindness creates in his acquisition of language, his confinement to stimulation through touch and sound, his egocentric trends, his verbal unreality, and the developmental retardation that may be a result of all these factors. He considered the reasons for verbalism in blind and deaf-blind children and he held teachers who imposed visual experiences upon children without sight responsible for it. He wanted to have the blind child educated "into his own world of experience so that he may live in harmony with himself and his world, whether it be among the blind or the seeing" (p. 70). Cutsforth classified fantasies of the blind into three categories;

(1) Phantasies in which the individual eradicates the source of social annoyance; (2) phantasies in which the individual attains marked superiority or security; (3) phantasies in which the individual withdraws from the active situation in a surrender to a simple, regressive preoccupation, largely emotional in nature (p. 75).

In considering voice and speech and its value for the blind, he emphasized the psychogenic character of many of their speech defects. In a chapter on emotional problems, he discussed false attitudes toward the blind and false attitudes adopted by the blind, and denied that there is anything like a "world of darkness" for the blind. "The dark experiential world of the totally blind from birth consists of visual nothingness so far as its nature can be discovered" (p. 130). He also denied that the blind suffer because they cannot see or have a yearning for sight unless they adopt these attitudes under social pressure. He considered the fear of being watched an important factor in creating an emotional strain, particularly for pupils in schools for the blind, and believed that this phobia of being watched may persist long after the pupil has left the institution.

Cutsforth's book includes the only extensive treatment of sex behavior of the blind, on which information was and is quite meager. His basic assumption is that the blind child does not have as normal a sexual development as the seeing child. Because sexual growth takes place to the very limit that the environment provides, the environmental conditions and attitudes determine to a large extent the blind child's sexual growth. He does not have the same expanding social or the same stimulating objective environment and is confined to a much greater degree to stimulations which the self provides. The problems of masturbation and of homosexuality are discussed, and the need for a larger heterosexual environment is stressed. Cutsforth is very critical of the practice of segregation of boys and girls in schools for the blind and wants it replaced by a social environment in which the opposite sex is included.

In general it is Cutsforth's conviction that "blindness changes and utterly reorganizes the entire mental life of the individual" (p. 2), and that this reorganization, and its support or frustration, determines the influence blindness has on the individual.

Among the first studies that deal with the influence of blindness on certain personality traits are those of Brown (1938, 1939). He found a higher incidence of introversion among blind girls than among blind boys, and a higher incidence of "neurotic tendency" among the blind than among the seeing. According to the results of the study, the groups seemed to arrange themselves in order of decreasingly desirable adjustment, as follows: seeing boys; blind boys; seeing girls; blind girls.

McAndrew (1948a,b) investigated the problem of rigidity in the deaf and the blind. She explained that she was using "a broad Lewinian-type concept of rigidity" and defined it as a lack of variability and adaptability resulting in persistent repetition or continuation of an activity, and interfering with the ability to adjust to small changes in a situation. According to McAndrew's results, the blind are more rigid than the nor-

mal; the deaf more rigid than the blind and the normal. She concluded:

> All of the data suggest that the deaf and the blind have smaller life spaces than the normal, being partially isolated from the objective environments in which they live by the barrier qualities of their handicaps; and that they, therefore, develop less-differentiated and more rigid personalities (1948b, p. 77).

Jervis and Haslerud (1950) placed blind, blindfolded, and sighted adolescents in a masked experimental situation that induced frustration. The blind group acted in a significantly different manner from the sighted group: they exceeded the sighted significantly in the quantity of their physiological and verbal reactions. The authors conclude:

> The apparent volubility and large amount of overt emotional expression in the blind do not reduce tension because in an unhealthy and immature way they generally have intropunitive reference. The desirability of promoting more direct outlets for tensions would seem indicated in the education of the blind (p. 75).

Brieland (1950, p. 102) gave the Bell Adjustment Inventory to eighty-four matched pairs of blind and seeing pupils 12 to 18 years old. The test items were recorded and played back. The blind students were significantly inferior in health and in social and emotional adjustment; the home adjustment did not show any significant difference.

A scale specifically designed to evaluate adjustment to blindness was developed by Fitting (1954). He interprets adjustment to blindness as including six areas: (1) morale, dealing with the individual's confidence in himself, his hopes, and his aspirations; (2) outlook toward sighted people, dealing with the individual's concept of others; (3) outlook on blindness, dealing with the individual and his concept of himself as a blind person; (4) family relationships, dealing with the attitudes toward members of the family in the home situation; (5) attitudes toward training, including the anticipated degree of success in adjustment training and outlook toward education in general; (6) occupational outlook, dealing with the individual's concept of himself as an employee, his expectations in an employment situation, and his feelings about expected concessions because of his disability. The scale includes forty-two items that were standardized on a sample of 144 trainees in nine adjustment centers. Among other results, "the study indicated that there was a direct relationship between the amount of education, such as at a school for the blind, and the level of adjustment" (p. 73).

Land and Vineberg (1965) used the concept of locus of control as employed in the Bialer-Cromwell Children's Locus of Control Scale, which they applied to eighteen residential-school blind children, eighteen public-school blind children, and eighteen sighted children, matched according to certain criteria. Internal locus of control exists if an individual perceives himself as instrumental in the successful outcome of a situation; external locus of control means that an individual feels dependent upon external factors and perceives himself as ineffective. Differences based on mental age as well as differences between the blind and the sighted were found to be significant, with the blind scoring lower for internal control. The difference between the residential and public school group was found to be not significant. Also, no significant correlation was found between the degree of blindness and the locus of control. The scale was found to be a valid instrument for the purposes of this study.

Many authors have considered increased anxiety a personality characteristic of the blind, but no research had been undertaken on this problem. Hardy (1967) recognized that "a general anxiety scale could be less useful with the blind than an instrument constructed specifically for the blind" (p. 51). He constructed the Anxiety Scale for the Blind (1968a), consisting of seventy-eight items, and used it (1968b) with a sample of 122 "normal" blind children, 13 to 22 years of age, in two residential schools. Taylor's Manifest Anxiety Scale was also administered to these students. The data showed that both anxiety scales measure about the same characteristics and are equally useful, at least with the group of students tested. The anxiety level of totally blind students and of those with relatively useful vision did not vary with age, whereas students with light perception and projection showed significantly higher anxiety test scores as their ages increased. There was a significant inverse relationship between verbal intelligence and anxiety scores but no significant relationship between sex and anxiety scores. This study reveals some facts concerning the correlation of anxiety and certain characteristics of blind students in residential schools. A comparative study between anxiety levels of blind and sighted students, in which blind students in residential as well as public schools are represented, is still a project for further research.

Miller (1970) also used Hardy's Anxiety Scale for the Blind and concluded that the population "was anxious and concerned regarding future events, occupational security, and related social implications" (p. 94). Differences between totally blind and partially sighted groups were not significant, but the anxiety level of eleventh- and twelfth-grade students was significantly higher than that of the ninth and tenth graders.

As noted before, tests for the personality assessment of the seeing are of questionable value when used with the blind. Recognizing this, Bauman, Platt, and Strauss (1963) developed the Adolescent Emotional Factors Inventory. Its final form is made up of ten subscales (sensitivity, somatic symptoms, social competency, attitudes of distrust, family adjustment, boy-girl adjustment, school adjustment, morale, attitudes toward blindness, validation), each consisting of roughly fifteen items. This scale has proven itself effective in clinical use. A comparison between adolescent students in residential schools and those in integrated classes in public schools shows significant differences between the mean scores of girls in these two types of school settings for seven of the subscales; there were practically no differences of significance for the boys.

Bauman (1964) administered the Adolescent Emotional Factors Inventory to a group of 150 boys and girls attending residential schools and to an equal number attending integrated classes. Various differences were determined between boys and girls, between partially seeing and totally blind students, and between students from residential schools and integrated schools. For instance, the partially seeing students showed significantly higher anxiety and insecurity than the blind; the residential school group indicated more anxiety and insecurity, more difficulties in relating to the home and parents, and more problems of social and emotional adjustment than the integrated school group. Bauman noted that further research is needed to determine whether the differences between the students attending the two different types of school setting are due to direct effects of the residential school environment, to the separation from the family, or to other socioeconomic differences.

Projective tests for use with the blind obviously cannot offer visual stimuli such as inkblots or drawings, but must make use of stimulus situations that are either auditory, tactile-kinesthetic, or ideational-verbal. Lebo and Bruce (1960) published a then-current evaluative review of projective tests. For example, Wilmer and Husni (1953) have used an auditory projective test with blind children which presented a recorded variety of sound sequences. The Twitchell-Allen Three-Dimensional Apperception Test is a tactile-kinesthetic projection test that makes use of twenty-eight plastic pieces with ambiguous shapes. McAndrew (1950) used this test with blind, deaf, and normal children and concluded that it is "applicable to the

blind but must be interpreted cautiously." The Rotter Incomplete Sentences Blank is an example of an ideational-verbal projective test. In this test parts of sentences are presented, and the person is asked to complete them in a way that expresses his own feelings. Dean (1957) used this test among others with blind persons and found that its value with the blind is more likely in the qualitative rather than in the quantitative evaluations.

Cholden (1958) mentioned three special preoccupations of the adolescent that make acceptance of blindness particularly difficult: (1) The importance of bodily attractiveness in the female, and masculine strength and independence in the male. These preoccupations are of course related to sexual fears that are accentuated in the blind adolescent; (2) The problems of developing independence in an adolescent who must accept certain dependencies that are characteristic for blindness; (3) The exhibitionism accompanied with the desire for anonymity of the adolescent (p. 56).

Cole and Taboroff (1955) reported the successful therapy of a disturbed congenitally blind adolescent girl. They distinguish three categories of special problems of congenitally blind children: the cultural pressures that create a charged atmosphere in which the blind person must make his adjustment; the effects that blindness may have on personality and emotional development; and the problem of semantics of those blind from birth, since "their means of conceptualizing, their orientation, their perception of reality, may be different but also is poorly transmitted in a language manufactured by the seeing" (p. 630).

Abel (1961) discussed the special needs of the blind adolescent. He needs to be understood and respected as an adolescent who is blind; because he cannot observe visually, he needs to have his questions answered honestly and specifically by people around him and by professional persons; he needs to be a participating member of his family and of his peer group; he needs to acquire an optimistic outlook toward his future; he needs expert instruction in independent modes of travel; and he needs educational facilities and special equipment based on good practice and sound research.

Lowenfeld (1959) examined some difficulties that blindness creates for the adolescent in the areas of sex curiosity, dating, mobility, and concern for the future. These difficulties may influence the blind adolescent's self-concept and his attitudes toward interpersonal relations, but "may be simply different but no more severe or serious manifestations of the process of maturation which goes on in all adolescents" (p. 315).

Hooft and Heslinga (1968) discussed the sex education of congenitally blind children, which, though essentially not different from that of the seeing, poses some special problems. They point out the likelihood that blind children learn later about sex differences and are, therefore, more prone to harbor erroneous ideas about them and also about the sex act. Stressing the fact that literature which deals frankly with sex and the sexual organs is far less accessible to blind than to seeing children, they recommend realistic teaching models of male and female nudes and opportunities for frank discussion with educators in whom the blind child has confidence.

Foulke and Uhde (1975) and Scholl (1974) discuss the reasons why visually handicapped children are in special need of sex information and sex education. Their lack of visual input and of ready access to information and experiences about physical characteristics deprives them of adequate knowledge and causes them to harbor often bizarre ideas about anatomical facts and functions. Sex education of the visually handicapped is an essential part of their education, and the home as well as the school is responsible for it. Another side of this problem, traumatic effects of abnormal sexual experiences inflicted on the child, is discussed by Elonen and Zwarensteyn (1975).

In order to meet the demands for useful material in this long-neglected field, the Sex Information and Education Council of the United States and the American Foundation for the Blind published a well-organized and psychologically oriented resource guide edited by Dickman (1975).

Teen-age discussion groups have been suggested and arranged (Bucknam, 1967), as a prophylactic measure to avoid some of the difficulties blind adolescents must face in a residential school setting. Group therapy techniques were used with junior high school age groups, separated according to sex. Sex problems arose for discussion only after many months, but when they did, they became a predominant topic during the year in which each group met. The group setting provided opportunities for reality testing of some of the concepts students had about their sexual role.

A growing interest in dynamically oriented research in the field of adjustment to blindness on the adult level is evidenced by such studies as those by Bauman (1954); Cowen, Underberg, and Verillo (1958); Gowman (1957); and Lukoff and Whiteman (1961, 1970). Bauman and Yoder (1966) reviewed the literature on adjustment to blindness and included a followup of Bauman's study (1954), which deals with problems of adjustment of the adult blind population. They also discussed and reviewed some literature dealing with various adjustment problems of the growing child and adolescent, and covered such topics as blindness, frustration, and conflict; blindness and anxiety; blindness as an assault on the ego; blindness as physical stress; and learning, motivation, and blindness. Pringle (1964) reviewed the literature published on the emotional and social adjustment of blind children during the previous thirty-four years. The main contribution in the general field of physical disability is Wright's thought-provoking work (1960), which integrates findings from all areas of disability, including blindness.

A major publication on the adjustment to blindness in adolescence reported on the three-year research program that had been carried on under Emory L. Cowen at the University of Rochester, New York (Cowen, Underberg, Verillo, and Benham, 1961). Because the available research studies on attitudes toward the blind and adjustment to blindness had resulted in ambiguous and contradictory findings, the University of Rochester research group set out to examine afresh the essentially unresolved question of the comparative adjustment of visually disabled and sighted adolescents. They also wanted to test the proposition that characteristics of parent behavior (attitudes and understanding) are related to the adjustment of the visually disabled adolescent. They hoped that, in addition, their studies would clarify some other problems, such as the difference in adjustment between adolescents attending a residential school for the blind and those attending public school programs for the blind while living at home.

In their efforts to develop suitable measuring instruments for their research, the research team considered three factors as essential besides those that are required for all studies (reliability and validity): direct applicability to the visually disabled, objectivity of the indices of adjustment, and representation of a variety of situations. They developed, adapted, and adopted instruments to be used for the measurement of child adjustment, parental attitudes, and parental understanding. The child adjustment indices, which yielded seven global measures of adjustment were: A Self-Concept and Ideal-Concept Sort, a Teachers' Behavior Rating Scale, and a newly developed, objectively scorable projective type device, the Situations Projective Test B (SPT-B). Measures of Parental Attitude consisted of the Master Scale of 150 items, testing generalized attitudes toward child-rearing, sociopsychological attitudes toward minority groups and toward authority, and specific attitudes to blindness; and the Situa-

tions Projective Test A (SPT-A). Measures of Parental Understanding were in part the same as those used in measuring the adjustment of the children—the Predicted Self-Concept Sort and the Predicted SPT-B—so that the child's responses and the responses his parents predicted for him could be compared; and a "Dummy" Sort control in which the parent was asked to rank certain statements as he thought an "average teenager" would rank them.

The population of the study consisted of 167 adolescents aged 13 to 18 years, in the seventh through twelfth grades. Of these, 71 were visually disabled adolescents attending public day-school facilities, and 56 were visually disabled adolescents from residential schools for the blind. The control group consisted of 40 sighted adolescents matched as closely as possible to the experimental group in age, grade placement, intelligence, and socioeconomic status. The mothers of all 167 adolescents and the fathers of 66 were tested independently. The experimental groups were also broken down according to their degree of visual disability, and the sex distribution of all three groups was equated. The children were tested in their schools in two sessions of at least 45 minutes duration; parental tests were administered during individual home visits, in one session of about two hours.

So far as the problem of adjustment is concerned, the outstanding result of this study is that no systematic or consistent differences in personality attributes or adjustment were found among the three major groups tested. Elsewhere the authors (Underberg, Verillo, and Benham, 1961) state that their findings "cast an important shadow of doubt on beliefs about inherent associations between visual disability and maladjustment" (p. 257). Although there were no significant differences, partially sighted adolescents ranked slightly lower in adjustment than the legally or totally blind. There were no sex differences found, except that within the residential school sample, male adolescents were significantly better adjusted than their female fellow students. The study revealed no differences in adjustment between those living in residential schools for the blind and those living at home and attending public schools.

In their study of the relationship between attitudes of parents and child adjustment, the authors compared the mothers of the three major groups. They found mothers of adolescents in the residential school group to have more favorable attitudes toward their children than did the other mothers. This they interpret as "a powerful contra-indicant" for the belief that children are placed in residential schools because of unfavorable parental attitudes. To their concern, the authors found that their data failed to show any relationship between maternal attitudes and child adjustment, a finding contrary to past research as well as to clinical observation and psychological theory. They call attention to the fact that their research used the questionnaire method, which depends heavily on what a parent is willing to verbalize publicly, and they conclude that continued exploration of this problem is needed.

The third problem area, that of the relationship between parental understanding and adjustment of the visually handicapped child, has not previously been explored. The mothers of the three experimental groups showed no significant intergroup differences in the indices of understanding. However, a high degree of parental understanding (that is, accuracy in predicting the child's test behavior) correlated significantly and consistently with good adjustment of the child for all three experimental groups. This ability to predict apparently indicates an empathy and reality perception that is an essential condition for good child adjustment. The same pattern of relationship, though less clear-cut, was found for fathers.

The study also includes a preliminary attempt toward the construction of a prediction formula for adjustment. The adoles-

cent who perceives a high degree of parental acceptance, who is seen by his mother as well adjusted and similar to other adolescents, and who has a relatively high socio-economic status, is likely to be a well-adjusted individual.

The authors display rigorous self-criticism in the appraisal of their research methods and results. This makes the reading of their study a stimulating intellectual excercise, and the study itself a good one from which to learn scientific objectivity.

Jervis (1959) used the self-concept for a comparison of blind and sighted adolescents. His subjects were twenty students, 17 to 19 years of age, from two residential schools. All were totally blind since their third birthday or before, were of normal intelligence, and were free from additional physical or severe emotional problems. As a control group Jervis selected twenty sighted students, matched in all essential characteristics except blindness. Each subject had two open-ended interviews to yield a qualitative measure, and was given a modification of the Chicago Card-sort to yield a quantitative measure. The interviews were used to explain the purpose of the study, to establish a good relationship, and to encourage the subject to talk freely about himself and his feelings—in response to a set of twelve stimulus questions, such as "How would you describe yourself to a stranger? What do you consider some of your strengths? What do you see yourself doing in five or ten years?" In the Q-sorts the subjects were asked to sort statements twice concerning their feelings or attitudes toward themselves—once as they would best describe themselves, and once as they would describe their ideal selves. The interviews were independently judged by two psychologists, and no significant differences were found between the self-concepts of the two groups. A breakdown of the data revealed that blind subjects tended to be more apprehensive about their future, more aware of the need to get along with others, and felt less able to control outbursts of temper or aggression. Also, more of them felt that people in general did not expect enough of them. The Q-sort data also showed no significant differences between the two groups in their actual self-concept or in their idealized concept. However, more blind subjects had either high positive or high negative attitudes toward themselves, and the blind as a group exhibited a greater amount of variation. Jervis observes that

> blindness may be considered more than sight-deprivation but not a completely crippling factor. The fact that the blind subjects pushed either to an extreme negative or an extreme positive attitude toward themselves would indicate that they have difficulty in normal adjustment (p. 23).

In general, the studies of the University of Rochester group and of Jervis agree that there are no essential and consistent differences between blind and sighted adolescents as a group, but there appear to be individual differences—and these should be further explored.

Davis (1964) and Jervis (1964) discussed the development of the self-concept and the process of obtaining and maintaining self-esteem in blind children and adolescents, which must be considered issues of central importance in the personality development of blind individuals.

Zunich and Ledwith (1965) compared the self-concept of visually handicapped children with those of sighted children. They used the self-concept scale designed by Lipsitt with twenty-nine sighted and twenty-nine visually handicapped subjects. They found that the visually handicapped tended to use extremes, such as *not at all* and *all of the time* more than sighted subjects, as Jervis (1959) had also stated. Of the twenty-two trait-descriptive terms, significant differences, with the visually handicapped rating higher, were found in only four; namely, trusted, jealous, loyal, and obedient. Only in popu-

larity did nonsighted boys rate themselves significantly lower than the sighted.

Meighan (1971) used the Tennessee Self Concept Scale with 203 adolescents from residential schools. He found that, compared with the norms, they are "a very deviant and homogeneous group whose scores on the basic dimensions of self-concept were all found to be in an extremely negative direction" (p. 35). Among these were the identity, physical self, moral-ethical self, and behavior scores. No significant differences were found between the subgroups (females–males, white–black, blind–partially seeing), and no significant correlation was found between self-concept and academic achievement. Their unique self-concept is interpreted as the result of the appraisal of significant others. The results prove "that blindness has a definite and distinct effect upon the development of personality" (p. 31).

Blank (1957) observed that

> Psychoanalytic literature abounds in references to the symbolism of the eye, scoptophilia and exhibitionism, hysterical visual disturbances, and Oedipus and his blindness. . . . Yet contributions on the psychic problems of the blind are scant (p. 1).

Burlingham (1941) reported two case histories of blind children and concluded that the lack of sight disturbs and diminishes the testing of reality, one of the most important functions of the ego. Instead of compensating for this, the blind child turns to fantasy—which leads to denial of reality and to wishful thinking. She stated that there was little new material concerning the early sexual development of the two children and concludes that "the instinctual processes and the attempts to repress them which cause anxiety, act independently of sight" (p. 81). Her observations agree with those of Deutsch (1940), who also noticed a striking readiness to give up reality and escape into fantasy.

Blank (1957) believes that congenital

blindness does not always cause ego defect, but blindness which occurs when ego functions are already developed is inevitably traumatic. He distinguishes three factors that underlie personality disturbances of the visually handicapped:

(1) The unconscious significance of the eye as a sexual organ, including the equation of eye with mouth and with genital. (2) The unconscious significance of the eye as a hostile, destructive organ, including the equation of eye with piercing phallus and with devouring mouth. (3) The unconscious significance of blindness as castration, as punishment for sin (p. 1).

In two case presentations Blank demonstrated the problems of congenitally blind disturbed children and stressed that their ego development "depends primarily upon the physical contacts, consistent communication, and other components of mother love" (p. 6). Therefore, psychotherapy with the mother and assistance to the whole family are important prerequisites for helping the child.

In his discussion of acquired blindness, Blank comes to the same conclusions as Cholden (1958), who distinguished two stages in the reaction of healthy personalities to the loss of sight. The shock stage is a state of "psychological immobility," which can be thought of "as a period of protective emotional anesthesia which is available to the human organism under such stress" (p. 74). The degree of ego strength and maturity will determine the individual's capacity to recover from this initial shock and to enter the next stage, that of depression. This stage is interpreted as a mourning for the loss of a loved object, and "the patient must die as a sighted person in order to be reborn as a blind man" (p. 76). This stage must be lived through before blindness can be accepted; attempts to prevent or prematurely shorten this depression may impede the rehabilitation process. Also, the raising of false hopes for the return of sight or, on the other hand,

the premature offer of braille can prevent the acceptance of blindness as a reality. The problem of reactions to misfortune, such as mourning, was more thoroughly examined by Dembo, Leviton, and Wright (1956).

Lowenfeld (1975) distinguished three subsequent but overlapping phases in the history of the blind in the United States and psychological research on blindness: psychometric, psychosocial, and sociological. The sociological phase can be traced back to Cutsforth who wrote in 1933 that "the blind must either retain their self-respect by becoming socially distasteful" or "gain social approval by selling their self-regarding attitudes for conformity with the attitudes and concepts of the seeing. They become precisely the defectives that society conceives them to be" (1951, p. 125).

This is the thesis of Robert A. Scott's important book *The Making of Blind Men* (1969a):

The disability of blindness is a learned social role. The various attitudes and patterns of behavior that characterize people who are blind are not inherent in their condition but, rather, are acquired through ordinary processes of social learning (p. 14).

In Scott's analysis the self-concept plays a central role. Three contexts in which role-learning occurs in the blind person's life are distinguished: (1) In childhood attitudes, beliefs, and values about stigmatized people such as the blind are learned. If one is blind these become internalized and one learns to play the role of a blind person. (2) Personal interactions in encounters between seeing and blind people impress upon the latter negative and devaluing assumptions about blindness, and they are internalized as a part of the blind person's self-concept. (3) The network of service organizations for the blind and the practitioners active in them play an overridingly important role in the socialization of the blind. This service system instills in the blind certain model behavior patterns and attitudes based on its own beliefs and assumptions, and thus makes them into blind men. Obviously, the first context concerns childhood experiences; the second affects individuals from childhood on, and so does the third, particularly if schools and their personnel act similar to service agencies, as some undoubtedly do. Scott (1969*b*) deals at greater length with the socialization of blind children and its psychological causes.

Among the few studies investigating the social role concept are those of Mayadas (1972) and Mayadas and Duehn (1976). In the first study, Mayadas states:

It was an assumption of this study that discrepancy between role expectations and role performance is a function of the lack of familiarity on the part of the expectation holders who are sighted with the subculture within which the blind role is performed (pp. 46, 47).

The analysis of the data revealed role synchrony between the performance of blind children and (1) the expectations of significant others, (2) the children's perception of the expectations of significant others, and (3) the children's self-expectations. Role asynchrony (that is, no relationship) was found between the children's role performance and the expectations of strangers. Mayadas recommends the use of blind children's tendency for compliance to produce desirable behavior changes. The findings of the second study indicate that females are more receptive to environmental expectations than males, though both sexes acted independently of these expectations in their social interactions with the opposite sex. Also, nonresidential students demonstrated greater social assertiveness than residential students. The general findings "tend to negate the overall prevalence of the 'blind role' as the central organizing concept for the visually handicapped personality" and "reinforce the treatise that blindness is not an all-encompassing behavior trait, but that

sociocultural variables do affect the behavior of blind people just as they affect the sighted" (p. 289). Mayadas (1975), in another report, stressed the importance of selecting houseparents for residential schools for the blind, because as significant others they are instrumental in shaping each pupil's self-concept, so important for his strength in facing the world.

Facial Expressions

The problem of facial expression and of its development in the blind is of practical as well as theoretical importance. The questions of the innateness of certain expressions and of the cultural determination of expressive mimicry have received considerable attention. The social value of "normal" facial expression for blind children and adults has been stressed by many educators. Thompson (1941) studied this problem in twenty-six blind children, from 6 weeks to 13 years of age, who had been blind from birth or shortly thereafter. She compared them with a matched group of twenty-nine seeing children. The children were observed and photographed in naturally occurring situations of an emotional nature. The purpose of the study was to determine the effects of maturation and of social mimicry upon the innate neuromuscular mechanisms of emotional expression. Expressions of laughing, smiling, and crying were observed in blind, deaf-blind, and seeing children, although there were certain differences between them. The effect of maturation showed itself in a decrease of facial activity in smiling in older blind children; it showed an increase in facial activity in crying blind and sighted children. The emotional responses in blind and deaf-blind children were, in general, appropriate to the situation, but did not occur as uniformly among the blind as among the seeing children. These changes were considered to be maturational, because they could not have been brought about in blind children in any other way. The development of facial expressions in seeing children seems largely to be determined by mimicry. Thompson concluded: "Since it is believed that the facial musculature is under a dual neural control, it seems that maturation effects the 'emotional' expressions whereas mimicry effects 'voluntary' expression" (p. 41).

Fulcher (1942) asked 118 seeing subjects from 4 to 16 years of age and 50 blind subjects from 6 to 21 years of age to form facial expressions of emotions. These were photographed by a motion picture camera. The analysis of the requested expressions revealed: (1) the blind show less facial activity than the seeing in expressing every emotion; (2) the relative amount of facial activity in expressing emotions is about the same for the blind as for the seeing; (3) facial activity increases with age in the seeing but decreases with age in the blind; (4) the blind show slighter, though similar, differences of facial movement in expressing different emotions; (5) the expressions of the seeing are more adequate than those of the blind. He concluded, therefore, that vision is an important means of acquiring the ability to form appropriate facial expressions, but that there are other ways of acquiring them besides visual imitation.

After reviewing the literature on innate versus acquired facial expressions, Freedman (1964) reported observations on four congenitally blind infants. He observed that all four babies reacted to touch and voice stimuli with smiles which were extremely fleeting. In two cases, who were observed through 6 months of age, these fleeting smiles gradually changed to normal prolonged smiling. These observations led him to two interim hypotheses: "(1) the initial elicited smiles were reflexive in nature, since there was the typical sharp onset and almost immediate waning; (2) in these early months prolonged social smiling seems to require visual regard as a maintaining stimulus" (1967, p. 162).

Apple (1972a) recommended kinesic train-

ing for congenitally blind persons, which "should attempt to acquaint them with facial expressions and gestures that are common to everyday situations, but flexible enough to allow for the molding of behavior patterns to fit the individual" (p. 207). She also described (Apple, 1972b) the successful conduct of such a nonverbal communications training program with seven congenitally blind adolescents at a residential school.

Dreams

How blind individuals dream is a topic of frequent discussions and numerous observations, but there are few studies available that investigate the dreams of blind children. Deutsch (1928) presented descriptions of dreams of various children and also her own dreams, without discussing the symbolism contained in any of the dreams. She found that children often said that they "saw" an object when they actually meant that they only heard or felt it, or just knew that it was present. Therefore, she based her conclusions only on her own dreams and found that the imagery in them is "entirely auditory, kinesthetic, static, and tactile. The sense of hearing usually plays the most important part, while the other three sense modalities seem to be of about equal moment" (p. 293). Taste and smell imagery did not play any part in her dreams. She often carried on long conversations and actually heard what was being said to her by voices, which had all their usual inflections. An Italian study by Costa (1937) also showed that the dreams of totally blind children are predominantly of a tactual and auditory nature. A French study by Bolli (1932) agrees with this observation and also stresses that the dreams of those born blind are not lacking in variety or richness. In persons blinded later in life, visual imagery deteriorates in proportion to the age of the subject and the duration of his blindness. Schumann (1959), in a German treatise, made prodigious comments on the dreams of those born blind, blind at an early age (2 to 14 years), and at a later age. He agreed essentially with other writers, but his thorough review of the blind in mythology and in various arts is of special value (pp. 61–109).

That the congenitally blind and those who became blind before the age of about 5 do not have visual dreams was confirmed by the reports of Blank (1958). He concurred with Deutsch and others that hearing ranks first in importance, tactile and kinesthetic perceptions next—but also found that sometimes blind people's dreams include taste, smell, and temperature perceptions. He described five cases (three of whom were congenitally blind) and their dreams, and concluded:

> The typical dream of the blind is a dream "from above," one that is determined primarily by serious reality problems and it usually contains some prominent spoken statement, or other superego elements more closely related to the day's residue than to deeply repressed conflicts. . . . The phenomenological differences between the dreams of the blind and the seeing are not fundamental. They require no revision of the psychoanalytical theory of dreams (p. 173).

Imaginativeness in dreams and in fantasy plays of blind and sighted children was studied by Singer and Streiner (1966). Blind children showed themselves less imaginative or flexible than their sighted peers of comparable intelligence and socioeconomic status, except for their greater use of imaginary companions. These results confirmed Blank's (1958) findings on the poverty of content and concreteness in the dream reports of blind children.

Kirtley (1975) devotes two substantial chapters of his book *The Psychology of Blindness* to the dreams of the blind. He first reviews the empirical studies of dreaming in the blind and reports the content analysis of the dream diaries of seven visually handicapped men and women, kept over a 2- to 4-month period. It was found that, so far as imaginal content is concerned, "the dream reports of persons blinded after age seven are scarcely distinguishable from those of the seeing" (p. 307). The congenitally or early blind did not report dream vision, but the thematic content of their dreams and personality factors affecting dreams also did not differ from the seeing. The impact of visual impairment upon dream content is not determined by any shared trait of blindness, but rather by the unique characteristics of each subject. In a final chapter, the results of a content analysis of 307 dream reports of an adventitiously blind man are presented and interpreted.

Developmental Aspects

There is a large and growing literature that deals with descriptions, observations, and generalizations concerning the development of blind children. In many cases it also includes advice to parents on their functions in rearing a blind child. The number of scientific studies in this area, however, is rather small, although many of the research studies that were reported here have direct or indirect implications of a developmental nature.

Gesell, Ilg, and Bullis (1950) followed the development of a child born with clinically complete bilateral anophthalmia (congenital absence of both eyes) up to the age of 4 years. Their observational data demonstrated that in general the sequences of development in this blind child were comparable to those of seeing children. The blind child progressed in the basic patterns of posture, manipulation, locomotion, exploration, language, and social behavior, thus confirming the basic role of maturation in the blind infant's growth. Due to the lack of visual control, the child showed atypical orientational behavior, established no eye-hand coordination, and his head remained in a consistently maintained midposition. The authors concluded that blindness "profoundly alters the structure of the mental life but not the integrity of a total growth complex" (p. 273).

Although Gesell and his associates found that blindness by itself does not produce a serious degree of retardation (at least up to 4 years of age), another study (Wilson and Halverson, 1947) reached a different conclusion. In this study, a totally blind child was observed and tested with a battery of tests including the Gesell Schedules, the Cattell Infant Scale, and the Vineland Social Maturity Scale. The data indicated a general developmental retardation that was greatest in his motor and adaptive behavior—particularly in all activities involving prehension and locomotion—and least in language. In contrast to the aggressive attitude of seeing children, the child also showed a lack of initiative and spontaneity in his movements. The authors believe that much of the value of touch as an informative sense in early childhood is due to its association with vision and conclude that the blind child's retardation was for the most part caused by inadequate perception of space.

The difference in the findings of these two studies concerning the retarding influence of blindness may be due to a difference in innate potentialities of the two children, although the authors of the latter study do not consider this a possible cause. It must, however, be recognized that even a single case of a blind child with essentially normal development is sufficient proof that blindness does not necessarily retard a child. As a matter of fact, there are innumerable blind children who have demonstrated normal growth in spite of total blindness.

Maxfield and Fjeld (1942) used the Vineland Social Maturity Scale with 101 visually handicapped children ranging in age from 9 months to 6 years and 10 months. Of great importance in this study are the qualitative results that led to a tentative revision of the Vineland Social Maturity Scale for use with visually handicapped preschool children. Maxfield and Fjeld used the first seventy-seven items of the whole scale and found that fourteen items were relatively more difficult for visually handicapped children than for the seeing. Among them were eating with spoon and fork, buttoning coat or dress, marking with pencil, fetching or carrying familiar objects, cutting with scissors, reaching for familiar person, and playing simple table games. Of the fourteen items, at least four, such as marking with pencil and cutting with scissors, were obviously more difficult for visually handicapped children. Among fifteen items found to be relatively easier for visually handicapped children were: sitting unsupported, discriminating foods, washing hands unaided, initiating own play activities, using names of familiar objects, and playing with other children. Thus the blind children revealed a tendency to succeed better on items requiring less initiative, less activity, and less aggressiveness. Maxfield and Fjeld, in their adaptation of the scale, adhered to the categories and age levels of the original scale, but included new items and revised some others. They concluded that visually handicapped children as a group appeared to be more docile, less active, and to have less initiative than seeing children of corresponding ages. This trend was more striking in the blind than in the partially seeing. Hayes (1952) used the Maxfield-Fjeld Adaptation of the Vineland Social Maturity Scale with 300 blind babies and reported results closely corresponding to the findings of Maxfield and Fjeld.

Maxfield and Kenyon (1953) prepared a guide for the use of the Maxfield-Fjeld scale. Finally, Maxfield and Buchholz (1957) presented their Social Maturity Scale for Blind Preschool Children. The new scale consists of ninety-five items and is based on data and observations of 484 children. The authors aim at providing "as objective a means as possible for comparing the present status, or the progress, of a given blind child, in his acquisition of personal and social independence and competence, with that of other blind children of corresponding chronological age" (p. 8).

Sands (1952) stressed the importance of qualitative observation in connection with any use of preschool tests with blind children; these observations should include:

. . . the child's spontaneous play activities, his awareness and alertness; his methods of discrimination, exploration, and localization; his means of communication and use of language; his attention span and learning ability; his reactions to routine, and to people he knows as well as to new people (p. 26).

Sound and practical discussions on the psychological evaluation of young blind children are offered in articles by Hepfinger (1962) and Kenyon (1959).

Lowenfeld (1950) distinguished three objective effects of blindness: (1) the limitation in the range and variety of experiences; (2) the limitation in the ability to get about; and (3) the limitation in the control of the environment and the self in relation to it. From these limitations he derives the following basic principles in methods of teaching blind children: individualization, concreteness, unified instruction, additional stimulation, and self-activity. The first two limitations have already been discussed here, but the third one, in the control of the environment and the self in relation to it, needs further elaboration.

Sight is the human sense that overcomes distance and, at the same time, gives details and relationships of form, size, and position. This "object quality" of vision permits more effective contact with and control of the environment than are achieved by the other senses. Therefore, lack of sight causes a detachment from the physical and, to a lesser degree, from the social world. As a result, the blind individual is affected in different ways during his development. It has been noted, for instance, that the blind infant does not reach out for objects or crawl toward them, because he is not attracted by them unless they emit sounds. Some blind children omit

the crawling stage, although they follow in general the same sequence of development as seeing children do. Also, the blind child cannot acquire certain behavior patterns on the basis of visual imitation. This factor plays an important role in his learning to walk, to talk, to play, to acquire expressive movements, and to perform the many other actions in which learning by imitation is important. Dressing, eating, and many daily activities are considerably more complicated when they must be learned and performed without sight. For this reason, it is generally agreed that some retardation in the blind child's rate of development as compared with that of seeing children can be expected.

The blind child's inability to control his environment by sight also is responsible for his fear of being observed, which has been reported by many observers. He cannot determine whether he is being observed or when the observation begins or ends unless the observer makes himself known by some nonvisual means. This fear by itself is liable to produce tension and self-consciousness. The question of how blind children learn to understand what it means to be watched has not yet received scientific attention. Reported observations have shown that the blind child realizes at an early age that people can tell what he is doing without having bodily contact with him. Thus he learns that others can do something to him which he cannot do to them. Also, he finds out at an early age that he must grope around for something he has lost, whereas his seeing brother, sister, or friend can locate it immediately. Thus he learns by experience that he is in some way different from the others, although he may not know or may not be able to verbalize until much later that this is due to his blindness.

A research volume by Norris, Spaulding, and Brodie (1957) reports a 5-year longitudinal study conducted under the University of Chicago clinics by an ophthalmologist-psychologist–social worker team that cooperated with available community resources. Sixty-six of the 259 blind children in the study were studied intensively. Fifty-six of the former and 209 of the latter were blind as a result of retrolental fibroplasia. The first part of the study describes its research methods and findings; the second part presents case histories of six RLF children illustrating adjustment "ranging from very favorable to very unfavorable." The Cattell Infant Intelligence Scale, supplemented by certain items from the Kuhlmann Scale of Intelligence, and the Maxfield-Fjeld tentative adaptation of the Vineland Social Maturity Scale were used with children up to 3 years. The Interim Hayes-Binet Intelligence Tests for the Blind were used with children above the 3-year level. Detailed item analyses are reported for the Cattell and for the Maxfield-Fjeld scales. In interpreting the test results, it is stated that "in the experience of the project staff, any expectation that a psychological test result in itself could be regarded as a valid measure either of a child's capacity or of his functioning level proved unfounded" (p. 15). The importance of readiness is recognized, and the results of the study suggest "that the more time that elapses between the time of optimum readiness and the time when the opportunity for learning is provided, the greater the difficulties in learning become" (p. 23). Therefore, favorable opportunities for learning "are more important in determining the child's functioning level than such factors as his degree of blindness, his intelligence as measured by psychological tests, or the social, economic, or educational background of his parents" (p. 65).

The general conclusions of the study can be summed up by stating that under favorable conditions "the blind child can develop into an independent, responsible, freely functioning child whose use of his potential compares favorably with that of most sighted children of his age" (p. 65). This result confirms what Gesell and his associates (1950) found in their study of a child with congenital absence of both eyes. But whereas Gesell states that blindness "profoundly alters the structure of the mental life, but not the in-

tegrity of a total growth complex" (p. 273), the University of Chicago study asserts: "There are no special problems or 'handicaps' which can be attributed directly to the blindness" (p. 65)—a statement with which many would take issue.

Cohen (1966b) undertook a follow-up study of 57 of the 66 subjects in the University of Chicago study. Some 8 to 12 years later about half of these children were either untestable (4), in institutions (5), or had IQ scores below 80 (18). Of the remaining children, 24 scored between 80 and 120, and 6 scored above 120. Though most of the children had caught up with the height and weight norms for their ages, this cannot be said for their intellectual functioning. As a result, Cohen contends: "However, blindness from birth so limits the ordinary information flow available to the person that, in the absence of compensatory experiences, the child is not likely to reach the same functional level as he might have done with normal vision" (p. 151).

Referring to the studies of Norris et al. (1957) and of Cohen (1966b), Gillman (1973) observes: "In retrospect, it seems that the delays noted in the original study were significant, were not 'caught up,' and may well have been related to central nervous deficits, rather than sensory deficit per se" (p. 310).

McGuire and Meyers (1971) gathered information about twenty-seven congenitally totally blind children who were followed for at least one year and up to eight years. Fifteen of them were blind as a result of RLF. The authors found that "to be congenitally blind puts the child in the high risk category for personality problems" (p. 139) and they concluded "that the behavior disturbances have a psychogenic base" (p. 142). They explain the behavior disturbances as results of the difficulties in testing, controlling, and adapting to the environment without visual input; also, the anxiety of parents causes disturbed interpersonal relations.

Imamura (1965) compared the behavior of preschool blind children and sighted children, and sought to determine what relationship, if any, exists between the children's behavior and that of their mothers. Her results are based on systematic observations of the behavior of children and their mothers in their natural home environment. The study parallels cross-cultural investigations, conducted jointly by Harvard, Yale, and Cornell universities, by using the same observational methods and by matching its blind subjects on certain variables with a group of sighted children in the larger study. Imamura found that, compared with sighted children of the same ages, blind children are more dependent (the author uses the term "succorant") on the nurturance of their mothers, are less aggressive toward their mothers, are more succorant and less aggressive toward other children, have excessive social interaction with their mothers and proportionately less with other children, and are more verbal. So far as the behavior of mothers toward their children is concerned, mothers of blind children performed approximately five times as many responses as the mothers of sighted children. They reacted, in response to the children's request for help, significantly more frequently by compliance, by refusal, and by ignoring. The difference in the category of ignoring was the largest. The correlational data indicated that:

(a) more succorant mothers tend to have more nurturant children; (b) less sociable mothers tend to have more sociably aggressive children; and (c) extremely compliant and extremely noncompliant mothers tend to have children who are more self-reliant, while moderately compliant (equal amount of compliance and noncompliance) mothers tend to have children who are less self-reliant (p. 50).

Thus, in general, the study asserts that blind children are much more dependent than sighted children; that mothers of blind children treat their children's succorant behavior differently than mothers of sighted children by ignoring rather than refusing it;

and, finally, that there is a relationship between the children's behavior and the way their mothers react to it. Succorance is the behavior characteristic that most clearly distinguishes blind from sighted children. The author concluded: "Although we cannot ignore the significant effect lack of sight has on the blind child's development and behavior, the dependency of the blind child bears a strong relationship to the differential treatment he receives from his mother" (p. 57).

The play behavior of twenty-nine blind and twenty-nine seeing children was compared by Tait (1972). Blind children engaged more in manipulative play and were found to be much more inclined to become personally involved with the observer. This is considered a result of their greater experience in developing relationships with adults. Degree of blindness, and residential-school or at-home living, had no significant effects.

Cutsforth (1951) discussed "blindisms," which are acts of automatic self-stimulation such as rolling or tilting the head, thrusting the fingers into the eyes, and swaying the body. He explains that, in contrast to the seeing child, the blind child must find his stimulation without bodily reach and turns to his own body as the source and the object of stimulation. Thus, lack of stimulation from the external world furthers the blind child's concentration on the self and encourages the exercise of self-stimulation. Totman (1947) believes, on the basis of experience, that like any undesirable activity, blindisms must be replaced by more socially acceptable activities that give pleasure and satisfaction to the child.

Morse (1965) argues that the term *blindism* implies that the behavior described is exhibited only by those who are blind, whereas seeing children actually show the same behavior. Therefore, he suggests the term *mannerisms*. He also believes that anxiety and frustration are causal factors in these mannerisms. These and similar behavior patterns, such as thumb-sucking, nail-biting, leg-swinging, increase in sighted people as expressions of anxiety or frustration. He recommends finding substitutes for these expressions through the establishment of rewarding relationships with people in the child's environment.

An interesting distinction concerning blindisms was made by Stone (1964). He distinguished "withdrawal" and "alerting" blindisms. Withdrawal blindisms constitute intense rhythmic behavior that is completely involving and repetitive, thus resulting in a blocking out of environmental stimuli. Alerting blindisms employ small muscle masses and involve often ritualized behavior such as hand-clapping. Children engaged in these blindisms are aware of and responsive to the environment. He found that alerting blindisms resulted always in an increase of rate of a previously slow electroencephalogram. The results of his study suggest that blindisms of retarded blind children are accompanied by changes in the level of consciousness and "must represent an important method for the child in the alteration or regulation of his contact with a stressful reality" (p. 18).

In examining eye rubbing as one of the stereotyped behaviors in blind children, Thurrell and Rice (1970) found that the group with minimal vision showed significantly more eye rubbing than did either the totally blind or the more useful vision groups. They also noted that eye rubbing decreased with the increase of age, which might be due to training, increasing social maturity, and social feedback. They conclude their study by stating that, "given sensory social deprivation as a critical ingredient, plentiful substitute stimulation within an appropriate social context appears to diminish, if not eliminate, the blind mannerisms" (pp. 329–330).

Smith, Chethik, and Adelson (1969) describe three cases of blind children with behavior patterns of "blindisms." They trace them to individual problems in the child's development and to his particular life situa-tion, and they call attention to the complexity of the origin and meaning of these "blindisms" for each individual child. The behavior syndromes were in one case caused by inadequate environmental stimulation and persistence of a behavior pattern that had become useless; in the second, by difficulties in the transition from sitting to walking; and in the third, by a severe disruption in the parent-child relationship that affects other children in a similar way.

Hoshmand (1975) observed that past studies concerned themselves largely with the etiology of blindisms, but only in a few instances with their treatment. He concludes: "Given that the behavioral phenomenon of 'blindism' exists in some cases, direct ways of intervention on these target behaviors should be a research priority" (p. 59).

Two studies report on direct ways of intervention. Caetano and Kauffman (1975) effectively used elements of the Foxx and Arzin Overcorrection treatment strategy to reduce rocking mannerism in two blind girls, 9 and 10 years of age. Miller and Miller (1976) extinguished rapid horizontal head-wagging in a 13-year-old blind girl by a comprehensive, longitudinal, and tightly coordinated behavior modification. They concluded that "a generalization paradigm has been established whereby this subject-centered mode of intervention may be effectively utilized to remediate or extinguish a broad range of 'blindisms' and inappropriate behaviors" (p. 14).

Blindisms in their children are often quite disturbing to the parents because of the unfavorable reactions of other people to them. In most cases, blindisms disappear as the child grows up, although observers agree that emotionally disturbed children or those of low mentality may continue to practice them for a long time. This, however, is characteristic not only of blind but also of seeing children who are thus affected.

Some of the most valuable contributions to our knowledge of the influence of blindness on the development of children are coming from the staff of the Educational Unit of the Hampstead Child-Therapy Course and Clinic in London, of which Anna Freud is the head. The research group on blind children is directed by Mrs. Dorothy Burlingham. Burlingham (1961), in reporting her observations on the development of these children, stated that "retardation and restriction of muscular achievement are the order of the day. . . . The blind baby although not intentionally restricted yet behaves in many respects like a restricted sighted child" (p. 123).

Burlingham considers blindness responsible for this because it prevents stimulation to reach out and causes lack of some incentive, such as the observed approval of the mother, to repeat achievements. The dependency stage of the blind child is enlarged and prolonged; frequent persistence of mouth pleasure is characteristic. Blind children are observed as showing much less aggressive expression and more fear of external aggression. They feel the need for controlling their aggression because they realize how dependent they are on the seeing. Burlingham also observed that blind children often ask strangers immediately for their names, where they live, and so forth. She believes that people are far more attractive to them than objects, and imputes frequently occurring faulty methods of verbalization to such factors as speech, which is less firmly connected with sensory experiences, and to lack in ego achievement. She raises the question whether this will affect later superego formation and produce "certain ego characteristics such as superficiality, hypocrisy, overcompliance, which are often considered to be connected with blindness" (p. 137). Many of Burlingham's other observations are similar to those made in the United States on disturbed RLF children, but the research on blind adolescents fails to confirm the presence of any of the ego characteristics that she alleges are with blindness.

Burlingham (1964) also discussed the role of hearing and sound in the development of blind infants. Her observations are limited to a few blind children only, as she herself recognized. She stressed that the lack of visual contact between mother and child cannot be made up for by voice and listening. Thus, mother and infant cannot develop the close relationship that is established otherwise by the reciprocal effects of visual response. Mothers frequently do not understand the importance of silence and sounds for their blind infants. What may appear in the child as passivity may actually mean that he is listening to whatever goes on in his environment. The fact that the blind child later imitates something that he can only have heard during such periods of "passivity" is cited by her as evidence. However, stillness can also be frightening to the child, as for instance, if somebody leaves the room and the child feels that he is left alone. Burlingham believes that any continual auditory stimulation, such as the playing of the radio, has detrimental effects, not only because it blocks out environmental noises which might interest the child but also because it invites passivity and self-stimulation.

In another contribution, Burlingham (1965) dealt with problems of the ego development in blind children. She calls attention to the immobility of the blind child, except where conditions of absolute safety are provided, and contrasts this with the spontaneous active behavior of seeing children. She claims that this "immobilization is displaced from the motor area to other ego functions." She considers verbalization as a problem of the blind and states: "There is, thus, a comparative void left in the minds of those who have to build up their world image without visual impressions," and "from our observations of the blind it appears that this void is filled in part by the child's attentiveness to the sensations arising from his own body" (pp. 203–204). She also observed that blind children possess to an extraordinary degree an excellent memory. This memory plays a role in the impasse that results from the increase in his vocabulary of essentially meaningless words and his frustration in not understanding words which are spoken by people important to him. She gives some examples of speech observed in the Hampstead Nursery School and classifies them as follows: words acquired normally on the basis of sense experience; verbalizing by sense association; using words of the sighted world; associating from memory to unknown words; confusion between word and thing; and undigested parroting (pp. 207–208).

In her discussions of childhood occupations, Burlingham (1967) gives copious examples of plays and games, and professes that she cannot understand why, in view of the great variety of toys and activities which blind children can use, so many of them spend hours of inactivity and boredom and why mothers find it so difficult to keep them happily and satisfactorily occupied. She presents the following important comment:

> There is, of course, the possibility that we are wrong in judging the development of the blind child on the basis of comparisons with the sighted. What in this light appears as backwardness or a slowing up may turn out to be a matter of much greater basic difference in kind. To deal with visual representations of things, as the seeing do, is probably a much easier process than to deal with the verbal abstractions to which the blind are confined and for which they depend wholly on the progressive development of verbalization and its ramifications—inevitably later occurrences (p. 188).

The five papers of Burlingham discussed here have been included in her book *Psychoanalytic Studies of the Sighted and the Blind* (1972).

The most elaborate narrative of the psychoanalytic treatment and the recovery of a severely disturbed blind girl was presented by Omwake and Solnit (1961). Their contact with this child began when she was 3½ years old. Treatment continued to age 7.

They selected for discussion in this presentation four of the child's difficulties: an arrest of libidinal and ego development; the development of an inhibition of touching; the disorganizing effect of memories of painful experiences from the first 3 years of life; and the gradually developing comprehension of her sensory defect.

Klein (1962) further discussed the case presented by Omwake and Solnit and stressed that blindness must be understood "not in terms of the loss of visual function, but in the manner of organization of the information provided by the residual modalities" (p. 90). In modification of Omwake and Solnit's conclusions, he assures that the cognitive style that a blind child can develop may correspond essentially to that of a seeing child. In other words, vision does not appear to be indispensable for ego functioning. Maladjustments as a result of blindness are seen as consequences of a vacuum created by inadequate ego surrogates.

Passivity and ego development in blind infants was discussed by Sandler (1963). She proposed to provide a tentative theoretical model, since psychoanalytic theory gives a basic frame of reference but no specific theory accounting for the peculiarities of the blind child's development.

> Briefly, the thesis to be advanced is that the development of blind and sighted children follows roughly parallel courses for about twelve to sixteen weeks after birth, but that at the time of transition from the first (predominantly passive) oral phase to the second (predominantly active) phase, the ego development of the blind child pursues a course which results in his passive self-centeredness and lack of striving toward mastery at later ages (p. 346).

While in the first phase the mouth is the most important organ of exploration for blind as well as seeing children, in the second phase the hand takes over and sight plays an all-important role in directing the hand's exploratory functions. This leads during the second and third quarters of the first year to a differentiation between the child's own body and the outside world. The blind child is hindered and retarded in this process of turning from the self to the outer world. Although sounds can play some role in this process, the blind child by necessity lacks the sensory continuity of visual impressions. Thus, the blind infant is to a large extent deprived of the satisfactions of external stimulation and turns to repetitive self-stimulating behavior. Sandler notes that even the mother's best handling of her child cannot avoid the basic retardation in ego development. "It is inevitable that this must have a profound effect on later stages of development" (p. 356).

Sandler's theory about the blind child's divergent development is supported by Fraiberg (1968) on the basis of long-term observation of eight "normal" congenitally blind babies. She agrees with Sandler that the delay in locomotion observed in blind babies is linked to their prehension problems and to their difficulties in reaching out and attaining objects on sound cues alone. Only after the baby succeeds in this, will he begin to creep. This occurs, as Wills (1970) also observed, between the seventh and twelfth month. In continuing her observations into the second year, Fraiberg finds impressive parallels between the achievements of blind and sighted children, particularly in mobility, in exploration, in tracking objects by sound, in self-feeding, and in speech. But serious adaptive problems exist in such areas as human relations, gross-motor activities, cognitive development, and particularly in the vulnerability of his ego and his ego-defense mechanisms.

Adelson and Fraiberg (1974) described the patterns of gross-motor development in congenitally blind infants, which they had reported in previous studies. Fraiberg (1971) and Fraiberg, Smith, and Adelson (1969) report in detail, and with great warmth and insight, an intervention program by which she and her co-workers were able to reduce in nine blind children the delay in mobility

achievements and its effects, as compared with another group of blind children.

Three periods of particular vulnerability in blind children were described by Wills (1970): (1) the period before the blind infant reaches for an object on sound cue alone, (2) the prolonged period when the blind child remains tied closely to the familiar and to routine, and (3) the period when the fate of the blind child's aggressive impulses to the object is being decided.

Sandler and Wills (1965) reported many observations on totally blind children at the Hampstead Unit in an effort "to trace the baby's early difficulties in moving away from passive instinctual aims to exploration of the world around" (p. 18). They stress the importance of the mother and her body in this process and the significant role that hearing and sound assume. Evidence of this they find in the children's recall of conversations and in their frequent and repetitive imitation of sounds. In role-playing situations, copying adult activities is mostly on the verbal level while the child has difficulties in acting the adult role. The authors suggest that the poor cathexis of adult activities raises the whole question of later sublimation.

Wills (1968) examined the reasons why blind children so easily withdraw from age-adequate playing into simple primitive activities. In the case of 5-year-old Sam, she explains the importance of repetitive play in discharging affects, the occurrence of phobic anxieties and the resultant withdrawal, and the role of repetitive play in mastering certain fears of external reality.

Observations on six blind children, illustrating Burlingham's (1961) comments on blind children's conceptualization of the world around them, were presented by Wills (1965). She concluded that it takes blind children much longer to gain a knowledge of the world around them, that they have difficulties in distinguishing reality from fantasy, that they frequently gain only partial and insufficient knowledge of objects, that they have a tendency toward animistic thinking long after seeing children have overcome it, and that they need help in establishing their own way of thinking and their own methods of understanding and adaptation in order to integrate with the sighted world around them.

There are other psychoanalytically oriented studies that deal with the development of blind children. Fraiberg and Freedman (1964) reported the illuminating case of a 9-year-old blind child with arrested ego development, which they consider typical of deviant blind children. They call attention to the importance of the functions of the mouth as a leading organ of discrimination and perception throughout the blind person's life. The blind child's development proceeds by the hand gradually taking over perceptual functions that were centered in the mouth. Deviant blind children may fail to develop this "hand autonomy."

The importance of the search for the source of sound in the ego development of blind infants was stressed by Fraiberg, Siegel, and Gibson (1966).

Nagera and Colonna (1965) examined the ego and drive development of six blind children aged 4 to 8½ years. The authors distinguished two types among the blind children: some who are not far behind sighted children of similar ages in their ego processes, drive development, and object relationships; and others whose developmental processes are atypical, lagging behind in different degrees in the different areas and giving in some extreme cases the impression of marked mental retardation. They dealt mainly with the latter group, and reported many observations in line with those made by others analytically oriented.

Psychoanalytic studies are almost exclusively concerned with ego-development disturbances caused by the effects of blindness. Chase (1973, 1974) studied retrospectively several groups of variables that could have contributed to cause some RLF children to show autistic symptoms, and others not. Her findings suggest a multifactor theory of eti-

ology because no single factor could be identified. But "the evidence suggests physiological (biogenic) influence. Parental factors, although relevant to some degree, must be viewed as only one element of the total picture in the development of blind children" (1974, p. 69). Chase also expressed the hope that professional workers will take this into consideration in the counseling of parents.

A broadly conceived research study by Gomulicki (1962), sponsored by the Royal National Institute for the Blind, London, the Cambridge Institute of Education, and the Mental Health Research Fund, has been reported only in a preliminary way with some of its conclusions. The experimental tasks used in this research were designed to throw light on the developmental patterns of perceptual learning in blind children. According to the report:

. . . Details differed, but in experiment after experiment, regardless of the perceptual modality concerned, much the same picture emerged. At the age of five, the blind child was at a distinct disadvantage as compared with the sighted one, taking decidedly longer to produce results that were markedly inferior. By that age, the sighted child had already achieved the major part of his perceptual development; the blind child still had far to go. But the further progress of sighted children from five onward is, in general, slower than that of the blind, who, over a period varying from about four years to ten or more, manage to draw approximately level . . . by their mid-teens or thereabouts, the blind children become, to all intents and purposes, as good as the sighted children of the same age (p. 120).

The author asks at what cost this is achieved, and states that the data of his experiments suggest "that a prolonged effort of the intellect is part of the cost to the blind of a degree of perceptual skill that for the sighted is a relatively effortless product of maturation" (p. 120). Gomulicki believes that parent education is essential in fostering attitudes that would enable them to deliberately encourage their blind child to be active and self-reliant and to provide them with ample opportunities to develop the effective use of their senses. Also, methods of training the children in the various perceptual skills should be cultivated during their school years, because for the blind it cannot be taken for granted—as it safely can be for the sighted—that their "normal" senses will achieve the required efficiency without aid.

If the results of Gomulicki's research could be satisfactorily documented, they would provide an explanation for the contradictory findings of frequent problems in young blind children and generally good adjustment and success among blind adolescents and adults.

MULTIHANDICAPPED BLIND CHILDREN

Since the second and third editions of this book appeared, retrolental fibroplasia as a cause of blindness has become an issue of historical importance so far as psychological problems of blind children are concerned. The second edition of this book dealt with it extensively (pp. 289–294). This chapter has incorporated some of the research of general importance in its preceding treatment of developmental aspects.

For many years to come, it is certain that comparatively large numbers of multihandicapped blind children will need educational facilities and psychological services geared to their special needs. An indication of the extent to which blind children have additional handicapping conditions can be found in two studies. Wolf (1967) secured in 1965 data from forty-eight residential schools for the visually impaired. Thirty-five of these schools with a pupil population of 4,711 reported 1,170 mentally retarded children, which is a prevalence rate of 250 mentally retarded per 1,000 visually impaired children. His investigation indicated that there

was a combined average of 3.18 disabilities for children enrolled in special classes for the mentally retarded blind in residential schools.

Lowenfeld (1968) surveyed educational and other facilities throughout the state of California to determine the prevalence of multihandicapped blind and deaf-blind children in that state. According to his conservative estimate, 80 to 90 percent of the multihandicapped blind children's population is included in his data. He concluded:

> It can, therefore, be stated that for the school age population, normal blind children (1,111) outnumber the multihandicapped blind children by 11 to 9. If we include the State Hospital population of multihandicapped blind children, multihandicapped blind children of school age (1,919) outnumber 'normal' blind children (1,111) by 19 to 11 (p. 32).

In Lowenfeld's study, children enrolled in residential or public school facilities for the visually handicapped (the deaf-blind not included), had a combined average of 3.0 handicaps per child. The additional handicaps in order of their frequency were: mental retardation, emotional, speech, cerebral palsy, communication, orthopedic, epilepsy, and others.

In 1966 Graham (1968) collected descriptive data on 8,887 multiply impaired blind children and estimated that there are about 15,000 such children in the United States.

The number of multihandicapped blind children shows a dramatic increase, largely because of the following factors: (1) there are still some retrolental fibroplasia children; (2) maternal rubella epidemics (Wagner, 1967) have caused comparatively large numbers of multihandicapped blind and deaf-blind children; (3) prenatal causes of blindness, many of which affect not only the eye but also cause additional abnormalities, have increased while other causes such as infectious diseases and accidents—many of which affect only the eye and leave the child's other sensory, intellectual, and physical capabilities intact—have decreased.

The rubella epidemics released a veritable flood of articles, pamphlets, and reports dealing with psychoeducational problems of blind children with additional handicaps. They all stressed the importance of emotional acceptance of the child by his parents, of providing early and suitable opportunities for learning at the right time, and of environmental influences—principles that are accepted for children in general but that need to be specially stressed with blind children who have additional handicaps.

Some books, widely acclaimed by parents and professional workers, have been found helpful. Lowenfeld's *Our Blind Children— Growing and Learning With Them* (1971) is a psychologically oriented book dealing with the education of blind children. Spencer's *Blind Children in Family and Community* (1960) is a more sociologically oriented picture story of preschool blind children. Halliday's *The Visually Impaired Child: Growth, Learning, Development—Infancy to School Age* (1971) is concerned with learning processes and intended for readers acquainted with children through experience and/or formal education. *The Visually Handicapped Child in School,* edited by Lowenfeld (1973), is a text for students and teachers, and a practical guide for parents in need of more advanced information.

One of the pivotal elements in the placement and provision of education for multihandicapped blind children is that of evaluation or assessment. Intelligence tests, which are only reasonably satisfactory in use with normal blind children, are practically useless with many of the multihandicapped blind children, particularly those who are retarded or emotionally disturbed. These tests are largely verbal, and this is precisely the area in which many multihandicapped blind children are most deficient. For this reason, assessment based on long-term observations is regarded by many teachers and psychologists working with these children as

the best way to determine whether an individual child is likely to make progress. It is not the present status of performance of a child that must be considered, but his ability to improve and to progress.

Chase (1975) discussed the more formal early developmental assessment and the measures widely used in it. She also recommends techniques and informal materials that can be applied. Weiner (1967) identified five characteristics as the most relevant dimensions of educability: level, rate, range, efficiency, and autonomy. *Level* is to be understood as the amount of development or achievement in terms of degree of difficulty or complexity; *rate* refers to the time required for different tasks; *range* means the curriculum and in which parts of it the child is able to function; *efficiency* refers to economy and speed of performance in a wide range of socially and educationally meaningful tasks; *autonomy* is described as evidence of independence, self-actualizing behavior, and how the child chooses, initiates, and executes tasks he has selected for himself, and whether he experiences satisfaction from his activity. Weiner comments: "These characteristics reflect the response of the child to the demands made of him in out-of-school as well as in-school activities. They are observable in all stages of development, across the conventional categories of handicaps, and in all social and cultural groups" (p. 74).

Because assessment can often be carried out only over prolonged periods of time, various programs serving multihandicapped children include assessment as one of their functions. There are many descriptions of such facilities available, as for instance those of Blanchard, Bowling, and Roberts (1968); Brodey (1962); Cicenia, Belton, Myers, and Mundy (1965); Donlon (1964); Goodman (1967); Mattis (1967); Tretakoff (1966); and Williams (1964).

The short description of only one of these programs can be given here—that of the Children's Division of the Syracuse Psychiatric Hospital in Fairmount, New York (Ross, Braen, & Chaput, 1967). It carried on a program for twenty severely disturbed blind children, 6 to 12 years of age, in a residential setting. In the beginning, these children were without any interest in the external world and in learning, and they had a short attention span and extremely low frustration tolerance. None of them had had any successful school experience.

> The heart of the program lay in an expectation that each staff member would show the same respect to each child regardless of his individual developmental level; would provide the child with interpersonal and other kinds of experiences to help guide him to the next step in development; and would patiently allow him to achieve that step at a speed consistent with his specific needs (p. 218).

The difficult and complex progress of some of these children from regression as a reaction to admission, to slowly developing interest in others, use of language, lessening of anxiety and consequent decrease in aggression, and finally to participation in an educational curriculum is described.

As these blind children with additional handicaps grow into adolescence they may be in need of further training, either to become independent and vocationally placeable or to become less dependent within their family or in a special facility. Such training, including individual and group instruction in mobility skills, communication, recreation, and social relations, has been described by Hatlen, Le Duc, and Canter (1975).

Para-analytic group therapy in which the therapist, whose basic role is analytical, also functions as a counselor and supplies accurate factual information (on sex matters and reproduction), was described by Avery (1968a).

In another report, three cases of multihandicapped blind children received mobility training in order to prove that this kind of training, with some modifications in technique according to the individual student's needs, was possible and beneficial (Seelye and Thomas, 1966). Though the students were not able to participate in every phase of mobility, the value of the program was demonstrated.

Various reports by Elonen and her coworkers described the arrangements, experiences, and results of programs carried out by the Michigan School for the Blind. Elonen and Polzien (1965) described summer-session programs for multihandicapped blind children and the very favorable results that were obtained with extremely deviant blind children by individual, intensive therapy.

As a result of this success, the Michigan School for the Blind established a full program to which some children, formerly committed to institutions for the retarded, were admitted (Elonen, Polzien, & Zwarensteyn, 1967). These children reacted to their frustrations with such aggressive violence that their families had removed them from their homes. Frequently long periods of institutionalization had prevented any developmental progress. The provisions at the school include psychological therapy, speech and language training or speech therapy, physical and occupational therapy, music therapy, remedial reading, and special living conditions with handpicked, understanding housemothers. The cases of six children were reported in some detail.

Elonen and Cain (1964) and Elonen and Zwarensteyn (1964) discussed in greater detail the methods applied in the Michigan programs. In the first paper, they stress that the therapist needs to have a deep personal commitment toward these children and must work with them in the same way in which he works with psychotic children. They warn that in this process the therapist may overidentify with a blind child to the extent that he negatively interprets actions of other people in the child's environment. The relationship is usually on a one-to-one basis and demands a high degree of skill and dedication on the part of the therapist.

In the second paper, the authors discuss in detail the deviations that may occur in the development of the young blind child. They believe that in many of the deviant children retarded development, autistic behavior, and apparent brain damage may be only pseudoconditions. For the prevention of such pseudoconditions, they recommend intensive counseling for parents, information and demonstration of techniques in managing the child, information about developmental expectations for each individual child, and support for the parents on the basis of long-term observation of the child through his various developmental stages. Preconceived attitudes of parents and also of many professional people to whom the parents turn may affect the development of these children so severely that pseudoconditions become irreversible. More research is needed to ascertain this point of irreversibility and the indications for it. "Certainly, the earlier the parents can be encouraged to provide maximal nurture, motivation, and opportunity for growth, the more hopeful are the children's chances for attaining normal development" (pp. 609–610).

The cases of three blind children and their psychiatric therapy were presented by Green and Schecter (1957). Two were RLF cases showing severe disorders; the third, blind from early infancy, was not as autistic or retarded as the other two. Four phases of the therapeutic program are described:

(1) The individual work of the psychiatrist with the child. (2) Consultations with parents by the psychiatrist and the psychiatric social worker. (3) Placement of the child in daytime school programs, with regular consultations with the teachers. (4) Placement in institutions for disturbed blind children for those who could not be treated on a once-a-week clinic basis.

Attention is called to the need for early detection of such emotional disturbances, and the authors warn of "the danger of explaining, all too easily, the psychological deviations on the basis of a child's handicap, rather than exploring the severe child-parent disturbances which have become organized around the handicap" (pp. 645–646).

To the many case studies that have already been mentioned, Cohen's (1966a) report on a blind spastic child must be added. He presented this case as an example of how a child can overcome the severe disadvantages of gross multiple handicaps (blindness, spastic quadriplegia, and hearing disorder) and early emotional deprivation. A stimulating school environment, a good program of physical therapy, special attention and help for specific problems, an accepting foster home, and above all, the child's own inner courage and drive toward growth were instrumental in achieving a healthy psychological and physical development despite a gloomy early picture.

Play therapy has also been found to be successful in restoring a measure of mental health to many blind children (Avery, 1968b; Axline, 1947; Raskin, 1954; Rothschild, 1960). Behavior modification and some ways of applying its techniques to multihandicapped blind children were discussed by Larsen (1970).

There are some reports that deal with electroencephalographic findings of multihandicapped blind children. Akiyama, Parmelee, and Flescher (1964) studied the electroencephalograms of children who had varying degrees of visual handicaps. The frequency of abnormal EEGs was higher when the visual handicap was more severe, but there was no relationship between abnormal EEGs and the occurrence of seizures or the intellectual development. The authors conclude, "These EEGs should not be interpreted as indication for a poor prognosis in terms of behavioral development" (p. 241). Similar observations are made in studies by Boshes, Cohen, Alfano, and Lee (1967), and by Cohen (1970).

There is very useful material available on the education of deaf-blind children (Robbins, 1960, 1963; Robbins and Stenquist,

1967; Stenquist, 1974; American Association of Workers for the Blind, 1967) that has psychological implications; and there is a valuable chapter on deaf-blindness in the adult population by Rothschild (1962). But only a few psychological research studies dealing with this highly challenging group of multihandicapped children can be reported. This may be due to the fact that in the past their numbers were very small, though during the more recent years they have greatly increased due to the unfortunate results of rubella epidemics.

Curtis, Donlon, and Wagner (1970) give a detailed description, written by experts in each field, of the evaluation techniques useful in the psychoeducational, speech and language, casework, pediatric, audiological, ophthalmological, and neurological examination of deaf-blind children. The Callier-Azusa Scale (Stillman, 1976) evaluates the developmental status of deaf-blind children, particularly low-functioning ones.

Positive and negative experiences in using operant conditioning with twenty children under age 6, legally deaf-blind as a result of maternal rubella, were reported by Calvert, Redell, Jacobs, and Baltzer (1972). They concluded that "operant conditioning procedures have limited value for testing and training severely involved deaf-blind children but hold some promise for those having good organization of the central nervous system" (p. 420). They also discuss evaluation of progress for this group of children.

Curtis, Donlon, and Tweedie (1974, 1975) gave an account of examination procedures, communicative, adjustive, and learning behavior of twenty deaf-blind children. Their results are highly interesting but not yet final because they plan to study a total of fifty children.

Jordan (1964) draws attention to differences within the group of the deaf-blind, distinguishing those who are deafened-blind, blinded-deaf, and those who lack both senses from birth or early childhood on.

These groups should be clearly distinguished in any future research.

H. and R. Rusalem (1964) examined the reactions of high school students, and H. Rusalem (1965) those of college students (freshmen) to deaf-blindness. Both groups reported that they had practically no contact with any deaf-blind person—which was not surprising, considering their small numbers. They tended to maintain a social distance from deaf-blind individuals, which prevented correction of their negative percept of deaf-blindness. The high school students were exposed to an unusually gifted deaf-blind speaker at a school assembly, which produced more accepting verbalized feelings that could, if reinforced, lead to attitude changes.

In summing up the discussion of multihandicapped blind children, some facts stand out as a result of experiences with them reflected in the literature. Any effective program to assist these children therapeutically must be based on a clinical approach. Ashcroft (1966, p. 93) stressed this by saying: "The therapeutic intervention must be rather drastic as compared to conventional educational programs. The program should be 'clinical' in nature—that is, it should be conducted virtually on a one-to-one basis" (p. 93). Cruickshank and Trippe conducted a very extensive study of blind children in New York State (1959). They present extensive data on all aspects of blindness, but especially, they illustrate the magnitude of the issue of multiple problems of blindness in relation to mental retardation, impaired hearing, cerebral palsy, and other physical disabilities. Cruickshank (1964) warned that in order to understand multihandicapped children, one cannot think of them in a generic sense. Each one is an individual and his special condition must be considered in clinical terms in order to find a workable solution, only after careful and frequently long, exhaustive periods of study.

The effects of multiple handicaps cannot

be understood by simply adding those of every handicap found in an individual child. They lead to something more and different than would be the result of a mere addition of the handicapping conditions. This idea has been expressed by Curtis (1966):

> It is necessary for the examiner to recall throughout the interview and examination process that the list of characteristics which we associate with a certain degree of hearing loss, type of brain injury, or particular physical disability, when viewed in isolation, does not have the same significance when that particular disability occurs simultaneously with one or more other severe disabilities (p. 374).

So far as the causes of the problems in many of these children are concerned, Guess (1967) summed them up well in reviewing Sandler's (1963) study:

> The blind child turns inward because he receives less stimulation in quantity and variety from his environment. Moreover, the blind child does not receive emotional feedback from his mother to reward and stimulate him. He lacks the continuity with environment afforded by vision and consequently directs his attention to his own bodily experiences. This drive for bodily gratification impairs his relationships to things and people around him (p. 473).

Finally, there is a noticeable difference between the writings of psychoanalysts and those of others concerning the outlook for successful improvement in the condition of retarded or disturbed blind children. The psychoanalytically oriented group is far less optimistic about it than the clinical-educationally oriented group. Most of the psychoanalytically oriented studies consider the ego damage resulting from congenital blindness either as irreversible or at best as only partially compensable. The clinical-educational group believes more optimistically that therapy and a wholesome environment can successfully restore the child's mental health, though they recognize that at a certain not-yet-determined point conditions caused by environmental deprivation may become irreversible.

Effects of Physical Factors

A number of physical factors related to the eyes doubtlessly affect the individual, although no research has clarified the extent and kind of this influence. Facial disfigurement is a frequent result of eye defects. The eyeball may be enlarged (as in congenital glaucoma) or abnormally small (microphthalmia), or there may be no eyeball at all (anophthalmia); the muscles controlling the movements of the eyeball or the eyelids may not function normally and thus cause strabismus, nystagmus, or ptosis (dropping of the upper lid); X-ray treatment of the eyes to control malignant growths may have resulted in disfiguring burns; pathological changes in the eyeball or parts of it may be quite apparent. All these and other disfigurements are liable to make the individual quite self-conscious and ill-at-ease. The eye condition responsible for the visual defect may not be static but progressive, and this may cause anxiety and feelings of insecurity. There may be actual pain as a result of the eye defect (as, for instance, in glaucoma), or discomfort and irritation may make the child acutely conscious of his eye trouble. Also, frequent and prolonged hospitalization because of eye pathology exerts its influence on the child, particularly if it necessitates separation from the mother during the earlier years of life. It may result in developmental retardation as well as in emotional reactions characteristic of deprivation of maternal care (Kanner, 1972; Spitz, 1946). Prolonged treatment of eye diseases by medication also has emotional effects on the child and his environment. Finally, any blindness that occurs late in life results in an emotional trauma which may manifest itself in various reaction forms.

CONCLUSION

Blindness is a defect of one sense, but it affects the individual in various ways. Though studies on the psychological implications of blindness have increased, research to connect behavior with specific effects of blindness is still needed. Personality inventories, scales, and interviews record only reported behavior, judgments (often about oneself), and opinions. Therefore, any analyses of these must be accepted with caution, no matter how refined and objective the statistical treatment may be. The problem of a blindness-adequate intelligence test still awaits solution.

The distinction between those who are totally and congenitally blind and those who are only partially blind, or partially seeing, or those who became blind later in life, has not received due attention. The lack of this distinction is responsible for ambiguity in the results of many studies and for contradictions among the results of some of them.

Behavioral studies (research as well as observations) provide increasing evidence that blindness, uncomplicated by other disorders of either organic or environmental nature, does not cause developmental disturbances. However, the chances that these may occur are heightened by the effects that the child's blindness may have, from early infancy on, on his social environment, particularly in the mother-child relationship. The effects of blindness modify some cognitive functions, and this may have a retarding influence, more noticeable during the preadolescent period. All this, however, does not prevent normal achievement according to the individual's capacity.

REFERENCES

ABEL, G. L. The blind adolescent and his needs. *Exceptional Children,* 1961, *27,* 309–310, 331–334.

ADELSON, E., & FRAIBERG, S. Gross motor development in infants blind from birth. *Child Development,* 1974, *45,* 114–126.

AKIYAMA, Y., PARMELEE, A., & FLESCHER, J. The electroencephalogram in visually handicapped children. *The Journal of Pediatrics,* 1964, *65,* 233–242.

American Association of Workers for the Blind. *Contemporary papers.* Vol. 2. Washington, D.C., 1967.

AMMONS, C. H., WORCHEL, P., & DALLENBACH, K. M. "Facial vision": The perception of obstacles out of doors by blindfolded deafened subjects. *American Journal of Psychology,* 1953, *66,* 519–553.

APPLE, M. M. Kinesic training for blind persons: A vital means of communication. *New Outlook for the Blind,* 1972, *66,* 201–208. (*a*)

————. Kinesic training for the blind: A program. *Education of the Visually Handicapped,* 1972, *4,* 55–60. (*b*)

ASHCROFT, S. C. Delineating the possible for the multi-handicapped child with visual impairment. *Sight-Saving Review,* 1966, *36,* 90–94.

AVERY, C. Para-analytic group therapy with adolescent multi-handicapped blind. *New Outlook for the Blind,* 1968, *62,* 65–72. (*a*)

————. Play therapy with the blind. *International Journal for the Education of the Blind,* 1968, *18,* 41–46. (*b*)

————, & Streitfeld, J. W. An abbreviation of the Haptic Intelligence Scale for clinical use.

Education of the Visually Handicapped, 1969, *1,* 37–40.

AXELROD, S. *Effects of early blindness: Performance of blind and sighted children on tactile and auditory tasks.* New York: American Foundation for the Blind, 1959.

AXLINE, V. M. *Play therapy.* Boston: Houghton Mifflin Company, 1947, Chap. XXI.

BACHELIS, L. A. Developmental patterns of individuals with bilateral congenital anophthalmos. *New Outlook for the Blind,* 1967, *61,* 113–119.

BALL, M. J. Mobility in perspective. *Blindness 1964.* Washington, D.C.: American Association of Workers for the Blind, pp. 107–141.

BARKER, R. G., WRIGHT, B. A., MEYERSON, L., & GONICK, M. R. *Adjustment to physical handicap and illness: A survey of the social psychology of physique and disability* (rev. ed.). New York: Social Science Research Council, 1953.

BARRAGA, N. *Increased visual behavior in low vision children.* New York: American Foundation for the Blind, 1964.

———. Utilization of sensory-perceptual abilities. In B. Lowenfeld (Ed.), *The visually handicapped child in school.* New York: John Day, 1973.

———. *Visual handicaps and learning: A developmental approach.* Belmont, Calif.: Wadsworth, 1976.

——— (Ed.). *Visual Efficiency Scale.* Louisville, Ky.: American Printing House for the Blind, 1970.

BATEMAN, B. Sighted children's perception of blind children's abilities. *Exceptional Children,* 1962, *29,* 42–46.

———. The modifiability of sighted adults' perceptions of blind children's abilities. *New Outlook for the Blind,* 1964, *58,* 133–135.

BAUMAN, M. K. Studies in the application of motor skills techniques to the vocational adjustment of the blind. *Journal of Applied Psychology,* 1946, *30,* 144–154.

———. *Adjustment to blindness.* Harrisburg, Pa.: State Council for the Blind, 1954.

———. Group differences disclosed by inventory items. *International Journal for the Education of the Blind,* 1964, *13,* 101–106.

———. An interest inventory for the visually handicapped. *Education of the Visually Handicapped,* 1973, *5,* 78–83. (*a*)

———. Psychological and educational assessment. In B. Lowenfeld (Ed.), *The Visually Handicapped Child in School.* New York: John Day, 1973, pp. 93–115. (*b*)

———. (Comp.) *Blindness, visual impairment, deaf-blindness: Annotated listing of the literature, 1953–75.* Philadelphia: Temple University Press, 1976.

———, & HAYES, S. P. *A manual for the psychological examination of the adult blind.* New York: The Psychological Corporation, 1951.

———, PLATT, H., & STRAUSS, S. A measure of personality for blind adolescents. *International Journal for the Education of the Blind,* 1963, *13,* 7–12.

———, & YODER, N. M. *Adjustment to blindness—reviewed.* Springfield, Ill.: Charles C Thomas, 1966.

BERG, J., & WORCHEL, P. Sensory contributions to human maze learning: A comparison of matched blind, deaf, and normals. *Journal of General Psychology,* 1956, *54,* 81–93.

BERLA, E. P. Effects of physical size and complexity on tactual discrimination of blind children. *Exceptional Children,* 1972, *39,* 120–124.

BERRY, M. F., & EISENSON, J. *The defective in speech.* New York: Appleton-Century-Crofts, 1942, pp. 340–353.

BLANCHARD, I., BOWLING, D., & ROBERTS, R. L. Evaluation of an educational testing program for retarded blind children. *New Outlook for the Blind,* 1968, *62,* 131–133.

BLANK, H. R. Countertransference problems in the professional worker. *New Outlook for the Blind,* 1954, *48,* 185–188.

———. Psychoanalysis and blindness. *The Psychoanalytic Quarterly,* 1957, *26,* 1–24.

————. Dreams of the blind. *The Psychoanalytic Quarterly*, 1958, *27*, 158–174.

BOLDT, W. *Blinde und hochgradig sehbehinderte Kinder in der physisch-technischen Welt.* Ratingen, Germany: Aloys Henn, 1966.

————. The development of scientific thinking in blind children and adolescents. *Education of the Visually Handicapped*, 1969, *1*, 5–8.

BOLLI, L. La rève et les aveugles. *Journal de Psychologie*, 1932, *29*, 2–73, 258–309.

BOSHES, L. D., COHEN, J., ALFANO, J. E., & LEE, W. C. Longitudinal appraisal of school-age children with retrolental fibroplasia. *Diseases of the Nervous System*, 1967, *28*, 221–230.

BRAVERMAN, S. The psychological roots of attitudes toward the blind. In *Attitudes Toward Blindness*. New York: American Foundation for the Blind, 1951, pp. 22–32.

BREKKE, B., WILLIAMS, J. D., & TAIT, P. The acquisition of conservation of weight by visually impaired children. *Journal of Genetic Psychology*, 1974, *125*, 89–97.

BRIELAND, D. M. A comparative study of the speech of blind and sighted children. *Speech Monographs*, 1950, *17* (1), 99–103.

BRODEY, W. M. Normal developmental learning and the education of the child born blind. *Gifted Child Quarterly*, 1962, *6*, 141–149.

BROWN, P. A. Responses of blind and seeing adolescents to an introversion-extroversion questionnaire. *Journal of Psychology*, 1938, *6*, 137–147.

————. Responses of blind and seeing adolescents to a neurotic inventory. *Journal of Psychology*, 1939, *7*, 211–221.

BUCKNAM, F. G. Preventive child psychiatry at a residential school. *New Outlook for the Blind*, 1967, *61*, 232–237.

BUELL, C. E. *Motor performance of visually handicapped children.* Berkeley: Charles Edwin Buell, 1950.

BÜRKLEN, K. *Blinden-Psychologie.* Leipzig: Johann Ambrosius Barth, 1924.

————. *Touch reading of the blind.* Trans. by F. K. Merry. New York: American Foundation for the Blind, 1932.

BURLINGHAM, D. Psychic problems of the blind. *American Image*, 1941, *19*, 95–112.

————. Some notes on the development of the blind. *The Psychoanalytic Study of the Child.* New York: International Universities Press, Inc., 1961, *16*, 121–145.

————. Hearing and its role in the development of the blind. *The Psychoanalytic Study of the Child.* New York: International Universities Press, Inc., 1964, *19*, 95–112.

————. Some problems of ego development in blind children. *The Psychoanalytic Study of the Child.* New York: International Universities Press, Inc., 1965, *20*, 194–208.

————. Developmental considerations in the occupations of the blind. *The Psychoanalytic Study of the Child.* New York: International Universities Press, Inc., 1967, *22*, 187–198.

————. *Psychoanalytic studies of the sighted and the blind.* New York: International Universities Press, Inc., 1972.

CAETANO, A. P., & KAUFFMAN, J. M. Reduction in rocking mannerisms in two blind children. *Education of the Visually Handicapped*, 1975, *7*, 101–105.

CALDWELL, F. F. *A comparison of blind and seeing children in certain educational abilities.* New York: American Foundation for the Blind, 1932.

CALVERT, D. R., REDELL, R. C., JACOBS, U., & BALTZER, S. Experiences with preschool deaf-blind children. *Exceptional Children*, 1972, *38*, 415–421.

CANTRIL, H., & ALLPORT, G. W. *The psychology of radio.* New York: Harper & Row, 1935.

CHASE, J. B. Cognitive patterns in subjects blinded by retinoblastoma. In *Selected Papers, Association for Education of the Visually Handicapped—Fiftieth Convention.* Philadelphia: Association for Education of the Visually Handicapped, 1970, 166–171.

————. *Retrolental fibroplasia and autistic symptomatology.* New York: American Foundation for the Blind, 1973.

————. A retrospective study of retrolental fibroplasia, *New Outlook for the Blind,* 1974, *68,* 61–71.

———. Developmental assessment of handicapped infants and young children: With special attention to the visually impaired. *New Outlook for the Blind,* 1975, *69,* 341–349, 364.

CHEVIGNY, H., & BRAVERMAN, S. *The adjustment of the blind.* New Haven: Yale University Press, 1950.

CHOLDEN, L. S. *A psychiatrist works with blindness.* New York: American Foundation for the Blind, 1958.

CICENIA, E. F., BELTON, J. A., MYERS, J. J., & MUNDY, G. The blind child with multiple handicaps: A challenge. *International Journal for the Education of the Blind,* 1965, *14,* 65–71, 105–112.

COHEN, J. Development of a blind spastic child: A case study. *Exceptional Children,* 1966, *32,* 291–294. (a)

———. The effects of blindness on children's development. *New Outlook for the Blind,* 1966, *60,* 150–154. (b)

———. Brain waves and blindness. In *Proceedings of the Conference on New Approaches to the Evaluation of Blind Persons.* New York: American Foundation for the Blind, 1970, pp. 112–125.

COLE, N. J., & TABOROFF, L. H. The psychiatric problems of the congenitally blind child. *The American Journal of Orthopsychiatry,* 1955, *25,* 627–639.

COSTA, A. Sogni di fanciulli ciechi e semiveggenti. *Rivista de Psicologia,* 1937, *33,* 44–52.

COTZIN, M., & DALLENBACH, K. M. "Facial vision": The role of pitch and loudness in the perception of obstacles by the blind. *American Journal of Psychology,* 1950, *63,* 485–515.

COVENY, T. E. A new test for the visually handicapped: Preliminary analysis of the reliability and validity of the Perkins-Binet. *Education of the Visually Handicapped,* 1972, *4,* 97–101.

COWEN, E. L., UNDERBERG, R. P., & VERILLO, R. T. The development of an attitude to blindness scale. *Journal of Social Psychology,* 1958, *48,* 297–304.

———, & BENHAM, F. G. *Adjustment to visual disability in adolescence.* New York: American Foundation for the Blind, 1961.

CRANDELL, J. M., & WALLACE, D. H. Speed reading in braille. *New Outlook for the Blind,* 1974, *68,* 13–19.

CRATTY, B. J. *Perceptual-motor behavior and educational processes.* Springfield, Ill.: Charles C Thomas, 1969.

———. *Movement and spatial awareness in blind children and youth.* Springfield, Ill.: Charles C Thomas, 1971.

———, PETERSON, C., HARRIS, J., & SCHONER, R. The development of perceptual-motor abilities in blind children and adolescents. *New Outlook for the Blind,* 1968, *62,* 111–117.

———, & SAMS, T. A. *The body-image of blind children.* New York: American Foundation for the Blind, 1968.

CRUICKSHANK, W. M. The multiple-handicapped child and courageous action. *International Journal for the Education of the Blind,* 1964, *13,* 65–76.

———, & TRIPPE, M. J. *Services to Blind Children in New York State.* Syracuse: Syracuse University Press, 1959.

CUNDICK, B. P., CRANDELL, J. M., & HENDRIX, L. A new method for the group testing of blind persons. *New Outlook for the Blind,* 1974, *68,* 398–403.

Curriculum guide: Pre-cane mobility and orientation skills for the blind. Lansing: Michigan School for the Blind, 1966.

CURTIS, W. S. The evaluation of verbal performance in multiply handicapped blind children. *Exceptional Children,* 1966, *32,* 367–374.

———, DONLON, E. T., & TWEEDIE, D. Deaf-blind children: An examination procedure for behavior characteristics. *Education of the Visually Handicapped,* 1974, *6,* 67–72.

———. Communication behavior of deaf-blind children. *Education of the Visually Handicapped,* 1974, *6,* 114–118.

———. Adjustment of deaf-blind children. *Education of the Visually Handicapped,* 1975, *7,* 21–26.

———. Learning behavior of deaf-blind children. *Education of the Visually Handicapped,* 1975, *7,* 40–48.

CURTIS, S., DONLON, E. T., & WAGNER, E. (Eds.). *Deaf-Blind Children: A program for evaluating their multiple handicaps.* New York: American Foundation for the Blind, 1970.

CUTSFORTH, T. D. The unreality of words to the blind. *The Teachers Forum,* 1932, *4,* 86–89.

———. *The blind in school and society* (rev. ed.). New York: American Foundation for the Blind, 1951.

DAUGHERTY, K. M. Listening skills: A review of the literature. *New Outlook for the Blind,* 1974, *68,* 363–369, 415–421, 460–469.

DAUTERMAN, W. L., SHAPIRO, B., & SUINN, R. M. Performance tests of intelligence for the blind reviewed. *International Journal for the Education of the Blind,* 1967, *17,* 8–16.

DAVIS, C. J. The assessment of intelligence of visually handicapped children. *International Journal for the Education of the Blind,* 1962, *12,* 48–51.

———. Development of the self-concept. *New Outlook for the Blind,* 1964, *58,* 49–51.

———. New developments in the intelligence testing of blind children. In *Proceedings of the Conference on New Approaches to the Evaluation of Blind Persons.* New York: American Foundation for the Blind, 1970, pp. 83–92.

DEAN, S. I. Adjustment testing and personality factors of the blind. *Journal of Consulting Psychology,* 1957, *21,* 171–177.

DEMBO, T., LEVITON, G. L., & WRIGHT, B. A. Adjustment to misfortune: A problem of social-psychological rehabilitation. *Artificial Limbs,* 1956, *3,* 4–62. Also in *Rehabilitation Psychology,* 1975, *22,* 1–100.

DEMOTT, R. M. Verbalism and affective meaning for blind, severely visually impaired, and normally sighted children. *New Outlook for the Blind,* 1972, *66,* 1–8, 25.

DEUTSCH, E. The dream imagery of the blind. *Psychoanalytic Review,* 1928, *15,* 288–293.

DEUTSCH, F. The sense of reality in persons born blind. *Journal of Psychology,* 1940, *10,* 121–140.

DICKMAN, I. R. (Ed.). *Sex education and family life for visually handicapped children and youth: A resource guide.* New York: Sex Information and Education Council of the United States and American Foundation for the Blind, 1975.

DIDEROT, D. *Letter on the blind for the use of those who see.* Chicago: Open Court Publishing Co., 1916, pp. 88–104. Reprinted: *Blindness 1966.* Washington, D.C.: American Association of Workers for the Blind, pp. 210–230.

DOKECKI, P. R. Verbalism and the blind. A critical review of the concept and the literature. *Exceptional Children,* 1966, *32,* 525–530.

DOLANSKI, V. Les aveugles possèdent-ils le "sense des obstacles"? *L'Année Psychologique,* 1930, *31,* 1–50.

DONLON, E. T. An evaluation center for the blind child with multiple handicaps. *International Journal for the Education of the Blind,* 1964, *13,* 75–78.

DREVER, J. Early learning and the perception of space. *American Journal of Psychology,* 1955, *68,* 605–614.

DUNCAN, B. K. A comparative study of finger-maze learning by blind and sighted subjects. *Journal of Genetic Psychology,* 1934, *44,* 69–94.

EAGLESTEIN, A. S. The social acceptance of blind high school students in an integrated school. *New Outlook for the Blind,* 1975, *69,* 447–451.

EAVES, L., & KLONOFF, H. A comparison of blind and sighted children on a tactual and performance test. *Exceptional Children,* 1970, *37,* 269–273.

EICHORN, J. R., & VIGAROSO, H. R. Orientation and mobility for pre-school blind children. *International Journal for the Education of the Blind,* 1967, *17,* 48–50.

ELONEN, A. S., & CAIN, A. C. Diagnostic evaluation and treatment of deviant blind children. *The American Journal of Orthopsychiatry,* 1964, *34,* 625–633.

————, & POLZIEN, M. Experimental program for deviant blind children. *New Outlook for the Blind*, 1965, *59*, 122–126.

————, & ZWARENSTEYN, S. B. The "uncommitted" blind child: Results of intensive training of children formerly committed to institutions for the retarded. *Exceptional Children*, 1967, *33*, 301–7.

ELONEN, A. S., & ZWARENSTEYN, S. B. Appraisal of developmental lag in certain blind children. *The Journal of Pediatrics*, 1964, *65*, 599–610.

————. Sexual trauma in young blind children. *New Outlook for the Blind*, 1975, *69*, 440–442.

ENC, M. E., & STOLUROW, L. M. A comparison of the effects of two recording speeds on learning and retention. *New Outlook for the Blind*, 1960, *54*, 39–48.

ESCOVAR, P. L. Another chance for learning—the Assessment Class. *Teaching Exceptional Children*, 1976, *9*, 2–3.

EWART, A. G., & CARP, F. M. Recognition of tactual form by sighted and blind subjects. *American Journal of Psychology*, 1963, *76*, 488–491.

FAIRBANKS, G., GUTMAN, N., & MIRON, M. Effects of time compression on auditory comprehension of spoken messages. *Journal of Speech and Hearing Disorders*, 1957, *22*, 10–19.

FELDEN, H. W. *Die Ganzwortmethode im Erstleseunterricht der Blindenschule (The whole-word method in the beginning reading instruction in the school for the blind)*. Hannover-Kirchrode: Verein zur Förderung der Blindenbildung, 1955.

FERTSCH, P. An analysis of braille reading. *New Outlook for the Blind*, 1946, *40*, 128–131.

————. Hand dominance in reading braille. *American Journal of Psychology*, 1947, *60*, 335–349.

FINESTONE, S., LUKOFF, I. F., & WHITEMAN, M. *Aspects of the travel adjustment of blind persons*. New York: American Foundation for the Blind, 1960.

FISHER, G. H. Spatial localization by the blind. *American Journal of Psychology*, 1964, *77*, 2–14.

FITTING, E. A. *Evaluation of adjustment to blindness*. New York: American Foundation for the Blind, 1954.

FOULKE, E. A language of the skin. *New Outlook for the Blind*, 1963, *57*, 1–3.

————. Time compressed recorded speech and faster aural reading. *Blindness 1967*. Washington, D. C.: American Association of Workers for the Blind, pp. 11–20.

————, AMSTER, C. H., NOLAN, C. Y., & BIXLER, R. H. The comprehension of rapid speech by the blind. *Exceptional Children*, 1962, *29*, 134–141.

FOULKE, E., & UHDE, T. Do blind children need sex education? In *Sex Education for the Visually Handicapped in Schools and Agencies—Selected Papers*. New York: American Foundation for the Blind, 1975, pp. 20–28.

FOULKE, E., & WARM, J. Effects of complexity and redundancy on the tactual recognition of metric figures. *Perceptual and Motor Skills*, 1967, *25*, 177–187.

FRAIBERG, S. Parallel and divergent patterns in blind and sighted infants. *Psychoanalytic Study of the Child*, 1968, *23*, 264–300.

————. Intervention in infancy: A program for blind infants. *The Journal of The American Academy of Child Psychiatry*, 1971, *10*, 381–405.

————, & FREEDMAN, D. A. Studies in the ego development of the congenitally blind child. In *The Psychoanalytic Study of the Child*. New York: International Universities Press, Inc., 1964, *19*, 113–169.

————, SIEGEL, B. L., & GIBSON, R. The role of sound in the search behavior of a blind infant. In *The Psychoanalytic Study of the Child*. New York: International Universities Press, Inc., 1966, *21*, 327–357.

————, SMITH, M., & ADELSON, E. An educational program for blind infants. *Journal of Special Education*, 1969, *3*, 121–139.

FREEDMAN, D. G. Smiling in blind infants and the issue of innate versus acquired. *Journal of Child Psychology and Psychiatry,* 1964, *5,* 171–184. Reprinted in *New Outlook for the Blind,* 1967, *61,* 156–163, 194–201.

FRIEDMAN, J., & Pasnak, R. Attainment of classification and seriation concepts in blind and sighted children. *Education of the Visually Handicapped,* 1973, *5,* 55–62.

FULCHER, J. S. *"Voluntary" facial expression in blind and seeing children.* New York: Archives of Psychology, no. 272, 1942.

GARRY, R. J., & ASCARELLI, A. "Teaching topographical orientation and spatial organization to congenitally blind children. *Journal of Education,* 1960, *143,* 1–48.

GESELL, A., ILG, F. L., & BULLIS, G. E. *Vision: Its development in infant and child.* New York: P. B. Hoeber, Inc., 1950.

GILLMAN, A. E. Handicap and cognition: Visual deprivation and the rate of motor development in infants. *New Outlook for the Blind,* 1973, *67,* 309–314.

GOMULICKI, B. R. The development of perception and learning in blind children. *The New Beacon,* 1962, *46,* 118–121.

GOODMAN, L. A treatment program for multiply-handicapped blind young adults. *Blindness 1967.* Washington, D.C.: American Association of Workers for the Blind, pp. 89–103.

GOTTESMAN, M. A comparative study of Piaget's developmental schema of sighted children with that of a group of blind children. *Child Development,* 1971, *42,* 573–580.

———. Conservation development in blind children. *Child Development,* 1973, *44,* 824–827.

———. Stage development of blind children: A Piagetian view. *New Outlook for the Blind,* 1976, *70,* 94–100.

GOWMAN, A. G. *The war blind in American social structure.* New York: American Foundation for the Blind, 1957.

GRAHAM, M. D. *Multiply impaired blind children: A national problem.* New York: American Foundation for the Blind, 1968.

GREEN, M. R., & SCHECTER, D. E. Autistic and symbiotic disorders in three blind children. *The Psychiatric Quarterly,* 1957, *31,* 628–646.

GRIFFIN, D. R. Echolocation by the blind. In *Listening in the dark.* New Haven, Conn.: Yale University Press, 1958, pp. 297–322.

GUESS, D. Mental retardation and blindness: A complex and relatively unexplored dyad. *Exceptional Children,* 1967, *33,* 471–479.

HALLIDAY, C. *The visually impaired child: Growth, learning, development—Infancy to school age.* Louisville, Ky.: American Printing House for the Blind, 1971.

HAMPSHIRE, B. E. Tactile and visual reading. *New Outlook for the Blind,* 1975, *69,* 145–154.

HAPEMAN, L. B. Developmental concepts of blind children between the ages of three and six as they relate to orientation and mobility. *International Journal for the Education of the Blind,* 1967, *17,* 41–48.

HARDY, R. E. Prediction of manifest anxiety levels of blind persons through the use of a multiple regression technique. *International Journal for the Education of the Blind,* 1967, *17,* 51–55.

———. *The anxiety scale for the blind.* New York: American Foundation for the Blind, 1968. (*a*)

———. A study of manifest anxiety among blind residential school students. *New Outlook for the Blind,* 1968, *62,* 173–180. (*b*)

HARE, B. A., HAMMILL, D. D., & CRANDELL, J. M. Auditory discrimination ability of visually limited children. *New Outlook for the Blind,* 1970, *64,* 287–292.

HARLEY, R. K. *Verbalism among blind children.* New York: American Foundation for the Blind, 1963.

———, MERBLER, J. B., & WOOD, T. A. The development of a scale in orientation and mobility for multiply impaired blind children. *Education of the Visually Handicapped,* 1975, *7,* 1–5.

———, & SPOLLEN, J. A. A study of the reliability and validity of the Visual Efficiency Scale with low vision children. *Education of the Visually Handicapped,* 1973, *5,* 110–114.

——. A study of the reliability and validity of the Visual Efficiency Scale with first grade children. *Education of the Visually Handicapped,* 1974, *6,* 88–93.

——, & LONG, S. A study of the reliability and validity of the Visual Efficiency Scale with preschool children. *Education of the Visually Handicapped,* 1973, *5,* 38–42.

HARRIS, J. C. Veering tendency as a function of anxiety in the blind. *Research Bulletin No. 14.* New York: American Foundation for the Blind, 1967, pp. 53–63.

HARTLAGE, L. C. Differences in listening comprehension of the blind and the sighted. *International Journal for the Education of the Blind,* 1963, *13,* 1–6.

HARTLAGE, L. C. Verbal tests of spatial conceptualization. *Journal of Experimental Psychology,* 1969, *80,* 181–182.

——. Development of spatial concepts in visually deprived children. *Perceptual and Motor Skills,* 1976, *42,* 255–258.

HARTONG, J. R. A special orientation and mobility project at a residential school. *New Outlook for the Blind,* 1968, *62,* 118–121.

HATFIELD, E. M. Why are they blind? *Sight-Saving Review,* N.Y.: National Society for Prevention of Blindness, 1975, *45,* 3–22.

HATLEN, P. H., LE DUC, P., & CANTER, P. The Blind Adolescent Life Skills Center. *New Outlook for the Blind,* 1975, *69,* 109–115.

HAYES, S. P. *Facial vision, or the sense of obstacles.* Watertown, Mass.: Perkins Institution for the Blind, 1935.

——. *Contributions to a psychology of blindness.* New York: American Foundation for the Blind, 1941.

——. Alternative scales for the mental measurement of the visually handicapped. *Outlook for the Blind and the Teachers Forum,* 1942, *36,* 225–230.

——. Measuring the intelligence of the blind. In P. A. Zahl (Ed.), *Blindness.* Princeton,

N.J.: Princeton University Press, 1950, pp. 141–173.

——. *First regional conference on mental measurements of the blind.* Watertown, Mass.: Perkins Institution for the Blind, 1952, pp. 26–30.

HECHT, P. J., & Newland, T. E. Learning potential and learning achievement of educationally blind third–eighth graders in a residential school. *International Journal for the Education of the Blind,* 1965, *15,* 33–38.

HELLER, T. *Studien zur Blinden-Psychologie.* Leipzig: Wilhelm Engelmann, 1895.

HENDERSON, F. The rate of braille character recognition as a function of the reading process. *48th Bienniel Conference of the American Association of Instructors for the Blind,* 1966, pp. 7–10.

HEPFINGER, L. M. Psychological evaluation of young blind children. *New Outlook for the Blind,* 1962, *56,* 309–315.

HIGGINS, L. C. *Classification in congenitally blind children.* New York: American Foundation for the Blind, 1973.

HIMES, J. S. Some concepts of blindness in American culture. In *Attitudes toward blindness.* New York: American Foundation for the Blind, 1951, pp. 10–22.

——. Changing attitudes of the public toward the blind. *New Outlook for the Blind,* 1958, *52,* 330–335.

HOLLAND, B. F. Speed and pressure factors in braille reading. *The Teachers Forum,* 1934, *7,* 13–17.

——, & EATMAN, P. F. The silent reading habits of blind children. *The Teachers Forum,* 1933, *6,* 4–19.

HOOVER, R. E. The cane as a travel aid. In P. A. Zahl (Ed.) *Blindness.* Princeton, N.J.: Princeton University Press, 1950, pp. 353–365.

HORBACH, H. *Taktiles Lesen.* Hannover, Germany: Verein zur Förderung der Blindenbildung, 1951.

Hoshmand, L. T. "Blindisms": Some observations and propositions. *Education of the Visually Handicapped,* 1975, *7,* 56–60.

HUNTER, W. F. An analysis of space perception in congenitally blind and in sighted individuals. *Journal of General Psychology*, 1964, *70*, 325–329.

HURLIN, R. G. Estimated prevalence of blindness in the U.S., 1960. *Sight-Saving Review*, 1962, *32*, 4–12.

IMAMURA, S. Mother and blind child. New York: American Foundation for the Blind, 1965.

JEROME, E. A., & PROSHANSKY, H. Factors in the assay and use of guidance devices. In P. A. Zahl (Ed.), *Blindness*. Princeton, N.J.: Princeton University Press, 1950, pp. 462–494.

JERVIS, F. M. A comparison of self concepts of blind and sighted children. In C. J. Davis (Ed.), *Guidance programs for blind children*. A report of a conference. Watertown, Mass.: Perkins Institution for the Blind, 1959, pp. 19–25.

———. The self in process of obtaining and maintaining self-esteem. *New Outlook for the Blind*, 1964, *58*, 51–54.

———, & HASLERUD, G. M. Quantitative and qualitative difference in frustration between blind and sighted adolescents. *Journal of Psychology*, 1950, *29*, 67–76.

JOHNSON, D. E., & GILSON, C. Teenagers evaluate mobility training. *New Outlook for the Blind*, 1967, *61*, 227–231, 237.

JONES, R. L., & GOTTFRIED, N. W. The prestige of special education teaching. *Exceptional Children* 1966, *32*, 465–468.

———, & OWENS, A. The social distance of the exceptional: A study at the high school level. *Exceptional Children*, 1966, *32*, 551–556.

JONES, R. L., LAVINE, K., & SHELL, J. Blind children in classrooms with sighted children: A sociometric study. *New Outlook for the Blind*, 1972, *66*, 75–80.

JORDAN, S. The deaf-blind: A clarification. *Perceptual and Motor Skills*, 1964, *18*, 503–504.

JUURMAA, J. *Ability structure and loss of vision*. New York: American Foundation for the Blind, 1967.

———. Transposition in mental spatial manipulation: A theoretical analysis. *American Foundation for the Blind Research Bulletin*, 1973, *26*, 87–134.

KANNER, L. *Child Psychiatry* (4th ed.). Springfield, Ill.: Charles C Thomas, 1972.

KEDERIS, C. J., NOLAN, C. Y., & MORRIS, J. E. The use of controlled exposure devices to increase braille reading rates. *International Journal for the Education of the Blind*, 1967, *16*, 97–105.

KENYON, E. L. Diagnostic techniques to be applied with blind children. In C. J. Davis (Ed.), *Guidance programs for blind children*. A report of a conference. Watertown, Mass.: Perkins Institution for the Blind, 1959, pp. 31–40.

KEPHART, J. G., KEPHART, C. P., & SCHWARZ, G. C. A journey into the world of the blind child. *Exceptional Children*, 1974, *40*, 421–427.

KIRTLEY, D. D. *The psychology of blindness*. Chicago: Nelson-Hall, 1975.

KLEIN, G. S. Blindness and isolation. In *The Psychoanalytic Study of the Child*. New York: International Universities Press, Inc., 1962, *17*, pp. 82–93.

KNOTTS, J. R., & MILES, W. R. The maze-learning ability of blind compared with sighted children. *Journal of Genetic Psychology*, 1929, *36*, 21–50.

KOCH, H. L., & UFKESS, J. A comparative study of stylus maze learning by blind and seeing subjects. *Journal of Experimental Psychology*, 1926, *9*, 118–131.

KUSAJIMA, T. *Visual reading and braille reading: An experimental investigation of the physiology and psychology of visual and tactual reading*. New York: American Foundation for the Blind, 1974.

LAND, S. L., & VINEBERG, S. E. Locus of control in blind children. *Exceptional Children*, 1965, *31*, 257–260.

LARSEN, L. A. Behavior modification with the multi-handicapped. *New Outlook for the Blind*, 1970, *64*, 6–15.

LEBO, D., & BRUCE, R. S. Projective methods recommended for use with the blind. *Journal of Psychology*, 1960, *50*, 15–38.

LENDE, H. *Books about the blind* (new ed.). New York: American Foundation for the Blind, 1953.

LEVITT, E. A., ROSENBAUM, A. L., WILLERMAN, L., & LEVITT, M. Intelligence of retinoblastoma patients and their siblings. *Child Development*, 1972, *43*, 939–948.

LEZAK, R. J., & STARBUCK, H. B. Identification of children with speech disorders in a residential school for the blind. *International Journal for the Education of the Blind*, 1964, *14*, 8–12.

LORD, F. E. Development of scales for the measurement of orientation and mobility of young blind children. *Exceptional Children*, 1969, *36*, 77–81.

LOWENFELD, B. *Braille and talking book reading: A comparative study*. New York: American Foundation for the Blind, 1945.

————. Psychological foundation of special methods in teaching blind children. In P. A. Zahl (Ed.), *Blindness*. Princeton, N.J.: Princeton University Press, 1950, pp. 89–108.

————. Psychological problems of children with impaired vision. In W. M. Cruickshank (Ed.), *Psychology of exceptional children and youth* (1st ed.). Englewood Cliffs, N.J.: Prentice-Hall, 1955, pp. 214–283.

————. The blind adolescent in a seeing world. *Exceptional Children*, 1959, *25*, 310–315.

————. *Multihandicapped blind and deaf-blind children in California*. Sacramento: State Department of Education, 1968.

————. *Our blind children: Growing and learning with them* (3rd ed.). Springfield, Ill.: Charles C Thomas, 1971.

————. *The changing status of the blind: From separation to integration*. Springfield, Ill.: Charles C Thomas, 1975.

————. (Ed.). *The visually handicapped child in school*. New York: John Day, 1973.

————, ABEL, G. L., & HATLEN, P. N. *Blind children learn to read*. Springfield, Ill.: Charles C Thomas, 1969.

LOWENFELD, V. *The nature of creative activity*. New York: Harcourt, Brace & World, Inc., 1939.

————. *Creative and mental growth* (3rd ed.). New York: The Macmillan Company, 1957.

LUKOFF, I. F. Attitudes toward the blind. In I. F. Lukoff, O. Cohen, et al., *Attitudes toward blind persons*. New York: American Foundation for the Blind, 1972, pp. 1–15.

————, & WHITEMAN, M. Attitudes toward blindness—some preliminary findings. *New Outlook for the Blind*, 1961, *55*, 39–44.

————. *The social sources of adjustment to blindness*. New York: American Foundation for the Blind, 1970.

MACFARLAND, D. C. An exploratory study comparing the maze learning ability of blind and sighted subjects. *New Outlook for the Blind*, 1952, *46*, 259–263.

MANDOLA, J. A theoretical approach to graphic aids for the blind. *International Journal for the Education of the Blind*, 1968, *18*, 22–24.

MATTIS, S. An experimental approach to treatment of visually impaired multi-handicapped children. *New Outlook for the Blind*, 1967, *61*, 1–5.

MAXFIELD, K. E. *Adaptation of educational tests for use with blind pupils*. New York: American Foundation for the Blind, 1927.

————. *The blind child and his reading*. New York: American Foundation for the Blind, 1928.

————. *The spoken language of the blind preschool child*. New York: Archives of Psychology, 1936, No. 201.

————, & BUCHHOLZ, S. *A social maturity scale for blind preschool children: A guide to its use*. New York: American Foundation for the Blind, 1957.

MAXFIELD, & FJELD, H. A. The social maturity of the visually handicapped preschool child. *Child Development*, 1942, *13*, 1–27.

MAXFIELD, & KENYON, E. L. *A guide to the use of the Maxfield-Fjeld tentative adaptation of the Vineland Social Maturity Scale for use with visually handicapped preschool children.* New York: American Foundation for the Blind, 1953.

MAYADAS, N. S. Role expectations and performance of blind children: Practice and implications. *Education of the Visually Handicapped*, 1972, *4*, 45–52.

——. Houseparents' expectations: A crucial variable in the performance of blind institutionalized children. *New Outlook for the Blind*, 1975, *69*, 77–85.

——, & DUEHN, W. D. The impact of significant adults' expectations on the lifestyle of visually impaired children. *New Outlook for the Blind*, 1976, *70*, 286–290.

McANDREW, H. Rigidity and isolation: A study of the deaf and the blind. *Journal of Abnormal and Social Psychology*, 1948, *43*, 476–494. (a)

——. Rigidity in the deaf and the blind. *Journal of Social Issues*, 1948, *4*, 72–77. (b)

——. The use of projective techniques in the personality evaluation of the blind. *American Psychologist*, 1950, *5*, 340.

McBRIDE, V. G. Exploration in rapid reading in braille. *New Outlook for the Blind*, 1974, *68*, 13–19.

McCARTHY, B. M., & WORCHEL, P. Rate of motion and object perception in the blind. *New Outlook for the Blind*, 1954, *48*, 316–322.

McGUIRE, L. L., & MEYERS, C. E. Early personality in the congenitally blind child. *New Outlook for the Blind*, 1971, *65*, 137–143.

McREYNOLDS, J., & WORCHEL, P. Geographic orientation in the blind. *Journal of General Psychology*, 1954, *51*, 221–236.

MEIGHAN, T. *An investigation of the self concept of blind and visually handicapped adolescents.* New York: American Foundation for the Blind, 1971.

MERRY, R. V. Adapting the Seashore Musical Talent Tests for use with blind pupils. *The Teachers Forum*, 1931, *30*, 15–19.

——. The tactual recognition of embossed pictures by blind children. *Journal of Applied Psychology*, 1933, *17*, 148–163.

——, & MERRY, F. K. The finger maze as a supplementary test of intelligence for blind children. *Journal of Genetic Psychology*, 1934, *44*, 227–230.

MEYERSON, L. The visually handicapped. *Review of Educational Research*, 1953, *23*, 476–491.

MILLER, B. S., & MILLER, W. H. Extinguishing "blindisms": A paradigm for intervention. *Education of the Visually Handicapped*, 1976, *8*, 6–15.

MILLER, C. K. Conservation in blind children. *Education of the Visually Handicapped*, 1969, *1*, 101–105.

MILLER, W. H. Manifest anxiety in visually impaired adolescents. *Education of the Visually Handicapped*, 1970, *2*, 91–95.

MINER, L. E. A study of the incidence of speech deviations among visually handicapped children. *New Outlook for the Blind*, 1963, *57*, 10–14.

MONBECK, M. E. *The meaning of blindness: Attitudes toward blindness and blind people.* Bloomington: Indiana University Press, 1973.

MORRIS, J. E. The 1973 Stanford Achievement Test series as adapted for use by the visually handicapped. *Education of the Visually Handicapped*, 1974, *6*, 33–40.

——, & NOLAN, C. Y. Minimum sizes for areal type tactual symbols. *International Journal for the Education of the Blind*, 1963, *13*, 48–51.

MORSE, J. L. Mannerisms, not blindisms: Causation and treatment. *International Journal for the Education of the Blind*, 1965, *15*, 12–16.

MURPHY, A. T. Attitudes of educators toward the visually handicapped. *Sight-Saving Review*, 1960, *30*, 157–161.

NAGERA, H., & COLONNA, A. E. Aspects of the contribution of sight to ego and drive development: A comparison of the development of some blind and sighted children. In *The Psychoanalytic Study of the Child*. New York: International Universities Press, Inc., 1965, *20*, pp. 267–287.

NEWLAND, T. E. The blind learning aptitude test. *Report Proceedings of Conference on Research Needs in Braille.* New York: American Foundation for the Blind, 1961, pp. 40–51.

————. Prediction and evaluation of academic learning by blind children, II: Problems and procedures in evaluation. *International Journal for the Education of the Blind,* 1964, *14,* 42–51.

NEWMAN, J. Faculty attitudes toward handicapped students. *Rehabilitation Literature,* 1976, *37,* 194–197.

NOLAN, C. Y. On the unreality of words to the blind. *New Outlook for the Blind,* 1960, *54,* 100–102.

————. Evaluating the scholastic achievements of visually handicapped children. *Exceptional Children,* 1962, *28,* 493–496.

————. Perceptual factors in braille word recognition. *48th Biennial Conference of the American Association of Instructors for the Blind,* 1966, 10–14.

————, & KEDERIS, C. J. *Perceptual factors in braille word recognition.* New York: American Foundation for the Blind, 1969.

————, & MORRIS, M. E. Development and validation of the Roughness Discrimination Test. *International Journal for the Education of the Blind,* 1965, *15,* 1–6.

NORRIS, M., SPAULDING, P. J., & BRODIE, F. H. *Blindness in children.* Chicago: University of Chicago Press, 1957.

NORTON, F. M. *Training hearing to greater usefulness, a manual.* Cleveland: Cleveland Society for the Blind, 1960.

OHWAKI, Y., TANNO, Y., OHWAKI, M., *et al.* Construction of an intelligence test for the blind. *Tohoku Psychologica Folia,* 1960, *18,* 45–65.

OMWAKE, E. G., & SOLNIT, A. J. It isn't fair: The treatment of a blind child. *The Psychoanalytic Study of the Child.* New York: International Universities Press, Inc., 1961, *16,* 352–404.

PIAGET, J. *Genetic epistemology* (trans. E. Duckworth). New York: Columbia University Press, 1970.

PICK, A. D., THOMAS, M. L., & PICK, H. L., JR. The role of grapheme-phoneme correspondences in the perception of braille. *Journal of Verbal Learning and Verbal Behavior,* 1966, *5,* 298–300.

PITMAN, D. J. The musical ability of blind children. *Review of Psychology in Music,* 1965, *2,* 19–28. Also in *Research Bulletin No. 11.* New York: American Foundation for the Blind, 1965, pp. 63–79.

PRINGLE, M. L. K. The emotional and social adjustment of blind children. *Education Research,* 1964, *6,* 129–138.

PSATHAS, G. Mobility, orientation, and navigation: Conceptual and theoretical considerations. *New Outlook for the Blind,* 1976, *70,* 385–391.

RASKIN, N. J. Play therapy with blind children. *New Outlook for the Blind,* 1954, *48,* 290–292.

————. Visual disability. In J. F. Garrett and B. S. Levine (Eds.), *Psychological practices with the physically disabled.* New York: Columbia University Press, 1962, pp. 341–375.

REVESZ, G. *Psychology and art of the blind* (trans. H. A. Wolff). New York: Longmans, Green, 1950.

ROBBINS, N. *Educational beginnings with deaf-blind children.* Watertown, Mass.: Perkins Institution for the Blind, 1960.

————. *Speech beginnings for the deaf-blind child: A guide for parents.* Watertown, Mass.: Perkins Institution for the Blind, 1963.

————, & STENQUIST, G. *The deaf-blind rubella child.* Watertown, Mass.: Perkins Institution for the Blind, 1967.

ROSENCRANZ, D., & SUSLICK, R. Cognitive models for spatial representations in congenitally blind, adventitiously blind, and sighted subjects. *New Outlook for the Blind,* 1976, *70,* 188–194.

ROSS, J. R., BRAEN, B. B., & CHAPUT, R. Patterns of change in disturbed blind children in residential treatment. *Children,* 1967, *14,* 217–222.

ROTHSCHILD, J. Play therapy with blind children. *New Outlook for the Blind,* 1960, *54,* 329–333.

———. Deaf-blindness. In J. F. Garrett and B. S. Levine (Eds.), *Psychological practices with the physically disabled.* New York: Columbia University Press, 1962, pp. 376–409.

ROUSE, D. L., & WORCHEL, P. Veering tendency in the blind. *New Outlook for the Blind,* 1955, *49,* 115–119.

ROWE, E. D. *Speech problems of blind children: A survey of the North California area.* New York: American Foundation for the Blind, 1958.

RUBIN, E. J. *Abstract functioning in the blind.* New York: American Foundation for the Blind, 1964.

RUSALEM, H. The environmental supports of public attitudes toward the blind. *New Outlook for the Blind,* 1950, *44,* 277–288.

———. Research in review. *New Outlook for the Blind,* 1962, *56,* 66–68.

———. A study of college students' beliefs about deaf-blindness. *New Outlook for the Blind,* 1965, *59,* 90–93.

———, & RUSALEM, R. Students' reactions to deaf-blindness. *New Outlook for the Blind,* 1964, *58,* 260–263.

SANDLER, A. M. Aspects of passivity and ego development in the blind infant. In *The Psychoanalytic Study of the Child.* New York: International Universities Press, Inc., 1963, *18,* 343–360.

———, & WILLS, D. M. Preliminary notes on play and mastery in the blind child. *Journal of Child Psychotherapy,* 1965, *1,* 7–19.

SANDS, H. H. The psychological appraisal of young blind children. In S. P. Hayes (Ed.), *First regional conference on mental measurements of the blind.* Watertown, Mass.: Perkins Institution for the Blind, 1952, pp. 25–26.

SCHAUER, G. Motivation of attitudes toward blindness. In *Attitudes toward blindness.* New York: American Foundation for the Blind, 1951, pp. 5–10.

SCHIFF, W., & ISIKOW, H. Stimulus redundancy in the tactile perception of histograms. *International Journal for the Education of the Blind,* 1966, *16,* 1–11.

SCHLAEGEL, T. F., Jr. The dominant method of imagery in blind as compared to sighted adolescents. *Journal of Genetic Psychology,* 1953, *83,* 265–277.

SCHOLL, G. T. The psychosocial effects of blindness: Implications for program planning in sex education. *New Outlook for the Blind,* 1974, *68,* 201–209.

———, & SCHNUR, R. *Measures of psychological, vocational, & educational functioning in the blind & visually handicapped.* New York: American Foundation for the Blind, 1976.

SCHULZ, P. J. Psychological factors in orientation and mobility. *New Outlook for the Blind,* 1972, *66,* 129–134.

SCHUMANN, H. J., VON. *Träume der Blinden, vom Standpunkt der Phänomenologie, Tiefenpsychologie, Mythologie und Kunst.* Basel und New York: S. Karger, 1959.

SCOTT, R. A. *The making of blind men.* New York: Russell Sage Foundation, 1969. *(a)*

———. The socialization of blind children. In D. A. Goslin (Ed.), *Handbook of socialization theory and research.* New York: Rand McNally, 1969, pp. 1025–1045. *(b)*

SEASHORE, T. E., & LING, T. L. The comparative sensitiveness of blind and seeing persons. *Psychological Monograph,* 1918, *25,* 148–158.

SEELYE, W. S., & THOMAS, J. E. Is mobility feasible with multiply handicapped blind children? *Exceptional Children,* 1966, *32,* 613–617.

SENDEN, M., VON. *Space and sight.* Glencoe, Ill.: The Free Press, 1960.

SHURRAGER, H. C., & SHURRAGER, P. S. Haptic Intelligence Scale for adult blind. Chicago: Psychology Research, 1964.

SIEGEL, I. M. *Posture in the blind.* New York: American Foundation for the Blind, 1966.

SILLER, J., CHIPMAN, A., FERGUSON, L., & VANN, D. H. *Attitudes of the nondisabled toward the disabled.* New York: New York University School of Education, 1967.

———, FERGUSON, L., VANN, D. H., & HOLLAND, B. *Structure of attitudes toward the physically disabled; disability factor scales—amputation, blindness, cosmetic conditions.* New York: New York University School of Education, 1967.

SINGER, J. L., & STREINER, B. F. Imaginative content in the dreams and phantasy play of blind and sighted children. *Perceptual and Motor Skills,* 1966, *22,* 475–482.

SMITH, M. A., CHETHIK, M., & ADELSON, E. Differential assessments of "blindisms." *American Journal of Orthopsychiatry,* 1969, *39,* 807–817.

SMITS, B. W. G. M., & MOMMERS, M. J. C. Differences between blind and sighted children on WISC verbal subtests. *New Outlook for the Blind,* 1976, *70,* 240–246.

SOMMERS, V. S. *The influence of parental attitudes and social environment on the personality development of the adolescent blind.* New York: American Foundation for the Blind, 1944.

SPENCER, M. B. *Blind children in family and community.* Minneapolis: University of Minnesota Press, 1960.

SPITZ, R. A. Anaclitic depression. In *The Psychoanalytic Study of the Child.* New York: International Universities Press, Inc., 1946, *2,* 313–342.

STEINBERG, W. *Die Raumwahrnehmung der Blinden.* Munich: Reinhardt, 1920.

STEINZOR, L. V. School peers of visually handicapped children. *New Outlook for the Blind,* 1966, *60,* 312–314. (a)

———. Visually handicapped children: Their attitudes toward blindness. *New Outlook for the Blind,* 1966, *60,* 307–311. (b)

———. Siblings of visually handicapped children. *New Outlook for the Blind,* 1967, *61,* 48–52.

STENQUIST, G. *The story of Leonard Dowdy: Deaf-blindness acquired in infancy.* Watertown, Mass.: Perkins School for the Blind, 1974.

STILLMAN, R. D. *Assessment of deaf-blind children: The Callier-Azusa Scale.* Reston, Va.: Council for Exceptional Children, 1976.

STINCHFIELD, S. M. *Speech disorders.* New York: Harcourt, Brace & World, Inc., 1933, pp. 62–76.

STONE, A. A. Consciousness: Altered levels in blind, retarded children. *Psychosomatic Medicine,* 1964, *26,* 14–19.

STREITFELD, J. W., & AVERY, C. D. The WAIS and HIS as predictors of academic achievement in a residential school for the blind. *International Journal for the Education of the Blind,* 1968, *18,* 73–77.

SUINN, R. M., DAUTERMAN, W., & SHAPIRO, B. The Stanford Ohwaki-Kohs Tactile Block Design Intelligence Test for the Blind. *New Outlook for the Blind,* 1966, *60,* 77–79.

SUPA, M., COTZIN, M., & DALLENBACH, K. M. "Facial vision": The perception of obstacles by the blind. *American Journal of Psychology,* 1944, *57,* 133–183.

SUTERKO, S. Life adjustment. In B. Lowenfeld (Ed.), *The Visually Handicapped Child in School.* New York: John Day, 1973, pp. 279–317.

SWALLOW, R. Piaget's theory and the visually handicapped child. *New Outlook for the Blind,* 1976, *70,* 273–281.

'T HOOFT, F., & HESLINGA, K. Sex education of blind-born children. *New Outlook for the Blind,* 1968, *62,* 15–21.

TAIT, P. Behavior of young blind children in a controlled play session. *Perceptual and Motor Skills,* 1972, *34,* 963–969.

TAYLOR, J. L. Educational programs. In B. Lowenfeld (Ed.), *The visually handicapped child in school.* New York: John Day, 1973, pp. 155–184.

THOMPSON, J. *Development of facial expression of emotion in blind and seeing children.* New York: Archives of Psychology, No. 264, 1941.

THURRELL, R. J., & JOSEPHSON, T. S. Retinoblastoma and intelligence. *Psychosomatics*, 1966, *7*, 368–370.

THURRELL, R. J., & RICE, D. G. Eye rubbing in blind children: Application of a sensory deprivation model. *Exceptional Children*, 1970, *36*, 325–330.

TILLMAN, M. H. The performance of blind and sighted children on the Wechsler Intelligence Scale for Children. *International Journal for the Education of the Blind*, 1967, *16*, Study 1, 65–74; Study 2, 106–112.

———, BASHAW, W. L., & BRADLEY, M. Reanalysis and critique of "Sensory Discrimination" as an ability component of the blind. *Perceptual and Motor Skills*, 1969, *29*, 283–288.

———, & OSBORNE, R. T. The performance of blind and sighted children on the Wechsler Intelligence Scale for Children. *Education of the Visually Handicapped*, 1969, *1*, 1–4.

———, & WILLIAMS, C. Associative characteristics of blind and sighted children to selected form classes. *International Journal for the Education of the Blind*, 1968, *18*, 33–40.

TOBIN, M. J. Conservation of substance in the blind and partially sighted. *British Journal of Educational Psychology*, 1972, *42*, 192–197.

TOTH, Z. *Die Vorstellunswelt der Blinden*. Leipzig: Johann Ambrosius Barth, 1930.

TOTMAN, H. E. Training problems and techniques. In B. Lowenfeld (Ed.), *The blind preschool child*. New York: American Foundation for the Blind, 1947, pp. 57–72.

TRETAKOFF, M. What they are all doing. *American Association of Instructors for the Blind Convention Report*. Washington, D.C.: 1966, 42–44.

TRISMEN, D. A. Equating braille forms of the sequential tests of educational progress. *Exceptional Children*, 1967, *33*, 419–424.

UMSTED, R. G. Improving braille reading. *New Outlook for the Blind*, 1972, *66*, 169–177.

UNDERBERG, R. P., VERILLO, R. T., & BENHAM, F. G. Factors relating to adjustment to visual disability in adolescence. *New Outlook for the Blind*, 1961, *55*, 252–259.

VILLEY, P. *The world of the blind*. Trans. by A. Hallard. New York: The Macmillan Company, 1930, pp. 101–117.

VOSS, W. *Das farbenhören bei erblindeten*. Hamburg. Psychologisch-Aesthetische Forschungsgeselleschaft, 1930.

WAGNER, E. M. Maternal rubella: A general orientation to the disease. *New Outlook for the Blind*, 1967, *61*, 97–105.

WARREN, H. C. (Ed.). *Dictionary of psychology*. Boston: Houghton Mifflin Company, 1934.

WATTRON, J. B. A suggested performance test of intelligence. *New Outlook for the Blind*, 1956, *50*, 115–121.

WEINBERG, B. Stuttering among blind and partially sighted children. *Journal of Speech and Hearing Disorders*, 1964, *29*, 322–326.

WEINER, B. B. A new outlook on assessment. *New Outlook for the Blind*, 1967, *61*, 73–78.

WHEELER, R. H., & CUTSFORTH, T. D. The role of synaesthesia in learning. *Journal of Experimental Psychology*, 1921, *4*, 448–468.

———. Synaesthesia and meaning. *American Journal of Psychology*, 1922, *33*, 361–384.

———. Synaesthesia in the development of the concept. *Journal of Experimental Psychology*, 1925, *8*, 149–159.

WILLIAMS, D. Sunland's Program for the blind. *Mental Retardation*, 1964, *2*, 244–245.

WILLIAMS, M. *Williams Intelligence Test for children with defective vision*. Birmingham, England: University of Birmingham, 1956.

———. Superior intelligence of children blinded from retinoblastoma. *Archives of Disease in Childhood*, 1968, *43*, 210–214.

WILLS, D. M. Some observations on blind nursery school children's understanding of their world. In *The Psychoanalytic Study of the Child*. International Universities Press, Inc., 1965, *20*, 344–364.

———. Problems of play and mastery in the blind child. *British Journal of Medical Psychology*, 1968, *41*, 213–222.

————. Vulnerable periods in the early development of blind children. *The Psychoanalytic Study of the Child*, 1970, *25*, 461–480.

WILMER, H. A., & HUSNI, M. A. The use of sounds in a projective test. *Journal of Consulting Psychology*, 1953, *17*, 377–383.

WILSON, E. L. A developmental approach to psychological factors which may inhibit mobility in the visually handicapped person. *New Outlook for the Blind*, 1967, *61*, 283–289.

WILSON, J. W., & HALVERSON, H. M. Development of a young blind child. *Journal of Genetic Psychology*, 1947, *71*, 155–175.

WITKIN, H. A., BIRNBAUM, J., LOMONACO, S., LEHR, S., & HERMAN, J. L. Cognitive patterning in congenitally totally blind children. *Child Development*, 1968, *39*, 767–786.

WOLF, J. M. *The blind child with concomitant disabilities*. New York: American Foundation for the Blind, 1967.

WORCHEL, P. Space perception and orientation in the blind. *Psychological Monographs*. Washington, D.C.: American Psychological Association, 1951, *65* (332).

————, & DALLENBACH, K. M. "Facial vision": Perception of obstacles by the deaf-blind. *American Journal of Psychology*, 1947, *60*, 502–533.

————, & MAUNEY, J. The effect of practice on the perception of obstacles by the blind. *Journal of Experimental Psychology*, 1951, *41*, 170–176.

————, & ANDREW, J. G. The perception of obstacles by the blind. *Journal of Experimental Psychology*, 1950, *40*, 746–751.

WRIGHT, B. A. *Physical disability—a psychological approach*. New York: Harper & Row, 1960.

WYDER, F. T., WILSON, M. E., & FRUMKIN, R. M. Information as a factor in perception of the blind by teachers. *Perceptual and Motor Skills*, 1967, *25*, 188.

ZUNICH, M., & LEDWITH, B. E. Self-concepts of visually handicapped and sighted children. *Perceptual and Motor Skills*, 1965, *21*, 771–774.

ZWEIBELSON, I., & BARG, C. F. Concept development of blind children. *New Outlook for the Blind*, 1967, *61*, 218–222.

PART THREE

Psychological Components
of Physical Disabilities

A myriad of distinct clinical problems can be grouped under the headings of "physical disabilities," "crippling conditions," or "chronic medical problems." The authors writing in Part Three of this book have, of necessity, had to be selective in their choices of disabilities to include in their chapters. Lawrence J. Lewandowski and William M. Cruickshank, in their chapter, have chosen to be somewhat generic, discussing the dynamics of crippling conditions of whatever nature, and their impact on the adjustment of children and youth. If the generalizations that they make hold true, it is possible that they may also apply to the types of disabilities discussed in Parts Two and Four of this volume. It is doubtful that specific clinical categories have specific adjustment characteristics associated with them.

Joseph Newman has prepared a classic chapter dealing with the problems of children and youth with chronic medical problems. In many of their observations, he and Franklin C. Shontz (Chapter 1) reinforce one another; the two chapters should be read and reread together. Newman's concern with the rehabilitation of those with chronic medical problems long antedated the appearance of the first edition of *Psychology of Exceptional Children and Youth*. Working originally with patients with tuberculosis, Newman has kept pace with the developing field of chronicity, in disability, and has always provided an important contribution to the field and to the contemporary nature of this book. Illness, hospitalization, separation, chronicity—each of these is thoroughly discussed in relation to four long-term problems that Newman has chosen as the central themes of his chapter.

W.M.C.

Editor's Note:

As an author, the editor of this book has always been closely related to this chapter. In the original edition of this book, he was the chapter's sole author; in subsequent editions, he served as a coauthor, and his material was expanded upon by Frances P. Connors of Columbia University (second edition) and by Connors along with Herbert Rusalem of Columbia University (third edition). The mixture of writing by the three authors is difficult, if not impossible, to separate as to specific authorship. Drs. Connors and Rusalem were unable to contribute together to this textbook, which has long been recognized as a definitive volume in the field of psychology of exceptional children and youth. They graciously permitted the editorauthor to utilize whatever was appropriate from the second and third editions, and to integrate this as desired, into revised writings for the present edition. Joining the original author of the chapter is a new professional, Lawrence J. Lewandowski, whose debut coincides with the publication of this chapter. Writing with his professoradvisor, he has given a different slant to portions of the original and its two revisions, bringing into focus, not only some of the quantitative data retained from earlier versions, but current theoretical and qualitative concepts, particularly from ego psychology and the writings of Jean Piaget.

Portions of this chapter should be considered carefully in relation to Chapter 12, which pertains to the psychological problems of children with specific learning disabilities. There is considerable application of the material presented in Chapter 12 to the psychoeducational problems of learning in children and youth with cerebral palsy discussed in the present chapter. The same may be said for discussions which appear in this volume and are concerned with the perceptual processing deficits of some children and youth with epilepsy or with other forms of central neurological malfunction; for example, post-encephalitis, post-meningitis, aphasia.

8 Psychological Development of Crippled Children and Youth

Lawrence J. Lewandowski

Ph.D., Psychologist, Southgate Regional Training Center for the Developmentally Disabled, Michigan Department of Mental Health.

William M. Cruickshank

Ph.D., Director, Institute for the Study of Mental Retardation and Related Disabilities, Professor of Maternal and Child Health, Professor of Psychology, Professor of Education.

Although the basic adjustment problems of the crippled child are the same as those of physically normal children of comparable chronological and mental development, disability does introduce psychologically significant variables. This viewpoint was expressed in a phenomenological frame of reference:

> It is seen that the physically handicapped child in his social relationships is, as are all children, attempting to insure not his physical organic self, but his phenomenal self, the concept of himself of which he is cognizant. Two types of problems are to be observed in the handicapped child from this point of view: (1) adjustment problems which might occur in the normal developmental progress of any individual who is simultaneously striving for expansion of self and for the maintenance of the self-concept already developed, and (2) adjustment problems which are solely resultant from the fact that a physical handicap is inserted between the goal and the self-desire to achieve such a goal (Cruickshank, 1948, pp. 77–83).

Although such a dichotomy is useful for the sake of discourse, no clear-cut separation ever exists in reality. However, "the failure to recognize the duality of the problem accounts for much current misunderstanding with reference to the handicapped" (Cruickshank, 1971, p. 309).

Development, as depicted in Figure 8–1, refers to the physiological, cognitive, social, and psychological growth of an individual as a result of all experiences and interactions that the person has with the environment. Since all aspects of growth and development are interrelated and interdependent, and since physical development is one of these aspects of overall development, one can understand how a crippling condition might influence the cognitive and affective aspects of development. A crippling condition can alter and continually modify any or all of these developmental dimensions to varying degrees. It is not uncommon to note a chain reaction beginning with the impairment of selected sensory-motor functions, followed by attenuation of cognitive development and emotional stress resulting in environmental maladaptation.

JEAN PIAGET

For a closer examination of the development of crippled children it may be helpful to consider parts of the developmental framework

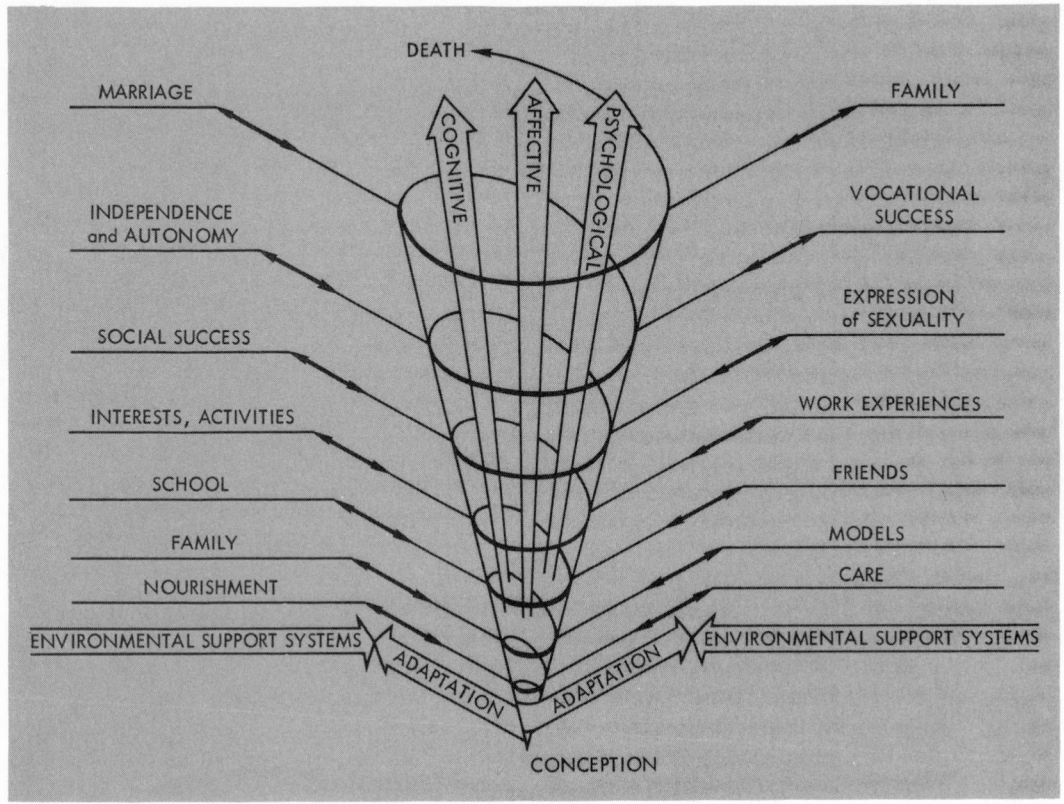

FIGURE 8–1. Schema illustrating human development.
Figure 8–1 is a hypothetical visual representation
of the developmental process. Although a simplified
schematic, it warrants some explanation. The figure
is a three-dimensional cone intended to depict the
development of an individual from conception to
death. The outer wall of the cone serves to differentiate
the organism from the rest of the environment. Within
this outer wall extend three developmental lines—
cognitive, affective, and psychological—which represent
the dimensions of overall development. The spiral
inside the cone represents the synthesizing function
of the organism throughout development—
illustrating isomorphically the autonomy and
interdependency of the three developmental
dimensions. Outside the cone are shown some
examples of environmental support systems that are
necessary to human development. The arrows
pointing toward the cone signify environmental
forces that are available for the individual to adapt
to. The quantity and quality (strength) of these
forces will have a dictatorial effect on the way a
person actualizes his potential. The arrows extending
from inside the cone reflect the internal forces of the

of Jean Piaget. In Piagetian terms, the process of development involves adaptation. The organism must adapt to its environment in order to achieve some kind of equilibrium, or homeostasis. Adaptation is not only the key to survival, but also accounts for differences in quality of life. Adaptation itself is an inherent determinant for all human organisms. However, what the organism adapts to, and the equipment with which it adapts, may vary greatly among individuals. Therefore, the two most significant variables on which development hinges are (1) the environment and (2) the biological potentials of the individual, as noted in Figure 8–1.

Adaptation to the environment involves ongoing interplay of two cognitive schemas, (a) *assimilation* and (b) *accommodation*. Assimilation is the process by which the organism contours reality or the environment to fit its cognitive structure. For example, the infant has a schema to chew, and thus brings all objects to its mouth. This is a form of adaptation.

Accommodation takes place at the same time. This is the process by which the organism's cognitive structures are altered by contact with something in the environment. For example, by bringing objects to its mouth the infant may learn certain properties about the object (i.e., the milk bottle is a warm and satisfying stimulus). Adaptation is the interaction of assimilation and accommodation. Although at times one process

has primacy over the other (i.e., in infancy assimilation has primacy over accommodation), the ultimate goal in development is to achieve equilibrium between these processes.

Piaget suggests that through adaptation the organism develops in a variety of ways. However, through careful observation, Piaget and others have found patterns which characterize stages of development; for example, the myelinization of the nervous system during the first year of life, or the progression of motor schemas in infancy from head control to grasping, to crawling, and to walking. The stages at which many such developmental milestones have been achieved are well documented for the first 36 months of life (Rogers & D'Eugenio, 1977; Gesell, 1940). Piaget also found that continuing development almost always depends on successful development at earlier stages. In this way, development is seen as a logical progression of steps.

With these Piagetian concepts in view, one has a framework that can assist in the analysis of the development of crippled children. The conditions under which successful development takes place are (1) a stimulating and supportive environment and (2) a physically (biologically) intact individual. The effects of a noxious environment have been studied intensively. Well known in psychological literature are the various types of psychological damage which can be experienced when the latter situation occurs.

---

individual as proportional to that person's ability to adapt to the environment. When the two arrows meet head on, this indicates equilibrium between the mutual influences of internal and external stimuli. This makes for successful adaptation and development favorable to the ego. For example, if an individual has one or more developmental lines attenuated (such as the atypical physiological development of a dwarf), is lacking support systems, or is unable to utilize the environment in an adaptive way, then such an individual will be prone to delayed or maladaptive development.

However, little is known definitely regarding the effects of a crippling condition on the development of an individual. At this point one can only hypothesize as to how the Piagetian notion of development applies to crippled children.

This idea highlights the duality of development in that it must proceed simultaneously from the internal and external, or from the organism and the environment. An organic inferiority is as likely to cause an arrest in development as the deprivation of some needed environmental stimulation. In these cases the child is either unable to take the next step in the developmental process or is prevented from doing so by not encountering the environmental requisites.

Whether a child is afflicted by cerebral palsy, myelomeningocele, or other crippling conditions, that child will encounter biological interference to its development. In many cases the interference causes a deficit in motoric ability. For example, a young child with cerebral palsy cannot walk and has a difficult time grasping objects. These limitations drastically constrict this child's life space. In Piagetian terms, this child is unable to acquire new schemas of adaptation at a normal developmental rate. The developmental delay, which started with restriction of simple motor functions, affects normal exploration of the environment. In most cases this will impede cognitive growth. Over time, the discrepancy between normal development and this child's delayed development will become more apparent. Parents or other significant people may react unfavorably or without understanding toward the child, who may then incorporate within the cognitive self negative affective schemas. The child will soon learn that it is limited and is different from others. The child undergoes many frustrations and feelings of inadequacy in an attempt to establish a positive self-concept. These children must adapt to their own awareness of themselves. This is a difficult task in the psychological development of all individuals, but it is made harder for the handicapped child. Often it is here that psychological maladaptation really begins, and a defensive posture takes over. The ego must defend against frustration, criticism, and inadequacy. How the child deals with these influences, coupled with the amount of support received from family, teachers, therapists, and others, largely will dictate the course of psychological development for this child. These issues will be discussed further in a later section on ego development. Here the authors have provided a "developmental" frame of reference for examining the problems of crippled children.

Figure 8–1 is a schematic representation of the developmental process. It attempts to capture some of the salient features of development which pertain to this chapter. Emanating from the vertex of the cone are three developmental lines symbolizing cognitive, affective, and psychological growth. Each of these aspects of development has inherent in it genetically determined biological givens within which all individuals vary to a degree. These biological givens reflect the potential of the organism to develop, providing no environmental accident (whether physical or mental trauma) occurs. Within these biologically programmed developmental lines are developmental stages which individuals successively pass through. Such stages have been identified by Piaget in young children. Less is known about the course of these developmental lines after the individual is fully equipped to function autonomously.

The reason why biological givens are expressed in terms of potentials is that the environment plays the key role in actualizing potential. Having received one's genetic endowments, it is up to the individual to develop them. Development, or growth, is made possible by an environment that has the ingredients needed to actualize the potential. Some of these requisites are listed around the periphery of the cone in Figure 8–1.

These environmental factors, not an exhaustive list, are often called *support systems*. These systems provide the love, care, guidance, education, success, and other ingredients which make possible the actualization of one's potential. Not only do the support systems have to be there, but the individual has to reach out and make good use of them. That means not rejecting the environmental support, or becoming overly dependent on it. This process of assimilation and accommodation to the environment is what Piaget means by *adaptation*, noted in Figure 8–1.

If the organism is biologically intact and adapts well to the environment, then that individual should develop at a normal and expected rate. There should be no obstruction to any developmental line, and the individual will continue to grow and expand, as shown in the representation. However, when one or more of the developmental lines are impeded or if the environmental support is lacking, then the individual incurs a setback. In such a case, development may be attenuated or maldevelopment may occur. Another alternative is to rely more heavily on internal or external resources, and continue to develop in whatever way possible.

Following are some examples of the development of crippled children and youth which constitute exceptions to normal development, extrapolations from the schema provided in Figure 8–1:

J.K. is a 6-year-old mentally impaired boy who has cerebral palsy. He is in a special education class and receives physical therapy every day. J.K. has devoted parents and five older siblings who also take good care of him. J.K. appears to be a happy, affectionate boy who likes to be around people. Figure 8–2 is representative of J.K.'s development. As one can see, the rate of growth is not even, and only affective development seems on course at this time. The degree to which the environmental support systems appropriately interface with the developmental

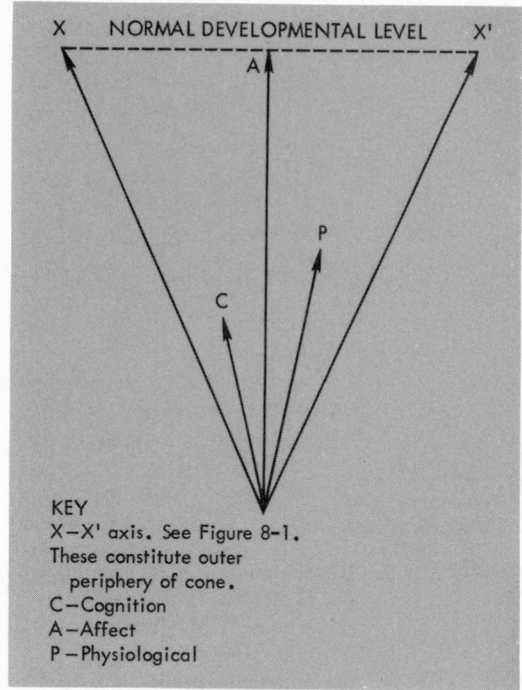

FIGURE 8–2. Development of J.K. In relation to Fig. 8–1 this schema illustrates the subnormal development in physiological (P) and cognitive (C) areas of J.K., a mentally retarded boy. His emotional growth (A) has been surprisingly good, due in large measure to the presence of existing support systems. There is no way to predict that his affective development will continue to progress positively as he grows older and more fully realizes his disability.

lines will determine the normalcy of future adaptation.

L.M. is a 14-year-old girl who has never been able to walk, because of congenital arm and leg deformities. She has been in a wheelchair most of her life. Her parents would do anything for her (largely out of guilt).

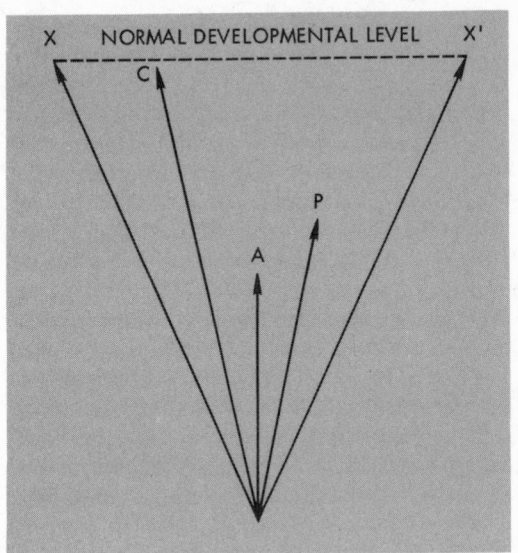

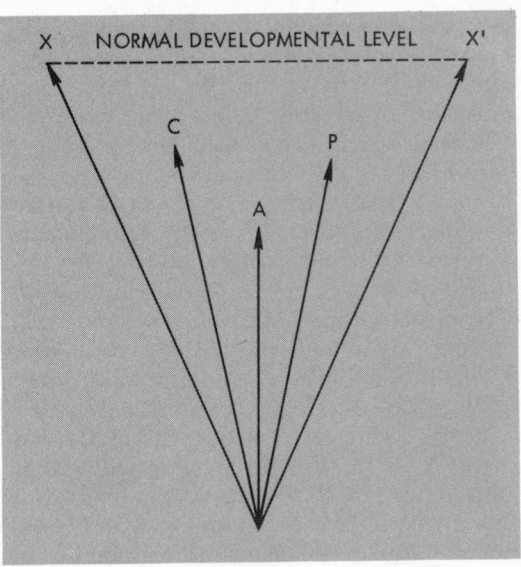

FIGURE 8–3. Development of L.M. (See Figure 8–2 for KEY.) As observed in this schema, L.M. shows irregular aspects of development. Intellectually (C) she is normal with adequate problem-solving abilities and learning potential. However, L.M. lacks motivation. In addition to her visible physical disability (P), L.M. has maladapted (A) to her environment. By doing as, little as possible for herself, she has gotten others to respond to her wishes. Her ego structure seems to be centered around infantile relationships with people in which she takes but does not give.

FIGURE 8–4. Development of P.W. (See Figure 8–2 for KEY.) This is another example in which a physical disability (P) has dramatic effect on all aspects of development. P.W. is limited in physical achievements because of his crippling condition. This has a domino effect on his affective (A) (ego) development as illustrated by his low self-esteem and insecurity. When others perceive his poor self-concept, a cycle begins that only worsens the problem. These predisposing factors slant P.W.'s entire attitude toward life. He now avoids and defends against any situation that may end in failure or embarrassment. He particularly avoids heterosexual relationships, because he fears that he is physically inadequate and would fail ultimately in sexual relations.

Thanks to early intervention, she has had an adequate education and has average cognitive skills. However, L.M. is very demanding and extremely narcissistic. She is easily frustrated when things do not come easily. Her relationship with people is manipulative so she can satisfy her needs. (See Fig. 8–3.)

P.W. is a 15-year-old boy (See Fig. 8–4)

suffering from gout. He often gets swelling of the joints and sluggishness, which keep him from most of the sports activities of his peers. P.W. has evolved a personality of an outcast and scapegoat. He is picked on by his classmates and has developed a poor self-concept, marked by insecurity and lack of confidence. P.W. is of normal intelligence, but is failing in school (See Fig. 8–4, (c)).

These are but a few examples which help visualize the range of crippling conditions, and the varying ways in which the aspects of development are affected.

VARIABLES AFFECTING PSYCHOLOGICAL DEVELOPMENT OF CRIPPLED CHILDREN AND YOUTH

Numerous theoretical positions have been taken regarding the impact of physical disability upon social and emotional adjustment. Although considerable thought has been given to this problem, little research in support of these positions has provided consistent verification of any of them. Thus, relatively little is known about the effects of the degree of disability, the age of onset, the visibility of the conditions, and the family and home situation on the development of crippled children.

Although the basic adjustment problems of the crippled child apparently are the same as those of physically normal children of comparable chronological and mental development, disability does introduce psychologically significant variables.

Degree of Disability

Although it may be argued that disability imposes extra burdens upon children and thus renders them more vulnerable to adjustment problems, conclusive evidence supporting this position has not yet emerged from studies comparing groups of physically exceptional children with normal children.

Conversely, the position that disability constitutes an adequate defense against frustration, and thus shields the individual from marked adjustment problems, also lacks unequivocal research support. Consequently, at this point in psychological research, it must be conceded that physically disabled children as a group do not appear to differ *qualitatively* in adjustment from other children. Also lacking is conclusive evidence to support the belief that mental-health problems occur with greater frequency among the disabled.

Nothwithstanding their equivocal character in certain instances, the data on social and emotional adjustment of crippled children suggest that the disability experience renders the goal of sound mental health difficult but not impossible to attain. The barriers created by the physical limitations themselves are not inconsiderable, but the core of the matter seems to be treatment accorded to crippled children by the nondisabled.

Not only have there been no significant differences found between crippled and normal children regarding mental health problems, but there has been no greater incidence of emotional disturbance within any specific group of children. It seems that no particular type of crippling condition predisposes a child or youth to emotional disturbance. There is no evidence to sustain a hypothesis that more severely crippled children will have more serious affective problems. Dreikurs (1948) made the following statement about these concerns:

> Each handicapped individual formulates his own response to his disability in accordance with his life style, which can only be determined through dynamic psychological investigation. Alfred Adler developed a specific technique to determine the life style of each individual. This life style is developed in early childhood through the interpretation which the child makes of all the experiences and difficulties with which he is confronted. The disability is only one, although often an im-

portant factor. Not what he has—in heredity endowment and environment—but what he does with it is important. Courage and social interest, or the lack of them, determine whether a disability permits a good social adjustment or leads to permanent failure (Dreikurs, p. 50).

Another study by Cruickshank *et al.* investigating the effects of cerebral palsy, although inconclusive, suggests that cerebral palsied children and adolescents are subject to a multiplicity of negative developmental influences in the personality area and run greater risks of having adjustment problems. However, such problems seem more closely related to the social response to cerebral palsy than to the disability itself. This position is supported in the finding that cerebral palsy does not necessarily engender adjustment problems, and that favorable social conditions tend to neutralize aspects of the disability.

Although research shows no significant relationship between degree of crippling impairment and affective development, this does not mean a relationship does not exist. A consideration of the development theory of Piaget and a look at the schematic representation of development in Figure 8-1, leads one to seriously question the research. It would seem that according to Piaget, the greater the restriction on the child's ability to assimilate and accommodate to the environment, as well as resulting limitations in cognitive growth, the greater the increased strain on the child's existing resources and concomitant reduction on the child's chances for successful adaptation.

The difference between research and theory on this issue seems to lie in the following explanation. Research says that crippled children have no more mental health problems than normal children, and that the degree of impairment appears to have no effect on mental health status. Developmental theory says this is possible, because even though development is slower and impeded

in some way, the child has the same chances to adapt to the environment no matter what his developmental level. Development in a global sense may be considerably affected or attenuated by the degree of impairment, but does not necessarily result in psychopathology. However, even greater environmental support is needed in order for the crippled child to develop as fully as possible and avoid maladjustment.

Age of Onset of Crippling Condition

Again, research shows no remarkable differences in the psychological development of crippled children, regardless of when they became crippled. Some say that early onset is the most debilitating because it impedes the acquisition of skills and overall normal functioning, whereas a later-acquired disability gives one a chance to develop normally at least up to that point. On the other hand, some feel that a crippling condition acquired later in life has even more impact since such individuals see themselves regress. They can't do what they once did, and they know what it was like to be normal. Accepting the disability becomes a rough task.

It is not that one side is right and one wrong. It appears there are two separate issues begging the question. Up to a certain early age, a crippling disability will affect one's rate of development and the type of development (psychologically and otherwise). An acquired disability will have less of an effect on the rate of development, but will trigger a psychological reaction to the condition.

Using the Rosenzweig Picture Frustration Test, Lange (1959) found frustration reactions of handicapped children with congenital disabilities did not differ from children with acquired ones. The generalization emerging from this study was that when they reach the age when denial of freedom and independence becomes important to them, congenitally disabled children suffer as much frustration as their adventitiously disabled peers.

Visibility of a Crippling Condition

Visibility of a disability is a variable that does seem to have a significant effect on both the attitude of the crippled person and the attitudes of others toward that person. Cruickshank (1952) reported a study comparing cardiac children, as a subset of physically handicapped children, with non-handicapped children. In general, it was observed that the cardiac children (using a sentence completion task) did not show the degree of difficulty in adjusting to society that the total group of crippled children did. It was hypothesized that this is because the cardiac children are characterized by a handicap which, socially, is hidden. From an external point of view nothing of a visible nature sets cardiac children apart, and society accepts them as normal members. The cardiac children do not have to feel different because of any barrier that their culture establishes. It is only when the defect becomes a visible one that the handicap per se begins to have a serious effect on the adjustment process.

A study of the psychological effects of facial deformity by Lansdown and Polak (1975) also suggests that a visible handicap has a relationship to the crippled child's acceptance or rejection by other children. Among the most rejected conditions were those involving deformity of the mouth (harelip, protruding teeth).

Cruickshank, Wiberley, and Summers, in an unpublished study, investigated the social acceptance of crippled children by their physically normal peers (1955, p. 318). Twenty-eight classrooms were located within a series of public school systems wherein no special programs differing from those planned for all of the children of a particular class were prepared for the crippled child. Included on the total class registers were 29 crippled children and 807 physically normal children.

Two crippled children were registered in one of the classes and the remaining twenty-seven classes each contained one crippled child. To all of the children in the seventh grade groups, the investigators administered a sociometric test to determine the degree of social acceptance or rejection of each child. The crippled children included those with poliomyelitis, cerebral palsy, congenital amputation, Perthe's disease, and other categories of disability.

One finding of the study is pertinent at this point. Three classifications were made for the positions achieved by the children on the sociometric test through the responses given; that is, stars, neutral groups, and isolates. Among the physically handicapped children there were 7 stars, 7 neutrals, and 15 isolates; among the physically normal children, 205 stars, 227 neutrals, and 375 isolates. When these two sets of figures are compared statistically, there appears to be no significant difference in the rate of acceptance or rejection between the crippled and noncrippled children of these classrooms as demonstrated by the children's own choices. The factor of visible physical disability alone, in other words, is apparently not the basis on which acceptance or rejection of a crippled child is made. This study is one of the earliest statements basic to a logical concept of normalization or "mainstreaming" of selected children with handicaps.

Although the presence of a visible crippling condition does not seem to affect whether or not a child is accepted or rejected by peers, it does seem to have an impact on the self-concept of the crippled child. Projective techniques have been used to assess discrepancies between the goals that crippled children set for themselves and their measured capacities. A study by Harway (1952) revealed that exceptional children tend to overestimate and to be inconsistent in their self-evaluations in some, but not all, situations. One of the areas of the crippled child's self-evaluation that has relevance for professional workers is that of body-image. Through the use of a draw-a-person test developed by Machover (1949), Wysocki (1965) found that crippled children can be differentiated from noncrippled children in terms of their higher levels of feelings of inferiority, anxiety, and aggression. Physical insults appearing in the figure drawings tended to correspond with the child's own disability. Also using figure drawings in an earlier study, Centers and Centers (1963) reported that the figures produced by amputee children provided clues to their perceptions of their own disabilities in drawing a deformed limb or omitting a limb entirely.

In drawing nondisabled persons, crippled children tend to be realistic about the differences that exist between themselves and others. This sense of reality is not accompanied by extreme anxiety or conflict. Machover (1949) reports on the drawings of twenty orthopedically handicapped persons. She states that the preliminary findings were notable, and that the individual's projections of the disability into the drawings varied "according to the basic personality of the individual afflicted, the degree of disability, and the duration of the disease, but important features of the subject's reaction to the disease were made graphically explicit in most of the cases."

It is hypothesized that, until the child has a coordinated and coherent understanding of the body-image, learning in the form of reading and number concepts, for example, will either not take place or will be severely retarded. In working with a small group of hyperactive children, some with and some without the diagnosis of central nervous system impairment, Cruickshank (1963) observed a close relationship in several children between the developing body-image concept as depicted in the children's drawings of a person and their initial development of reading and number concepts. In a group of forty such children, those who achieved most academically had well-developed body-image concepts, and were able to depict these with accuracy. Those who did not achieve in reading and related learning areas, on the contrary, were those whose body-image concepts were immature or almost nonexistent. The author suggests that a very close relationship exists between the two types of learnings. Until the child realizes his total body functions in a coordinated way, that there is meaning and reason to the relationship of the several parts, and that each part has its separate and appropriate functions in relation to the total, learning of a socially acceptable nature may not take place.

Bender (1934), and Bender and Silver (1948) point out that a disturbance in the body-image may occur at any period in the development of the individual or at any level in the perceptual or integrative growth of the person. "In its early development, emphasis upon one particular part of the body by disease or by the attention of others, creates an increased psychological value to that part which disturbs the body-image."

Family and Social Support

As has already been observed in Figure 8-1, the family and social support system is tremendously important to child development. In the case of a child limited by a crippling condition, the reliance on outside support is even greater. If the environment fails to meet the child's social and emotional needs, or overindulges the child's dependency situation, then maladjustment may easily occur. This sensitive relationship has been observed to be a critical variable affecting the adjustment of crippled children and youth.

Freedman (1967), among others, in a comprehensive review of the subject, observed that environmental factors are at least as important in the genesis of emotional disturbances as is the handicap itself. Parent-child relationships are often viewed as the central consideration in the adjustment of the physically limited child. A study by Fitzgerald

(1951), through the use of the Thematic Apperception Test, found that family reactions appeared to be a source of more frustration in orthopedically handicapped adolescents than the disability per se. Allen and Pearson (1938) state that behavior problems of crippled children are directly related to inadequate parental attitudes rather than to the child's inability to encompass psychologically the physical disability. These points of view are also reported by McMichael (1971) in her study of the impact of disability on personal, social, and family adjustment. Most importantly, she notes the presence of emotional stress and maladjustment on individual members and in the family as a whole coincident with the presence of a handicap in the child.

Nussbaum's work (1962) suggests that the personality development of cerebral-palsied children is related to the attitudes of significant adults in their lives. Generally, however, these children revealed less of a reality orientation to themselves than did the adults around them.

Miller's study (1958) of clients in a child-guidance clinic, although cautious in generalizing her findings to all children with cerebral palsy, notes that disturbed parent-child relationships tend to play a more significant role in personality development among such children than the severity of the disability. Although the disability may "trigger" the emotional response, the troubled child with a physical disability functions in a manner similar to that of his nondisabled counterpart.

If real and consistent differences in adjustment do exist between the crippled and nondisabled, they probably are a product of the negative and inconsistent attitudes of the latter group. To the degree that this is so, social maladjustment is preventable and, in all probability, remediable if only the perceptions of disability in the social milieu could be modified in a favorable direction.

In a consideration of differences in adjustment between physically limited and other persons, Michal-Smith (1962) observed that the status that a physically handicapped individual has in society contributes to feelings of inadequacy, rejection, frustration, hostility, and guilt. Social perceptions of the disability accentuate feelings of social devaluation and deter the individual from making an adequate social adjustment. At times, however, the disabled person may turn this social devaluation to his own advantage, using his perceived helplessness to avoid responsibilities and to project blame for failure upon others. The critical role of interaction with others in an unstructured social field in creating problems for disabled individuals was underscored in Meyerson's study (1948) in which an artificial injury was imposed upon a group of children and adults for a period of twenty-four hours. The subjects in this experiment reported that the difficulties they experienced were due not so much to the limitations associated with the physical condition as to the quality of their life experiences.

The human response to crippled children or youth is not the only aspect of environment that has a dramatic impact on their development. Socio-cultural attitudes as reflected by schools, politics, business, and other factors play a significant role in shaping the crippled person's development and adjustment. These factors are too numerous and complex to deal with here beyond their mere mention.

Another factor that has attracted some psychological interest is the effect of experience deprivation. Evidence is accumulating, suggesting that a restriction of sensory input and exploration during the formative years both to amount and variety of stimuli, exercises an adverse effect upon human development. The literature suggests that sensory (and probably experiential) deprivation plays a part in infant growth, and has pervasive ramifications for a child in the intellectual, social, and affective domains. Although this approach to understanding crippled children is gathering momentum, deprivation theory formulation is in its early stages insofar as psychology and education of the handicapped is concerned. Yet, important clues to the effects of deprivation can be found in the literature. Lemkau (1961) holds that prolonged stimulus deprivation is a relevant variable in the development of the handicapped child and that restoration of stimulus input is required to prevent disordered personality formation. Attempts have been made to coordinate data concerning the lack of mothering with experience deprivation among exceptional children. The one-time maternal deprivation hypothesis of Rene Spitz (1945), as an explanation for observed physical, mental, and emotional anomalous development among infants in institutional settings, has been challenged by the sensory, experiential-deprivation hypotheses. Studies involving children who experienced the Dutch famine of 1944–45, however, do not support some of the findings or theoretical positions regarding deprivation (Stein *et al.*, 1975). Thus additional research is needed on this issue.

Attitudes Toward the Crippled Child

Clinical work with crippled children has revealed that the attitudes of family, peers, schoolmates, and people in general play an important role in the shaping of the crippled children's self-concepts and their responses in social situations. There is a tremendous amount of circularity in this issue which complicates matters. For instance, a crippled child who is a financial burden on a poor family may get occasional negative feedback and in response feels guilty, internalizes the guilt, and feels rejected by the parents. Another example is the child who cannot participate in sports or other peer activities. These children perceive themselves as being different and not fitting in; the children thus withdraw from peer contacts. Other circumstances such as teasing or criticism from schoolmates set up an antithetical relationship instead of a coopera-

tive one. It is plain to see that these situations apply to children generally, but because of disabling conditions and resulting affective sensitivity in crippled children, the latter more often proves to acquire negative feelings. This can spiral into mutually negative attitudes and responses between normal and crippled children and youth.

Not all societies view the disabled in a similar manner. In reviewing the situation in some non-Occidental areas, Hanks and Hanks (1948) concluded that attitudes toward them are more favorable in those societies which maintain higher levels of industrial productivity, have a more equitable diet, minimize competitive factors in individual and group achievement, and maintain a concern for individual capacity rather than setting formal standards of attainment. Reiterating the role of social attitudes in fashioning the behavior of exceptional children, Trippe (1959) observed that America's cultural dedication to success, coupled with the opening of more limited channels for the disabled to achieve that success, creates anxiety and insecurity with possible personality disorganization. In attempting to cope with this situation, disabled children adopt different means, one of which is to abandon the goal of social success while retaining the accepted means of achieving success. The consequence of this adjustive mechanism often is rigidity, compulsivity, and personality constriction. Pressed into this life style by their lack of access to opportunities to become successful, disabled children are forced into deviant behavior associated with poor reality testing and unrealistic goals. In addition, the problem for the disabled child starts quite early in his life. Silberberg and Silberberg (1967) found that nondisabled children evidence consistent and negative perceptions of orthopedic disability by age four years.

Gellman (1959) observed that prejudice toward the disabled exists at all socioeconomic levels in all regions of the United States. Stereotypical behavior toward the exceptional in our society has its roots in child-rearing practices which stress normalcy, social customs, and norms that institutionalize pity, the arousal of neurotic childhood fears among nondisabled persons under stress, and the impact of behaviors exhibited by the disabled which invite discrimination. Through emphasizing the concept that difference among people is acceptable and normal, schools and other social institutions can improve the social climate in which the disabled child lives.

In exploring attitudes of first-, third-, and sixth-grade nondisabled children toward the crippled, Billings (1963) used two projective techniques, one requiring a written story in response to a picture stimulus and the other, a picture-completion test. The attitudes of these fifty-four children toward the crippled were significantly less favorable than their attitudes toward the nondisabled. Negative attitudes, even among educators, are often engendered merely by identifying an individual as exceptional. In this regard, Combs and Harper (1967) found that teachers in their sample reacted more negatively to descriptions of cerebral-palsied children than they did to the same descriptions presented without the disability label. Reporting a comparable finding in a sample of disabled high-school seniors, Jaffe (1967) concluded that when the disability as a stimulus appears in the context of a disabled person's other traits, it is accorded more favorable attitudes. Jones, Gottfried, and Owens (1966), noted that their nondisabled subjects expressed greater acceptance of exceptionalities that reflect mild handicaps, that is, promise greater compensation potential.

Investigations of attitudes toward the physically exceptional do not agree in all details concerning the incidence of avoidance and rejection in society. Undoubtedly, these differences stem, in part, from variations in the reference groups and the instrumentation used in these studies. It may be hypothesized that young elementary-school-aged children find themselves subject to fewer negative attitudes from peers than do physically disabled teenagers. Furthermore,

college students probably encounter fewer negative attitudes on campuses than they do in seeking employment. The most valid conclusion regarding attitudes seems to be that physically disabled children will experience such attitudes from time to time, but because the attitudes vary from situation to situation and are applied inconsistently to the same disabled individual, uncertainty in new situations is engendered whenever a disabled child enters unfamiliar sectors of life. Somatopsychologists have studied this problem in depth, and Barker and his associates suggest that the phenomenon accounts for some of the tensions felt by disabled individuals in social situations. Meyerson also emphasizes this point of view.

The most hopeful note about attitudes is that educators and other professional persons can influence the disabled under selected conditions. The most promising approach seems to be planned interaction between disabled and nondisabled children under conditions favorable for both groups. Such arrangements require both social-psychological sophistication and educational engineering. Yet the stakes are sufficiently high for the adjustment of the exceptional child to warrant carefully planned interventions. Thus far, group encounters under adult leadership seem to offer the most productive approach to attitude modification in this context. Other approaches merit further study.

Social Status with Peers

As increasing proportions of physically disabled children participate in classes with the non-disabled peers, the quality of their relationships with such children is being studied. As a result of using incomplete sentences with physically limited and nondisabled children, Cruickshank (1952) reported that handicapped children reveal insecurity relative to the negative feelings expressed about them by their nondisabled peers. Despite this, however, the relationships between the two groups are, in most instances, favorable. Comparing cardiac and orthopedic with nonhandicapped adolescents, Giovannoni (1967) found that the two groups were not differentiated on the basis of membership in informal social groups or social relations with the opposite sex. However, the disabled indicated less participation in formal social groups. Giovannoni concluded that the disabled do not constitute a deviant group in society and that the disability is not useful in determining social role behavior or level of social participation.

On the other hand, at least one investigation resulted in sociometric data suggesting that disability constitutes an important variable in determining children's social status. Non-disabled subjects aged 10 to 12 were asked by Richardson and Royce (1968) to rank preference for drawings in which skin color and physical handicap were systematically varied. The authors concluded that physical handicap is such a powerful determiner of attitudes that it masks skin color in children's social preferences.

At least one group of physically limited children, the homebound, expressed their own needs in relation to non-disabled students. Responding to questions put to them by Rusalem and Jenkins (1961) relating to their home instruction experience, these homebound teenagers noted that special deprivation and isolation from peers constituted the most important limitation imposed upon them by their inability to attend classes in a regular school building. In considering a possible return to classroom instruction, they expressed their greatest degree of anxiety about the manner in which other students would accept and integrate them into their social fields.

THEORIES ON THE PSYCHOLOGICAL EFFECTS OF A CRIPPLING CONDITION

The importance that Allen and Pearson place upon the parental attitudes as being basic in the development of healthy adjust-

ment among handicapped children has been mentioned. Similarly, numerous other authors have made contributions to psychological theory relating to crippled individuals. Among these should be recorded the writings of Phelps (1948), Dembo (1948), Winkler (1931), Landis and Bolles (1942), Menninger 1949), Meyerson (1948), and Barker (1948). Clark (1934), also in psychoanalytic terms, has pointed out that the ego loss due to a somatic defect resolves itself in emotional compensatory behavior, whereas Kubie (1945), in the same frame of reference, points out that the impact of the handicap will be the result of the interaction of three factors—reality, conscious fantasy, and unconscious fantasy and feeling. Several studies based upon small samples of twins have in large measure supported the conclusion of Allen and Pearson, namely, that the impact of the disability is closely related to the adequacy or inadequacy of the parental attitudes that surround the child (Jenkins, 1934; Klapper & Werner, 1950; Bradway, 1937; Newell, 1930). Barker and his associates have summarized the theoretical assumptions that are proposed as etiological problems in individuals with physical disability to which the present writers have made additions:

1. Compensation for inferiorities (Adler, 1926).
2. Easy narcissistic satisfactions from pain and uniqueness (Meng, 1938; Clark, 1934).
3. Parental rejection or anxiety and overprotection (McMichael, 1971).
4. Impeded development (Piaget & Inhelder, 1969).
5. Lack of normal plan and expressive actions (Meng, 1938; Wurtz, 1932).
6. Easy cathexis to disabled body part (Meng, 1938).
7. Blame of parents (Meng, 1938: Allen & Pearson, 1938).
8. Unrelated anxieties transferred to bodily handicap (Meng, 1938).
9. Feeling of guilt for hostility toward parents (Meng, 1938; Winkler, 1931).

10. Efforts to achieve social acceptance (Meng, 1938; Lowman, 1942; Allen & Pearson, 1938).

11. Body-image at variance with reality (Schilder, 1950; Bender, 1934).

12. Conflict between withdrawal and compensatory tendencies (von Baeyer, 1928).

13. Goals beyond achievement possibilities due to pressure from parents, and to physical, social, and economic restrictions (Lord, 1930; Landis & Bolles, 1942).

14. Variable, conflicting behavior in response to variable, inconsistent attitudes of others (Allen & Pearson, 1938).

15. Dependent, demanding apathetic behavior deriving from oversolicitous protective situation (Meng, 1938; Allen & Pearson, 1938).

16. Psychopathological responses (Verwoerdt, 1972).

17. Acceptance of disability as a punishment for sin (Winkler, 1931).

18. Retaliatory behavior for "unjust" treatment by nature (Meng, 1938).

19. Self-concept (Fishman, 1949).

20. Value systems of disabled person and his associates (Dembo et al., 1948).

21. Degree of acceptance of disability by disabled person (Fielding, 1950).

22. Cultural role of disabled person (Schneider, 1947; Fitzgerald, 1951).

23. Intergroup dynamics (Schneider; Barker et al., 1953).

One theoretical view not listed above is the more recent theory of ego psychology. This school of thought makes no specific applications to crippled children. However, just as Piaget's concepts were used to explain development, ego-psychological concepts will be employed to discuss the affective development of crippled children and youth.

The ego is that often-mentioned hypothetical construct which Freud established as the mediating device among psychic structures. In psychoanalytic theory, ego is defined in terms of its functions. The development of the ego, therefore, can only be described in terms of the development of its separate functions. Hartman (1950) calls the ego "man's specialized organ of adaptation." It mediates between inner and outer reality with the goal being adaptation to reality. The ego grows over time in relation to what is learned, and the ego functions emerge with thought. An ego-psychological approach assumes a progressive process of development and maturation in all areas of psychic functioning, as well as regressive manifestations, which may be normal or pathological. In this respect ego psychology has a commonality with Piaget's explanation of cognitive, physiological, and affective development (see Figure 8–1). In this section, ego development will be analyzed in terms of seven major ego functions. Examples will be presented to highlight differences in the ego functioning of three crippled children.

Ego Development

Ego psychology assumes that a child is born in an undifferentiated state. This means the newborn child is in an unconscious psychological state. The child can lay down memory traces, but cannot yet organize them. The infant is governed by the pleasure principle (the *id*) in efforts to satisfy its needs. From this undifferentiated state emerges the primary autonomous ego along with increasing consciousness, control of drives, and use of the reality principle. The *primary autonomous ego* refers to the biological aspects of the organism's functioning which can be achieved well before the acquisition of higher level cognitive functions. These biological determinants are perception, motility, language, physical growth, thought, and memory. They are all different processes of the central nervous system. Theorists believe that if there is impairment of primary autonomous ego, the ego will not develop normally.

As the child continues to differentiate himself from reality, begins to think logically rather than magically, and starts to regulate his drives purposefully, there is marked the emergence of the *secondary autonomous ego*. The appearance of the secondary autonomous ego, referred to as *ego,* demarcates the period when ego functions begin to differentiate and to develop, and become resistant to regression. The secondary autonomous ego's goal is to maintain a steady state (equilibrium) between self and the environment (similar to the developmental view depicted in Figure 8–1). In ego-psychological terms, these developing ego functions keep the organism stable, yet open to adaptation with the environment. In this way the ego continues to grow in a normal and healthy manner.

Psychologists have suggested a wide variety of ego functions too exhaustive to discuss at length here. Much of the literature arbitrarily has accepted the seven major ego functions which serve as reasonably comprehensive components of the ego. A brief summary of these ego functions will be helpful before profiling them in three examples of ego development in crippled children.

Object Relations refers to the development of psychological relationships to objects. From birth, the relation to mother regarding feeding and fondling is an important precursor to later cathexes of people. After several months the child internalizes primitive mental representations. Gradually object constancy develops and images can be recalled without seeing them (cue reduction in behaviorist terms). The function of object relations encompasses all relationships, but most importantly those involving family, friends, and loved ones. This function serves the individual's ability to seek, establish, and maintain relationships, and varies qualitatively from one person to another.

Relation to Reality is that function of the ego which involves: (a) the individual's differentiation of self from reality, (b) the ability to judge and test reality and to be aware of its exigencies, (c) the selection and organization of perception, (d) the capacity to maintain contact with reality and adapt to it, and (e) orientation in time, place, space, and person.

Regulation and Control of Drives is that function which governs the organism's response to physiological and psychological needs. For instance, the ability to delay gratification or engage in detour behavior, and the capacity to tolerate frustration or anxiety. Whether the person's self-control tends to be rigid or impulsive is a characteristic of this function. The parameters of this function are quite dependent on the socialization process and the development of superego.

Thought Processes refers to the function which covers an individual's style of thinking, abstracting, capacity to concentrate and memorize, and ability to develop logical thought from fantasy. This function seems to develop with increasing consciousness and cognitive skill, and is closely related to the synthetic ego function dealing with mental organization.

Defense Functions are those mechanisms which individuals employ in varying ways and degrees to maintain equilibrium among instinctual drives, reality demands, and superego pressures. Some examples of common defenses are denial, projection, repression, reaction formation, isolation, and rationalization. The degree to which defensive functions are employed and their effectiveness are crucial determinants of an ego-syntonic personality, or one who adapts easily and willingly to reality.

Autonomous Functions have been discussed as being those attributes of an individual which depend greatly on initial biological endowments. Such functions include perception, intelligence, language, motor development, and memory. These biological givens start out as primary autonomous functions on which the organism relies, but over which it has little control. Over time, these and all other ego functions develop in the service of the ego.

The Synthetic Function refers to the ego's ability to receive input from the environment and unite, organize, and synthesize these data in a meaningful way. This function also serves to bind energy in order to make purposeful and adaptive responses to the environment. The synthetic function governs the integrating process of all other ego functions; for instance, organizing perceptions, setting realistic responses to the environment, exercising the proper controls and defenses, and maintaining equilibrium throughout the adaptation process.

Even though these ego functions apply to all individuals, no two people have the same ego profile. Ego functions develop to varying degrees and differ qualitatively as well from individual to individual. By analyzing ego functions one has a somewhat systematic reference for examining psychological development and making comparisons. This shall be the approach taken below in considering three examples of crippled children and youth, and constructing profiles of their ego functions based on some clinical information.

Example 1. Joey, age 6, was born with a tumor on his lower spine. He had several major operations before the age of 3, including long periods of hospitalization. Joey is now paralyzed from the hips down. He is incontinent. Joey has learned to walk with the use of a walker. He is a seemingly happy child with normal intelligence. He does get frustrated rather easily. His parents are devoted, loving people who assist him in any ways they can.

Example 2. Sally, age 11, was in a car accident a year ago and suffered brain damage to her right hemisphere. Sally has recovered well, but still has a left hemiplegia and some difficulty with visual-perception tasks. In addition, her school achievement has declined and she has become quite inhibited in peer interactions. Sally has become much more dependent on other people to do things for her, and often takes a position of helplessness. Her parents both work and cannot find the time to meet all of Sally's requests. Additionally, the parents are seeking marital counseling for the many strains on their relationship.

Example 3. Kurt is a 15-year-old boy born with malformed shoulders and abnor-

mally short arms, one hand having two fingers and no thumb; the other hand, with digital stubs. His mother believes that his prenatal deformity had been caused by her mother-in-law with whom she quarreled frequently. Nocturnal enuresis appeared at age 8 and continues. Underachievement at school was another problem. Foremost was an emotional disturbance expressed in a continuous evasion of factual truth, and in the creating of a fantasy life of remarkable complexity. There were some depressive tendencies, also. Kurt tried to push his handicap out of existence by denying it; he built a fantasy world from which he excluded his physical handicap; and he developed certain reaction formations as defenses against insecurity and impropriety.

In Table 8–1, the seven ego functions discussed earlier are seen in relationship to the developmental progress of the three crippled children just described.

By analyzing Table 8–1 it is possible to obtain an appreciation for the wide range of crippling conditions and the diverse effects on ego development. This is not to imply that all crippled children have poor ego development. In fact, the example 1, Joey, is a fairly common ego profile. Many children are narcissistic, infantilized, and have low frustration tolerance. But surely these characteristics are exacerbated by Joey's condition. Example 2, Sally, demonstrates the pervasive effect of a crippling condition across physiological, cognitive, and affective dimensions. Her ego profile points out neurotic processes with which she defends against her disability. On the other hand, Kurt in example 3 presents the most maladaptive response to his crippling condition. Following in the confusion and misunderstanding of his mother, Kurt builds a fantasy world where his disability does not exist. The psychotic processes of this boy have been unchallenged for years, and now dominate his ego functioning.

Clearly there is no one pattern of ego development for crippled children. These profiles show that ego functioning is a com-

TABLE 8–1
PROFILES OF THREE CRIPPLED CHILDREN IN RELATION
TO SEVEN EGO FUNCTIONS

Ego Functions	Example 1: Joey	Example 2: Sally	Example 3: Kurt
Object Relations			
a. Capacity to form relations	Forms stable relations with adults.	Clings to adults. Insecure.	Avoids human relationships.
b. Type of relationships formed and how well they are maintained	Competes with peers and is frustrated when they run off. Maintains narcissistic relationships.	Relations are characterized by inconsistency.	Mother is only relation; mutual dependency.
Autonomous Functions			
a. Perception	Very good.	Impaired.	Distorted.
b. Intelligence	Very good.	Functioning below premorbid potential.	Average.
c. Language	Very good.	Intact.	Normal.
d. Motor development	Strong, agile and mobile; cannot run or climb.	Hemiplegia obstructs play and self-help.	Abnormal upper trunk (strength coordination).
Relation to Reality			
a. Adaptation (coping with environment)	Copes well when environment is kind to him.	Constriction of life space more and more withdrawal.	Creates fantasy environment.
b. Reality testing (judgment)	Intact.	Reasoning seems distorted.	Impaired judgment.
c. Sense of reality (differentiate self from world)	Has differentiated.	Distorts impressions people have of her.	Very poor/fragmented.
Control of Drives			
a. Frustration tolerance	Frustrated easily.	Avoids frustrating situations.	Able to control drives or escape from them.
b. Delay gratification	Seeks immediate gratification.	Relies on sure means of gratification.	Created grandiose ways of self-gratification.
c. Control of impulses	Shows temper when frustrated.	Overcontrol; keeps feelings in.	Channeled into games and fantasy.

TABLE 8-1 (Cont.)

Ego Functions	Example 1: Joey	Example 2: Sally	Example 3: Kurt
Defenses			
a. Denial, withdrawal	Denial and projection.		Denial.
b. Projection-sublimation	Blame someone else.	Projects her anger on others and says everyone hates me.	
c. Reaction formation, repression	Upset when adults disapprove.	Represses and isolates feelings.	Reaction formation.
Thought Processes			
a. Thought organization	Increased secondary process logical and organized.	Disorganized; gaps in thinking.	Preoccupied with fantasy.
b. Memory and concentration	Good; sometimes short attention; boredom.	Poor visual memory.	Easily distracted.
Synthetic Functions			
a. Unite, organize, create	Tends to be impulsive.	Little initiative to create.	Creates fantasy.
b. Ability to manage	Jumps from one thing to another	Only passive involvement in activities.	Little involvement in normal activities.

plex multifaceted process in all individuals. The way in which one adapts (See Figure 8–1) is contingent on a combination of biological endowments interacting with environmental supports across all life experiences (Thomas & Chess, 1977). The ego-function framework and profiles provided in this section were used to give the reader a tool in grasping the complexity of ego functioning and ego development.

Human Sexuality

In Figure 8–1 it was noted that expressions of sexuality constitute one of many environmental resources supporting the individual's total development. From the earliest activities leading from gender identity to the complete fulfillment of self in sexual behavior of one form or another, the physi-

cally normal individual cautiously, often with a minimum of guidance of modeling, makes his way. Such an individual has almost complete latitude to explore, experiment, and to obtain self-satisfaction. Only the mores of the society in which he lives constitute limitations to the person's behavior. In recent years these limitations have been relaxed by societies almost everywhere, and the individual is permitted an even greater arena within which to learn what his sexual role is. That human sexuality is an aspect of human development which encompasses the total life span is a fact now widely recognized. On the purely physical side, primitive masturbatory movements may indeed often be observed in X-ray or fluoroscopic techniques to be a prenatal fetal behavior. From these primitive conditioned learnings, the physical sexual behavior in varying ways characterizes all growth stages and is itself often a characterization of a specific growth process, that is, puberty and menopause among others.

One of the primary aspects of human fulfillment in the physically normal person is that of physical freedom to explore and to experiment. Ordinary persons, within the limitations created by themselves, their families, friends, school, church, or social groups, are free and capable of making their own decisions. Such is not to say that the way has always been easy for people; the Puritan ethic, guilt feelings, misinformation, and fears have often produced conflict and personal disturbances. However, for this discussion it is necessary only to point out the fact that no physical impediment serves to limit the achievement of complete sexuality in the ordinary person, albeit one of heterosexuality or homosexuality.

Human sexuality for the child and youth with a crippling condition is a problem of a different order. As has been pointed out elsewhere in this chapter, the affective, cognitive, and physiological growth of such individuals is not only a reflection of the social constraints imposed by society, but may also be intensified by them. For example, parental guidance or lack of it may blunt the sexual exploration of normal youth. For the crippled youth, parental attitudes may stop exploration entirely. A mother reported to the authors on one occasion, "Thank goodness I won't need to worry about girls when he gets to that age. He can't get out of his wheelchair; but then I guess the handicapped don't have those needs anyhow." In this instance, parental concern regarding normal sexual exploration, a fact which alone would cause this mother concern, was solved by the confinement represented by a wheelchair. The parent failed to recognize, or ignored, the human needs of the developing youth.

If one refers again to Figure 8–1, the numerous components of the support system are observed. In the normal child and youth these have an almost spontaneous impact on his development. In the instance of those with physical disability, many or all of these components may have to "volunteer" support to the individual. Greater exertion on the part of family, school, models of care and behavior toward the individual may need to be made. In the area of human sexuality, what does this mean?

In small children it is essential that exploration of their bodies be undertaken as a significant aspect of self-knowledge. Many children with perceptual-processing deficits are deficient in their understanding of body parts, orientation of body in space, and directionality. The boy or girl with quadriplegic cerebral palsy may indeed not have the privilege of physically exploring their own bodies, and through such play and exploration come to know who "I am." The need and interest is still there. The presence of a disability does not mean a reduction in the wish of the person to be sexually active. At a very early age, sexual activity may be a reflection of a need to know the body, its function, and the interesting and physically satisfying roles which many body parts play. Hence, as we have stated before, the child's environment may have to support it more. We have advised parents to be willing to caress their crippled child, to manipulate genitalia, to recognize at the same time the pleasant emotions this produces, and the sense of well-being which ensues. During the bathing, changing, or dressing of young children, comments and conversation with meaning can accompany the physical handling by the adult, and in so doing the normalcy of the human body and its emotional responses can be established in a secure and healthy climate.

As the seriously physically handicapped child grows older, the attendant care provided them by their parents or other adults of necessity will have to become more specific. Their sexual growth needs will progress normally, even if their physical activity potential does not. One parent stated the complete misconception when he reported, "Johnny won't ever have to go through the agonies of masturbation I did. His hands are completely useless. No one will ever tell him that to masturbate is to become crazy like my father did to me. But then again what are his needs here?"

This father has almost missed the essential fact. His question, however, opened up a major opportunity for him and his seriously handicapped adolescent son. He was urged either to teach his son how to masturbate, so that in privacy he could fulfill his needs, or himself to respond to the son's request to be masturbated. This takes a secure parent. But parents can be secure. They can be supported in their efforts truly to meet the needs of their children. They can, as has been stated elsewhere, bring to the child the supporting system needed for complete fulfillment. There may be other ways to assist physically disabled youth, but the issue here is not so much technique as a recognition of a need somehow to be met.

One may legitimately ask how far this goes in the support of human sexuality in the disabled. The authors feel that one goes a long way if there is a commitment to the concept of total human fulfillment. The problem we are discussing too long has been exacerbated by guilt-ridden adults or by those who feel the issue can be ignored as a matter that need not be pursued because of the handicap itself. One set of parents exemplifies a degree of personal courage that might be a model for many others. Two brothers with progressive Friedreich's ataxia were confined to wheelchairs. Their lower extremities were essentially useless. They occupied large twin beds in the same room. At the ages of seventeen and nineteen the boys' mother inadvertently entered their bedroom to find them in the same bed in a sexual embrace. The older son had apparently dragged himself across the room to his brother's bed, and by sheer strength of his arms and shoulders and with his brother's help had raised himself to the bed level.

The mother left the room to regain her composure, and also left two anxious young men whose secret was now a family matter.

Mrs. S. talked with her husband who was equally concerned, but reminded his wife that they had always urged the boys, as well as themselves, to accept others in terms of the facts, not on an emotional first-reaction basis. With this orientation, the two parents went to the boys' room, the mother apologizing for invading their privacy, and assuring the sons that indeed the long-standing rule of privacy and acceptance was to be honored. Following an expected emotional reunion, the parents, leaving the young men in the same bed, suggested a calmer conversation the next evening, which the sons agreed would be welcome. No outside counseling was sought at this point, but as all parties later reported, there was much individual planning and thinking done by the four people during the night and next day.

The crucial family session took place with the boys taking the lead, expressing their need for sexual release, and bemoaning their inability to obtain a free sexual life outside the home. Their mutual sexual activities had been going on for several months before it was discovered the previous night. The parents acknowledged the boys' problems and expressed a willingness to talk more to seek solutions. "Put our beds together as a first step," said the younger son. "Easily done," said the mother to two astonished young men. "You have a right to express your needs as you see fit," was the comment reported to the authors by the father during a later conference.

At this point, the father turned the family discussion to the broader issue of sexual adjustment and preferences. Homosexuality as a matter of adult adjustment was rather thoroughly discussed. For several months previously there had been discussions within the family around the wisdom of employing a live-in companion and aide for the sons. The matter was brought up again, and the father asked the boys directly if they wished to pursue this plan and, if so, did they desire to have someone near them with heterosexual or homosexual preferences. Time out was called, and the boys asked time to consider this rather radical outcome to the conversation.

A week later, according to the father, the sons had made their decision and asked that a "well-adjusted gay guy" be employed. At this point the parents sought both advice and reinforcement from professional counseling. They also asked the counselor for assistance in locating a person to meet both the needs of their sons and of the family as a whole on a non-sexual basis. Through a local university, a splendid male student was located who ultimately entered into the employment of the family.

In this report, there is to be observed a set of well-adjusted parents, two who honored the needs and privacy of their sons and who recognized what the "whole person" means. It provides not a completely unique example of the external support suggested in Figure 8–1, which may be needed by crippled youth in their attempts to reach the full life. Certainly it recognizes the validity of both the homosexual and heterosexual life patterns of our society.

Another example of external supports provided to crippled youth in the area of human sexuality concerns a physician's family in an eastern community. A 20-year-old son was seriously incapacitated with the early onset of progressive muscular dystrophy, and was essentially confined to a wheelchair. On frequent weekends this family employed a young lady, not only to provide attendant care, but to serve him sexually. The parents almost always used these occasions to be away from the home for at least a portion of the weekend so as not to intrude on the privacy of their son. In preparation for this decision, the parents, although both professional persons, wisely sought counseling as a means, not only of thoroughly voicing their own feelings about what they saw as a radical step, but as a method whereby with a third party present they could assure each other of their complete acceptance of the situation. Recog-nizing that their son would never have a full life and would undoubtedly also have a short life, they were determined that his physical condition would not serve as a complete limitation to the full experiencing of one of the most significant aspects of human behavior.

It is unfortunate that, in spite of the more recent and liberal attitudes regarding sexual behavior, this significant aspect of human development is still, in the United States and often elsewhere, cloaked in secrecy, fear, outmoded attitudes, and is relegated to the closet. Other countries have often adopted a much more liberal position regarding human sexuality, and accept it as a normal aspect of planning for the physically handicapped as it is for the physically normal individual.

A group of youths, male and female, with serious upper extremity disabilities, exists for whom external social supports in the area of human sexuality are a necessity unless this area of developmental need is completely ignored by parents, friends, and professional persons. These include the seriously handicapped cerebral-palsied youth, those with congenital (or accidental) amputations, with growth anomalies involving the upper extremities, those with paralysis stemming from accidents or disease, and other similar conditions.

An 18-year-old young man who had been sexually active for three or four years was in a water skiing accident, and came through it as a lower extremity paraplegic with upper-right-arm paralysis. He was confined to a wheelchair. Having experienced the fullness of sexual behavior, he knew what he wanted and needed. Now confined to a wheelchair, his self-obtained outlets for them, which had been a secret of his and his close friends heretofore, needed to be shared first with his father and then with his mother. Although there was protest on the part of the parents, they came to understand that the accident per se did not change the growth processes for their son. Reluctantly they agreed that as an adult he was free to make his choices. "It was a rough evening," reported the mother, "when we saw two of his friends lift him into their car and drive off, and we knew what the activity of that night would be. Since then we have grown to accept that behavior as a necessary part of his adjustment, and we hope one day he will be married." This person's problem is not as great either psychologically or physically as the individuals mentioned earlier with total amputations of arms and legs, or who, for other reasons, have no use of upper extremities. The external world must play the same part as the young man's friends.

*Use of mechanical devices.** Professional people are often guilty of paying an inordinate amount of attention to the physical disability per se, and frequently have ignored the sexual needs and life styles of seriously disabled youths. With this in mind, there have been brought to our attention three youths in a community hospital setting located in the rural midwest part of the United States.

Two young men and one young woman, all quadraplegics, were recovering from neck injuries and spinal cord severations. All had injuries resulting from swimming accidents. These three young people were made as comfortable as possible by professional people who were sensitive to their needs. They were cared for within the medical care facility, but their recovery was painful and lengthy both physically and psychologically. Substantial physical deterioration of the muscles and general appearance of these individuals resulted. All three youths were psychologically depressed a great deal of the time during this period.

* The examples used in this section have been provided to the authors by Mr. David Rinckey, to whom appreciation is extended.

During a counseling session with one of the two men, Tom, a 17-year-old who had now been hospitalized for more than 6 months, said, "During times when I lie here in bed, particularly when I've just seen or talked with one of the young female nurses, I get these terrible (genital) aches. These aches irritate me, and I feel very much like I'm being tortured while I lie here. Can and will you help me?" Tom indicated during an early interview that he had been sexually active with a young woman prior to his accident. With this in mind, the young woman was contacted by one of the hospital psychiatrists. This was Tom's first request, and it had taken place before he made the above comment to his counselor. It was learned, however, that the young woman was 15 years of age, and had seen the result of much of Tom's physical deterioration through hospital visitations. She was insistent on not seeing Tom ever again—"I can't accept him now the way he is," she stated.

With this in mind, the hospital staff met with several specialists and had many briefings to discuss the sexual needs of Tom as well as of Peter and Lisa, who had similar physical problems. The suggestion was made to contact an organization which was developing a unit for sexual self-pleasuring. When the organization heard of the hospital personnel's interests and needs, they immediately sent them a demonstration unit designed for use by males only. There is now a unit for women as well as men.

This unit was employed as an experiment, and of the two male quadraplegic patients, Tom volunteered to participate in the endeavor. After fittings (for penis size), were carried out by a male nurse, the equipment was installed into the patient's room for whatever length of time he desired. All installations were carried out by a male nurse upon Tom's request. Tom's privacy was insured during these times by moving him to a private room with a closed-door policy.

Further, at his request he was provided with sexually explicit materials of a heterosexual nature to assist with fantasy.

After one month, Tom reported a disappearance of his genital discomfort; improvement in self-adjustment could be observed; and he was fascinated by how quickly he became sexually stimulated when the unit was installed. He further stated that he achieved not only orgasm, but also ejaculations. In the meantime his body was beginning to put on weight and his physical appearance was showing a dramatic improvement.

Following these events with Tom, the hospital director and chief psychiatrist arranged for an in-service program pertinent to these matters for all related hospital staff. All staff personnel (from physicians to custodians) were oriented with regard to Tom's situation and the type of equipment being used. The staff was found to be in accord with the development of this type of program for patients. Further, the state provided funds and purchased the equipment as necessary rehabilitative equipment for Tom. The hospital continued to provide the mechanical device as an optional sex-style to disabled patients both for men and women. This hospital also finds female patients who choose to use the device equally improved in their health and attitudes.

QUANTITATIVE INFORMATION

In the previous section, the psychological problems related to those with crippling conditions was approached from a dynamic, ego-psychology point of view. Some quantitative data, when such were available, were provided. The intent of that section, however, was to present a theoretical orientation which would serve as a point of view regarding the impact of physical disability on growth and adjustment. In this section of the chapter, attention will be given to several matters which serve further to differ-

entiate physically handicapped children and youth from their peer groups, and on which some, albeit often incomplete, quantative data are available.

STUDIES OF INTELLIGENCE OF CRIPPLED CHILDREN

Few recent investigations have been conducted regarding the intelligence of crippled children as a group. Those which are available deserve reporting and consideration in a text of this nature. These studies are reported as important in the full recognition of the variety or lack of variety of tests and testing with the physically handicapped. Data of the nature included here are important irrespective of their limitations in the orientation of personnel who work with crippled children.

Lee (1931) reports the results of a study of intelligence of 148 crippled children in the Children's Orthopedic Hospital in Seattle, Washington. She utilized the Binet Test. The age range of her group was between 3 and 16 years; the intelligence quotient range, 35 to 138, with a mean of 86.8. Lee found that the children with poliomyelitis had the highest mean intelligence quotient score, 92. Children with "spastic paralysis" (her term) had a mean intelligence quotient of 69; tuberculosis of bone and joint, 88; congenital deformities, 61; and central nervous system involvements, 74. Of particular interest is a comprehensive study of hemophiliac boys in Los Angeles (Dietrich, 1968). Their mean IQ on the WISC was 121. Yet, as a group, they suffer both academic and vocational frustration.

Witty and Smith (1932) have reported a study which included 1,480 crippled children. They obtained a mean intelligence quotient of 84.5 with a range of from 50 to 130. Pintner, Eisenson, and Stanton (1941) and Gordon, Roberts, and Griffiths (1939) present differing results with two populations of crippled children. The former, utilizing a group of 300 crippled children (which excluded cerebral-palsied children), obtained a mean intelligence quotient of 88; the latter, a mean quotient of 103.9 from a group of 98 children with poliomyelitis. Fernald and Arlitt (1925), in one of the earliest studies reported, found a mean intelligence quotient of 82.35 and a range of 30 to 138 in a group of 194 crippled children, representing many different types of physical conditions, including cerebral palsy. Donofrio (1952) reported that the distribution of Stanford-Binet scores obtained with 157 crippled children were skewed toward the lower end of the curve.

Practically all of the studies mentioned appeared prior to the publication of even the 1937 revision by Terman and Merrill of the Stanford-Binet Intelligence Scale. The 1960 revision of the scale has somewhat more adequate standardization and, in general, is a great improvement in terms of items and administrative procedures over earlier forms of the same test. New studies need to be completed to provide information regarding the intelligence of crippled children on this scale. Other intelligence tests, some with better statistical foundations than the Binet, have subsequently been developed. New studies are needed using these tests. It has previously been pointed out that the intelligence range of children with cerebral palsy is apparently considerably different from that of the normal population and may, as well, be different from that of other types of crippled children. Hence, those studies which included cerebral-palsied children within their populations need to be considered tentative and need to be reevaluated with populations which exclude this group of children. Crippled children cannot be considered a homogeneous group insofar as psychological characteristics are concerned. Cardiac children, often included in group studies of crippled children, for example, appear to be characterized in many instances quite differently from other crippled children. Cerebral-palsied children have already been

discussed in this respect. It is likely that other groups of crippled children will likewise have characteristics that distinguish one from the other. The impact of congenital defects on intelligence and personality *versus* adventitious disabilities needs to be seriously investigated and has not been done adequately to date.

It can undoubtedly be expected that the intelligence level of some groups of crippled children will be below national norms or will have a different curve from that of the general population. Although Briggs (1960) reported that scores achieved on the WAIS Performance Scale when only the dominant hand is available do not suffer significant decrements, the same probably does not hold true if the dominant hand is affected. Consequently, limitations in manipulation should be taken into account in assessing intelligence test performance when the stimulus tasks require dexterity or rapid movement. In considering the multitudinous factors that may depress the intelligence test scores of physically exceptional children, Braen and Masling (1959) question the indiscriminate application of general population norms to handicapped children and advocate modifications devised for each case. Children who have been markedly restricted in their experiences and activities will, with the present instruments of evaluation, achieve lower-than-average scores. Children who have been restricted in their experiences through long periods of hospitalization and convalescence may be expected to show differences in intelligence scores and personality factors. Children who have suffered a cerebrospinal involvement may be expected to achieve lower scores on tests because of the interaction in function of the cerebral cortex. However, studies which continue to group all types of handicapped children together, regardless of etiological factors or type of involvement, will add little to the present meager fund of knowledge of this problem.

The Binet-type tests and the revisions of

them have limitations in their application to disabled children. The preponderance of verbal material serves as a disadvantage to children with speech disorders or auditory impairments, whereas the heavy emphasis on motor activities in the remaining items often makes the test inappropriate for children with severe motor involvements. Such factors as these are basic to the criticism heard of the studies of the intelligence of cerebral-palsied children noted earlier. Several authors have made serious attempts to circumscribe the criticisms of the Binet materials. Chief among these are Ammons and Ammons (1949), and Blum, Burgemeister, and Lorge (1951). These investigators have attempted to develop scales that require little or no verbalization and which can be completed through the utilization of gross-motor activities rather than through the fine muscle movements required on most intelligence scales. The attempt in each instance is to produce a scale that permits a more accurate evaluation of the innate ability of the crippled child and that reduces to a minimum the impact of the disability on test performance. However, the statistical characteristics of these tests leave much to be desired. Other tests in current use include Haeussermann's test of the educability of young handicapped children, the Illinois Test of Psycholinguistic Abilities, and the Peabody Picture Vocabulary Test. The Illinois Test of Psycholinguistic Abilities is particularly being questioned by some regarding its statistical adequacy. The Leiter International Intelligence Scale was developed with the assessment of intelligence of physically handicapped children as one of its major goals. The test is ingenious in several of its parts; however, the scale consists of dozens of items, many of which are composed of many tiny pieces to be placed together in a variety of ways. These pieces are so small that subjects with almost any degree of motor incoordination involving the hands are seriously restricted in their ability to participate in the test. As a test of motor performance, the Leiter not only has all of the restrictions of performance tests generally, but has intensified some of them to a point that renders almost useless an interesting and potentially useful instrument. These tests, however, together with careful modifications still required on Raven's Progressive Matrices, provide resources for clinical psychologists which in the future will permit more accurate research and greater understanding of the intellectual potential of individual crippled children.

Special Consideration in Cerebral Palsy

Most crippling conditions do not alter directly the learning mechanism of the disabled individual. With few exceptions, the damage is localized in the limbs, the spine, the joints, or the trunk. Learning deficits, if they occur at all, result from environmental influences. On the other hand, the neurological damage which causes cerebral palsy lies in the brain of a child and, not infrequently, involves neurological structures and processes which influence perception and intellectual capacity. Although direct neurological involvement of this type is not inevitable, it happens often enough to justify separate consideration of the special psychological problems of cerebral-palsied children who do suffer an insult to the learning mechanisms. Obviously, their adjustment problems are even more complex than those of other crippled children, because the whole gamut of human response—communication, perception, and controlled movement—may be impaired. Consequently, a special section is devoted to a review of the intellectual and perceptual problems of cerebral palsy within the larger population of those with developmental disabilities.

Intelligence. In 1946 McIntire reported the results of a study to which Phelps and others have referred. Phelps (1948) suggests that approximately 30 percent of the cerebral-palsied group is mentally retarded as a result of brain damage; the remaining 70 percent is normal "in the sense that these individuals show the normal spread of the population seen at large." This statement had been widely accepted until about 1950 when, simultaneously and independently, several studies appeared, each of which is markedly similar to the others in methodology, treatment of data, and results (Asher & Schonnel in Figure 8–5, 1950; Holoran, 1952; Miller & Rosenfeld, Figure 8–6, 1952; Heilman, 1952; Hopkins *et al.*, 1954; Bice & Cruickshank, 1966). Heilman has compared the results of these studies in Table 8–2.

It is interesting to observe the close similarity of the results of the five investigations and to note the results of the combined data. Among the 1,002 children included in the studies, 25 percent have average or above average intelligence; 30 percent, borderline-

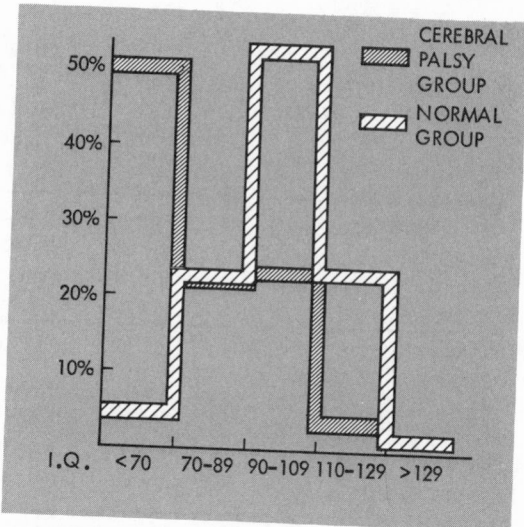

FIGURE 8–6. Distribution of intelligence quotients of normal and cerebral-palsied populations, Buffalo (N.Y.). Children's Hospital study [from Miller & Rosenfeld, *Journal of Pediatrics,* XLI (November 1952). Reproduced with permission.]

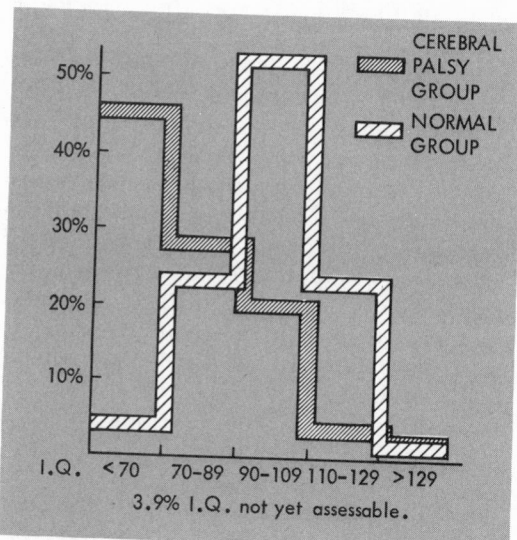

FIGURE 8–5. Distribution of intelligence quotients of normal and cerebral-palsied populations, British study [from Asher & Schonnel. *Archives of Diseases of Children,* XXV (1950). Reproduced with permission.]

dull intelligence; and 45 percent are in the mentally defective range. Fouracre and Theill (1953) reports similar findings in still another study, although his population was considerably smaller than those previously mentioned. Likewise, Hopkins *et al.* (1954), in a study involving *992 additional cerebral-palsied children,* report 487 children, or 49.0 percent, with intelligence quotients between 0 and 69; 224 children or 22.5 percent, between 70 and 89; 212 children or 21.9 percent, between 90 and 109; and 69 children or 6.6 percent, with IQs above 109. Cruickshank and Bice later increased this figure to 1000 subjects and subjected the data to intensive analysis according to clinical subtype of cerebral palsy (1966). All these studies have employed the 1937 Stanford revision of the

TABLE 8–2

COMPARISON OF INTELLIGENCE TEST RATINGS OF CEREBRAL-PALSIED
CHILDREN FOR WHOM RATINGS WERE DETERMINED
IN FIVE RECENT STUDIES

	Miller and Rosenfeld	Strong Memorial Hospital Staff	Asher and Schonnel	Holoran	Heilman	Combined Data
	% of	% of	% of	% of	% of	% of
Estimated intellectual level	261	90	340	133	178	1,002
Mentally defective	49	43	47	36	47	45
Borderline dull	25	30	28	38	30	30
Average and above	26	26	25	26	23	35

SOURCE: From A. Heilman, Intelligence in cerebral palsy. *The crippled child*, 1952, *30*, 12. By permission.

Binet Intelligence Scale as a basis of their evaluations. It is recognized that the Binet-type tests are not the most satisfactory measures of intellectual evaluation for severely disabled children. However, the independent nature of the studies which have been cited, the knowledge that the psychologists involved in the studies were exceedingly well prepared for their responsibilities, and the increased understanding which clinical psychologists now have regarding the problems of mental measurement with handicapped children lend stature to these studies and credence to their collective findings.

The large population of cerebral-palsied children reported by Hopkins, Bice, and Colton, and later analyzed in greater statistical detail by Bice and Cruickshank, supports the other studies with respect to the percentages of cerebral-palsied children in the several classifications of intelligence. Some minor differences were noted particularly relating to the triplegia spastic group, but the meaning of these differences is not clear and is certainly not basic to psychological or educational planning.

Taibl (1951), utilizing Raven's Progressive Matrices Test, examined 115 cerebral-palsied children who ranged in age from 6 years to adulthood. The school-grade placement of the subjects was from grade one through grade eight with the exception of grade five. No high-school students were represented in his study, although two university students were included. The group consisted of sixty-nine spastics, six ataxics, one rigidity, and four mixed types. Seventy-two of the children were educationally classified as either "special class" or "ungraded group." The findings indicated that the cerebral-palsied children of Taibl's population ranged from intellectually superior to mentally defective, the distribution not being a "normal" one. The performance of the spastic group was in keeping with the distribution of intelligence scores in earlier studies cited. The athetoid group, however, showed a close relationship to normal comparative groups. In general the author concludes that the cerebral-palsied children perform on Raven's Progressive Matrices in a manner closely similar to that of other North American children. This points to the need for further examination of the problem, because his findings are in contrast to those of Bice, Holoran, Heilman, Asher, Miller, and others. Taibl also states that he is encouraged in the use of Raven's Progressive Matrices as a test for cerebral-palsied children. A later statement by Banks and Sinha (1951), however, indicates that the average reliability (0.88) of the matrices is considerably smaller than that given by Raven and "appreciably below the minimum needed for a satisfactory test of intelligence. Since the date of this comment, no rigorous statistical treatment of the matrices has taken place, although they are widely used. The Taibl data are open to question.

Because cerebral palsy is not a homogeneous system of symptoms, and because persons with this diagnosis vary one from another in numerous ways, attempts have been made to differentiate the intellectual functioning of various subgroups. Comparing intelligence-test scores after a fourteen-year lapse, Klapper, Zelda, and Birch (1967) found that, in general, retest scores indicated a significant increase in IQ for the sample. However, the greatest variability occurred in the paraplegic and monoplegic subgroups, and the least variability in those having hemiplegia and athetosis. Prediction of retest scores was most difficult in those who had originally tested in the 75 to 89 IQ range. Wedell's (1961) retesting perceptual ability of spastic hemiplegic children after six years indicated considerable rise in performance levels. All children improved on at least one test, and more than half improved on four or more tests. He noted that superiority of right hemiplegics over the left group persisted. Additional support for age differences in performance was provided by Delaney (1962), who reported that younger subjects (aged 4 to 10 years) taking four perceptually oriented tests scored higher than an older group (aged 10 to 18 years) on all subtests, total score, and mental age. However, when the scores were translated into IQs, the younger group was found to be superior. Spastic children and those with extra-pyramidal tract injuries could not be differentiated on three of the four subtests. However, the extrapyramidal group

did perform better on the Goldstein-Scheerer Test. In this instance, visual and visual-motor perception were found to be positively related to mental age. The role of chronological age is suggested by Hirschenfang and Benton (1965), indicating that the intelligence-test scores of cerebral-palsied children tend to rise with age. They concluded that it takes a longer time for such children to reach maturity mentally.

In performance comparisons of spastic and athetoid children, Katz noted no differentiation on Stanford-Binet scores in either mental age or IQ terms. In an investigation of reading skills, Jones (1966) found that athetoids tend to suffer more severely from disordered eye movements, but that the frequency of such defects was greater among spastics. Consequently, measures of intellectual ability that rely upon some degree of reading speed may be influenced by the visual factors described in this study.

Psychologists have been troubled by the sources of invalidity that may lie even within the best-designed measures of intellectual ability when such measures are used with cerebral-palsied children. In addition to exercising great caution in using the standardized instructions, time limits, and test materials, examiners have been comparing the disabled child with the normal groups assembled by the test-makers. As a consequence, great reliance has been placed on the judgment of the well-trained and experienced examiner whose observations during the testing session are considered more appropriate than are indiscriminate uses of numerical scores. Simultaneously, the search for valid and functional instruments goes on. This search often takes the form of comparisons among respected standarized instruments in the hope that one or another, in original or adapted form, will provide a ready yardstick of intellectual functioning, especially for individuals with cerebral palsy. Dunn and Harley (1969) in a comparison of the results yielded by the Peabody Picture Test, the Ammons, the Van Alstyne, and the Columbia Mental Maturity Tests, concluded that all four tests had utility as predictors of the school success of children with cerebral palsy, correlating as they did in the .80s with teacher ratings. The Peabody and the Ammons tests were more useful with a wider range of age groups than the other two tests examined. In fact, the Van Alstyne seemed applicable to children whose mental age was below 8.0, whereas the Columbia had its greatest value in use with children with MAs above 4.0. Similarly, Ando (1968), comparing the values for the cerebral-palsied on the Peabody Picture Vocabulary Test with the Verbal Scale on the Wechsler Intelligence Scale for Children, found the two instruments to be highly correlated. If anything, the Peabody scores were less affected by the degree of physical and speech limitations in cerebral-palsied children. In another study with a sample of cerebral-palsied children, Hammill and Orvis (1966) noted that the Peabody Picture Vocabulary Test does not overlap, but is supplementary to scores obtained on tests of sound discrimination and abstraction.

In assessing the values of the Gesell Developmental Scale for young cerebral-palsied children, Sievers and Norman (1961) conclude that physical, visual, and speech handicaps and limited life experiences tended to depress children's scores and to give evidence of retardation. Older cerebral-palsied children who were given the Stanford-Binet seemed to do less well than expected in verbally describing objects, forming blocks into a bridge, and working with picture stimuli, owing to problems of perception, life experience, and limited environments. Finally, with cerebral-palsied children aged 14 years and older, these authors found the Wechsler-Bellevue Verbal to be relatively accurate in assessing intellectual ability. As a caution to examiners and teachers, they advise intra-individual rather than inter-individual comparisons, and selective alteration of the standarized testing conditions in accordance with the needs of the child. In still another

comparison study concerning three well-known tests, Richardson and Kobler (1955) concluded that the Binet, the Ammons Full-Range Picture Vocabulary Test, and the Raven's Progressive Matrices correlated quite well with each other when used with a sample of thirty-two cerebral-palsied children 61 to 138 months of age. The Raven's and the Ammons were recommended for use with severely handicapped children because they both elicit nodding and pointing responses. However, it was noted that the Binet produced an acceptable score in the cases in this sample, including a basal age.

Discussion about the most favorable techniques of assessing the intellectual functioning of cerebral-palsied children continues. Allen (1960) focused upon the biological fact of neurological impairment, considering it an important, but not the only, factor to be taken into consideration in evaluating the individual. Thus, perceptual processes are significant as reflected in test behaviors. Because these test behaviors in the cerebral-palsied constitute an atypical situation, the psychological evaluation is useful when regarded as an approximation of individual potentialities and current efficiency. In line with the thinking of some specialists in the field, Cotton (1941) departed from standardized batteries and worked with a custom series in testing spastic children in his sample. This series consisted of a sorting technique, a string pattern test, completion tests, and pattern-memory tests. As the author views it, this series constitutes an effective mental test that is especially adapted for spastic children.

Other investigators have attempted to adapt standardized instruments for use with cerebral-palsied children. In working with the Stanford-Binet, using a "pointing modification method," Katz (1955) prepared tables indicating the physical capacities required for various test items, enabling an examiner to select those items that are within the physical range of the subject. Allen and Collins reported on the selection of tests that were found suitable for psychological evaluation purposes by a cerebral palsy clinic team. Among the tests they selected were: the Ammons Full-Range Picture Vocabulary Test, the Columbia Mental Maturity Test, Raven's Progressive Matrices, the Leiter International Performance Scale, the Cattell Infant Intelligence Scale, the Gesell Preliminary Behavior Inventory Scale, and the Stanford-Binet. In light of the nature of the limitations found in any sample of cerebral-palsied children, adaptations may be required in these instruments from time to time.

In accordance with the feeling of some examiners that special tests are needed for severely disabled children, Haeussermann (1952) developed test items that require minimal response from the child—usually affirmation or negation. Although the level of abstractness of these test items increases progressively, the response modality remains the same. Presenting items to the child that are either life-size concrete objects or large, clear pictures, the examiner offers him at least two alternatives to be indicated in any manner possible. This individualized approach, relying heavily upon observations of the examiner rather than upon standardized procedures, is based upon the tester's knowledge of the child (familiarity with the case record is recommended) and awareness of such problems as immaturity and infantilization, negation, experience deprivation, concretization, mental retardation, visual difficulties, inaccessibility to human speech, delayed responses, and behavior deviations. In another attempt to develop a custom-made battery, Peters (1964) combined nine subtests into an instrument that presents stimulus tasks on graduated levels of concreteness until relative abstractness of objects, agents, and actions are reached. This battery is thought to measure developmental aspects of the conceptual components of presymbolic behavior.

Although the references noted above do not designate solutions to all testing problems in cerebral palsy, they do suggest that standardized measurement may be less informative about the cerebral-palsied child than other children. The pervasive physical, social, and neurological effects of this disability usually generate such great differences from the usual in the testing situation that comparisons with non-disabled norms and the imposition of ordinary testing procedures become exceedingly risky. In place of definite quantitative mental ages, IQs, and other test score variants, the psychologist and educator are well advised to think in terms of ranges and qualitative assessments. Generally, the most useful product of a testing experience is a workable estimate of both current intellectual functioning and estimated potential. In time, as experience with the child accumulates in the service situation and as repeated contacts are made with the examiner, these estimates can be revised. However, for the present, they serve as functional hypotheses concerning the child and allow tentative program decisions to be made for him. Although reports in the literature generally indicate a higher incidence of low intelligence-test scores among other children, it is probable that some part of this finding can be traced to the concepts and procedures used in assessing the handicapped group and to a changing population seeking community service. Classification is difficult because performance is influenced by all factors that enter into any testing situation, coupled with the physical, neurological, and environmental factors that make cerebral palsy such a complex condition.

This complex condition makes for a good example of all the issues being examined in this chapter. It is true that cerebral palsy cannot be viewed as a stereotype of crippling conditions, but for the purpose of study, this problem encompasses and illustrates the following concepts:

1. Cerebral palsy is affected differentially in the three major developmental areas—cognitive, affective, and physiological.

2. Cerebral palsy demonstrates the impact of certain variables on four developmental areas—visibility of condition, degree of crippling condition, attitudes of society, and environmental support systems.

3. Due to its usual early origin, the cerebral-palsy condition lends itself to analysis of ego functions which develop under the influence of many atypical circumstances.

4. The various physical, cognitive, and emotional involvements of cerebral palsy create a challenge for health professionals in terms of adapting a suitable means of quantitative and qualitative assessment, as well as providing for the uniquely individualized needs of such children.

For these reasons, the last section of the chapter has stressed the multifaceted problems of cerebral palsy. It is hoped that the reader can apply the information in the first section to the cerebral-palsy condition. In so doing, the reader should be more aware of and sensitive to the psychological development of cerebral-palsied children, and be able to generalize this acquired knowledge in all cases of crippled children and youth.

There is quite a contrast between the two sections of this chapter. The first, dealing with conceptual and theoretical frameworks relating to the psychological development of crippled children; the second, providing research data on psychometric variable of cerebral palsy, i.e., intelligence. It was felt that professionals and students working with crippled individuals should be exposed to information of both these types.

REFERENCES

ADLER, A. *The neurotic constitution.* New York: Dodd, Mead & Co., 1926.

——. *Study of organ inferiority and its physical compensation: A contribution to clinical medicine.* New York: Nervous and Mental Disease Publishing Co., 1917.

ALLEN, F. H., & PEARSON, G. H. J. The emotional problems of the physically handicapped child. *British Journal of Medical Psychology,* 1938, *8,* 212–235.

ALLEN, R. M. One point of view: Intellectual evaluation in cerebral palsy. *Exceptional Children,* 1960, *22,* 202–204.

ALLEN, R. M., & COLLINS, M. G. Suggestions for the administration of intelligence tests for those with cerebral palsy. Part I, *Cerebral Palsy Review,* 1955, *16,* 11–14.

AMMONS, R. B., & AMMONS, H. S. The Full-Range Picture Vocabulary Test: 1, preliminary scale. *Journal of Psychology,* 1949, *28,* 51–64.

ANDO, K. A comparative study of Peabody Picture Vocabulary Test and Wechsler Intelligence Scale for Children with a group of cerebral palsied children. *Cerebral Palsy Journal,* 1968, *29,* 7–9.

ASHER, P., & SCHONNEL, F. E. A survey of 400 cases of cerebral palsy in childhood. *Archives of Diseases of Children,* 1950, *25,* 360–379.

BANKS, C., & SINHA, U. An item analysis of the Progressive Matrices Test. *British Journal of Psychology, Statistical Section,* 1951, *4,* 91–94.

BARKER, R. G. The social psychology of physical disability. *Journal of Social Issues,* 1948, *4,* 28–38.

——, WRIGHT, B., & GORICK. *Adjustment to physical handicap and illness: A survey of the social psychology of physique and disability.* Bulletin 55. New York: Social Science Research Council, 1953.

————. Psychoses associated with somatic diseases that distort the body structure. *Archives of Neurology and Psychiatry,* 1934, *32,* 1000–1024.

BENDER, L. Psychoses associated with somatic diseases that distort body structure. *Archives of Neurology and Psychiatry,* 1934, *32,* 1000–1024.

————, & SILVER, A. A. Body image problems of the brain injured child. *Journal of Social Issues,* 1948, *4,* 84–89.

BICE, H., & CRUICKSHANK, W. M. Evaluation of intelligence. In W. M. Cruickshank (Ed.), *Cerebral palsy, its individual and community problems.* Syracuse, N.Y.: Syracuse University Press, 1966.

BILLINGS, H. K. An exploratory study of the attitude of non-crippled children toward crippled children in three selected elementary schools. *Journal of Experimental Education,* 1963, *31,* 381–387.

BLUM, L. H., BURGMEISTER, B., & LORGE, I. The Mental Maturity Scale for the Motor Handicapped. *School and Society,* 1951, *73,* 232.

BRADWAY, K. Birth lesions in identical twins. *American Journal of Orthopsychiatry,* 1937, *7,* 194–203.

BRAEN, B., & MASLING, J. M. Intelligence tests used with special groups of children. *Exceptional Children,* 1959, *21,* 42–45.

BRIGGS, P. F. The validity of WAIS Performance Subtests completed with one hand. *Journal of Clinical Psychology,* 1960, *16,* 318–320.

CENTERS, L., & CENTERS, R. A. A comparison of the body images of amputee and non-amputee children as revealed in figure drawings. *Journal of Projective Personality Assessment.* 1963, *27,* 158–165.

CLARK, L. P. What is the psychology of Little's Disease? *Psychoanalytic Review,* 1934, *21,* 131–145.

COMBS, R., & HARPER, J. Effects of labels on attitudes of educators toward handicapped children. *Exceptional Children,* 1967, *34,* 399–403.

COTTON, C. B. A study of the reactions of spastic children to certain test situations. *Journal of Genetic Psychology,* 1941, *58,* 27–44.

CRUICKSHANK, W. M. The impact of physical disability on social adjustment. *Journal of Social Issues,* 1948, *4,* 78–83.

————. A study of the relation of physical disability to social adjustment. *American Journal of Occupational Therapy,* 1952, *6,* 100–109.

————. *Psychology of exceptional children and youth.* Englewood Cliffs, N.J.: Prentice-Hall, Inc., 1963, 1971.

————, & BICE, H. V. Evaluation of Intelligence, Chapter 3 in W. M. Cruickshank (Ed.) *Cerebral Palsy,* 2nd Edition, pp. 101–134.

————, & HALLAHAN, D. P. *Perception and learning disabilities in children.* Syracuse: Syracuse University Press, Vols. 1 and 2, 1975.

DELACOTO, C. H. *Neurological organization and reading.* Springfield, Ill.: Charles C Thomas, 1966.

DELANEY, F. I. Cerebral palsy—An investigation into certain aspects of visual and visio-motor perception in children with cerebral palsy. *Dissertation Abstracts,* 1962, *28* (4-A).

DEMBO, T., LADIEU, G., & WRIGHT, B. A. *Adjustment to misfortune: A study in social-emotional relationships between injured and non-injured people.* Washington, D.C.: War Department, Office of the Surgeon General, 1948.

DIETRICH, S. *Hemophilia: A total approach to treatment and rehabilitation.* Los Angeles: Orthopedic Hospital, 1968.

DOLPHIN, J. E. Pathology of concept formation in children with cerebral palsy. *American Journal of Mental Deficiency,* 1951, *41,* 392–336.

DONOFRIO, A. F. A study of crippled children in an orthopedic hospital school. *Exceptional Children,* 1952, *18,* 33–38.

DREIKURS, R. The social psychological dynamics of physical disability. *Journal of Social Issues*, 1948, *4*, 39–54.

DUNN, L. M., & HARLEY, R. K. Comparability of Peabody, Ammons, Van Alstyne, and Columbia test scores with cerebral palsied children. *Exceptional Children*, 1969, *35*, 5–21.

FERNALD, M. R., & ARLITT, A. H. Psychological findings regarding crippled children. *School and Society*, 1925, *21*, 449–452.

FIELDING, B. B. *Attitudes and aspects of adjustment of the orthopedically handicapped woman.* Unpublished doctoral dissertation, Columbia University, 1950.

FISHMAN, S. *Self-concept and adjustment to leg protesis.* Unpublished doctoral dissertation, Columbia University, 1949.

FITZGERALD, D. C. Success-failure and TAT reactions of orthopedically handicapped and physically normal adolescents. *Personality*, 1951, *1*, 67–83.

———, & THEILL, E. A. Education of children with mental retardation accompanying cerebral palsy. *American Journal of Mental Deficiency*, 1953, *57*, 401–414.

FOURACRE, M. H., & THEILL, E. A. Education of children with mental retardation accompanying cerebral palsy. *American Journal of Mental Deficiency*, 1953, *57*, 401–414.

FREEDMAN, R. D. Emotional reactions of handicapped children. *Rehabilitation Literature*, 1967, *19*, 274–282.

GELLMAN, W. Roots of prejudice against the handicapped. *Journal of Rehabilitation*, 1959, *25*, 4–6.

GESELL, A., HALVERSON, H., THOMPSON, H., ILG, F., CARTNER, B., AMES, L., & AMATRUDA, C. *The First Five Years of Life.* New York: Harper & Row, 1940.

GIOVANNONI, J. Social role behavior and extent of social participation in disabled and non-disabled adolescents. *Dissertation Abstracts*, 1967, *27* (11-A).

GORDON, R. G., ROBERTS, J. A. F., & GRIFFITHS, R. Does poliomyelitis affect intellectual capacity? *British Medical Journal*, 1939, *2*, 802–805.

HAEUSSERMANN, E. *Evaluating the developmental level of preschool children handicapped by cerebral palsy.* New York: United Cerebral Palsy Association, Inc., 1952.

HAMMILL, I., & ORVIS, C. Relations among measures of language of cerebral palsy and mentally retarded children. *Cerebral Palsy Journal*, 1966, *1*, 8–9.

HANKS, J. R., & HANKS, L. M. The physically handicapped in certain nonoccidental societies. *Journal of Social Issues*, 1948, *4*, 11–20.

HARTMAN, H. Comments on the psychoanalytical theory of the ego. In *Psychoanalytic Study of the Child.* New Haven: Yale University Press, Vol. 5, 1950.

HARWAY, V. T. *Self-evaluation and reactions to success and failure experiences in orthopedically handicapped children.* Unpublished doctoral dissertation, University of Rochester, 1952.

HEILMAN, A. Intelligence in cerebral palsy. *The Crippled Child*, 1952, *30*, 11–13.

HIRSCHENFANG, S., & BENTON, J. Delayed intellectual development in cerebral palsy children. *Journal of Psychology*, 1965, *60*, 235–238.

HOLORAN, I. M. The incidence and prognosis of cerebral palsy. *British Medical Journal*, 1952, *4751*, 214–217.

HOPKINS, T. W., BICE, H. V., & COLTON, K. C. *Evaluation and education of the cerebral palsied child.* Washington, D.C.: Council for Exceptional Children, 1954.

JAFFE, J. What's in a name: Attitudes toward disabled persons. *Personnel and Guidance Journal*, 1967, *45*, 57–60.

JENKINS, R. L. Dissimilar identical twins: Result of brain injury at birth. *American Journal of Orthopsychiatry*, 1934, *5*, 39–42.

JONES, M. H. Pilot study of reading problems of cerebral palsied adults. *Developmental Medicine and Child Neurology*, 1966, *8*, 417–427.

JONES, R., GOTTFRIED, N. W., & OWENS, A. The social distance of the exceptional: A study at high school level. *Exceptional Children*, 1966, *32*, 551–556.

KATZ, E. Intelligence test performance of athetoid and spastic children with cerebral palsy. *Cerebral Palsy Review*, 1955, *16*, 17–19.

———. Method of selecting Stanford-Binet Intelligence Scale Tasks for evaluating the mental abilities of children severely handicapped by cerebral palsy. *Cerebral Palsy Review*, 1955, *16*, 14–17.

KLAPPER, R., ZELDA, A., & BIRCH, H. G. A fourteen-year follow-up study of cerebral palsy: Intellectual change and stability. *American Journal of Orthopsychiatry*, 1967, *37*, 540–547.

KLAPPER, Z. S., & WERNER, H. Developmental deviations in brain-injured (cerebral palsied) members of pairs of identical twins. *Quarterly Journal of Child Behavior*, 1950, *2*, 288–313.

KUBIE, L. S. Motivation and rehabilitation. *Psychiatry*, 1945, *8*, 69–78.

LANDIS, C., & BOLLES, M. M. *Personality and sexuality in the physically handicapped woman.* New York: Paul B. Hoeber, Inc., 1942.

LANGE, P. Frustration reactions of physically handicapped children. *Exceptional Children*, 1959, *25*, 355–357.

LANSDOWN, R., & POLAK, L. A study of the psychological effects of facial deformity in children. *Child Care and Health Development*, 1975, *1*, 85–91.

LEE, M. V. The children's hospital: a survey of the intelligence of crippled children. *Journal of Educational Research*, 1931, *23*, 164–167.

LEMKAU, P. V. Influence of handicapping conditions on child development. *Children*, 1961, *8*, 43–47.

LORD, E. E. *Children Handicapped by Cerebral Palsy.* New York: Commonwealth Fund, 1930.

LOWMAN, C. C. *Survey of the vocational, educational and social status of poliomyelitis patients.* New York: National Foundation for Infantile Paralysis, 1942.

MACHOVER, K. *Personality projection in the drawing of the human figure.* Springfield, Ill.: Charles C Thomas, 1949.

MCINTIRE, J. T. The incidence of feeblemindedness in the cerebral palsied. *American Journal of Mental Deficiency*, 1946, *50*, 491–494.

MCMICHAEL, J. K. *Handicap: A Study of Physically Handicapped Children and Their Families.* London: Stoples Press, 1971.

MENG, H. Zur socialpsychologie der korperbeschadigten: Ein beitrag zum problem der praktischen psycholhygiene. *Schweizer Archiv fur Neurologie und Psychiatrie*, 1938, *40*, 328–344.

MENNINGER, W. C. Emotional adjustments for the handicapped. *The Crippled Child*, 1949, *27*, 4.

MEYERSON, L. Physical disability as a social psychological problem. *Journal of Social Issues*, 1948, *4*, 2–10. (a)

———. Experimental injury: An approach to the dynamics of disability. *Journal of Social Issues*, 1948, *4*, 68–72. (b)

MICHAL-SMITH, H. Psychological factors in the therapist-patient relationship in the rehabilitation process. *Rehabilitation Literature*, 1962, *23*, 66–69.

MILLER, E. A. Cerebral palsied children. *Exceptional Children*, 1958, *24*, 298–302.

———, & ROSENFELD, G. The psychological evaluation of children with cerebral palsy and its implications for treatment. *Journal of Pediaatrics*, 1952, *61*, 613–622.

NEWELL, H. W. Differences in personalities in the surviving pair of identical triplets. *American Journal of Orthopsychiatry*, 1930, *1*, 61–80.

NUSSBAUM, J. An investigation of the relationship between the self-concept and reality orientation of adolescents with cerebral palsy. *Dissertation Abstracts*, 1962, *22*, 4410–4411.

PETERS, D. M. Developmental and conceptual components of the normal child: A comparative study with the cerebral palsy child. *Cerebral Palsy Review*, 1964, *25*, 3–7.

PHELPS, W. M. Characteristic psychological variations in cerebral palsy. *Nervous Child*, 1948, *7*, 10–13. (a)

————. Description and differentiation of types of cerebral palsy. *Nervous Child*, 1948, *8*, 107–127. (*b*)

PIAGET, J., & INHELDER, B. *The Psychology of the Child.* New York: Basic Books, 1969.

PINTNER, R., EISENSON, J., & STANTON, M. *The psychology of the physically handicapped.* New York: Appleton-Century-Crofts, 1941.

RICHARDSON, E., & KOBLER, F. Testing the cerebral palsied—A study comparing the Binet, Raven, and Ammons. *Exceptional Children*, 1955, *21*, 101–103; 108–109.

RICHARDSON, S. A., & ROYCE, J. Race and physical handicap in children's preference for other children. *Child Development*, 1968, *39*, 2, 467–480.

ROGERS, S., & D'EUGENIO, D. *Assessment and Application in Developmental Programming for Infants and Young Children*, D. S. Shafer and M. Moersch, Eds., Vol. 1. Ann Arbor: University of Michigan Press, 1977.

RUSALEM, H., & JENKINS, S. Attitudes of homebound students towards return to regular classroom attendance. *Exceptional Children*, 1961, *28*, 71–74.

SCHILDER, P. *The Image and Appearance of the Human Body.* New York: International Universities Press, 1950, pp. 14–15.

SCHNEIDER, D. M. The social dynamics of physical disability in army basic training. *Psychiatry*, 1947, *10*, 323–333.

SIEVERS, D. J., & NORMAN, R. D. Some suggestive results in psychometric testing of the cerebral palsied with Gesell, Binet, and Wechsler Scales. *Genetic Psychology*, 1961, *82*, 69–90.

SILBERBERG, N., & SILBERBERG, M. Hyperplexia-specific word recognition skills in young children. *Exceptional Children*, 1967, *34*, 41–42.

SPITZ, R. Hospitalization: An inquiry into the genesis of psychiatric conditions in early childhood. In *Psychoanalytic study of the child.*

New Haven: Yale University Press, Vol. 1, 1945.

STEIN, I., SUSSER, M., STAENGER, G., & MOROLDO, F. *Famine and human development: The Dutch hunger winter, 1944–45.* New York: Oxford University Press, 1975.

STRAUSS, F. The initiative of the crippled child. *The Crippled Child*, 1936, *13*, 164–165.

TAIBL, R. M. *An investigation of Raven's "Progressive Matrices" as a tool for the psychological evaluation of cerebral palsied children.* Unpublished doctoral dissertation, University of Nebraska, 1951.

THOMAS, A., & CHESS, S. *Temperament and Development.* New York: Brummer/Mazel Publishers, 1977.

TRIPPE, M. J. The social psychology of exceptional children, part II, in terms of factors of society. *Exceptional Children*, 1959, *26*, 71–75.

VERWOERDT, A. Psychopathological responses to the stress of physical illness. In Z. J. Lipowski (Ed.), *Advances in Psychosomatic Medicine.* Basel, Switzerland: Karger, 1972.

VON BAEYER, W. "Zur psychologie verkrüppelter kinder und jugendlichter," *Zeitschrift für Kinderferschung*, 1928, *34*, 229–292.

WEDELL, K. Follow-up study of perceptual ability in children with hemiplegia. *Little Clubs Clinic in Developmental Medicine*, 1973, *4*, 76–85.

WINKLER, H. *Psychische entwecklung and kruppeltum.* Leipzig: Leopold Voss, 1931.

WITTY, P. A., & SMITH, M. B. The mental status of 1,480 crippled children. *Educational Trends*, 1932, *1*, 22–24.

WURTZ, H. *Zerbrecht die krucken.* Leipzig: Leopold Voss, 1932.

WYSOCKI, B. Body image of crippled children as seen in Draw-a-Person Test behavior. *Perceptual and Motor Skills*, 1965, *21*, 499–504.

9 Psychological Problems of Children and Youth with Chronic Medical Disorders

Joseph Newman

Ph.D., Professor of Education and Psychology, Rehabilitation Counseling Program, School of Education, University of Pittsburgh.

Since the earlier editions of this book, there have been an increased number of published works in the psychological literature on chronic disorders among children and youth. With this growth, theoretical concepts guiding research have become diversified, and the once dominant psychoanalytic approach, as Shontz earlier stated, has receded into a more general psychodynamic influence.

The literature on chronic medical disorders among children and youth emphasizes the general elements present in all disorders, but with recognition that there are characteristics specific to certain conditions. Thus, a fundamental postulate is affirmed—that there are more similarities in the psychological aspects of different chronic disorders than dissimilarities. Also, it is important to note the increased psychological sophistication of the pediatrician and other medical specialists who report on childhood chronic disorders. Child psychiatrists apply a wide range of psychological concepts, including behavioral theories, to their studies.

THEORETICAL MODELS IN THE PSYCHOLOGY OF ILLNESS

In the early period of psychological study of chronic disorders, when the influence of *psychoanalytic theory* was dominant, the chief focus of research efforts was on parent-child relationships. However, variables developed proved to be complicated and studies were both time consuming and expensive, with the result that research was limited in both output and impact. The generalizations derived from the psychoanalytic frame of reference had less than adequate empirical foundations. Nevertheless, psychoanalysis continues to influence research among chronically ill children. The explanation for this phenomenon would seem to be the medical context in which much of the research is conducted by investigators with medical backgrounds, principally psychiatrists and pediatricians. Frequently, the research is collaborative between medical men and non-medical professionals, usually psychologists and social workers.

A later research influence came from the general field of psychology, especially from learning theory. The attractiveness of this approach was in the ready availability of testable hypotheses and developed techniques, particularly from studies in developmental psychology. There was interest in the effects of stress or strong simulation during infancy and early years. The importance of this psychological influence is that it enlarged research activities from an almost exclusive focus on intrapsychic phenomena to include the social environment.

When there is an involvement of psychological factors in an illness, the illness is generally referred to as a *psychosomatic disorder*. Such psychosomatic or psychophysiologic disorders represent a continuum of physiological reactions that occur in response to a variety of life experiences or in association with emotional status, whether as a cause or a consequence. The reactions may range from minor physiological changes to those resulting in severe tissue damage. Everyone has had symptoms such as heartburn, palpitations, or dry mouth as consequences of emotional experience without pathology in the gastrointestinal, cardiovascular, or secretory systems. Psychosomatic considerations are generally recognized in contemporary pediatrics. Prugh (1963) states:

> The concept of comprehensive pediatric care rests upon two basic assumptions: (1) both somatic and psychologic factors may act as predisposing, contributory, precipitating, and perpetuating forces in illness; (2) the prevention of disease and the promotion of healthy growth and adaptation must include attention to all aspects of the developing child's psychobiological equipment as well as the psychological setting in which he exists (p. 246).

Within this context, there is no dichotomization of wholly somatic or completely psychological disease. At one time, psychosomatic disease was thought to represent a group of specific diseases, each of which had its own psychodynamic constellation. Such specificity is no longer advanced; rather, a more general "specificity" is advanced which links a number of specific dysfunctions. Some studies suggest that all "psychosomatic" patients, regardless of their bodily disorders, have some personality characteristics in common (Green, 1968).

In the past, most of the literature in psychosomatic disorders was based upon studies of adults. This is less true today with a growing literature dealing specifically with children and youth. It is possible that psychosomatic disorders are more prevalent among adults and that they are more readily identified. On the other hand, there is little question that psychosocial stresses in children may be associated with significant physiological changes.

Theoretically, the questions confronting workers in the field may be stated as follows: (1) How are life experiences translated into physiological changes? (2) What factors determine which persons are most likely to develop psychosomatic disorders? and (3) What factors determine the "choice" of the organ system? (Lipton, Steinschneider, & Richmond, 1966).

Several theoretical models have been developed to explicate these problems. Already mentioned are the approaches derived from psychoanalytic concepts. One approach postulated that psychosomatic disorders are basically conversion reactions and represent symbolic expressions of repressed feelings. For any individual, the process whereby this takes place may be understood only after knowledge is gained of repressed thoughts and feelings with elaboration of the symbolic meanings associated with them. There is little support for this formulation.

Departing from the orthodox Freudian approach, Dunbar (1948) attempted to develop personality profiles in which specific personality constellations were associated with specific disorders. Again, *specificity theories* have not been supported in research studies.

Alexander (1950) presented a model in which he hypothesized that each conflict situation and emotional state are accompanied by a specific pattern of physiological alteration. Persisting strong unresolved conflicts may lead to psychophysiological disorders. The nature of the conflict situation determines to some extent the selection of the disorder organ; predisposition also plays a role. Alexander's model is also a specificity theory that has not been substantiated.

More prevalent currently are the *non-*

specific theories that attribute psychosomatic disease to general psychological stress reactions. Some writers emphasize the common origins of many diverse psychosomatic symptoms (Kubie, 1954). Thus, psychosomatic disturbances are multiplexly expressed in various systems of the body and not in just one organ system. They are the end results of series of events. These series of events may appear to have been initiated by some easily visible life stress such as school failure, injury, or death. However, the way in which a person reacts to stress is a highly individual matter, which can be understood only by appreciation of the many factors operating in that person's situation (Ehrentheil, 1959; Stevenson & Matthews, 1953).

Hence, the psychological component in any illness is variable; it may range from incidental to central importance. Starr (1955) has conceptualized a schema, a psychosomatic spectrum, in which he describes a continuum of psychological complications as they may occur in all types of clinical illness. The range is from illnesses in which the psychological factor is regarded as causative to those illnesses in which it is incidental.

In recent years, the *role of the family* has come to receive greater emphasis and this attention has developed from recognition of the family unit as a significant force in the life of the chronically ill child to a central position (Mattson, 1972; Prugh, 1971; Steinhauser, Mushin, & Rae-Grant, 1974). A particularly influential approach is that of Minuchin, who has applied systems theory to therapeutic work with families. These considerations are applicable to every type of medical disorder affecting children and youth (Minuchin, 1974).

In the explication of the complexly related somatic and psychological states, it is not necessary to analyze an example of each variety of disorder along the continuum of psychosomatic reactions. From among the chronic disorders, we have chosen four severe and common disorders: asthma, diabetes mellitus, heart ailments, and tuberculosis.

Asthma, diabetes, and heart ailments are the more common physical conditions for children (Mattson, 1972). These disorders illustrate two psychosomatic relationships—psychophysiological and somatopsychological. However, before discussing these specific diseases, some observations and findings should be presented about significant psychological factors in illness in general among children. Basic to our approach is Thompson's observation (1959) that "the living organism is a dynamic and developing system, variable in its functioning according to inherent genetic characteristics which interact with selected environmental antecedents. We now know that alteration in one part of this system can have widespread and enduring consequences" (p. 1).

INFLUENCE OF EARLY EXPERIENCE IN CHRONIC DISORDERS

Noted previously was the theoretical and research interest in the effects of early experience on individuals. Practically no one today denies the importance of early experience. Much of this interest, to be sure, stemmed from Freud's writings and led to investigations of the effects of trauma, such as the effects of inadequate mothering, but with the research sophistication and theoretical refinements derived from experimental psychology. Both of these research areas are significant to a psychology of illness.

A crucial component of Freud's notions about early experience was that the primary effects of trauma were on emotional development. One avenue of investigation was to relate psychosomatic disorders to emotional traumas having their origin in the very early life of the individual. Mohr and others (1955) studied a group of psychosomatically ill children. They found that these children were consistently exposed to inadequate mothering care during the first year of life.

In a later report, Garner and Wenar

(1959) more systematically explored the hypothesis that susceptibility to psychosomatic illness in children develops in the first year of life when somatic response patterns are laid down in an atmosphere of close but mutually frustrating mother-child interaction. Thus, mothers of physically ill children had positive attitudes toward pregnancy and early child care; mothers of neurotic children had negative attitudes in those respects; and mothers of psychosomatically ill children had positive attitudes toward pregnancy but not toward child care. Mothers in this last group were seen as ambitious, controlling, driving women who victimized their children. They expected conformity but lacked tenderness and the spontaneous enjoyment of children. They were mothers who "loved" their children and did all the "right" things. Although this study did not have a control group and the number of subjects was relatively small, it is regarded as a contribution to the literature about psychosomatically ill children.

In a study (Carter & Chess, 1951) of factors influencing the adjustment of organically handicapped children, the most prominent single factor in determining whether anxiety would become an important element seemed to be parental attitude. It was found that the amount of anxiety and the manner in which it found expression bore no predictable relationship to the handicap per se. There was no predictable relationship between the severity of the handicap and parental attitudes, such as overprotection or underprotection. The amount of parental anxiety and the manner in which it found expression seemed more related to the parents' own particular emotional needs and basic attitudes toward the child than to realistic elements of the handicap.

Again, Tuttman (1955), in an investigation of the influence of the severity of disability and parental authoritarianism in the child's acceptance of disability, found that children of authoritarian parents had more difficulty in accepting disability than did children of less authoritarian parents.

Parsons (1952) has emphasized that the concept of illness as applied to the sick adult cannot be applied to the sick child. The immature child cannot be expected to assume the same roles and levels of responsibility as the adult. For example, the child cannot be held responsible for getting out of his condition by act of will. He is not held responsible in usual dealings with others and, therefore, is not to be held responsible for recognition of his own condition, its disabilities, and his need for help. Therefore, third parties—parents—must play an especially important role in the child's illness.

The most severe trauma faced by the chronically ill child is separation from parents, especially the mother, when hospitalization becomes necessary. This trauma is indeed a common experience. The earlier research on maternal separation led to broad generalizations, many of which are now regarded as oversimplified interpretations. Yarrow (1964) does not regard separation from the mother as a simple, delimited event with simple predictable consequences.

> The meaning to the child of the event of separation and the experiences subsequent to separation will also vary with individual and experiential factors, such as the child's unique vulnerabilities and sensitivities, his developmental stage, and his experiences prior to separation. Separation that occurs after a long period of indifferent parental care or overt rejection and hostility is likely to have a different meaning to the child from that representing a break in an intimate, protective, gratifying relationship. It is also likely that the meaning of separation to the child will vary with such characteristics of the experience as: the degree of concomitant trauma; whether it is permanent or temporary; and if temporary, whether it is of long or short duration; whether any contact is maintained with the parents; and whether it is the first or one in a series of similar experiences (p. 91).

Similarly, Rutter (1974) believes that early attitudes toward the concept of maternal deprivation were uncritical. He emphasized the importance of the conditions during the period of separation—its duration and the presence of another person to whom the child can relate. A distinction must be made between the failure to form affective bonds and bond disruption, if the child has a stable figure with whom a relationship can be formed during the separation. Rutter questions whether the bond has to be specifically with the natural mother and whether it could be someone else, not necessarily a female. Thus, separation does not have to be a deprivation, especially a loss of "mothering."

In summary, the effects of separation from the mother have been the subject for much reassessment. It may be said that a more balanced orientation exists in that the effects of maternal deprivation do not inevitably and inexorably lead to psychologically disastrous consequences, nor is there a negation of the importance of early maternal care. It seems clear that all separation experiences cannot be equated as to their consequences. Such experiences vary widely from minor events with which most children are able to cope to very traumatic disruptions of relationships. Important here are the situational circumstances.

HOSPITALIZATION

Studies of hospitalization for children emphasize that separation from parents and from familiar surroundings is but one element in the total experience. The other elements identified are feelings of helplessness and the increased dependency associated with illness, threats to bodily integrity through medical and surgical procedures, and, finally, effects of a strange environment filled with strange people (Shore, 1967).

Interest in the effects of hospitalization was stimulated by the studies of Spitz & Wolf (1946) and Goldfarb (1947). They showed that favorable conditions of shelter, food, medical care, schooling, and supervised social life were not in themselves sufficient to assure adequate physical growth and emotional development. Developmental retardation, emotional disturbances, and language dysfunctions were reported. Influential also were reports of World War II experiences in England with children separated from their families. Evacuated children displayed evidences of severe personality damage (Freud & Burlingham, 1944).

The lack of intellectual and social stimulation was judged to be critical in the institutional situation, not separation from the mother. It was this observation that led to efforts to modify institutional circumstances to prevent harmful effects to whatever extent possible. Both the age of the child and the duration of institutional care were found to be significant; the earlier the age of placement and the longer the duration, the greater the deleterious effects.

These findings had face validity in application to hospitalized children and spurred investigations of the effects of hospitalization (Bowlby, 1951). The hospitalized child usually has a different psychological situation than the institutionalized child; he has a family, an illness, and continued contact with parents. It was the work of Bowlby et al. (1952, 1956) in England and particularly that of his associate, Robertson (1959, 1962), that advanced the hypothesis that maternal separation experiences during hospitalization were pathogenic. Robertson stated that when hospital admission deprives a child of a warm, intimate, and continuing relationship with his mother, particularly before the age of 4, he reacts emotionally in a characteristic manner. The child will first protest, strongly and consciously demonstrating his grief. Next he will be in despair; that is, less active in showing a conscious need of his mother but experiencing an increasing hopelessness. He may become withdrawn, apathetic, and may make no demands. Sometimes this stage is presumed to indicate that distress has lessened. A common remark is, "He was quite settled until his mother came." With short hospitalization, some children just reach this stage or may go home in the stage of protest. In the next phase, denial, the child shows more interest in his surroundings. He may appear stable and sociable. However, this is believed to be a superficial impression and actually is a manifestation of a defensive or adaptive maneuver. When the previously lamented mother comes, the child will hardly know her and will no longer cry when she leaves. He is reluctant to leave the hospital. Robertson believes that the aftermath of long hospitalization in the early years is an extended period of serious emotional maladaptation. The two main dangers of hospitalization are the traumatic (shock of losing the mother and the pain and fright of treatment) and the deprivational—a function of lengthy separation.

In this country, studies were also stimulated, and the most notable were those by Prugh and his associates (1953, 1954, 1955). The purpose of the studies was to investigate the nature of the effects of brief hospitalization upon both children and parents. Two groups of 100 children, matched for age, sex, and diagnosis and hospitalized for relatively acute illnesses and for relatively short periods of time, formed the basis of one investigation. The results supported the impression of other investigators that children under three years of age are the most susceptible to the negative aspects surrounding hospital care. Separation from the mother is often interpreted as a punishment or desertion. This reaction, separation anxiety, was most frequent among the younger children. It was also common in older age groups but in less severe form and not as frequently. Among the older children, anxiety was the most common persisting posthospital reaction. Depression and various disturbances, such as in feeding, sleeping, and toilet behavior, were noted. Regressive phenomena constituted the most common defense. Among older children, withdrawing behavior became common. Frequent among all children was the reaction to treatment and diagnostic procedures as punishment. In the main, children who showed the most successful adjustment to hospitalization were those who seemed to have the most satisfying relationship with their parents, especially the mother. The highest positive correlation was reported between apparent adaptive capacity and adjustment to hospitalization. Children with limited adaptive capacity showed the most severe reaction to the total experience of hospitalization. The reactions of the parents to hospitalization were found to be dependent upon the adjustment of the parents and the nature of their relationships with the child.

Other studies revealed essentially similar findings. Gofman, Buckman, and Schade (1957) undertook to assess the preparation for hospitalization among 100 children, ages 3 to 15 years, as well as their understanding of illness and their reaction to hospital care. They found that 75 percent of their group were not prepared for hospitalization. It was felt by these investigators that children as young as 3 or 4 years of age could understand something of their illness and the necessary treatment if explanations were made in terms suited to their levels. Marlens (1960) compared emotional attitudes toward self and the environment for a group of children hospitalized and a group with similar complaints but not hospitalized. The hospitalized children were significantly higher in feelings of rejection and punishment, in somatic preoccupation, and in anxiety and depression. There was no difference between the groups in feelings of hostility.

At the University of Maryland Hospital, Glaser (1960), by means of group discussions with mothers, elicited descriptions of the reactions of their children to hospitalization. These reactions included: increased dependency needs and physiological regression in behavior; withdrawal from others; and need for continued contact with the outside world. This last reaction made mothers fearful that mention of friends, pets, and other familiar aspects of home life would make the child homesick. Actually, it was found that talking about these matters was helpful. The technique of group discussions for mothers was found to be useful in dealing with the mother's anxieties, fears, and misconceptions about the illness and the hospitalization.

In another study, Vaughan (1957) undertook to investigate the attitudes toward hospitalization and an impending operation for correction to strabismus in a group of twenty children and a group of twenty controls. He found that all children had varied, bizarre, and sometimes frightening ideas about the hospital. The children reflected the parents' anxieties. However, Vaughan provided (to his experimental group) simple and brief explanations and reassurances of what to expect. He found that this was enough to result in a significant benefit.

Schaffer and Callender (1959) studied twenty-five infants hospitalized less than two weeks. They found distinct differences between infants under 7 months of age and infants between 7 and 12 months of age. The younger infants adapted to the hospitalization with little evidence of disturbance. The older infants showed a variety of disturbances associated with maternal separation—marked anxiety with strangers, desperate clinging to mothers, and vigorous crying when the mother left.

These and similar experiences led to actions to minimize, if not eliminate, the hazards of hospitalization for children. This subject was the concern of a study group of the World Health Organization (WHO) in meetings held in Stockholm in September 1954. It was pointed out that the best place to care for the ill child is at home, that the child under five finds it difficult to understand the meaning of illness. Even for an adult, going to a hospital is a major event. For the small child, the break in relationships occasioned by hospitalization seems final and irrevocable.

The remedial efforts suggested by the WHO meetings (Capes, 1956) proceeded along three lines: elimination of force or actual pain in contact between staff and child; preparation for hospitalization; and

continuing close contact between the mother and child. This last proved to be most controversial and has met the most resistance.

In England these recommendations were incorporated in the Platt Report of 1959 (Robertson, 1962). This report encouraged hospitals to provide unlimited visiting to all children in hospitals and to develop living-in arrangements for mothers of preschool patients.

Students of the problem insisted that the deleterious effects were not inevitable. Further, they were agreed that, with preventive measures, hospitalization could be a constructive experience (Solnit, 1960). The result has been that, today, children's hospitals and pediatric units in general hospitals do not emphasize medical care alone; they pay attention to psychosocial and developmental factors as well. Programs have been instituted to prepare children and parents for admission (Belmont, 1970; Green & Haggerty, 1968; Magnus, 1974).

On the other hand, Illingworth (1958) has questioned whether the case has been overstated, that children who experience institutionalization and similar forms of deprivation, especially in early life, commonly develop psychopathic or affectionless characters. He believes that exaggeration of the risk can cause much unnecessary anxiety in parents and might possibly delay necessary hospital treatment; it can also lead to the minimizing of risk or denial of its existence. On the basis of his experience in the follow-up of all children discharged from a medical ward in an English hospital, Illingworth found that it was exceptional for the child to show behavior problems which could be ascribed directly to hospital stay and experiences. Certainly, the majority of children cry in hospitals, especially young children, when parents leave at the end of visiting time. Some may show other types of emotional behavior. But the existence of this sort of behavior does not mean that the hospital experience leads to behavior problems which persist for weeks or months after discharge. Indeed, it would be surprising if young children below 4 years of age were not upset by hospital admission. Nevertheless, Illingworth believes that the problem of psychological trauma is significant, and the fact that "only a small majority" show any lasting ill effects must not be a basis for minimizing it.

At this point in discussing remedial and preventive measures for the harmful consequences of hospitalization, it would be instructive to scan briefly similar actions with regard to the broader problems of institutionalization. Certainly, the findings on the destructive effects of institutional care on young children led to an avoidance, if not rejection, of all forms of group care for young children. However, since alternatives were not easy to find, exploration of changes in institutional child care was begun. This development was reinforced by reevaluations and reinterpretations of the early studies. The new findings provided a more precise understanding of the parameters of institutional environments that are associated with deleterious effects of institutional life. Thus, bases were established for changes in institutional care.

A report of one such institutional effort concerned eighty-five children between the ages of 3 months and 3 years (Flint, 1966). Despite numerous difficulties and resistances, many and varied changes were introduced. Marked alterations were made in the physical environment to increase the quality and variety of sensory stimulation. Especially significant were the attempts to create an environment conducive to the development of feelings of individuality in the children. Each child was given special possessions—clothes, bedcovers, toys—with some unique characteristics. The management of routines was altered to provide greater flexibility and recognition of the role of the caretakers to emphasize individualized relationships with the children. The number of caretakers was increased to enhance the possibility of closer relationships. A central element in those relationships was the effort to elicit initiative and to encourage persistence in mastering simple defined tasks.

Several factors have been identified as contributing to behavior problems encountered in hospital stays. First is the disturbance in parent-child relationship before admission or after; the better this relationship, the less likely the development of disturbance. Lack of or inadequate preparation for admission is another factor. A third is unwise or excessive preparation as a result of anxiety on the part of the parents. Frequently encountered are threats to the child—to do as they are told or lose love. Also implicated is a lack of daily visiting. Parental anxiety during visits, along with unkept promises, are potent in creating problems. Parental attitudes on discharge, overindulgence and the like, especially after serious illness, are important. Age at hospitalization is a critical factor; children are likely to be susceptible to psychological damage from about 7 months to 7 years, with the most vulnerable period from 7 months to 3 years. Hospital procedures also stimulate anxieties regarding bodily injury.

Unquestionably, there is broad recognition of the problem of psychological trauma for hospitalized children and the realization that many areas of hospital procedure should be modified for the welfare of the child. The measures recommended are implicit in the discussion of factors believed to be causative of disturbance. But the very first consideration should be to determine whether hospitalization could be avoided, if the illness could be treated at home. When admission to a hospital becomes necessary, then there should be appropriate preparation for admission. Such preparation would depend upon the age, experience, cultural background, and the type of illness of the child (Green & Haggerty, 1968). Where possible, admission should be to a children's hospital rather than to a general hospital and certainly never to an adult ward. Upon admission, the child should not be separated from the mother;

the mother should go up to the ward with him. Daily visiting should occur. Routines should be explained to the child. Unpleasant sights and sounds should be avoided, and painful procedures should be carried out in treatment rooms away from the observations of children. Ward routines should be conducted with some consideration of the child as an understanding individual with feelings. Educational and recreational facilities should be available. Staff contacts with family, especially the mother, should be maintained either through individual or group meetings. Mason (1968) suggests the use of "worry work," a concept developed by Irving Janis, in which attention is paid to the anxieties of the child, and those of the parents. They are encouraged to express emotions and feelings, to ask questions, to participate actively in every way. They are given information as the occasion arises. The relationship with the physician is strengthened and his role as a psychotherapist is strongly encouraged (Belmont, 1970; Solnit, 1968).

These measures, pediatric authorities are convinced, would contribute to positive experiences as a result of the hospital stay— in that the solution of mother-child problems would be furthered and healthy maturational forces encouraged. There are many constructive forces within the hospital, and with the aid of these forces (for example, parent substitutes and family substitutes) the child may grow emotionally (Blom, 1958).

A study incorporating such preventive measures was conducted by Faust (1952), involving 140 children hospitalized for tonsillectomies. The preventive procedures included preparation for the hospital experience through discussion with parents, helping the parents prepare the children for the hospitalization, careful timing, and elective hospitalization in terms of the child's developmental stage and emotional state in relation to other experiences in the home, such as the arrival of a sibling or a move to a new home or school. In the hospital itself,

changes permitted the mother to remain with the child. Potentially traumatic procedures such as enemas and venipunctures were kept to a minimum. Most of the children in the immediate postoperative period, and again three months later, showed no adverse effects. Only a small number, thirteen, displayed changes indicative of emotional trauma. Generally, younger children showed more adverse behavior changes but these were considered essentially mild in nature. The children more seriously affected were those who had been sensitized to separation through previous traumatic experiences and those who had poor relationships with their parents prior to hospitalizations.

A more recent study by Wolfer and Visintainer (1975) demonstrated the effectiveness of a systematic preparation program for children and their parents. Eighty children were divided into an experimental group and a control group as they were admitted for surgery. The experimental group and parents received a continuing program of psychologic preparation and support. The experimental group displayed significant gains over the control group in indices of upset behavior, potential anxiety, cooperation, recovery of functions, and posthospital adjustment.

As a concluding note on hospitalization, two related developments should be recorded. One is the trend toward restricted use of hospitalization for an ever-narrowing set of conditions which can be regarded as "absolutely necessary." Conditions for which hospitalization was formerly required are now treated on an outpatient basis. This is the second development—the growth of outpatient facilities or ambulatory pediatrics (Green & Haggerty, 1968). It is to be expected that there will be further attention and development in ambulatory pediatrics since more than half of the children in hospitals are there for surgical conditions, and it is estimated that there is an annual average of about 14 million children under the age of 17 years with chronic conditions.

GENERAL PSYCHOLOGICAL ELEMENTS IN CHRONIC ILLNESS

The significance of a specific illness to a particular child depends upon a large number of interacting factors coming out of past experiences as well as ongoing experiences (Prugh *et al.*, 1953; Prugh, 1971; Stocking *et al.*, 1974; Szurek, 1951). These factors are general and relate to parental, familial, social, and physical circumstances as well as to the long-term and/or chronic character of the disorder and whether it is life-threatening or not. In addition, there are specific stress factors such as those that occur in diabetes, asthma, and heart disease (Freud, 1952; Green, 1968; Josselyn *et al.*, 1955; Korsch, 1958; Langford, 1948; Mattson, 1972; Prugh, 1971).

A particularly useful and unifying frame of reference in understanding the effects of chronic illness is in terms of the self. The self-concept is one approach to gain insight as to how the individual sees himself (Lowe, 1961; Wright, 1960). While no firm cause and effect inferences can be drawn, it seems reasonable to relate the self-concept to physical health and to illness. Wylie (1974), in her review of the self-concept, states that there is no strong support for assuming that low self-regard is an invariant consequence of poor physical health. Wright (1960) also does not believe there is a consistent relationship between the self-concept and physical disability; the effects of physical disability for any individual are related to the personality characteristic existing prior to disability. While physical disability has a profound effect upon the individual, that effect is not necessarily negative—it may be positive.

However, the attitudes of a disabled person toward self are frequently devaluating (Barker & Wright, 1954). In a similar way, Shelsky (1957) found that disabled and chronically ill patients are more self-rejecting and less self-accepting. This process is affected by the nature of the disability; persons with tuberculosis are more negatively affected than amputees. In a study by Kimmel (1959), the kind of personality problems created by orthopedic disability was related to the period in life in which the handicap occurred. Children with acquired orthopedic handicaps have greater confidence in and more esteem for their bodies and they can cope more adequately with anxiety than children with congenital handicaps. Kimmel felt that the results supported theories of personality development that emphasized the importance of motor maturation in the development of body confidence and ability to cope with anxiety.

Various surveys report higher incidences of social and psychological problems among chronically ill children than among normal children (Pless, 1968; Sultz, Schlesinger, Mosher, & Feldman, 1972). Dibner and Dibner (1973) found the self-concept of physically handicapped children to be adversely affected by their conditions. Green (1968) notes the existence of emotional problems in handicapped children and sees them as secondary to the handicap.

ASTHMA

The Nature of Asthma

Asthma is a common chronic disorder of respiration affecting persons of all ages with repeated episodes of difficulty in breathing, characterized by wheezing, labored breathing, cough, and sputum. These symptoms may range from the mildest cough and wheeze to respiratory distress of such severity as to obstruct breathing with fatal consequences. The asthmatic condition has a physiological substrate, tissue sensitivity to certain substances (food, dust, drugs, bacteria); these are called immunologic factors and in themselves are not sufficient to explain the asthmatic attack (Williams & McNicol, 1975). The inciting factors, once the immunologic reaction is established, are extremely varied and the severity of symptoms and their effects are greatly influenced by a multiplicity of interacting factors (Pinkerton & Weaver, 1970). There is no common agent, such as in tuberculosis, through which many quite different manifestations may be related; there are instead a number of nonspecific factors which include infection, and social and psychological stress. Pinkerton (1973) states no single factor is of overriding importance in symptom production; he speaks of the principle of summation. Thus, when the bronchus is labile, it may become sensitized by allergenic, physiologic, infective, and psychologic factors and once activated, it will react to a number of stimuli, resulting in an asthmatic attack. Pinkerton's view expresses that held by virtually all writers in the field. That literature, especially those dealing with the psychological forces in the asthmatic, has grown tremendously since the previous chapter was written in 1971 (chapter 9).

Pinkerton sees asthma as "perhaps the example *par excellence* of psychosomatic illness, the clearest demonstration of that complex interrelationship of body, intellect, and emotion, which links patient, family, doctor. . . ." He does not believe that on the basis of present understanding that a differentiation can be made between "organically" determined asthma and "psychogenic" asthma. He is opposed to such a dichotomy particularly when "there is no evidence for primary psychogenesis in asthma" (Pinkerton, 1973). Again, Pinkerton's position reflects that of the majority of writers in the field.

Some Statistics

There is no agreement about statistics on the incidence of allergic disorders. Part of the difficulty lies in the matter of definition. If a liberal definition is followed, the incidence would be estimated to be about fifty percent of the population; this figure is indicative of the wide prevalence of allergic reactions. While there is no sure evidence that allergic disorders are on the increase, one may infer an increase from the National Health Survey report on "Limitations of Activity Due to Chronic Conditions," which added asthma and hay fever to its list of leading causes of activity limitations in 1969–70 (USDHEW, 1973). One writer has pointed to the observations that as wealth in a community rises so does the incidence of allergic disorders.

It is estimated that there are about 8.6 million persons handicapped by asthma in the United States (Creer, Renne, & Christian, 1976), and of these, 3 million are children. Asthma is the leading cause of chronic disease among children under seventeen years of age as well as the primary reason for school absence among children with chronic disease (Creer *et al.*, 1976). Most children who develop asthma do so before the age of 5 years. There is a 2:1 ratio of boys over girls in asthma prevalence rates. About 10 percent of children with asthma have the intractable form. In a study of 2,169 children under the age of 15 years, it was found that 20 percent had major allergic disorders but only one-third of this group was receiving treatment. The investigators felt that this situation pointed to a public health problem. If two-thirds of the allergic children are untreated, how many learning problems and how much school difficulty and absenteeism may have roots in allergy? (Rappaport, Appel, & Szanton, 1960)

Psychological Determinants in Asthma

Studies of the psychological factors in asthma have grown at an accelerated rate and constitute the largest and most active literature of the four disorders considered in this chapter. Although the literature began with a psychoanalytic frame of reference, there are a growing number of reports which reflect psychodynamic points of view that are not necessarily psychoanalytic. Maurer

(1965) has published a comprehensive assessment of the relative importance of emotional factors in asthma that contains discussions of the various psychological views about asthma.

Impetus to the psychoanalytic approach came from the work of French and Alexander (1941), who pointed out the particular significance of the interrelationships between the mother and the asthmatic child. They found that the child is more or less rejected by the mother or both parents and that the mother is much too preoccupied with her own problems to give adequate love to the child, although she overcompensates for this unconscious rejection by an overprotective attitude. They also noted the overambition of the mother for the child and the overdependence of the child upon the mother, with the result that the child is immature and lacking in self-confidence in most situations. Thus, French and Alexander formulated their hypothesis that the psychological conflict in asthma is basically a repressed longing for the mother. When this desire is frustrated or threatened with frustration, an asthmatic attack is precipitated. The asthmatic attack becomes, symbolically, the protest of a crying spell.

This hypothesis formed the basis of further investigations which followed psychoanalytic formulations and supported French and Alexander's observations. Miller and Baruch (1957), in an extensive series of studies, observed and treated some 201 clinically allergic children since 1946. Similarly treated was a group of 110 children with no allergic disorder but with behavior problems. They reported that 97 percent of the allergic children had mothers who verbally expressed rejecting attitudes, whereas 37 percent of the mothers of nonallergic children did so, the difference being highly significant. This theme of maternal rejection became a dominant one in the literature of asthma.

Miller and Baruch believe that maternal rejection preceded the development of symptoms. They studied hostility in allergic children as a reaction to the experience of rejection. The allergic child did not dare to express his hostile feelings to the same extent or as freely as the nonallergic child. He developed guilt and anxiety in relation to his hostility and was more frequently in conflict about bringing out his hostile feelings. Miller and Baruch likened the allergic child to a cornered animal who feels and hates the impact of his mother's rejection, as all children would. But he is not able to express this hostility in either direct or indirect fashion and, consequently, he cannot get release from the tension of hostile feeling. He turns his resentment on himself and uses his allergic condition as satisfaction for his conflicting needs.

An elaboration of Miller and Baruch's thesis is the concept of mutual engulfment, advanced by Abrahamson (1954). The rejecting mother is found to be ambitious, willful, and oversolicitous of her child. She wants to mold the child along the lines she wishes. When the child rebels, as frequently happens, she rejects him. This raises anxiety for the child. Thus, the basic conflict is dependence-independence, and the anxiety emerging from this conflict is expressed through a somatic response—asthma.

A more broadly conceived factor is advanced by Rees (1963), who found faulty parental attitudes to be significantly higher among parents of asthmatic children than among parents of a control group. Rees did not find parental rejection to be the significant factor reported by Miller and Baruch. Similarly, Jacobs (1963), in a study of fantasies among children with hay fever, found significant differences for stories of maternal domination than for stories of maternal rejection.

Maternal rejection concepts have found support in a number of studies which sought to verify the frequent observation that asthmatic children invariably showed an abatment of their symptoms when they were away from homes and families, for example, in a hospital or a camp. Equally invariably, the symptoms recurred when the children returned home (Jessner *et al.*, 1955).

Long and his co-workers (1958) undertook to investigate this phenomenon in a study of eighteen children hospitalized for asthma. After their symptoms had been relieved while in the hospital, the children were exposed to heavy concentrations of house dust from their homes but showed no demonstrable reaction. This finding was interpreted to indicate that allergy is not the only necessary factor to produce asthma and to point to the complex etiology of asthmatic episodes.

The results of the various studies that support the fact of maternal rejection are generally accepted. However, what is challenged is the specificity of the concept itself —that it is primary psychological conflict and trauma leading to the asthmatic reaction. Harris and Shure (1956), Leigh (1953), Lipton, Steinschneider, and Richmond (1966), and others raise the question of whether the psychological reactions observed are the results of the asthma, not the causes. For example, Fitzelle (1959), in a controlled study involving 100 mothers of asthmatic children and 100 mothers of children with other ailments, found no differences in personality tests and child-rearing attitude surveys between the two groups; both groups deviated from the normal. Dubo and her co-workers (1961) report similar negative results as to severity, cause, response to treatment, and family situations.

Margolis (1962) failed to find support for the psychosomatic interpretation of asthma, using the PARI scales. However, the use of the Blacky test indicated that mothers of asthmatic children are more psychologically disturbed.

Coolidge (1956) observed that the conflictual mother-child relationship is not specific for asthma but that ambivalence conflict is a basic characteristic of development.

Implicit in the challenge to the concept of maternal rejection as a causative factor is the questioning of the existence of a unique or specific personality pattern in the child as a significant etiological element. There have been a number of studies that bring into question the generality of the concept (Harris & Shure, 1956; Knapp & Nemetz, 1957; 1960; Rees, 1959; Purcell, Turnbull, & Bernstein, 1962; Resh, 1970; Block, *et al.*, 1964; Luparello, *et al.*, 1971). The current prevailing view is that no single etiologic statement can be made for all asthmatics (Weiss, 1973), that asthma is a heterogeneous condition with wide variation in the importance of the different causative factors (Block *et al.*, 1964), that one cannot generalize from one study group to another (Luparello *et al.*, 1971). This heterogeneity is especially emphasized for psychological factors (Freeman *et al.*, 1964; Resh, 1970; Weiss, 1973).

The studies of asthma as a learned response, stemming from classical conditioning theory, have aroused interest (Dekker & Groen, 1956; Dekker, Pelser, & Groen, 1957; Stubblefield, 1966). Purcell advanced the hypothesis that children with rapidly remitting disease may have learned asthma as a defensive-adaptive response. Turnbull (1962) developed a theoretical model to explicate asthma within a classical conditioning frame of reference. Thus, asthmalike behavior could be learned and would persist as a means of resolving conflicts and problems. He hypothesized that asthma is triggered initially by an allergy or infection and attacks may be provoked by external stimuli, environmental or emotional, and thus become associated as in classical conditioning. Later, attacks may be precipitated or intensified by any one of a number of social or psychological situations with which the attack had been associated in the past.

Lachman (1972) develops a similar approach. He cites experimental evidence that modifications in breathing can be learned. The child can learn to use such breathing patterns in stressful situations. Thus a child who could not elicit a parental response by being silent or by crying and screaming finds that sighing, gasping, and wheezing can do so. In later life, in problem situations, the individual may utilize these early-established and frequently practiced habits.

Behavioral approaches have been utilized in therapeutic endeavors and will be considered in a later section. Friend and Pollock (1954) were early critics of the predominant focus on intrapsychic elements in the study of the asthmatic child. They believed that situational and social factors had been neglected. Pinkerton (1970) states that exclusively intrapsychic formulations, such as the psychoanalytic, fail to consider the "somatic substrate" which he regards as fundamental and this failure "forfeits [the] validity" of that approach. Certainly the literature up to a decade ago justified these criticisms. The probable explanation is that psychoanalytic theory was the prime source of hypotheses for the study of asthma. However, this theoretical ascendancy is not evident today, as we have pointed out. If there is a major psychological focus then it is in the systematic identification of the various groups of asthmatic patients and the delineation of their special characteristics to provide the bases for therapeutic intervention.

Psychological Effects of Asthma

The approach to psychological variables suggested by Pinkerton (1970) is to regard them as somatopsychological phenomena. There is, as we have seen, virtually complete acceptance of the fact that psychological variables influence the frequency and severity of asthmatic episodes in children. The earlier discussion of the characteristics of chronically ill children will be pertinent here. Mattson (1972) emphasizes the realistic aspects of asthma in its effects upon the child and the family. An asthmatic attack causes anxiety and embarrassment for the child, arouses fears of suffocating and dying. If hospitalization becomes necessary, the child is separated from family and friends, is subjected to painful and poorly understood treatments, is absent from school, and is away from usual activities. For the family, fear, helplessness, irritation, self-blame, guilt, resentment are provoked in addition to the financial burden. Thus a situation is created, and repeated, which is fraught with a high potential for psychological disturbances. To be sure there are wide differences in the effectiveness with which the child and family cope with the stresses produced. We have considered the position that, regardless of these realistic experiences, psychological disturbances are implicated in the etiology of asthma. One must recognize the difficulty in determining whether psychological problems are primary or secondary to the illness, or any other illness for that matter. Certainly, psychological problems are not unique among asthmatic children and their problems are reportedly similar to those observed in other chronic childhood disorders (Mattson, 1972). Moreover there is the growing opinion that etiological factors have little or limited usefulness in dealing with psychological problems in asthma. This is emphasized especially in behavioral approaches.

These considerations are intended to emphasize that we are on surer grounds when the psychological problems observed are looked upon as concomitants of illness and not necessarily as either causative or consequence. Thus we may proceed to examine the nature of the psychological problems observed among asthmatic children; the realistic aspects of those problems have been noted. The severity of emotional problems is thought to provide a clue to the nature of the asthmatic condition. Bakwin (1954) felt that when asthmatic attacks occur frequently and are difficult to control, emotional factors should be suspected. Related findings were reported by Williams and McNicol (1975) in a study of 400 asthmatic children and 100 normal controls. While most of the asthmatics did not display behavioral disturbances, those disturbances did occur significantly for the severely involved children. These children were described as immature, demanding, and showed displaced aggression; their families showed more evidence of stress than the families of less severe asthmatics. Similarly, Straker and Tamerin (1974) and Ghory (1972) reported that the severely affected asthmatic children in their studies displayed significant psychological problems. Purcell divided asthmatic children admitted to the hospital into one group composed of the children who obtained rapid remission of symptoms after admission, and into a second group of those who did not remit symptoms rapidly. This symptom response to institutionalization, Purcell believed, occurred among those whose asthma had greater emotional components (Purcell et al., 1969). Sperling (1968), using Purcell's classification, regarded the non-rapidly remitting group as having a significant degree of psychopathology. Similar findings were made by Block and his associates (1964), which indicated that children with low somatic predisposition to asthma had greater psychopathological involvements. Resh (1970) compared children with asthma of unknown origin and children with asthma on an allergic basis, and found that the children with asthma of unknown origin were psychologically different. Lest these results become confusing, it is important to point out that the studies are reporting upon different groups, a caution we had expressed earlier.

There are differences of opinion about the prevalence of emotional disturbances among asthmatic children, and we do not have clear answers to such questions: Are all asthmatic children affected? Only selected groups? Are the identified problems peculiar to asthma? Or are they common to all chronic illness? Are they etiologic or sequelae? There is little question that the main contributors to the reported differences are the differences in the studies, differences in populations involved, methodologies, and objectives. These are the judgments of Freeman and his colleagues (1964) on the basis of their extensive review of the psychological literature in allergic disorders. It has also been pointed out that most studies deal

with severely involved asthmatics in clinics or hospitals. What of the "garden-variety" —those who are under the care of the private physician? Two studies of illness in several populations of children present contrasting results: Mitchell and Dawson (1973) found no greater incidence of "psychiatric difficulty or neurotic behavior" among asthmatic children than in the general population; and Sultz et al. (1972) report asthmatic and allergic children in general had more behavioral deviations than physically healthy children.

If issues of etiologic significance are put aside as well as definitional questions such as "psychiatric difficulty" as against "behavioral deviations," it would seem that most studies indicate the probability of greater psychological disturbance among asthmatics than non-asthmatics (Hahn & Clark, 1967; Williams, 1975) especially among those who cope poorly with their illness. Much clearer is the fact that no asthmatic personality type has been established; whatever common or group characteristics that appear are attributed to the experience of the disease itself.

It is a truism in dealing with psychological problems among children that the families must be involved. This has been especially emphasized in recent years with the growth of ecological concepts and the interest in systems theory (Koch, Minuchin, & Donovan, 1974; Mattson, 1972). The traditional diagnostic categories are being challenged and questions are being raised about the validity of therapeutic procedures carried out in the isolation of the doctor's office. The necessity to actively involve families is emphasized. The views of Minuchin (Combrinck-Graham, 1974) are put forth in this regard; the child's symptoms are seen as being produced by dysfunctional family interactions, and these symptoms help in maintaining those dysfunctions in the family system. The object of intervention then is to alter or restructure the patterns in the family system to improve the child's condition; cases are cited to demonstrate the effectiveness of Minuchin's approach, structural family therapy (Liebman, Minuchin, & Baker, 1974).

Whether or not one subscribes to the above techniques, there is little question that asthma presents severe problems to parents (McLean, Schrager, & Stoeffler, 1968). This is experienced in two ways; namely, handling the physical and concrete realities of the disease, and handling the behavior of the child within that context. The parents must follow a medical regimen. The house must be kept clean and dust-free. Certain foods must be avoided because of potential allergenic nature. Household pets are given away. Desensitization shots are administered to decrease allergic reactions to pollens and molds. There is curtailment of peer group relations, extracurricular activities, competitive sports, and exercise.

This regimen affects the entire family, but the brunt of maintaining it is usually assumed by the mother. This may create situations for conflict and stress among family members. For one, different standards of behavior are adopted for the asthmatic children than for non-asthmatic siblings. Also, there may be neglect of other family members and perhaps of marital relationships. Usually, if hostility and resentment are present, these are submerged to be acted out in diverse and covert ways. The entire family becomes organized around emergencies. Family activities, trips, vacations suffer because of apprehension about an acute attack.

The asthmatic child becomes labeled as being sick and weak, and more often than not develops feelings of low self-esteem, low self-confidence, and hesitancy in coping with problems. In such a setting, the asthmatic child learns that his symptoms give him power to control and manipulate the family. The reports in the literature attest to the effectiveness of this learning.

A frequent later complication is that the child will rebel, usually in adolescence (Johnson, Baker, & Alexander, 1971). In doing so, he defies and violates the prescribed regimen—an action with high risk.

Moreover, the parents of asthmatic children, especially of severely affected children, tend to become overdependent upon physicians; they relinquish much responsibility. Liebman, Minuchin, & Baker (1974) find that the family members become intrusive, overinvolved, and overresponsive to one another, and thus decrease autonomy and privacy for each individual. There is a high degree of overprotective concern for each other, especially parental overprotectiveness. Usually the family presents itself as completely normal except for the child's condition. Conflict and unpleasantness are avoided. Such an unreal family setting is a detouring process; it does not resolve disagreements and problems and leads to perpetuation of stress and tension. It is the kind of situation that intensifies and expands the psychological components of the asthmatic disorder.

These problems have long been recognized and form the basis for family intervention methods. The earliest of these is parentectomy, a procedure developed by Peshkin (Robinson, 1972), which is the removal of the asthmatic child from the home to a residential treatment center for a period of six to nine months. This procedure was advised for intractable cases—those children who did not respond to treatment completely. The result usually was remission of symptoms; one residential treatment center in Denver reported that of 500 children admitted over a period of years, only 10 percent did not improve (Peshkin, 1960; Tuft, 1957). These reported successes led to a growth of residential treatment facilities throughout the country; at present there are about nineteen (Robinson, 1972).

A study by Purcell et al. (1969) demonstrates the potent influence of family problems in producing asthmatic symptoms. He removed parents and siblings from the home, leaving the asthmatic child there in care of surrogates. The removed relatives were placed in motels. Two groups were formed, one in which emotional factors were judged to be important and one in which they were regarded as being minimal or irrelevant. The emotional factor group showed significant improvement and the minimal or irrelevant emotional factor group did not but their symptoms did not get worse. While Purcell regarded this study as support for the concept of parentectomy, it is also support for the notion of heterogeneity of asthmatic conditions. Few will challenge the primacy of family factors in emotional aspects of asthma but this is not to say that parentectomy in the form of placement in a residential treatment center is *the* therapeutic approach.

Falliers (1970) presents statistics of treatment success, remission of symptoms, at one residential center. Over a fifteen-year period, the success rate dropped from 98 percent in 1953–1955 to 12 percent in 1968–1969. While the reasons for this decline are not altogether certain, there was a change in the population sources from which the asthmatic children came. Formerly, most came from the northeastern states, particularly New York City, and in later years, more and more children came from an ever wider geographic distribution. Simultaneously in this period, great progress was made in the understanding of the immunologic, physiologic, biochemical, psychological, and other aspects of asthma. Treatment at home became more common and outpatient programs appeared that offered comprehensive services. Moreover, outpatient facilities were able to save about one-third of costs as compared with inpatient facilities without sacrificing effectiveness of services while serving greater numbers (Robbins & Finklestein, 1973). The net result of these various factors has undoubtedly been to change the kind of asthmatic child who was sent to residential centers. One may speculate that the more severely affected and refractory asthmatic was the one being referred; we do not have data to support this speculation.

Parentectomy has also been examined critically on therapeutic grounds. It is seen "as a process that is emotionally traumatic and deleterious to the family and particu-

larly to the patient" (Liebman *et al.,* 1974). Frequently the child will have remission of symptoms while in treatment away from home but will suffer a relapse upon return. These critics insist that the family is the basic unit toward which attention must be paid. The importance of the family situation in the treatment of the asthmatic child is stressed in the study by McLean and Ching (1973), who followed some seventy-one asthmatic children for more than ten years after discharge from the hospital. They found that the deciding factor in the improvement of the asthmatic symptoms was not the severity of the asthma, but the emotional status of both the child and the family. While one may infer that family treatment should proceed as a unit including the child, it would seem that a range of treatment possibilities should be available and the parentectomy should be one of those possibilities. Unquestionably, there is a place for residential centers (Mattson, 1972).

Also to be recognized in the changing therapeutic scene for asthma is the increasing interest in behavioral approaches. Essentially these approaches view asthma as a learned phenomenon and as such can be modified by new learning (Wohl, 1971). The emphasis on current situations usually followed by behavioral theorists is advocated by Weiss (1973) who does not believe etiological factors are useful in treatment. Khan (1973) has used conditioning methods in treatment of asthmatic symptoms—biofeedback is the basis for his work.

Creer, Renne, and Christian (1976) have described their behavioral methods in treating asthmatic children in a residential treatment center, the Children's Asthma Research Institute and Hospital in Denver, Colorado. An interesting feature of the center is the encouragement for children to enter into physical activities. This is a departure from the usual apprehensiveness and restriction of physical activities, since exercise is known to produce airway obstruction in asthmatics. Ghory (1974) opposes the routine elimination of exercise. He recommends the use of athletics and exercise for asthmatics. Sly, Harper, and Rosselot (1972) instituted a physical conditioning program and found that over a three-month period frequency of wheezing was reduced but there was no worsening of pulmonary function. The main effects were subjective feelings of improvement and parental reports that the children were "less anxious."

The available data on the school adjustment of asthmatic children indicate they were often retarded in their grade placement mainly as a result of frequent absence. One report (Sultz et al., 1972) states that 22 percent are below grade and 20 percent have school problems. Other reports characterize the asthmatic child as an underachiever. The residential treatment centers report similar experiences (Bakwin & Bakwin, 1948; Creer et al., 1976).

DIABETES

The Nature of Diabetes

The history of diabetes has been described as illustrative of the progressive refinement of medical concern and care in a disease from a focus on physical aspects, reduction of mortality, and lessening of morbidity to increasing awareness and acceptance of the psychological aspects. In the preinsulin era, the central objective of the physician was quite simply that of the patient's survival. The early 1920s ushered in the insulin era, a development whose promise to help achieve mastery of the illness has not been realized. Little progress in coping with diabetes has been made in the more than fifty years since the discovery of insulin (USDHEW, Vol. III, 1976). The availability of insulin for treatment prevented death from diabetic coma and controlled the overt symptoms of the disease and so was mistakenly believed to be a "cure" for diabetes. Ironically, the prolonging of life made possible by insulin brought with it an array of complications such as blindness, kidney disease, and cardiovascular disease. The recognition that diabetes is a growing major health problem presently affecting about ten million Americans led the United States Congress to establish a National Commission on Diabetes in 1974 with the charge to formulate a long-range plan to combat the disease. Its report was made in 1975.

Diabetes mellitus is a complex, life-threatening disorder of metabolism, a defect in the metabolism of carbohydrates. The disease is characterized by abnormal concentrations of sugar in the blood (hyperglycemia) and in the urine (glycosuria), and by relative or absolute insulin deficiency. Diabetes affects virtually every organ in the body, and it is unique in the fact that it is accompanied by severe and debilitating complications: blindness; renal disease; vascular disease; gangrene and amputation; heart disease; and decreased life expectancy.

Health officials are alarmed at the rate the prevalence of diabetes is increasing; there was a 50 percent increase between 1965 and 1973. Its incidence is rising by 6 percent per year and it is anticipated that the number of people with diabetes will double every fifteen years. The average American has one chance in five of developing diabetes. It is estimated that diabetes and its complications account for more then 300,000 deaths annually and is the third ranking cause of death (USDHEW, Vol. 1, 1976).

Diabetes among children, juvenile diabetes, constitutes a special problem; one half of diabetic children now living will die twenty-five years after diagnosis of diabetes and 63 percent will develop eye problems. Many diabetics are bedridden for an average one and a half months each year; no other chronic disease causes so many days in bed among noninstitutionalized population. The most common age period for occurrence is ten to twelve years. The juvenile diabetic requires intensive initial support and treatment and continuous, long-term care. The number of children with diabetes in the

United States is unknown; it is roughly estimated to be from 51,000 to 85,000; other estimates place the number of juvenile diabetics, up to the age of 21 years, at 90,000 to 150,000 (USDHEW, Vol. III, 1976).

Despite considerable research, the biochemical basis of diabetes remains unknown. The National Commission on Diabetes believes diabetes should be considered a syndrome rather than a specific condition; it is unlikely that a single abnormality will explain all cases and all complications. Twin studies in diabetes have led to the conclusion that both genetic and environmental factors are involved. Predictions for the occurrence of diabetes for any specific individual is not regarded as possible. Nutritional factors play a major role in determining the risk of diabetes; obesity has the strongest relationship.

However for diabetes in young persons, hereditary factors are primary. Research pursuing a single factor of causation has not been productive. It is probable that there is more than one causative factor in diabetes (Knowles, 1971), and such multifactorial etiology is now beginning to be understood (USDHEW, Vol. II, 1976). The role of psychosocial factors is believed to be significant but they have not been easy to study. Hinkle and Wolf (1952), pursuing the hypothesis that diabetes is a disease precipitated by emotional factors, believed that the kind of stress which represented a lack of affection and security activated the metabolic derangement in diabetes. Their results have not been replicated, and Baker and Barcai (1970) state quite positively that the instigation of diabetes as a permanent state in a totally non-diabetic individual has not been confirmed by clinical data. They state that there is considerable direct support and evidence for the view that stress intensifies known pre-existent diabetes and brings to clinical recognition previously unrecognized diabetes, and may convert a pre-diabetic state to actual diabetes. The National Commission also takes the position that while emotional factors do influence the clinical course of dia-

betes, a cause-and-effect relationship has not been demonstrated in the sense that emotional stress can produce the illness in a previously non-diabetic.

Diabetics do not constitute a homogeneous group (Baker & Barcai, 1970). This kind of issue is being raised in all so-called psychosomatic children. A differentiation is made between juvenile diabetes and adult diabetes, that the disease mechanism is different in each. Among the differences between the two types is the fact that diabetes tends to be more severe in the child and runs a notoriously stormy course. It stabilizes as the child gets older but often becomes stormy again during adolescence. There is great frequency of symptoms among juvenile diabetics (Forbes, 1956), and greater fluctuations prevail in day-to-day control. Psychologically there are important differences. As a growing, maturing, and developing organism, the child is affected in a much more comprehensive and complex fashion. In addition, the child has the problem of rationalizing a regimen of living—an infinitely more difficult task for younger age groups than for older age groups (Collier & Etzwiler, 1971; LaHood, 1970).

The Diabetic Regimen

Diabetes is unique among chronic diseases in its demands upon the diabetic youngster and the family—daily medication, adherence to dietary requirements, frequent testing of urine specimens, regulation of activity, frequent visits to the physician, and, in addition, long-term concerns such as insulin reactions, acidosis and possible coma, potential blindness, kidney failure, and premature death. Thus, many stresses are placed upon the family group in order to maintain disease control, in the center of which are the psychological stresses.

The family may be further troubled by the fact that the treatment of juvenile diabetes has not "been sufficiently standardized or outcomes followed long enough to provide . . . certainty in choosing one or another course or modality of management" (USDHEW, Vol. III, 1976). Moreover, there is the expense to the family, since the services necessary are of relatively high cost.

Basic to following the diabetic regimen is knowledge about the disease and the rationale for the treatment. But education alone is not sufficient to insure adequate management. For example, Bloodgood (USDHEW, Vol. II, 1976) found that knowledge about diabetes was not enough to bring about compliance with the regimen, that motivational and situational factors along with ability to make decisions were influential. Generally, there is a close correlation between the children and their parents in knowledge about diabetes (Collier & Etzwiler, 1971). The objective of treatment of the diabetic child is to enable the child to compete with his peers physically, mentally, and socially. Insofar as he is not able to do so, to that degree he is considered inadequately treated.

There is not complete agreement among physicians as to the degree of control necessary in the management of diabetic patients —whether there should be chemical control or clinical control. Those who favor chemical control have rigid rules and procedures to be followed very strictly and carefully, such as frequent urine examinations, keeping of daily records, and others. Those physicians who favor clinical control usually recommend liberal handling of diabetic patients. Their patients have only a few rules to follow, one of which is never to omit insulin. These physicians emphasize psychological elements in the treatment of diabetes (Forsyth & Payne, 1956; Tolstoi, 1948). The type of control over diet is not agreed upon, whether it should be strict or flexible. In general, there is recognition of the difficulty in maintaining a program of rigid control, especially among juvenile diabetics, and the need for more attention to the interpersonal elements of the doctor-patient relationships to achieve effective management of the diabetes.

Psychological Ramifications

The importance of psychological factors in diabetes has been recognized for a long time. However, in the preinsulin era, it was quite impractical to be concerned with the emotional health of diabetics when the physician was struggling to stem the death-dealing effects of unregulated diabetes. With the discovery of insulin, systematic attention to psychological variables slowly evolved.

The work of Menninger (1935), pointing out striking temporal correlations between changes in diabetes and changes in the mental states of a number of psychotic patients, helped to stimulate interest in the importance of psychological experiences. Other investigators noted that the severity of the metabolic disturbances in diabetes can be aggravated by emotional disturbances. Hinkle, Evans, and Wolf (1951) have demonstrated that emotional stress factors can produce undesirable changes in diabetic regulation, which clear up upon the removal of stress. Virtually every writer recognizes the significance of emotional factors in the clinical cause of diabetes, and the National Commission on Diabetes clearly affirms this position.

However, as we have indicated, to move to the position that diabetes can be caused by emotional factors is another matter. Early, Danowski (1957) stated: "There is no extensive support for the suggestion that diabetes actually originates as a result of such stress." The data may tell why an individual becomes ill at the time he develops symptoms, but they do not tell why he becomes ill with diabetes. Hinkle and Wolf (1952) attempted to do so, but the stresses they described were no different from the types of stresses that many individuals encounter without developing diabetes. On the other hand, Danowski believes it is wise to keep an open mind on this issue since emotional conflicts have very specific meaning for individuals. Nevertheless, the position of most of the investigators in the field would be in agreement with that of the National Commission on Diabetes that it is "unlikely that emotional stress alone can produce the illness in a previously non-diabetic."

Dunbar (1948) has been especially positive in asserting that the diabetic has a distinctive behavioral pattern. However, her hypothesis has not been supported in subsequent research (Falstein & Judas, 1955). It seems well accepted that diabetics, adult or juvenile, do not have distinctive personality patterns that are different from those in other disease entities, for example, rheumatic fever (Crowell, 1953; Neuhaus, 1958). The view of the National Commission that there is no distinctive personality pattern for diabetics would reflect the prevailing opinion of current investigators.

Starr (1955) places diabetes among the psychopathophysiological reactions in his psychosomatic spectrum. The somatic component is dominant and psychological factors would exacerbate and/or perpetuate the somatic manifestations. This point of view would be supported by most writers in the field. As a matter of fact, Hinkle's extensive investigation precisely demonstrates the influence of emotional stress on the diabetic's course. Emotions acting through the autonomic nervous system affect blood glucose and severe disturbance can precipitate acidosis. The carbohydrate-regulating mechanism can break down under the influence of stress (USDHEW, Vol. III, 1976).

In some early studies, a marked incidence of mental retardation among diabetic children was reported. However, the work of Kubany, Danowski, and Moses (1956) found that the intelligence of diabetic children is like that of the nondiabetic population. They are of the opinion that the differences found in the past were mainly due to sampling biases.

Developmentally, the diabetic is not different from nondiabetic children except in height and weight. Hormonal secretions also are not strikingly variant from normals (Danowski, 1957).

Psychological Elements in Treatment

Despite the fact it is not possible to make precise statements as to ways in which emotions do or do not affect the course of diabetes, virtually every writer will subscribe to the opinion that emotional factors touch on every problem connected with understanding and treatment of diabetes (Bruhn, 1974; Rome & Robinson, 1959). Kimball (1971) states that there are four points to be kept in mind: (1) the individual and the disease process are not separate entities but are intimately related with one another—the earlier the onset, the more intimate the interrelationship; (2) both onset and exacerbation are frequently related to events in the broad psychosocial environment; (3) effects of diabetes will depend upon many factors within and outside the individual; (4) the individual's adaptive capacities and resources affect the psychological aspects of diabetes.

In addition to its effects as a chronic illness in general, diabetes has its specific implications. First of all, diabetes in childhood is a severe, lifelong, life-threatening disease (Bruch, 1949). Diabetic children can become desperately ill. With insulin, their outlook has changed, but the disease means constant awareness of danger. Ever present is the fear of hypoglycemic shock and possible coma. Avoidance of infections because they affect the physiology of the body cells for special vigilance. Blood-vessel complications are always a danger. Consequently, a feeling of apprehension surrounds the life of the diabetic child. Complicating these fears are the usual bewilderment and lack of understanding of the illness on the part of both the family and the child.

The responses of the family to chronic illness, previously discussed, have special pertinence here because of the critical responsibility of the mother in the daily management of the diabetes. The mother has the realization that the health and the life of her child depend upon her ability to get the child to follow the prescribed regimen. To be sure, the entire constellation of psychological elements in the family is involved, and, as shown by Bruch and Hewlett (1947) and by Kaye's analysis of family participation in the management of diabetes (USDHEW, Vol. III, 1976), the extent of success or failure in the daily management of the diabetic child is dependent upon the psychological elements in the home.

The concept of parentectomy has been borrowed from treatment in asthma. Baker and his co-workers believe that certain diabetic children can benefit from parentectomy, such as those who have repeated bouts of diabetic acidosis for which no explanation can be found. When control is achieved in the hospital and when a relapse occurs upon return home, parentectomy should be considered. Such a sequence of events lead Baker and his colleagues to regard the family as having pathological characteristics that must receive attention. In a study of the families with such diabetic control problems, they found a correlation between pathological family characteristics—overprotectedness, enmeshment, rigidity, lack of conflict resolution—and the occurrence of acidosis (Baker et al., 1975).

Crain, Sussman, and Weill (1966), pursuing an interest in effects of the illness of one family member upon other members, studied fifty-four diabetic children and seventy-six controls. The investigation found that parents of diabetic children have inferior marital integration, less agreement on how to handle the child, and greater marital conflict. The authors believed that the diabetes produced an intrafamiliar crisis.

The prescribed regimen for the diabetic contains fertile sources for psychological disturbance (Podolsky, 1955). Fischer (1948) studied such factors in the families of a group of diabetic children followed for ten years. The necessity for dietary restriction, although made more liberal with the advent of insulin, is a critical part of the daily routine. Thus, parents develop many anxieties about food, fearing carbohydrates in particular, and hesitate to give sugar. They tend to repeat the same foods day after day and the lack of variety often provokes resistance. The children commonly become hungry after meals and extra between-meal snacks are permitted. Not infrequently, diabetic children do their own supplementing and this provokes violent reactions from the parents because of "cheating" or "stealing." The parents become overzealous in enforcing the diet and begin to use detective methods. The work of Hinkle and his associates suggests that the attempt to regulate the diets of many diabetic children is fruitless because such attempts become entangled with strong psychological drives; food becomes an arena of struggle. The accusations of the parents bring guilt feelings and induce more concealment and a vicious circle is set up—more guilt, more anxiety, and more conflict. Thus, food acquires the character of poison, which not only intensifies the child's anxieties, but may also cause it to be used as a weapon in his relationships to the environment.

Probably the most important aspect of daily routine is the necessity for insulin injections. This necessity most pervasively affects the emotions of the diabetic child. The use of the hypodermic syringe cannot be avoided even though the frequency of its use is reduced with slower-acting insulin preparations. The emotional effects of the injections are often traumatic; some children regard them as punishment. Physiological reactions from insulin (pallor, sweating, fainting), when they occur, are very disturbing, and after such experiences, the child becomes fearful and may seek to avoid or in some way weaken the insulin injection. The latter may occur when the child administers his own injection. Dread of insulin reactions may upset parents even more, particularly if the reactions come at night.

Hypoglycemia produces such effects as irritability, sleepiness, crying, temper tantrums, and behavioral disturbances. The child may fall asleep in the classroom or become unconscious after heavy exercise. Not infrequently, these symptoms are misunderstood by teachers and the children are punished for "bad" behavior (Fischer, 1948). In the National Commission on Diabetes report, Schwartz comments on some of the implications of syringe use. The necessity for insulin injection has made juvenile diabetics syringe-oriented, and syringe use has special contemporary meaning in the eyes of the peer culture because of its association with drugs. He emphasizes the hazards implicit in this situation because the influence of the adolescent culture has a destructive potential for the diabetic youngster (USDHEW, Vol. II, 1976).

A third aspect of the diabetic regimen is the necessity to test the urine. Although testing of every voided specimen is unnecessary, urination takes on much emotional color. Aside from any diabetic disorder, this eliminative function seems to have an especially high potential for involvement in emotional disturbances. Added to this sensitivity is the anxiety surrounding the urine specimen and analysis. There is, not infrequently, bedwetting among diabetic children because of a greater necessity for frequent voiding (polyuria) as a result of increased thirst and water intake (polydipsia). This bed-wetting is an aspect of the diabetes, but, of course, it may become involved with bed-wetting that is symptomatic of emotional disturbance. In any event, the parents and the child are upset and embarrassed by bed-wetting when it occurs. Here again, the relationships and the attitudes that exist in the family are important.

Anna Freud (1952) discusses an inherent conflict in the management of the diabetic. The goal is to teach the child the various requirements of self-care. The young child who is slowly and uncertainly moving away from dependence on the mother suffers a blow to this developmental progress when he falls ill with diabetes. The regimen of treatment requires that he begin to learn how to take care of himself. Freud believes this burdens the child with excessively grave responsibilities. To be sure, the young diabetic is expected to become his own diagnostician, laboratory technician, and nurse, to attend classes, and to monitor his diet.

In contrast, however, some recent studies indicate that the early assumption of these responsibilities is not necessarily deleterious to developmental progress. Partridge and his co-workers (1972) compared a group of adolescent diabetics with a group of normal controls and found that the diabetics tended to assume responsibilities in other areas of life, in addition to those associated with their illness, at an earlier age than did the controls. They did not display evidence of being infantilized and overdependent, as is often stated. Other investigators (Linde et al., 1967) have reported similar results that nondiabetics felt that they were given responsibilities (choice of clothing, use of money, hours of curfew, and so on) at too early an age whereas the diabetics did not think so. In fact, the diabetic youngsters sought to assume such responsibilities early. It was the opinion of the investigators that the diabetics could understand their condition in a realistic way and could appraise the degree of control achieved. It was found that they were ready to assume total responsibility by the age of 15. One study of diabetic adolescent girls showed them to be "well adjusted" despite worries and fears about the disease; all of them wanted to learn more about control of the illness (Khurana & White, 1971). Others (Baker & Barcai, 1970) believed that most diabetic children adjust reasonably well to the disease, given sensible parents, and present no problems to physicians, parents, and teachers.

Limitation of activity occupies a prominent place in the daily routine of the diabetic child. The first limitation is in physical activity because of the fear of shock due to rapid depletion of blood sugar as the result of heavy exercise. Although physical restriction is observed when the child is young and not fully capable of self-regulation, it is frequently carried over and extended in later years, particularly in social life. For example, a child is not permitted to attend parties because it is feared he may indulge in the excessive eating of sweets. In addition, parents may be fearful of letting the child out of sight for any length of time for fear of insulin reactions. Excursions and visits away from home are difficult because of insulin and meals. These difficulties serve to impress on the child the fact that he is different.

The many and complex problems of the diabetic's life led Bennett and Johannesen (1954) to conclude that the disease may make a real and tangible impact on the child. They are of the opinion that the child may never get used to diabetes and its restrictions, and the results of the restricted life are a constricted passive-dependency.

Starr (1955), in a comprehensive discussion of the psychosomatics of juvenile diabetes, points out that the child's adjustment to the "sudden" diagnosis of diabetes depends upon the premorbid emotional state of affairs for the child and his family. Given the same degree of life stress, that is, the appearance of diabetes, afflicted children and their families will react varyingly. Where the intrafamilial adjustment has been adequate, the diabetic illness, after a short period of reactive disturbance, will be taken in stride. On the other hand, where faulty interpersonal relationships and extensive conflicts existed, diabetes will result in emotional upheavals.

In families with histories of psychological strains and problems or with tenuous control over such troubles, diabetes can be disruptive and cause intensified or open expression of the problems. Those situations are sure to contaminate the different aspects of the diabetic regimen. Parent-child conflicts may become accentuated. The entire family may regard itself as under stigma (Etzwiler, 1962). The specific reaction of the diabetic child depends largely upon the idiosyncratic history of the family. The adverse reactions may include excessively anxious and endangered personalities, compulsive, overly regulated, and regimented personalities, depressive and self-destructive personalities, delinquent and rebellious personalities, and submissive, passive, and excessively dependent personalities. Some of these may comprise a "super-labile" group who clearly show diabetic decompensation after emotional arousal (Baker & Barcai, 1970; Rome & Robinson, 1959; Starr, 1955).

The Adolescent Diabetic

In adolescent years especially, the diabetic seems to become psychologically vulnerable because of the many changes and stresses associated with those years in our culture. The usual adolescent struggles are complicated by diabetes and, in turn, the problems created by the disease are exaggerated. The social stigma of being diabetic becomes more apparent; awareness grows that the diabetic care routine does not make for social success. There is general agreement among diabetes specialists that adherence to the prescribed regimen becomes a problem (Baker & Barcai, 1970; LaHood, 1970; USDHEW, Vol. III, 1976). Young people will strive to hide their illness; rebellion is not uncommon.

This rebellion is short-lived because there is no escape from diabetes. We do not have information as to the consequences of this defeat. There are suggestive data, as reported by Fischer (1948), that many diabetic children begin to fail in studies after elementary school. Whether this is due to physical or psychological factors is not known. Still fewer diabetics go on to college, and fewer of these complete college and go on to professional careers.

There is evidence that diabetic control in young children, say under the age of nine, is less reactive to group participation than among older children. Crain, Sussman, and Weill (1966) found that participation in group activities, especially the conditions of that activity, has an important effect on diabetic control. The less competitive and more crisis-free groups tend to have more stabilizing effects.

During adolescence, problems involving future aspirations arise—problems of marriage, parenthood, and career (Kennedy, 1955). As for marriage and parenthood, there are many risks to be faced by the future mothers with diabetes. There is a high rate of abortions, stillbirths, and neonatal deaths. The risk of pregnancy to the diabetic woman herself is not appreciable, but the infant is at risk after birth even under the best of circumstances (USDHEW, Vol. III, 1976).

These are matters for skilled and wise counseling. There is no agreement about the advice that should be given to diabetic women. One writer states that diabetes should not be a bar to pregnancy (Frankel, 1975). The National Commission on Diabetes report emphasizes the hazards of pregnancy and the need for careful and informed consideration of those hazards. The report expresses the hope that "research will yield tools which will permit a better chance of successful outcome in pregnancy for women with diabetes" (USDHEW, Vol. III, 1976).

The employment of diabetics is a problem that is being given systematic attention. Surveys of the employment practices of industry pertaining to diabetics have been carried out, the most recent is that prepared by Krosnick for the National Commission on Diabetes (USDHEW, Vol. III, 1976). In a sense, employability depends upon the diabetic. If control is achieved by diet alone,

then the problem is relatively simple. If insulin is required, then questions arise, and if control is precarious with insulin, problems are created for employment potential; if the factor of "uncooperativeness" is introduced, the exclusion results.

The American Diabetes Association takes the position that although the poorly controlled, uncooperative diabetic should be refused employment, the well-controlled, cooperative diabetic is a good employment risk. The results of studies in industry show that the diabetic may be compared to the nondiabetic in his ability to work, in caliber of work, and in absentee record. The National Commission report does believe that insurance rates consideration play a part, directly or indirectly, in hiring practices. For example, second-injury laws, protection of employers who hire handicapped persons from excessive health and insurance rates in the event of second injury to the handicapped persons which result in permanent disability, do not cover diabetics on the grounds that diabetes is a progressive disease which may result in total disability without second injury. This is, of course, a serious obstacle to employment.

Krosnick (1976) reviewed studies of hiring practices of both public and private employers. While employment opportunities have improved, there is "ample evidence of discriminatory practices . . . observed over the last decade or two." The improvement in job opportunities has been mainly for milder cases, and the severe cases, those that are poorly controlled, are universally rejected. Krosnick cites a World Health Organization report to the effect that the restrictions on the employment of diabetics are often "purely negative and are based on prejudice or ill-informed opinion about the effects of diabetes on a person's working ability or capacity."

These serious vocational problems of the diabetics point to the need for extensive and systematic education of employers and the public in general about diabetes. Again, the

National Commission has made recommendations for this purpose. More pressing, perhaps, is the provision of skilled and knowledgeable professional counseling, both vocational and personal, for the diabetic adolescent—a service that is usually absent.

The Education of Diabetic Children

In contrast to other disorders, there is no mention in the literature of special education facilities for the diabetic child. Certainly there do not seem to be compelling medical or psychological reasons for such. His educational needs apparently can be met most adequately in regular classes (USDHEW, Vol. III, 1976).

Diabetes requires a life style that serves to set the diabetic apart, most of all in his own eyes. Because of the necessity to train the child in this style of life and yet to make him feel part of a group, summer camps for diabetics have been developed in many parts of the country. The stated values of these camps are to train the diabetic child in the prescribed diabetic regimen, but to do so in an atmosphere of recreation, companionship, and emotional support. Such camps seem to be well established as a part of the educational program in the disease. The therapeutic evaluation of the camps are mainly impressionistic and generally favorable. Camp sessions have been utilized as occasions for studies of diabetic children. As elements in the treatment scheme, the camps are not only pleasant interludes but desirable and important facilities in the total treatment scheme (Frankel, 1975; Geist, 1964; Jacobi, 1954; Marble, 1957; Skyler et al., 1975; Wentworth & Gregory, 1972).

Finally, psychological attention is recommended consistently for the diabetic child. Throughout the literature, there is the theme that measures should be observed to prevent emotional problems and, when needed, psychotherapeutic programs should be set up for both child and parents. Group programs are also reported (Luzzati & Dittman, 1954), and the fundamental value of family treatment has been recognized.

HEART DISORDERS

Nature of Heart Disorders Among Children

Heart disorders among children and youth comprise for the most part congenital heart disease and rheumatic heart disease. Remarkable advances in diagnostic and surgical techniques in recent decades have altered the prognosis in most forms of congenital heart disease from hopeless to appreciable improvement (Rowe et al., 1974). The changes in the epidemiology of rheumatic fever have reduced the disease incidence over the past thirty years (Kaplan, 1975). Despite this progress, both conditions remain important health problems which produce heart disease in children. Congenital heart disease is the greater of the two problems and is seen about ten times more frequently among new patients in centers for the treatment of heart disease (Nelson, Vaughan, & McKay, 1969).

There are many types of congenital heart defects; each may occur alone or in combination with other defects. The various anatomical subdivisions of the heart or of the great vessels leaving the heart may be affected. Some are more lethal or disabling than others; some produce little obvious handicap in childhood, but may cause difficulty at a later age.

The causes of congenital heart defects are not known. Some implicate occurrence of German measles (rubella) during the first three months of pregnancy. Other virus diseases are also believed to be involved. A more recent view attributes congenital heart disease to a combination of adverse genetic and environmental interactions (Neill, 1972). Approximately 5 to 8 babies in 1,000 live births are born with congenital heart disease; another author estimates this to amount to 30,000 to 45,000 children per year.

Many youngsters with congenital heart disease have undergone open-heart surgery with spectacular results (Kaplan, 1974). For severely affected children, by the end of the first year of life most have either had successful surgery or had died. However, successful surgery does not mean ability to pursue "normal" activities. Restriction of physical activities is necessary and careful checkup is essential. Drug therapy is recommended as a prophylactic measure whenever infection is possible in order to prevent infective endocarditis. This regimen is a life-long matter because generally, even with the improvement achieved through surgery, there are residual abnormalities. Despite these measures, physical growth in children with heart malformations is not optimal.

Rheumatic fever is a clinical syndrome whose chief manifestations are heart disease, arthritis, chorea, skin rashes, and subcutaneous nodules. The importance of the disease centers around the fact that it produces heart damage. Until the 1930s it was one of the chief causes of illness and death in childhood and early adult life. It is now much less common and mortality and incidence rates have decreased (Kaplan, 1975). Typically, physicians today see fewer cases and many have the impression that rheumatic fever has been eradicated (Brownell & Bailen-Rose, 1973). Unfortunately, it is still a major health problem—"a disease of crowding, inadequate medical care, and in general of low socioeconomic environment" (Noonan, 1974), and remains concentrated in the groups it has always predominantly affected —three times greater in low-income areas than in higher-income areas (Brownell & Bailen-Rose, 1973). Some authorities are of the opinion that the decline is due more to the improvement in socioeconomic status of formerly depressed groups than to the effect of antibiotics, hence, the continued high

prevalence rates for disadvantaged groups (Nelson et al., 1969).

The specific important causative factor is accepted to be streptococcus bacteria. The disease rarely begins in the first four years of life; as adolescence is approached, the incidence rises. Thus the disease strikes mainly during the school years, from ages 5 to 19 years, with a peak at 8 years.

Rheumatic heart disease is found in only 1 or 2 school children per 1,000 (Nelson et al., 1969). An approximately equal number have rheumatic fever but no residual heart involvement. Of children who have recovered from an attack of rheumatic fever, 95 percent are able to lead an average existence. Perhaps 5 percent are semi-invalid and lead restricted lives. The vast majority are able to go to school and take part in ordinary activities that do not involve strenuous effort. In a study of 699 surviving patients out of 1,000 rheumatic fever patients who twenty years before had acute attacks, it was found that 3 out of 4 had little or no limitation in their activities (Keith, Rowe, & Vlad, 1958.)

The periods of illness in rheumatic fever are usually prolonged despite the fact that the earliest infection is often mild. In addition, the child with rheumatic fever is subject to repeated attacks of acute infection, and if the heart escapes damage during earlier attacks, it rarely escapes as the result of repeated attacks. The greater the number of recurrences, the greater the heart damage. In the past, once the acute infection phase was over, convalescent care was recommended for long periods of time, sometimes for years. No one strongly advocates the prolonged and rigid regimen once employed. Authorities question the value of bed rest in preventing or minimizing heart damage. Thus bed rest, although still widely used, is not prescribed routinely, and adaptation to individual needs, both clinically and psychologically, is recommended. Penicillin is the effective treatment and it is also used to prevent recurrences of the illness. There are no preventive measures for initial infection such as in polio and measles, nor is penicillin a cure.

Many children with rheumatic fever may be regarded as being cardiac, even though they do not have heart disease, because of the necessity for close health supervision and prophylactic medication. The prognosis in rheumatic fever has improved, mortality is falling, recurrences are less common, initial attacks are less severe, streptococcal disease is more readily treated, and increasingly successful surgical techniques for valvular damage are available. Ultimately, the prognosis is related to the development and persistence of heart disease.

Psychological Sensitivity of the Cardiovascular System

Psychological factors have been associated with the functioning of the heart since time immemorial. There are numerous allusions in literature to the particular vulnerability of the heart to emotional influence, if not to its being the actual seat of emotion. In view of the critical importance of the heart for life or death, it is not at all surprising that the heart has been probably the most heavily emotionally invested organ of the body. Any threat to the heart is a threat to life itself. Thus, the accumulated folklore concerning the heart would be expected to cause immediate psychological repercussions whenever there is the slightest implication of heart disease.

Interest in the psychosomatic aspects of heart disease has been accompanied with the general development of psychosomatic medicine (Garner & Wenar, 1959). Dunbar (1948), in particular, has formulated psychosomatic hypotheses in many forms of heart disease, including one for a psychosomatic predisposition to rheumatic heart disease. Except for rheumatic heart disease, the diseases implicated are those of adulthood and so do not directly concern the age groups under study. Moreover, the evidence presented is based almost entirely on adult groups. Nevertheless, her hypotheses have not been supported—no distinct personality has been found for children with heart disease (Crowell, 1953; Neuhaus, 1958; Wrightstone et al., 1961).

In patients with structural heart defects, there is a basic physiological problem that can be stated in terms of supply and demand. As long as it is possible for the heart to maintain circulation at an adequate level, the patient is compensated; that is, an adequate blood supply is maintained to tissues in response to varying functional demands. Whenever the balance between circulatory demands and the capacity of the heart to meet these demands cannot be maintained, heart failure develops. This balance may be disrupted by factors which increase the demand to a level greater than can be met or by factors that lead to reduction of the capacity of the heart to meet demands. In both these situations, psychological stress may operate to increase demand and/or decrease available supply.

Many studies have been conducted that demonstrate this. Wolf and Wolff (1946) and the various studies of the Cornell group have shown that variations in pulse rate, cardiac output, and blood pressure, as well as other cardiovascular changes, may be induced under conditions of psychological stress having specific meaning for the individual. These stress conditions include the persistent low-grade strains of everyday living. Insofar as the patient with heart disease is concerned, there is little doubt as to the influence of psychological stress on the course of his disease (Boshes, 1958). However, the etiological role of psychological stress is not firmly established.

Anxiety is an inevitable consequence of heart disease, as of disease in general. Koenig (1959) studied this phenomenon in children with rheumatic fever. She investigated the relationship between recurrences of rheumatic fever and Rorschach indices of anxiety. She found that children with recurrences of rheumatic fever exceeded normal children in degree of anxiety. Children who had experienced several attacks exhibited more marked anxiety than those who had suffered a single attack. She also found that the younger the child during the first and ensuing attacks, the greater the anxiety in extent of indicators and intensity.

Green and Levitt (1962), using drawings of human figures by a group of children with congenital heart disease, found that those children tended to depict themselves as graphically smaller than did a group of normal children. Reed (1959) compared a group of children with congenital heart disease with non-disabled controls and found no significant differences in intelligence-test scores, social-maturity scores, and judgments about personal adjustment.

Josselyn, Simon, and Eells (1955) describe rheumatic children who came to a convalescent home after hospitalization as having "unwarranted anxiety in regard to their heart." They point out that anxiety may persist where damage to the heart is severe. Among their children, anxiety was also provoked by other factors than the actual cardiac condition—factors they classify under neurotic anxiety. Neurotic anxiety includes such sources of disturbances as the nature of the parent-child relationships and utilization of the illness for secondary gain—for attention, avoiding responsibility, controlling and tyrannizing the family, and the like.

In a group of 262 cardiac adolescents who responded to a questionnaire, about one-half reported worries about their heart condition. About two-thirds of the rheumatic heart cases reported a higher incidence of worries. In every group of this study, the adolescent felt that his parents were much more concerned about the cardiac limitation than he was (Wrightstone *et al.*, 1961).

Whitehouse (1964) has explicated the problems of the cardiac adolescent. These are emotional immaturity, cultural isolation. academic deficiency, and vocational ineptitude. Together, these problems constitute a social handicap. These problems, of course, refer to children with long-standing heart disorders.

Neuhaus (1958) compared the personalities of asthmatic, cardiac, and normal children. The cardiac children exceeded the normals in degree of neuroticism and in dependency feelings but were not significantly different from asthmatic children. The younger sick children in the study groups showed more intense maladjustment.

It seems clear that anxiety among cardiac children is invariably aroused. Once aroused, it cannot fail to reverberate to the cardiovascular system as a stress factor. Inevitably, the physiological reserve and heart function will be taxed—and possibly contribute to further disability. Finally, symptoms that are psychogenic in origin, the results of anxiety, may be misinterpreted as being based on heart disease (Bellak & Haselkorn, 1956).

Psychological factors have been found to be influential in determining the continuation of recommended prophylactic treatment to prevent recurrent rheumatic fever attacks. A group of 284 college students with histories of rheumatic fever were interviewed, and it was found that their conscientiousness in maintaining prophylaxis depended upon beliefs and attitudes rather than objective experiences (Heinzelman, 1962).

Psychological Factors in the Home

The outcome of these psychological forces is to place the heart in a central position in the phenomenological schema of patients. With children, the intensity and content of anxiety about the heart seem to be derived from parental influences rather than from self-awareness except, of course, as children grow older. Brazelton, Holder, and Talbot (1953) found that parent-child relationships, particularly before illness, greatly influenced the way in which the child subsequently handled his disease. This fact is emphasized by most investigators. It must be remembered, too, that anxiety in cardiac disease is realistic to a certain extent. The potential dangers of heart damage and death are constantly in the awareness of the parents, who in turn impress them upon the child. As a result, these authors believe that rheumatic fever is a real trauma which, because of these threats, lowers the capacity of the child to withstand daily stresses.

Intensifying these effects is confusion about the nature of heart disease (Bauer, 1952). Children found it especially difficult to comprehend the concept of heart disease; their concepts were as vague as those of their mothers. Kennell and his co-workers (1960) similarly report a "remarkable" lack of understanding about rheumatic fever and the prevention of recurrences among parents despite the fact that they had been attending a rheumatic fever clinic with their children regularly for long periods. The parents, moreover, were quite ignorant of health matters in general. Their level of anxiety was high.

Psychologically, another complication is that treatment programs in heart disorders usually have been guided by the demands of the pathologic process. Generally this meant adherence to strict bed rest with gradual resumption of activity. Emphasis was placed on lessened participation. Furthermore, most children with rheumatic heart disease were hospitalized because of the need for nursing care and close medical supervision. This experience of hospitalization can be a very significant one, as we have seen.

In contrast, for his group of children, Bauer (1952) found that the anxiety coming out of separation was usually of short duration. To be sure, adjustment to hospitalization depended upon the nature of developmental relationships with parents; those who adjusted best had experiences of emotional security and growth with their parents. Other factors in hospital adjustment were found in the nature of specific prac-

tices of the hospital to provide for emotional needs of the children, such as frequency of visits, and opportunities and encouragement to form attachments to parental substitutes. As we have noted, the aseptic and impersonal atmospheres in hospitals have served to enhance anxiety feelings.

The recognition among cardiologists of the importance of psychological factors in the care of children with long-term illness has led to increased attention to the extramedical aspects of treatment. One study, for example, undertook to investigate the suitability of home care for children with active rheumatic fever (Young & Rodstein, 1953). It was found that children could be cared for at home as well as in the hospital, provided certain initial criteria were met. The most important criterion was the willingness and ability of the parents to undertake a long, exacting regimen of unpredictable duration and outcome. Both children and parents preferred home treatment to that in a hospital. There seems little doubt that the homes in this study were in many ways superior to those ordinarily found among cardiac children. As such, this study is limited in its usefulness. Nevertheless, as noted above, there have been changes in the rigid activity restrictions formerly practiced. Indeed, Gasul, Arcilla, and Lev (1966) state that "no proof [exists] . . . that [rest] prevents or minimizes heart damage."

Thus, the trend toward home care in rheumatic fever presupposes optimal living circumstances but this is a questionable expectation. Most of the families with rheumatic fever patients, in view of the highest prevalence rates, derive from poor and disadvantaged populations. Is it reasonable that such families could be counted on to observe the many recommendations for the management of their sick children? With the numerous economic and psychological pressures upon those groups, how effectively can they cope with the added stresses of a chronically ill child at home? There are no reported studies on this matter except mention of high occurrence of poor adjustment among children with heart defects and the need for psychological support (Rowe *et al.*, 1974).

Restriction of Physical Activity

The single element running through every phase of the care of children with heart disorders is the necessity for *some* degree of restriction of physical activity. This necessity dictates the need for extended convalescence and continued efforts to teach the child to live within his limitations. In the past, it dictated the policy of many school systems to make arrangements for the education of children with heart disease in other than regular classes. It is important, therefore, that the psychological implications of restricted activity be considered.

Holder (1953) found that the restrictions placed upon children because of heart disease impressed upon them that they were sick and were constant reminders of their illness. The child finds it difficult to understand the necessity for limited activity beyond the acute phases of illness, when he readily accepts restrictions. As he begins to feel better, the restrictions become onerous. Hence, it is necessary to use pressure to maintain restricted activity, and this is a persistent source of conflict. The parents' anxiety may lead them to overcontrol. Bauer (1952) felt that much overemphasis on restrictions was an unconscious expression of the parents' hostility engendered by the hardships the illness caused the family.

It is to be expected that cardiac children would dislike the restrictions placed on their activity (Wrightstone, Justman, & Moscowitz, 1953). They resent segregation at school; they feel singled out and "different." They regard themselves as adequate and not different from other children. They miss identification with peers and the competitive outlets afforded in their relationships both at school and in their neighborhoods. The net effect of these restrictions is to arouse

hostility, anxiety, and feelings of low self-esteem and insecurity. Passive children accept the restrictions, and the others become resigned despite initial resistiveness.

On the other hand, a group of adolescent cardiac students on a self-report questionnaire tended to minimize the consequences of the restrictions imposed by the physicians. In distinction to the findings reported among elementary school cardiacs, very few of the adolescents felt that their limitation had affected their ability to make friends. Virtually none of the students reported having no friends. Two factors should be kept in mind in interpreting these findings. One is that the data are based on self-reports, and two, adolescents would be loath to admit they have few or no friends. This is a reflection of the cultural stereotype of popularity (Wrightstone *et al.*, 1961).

A committee of the American Heart Association has studied the problem of restriction of physical activity both for vocational guidance and recreational purposes. The committee developed the concept of peak loads which correspond to the usual definitions of sedentary, light, medium, and heavy physical activity. The importance of intensity of participation in recreational activity is emphasized. Severe restriction would limit the individual to activities requiring low levels of energy expenditures such as golf, bowling, walking, swimming—all on a non-competitive basis. Mild restriction would avoid intensive effort (peak loads) lasting more than one-half minute at any one time. The work of the committee provides a schema and guidelines in this fundamental but troublesome area (Rowe *et al.*, 1974).

The advisability for a regimen of limited activity and graded steps in increasing activity at one time meant that the cardiac child went to a convalescent home where he stayed perhaps up to a year after discharge from the hospital; the procedure is not commonly practiced today. Here again, lack of understanding on the part of the child of the need for a convalescent period was found. The reactions noted among the children were accentuated guilt feelings and anxiety. During the period of convalescent care, the concepts of controlling and limiting his activity are emphasized as are the precautions necessary to avoid infection. Summer camps for cardiac children were also utilized to help these children adapt to the regimen imposed by their illness.

Adjustment Problems of the Cardiac Child

If the child has been hospitalized, all observers agree that the return home is fraught with difficulties. After a long absence, the child may have developed feelings of rejection and, hence, hostility toward his parents and siblings (Taran & Hodsdon, 1949). In a sense the child has grown away from the family. Bauer found that whereas the home could do much to help the child in this difficult period, more often than not the child's problems are enhanced. The parents' anxieties tend to maintain the child's separation from his age group; overprotectiveness and overcontrol are common. Without the experience in relationships with healthy peers, the child hesitates in or withdraws from competition with his playmates. Holder saw the uncertainties of outlook and the possibility of recurrence of rheumatic fever as leading parents to curb and hamper the expression of positive social interactions.

Another contributing element to negative psychological development in the cardiac child is the ambivalent attitude of parents, as shown in a New York City Board of Education study. There was a limited acceptance of the child. The attitude of the parents was related to the degree of marital harmony existing between them. When the marriage was harmonious, the attitudes toward the child were positive, and when disharmony prevailed, negative attitudes were the rule (Wrightstone, Justman, & Moscowitz, 1953).

The net result of these forces seems to be to encourage passive, dependent reactions. One study found that cardiacs exceed normal children in degree of neuroticism and dependency (Neuhaus, 1958).

The picture of the cardiac child, as drawn by the study of the New York City Board of Education, portrays him as one who has come to accept his disability with persistent withdrawal behavior. As a group, the cardiac children tend to be unresponsive. They are unable to cope with many situations in which they find themselves. They are passive and lacking in initiative and drive for achievement. They do not make adequate use of their intellectual capacity; they require that effort to be made to stimulate them to be productive. Emotionally, the children are immature, constricted, and regressed. They are given to daydreaming and brooding. As in other studies, a high percentage of children are judged to be maladjusted. They have few friends and do not engage in organized play activities outside the home.

On the other hand, a later study of adolescents in New York schools reported that the cardiac group was similar to the general adolescent population. Dependency was not a significant factor. The great amount of deviation from average was in sex anxiety. This finding was adjudged to be not unusual because one of the outstanding changes in adolescence is sexual maturity. The investigators in this study of adolescents felt that the evidence did not indicate that cardiac illness per se was related to any of the personality traits investigated. When disturbances were found, it was not believed they were the results of cardiac illness. It is difficult to evaluate these results, whether they are the outcomes of the techniques and criteria of investigation or whether they represent developmental change. They stand in contrast to the findings of other investigations (Wrightstone et al., 1961).

In the New York City study, teachers of children in special cardiac classes evaluated their adjustment by means of a rating scale. It was observed that the teachers were biased in favor of the children, tending to assign more favorable ratings in practically all categories of the scale. In contrast to the ratings by specialists, the children showed the best adjustment in (1) relationship to parents, (2) relationship to other children, (3) attitude to group control, and (4) adjustment to leadership. Their poorest adjustments were reported in (1) leadership, (2) work habits, (3) nervous habits, (4) self-confidence, and (5) responsibility. Furthermore, according to the teachers, the children tended to adopt aggressive, rather than withdrawing, mechanisms of adjustment.

In the study of adolescents, the teachers reported the majority of students as socially adjusted. Psychologists were in agreement with this group.

It is not easy to reconcile these contradictory findings within the same study and between studies; the reports do not attempt to do so. In addition to the probably different frames of reference for the teachers and specialists in rating the cardiac children, it seems that the biases of the teachers in favor of the children were potent factors in contributing to much of the difference.

In the high school, the situation is altered. The student is less well known to any single teacher. The teacher usually feels competent to provide information on academic achievement but less able to provide personal information. The majority of students were reported as socially adjusted. Academic adjustment was rated as wholly positive for 48 percent of the students and wholly negative for 20 percent in the tenth grade. The majority of teachers felt that the cardiac students showed interest in the classroom and possessed other positive attributes about school.

On both group and individual tests of intelligence, the cardiac children in elementary schools were found to fall into the low-average category. The distribution of scores showed a wide range of variability. There were no data available to evaluate this finding, but it seemed to be due mainly to sociocultural phenomena. Most of the children came from below-average socioeconomic homes, and the deficit may be a function of cultural factors. It may be speculated, also, that the restriction of activities due to illness, with limited opportunities for social, cultural, and intellectual stimulation, was contributory. Certainly, the data presented previously on personality evaluation, indicating mental apathy and lack of drive, tend to support these speculations.

Eighth-grade cardiacs attained an average IQ of 95.3 on a group intelligence test; the city-wide average for eighth-graders was 101.8. Here again, the cardiacs as a group fell into the low-average category.

As part of the New York City study, a group of 180 cardiac students in the eleventh grade were given individual intelligence examinations. The average IQ for this group was 105.7. This places them in the slightly above-average group and compares favorably to the level achieved by the noncardiac New York City eleventh-grade population. The latter had achieved an average IQ of 103.7 on a group intelligence test when they were in the eighth grade.

The discrepancy between the mean IQs of the eleventh graders and eighth graders is believed to be due to selective factors. Most of the school dropouts occur in the tenth and eleventh grades, and generally result from poor scholarship. Hence, the eleventh graders are superior students. The proportion of dropouts by school year is much the same in the cardiac and in the total school population.

There have been studies of special psychological issues among children with heart disease. One relates to children with chorea, a disorder associated with rheumatic fever, which is characterized by abrupt, spontaneous, uncoordinated movements. On the basis of long-term observation, there have been reports of high percentages of behavioral disturbances or emotional problems among persons with chorea (Nelson et al., 1969). It is not clear, however, whether those problems were implicated in the etiology of chorea or they were the consequences of the condition. Stehbens and MacQueen (1972) undertook to study whether patients with chorea are more tense and anxious, hence more prone to develop chorea. Using the MMPI, they studied sixty-five patients with chorea and sixty-five without chorea ten years after the onset of the illness. They found no differences between the choreics and nonchoreics.

A second psychological issue revolves about the effect of congenital heart disease, in particular cyanotic congenital heart disease, upon the functioning of children. Linde, Rasoff, Dunn, and Rabb (1966) and Linde, Rasoff, and Dunn (1967) studied the adjustment problems and intellectual functioning of children with cyanotic heart disease. The study included two groups of children with congenital heart disease, 98 with cyanosis and 100 without cyanosis, and two control groups of normal children, 81 siblings of the cardiac children and 40 children who were not relatives. In all there were 319 children ranging in age from 3 to 5 years. The instruments used were the Cattell Infant Series, the Gesell Development Schedule, the Stanford-Binet, and interviews with the mothers. The results indicated that the cyanotic children scored significantly lower on the Stanford-Binet than did the non-cyanotic children and both heart disease groups achieved lower scores than the normal groups. Also, retardation was found in physical capacities such as a later age of walking and poor motor ability. However in subsequent years these differences disappeared. The investigators concluded that the intellectual retardation was related to the physical incapacities which were judged to be the result of limitations on physical activity. Once the children began to walk and be more active, they caught up. Nevertheless, even in later years, the cyanotic group fell into the lower end of the range of obtained scores for all the children in the study. This was determined to

be the consequence of the altered and reduced environmental experiences for the cyanotic group; the lower scores were not believed to be due to cultural, socioeconomic, or other family characteristics, but to a developmental phenomenon related to the heart condition. The study found most of the cardiac children to be fairly well adjusted, and that their adjustment was independent of the severity of the disease. Maternal pampering and overprotectiveness were more common for the cardiac groups than they were for the normals, and were highest for the cyanotic group. These actions by mothers were felt to be due more to anxiety than to severity of disease. In the same manner, when poor adjustment occurred, it was taken to be due to maternal anxiety rather than to an incapacity on the part of the cardiac child.

In another study of children with cyanotic heart disease, Silbert and his co-workers (1969) examined the effects of chronic hypoxia, insufficiency of blood oxygen, which is characteristic in cyanosis, on the perceptual, motor, and intellectual development of those children. Three groups were formed: cyanotic children; non-cyanotic children with congestive heart failure; and non-cyanotic children with heart disease but without congestive heart failure. There were forty-two children with heart disease studied, ranging in age from 4 to 8 years, and all the children had similar socioeconomic backgrounds. The test instruments used were the Stanford-Binet, the Frostig Development Test, the Five Figure Formboard, the Wallin Pegboard, and the Draw-a-Person Test. On all measures, the cyanotic children attained significantly lower scores than the two other groups. The investigators felt that the results showed the effects of chronic cerebral hypoxia and that the inferior performances of the cyanotic children were not due to the activity restrictions during early years; there is no specific statement as to the probable permanence of this result. This is the major point of difference from the somewhat similar finding by Linde and his co-workers; Linde found that the differences disappeared in later years with increased activity.

On tests of achievement, the New York City study found that cardiac children showed retardation, although wide variability was seen; they performed below the level of nonhandicapped children in the same grade level. Analysis indicated that the cardiac children, as compared to the total school population of New York City in the grades studied, were in far larger proportion overage for their grade. This high percentage of overageness was believed to be due, mainly, to irregular attendance and consequent nonpromotion.

It is appropriate at this point to discuss the advisability of special educational arrangements for cardiopathic children. In the past there have been three types of school provisions for these children: (1) day schools —special provisions in regular classes, special classes in regular schools, special centers for the handicapped in schools for normal children, and special schools; (2) residential provisions in institutions, sanatoria, convalescent homes, and hospitals; (3) homebound provisions for those children who are too handicapped to go to school, who cannot be transported, or who are excluded for whatever reasons.

In the past, these educational provisions were dictated by purely medical considerations so as to provide for limited activity. Usually, the anxieties of the school administrator and the teacher caused the child to be set apart. Furthermore, it has been customary to stress cardiac damage and resulting cardiac disability as the starting points in the education of the cardiopathic child. In other words, once the child was sick, he was to be trained for a life of cardiac disability. From this frame of reference, segregation in special classes and training in the realization of limitations were logical developments.

However, current medical thinking and educational thinking does not accept this point of view. The child is either completely handicapped because of rheumatic activity and cannot attend classes, or, as in the vast majority of cases, he can participate in all childhood activities when his illness is quiescent (Levitt & Taran, 1948). White (1951) shares this view and believes that most children with heart disease at any age, once the disease is not active, can safely attend school and need not or should not be separated in special categories or classes. The exceptions would be those children with such congenital or organic defects as to make them actual cardiac cripples. Thus, with the medical necessity for special facilities for the education of cardiac children placed in doubt, it is not surprising that many educational authorities took another look at their special education facilities. This, of course, does not take into consideration the many compelling psychological arguments and findings against such segregation. These have been indicated throughout the present discussion.

In New York City, the Board of Education undertook to determine whether its program was meeting adequately the needs of children with physical limitations. This study was extremely broad and comprehensive, and delved into every aspect of education of cardiopathic children. One part of the study was an evaluation of a sampling of special classes for physically handicapped children, not only for cardiac children. The physical and recreational facilities of these classes seemed to be adequate. The classroom climates in less than one-third of the rooms observed were regarded as attractive; the others were "neat, staid, static." The large majority of the classes were friendly in atmosphere. About one-third of the classes were conducive to the development of pupil initiative. Few were stimulating for the children; in most, interest was either forced, passive, or indifferent. Formal control by the teacher was the practice in the great majority of classes. However, in most classes, the pupil-teacher attitudes were friendly and sharing. From these data, it does not seem that these classes reflect the best practices for providing the stimulation and opportunities for emotional growth. They tend to reinforce the trends toward passivity and lack of initiative.

Studies such as these are difficult to evaluate because their results provide no frame of reference against which they may be evaluated. For example, with regard to special classes, it is necessary to know something of the regular classroom facilities and practices to learn whether the results are typical of the schools themselves or are specific for the special classes. This situation serves to point out again the need for controlled study.

TUBERCULOSIS

Nature of the Disease

Tuberculosis is an infection to which apparently all humans are susceptible. It is caused by the tubercle bacillus, which can and does infect almost any tissue or organ in the body; the most common site of infection is the lungs.

In this country, the tuberculosis situation has undergone a remarkable change during the past five decades. In the early 1930s, large numbers of children contracted tuberculosis and many died in infancy and early childhood from tuberculosis. Since 1930, a marked decline has been observed in the prevalence of tuberculosis among children in nearly every region in this country. In the age groups under 25 years, 5 percent have a positive reaction to tuberculin skin tests as compared with a rate of 90 percent prior to 1930 (Johnston & Wildrick, 1974). (Arango, Brewin, & Murray, 1973; Charney, 1968; *Statistical Bulletin,* 1974). The rates are higher in urban centers, mainly among indigent groups; they are also higher for older adults, especially men. In general, there is a direct but inverse relation between tuberculosis morbidity and mortality rates in any geographic area and the socioeconomic level of the people who live in that area. Where incomes are low and living conditions are poor and crowded and the diets are inadequate, the tuberculosis rates are higher. This is seen particularly among American Indian groups. Thus tuberculosis remains an important health problem for the poor and disadvantaged.

With the overall dramatic decline in tuberculosis rates and the great effectiveness of therapeutic measures, treatment programs gradually shifted from hospital to ambulatory care. Hospitals devoted only to tuberculosis treatment have been disappearing; the reduction in both number of patients requiring hospitalization and the length of time of hospitalization have made it feasible and advantageous to use general hospitals for the short periods required and for ambulatory care. Authorities expect that the tuberculosis hospital will disappear soon and tuberculosis care will be part of the mainstream of medicine (Bates, 1974).

As a chronic disease, tuberculosis requires regular drug treatment for a period of a year or more. Such extended treatment creates patient-management problems since a large proportion of the young patients avoid taking medication regularly—a phenomenon encountered in all chronic diseases which demand adherence to a prescribed regimen. Hence tuberculosis treatment becomes vulnerable to conflict when strict following of a treatment schedule is required. A positive reaction to the tuberculin test does not mean active clinical disease—it is an indication of previous contact with the tubercle bacillus.

There has been a continued and marked decline in the mortality rate of tuberculosis since 1900 and a precipitous drop since 1947, corresponding to the introduction of antibiotic and chemical therapy. In 1900 the tuberculosis death rate in the United States was about 200 per 100,000; in 1945, the death rate was less than 50 per 100,000; in 1965, 4.2 per 100,000, and in 1972 the death rate was 1.9 per 100,000 (Johnston & Wildrick, 1974. Some tuberculosis workers felt this decline heralded the beginning of the complete eradication of tuberculosis, but that goal is now recognized as a premature aspiration. Tuberculosis is still a major public health problem, and much work still must be done if that prospect of complete eradication is ever to become a reality (Charney, 1968).

The decline in mortality rate reflected a corresponding decline in the incidence of the disease; the active case rate in 1950 was estimated at 80 per 100,000; in 1965 the active case rate was 25.3 per 100,000; and in 1972 the active case rate was 16.1 per 100,000 (Johnston & Wildrick, 1974). These downward trends are seen in every industrialized country—a phenomenon observed over the past century (Bates, 1974). Current therapeutic and public health techniques make tuberculosis both curable and preventable. Other contributing factors to the fall in morbidity and mortality rates are improved standards of living with less crowding, and hence reduced likelihood for transmission of infection.

However, the decreases are not uniform for all population groups. They are greatest for the white population, but not for non-whites.

Psychological Sequelae of Tuberculosis

Psychological study in tuberculosis has been mainly carried out with adults; the number of studies dealing with children specifically has been very few, and in recent years, we have found none. The current literature in tuberculosis is restricted mainly to the medical and public health aspects.

The changes in the epidemiology and advances in the treatment of tuberculosis have modified the psychological ramifications surrounding the illness. The greater control over contagiousness, the shortening, and often the avoidance, of hospitalization lessen the psychological impact of tuberculosis; it becomes more generally akin to the other disorders considered in this chapter. Because

the historical life-threatening reputation is still associated with the disease, it is important to explicate some of its characteristics.

First is the chronic nature of tuberculosis. The disease process, once brought under control, lies dormant. This dormancy is termed "inactive" or "arrested," but not "cured." Thus, there is always the potential for reactivation, but the probability of reactivation is radically reduced with drug therapy.

This fact leads to the second aspect of tuberculosis, which is important psychologically. Reactivation of dormant lesions is ever a possibility and can be caused by a variety of factors as apparently unrelated as puberty, fatigue, malnutrition, uncontrolled diabetes, and emotional disturbances.

Third is the contagious nature of the disease. In the pre-antituberculosis drug era, this led to isolation usually in a hospital. Isolation, entailing separation from family and friends, was maintained until noncontagiousness was established and maintained and the disease process was rendered inactive. With antibiotics and chemotherapy the period of hospitalization, when necessary, has been reduced from an average of ten months in the 1950s to an average of three months in the 1970s. Contagiousness is controlled by drugs (Comstock, 1975). These specific changes have implications for two traditional aspects of tuberculosis—the stigma of contagiousness and the avoidance of prolonged stays in hospitals and sanitoria. The tuberculosis patient was regarded as a kind of "social menace" who was removed from contact with the public and who was required to pursue a life of complete inactivity for long periods of time. The artificiality and psychological complexities of hospital and sanatorium life have been portrayed in literary works as, for example, in *The Magic Mountain* by Thomas Mann. The one-time threat of lung surgery is rarely present today. Paradoxically, the patient usually feels fine from the outset of treatment.

Fourth, tuberculosis was historically a leading cause of death. To this statistical fact must be added the folklore about consumption as a wasting disease leading to certain fatality.

Fifth, in considering the folklore of tuberculosis, the sense of ostracism must be recorded. Further, tuberculosis is a disease, in the main, of the least-favored social classes. As one writer put it, "Tuberculosis is not a disease which spells retirement with honor." It is often felt by patients, and to a certain degree by society, to be evidence of failure.

Sixth, the susceptibility to tuberculosis increases shortly after puberty and during early adulthood. Thus, for some young people, tuberculosis comes at a period of life in which important adjustments are being made, and the extended treatment serves to complicate these processes.

The literature on the psychological aspects of tuberculosis is extensive and has been reviewed by several authors (Barker et al., 1953; Berle, 1948; Derner, 1953; Harris, 1955; Korkes & Lewis, 1955; Merrill, 1953; Wittkower, 1952). It has been concerned almost exclusively with adult groups. As we stated above, although there are references to add since our previous review, we have not been able to find any new studies involving age groups below adults.

Up to about 1940, the literature was mainly the result of subjective observation and clinical experience. Observations were usually made on small numbers of cases; contradictory conclusions were frequent; and systematic work with adequate experimental designs was virtually nonexistent. In sum, this work served as a source of hypotheses for study, but it did not provide useful knowledge.

In post–World War II years, studies of a systematic and experimental nature appeared, and a more consistent body of knowledge evolved. Despite its hoary tradition, the notion of a "tuberculosis personality" has been discarded. Differences in scores on psychological tests of tuberculosis patients and non-ill people did occur, but these were seen in the context of the patients' experience of hospitalization; in other words, the effects seen in the tuberculosis patient were reactive to the illness and its treatment. A number of studies reported specific emotional characteristics such as depression and anxiety, and it was concluded that these were frequently found in tuberculosis patients. Some relationship between psychological factors and response to treatment has been suggested (Vernier et al., 1961).

Attempts have been made to relate the onset of tuberculosis or its relapses to emotional stress (Hartz, 1944). This association has been noted by nonpsychiatric observers such as Dubo (1950). The exact relationship of emotional factors to the onset of active disease has not been established. The various efforts to formulate tuberculosis as a psychosomatic disease have served to offer some explanation as to why a person falls ill and why he falls ill when he does, but have failed to explain why he falls ill with pulmonary tuberculosis (Wittkower, 1959).

A thoroughgoing psychological study has been reported by Vernier and her associates (1961). For some 814 adult patients in eighteen hospitals, several psychological variables were related to hospital adjustment, response to medical treatment, and posthospital adjustment. One psychological variable, anxiety, was found to be related to all three criteria.

> Anxiety appears to play an important role in poor adjustment as seen both in the hospital and in the posthospital situations. Further, among those hospitalized patients with far advanced disease, the presence of anxiety was significantly related to less satisfactory response to the medical treatment of the disease process itself. These results lend some confirmation to the concept that anxiety is a central psychological variable in determining a wide variety of behaviors (p. 28).

These investigators felt that in this disease, "the need to maintain anxiety at a minimal state makes sense both logically and psychologically."

This last study dealt essentially with the somatopsychological effects of tuberculosis. From a practical point of view, these are especially significant. In addition, there is much agreement among the various studies on such psychological effects of the disease.

Somatopsychological Aspects

The effect of the diagnosis of tuberculosis is a traumatic one—a reaction of shock, followed by anxiety and depression. One may raise the question whether the impact of this effect has been diminished with the advances in treatment and prognosis—there are no reports on this issue. The significance of the disease is still emphasized and with its highest incidence occurring in urban, nonwhite, and poverty groups, the traditional attitudes of fear and fatalism are to be expected. However, this is a matter that should be investigated. To be sure, the length of hospitalization required for the average patient is three months and this is a significant period of time.

Derner (1953) found that the specific reaction for each individual was related to the individual's perception of the meaning of the disease. The defenses against anxiety and depression are frequently seen in defiance, cheerfulness, resentment, and apathy. The feelings of anxiety and depression are usual and expected so long as they are consistent with the nature and degree of the disease itself and with the repercussions that the illness has for the individual's life situation. If, however, the situation becomes complicated by existing conflicts and disturbances, neurotic anxiety may be superimposed on justifiable fear.

Psychological Effects in Children

The psychological effects of tuberculosis upon children have been the concern of several investigators. Kramer (1948) did not find any specific personality type among children suffering from tuberculosis, a finding consistent with other tuberculosis workers (Demuth, 1951; Derner, 1953). Kramer also was of the opinion that the psychopathology of tuberculous children did not differ essentially from the psychopathology of those who were nontuberculous. In addition, infection with tuberculosis did not necessarily lead to psychopathology; it was dependent on the reactions to the disease, not on the disease itself. Kramer found no specific reaction pattern among the tuberculous children. This last finding was at variance with the results of Dubo's study (1950).

Dubo studied twenty-five tuberculous children, ages 6 to 13 years, in Bellevue Hospital, New York City. These children came from deprived homes of low economic status in congested neighborhoods where the tuberculosis incidence was high. Data were gathered through individual interviews, group sessions, and psychological tests.

It was found, despite wide diversity of premorbid personalities, that there was a remarkable similarity of specific reactions. These reactions appeared to be closely linked with the difficulties in medical management encountered with these children. Ward behavior was characterized by diffuse motor activity, aggressive outbursts, and inability to cooperate in bed rest. The necessary limitation of activity was intolerable. These reactions were believed to stem from the intense anxiety that characterized the children's reactions to tuberculosis. Their thinking was preoccupied with death and other morbid content. Tuberculosis was equated with death. Dreams, fantasies, and drawings were filled with morbid and threatening symbols.

To these children, tuberculosis was a highly abstract phenomenon. It was symptomless and yet terrible because they had seen relatives and other patients die of it. In the face of this terrifying threat, the children were not allowed to react with the usual psychological response—fight or flight.

They were forced to remain inactive and passive. It is not surprising, therefore, that Dubo found that the fantasies of these children were filled with constant motion— running, dancing, roller-skating.

Regressive phenomena were observed but were expected in a prolonged, confining, and anxiety-producing illness. Yet strong resistance was found to these regressive trends. Another source of disturbance was the necessity for isolation. The children could not comprehend the abstract concept of contagion, much less the measures utilized to reduce contagion. They felt different and stigmatized; the most forceful term of opprobrium was to be called "TB patient." They believed that tuberculosis was contracted through lack of cleanliness and, therefore, was shameful. In addition, the children tended to assume personal responsibility for being ill and looked upon the illness as punishment. The reactions to these feelings of guilt and shame were resentment and feeling of being wronged. Aggression and defiance of authority were frequent problems.

The results of Dubo's study fit in with some of the findings of research with the adult tuberculous, particularly the reaction of anxiety. To be sure, this appeared to be the basic generalized reaction to great threat. Important to note was the failure of the children to comprehend the meanings of tuberculosis and contagion, which remained abstract concepts. We may wonder, indeed, if adults do not have the same difficulty (Hartz, 1950). It is quite likely that many of the attitudes and reactions expressed by these children reflect their sociocultural backgrounds.

Bowlby *et al.* (1956) conducted an investigation of sixty children who were under treatment for tuberculosis. The children were between 6 and 14 years of age, and had been hospitalized at various times before their fourth birthday for treatment of tuberculosis. They received the standard tuberculosis treatment while visits from parents

were maintained. No special attention was given to the problems of separation.

The findings indicated that these children suffered no significant damage to intellectual functions. There were, however, some indications of personality damage. On the basis of teachers' reports and interviews with the parents, the sanatorium children were judged to be showing tendencies toward withdrawal and apathy, as well as aggressiveness. Contrary to expectation, however, disturbance in the capacity to establish relationships with peers was not found in any significant number of these cases. On the basis of judgments of overall adjustment, a fairly high proportion of the children who had been hospitalized during their preschool years were considered maladjusted (63 percent of the sanatorium children as compared with 40 percent of the control group of 8-year-olds). In the interpretations of findings, the authors felt that factors in addition to separation may have influenced these outcomes, for example, concomitant deprivation of maternal care. These children were not only ill and hospitalized, but in many there were also histories of disruption and stress in their families—factors which were undoubtedly important for their subsequent adjustment.

In summing up the findings of this study, the investigators emphasized the great variations in personality patterns among the hospitalized children and pointed out that only a small minority developed very serious personality disabilities. On the other hand, they stressed that the potentially damaging effects of this kind of experience should not be minimized and felt that there were similarities in persisting personality deviations in some of these children reminiscent of those found in studies of severely deprived institutionalized children.

Bellak (1950), in a study of forty-six patients, emphasized the problems of the tuberculous adolescent. These patients faced many problems upon their return home after long absence. In the hospital sanatorium, they had lived under altogether different conditions in a sexually mixed group of all ages, and had been exposed to many ideas. Thus, with the usual problems of adolescent growth, they encountered special difficulties at home and in their social relationships. Instead of growing up with their problems, absorbing changes in small doses, there were sudden changes and clashes. Bellak called attention to these difficulties as one of the most clear-cut results of his study.

There may be some question of the continued relevance of the concerns expressed in studies of the effects of separation through hospitalization for children with tuberculosis. Until recent years, the tuberculosis hospital was the foundation upon which the treatment regimen was built. The effectiveness of chemotherapy brought to a climax the many dissatisfactions with hospital treatment in tuberculosis. Ambulatory treatment has become the practice and the tuberculosis hospital is disappearing.

Tuberculous Children in School

A practical issue in the care of tuberculous children, of particular interest to school authorities, is the provision of special facilities for education. At one time there was much enthusiasm about the treatment of children with primary tuberculous infections by removal from the home to preventoriums and camps. For those at home, attendance in special buildings, special schools, and "fresh-air" classes were recommended. In addition, as measures to prevent tuberculosis, malnourished and anemic children were sent to institutions set up for the purpose.

Experience, however, had shown that these facilities made no difference in treatment, and the results were the same whether the children were treated at home or in any of these special facilities. Consequently, most of these facilities were discontinued. The prognosis in primary tuberculosis is excel-

lent. For those with active reinfection tuberculosis, the proper place is to be decided by medical authority. If hospitalization is necessary, hospitals with patients of school age usually provide bedside instruction. This hospitalization is usually of relatively short duration. Upon discharge, the physician will prescribe a regimen for return to school. Contagion will usually not be a problem; tuberculosis is not really highly communicable (Comstock, 1975).

Segregation in special classes is not warranted medically or psychologically. This is not to say that there will not be problems arising from the integration of children with inactive tuberculosis in class activities. However, to the interested teacher, these problems are no greater than for the child who requires some adjustment in classroom routine. The problem of tuberculosis among children, which at one time appeared to be a vanishing one, persists, but it is, in the main, a public health and medical issue.

CONCLUSIONS
AND IMPLICATIONS

The study of these four chronic disorders serves to emphasize that the psychology of the ill and the disabled is to be understood in terms of the psychology of other groups, the normal and the deviant. The reactions of any child or youth to the stress of illness and disability depend upon a complex interplay of many forces, both internal and external. There is no simple, predictable relationship between any single factor and the reaction displayed by the individual, whether this relationship is between a psychological variable and a physical response or between a physical event and a psychological response. Rather, the evidence is in the direction of interactional effects which, in turn, are influenced by situational, developmental, and psychosocial elements. It is in this sense that psychosomatic factors are coming to be defined; at the same time there is critical examination of the value of etiologic considerations. The term *psychosomatic* is regarded as being descriptive of the interrelationships between the physical and the psychological, without concern for the direction of those relationships, whether causes or effects.

There are, to be sure, psychological reactions that occur with sufficient frequency to be regarded as being common, but those are by no means inevitable or invariant. Prominent among the common reactions to illness are anxiety and guilt feelings. Children often feel that their illness is a punishment. For them, illness is a poorly understood phenomenon and is clouded by subjective and irrational forces.

Inextricably implicated and strongly influential in these reactions are the family, and particularly the parent-child relationships. There is a continuing interplay between familial and subsequent experiences. Consequently, even though we are concerned with children and youth, it is appropriate to consider the reactions of adults to illness because the content of those reactions are communicated and provide the core of the children's reactions.

Hospitalization is not inevitably a negative experience, certainly not with the changes in hospital practices initiated to insure positive reactions. However, alternate treatment modalities to hospitalization are being developed, especially ambulatory units which provide comprehensive services of both medical and non-medical kinds.

In educational settings, chronically ill children are likely to appear in any classroom. As adults, teachers show the lack of knowledge, limited understanding, and distorted attitudes about chronic illness that adults as parents demonstrate.

Although there is much we still have to learn about the psychological aspects of chronic medical disorders among children, considerable interest and activity are apparent. There is general recognition of the fundamental importance of psychological forces in chronic medical disorders.

Finally, we should note the implication of sociocultural and socioeconomic factors in chronic medical disorders. In each of the conditions considered in this chapter, there is attention and concern with situational, environmental, and ecological factors—a point of view that has been gaining increasing importance and influence over the past thirty years.

REFERENCES

ABRAHAMSON, H. A. Evaluation of maternal rejection theory in allergy. *Annals of Allergy,* 1954, *12,* 129–140.

ALEXANDER, F. *Psychosomatic medicine. Its principles and applications.* New York: W. W. Norton & Company, 1950.

ARANGO, L., BREWIN, A. W., & MURRAY, J. F. The spectrum of tuberculosis as currently seen in a metropolitan hospital. *American Review of Respiratory Diseases,* 1973, *108,* 805–812.

BAIN, A. W. (Ed.). Symposium on chronic disease in children. *The Pediatric Clinics of North America,* 1974, *21,* 871–884.

BAKER, L., & BARCAI, A. Psychosomatic aspects of diabetes mellitus. In C. W. Hill (Ed.), *Modern Trends in Psychosomatic Medicine.* London: Butterworths, 1970.

——, MINUCHIN, S., MILMAN, L., LIEBMAN, R., & TODD, T. Psychosomatic aspects of juvenile diabetes mellitus; A progress report. In Z. Laron (Ed.), *Diabetes in Juveniles.* Basel: S. Karger, 1975, 332–343.

BAKWIN, R. M. Essentials of psychosomatics in allergic children. *The Pediatric Clinics of North America,* 1954, *1,* 921–928.

———, & BAKWIN, H. The child with asthma. *Journal of Pediatrics,* 1948, *32,* 320–323.

BARKER, R. G., & WRIGHT, B. A. Disablement: The somatopsychological problem. In E. D. Wittkower and R. A. Cleghorn (Eds.), *Recent developments in psychosomatic medicine.* Philadelphia: J. B. Lippincott Co., 1954, 419–435.

———, MEYERSON, L., & GONICK, M. R. *Adjustment to physical handicap and illness: A survey of the social psychology of physique and disability.* Bulletin 55 (rev. ed.), New York: Social Science Research Council, 1953.

BATES, J. H. Ambulatory Treatment of Tuberculosis: An idea whose time is come. *American Review of Respiratory Diseases,* 1974, *109,* 317–319.

BAUER, I. L. Attitudes of children with rheumatic fever. *Journal of Pediatrics,* 1952, *40,* 796–806.

BELLAK, L. Psychiatric aspects of tuberculosis. *Social Casework,* 1950, *31,* 183–189.

———, & HASELKORN, R. Psychological aspects of cardiac illness and rehabilitation. *Social Casework,* 1956, *37,* 483–489.

BELMONT, H. S. Hospitalization and its effects upon the total child. *Clinical Pediatrics,* 1970, *9,* 472–483.

BENNETT, E. W., & JOHANNESEN, D. E. Psychodynamics of the diabetic child. *Psychological Monographs,* 1954, *68,* 1–23.

BERLE, B. B. Emotional factors and tuberculosis. *Psychosomatic Medicine,* 1948, *10,* 366–373.

BLOCK, J., JENNINGS, P. H., HARVEY, E., & SIMPSON, E. Interaction between allergic potential and psychopathology in childhood asthma. *Psychosomatic Medicine,* 1964, *26,* 307–320.

———. Clinician's conceptions of the asthmatogenic mother. *Archives of General Psychiatry,* 1966, *15,* 610–618.

BLOM, G. E. The reactions of hospitalized children to illness. *Pediatrics,* 1958, *22,* 590–600.

BOSHES, B. Emotions, hypothalamus, and the cardiovascular system. *American Journal of Cardiology,* 1958, *1,* 212–223.

BOWLBY, J. *Maternal care and mental health.* Geneva: World Health Organization, 1951.

———, ROBERTSON, J., & ROSENBLUTH, D. A two-year-old goes in the hospital. In *The psychoanalytic study of the child, Vol. 7.* New York: International Universities Press, 1952, 82–94.

———, AINSWORTH, M., BOSTON, M., & ROSENBLUTH, D. The effects of mother-child separation: A follow-up study. *British Journal of Medical Psychology,* 1956, *29,* 211–247.

BRAZELTON, T. B., HOLDER, R., & TALBOT, B. Emotional aspects of rheumatic fever in children. *Journal of Pediatrics,* 1953, *43,* 339–358.

BROWNELL, K. D., & BAILEN-ROSE, R. Acute rheumatic fever in children. *The Journal of the American Medical Association,* 1973, *224,* 1593–1597.

BRUCH, H. Physiologic and psychologic interrelationships in diabetes in children. *Psychosomatic Medicine,* 1949, *11,* 200–210.

———, & HEWLETT, I. Psychological aspects of the medical management of diabetes in children. *Psychosomatic Medicine,* 1947, *9,* 205–209.

BRUHN, J. G. Psychosocial influence in diabetes mellitus. *Postgraduate Medicine,* 1974, *56,* 113–118.

CAPES, M. The child in the hospital. *Mental Hygiene,* 1956, *40,* 107–159.

CARTER, V. E., & CHESS, S. Factors influencing the adaptations of organically handicapped children. *American Journal of Orthopsychiatry,* 1951, *21,* 827–837.

CAVEY, K., & KOGAN, K. L. A pilot study of mother-child interactions in children with bronchial asthma. *Journal of Asthma Research,* 1974, *11,* 169–179.

CHARNEY, E. Screening tests: Birth to six years of age. In M. Green and R. J. Haggerty (Eds.), *Ambulatory Pediatrics.* Philadelphia: W. B. Saunders Company, 1968, 424–435.

COLLIER, B. N., & ETZWILER, D. D. Comparative study of diabetes knowledge among juvenile diabetics and their parents. *Diabetes,* 1971, *20,* 51–57.

COMBRINCK-GRAHAM, L. Structural family therapy in psychosomatic illness. *Clinical Pediatrics,* 1974, *13,* 827–833.

COMSTOCK, G. W. Frost revisited: The modern epidemiology of tuberculosis. *American Journal of Epidemiology,* 1975, *101,* 363–382.

COOLIDGE, J. C. Asthma in mother and child as a special type of intercommunication. *American Journal of Orthopsychiatry,* 1956, *26,* 165–178.

CRAIN, A. J., SUSSMAN, M. B., & WEILL, W. B., JR. Effects of a diabetic child on marital integration and related measures of family functioning. *Journal of Health and Human Behavior,* 1966, 7 (2), 122–127.

CREAK, M., & STEPHENS, J. M. The psychological aspects of asthma in children. *Pediatric Clinics of North America,* 1958, *5,* 731–747.

CREER, T. L., RENNE, C. M., & CHRISTIAN, W. P. Behavioral contributions to rehabilitation and childhood asthma. *Rehabilitation Literature,* 1976, *37,* 226–232.

CROPP, G. J. A. The problem of lung disease in children and adolescents. *American Lung Association Bulletin,* 1976, *62,* 10–14.

CROWELL, D. H. Personality and physical disease: A test of the Dunbar hypothesis applied to diabetes mellitus and rheumatic fever. *Genetic Psychology Monographs,* 1953, *48,* 117–153.

Current Status of Tuberculosis in the United States. *Statistical Bulletin* (Metropolitan Life Insurance Company), 1974, *55,* 9–11.

DANOWSKI, T. D. *Diabetes Mellitus.* Baltimore: The Williams and Wilkens Company, 1957.

DEKKER, E., & GROEN, J. Reproducible psychogenic attacks of asthma. *Journal of Psychosomatic Research,* 1956, *1,* 58–67.

————, PELSER, H. E., & GROEN, J. Conditioning as a cause of asthma. *Journal of Psychosomatic Research,* 1957, *2,* 97–108.

DEMUTH, E. L. Is there a specific personality in tuberculosis patients? *Archives of Neurology and Psychiatry,* 1951, *66,* 30–37.

DERNER, G. F. *Aspects of the psychology of the tuberculous.* New York: Paul B. Hoeber, 1953.

DIBNER, S. S., & DIBNER, A. S. *Integration or segregation for the physically handicapped child.* Springfield, Ill.: Charles C Thomas, 1973.

DUBO, S. Psychiatric study of children with pulmonary tuberculosis. *American Journal of Orthopsychiatry,* 1950, *20,* 520–528.

————, MCLEAN, J. A., CHING, A. Y., WRIGHT, H. L., KAUFFMAN, P. E., & SHELDON, J. M. A study of relationships between family situations, bronchial asthma and personality adjustment in children. *Journal of Pediatrics,* 1961, *59,* 402–414.

DUNBAR, F. *Psychosomatic diagnosis.* New York: Paul B. Hoeber, 1948.

EHRLICH, R. M. Diabetes mellitus in childhood. *Pediatric Clinics of North America,* 1974, *21,* 871–884.

EHRENTHEIL, O. F. Some remarks about somatopsychic compared to psychosomatic relationships. *Psychosomatic Medicine,* 1959, *21,* 1–7.

ETZWILER, D. D. What the juvenile diabetic knows about his disease. *Pediatrics,* 1962, *29,* 135–141.

FALLIERS, C. J. Treatment of asthma in a residential center: A fifteen year study. *Annals of Allergy,* 1970, *28,* 513–521.

FALSTEIN, E. I., & JUDAS, I. Juvenile diabetes and its psychiatric implications. *American Journal of Orthopsychiatry,* 1955, *25,* 330–342.

FAUST, O. A. *Reducing emotional trauma in hospitalized children.* Albany, New York: Albany Research Project. Albany Medical College, 1952.

FINE, R. The personality of the asthmatic child. *Abstracts of Dissertation.* New York: University Publishers, 1948, 165.

FISCHER, A. E. Factors responsible for emotional disturbance in diabetic children. *The Nervous Child,* 1948, *7,* 78–83.

FITZELLE, G. T. Personality factors and certain attitudes toward child rearing among parents of asthmatic children. *Psychosomatic Medicine,* 1959, *21,* 208–217.

FLINT, B. M. *The child and the institution: A study of deprivation and recovery.* Ontario: University of Toronto Press, 1966.

FORBES, G. B. The juvenile diabetic, *G.P.,* 1956, *13,* 99–110.

FORSYTH, C. C., & PAYNE, W. W. Free diets in treatments of diabetic children. *Archives of Diseases of Childhood,* 1956, *41,* 245–253.

FRANKEL, J. J. Juvenile diabetes: The look from within. In Z. Laron (Ed.), *Diabetes in Juveniles,* Basel: S. Karger, 1975, 358–360.

FREEMAN, E. H., FEINGOLD, B. F., SCHLESINGER, K., & GORMAN, F. J. Psychological variables in allergic disorders: A review. *Psychosomatic Medicine,* 1964, *26,* 543–575.

FRENCH, T. M., & ALEXANDER, F. Psychogenic factors in bronchial asthma. *Psychosomatic Medicine Monographs.* Washington, D.C.: National Research Council, 1941, Parts 1 and 2.

FREUD, A. The role of bodily illness in the mental life of children. *The psychoanalytic study of the child. Vol. 7.* New York: International Universities Press, 1952, 69–81.

———, & BURLINGHAM, D. I. *Infants without families.* New York: International University Press, 1944.

FRIEND, M. R., & POLLOCK, O. Psychosocial aspects in the preparation for treatment of an allergic child. *American Journal of Orthopsychiatry,* 1954, *24,* 63–72.

GAMBRILL, E. Post-hospitalized disabled children. *Journal of Health and Human Behavior,* 1963, *4,* 206–210.

GARNER, A. M., & WENAR, C. *The mother-child interaction in psychosomatic disorders.* Urbana: University of Illinois Press, 1959.

GASUL, B. W., ARCILLA, R. A., & LEV, M. *Heart disease in children.* Philadelphia: J. B. Lippincott Co., 1966.

GEIST, H. *The psychological aspects of diabetes.* Springfield, Ill.: Charles C Thomas, 1964.

GHORY, J. E. The adolescent in an asthmatic rehabilitation program. *Journal of Asthma Research,* 1972, *16,* 55–60.

———. The allergic child in school. *Journal of Asthma Research,* 1974, *11,* 109–111.

GLASER, H. H., HARRISON, G. S., & LYNN, D. B. Comprehensive medical care for handicapped children: 1. Patterns of anxiety in mothers of children with rheumatic fever. *American Journal of Disease of Children,* 1961, *102,* 344–354.

———. Emotional implications of congenital heart disease in children. *Pediatrics,* 1964, *33,* 367–379.

GLASER, K. Group discussion with mothers of hospitalized children. *Pediatrics,* 1960, *26,* 132–140.

GLUCK, R. *Diagnosis of congenital cardiac defects in general practice.* New York: American Heart Association, 1961.

GOFMAN, H., BUCKMAN, W., & SCHADE, G. H. The child's emotional response to hospitalization. *American Medical Association Journal of Diseases of Children,* 1957, *93,* 157–164.

GOLDFARB, W. Variations in adolescent adjustment in institutionally reared children. *American Journal of Orthopsychiatry,* 1947, *17,* 449–457.

GREEN, M. The management of long-term, non-life-threatening illnesses. In M. Green and R. J. Haggerty (Eds.), *Ambulatory Pediatrics,* Philadelphia: W. B. Saunders Co., 1968, 443–550.

———. The care of the child with a long-term, life-threatening illness. In M. Green and R. J. Haggerty (Eds.), *Ambulatory Pediatrics,* Philadelphia: W. B. Saunders Co., 1968, 659–665.

———, & LEVITT, E. E. Constriction of body image in children with congenital heart disorders. *Pediatrics,* 1962, *29,* 438–441.

———, & HAGGERTY, R. J. (Eds.), *Ambulatory Pediatrics.* Philadelphia: W. B. Saunders Company, 1968.

HAHN, W. W., & CLARK, J. A. Psycho-physiological reactivity of asthmatic children. *Psychosomatic Medicine*, 1967, *29*, 526–536.

HARRIS, M. C. Is there a specific emotional pattern in allergic disease? *Annals of Allergy*, 1955, *13*, 654–661.

————, & SHURE, N. A study of behavior patterns in asthmatic children. *Journal of Allergy*, 1956, *27*, 312–323.

HARTZ, J. Human relationship in tuberculosis. *Public Health Reports*, 1950, *65*, 1293.

————. Tuberculosis and personality conflicts. *Psychosomatic Medicine*. 1944, *6*, 17–22.

HEINZELMAN, F. Factors in prophylaxis behavior in treating rheumatic fever: An exploratory study. *Journal of Health and Human Behavior*, 1962, *3*, 73–81.

HEROLD, A. A., JR. Juvenile diabetes. *Journal of Louisiana Medical Society*, 1966, *118*, 429–432.

HINKLE, L. E., EVANS, F. M., & WOLF, J. Studies in diabetes mellitus. *Psychosomatic Medicine*, 1951, *13*, 184–202.

————, & WOLF, S. A summary of experimental evidence relating to life stress to diabetes mellitus. *Journal of the Mount Sinai Hospital*, 1952, *19*, 537–570.

HOLDER, R. *Rheumatic fever project* (typescript). Boston: Massachusetts General Hospital, 1953.

ILLINGWORTH, R. S. Children in hospital. *Lancet*, 1958, *2* (7039), 165–171.

JACOBI, H. G. Nutritional studies of juvenile diabetics attending summer camp. *Journal of Clinical Nutrition*, 1954, *2*, 22.

JACOBS, M. A. Fantasies of mother-child interaction in hay-fever sufferers. *Dissertation Abstracts*, 1963, *24* (4), 1698–1699.

JESSNER, L., LAMONT, J., LONG, R. T., ROLLINS, N., WHIPPLE, B., & PRENTICE, N. Emotional impact of nearness and separation for the asthmatic child and his mother. *The psychoanalytic study of the child. Vol. 10*. New York: International Universities Press, 1955, 353–375.

JOHNSON, F. K., BAKER, G., & ALEXANDER, A. A. A psyche and soma reunited. *Clinical Pediatrics*, 1971, *10*, 719–725.

JOHNSTON, R. F., & WILDRICK, K. H. The impact of chemotherapy on the care of patients with tuberculosis. *American Review of Respiratory Diseases*, 1974, *109*, 636–664.

JOSSELYN, I. M., SIMON, A. J., & EELLS, E. Anxiety in children convalescing from rheumatic fever. *American Journal of Orthopsychiatry*, 1955, *25*, 109–119.

KAPLAN, E. L. Epidemiology and pathogenesis of acute rheumatic fever. *Minnesota Medicine*, 1975, *58*, 592–597.

KAPLAN, S. The adolescent with operated or unoperated congenital heart disease. *Postgraduate Medicine*, 1974, *56*, 147–152.

KAYE, R. Psychological aspects of management of juvenile diabetics. In U.S. Department of Health, Education, and Welfare. *Report of the National Commission on Diabetes*. Vol. III, Pt. 4, 1976, 129–136.

KEITH, J. D., ROWE, R. D., & VLAD, P. *Heart disease in infancy and children*. New York: Macmillan Company, 1958.

KENDIG, E. L. Tuberculosis. In E. L. Kendig (Ed.), *Disorders of the respiratory tract in children*. Philadelphia: W. B. Saunders Company, 1967, 656–701.

KENNEDY, W. B. Psychologic problems of the young diabetic. *Diabetes*, 1955, *4*, 207–209.

KENNELL, J. H., SOROKER, E., THOMAS, P., & WASMAN, M. What parents of rheumatic fever patients don't understand about the disease and its prophylactic management. *Pediatrics*, 1960, *43*, 160–167.

KHAN, A. U. Present status of psychosomatic aspects of asthma. *Psychosomatics*, 1973, *14*, 195–200.

KHURANA, R. C., & WHITE, P. Attitudes of the diabetic child and his parents toward his illness. *Postgraduate Medicine*, 1970, *48*, 72–76.
————. Juvenile-onset diabetes: problems in managing 16 to 22 year olds. *Postgraduate Medicine*, 1971, *49*, 118–123.

KIMBALL, C. P. Emotional and psychosocial aspects of diabetes mellitus. *Medical Clinics of North America,* 1971, *55,* 1007–1018.

KIMMEL, J. A. A comparison of children with congenital and acquired orthopedic handicaps on certain personality characteristics. *Dissertation Abstracts,* 1959, *19,* 3023–3024.

KNAPP, P. H., & NEMETZ, S. J. Personality variations in bronchial asthma. *Psychosomatic Medicine,* 1957 (a) , *19,* 443–465.

———. Acute bronchial asthma. *Journal of Psychosomatic Medicine,* 1960, *22,* 42–56.

KNOWLES, H. C. Diabetes mellitus in childhood and adolescence. *Medical Clinics of North America,* 1971, *55,* 975–987.

KOCH, C. R., Minuchin, S., & Donovan, W. M. A case of somatic expression of family and environmental stress. *Clinical Pediatrics,* 1974, *13,* 815–818.

KOENIG, F. G. A study of anxiety in children with rheumatic fever. *Dissertation Abstracts,* 1959, *20,* 1438–1439.

KORKES, L., & LEWIS, N. D. C. An analysis of the relationship between psychological patterns and outcome in pulmonary tuberculosis. *Journal of Nervous and Mental Disease,* 1955, *122,* 524–563.

KORSCH, B. M. Psychological principles in pediatric practice: The pediatrician and the sick child. In S. L. Levine (Ed.) , *Advances in Pediatrics.* Chicago: The Year Book Medical Publishers, 1958, 11–73.

KRAMER, H. D. Psychopathology of childhood tuberculosis. *The Nervous Child,* 1948, *7,* 102–114.

KROSNICK, A. Diabetes and employment: Is there discriminatory practice? U.S. Department of Health, Education, and Welfare. *Report of the National Commission on Diabetes,* 1976, Vol. III, Pt. 5, 279–290.

KUBANY, A. J., DANOWSKI, T. S., & MOSES, C. The personality and intelligence of diabetics. *Diabetes,* 1956, *5,* 462–467.

KUBIE, L. S. The problem of specificity in the psychosomatic process. In E. D. Witttkower and R. A. Cleghorn (Eds.) , *Recent develop-*

ments in psychosomatic medicine. Philadelphia: J. B. Lippincott Co., 1954, 29–40.

LACHMAN, S. J. *Psychosomatic disorders: A behavioristic interpretation.* New York: John Wiley & Sons, 1972.

LaHOOD, B. J. Parental attitudes and their influence on the medical management of diabetic adolescents. *Clinical Pediatrics,* 1970, *9,* 468–471.

LANGFORD, W. S. Physical illness and convalescence: Their meaning to the child. *Journal of Pediatrics,* 1948, *33,* 242–250.

LEIGH, D. Asthma and the psychiatrist: A critical review. *International Archives of Allergy,* 1953, *4,* 227–246.

LEVITT, J., & TARAN, L. M. Some of the problems in the education of rheumatic children. *Journal of Pediatrics,* 1948, *32,* 553–557.

LIEBMAN, R., MINUCHIN, S., & BAKER, L. The use of structural family therapy in the treatment of intractable asthma. *American Journal of Psychiatry,* 1974, *131,* 535–540.

LINDE, L. M., RASOFF, B., & DUNN, O. J. Mental development in congenital heart disease. *The Journal of Pediatrics,* 1967, *71,* 198–203.

———, & RABB, E. Attitudinal factors in congenital heart diseases. *Pediatrics,* 1966, *38,* 92–101.

LIPTON, E. L., STEINSCHNEIDER, A., & RICHMOND, J. B. Psychophysiologic disorders in children. In L. W. Hoffman and M. L. Hoffman (Eds.) . *Review of Child Development Research.* New York: Russell Sage Foundation, 1966, 169–220.

LITTLE, S. W., & COHEN, L. D. Goal setting behavior of asthmatic children and of their mothers for them. *Journal of Personality,* 1951, *19,* 376–389.

LONG, R. T., LAMONT, J. H., WHIPPLE, B., BANDLER, L. BLOM, G. E., GURGIN, L., & JESSNER, L. A psychosomatic study of allergic and emotional factors in children with asthma. *American Journal of Psychiatry,* 1958, *114,* 890–899.

LOWE, C. M. The self-concept: Fact or artifact. *Psychological Bulletin,* 1961, *58,* 325–336.

LUPARELLO, T. J., McFADDEN, E. R., LYONS, H. A., & BLEECHER, E. R. Psychological factors and bronchial asthma. *New York State Journal of Medicine,* 1971, *71,* 2161–2165.

LUZZATI, L., & DITTMAN, B. Group discussion with parents of ill children. *Pediatrics,* 1954, *13,* 269–272.

MAGNUS, R. A. Parent involvement in residential treatment programs. *Children Today,* 1974, *3,* 25–27.

MARBLE, A. The future of the child with diabetes. *Journal of the American Diabetic Association,* 1957, *33,* 565–574.

MARGOLIS, M. A psychological study of mothers of asthmatic children. *Dissertation Abstracts,* 1962, *23* (1) , 311–312.

MARLENS, H. S. A study of the effect of hospitalization on children in a metropolitan municipal institution. *Dissertation Abstracts,* 1960, *20,* 3385–3386.

MASON, E. A. Preparation of children for hospitalization. In M. Green and R. J. Haggerty, (Eds.) , *Ambulatory Pediatrics,* Philadelphia: W. B. Saunders Co., 1968, 139–142.

MATTSON, A. Long-term physical illness in childhood: A challenge to psychosocial adaptation. *Pediatrics,* 1972, *50,* 801–811.

————. Psychologic aspects of childhood asthma. In R. Ellis (Ed.) , *Pediatric Clinics of North America,* Philadelphia: W. B. Saunders Co., 1975, 77–78.

MAURER, E. The child with asthma: An assessment of the relative importance of emotional factors in asthma. *Journal of Asthma Research,* 1965, *3,* 25–79.

McLEAN, J. A., & CHING, A. Y. Follow-up study of relations between family situations and bronchial asthma in children. *Journal of the American Academy of Child Psychiatry,* 1973, *12,* 142–161.

————, SCHRAGER, J., & STOEFFLER, V. R. Severe asthma in children: A study of its effects in fifty families. *Michigan Medicine,* 1968, *67,* 1219–1226.

MEEK, H. W., SR. An investigation of certain psychological variables in diabetes mellitus. *Dissertation Abstracts,* 1960, *20,* 4176.

MENNINGER, W. C. Psychological factors in the etiology of diabetes mellitus. *Journal of Nervous and Mental Disease,* 1935, *81,* 1–13.

MERRILL, B. R. Some psychosomatic aspects of pulmonary tuberculosis. *Journal of Nervous and Mental Disease,* 1953, *117,* 9–28.

MILLER, H., & BARUCH, D. W. The emotional problems of childhood and their relation to asthma. *American Medical Association Journal of Diseases of Children,* 1957, *93,* 242–245.

MINUCHIN, S. *Families and family therapy.* Cambridge, Mass.: Harvard University Press, 1974.

MITCHELL, R. G., & DAWSON, B. Educational and social characteristics of children with asthma. *Archives of Diseases in Childhood,* 1973, *48,* 467–471.

MOHR, G. J., RICHMOND, J. B., GARNER, A. M., & EDDY, E. J. A program for the study of children with psychosomatic disorders. In G. Caplan (Ed.) , *Emotional Problems of Early Childhood.* New York: Basic Books, 1955, 251–268.

MORRIS, R. P. Effect of mother on goal-setting behavior of the asthmatic child. *Dissertation Abstracts,* 1959, *20,* 1440.

NEILL, C. A. Etiology of congenital heart disease. In M. A. Engle (Ed.) , *Pediatric Cardiology.* Philadelphia: F. A. Davis Company, 1972, 137–147.

NELSON, W. E., VAUGHAN, V. C., III, & McKAY, R. J. *Textbook of Pediatrics.* Philadelphia: W. B. Saunders Company, 1969.

NEUHAUS, E. C. A personality study of asthmatic and cardiac children. *Psychosomatic Medicine,* 1958, *20,* 181–186.

NOONAN, J. A. Natural history of rheumatic heart disease in adolescents. *Postgraduate Medicine,* 1974, *56,* 107–114.

ONGLEY, P. A. and DuSHANE, J. W. Rehabilitation of the child with congenital heart disease. *American Journal of Cardiology,* 1961, *7,* 335–339.

OWEN, F. W. Asthma and maternal stimuli. *Dissertation Abstracts,* 1961, *22,* 644.

Parsons, T. Illness and the role of the physician: A sociological perspective. *American Journal of Orthopsychiatry*, 1952, *21*, 452–460.

Partridge, J. W., Garer, A. M., Thompson, C. W., & Cherry, T. Attitudes of adolescents toward their diabetes. *American Journal of Diseases of Children*, 1972, *124*, 226–229.

Peshkin, M. W. Management of the institutionalized child with intractable asthma. *Annuals of Allergy*, 1960, *18*, 75–79.

———. The emotional aspects of asthma in children. *Journal of Asthmatic Research*, 1966, *3*, 265–275.

———, & Friedman, I. Residential asthma treatment centers in U.S. and problems in relation to them. *Journal of Asthma Research*, 1975, *12*, 129–174.

Pinkerton, P. The influence of *sociopathy* in childhood asthma. *Psychotherapy and Psychosomatics*, 1970, *18*, 231–238.

———. The enigma of asthma. *Psychosomatic Medicine*, 1973, *35*, 401–463.

———, & Weaver, C. M. Childhood asthma. In C. W. Hill (Ed.), *Modern trends in psychosomatic medicine*. London: Butterworths, 1970, 81–104.

Pless, I. B. Epidemiology of chronic disease. In M. Green and R. J. Haggerty (Eds.), *Ambulatory Pediatrics*. Philadelphia: W. B. Saunders Co., 1968, 760–768.

Podolsky, E. Physical ailments and the frightened child. *Mental Hygiene*, 1955, *39*, 489–497.

Prugh, D. G. Investigations dealing with reactions of children and families to hospitalization and illness: Problems and potentialities. In G. Caplan (Ed.), *Emotional Problems of Early Childhood*. N.Y.: Basic Books, 1955, 307–321.

———. Toward an understanding of psychosomatic concepts in relation to illness in children. In A. J. Solnit and S. A. Provence (Eds.), *Modern Perspectives in Child Development*. New York: International Universities Press, 1963, 246–339.

———. Children's reactions to illness, hospitalization and surgery. In A. M. Freedman and H. I. Kaplan (Eds.), *The child—his psychological and cultural development*. New York: Atheneum, 1971, 181–194.

———, & Cath, S. Psychosocial stress: children's reactions to hospitalization and the use of the respirator. *Journal of Nervous and Mental Disease*, 1954, *120*, 339–400.

———, Staub, E. M., Sands, H. H., Kirschbaum, R. M., & Leniham, E. A. A study of the emotional reactions to hospitalization and illness. *American Journal of Orthopsychiatry*, 1953, *23*, 70–106.

Purcell, K. Distinction between sub-groups of asthmatic children: Children's perceptions of events associated with asthma. *Pediatrics*, 1963, *31*, 486–494.

———, Bernstein, L., & Bukantz, S. C. A preliminary comparison of rapidly remitting and persistently "steroid-dependent" asthmatic children. *Psychosomatic Medicine*, 1961, *23*, 305–310.

———, Brady, K., Choi, M., Muser, J., Molk, L., Gordon, N., & Means, J. Effect on asthma in children of experimental separation from the family. *Psychosomatic Medicine*, 1969, *31*, 141–164.

———, & Metz, J. R. Distinctions between sub-groups of asthmatic children: Some parent attitude variables related to age of onset of asthma. *Journal of Psychosomatic Research*, 1962, *6*, 251–258.

———, Muser, J., Miklich, D., & Dietker, K. E. A comparison of psychologic findings in variously defined asthmatic sub-groups. *Journal of Psychosomatic Research*, 1969, *13*, 67–75.

———, Turnbull, J. W., & Bernstein, L., Distinctions between subgroups of asthmatic children: Psychological tests and behavior rating comparisons. *Journal of Psychosomatic Research*, 1962, *6*, 283–291.

Rappaport, H. G., Appel, S. J., & Szanton, V. L. Incidence of allergy in a pediatric population. *Annals of Allergy*, 1960, *18*, 45–49.

Reed, M. K. The intelligence, social maturity, personal adjustment, physical development, and parent-child relationships of children with congenital heart disease. *Dissertation Abstracts*, 1959, *20*, 385.

REES, L. The role of emotional and allergic factors in hay fever. *Journal of Psychosomatic Research*, 1959, *3*, 234–241.

———. The significance of parental attitudes in childhood asthma. *Journal of Psychosomatic Research*, 1963, *7*, 181–190.

RESH, M. G. Asthma of unknown origin as a psychological group. *Journal of Consulting and Clinical Psychology*, 1970, *35*, 429.

ROBBINS, S. M., & FINKLESTEIN, J. Reducing the emotional and economic costs of hospitalization of acutely ill asthmatics. *Clinical Pediatrics*, 1973, *12*, 550–554.

ROBERTSON, J. *Young children in hospitals*. New York: Basic Books, 1959.

——— (Ed.). *Hospitals and children*. London: Victor Gollancz, Ltd., 1962.

ROBINSON, G. The story of parentectomy. *Journal of Asthma Research*, 1972, *9*, 199–205.

ROME, H. P., & ROBINSON, D. B. Psychiatric conditions associated with metabolic, endocrine and nutritional disorders. In S. Arieti (Ed.), *American Handbook of Psychiatry, Volume II*. New York: Basic Books, 1959, 1260–1282.

ROWE, R. D., KIDD, B. S. L., FOWLER, R. S., OLLEY, P. M., IZUKAWA, T., ROSE, V., & TRUSLER, G. A. Long term management of heart defects. *Pediatric Clinics of North America*, 1974, 841–869.

RUTTER, M. *The Qualities of Mothering: Maternal Deprivation Reassessment*. New York: Aronson, 1974.

SANDLER, L. Child-rearing practices of mothers of asthmatic children, Part I. *Journal of Asthma Research*, 1964, *2*, 109–142.

———. Child-rearing practices of mothers of asthmatic children, Part II. *Journal of Asthma Research*, 1965, *2*, 215–256.

SCHAFFER, H. A., & CALLENDER, W. M. Psychologic effects of hospitalization in infancy. *Pediatrics*, 1959, *24*, 528–539.

SHELSKY, I. The effect of disability on self concept. *Dissertation Abstracts*, 1957, *17*, 1598–1599.

SHORE, M. F. (Ed.). Red is the color of hurting. *Public Health Service Bulletin, No. 1583*. Washington, D.C.: Government Printing Office, 1967.

SILBERT, A., WOLFF, R. H., MAYER, B., ROSENTHAL, A., & NADAS, A. S. Cyanetic heart disease and psychological development. *Pediatrics*, 1969, *43*, 192–200.

SKYLER, J. S., ELLIS, G. J., III, & DELCHER, H. K. The value of summer camps for diabetic children. In Z. Laron (Ed.), *Diabetes in Juveniles*, Basel: S. Karger, 1975, 382–384.

SLY, R. M., HARPER, T. T., & ROSSELOT, I. The effect of physical conditioning on asthmatic children. *Annals of Allergy*, 1972, *30*, 86–94.

SOLNIT, A. J. Hospitalization: An aid to physical and psychological health in childhood. *American Medical Association Journal of Diseases of Children*, 1960, *99*, 155–163.

———. Psychotherapeutic role of the pediatrician. In M. Green and R. J. Haggerty (Eds.), *Ambulatory Pediatrics*, Philadelphia: W. B. Saunders Co., 1968, 159–167.

SONTAG, L. W. The genetics of differences in psychosomatic patterns of childhood. *American Journal of Orthopsychiatry*, 1950, *20*, 479–489.

SPERLING, M. Asthma in children. *Journal of the American Academy of Child Psychiatry*, 1968, *7*, 44–58.

SPITZ, R. A., & WOLF, K. Anaclitic depression. *Psychoanalytic Study of the Child*, 1946, *2*, 313–342.

STARR, P. H. Psychosomatic considerations of diabetes in childhood. *Journal of Nervous and Mental Disease*, 1955, *121*, 493–504.

STEHBENS, J. A., & MACQUEEN, J. C. The psychological adjustment of rheumatic fever patients with and without chorea. *Clinical Pediatrics*, 1972, *11*, 638–640.

STEINHAUSER, P. D., MUSHIN, D. N., & RAE-GRANT, Q. Psychological aspects of chronic illness. *Pediatric Clinics of North America,* 1974, *21,* 825–840.

STEVENSON, I., & MATTHEWS, R. A. Fact and theory in psychosomatic medicine. *Journal of Nervous and Mental Disease,* 1953, *118,* 289–306.

STOCKING, M., ROTHNEY, W., GROSSER, G., & GOODWIN, R. Psychopathology in the pediatric hospital—Implications for community health. In S. Chess, and J. Thomas, (Eds.), *Annual progress in child psychiatry and child development.* New York: Brunner/Mazel, 1974, 654–666.

STRAKER, N., & TAMERIN, J. Aggression and childhood asthma: A study in a natural setting. *Journal of Psychosomatic Research,* 1974, *18,* 131–135.

STUBBLEFIELD, R. L. Psychiatric observations of asthma in children. *Southern Medical Journal,* 1966, *59,* 306–310.

SULTZ, H. A., SCHLESINGER, E. R., MOSHER, W. E., & FELDMAN, J. G. *Long-term childhood illness.* Pittsburgh: University of Pittsburgh Press, 1972.

Symposium on rehabilitation in cardiovascular disease. *American Journal of Cardiology,* 1961, *7,* 315–319.

SZUREK, S. A. Comments on psychopathology of children with somatic illness. *American Journal of Psychiatry,* 1951, *107,* 844–849.

TARAN, L. M., & HODSDON, A. F. Social and psychologic problems associated with prolonged institutional care for rheumatic children. *Journal of Pediatrics,* 1949, *35,* 648–661.

THOMPSON, G. G. Developmental psychology. In P. R. Farnsworth (Ed.), *Annual review of psychology.* Palo Alto, Calif.: Annual Reviews, Inc., 1959, 1–41.

TOLSTOI, E. The objectives of modern diabetic care. *Psychosomatic Medicine,* 1948, *10,* 291–294.

TUFT, H. S. The development and management of intractable asthma of childhood. *American Medical Association Journal of Diseases of Children,* 1957, *93,* 251–254.

TURNBULL, J. W. Asthma conceived as a learned response. *Journal of Psychosomatic Research,* 1962, *6,* 59–69.

TUTTMAN, S. Children's reactions to their physical disabilities in relation to parent's personalities. *Dissertation Abstracts,* 1955, *15,* 1909–1910.

U.S. Department of Health, Education and Welfare. *Limitations of Activity Due to Chronic Conditions.* (D.H.E.W. Publication No. (HSM) 73-1506.) Washington, D.C., 1973.

————. *Report of the National Commission on Diabetes* (D.H.E.W. Publication No. [NIH] 76-1018, No. 1, Long-range plan to combat diabetes) Washington, D.C., 1976.

————. *Report of the National Commission on Diabetes* (D.H.E.W. Publication No. [NIH] 76-1019, Vol. II, Pt. 2, A, Public Testimony) Washington, D.C., 1976.

————. *Report of the National Commission on Diabetes* (D.H.E.W. Publication No. [NIH] 76-1022, Vol. III, Pt. 2, Scope and impact of diabetes) Washington, D.C., 1976.

VAUGHAN, G. F. Children in hospital. *Lancet,* 1957, *272,* 1117–1120.

VERNIER, C. M., BARRELL, R. P., CUMMINGS, J. W., DICKERSON, J. H., & HOOPER, H. E. Psychosocial study of the patient with pulmonary tuberculosis. *Psychological Monographs,* 1961, *75,* 1–32.

VERNON, D. T., FOLEY, J. M., SIPOWICZ, R. R., & SCHULMAN, J. L. *The psychological responses of children to hospitalization and illness: A review of the literature.* Springfield, Ill.: Charles C Thomas, 1965.

WEISS, J. H. Mood states associated with asthma in children. *Journal of Psychosomatic Research,* 1966, *10,* 267–273.

————. Letter to editor. *Psychosomatic Medicine,* 1973, *35,* 461–463.

WENTWORTH, S. M., & GREGORY, R. H. Indiana's camp for diabetic children: A sixteen year follow-up. *Journal of the Indiana State Medical Association,* 1972, *65,* 316–319.

WHITE, P. D. *Heart disease.* New York: The Macmillan Company, 1951.

WHITEHOUSE, F. A. Problems of the cardiac adolescent. *New York State Journal of Medicine,* 1964, *64,* 1108–1111.

WILLIAMS, H. E., & McNICOL, K. N. The spectrum of asthma in children. *The Pediatric Clinics of North America,* 1975, *22,* 43–52.

WILLIAMS, J. S. Aspects of dependence and independence conflict in children with asthma. *Journal of Child Psychology and Psychiatry,* 1975, *16,* 199–218.

WITTKOWER, E. Psychology of the tuberculosis patient. In T. H. Sellors and J. L. Livingstone (Eds.), *Modern practice in tuberculosis.* London: Butterworths, 1952.

———. *A psychiatrist looks at tuberculosis.* London: National Association for the Prevention of Tuberculosis, 1959.

WOHL, T. A. Behavior modification: Its application to the study and treatment of childhood asthma. *Journal of Asthma Research,* 1971, *9,* 41–45.

WOLF, G. A., & WOLFF, H. G. Studies on the nature of certain symptoms associated with cardiovascular disorders. *Psychosomatic Medicine,* 1946, *7,* 293–319.

WOLFER, J. A., & VISINTAINER, M. A. Pediatric surgical patients' and parents' stress responses and adjustment as a function of psychologic preparation and stress-point care. *Nursing Research,* 1975, *24,* 244–255.

WRIGHT, B. *Physical Disability: A psychological approach.* New York: Harper & Row, 1960.

WRIGHTSTONE, J. W., JUSTMAN, J., & MOSCOWITZ, S. *Studies of children with physical handicaps. No. 1. The child with cardiac limitations.* New York: Board of Education, 1953.

———. *No. 6. The adolescents with cardiac limitations.* New York: Board of Education, 1961.

WYLIE, R. C. *The self-concept.* Lincoln: University of Nebraska Press, 1974.

YARROW, L. J. Separation from parents during early childhood. In M. L. Hoffman and L. W. Hoffman (Eds.), *Review of Child Development Research.* New York: Russell Sage Foundation, 1964, 89–136.

YOUNG, D., & RODSTEIN, M. Home care of rheumatic fever patients. *Journal of the American Medical Association,* 1953, *152,* 987–990.

PART FOUR

Psychological Factors in Intellectual, Perceptual, and Emotional Disabilities

The manner in which the mind of man operates has fascinated writers of both popular and scientific publications for hundreds of years. Grouped in Part Four of *Psychology of Exceptional Children and Youth* are four chapters that deal with four different aspects of man's use of the mind.

Lynn Kay Brown, a new author to this writing team, has approached mental retardation, not from a traditional point of view of classification by intelligence, clinical type, or subtype, but by selecting the generic problems of mental retardation with which to deal; namely, intelligence as a major construct, cognition, and personality.

E. Paul Torrance, long recognized as an authority on the superior and gifted pupil, has also chosen to approach the discussion of these children and youth from the point of view of their essential characteristics; namely, general intellectual abilities, creative or productive thinking, psychomotor ability, and others. His chapter and Brown's chapter accentuate the exceptional children at either end of the intellectual spectrum.

Two other chapters are included in Part Four, emphasizing the different impacts of intellect and the central nervous system on individual adjustment and learning when they function in abnormal ways.

The popular term *learning disabled,* inefficient as it is, has replaced a myriad of other terms. In the chapter by William M. Cruickshank and James L. Paul, the term *brain-injured,* which the authors had utilized in earlier editions generally is dropped and the two terms have been used interchangeably in this edition. A reviewer in another instance commenting on our writing said that the writing in a chapter dealing with learning disabilities sounded like the author was referring to brain-injured children. This was insightful but illustrative of the general failure to understand the historical and accurate definition of learning disabilities. So much popular misconception of the problem has been pushed under the umbrella-like term *learning disabilities* that the central issue, which unfortunately produced a new category, has been lost to many people. Learning disabilities here is defined in the chapter by Cruickshank and Paul as a plural noun, and it is presented in its historical and rightful relationship to the malfunction of the central nervous system.

Culminating several years of work begun in 1972, William C. Rhodes and his associates have produced a series of major publications under the general rubric of "child variance." Peter Knoblock recognizes these publications and this work as providing new dimensions to an understanding of the emotionally disturbed child and youth. They form the basis for his discussion of the varying perspectives—often not in harmony with one another—by which the emotionally disturbed individual can be viewed and perhaps better understood.

The four chapters included in Part Four need to be viewed in relation to the chapters in Parts Two and Three, as there are intellectually retarded children who are blind, deaf, or crippled as well; *there are learning-disabled children and youth among the mentally retarded as well as among the gifted* and emotionally disturbed, in contradiction to popularly held beliefs. Emotional disturbance may be a secondary characteristic to any or all of the other disabilities discussed in this volume. Likewise, giftedness is not a thing unto itself, but may occur in relation to all of the clinical categories that have been mentioned except mental retardation. As with Part One, these chapters in Part Four should be seen as serving to integrate the total volume in a meaningful manner.

W.M.C.

10 Psychology and Mental Retardation

Lynn Kay Brown*

*Ph.D., Program Associate in Psychology, Institute for the Study
of Mental Retardation and Related Disabilities;
Assistant Professor of Psychology, University of Michigan.*

A major direction in the writing on mental retardation and the retarded is the concern with definition and description of the various subgroups composing this exceedingly heterogeneous population. Instead of focusing on population characteristics per se, however, it is the intent of this chapter to select for discussion a number of major psychological constructs related to human development and performance. The exploration of each of these constructs will be aimed at examining pertinent issues in their measurement and application within the field of mental retardation. Part of the task in bringing these psychological constructs into perspective is to view them as intimately involved with other levels of human functioning. Psychological constructs were evolved to deal with mental states and processes, and are inferred from direct observations of behavior. While complex theories have been built around these hypothetical constructs, it is important to recognize that overt behavior reflects forces and processes spanning a wide range of levels of functioning extend-

ing from the biological through the psychological to the social levels. Across all these levels, the individual is constantly changing in a changing world. There is a natural tendency in the process of attempting to study aspects of human performance to become reductionistic and to simplify, which tends to lead eventually to the reification of the constructs. This trend becomes even more powerful when investigators use populations of subjects in research aimed at detecting group differences. Furthermore, when a population is almost exclusively characterized as deviant along one salient socially negative dimension, the trend is even further enhanced. Therefore, this discussion will examine factors which contribute to the *relativity* of several psychological constructs and will highlight issues of individual variation. Concomitantly, it will provide a framework for examining the process of inquiry into human functioning, since the very process of investigation itself shapes and changes that which is studied.

A dynamic comprehensive psychology of the changing individual in a changing world must ultimately deal simultaneously with the *data* generated by the many different psychological theoretical perspectives. The

* The author would like to thank her colleagues, Professor Bettie Arthur and Professor William Rhodes, whose comments on this chapter have clarified and contributed to the contents.

435

study of psychological constructs as they are reflected in behavior and as they shape and are shaped by the external and internal conditions of the behaving individual constitutes one productive approach. This discussion, therefore, will be organized around a subset of psychological constructs which have in the past formed major foci of interest for persons working in the field of mental retardation. This subset does not by any means make up an holistic view of the individual, but it does provide a theoretical base for raising questions about the role of psychology in mental retardation.

INTELLIGENCE

This construct has been a major defining variable for classification of the mentally retarded. As measured psychometrically, it has traditionally been considered one of the most potent mediators between the external environment and behavior. There is, however, evidence accruing that questions the nature of intelligence and its role in personality development (e.g., Resnick, 1976). Yet, at an operational level and with regard to clinical and educational decision making, a subaverage IQ is oftentimes used to make predictions concerning limitations in future personality development, social adjustment, and the ability to profit from experience. Every practicing psychologist has seen people operate as though an individual, when found to be below a certain level of psychometrically assessed intelligence, is qualitatively different from those individuals whose intelligence is assessed to be above that level. In examining this issue, a number of factors contributing to the relativity of psychometrically assessed intelligence must be taken into consideration.

Cultural Relativity

There are strong statements currently being put forth regarding the cultural-relativism of various problems that were previously thought to reside mainly within the individual (cf. Becker, 1964, 1966; Rubington & Weinberg, 1973; Scheff, 1966; Szasz, 1961). The problem of intelligence and its implications for behavior is one of these. Dexter (1964), in arguing from a cultural-relativism point of view that society creates its own problems, suggested in an often quoted example that if our schools made gawkiness unacceptable, gawky children would suddenly become problem children. It is obvious that our society does place a high value on intellectual competence and that the school system is the major forum for highlighting the intellectual competence of each individual. Mercer (1973) has studied systematically and in illuminating detail the role of the school personnel in the process of labeling individuals as retarded. Evidence has been presented which suggests that when individuals who have been labeled mildly retarded by the schools leave the educational system, they function normally within society and their "careers" as retardates come to an end (Mercer, 1973; Cobb, 1972).

A cultural-relativistic position with regard to problems of intelligence appears to find support in explications of the genetic mechanisms of intelligence. Since an understanding of this mechanism is necessary for appreciating much of the current debate on labeling and mental retardation, it will be presented briefly here.

Much of the variability between individuals in intelligence can be attributed to the mechanism of polygenic inheritance. The variations of intelligence in a large population sampled at random would, according to this theoretical model, show a continuously smooth gradation on both sides of the population mean. This bi-symmetric bell-shaped curve of the normal distribution of intelligence is assumed to be the result of multiple genetic factors (each child receives a pool of many genes from each parent) interacting with multiple environmental factors. Each gene and each environmental factor has, it is assumed, under normal circumstances only a small additive effect, and it is the additive nature of these multiple factors that leads to potentially infinitely small differences between measurements resulting in the theoretically derived continuous distribution of intelligence.

When, however, the empirically derived distribution of intelligence from a sampled population is compared to this theoretical distribution, it is found that there is an overrepresentation at the lower end of the curve (Dingman & Tarjan, 1960). Zigler (1967) has argued that this situation can best be understood as two superimposed curves. One curve represents the normal polygenic mechanism and is distributed from approximately IQ 50 to IQ 150. The second curve has a mean of approximately 35 and ranges from 0 to 70. Individuals represented by this second curve are those who have been impacted upon by one or more factors, for example, rare but debilitating single gene effects, chromosomal abnormalities, exogenously derived damage. Although the second curve is essentially normal, it may be skewed to the right since some degree of damage or defect is possible at all levels of intellectual functioning. When individuals with known organic defect are removed from the total distribution, the remaining distribution closely approximates the distribution predicted by the theory of polygenically determined intelligence. The individuals in that distribution can be thought to be normal in that they represent the normal expression of their gene pools and additive environmental factors. Thus, many professionals view the cutoff point of 70 for the label *mental retardation* as an arbitrary societal decision. They would consider, therefore, the person with no known organic defect and an IQ 70 as no more abnormal in terms of the population distribution than the person with IQ 130.

On the other hand, Robert Edgerton, an anthropologist, has questioned the notion of cultural relativism by suggesting that the arbitrary cutoff point of IQ 70 might not be so arbitrary (Edgerton, 1968). His argument is that there is a minimum level of social competence necessary to conform to societal mores and to negotiate successfully the rigors of day-to-day societal transactions. "Even the least elegant of cultures establishes forms of interpersonal conduct that require no little subtlety, tact, deceit and verbal skill—indeed these traits may be more highly valued among primitives than they are in our Western World" (p. 86). Edgerton suggests that the threshold between competence and incompetence in *any* society lies between IQ 60–70. In addition to providing examples from more "primitive" cultures in which intellectual retardation does seem to cause problems for some individuals, Edgerton has provided us with a most interesting follow-up study of forty-eight mildly retarded adults in this country who were returned from institutional placements to their community (Edgerton, 1967).

Edgerton's methodology consisted of informal interviews and participation in virtually all aspects of the lives of these individuals who, at the time of study, had been in the community an averge of six years. Edgerton reported that although at first glance they appeared to be coping successfully, careful study of each individual revealed similar characteristics of functioning which Edgerton took to be signs of less than successful coping. For example, each person had acquired the assistance of one or more normal persons (called benefactors) who helped provide them with a sense of social competence and self-esteem. Despite such help, Edgerton noted, each subject appeared handicapped in dealing with the abstract relationships of time, space, and number. The lack of intellectual grasp of such concepts posed difficulties in daily social transactions and the subjects developed elaborate and clever ways of attempting to hide their difficulties. In other words, these people tried to appear normal (that is, non-retarded) to others, an activity that

Edgerton termed "passing." For example, some of the subjects who could not tell time wore old, broken watches, which then justified their telling other people that their watches were not working and provided them a socially acceptable excuse for asking the time of day. Edgerton takes examples such as these as evidence against cultural relativism.

These findings, however, are not incompatible with a position of cultural relativism, even though there undoubtedly is a minimum level of intellectual competence necessary to function in any society. The more a society prescribes specific social expectations and proscribes a limited repertoire of means for approaching goals, the higher the intellectual competence necessary to fit acceptably into society. Edgerton's view of these subjects was in itself a culturally relativistic one. His subjects could be considered to be functioning quite ingeniously in meeting societal expectations while functioning "normally" for their own ability levels in these situations. It is interesting to speculate, for example, that the new popularity of digital readout watches may well provide a better way of solving the problem of telling time faced by Edgerton's subjects, thereby removing one problem for their functioning in complex technological society. We have, as a society, a technological capacity to program for difference but we do not have an attitudinal climate that facilitates the productive use of that technology for such ends. True normalization, which is often taken to mean providing an "average expectable environment," can come about in this society only when there is: (1) a recognition of the tremendous human variability which is the normal product of genetic and environmental factors (cf. Williams, 1963); (2) a natural respect for difference; and (3) a concerted effort to program society, as well as the individual, in order to facilitate multiple avenues of development.

In examining issues of individual differences and subaverage intelligence, Jensen (1971) has pointed out that individual psychometric tests of intelligence have their highest reliability and concurrent validity in the IQ range between 50 and 80. Yet, he points out, within this group which is relatively homogeneous with regard to IQ, there is a very great range of cognitive and social abilities. If we have not been overly aware of these individual differences, it may be because we have not facilitated their expression. For example, Edgerton (1968, p. 81) has pointed out the tendency to simplify and slow down social interaction when communicating with someone who is considered to be retarded. The issue of the negative and restricting aspects of labeling is a matter of concern and debate (e.g., MacMillan et al., 1974; Hobbs, 1975).

The relativity issue is more complex than cultural relativism itself implies. There is a multitude of factors relating to the assessment problem which contributes to relativity. Among these is the tacit assumption that using a standardized test of intelligence somehow insures accuracy of measurement and that all examinations with such tests are valid and reliable under all circumstances. It is uncommon to see psychological test reports wherein time and space are devoted to analyses of these issues as they bear on the evaluation of the individual being assessed.

Relativity Related to the Assessment Process

The standardized-testing situation has a number of parameters relevant to the relativity issue as it pertains to intellectual assessment.

Standardized testing necessitates a controlled testing context: for example, the room, materials, order of presentation, and examiner instructions are uniformly prescribed. With the testing context held constant, variations in child performance should ideally be attributable to differential responses to specific test items mediated by differential intellectual abilities. There is, however, much evidence indicating that children vary tremendously in their reactions to the standardized testing situation itself, and that these differential responses, based on experiential, emotional, and motivational differences, affect performance outcome on test items. In addition, the individual child is a stimulus with tremendous demand characteristics who impacts differentially on different diagnosticians, despite the diagnostician's attempts to adhere to the standardized 'script.' The testing situation is therefore a complicated interaction between a child who brings unique experiences, expectations, and responses and a diagnostic examiner who also brings unique experiences, expectations and responses. The test is a tool around which this very complicated interaction takes place. Also, the tools themselves (different tests and test items) change the context of the interaction. The diagnostician's very difficult problem is to figure out *why* the child performed the way he or she did in this very complicated situation (Brown, 1977, pp. 49–50).

Is there empirical evidence that demonstrates the concept of relativity as it applies to the testing situation? One line of evidence comes from the early study of Sachs (1952), who demonstrated that there was an improvement in test performance by some children when they were administered a test by an adult with whom they had had a prior positive experience. Along the same line, Zigler and Butterfield (1968), using culturally deprived children of nursery school age, demonstrated that a nonstandard testing situation designed to optimize success experience significantly facilitated intelligence test performance. Through a comparison of standard and optimally designed testing situations presented in both the fall and spring of the year to the same children, the authors demonstrated that improved performance in the standard testing from fall to spring could be interpreted on the basis of motivational factors. "By the end of the year they were better able to use their intelligence in a standard testing situation"

(p. 10). Zigler *et al.* (1973) with economically deprived children found substantial gain on a retest of the Peabody Picture Vocabulary Test administered one week after the original testing *when* attempts were made to reduce test anxiety through a familiar experimenter on a pretest play situation. These studies indicate that, for some children, changing the parameters of the testing situation can lead to improved test performance.

In view of these considerations regarding standardized testing, some critics have advocated moving away from standardized testing altogether. Bersoff (1973), for example, has argued that "psycho-situational assessment," defined as the analysis of a child's behavior in its natural context, yields more valid data than standardized psychometric testing. Some areas have declared a moratorium on the use of standardized psychological tests as the sole basis for pupil classification. The American Association on Mental Deficiency has required that a diagnosis of retardation involve documentation of sub-average intellectual as well as sub-average adaptive functioning. Also, modifications of the standardized testing situation have been used to advantage. This author, for example, has written about the value of bringing parents into the psychological testing situation (Brown, 1975). Efforts such as these are based upon a growing recognition that the *context* has a tremendous impact on behavior. Psychologists are moving away from a static description of intelligence and personality as a set of characteristics and abilities that are likely to be expressed in similar ways under a wide variety of life situations to a much more dynamic concept of differential functioning in different contexts. Thus, intelligence test performance might begin to tell us a great deal about an individual when it is viewed in relation to that individual's functioning in a wide variety of situations, including those more closely approximating real life situations.

Thus far, this discussion of factors contributing to the relativity of psychological assessment has focused primarily on the psychological and social levels of functioning. The biological level of functioning is also a consideration and has been taken into account most commonly in infant testing in which the "state of the organism" is considered to affect performance outcome. Some of the older retarded individuals who receive diagnostic testing have known physiological deficits and many are on drug regimes. Sorting out the contributions of these factors to test performance is exceedingly complicated. Further, there are less obvious issues of potential biological impact. For example, one recent study has found that allergic children with neurologic symptoms (learning disabilities, hyperactivity, fatigue, incoordination, and irritability) showed marked improvement on WISC performance after allergy therapy (Millman *et al.*, 1976). Nutritional status has certainly been shown to affect intelligence test performance and ability to attend. There are probably a variety of sub-clinical conditions which are not immediately obvious but affect ability to perform in a testing situation.

In addition to factors contributing to relativity in the assessment process itself, another problem relates to the *selection* of those individuals who ultimately receive assessment. One of the most important findings of the Mercer (1973) investigation has been that all of those who are eligible to be labeled retarded are not so labeled. This stems from, among other things, behavioral differences of the children (rather than overall academic performance alone) which influence teachers' judgments with regard to who should be referred for psychometric testing. Since psychometric testing is a necessary criterion for being labeled retarded, children whom the teachers do not refer do not get so labeled. Teacher judgments are not, it appears, always based upon intellectual factors alone, and the judges are not always aware of the factors which contribute to their decisions.

The findings of Mercer are supported by other investigators such as Caplan (1973) who documented the existence in the school system of children of similar low academic performance levels who received differential disposition with regard to being passed on to the next grade. Those who were passed on and those who were retained differed on behavioral dimensions in the classroom and the school was not aware that such disparity existed.

The foregoing considerations have attempted to highlight only a few factors which contribute to the relativity of the psychological construct of intelligence as it is assessed and applied within our society. Although the issues have been documented by many professionals who have written about them, what is "known" and what is "practiced" are not always in synchrony. A personal example provides an illustration of the problems we face.

I presented to a group of professionals a lecture that covered many of the same points made in this section. A colleague approached me after the lecture to express her agreement with the points I had made. Yet, weeks later this same person came to me asking that I look for clerical errors in the protocol of a young boy I had recently tested. When I asked why, she said: "Well, you gave him an IQ of 69. If there was an error of only two points, his IQ might be 71. I have to meet with his parents this afternoon and I don't want to have to tell them that their son is retarded." It is obvious that, despite her beliefs about the relativity of assessments of intelligence, she was operating on the assumption that a child with an IQ score of 69 was qualitatively different from a child with an IQ score of 71. This unfortunately is not an isolated example, since professionals, like all other human beings, seem to feel more comfortable working with limiting categories than with diffusely defined contexts.

The cultural relativity of definitions of intellectual competence and the contextual variability of intellectual assessment do not by any means exhaust the parameters of mental functioning in need of consideration in working with individuals whether retarded or not. Today there is agreement that the most commonly used intelligence tests, such as the Binet and Wechsler, measure, to a large extent, acquired knowledge. Such tests do not systematically measure the *processes* by which that knowledge was acquired. An understanding of the processes by which knowledge is acquired, as well as stored and utilized, should add to the understanding of intellectual differences. The acquisition, storage, and utilization of information is, in fact, a broad definition of cognition (Kessler, 1970) (cf. Newlands also, Chapter 3).

COGNITION

Suppes (1974) points out that the definition of cognition has continued to widen until it now encompasses all the major academic skills and overlaps with that which has classically been considered part of the area of perception. Although any delimitation of cognition would be a matter of debate, Mussen, Conger, and Kagan (1974) provide a working definition that helpfully indicates a number of areas of inquiry that are pertinent to a discussion of cognition. They suggest that cognition consists of a minimum of five processes: (1) perception, (2) memory, (3) generation of ideas, (4) evaluation, and (5) reasoning, and that these processes involve the manipulation, in thought, of a number of units, among which are included schemata, images, symbols, concepts, and rules. Many investigators in cognition have been interested in orderly sequential changes in cognitive processes which are related to age and experience. Developmental psychologists especially have attempted to understand the mechanisms of cognitive change and have assessed the influence of the various stages of cognitive development over a wide range of behavior.

It is obvious that cognition is a broad and diversified field of inquiry and it is not uncommon for an investigator to concentrate on one cognitive process in one portion of the age span. Church (1970) has warned that such fragmentation can lead to the reification of the abstractions we attempt to study and that in studying these "we sometimes lose sight of our basic subject matter, human organisms making their way through space, society, and life" (p. 2). It may be difficult, therefore, to keep in mind that cognitive processes are psychological *constructs* not only because of the fragmentation of inquiry but also perhaps because there is the impression that these constructs are more fundamental (and, therefore, supposedly more real) than an elusive construct such as intelligence. How susceptible to factors contributing to relativity are the psychological constructs of cognition likely to be?

> . . . We have become aware that our knowledge of human cognition is inescapably relativistic, that is, we know that there are radical individual and group differences in the way self and world are perceived, thought about, talked about, valued, categorized, and acted with and toward. Thus, the quest for universals has proven largely futile (Church, pp. 1.2).

Cognition and Intelligence

What is the expected relationship between cognition and intelligence? The retarded, by definition, display in the testing situation a deficit in acquired knowledge. Since cognition involves the processes by which knowledge is acquired, stored, and utilized, any intellectual deficit should be reflected in one or more of the cognitive processes. Deficits have, in fact, been demonstrated in all of the cognitive processes included in the working definition of Mussen *et al.* (perception, memory, generation of ideas, evaluation, and reasoning) when the retarded are compared to non-retarded individuals of the same chronological age.

Less clear are the expectations when the retarded are matched with non-retarded individuals of the same *mental age*. The debate over chronological versus mental age matches has been vigorous with regard to cognition and has helped to highlight some factors contributing to the relativity of cognitive performance of the retarded. This debate has been characterized as a developmental versus a defect orientation.

Zigler (1967, 1969) has presented a developmental orientation to cognitive development of the retarded. In this view, when individuals with known physiological defects are removed from consideration, the remaining individuals on the lower end of the polygenic distribution of intelligence (whom Zigler refers to as familial retardates) are simply normal individuals with low intelligence. These individuals pass more slowly through the same cognitive sequences as do non-retarded individuals although they reach a lower final level of development. Thus, when compared with their chronological-age peers, they will be cognitively delayed, but when compared to non-retarded peers of the same mental age, the two groups theoretically should function similarly. The defect orientation, on the other hand, would predict that even when matched for mental age there would be dissimilarity of cognitive functioning.

A less parsimonious developmental position might also predict mental-age differences. In our current conceptualizations of human development we are moving away from the notion of a passive developmental "unfolding" to a view of the individual as actively constructing his or her own internal structures through interaction with the environment. Since the retarded have very different experiential histories from their mental-age non-retarded peers, one could predict that the evolving cognitive structures would also eventually be different.

The data which speak to this debate have been equivocal. In support of Zigler's developmental position, the retarded who have no known physiological defects have been shown to progress more slowly through the same sequence of Piagetian stages of cognitive development than do non-retarded children, though reaching lower final levels of cognitive development. When the research sample has included those individuals with known physiological defects, the findings have been much less consistent (Weisz, 1976). Weisz points out that Inhelder's (1968) research on reasoning in the retarded indicated distinct differences between the cognitive development of brain-damaged and non-brain-damaged mentally retarded persons. He cites studies of conservation which have demonstrated MA-match similarities of functioning *only* when organicity is ruled out. Kahn (1976) cites similar findings with regard to moral development. Wohlhueter and Sindberg (1975) provide an interesting longitudinal study of object concept development in profoundly and severely retarded subjects (subjects expected to have organic defects) and some moderately retarded subjects with physical handicaps. Repeated assessments revealed much variability in object concept performance and this variability included both upward and downward movement as well as skipping of stages of development. Such variability has not been found in normal subjects nor has it been demonstrated with non-organically defective retarded individuals. These investigations all lend support to Zigler's contention that the organically defective must be studied separately from the non-organically defective. When specific mental-age comparisons are made with organicity ruled out, however, similarities of functioning between retarded and non-retarded subjects are still not always found (Zigler & Balla, 1971). Zigler and his associates have argued that when such differences are found they are likely to be attributed to emotional and motivational differences related to the differential experiential histories of the retarded rather than cognitive defects or deficits. They have had much success in demonstrating that changes in the motivational and emotional demand characteristics of the cognitive task can enhance the cognitive performance of the retarded and often bring that cognitive performance in line with that of non-retarded mental-age matched peers. One example of a contextual variable found to be pertinent to performance of the retarded has been the nature of the reinforcer (e.g., Zigler, 1966). It was hypothesized that being "correct" or "right" does not have the same meaning for subjects who fail often as it does for subjects who do not. Thus, as one example, the introduction of a tangible reinforcer removed the mental-age differences that had previously been demonstrated in a concept-switching task (Zigler & deLabry, 1962). The reinforcement hierarchy is just one (and perhaps the least dynamic) of many variables contributing to the relativity of the cognitive functioning of the retarded that have been highlighted by Zigler's research. Other variables will be discussed in more detail in the next section of this chapter when dealing with personality. While mental age is a crude basis of comparison that does not insure homogeneity of subjects, whether or not all mental-age matches ultimately reveal similarity of cognitive functioning, the heuristic value of Zigler's work is obvious.

A Component of Cognition— Memory

With this discussion of cognition as background, the focus will turn to one specific cognitive process, memory, which was chosen for several reasons. Interest in memory and retardation is longstanding (Galton, 1887) and memory items are incorporated into most intelligence tests (for example, digit span and sentence recall). Findings from the work on memory speak to the interrelatedness of the various cognitive processes. Some recent investigations of retardation bearing upon such interrelationships have dealt with the role of memory in language production (Walker *et al.,* 1975) and in reading and

arithmetic (Blackman *et al.,* 1976). Findings from the work on memory also speak to the interrelatedness of different levels of functioning (biological, psychological, and social). Finally, the issues of relativity with regard to memory seem particularly pertinent. For example, life-history information is notoriously susceptible to distortion by contextual factors. Similarly, in the laboratory, a seemingly neutral nonsense syllable may be linked consciously or unconsciously to other variables in the test situation which may result in differential memory performance (see Jenkins, 1974, for a discussion of the impact of context on the laboratory memory performance of college students). If relativism affects mature memorizers in what would seem to be a rather neutral learning situation, the question may be raised whether a greater impact might be expected for the less mature memorizer for whom the learning situation is anything but neutral. There is a body of research dealing directly with memory and mental retardation which provides data for further exploration of these issues.

When retarded memorizers are compared with non-retarded memorizers they do *not* seem to differ with regard to long-term memory. In other words, once the retarded have taken information into the memory system, their retention is similar to non-retarded individuals. There is, on the other hand, evidence that the retarded do differ from the non-retarded in immediate recall (that is, in terms of what gets into the memory system). Several explanations of this short-term retention deficit have been closely allied with neuro-biological concepts.

Spitz (1963) applied a cortical satiation theory to mental retardation. His hypothesis is that cortical cells of the retarded are slower to show chemical, electrical, and physical changes. Temporary changes in cortical cells, once they do occur, are slower to return to their original state. Once permanent changes do occur in cortical cells modification is more difficult and there is less spread of activity from the stimulated cells to the surrounding cells. Because of less neural flexibility the retardate is also less able to organize and isolate material to be learned (Spitz, 1966). Although there is no direct physiological evidence with human subjects to support these hypotheses, Kessler (1970) cites as indirect support the EEG studies of Baumeister and Hawkins (1967) which found that more intelligent subjects show more EEG responsivity to a light stimulus than do less intelligent subjects.

Ellis (1963) posited a stimulus trace theory to explain the short-term memory retention deficits of the mentally retarded. The stimulus trace is an hypothesized neural event which varies with the intensity, duration, and meaning of the stimulus event. According to this position a low IQ reflects a lack of neural integrity which impacts adversely on the amplitude and duration of the stimulus trace activity resulting in a more rapidly fading stimulus trace. Again, direct physiological evidence is not possible in humans, but Kessler (1970) cites indirect support from the animal studies of Thompson (1958) and from the intercorrelations and factor analyses of WISC scores for 13-to-14 year-old retarded and non-retarded public school students carried out by Baumeister and Bartlett (1962). This factor analysis identified, in addition to a Verbal and Performance factor for both groups, a third factor for the retarded group which was labeled a Trace (memory) factor involving particularly the Digit Span, Coding, and Arithmetic subtests.

Even though there appears to be no basis on which to choose one theoretical framework over another, one important contribution of these theories is the postulation of a relationship between the biological and psychological levels of functioning which can lead to different ways of conceptualizing and investigating the problems. These theories have, however, been criticized as being "defect theories" since they infer an inborn or acquired defect in brain functioning (Zigler, 1966, 1967). A wide variety of performance differences are predicted from the inferred physiological differences. Since physiological evidence for such theorizing cannot be readily obtained from the human brain given our present availability of technology, there is a tendency for the positions to lead initially to attempts to catalogue group differences. Once differences have been identified (particularly when these are qualitative differences due to brain damage), investigators in the early stages of empirical investigation are not as likely to see as pertinent the search for multiple contributing factors that influence performance. In other words, the issues of relativism are not as likely to be explored. Kessler (1970) has summarized this issue in her discussion of memory and retardation.

It appears that [the] mentally retarded suffer mainly in the very first stage of information processing. This would seem to suggest some differences in synaptic transmitter mechanisms rather than a primary defect in protein synthesis necessary for RNA. *However, it must be kept in mind that the neurophysiological aspects of learning are correlates, not causes, so that the ultimate "cure" may be either environmental or neurochemical manipulations, or both* (p. 124; emphasis added).

Kessler's statement could be enhanced by also taking into account the contribution made at the psychological level by thought processes themselves. A difference or abnormality in one level of functioning will certainly be reflected in some ways at other levels of functioning. It does not, however, imply difference in every area of functioning at every level. Psychological constructs are applicable across the entire distribution of intelligence, just as neurophysiological constructs underlie and social constructs overlie that same distribution. Advances in understanding at the neurophysiological, psychological, and social levels should contribute to a broader understanding and conceptualization of the functioning of the total individual. This ultimately should result in benefit for all learners.

To return to the issue of memory, the deficiency of the retarded has been shown to be a problem of getting information into storage rather than a problem of long-term retention. Wickelgren (1974) points out that these differences can be attributed to coding capacity or coding strategy. This would seem to be in line with the theorizing by Spitz, who postulated both a capacity and an organizational component, and it is in line with more recent hypotheses by Ellis (1970) in which he points to a rehearsal strategy deficiency in memory performance of the retarded. The exciting aspect of investigating strategy deficiencies, as Wickelgren suggests, is that such deficiencies may be eliminated by teaching strategic behavior. A capacity (biological) deficit, on the other hand, does not give much clue as to environmental or psychological factors which might be manipulated to enhance performance.

Campione and Brown (1977) have presented a review of memory research with the retarded that bears upon the capacity-strategy distinction. They have limited their review to mildly and moderately retarded individuals with no known organic etiological compenent (the group Zigler has referred to as familial retardates). The comparisons with which they deal are based upon chronological rather than mental age. They point out that comparative differences in memory tasks between the retarded and non-retarded seem to be found most particularly in tasks in which a strategy is necessary or helpful. In memory tasks, mnemonic strategies include rehearsal, organization, and elaboration. Campione and Brown cite work which consistently shows that the retarded are deficient in their use of these mnemonic strategies. Specific training in the use of these strategies does result in marked performance increment and maintenance of strategy usage can be attained given sufficient training. Yet there does not seem to be evidence of generalization of the use of strategies to new situations. Thus, the retarded have the ability to use strategies but they appear deficient in the spontaneous *intent* to use strat-

egies. As is usually the case when generalizing from group findings, there are exceptions. The authors point out that there are retarded individuals who do spontaneously utilize strategic behavior. Further study of these individuals would appear to have promise.

The conclusion of Campione and Brown is that there must be some "more general factors that underlie both the use of strategies and the failure to show generalization of training" (p. 12). They discuss a number of potential "metamemorial" factors which include the subject's estimating task difficulty and self-monitoring of strategy usage. The notion is that if a learner does not recognize a task as difficult he or she may not be moved to utilize learning strategies. Research is presented which indicates that retarded children do have trouble estimating their own performance both prior to the task and during the task itself. Training for task estimation has been shown to improve performance but again not to generalize to new situations. This would seem to be a depressing finding, but the search for contextual factors need not be over. At the conclusion of the review, the authors suggest that the experimental research may not have been designed to facilitate optimal generalization. They make the important observation that, in training for strategies, researchers have made little attempt to explain to subjects just why strategies may be useful: "It generally is the case that the experimenter simply tells the subject what to do and leaves the subject to infer why he should do it." Thus, Campione and Brown have touched upon an issue which will be of central concern in the next section of this chapter which deals with personality. That issue concerns the active involvement of the subject in the exploration of his or her own situation. Mischel (1977) has referred to this as "the subject as expert and colleague" and has pointed out "that the individual's awareness of the contingencies in the situation—his or her understanding (not the psychologist's) of what behavior leads to what outcome—is a crucial determinant of the resulting actions and choices, including behavior in the classical and instrumental conditioning paradigms" (p. 253).

It is obvious, even in this brief discussion of memory, that there is much overlap between memory and the other cognitive processes. Wickelgren provides a statement which speaks not only to this interrelationship but which also relates these to the biological level of functioning:

> For a while some people thought that memory might be in a modality of its own, separate from the various sensory, motor, and cognitive modalities. Lesion studies have failed completely to discover an area of the brain that is the respository of memories, which is not also concerned with perceptual, motor, or cognitive aspects of functioning (1974, p. 89).

As one example of interrelatedness, the identification and utilization of mnemonic strategies would seem to overlap with concept identification and utilization. In support of this interrelatedness, concept studies have shown that the retarded are deficient in the initial stages of learning (which involves learning to attend to the relevant dimensions of a problem), but they are not deficient in learning appropriate associations after they have once successfully attended to those relevant dimensions (Zeaman & House, 1963). This parallels the observed mental-age differences in memory in relation to which the problem for the retarded involves getting information into the memory system rather than retaining information once it has entered the system. These findings on memory have complex interrelationships with such areas of functioning as perception and language, the discussion of which would take us beyond the scope of this chapter. The interested reader is referred to the review of cognition and the handicapped child by Suppes (1974).

The psychological constructs of intelligence and cognition have been used repeatedly to identify and compare groups and subgroups of people. Most particularly, they have been employed in studying and discussing the retarded. Each construct deals with limited aspects of human behavior which contribute to and are influenced by personality. Personality can be thought of as the individual's immediate inner context which interacts with the contexts of the social milieu.

PERSONALITY

Personality is a psychological construct formulated to explain the behavioral consistency displayed by an individual across a variety of stimulus situations. This behavioral consistency leads to an ascribed identity which is potentially recognizable by more than one observer. Personality theories acknowledge, to varying degrees, the impact of the context on behavior but the major cause of behavioral consistency is generally seen as coming from within the individual. Behavioral inconsistencies also can be seen as reflective of underlying personality structures. In projective testing, for example, a break in defenses resulting in atypical responses may be adjudged a more pertinent representative of underlying personality structure than the individual's typical behavioral repertoire. This certainly occurs in everyday social interactions where a very infrequent but socially significant behavior (such as impulsive, aggressive outbursts) may become a central part of the socially perceived identity of a more usually docile person. Personality theories, therefore, must deal both with the generality and the specificity of behavior.

There are numerous theories of personality and each utilizes a subset of psychological constructs. It is not the intent of this chapter to examine personality theories per se, for there are available several comprehensive surveys (e.g., Millon, 1973; Levy, 1970). Instead, the present discussion will examine a few personality constructs that have been most typically utilized in the discussion and study of mental retardation, and will also suggest constructs that perhaps have not been emphasized enough. It will be helpful first, however, to examine the general relationship of the construct of personality to intelligence and cognition.

Personality and Intelligence

There is strong agreement that personality is interrelated with intelligence. Eisenberg (1958) as quoted in Webster (1970) has stated that "the interdependence of emotion and intelligence is a *fundamental fact* of human behavior, at the psychological and the biological levels of integration" (p. 6; emphasis added). The cognitive processes underlying intelligence are also considered to be interrelated with personality. Chess (1970), writing on emotional problems in mental retardation, points out that "specific aspects of cognitive functioning such as retentive memory and imitative ability, may be influential in determining the child's adaptive abilities" (p. 58). There are stronger statements of the interdependency of cognition and personality and, in fact, theories of personality exist in which cognition is the central basis of personality differences (e.g., Levy, 1970, pp. 249–306). According to these theories, therefore, one would definitely expect to see correlates of sub-average intellectual functioning in personality functioning.

In focusing on personality issues of people of sub-average intelligence, Webster (1970, p. 3) poses two questions: (1) "What is unique in the personality development of mentally retarded children?" and (2) "What is 'normal' or optimal emotional development for a retarded child?" Each of these questions will be explored.

The first question can lead to the chronological/mental age argument that was raised with regard to cognition. A developmental as opposed to defect expectation might be that personality, like intelligence, develops more slowly for the non-physio-logically defective retarded and reaches a lower final level of development. Therefore, personality differences would be expected between retarded and non-retarded individuals of the same chronological age but no personality differences would be expected when the retarded and non-retarded are matched for mental age. There would be, according to a developmental orientation, no personality factors expected to be unique to familial mental retardation.

Again, although there would be general agreement about the personality differences resulting from chronological-age comparisons, there would be considerable debate surrounding the expectations using a mental-age match. Much of the data on retardation that pertain to this question come from psychiatric and residential facilities and there is therefore, as Chess (1970) points out, the potential problem of a sample biased toward behavioral and personality disorders. With such samples one of the ways in which personality factors have been examined is by tabulating the frequency and quality of emotional disturbance in the retarded as compared to the non-retarded population.

In terms of frequency of emotional disturbance, it is generally agreed that there is a higher incidence of behavioral and personality disorders among the retarded although not everyone would agree as to the cause or extent of the reported incidence. Webster (1963, p. 38) has written, for example, that the "slow and incomplete unfolding of the personality is associated with partial fixations that result in an infantile or immature character structure." Thus, Webster is hypothesizing that personality development of the retarded is more than simply slower than in the non-retarded. From a study of 159 retarded children living with their parents, all of whom were applicants for a preschool program for the retarded, Webster found that all of the retarded children showed some degree of emotional disturbance when compared to non-retarded children of the same mental age.

Chess, in contrast to the findings of Webster, reports from her own clinical and research experience that not all retarded children have emotional problems. Further, she cites findings which suggest that, under proper environmental circumstances, the *majority* of the retarded can develop personality patterns compatible with their mental age peers (Cytryn & Lourie, 1967). The sampling bias may be a principal factor in the discrepancy between these findings. Chess also points out that little consideration is typically given to the heterogeneity of the retarded population with regard to etiology, degree of "defect," individual temperament and environmental setting—all factors which would lead to diversity in personality functioning.

A better way to look for *unique* factors in personality functioning would be to look for qualitative differences in structure and/or cause of emotional disturbance in the retarded as compared to the non-retarded. Philips and Williams (1975, 1977) studied 100 mentally retarded children referred to a psychiatric clinic and found that their symptoms did not differ in kind from the referred non-retarded. Also, there was no evidence that the symptomatology of the retarded fit into unique patterns. Although the symptomatology of the retarded did fit into established diagnostic categories, there was a difference in the incidences with regard to referral question and diagnostic category.

In general, these findings are supported by those of others such as Rutter (1975) and are in agreement with Chess (1970) who states that "there are no emotional or behavioral characteristics that are invariably associated with mental retardation (p. 56)." Further support comes from studies of non-clinic retarded children who were shown to have average ratings of temperament that did not differ from non-retarded children matched on mental age (Chess and Korn, 1970). There is, therefore, much evidence that argues against unique personality factors in the retarded.

In personality, as was true of cognition, the issue of chronological versus mental age comparisons is not easy to resolve. It will be recalled that Zigler utilized a personality construct (i.e., motivation) to point to differences between the retarded and non-retarded of the same mental age in his attempt to show that experiential differences impacted upon cognitive performance. This alone might seem to support basic personality differences between retarded and non-retarded children. Zigler also, however, found that there were motivational differences between the institutionalized and non-institutionalized retarded (Zigler, 1966). We know that the institutional environment has a decided impact upon personality development but, now that the retarded are more likely to be reared in a home environment, it does not necessarily mean that their environment is at all comparable to that of the non-retarded. To take one speculative example out of numerous possibilities, most parents of the retarded are not able to expect with confidence that their retarded child will grow to be independent of the family situation. The lack of such expectation would likely influence the parent-child interactions in ways that could have impact on the personality development of the child. When and if such attitudes can be alleviated (such as by parents having the knowledge that community-living arrangements can be made for their child), some differences in personality that were thought to be related to intellectual level may be alleviated.

It is likely that when the environmental stresses are relieved by changing societal systems to better meet the individual needs of the retarded, mental age comparisons of personality functioning will be better controlled. This does not necessarily mean that all differences related to environmental stresses will be eliminated. Many people suggest, for example, that the physiological growth of the retarded which proceeds ahead of mental development creates internal stress. A body size which does not match mental functioning may create stressful initial interactions between the retarded person and people who are not at first aware of the disparity. For such reasons many people consider the retarded to be more vulnerable to stress and more likely to be stressed. For example, Philips & Williams (1975) state one viewpoint:

> The development of emotional disorder in retarded children often begins with transient situational problems that become more fixed as the child's development is distorted. Such difficulties, coupled with negative social attitudes, may make less acute problems intense as the child encounters each developmental level. In addition, the birth of a retarded child obviously arouses reactive problems in the family that will result in difficulties in caring for the offspring. This has been noted by other authors . . . and may account for the high incidence of behavioral and personality disorders among retarded children (p. 1269).

Another complication to be considered concerns the heterogeneity of the retarded population. Zigler (1967) has argued that for cognitive comparisons, those individuals with known organic defects should be viewed separately. Similar considerations pertain to personality research. Not only should the individuals with known organic defects be viewed separately, but the heterogeneity within that particular group should be further sorted out. To take brain damage as an example, the type of insult, site of insult, age at insult and degree of tissue damage are important factors which have been shown to be related to differential patterns of gross personality functioning (Lezak, 1976).

Webster's second question concerning normal or optimal functioning of the retarded might be rephrased as "normal *and* optimal functioning," since normal functioning and optimal functioning are not synonymous, particularly for the retarded. The pursuit of this general question has

particular heuristic value for the field of mental retardation.

To begin this discussion we can turn once more to the polygenic distribution of intelligence. It is hypothesized that an individual, at any point on the distribution of intelligence, has a range of potential intellectual functioning. This range is determined by the particular genotype and different genotypes may have different ranges (Gottesman, 1963). Further, it is hypothesized that individuals on the high end of their distribution of intelligence are likely to be functioning at the higher potential range of functioning. This may be because, having better cognitive equipment, these individuals are more likely to make use of their environment, and the environment is also more likely to be growth facilitating. On the other hand, individuals at the low end of the distribution are likely to be functioning at the lower end of their potential range of functioning. This lowered functioning may be accounted for by less adequate equipment to maximize environmental interactions and the probability of a less adequate environment. Support for these theoretical assumptions can be taken from work such as that of Heber (1972), who has demonstrated massive intelligence gains for retarded children of retarded mothers after a comprehensive intervention effort. Given the interdependence of intelligence and personality, can we point to comparable examples of personality change toward better integrative functioning?

Edgerton and Bercovici (1976) have presented a 12–14 year follow-up of Edgerton's original study of institutionalized retarded adults who had been returned to their community. It will be recalled from the discussion of his original study that these individuals were first studied after having been in the community for an average of six years. Thirty of the original forty-eight individuals were located for this second follow-up. Among the findings were the following:

1. The lives of the majority of the individuals were marked by major fluctuations. These fluctuations included changes in mood and aspirations (personality constructs) as well as social adjustment practicalities (goals of personality functioning).
2. Concern with "passing" was no longer a major issue for the majority of the individuals.
3. The benefactors played a less significant role.
4. The lives of the subjects were more varied and were reported to be more pleasurable than in the first follow-up study.
5. Many of the sample defined themselves as normal despite the fact that many did not have vocational success.
6. Edgerton's own predictions of community adjustment based upon the first follow-up proved to be quite inaccurate, which Edgerton points out is in line with the general literature which fails to support the predictability of community adjustment.

Edgerton's findings suggest that with intervention (i.e., time, experience, and opportunity) personality changes do continue and many of these changes can be considered to consist of movement toward more optimal functioning.

This discussion of normal and optimal functioning has been posed as a present-future distinction. Chess (1970) provides a very important discussion of normal and optimal functioning within the time frame of the present. It is not uncommon for the retarded individual to display discrepant behavior within a particular area of functioning. Such discrepancies are not necessarily, according to Chess, indicative of motivational or emotional factors. She makes a distinction between routine accomplishments and behaviors which can be carried out *only* under certain optimal circumstances. Many diagnosticians attempt to demonstrate optimal functioning of the retarded client and then attempt to find ways to restructure the environment to elicit and support this optimal functioning. Chess's caution that overstressing the optimal behavior may put unwarranted stress on the retarded is one

which should definitely be taken into consideration in dealing with the mentally retarded individual.

In summary, there is a range of functioning possible for all people. It is likely that the lower on the intelligence continuum the individual, the more limited will be the forms of expression possible for variability, but this does not eliminate the fact that human variability does exist at all levels of intelligence. The search for personality factors unique to sub-average intelligence has not progressed sufficiently for the questions to be answered, but there is some evidence that argues against unique personality factors being found, particularly for retardation of non-organic etiology.

Specific Components of Personality

If the level of intelligence is not as highly predictive of adjustment as was once thought and if, as Edgerton and others have suggested, there is personality change throughout the life span, it is critical to explore the dimensions of personality that may be involved in this process of growth and change. In the multiplicity of theories of personality, most authors give a central role to affective experience in personality growth and development.

Affects (emotions) are phenomenological aspects of personality functioning which are hypothesized to serve as mediators and motivators of behavior. They are descriptive of aspects of inner experience which are considered to lend meaningfulness, substance, and force to that experience. It is generally assumed that all human organisms are born with the capacity to experience basic affects and that these basic affects, like all mental processes, are subject to development and differentiation (Bakwin & Bakwin, 1972). Some approaches to understanding affective experience have attempted to bridge the different levels of functioning. Thus Schacter (1962), pointing to the similarities between affective responses at the physiological level, has emphasized the role of situational cues (i.e., context) in the labeling of one's own affective experience. Essentially, one major role of affects in behavior is that of an arousal mechanism which can serve an adaptive signal function by alerting the individual to take action. Although affects have a central role in theories of human development, there have been, to this author's knowledge, no systematic studies of affective development in the retarded. There have, however, been studies of the affective responses of the retarded in different situations, but even that work is limited.

One of the approaches to the elucidation of personality variables in the retarded has been the study of failure experiences. Most personality statements pertaining to the retarded begin with the assumption that the retarded fail more frequently than comparable groups of non-retarded individuals (again, of course, this expectation may differ depending upon whether the comparison group is matched for CA or MA). Further, most of these statements assume that such failure experiences elicit affective responses which may ultimately have a negative impact on personality development.

In evaluating the studies of failure experiences in the retarded, the tacit assumption that the retarded actually experience more failure can be questioned since there are no empirical studies which have explored the parameters and/or documented the actual incidence of failure experiences in the lives of the retarded. Although it may seem reasonable to assume that the retarded do fail frequently, it is also equally reasonable to assume that, in some environments, the retarded experience *less* failure than the non-retarded (whether or not the comparison is based on CA or MA). The most common strategy in working with the retarded has been to reinforce the individual for doing his or her best (i.e., reinforcing the successes and ignoring the failures) in an attempt to avoid the supposedly negative

consequences of failure. Ignoring the failures, however, may also have negative consequences. There are studies of non-retarded children which have shown that being signaled both when correct as well as incorrect results in better learning than being signaled only when correct (Meyer & Offenbach, 1962; Whitehurst, 1969). Harter, Brown, and Zigler (1971), as one example with retarded children, demonstrated that MA matched non-retarded and familial retarded children showed better learning when tangible rewards were combined with tangible penalties than when only rewards were presented. This effect did not hold for organically retarded children also matched for mental age. It is difficult to separate informational from motivational components of a signal of incorrectness such as a penalty. Most probably, both aspects are involved.

The implication of such studies is that, in those environments in which failures are ignored, the retarded may truly be deprived of important informational and motivational input through these attempts to protect them from failure. It should be noted, however, that the literature also provides examples in which success has been shown to be more facilitative of performance of the retarded than failure (Gardner, 1958; Heber, 1957). Differing theoretical orientations have been utilized to predict different outcomes based upon experiential history of success and failure. For example, in explanation of the Gardner and Heber findings, it may be reasoned that limited experience of success may give success a high motivational (almost novelty) impact when success does occur (Cromwell, 1967). On the other hand, it also might be reasoned that limited experience with success results in a less strong association of reinforcement with success and thus a reduced positive impact. Similarly, one might predict that multiple failure experiences have a highly motivating, aversive impact (Zigler, 1966). On the other hand, frequent failure experience might be predicted to lead to a blunting or desensitization of the motivating impact of failure (Cromwell, 1967). Zigler (1966) has pointed to some contextual variables that may lead to differential responses to success and failure. He found, for example, that responsivity to adults with regard to desire for approval led to differing effects of failure upon performance of the retarded. Certain social variables, subject characteristics, and task characteristics need to be taken into consideration in sorting out the differential impact of success and failure.

If the retarded are given a realistic orientation regarding their successes and failures, it could well be that their learning efforts would be more successful. A clearer reality orientation to success and failure might also better prepare the retarded for what is expected of individuals in the environment, give them a better sense of self in terms of their own limitations and capabilities, and provide them more opportunities to experience the sense of reward that is built upon trying and *finally* succeeding. The affective consequences of failure itself, irrespective of the frequency of failure, have important implications for personality development and functioning in the retarded.

Failure situations are capable of evoking a variety of responses in individuals. Associated with failure experience might be the threat of loss of control, loss of self-esteem, loss of gratification from the teaching adult, and so forth, all of which may be poorly conceptualized and differentiated by the retarded. The affective component of a vaguely perceived threat is called anxiety and, in the mental retardation literature, anxiety is often suggested as being a consequence of failure for these individuals. Anxiety is a stressful affect that has strong physiological correlates. Normally, anxiety serves as a signal to the organism; in moderate amounts it has an alerting and arousing function which helps individuals to avoid danger by preparing for action of some sort, including defensive behaviors. To the extent that the threat in the situation is vague and undifferentiated, it is difficult for the individual, especially when he or she is experiencing intense anxiety, to mobilize resources for appropriate actions. If the alerting and arousal properties of anxiety lead to clarification of the threat, the affect becomes more appropriately labeled "fear." Knowing the source and nature of the threat, the individual is better able to prepare for "fight or flight"; that is, action or withdrawal.

Because the retarded are slower in their cognitive development, they may be likely to experience more occasions of early forms of anxiety for longer periods of their development without cognitive concepts for ordering complicated events, differentiating self from other, assessing cause and effect, and taking action. This state of affairs could eventuate in different outcomes in different individuals. It is possible, for example, that prolonged experience with unresolved anxiety may result in a desensitization to that affect; that is, a blunting of the motivational impact of anxiety in some individuals. On the other hand, other retarded persons may continue to feel the affect intensely for the duration of the situation but may be unable to modulate it by action, in which case the individual may suffer physiological, psychological and/or social disruption. To the extent that anxiety continues to mount in a particular situation, it tends to reduce cognitive flexibility through inhibition so that problem-solving strategies are more limited. A third possibility is that some retarded individuals may continue to feel anxiety initially in threatening situations, but may not be able to convert that anxiety into an adaptive state of vigilant awareness. Some supporting evidence suggesting that this may be a factor in the functioning of the retarded is provided by Zigler (1966), who demonstrated that institutionalized retarded individuals display an initial wariness in interacting with supportive adults which rapidly gives way to a heightened motivation to interact with them. Thus, the initial signal function of anxiety may not be effectively utilized in such situations. Although in an instance of social interaction this may be adaptive, it would be less adaptive in a learning situation, for example, in which the first solution selected may reduce anxiety or fear but may not be the most efficient solution possible.

For a variety of reasons, therefore, it is likely that the retarded are less able to utilize adaptively the signal properties of anxiety. Campione and Brown stated, in the review of memory research cited earlier, that the retarded are not motivated to apply strategies to memory tasks, and this may well reflect, in part, a failure to respond to anxiety as a signal for action. In other words, difficulty in memorization should lead to arousal and alerting, which in turn should elicit a search for a better method of approaching the task and should eventuate in discovery of the best possible solution.

If anxiety is indeed a by-product of failure, if the retarded as a group are thought to fail frequently, and if they are not able to deal effectively with anxiety, then one might predict that there would be more anxiety in the retarded than the non-retarded. Although Robinson and Robinson (1976) summarize the literature as strongly supporting the assumption that the retarded are more anxious, Hutt and Gibby (1976) qualify the findings, suggesting that the assumption may hold true for manifest (overt) anxiety but that the results are more equivocal for covert and basic anxiety. Heber (1964), on the other hand, has strongly questioned whether the research literature supports any generalizations with regard to anxiety as well as other personality constructs attributed to the retarded. Butterfield (1970) analyzed the relationship between intelligence and anxiety and concluded that anxiety is not a chronic state, but is a function of specific situations, and it is this situation-specific nature of anxiety which may have contributed to the diversity of experimental and clinical findings. A further complication in the research in this area concerns the difficulty in measuring or assessing anxiety. To take one problematic example, if, as we suggested earlier, the retarded are desensitized to their own anxiety, self-reports of low anxiety levels might accurately reflect the psychological levels of functioning but not the biological and social correlates.

As has already been mentioned, anxiety is not the only expected affective consequence of failure. It is often stated in the mental retardation literature that failure results in frustration. Frustration is not usually defined as an affect but as a state of being blocked from a desired goal which in turn leads to affective arousal. While anxiety is one possible response, particularly when there is no clear understanding of the blocking event, frustration is most commonly expected to result in anger (Dollard et al., 1939) which is directed toward the cause of the disruption. Despite the interest in frustration experiences expressed in the literature, there is surprisingly little detailed analysis of anger and angry behaviors (aggression) in the retarded. Most commonly the literature appears to be aimed at discrediting the stereotyped expectation that the retarded are aggressive or in any way antisocial beings. Indeed, parents and professionals in their concern for socializing the retarded have often been observed to be more harsh in curbing impulsive behaviors than with the non-retarded (Kessler, 1970). Suppression of aggressive behaviors in the retarded, however, is likely to have negative developmental consequences.

Aggression is a form of behavior which has as its aim the domination of some aspect of the environment. As such, it can be either positive in its intent (mastery) or negative (destruction). Properly channeled aggression can work in the service of the individual to abet efforts to achieve. It is often overlooked that aggression is a normal response which, through its redirection during the process of socialization, begins to be carried out in more socially acceptable ways in relationship to the environment. If, rather than redirection of such energies, however, the entire generic class of aggressive behaviors is suppressed, it can lead to a withdrawal from active interchange with the environment. In a discussion of inhibition of spontaneous responses, Kagan (1971) has stated: "It is possible that the association of any urge to act and strong anxiety . . . may lead to the tendency to 'inhibit responding' *whenever* anxiety is experienced" (p. 303). Kessler (1970) has suggested, for example, that inhibition of aggression as a result of suppression can have negative implications for intellectual functioning which requires active confrontation and mastery of the environment. By reconceptualizing aggression in a broader sense, its facilitative role can be recognized. Active confrontation and mastery, therefore, may well be affected by the success or lack of success in the redirection of anger and this may be particularly pertinent to considerations of intellectual functioning in the retarded.

In clinical theorizing, aggression which is prohibited from expression, if it is not blocked, is not lost, but is thought to be turned against the "self." The "self" is generally thought to be a highly delineated concept abstracted from the cumulative experience of acting upon and reacting to the environment, but it also involves, as a core, earlier forms of "self" that are directly grounded in the body-image and ultimately in sensory-motor experience. The affective state resulting from this process of turning against the self is called depression, although depression also results from other causes as well, as will be discussed shortly. Failure experience and the resultant loss of self-esteem could produce depressive affect in the retarded but, again, there is surprisingly little discussion of depression in relation to mental retardation, even though withdrawal, a manifestation of depression, is cited as a common defense of the retarded (Sternlicht & Deutsch, 1972).

Depression is an affective response of the total organism characterized by a feeling of sadness or unhappiness and sometimes accompanied by a sense of real or imagined loss. Typically, it involves a feeling of disappointment over something that has already happened. This is in contrast to anxiety which is an affective response related to the anticipation of future events. There are differing forms of depressive reactions related to the level of personality differentiation and development. Although clinicians have conceded that children can experience unhappiness momentarily, Cytryn and McKnew (1974) have pointed out that in contrast to depressive affect and illness in adulthood:

> Depressive affect in childhood psychopathology has not been as widely accepted. Until recently the existence of depressive illness in children was denied by most people in the field and ignored in most authoritative textbooks . . . a noteworthy exception is the long-standing recognition of and interest in depressive states in infancy (p. 879).

It has been suggested that adults may tend to persuade the child that he or she is really not unhappy (Sandler & Joffe, 1965). This tendency may obscure recognition of depressive affect and states in childhood. It has been found, for example, that depression is an uncommon referral complaint when children are brought for diagnosis and treatment. The most common referral problems such as phobic and aggressive behaviors may be more difficult for referring adults to ignore or deny. Another possible reason for the lack of recognition of depression in childhood comes, again, from Cytryn and McKnew (1974), who suggest that children have defenses against depression which result in a "masking" of that depression (Toolan, 1974; Meyers 1974). That is, the depression is not overtly observable, but is expressed in such other ways as somatic complaints, accident proneness, disobedience, tantrums, running away and self-defeating behavior which, incidentally, can also be observed in the retarded. Berman (1967), for example, has reported that a number of retarded individuals referred for psychiatric interview because of misbehavior actually were suffering from severe underlying feelings of depression:

Rather than exhibiting the usual neurotic reactive symptoms of depression with verbalization of feelings of hopelessness, helplessness, and unworthiness, many retarded youngsters with poor ability to abstract, and poor impulse control, and for lack of alternatives, present initially as an angry, hostile patient. In order to avoid the unpleasant conscious experience of depression, these patients use the behaviors which are effective, such as stealing, destroying property, and fighting; all aversive behaviors which receive almost immediate and highly predictable reaction (i.e., some response) from the environment (p. 20).

Gardner (1967) has reviewed a number of surveys of institutionalized retarded individuals that report a very low incidence of depression. Three out of the four reports were explicitly cited by Gardner as having focused on psychotic manifestations (for example, manic-depressive psychosis) a syndrome which should be considered quite separately from the discussion of depression as an affective state or as a reactive symptom. Another factor that may contribute to the lack of recognition is the fact that the way in which depression is manifested is subject to developmental changes, as already mentioned. In this regard, the qualitative nature of the affect itself and the way it is handled will reflect the developmental level of the child. All of the above considerations are equally applicable to retardation and, in some instances, may be more pertinent to retardation because of the nature of the retarded individual's relationship to the environment. For example, parents who themselves are depressed about their retarded child, in their struggles to ward off their own depression, may find it particularly difficult to recognize that same affect in their child.

Yet depression and pessimism in the parents is felt to be one cause of depressive states in childhood (Malmquist, 1971).

The forms of depression that are recognizable in the early stages of development have been described by Spitz (1946). Those who claim that depression is not common in retardation because object loss and mourning require higher levels of cognitive development fail to take the differing origins of depression into consideration. There are a number of early forms of depression that appear to be particularly applicable to retarded children. Sandler and Joffe (1965) discuss depression as simply a "loss of a previous state." For the very young child or for the retarded such "previous states" might consist of nothing more than sensory-motor involvement with the environment. Sensory or motor functional variability and undependability may interfere with these transactions and produce only fleeting or unstable states, just as other disruptive experiences, such as seizures, may also cause a sense of loss. Suppression of aggression might also be thought to be interference with and/or a loss of state. For example, Cochrane (1975) presents evidence which suggests that drive frustration (interference) can cause depressive illness. With a somewhat different orientation, Bibring (1966) defines depression as a reaction of helplessness in the face of a difficult reality, with that helplessness leading to a withdrawal from interaction. Depression, in common with other psychological constructs, is therefore not a unitary phenomenon but has multiple causes and the construct appears applicable in some forms at all levels of development of the retarded. It is enlightening to examine descriptions of depression:

The bulk of the depressed person's activity is likely to be passive, derived from prompts, commands, or other aversive initiatives from other persons rather than freely emitted activities. The reinforcer in the interaction is more likely to be appropriate to the other person's repertoire than to the depressed person (Ferster, 1973. p. 859).

Such descriptions of depressed individuals seem to aptly describe many retarded individuals. Certainly depression, like anxiety, bears careful research in the field of mental retardation.

There is some work in the mental retardation field which concerns second order constructs that would have relation to depression. For example, Floor and Rosen (1975) have indicated that "helplessness" (i.e., inability to take effective action in a problem situation) was a meaningful personality dimension found to have behavioral-motivational and competence factors pertinent to mentally retarded adults in a vocational rehabilitation program. Peters, Pumphrey and Flax (1974) as another example, found that the dimension of Interest-Participation versus Apathy-Withdrawal differentiated retarded from the non-retarded youngsters in a recreation group (although there was overlap in the distributions), with the retarded tending toward depression.

Affects are difficult to define and, as has been pointed out, have been shown to be situation specific. When affects are referred to in the mental retardation literature, it is often without reference to the massive literature which attempts to define these constructs and place them in theoretical perspective. The importance of a thorough understanding and flexible use of these frameworks lies in the consequent rethinking of the behavior of the retarded and the highlighting of features that require further investigation.

Part of the difficulty in defining affects stems from the abstract nature of the constructs as they are now conceptualized (Arnold, 1960, 1970). Many investigators in the field of mental retardation have focused not on affect per se, but on psychological constructs which are assumed to have strong affective investment such as self-concept and self-esteem. It is generally assumed that the retarded have negative self-concepts and lowered self-esteem because they are also assumed to experience more frustration and failure. Although some psychologists have contended that, "what a person does and how he behaves are determined by the concept he has of himself and his abilities" (Snygg & Combs, 1949, p. 78), others have not agreed. Mischel (1968), for example, has summarized the personality literature as indicating that "the trait categories people attribute to themselves and others may be relatively permanent and may be *more enduring than the behaviors to which they refer*" (p. 36; emphasis added). Thus, the utility of self-concept for understanding specific behavior in specific situations is a matter for further study. The measurement problems that plague studies of self-concept and self-esteem may be intensified when the subjects have sub-average intellectual ability. Lawrence and Winschel (1973) have summarized self-concept studies in mental retardation as being generally inconclusive. They make the suggestion that longitudinal studies of the emergence of self-concept in the retarded may help to answer whether or not there are unique components to the self-concepts of the retarded.

As the foregoing discussion indicates, the mental retardation literature suggests a number of negative consequences of failure experience. One way of experimentally exploring this issue would be to find out directly from the retarded the nature of their immediate reactions and feelings to actual success and failure experiences. As an example of this type of research, MacMillan (1975) compared a group of retarded subjects with two groups of non-retarded subjects (one matched for MA and one for CA). The three groups were found not to differ on their predictions of success and failure *prior* to the experimental tasks. After the interpolated success/failure manipulations, the three groups again did not differ in their predications of success and failure for a subsequent task. The author interpreted his results as supporting Cromwell's (1963) suggestion that expectancy of success on a given task is both a product of generalized expectancy (based upon history) *and* a situational expectancy (based upon specific situations). MacMillan further characterized his findings as indicating that the situational expectancy in his particular experiment exerted more control over the predictions of all subjects than did past histories of success and failure. MacMillan's findings also might be interpreted as support for the suggestion made earlier in this discussion that the retarded do not necessarily experience more failure than the non-retarded and may indeed experience less.

While MacMillan's study dealt with the cognitive aspects of success/failure in the form of predictions about future success and failure, it did not speak to the issue of the affects associated with these events. An example of research directed to this question is found in the work of Hayes and Prinz (1976) who asked retarded and non-retarded subjects to point to photos showing various affective responses as a way in which they could indicate their feelings and their perceptions of their teachers' feelings about them after they experienced experimentally manipulated success and failure. In general, subjects from both groups indicated positive affect within themselves and on the part of their teacher in response to success. After they had failed, the retarded indicated *less* negative feelings about themselves than did the non-retarded (i.e., they did not appear to judge themselves as harshly). The retarded, after failure, particularly indicated less negative response on the part of their teacher. This was taken by the authors to be a possible indicator that classrooms for the retarded tend to be oriented to reinforce success and minimize failures. Somewhat different findings were reported by Miller and Gottlieb (1972), who constructed a complicated social situation in which a non-retarded child was asked to choose either a retarded or non-retarded child for a partner

in a ring-toss game. Photographs were used for participants to indicate their feelings after the game and to indicate the feelings of a child they did not know who was said also to have participated in the game. The quality of the actual ring-toss performance of the retarded children was related to their ratings of the feelings of the "other child" but not to their ratings of their own feelings. The authors tended to reject the hypothesis that the retarded were projecting their own (unacceptable) angry feelings onto another person and suggested instead that these findings reflect a reality in the world of the retarded; that is, that when they do well "others" (in this case peers as opposed to teachers) are pleased, and when they don't do well "others" are angry. What is most salient for the retarded, according to this hypothesis, are the feelings of peers rather than their own feelings. The above three studies, though limited by particular contexts, subjects and methodologies, do raise important, unanswered questions concerning the experiences of failure by the retarded that bear further investigation.

A variable that may be of particular importance to an understanding of differential impact of success and failure is the subject's ability to understand those experiences in terms of his or her own efforts rather than in terms of external circumstances. This ability is a product of development that has been shown to be more related to MA than to CA (Robinson & Robinson, 1965), and has been studied as a general-personality disposition called locus of control. This is a bipolar personality dimension reflecting the extent to which an individual feels that he or she can manipulate events as opposed to being manipulated by events (internal versus external locus of control). In addition to its relation to MA, this personality dimension is influenced by contextual variables. For example, Horai and Guarnaccia (1975) have presented evidence to suggest that locus of control may be influenced by the subject's perception of the importance of the particular task in question. Outer-directed behavior, the degree to which an individual turns to external cues to guide behavior rather than rely on internal problem-solving ability, would obviously be related to locus of control and has been cited as a factor pertinent to cognitive functioning of the retarded (Zigler, 1966). Outer-directed behavior has been related to a number of task variables including level of difficulty (Zigler, 1966), amount of failure experienced in a particular task (Maguire, 1976), and the particular response demands of the task (Gordon and MacLean, 1977).

This discussion of responses to success and failure has been couched in terms that may seem to put the retarded individual in the position of being quite passive vis-a-vis his or her own biology, psychology and environmental circumstances. Current conceptualizations of intellectual, cognitve and personality development, however, are based upon the notion that the individual actively participates in and uniquely shapes his or her own growth. In this active interchange, the environment, as well as the individual, is modified in a continuing series of mutual interactions. Affects, under minimally optimal circumstances, function to help keep the individual in adaptive interactions with the withdrawal and passivity. Even in those states of withdrawal in which the environment becomes more or less limited to one's own body, there are still remnants of this active interchange and the creation of predictable events (e.g., repetitive patterns of self-stimulation). The energy which brings organisms into this continual contact with the environment has been labeled effectance (White, 1959), which is assumed to be a fundamental aspect of all living organisms. Human beings are born with an innate propensity to interact with their environment and it is assumed that derived from this is a need to seek out and master particular aspects of the stimulus environment. From the active organization of stimulus variables comes predictability, which is also

rewarding and which appears under optimal circumstances to free the organism to seek out levels of complexity and novelty appropriate to the new levels of organization. The fate of this tendency after prolonged failure or deprivation has important implications for the study of mental retardation. As an illustration of effectance under debilitating circumstances, an example will be presented from personal experience.

Under Michigan's Mandatory Education Act (which requires the provision of educational services from birth to 26 years of age) , a 22-year-old woman living in a private institution was identified as eligible for educational services. She had a limited repertoire of behavior for she had spent most of her life lying on the floor engaged in self-stimulating activities. In order to explore the intactness of her sensory modalities an audiologist put her into a behavior modification situation in which the response to be trained was putting out her hand to receive a piece of sandwich at a signal of a tone. The audiologist was most excited when he was able to successfully teach her the connections and document her hearing levels. That she could be trained, even at so basic a level, was more than many had expected of her. When I observed her in the auditory training situation, I was most struck by the affective reaction she displayed in the situation. When she heard the tone she grinned broadly, extended her hand almost with an air of bravado and awaited the anticipated result. When the sandwich was placed in her hand she laughed and then, more often than not, set it down on the table and maintained an alert posture aš though waiting for the next signal. It was obvious that it was not the consuming of the sandwich that was reinforcing. The reinforcing event seemed to be her recognition that operating upon the environment (i.e., extending her hand in response to a signal) she could effect a predictable result. This appears to me to be an example of effectance, and that such joy of mastery could exist after so many years of deprivation of experience is most impressive and most encouraging.

There is a burgeoning experimental and theoretical literature that bears directly on the understanding and further development of the example just presented. Since the situation of that young woman encompasses many issues that frequently face workers in mental retardation, it is worthwhile to explore further the example in relation to current conceptualizations of human development. The ensuing discussion will rely heavily upon the comprehensive presentations of Eleanor Wertheim (1975 a,b,c,d).

While the innate *energy* which keeps organisms in interaction with the environment has been labeled "effectance," the *capacity* of an individual to interact effectively with the environment at any given time has been called "competence" (White, 1963). Wertheim (1975a) has pointed out that the construct of competence has been applied by White to all individual action systems irrespective of the object(s) being acted upon. She suggests that there is a need for a distinction between effective action directed toward the *physical* environment (including one's own body) and effective action directed toward the *interpersonal* environment. The former class of behaviors are grouped by Wertheim under the construct of competence, while the latter class of behaviors are grouped under the construct of autonomy.

Wertheim suggests that competence and autonomy have different biological roots and different courses of epigenetic development, with the specific forms of each class of behaviors shaped socioculturally. Although these behaviors are seen as parallel classes, Wertheim points out that they are interdependent and that the patterns of interdependence may change with development. There is much evidence to suggest that effective interpersonal interactions in early infancy are important precursors to effective competence with the world of inanimate objects. In order to explore this early interdependence of autonomy and competence,

it is helpful to first examine another distinction emphasized by Wertheim (1975a, pp. 1–2) who quotes Stierlin (1969):

> In order to survive, even the lowest organism must be able to reconcile these features: All living things must *do;* they must exercise their powers, they must initiate action and actively impinge upon their environment. But all living things must also *undergo,* they must make themselves accessible to being influenced, they must let the environment affect them.

Piaget has provided a framework for viewing the balance between "doing" and "undergoing" with regard to inanimate objects. Central to his model of cognitive development are the processes of assimilation (doing) and accommodation (undergoing), which are in dynamic interchange throughout the course of development. With regard to the interpersonal environment, however, the relationship between "doing" and "undergoing" has typically been viewed as a less immediately dynamic uni-dimensional process in which a relatively passive, dependent infant who is "undergoing", slowly develops into a relatively active, independent child who is "doing." Current data indicating that the infant is already actively seeking, selecting, organizing, and communicating information in relation to the caretaker as well as to inanimate objects has helped to force a reconceptualization which Wertheim describes in the following manner: "Dependence and independence, or undergoing and doing are components of a *circular feedback process throughout life.* Only their balance varies with age" (1975a, p. 4, emphasis added).

The recognition of this circular feedback process of dependence and independence of the infant in interaction with the caretaker has been facilitated by current trends toward studying the micro-units of interactions. A micro-unit involves shorter temporal periods and subtle response units which are made more salient by technological amplification such as slow motion films, physiological recording, and so forth. Findings from different areas of developmental focus have indicated that consistent responses with short latencies from the interpersonal environment in relation to signals from the infant contribute to the development of autonomy. In examining the quality of these interpersonal responses, investigators have described what Wertheim (1975c) has called "rhythmic calibration" between infant and caretaker, which appears easily disrupted by a mismatch or subtle negation on the part of the caretaker. The development of this rhythmic calibration is influenced by biological differences (temperament, for example) in both the infant and caretaker, as well as contextual variables in specific situations of interaction.

Thomas and Chess (1977) have reported a long-term follow-up of individuality of temperament in children with developmental deviations including mild mental retardation, perinatal brain damage, and congenital rubella. Their findings indicated that healthy development in these children required special concern for consonance between temperament characteristics and environment demands. The findings also suggest that the type of handicap may change the type of management that is optimal for a particular temperament constellation, as compared to a non-handicapped child.

The primary autonomy which is said to develop in the first nine months of successful interpersonal interaction facilitates subsequent competence in the world of objects, primarily through its concomitant influence on the motivational and organizational structures of attention. The retarded, it will be recalled, do have a deficit in selective attention and certainly can be considered to be at a risk for developing primary autonomy. Wertheim (1975d) suggests that primary autonomy that is not successfully achieved can lead to a helplessness that precludes effective interaction with inanimate objects, or it may

lead to the use of objects, not for active exploration of the objects per se, but for the blocking out of interpersonal interactions. Harter and Zigler (1974) have, for example, demonstrated that institutionalized retarded children show less competence motivation with a variety of tasks utilizing inanimate objects than do non-retarded children matched for mental age.

It is possible to consider a number of ways in which a handicapped child might, because of biological, psychological and/or social factors, be out of "rhythmic calibration" with the environment. From this one might envision an escalating series of mismatches at successive developmental levels. Sameroff (1975), however, points out in a discussion of deviant development that, "despite the great variety and range of influences on development, there are a surprisingly small number of developmental outcomes" (p. 283). He posits a self-righting, self-organizing tendency in the human organism which counteracts the tendency to progressive deviations in development. In support of this supposition, Sameroff discusses recent longitudinal evidence indicating that the effects of severe physiological trauma disappear over long periods of time. Thus, when the self-righting, self-organizing tendency does not occur in successive stages of development, Sameroff suggests that either the integrative mechanisms necessary for self-righting and self-organizing have been impaired or the environment is organized in a way that supports a continuous malfunction between the individual and the environment across time. It has been suggested in the earlier discussions of defect versus developmental orientations in this paper that a particular heuristic gain in the field of mental retardation comes from the search for ways to restructure the environment to facilitate development.

Bearing in mind the distinctions between autonomy and competence, doing and undergoing, and the notion of the self-righting capacity, let us return to the example of the 22-year-old woman whose response to the auditory training paradigm was described earlier. Although it was never fully documented until age 22, this girl had both visual and auditory impairment and had been functioning for a large part of her life at the profound level of mental retardation. Her early years were spent at home, where perhaps her unpredictable behavior promoted unpredictable responses from her caretakers. Her mother reported, for example, that in response to her cries this girl as an infant sometimes received physical contact in the form of cuddling and sometimes in the form of spanking. After being sent to a number of schools in a period of one or two years, this girl was permanently institutionalized in what was described earlier as a very barren environment and was not seen again by her parents. No analysis of micro-units is necessary to realize that this girl had always been at great risk in terms of the development of autonomy and competence. How does one begin to promote the opportunities for adaptive self-righting transactions between this girl and her environment?

If we look to the discussion of early infant development, we might conclude that it would be necessary to get into "rhythmic calibration" with this individual. Under normal circumstances, mothers and their infants come prepared biologically for this mutual adaptation. How does a stranger bridge unknown experiences and approach this type of equilibrium? It seems to be of critical importance to first realize that all responses, no matter how unusual or primitive they may be from another's point of view, are normal for that individual in terms of his or her biological, psychological, and social realities, although they may not be optimal for that individual in the interaction. If the normality of these behaviors for the individual is *not* taken into account, interpersonal interaction may subtly or not

so subtly interfere with or negate that individual's behavior in a way that may be incompatible with the development of autonomy and competence. In order to get into "rhythmic calibration" with that individual, we may also need to identify with the behavior—something that becomes quite difficult when the behavior is aberrant, primitive and/or unpleasant. This difficulty in identification may contribute to the infrequency of provision of psychotherapeutic services to the retarded. An approximation of a micro-unit analysis of the process of identification is found in a book written by a parent (Kaufman, 1976) in which descriptions are provided of the way in which that particular family attempted to get into rhythm with their autistic child. It was through these attempts that the family sought the meaning of their child's behavior within a transactional framework designed to reinforce and amplify the normality of that behavior.

It was discussed earlier that the meaning an individual imposes upon a situation influences his or her behavior, even when it is a fairly neutral laboratory learning situation. We also tend not to look for that meaning in very young or retarded children. Wertheim has pointed out, for example, that even in infancy, "how an infant responds to maternal behavior depends on his perception of the meaning of this behavior. The latter, in turn, changes with age as a function of increasing cognitive differentiation and past experience" (1975*b*, p. 101). Thus, in order to attempt to achieve rhythmic calibration with the retarded, we may need to understand the normality of their behavior, identify with that behavior, and search for meaning in that behavior within an interpersonal framework.

An example of the tendency not to search for meaning in the communications of the retarded is provided by Muhlfelder (1969), who described a mentally retarded, speech-impaired, therapy patient who began each therapeutic session with the question, "Wa huppen?" This question could easily be considered a stereotyped conversational "filler," and it was not until the therapist began to respond to this question as though it contained dynamic meaning (i.e., What happened to me that I am this way?) that the therapeutic interaction elicited meaningful elaboration of the patient's experience.

In essence, it is suggested that by providing experiences based upon general principles of human development, it may be possible to promote a more continuous, productive use of that innate energy to interact effectively with the environment. Specifically, some current thinking in human development suggests that without attention to issues of primary autonomy, the retarded may simply be provided specially designed incentive situations in which they become motivated situationally to respond, but then become "revved down" outside of those specific situations.

As a final part of this discussion, I would like to describe the difficulties I had as a psychologist trying to relate to the above-mentioned young woman. When I saw her for a psychological evaluation, I brought her into an examination room and seated her in front of a table on which I had placed three common objects. I spoke loudly into her best ear (since she needed but had not yet received a hearing aid), making comments that I hoped would communicate my understanding and acceptance of her reality. Although I did not know what she could understand, if anything, I tried many different ways of communicating that it must be confusing and frightening not to understand what people expected of her; that it must seem puzzling to be in that room with a stranger; and so forth. I suggested that when she felt more comfortable with me she might be willing to explore the objects on the table and find the comb. I reassured her that as we spent more time in the room together, she would indeed become more comfortable. During my entire monologue, the young woman was engaged in mild rocking and the only clue that we were in rhythmic calibration was the fact that she remained in her chair. During this time I could hear the observers behind the one-way mirror become increasingly restless because it appeared to them that nothing was happening in the psychological evaluation. After about forty-five minutes of commentary by me, the girl suddenly reached out toward the objects, grabbed the comb and jumped into my lap displaying diffuse affective excitement in the form of motoric and vocal activity.

The above example provides a complicated interplay of: autonomy and competence; doing and undergoing; cognitive and affective expression; and perhaps the self-righting tendency. That this young woman ultimately responded makes a nice capstone for the example, but is really not necessary to make the point. All psychotherapists, perhaps particularly those who work with the retarded, know the difficulty in finding the appropriate mode of communication (getting into rhythmic calibration) with the client. They have experienced the length of time that it sometimes takes to effectively communicate the predictability, acceptance, and nurturance that helps an individual to *initiate* new behaviors.

In essence, the attempts to engage in rhythmic calibration with another human being, to understand the normality of behavior for that particular individual in that particular situation, to identify with that behavior, and to search for the meaning of that behavior within an interpersonal framework are all steps toward first utilizing the subject more actively in the study of his or her own situation. It is out of the dynamic interpersonal interaction of subject and object that new synthesis in understanding can develop. The professional, student, and parent all need to realize that their own theoretical and conceptual frameworks, their own philosophic and attitudinal bases and biases, contribute to the contextual relativity and thereby influence the nature of interpersonal interaction, and ultimately influence that which is known or not known and that which is achieved or not achieved.

REFERENCES

ARNOLD, M. *Emotion and personality. Vols. I and II.* N.Y.: Columbia University Press, 1960.

——— (Ed.), *Feelings and emotions.* New York: Academic Press, 1970.

BAKWIN, H., & BAKWIN, R. M. *Behavior Disorders in Children* (4th ed.). Philadelphia: W. B. Saunders Company, 1972.

BAUMEISTER, A. A., & BARTLETT, C. J. A comparison of the factor structure of normals and retardates. *American Journal of Mental Deficiency,* 1962, *66,* 641–646.

———, & HAWKINS, W. F. Alpha responsiveness to photic stimulation in mental retardates. *American Journal of Mental Deficiency,* 1967, *71,* 783–786.

BECKER, H. S. (Ed.). *The other side: Perspectives on deviance.* N.Y.: Free Press, 1964.

———. *Outsiders: Studies in the sociology of deviance.* N.Y.: Free press, 1966.

BERMAN, M. I. Mental retardation and depression. *Mental Retardation,* 1967, *5,* 19–21.

BERSOFF, D. N. Silk purses into sow's ears. *American Psychologist,* 1973, *28,* 892–899.

BIALER, I. Emotional disturbance and mental retardation: Etiologic and conceptual relationships. In *Psychiatric Approaches to Mental Retardation.* Ed. F. J. Menolascino. New York: Basic Books, Inc., 1970.

BIBRING, E. The mechanism of depression. In *Affective Disorders.* Ed. P. Greenacre. New York: International Universities Press, 1966.

BLACKMAN, L. S., BILSKY, L. H., BURGER, A. L., & MAR, H. Cognitive processes and academic achievement in EMR adolescents. *American Journal of Mental Deficiency,* 1976, *81,* 125–134.

BROWN, L. K. Familial dialectics in a clinical context. *Human Development,* 1975, *18,* 223–258.

———. Parent involvement in diagnostic testing. In *Special study institute #9—Alternatives to litigation: The necessity for parental consultation.* Eds. W. C. Rhodes and D. P. Sweeney. Lansing: Michigan Department of Education, 1977.

BUTTERFIELD, E. C. The roles of motivation and personality in the development and expression of intelligent behavior. In *Psychometric intelligence.* Ed. H. S. Haywood. New York: Appleton-Century-Crofts, 1970.

CAMPIONE, J. C., & BROWN, A. Memory and metamemory development in educable retarded children. In *Perspectives on the development of memory and cognition.* Eds. R. V. Kail & J. W. Hagen. Hillsdale, N.J.: Lawrence Erlbaum Associates, 1977.

CAPLAN, P. J. The role of classroom conduct in the promotion and retention of elementary school children. *The Journal of Experimental Education,* 1973, *41,* no. 3.

CHESS, S. Emotional problems in mentally retarded children. In *Psychiatric Approaches to Mental Retardation.* Ed. F. J. Menolascino. New York: Basic Books, Inc., 1970.

———, & KORN, S. Temperament and behavior disorders in mentally retarded children. *Archives of General Psychiatry,* 1970, *23,* 122–130.

CHURCH, J. Techniques for the differential study of cognition in early childhood. In *Cognitive Studies 1,* Ed. J. Hellmuth. New York: Bruner/Mazel, Inc., 1970.

COBB, H. *The forecast of fulfillment: A review of the research on predictive assessment of the adult retarded for social and vocational adjustment.* New York: Teachers College Press, 1972.

COCHRANE, N. The role of aggression in the psychogenesis of depressive illness. *British Journal of Medical Psychology,* 1975, *48,* 113–130.

CROMWELL, R. L. A social learning approach to mental retardation. In *Handbook of Mental Deficiency: Psychological Theory and Research.* Ed. N. R. Ellis. New York: McGraw-Hill, 1963.

————. Success-failure reactions in mentally retarded children. In *Psychopathology of mental development.* Eds. J. Zubin & G. A. Jervis. New York: Grune & Stratton, 1967.

CYTRYN, L., & LOURIE, R. S. Mental Retardation. In *Comprehensive Textbook of Psychiatry.* Eds. A. M. Freedman & H. I. Kaplan. Baltimore: Williams & Wilkins, 1967.

————, & MCKNEW, D. H. Factors influencing the changing clinical expression of the depressive process in children. *American Journal of Psychiatry,* 1974, *131,* 879–881.

DEXTER, L A. On the politics and sociology of stupidity in our society. In *The Other Side.* Ed. H. S. Becker. Glencoe, Ill.: The Free Press, 1964.

DINGMAN, H. F., & TARJAN, G. Mental retardation and the normal distribution curve. *American Journal of Mental Deficiency,* 1960, *64,* 991–994.

DOLLARD, J., DOOB, L. W., MILLER, N. E., MOWRER, O. H., & SEARS, R. R. *Frustration and aggression.* New Haven: Yale University Press, 1939.

EDGERTON, R. B. *The cloak of competence. Stigma in the lives of the mentally retarded.* Berkeley: University of California Press, 1967.

————. Anthropology and mental retardation: A plea for the comparative study of incompetence. In *Behavioral Research in Mental Retardation.* Eds. H. J. Prehm, L. A. Hamerlynck, & J. E. Crosson. Eugene, Oregon: Rehabilitation Research and Training Center in Mental Retardation, University of Oregon, 1968.

————, & BERCOVICI, S. M. The cloak of competence: Years later. *American Journal of Mental Deficiency,* 1976, *80,* 485–497.

EISENBERG, L. Emotional determinants of mental deficiency. *Archives of Neurology and Psychiatry,* 1958, *80,* no. 1.

ELLIS, N. R. The stimulus trace and behavioral inadequacy. In *Handbook of mental deficiency: Psychological theory and research.* Ed. N. R. Ellis. New York: McGraw-Hill, 1963.

————. Memory processes in retardates and normals. In *International review of research in mental retardation. Vol. 4.* Ed. N. R. Ellis. New York: Academic Press, 1970.

FERSTER, C. B. A functional analysis of depression. *American Psychologist,* 1973, *28,* 857–870.

FLOOR, L., & ROSEN, M. Investigating the phenomenon of helplessness in mentally retarded adults. *American Journal of Mental Deficiency,* 1975, *79,* 565–572.

GALTON, F. Supplementary notes on 'prehension' in idiots. *Mind,* 1887, *12,* 79–82.

GARDNER, W. I. *Reactions of intellectually normal and retarded boys after experimentally induced failure: A social learning theory interpretation.* Unpublished Doctoral Dissertation, George Peabody College for Teachers, 1958.

————. Occurrence of severe depression in the mentally retarded. *American Journal of Psychiatry,* 1967, *124,* 142–144.

GORDON, D. A., & MACLEAN, W. E. Developmental analysis of outerdirectedness in noninstitutionalized EMR children. *American Journal of Mental Deficiency,* 1977, *81,* 508–511.

GOTTESMAN, I. I. Genetic aspects of intelligent behavior. In *Handbook of mental deficiency: Psychological theory and research.* Ed. N. R. Ellis. New York: McGraw-Hill, 1963.

HARTER, S., BROWN, L., & ZIGLER, E. Discrimination learning in retarded and nonretarded children as a function of task difficulty and social reinforcement. *American Journal of Mental Deficiency,* 1971, *76,* 275–283.

———, & ZIGLER, E. The assessment of effectance motivation in normal and retarded children. *Developmental Psychology,* 1974, *10,* 169–180.

HAYES, C. S., & PRINZ, R. J. Affective reactions of retarded and nonretarded children to success and failure. *American Journal of Mental Deficiency,* 1976, *81,* 100–102.

HEBER, R. *Expectancy and expectancy changes in normal and mentally retarded boys.* Unpublished Doctoral Dissertation, George Peabody College for Teachers, 1957.

———, HARRINGTON, S., GARBER, H., & THELAN, M. *An experiment in prevention of sociocultural retardation: The Milwaukee Project.* Unpublished symposium, 96th Annual Meeting, AAMD, Minneapolis, May 18, 1972.

———. Personality. In *Mental retardation: A review of the research.* Eds., H. A. Stevens & R. Heber. Chicago: University of Chicago Press, 1964.

HOBBS, N. (Ed.). *Issues in the classification of exceptional children. Vol 1.* San Francisco: Jossey-Bass, 1975.

HORAI, J., & GUARNACCIA, V. J. Performance and attributions to ability, effort, task, and luck of retarded adults after success or failure feedback. *American Journal of Mental Deficiency,* 1975, *79,* 690–694.

HUTT, M. L., & GIBBY, R. G. *The mentally retarded child: Development, education and treatment* (3rd ed.). Boston: Allyn & Bacon, Inc, 1976.

INHELDER, B. *The diagnosis of reasoning in the mentally retarded.* New York: The John Day Company, 1968.

JENKINS, J. J. Remember that old theory of memory? Well forget it! *American Psychologist,* 1974, *29,* 785–795.

JENSEN, A. R. A two-factor theory of familial mental retardation. Paper presented at the 4th International Congress of Human Genetics, Paris, France, September 9, 1971.

KAGAN, J. Personality development. In *Behavioral science in pediatric medicine.* Eds. N. B. Talbot, J. Kagan, & L. Eisenberg. Philadelphia: W. B. Saunders Company, 1971.

KAHN, J. V. Moral and cognitive development of moderately retarded, mildly retarded, and nonretarded individuals. *American Journal of Mental Deficiency,* 1976, *81,* 209–214.

KAUFMAN, B. N. *Son-Rise,* New York: Harper & Row, 1976.

KESSLER, J. W. Contributions of the mentally retarded toward a theory of cognitive development. In *Cognitive Studies 1.* Ed. J. Hellmuth. New York: Bruner/Mazel, Inc., 1970.

LAWRENCE, E. A., & WINSCHEL, J. F. Self-concept and the retarded: Research and issues. *Exceptional Children,* 1973, *39,* 310–319.

LEVY, L. H. *Conceptions of personality: Theories and research.* New York: Random House, Inc., 1970.

LEZAK, M. D. *Neuropsychological assessment.* New York: Oxford University Press, 1976.

MACMILLAN, D. L. Effect of experimental success and failure on the situational expectancy of EMR and nonretarded children. *American Journal of Mental Deficiency,* 1975, *80,* 90–95.

———, JONES, R. L., & ALOIA, G. F. The mentally retarded label: A theoretical analysis and review of research. *American Journal of Mental Deficiency,* 1974, *79,* 241–261.

MAGUIRE, M. Failure effects on outerdirectedness: A failure to replicate. *American Journal of Mental Deficiency,* 1976, *81,* 256–259.

MALMQUIST, C. P. Depressions in childhood and adolescence. *New England Journal of Medicine,* 1971, *284,* 887–893, 955–961.

MERCER, J. R. *Labeling the mentally retarded.* Berkeley: University of California Press, 1973.

MEYER, W. J., & OFFENBACH, S. I. Effectiveness of reward and punishment as a function of task complexity. *Journal of Comparative and Physiological Psychology,* 1962, *55,* 532–534.

MEYERS, D. I. The question of depressive equivalents in childhood schizophrenia. In *Masked Depression*. Ed. S. Lesse. New York: Jason Aronson, 1974.

MILLER, M. B., & GOTTLIEB, J. Projection of affect after task performance by retarded and non-retarded children. *American Journal of Mental Deficiency*, 1972, 77, 149–156.

MILLMAN, M., CAMPBELL, M. B., WRIGHT, K. L., & JOHNSTON, A. Allergy and learning disabilities in children. *Annals of Allergy*, 1976, 36, 149–160.

MILLON, T. *Theories of psychopathology and personality* (2nd ed.). Philadelphia: W. B. Saunders Company, 1973.

MISCHEL, W. Personality and assessment. New York: John Wiley and Sons, Inc., 1968.

———. On the future of personality measurement. *American Psychologist*, 1977, 32, 246–254.

MUHLFELDER, W. J. Mental retardation and the anatomy of existential therapy. *Pennsylvania Psychiatric Quarterly*, 1969, 9, 25–32.

MUSSEN, P. H., CONGER, J. J., & KAGAN, J. *Child development and personality* (4th ed.). New York: Harper & Row, 1974.

PETERS, E. N., PUMPHREY, M. W., & FLAX, N. Comparison of retarded and nonretarded children on dimensions of behavior in recreation groups. *American Journal of Mental Deficiency*, 1974, 79, 87–94.

PHILIPS, I., & WILLIAMS, N. Psychopathology and mental retardation: A study of 100 mentally retarded children: I. Psychopathology. *American Journal of Psychiatry*, 1975, 132, 1265–1271.

———, WILLIAMS, N. Psychopathology and mental retardation: A statistical study of 100 mentally retarded children treated at a psychiatric clinic: II. *American Journal of Psychiatry*, 1977, 134, 418–419.

RESNICK, L. B. (Ed.). *The Nature of Intelligence*. Hillsdale, N. J.: Lawrence Erlbaum, 1976.

ROBINSON, H. B., & ROBINSON, N. M. *The mentally retarded child: A psychological approach*. New York: McGraw-Hill, 1965.

———. *The Mentally Retarded Child* (2nd ed.). New York: McGraw-Hill, 1976.

RUBINGTON, E., & WEINBERG, M. S. *Deviance: The interactionist perspective*. New York: Macmillan, 1973.

RUTTER, M. L. Psychiatric disorder and intellectual impairment in childhood. *British Journal of Psychiatry*, 1975, Spec. Pub. #9, 344–348.

SACHS, E. L. Intelligence test scores as a function of experimentally established and social relationships between child and examiner. *Journal of Abnormal and Social Psychology*, 1952, 47, 354–358.

SAMEROFF, A. Early influences on development: Fact or fancy? *Merrill-Palmer Quarterly*, 1975, 21, 267–294.

SANDLER, J., & JOFFE, W. G. Notes on childhood depression. *International Journal of Psychoanalysis*, 1965, 46, 88–96.

SCHACTER, S., & SINGER, J. E. Cognitive, social, and physiological determinants of emotional state. *Psychological Review*, 1962, 69, 379–399.

SCHEFF, T. J. *On being mentally ill: A sociological theory*. Chicago: Aldine, 1966.

SNYGG, D. S., & COMBS, A. W. *Individual behavior: A new frame of reference for psychology*. New York: Harper, 1949.

SPITZ, H. H. Field theory in mental deficiency. In *Handbook of mental deficiency: Psychological theory and research*. Ed. N. R. Ellis. New York: McGraw-Hill, 1963.

———. The role of input organization in the learning and memory of mental retardates. In *Research in mental retardation, Vol. 2*. Ed. N. R. Ellis. New York: Academic Press, 1966.

SPITZ, R. Anaclitic depression. *Psychoanalytic Study of the Child*. 1946 2, 313–342.

STERNLICHT, M., & DEUTSCH, M. R. *Personality development and social behavior in the mentally retarded*. Lexington, Mass.: D. C. Heath & Company, 1972.

STIERLIN, H. *Conflict and reconciliation*. New York: Anchor Books, 1969.

SUPPES, P. Cognition: A survey. In *Psychology and the handicapped child*. U.S. Department of Health, Education and Welfare, Publication No. (OE) 73-05000. Washington: U.S. Government Printing Office, 1974.

SZASZ, T. S. *The myth of mental illness: Foundations of a theory of personal conduct*. New York: Hoeber-Harper, 1961.

———. *The Manufacture of Madness*. New York: Harper & Row, 1970.

THOMAS, A., & CHESS, S. *Temperament and development*. New York: Brunner/Mazel, Inc., 1977.

THOMPSON, W. R. An analysis of the differential effects of ECS on memory in young adult rats. *Canadian Journal of Psychology*, 1958, *12*, 83–96.

TOOLAN, J. M. Masked depression in children and adolescents. In *Masked Depression*. Ed. S. Lesse. New York: Jason Aronson, 1974.

WALKER, H. J., ROODIN, P. A., & LAMB, M. J. Relationship between linguistic performance and memory deficits in retarded children. *American Journal of Mental Deficiency*, 1975, *79*, 545–552.

WEBSTER, T. G. Problems of emotional development in young retarded children. *American Journal of Psychiatry*, 1963, *120*, 37–43.

———. Unique aspects of emotional development in mentally retarded children. In *Psychiatric approaches to mental retardation*. Ed. F. J. Menolascino. New York: Basic Books, Inc., 1970.

WEISZ, J. R. Studying cognitive development in retarded and nonretarded groups: The role of theory. *American Journal of Mental Deficiency*, 1976, *81*, 235–239.

WERTHEIM, E. Person-environment interaction: the epigenesis of autonomy and competence, I.: Theoretical considerations (normal development). *British Journal of Medical Psychology*, 1975a, *48*, 1–8.

———. Person-environment interactions: The epigenesis of autonomy and competence, III: Review of developmental literature (normal development). *British Journal of Medical Psychology*, 1975b, *48*, 95–111.

———. Person-environment interaction: The epigenesis of autonomy and competence, III: Autonomy and para/pre-linguistic and linguistic action systems: Review of developmental literature (normal development). *British Journal of Medical Psychology*, 1975c, *48*, 237–256.

———. Person-environment interaction: The epigenesis of autonomy and competence, IV: Their interrelationship: Theoretical considerations and review of developmental literature (normal development). *British Journal of Medical Psychology*, 1975d, *48*, 391–402.

WHITE, R. W. Motivation reconsidered: The concept of competence. *Psychological Review*, 1959, *66*, 297–333.

———. Ego and reality in psychoanalytic theory: A proposal regarding independent ego energies. *Psychological Issues*, 1963, III, no. 3.

WHITEHURST, G. J. Discrimination learning in children as a function of reinforcement condition, task complexity, and chronological age. *Journal of Experimental Child Psychology*, 1969, *7*, 314–325.

WICKELGREN, W. A. Memory. In *Psychology and the handicapped child*. U.S. Department of Health, Education, and Welfare, Publication No. (OE) 73-05000. Washington, D.C.: U.S. Government Printing Office, 1974.

WILLIAMS, R. J. *Biochemical individuality*. New York: John Wiley, 1963.

WOHLHUETER, M. J., & SINDBERG, R. M. Longitudinal development of object permanence in mentally retarded children: An exploratory study. *American Journal of Mental Deficiency*, 1975, *79*, 513–518.

ZEAMAN, D., & HOUSE, B. J. The role of attention in retardate discrimination learning. In *Handbook of mental deficiency: Psychological theory and research*. Ed., N. R. Ellis. New York: McGraw-Hill, 1963.

ZIGLER, E. Research on personality structure in the retardate. In *International review of research in mental retardation, vol. 1*. Ed.,

N. R. Ellis. New York: Russell Sage Foundation, 1966.

———. Familial mental retardation: A continuing dilemma. *Science,* 1967, *155,* 292–298.

———. Developmental versus difference theories of mental retardation and the problem of motivation. *American Journal of Mental Deficiency,* 1969, *73,* 536–556.

———, ABELSON, W. D., & SEITZ, V. Motivational factors in the performance of economically disadvantaged children on the Peabody Picture Vocabulary Test. *Child Development,* 1973, *44,* 294–303.

———, & BALLA, D. Lurias' verbal deficiency theory of mental retardation and performance on sameness, symmetry, and opposition tasks: a critique. *American Journal of Mental Deficiency,* 1971, *75,* 400–413.

———, & BUTTERFIELD, E. C. Motivational aspects of changes in IQ test performance of culturally deprived nursery school children. *Child Development,* 1968, *39,* 1–14.

———, & deLABRY, J. Concept-switching in middle-class, lower-class, and retarded children. *Journal of Abnormal and Social Psychology,* 1962, *65,* 267–273.

11 Psychology of Gifted Children and Youth

E. Paul Torrance

Ph.D., Alumni Foundation Distinguished Professor of Educational Psychology, University of Georgia, Athens.

Psychology during recent years has witnessed the emergence and beginning implementation of new and broadened concepts of gifted children and youth. Paul A. Witty (1953) earlier had prepared the way for this broader concept by defining as gifted children and youth those whose performance is consistently remarkable in music, art, social leadership, and any other activity valued by society. National and international needs and research productivity in the 1960s combined to bring about a widespread acceptance of a broadened concept of giftedness and make possible some exploratory implementations. Official recognition and a definition of this broadened concept of giftedness came from a careful and intensive study of the Commissioner of Education of the United States Office of Education, culminating in a report to the United States Senate in 1972. In this report, giftedness was defined to include those with demonstrated achievement and/or potential ability in any of the following areas, singly or in combination:

1. General intellectual ability
2. Specific academic aptitude
3. Creative or productive thinking
4. Leadership ability
5. Visual and performing arts
6. Psychomotor ability.

Since 1972, the Office of the Gifted and Talented within the United States Office of Education has sought to implement this definition of giftedness through guidelines and support. Some state legislatures and state departments of education have also accepted this broadened concept of giftedness and have provided guidelines for its implementation. However, other states have clung to traditional definitions of the gifted as those with high intelligence quotients. The report presented to the United States Senate Committee also detailed several dimensions of the new concept of giftedness. Among the more important of these are the following:

1. Evidence of gifted and talented abilities are to be determined by multiple criteria and should include objective measures and professional evaluation measures.
2. The application of criteria in the six areas identified should lead to differentiated pro-

469

grams for 3 to 5 percent of the school population.

3. Differentiated educational programs for the gifted should be characterized by
   a. a differentiated curriculum emphasizing higher cognitive concepts and processes (problem solving, creative thinking, evaluation, decision making, etc.)
   b. instructional strategies which accommodate the learning styles of the gifted and talented, and curriculum content
   c. special grouping arrangements which include a variety of administrative procedures appropriate to particular children, i.e., special classes, honor classes, seminars, resource rooms, and the like (*Education of the gifted and talented,* report to the Congress of the United States by the U. S. Commissioner of Education, 1972, pp. 2–3).

Along with the development and refinement of these new conceptualizations of giftedness, there have arisen new interests in finding and developing "hidden giftedness" among children born and reared in poverty and deprivation, and among children from culturally different groups. These interests, in turn, have given rise in psychology to issues of early identification and educational stimulation and of identifying and cultivating those talents that are highly valued by different cultures and subcultures. Interest in the problems of giftedness among disadvantaged groups has continued to stimulate renewed interest and controversy concerning the roles of heredity and environment. In the middle and late 1960s, protesting and dissident high-school and college students brought about a new interest in sociocultural concepts of divergent behavior as they relate to gifted children and youth. This seems to have given us a generally more favorable climate for those who are different as a result of their giftedness in the six broad areas identified in the report of the United States Commissioner of Education.

CONTEMPORARY CONCEPTS OF GIFTEDNESS

For many years, numerous psychologists and educators have tried to change the predominant concept of a single type of giftedness. Many of them sensed that an adherence to this concept deprived many highly gifted and talented children and young people of opportunities to develop their potentialities. Other psychologists and educators have firmly opposed this change and have held to the adequacy of general intelligence tests for identifying the gifted. For example, Sir Cyril Burt (1975), even in his last published work, opposed the use of the concept of creativity in identifying gifted students, declaring, "There is no genuine creativity without an equally high degree of general intelligence" (p. 143).

A major problem in the psychology of giftedness has been finding ways of conceptualizing the various kinds of giftedness and developing measures of the different kinds of abilities and personality qualities involved. Some bold attempts have been made, and some of them have had considerable influence upon educational policies and practices. Some of the contemporary conceptualizations will be reviewed here.

STRUCTURE OF INTELLECT MODEL

There are current today a number of models that have been giving a more psychologically sound and adequate basis for designing differentiated educational programs for gifted children and youth. Many of these models have been inspired by Guilford's Structure of Intellect Model (1956, 1959, 1967). As late as 1958, leaders in the study of giftedness, such as Strang (1958, p. 64), were struggling with such categories as scientific, artistic, musical, and leadership giftedness, saying that "giftedness may take many forms, depending upon the circumstances."

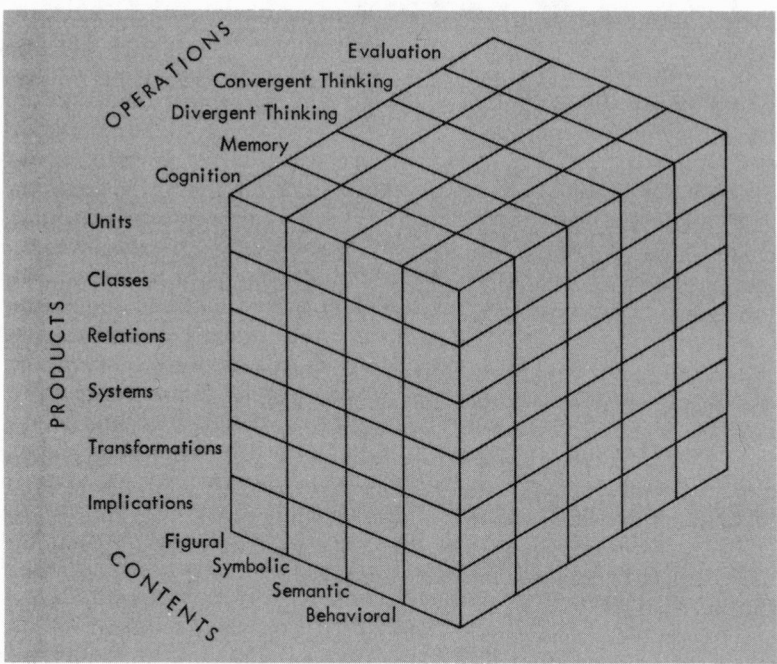

FIGURE 11–1. Guilford's Structure of Intellect Model
Used by permission from J. P. Guilford.

Guilford's work marks a turning point because it directed both psychologists and educators away from dependence upon a single measure of giftedness. In his Structure of Intellect Model depicted in Figure 11-1 in the shape of a cube, Guilford has given us what virtually amounts to a periodic table of different kinds of intelligence. As shown in Figure 11-1, the model has three dimensions: operations, contents, and products.

In the model, the operations are the major kinds of intellectual activities or processes that a person does with the raw materials, or information. The first, *cognition,* includes discovery, awareness, recognition, comprehension, or understanding. The second, *memory,* refers to retention or storage, with some degree of availability of information. Then there are two types of

productive thinking in which something is produced from what has been cognized and memorized: *divergent production* or the generation of new information from given information where emphasis is upon variety and quantity of output from the same source, and *convergent production,* or the generation of information where emphasis is upon achieving conventionally accepted best outcomes (the given information fully determines the response). The fifth operation is *evaluation,* making decisions or judgments concerning the correctness, suitability, adequacy, desirability, and the like of information in terms of criteria of identity, consistency, and goal satisfaction.

These five operations act upon each of the kinds of content (figural, symbolic, semantic, and behavioral) and products (units, classes, systems, transformations, and implications). Theoretically, this yields 120 different kinds of mental ability. Ever since the formulation of this model, Guilford and others have been quite productive in developing and validating instruments for assessing these abilities (Guilford, 1967; Guilford, Hendricks, & Hoepfner, 1968; Guilford, 1971; Biondi & Parnes, 1976) and developing instructional materials for the development of these abilities (Meeker, 1969; Williams, 1970; Feldhusen & Treffinger, 1976).

Two-Mode Models

Guilford's monumental work remained neglected by both educators and psychologists until Getzels and Jackson (1962) showed that highly creative adolescents achieved as well as their highly intelligent peers, in spite of the fact that their average IQ was 23 points lower. This study attracted widespread national and international attention and was vigorously and widely criticized. The study had many acknowledged limitations, but it and the other investigations that it inspired showed quite clearly that creatively gifted children and youth could not be equated with highly intelligent ones. In eight partial replications of the Getzels and Jackson study, Torrance (1962) found that if one identified as gifted the upper 20 percent of a given population on an intelligence test alone, he would miss 70 percent of those who would be identified as gifted by a test of creative thinking. In his eight partial replications of the Getzels-Jackson study, Torrance (1962) obtained results similar to the original study, and in the other two cases the results were dissimilar. These studies gave clues about the conditions that generate the Getzels-Jackson effect and those that do not. Torrance then conducted seven additional partial replications of the Getzels-Jackson study to pursue these clues further. In these partial replications, all subjects in the upper 20 percent on the measure of intelligence and all in

the upper 20 percent on the creativity measure were included, whereas Getzels and Jackson included only those not in the upper 20 percent on some other ability. In ten of a total of fifteen studies, the Getzels-Jackson effect was found. In the schools where this effect did not occur, two conditions seemed to be common and may help explain the exceptions: (1) the children were taught primarily by methods of authority and had little chance to solve problems and use their creative abilities, and (2) the average IQ of the children was considerably lower than in the other ten situations and in the Getzels-Jackson study.

Still almost unnoticed is that part of the Getzels-Jackson study (1962) dealing with two kinds of psychosocial excellence—that is, high social adjustment and high moral courage. It was found that just as the highly intelligent student is not always highly creative, the highly adjusted student is not always high in moral courage. Further, it was found that although the students high in moral courage achieved at a higher level than highly adjusted students, the teachers perceived the highly adjusted students as the leaders, rather than those high in moral courage. This is especially significant in a peer-oriented culture such as predominates in the United States.

Rather than going beyond the intelligence-creativity distinctions in searching for giftedness among children and youth, however, researchers have had a kind of fixed interest in this distinction, and hundreds of studies have dealt with it (Torrance, 1967a). Perhaps the most notable work concerning this distinction is that of Wallach and Kogan (1965) and Wallach and Wing (1969). Wallach and Kogan's criterion tests for creativity were five tasks, each requiring the generation of different kinds of associates. The tests were administered individually in a gamelike atmosphere without time limits. The associates generated were scored for uniqueness and number. Five measures of general intelligence were also used. These included verbal and perfor-mance subtests from the Wechsler Intel-ligence Scale for Children, the School and College Ability Tests (verbal and quantita-tive), and the Sequential Tests of Educa-tional Progress. A single index of creativity and a single index of intelligence were de-rived for each child on the basis of these ten measures. Wallach and Kogan then composed four groups within each sex: those in the top half of the distribution on intel-ligence and also in the top half on creativ-ity; those in the top half on intelligence and in the lower half on creativity; those in the lower half on intelligence and in the top half on creativity; and those in the lower half on both intelligence and cre-ativity.

Only limited work thus far has been com-pleted to validate the intelligence-creativity distinction using the Wallach and Kogan measures. Wallach and Wing (1969) con-ducted a study with college students as sub-jects, and academic and extracurricular achievement as criteria. They found that level of intelligence was strongly related to academic grades, but only to grades. In-telligence was not at all related to the level or quality of achievement in any of the forms of extracurricular activities studied. Performance on the measures of creativity, however, were unrelated to grades but strongly related to non-academic achieve-ments, especially those in which innovation plays a major role.

At the present time, still another two-factor model of talent seems to be emerging from the interest and research now current concerning the specialized cerebral functions of the right and left hemispheres of the brain (Ornstein, 1972, 1973; Samples, 1975, 1976; Brandwein & Ornstein, 1977). People have long been interested in the specialized functioning of the right and left hemi-spheres of the brain, and there has been a great deal of folklore associated with the topic. Until recently, however, the matter was shrouded in mystery and speculation.

Research in a great many disciplines, includ-ing psychology and education, is now remov-ing much of the mystery and reducing the need for speculation.

It now seems reasonably clear, at least among adults, that the cerebral hemispheres have independently specialized their func-tions. These specialized functions of the cerebral hemispheres seem to represent two different modes of processing information. The left cerebral hemisphere seems to be the locus of logical, analytical, linear, prop-ositional thought. It is the locus of almost all language, order, and time sense. In other words, the left hemisphere seems to process information linearly, sequentially, and log-ically. In contrast, the right hemisphere seems to be the locus of visuospatial and appositional thought and imagination. It is virtually nonverbal, and most often makes itself known through dreams and fantasy. In other words, the right cerebral hemisphere seems to process information nonlinearly, simultaneously handling a variety of kinds of information, relating and associating bits of information, rather than logically and sequentially.

In schools, especially in Western cultures, most activities have required primarily the kinds of information processing performed by the left hemisphere. Thus, schools have developed primarily the left-hemisphere functions. This has caused some critics of education to charge that schools have been educating "only half of the mind" (Samples, 1975; Brandwein & Ornstein, 1977) and giv-ing attention to those kinds of giftedness associated with the left hemisphere func-tions. It is predictable that intelligence and other future tests of giftedness will include tasks which will call for both right- and left-hemisphere functions.

Multiple-Talent Models

Whereas Guilford's Structure of Intellect Model (1967), with its 120 abilities, and even Thurstone's 20 primary mental abilities

(1938), are too complex for practical use in providing guides to identification and program design, the various two-way distinctions may be too simplified. Some of the moderately complex models now being considered may provide a more practical, working conceptualization to guide identification and development of the many different types of gifted children and youth. Some of the more promising of these will now be considered.

One of the more promising multiple-talent models has been suggested by Calvin W. Taylor (1968) and is represented graphically in Figure 11–2. Taylor's groupings of talents are based on world-of-work needs and specify at present academic talent and five other important types: creative (and productive) talent, evaluative or decision-making talent, planning talent, forecasting talent, and communication talent. Taylor argues that

if we consider only the upper 10 percent on each talent group as gifted, the percentage of gifted will increase from 10 percent for one talent area to 30 percent across the six talent areas. He argues further that if we limit ourselves to cultivating one of these talent groups, only 50 percent of our students will have a chance to be above average (the median) in classes. If all six talent groups are considered, about 90 percent will be above average in at least one group, and almost all others will be nearly average in at least one of them.

Taylor (1968) believes that we now know enough about measuring and fostering multiple talents to find ways of cultivating most of them in school rather than letting them lie largely dormant. He also believes that in classrooms where multiple talents are cultivated all students will learn more. In other words, by having many pathways

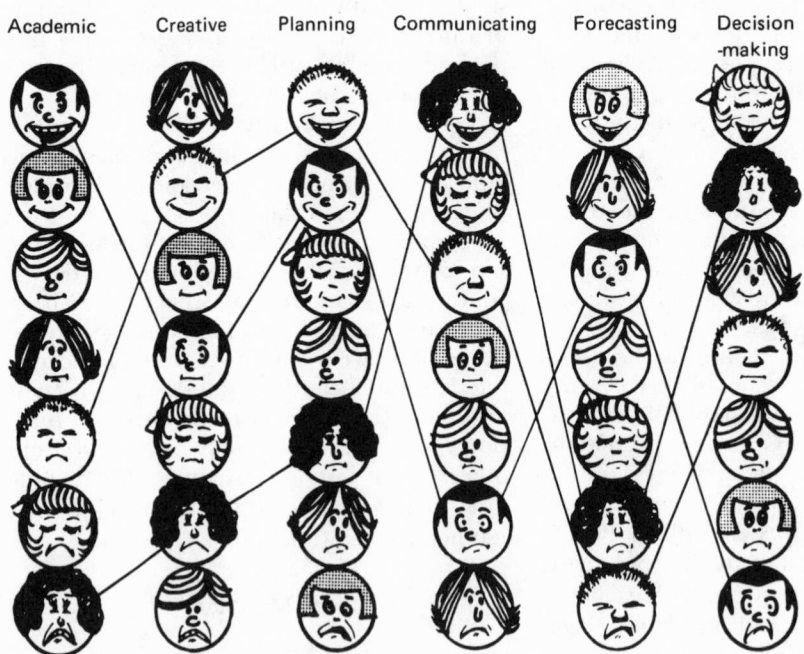

FIGURE 11–2.   The Taylor Multiple Talent Totem Poles
Used by permission from Calvin W. Taylor, University of Utah.

through their complex nervous systems, students can use several different abilities at one time or another to process information during the school week. He believes that this will happen if teachers sharpen their abilities to cultivate these talents and deliberately work across a greater number of these talents.

Taylor recommends that teachers give greater emphasis to their talent-developer role and less emphasis to their role as information dispenser. He suggests further that each teacher might specialize to become expert in developing particular talents, and that students could study under each of these separate talent development specialists. He proposes that educational programs be evaluated by determining how much students have developed each of these talents as well as how much they have gained in subject mastery. He suggests that the best place to begin is by cultivating the creative and productive type of talent, because creative teaching approaches do most to expand the narrow band of talents with which schools now concern themselves.

Taylor's Multiple-Talent Model (1968) represents one of the cleanest departures yet offered from traditional conceptualizations of talents in terms of subject matter content such as science, art, music, dramatics, creative writing, mechanics, social leadership, and the like. The latter model is perhaps best represented by the Quincy, Illinois, and Portland, Oregon, gifted-child projects of the 1950s (De Haan & Wilson, 1958). Although Taylor's Multiple-Talent Model is based on world-of-work needs, it also seems to be a departure from the vocational-guidance-oriented models born largely in the 1940s and thrust into prominence in the 1950s. These models are represented by test batteries such as the Differential Aptitude Tests (Bennett *et al.*, 1959), the General Aptitude Test Battery (Bureau of Employment Security, 1958), the Multiple Aptitude Tests (Segel & Raskin, 1959), and the Flanagan Aptitude Classification Tests (Flanagan, 1959). Although the models upon which these test batteries were designed guide job selection and personnel selection, Taylor's model seems to be designed for talent development in education.

A number of somewhat similar models have been proposed, but none of them have been developed and instrumented to the extent that Taylor's has. Major programs that have instrumented and implemented this model include Project Implode at Salt Lake City, Utah (Stevenson, 1971; Taylor, Lloyd, & Rollins, 1971) and Project Talents Unlimited in Mobile, Alabama (Project Talents Unlimited, 1974*a,b,c*).

The National Model

Both because of its national status and its reasonableness, the national model represented by the six categories of giftedness recognized by the Office of Gifted and Talented (Commissioner of Education, 1972) is likely to continue for some years to influence policies, practices, research, and development. Perhaps no school system has yet implemented a comprehensive program to provide differentiated programs for all of these six types of giftedness. There are enormous gaps in the development of identification instruments and procedures and in curriculum materials and instructions. These will be reviewed in later sections of this chapter.

CHARACTERISTICS OF GIFTED PEOPLE

Psychologists have continued to struggle to delineate the characteristics of gifted people. For example, Albert (1975) has continued to strive for a behavioral definition of genius or the outstandingly gifted person. The following definition is provocative and illuminating, and has implications for both identification procedures and educational programs:

A person of genius is anyone who, regardless of other characteristics he may possess or have attributed to him, produces, over a long period of time, a large body of work that has a significant influence on many persons, for many years; requiring these persons, as well as the individual in question, to come to terms with a different set of attitudes, ideas, viewpoints, and techniques before all can have "peace of mind," that is, a sense of resolution and closure (Albert, 1975, p. 144).

Albert (1975) has used evidence from research, theory, and the life histories of eminent people to support his definition. The definition may be generalized to each of the six types of giftedness included in the "national model." Ultimately, it might serve as a guide in evaluating existing instruments and programs, inventing and validating new instruments, programs, and the like.

From studies of eminent creative adults and other highly productive, creatively gifted adults, there has emerged a fairly consistent profile. One of the most intense and comprehensive investigations of the productively creative personality was carried out by MacKinnon (1961) and his associates at the Institute for Personality Assessment and Research (IPAR) at the University of California at Berkeley. Most of their studies were based on investigations of highly productive persons, in various occupations, who have achieved eminence because of their creativity. These groups included: scientists, architects, writers, artists, students, and others. In summarizing this work, MacKinnon identified the following characteristics of the productively creative person:

1. Intelligent—but the most intelligent persons are not always the most creative (Concept Mastery Test and creativity correlate .08 among architects and .07 among scientists).

2. Original.

3. Seeks deeper meanings, implications, possibilities.

4. Independent in judgment and in thought and action.

5. Often chafes and rebels; a high level of energy is channeled toward activities and goals the individual has set for himself.

6. Perceptive, open to experience both of the inner and outer world.

7. Intuitive, both in perceptions and in thought processes.

8. Has an image of himself as a responsible person, and a sense of destiny about himself as a human being; has a belief in the worth and validity of one's creative efforts.

9. Entertains both theoretical and aesthetic values; has the capacity to tolerate the tension created in him by conflicts, and effects some reconciliation.

10. Similarly, concerning masculinity-feminity, there is a resolution of the conflict with creative male subjects appearing to give more expression to the feminine side of their nature than do less creative persons.

11. Is not stimulus and object bound in perceptions, but is ever alert to the as-yet-not-realized.

Barron (1963), one of the members of MacKinnon's research team at IPAR, called attention to certain other aspects of the personality of the productively creative individual. One of these is the creative person's preference for complexity and his tolerance for disorder, imbalance, ambiguity, and incompleteness. Barron (1963) also emphasized the idea that the creative individual not only respects the irrational in himself, but courts it as the most promising source of originality in his thought. According to Barron, the creative person rejects the demands of society that he should shun in himself the primitive, the uncultured, the naïve, and the nonsensical. He rejects this demand because he wants to own himself totally and because he perceives a shortsightedness in the claim of society that all its members should adapt themselves to a norm for a given time and place. Barron maintains that this type of imbalance is more likely to be healthy than unhealthy. The truly creative person is ready to abandon old classifications and to acknowledge that life, particularly his own unique life, is rich with new possibilities; disorder offers the potentiality of order.

IDENTIFYING GIFTED CHILDREN AND YOUTH

The New Problem

The emergence of new and broader concepts of giftedness has been quite confusing to teachers, administrators, and parents who insist upon strict adherence to rules and demand precision. Man's enormously strong need for simplicity of structure has perhaps, more than any other factor, impeded the emergence and implementation of appropriate complexity in educating gifted children and youth. For example, Guilford and his associates, to implement the Structure of Intellect Model, have developed tests for about 90 of the 120 hypothesized abilities that have been completed and validated, and there are several tests for each ability. Furthermore, most of Guilford's tests were initially designed for superior adults. Some progress has been made, however, in adapting the test tasks for use with school children and youth (Merrifield, Gardner, & Cox, 1964; Guilford, 1971; Hoepfner & Guilford, 1965; Merrifield, Guilford, & Gershon, 1963).

Reinterpretation of Old Measures

One hope has been that out of the complexity of the Structure of Intellect Model and the great mass of test devices that have been invented to implement it would come simpler, practical procedures that will distill most of the essence of the more complex model. One approach to this goal has been the reinterpretation of data from existing psychometric procedures such as the Binet and Wechsler in terms of Structure of Intellect concepts, and the other has been

efforts to invent complex tasks that can be scored in a variety of ways and in terms of Structure of Intellect concepts. The efforts of Meeker (1969) and Bruch (1969) are perhaps the best exemplars of the former, and the work of Torrance and his associates (Torrance, 1962, 1965, 1966, 1968), the latter.

Meeker (1969) has made a systematic attempt to develop practical ways to translate the Stanford-Binet, the Wechsler Intelligence Scales for Children, and the Wechsler Pre-Primary Scales of Intelligence into Guilford's Structure of Intellect Model so that a graphic profile of a child's intellectual abilities becomes evident. In her book, Meeker provides specific profiles of gifted children and discusses how the information from these profiles can be used as guides for tailoring programs.

Case-Study and Multiple-Criteria Approaches

In recent years, increased emphasis has been placed on the use of multiple criteria approaches in identifying gifted students. For example, Georgia state guidelines for comprehensive planning for the gifted (Bynum, 1976) suggest that the identification and placement program include utilization of the following kinds of information:

Teacher referral

Behavioral checklists

Parent referral

Peer referral

Referral by others such as principal, counselor, etc.

Review of student folders

Group intelligence testing

Individual intelligence testing

Standardized achievement testing

Specific aptitude testing

Teacher grades

Creativity testing

Biographical data.

These guidelines suggest that placement in the program for the gifted should be determined by a screening and placement committee which will review case studies that include these kinds of information. It is specified further that the identification and placement process should be systematic and continuous.

Thus far, there have been only a few systematic studies to test the validity of this approach. A study reported by Renzulli and Smith (1977) tested the validity of the case study approach to the identification of academically gifted students in the elementary grades. Time and cost analyses were conducted, as was an examination of the usefulness of various types of information included in the case studies. These case studies included the following types of information:

Aptitude and achievement test scores

Ratings by present and/or past teachers

Past performance as shown in the cumulative records

Parent ratings and student self ratings.

In the traditional approach, performance on individually administered intelligence tests was the basis for identification. The results indicated that the case-study approach is generally superior to the traditional approach because of its consideration of multiple sources of information. The case-study approach was especially effective in identifying gifted minority group students, and was found to be less costly and time consuming than others have suggested.

Another alternative criteria selection study was reported by Cummings (1976). Cummings and his associates in the San Francisco Unified School District developed a checklist of characteristics of gifted and talented children based primarily upon the research of Torrance. At the end of the school year, a research project was conducted to determine how well those students placed in the program by alternative criteria fared when compared with students placed in the program as a result of having scored at or above the 98th percentile on an individual test of intelligence. There were no statistically significant differences between the two groups of children with regard to achievement test scores, supporting again the use of varied criteria for selection to gifted programs.

Identification to Fit the New National Model

Psychologists are challenged now to develop and validate special identification instruments and procedures to select participants for the six types of programs specified in the 1972 report of the Commissioner of Education. In some of the areas, there are fairly adequate instruments for identification, but in others carefully developed and tested instruments are almost totally lacking.

1. The Intellectually Gifted. Identification procedures for selecting the *intellectually gifted student* are fairly well established. The most frequently used and respected instruments are the Stanford-Binet and Wechsler scales. Since testing with these individually administered instruments is expensive, it is likely that there will continue to be heavy reliance upon group tests such as the Lorge-Thorndike, the Concept Mastery Test, the Otis-Lennon Mental Ability Test, the Raven Progressive Matrices, the Primary Mental Abilities Tests, Flanagan's Tests of General Ability, the Kuhlmann-Anderson, the California Tests of Mental Maturity, the Slosson, and others.

Generally, these measures are acknowledged to be racially and socioeconomically biased. However, if scores derived from these measures are used in case-study approaches, such as the one reported by Renzulli and Smith (1977), corrections may be made for this bias. For example, in the Renzulli and Smith study some of the school districts rated intelligence test information as highly important in decision making, while one school district rated such information as the least useful piece of information in the case study. This latter district, it was noted, served a large proportion of minority group youngsters. Apparently, the case study files contained more valid indicators of giftedness than the intelligence-test scores for children in this district.

2. Specific Academic Aptitude. There is also available a great variety of measures of *specific academic aptitude*. Most frequently used measures in this area are anchored in subject matter areas such as mathematics, science, languages, social sciences, and the like. One of the more ambitious research projects in this area at the present time is the Study of Mathematically Precocious Youth (SMPY) at The Johns Hopkins University directed by Julian C. Stanley and assisted by Daniel P. Keating and Lynn H. Fox (1974). On the basis of this program of research, Stanley (1976) has concluded that tests are "a prime way—probably *the* prime way—for initially finding high-level developed aptitude or achievement" (p. 179). Furthermore, he concluded that it is even more important than generally realized for tests to have enough "ceiling" for each individual tested, and this means bold use of tests designed for older persons. Stanley has argued that critics of testing who allege that instruments such as the Scholastic Aptitude Test serve mainly to discriminate against low scorers, do not take into account the talent-finding aspects of tests.

3. Creative or Productive Thinking. There has also been considerable developmental work in the area of testing for giftedness in *creative or productive thinking*. Over a period of almost twenty years, Torrance and his associates (1962, 1965, 1966, 1968, 1972a,b, 1974) have developed and published alternate batteries of tests of creative thinking that have been used successfully in a variety of cultures and subcultures and at all educational levels from kindergarten through graduate school. Deliberate efforts were made to construct test tasks that are models of the creative thinking process, each involving different kinds of thinking and each contributing something unique to the batteries, both verbal and figural. These batteries, or test tasks from them, have been used in over 800 investigations and have been translated into more than 30 different languages. A great variety and bulk of validity and reliability data are presented in the norms-technical manual (1966, 1974). Torrance (1972a) has reviewed fifteen predictive validity studies of the TTCT that seem to link test performance with real-life behavior. In a long-range predictive validity study involving high school students tested in 1959 and followed up in 1971, a canonical correlation of .51 was obtained for the combined scores on the creativity test battery to predict the combined creative achievement criteria in the total sample of 236. For men, the canonical correlation coefficient was .59 and for women, .46. The following additional findings provide encouraging support (Torrance, 1972b):

a. The class of 1960 was followed up both in 1966 and in 1971 and there was a consistent trend for the validity coefficients to increase from 1966 to 1971. Using the measures of Fluency, Flexibility, Originality, and Elaboration and measures of Quantity and Quality of Creative Achievements and Creative Motivation, the mean validity coefficients was .40 for 46 subjects in 1966 and .51 for 52 subjects in 1971.

b. The present and projected occupations of 252 respondents were classified as conventional according to criteria developed by Getzels and Jackson (1962). Using a median split within grade and sex on the original population, 113 subjects were classified as high creatives and 138 as low creatives. Sixty-two (55 percent) of the high creatives and 13 (9 percent) of the low creatives were in unconventional occupations in 1971. When projected occupations or future aspirations were classified, 71 percent of the high creatives and 32 percent of the low creatives chose unconventional occupations.

c. Creative achievements in writing were most easily predicted, followed by creative achievements in science, medicine, and leadership, perhaps because the criteria in these areas are clearer and more obvious than in such fields as business, music, art, and the like.

Torrance and Khatena (1969) reported a study to validate the originality score of *Sounds and Images* (Cunnington and Torrance, 1965) for identifying creative talent in music. A total of 137 students enrolled at Westminster Choir College were administered both Forms A and B of the test, and information was obtained concerning their creative achievements in music. Both forms of the test successfully discriminated between the music students as a group and a sample of education students. Scores also satisfactorily differentiated those who had had experience in original composition of music, those who had composed in different performance media, and number of awards for outstanding music achievement (Khatena & Torrance, 1973).

One must ask what are reasonable and acceptable standards of validity for tests of creative thinking ability. Some critics (Crockenberg, 1972; Baird, 1972) have stated that the problem is not a lack of validity data on the TTCT but that these data are weak. When confronted by the fact that creative functioning involves a variety of phenomena which occur simultaneously and interact with one another, how much weight should we expect measures of general creative abilities to carry? Research evidence indicates that the motivation of the subject, his early life experiences, the immediate and long range rewards, the richness of the environment, and other factors are all important enough to make a difference in creative functioning and, furthermore, that these phenomena interact with one another.

When Torrance and his associates found that women in the long-range prediction study were less predictable than the men, they tried to obtain responses to the *Alpha Biographical Inventory* for as many of the women respondents as possible. With a sample of forty-five of these women, they (Torrance, Bruch, & Morse, 1973) combined the *Alpha Biographical Inventory* score with the creativity score derived in 1959. A canonical correlation of .60 resulted. The coefficients of correlation between the *Alpha Biographical Creativity Scale* and the criteria of creative achievement are .38, .39, and .37; the mean coefficients of correlation between the *Alpha Biographical Score* and the creative ability measure is .15.

A variety of procedures are being used regarding the function of the *Torrance Tests of Creative Thinking* in the selection of students for participation in special programs for gifted and talented students. Some programs have relied entirely upon measures derived from the TTCT to select participants. Most programs, however, use multiple criteria, and use the TTCT along with measures of intelligence, achievement on tests, life achievements, demonstrations of special talents in the arts, and the like. For example, one very large school system used the figural form of the TTCT to supplement the use of a group intelligence test. Students in Grades three through eight were administered a group intelligence test. Those who achieved IQs in excess of 130 were placed in the special program. Those with IQs between 115 and 130 were then administered the figural form of the TTCT. New streamlined scoring procedures yield a Creativity Index in addition to a variety of indicators of creative strength. These data were then used to select an additional number of gifted/talented students. In multiple criteria approaches, creativity tests may be used in selecting participants for any of the six types of differentiated programs for gifted children and youth.

Among other published tests of creativity are: (1) a battery for children by Guilford (1971), (2) a test of creativity in machine design by Owens (1968), (3) the *Remote Associates Test* by Mednick (1968), and (4) Flanagan's (1959) *Ingenuity Test*. Owens' test has been used primarily with engineering students; Mednick's with college students; and Flanagan's with high school students.

Taylor and his associates (Taylor, 1960, 1961, 1963; Taylor *et al.* 1961) have been engaged for over fifteen years in the development of measures to implement the Multiple-Talent Model presented in the first section of this chapter. These ability measures, however, have not been published and made generally available to schools.

4. Leadership Ability. In the past, there seems to have been relatively little attention to the identification and development of children gifted in leadership ability. Social psychologists, however, have been aware for a long time of the early emergence of giftedness in leadership even in the pre-primary school years. During the 1950s, there was considerable interest in business, industry, and in military organizations concerning the identification and development of leadership ability. Although never very widespread, there were also a few efforts in education to identify and develop this type of giftedness. DeHaan and Havighurst (1957) have described one such project in Quincy, Illinois schools in 1951–52. The primary identification procedures in this project involved teacher and peer nominations. For example, teachers were asked to list the names of students to whom others came for help. The following items were used in their peer nomination instrument which was called the "Who Are They?" technique:

a. Who are the boys and girls that make good plans?

b. Who are the good leaders? They are leaders in several things.

c. Who are the ones that seem to understand things most easily, out of school and in school?

d. Who are the boys and girls that always work

for the good of their class, or their team, or their playmates?

e. Who are the most popular boys and girls?

f. Who are the ones that are sure to have ideas for games and other interesting things to do, both out of school and in school?

Somewhat later, Elizabeth M. Drews (1961, 1963) studied gifted social leaders as one of her four types of gifted adolescents. She found that these social leaders were popular and well liked by their peers. They tended to conform more to teen-age mores than to teachers' expectations. They were generally quite successful academically. Drews found that while the studious gifted students are preparing for examinations and the creative intellectuals are reading about such things as existentialism, the social leaders are out electing someone to office or getting themselves elected. Although they received good grades, they did not achieve very well on difficult scholarship examinations.

Although the literature related specifically to the psychology of children and youth gifted in leadership, there is a considerable body of research and development from which we may draw clues in both identification and the development of differentiated educational experiences. Much of the work of Calvin W. Taylor and his associates (1974) in their multiple talent approach would seem to be relevant. This is especially true of their work on giftedness in planning, communicating, and decision making. Much of the work of the 1950s on leadership in business, industry, and military organizations also provides a rich resource. One of the richer keys to this leadership literature will be found in *Leadership and Interpersonal Behavior* edited by Petrullo and Bass (1961). In designing programs, a helpful source is *Leadership Development: Theory and Practice* edited by Cassel and Heichberger (1975). This book is an attempt to adapt for use in high schools some of the search and development work in the military, business, and industry.

5. Visual and Performing Arts. Differentiated educational programs for children and youth gifted in the visual and performing arts have experienced a phenomenal upsurge in the 1970s. In addition to the older schools for students gifted in the visual and performing arts, such as the ones in New York City and in the state of North Carolina, new schools have emerged in such cities as Houston, Texas; New Orleans, Louisiana; Columbia, South Carolina; New Haven, Connecticut; West Chester, Pennsylvania; and other cities. Another recent movement that has provided new opportunities for children gifted in the visual and performing arts has been artist-in-residence programs in schools. One of the special benefits reported in many of these programs is that children and youth gifted in the arts and displaying behavior and learning problems, when given opportunities in these and similar programs, cease to present behavior problems and begin achieving in gifted ways in other areas such as mathematics, reading, science, and the like (Seides, 1967; Giannini, 1968).

In selecting students for differentiated programs for those gifted in the visual and performing arts, performance and product criteria have been used. Although considerable attention has been given by the Aesthetic Education Program of the Central Midwestern Regional Educational Laboratory (Davis, 1973) to the development of criteria for evaluating the aesthetic qualities for both products and performances, major attention in measurement has been given to such quantifiable characteristics as originality, uniqueness, elaboration, and the like. In practice, greatest reliance seems to have been placed upon the tools and procedures used in selecting students for postsecondary schools and colleges in the arts—the use of auditions, portfolios, and the like.

Where children have had opportunities, either in school or through private instruction, to develop their talents in the visual arts, music, drama, and the like, the audition approach may be satisfactory. However, there is also concern for undeveloped talents among children in schools having no programs in the arts and among families that live in poverty. Psychometric procedures have been developed and used in many of these areas and have been useful in making teachers and parents aware of talents that had otherwise been unnoticed.

Some of the more widely used tests of musical ability are: the *Seashore Measures of Musical Talents* (Seashore, 1960), *Aliferis Music Achievement Tests* (1957), *Drake Musical Aptitude Tests* (1954), and the *Musical Aptitude Profile* (Gordon, 1965). There are also measures such as *Sounds and Images* (Torrance, Khatena, & Cunnington, 1973) and Vaughan's (1971) test of musical creativity, which seem to predict creative achievement in music. Similarly, there are tests for assessing giftedness in the visual arts, dramatics, dance, creative writing, and the like. Such tests have never been used widely and few teachers and school psychologists are skilled in their use. Perhaps the most promising approach would be for school programs to provide opportunities for performance in the various arts and train teachers to make observations of exceptional performance. Torrance (1976a), in his work on giftedness among culturally different children, has developed observation guidelines in these areas. For example, the following indicators are suggested for identifying giftedness in the area of dramatics:

Expresses ideas powerfully and accurately through gestures and body language

Combines speech with gestures and body language to communicate nuances that cannot be expressed by words alone

Skilled in mimicry, imitations, impressions, etc.

Uses gestures and body language to "tell a story"

Skilled in charades that rely upon the use of gestures and body language

Reads orally "as though the thing were happening"
Skilled in role playing.

6. Psychomotor Ability. An examination of over twenty textbooks on gifted children and youth revealed no consideration of the psychology of giftedness in the psychomotor area. This does not mean that there have been no programs for children and youth gifted in the psychomotor domain. Communities, schools, and colleges have invested heavily in the identification and development of outstanding athletic ability. This kind of activity has been widespread in the United States and many other countries. Less widespread has been the identification and development of giftedness in dance, calisthenics, figure skating, and similar psychomotor talent areas. Some countries, such as the U.S.S.R., have given systematic national attention to these kinds of talents (Beck, 1960). Even less attention has been given to the mechanical genius, the youngster gifted in mechanical manipulation, invention, and improvisation—unless, of course, they were also gifted academically. There have been virtually no schools for inventors. Generally, young inventors have been discouraged from messing up their homes and schools with their inventions.

As in the visual and performing arts, recruiting of gifted athletes, dancers, calisthenists, figure skaters, and the like has been on the basis of skilled performances. Outstanding high-school athletes are scouted quite heavily by college coaching staffs. Generally, a scout will have very clear notions about the physical size, strength, agility, stamina, and motivation he is searching for and will evaluate candidates according to these criteria.

In the fields of physical education, psychology, and educational evaluation, there has been considerable research and development from which developers of programs for children and youth gifted in psycho-motor abilities can draw. Taxonomies of the psychomotor domain have been developed by Harrow (1972) and others, and these provide a rich source of guidance for instrument development, identification of outstanding talent, and program development. A number of tests and observational procedures have been developed and are being refined. Again, however, it is likely that giftedness in the psychomotor areas will be identified primarily through scouting for outstanding performers. However, there is a need for testing and/or observational procedures for use with children who do not have opportunities for early training and encouragement in psychomotor development. Torrance (1976a), out of his search for giftedness among disadvantaged and culturally different young children, has suggested a set of checklists for this purpose. Examples of a few of these will be given to illustrate their nature.

The following are examples of items included in the checklist for giftedness in creative movement and dance:

Experiences deep enjoyment in creative movement/dance
Becomes completely absorbed in creative movement/dance
Can interpret songs, poems, stories, etc. through creative movement, dance, etc.
Movement facilitates child's learning and understanding
Spends unusual amounts of time in perfecting movement/dance.

The following items illustrate the kinds of observations suggested for identifying giftedness in responsiveness to the kinesthetic:

Skillfully communicates ideas through movement
Skillfully interprets meaning of movement
Displays skillful manipulative movement in crayon work, typing, piano playing, etc.

Makes quick, precise movements in mime, creative dramatics, etc.

Shows skilled movements in drawing and other visual art products

Makes fine discriminations of kinesthetic phenomena

Has excellent memory for kinesthetic information

Displays total bodily involvement in interpreting a poem, story, etc.

The following items from Torrance's checklist for identifying giftedness among young children in improvisation with common materials will illustrate the kinds of observations that may be used in the mechanical manipulativeness and invention area:

Makes toys from common materials

Uses common materials to modify or repair toys

Makes games from common materials

Uses common materials for unintended uses in the home, the school, etc.

Uses common materials in inventions.

In other sources, Torrance (1973, 1977) has provided a great variety of suggestions for identifying giftedness in several psychomotor areas and using these abilities in the curriculum and in developing careers. While these suggestions require additional validation and amplification, they suggest many exciting ideas for developing a psychology of giftedness in the psychomotor domain. The autobiographies and biographies of people who have been acclaimed for giftedness in these areas also provide rich and stimulating materials for this purpose. Artistic and literary studies of gifted children in the process of developing their giftedness in the psychomotor areas are also useful.

Although there has not yet been a great deal of response to the psychomotor ability category of the new national model, it is anticipated that there will be increased attention in the psychology of psychomotor gifted children and youth.

Issues in Identifying Gifted Disadvantaged Children and Youth

Increased concern about the education of disadvantaged children in the late 1960s brought about increased interest in the identification of giftedness among disadvantaged groups and the search for hidden talents. The theme of this increase is rather well summarized in the following quotation from Wolfle's introduction (1969) to the Walter Van Dyke Bingham Lectures on the Development of Exceptional Abilities and Capacities:

There has come to be widespread recognition of the huge social loss we suffer in all ranges of the ability distribution. Far too many children are born into homes that give them no intellectual stimulation, in which their potentialities cannot mature, in which attitudes and customs are so rigid that originality and creativeness cannot flourish, in which the traits and abilities required for effective participation in a complex technological society have little chance to develop (p. xx).

Before this, numerous scholars (Anderson, 1960; Riessman, 1962; Taba and Elkins, 1966) had written of the hidden talents among disadvantaged children. There has long been a general recognition that existing methods of psychological assessment fail to discover these talents (Terman, 1925, 1954; Davis, 1948). Attempts to develop culture free (Cattell, 1949) and culture fair (Davis and Eels, 1953) tests of intellectual talent have not been very successful.

As the author perceives the situation, there are three major issues:

1. Should we seek to identify and cultivate those kinds of talents that the dominant society values or look for talents of the type that are

highly valued in the particular disadvantaged subcultures?

2. Are there important kinds of talents found in abundance among disadvantaged subcultures?

3. How early should attempts be made to identify and give special encouragement to outstandingly gifted children among disadvantaged subcultures? Is the time of college admission too late?

Common Strengths of Disadvantaged Children

On the basis of ten years of exploratory work with disadvantaged groups, primarily blacks, the author (1977) has suggested a set of creative positives that exist to a high degree among disadvantaged children and upon which he believes we can build successful educational programs and, ultimately, successful lives:

1. Ability to express feelings and emotions in communication through creative writing, music, creative movement, interpersonal relations, etc.

2. Ability to improvise with commonplace materials

3. Articulateness in role playing, sociodrama, and storytelling

4. Enjoyment of and ability in the visual arts—drawing, painting, sculpture, etc.

5. Enjoyment of and ability in creative movement, dance, dramatics, etc.

6. Enjoyment of and ability in music, rhythm, etc.

7. Expressiveness of speech, richness of imagery, colorfulness of language, etc.

8. Fluency and flexibility in nonverbal media (figural, motor, etc.)

9. Enjoyment of and skills in small group activities, problem solving, etc.

10. Responsiveness to the concrete

11. Responsiveness to the kinesthetic

12. Expressiveness of gestures, "body language," etc. and ability to "read body language" and non-verbal communication

13. Humor and ability to create surprise

14. Originality of ideas in problem solving

15. Problem-centeredness and persistence in problem solving

16. Emotional responsiveness and responsiveness to emotion

17. Quickness of physical and emotional warm-up.

It appears that these creative positives can be observed with high degrees of frequency among black disadvantaged children when they are engaged in challenging and exciting learning activities that give them a chance to use such abilities (Torrance, 1976a).

Since funding agencies have been willing to support only compensatory programs for disadvantaged children, there have been few systematic demonstrations to support these conclusions. One such program was one conducted by Witt (1971) in New Haven, Connecticut. This program (Witt, 1968) involved sixteen highly creative, lower-class black children in a ghetto setting. They were selected in 1965 solely on the basis of tests of creative thinking (the Torrance figural tests and one test task developed by Witt). Twelve of them continued in this program which continued to change to meet the children's changing needs. As truly high level talents were manifested, opportunities were provided for them to have music, art, ballet, and other kinds of lessons from excellent teachers. Many of the children's parents were assisted in upgrading their job skills. Sponsors were arranged both for the children and their families. Fellowships were arranged for participation in science and arts camps, and scholarships were obtained for some of them in private schools. These children have competed successfully with affluent gifted children in both types of settings. The competencies with which they have succeeded in such competition were attained as an outgrowth of activities that made use of their creative positives rather than as a direct result of deliberate attempts to develop these competencies.

Early Identification and Encouragement

Most talent searches have been leveled at high-school seniors. In recent years the Upward Bound and similar programs for disadvantaged youths have been designed to appeal to younger groups. Now there are some talent searches aimed at the junior-high-school level group. The younger the person, the better the chance he has of overcoming the deficits he has developed along the way, and the better the chance he has of developing his positives more fully. Even junior high school, however, is rather late.

Studies in recent years by Bloom (1964) and others have shown that it is extremely difficult to overcome deficits acquired after age 5 or so. Insights arising from these findings did much to inspire Head Start and other preprimary programs. The author knows of no instances, however, where deliberate efforts have been made to identify outstanding talent among disadvantaged preprimary age children and give special encouragement to the development of this outstanding talent.

NEW CONCERN ABOUT ROLES OF HEREDITY AND ENVIRONMENT

New interest in improving the education of disadvantaged and minority subculture children has brought renewed concern about the roles of heredity and environment in giftedness. The problem is indeed a complex one, and as evidence concerning the issue has been presented and discussed, teachers and parents with low tolerance for complexity have been disturbed and professed confusion. This state of affairs is reflected in the following quotation from a letter by an Alabama teacher (Carswell, 1969) to the editor of *The Instructor* magazine:

One article I read recently said that "the maximum contribution of the best environment to intelligence is about 20 IQ points." The next book I took from the shelf said, "It is possible to envision a 40- to 60-point difference produced by a minimum negative environment and a maximum positive environment."

The IQ boys don't seem to be able to get together. Some insist that the IQ is fixed by the time a child is four, others by the time he is seven, and still others that it can change throughout childhood. I think it's time we should throw out the IQ scores (p. 12).

Actually there is not as much discrepancy between this teacher's two sources as she implies. If a maximum positive environment can serve to raise the IQ 20 points and an extreme negative environment can lower the IQ 20 points, it could be argued that environment might possibly make a 40-point difference. This, in fact, was rather close to the facts in the well-known study of Skeels (1936, 1940, 1966) conducted in the 1930s and followed up in the 1960s. In this study, the children placed in the stimulating care of mentally retarded adolescents gained an average of 27.5 IQ points, whereas the comparison group placed in an institution lost an average of 26.2 IQ points. This experiment yields a difference of 53.7 IQ points between what was far from the maximum positive environment and the negative environment of a state institution for mentally defective children in the 1930s.

One center of the controversy has been the work of Jensen (1966, 1968, 1969). The most controversial of his papers is his lengthy article in the *Harvard Educational Review* (1969). In this paper he argued that the failure of recent compensatory education efforts to produce lasting effects on children's IQ and achievement called for a reexamination of the premises on which these efforts have been based. He especially questioned the idea that IQ differences are almost entirely a result of environmental differences and the cultural bias of intelligence tests. As in his earlier papers, he argued that environmental factors are less important in determining IQ than genetic factors. After examining the recent research concerning compensatory educational programs for young children, Jensen concluded that extreme environmental deprivation can keep a child from performing up to his genetic potential, but an enriched educational program cannot push the child above that potential. Jensen argues, however, that there are other mental abilities not included in intelligence tests that might be capitalized upon in educational programs. He believes that current educational attempts to boost IQ have been misdirected, and he advocates the development of educational methods that are based on other mental abilities besides IQ. The controversial work by Rosenthal and Jacobson (1968), and the many variations of their work which followed, and the work of Arthur and Linda Shaw Whimbey (1975) present a more optimistic view. The Rosenthal and Jacobson study suggests that intellectual development may be stimulated or inhibited by the attitudes that teachers have concerning the abilities of children and their expectations of them. The work of the Whimbeys suggests that intellectual abilities can be increased by deliberate, systematic teaching of better strategies of processing information and training basic-thinking skills.

A new element has been introduced into the heredity-environment controversy by a series of the classical type twin studies. A study of Pezzullo, Thorsen, and Madaus (1972) showed no evidence of hereditary variation in either the figural or verbal forms of the TTCT. Their subjects were thirty-seven pairs of fraternal and twenty-eight pairs of identical twins carefully tested. These investigators found that short-term memory (Jensen's Level I abilities) has only a moderate index of heritability, .54; the general intellective factor (Jensen's Level II abilities) has a relatively high index of heritability, .85. The heritability index for the figural and verbal measures of the TTCT

approached zero. Another twin study by Richmond (1968) similarly found no evidence of heritability for the abilities assessed by the TTCT. Davenport (1967), using the Getzels and Jackson (1962) measures, did find weak evidence for heritability on most of these measures of creativity. The indications were so weak, however, that Davenport concluded that there was a wide margin in which experience could influence the creative thinking abilities.

An important implication of the finding that creative abilities are not heritable is that educators can expect to be able to do more to modify the creative abilities than they can the abilities assessed by intelligence tests. Thus, educational programs that build competencies in creative thinking and build upon the creative positives of disadvantaged children are likely to be more successful than are those programs that seek to improve intelligence and compensate for deficiencies in this area.

CHARACTERISTICS OF GIFTED CHILDREN AND YOUTH

In the past, teachers and other educators have not found studies of the psychological characteristics of gifted children and youth to be very helpful. Perhaps a major reason is that these studies had not differentiated the various types of giftedness and had not specified the type of gifted children or youth being studied. Certainly the acceptance of a more complex concept of giftedness requires a reorientation of studies in this area. Thus far, few such studies have been reported and these have been primarily concerned with differentiations between highly creative children and youth and highly intelligent ones, and between different types of creatively gifted children and youth.

With the recognition that has been given to the six categories of gifted children and youth, it may be expected that the next ten to twenty years will produce useful studies of the psychological characteristics of children and youth gifted in the various categories.

SPECIAL PROBLEMS OF ADJUSTMENT OF GIFTED CHILDREN AND YOUTH

Those who have been interested in special provisions for gifted children and the improvement of the skills of all teachers for working with gifted children have usually met with opposition and discouragement. Critics of proposals for improving the education of gifted children and youth have said that the plight of the mentally retarded, the blind, the deaf, and the crippled arouses sympathy but that the gifted are well endowed and can take care of themselves. They generally believe that gifted children who do not succeed are morally delinquent and should be punished.

These critics may express shock when the town's "model" honor student commits murder, arson, or rape and express delight when the town's brilliant but nonconforming young artist, scientist, musician, or writer is imprisoned for a minor misdemeanor. They may express surprise when some young prisoner is acclaimed for a great novel, work of art, or important invention executed while in prison. They will still say, "If a child has any spark of creativity or anything good in him, it will come out regardless of what happens to him." They fail to recognize the compelling fact that the gifted young child is frequently completely unable to help himself and to cope with hate, aggression, coercion, poverty, and other negative forces.

Self-Concepts of Gifted Children and Youth

The search of gifted children and youth for their identity and for a realistic and favorable self-concept is frequently painful and prolonged. The feedback that the gifted child receives is conflicting and confusing. He is puzzled. He performs outstandingly and is punished rather than rewarded. He is taught that the good child is a modest child. He is also taught that he should at all times "do his best." In doing his best, however, he breaks norms, and this brings punishment, hostility, and rejection. He is made to feel ashamed and unworthy. Thus, the gifted child frequently derogates himself and is severely handicapped by his low estimate of himself.

Torrance (1960) studied a group of underevaluating gifted college freshmen (students actually ranking in the upper 10 percent in scholastic ability but estimating their ability as below average). The portrait developed through this study of the underevaluating gifted college freshman is that of an intellectually sublimating, over-rational, self-punishing individual who sees himself basically as a little boy. In spite of the great energy invested in intellectual control, he occasionally gives way to emotional outbursts and tries to hide his inner disturbance by isolation and intellectual achievement. He thus avoids group participation and association with the opposite sex. He sees himself as stubborn, reserved, bashful, impetuous, tactful, conscientious, nervous, anxious, and depressed. As a function of his immaturity, he is unable to picture himself in any mature vocational role. He is socially conforming, represses his aggression and hostility, and is generally inhibited in the sphere of emotion and will. Basically, he is dependent but, because of previous disappointments, he cannot accept his need for dependence.

Purkey (1967), reviewing research concerning the self-concepts of gifted children and youth, found that the evidence refutes the popular idea that gifted individuals see themselves as superior, are filled with self-satisfaction, or have contempt for their less able peers. Purkey (1966) himself conducted a study of intellectually gifted high school students and compared their test-estimated and self-estimated personality characteristics. The results of this study showed that gifted high school students are markedly above average in personal adjustment. They saw themselves as simply average on these qualities, however.

Werblo and Torrance (1966) conducted a study of gifted upper-elementary children to test the hypothesis that the gifted who engage in research, using the process of historiography to investigate their own development, will achieve more realistic self-evaluations in such areas as size of vocabulary, reading speed, and curiosity. The study involved sixty-nine sixth-graders in three classes for high achievers in a public school system. As a part of a unit taught by Torrance on how to do research, these gifted children were asked to estimate on a set of graphs their own growth, including height, curiosity, reading speed, imagination, spelling, independence in thinking, and arithmetic computation. Next, they were asked to indicate the point on their graph where they thought average boys and girls their age would be. Then they were encouraged to collect as much data from witnesses and records as possible to test their hypotheses and to modify them, if necessary.

Results of the study showed that self-evaluations of vocabulary, curiosity, and reading speed showed significant changes at the end of the research training, all in the direction of higher self-evaluations. For example, in curiosity, of fifty-three students rating themselves as average or below average at the start of the unit, only twenty-eight remained the same at the end, with fifteen changing to above average.

It was clear from this study that even gifted, high-achieving, and socially well-adjusted children tend to underevaluate themselves on such variables as size of vocabulary, reading speed, and curiosity, even after thorough testing and segregation from regular classes. Werblo and Torrance suggest that gifted students can apply the concepts and methods of research to attain more realistic self-evaluations in the areas discussed and perhaps in others. One can only imagine the plight of emotionally disturbed and low achieving gifted children and youth.

Creatively Gifted Children and Youth

Many creatively gifted children and youth are so severely handicapped in adjusting and learning in the typical school that this author has suggested that such children and youth be recognized as a new category in the field of special education. There are many children in this category whose behavior problems stem from the differences their abilities create between them and their teachers. Their learning difficulties arise from the incompatibility between their abilities and learning preferences on one hand and the teaching methods and system of rewards of the school on the other. If brought together with other creatively gifted youngsters, they would no longer be misfits. If taught in ways compatible with their abilities and interests, their achievement might soar.

Out of a series of studies dealing with mental health problems, the author (Torrance, 1963) has offered the following conceptualization for investigating and ameliorating the problems of highly creative children and youth. Because almost all definitions of creativity involve the production of something new, original, or divergent, it is inescapable that the creatively gifted person repeatedly will find himself a minority of one. Even when matters of fact are involved, as in Asch's (1955) famous experiments in social psychology, there are few people who can endure being a minority of one. Being a minority of one leaves a person with too few anchors in reality or guides to behavior. Because creative behavior requires independence of mind, divergence from group norms, or unusualness, it is inevitable that highly creative persons will experience many problems of adjustment. The highly creative child must either repress or sacrifice his creativity or learn to cope with or reduce the tensions that arise from being so frequently a minority of one. Repression, if prolonged or severe, leads to uncertain or inadequate self-concepts, learning difficulties, behavior problems, neurotic distortions, or even psychotic breakdowns. The continued expression of creative needs in spite of tensions and pressures may lead to loneliness, conflicts, or other types of alienation.

It now seems that different types of creatively gifted children and youth experience different kinds of mental health problems. In a population of 712 high school seniors, Torrance and Dauw (1965) studied the mental health problems of youths characterized by high originality, high elaboration, and high originality and elaboration. Their findings confirmed the findings of other studies that highly creative youths frequently experience rather intense and prolonged stresses that reduce creativity and that the stresses of the highly original youth differ in important ways from those characteristically experienced by those who excel in elaboration. Those high on both originality and elaboration share many of the vicissitudes of the high originals but apparently escape some of the discomforts and strains that result from nonconformity.

The high originals and those high on both originality and elaboration tend to be characterized by concern about ridicule, restriction of freedoms, and pressures of time, whereas the high elaborators are more frequently concerned about possible failure and inability to meet the expectations their parents and teachers have of them. The high originals and those high on both seem to cope with stresses by changes in strategies and the initiation of new projects whereas the high elaborators more frequently report using withdrawal strategies and resort to eating, sleeping, and drinking. All three groups rely rather frequently on absorption in work and creative activities and discussion of their problems with others.

The high originals reported more frequently than the other groups special problems involving parental disagreements and estrangement, whereas the other groups reported concerns about meeting the high expectations of their environment. In general, the environment of the high originals does not seem to hold very high expectations of them, tending instead to disparage them and to frustrate their craving for independence and achievement. At least, this is the way that the highly original high school seniors in the Torrance and Dauw study perceived the situation.

NEW KINDS OF GIFTEDNESS

Psychologists do not know what new kinds of giftedness will be needed in the future. It seems likely that many abilities, not now measured or even acknowledged by current methods, will be important in the future. Certainly the ability to construct images of the future will be important. Polak (1973, 1976), in fact, has shown that images of the future have always been important in human achievement. He has also maintained that these images of the future have always come from the gifted members of a society (the prophets and projectors of images). He believes that the strength of a culture can be measured by the intensity and energy of its images of the future. Torrance (1976bc) has recently given considerable attention to measuring the ability of gifted students to project images of the future through scenario and soliloquy techniques, a device he calls "20 Questions About the Future," and one he called the "Future of the World of Work." It may be that, in the future, the education of gifted children and youth will be concerned about developing differentiated programs which will enlarge, enrich, and make more accurate their images of the future.

Recent years have seen an interest in various kinds of psychic ability. However, there has not yet been very much real research concerning these psychic or paranormal abilities. What research there has been, however, indicates that these abilities emerge in very young children but are discouraged by adults. Peterson (1975) has called attention to the following paranormal abilities: telepathy (the ability to read another's thoughts), precognition (having an awareness of the future), clairaudience (hearing "inaudible" voices, or music), psychometry (obtaining facts about the history of an object by touching it), clairvoyance (seeing "superphysical" sights), and the like. In the professional field of the psychology of gifted children and youth, John Gowan (1974, 1975) has been especially active in calling attention to these kinds of giftedness and the conditions that facilitate their development and manifestations. The research of Jerome Singer (1973, 1975) on the imaginative play of young children and the inner world of daydreaming has also emphasized the constructive role of these aspects of experiencing.

In attempts to transcend the complexities of evaluating the kinds of abilities identified by psychologists such as J. P. Guilford, the Thurstones, C. W. Taylor, and others, psychologists continue to search for some ability which will capture the essence of "giftedness," "creativity," or "genius." Some have sought to capture this essence through instruments designed to elicit associations, basing their work on associationist theories. Among these have been Wallach and Kogan (1965) and Mednick (1968). More recently, Getzels and Csikszentmihalyi (1976) have suggested that the essence of giftedness is the ability to find and formulate problems. They maintain, on the basis of ten years of study, that the essence of "gifted-

ness" or "genius" may be the sensitivity and imagination for finding problems. They point out that the copyist in art, the technician in science, the pedant in scholarship, and the bureaucrat in government deal with problems that have already been identified. The really gifted people—the fine artists, the inventive scientists, the creative scholars, the innovative statesmen, the self-actualizing persons—are also aware of unformulated problems potentially present in the conflicts of their own experience. Getzels and Csikszentmihalyi argue further that this ability is not based on superiority in memory, reasoning, or conventional cognitive abilities. It involves a process more in touch with the deeper layers of personality; is far more holistic; is goal-directed but often pursues goals beneath the threshold of awareness; and uses symbolic means to express formless feelings, disclosing what otherwise would go unperceived and articulating what would otherwise remain unarticulated.

CONCLUSION

It is obvious from the analysis that has been presented in this chapter on gifted children and youth that the acceptance of new concepts of giftedness creates many new problems and calls for a re-examination of much of the research and development of the past. The new concepts provide exciting ways of examining the problems of gifted children and youth, however, and offer hope for a more humane and liberating approach to their problems and their education.

REFERENCES

ALBERT, R. S. Toward a behavioral definition of genius. *American Psychologist*, 1975, *30*, 140–151.

ALIFERIS, J. Aliferis music achievement test, college entrance level. Minneapolis: University of Minnesota Press, 1957.

ANDERSON, J. E. The nature of abilities. In E. P. Torrance (Ed.), *Talent and education.* Minneapolis: University of Minnesota Press, 1960, pp. 9–13.

ASCH, S. E. *Studies of independence and submission to group pressure. I. A minority of one against a unanimous majority.* Swarthmore, Pa.: Swarthmore College, 1955.

BAIRD, L. J. The Torrance tests of creative thinking. In O. K. Buros (Ed.), *The seventh mental measurement yearbook.* Highland Park, N.J.: Gryphon Press, 1972, pp. 836–838.

BARRON, F. *Creativity and psychological health.* Princeton, N.J.: D. Van Nostrand Co., Inc., 1963.

BECK, R. H. The treatment of individual differences in Russian schools. In E. P. Torrance (Ed.), *Talent and education.* Minneapolis: University of Minnesota Press, 1960, pp. 134–146.

BENNETT, G. K. The DAT—a seven year followup. *Test Service Bulletin No. 49.* New York: The Psychological Corporation, 1959.

——— et al. *Differential aptitude tests: Manual.* New York: The Psychological Corporation, 1959.

BIONDI, A. M., & PARNES, S. J. *Assessing creative growth: The tests—Book one.* Great Neck, N.Y.: Creative Synergetic Associates, 1976.

BLOOM, B. S. *Stability and change in human characteristics.* New York: John Wiley & Sons, Inc., 1964.

BRANDWEIN, P., & ORNSTEIN, R. The duality of the mind. *Instructor,* 1977, *86* (5), 54–59.

BRUCH, C. B. A creativity score from the Stanford-Binet and its applications. Paper presented at the meetings of the Council on Exceptional Children International, Denver, Colorado, April 10, 1969.

Bureau of Employment Security. *General aptitude test battery: Section III, development: Guide.* Washington, D.C.: U.S. Department of Labor, 1958.

BURT, C. L. *The gifted child.* New York: John Wiley & Sons, Inc., 1975.

BYNUM, M. O. Needs assessment instrument for comprehensive planning—Gifted. Atlanta, Ga.: Georgia State Department of Education, 1976. (Mimeographed)

CARSWELL, F. D. IQ scores. *Instructor,* 1969, *79* (1), 12.

CASSEL, R. N., & HEICHBERGER, R. L. (Eds.). *Leadership development: Theory and practice.* North Quincy, Mass.: Christopher Publishing House, 1975.

CATTELL, R. B. *The culture-free intelligence test.* Champaign, Ill.: Institute for Personality Assessment and Testing, 1949.

CROCKENBERG, S. B. Creativity tests: A boon or boondoggle for education? *Review of Educational Research,* 1972, *42,* 27–45.

CUMMINGS, W. B. No significant difference found between alternative criteria selection and 98th percentile. *N/S-LTI-G/T Bulletin,* 1976, *3* (1), 3.

CUNNINGTON, B. F., & TORRANCE, E. P. *Sounds and images.* Lexington, Mass.: Personnel Press, 1965.

DAVENPORT, J. D. A study of monozygotic and dizygotic twins and siblings on measures of scholastic aptitude, creativity, achievement motivation, and academic achievement. Doctoral dissertation, University of Maryland, 1967. (*Dissertation Abstracts* 28: 3865-B; University Microfilms Order No. 68-3350)

DAVIS, A. *Social class influence on learning.* Cambridge, Mass.: Harvard University Press, 1948.

———, & EELS, K. *Davis-Eels games.* New York: Harcourt, Brace & Jovanovich, 1953.

DAVIS, D. J. Characteristics of the creative product. In Sells, S. B. (Ed.), *Needed research on creativity.* Ft. Worth, Texas: Institute of Behavioral Research, Texas Christian University, 1973.

DEHAAN, R. F., & HAVIGHURST, R. J. *Educating gifted children.* Chicago: University of Chicago Press, 1957.

DEHAAN, R. F., & WILSON, R. C. Identification of the gifted. In N. B. Henry (Ed.), *Education for the gifted.* Chicago: University of Chicago Press, 1958, pp. 166–192.

DRAKE, R. M. *Drake musical aptitude tests, grades 3 through college.* Chicago: Science Research Associates, 1957.

DREWS, E. M. A critical evaluation of approaches to the identification of gifted students. In A. Traxler (Ed.), *Measurement and research in today's schools.* Washington, D.C.: American Council on Education, 1961, pp. 109–121.

————. The four faces of able adolescents. *Saturday Review,* 1963, *46,* 68–71.

FELDHUSEN, J. F., & TREFFINGER, D. J. *Teaching creative thinking and problem solving.* Dubuque, Iowa: Kendall/Hunt, 1976.

FLANAGAN, J. C. *Flanagan aptitude classification tests: Technical report.* Chicago: Science Research Associates, 1959.

GETZELS, J. W., & CSIKSZENTMIHALYI, M. *The creative vision: A longitudinal study of problem finding in art.* New York: John Wiley & Sons, Inc., 1976.

————, & JACKSON, P. W. *Creativity and intelligence.* New York: John Wiley & Sons, Inc., 1962.

GIANNINI, V. Nurturing talent and creativity in the arts. In P. Heist (Ed.) *The creative college student: An unmet challenge.* San Francisco: Jossey-Bass, 1968, pp. 73–83.

GORDON, E. *Musical aptitude profile, Grades 4–12.* Boston: Houghton Mifflin, 1965.

GOWAN, J. C. *Development of the psychedelic individual.* Buffalo, N.Y.: Creative Education, 1974.

————. *Trance, art and creativity.* Buffalo, N.Y.: Creative Education Foundation, 1975.

GUILFORD, J. P. Creativity. *American Psychologist,* 1950, *5,* 444–454.

————. Structure of intellect. *Psychological Bulletin,* 1956, *53,* 267–293.

————. Three faces of intellect. *American Psychologist,* 1959, *14,* 469–479.

————. *The nature of human intelligence.* New York: McGraw-Hill Book Company, 1967.

————. *Creativity tests for children.* Beverly Hills, Calif.: Sheridan Psychological Services, 1971.

————, HENDRICKS, M., & HOEPFNER, R. Solving social problems creatively. *Journal of Creative Behavior,* 1968, *2,* 155–164.

————, MERRIFIELD, P. R., & COX, A. B. *Creative thinking in children at the junior high school level.* Los Angeles: Psychological Laboratory, University of Southern California, 1961.

HARROW, A. S. *A taxonomy of the psychomotor domain.* New York: David McKay, 1972.

HOEPFNER, R., & GUILFORD, J. P. *Figural, symbolic, and semantic factors of creative potential in ninth-grade students.* Los Angeles: Psychological Laboratory, University of Southern California, 1965.

JENSEN, A. R. Verbal mediation and educational potential. *Psychology in the Schools,* 1966, *3,* 99–109.

————. Social class and verbal learning. In M. Deutsch, I. Katz, & A. R. Jensen (Eds.), *Social class, race, and psychological development.* New York: Holt, Rinehart & Winston, Inc., 1968, pp. 115–174.

————. How much can we boost IQ and scholastic achievement? *Harvard Educational Review,* 1969, *39,* 1–123.

KHATENA, J., & TORRANCE, E. P. *Norms-technical manual: Thinking creatively with sounds and words.* Lexington, Mass.: Personnel Press/Ginn and Company, 1973.

MACKINNON, D. W., & ASSOCIATES. *The creative person.* Berkeley, Calif.: University of California Extension Department, 1961.

MEDNICK, S. A. *Remote associates test.* Boston: Houghton Mifflin, 1968.

MEEKER, M. N. *The structure of intellect: Its interpretation and uses.* Columbus, Ohio: Charles E. Merrill, 1969.

MERRIFIELD, P. R., GARDNER, S. F., & COX, A. B. *Aptitudes and personality measures related to creativity in seventh-grade children.* Los Angeles: Psychological Laboratory, University of Southern California, 1964.

————, GUILFORD, J. P., & GERSHON, A. *The differentiation of divergent production abil-*

ities at the sixth-grade level. Los Angeles: Psychological Laboratory, University of Southern California, 1963.

ORNSTEIN, R. E. *The psychology of consciousness.* San Francisco: W. H. Freeman, 1972.

——— (Ed.) *The nature of human consciousness.* San Francisco: W. H. Freeman, 1973.

OWENS, W. A. The predictive validity of certain measures of creativity in machine design. *Journal of Creative Behavior,* 1968, *2,* 211–212.

PETERSON, J. Extrasensory abilities of children: An ignored reality? *Learning,* 1975, *4* (4) , 10–14.

PETRULLO, L., & BASS, B. M. (Eds.) *Leadership and interpersonal behavior.* New York: Holt, Rinehart, and Winston, Inc., 1961.

PEZZULLO, T. R., THORSEN, E. E., & MADAUS, G. F. The heritability of Jensen's level I and II and divergent thinking. *American Educational Research Journal,* 1972, *9,* 539–546.

POLAK, F. L. *The image of the future.* San Francisco: Jossey-Bass, 1973.

———. Responsibility for the future. In R. Bundy (Ed.) , *Images of the future: The twenty-first century and beyond.* Buffalo, N.Y.: Prometheus Books, 1976, pp. 9–15.

Project Talents Unlimited. *Multiple talent teacher training.* Mobile, Ala.: Mobile County Public Schools, 1974*a.*

———. *Multiple talent evaluation.* Mobile, Ala.: Mobile County Public Schools, 1974*b.*

———. *Multiple talent instruction.* Mobile, Mobile County Public Schools, 1974*c.*

PURKEY, W. W. Measured and professed personality characteristics of gifted high school students and an analysis of their congruence. *Journal of Educational Research,* 1966, *60,* 99–104.

———. *The self and academic achievement.* Gainesville, Fla.: Florida Educational Research and Development Council, College of Education, University of Florida, 1967.

RENZULLI, J. S., & SMITH, L. H. Two approaches to identification of gifted students. *Exceptional Children,* 1977, *43,* 512–518.

RICHMOND, B. O. Creativity in monozygotic and dizygotic twins. Paper presented at the meetings of the American Personnel and Guidance Association, Detroit, Michigan, April, 1968.

RIESSMAN, F. *The culturally deprived child.* New York: Harper & Row, 1962.

ROSENTHAL, R., & JACOBSON, L. *Pygmalion in the classroom.* New York: Holt, Rinehart & Winston, Inc., 1968.

SAMPLES, R. E. Are you teaching only one side of the brain? *Learning,* 1975, *3* (6) , 24–28.

———. *The metaphoric mind.* Reading, Mass.: Addison-Wesley, 1976.

SEASHORE, C. E. *Seashore measures of musical talent.* New York: The Psychological Corporation, 1960.

SEGEL, D., & RASHKIN, E. *Multiple aptitude tests.* Monterey, Calif.: California Test Bureau, 1959.

SEIDES, E. The effect of talent class placement on slow learners in the seventh grade of a New York City junior high school. Doctoral dissertation, New York University, 1967. (*Dissertation Abstracts* 28: 4011; University Microfilms Order No. 68-4821)

SINGER, J. L. *The child's world of make-believe.* New York: Academic Press, 1973.

———. *The inner world of daydreaming.* New York: Harper & Row, 1975.

SKEELS, H. M. The mental development of children in foster homes. *Journal of Genetic Psychology,* 1936, *49,* 91–106.

———. Some Iowa studies of the mental growth of children in relation to differentials in the environment: A summary. In *Intelligence: Its nature and nurture.* 39th yearbook, Part II. Chicago: National Society for the Study of Education, University of Chicago Press, 1940, pp. 281–308.

———. Adult status of children with contrasting early life experiences. *Monographs of the Society for Research in Child Development,* 1966, *31* (3) , 1–65.

STANLEY, J. C. Accelerating the educational progress of intellectually gifted children. In

W. Dennis & M. W. Dennis (Eds.), *The intellectually gifted: An overview*. New York: Grune & Stratton, 1976, pp. 179–196.

———, KEATING, D. P., & FOX, L. H. *Mathematical talent: Discovery, description, and development*. Baltimore, Md.: The Johns Hopkins University Press, 1974.

STEVENSON, G. M. Implode. *Journal of Research and Development in Education*, 1971, *4* (3), 51–56.

STRANG, R. The nature of giftedness. In N. B. Henry (Ed.), *Education for the gifted*. Chicago: University of Chicago Press, 1958, pp. 64–86.

TABA, H., & ELKINS, D. *Teaching strategies for the culturally disadvantaged*. Chicago: Rand McNally & Co., 1966.

TAYLOR, C. W. The creative individual: A new portrait in giftedness. *Educational Leadership*, 1960, *18*, 7–12.

———. Finding the creative. *Science Teacher*, 1961, *28*, 593–606.

———. Some possible relations between communication abilities and creative abilities. In C. W. Taylor & F. Barron (Eds.), *Scientific creativity: Its recognition and development*. New York: John Wiley & Sons, Inc., 1963, pp. 365–371.

———. Be talent developers as well as knowledge dispensers. *Today's Education*, 1968, *57* (9), 67–69.

———. Developing effectively functioning people—the accountable goal of multiple talent teaching. *Education*, 1974, *94*, 99–111.

——— et al. *Explorations in the measurement and prediction of contributions of one sample of scientists*. USAF Personnel Research Laboratory Report No. ASD-TR-61-96. Lackland Air Force Base, Texas: USAF Personnel Research Laboratory, 1961.

———, LLOYD, B., & ROLLINS, J. Developing multiple talents in classrooms through the implementation of research. *Journal of Research and Development in Education*, 1971, *4* (3), 42–50.

TERMAN, L. M. *Mental and physical traits of a thousand gifted children*. Stanford, Calif.: Stanford University Press, 1925.

———. The discovery and encouragement of exceptional talent. *American Psychologist*, 1954, *9*, 221–230.

THURSTONE, L. L. Primary mental abilities. *Psychometric Monographs*, 1938, *1*, 1–121.

TORRANCE, E. P. Personality dynamics of under-self-evaluation among intellectually gifted college freshmen. In E. P. Torrance (Ed.), *Talent and education*. Minneapolis: University of Minnesota Press, 1960, pp. 165–172.

———. *Guiding creative talent*. Englewood Cliffs, N.J.: Prentice-Hall, Inc., 1962.

———. *Education and the creative potential*. Minneapolis: University of Minnesota Press, 1963.

———. *Rewarding creative behavior*. Englewood Cliffs, N.J.: Prentice-Hall, Inc., 1965.

———. *The Torrance tests of creative thinking*. (Research Edition) Lexington, Mass.: Personnel Press, 1966.

———. The Minnesota studies of creative behavior: National and international extensions. *Journal of Creative Behavior*, 1967, *1*, 137–154. (a)

———. Examples and rationales of test tasks for assessing creative behavior. *Journal of Creative Behavior*, 1968, *2*, 165–178.

———. Predictive validity of the Torrance Tests of Creative Thinking. *Journal of Creative Behavior*, 1972, *6*, 236–252. (a)

———. Career patterns and peak creative achievements of high school students twelve years later. *Gifted Child Quarterly*, 1972, *16*, 75–88. (b)

———. Non-test indicators of creative talent among disadvantaged children. *Gifted Child Quarterly*, 1973, *17*, 3–9.

———. *The Torrance tests of creative thinking*. (Revised) Lexington, Mass.: Personnel Press, 1974.

———. *Discovering and using the strengths of the disadvantaged and culturally different in career education.* Athens, Ga.: Career Education Project, College of Education, University of Georgia, 1976. (a)

————. Today's students' images of the future. Paper presented to the Eighth Western Symposium on Learning, Western Washington State College, Bellingham, Washington, October 8, 1976. (b)

————. Career education and the gifted and talented: Images of the future. Paper presented to the Commissioner's National Conference on Career Education, Houston, Texas, November 9, 1976. (c)

————. *Discovery and nurturance of giftedness in the culturally different.* Reston, Va.: Council for Exceptional Children, 1977.

————, BRUCH, C. B., & MORSE, J. A. Improving predictions of the adult creative achievement of girls by using autobiographical information. *Gifted Child Quarterly,* 1973, *17,* 91–95.

————, DAUW, D. C. Mental health problems of three groups of highly creative high school seniors. *Gifted Child Quarterly,* 1965, *9,* 123–127f.

————, & KHATENA, J. Originality of imagery in identifying creative talent in music. *Gifted Child Quarterly,* 1969, *8,* 3–8.

United States Commissioner of Education. *Education of the gifted and talented.* (Report to the Congress of the United States) Washington, D.C.: U.S. Government Printing Office, 1972.

VAUGHAN, M. M. Test of musical creativity. Victoria, B. C., Canada, 1971. (Unpublished manuscripts and videotapes)

————, KHATENA, J., & CUNNINGTON, B. F. *Thinking creatively with sounds and words.* Lexington, Mass.: Personnel Press/Ginn and Company, 1973.

WALLACH, M. A., & KOGAN, N. *Modes of thinking in young children: A study of the creativity-intelligence distinction.* New York: Holt, Rinehart & Winston, Inc., 1965.

————, & WING, C. W., JR. *The talented student: A validation of the creativity-intelligence distinction.* New York: Holt, Rinehart & Winston, Inc., 1969.

WERBLO, D., & TORRANCE, E. P. Experiences in historical research and changes in self evaluations of gifted children. *Exceptional Children,* 1966, *33,* 137–141.

WHIMBEY, A., & WHIMBEY, L. S. *Intelligence can be taught.* New York: E. P. Dutton & Co., Inc., 1975.

WILLIAMS, F. E. *Classroom ideas for encouraging thinking and feeling.* Englewood Cliffs, N.J.: Educational Technology Publications, 1970.

WITT, G. *The life enrichment activity program: A brief history* (mimeographed) . New Haven, Conn.: LEAP, Inc., 1968.

————. The life enrichment activity program, inc.: A continuing program for creative, disadvantaged children. *Journal of Research and Development in Education,* 1971, *4* (3), 67–73.

WITTY, P. A. How to identify the gifted. *Childhood Education,* 1953, *29,* 313.

WOLFLE, D. *The discovery of talent.* Cambridge, Mass.: Harvard University Press, 1969.

12 The Psychological Characteristics of Children with Learning Disabilities

William M. Cruickshank

Ph.D., Director, Institute for the Study of Mental Retardation
and Related Disabilities, Professor of Maternal and Child
Health, Professor of Psychology, Professor of Education.

James L. Paul

Ed.D., Professor of Education, Chairman, Division of Special
Education, School of Education, University of North Carolina.

No presentation of the psychological characteristics of learning disabled children would be complete without specific acknowledgment of the confusion surrounding the term *learning disabled*. This chapter might have been titled "Psychological Characteristics of Brain-Damaged Children," or "The Psychological Characteristics of Perceptually Handicapped Chilren," or "The Psychological Characteristics of Brain-Injured Children" as in an earlier edition of this book. Any one of more than forty labels that have been used interchangeably to designate these children could have been used. The words *brain, damage, neurological, injury, organic, minimal, disorder, learning, disability, handicap,* and others have been used in a variety of combinations. Russian literature often refers to this same group as "children with temporary psychological retardation" (Wozniak, 1975).

TERMINOLOGY AND LABELS

In 1964 a task force, cosponsored by the National Society for Crippled Children and Adults, Inc., and the National Institute of Neurological Diseases and Blindness of the National Institutes of Health, was appointed to study the issues of terminology and identification. A report (Clements, 1966, p. 9) of the work of this task force, which adopted the term *minimal brain dysfunction,* included the following statement:

A review of selected literature revealed a total of 38 terms used to describe or distinguish the conditions grouped as minimal brain dysfunction in the absence of findings severe enough to warrant inclusion in an established category, e.g., cerebral palsies, mental subnormalities, sensory defects. Several methods of grouping these terms are possible, such as:

Group 1-Organic Aspects

Association Deficit Pathology

Organic Brain Disease

Organic Brain Damage

Organic Brain Dysfunction

Minimal Brain Damage

Diffuse Brain Damage

Neurophrenia

Organic Driveness

Cerebral Dysfunction

Organic Behavior Disorder

Choreiform Syndrome

Minor Brain Damage

Minimal Brain Injury

Minimal Chronic Brain Syndromes

Minimal Cerebral Damage

Minimal Cerebral Palsy

Cerebral Dys-synchronization Syndrome

Group II-Segment or Consequence

Hyperkinetic Behavior Syndrome

Character Impulse Disorder

Hyperkinetic Impulse Disorder

Aggressive Behavior Disorder

Psychoneurological Learning Disorders

Hyperkinetic Syndrome

Dyslexia

Hyperexcitability Syndrome

Perceptual Cripple

Primary Reading Retardation

Specific Reading Disability

Clumsy Child Syndrome

Hypokinetic Syndrome

Perceptually Handicapped

Aphasoid Syndrome

Learning Disabilities

Conceptually Handicapped

Attention Disorders

Interjacent Child.

Cruickshank (1966, pp. 10–18) convened a distinguished panel of professional leaders who had had specific interest in these children and suggested that they address themselves to the question, among others, of labels. There was, predictably, reasonable professional defense for several of the labels already listed. In addition, the term, *developmental imbalances,* was suggested by Gallagher at this meeting.

It was recognized by this group as by previous groups that no single term would serve all purposes. Cruickshank suggested that in the absence of a completely adequate label, the term *brain-injured* be used.

This label did not satisfy all the logical criteria required for a label, but it was hoped that it might be used to obtain a professional meeting of the minds until a more generally acceptable label could be adopted. For those who for good reasons preferred other labels, at least the general characteristics of the children being discussed would be understood and planning discussions could proceed. This has not occurred. In 1963 learning disabilities was put forward and adopted, still an unsatisfactory term.

Other labels have been suggested since 1966, each failing to unify professional opinion. Nellhaus (1968, p. 536), for example, suggests the term *dyssynchronous child* as being more generic and providing a better basis for communication between parents and professionals. Cruickshank (1977) suggests that from a psychoeducational perspective, the most accurate term would be to describe these pupils as children or youth with *perceptual processing deficits*—an issue to be described more fully later.

The problem of terminology should not be considered simply a semantic lag, an annoying hang-up in the interest of a better name, which will placate the idiosyncrasies of different disciplines and interest groups. The issue is grossly oversimplified if one assumes that the existing conceptualizations of etiology and the complex learning and behavior problems presented by this group of children are waiting for a uniting banner or a magical solution to the difficult problems by the genius of a better name. The hard-core problems are conceptual and empirical. The energy dissipated in disagreement over a name for the child may serve to keep the child in the corridors waiting for a more adequate treatment or educational program. This is not to suggest that terminology is unimportant. We often act, however, as though the resolution of problems lies primarily in the clarification of language. If we could find the correct label, then it follows that we could in some important sense advance in treating these children. This lies rather in the clarification of concepts, their accurate description, and their social consequences. A more acceptable label may well communicate our solution; it will never be the solution.

The ultimate resolution of the terminology issue, like that of definition, must satisfy certain criteria. The task force (Clements, 1966, p. 8) on terminology and definition states that certain professional and interest groups with their own built-in criteria must be satisfied: clinicians, researchers, other professionals, and parents. Cruickshank (1966, pp. 17–18) indicated that a definition should include the concepts of etiology, developmental imbalances, ego problems, and interdisciplinary interest. Obviously, a satisfactory label would be judged by its adequacy to reflect these issues and, at a minimum, to not exclude by implication one of these aspects. An example of exclusion by implication would be a strictly medical label, such as brain damage, which might not suggest an interdisciplinary point of view and consequently could exclude the non-medical interest, such as that of teachers.

One aspect of the terminology question is essentially phenomenological. It is useful to distinguish between the act of naming what is seen or what is thought to be seen or what is decided upon as the salient view. Elementary concerns in a philosophy of science ought to force a rejection of the assumption that a one-to-one correspondence exists between what is there and what we see as being there. This is at the center of the interdisciplinary question and the implications for terminology. Whether a reductionistic psychological point of view or an existential psychological perspective is utilized makes an important difference in the kind of reality under consideration. The assumptions, the priorities of interest, the view of man, the rules for discovery, and so forth are different. Similarly, the

language for describing and explaining is different.

Professional groups only partially represent the different philosophic orientations. There is much overlap. Rhodes (1966), Hewett (1968, pp. 8–41), and Bateman (1967) have described these orientations. They may be grouped in terms of the psychoanalytic, behavioral, neurosensory or communicative, and ecological.

The way in which a disability is named, described, explained, and treated usually betrays the set of assumptions we employ and the general view we accept as most valid or useful. The reader should recognize that these are not pure or mutually exclusive positions but rather represent general philosophic stances. The learning-disabled child has been named, described, and treated as such primarily within the neurosensory or communication frame of reference. This point of view is essentially the basis of discussion in this chapter. It provides a specific view of the child as a receiver and processor of stimuli with consequent behavioral acts or responses. The adequacy of these perceptual and perceptual-motor acts are the specific clinical concerns. Treatment is specified in terms of work with the specific dysfunction. There is not complete agreement in the field as to whether the clinician or teacher identifies and exploits the appropriately engaged processes or whether he focuses specifically on the disabled or disengaged processes. Similarly, there is some difference in professional opinion as to whether the child is viewed and worked with as a whole or unity, or whether he is viewed as a complex interaction of parts, some of which are working appropriately and some of which are not.

The neuro-sensory position has two aspects: descriptive and explanatory. The descriptive aspect focuses upon the process of describing, in objective behavioral terms as much as possible, the abilities and disabilities of the child. The explanatory aspect is more difficult. Explanations are postulated in terms of the integrity of the central nervous system. The distinction between description and explanation is essentially the same as the distinction between what and why.

The phenomenological question is no less relevant in the more apparent aspect of describing the behavior. It is, however, the explanatory aspect that is more difficult in terms of empirical defense. It is this aspect that provided the basis for many of the labels applied to these children; for example, brain damage, brain injury, and so forth. Explanations or attempts to formulate answers to the questions of cause have always been difficult in the behavioral sciences. With human behavior we do not have the kind of freedom in experimental design to deal effectively with the question of causality. Behavioral data is based, for the most part, on correlational analyses. It should be noted, however, that even with freedom in design to control and manipulate experimental variables, the philosophic issues of causality would still be extremely difficult to manage.

For the most part, our understanding of disabilities is based on experimental laboratory research with animals and studies of adults, much of which is based on studies of casualties in wars. Neither of these translates directly to children. The study of learning disabilities in children, their characteristics, and their treatment is very new compared to the other disability groups described in this volume. Much of the original work was with captive institutionalized retarded residents.

The importance of labels should not be underestimated. The academic concern is only one aspect, perhaps even the least important in terms of the child. Different labels have different public meanings and associations. They do communicate something to the parent, the teacher, the neighbor, the minister, and the child, who will hear the label eventually assigned. The label

affects what is expected of the child, elicits feelings in the adult about the child, often even before the child and the adult have interacted, and can subvert the child's chance to interact as a child with an adult who chooses to interact with the child as being learning disabled, in which case the child is the victim of whatever myths, fantasies, or associations that adult may have about brain injury and related learning problems. The whole issue of expectancy is extremely important. The influence value of the researcher on the outcomes of his work is one way of thinking about the determinate influence of the teacher on the outcomes of her teaching. The outcomes of the former are expressed in data terms. The latter are expressed in human-life terms, that is, educational gains of students.

The expectancy phenomenon is not new to literature on experimental design. The Hawthorne effect, for example, was described by Roethlisberger and Dickson in 1939. More recently, the work of Rosenthal and Jacobson (1968) has dealt specifically with the question of teacher expectancy on pupil gain. They concluded that "teachers' favorable expectations can be responsible for gains in their pupils' IQs and, for the lower grades, that these gains can be quite dramatic" (p. 98).

Their work has been seriously questioned (Barber & Silver, 1968a, 1968b; Snow, 1969; Thorndike, 1968). The criticisms have been leveled primarily in terms of measurement and data analysis questions. Thorndike (1968) who considered the Rosenthal and Jacobson study "so defective technically that one can only regret that it ever got beyond the eyes of the original investigators!" went on to point out in his review that "the general reasonableness of the 'self-fulfilling prophecy effect' is not at issue." He concluded, "the indications are that the basic data upon which this structure has been raised are so untrustworthy that any conclusions based upon them must be suspect. The conclusions may be correct, but if so it must be considered a fortunate coincidence" (p. 711).

Snow (1969), who raised serious measurement and data analysis questions and suggested that Rosenthal and Jacobson may be guilty of the bias they describe, further indicated that "teacher expectancy may be a powerful phenomenon which, if understood, could be used to gain much of positive value in education."

The salient point for the present writing is that, in the opinion of the authors, teacher expectancy is a real phenomenon and possibly never more dramatically evident than in the teacher-handicapped child relationship. The extent to which the labels we assign communicates what is to be expected of a child indicates the seriousness of the issue. This is not easily rationalized by supposedly positive statements such as, "we reduce our expectations to what is more reasonable in terms of the child's abilities." The child's abilities and disabilities are appropriately communicated by a careful and thorough diagnosis, not a label. The label communicates a total picture of all the retarded, the emotionally disturbed, the brain-injured, and so forth. This total picture is never a portrait of the individual child.

The hazards of expectancy and labels are not limited to the public without relevant professional training. Gallagher (1966, p. 27) has suggested that professionals, who sit around the conference table representing different disciplinary points of view, often relax when the results of their different evaluations of the child are brought together and a label is selected and agreed upon. In such an instance, the label might be expected to do what only the diagnosis can do. It might be expected to communicate what only the complete diagnostic study could communicate.

Trippe (1966), writing about the emotionally disturbed child, has suggested that the purpose of the label is often to get the child somewhere. This is not less true of the retarded, the learning disabled, or any other special child. Clinical evaluations of children generally are initiated following the child's exhibition of his incompetence or his noncompliance with certain performance standards or regulations. This is always in a context or a system that has a purpose and a set of expectations and values. When there are resistances or experienced frustration—that is, the incompetent, the incompatible, the incongruous, the non-compliant, and so forth. The alternatives in terms of modifying the system in which the stress or the concern is experienced are almost never as well developed.

This is most clearly evident in the public school system. Hence, the question What is to be done with the child? is answered by a pursuit of an answer to the question What is wrong with the child? or Why does he act that way? or Why can he not learn? An alternative set of questions might involve the appropriateness of the teaching methods and materials, what is wrong with the teaching space, the teacher, and so forth. Whereas the most honest appraisals involve answers that reflect an interaction of these two sets, the relevant point here has to do with the purpose of labeling which goes beyond academic questions of accuracy.

The implications of labels are profound for parents. Some labels subtly communicate parental responsibility—not because of the label but the parents' associations with it. The term "emotionally disturbed" is a good example. Many parents have read popular journal articles and books written for lay consumption on the psychosexual development of children. Their translations of these concepts are within the guilt and concern and disturbed relationships that already exist.

Another communication is that of futility. Brain injury or damage communicates irreversibility which may be construed that little or nothing can be done. Rappaport (1966) has attacked the irreversibility notion from an ego psychological (not neurological) point of view. The label, however, is neurological in its reference and, consequently, in the associations it generates.

Learning disabilities, however, as a term, while focusing the problem on the school's responsibilities, provides confusion to those who are unaware of its historical antecedents, and often is used synonymously with remediation.

The concept of degree has been reflected in labels by the use of the word *minimal*. Cruickshank (1966, p. 13; 1967, pp. 5–6) has criticized this concept because the psychological problems are anything but minimal, and also because of the fact that injury either exists or it does not. The concept of minimal distorts the picture. Birch (1964, p. 5) similarly pointed out that minimal, as a descriptive adjective, does not increase the descriptive accuracy or add to the validity or utility of terms such as "brain injury," "brain damage," or learning disabilities.

The concept of the brain-damaged child has been used to indicate a pattern or set of patterns of behavioral aberrance. Birch (1964, pp. 3–11) and others have criticized this concept because of the problem of evidence with reference to the question of causality. There are children with learning disabilities who manifest the patterns of behavior associated with brain injury or brain damage who cannot be diagnosed with the procedures and instruments available as in fact having an injury to the brain. Also, there are children who have diagnosable injury who do not display the behavioral pattern. The position is argued both ways, and solid empirical support is yet to be obtained for either. The relevant immediate point is that brain damage is applied to some children in which there is no demonstrable damage to the brain. Using the label in this way rests on the assumption that aberrations in the normal functions of the central nervous system become manifest in certain patterns of behavior and learning. Hence, the existence of such patterns which, some (for example,

Cruickshank 1966, pp. 13–14; Cruickshank, 1967a, pp. 3–4; Strauss and Kephart, 1955, pp. 41–42) have argued, are symptomatic of injury or damage to the brain. When such injury is not verified in clinical assessment of learning disabled children, it is assumed to be due to the lack of sophistication and precision in our methods and procedures.

It may be argued, and many have done so (Bateman, 1964; Hanvik, 1966; Hewett, 1968, p. 77), that the question is academic. In settings where the pragmatic concern dominates, such as in a classroom where the teacher is faced with the decision as to what will be done in teaching the child how to read, the behavioral characteristics are obviously the most crucial. That is, the fact that a child is reversing figure and background and that he perseverates is much more important to the teacher in teaching the child to read than the most basic cause of these behaviors. The child may in fact have suffered insult to the brain, but it is not this fact that answers the practical methodologic question. This kind of rationale has precipitated the use of such labels as learning disabled. Some (Hanvik, 1966) have suggested that the child should be described behaviorally and not labeled. This is not to say that the question of cause is in any sense unimportant. It is to suggest that the setting in which the child is identified and eventually labeled has something to do with the label, has some implications for the relevant action to be taken and who is most responsible for taking that action.

More than a decade after the 1966 Task Force report (Clements), the problem of terminology is still with us. Indeed with the advent of the term *learning disabilities,* the issue has become much more confused and the literature more cluttered with the personal terminology of authors recently arrived on the scene with little or no perspective regarding either the historical antecedents to this problem of child growth

and development or of the neurophysiological and resulting neuropsychological
problems central to the issue.

We have stated elsewhere (Cruickshank,
1977, 1978) that learning disabilities, exactly defined, are the manifestations of more
elusive problems of perceptual processing
deficits which may impact on one, several,
or all of the sensory modalities. The student who has been well-founded in the
psychology of perception is well aware that
perceptual processing is not a function in
and of itself, but is a function inherent in
the central nervous system. It is this assumption which Wepman and his associates recognized in defining learning disabilities (1975). Paraphrasing, restating, and
expanding the Wepman Committee definition, *learning disabilities can be defined*
(from the point of view of a psycho-educa-
tional orientation) *as resulting from perceptual processing deficits which are in
turn the result of a malfunction in some
aspect of the central nervous system. Learning disabilities may occur in a child or
youth of any age, of any intellectual level,
and be of widely diversified etiologies.* We
emphasize, as others have done, that learning disabilities and mental retardation are
not synonymous terms, but we emphasize that
there are many mentally retarded children
and youth who have perceptual processing
deficits and are, therefore, *mentally retarded
children with learning disabilities.* To ignore this fact and to classify all learning
disabled children as being within the normal limits of intelligence, as is frequently
done, is to ignore research, history, and
logic. This problem is to be found at all
levels of intelligence, and is a respector of
no single group of young people.

Discrimination, Memory,
and Sequencing

The Wepman Committee (1975), in defining children with learning disabilities
(See also Cruickshank, 1978), pointed out

that these were children and youth with a
pronounced inability to discriminate fine
differences between the "orthographic forms
used in reading and writing and sounds
used in speech." The committee members
further indicate that once discrimination
is made, these same subjects also have deficiencies in both long- and short-term memory. If both discrimination and memory
are under control, the child may be unable
to sequence that which is discriminated
and remembered into a socially acceptable
response or action. There is little question
in the minds of these present writers that
such disability manifestations are related
to the pervasive impact of sensory hyperactivity and over-responsiveness to stimuli
which almost universally characterize children and youth with perceptual processing
deficits and resultant learning disabilities.

Lability of Affect

Hirt (1964) refers to this as "an emotional instability in which the child over-
reacts to minimal stimulation either by an
inordinately intense or mobile response. For
example, upon accomplishing a task at
which she had been working for several
days, a 10-year-old girl burst into tears accompanied by loud sobs. Another example
is an 11-year-old boy who begins to giggle
and speak rapidly as soon as he feels un-
sure of himself" (p. 52). Morse discussed
this also in connection with his analysis of
the life-space interview as applied to children and youth with learning disabilities
(1976).

Motor Dysfunction
and Disinhibition

This refers to difficulties in both gross
and fine motor movement. These problems
are considered by Rappaport and his associates from the point of view of segmenta-
tion and inadequate laterality and directionality. The former is "the inability to

move one's body or its parts in a synchronized and integrated fashion" (Hirt, 1964). The latter refers to problems in crossing the body midline, reversals of figures, and lack of discrimination of left from right.

Motor dysfunction and perceptual dysfunction of a sensory nature are closely related. As a matter of fact, the former may be the result of the latter, except in those instances where major motor problems resulting from brain damage cause cerebral palsy. In the area of learning disabilities, however, we are dealing with a psychological process based on neurological dysfunction, i.e., the inability of the child to refrain from reacting to stimuli. Stimuli which result in a gross-motor response can be equally as distracting to the learner as when the child responds in an uncontrolled manner to visual, auditory, tactile, or stimuli involving other sensory modalities. Disinhibition and distractibility result, and failure experiences are constantly observed in the child.

The present writers consider distractability to be the more central of the above characteristics. Rappaport's characteristics of hyperactivity, disinhibition, impulsivity, and perseveration may all be explained, to some extent, by the child's distractibility, that is, his inability to filter out extraneous stimuli and focus selectively on a task. Cruickshank (1967*b*, pp. 252–253; See also 1977) gives the following example:

It can be argued, however, that hyperactivity, as Rappaport describes it, is a function of hyperdistractibility and that disinhibition and impulsivity are also manifestations of the same factors, namely, the inability of the child to refrain from reaction to extraneous external or internal stimuli is a characteristic of the brain-injured (perceptual processing deficit) which has been commented upon frequently by many writers. Werner and Strauss (1942) often refer to this phenomenon. It is called being "stimulus-bound" (tied to stimuli) by Homberger (1926). Others have mentioned a "drive" to respond to unessential stimuli.

Goldstein (1939) speaks of the behavior as hyperactivity in the face of being unable to do other than to react to stimuli on an unselective basis. Dolphin and Cruickshank (1951) report this factor an essential one in the inability of their large groups of spastic and athetoid cerebral palsy children to function in a variety of experimental test situations (Cruickshank, 1967*b*, pp. 252–253).

Although the statement of the problem by Cruickshank and his associates is perhaps the more parsimonious, there is no real fundamental difference among these authors on this matter. It is largely a matter of semantics. They view the same behavioral characteristics from slightly different perspectives.

STUDIES OF INADEQUATE IMPULSE CONTROL IN CHILDREN WITH LEARNING DISABILITIES*

Williams, Gieseking, and Lubin (1961) compared groups of normal, dull normal, and brain-injured subjects using the Block Design Rotation Test (Shapiro, 1951). It was found that, under conditions of reduced peripheral cues, the normals and dull normals rotate the figures more but the brain-injured group rotate less. It is hypothesized, by the authors, that with the reduction of peripheral cues there is also a reduction of

* Undoubtedly the most complete review of the literature related to learning disabilities, from both psychological and educational points of view, is included in *Perceptual and Learning Disabilities in Children* (Syracuse, Syracuse University Press, 1975), Vol. 1, *Psychoeducational Procedures;* Vol. 2, *Research and Theory,* W. M. Cruickshank and D. P. Hallahan (Eds.). The reader is referred to this source, the contents of which will not be extensively reviewed in this chapter because of limitations of space. Therein, however, the reader will find exceedingly complete chapters by more than twenty international authorities on most topics germane to children and youth with learning disabilities.

distracting stimuli. Thus, when the range of possible distracting stimuli is reduced, the brain-injured subject is better able to focus his attention on the more essential stimuli. *It is important to note that what prove to be extraneous stimuli for the brain-injured are actually an aid to the non-brain-injured groups.* They are able to integrate the additional information from the peripheral cues and this lessens their tendency to rotate; whereas this extra information is a burden for the brain-injured subjects and leads them to errors in rotation. These and the authors included below, refer to the "brain-injured" as Cruickshank originally did; that is, corresponding to the child with perceptual processing deficits whose deficits result in learning disabilities.

Other authors (Garfield, Benton, & MacQueen, 1966) compared a group of brain-injured children with a group of familial retarded children, matched for age and IQ, on eight tasks of "motor impersistence." The eight tasks were: keeping the eyes closed; protruding the tongue, both blindfolded and with eyes open; fixation of gaze in lateral visual fields; keeping the mouth open; fixation on the examiner's nose during confrontation testing; head turning during sensory testing; and holding a prolonged "ahh" sound. It was found that the brain-injured children performed significantly poorer than the familials on all but the last two of the eight tasks. In both groups, there was a greater tendency for the young subject (Ss) to be impersistent. No relationship between motor impersistency and IQ was found. Because the investigators included only those brain-injured Ss with no apparent damage to the muscles involved in the tasks, it may be concluded that the brain-injured Ss were displaying disturbances of a central nature.

Rosvold *et al.* (1956) compared three groups on a continuous performance test (CPT): Defective Group, brain-damaged and familials; Child Group, brain-damaged and normals; Adult Group, brain-damaged and normals. Analysis of covariance was performed in order to control for significant age difference between the child subgroups and significant IQ difference between the adult subgroups. The CPT allowed S to choose his own time to respond and required a high level of continuous concentration. There were two tasks: X Task–letters were presented approximately every 0.92 second. Every time an X was presented, the S was to press a response key. AX Task–S was to respond to an X every time it was presented after an A. The results indicated that the brain-injured Ss perform poorer than the non-brain-injured Ss. This difference is greater on the more complex AX Task and between the two children subgroups.

Rosvold notes that it has been shown that brain-injured Ss generally show either random bursts of hypersynchronous activity or a general hypersynchrony on their EEGs. The authors suggest that if hypersynchrony is associated with reduced attention, as suggested by its presence in sleep, then hypersynchrony might be an indication of inattention when an individual is awake. The authors admit that this is only a hypothesis and that this study does not really measure this directly. What would be needed is a measure of the Ss EEG while he is responding to such a vigilance task.

Schulman *et al.* (1965) found in a study of brain-injured children that the level of total day activity did not correlate significantly with any of the diagnostic or behavioral clusters of brain damage. These authors are convinced that the majority of brain-injured children have total activity levels, as measured by an actometer, that are similar to normal children. However, in a highly social situation which requires the child to prescribe to rigid rules of behavior, the brain-injured child becomes either hypoactive (he overcompensates for his not being able to control his behavior) or hyperactive. The Ss in this study became hypoactive, but the authors suggest that this was probably due to selection by the school from which they were drawn. To summarize, no evidence was found that hyperactivity is a correlate of brain injury except in highly socially structured situations (for example, a testing situation). Distractibility, however, did correlate significantly with measures of brain injury.

Activity was measured by means of an instrument called an actometer. This instrument consists of an automatically winding calendar wrist watch modified so that there is direct drive from pendulum to hands. The amount of "time" recorded on the watch indicates the amount of activity the child undergoes. Each child wore two actometers, one on the wrist and one on the ankle, both on the dominant side. The validity and reliability of this instrument have been demonstrated.

There were four different tests of distractibility:

1. The Clock Test. Briefly, this test consists of a toy mouse, a piece of cheese, and a mousetrap attached to a clock. S's task was to allow the mouse to reach the cheese, which was placed at position twenty-two, but to push a lever to return the mouse to the start before it reached the mouse-trap affixed to a position between positions twenty-three and thirty-two.

2. The Box Test. Three boxes each with a figure of a different color and shape painted on the front (red circle, yellow triangle, and blue square) were placed before S. At varying intervals, E exposed a hand puppet to view above one of the boxes. The child was to name, by shape, color, or position, which box the puppet came from after each time it was shown.

3. The Card Test. Two hundred cards were shown to each S at one-second intervals. On 180 of the cards, there was a picture of a rabbit. Interspersed randomly were 20 cards with a picture of a baby. S was to indicate whenever he saw a "baby" card.

4. The Tone Test. Twenty-five tones of 2,000 cycles per second were randomly dis-

tributed among 50 tones of 750 cycles per second. The interval between tones was varied throughout the tape. S's task was to raise his hand whenever he heard a 2,000 cps tone.

Each of the above tests was administered to each S twice. On one administration there was an external distractor and on the other administration there was not. The external distractor for the Clock and Box tests was a tape recording of Winnie the Pooh. On the card and tone tests, a sound track of a Yogi Bear cartoon and another reading from Winnie the Pooh served as the distractors.

Thus, the measure of hyperactivity used by Schulman *et al.* is primarily a measure of gross motor activity, whereas the measures of distractibility are concerned with the S's ability to concentrate and attend to a task. The finding that distractibility correlated with brain-injury, whereas hyperactivity did not, lent support to the contention of the present authors, mentioned earlier, that distractibility is the more central of the two characteristics.

Cruse (1961) compared brain-injured and familial (endogenous) children matched for MA and CA on a reaction-time task under low stimuli and distractible conditions. The highly distracting condition consisted of a room filled with balloons, toys, and a mirror. No differences in reaction time performances were found between the two groups. However, he further subdivided the brain-injured group. Brain-injured children with "determinate" and known etiologies were compared with children whose brain injury was considered definitely prenatal but with no differentiating clinical characteristics. The brain-injured Ss with known etiologies were more distractible (that is, had slower reaction times) than the group with unknown etiologies or the familial group of subjects. Both groups, the determinate brain-injured and familial, benefited the same amount from the reduction of the external distractions.

In terms of the possible neurological

pulse control, many authors have suggested cerebral inhibition (Birch, Belmont, & Karp, 1965; Eisenberg, 1964; Paine, 1966). For example, Eisenberg (1964), although he presents no data on the subject, states the following:

Pathways from cortex to reticular system provide for cortico-reticulo-inhibition. In this way, signals arriving at a primary receptive zone can initiate a depression of response in other cortical zones. Interference with these precisely interdigitated inhibitory systems might very well be the basis for the attention deficits observed in so-called minimal brain damage, in which no gross lesion with motor or sensory consequences can be identified (p. 64).

Birch and his associates conducted a study of brain-injured adults that has significance for children, particularly in terms of a hypothesis that distractibility is due to defects in cortical inhibition. It was shown that brain-injured Ss, when presented with two tones of equal intensity 3 seconds apart, underestimated the loudness of the second tone in contrast to the non-brain-injured Ss who tended to overestimate the second tone or say the two tones were equal. As the interval between the two tones was increased, the brain-injured Ss gradually approached normal levels of responsiveness until at 9 seconds they were responding as the non–brain-injured did at the 3-second interval. Thus, the first tone seems to be interfering with the judgment of the second tone. The neural impulses to be fired by the second tone seem to be inhibited by the neural impulses fired by the first tone. The authors suggest that this prolonged inhibition in the subject with the brain-injury is due to a defect in the recovery mechanisms of the reticulo-cortical system or changes in the rate of decay or spread of inhibition of a local excitation.

The above findings are quite interesting in that, at first glance, they go counter to what might be expected of the brain-injured

group. It would seem, as the interval between the two tones is increased, that there would be more chance for the brain-injured S to become distracted from the task. Instead, an increase in interval leads to a level of responsiveness indistinguishable from that of the normal S.

It would be interesting to conduct a developmental study of this task on normal children and children with perceptual processing deficits in order, first of all, to see if the results above found with brain-injured adults could be replicated with children. Secondly, a developmental study would allow one to determine whether the effects of the increased interval were peculiar only to adult Ss with perceptual deficits or whether younger normal Ss would also respond in the same way.

Numerous investigators have noted that the learning disabled individual's impulsive, hyperactive behavior tends to diminish with time (Menkes, Rowe, & Menkes, 1967; Pincus & Glasser, 1966; Rappaport, 1965). They all agree that by adolescence there is considerable likelihood that the "brain-injured child" will no longer manifest extremely hyperactive behavior.

Menkes, Rowe, and Menkes (1967) conducted a follow-up study on individuals 14 years to 27 years (X = 24 years) after they had originally been seen in a clinic and had been described as displaying hyperkinetic behavior and neurological abnormalities. The follow-up study revealed that only three of the original fourteen Ss were still hyperactive. The disappearance of hyperactivity had occurred between the ages of 8 and 21 in the others.

Cruickshank, in following up on a group of severely hyperactive and learning disabilities children with whom he worked when they were 7, 8, and 9 years of age, finds no evidence of hyperactivity insofar as gross behavior is concerned when they are 12 years older, that is, 19–22 years old.

Rappaport (1965) asserts that psychological and educational concern for these children should not decrease as the hyperactive behavior decreases. He notes that hyperkinesis may decline with age, but also warns that, if proper educational measures are not provided early in this child's life, he may become antisocial.

Perseveration is another frequently observed psychological characteristic of the brain-injured child. Hunt and Patterson (1958), for example, in comparing brain injured and familial children matched for IQ, MA, CA, and sex, found that the brain-injured Ss perseverated more on an auditory-sequence task where the child was required to repeat a story told to him by the experimenter. Perseveration is included under "inadequate impulse control" by Rappaport. Perseveration, however, seems to be more of an independent psychological factor than the others already discussed under inadequate impulse control. As Cruickshank *et al.* (1961, pp. 7–8) state:

> Perseveration is the inability to shift with ease from one psychological activity to another. More precisely, it is the apparent inertia of the organism which retards a shift from one stimulus situation to another, and it results in a prolonged after-effect of a given stimulus to which the individual has made an adjustment. There is an overlap in time between a shift from an old situation to a new situation. As is the case with many other characteristics which have been mentioned, perseveration is not restricted solely to children with central nervous system disorders. While it may be observed frequently in such patients, it is also a characteristic of psychopathology in many other clinical groups. It is difficult to understand how perseveration could be related to hyperactivity and distractibility, although Werner and Strauss on one occasion intimated that this might be possible.
>
> Perseveration appears to be an independent psychological variable whose presence may impede learning in as significant a way as can distractibility in all of its various forms (1961, pp. 7–8; see also Cruickshank, 1977).

One might also think of perseveration as another manifestation of defective cortical inhibition, which was discussed above. For example, two different stimuli, A and B, impinge on the organism at Time 1 and Time 2, respectively. It might be hypothesized, following a prolongation of inhibition model, that Stimulus A fires a neural impulse which inhibits for an abnormal amount of time the firing of an impulse to Stimulus B. Thus, the response to the first stimulus remains salient for a longer period of time than normal. In other words, the child perseverates.

Figure-Ground Disturbances

Figure-ground disturbances may be characterized by any one or a combination of the following: (1) confusion of figure and background, (2) reversal of figure and background, (3) inability to see any difference between figure and background. This disturbance can be considered as closely related to those under inadequate impulse control. The brain-injured child is unable to attend to the figure. The background becomes highly distractible to the child and he is forced to respond to it. He is unable to selectively respond to the essential stimuli while filtering out the unessential stimuli.

This disturbance has been demonstrated with cerebral palsy children in the visual modality (Dolphin & Cruickshank, 1951a) and in the tactual sense (Dolphin & Cruickshank, 1952; Cruickshank, Bice, & Wallen, 1957).

This disturbance is also well documented in non–cerebral-palsied brain-injured children in both the tactual (Werner & Strauss, 1941) and the visual modalities (Vegas & Frye, 1963; Werner & Strauss, 1941). Vegas and Frye (1963) compared groups of brain-injured and familial retardates matched for MA on their abilities to name as many objects as possible in pictures containing nonhidden and hidden objects. Although the total response rate was much greater for the familials, there was a greater percentage of responses for hidden objects for the brain-injured children as compared to the familial children. Thus, the brain-injured child manifested a forced responsiveness to the hidden objects, that is, the background stimuli.

Birch and Lefford (1967) have obtained results which indicate that the ability to separate figure from background is of a developmental nature. They presented different age groups of children of above average intelligence with tasks that required them to copy geometric figures. In one condition, the geometric forms were presented on blank sheets of paper and the S was asked to draw the form on a separate blank sheet of paper. In another condition, the forms were presented on sheets of paper with a grid-line background and the child was also given a response sheet with these grid lines. It was found that the youngest group of children (5 years old) performed more poorly when the grid lines were presented than when the forms were presented on blank sheets of paper. The seven year and older groups of children, however, performed better when the grid lines were presented than when they were not. Apparently, the older children were able to use the extra structure provided by the guidelines whereas, perhaps because of figure-ground disturbance, the grid lines distracted the younger children.

Grube (1978), using the same figure-ground two-and-three dimensional slides as were employed by Cruickshank and Bice, has also found that figure discrimination is developmental in children between 4 and 8 years of age.

Visual-Motor Disturbances

Studies have shown that the brain-injured child, compared to the endogenous retarded and the normal child, has an impaired ability to coordinate the visual system and the motor system. This child, for example, is unable to draw what the eye sees. Thus, when asked to copy a figure,

his representation is a distortion of the true figure. One can also hypothesize that he draws what he sees all right, but what he sees is so distorted by cerebral disorganization that his drawing results in what to us is a distorted figure.

Frostig, Lefever, and Whittlesey (1961) compared a group of children with learning disabilities, many of whom were diagnosed as neurologically handicapped, with a group of normal children on five areas of visual perception—eye-motor coordination, constancy of form, figure-ground relationships, position in space, and spatial relations. They found that the overall perceptual quotient (PQ) obtained from these tests was lower for the group with probable brain damage. Frostig (1962) also found that the average PQ was significantly lower than the average IQ for those children with probable brain injury.

Bensberg (1950) found familials superior to brain-injured Ss on reproducing designs on a marble board task. The brain-injured children were characterized by their inability to construct the design as a totality. They had a tendency to jump from one part of the design to another. This mode of construction was first observed by Werner and Strauss (1939) and has been named "dissociation" by Cruickshank (1961). As noted previously (Cruickshank, 1961 and 1977), this characteristic is thought to be closely related to distractibility. Placing two boards, each containing one hundred holes, and a few dozen marbles in front of the child creates a highly stimulating and potentially distracting testing situation.

Bensberg (1952), among many others, has also found that children with perceptual-processing deficits are deficient in performance on the Bender Gestalt Test. This visual-motor test requires the child to copy various designs. He found that a group of familial retardates were more accurate in their reproductions than a group of perceptual processing deficit children (PPD). The latter children were characterized, in particular, by their tendency to reserve figures, repeat parts of the designs, and to use lines when dots were required.

Performance on visual-memory tests may also be included as indicators of visual-motor disturbances. When an individual is required to reproduce a design that was previously presented to him, he must be able to both remember what the design looked like and then be able to reproduce it using his visual-motor skills.

Cassel (1949) compared brain-injured and familial children, matched for MA and CA, on their abilities to reproduce geometric designs. The experimenter then asked these two groups of children to identify these same designs when seen in a different context. The familials and the brain-injured children did not differ in their ability to do this. It was therefore concluded by Cassel that lower scores of brain-injured subjects on reproduction from memory tasks must be interpreted with caution. The poorer performance may be due to an inability to express what has been apprehended. In other words, poor performance of brain-injured children in reproducing designs from memory may be due, in large part, to a visual-motor deficit rather than a memory deficit.

It is possible that, just as with the Marble Board Task discussed by Cruickshank (1961 and 1977), perceptually handicapped children studied in the aforementioned investigations perform poorly on copying and reproducing designs because they are distracted by extraneous stimuli and are unable to attend to the task. Although there are no doubt more extraneous stimuli presented to Ss in the Marble Board Task, some general concentration deficit may still be hindering their performance on tests like the Bender Gestalt Test.

Rowley and Baer (1963) attempted to determine the influence or lack of attention and concentration on performance on the Benton Visual Retention Test. Assuming that emotionally disturbed youngsters ex-

hibit the same lack of concentration as brain-injured children, they compared a group of each of these kinds of children matched for age and IQ. Grossly defective performances were displayed by 28 percent of the brain-injured group but by only 4 percent of the emotionally disturbed group. Rowley and Baer thus concluded that poor performance on the Benton Visual Retention Test is not caused by attention or concentration difficulties but by more specific disabilities; for example, visual-motor coordination, visual memory, and spatial relations.

That emotionally disturbed and brain-injured children display the same kind and degree of inattention, however, is an assumption that the present writers feel should be viewed with some caution.

More research is needed into the relative affects of distractibility and visual-motor defects in the poor performance of brain-injured children on visual-motor tasks. Until such research is done, distractibility should not be discounted as at least a partial determiner of such defective performance.

It has been noted by many that there are large individual differences in the scores of brain-injured children on the various visual-motor tests (Colman & Com, 1966; Hunt, 1959; Koppitz, 1962).

Colman and Com (1966) compared the performances of brain-injured, emotionally disturbed, and normal groups of children matched for age and IQ on the Marble Board Test and Ellis Visual Designs Test. They found that 10 of the 28 brain-injured Ss received 3 or more ratings of both incoherent procedure and linear organization on the Marble Board Test and scores of less than 4.5 on the Ellis Visual Designs Test. This was in sharp contrast to the other 2 groups where none of the Ss in either of these 2 groups scored this poorly. However, as Colman and Com point out, 18 of the 28 brain-injured children did not receive such poor scores, indicating that one should not attribute the same behavioral characteristics to all brain-injured children.

Hunt (1959) compared groups of familial and brain-injured children on their abilities to construct three-dimensional designs from pictures. In addition, the brain-injured group was further broken down into two subgroups depending, on the basis of observable behavior displayed in the classroom, on whether they had visual-motor problems or auditory problems. The brain-injured group with visual-motor deficits performed the poorest on the task. The brain-injured group that displayed severe auditory disturbances, however, obtained the highest scores on these visual-motor tasks. Such results should caution one from attempting to describe "a typical brain-injured child," particularly with respect to his visual-motor abilities.

Koppitz (1962) also concludes that, when attempting to diagnose brain injury, it is unwise to rely upon the performance score of only one test. She has observed, for instance, that some brain-injured children may score well on the Bender Gestalt Test by compensating for their difficulties. This is often done by taking an unusually long time to complete the test. Also, some may anchor the design with their hands while copying it; some trace the design with a finger first before attempting to copy it; some may even turn both the stimulus card and paper upside down and then draw the design in this way.

Such methods of attacking the task differ from those of normal children. In light of the evidence cited above that a score on a visual-motor test may not always discriminate the brain-injured from the non-brain-injured child, more attention should be given to the way in which the child goes about accomplishing the task. In other words, instead of considering only the quality of the finished product, research also needs to be focused on how the brain-injured child accomplishes this final product, whether it be equal in quality to that of the non-brain-injured child or not.

Visual-Perceptual Disturbances

Size-distance Judgment. Jenkin and Morse (1960) compared the abilities of brain-injured, mentally retarded adolescents; familial adolescents; normal adolescents and normal adults to make size-distance judgments. It was found that, whereas the latter three groups tended to overestimate, the brain-injured retarded subjects tended to underestimate the size of a distant object in comparison to a proximal object. In this respect, Jenkin and Morse point out that the brain-injured adolescents in this study perform similarly to the youngest children (7 to 8 years) in Piaget and Lambercier's study (1951) of normal children. Piaget and Lambercier found that the youngest group made judgments that fell short of size constancy and that their older groups, starting from eight to ten years, progressively overestimated the size of the object. It may thus be concluded that the brain-injured adolescents, in contrast to familial adolescents, have not proceeded beyond the developmental level of 7 or 8 years with respect to their ability to make size-distance judgments.

The authors conclude that the brain-injured Ss fail to combine several sources of information in making their judgments. It is pointed out that in making size-distance judgments, various depth cues and the integration of these with other sources of information (for example, size of the proximal stimulus) must be taken into account by the individual. The brain-injured S is unable to integrate this information and thus tends to be "stimulus bound."

Apparent Movement. When a person placed in a dark room is presented with a stationary point of light, he will perceive this light as moving. This is referred to as the "autokinetic phenomenon." It is generally accepted that this phenomenon has a cerebral rather than a retinal basis (Haggard & Rose, 1944; Werner & Thuma, 1942). Werner and Thuma employed exogenous versus endogenous educable mentally retarded subjects in their studies; the exogenous subjects being mentally retarded learning-disabilities subjects within the definition of learning disabilities included in this chapter.

Bennett and Port (1963) compared brain-injured and familial children matched for age and IQ on their abilities to detect autokinetic movement. There was little differentiation between the two groups with regard to the total amount of movement seen. The brain-injured Ss, however, reported that the light moved for much shorter periods of time and that they saw the light start and stop more frequently than the familial control group. The authors explain these results as being due to disturbances in the neural pathways of brain-injured Ss resulting in more frequent interruptions in cerebral streaming. This finding is yet another explanation of the distractibility of the brain-injured child.

Mark and Pasamanick (1958) found higher asynchronism thresholds for two points of light in a group of brain-injured children compared to a control group matched for age, sex, and IQ. Such a finding indicates a loss of visual efficiency in brain-injured children in the detection of a pause between the onset time of two lights. Because the brain-injured children had no primary diagnosis of ophthalmologic disturbance, it may be concluded that the loss of visual efficiency is due to cerebral dysfunctioning of some kind.

Aftereffects. Levine and Spivack (1962) compared the reports of brain-injured, emotionally disturbed, and normal Ss on the Spiral Visual Aftereffects Test (SVA). The normal and emotionally disturbed Ss showed a decrease in SVA sooner than did those with brain injury. In addition, the normal and emotionally disturbed groups were characterized by an increase of failure to report SVA in later trials, whereas the brain-injured group did not. It is thus concluded by Levine and Spivack that the brain-injured Ss are characterized by a different adaptation pattern to the SVA. This finding may have explanatory value with regard to perseveration. The brain-injured individual may have a tendency to perseverate because of the prolonged aftereffect of a stimulus.

Day (1960) notes, however, that studies on SVA have obtained conflicting results. Some studies have shown that brain-injured Ss see little or no aftereffect. He points out that, in order for an individual to experience an aftereffect of seen movement for a rotating spiral pattern, it is necessary for him to fixate steadily on a stationary point in or near the moving stimulus pattern. Damage to a location in the brain that controls voluntary eye movement (for example, the frontal region) might render the individual unable to fixate on a stationary point and thus hinder his seeing an aftereffect. Day concludes that inconsistencies in results may be due to differences in the brain-injured Ss studied with regard to locus, extent, and nature of the injury.

Efstathiou and Morant (1966) lend some empirical support to Day's conclusions. They conclude from a study comparing brain-injured adults with normal adults that when proper measures are taken to assure fixation on the SVA test, brain-injured patients function at about normal level. Efstathiou and Morant also tested the two groups on the Waterfall Illusion Aftereffect (WIAE), a test that does not depend as critically on fixation as the SVA test. If one fixates on a stationary terrain after having looked at a waterfall, the terrain is then experienced as moving upwards. This phenomenon can be replicated in a laboratory situation with a moving set of parallel lines. On this WIAE test, where much less fixation is required, there were no significant differences between brain-injured and normal Ss.

Schein (1960) has also called into serious question cortical inhibition explanations of failure to report afterimages. He found in a study comparing brain-injured psychotic and normal individuals on their abilities to report an Archimedes Spiral afterimage that, whereas the brain-injured Ss failed to report any afterimage significantly more frequently than the control groups, when the afterimage was seen, none of the variables of age, intelligence, drugs, or diagnosis differentiated the groups with regard to the duration of the afterimage. He suggests, apparently as a result of the effect of instructions on the frequency of responses, that these findings indicate that the brain-injured Ss perceive the afterimage as frequently as the control groups but that the brain-injured individuals are more easily confused by the task and thus fail to report their perceptions more frequently.

Garner, Neuringer, and Goldstein (1966) found no differences between brain-injured and normal adults on duration of the spiral aftereffect. They suggest that some brain-injured individuals, particularly those with language disturbances, may be impaired in their ability to report subjective experiences.

From the above studies it would appear safe to conclude that the inconsistent findings may be resolved by considering the locus, extent, and nature of the lesion to the brain. It would also appear that in explaining the reason for no report of a visual afterimage in some brain-injured Ss there are at least three explanations more parsimonious than a cortical-inhibition explanation.

1. Failure of some brain-injured Ss to fixate on a steady point due to damage to brain centers controlling voluntary eye movements;

2. Failure of some brain-injured Ss to report subjective experiences;

3. Failure of some brain-injured Ss to understand the task.

It should be pointed out, however, that, because the latter studies were dealing with adults, these conclusions may not necessarily apply to brain-injured children. Furthermore, they do not explain the findings of Levine and Spivack (1962), discussed above, that the brain-injured Ss showed a longer SVA than normal and emotionally disturbed Ss. Research is now needed on brain-injured children, taking account of the pitfalls encountered in the adult studies.

Auditory Disturbances

Brain-injured children also frequently have problems of an auditory nature. Sabatino (1969), in fact, points out that one can often miss neurologically handicapped children if only the visual modality is tested.

Quirós (Argentina) (1978) as a matter of fact is of the opinion that the auditory modality may indeed be the most significant from a diagnostic point of view. His vestibular research, he states, produces important diagnostic data portending later learning disabilities in children when he performs his tests on very young infants.

Sabatino found that all of the subtests of his Test of Auditory Perception (TAP) correlated negatively with scores of the Bender Visual Motor Gestalt Test. The TAP's subtests are: recognition of sounds, recognitions of words, immediate memory for digits, immediate memory for speech, auditory integration, and auditory comprehension. He found that under conditions of background noise, a group of brain-injured children was significantly poorer on all six subtests than a non-brain-injured control group matched for age, sex, and verbal IQ. With normal background noise, the two groups were significantly differentiated on all but two subtests—immediate memory for digits and auditory integration. (The S was required to duplicate prerecorded patterns of tapping.) With regard to this finding, Sabatino concludes that meaningful language is necessary to differentiate normal and brain-injured children on auditory perception. It is also important to note that this finding is additional empirical evidence for the hyperdistractibility of the brain-injured child.

Schlanger (1958) found that varying the background noise made no difference in the performance of brain-injured children in discriminating pairs of words that were close in sound (for example, pin–pen). This task is highly similar to Sabatino's subtests of recognition of sounds and recognition of words. The findings of the two studies indicate that background stimuli may be distracting for brain-injured children only on certain kinds of auditory perceptual tasks. Schlanger concludes that the low performance of brain-injured children in discriminating sounds is of a psychological nature due to limited attention span, lack of concentration, and distractibility to internal factors rather than due to a general or specific auditory factor.

Other studies have shown brain-injured children to be deficient on tone-discrimination tasks (Birch, Belmont, and Karp, 1965; Stevens *et al.*, 1967). Closely related to this deficiency is the brain-injured child's problem in determining initial, final, and medial sounds of even short words (Kaliski, 1959). The separate sounds that go into making up these words tend to run into one another for the brain-injured child. If such a child is unable to discriminate the sounds of single words, it is evident that his problem is multiplied to an even greater extent when he is presented with a string of words in a sentence.

From the Birch, Belmont, and Karp study (1965) previously cited, in which it was found that a longer period of time between two tones was required for brain-injured as contrasted to normal Ss before the second tone was not interfered with by the first tone, we might posit that a disturbance in cerebral inhibition is a factor in the inability to discriminate sounds. Belmont, Birch, and Karp, furthermore, have concluded from a study of intersensory and intrasensory relations that brain-injured individuals are often characterized by a lack of spread of inhibition.

Either because of a prolongation of inhibition, as demonstrated in the Birch, Belmont, and Karp study, or because of a lack of inhibition, sounds run together and are not integrated into a meaningful sequence or pattern. Considering two sequential sounds—A and B—in the first case, sound A would interfere with sound B; in the latter case, B would interfere with A. To determine which of these two processes was working, one could set up an experimental situation in which brain-injured children with auditory disturbances and normal controls were presented verbally with a list of about seven random words and then asked to repeat the words they could remember. Looking at words 3, 4, and 5 in order to eliminate primacy and recency effects (assuming that the serial position curves are the same in the two groups), if prolongation of inhibition is occurring, the third word would tend to be remembered better than either the fourth or fifth word. If, however, there is a defect that was keeping inhibition from occurring at all, the fifth word would be remembered better than either the third or fourth word.

Intersensory Disturbances

Many investigators have concluded that organized behavior is the result of an integration of the different sensory systems (Birch, 1964; Maier & Schneirla, 1935; Scherrington, 1951). The ability to integrate information from more than one sensory system comes at a more advanced stage of development than the ability to integrate information from a single sensory system.

Referring to the classic writings of Goldstein (1939) in which he posits a "hierarchy of disintegration" whereby the higher, more complex behaviors of an organism are the first to be impaired by cortical injury, one can readily see why investigators have concluded that intersensory organization is more impaired than intrasensory organization in brain-injured individuals. Birch (1964), for example, has noted that, at the very least, the emergence of intersensory relations is delayed in the brain-injured child. As Birch points out, inadequate intersensory organization may not only result in the inability to organize input from two different sensory modalities, but may also predispose the child to develop bizarre types of integrations.

Frostig (1975), provides a very complete theoretical statement regarding intersensory organization and a thorough review of literature pertaining to this matter.

Hunt and Patterson (1958) found that brain-injured children, in contrast to familial controls, were characterized by an inability to coordinate information from two sensory modalities—auditory and visual. When given a task which required that they listen to a story read by the examiner and then rearrange a group of pictures to coincide with the story, they, instead of benefiting from the two different sources of cues, tended to select one or the other sensory modality as their sole base of operation.

The inability on the part of brain-injured children to integrate and organize inputs from more than one sensory modality may be viewed as another manifestation of distractibility. The neurologically impaired individual is limited in the amounts and sources of information he can deal with. It is difficult for him to attend to one stimulus at a time because so much of his attention is taken up with the impingement of other stimuli. But when he attends to these others, he is unable to integrate them in a meaningful way.

Conceptual and Abstract Thinking Disturbances

Another characteristic of the child with perceptual processing deficits that is often referred to in the literature is his inability to deal with objects and ideas on an abstract level. This inability requires that he operate on a concrete level (Paine, 1966). Goldstein (1939) in his investigation of brain-injured war patients noted that these patients could perform concrete tasks but were unable to function on tasks that required abstract thinking.

Hand in hand with this deficiency in abstract thinking goes the brain-injured child's inability to form concepts (Kaliski, 1959). He is often deficient in seeing the relationships and similarities in things; that is, he has conceptual difficulty (Burks, 1960; Rappaport, 1964). As Burks notes, poor conceptual ability usually leads to serious academic deficiences.

Strauss and Werner (1942) compared a group of familial children and a group of brain-injured children matched for MA and CA (MA = nine years) on a Sorting Test and a Picture-Object Test adapted from the still earlier work of Halsted. On the Sorting Test the S was required to sort fifty-six common objects into groups on the basis of their belonging together. On the Picture-Object Test, S was instructed to place objects in front of one of two pictures on the basis of the most appropriate matching. One picture was of a boy drowning and the other was of firefighters attempting to rescue a burning building.

On both tests the brain-injured Ss, compared to the familial controls, formed more groups and made far more uncommon responses. The principle by which the brain-injured children made their selections seemed to be based particularly upon unusual or accidental or apparently insignificant details. Furthermore, on the Picture-Object Test the brain-injured Ss more often than the familial Ss arranged the objects in circumscribed units, manifested formalistic behavior (for example, meticulosity, organic pedantry, arbitrary patterning), and dramatized the pictures in their selection of objects.

Dolphin and Cruickshank (1951b), comparing cerebral palsy children and non-brain-injured children matched for MA and CA, replicated the above results found by Strauss and Werner on the Picture-Object Test. The cerebral-palsy children chose significantly more objects than the controls, made more selections based on secondary qualities of the objects, chose a larger number of uncommon objects, and more often dramatized the pictures in their selection of objects.

Gallagher (1957) compared a group of familials and a group of brain-injured children matched for MA and CA on tasks requiring quantitative conceptual ability. He found no differences between the two groups on these measures of quantitative concepts. He did find, however, that the brain-injured group was inferior on a task that required the integration of verbal concepts. This task required that the S supply the missing word in a sentence.

Ernhart *et al.* (1963) compared a group of brain-injured preschool children with a group of normal preschool children. Scores on the measures were adjusted for age, sex, and socioeconomic status. Covarying for vocabulary subtest score on the Stanford-Binet, it was found that the brain-injured preschoolers performed poorer on a conceptual task requiring Ss to group blocks differing on the dimensions of color, size, and form.

However, Reed and Reed, Jr. (1967) found in a study of brain-injured and normal children (10 years to 15 years) that, when level of intellectual functioning is controlled, the two groups are indistinguishable with regard to abstract reasoning tasks and concept-formation tasks as measured by the Wechsler-Bellevue Block Design Test and Halstead Category Test, respectively. They have concluded that one accompanying characteristic of brain injury in older children is a general lowering of intellectual ability rather than specific deficiencies in nonverbal abstract reasoning or concept formation. They do not imply, however, that specific impairment does not occur. They point out that such variables as type of lesion, age of onset, lateralization, location, and rate of progression or severity need to be further investigated in order to determine their effects on selective impairment. The present writers would agree, if by "intellectual ability" Reed and Reed mean the functional use of intelligence as opposed to lowering of innate ability. It must be kept in mind that there is a generally heavier use of verbal content in most tests as the individual grows older, and neither raw nor weighted scores may realistically reflect the ability of the person with perceptual deficits which are manifested in verbal activities.

Language Disturbances

The authors mean to deal here briefly with the more common language disturbances of the child with neurological impairment. We shall exclude, in this study, those brain-injured children whose primary problem lies in the language area—the aphasics. Although, as Thelander, Phelps, and Kirk (1958) state, the most easily recognized disturbances of the learning-disabled child with brain injury are in the area of language, these children do not display the profound language aberrations that are characteristic of the child with aphasia. For a good account of the child with aphasia, see McGinnis (1963) and Wepman (1951).

As Luria (1966) states, speech is the result "of highly complex integration of nervous processes. All complex forms of human mental activity involve direct or indirect participation of speech." Because it is the higher mental processes in the hierarchy of complexity that are the most easily deranged by local or general brain lesions (Luria, 1966; Goldstein, 1939), it follows that language processes should be among those behaviors that are most significantly affected.

Fisichelli *et al.* (1966) have made extensive phonetic analyses of infants with brain injury. They found from the tape recordings of normal and brain-injured infants at three age levels—first week of life, approximately 6 months of age, and approximately 1 year of age—that the normal infants produce significantly more total sounds, significantly more vowel sounds, and significantly less nasal sounds than the brain-injured infants. Other studies cited by Fisichelli *et al.* have found significant differences between these two groups in regard to threshold (Karelitz & Fisichelli, 1962) and latency (Fisichelli & Karelitz, 1963). Another study (Karelitz, Karelitz, & Rosenfeld, 1960) has found that the cries of normal infants are more rhythmic and are characterized by earlier appearance of inflectional changes than those of brain-injured infants.

These infant studies have thus shown that the consequences of brain injury appear early in the area of language development. These findings reflect early disturbances in the motor area of speech production, however, and might best be considered as disturbances that might later be concomitant with language disturbances of a conceptual nature.

Sievers (1959) compared the performances of normal, brain-injured retardates, and familial retardates matched for MA on the Differential Language Facility Test. The MAs ranged from 2–0 years to 5–11 years. The normals were superior to the brain-injured and non-brain-injured groups in areas of language ability that require verbal production without semantic reasoning. However, a surprising finding was that the familial retardates were superior to normals on the subtest requiring semantic meaning but not verbal production. It was also found that the familials tended to perform better than the brain-injured group on subtests that required the subject to make semantic connections between visual objects as in the Object Association and Picture Series Description subtests.

Reed, Jr., Reitan, and Klove (1965) compared a group of brain-injured children ranging in age from 10 to 14 years with another group of children controlled for age but not for education or general intelligence. It was found that the brain-injured group was more frequently inferior in performance on tests directly dependent upon language functions. The authors note that this finding is in contrast to a previous study on adults (Reitan, 1959). The authors thus conclude that children and adults may differ quite significantly with respect to behavioral consequences of brain injury. The adult brain-injured Ss differ far more from their control group on tasks involving adaptive and problem-solving ability than on stored experience and memory abilities.

In reporting the various studies in this section, we have continued to utilize the terms which the original authors have employed; that is, for the most part "brain-injured." Whether that term is fully accurate or not is a question not to be solved here. Suffice to say that it is a term which was used comfortably by a large number of research personnel during the 1950s and 1960s, and has justification in precedent-setting earlier work. We have continued it here, not only because we too feel comfortable with the term, but because its neurological base, like the definition of learning disabilities, provides a comparable point of departure, and because the finding related to psychological characteristics of brain-injured children are fully comparable to those with learning disabilities. The proper use and definition of learning disabilities brings these two terms into basic functional harmony.

Socioemotional Disturbances

The learning-disabled child is engaged in a self-defeating cycle. His aberrant behavior is problematic in school and at home which results in rejecting or otherwise punitive responses from peers, teachers and family. The social and psychological consequences of the behavioral deficits of these children have been clearly delineated in the research literature (for example, McCartney, 1956; Jacobs & Pierce, 1968).

Rappaport (1964) and others have articulated the circuitry of development in which specific neurologically based competencies are learned in environments where those skills are practiced and valued. The match between successful learning and a positive, reinforcing, environment is the experience from which concept and worth of self is fashioned.

The behavior characteristics of these children, already described, place them in positions of high risk for social failure and alienation from significant others.

Wallace and Kauffman (1973) point out that when a child enters school his progress depends not only upon learning academic responses but upon building a repertoire of adequate emotional and social behavior. Children who have difficulty learning social and emotional responses which would contribute to success at school are more likely to develop maladaptive patterns of behavior such as tantrums, hitting or crying. Learning-disabled children as a group, manifest more problems with aggressive behavior than with immature or neurotic patterns. (Hallahan & Kauffman, 1976).

The behavior problems of these children that tend to set them apart or separate them from the nurturing environments available to others who can make more satisfactory adjustments result in a kind of social psychological exile. Kronick (1974), for example, has indicated that the child may feel alone in his experience since it is not shared with other family members. Kronick points out that these children tend to be less rewarding to their parents than their nondisabled siblings and peers and, hence, less rewarded. These children often fail to meet normal parental expectations in some of the earliest and most primary relationships. Feeding the infant can be traumatic and a failure experience for the mother, for example, when the infant cannot suck or sucks too briefly (Decker, 1964).

The pattern of excessive or inappropriate behavior often results in rejection by parents and by peer groups. The peer group conflict becomes particularly significant during the latency years when peer groups are so important. The consequences of the pattern of rejection by the most significant others over time can profoundly affect the child's personality development.

Bender (1956) has pointed out that all brain-injured children suffer from extreme anxiety. Anxiety is aroused by perceived threat and these children fail so consistently they come to expect it. Many of them become excessively dependent on teachers and parents for reassurance (Wallace & McLaughlin, 1975).

Gallagher (1957) in his comparison of brain-injured and familial children found the brain-injured poorer on all personality variables measured. On rating scales, the brain-injured Ss were judged to be more hyperactive, inattentive, fearful, unpopular, and uninhibited. Gallagher has proposed two possible explanations for the brain-injured child's poor personality ratings: (1) he does not perceive social situations correctly and consequently acts inappropriately; (2) his general lack of inhibition presents behavior that is unacceptable to peers.

Jacobs and Pierce (1968) analyzed responses to sociometric questions—"Which of the boys and girls in the class would you like most (least) to work with on some special project? Which of the boys and girls in the class would you like most (least) to play with outside of school?"—distributed to children in twelve public school classes for the educable mentally retarded. When the students were divided into those diagnosed as brain-injured and those diagnosed as familial, it was found that the brain-injured children were more often rejected by their peers than the familials were. The correlation of brain-damage characteristics with number of times rejected was .426 (significant at .001 level). Short attention span was the most commonly mentioned characteristic of those subjects who were most often rejected. Hyperkinesis, emotional liability, and impulsivity were also quite frequently associated with those students most often rejected. An insignificant correlation ($R=.14$) was found between IQ and number of brain injury associated characteristics, and thus IQ was not considered a significant variable.

Farnham-Diggory (1966) found that brain-injured children, in contrast to normals, have an immature view of life ahead and a lack of awareness of personal development and change. They also show a high degree of death imagery in their responses. She has concluded that their overall pictures suggest that of the "catastrophic" reaction observed by Goldstein (1939) in his war patients. This was particularly true of the younger children. Briefly, for Goldstein, a catastrophic reaction arises in a brain-injured patient when the whole organism is unable to function adequately. There is some degree of realization that time has slowed down and that death has, in a sense, already begun.

Farnham-Diggory did not find on a self-evaluation questionnaire (SE) that the brain-injured group made lower evaluations of themselves than the normal control group. (The subject indicated his evaluation on each item by moving a red wooden arrow along on a scale.) Also, a highly significant negative correlation ($R= -.54$) was found between the mean SE and IQ of the brain-injured group. Thus, the more intelligent the child, the less he thought of himself.

As with all findings based on questionnaires, there is the problem of how honest the reporter is when giving his answers. The fact that in this particular case the experimenter was present with the subject while he was responding to questions prefaced with "show me how good you are at . . ." makes the results even more questionable. Furthermore, the negative correlation found between IQ and SE may indicate that the more intelligent the child, the more honest he is in evaluating himself.

Perhaps because of his higher level of functioning, he does not feel as threatened when it comes to evaluating himself.

VARIABILITY OF PERFORMANCE AND ORDERLINESS

Many researchers and clinicians have observed the extreme variability in the behavior of these children. Their ability to attend to tasks and work successfully in a classroom, for example, varies markedly from day to day. This characteristic has been viewed as a function of the more basic problem of distractibility (Cruickshank, *et al.*, 1961) or hypersensitivity to variation within the environment (Francis-Williams, 1965). The inability of the child to make and maintain positive adjustment to relevant stimuli and negative adjustment to irrelevant stimuli, a characteristic described earlier in this chapter, make the child very dependent on the stability and structure of the environment. The child is, in this sense, a psychological captive of the environment having less ability than his normal peers to monitor and volitionally manage his own responses.

This aspect of the child's inability to succeed illustrates well the interactive nature of the learning disability or what Eisenberg, describing the behavior of brain-damaged children, called a psychobiological entity. Eisenberg (1957) noted that the outcome of the organic injury is determined by the interaction between: (1) qualitative and quantitative alterations in brain function produced by damage to its structure, (2) behavior influenced by reorganization of the previous personality of the patient in face of his functional deficit, and (3) influence of social environment on performance.

Another aspect of the child's variability in performance is in the affective domain. Lability of mood has been described by Eisenberg (1957), Rappaport (1964), Cruickshank (1967) and others. This child's tolerance threshold is very low and easily exceeded. Rapid changes in mood from laughter and happiness to tears and anger occur without apparent provocation or reason. This unpredictable shift in mood and behavior is alarming to parents, teachers and peers when it is not, and typically it is not, understood as one of the aberrant behavioral manifestations of a brain-injured child. Eisenberg has suggested that, in view of the disproportionate destructiveness and apparent lack of provocation, the behavior may be viewed as the "escape of the lower, more primitive rage mechanisms from cortical control" (1957, p. 74).

Investigators (Cruickshank *et al.,* 1961; Goldstein, 1939; Mackie & Beck, 1966) have also noted that individuals suffering from brain injury often display a tendency toward orderliness in their behavior. Goldstein (1939) suggests that this behavior is a reaction to avoid catastrophic situations already described. One might also consider the possibility that this ordered behavior is a reaction to the disordered perception and behavior of the child. The world can be a frightening place for a child who is constantly bombarded by stimuli that he is unable to organize and integrate into meaningful patterns. From the review of the studies above, it is evident that the brain-injured child is indeed unable to deal in an organized manner with the input of information. Considered from this point of view, then, the brain-injured child may frequently order his behavior to the point of becoming compulsive and rigid in defense against what is for this child an extremely disorganized environment.

There are many manifestations of the child's attempt to order his environment and, hence his experience. For example, he may compulsively arrange articles on a desk and be provoked into an excessive reaction such as a tantrum if the order is disturbed by others. It takes an inordinate amount of energy for the child to make this much psychological investment in maintaining his own order and structure.

Body-Image

Like the concept of self, the concept of body-image has resisted the operational clarity needed to significantly advance our knowledge in this area. Wylie (1961, p. 272) indicated that "Body image is a term with no clear literary or operational definition." Traub and Orbach (1964) have stated:

> Though broadly applied within the context of psychological, psychiatric, and neurological theory, the concept of body-image (body schema, postural model of the body, perceived body, body ego, body boundaries, etc.) has neither been satisfactorily defined nor rigorously measured in the clinic or laboratory (p. 53).

Current literature continues to recognize the vagueness of the body image construct (Hallahan & Kauffman, 1976). Yet, like the concept of self, the concept of body image has at least heuristic appeal and clinical utility. It remains, therefore, a major aspect of the conceptualization of development and a significant source of difficulty for learning disabled children.

Early formulations of the concept of body-image were made by neurologists in their attempts to explain certain phenomena associated with cerebral lesions. Poetzl, Critchley, Gerstmann, Bartlett, Head, and others did much of the beginning conceptual and experimental work on the organization and development of body attitudes. Head, a British neurologist, was the first to develop a rather elaborate theory in this regard. Since then considerable work has been done on the concept of body-image, and numerous definitions have been postulated.

Schilder (1950) has defined body-image as "the picture of our own body, that is to say the way in which the body appears to ourselves" (p. 11). Kephart (1960) has defined it as "a learned concept resulting from the observation of movements of parts of the body and the relationship of the different parts of the body to each other and to external objects" (p. 51). McAninch (1966) conceptualized body-image as a referential point, "a conceptual and operative image which includes an awareness of the body in relation to the physical world or, in other words, an image of the body and its boundaries, and an inner view of the self" (p. 140). Myers and Hammill (1976) have described body image as a fluid and dynamic internal conceptualization which, like the concept of self, is an important aspect of the learning ability of children. Horowitz (1966) views body-image as

a specialized, internal analogue data-center for information about the body and its environment. It is in constant transactional relationship with internal and external perceptions, memories, affects, cognition, and actions. It provides economical and specific information concerning the morphology, position and relationships of the body as well as the structure of the space, objects, and persons that are in some relation to it. This information has been compiled from all sources and is available to all mental mechanisms. Thus, while residues of prior sensations build the body-image, the momentary and immediate nature of the body-image affects the interpretations of current sense data and may even result in the apperceptive distortion of such sense data (p. 456).

Body-schema, the precursor to body-image, derives from early sensory experiences (Dubnoff & Chambers, 1966, p. 9). "From the point of view of sensory motor development, the child brings more or less isolated and uncorrelated experiences into a complete form by continual effort" (Schilder, 1950, p. 106).

Body-image development proceeds in terms of certain biologic laws of growth and the "integration of new experiences, physical and psychological, arising from one's self and from relationships and attitudes of others, into a gestalt" (Bender & Silver, 1948, p. 89). Continual modification

is required as new adaptive capacities are obtained by the organism as a result of its physical and psychological maturation. As abilities to perceive and integrate stimuli increase, so must prior judgments be modified on the nature of the body, how it works, and how its parts are interrelated in relation to its surrounding space and objects in that space.

Kessler (1966, p. 21), in a discussion of the discovery of physical self, noted that the distinction between self and nonself is first made on the basis of physical differences. The infant usually first notices his hands and experiences touching, being touched, and then seeing these simultaneously. Initially he views his hands as playthings and then moves quickly to viewing them as tools. After a sense of permanence and predictability about them is established, the eyes will lead and direct the hands, for example, in grasping and touching. During the first 6 months every object is given an oral trial, and later tactile and visual exploration is used. With this growing ability he learns what is self and what is nonself.

The baby does not become equally familiar with all physical boundaries of his body at the same time. He first becomes acquainted with the physical limits, capabilities, and sensations of his upper extremities: he must similarly discover his legs when he crawls and walks. In the development of a sense of reality, the conception of one's own body plays a very special role. It takes the better part of a year for the baby to form a complete image of his body (Kessler, 1966, pp. 21–22).

A differentiation in the body parts and their comparative relationship is required. This is a complex process which characterizes the neurosensory development of children. An adequate body-image provides the child with a dependable point of reference for his motor responses and the development of perception. It is the basis for purposeful body action in space and of complex goal directed behavior. An adequate body-image includes the almost infinite set of perceptual-motor linkages in the neurophysiological system of the organism which provides the preconditions for patterns of movement and associations on command.

There exists a degree of definitional confusion which has to do with the lack of clear delineation of the concept of body-image from the concept of self-concept. Freud (1960) states, "The ego is first and foremost a bodily ego; it is not merely a surface entity, but is itself the projection of a surface" (p. 38).

Since then, the clarification of either concept has, for the most part, increased the clarity of the relationship of the two. Wylie (1961) observed, "It seems safe to say . . . that self-concept theorists agree on the general idea that body characteristics which are lowly valued by S may be expected to undermine his general self-regard, while highly valued body characteristics should enhance self-regard" (p. 159). Prosen (1965) defines body-image with attached emotions—emotions concerned with self-esteem, feelings of adequacy, influence on or relations with others. "The body image is determined to a large extent by a person's sense of his own worth" (p. 1262).

Using a sample of 200 college freshmen women, Zion (1965) investigated certain relationships between self-concept and body-image. A significant linear relationship was found between self-description and body description, ideal self and ideal body, and self-description-ideal discrepancy and body description-ideal discrepancy. The self-acceptance and body-acceptance relationship was ambiguous. It was concluded that the security one has in one's body appears related to the security with which one faces one's self and the world (Zion, 1965, p. 494). Although extreme caution should be exercised in generalizing the results of this study to brain-injured children, the conclusion of the study is generally consistent with the view of the very close relationship between concepts of the self and the body.

Fisher and Cleveland (1958) considered the body-image a "summary in body terms of a great many experiences the individual has had in the course of defining his identity in the world . . . The body image is a sensitive indicator which registers many of the individual's basic social relationships, especially those early involved in his development of a sense of identity" (p. 111).

Although much conceptual work remains for researchers who will pursue new knowledge in this area, existing constructs have provided the practitioner with a useful frame of reference for the sequence and pace of developmental tasks of children. A basis has been established for analysis and understanding of behavior. An adequate body-image, for example, is essential to the development of laterality and directionality, which is so important in the development of integrity in body movement and increasingly complex competencies. (Myers & Hammill, 1976).

Laterality, which Radler and Kephart (1960, p. 33) describe as "the inner sense of one's own symmetry" is usually learned by the child's continual experimentation with movement—comparison of movements on the right side with movements on the left side with undifferentiated movements. Multiple proprioceptive, kinesthetic, tactile, visual, and other stimuli serve to inform the child of the consequences of his acts. Over time the child succeeds in movements of his own determination. This is vastly gratifying. Through this learning process the child begins "to build up an image of his own body, a visual and kinesthetic awareness of how he fills the space within his own skin. This awareness is basic to motor control; . . . fundamental to our perception of the world outside our skins, the left and right or up and down of things" (Radler & Kephart, 1960, p. 9).

The distinction between left and right and the simultaneous and separate control of the two sides is a crucial aspect of development dependent upon an adequately developed body-image. The human body is bilaterally symmetrical, anatomically and neurologically designed to develop right-left orientations (Kephart, 1960, p. 43). If it were not so, it would be very difficult, if not impossible, to sort and keep physical relationships in the world about us straight.

After developing body awareness and learning to control and integrate its parts, the child perceives the world around him—at first by relating all ideas of form to himself and his own body. "The first 'space world' develops within an arm's reach" (Radler & Kephart, 1960, p. 25).

Concepts of space outside the body are developed after laterality is established. Directionality is the projection of laterality into space (Radler & Kephart, 1960, p. 34). The relationship of an object to the self precedes the development of relationships between objects (Radler & Kephart, 1960, p. 39).

Spatial relations and directions in the environment, such as up, down, right, left, and behind, are established with reference to the body. They are not given in the physical construction of the environment. The human body must become oriented to the characteristics—space, gravity, form, motion, and so forth—of the world in which that body is to meaningfully and volitionally act. The functional relationship between the two, that is the body and its action space, must be developed and meaningfully conceptualized.

From the development of laterality and the concert of volitional movements, the child can develop balance. He begins to negotiate the innervation of one side against the other, the complex sensorimotor process that eventually involves countless linkages and message transmissions between sensory receptors and the motor neurons. The whole pattern of movement with reference to a specific task is developed through successive approximations of the goal in which self-corrective movements are required. Errors in posture, appendage position, speed, and so forth must be integrated into the movement pattern being executed

in walking, for example. As Barsch (1966, p. 184) has pointed out, this is occurring with reference to three ordinates: vertical, horizontal, and depth. A dynamic match between the demands endemic to the task and the capabilities of the organism is required for successful sensorimotor development.

The image of the body that is developed is, then, psychologically salient to the functional integrity of the organism. It has important implications, as has been indicated, for the feelings about self that are developed.

Events internal to the child do not completely explain the development of body-image and the feelings that derive from a satisfying, normative development of the sensorimotor system. The social aspects of self-concept development already discussed are very much relevant here because, as has been suggested, self-concept and body-image development are not mutually exclusive or discrete entities.

Interesting work has been done on some of the social-psychological implications, for example, of relative body-size perception. Beller and Turner (1964), investigating certain personality correlates of children's perception of human size, found that autonomous achievement striving was significantly correlated with accuracy of the child's estimation of his own and other people's sizes. Their sample included fourteen preschool normal children.

Although not typically discussed in the context of writing on body-image and brain-injured children, work on the social meaning or social stimulus value of the body provides an even broader sociological view. As an image of one's own body is developed, the adopted view gains social definition with reference, for example, to value.

In a study of social stereotype of body-image in normal male children (ages 6 to 10), Staffieri (1967) found a significant relationship between the adjectives of various behavior/personality traits assigned by children to body types (endomorph, mesomorph, and ectomorph). The adjectives assigned the mesomorph image were favorable, whereas those assigned endomorph and ectomorph images were not. The Ss in the study clearly preferred to look like the mesomorph image. The older the children, the more accurate the perception of their own body type. He obtained similar findings on the favorable social connotations of mesomorphs based on the adjectives assigned by thirty-three mentally retarded male Ss, ages 15 to 25 (Staffieri, 1968).

Discussion of body-image to this point has centered primarily on the sensorimotor development and social experience of all children. A child is born into a world with physical, psychological, social, and cultural demands already established. He brings with him a genetic endowment, a constitutional readiness and potential, and his own growth demands. The interaction between his demands and the demands of the world in which he happens to be born is the story of child growth and development. The characters in the story are in every instance different and the plot is infinitely varied. That variation is accounted for by the nature and extent of the demands in either and the capacity of coping in the other. The biological laws that govern child development and the principles of socialization are so carefully interwoven into the fabric of this interaction that aberrance in either is experienced as such by the other.

The learning-disabled child's neural maturation is aberrant, and hence his sensorimotor task negotiation is not always consonant with normative expectations. The predominance of harmony over disharmony in the interaction for most children may be reversed for these children. Such reversal constitutes failure both in the child and in the socializing system. The absorption of and recovery from experienced failure takes much less toll on the system than on the child.

Learning-disabled children may not establish adequate cerebral dominance or mature

at the expected rate (Gubbay et al., 1965). They may not be able to use kinesthetic feedback properly, such as in discriminating between similar and different sensations in various parts of the body, or to accurately classify motor responses to provide feedback necessary for the repetition of an act (McAninch, 1966, p. 153). Because of overall gross or fine motor skill disabilities, these children are often described as clumsy. (See, for example, Haring & Schiefelbusch, 1967, p. 366; Illingworth, 1968; Walton, Ellis, & Court, 1962). Gerstmann (1924, 1940), Strauss and Werner (1938, 1939), and others have described the phenomena of finger agnosia and deficiences in finger schema in these children.

Whether the activity is walking, jumping, or negotiating a pencil or a glass of milk, a body that does not work as a unity in response to a demand or goal will often fail. The very complex sensorimotor task involved in catching a ball when age peers are enjoying the game may keep this child on the bench. The concert of movement of eyes, hands, fingers, feet, head, and all other parts of the sensorimotor system in the interest of the organism's goal, the acquiescence of some body parts while other parts do their job—these are essential.

Many learning disabled children become convinced they cannot because they have learned their bodies will not. When rewards of adult approval, so important in the self-esteem of children, are forthcoming for those who are good at the act, these children often miss out and accept the fact that they are not because they have not. To be angry and seriously hurt is no uncertain human consequence of such human failure.

Self-Concept

The clinical and research literature on learning disabled children is no more clear or consistent on any issue than that the experience of these children is dominated by failure. As noted in the earlier discussion of psychopathology, there are different aspects of learning disabilities that contribute to that failure. Not all theoreticians are in agreement and the evidence is inconclusive, and in some instances inconsistent, regarding the specific neuropsychological mechanisms involved and their precise interactions contributing to inadequate or inappropriate performances. There are also differences in points of view regarding the most relevant theoretical frameworks and the most robust constructs to employ in understanding the performance of these children. There is no difference in the view, however, that these children fail in important areas where their developmental peers succeed and that, depending on the nature and extent of that failure, there are profound consequences for their psychological development.

A major aspect of development is that related to the definition and valuing of self. Much of the answer to the question, "Who am I?" is related to the answer to, "What can I do?" Similarly, how I feel about myself is related to how well I am able to do and how others respond to how well I do.

The concept of self is learned and is directly related to experience. Children who consistently fail and who have negative experiences with themselves in the world, particularly at a time when they are beginning to learn who they are, develop low and defeating self concepts. As that experience of failure continues, that low self-view is maintained and reinforced even more strongly. This low self-appraisal, then, becomes the foundation for the development of perceptions and behavior to protect a weak and fragile sense of self.

Knowledge about exactly how this process works, however, is limited. The research literature is weak for two major reasons. First, definitional problems, discussed earlier, have resulted in a lack of consistency and clarity in identifying the children to be studied. The second confounding aspect of the work has to do with the self construct. Wylie (1961) pointed out that constructs of

self have been applied to so many inferred cognitive and motivational processes that their analytic or predictive utility has been reduced. Lack of empirical evidence supporting theories of self-concept

> seems to be due in part to each of the following four factors: (1) the lack of proper scientific characteristics of the theories themselves; (2) the inevitable difficulties encountered in formulating relevant, well-controlled research in a new area; (3) the understandable fact that individual researches in a new area are not part of a planned research program and therefore cannot be easily synthesized; (4) avoidable methodological flaws (Wylie, 1961, p. 232).

While there are weaknesses recognized in research on the self-concept of learning disabled children, there is no more prominent theme in the professional literature than that poor self-concepts create serious difficulties for these children and result in particularly strong needs for successful experience. The authors have, therefore, included a substantial discussion of the meaning and status of the concept of learning disabilities and implications for the development of a concept of self.

That man, early in life, must accept a positive view and reject a negative view of himself—worthy, good, and valued rather than unworthy, mean, or unimportant—is not singularly a moral concept. It is a profound psychological concept in child development. Ross (1976) has pointed out that years of failure early in life will leave a mark in terms of the child's perception of himself, self-confidence, and response to the school situation.

Self-concept occupies a central position in several personality theories, for example, Rogers (1951). Self-concept is often considered the fundamental focus for behavioral change and for learning. Fennimore (1968, p. 448) has suggested that it is inconceivable that anyone could learn something inconsistent with his self-concept. Literature on early education is filled with the assumption that experiences to enhance the child's positive feelings about himself and to encourage the child's rejection of negative self-views are crucial (for example, Goodlad, 1964; Sears & Sherman, 1964).

Hawk (1976, p. 196) has stated, "To understand the behavior of a person, one must understand how that person sees himself." He summarizes the self as a dynamic unity of

> sensing, remembering, imagining, perceiving, wanting, feeling and thinking . . . The individual's idea of what he looks like and his ideas of how he affects other persons . . . the meaning of one's distinctive characteristics, abilities, and unique resources . . . attitudes, feelings, and values one holds about oneself, one's self-esteem or one's self-reproach or both (pp. 196–197).

Mead (1934, p. 164) has pointed out that "Selves can only exist in definite relationship to other selves." Davidson and Lang (1960, p. 107) state: "The child's self concept arises and develops in an interpersonal setting." Researchers (for example, Ausubel *et al.*, 1954; Coopersmith, 1968; Davidson & Lang, 1960) have accumulated support for the notion that significant adults affect the child's feelings about himself. These include his parents and, later, his teachers.

The first psychological task for the infant is the development of a basic sense of trust in himself and his environment (Erikson, 1960, p. 45). The social-psychological structure provided by the mother and later the family is elicited by the child. That is, normal maternal responses exist and are elicited by the child's behavior. The gross-motor activity and the variety of sounds produced, for example, by the healthy, happy baby bring the mother's relaxed attention. Her response is of equal delight—including her own gestures, verbal and physical—which is an important, total, affective communication. "I am very happy and my happiness has much to do with you. Right now you have my undivided attention. I will take

care of you and not abandon you." All are interwoven in the gestures. The infant's narcissim and omnipotence are then unchallenged. The lack of differentiation between the infant and mother for approximately the first six months makes the quality of this exchange particularly crucial. He learns to trust that his needs are cared for and that he can find pleasure in sensory and motor responses. The child's sense of trust is a reflection of his mother's sensitivity to his needs and her sturdy and realistic attitude (Rosenblith & Allinsmith, 1962, p. 206).

Mead (1934) has stated that "we have to distinguish ourselves from other people and this is accomplished by doing something which other people cannot do, or cannot do as well" (p. 208). The psychological saliency of the experience of competency, as already indicated in the most basic relationship, is a crucial concept. Importantly, as Mead pointed out, this experience is obtained in a social context. It is in relation to the perceived competency of others.

Parents and teachers know the requirements of children to have the adult recognize skills they have acquired. With siblings, for example, an older child may have learned to skip, to count to ten, to recognize certain letters of the alphabet, to print his name, or to perform any one of literally thousands of skills that are part of the natural growth and development of children. The younger child will often require equal time to display his skill for the adult's approval. The skill the younger child displays may not be a skill at all but an impromptu performance designed specifically to elicit reassurance from the adult. Equal state time and equal credit will not be based on equal performances. Importantly, the younger child fares well in skill comparison with age peers. He will not always be better than age peers, but he is competing on an equal footing and he knows it.

Learning disabled children do not compete so well. They consistently lose in some areas. Losing becomes even more devastating when the consistent winners are younger than he. The child knows when his relative performance is inferior. Caring and sensitive adults want so much for this child to also feel satisfied by his acts and may constantly reassure him of their love and his value to them. If, however, their reassurance is based on dishonest appraisal of his performance, both the child and the adult are locked into a futile engagement.

> How the child thinks about himself has a major influence on his behavior. The child's image of himself has two main sources: the way he sees others viewing him and what he sees himself as able to do—and hence to be. Others' views are first his parents' views. If they cannot provide the warm acceptance that underlies the sense of personal worth for the normal child, the inner core of his self-concept will be one of worthlessness. His extrafamilial experiences with peers and teachers often further self-depreciation as others display impatience with his limitations and shun his company. Even with the good fortune of having sympathetic parents and companions, he must daily face the painful realization of his incompetence at play and at work. No "reassurance" will satisfy him that he is capable as a person when he sees that he is not (Eisenberg, 1964, p. 70).

The child will have to continue to create pseudoskills, which often become either clownlike or defeatist in nature. The child may try to elicit genuine pride. Neither he nor his parents nor his teacher can feel good about his development as a "good" student, a responsible host to friends, a competent negotiator of the mealtime activities, and so on.

The development of the central nervous system is inextricably related to the psychological and social development of the child. The nature-nurture issue, although inviting in discussions of the psychological development of brain-injured children, has served, for the most part, to disguise or distort the real matter of complex interaction of the

two. Discussion of either one proceeds, at a minimum, with assumptions about the other.

Ego functions such as impulse control, frustration tolerance, ability to mediate between biological drives and environmental demands, and awareness of others are not present at birth. They are developed, rather, as an outgrowth of more primary ego functions, such as attention span, communication, perception, and motor control. These more primary functions emerge in the normal course of development according to a generally predictable pattern. This occurs if certain conditions are met, part of which are internal to the human organism. An intact central nervous system is one fundamental condition that provides the neonate an opportunity to develop those functions (Rappaport, 1966, p. 47). Although not a sufficient condition, this genetic endowment is necessary to normal growth and development and the acquisition of phase-specific competencies.

Rappaport (1964) has described the extrauterine epigenesis of the ego.

> Because ego development is first of all contingent upon the fetal development of the central nervous system and its extrauterine maturation, any neurological insult which the child experiences must interfere to some extent with his ego development. Only when born with his central nervous system intact does the child have the inborn capacities that develop, through growth, experience, and learning, to become the primary apparatuses of the ego. These include such important basic skills as motility, perception, concept formation, and language. Unlike the average child, the brain-damaged child is not born with these intact ego apparatuses which serve as the primary guarantees of the organism's adaptation to its environment (pp. 40–41).

The control of gross-motor discharges in the early phases of cephalocaudal neural maturation is an important source of gratification. This gratification is of primary value in the child's accomplishment of subsequent developmental tasks. The issue here is one of self-mastery, an aspect of his ego development.

> With further neural maturation, cortical inhibition takes place, allowing him the opportunity for volitional practice. That, in turn, provides him with greater opportunity for mastery and the resultant gratification of self-esteem. The first few years of life—in which a child learns such sensori-motor skills as to walk, talk, perceive, feed himself, and be toilet trained—provide literally hundreds of daily opportunities for being pleased with himself, for the budding of a positive identity which later will bloom into the conviction of "I am one who can!" (Rappaport, 1966, p. 48).

Rappaport (1964, pp. 49–51) has discussed reaction patterns associated with defective self-concept and narcissistic hypersensitivity in brain-injured children. His outline of these patterns will be used here. The patterns are not mutually exclusive in that discrete behaviors can always be identified as characterizing one pattern and not another. The outline is, however, very useful in providing a basis for discussion of the basic issues involved.

The first reaction pattern is *low frustration tolerance*. This is very much related to the gratification schedule required by the child who must succeed in his acts and whose success must be sufficiently gratifying to him. Delays in response, inadequate response, or negative response regarding his acts are often intolerable. It is his self-value that, to him, is at stake. The distinction between "I like you, but I do not approve of your behavior" frequently used by adults in managing aberrant behavior is very difficult for these children. No child is so devoid of a basic feeling of well-being and personal worth as the child whose books kept on success are almost always unbalanced and whose account is always in the red. The reasonable tolerance for failure or the positive use of the failure experience, so important in the realities of child growth and development, is predicated on assumptions of success histories and reasonable self-confidence. These children often do not fit the assumptions. The good they would, they do not. The essential equipment required for mastery—for example, of gravity, of behavioral expectations, of language, of one's own acts or patterns of movements—has not worked properly for them. This, coupled with our child-rearing practices, which are almost never aligned with the environmental and managerial needs of these children (to be discussed later), make them particularly vulnerable to failure.

These children become hyperaggressive in defense of self. This serves both to obtain some response, albeit usually negative, and also to protect their weaker selves from the aggression—such as the negative judgment of their acts—of stronger selves. This aggression is usually physical and becomes increasingly verbal as they acquire nonphysical aggressive capability.

Flight from challenge is the second reaction pattern. The last thing the child with a conviction of negative personal worth wants is social confirmation of unworthiness. He is convinced of low self-value and is equally certain that others will level their demeaning guns at him. He will find ways of avoiding the reality that he experiences as a challenge or threat. What he protects is an ego, short-changed in its primary gratification, and wounds to esteem too deep to risk another loss. The child who has always failed does not expect to succeed and probably cannot be expected to try.

Defending himself against the threat of failure, he may take other roles that remove him from the present days of performance in his real role. A barrage of verbiage is not uncommon if it keeps him from the task. He may attack others if this will head off expected attack from others and further reduction of personal esteem.

Wallace and McLaughlin (1975) have noted that poor self-concept, lack of self-reliance, and the feeling of being unable to accomplish anything correctly causes some children to refuse to complete assignments for fear of another failure. They become convinced of their inability to perform. Others have undue concern over what other people think because of their own lack of personal confidence.

The third reaction pattern listed by Rappaport is *overcompensation*. The child utilizing this defense will invest an inordinate amount of energy to excel in one area. This is often a skill or body of knowledge that has little payoff to the child except to provide him with a sense of pseudocompetence. It is usually something that other children his age typically do not know or cannot do and with which they are not likely to involve themselves sufficiently to become serious competitors. Rappaport describes two children to illustrate this pattern. One memorized all the Gilbert and Sullivan operettas and sang them when he was in a situation where he could compete successfully. Another memorized the names and complete records of every major league baseball player.

The fourth aspect is *control and manipulation of others*. These children who do not have sufficient mastery over themselves and are most frequently not able to obtain positive regard for age appropriate performance will often resort to the control of others. A child does battle with guts bared and both hands down when he must control those much larger and those much wiser than he. It is frightening for him to win, whereas the prospect of losing feels like devastation. This may be, after all, his sole engagement with the world from his point of view. If he does not withdraw from the world in which he has failed, he must control that world which will declare him unfit.

The fifth aspect listed by Rappaport (1964, p. 51) is *power struggle* or *negativism*. In this reaction pattern the child attempts to guard against a sensed impending loss of identity by total noncompliance. This pattern is characterized by the child's absence of regard for the wishes, requests, and feelings of others. His own sense of weakness and inadequacy is protected by his contu-

melious behavior aimed at the vulnerabilities of others. A child who is against everything has found too little he can safely be for. The reward of success he wants so much is precluded by his inability to risk failure.

To this point the discussion has centered on the child and his immediate and intimate relationships. The cultural issues are not separable from the view of the child already expressed. This is particularly true in terms of Mead's formulation (1934, pp. 173–78) of the concept of "me," the internalized attitude of the community, in the development of self. It would be a gross omission, however, to discuss these children and their appropriated self-feelings without more specific reference to the broader community. The error in reductionistic formulations is one well practiced in this area, many of the preceding statements in this chapter notwithstanding. Only a brief statement will be included here, though much more elaborate treatment is needed.

The community and its institutions have an essentially normative orientation. At certain ages certain things are expected, and the community reacts in terms of the congruence of the behavior and the expected behavior. An individual's need to test his worth or reestablish the trustworthiness of his world (the first task facing an infant during his first year of life) will be responded to as immaturity if he is, for example, 16 years old. Depending on the extent of the demand on the community, for example, violation of legal codes, the 16-year-old will be ignored, rejected, or punished, none of which are appropriate to the child's implied need statement. The community tolerance threshold is more or less age specific.

If the child feels too much mistrust, shame, uncertainty, or inferiority too long after he qualified by age to engage with adults to satisfactorily resolve these feelings, he has to deal with them in a special setting —special classes, special schools, clinics, hospitals, or correctional institutions. This is obviously not a conscious rational phenomenon with either the child or the culture that prescribes time bands and places.

The importance of this conceptualization here is that the development of learning disabled children is very uneven. Every child has a biologically and genetically determined ceiling rate of development. Rosenblith and Allinsmith (1962, p. 202) state that "Proper rate and normal sequence is necessary if functional harmony is to be secured." The interaction between his rate potential and his culture determines his actual development.

Gallagher (1966) has used the term developmental imbalances to describe the child who is *not* necessarily retarded in his measured intelligence but may be grossly retarded in one or more certain basic skills, such as perceptual-motor, or in his development of a positive self-concept.

Wallace and McLaughlin (1975) and others have pointed out the apparent relationship between self-concept and low achievement of these children. They note the results of a longitudinal study indicating that feelings of self worth consistently correlated with overall academic achievement among the variables designed to identify preschool children with learning disabilities (p. 228).

The interaction between the community's expectations, or those of any one of the community's child-socializing agents or agencies, and the child's response to those expectations constitutes the proving ground of mutual accord. The quality of the action of either has proportional consequences in the interaction. It is here that mutuality of regard is established. It is here that the self and personal values are presented and matched for fit with the perceptions, values, and expectations of the community. It is here that leaders are recognized and also where extrusion of certain members is accomplished. Rhodes (1967, p. 451) has described emotional disturbance in children as a crisis in the exchange between culture bearer and culture violator.

Learning-disabled children are often alien in a competence-oriented culture. The 9-year-old child may not, in fact, understand the parent's verbal request to hang up his coat because of other demanding and competing auditory stimulations, such as television, the dishwasher, and baby sister crying —all at once. He does, however, get the affective quality of the exchange that follows—"Are you absolutely stupid? Can't you do anything? You don't do anything you are told!"

This is a small sample of his failure in interactions in which his feelings and self were never really represented. This failure is augmented in the school and the community, where inaccurate or inappropriate responses interacting with his own feelings from a history of failure characterize his role in the engagement with the bearers of culture. The conviction that "I cannot" will over time be confirmed by significant others.

INTERVENTIONS

The complexity of the learning-disability area has been described. A completely satisfactory definition has yet to be developed, with the term itself representing a compromise of several legitimate professional interests. There is not agreement on the most appropriate way to conceptualize the functional deficits of learning disabled children. There is agreement on the fact that there are many such children and federal law (P.L. 94–142) now requires that they be provided an education in the least restrictive appropriate environment.

Given the substantive issues and the status of knowledge on the needs of these children already described, it is not surprising that there exist different approaches and varying perceptions of the relative efficacy of these approaches. Wiederholt (1974) has provided a helpful review of the history of the area and the several tributaries of influence that currently comprise the mainstream of the learning-disability movement. He projects a two-dimensional framework for the study and remediation of learning disabilities. One dimension involves the type of disorder and is divided into three areas: spoken language, written language, and perceptual and motor processes. He reviews the work of major contributors to the understanding of each disorder. The second dimension outlines the developmental phases of work in the field into three areas: foundation phase, transition phase, and integration phase. Wiederholt sees the integration phase, beginning in 1963, as bringing the three streams of concern for different disorders into a single major focus on learning disabilities. Of the integration phase, Wiederholt wrote:

Armed with the theories and programs of their professional progenitors, educators descended into the school and established programs for LD children during the integration phase. Interest in building theories and in developing assessment and remedial devices continues on the part of physicians, psychologists, and educators. However, the major characteristic of the field today is the rapid growth of school programs for LD children. The field is currently characterized by eclecticism . . . eclecticism (which) uses assessment and remedial or developmental materials borrowed from other areas of special education and regular education (1974, p. 327).

Decisions about interventions become increasingly complex when many are predicated on different assumptions about and views of the problem. Different data exist to support quite different historical streams of thinking. While research and clinical development have, as Wiederhold suggests, found a common conceptual roof, they have not been rationalized into a single body of theory and practice. He points out that the field has made great strides in the 1960s and 1970s in educational program development, teacher training, and the development of theory, research, and instructional materials and methods. Yet, as Wiederholt further states, the major problems remain, including definition, professional territoriality,

and efficacy research to provide a data base for improving services to learning disabled children. While developmental and behavioral psychology, and remedial education along with the more traditional theoretical and clinical developments in medicine, psychology and education, have generated rather substantial bodies of knowledge about interventions, "As an infant field (learning disabilities), has yet to clearly demonstrate its value in improving service to pupils with learning problems."

In reviewing the intervention approaches developed in the area, Ross (1976) argues for a different logic for developing interventions. He states: "A brief review of the history of the field that we now identify with the label 'learning disabilities' revealed that its origins in the study of brain-damaged adults have colored the approach to learning disabled children" (p. 15). Ross argues that the traditional approaches have failed because they reasoned inductively about these children based upon analogies drawn from work with the retarded, the cerebral palsied and the deaf. He proposes an alternative in developing interventions by reasoning deductively in which, according to his view, theorizing is based on empirical facts.

The field of learning disabilities has not grown in a systematic way based on the development and implementation of knowledge about these children and effective interventions. Like other special areas, it has been necessary to expand and apply intervention technologies before a sufficient base of knowledge about those technologies was developed. Much of what is now the large area of learning disability is the result of influences in the larger socio-legal and political system. It is important to understand that the threat and the fact of litigation involving rights to due process and rights to free appropriate education along with federal legislation requiring the education of all children in the least restrictive environment (P.L. 94–142), have forced the field to expand quickly.

In this environment, existing technologies will be disseminated. While this is not necessarily the ideal circumstance for program development, it is nevertheless one very familiar to those who are aware of the history of the development of services for handicapped children. The legislation that has created much of the recent imperative, however, has also specified some safeguards against certain potential abuses. Due process assurances in placement decisions and individual education plans, and the principle of least restrictive environment are examples. Social technology such as advocacy (Paul *et al.,* 1977) has emerged as an important aspect of the commitment to services and to accountability to consumers of services—in this instance, learning disabled children. The socio-political and legal environment is rich in opportunities for providing improved services to these children. In the presence of the massive bureaucracy, they will be required to implement services. In the absence of a sufficient data base of intervention, the rapid pace of change increases the risk and likelihood of interventions and delivery systems that either do not work or that work in the disinterest of the clients/consumers. Inappropriate labeling, and the inappropriate assessment procedures and use of data are examples (Hobbs, 1974).

There are very significant ethical questions involved in intervening to change the behavior of another person (Rhodes, 1974; Rhodes & Paul, 1978). The importance of professional standards, of monitoring treatment settings and of incorporating humanistic values in the philosophy of professional services are increasingly important.

A commitment to methodological research and quality training programs to produce the mature, well-trained professional corps that will be required must equal the commitment to program development and dissemination.

Much of the historical antecedent of the conceptualization of learning disabilities, as indicated earlier, was within the broad areas of neurology, neuropsychology, developmental psychology, and education. The basic brain-behavior paradigm guided the conceptual orientation of much of the research and the development of both facts and fancy about the nature of learning disabilities. While relatively little was known about brain-behavior relationships, the etiological die for understanding behavioral deficit was cast. That is, many behavioral deficits were presumed to be the result of deficits, damage, or injury to the central nervous system. While an interesting research question and important to our ultimately understanding the complex issues involved, an exclusive neuro-etiological focus was weak in generating interventions. If the etiological hypothesis were true, what then could be done about the functional disability?

This question, of course, mated selective research concerns of neurology and developmental psychology with education and, later, with behavioral psychology.

It is not unusual in periods of change and growth in a professional area for the strength of emerging perspectives to be overstated. Similarly, it is common for existing views to become defensive and resist change. The learning-disability area has developed very rapidly and many professional turfs have been challenged particularly around the issue of intervention: Who is going to work with these children? Wiederholt (1974), for example, notes the concerns of professionals in speech and remedial education over who will be responsible for handling language disorders in the schools.

This professional problem is well known. It is most basically a problem of growth and change in professional perspectives and practices. Each area seeks to replace other areas as the predominant view or the prevailing practice. Suffice it to say, in this context, the psychological problems of learning-disabled children are complex and require the creative and productive participation of different professional disciplines and different views within disciplines.

Behavioral theory, in its various applications with children in different settings, has had a profound impact on interventions with learning-disabled children. It helped conceptually with the isolation, identification and recording of behavior. It has had major empirical influence on interventions to change behavior more efficiently. This influence has been manifested in the clinic and in the classroom.

More recently, ecological views have had an important impact on understanding thinking about interventions. The ecological perspective places behavior and its neurological correlates within a larger sphere of interacting events. This view suggests that behavior disorders in children must be viewed as problems in interaction with reference to cultural rules. The cultural rites are protected; the cultural standard must be kept. It is the breach of these rites and rules or standards that constitutes the basis of discord and generates concern. Professionals are utilized in the reduction of tension between the standard bearer—parents, teachers, neighbors, peers, and so forth—and discordancy represented by the child. The problem of emotional disturbance, for example, has been conceptualized by Rhodes (1967) as a crisis in the interaction between culture bearer and culture violator.

The utility of this view is to avoid the dilemma of assigning responsibility entirely inside the organism, such as is suggested by a vigorous application of the medical, injury, disease, or sickness model. Szasz (1961), Trippe (1963, 1966), Albee (1969), Lewis (1965), Hobbs (1966), and others have clearly described the hazards of exclusive applications of medical constructs, including total assignment of responsibility for behavior to the brain. To view the child, rather, as a dynamic organism within dynamic systems with socializing responsibility is to suggest that aberrance in the child can also be accounted for by failures in the socializing systems. This view suggests a broader definition and analysis of problems and intervention on a broader basis. The questions now must include the nature of influences external to the child and responsibility for intervening to alter those influences when indicated as goals in a total treatment or intervention plan.

These points of view are not mutually exclusive, but provide important bases for understanding the multiple aspects of the problem any treatment or educational intervention program would attack. There are real differences in these views, and a smorgasbord approach justified by a banner of eclecticism based on a clear understanding of neither point of view will not work. The professional must have a solid technical base from which to work and must know what deviations from his orientation mean. Equally important is the rejection of an unquestioning commitment to his professional technical beliefs to the exclusion of other points of view. The therapy or treatment that must work and is viewed as adequate to all tasks for all children is simply unreasonable. A type of treatment which would be adequate for all children does not exist, and if a single method should be forced on all children, it would be unfortunate for many of them.

RESEARCH NEEDED

Throughout this chapter the authors have indicated major research needs related to different aspects of the problems associated with learning disabilities in children. Several of the major research problems in this area have already been described, including inconsistencies and lack of agreement in defining the population, weakness in the predictive validity of some of the constructs, and problems associated with low reliability of many of the instruments available for collecting data. The authors have also pointed out the relatively primitive level of integration of research from different behavioral and social science areas, and our failure to make substantial progress in developing truly interdisciplinary research.

Learning disabilities is one of the most complex problems facing child and family speciality areas. It is essential to conceptualize the problem in interdisciplinary terms and begin to develop knowledge from that perspective. A few of the research needs recently highlighted by researchers and clinicians will be mentioned here.

Denckla (1973) suggests that neurologists involved in research related to learning disabilities must develop the ability to detect neurological patterns of asymmetry and discrepancy which are deviations from developmental norms. She suggests developing neuro-metrical norms with normal children so that more sophisticated profiles for learning-disabled children could be developed with reference to this normative developmental data. Denckla argues that greater precision in syndrome classification should lead to better prediction, diagnosis, and treatment of certain learning problems.

Saphier (1973), in an overview of research on relationships between measurable perceptual motor skills in young children and academic success, has noted the relative "primitive state of the art." Future research on perceptual motor training, according to Saphier, should attempt to identify patterns or syndromes of performance in perceptual tests for children exhibiting early school failure. Research in this area should refine the spectrum of perceptual-motor skills, eliminate redundancy, and possibly generate hierarchical relationships among these skills.

Bryan, Wheeler, Felcan, and Henek (1976), in studying communication patterns to understand the sociometric rejection of learning disabled children, point out the need for research in this area, including examination of nonverbal communication with peers.

The need for studies on the impact of diet on perceptual and learning abilities is indicated. Extensive research is also needed to more fully understand the deleterious effects of noxious environmental agents on the performance of children (Perino & Erahart, 1974).

Considerable research is needed to determine the diagnostic utility of existing tests of perceptual functioning. Larsen, Rogers and Sowell (1976), investigating the use of several tests differentiating between normal and learning-disabled children, point out the need for research in this area. They also emphasize the importance of seeking a better understanding of the impact of situational factors within the regular classroom. The effect of teacher interaction upon achievement levels is particularly important in this research.

There remains the difficult task of developing an acceptable definition of learning disabilities. While this has many ramifications, Mercer and Forgnone (1976), as a result of their survey in forty-two states regarding different definitions of learning disabilities, point out the need for developing a definition that is useful to both practitioners and researchers.

REFERENCES

ALBEE, G. W. Emerging concepts of mental illness and models of treatment: The psychological point of view. *American Journal of Psychiatry*, 1969, *125*, 42–88.

AUSUBEL, D. P., *et al.* Perceived parent attitudes as determinants of children's ego structure. *Child Development*, 1954, *25*, 173–183.

BARBER, T. X., & SILVER, M. J. Fact, fiction, and

the experimenter bias effect. *Psychological Bulletin,* 1968, *70* (6) , 1–29. (*a*)

———. Pitfalls in data analysis and interpretation: A reply to Rosenthal. *Psychological Bulletin,* 1968, *70* (6) , 48–62. (*b*)

BARSCH, R. H. Teacher needs—Motor training. In W. M. Cruickshank (Ed.) , *The teacher of brain-injured children: A discussion of the bases for competency.* Syracuse, N.Y.: Syracuse University Press, 1966, 181–195.

BATEMAN, B. Learning disabilities—Yesterday, today and tomorrow. *Exceptional Children,* 1960, *27,* 18–26.

Behavioral status of young adolescents with iron deficiency anemia. *Journal of Learning Disabilities,* 1974, *7, 10* (December) , 19–20.

BELLER, E. K., & TURNER, J. L. Personality correlates of children's perception of human size. *Child Development,* 1964, *35,* 441–449.

BENDER, L. *Psychopathology of children with organic brain disorders.* Springfield, Ill.: Charles C Thomas, 1956.

———, & SILVER, A. Body image problems of the brain-damaged child. *Journal of Social Issues,* 1948, *4,* 84–89.

BENNETT, S. W., & PORT, C. H. The perception of autokinetic movement by brain-injured and familial retardates. *American Journal of Mental Deficiency,* 1963, *68,* 413–416.

BENSBERG, G. J. A test for differentiating endogenous and exogenous mental defectives. *American Journal of Mental Deficiency,* 1950, *54,* 502–506.

———. Performances of brain-injured and familial mental defectives on the Bender-Gestalt. *Journal of Consulting Psychology,* 1952, *16,* 61–64.

BIRCH, H. G. *A selective bibliography on brain-damaged children: The entity and its description; clinical and special diagnosis; characteristic mechanisms and natural history; etiology —Clinical, experimental, epidemiologic, treatment education, and management; reviews, overviews, and theories.* Presented through the courtesy of the Woods Schools and Residential Treatment Center. Longhorn, Pennsylvania, 1964.

———. *Brain damage in children: The biological and social aspects.* Baltimore: Williams and Wilkins, 1964.

———, BELMONT, I., & KARP, E. The prolongation of inhibition in brain-damaged patients. *Cortel,* 1965, *1,* 397–409.

———, & LEFFORD, A. Visual differentiation, intersensory integration, and voluntary motor control. *Monographs of the Society for Research in Child Development,* 1967, *32.*

BRYAN, T., WHEELER, R., FELCAN, J., & TOMACENE, H. "Come on Dummy": An observational study of children's communications. *Journal of Learning Disabilities,* 1976, *9, 10* (December) 661–669.

BURKS, H. The hyperkinetic child. *Exceptional Children,* 1960, *27,* 18–26.

CASSEL, R. H. Relation of design reproduction to the etiology of mental deficiency. *Journal of Consulting Psychology,* 1949, *13,* 421–428.

CLEMENTS, S. D. *Minimal brain dysfunction in children: Terminology and identification, phase one of a three-phase project.* U.S. Department of Health, Education, and Welfare. NINDB Monograph No. 3. Washington, D.C.: U.S. Government Printing Office, 1966.

COLMAN, P. G., & COM, B. A comparative study of the test performances of brain-injured, emotionally disturbed and normal children. *South African Medical Journal,* 1966, *40,* 945–950.

COOPERSMITH, S. Studies in self-esteem. *Scientific American,* 1968, *218,* 96–106.

CRUICKSHANK, W. M. *The teacher of brain injured children: a discussion of the bases of competency.* Syracuse, N.Y.: Syracuse University Press, 1966.

———. *Learning disabilities in home, school, and community.* Syracuse N.Y.: Syracuse University Press, 1977.

———. *The brain-injured child in home, school and community.* Syracuse N.Y.: Syracuse University Press, 1967. (*a*)

———. The education of the child with brain injury. In W. M. Cruickshank and G. O.

Johnson (Eds.), *Education of exceptional children and youth.* (2nd ed.). Englewood Cliffs, N.J.: Prentice-Hall, Inc., 1967, 238–283.

———, BENTZEN, F. A., RATZEBURG, F. H., & TANNHAUSSER, M. T. *Perception and cerebral palsy* (2nd ed.). Syracuse, N.Y.: Syracuse University Press, 1965, 1–172.

———, BICE, H. W., & WALLEN, N. E. *Perception and cerebral palsy: A study in figure background relationship.* Syracuse, N.Y.: Syracuse University Press, 1957.

———, & HALLAHAN, D. P. *Perceptual and learning disabilities in children.* (1st ed.). Syracuse University Press, 1975.

———, et al. *A teaching method for brain-injured and hyperactive children.* Syracuse, N.Y.: Syracuse University Press, 1961.

CRUSE, D. B. Effects of distraction upon the performance of brain-injured and familial retarded children. *American Journal of Mental Deficiency,* 1969, *66,* 86–92.

DAVIDSON, H. H., & LANG, G. Children's perceptions of their teacher's feelings toward them related to self-perception, school achievement and behavior. *Journal of Experimental Education,* 1960, *29,* 107–118.

DAY, R. H. The after effect of seen movement and brain damage. *Journal of Consulting Psychology,* 1960, *24,* 311–315.

DECKER, R. J. Manifestations of the brain damage syndrome in historical and psychological data. In S. R. Rappaport (Ed.), *Childhood aphasia and brain damage: A definition.* Narbreth, Pa.: Livingston Publishing Company, 1964.

DENCKLA, M. B. Research needs in learning disabilities: A neurologist's point of view. *Journal of Learning Disabilities,* 1973, *6,* 7 (August–September), 43–52.

DOLPHIN, J. E., & CRUICKSHANK, W. M. Pathology of concept formation in children with cerebral palsy. *American Journal of Mental Deficiency,* 1951, *56,* 386–392. *(b)*

———. The figure background relationship in children with cerebral palsy. *Journal of Clinical Psychology,* 1951, *7,* 228–231. *(a)*

———. Tactual motor perception of children with cerebral palsy. *Journal of Personality,* 1952, *20,* 466–471.

DUBNOFF, B., & CHAMBERS, I. A multifocal approach to the development of the concept of body image. In Council for Children with Behavioral Disorders (Ed.), *Yearbook 1966.* Washington, D.C.: Council for Children with Behavioral Disorders, 1966.

EFSTATHIOU, A., & MORANT, R. B. Persistence of the waterfall illusion after-effect as a test of brain damage. *Journal of Abnormal Psychology,* 1966, *71,* 300–303.

EISENBERG, L. Behavioral manifestations of cerebral damage in childhood. In H. G. Birch (Ed.), *Brain damage in children.* Baltimore: The Williams & Wilkins Co., 1964, 61–73.

———. Psychiatric implications of brain damage in children. *Psychiatric Quarterly,* 1957, *31,* 72–92.

ERNHART, C. B., GRAHAM, F. K., EICHMAN, P. L., MARSHALL, J. M., & THURSTON, D. Brain injury in the pre-school child: Some developmental considerations: II. Comparison of brain-injured and normal children. *Psychological Monographs: Genetic and Applied,* 1963, *77,* 16–33.

FARNHAM-DIGGORY, S. Self, future and time. *Monographs of the Society for Research in Child Development,* 1966, *31,* 1–63.

FENNIMORE, F. Reading and the self-concept. *Journal of Reading,* 1968, *11,* 447–451.

FERNALD, G. M. *Remedial techniques in basic school subjects.* New York: McGraw-Hill, 1943.

FISHER, S., & CLEVELAND, S. E. *Body image and personality.* Princeton, N.J.: D. Van Nostrand Company, Inc., 1958.

FISICHELLI, V. R., & KARELITZ, S. The cry latencies of normal infants and those with brain damage. *Journal of Pediatrics,* 1963, *62,* 724–734.

———, et al. The phonetic content of the cries of normal infants and those with brain damage. *The Journal of Psychology,* 1966, *64,* 119–126.

FRANCIS-WILLIAMS, J. Special educational problems of children with minimal cerebral dysfunction. *Spastics Quarterly,* 1965, *14,* 71.

FREUD, S. *The ego and the id.* Trans. by J. Strachley (Ed.), New York: W. W. Norton & Company, Inc., 1960.

FROSTIG, M. Visual perception in the brain damaged child. *American Journal of Orthopsychiatry,* 1962, *32,* 279–280.

——, LEFEVER, D. W., & WHITTLESEY, J. R. B. A developmental test of visual perception for evaluating normal and neurologically handicapped children. *Perceptual and Motor Skills,* 1961, *12,* 282–294.

——. *The Role of Perception in the Integration of Psychological Functions,* in Cruickshank, W. M., and Hallahan, D. P. (Eds.), Perceptual and Learning Disabilities in Children, Syracuse University Press, 1975, chapter 6.

GALLAGHER, J. J. Children with developmental imbalances: A psychoeducational definition. In W. M. Cruickshank (Ed.), *The teacher of brain-injured children.* Syracuse, N.Y.: Syracuse University Press, 1966, 22–43.

——. A comparison of brain-injured and non brain-injured mentally retarded children on several psychological variables. *Monographs of the Society for Research in Child Development,* 1957, *22,* 51.

GARFIELD, J. C., BENTON, A. L., & MacQUEEN, J. C. Motor impersistence in brain-damaged and cultural-familial defectives. *The Journal of Nervous and Mental Disease,* 1966, *142,* 434–440.

GARNER, F. E., NEURINGER, C., & GOLDSTEIN, G. The spiral aftereffect, extraneous stimulation and brain damage. *Cortel,* 1966, *2,* 385–398.

GERSTMANN, J. Fingeranosie: Eine unschriebene stoerund der orientierung am eigenen koerper. *Wiener Klinsche Wochenschrift,* 1924, *37,* 1010–1012.

GOLDSTEIN, K. *The organism.* New York: American Book Company, 1939.

GOODLAD, J. I. Understanding the self in the school setting. *Childhood Education,* 1964, *41,* 9–14.

GRUBE, M. M. *Visual Figure-Ground Perceptual Development in Four to Seven Year Old Normal Children.* Unpublished Doctoral Dissertation, University of Michigan, 1978.

GUBBAY, S., et al. Clumsy children: A study of apraxic and agnosic defects in 21 children. *Brain,* 1965, *88,* 295–312.

HAGGARD, E. A., & ROSE, G. J. Some effects of mental set and active participation in the conditioning of the autokinetic phenomenon. *Journal of Experimental Psychology,* 1944, *34,* 45–59.

HALLAHAN, D., & KAUFFMAN, J. *Introduction to learning disabilities.* Englewood Cliffs, N.J.: Prentice-Hall, 1976.

HANVIK, L. J. And the beanstalk grows. *Exceptional Children,* 1966, *32,* 577–578.

HARING, N. G., & SCHIEFELBUSCH, R. L. (Eds.). *Methods in special education.* New York: McGraw-Hill, 1967.

HAWK, T. L. Self-concepts of the socially disadvantaged. *The Elementary School Journal,* 1967, *67,* 196–206. (Permission to quote by the University of Chicago Press.)

HEWETT, F. M. *The emotionally disturbed child in the classroom.* Boston: Allyn & Bacon, Inc., 1968.

HIRT, J. B. Manifestations of the brain damage syndrome in school. In S. Rappaport (Ed.), *Childhood aphasia and brain damage: A definition.* Nabreth, Pa.: Livingston Publishing Co., 1964.

HOBBS, N. Helping disturbed children: Psychological and ecological strategies. *American Psychologist,* 1966, *21,* 1105–1115.

HOBBS, N. J. *Teaching children with behavior disorders: Personal perspectives.* Columbus, Ohio: Charles E. Merrill, 1974.

HOMBERGER, A. Vorlesungen uber psychopathologie des kindersaleters. Berlin: Julius Springes, 1926, 1–318.

HOROWITZ, M. J. Body image. *Archives of General Psychiatry,* 1966, *14,* 456–460.

HUNT, B. J. Performance of mentally deficient brain-injured children and mentally deficient familial children on construction from pattern. *American Journal of Mental Deficiency,* 1959, *63,* 679–687.

———, & PATTERSON, R. Performance of brain-injured and familial mentally deficient children on visual and auditory sequences. *American Journal of Mental Deficiency,* 1958, *63,* 72–80.

ILLINGWORTH, R. S. The clumsy child. *Clinical Pediatrics,* 1968, *7,* 539–543.

JACOBS, J. F., & PIERCE, M. L. The social position of retardates with brain damage associated characteristics. *Exceptional Children,* 1968, *34,* 677–681.

JENKIN, N., & MORSE, S. A. Size-distance judgment in organic mental defectives. *Journal of Consulting Psychology,* 1960, *24,* 139–143.

KALISKI, L. The brain-injured child: Learning by living in a structured setting. *American Journal of Mental Deficiency,* 1959, *63,* 688–695.

KARELITZ, S., & FISICHELLI, V. R. The cry thresholds of normal infants and those with brain damage. *Journal of Pediatrics,* 1962, *61,* 679–685.

———, KARELITZ, R., & ROSENFELD, L. S. Infants' vocalizations and their significance. In P. W. Bowman and H. V. Mautner (Eds.), *Mental retardation: Proceedings of the first international medical conference.* New York: Grune and Stratton, Inc., 1960.

KEPHART, N. C. *The slow learner in the classroom.* Columbus, Ohio: Charles E. Merrill Books, Inc., 1960.

KESSLER, J. W. *Psychopathology of childhood.* Englewood Cliffs, N.J.: Prentice-Hall, Inc., 1966.

KOPPITZ, E. M. Diagnosing brain damage in young children with the Bender Gestalt Test. *Journal of Consulting Psychology,* 1962, *26,* 541–546.

KRONICK, D. Some thoughts on group identification: Social needs. *Journal of Learning Disabilities,* 1974, *7, 3,* 144–147.

LARSEN, S. C., ROGERS, D., & SOWELL, J. The use of selected perceptual tests in differentiating between normal and learning disabled children. *Journal of Learning Disabilities,* 1975.

LEVINE, M., & SPIVACK, G. Adaptation to repeated exposure to the Spiral Visual Aftereffect in brain-damaged, emotionally disturbed, and normal individuals. *Perceptual and Motor Skills,* 1962, *14,* 425–246.

———. Rate of reversal of Necker Cube in diffuse brain injury. *Journal of Clinical Psychology,* 1962, *18,* 122–124.

LEWIS, W. W. Continuity and intervention in emotional disturbance: A review. *Exceptional Children,* 1965, *31,* 465–475.

MACKIE, J. B., & BECK, E. C. Relations among rigidity, intelligence, and perception in brain-damaged and normal individuals. *The Journal of Nervous and Mental Disease,* 1966, *142,* 310–317.

MAIER, N. R. F., & SCHNEIRLA, T. C. *Principles of animal psychology.* New York: McGraw-Hill, 1935.

MARK, H. J., & PASAMANICK, B. Asynchronism and apparent movement thresholds in brain-injured children. *Journal of Consulting Psychology,* 1958, *22,* 173–177.

McANINCH, M. Body image as related to perceptual-cognitive-motor disabilities. In J. Hellmuth (Ed.), *Learning Disorders.* Vol. II. Seattle: Special Child Publications of the Seattle Seguin School, Inc., 1966, 137–170. Quotations by special permission of Special Child Publications, Inc., Seattle, Washington.

McCARTNEY, L. D. Helping mentally deficient children of the exogenous type showing central nervous system impairment to make better social adjustments. *American Journal of Mental Deficiency,* 1956, *61,* 121–126.

McGINNIS, M. A. *Aphasic children: Identification and education by the association method.* Washington, D.C.: Volta Bureau, 1963.

MEAD, G. H. *Mind, self and society: From the standpoint of a social behaviorist.* C. W.

Morris (Ed.), Chicago: University of Chicago Press, 1934.

MENKES, M. N., ROWE, J. J., & MENKES, J. H. A twenty-five year follow-up study on the hyperkinetic child with minimal brain dysfunction. *Pediatrics,* 1967, *39,* 393–399.

MERCER, C. D., FORGNONE, C., & WOLKING, W. D. Definitions of Learning Disabilities Used in the U.S. *Journal of Learning Disabilities,* 9, 6, June-July, 1976, 376–386.

MYERS, P., & HAMMILL, D. *Methods for learning disorders.* New York: John Wiley, 1976.

NELLHAUS, G. What name for "these" children? *Developmental Medicine and Child Neurology,* 1968, *10,* 536–537.

PAINE, R. S. Neurological and grand rounds: Minimal chronic brain syndromes. *Clinical Proceedings of the Children's Hospital.* Washington, D.C.: 1966, *22,* 21–40.

PAUL, J. L., NEUFELD, G. R., & PELOSI, J. P. *Child advocacy in the system.* Syracuse, N.Y.: Syracuse University Press, 1977.

PERINO, J., & ERAHART, C. The relation of subclinical lead level to cognitive and sensorimotor impairment in black pre-schoolers. *Journal of Learning Disabilities,* December, 1974, 7 *(10),* 616–620.

PIAGET, J., & LAMBERCIER, M. La comparison des grandeurs projectives chez l'enfant et chez l'adulte. *Archives of Psychology,* 1951, *33,* 81–130.

PINCUS, J. H., & GLASSER, G. H. The syndrome of "minimal brain damage" in childhood. *The New England Journal of Medicine,* 1966, *275,* 27–35.

PROSEN, H. Physical disability and motivation. *Canadian Medical Association Journal,* 1965, *92,* 1261–1265.

QUIRÓS, DE, JULIO, *Neuropsychological Fundamentals in Learning Disabilities,* Academic Therapy Publication, San Rafael, California, 1978.

RADLER, D. H., & KEPHART, N. C. *Success through play.* New York: Harper & Row, 1960.

RAPPAPORT, S. R. *Childhood aphasia and brain damage. Vol. II. Differential diagnosis.* Narbreth, Pa.: Livingston, 1965.

———. *Childhood aphasia and brain damage: A definition.* Narbreth, Pa.: Livingston, 1964.

———. Personality factors teachers need for relationship structure. In W. M. Cruickshank (Ed.), *The teacher of brain-injured children.* Syracuse, N.Y.: Syracuse University Press, 1966, 45–55.

REED, J. C., & REED, H. B. C., JR. Concept formation ability and non-verbal abstract thinking among older children with chronic cerebral dysfunction. *The Journal of Special Education,* 1967, *1,* 157–161.

REED, H. B. C., JR., REITAN, R. M., & KLOVE, H. Influence of cerebral lesions on psychological test performance of older children. *Journal of Consulting Psychology,* 1965, *29,* 247–251.

REITAN, R. M. The comparative effects of brain damage of the Halstead Impairment Index and the Wechsler Bellevue Scale. *Journal of Clinical Psychology,* 1959, *15,* 281–285.

RHODES, W. C. Preface. In J. Hellmuth (Ed.), *Educational Therapy, Vol. I.* Seattle: Special Child Publications of the Seattle Seguin School, Inc., 1966, 16–26.

———. *A study of child variance, Vol. 4: The Future.* Ann Arbor, Michigan: University of Michigan, 1975.

———. The disturbing child: A problem of ecological management. *Exceptional Children,* 1967, *33,* 449–455.

———, & PAUL, J. L. *Theories of deviance: New views.* Englewood Cliffs, N.J.: Prentice-Hall, 1978.

ROGERS, C. R. *Client-centered therapy.* Boston: Houghton Mifflin Company, 1951.

ROSENBLITH, J. R., & ALLINSMITH, W. (Eds.). *The causes of behavior: Readings in child development and educational psychology.* Boston: Allyn & Bacon, Inc., 1962.

ROSENTHAL, R., & JACOBSON, L. *Pygmalion in the classroom, teacher expectation and pupils' intellectual development.* New York: Holt, Rinehart & Winston, Inc., 1968.

Ross, A. O. *Psychological aspects of learning disabilities and reading disorders.* New York: McGraw-Hill, 1976.

Rosvold, H. E., *et al.* A continuous performance test of brain damage. *Journal of Consulting Psychology,* 1956, 20.

Rowley, V., & Baer, P. Visual retention test performance in emotionally disturbed and brain damaged children. *American Journal of Orthopsychiatry,* 1963, *31,* 579–583.

Sabatino, D. A. The construction and assessment of an experimental test of auditory perception. *Exceptional Children,* 1969, *35,* 729–737.

Saphier, J. D. The relation of perceptual motor skills to learning and school success. *Journal of Learning Disabilities,* 6, *9,* November, 1973, 583–592.

Schein, J. D. The duration of the Archimedes Spiral Afterimage in the diagnosis of brain damage. *Journal of Consulting Psychology,* 1960, *24,* 299–300.

Scherrington, P. S. *Man on his nature.* Cambridge, England: Cambridge University Press, 1951.

Schilder, P. *The image and appearance of the human body.* New York: John Wiley & Sons, Inc., 1950.

Schlanger, B. B. Results of varying presentations to brain-damaged children of an auditory word discrimination test. *American Journal of Mental Deficiency,* 1958, *63,* 464–468.

Schulman, J. L., Kaspar, J. C., & Thorne, F. M. *Brain damage and behavior: A clinical experimental study.* Springfield, Ill.: Charles C. Thomas, 1965.

Sears, P. S., & Sherman, V. *In pursuit of self-esteem: Case studies of eight elementary school children.* Belmont, Cal.: Wadsworth Publishing Company, Inc., 1964.

Shapiro, M. B. Experimental studies of a perceptual anomaly: Vol. I. Initial experiments. *Journal of Mental Science,* 1951, *97,* 90–110.

Sievers, D. J. A study to compare the performance of brain injured and non-brain injured mentally retarded children on the Differential Language Facility Test. *American Journal of Mental Deficiency,* 1959, *63,* 839–847.

Snow, R. E. Unfinished Pygmalion. *Contemporary Psychology,* 1969, *14,* 197–199.

Staffieri, J. R. Body image stereotypes of mentally retarded. *American Journal of Mental Deficiency,* 1968, *72,* 841–843.

——. A study of social stereotype of body image in children. *Journal of Personality and Social Psychology,* 1967, *7,* 101–104.

Stevens, D. A., *et al.* Presumed minimal brain dysfunction in children: Relationship to performance on selected behavioral tests. *Archives of General Psychiatry,* 1967, *16,* 281–285.

Strauss, A. A., & Kephart, N. C. *Psychopathology and education of the brain-injured child. Vol. II. Progress in theory and clinic.* New York: Grune and Stratton, 1955.

——, & Werner, H. Deficiency in the finger schema in relation to arithmetic disability. *American Journal of Orthopsychiatry,* 1938, *8,* 719–725.

——. Disorders of conceptual thinking in the brain injured child. *The Journal of Nervous and Mental Disease,* 1942, *96,* 153–172.

——. Finger agnosia in children. *American Journal of Psychiatry.* 1939, *95,* 1215–1225.

Szasz, T. S. *The myth of mental illness.* New York: Hoeber-Harper, 1961.

Thelander, H. E., Phelps, J. K., & Kirk, E. W. Learning disabilities associated with lesser brain damage. *The Journal of Pediatrics,* 1958, *53,* 405–409.

Thorndike, R. L. Review. *American Educational Research Journal,* 1968, *5,* 708–711.

Traub, A. C., & Orbach, J. Psychophysical studies of body-image: I. The adjustable body distorting mirror. *Archives of General Psychiatry,* 1964, *11,* 53–66.

Trippe, M. J. Conceptual problems in research on educational provisions for disturbed children. *Exceptional Children*, 1963, *29*, 400–406.

———. Educational therapy. In J. Hellmuth (Ed.), *Educational therapy. Vol. I.* Seattle: Special Child Publications of the Seattle Seguin School, 1966, pp. 45–48.

VEGAS, O. V., & FRYE, R. L. Effects of brain damage on perceptual performance. *Perceptual and Motor Skills*, 1963, *17*, 662.

WALLACE, G., & KAUFFMAN, J. *Teaching children with learning problems.* Columbus, Ohio: Charles E. Merrill Publishing Company, 1973.

———, & McLAUGHLIN, J. *Learning disabilities.* Columbus, Ohio: Charles E. Merrill Publishing Company, 1975.

WALTON, J. N., ELLIS, E., COURT, S. D. M. Clumsy children: A study of developmental apraxia and agnosia. *Brain*, 1962, *85*, 603–612.

WEPMAN, J. M. *Recovery from aphasia.* New York: The Ronald Press Company, 1951.

———, CRUICKSHANK, W. M., DEUTSCH, C. P., MORENCY, A., & STROTHER, C. R. Learning Disabilities. In N. Hobbs (Ed.), *Issues in the classification of children, Vol. I.* San Francisco: Jossey-Bass, 1975.

WERNER, H., & STRAUSS, A. A. Disorders of conceptual thinking in the brain injured child. *Journal of Nervous and Mental Diseases,* 1952, *96*, 153–172.

———, & THUMA, B. D. Critical flicker frequency in children with brain injury. *American Journal of Psychology*, 1942, *55*, 394–99. (a)

———. A deficiency in perception of apparent motion in children with brain damage. *American Journal of Psychology*, 1942, *55*, 58–67.

WIEDERHOLT, J. L. Historical perspectives on the education of the learning disabled. In L. Mann & D. Sabatino, *The second review of special education.* Philadelphia: JSE Publisher, 1974.

WILLIAMS, H. L., GRIESEKING, C. F., & LUBIN, A. Interaction of brain injury with peripheral vision and set. *Journal of Consulting Psychology*, 1961, *25*, 543–548.

WOZNIAK, R. H. Psychology and Education of the Learning Disabled in the Soviet Union. In W. M. Cruickshank and D. P. Hallahan (Eds.), *Perceptual and Learning Disabilities in Children.* Syracuse: Syracuse University Press, Vol. 1, 1975, 407–479.

WYLIE, R. C. *The self concept: A critical survey of pertinent research literature.* Lincoln: University of Nebraska Press, 1961.

ZION, L. C. Body concept as it relates to self-concept. *The Research Quarterly*, 1965, *36*, 490–495.

13 Psychological Considerations of Emotionally Disturbed Children

Peter Knoblock

*Ph.D., Professor of Special Education and Area Coordinator,
Education for Emotionally Disturbed, Division of Special Education
and Rehabilitation, School of Education, Syracuse University.*

Revisions have been made in this chapter to reflect the several new developments in this field. Largely due to major efforts by Rhodes and Tracy (1972) and Hobbs (1975), there is now a greater recognition that emotional disturbance can be viewed from a variety of perspectives, and that each perspective carries with it a set of beliefs relative to causation and treatment. This chapter will not necessarily reconcile these varying perspectives, but rather expose the reader to them.

New material has been included on children labeled "severely emotionally disturbed," and often referred to as autistic or autistic-like. In the past, the majority of these children were in residential care, some form of institutional program, or were receiving no schooling at all (Cottle, 1976). New federal legislation under P.L. 94–142, the Right to Education for All Handicapped Children's Act of 1975 now mandates a free public education for *all* children, and a new consciousness among special educators attracts a new generation of teachers to respond to more seriously impaired children.

Another new section focuses on the mainstreaming or integration of emotionally disturbed (and other children with special needs) into the least restrictive setting or most normalized environment. As expected, this already is a controversial educational issue and this section attempts to specify the levels of integration possible and some successful programmatic approaches.

Despite some headway into the conceptualization of emotional disturbance from varying perspectives, the somewhat greater acceptance of individual differences and the successful integration of some children into the educational mainstream, there remain heated debate and differences between professionals and professions as to factors of definitions, causation, and treatment.

In many ways, the battle lines have been hastily and firmly drawn. Some professional workers place their diagnostic and intervention emphases on the behavior of the child. Others look for the psychodynamic explanations behind such symptomatic behaviors, or to the parents, who could be accountable for the genesis of disturbance in the child. Still others do not view emotional disturbance as a condition at all. To this group, emotional disturbance resides in the eyes of the beholder and is a reality only insofar as we are willing to label it as such. Closely related are those who feel that the environmental pressures under which children operate are overly burdensome to their psychosocial development.

Any or all of these perspectives may be useful as explanatory concepts or as points of view that allow for greater accessibility of assistance to the child. This chapter takes the point of view that any effort to understand emotional disturbance in its many manifest forms will need to view the child in the context of his environments. That the child labeled emotionally disturbed by adults, be they professionals or nonprofessionals, is capable of making an impact on those around him is well recognized, but not necessarily accepted or acceptable to those with whom he interacts. The reciprocal impact of the situational determinants on a child's emotional status and responsiveness is not nearly as well recognized. Yet we seem to operate on the basis that accurate understanding of environments can effectively assist a child in difficulty.

The interaction of the child we are referring to as emotionally disturbed and the many environments and people who inhabit those environments will be the central focus of this chapter. Explicit in such an approach is the fact that we need extensive understanding of both children and environments. As a matter of fact, there is much we do know of children's emotional development. To keep things in perspective, we should remind ourselves that we are still speaking of children and not necessarily referring to some irrational being who is helpless and who should be totally removed from society. Those serious students of child development and behavior are also encouraged to pursue studies in normal child development so as to gain some perspective on the prevalence of what we call childhood problem behavior (Macfarlane, Allen, & Honzik, 1954). This chapter attempts to convey the various frames of reference employed to understand the concept, "emotional disturbance," and a range of teaching, treatment, and environmental interventions used to respond to children who may experience inner conflict or are thought of as deviant by others. Those desiring other summaries of current research and descriptions of the field of educating disturbed children can refer to Kauffman (1977), Clarizio and McCoy (1976), Hewett and Blake (1973), and Anthony (1970).

PERSPECTIVES ON DEFINING EMOTIONAL DISTURBANCE IN CHILDREN

This section highlights a variety of perspectives that "explain" emotional disturbance as viewed from that particular point of view. Ideally, any approach to conceptualizing and understanding a concept such as emotional disturbance would focus on the total life space of a child, the environment and those in it. This could be formulated in Lewin's now classic statement, "Behavior (B) is a function of the Person (P) and the Environment (E)" (1936). The formula $B = f(P,E)$ represents this statement and when utilized by professional workers can allow for a more complete way of looking at a child and understanding the many forces impinging upon her. For example, we know from our clinical experiences that children may behave differently in different environments, and that they do not necessarily exhibit maladaptive behaviors in every situation and with every person they encounter. By including such a range of factors to help us look at emotional disturbance, we are taking a step toward acknowledging just how complex this thing is we have labeled emotional disturbance. To Lewin's social-psychological formulation we should add the many insights to be gained from a number of the behavioral sciences (Bower & Hollister, 1967).

The Conceptual Project in Emotional Disturbance

Just such an effort at pulling together the accumulated knowledge and research from the behavioral sciences has been attempted by Rhodes and Tracy (1972). They have served as director and principal investigator, respectively, on a federally funded project titled, "A Study of Child Variance." They and their colleagues have produced four volumes dealing with theories of emotional disturbance, interventions, service-delivery systems, and the future (University of Michigan, Publications Distribution Service). In addition, video tapes highlighting interviews with proponents of the various theories are available as is a manual of exercises to facilitate teacher training.

This project details five models or theories —behavioral theory, psychodynamic theory, biophysical theory, sociological theory, and ecological theory—and the phenomenon of child variation, and more specifically "emotional disturbance," within each. Reinert (1976) has written a textbook on emotional disturbance essentially organized around these theoretical viewpoints.

School Definitions

For many decades a rather awkward discussion raged in public schools as to whether teachers should be as concerned with the shy, withdrawn child as they are with the aggressive, acting-out child. This argument was awkward because a great many of the critics had insufficient information as to the shades and nuances of behavior in operation in a typical classroom. It is only within the decade that direct observation and recording of child behaviors and teacher-child interactions has assumed a degree of respectability (Smith & Geoffrey, 1968; Jackson, 1968; Good & Brophy, 1973; Rowen, 1973). As Beilin (1959) points out, there may be very appropriate reasons for teachers focusing on more overt, acting-out behaviors. These are the behaviors that directly subvert the instructional and management approaches of teachers. Of more subtle significance is Beilin's finding that over the years since the publication of the Wickman

study (1928), the correlation between clinicians' and teachers' judgments as to what constitutes problem behavior is increasing. One possible interpretation might be that teachers have become more like clinicians in their perceptions. Those of us involved in schools, however, do not see this. What is seen are teachers focusing very directly on those children manifesting deviant behaviors, usually those taking the form of physical or verbal aggression.

According to Gnagey (1965) "deviancy" is used synonymously with "misbehavior." "A deviancy occurs when a student takes actions which are prohibited by the teacher" (p. 4). It would seem, then, that a great number of school environments, while paying lip service to the quiet and shy, are labeling and focusing on aggressive children. It is this labeling of aggressive behavior as emotional disturbance and placing it in the realm of deviance that accounts for a large group of children being presented to special education for assistance.

The intrapsychic model for looking at emotional problems of children undoubtedly contributed to the placing of responsibility on the child for the control or mismanagement of his behavior. The locus of the problem, that of transgressing against the norms of the school, is viewed in this context as stemming from internal problems of the child. He is admonished to try harder, to respond to the interventions by adults, to re-set his behavioral goals, and, failing to do one or all of these, to suffer the consequences of his behavior.

A dramatically different approach to the defining of emotional disturbance in children is an ecological one in which environmental variables are viewed as possible determinants of children's emotional reactions and adjustments. Such a point of view would not rule out the psychodynamic forces operating within the child but, rather, place such forces within the context of the environment in which the child operates (Barker & Gump, 1964). Carried to a logical conclusion, such an emphasis upon the environmental pressures of schools should make us ask why some behaviors are considered deviant and disturbed. Have we redefined emotional disturbance in terms of what the school can and cannot tolerate without looking inward to examine the abrasive characteristics of our schools?

Out of an ecological orientation have come references to the disturbing child—one who may act out due to psychonoxious qualities in the environment. The matter becomes complex because it quickly leads to the observation that only some children are defined this way. The process of defining is rarely as clear as the above implies. School agents frequently believe that the child is doing things *to* the environment rather than acknowledging the reciprocal impact of school practices on the child (Trippe, 1963).

Rhodes (1966) pleads eloquently for a merger of education and ecological sciences, which would include behavioral, social, and mental-health approaches. He paints the picture of many ancillary workers flitting about in the school.

. . . whirling giddily around the outside periphery of the central instructional arena. All of these are patched onto the school as extraneous foreign bodies which are easily cast out, like the unassimilable appendages they are, every time it suits the administrators, the funding sources or reactionary power groups. In the center we see the regular teacher and the instructional program ploughing its way through the core of the curriculum, no matter what the balanced growth and learning needs of the children happen to be (p. 5).

Peer-Group Definitions of Emotional Disturbance

Some professional workers look to the peer group as a yardstick of who in the group represents deviant behavior and requires labeling as an emotionally disturbed child. Undoubtedly, this definitional stance has come about through the study of children who are scapegoated by groups. Not all of these observations are dramatically available to the observer, however. As children's groups develop greater cohesiveness, there is a greater tolerance for deviations from group norms, thus allowing for a greater range of behavior from individual members and less chance for clear labeling by adults. Studies of child group-behavior seem to point out that the environment in which behavior occurs defines certain limits as to the behavior of group members (Barker, 1963).

In an interesting study of social distance generated by the exceptional at the high school level (Jones, Gottfried, & Owens, 1966), it was found that acceptance was related to both interpersonal situations and the type of exceptionality. Using high-school students in grades nine through twelve, the acceptability of emotional disturbance varied according to the specific situation under consideration. Along with the importance of the interpersonal situation were the variables of sex and grades of the respondents. Thus, in response to the statement: "I would accept this person as a coworker in my occupation," the emotionally disturbed were rated very low. In contrast, this exceptionality fared much better when considered in the interpersonal situation, "I would accept this type of child as a playmate for my children."

We are just now gaining clear insights into how normal children view their age mates who are thought of as special. This information is coming to us through exciting efforts to integrate normal and handicapped children in regular elementary school settings (Hambleton & Ziegler, 1974). In this study integrating trainable retarded into a regular elementary school setting, Hambleton and Ziegler found a high degree of acceptance in behavior and attitudes on the part of normal children and the special children were known by name or had contact with normal children. This author's present involvement in a school for severely emotionally disturbed and typical children supports these findings with the added information that many of the special children, although thought of as autistic and autistic-like, clearly could recognize and identify by name or picture the other children in their classrooms. In addition, studies are being conducted to determine ways in which normal children can assist their handicapped peers. The message seems clear: if we hope to foster more positive attitudes on the part of normal children toward special children and help them define their peers in less stigmatizing ways, then both integration and specific helping interactions must be fostered.

Although it is of interest to know how normal children view deviant behavior, it is also of value for us to examine more direct forms of peer-group involvement to determine just how far children can go in their own groups before they are labeled deviant. Lesser (1959) reports on a study which supports the notion that groups of children are capable of making determinations as to which responses are acceptable and to be differentially rewarded or punished by peers. His study explored the relationships between different forms of aggression and peer-group approval or disapproval. In this sociometric approach he used five categories of aggression: provoked physical aggression; outburst aggression; unprovoked physical aggression; verbal aggression; and indirect aggression. His sample consisted of upper-lower-class boys, 10 to 13 years old. He found provoked physical aggression a relatively approved form of aggression, with indirect aggression ("to attack or injure indirectly through another person or object") strongly disapproved.

Not all children, however, will communicate their definitions to us quite so clearly. Redl (1949) has pointed out that individual members in a group will be drawn into acting-out behaviors, a phenomenon he refers to as contagion, depending on group psychological factors such as the status of the initiator. This would be an example, then, of deviant behavior displayed by a high-status group member, which would be followed by others and not singled out negatively by others in the group. This type of child, often referred to as the "master manipulator," has the power to pull deviant behavior from others while remaining almost unobtrusive to the untrained eye. It is the wise group-leader who focuses on the influence such a child may have on others. Many investigators find that the social-interactional systems operative in children's groups are not often recognized and channeled for constructive purposes. This inattentiveness to group process and dynamics would be as true for classroom groups as it is for institutional programs (Getzels & Thelen, 1960; Polsky, 1962). Polsky's participant observation study in a residential treatment center for disturbed boys clearly demonstrates that the peer culture of the center functioned in a powerful manner in terms of influencing children and, of course, the adults. The professional staff, concerned at the roadblocks thrown up by the children to the treatment program, sought an analysis of the peer social and emotional climate. Some of us joke with each other from time to time about the strong possibility that children plot and scheme against the kinds of notions we have for helping them. Ironically enough, Polsky's study shows how well-organized some delinquent subgroups can be in order to accomplish their own survival goals.

Parent Definitions of Emotional Disturbance

The prevalent notion that it is the professionals who seek out and define disturbance does not give credit to parent detection. Those responsible for clinic and child-welfare services will attest to the numerous requests for assistance made by parents.

Others would be willing to go a step further, such as Vogel and Bell (1960), who maintained that not only can some parents define emotional disturbance but that they may, in fact, create it. In such instances, the child's role is that of family scapegoat, and his problem is either created or exacerbated due to the marital conflicts and needs of the parents. In a study of disturbed children's parents, who were themselves disturbed, several definitional approaches were utilized by the parents. Such approaches revolved primarily around dynamic family-need patterns. Vogel and Bell indicate that the selection of a particular child as the scapegoat could be related to one or more of the following: value-orientation conflicts of parents, and the degree to which the child represents that conflict in the parents' minds; sibling order and sex of child; and physical, emotional, and intellectual resemblances or dissimilarities of child to parent.

Lest one come away with the notion that great numbers of parents deliberately set about to harm their children, the current attention being paid to the "direction of effects" research strategy (Bell, 1968, 1971) places this notion in proper perspective. As Bell points out, most research on parent-child relations has typically looked at the influence of the parent being directed at the child. He argues for a bidirectional model, which would then allow for the investigation of the impact the child's behavior may have on the parent and the relationship between parent and child.

Along with some of the research supporting the powerful influence of child behavior on adult behavior is the observation by many engaged in working with emotionally disturbed children that different children seem to "pull" rather dramatic behaviors from their parents. This is as true for professional workers as it is for parents. Professionals find themselves gravitating toward work with certain groups of disturbed children and often expressing, at the same time, the feeling that they couldn't really work with disturbed children manifesting certain behaviors.

At last, we seem to be entering a period of active cooperation between professional workers and parents. Hopefully, it is not too late to convey to the many concerned families desperately seeking services for their special children that we can work together as allies not as adversaries. Considerable evidence now exists for serious questioning of the long-assumed clinical posture of blaming the parent for a child's problem (Rutter, 1975). More important than causation is the issue of how can an appropriate program and set of interventions be developed for children in need.

Largely through the efforts of parents themselves offering insights into children's emotional concerns, we have seen this spirit of cooperation expanded (Park, 1972). Perhaps it is when parents are seen as competent that we are willing to actively involve them in the planning and implementation of a child's program; or when their participation can measureably assist professionals in the carrying out of educational and therapeutic plans that we view parents as allies. In any event, both of these factors exist: parents are indeed competent to assist professionals, and their active participation can be of great practical value in helping to implement a learning and treatment plan (Honig, 1975).

Through the public efforts of both parent groups and individual parents to define emotional concerns of children, we have made advances in both programming and fostering public awareness of the needs of disturbed children. For example, The National Society for Autistic Children* organized since 1965 by parents is now functioning as a clearinghouse for parents and professionals interested in better serving severely disturbed individuals. Along with a working definition of autism, they disseminate information, publish booklists of available materials and, perhaps most important of all, they are a visible support group to which parents can turn for ideas, materials and a host of services. There is now a magazine

* 169 Tampa Avenue, Albany, N.Y. 12208

*Exceptional Parent,** which contains many articles written by and for parents. It is a valuable source for other parents, and enables professional workers to gain a perspective on how parents experience their children's disabilities. Parents also function as advocates and both disseminate materials (as does "Closer Look,"** a federally funded project designed to make program information available to the public, and to actively push for the creation of new programs and services).

HOW DO THE EMOTIONALLY DISTURBED FEEL?

It can be seen from all that has been written so far that considerations of how emotional disturbance is defined are tied closely to the environment and the people within that environment. In this section an attempt will be made to describe how such children have come to see themselves or, in other words, define themselves. In the process of relating research and clinical information, some discussion of implications for changing negative self-perceptions will be presented.

Disturbed children are often seen as unpredictable, "bad," and presenting serious problems. But the disturbed are not necessarily the type of youngsters people would want to interact with professionally or socially. Certainly such attitudes are results of complex factors and are held by adults to different degrees and in different combinations. Such attitudes are communicated to disturbed children, and many professionals feel the children's responses reflect prevalent attitudes toward them. Just as society sees and prefers to place disturbed children apart from whatever it defines as the mainstream, there is evidence that disturbed child also see *themselves* as apart

* P.O. Box 4944, Manchester, New Hampshire 03108

** Box 1492, Washington, D.C.

from the mainstream. In an interesting methodological approach, Weinstein (1965) utilized concepts of social distance and had children organize social stimuli in a free-placement situation. This was accomplished by using flannelboards and felt figures representing humans and rectangles. Weinstein asked the question, "First, like normal adults, do emotionally disturbed children group humans closer than nonhuman objects?" The disturbed children, in contrast to a normal group, placed the human figures farther apart than they did rectangles. The interpretation of such findings is based upon conceptualizations of the importance of social schemata and their possible reflection of cultural norms (Keuthe, 1962). For example, we typically think of the closeness of certain relationships, such as the mother-child relationship, or perhaps, we even think of humans as belonging together in close proximity both emotionally and physically. Weinstein raises the question of whether physical distance can be equated with emotional distance. Findings similar to Weinstein's have been reported by Fisher (1967), and, with our concerns about changing negative self-concepts in children, perhaps we would do well to investigate social schemata as perceived by children. Some evidence for the impact of meaningful treatment environments on the restructuring of interpersonal space has been reported by Hobbs (1966). Comparisons of different studies reporting how disturbed children view psychological relationships must be made with some caution, and researchers need to consider methodology and impact of the particular stimuli used to measure social distance (Tolor, 1968).

Failure in school is often thought to reflect inadequate self-perceptions. After an investigation of high school students who were failing (Jan-Tausch & Granstrom, 1967, p. 14) stated: "School failure in these cases is symptomatic of neurotic behavior." Regardless of whether or not we agree with this, of importance for our purposes is their presentation of findings from interviews with the children. The children saw themselves at fault for not working hard enough; there was nothing the teacher could have done differently; and they felt guilty and ashamed when they came to class unprepared. And just as revealing was their inability to organize themselves to study and their very unclear perceptions of what teachers expected of them. These children seemed to be caught up in a cycle that rapidly spiraled them downward. They turned the burden of responsibility inward but at the same time expressed having inadequate skills and no clear guidelines as to expectations from school or home. Interviews with teachers showed essentially an undynamic view of these children. They were perceived as less intelligent than their IQ tests results showed, and, in effect, the teachers saw the children failing in much the same terms expressed by the children—lack of effort. One could hypothesize, based on surveys such as this, that as the external realities provided by negative teacher-feedback and internalized failure-feelings of the children move closer, there is less chance for a child to break out of such a failure cycle. Some ways to possibly avoid such a spiraling effect would be to view the school failure problems of children in more dynamic terms, by attempting to obtain the perceptions of the children and by looking to the expectations of the school environment and the teachers within it.

In line with the above discussion of school failure, one could conceptualize and explore the self of the disturbed child in terms of the child's self-image, which is being influenced by his observing his own behavior (Ganter, Yeakel & Polansky, 1967). This is just a short step from our discussion of how important other people's perceptions, such as the therapist's, are to the child, as seen in the Schwartz, Fearn, and Stryker study (1966). Farnham-Diggory (1966) makes the distinction between self-as-being and self-as-doing. She states (p. 13): "The best way

to avoid such confusions may be to limit self-image analysis to clear instances of imaged action to behavior that the child can observe in himself, just as he observes it in others." Using a sample of twenty-four psychotic children, twenty-four brain-injured, and forty-eight normal children, each normal was matched on sex, age, race, IQ and socioeconomic status with a non-normal. Her study explored concepts these groups held of self, future, and time.

Farnham-Diggory developed a self-evaluation scale using a wooden rating scale on which a child could show the answer to such questions as "When you're doing something you love to do, show me how good you are at it." By using a three-dimensional motor-activity stimulus, she hoped to prove that disorderly children need to observe themselves doing, and that their self-images would be defective. The scale measured their perception of skill, influence, independence, likability, dependability, judgment, decisiveness, and success. With the exception of "likability," the psychotic children were not distinguished from the other two groups. In other words, they saw themselves as less able to arouse affection in others. The profile similarities of the three groups lend support to the observation that those who designate and place children into categories, such as psychotic, brain-damaged, and normal, do so because they feel that there are distinct differences among children, though the children in all the groups saw themselves in similar terms. Apparently, our classification scheme does not always get through to the child! This is said only partly in jest. All too often, children in difficulty come to believe what is communicated to them by others. Perhaps more activities that would involve them in acquiring perceptions of themselves as they do things would provide them with more accurate and useful self-concepts. Although the implications for prognosis remain obscure, one could argue that as long as a child, or adult for that matter, continues to live under someone else's label and set of expectations, the less opportunity he has to be himself and to find out about himself.

Changing and Modifying Self-Concepts

What to change and how to do it remain perplexing questions, made even more difficult by the reluctance to change evidenced by some groups of children whose behavior, while maladaptive by some standards, serves useful purposes for the child. Groups of delinquent children might comprise such a resistant group. Further, it may be rather presumptuous of us to continue thinking of the problem as residing in the child (Ryan, 1971). Those practitioners who are exploring the impact of the school environment on the child prefer to think of some children as disturbing, that is, acting out in direct retaliation against a hostile and threatening environment.

Regardless of what we do, we had better do it rapidly. There is a sense of urgency to findings such as those of Morse (1964), who reports that children's concepts about themselves and about school become more negative with more time in school. A first line of attack used by many professional workers centers around the use of praise as a social reinforcer. In light of what we already know of the negative and alienated feelings many disturbed children have of themselves, the use of praise may have more limited effectiveness than we realize. In a conditioning study of fifteen emotionally disturbed boys, Levin and Simmons (1962) found that praise was not particularly effective as a reinforcer. In their study, patterns of operant response were unrelated to age, IQ, and psychiatric diagnoses. McDavid and Schroeder (1957) point up the dramatically different interpretations delinquent adolescents may have of approval and disapproval. Although approval and disapproval may be clear messages from the standpoint of the sender, McDavid and Schroeder found their delinquent sample to experience difficulty in adequately discriminating between positive and negative interpersonal events. Such interpretational difficulties may account for the lack of impact reinforcers such as approval and disapproval may have with this type of youngster.

Several lines of evidence regarding the difficulty disturbed children experience in understanding themselves in relation to their environment lend support to change efforts that focus on assisting the child to gain self-esteem in clearly definable environments. Basically, such evidence comes from the leads supplied by Weinstein (1965), who reports on how disturbed children organize their social relationships; increasingly negative self-concepts children have of their performance in school environments as reported by Morse (1964); and McDavid and Schroeder's findings (1957) concerning the difficulty that delinquent adolescents have in discriminating between approval and disapproval in interpersonal environments. A case could be made, in line with Farnham-Diggory's thesis (1966), that children need to function in environments which allow them to see changes in their performance and receive help in evaluating it.

Again, we are faced with the harsh reality that concepts of change are as elusive as definitions of emotional disturbance. From whose vantage point do we assess change? Issues revolving around improvement have major implications for the designing of school and community programs for disturbed children. Program designs such as the special class in public schools have failed to capture the imagination of children and parents (and an increasing number of professionals) mainly because these programs have not been able to establish their specialness. The same could be said for traditional child-guidance clinic programs, which have similarly failed to make significant enough differences with large enough numbers. But again, by whose standards have these approaches failed? For the teacher in the special class may feel that he is able to establish the kind of interpersonal relationship with individual children and design curriculum approaches that just would not be possible in larger regular classrooms. The staff in a particular school, however, may feel just as strongly about the preciousness of such a small intervention when their regular classrooms are filled with other youngsters equally in need of assistance.

But what about children's perceptions of change? Perhaps this dimension should be our guidepost. Redl (1965) cautions us that perceptions of improvement may, in fact, place a child, as well as adults, under great pressure. He mentions a child's concern for raised expectation levels of others toward him and whether he can match them; his concern in moving away psychologically from the peer group, based on improvement; and his difficulty in handling praise, a topic touched on earlier.

The only large-scale study of disturbed children's perceptions of change is incorporated in Morse, Cutler and Fink's (1964) research analysis of special-class programs. In line with this chapter's theme of the interdependence of environment and behavior, the authors were able to relate child change to the type of program the child was in. Those pupils involved in a program type referred to as psychoeducational generally reported the greatest number of gains. By "psychoeducational" we mean a design in which efforts are made to coordinate clinical and educational data by involving various disciplines, in which teachers' relationships with children are viewed as central to the learning process, and in which curriculum is placed in the context of a therapeutic classroom environment.

Pupils perceived themselves as improving more in general feelings, as experiencing reduced school anxiety, and as experiencing more positive perceptions of improved relationships with teachers. Also, as we might expect, changes in teachers' perceptions of pupil control were greater within psycho-

educational classroom environments. The authors conjecture that the progress of the children within this program aided the teachers' performance by making them more comfortable, and, in turn the teachers' changes in the direction of seeing children under greater control is a reflection of this reciprocal pattern. Such a pattern would involve the designing of an environment in which behavior is channeled in a firm and consistent manner so that children can feel safe to interact and learn. It is then hypothesized that when such child-behavioral changes occur, the teacher responds positively and is similarly able to cope with the situation more effectively and view the children more positively. The authors feel that pupil problems, teacher reactions, and program environments are intimately related. The authors (p. 129) go on to make a rather interesting statement: "the teachers' personal style and comfort in the setting is probably the major determiner of both operating program type and pupil responses." Their statement is interesting because, if we are really serious about facilitating change in children's self-concepts and responses, then we may need to focus on changing perceptions and behaviors of significant others in the disturbed child's life.

Further evidence for such a focus is found in a study of a nonclinical child and parent population by Medinnus and Curtis (1963). They and others found a correlation between parental self-acceptance and the parents' acceptance of their children. Many case-study descriptions of disturbed children allude to the rejection of the child by one or both parents. Certainly, the same could be said of some teachers with disturbed children and certain therapists with some patients (Schutz, 1966). In another study using normal elementary age boys, Weinstein (1967) found that the boys' positive views of human relationships reflected acceptance by parents. One of her points is that perceptions of human relationships are learned through social experience and that such experiences influence social behavior. Farnham-Diggory's (1966) emphasis on self-observation is also seen in a study of emotionally disturbed boys placed in a residential treatment hospital (Rosengren, 1961). In findings that Rosengren refers to as suggestive, it was found that those boys whose perceptions of self changed most positively also manifested improved overt behavior, and the converse was true for those whose perceptions of self changed the least. It could be inferred from this study that, in this therapeutic environment, disturbed boys were provided with the opportunity to test their concepts about themselves, and, in the process of looking at their behavior, they gathered more realistic feedback about themselves from their behavior. The interactional quality of self-evaluation and behavior seems apparent, and one could get into an endless discussion of which came first, the change in self-perception or the changes in behavior.

It should be emphasized again that it is not only the child who may be in need of modifying and changing. If we wish to bring about a more robust view of the world and the people in it, then our learning environments must foster such spontaneity. We have adequate research to show that children are more likely to change their self-evaluations when they experience success and positive feedback from others (Herndon, 1971; Dennison, 1969; Ludwig & Maehr, 1967).

This writer has become a firm believer in classroom organizational patterns that consider the student as a partner in the learning process (Knoblock, 1973). Such classrooms are often thought of as open classrooms or as examples of open education, but regardless of the designation, they are committed to children succeeding at their developmental level, and along with fostering a freedom-to-learn climate (Rogers, 1969), there is an expectation that no one fails! For many children labeled emotionally disturbed, there is a long history of failure, and this trend must be reversed if such children are to change the negative ways in which they see themselves and if others are to view them more positively.

EMOTIONALLY DISTURBED CHILDREN AS LEARNERS

At the outset it should be made clear that it may be virtually impossible to distinguish many children who are labeled emotionally disturbed from other children based on their learning characteristics. Both research studies (Hallahan and Kauffman, 1977) and observation support the difficulty in distinguishing between children with various labels (educable mentally retarded, learning disabled, and emotionally disturbed). In the Hallahan and Kauffman article, the point is made that the causative factors and appropriate educational interventions are similar and what may differentiate children termed emotionally disturbed is the greater frequency of certain behaviors, usually ones that the schools refer to as "acting-out" or socially maladaptive behaviors.

It is generally assumed that emotional disturbance is primarily a concept revolving around behaviors and feelings. As White and Charry (1966) point out, however, it would be a mistake not to realize that disorders in children, at least those in schools, are detected and defined often on the basis of learning behaviors. In their study of the relationship between school disorders, intelligence, and social class, the greatest number of children referred to school psychologists were singled out on the basis of learning difficulties. A second large group was singled out on the basis of behavior characterized by psychological disturbances. Further findings linked the educationally disturbed group with lower IQ, social class, and achievement, in contrast to the emotionally disturbed group. Such findings as these need to be looked at in the light of the referring persons (in this study they were all school personnel) and the age at referral, which was mostly ages 6 to 10. Also, several reasons could be given for each referral, thus making the dichotomy between the educationally and the emotionally disturbed less dichotomous.

Of interest in the White and Charry study was the differential intervention service patterns different groups were assigned to, based on school performance. In brief, those children designated as educationally disturbed had lower IQ, achievement, and social-class designations, with the emotionally disturbed being higher. Selective intervention practices tended to assist the former group with educational interventions and the latter with psychotherapy approaches. The authors (p. 80) state: "It appears that we are treating the potentially healthier pupils with psychotherapy, while the potentially sicker ones are treated with educational methods."

The above study attempted to look at school disorder in broad definitional terms, and found, as we discussed earlier, that in essence the particular environment, in this case the school, defines its concerns in its own terms and with concepts most relevant for its welfare.

Several studies have demonstrated that school-age children labeled as emotional problems (although various labels are assigned them) have low IQs, experience failure in one or more content areas such as reading and mathematics, and perform below expectancy for their age and ability (Kvaraceus, 1961; Powell & Bergen, 1962; Scarpitti, 1964).

Issues Related to the Learning Characteristics of Emotionally Disturbed Children

Before proceeding to a discussion of some of the specific learning problems experienced by disturbed children, three issues are deserving of mention. First, most analyses, clinical and experimental, make reference to the discrepancy between the potential of the disturbed child and his actual perfor-

mance. The majority of studies reported in the literature indicate that as a group, disturbed children possess at least average intelligence. In clinical investigations of individual children, however, we find many for whom the assumption of normal intelligence is less clear. What is typically done by clinical psychologists and clinical teachers is to speculate that many of these children possess greater potential than they show, and frequently base this on an inconsistent functioning pattern. For example, results on the Wechsler Intelligence Scale for Children might reveal areas of strength as well as weakness, thus lending support to definite skills in certain areas. Similarly, a child may excel in certain subject-matter areas and fail in others. Diagnosing a child's potential can be even more subtle, particularly when a child presents a flat learning-profile. In such instances, cues may need to be taken from the child's language pattern, nonverbal behaviors, motor skills, or other unobtrusive behaviors.

One assumption many of us continue to make, then, is that the personality and behavior traits of disturbed children contribute to discrepant achievement. In a review of the literature relating personality to discrepant achievement, Taylor (1964) investigated studies using many different populations and found seven factors contributing to achievement behavior: (1) ability to handle anxiety, (2) feelings of self-worth, (3) conformity to authority demands, (4) peer acceptance, (5) less conflict over independence, (6) engagement in activities of an academic nature, and (7) setting of realistic goals. Again, although these seven considerations represent a compilation of findings from many diverse populations, experience has shown that disturbed children lack many of the above attributes.

Second, the relatively new category of learning disabilities raises questions as to which youngsters can be grouped under this rubric. Is it to separate out children with degrees of emotional disturbance from those we are calling learning disabled? Of course it would be conceivable, depending on the definition we give to either term. What is of interest is the observation that many school and learning clinics identify large numbers of children referred to them for learning problems as manifesting emotional problems (Coleman & Sandher, 1967). The Coleman and Sandher study also highlighted the interaction of emotional status, intelligence, age, and sex in the learning condition of children. This study and others may give us cause to be cautious in our willingness to continue to carve youngsters up into mutually exclusive categories that in reality overlap considerably.

The third issue concerns our tendency to overlook very bright and creative disturbed children. These children remain an enigma to many professional workers, largely because of the dramatic discrepancy between ability and achievement. One useful way of developing a frame of reference for understanding the psychological and educational needs of bright underachievers is in a case-study approach. Kimball (1953) used a case-history approach to generate hypotheses and then tested her hypotheses by using results of psychological testing. Her results included a picture of bright underachievers as those who experience difficulty with relationships with fathers, demonstrated extreme passivity, demonstrated physical aggression toward inanimate objects, and showed feelings of inferiority. Those who have taught emotionally disturbed gifted children will attest to the challenge they present. For many of them, intellectualizing as a way of life can become so pronounced that enormous barriers are erected to prevent communication on an interpersonal basis. Often forgotten is the need on the part of the adult, be it therapist, teacher, or parent, to remain comfortable when confronted with flashes of brilliance and, in fact, to be intellectually able to respond so that the threat level of the adult does not interfere with the relationship.

Studies of the Learning Behavior of Emotionally Disturbed Children

As is the case with many problems attributed to emotionally disturbed children, there are many assumptions made about their reading status and really only descriptive evidence to carry us further. Those who have worked with disturbed children in educational settings are well aware of how discouraged many children become at not being able to read and of not being able to devote sufficient psychological energy to the learning of this skill. Their problems are exacerbated by increasing feelings of inadequacy as they grow older and feelings of remorse over not being able to meet peer and adult expectations in the area of learning to read. Often we see disturbed adolescents who refuse to even acknowledge that they have a reading problem.

Rabinovitch et al. (1956) identified a group of nonreaders who have proved to be almost completely resistant to remediation efforts. This writer recalls working in a remedial situation with an adolescent boy who absolutely denied that he could not read. Once having erected such a strong defense, he would not even go near the learning situation that had been developed for him. The erecting of self-preservation defenses tends to mask the potential for learning that a youngster may have as well as keep us from validating or even developing remedial interventions.

The literature on learning problems of the disturbed, scarce as it is, tends to focus on anecdotal statements such as the above, with little research available pointing to differences in learning behaviors of disturbed versus normal children. One problem, of course, is the lack of clarity as to just who is emotionally disturbed and who does the labeling. Despite the lack of available research, we have noted that large numbers of school children are labeled school disordered on the basis of learning problems.

One of the consistent findings that has turned up in descriptive and survey studies of normal and disturbed children has been the progressive decline in reading and arithmetic achievement as children identified as emotionally disturbed progress through the grades. Perhaps such findings gain importance and should attract our concern when we view them in light of Morse's (1964) finding, reported earlier, of diminished feelings of self-regard as children progressed in school.

The early California studies on an early identification process for emotionally handicapped children approached the problem at some points by comparing achievement of the normal and the disturbed. One such survey by Bower, Tashnovian, and Larson (1958) demonstrated that the differences in grade-level achievement in reading and arithmetic for the emotionally handicapped, in contrast to normal children, increased between grades four and six.

Another study attempting to link classroom behavior, intelligence, and achievement (Feldhusen, Thurston, & Benning, 1967) indicated that by the third grade, those children nominated by teachers as manifesting socially disapproved behavior (aggressive and disruptive) had already fallen far behind in both reading and arithmetic achievement. These researchers raise the need for exploring early interventions into the academic problems presented by such children, that is, before grade three.

Only a few studies have investigated the interrelationship of behavior and reading. As stated above, there are many clinical discussions but few attempts to clearly delineate the type or grouping of disturbed children under investigation.

One such attempt to find patterns between psychopathological labels and reading skills is found in a study by Wilderson (1967), which he labeled as exploratory. His study provided some valuable clues worthy of follow-up and showed that traditional psychiatric labels based on symptom ex-

pression still do not get us close enough to the reading behavior of disturbed children. Wilderson points out that the same problem plaguing our understanding of the emotionally disturbed is faced in understanding the reading process—namely, looking at reading as a unitary concept. In a factor analytic approach to reducing large numbers of symptomatic behaviors to fewer clusters or factors, he identified four factors: schizoid withdrawal, character disorder, borderline psychosis, and somatic complaints. Similarly, seven reading-skill deficiency factors were obtained: word recognition, perceptual efficiency, intellectual maturity, visual efficiency, auditory inflectional awareness, memory, and hyperactive style. Correlations among the two sets of factors—the psychiatric factors and reading-skill factors—yielded a number of low, but significant, correlations. The reader is encouraged to refer to Wilderson's study, for it is rich with clinical hunches. Perhaps if we could develop a system for more accurately describing and labeling children's behavior, an approach such as the one used in this study would yield even greater translation value for us in developing remedial programs. For example, Wilderson found that the factor *character disorder* correlated at or close to significance with *intellectual maturity* and *hyperactive style*. He considers these variables as representing inadequate impulse control. We can see, then, that the more specific we can become in dissecting the learning deficit and learning *style* of children, the closer we can come to responding appropriately to the deficit.

In line with this plea for more clearly defining the population of disturbed delinquent children, Graubard (1967) studied a group of disturbed delinquent children, using a variety of diagnostic instruments including the Illinois Test of Psycholinguistic Abilities (ITPA) and measures of auditory closure, right-left discrimination, and eye-hand coordination. In many ways Graubard's subjects would fall close to the group labeled as character disorders in Wilderson's study above. Graubard's group manifested, among other factors, a diffuseness in language structure and difficulty in right-left orientation and perceiving wholes from parts. Graubard (p. 366) states: "Much of the pathology of this sample lies in the fact that these subjects cannot delay gratification and have poor impulse control and a disturbed time sense."

Only a narrow band of findings has been pulled from these two studies, but they have served our purpose, namely, to demonstrate that the behavior of the child may have implications for the learning environment we create for him. The tragedy for many difficult and troubled youngsters has been that their behavior has had such an impact on their environments that we remain focused on the behavior to the exclusion of effecting remedial progress based on their learning deficits. These learning deficits are often considered secondary to the dramatic behavior, but in reality they serve as a constant reminder to the youngster that his world remains unmanageable. The assumption that many apparently operate under is that, first, we must cure the sickness, and then learning can take place. It may be just as valid to use a more reciprocal notion, which would maintain that accurate remediation of a child's learning deficits would go a long way toward modifying his behavior. After all, feeling of failure, diminished self-esteem, and lack of communication with adults arise from school failures and carry over into behavior styles that are manifested in many of the child's environments.

Understanding Children's Learning Processes

It might be more productive to explore the processes and approaches utilized by children termed emotionally disturbed than to seek out specific ways in which they represent a unique group of learners. For example, interesting work is being done on investigating just how a student learns and not necessarily what he learns. This can be done in a variety of ways. There are those who are looking at ways to diagnose children's learning styles. Dunn, Dunn and Price (1977) have developed a Learning Style Inventory which is really an attempt to specify a student's preference for the classroom conditions which are facilitative of learning. One interesting note in their study is that they compared student and teacher agreement on learning environment preferences. In one instance, both students and teachers recognized that for particular students there was a preference for learning through tactile and/or kinesthetic means, supplemented by a visual approach. We know from classroom observation research, however, that most instruction is done through a lecture method and thus could be inappropriate for the needs or learning style preferences of certain children.

We can see from the above discussion that there is much more of an interactionist point of view to the exploring of a learner's preferred style of learning and the teachers' or environment's ability and willingness to respond to that style and need-level. This means that the onus is not just on the learner, but that ideally there would be a match between learner needs and characteristics and environmental qualities. Hunt and Sullivan (1974) postulate the matching of a child's conceptual orientation with a responsive classroom environment. In addition, they feel that teachers could think of children in terms of "accessibility" channels, that is their cognitive, motivational, value and sensory orientation.

Another way to view the possible interaction between a child's learning style, teacher behavior, and environmental impact is the Aptitude Treatment Interaction (ATI) approach. This allows for the teacher to utilize a child's area of strength as the way to approach the teaching of skills or concepts. By using this approach, it is believed that there will be a successful interaction between the child's aptitude for learning with the treatment procedure (Lerner, 1976).

Very often, children termed emotionally disturbed are thought of as hyperactive and/or acting out. This has become a very casual designation; that is, it may often be used uncritically and to the eventual disadvantage of the child (Schrag & Divoky, 1975). Again, it would be more useful to utilize a process approach and understanding of impulsive behavior. The notion of a child's orientation to respond rapidly (tempo) and uncritically (impulsively) may reflect learning styles that lend themselves to study and, if necessary, modification. For example, a study of concept learning in hyperactive and normal children by Freibergs and Douglas (1969) suggested that any differences found in their experimental study between these groups could be attributed to attentional and motivational variables, and not necessarily to deficits in cognitive functioning.

SEVERELY EMOTIONALLY DISTURBED CHILDREN

As an earlier section clearly shows, there is much controversy as to just who defines a child as emotionally disturbed and which definition gains the most credence based either on empirical data or the weight of community and political activity. While this controversy presently exists, and probably always will, there is growing attention being paid to a relatively small, but behaviorally visible group of children who come under the broad heading of severely emotionally disturbed. In many instances, this term has become synonymous with children thought of as autistic, psychotic, or schizophrenic. As soon as we focus on the label we return to the same kind of debate seen in the previous sections. It is certainly possible to define the problem from a variety of perspectives and in this section some reference

will be made to questions of etiology. Of more immediate impact on the teacher and practitioner, however, are the implications of such extreme behaviors for the development of educational and community interventions. To be certain, we are obligated to continue to search for causative factors contributing to, or in fact causing, such a complex set of behaviors as autism, but in the meantime we are faced with an astounding array of behaviors and concerns that such children have, and the need for parent and professional intervention is great.

Perhaps because of the growing controversy over just who really is emotionally disturbed, there is an increasing emphasis on special education's responsibility to focus on the more severe handicapping conditions for which there is no question that a problem exists and a response is needed. This return to special education's earlier position of focusing on the severely and profoundly disabled implies that many of the more mildly involved children, while perhaps still in need of a response, can be aided as well by placement in regular education programs, or at least in more normalized settings. The increasing interest in mainstreaming has added fuel to the issue of the special educator's responsibility not to make youngsters "worse" by separating them out and away from the mainstream, and then not producing programs or results appreciably different from regular school programs (Bruinicks & Rynders, 1975).

An expanded funding effort by the federal Bureau of Education for the Handicapped (BEH) to develop educational programs for all categories of severe handicapping conditions has greatly increased the visibility and practicality of this new set of priorities. Of further interest is the fact that funding is also aimed at early childhood programs for the severely emotionally disturbed. In 1973 BEH organized a "Task Force on Severely Handicapped Children." Developing objectives for achieving the goal of educating *all* the severely handicapped and severely emotionally disturbed was part of their planning. The first funding of projects in this broad area began in 1974. In the funding year 1976 eleven projects were funded, and four of these were directed at programs and services for severely emotionally disturbed children and youth. One of those projects funded was for a model school demonstration program highlighting the integration of severely disturbed and typical children (Knoblock, in press). BEH estimates of the needs of such children are rather overwhelming in light of their figures of the existence of approximately 900,-000 seriously emotionally disturbed-autistic or schizophrenic children. Needless to say, only a small percentage of these children are receiving services.

Autism

Autism in children is thought of as one of the most severe forms of emotional disorder, both in terms of its impact on the behaviors of the affected child and on those who are involved in his or her life. The International Conference on Autism held in Switzerland in July 1976 highlighted autism as a social problem. One way of thinking of this is to consider the fact that each autistic child can be involved with at least four or five adults. These contacts ripple out so that in direct and indirect ways one child can affect the lives of a large number of adults.

As mentioned above, there is great disagreement over causes of such severe conditions in children and as to whether autism and childhood schizophrenia are one and the same (Miller, 1974). Each issue leads to another, and after thirty years of investigating childhood autism there is no clear answer as to whether it is a specific disease entity or rather a descriptive term that includes a number of conditions with enough behavioral disturbances in common that encourage us to group such behaviors into a syndrome. To add further to the confusion

is the question of nomenclature. Kessler (1966), in a review of psychosis in early childhood indicates that Childhood Psychosis can be thought of as the overall term of condition, and that autism is one manifestation of childhood psychosis but, in fact, the two terms are often used interchangeably.

Present-day practitioners generally pay credit to child psychiatrist Leo Kanner (1943) for defining a set of behaviors he believed formed a syndrome he labeled "early infantile autism." This condition, present at birth, was dramatic for: the affective estrangement of the infant from his or her caregivers; marked speech delay; noncommunicative use of speech, once it developed; the development of repetitive and stereotyped responses; and an inordinate need to maintain sameness in the environment.

Rutter (1975) has noted that the prevalence of particular behaviors may change depending on the age and developmental level of the child. He states:

> It has been demonstrated that, although the social abnormalities may involve lack of eye to eye gaze in infancy, in older children the defect is mainly shown by brief visual attention, by lack of postural accommodation when looking at someone, by lack of cooperative group play, and by a failure to develop persisting friendships. Physical withdrawal from people is not characteristic at any age. With respect to language, babble is often abnormal and there is a lack of response to sounds in infancy, echolalia which persists well beyond the usual age, pronominal reversal which is part of the echolalia, a lack of understanding of language, a failure to use gesture, and a poor use of words to communicate even after speech develops (p. 330).

Kanner's influence, along with others like Bettelheim (1967), was very strong for the next twenty years or so. The common thread running through much of the writing was one of explaining autism and childhood schizophrenia (often, but not always used synonymously), in psychodynamic terms, that is in using explanations that frequently focused on deviant interactions between parents and their child. There developed a "blaming the parent" orientation that appears to be largely unfounded but resistant to change in the minds of many practitioners and lay persons. In his recent book, Kauffman (1977) states:

> Attempts to pinpoint the origins of behavior disorders in family relationships have met with little success. Family relationships are best viewed as contributing factors in behavioral development. Although there are studies in which family members intervened in children's behavior disorders and changed the course of their development, convincing evidence that families cause children to behave abnormally in the first place is lacking (p. 97).

There are notable exceptions to using a psychodynamic explanation for autism. For example, the early writings of Loretta Bender (1947) made a strong case for an organic or biological basis for what she termed *childhood schizophrenia.*

Rimland (1964), Ornitz (1971), Ritvo (1976) and many others took great exception to the psychodynamic explanations of Bettelheim and others, postulating instead a range of biochemical, sensorimotor, neurological and cognitive deficits to account for the presence of such extreme behaviors.

They detail a planned set of activities designed to intrude on a child's world and help that child see the reasons for responding back to persons seeking to foster trust and warmth. Many of those activities are high-stimulation ones, often play experiences capitalizing on many of the developmental experiences that such children have apparently missed or failed to acquire.

Other workers are focusing on the possibility that autism in children may be primarily a language disorder. Certainly the position taken by The National Society for Autistic Children includes problems of communication as a central characteristic of many labeled children. Evidence at this time remains inconclusive, and it would not be possible to state with any certainty that language impairment is the primary disturbance in autism (Boucher, 1976), but the remediation of specific language problems is a promising trend in this field. Certainly, one of the implications is for the training of teachers with strong skills in language remediation. While the utilization of language specialists is important, it remains for classroom teachers to implement remedial programs and in some instances to design them. A recent article by Ricks and Wing (1975) summarizes much of the current literature on language and communication in autistic children. One of their conclusions, that the central problem is one of difficulty in handling symbols, again points to the potential impact a teacher can have with an autistic child.

This trend of more careful diagnostic assessment of autistic children, particularly when such assessments include a child's approach to learning, has great application for teachers. For years, the prevalent notion was that the major interventions in a severely disturbed child's life would be made by specialists outside the classroom. Now we are seeing renewed interest not only in language training that can be accomplished by teachers, but in ways of looking at information processing in autistic children (Bryson, 1972), the possibility of short-term memory deficits (Prior & Chen, 1976) and in utilizing sensory motor training approaches (Ayres, 1972). Gallagher and Weigerink (1976) have compiled a helpful summary of educational issues and remedial approaches that highlight the central role a skilled clinical teacher can play in an intervention program.

It is of interest to note that there are some practitioners, like DesLauriers and Carlson (1969), who are putting forth theories and intervention approaches that combine diverse approaches. For example, in their book *Your Child Is Asleep,* a neuro-physiological model highlights two arousal systems that can account for either high-arousal or low-arousal functioning in an autistic child. Their interventions, however, are extraordinarily humanistic in that they are couched in a deep respect for each child and are designed to respond in developmental terms to the needs of each child.

INTEGRATION OF EMOTIONALLY DISTURBED CHILDREN INTO REGULAR SCHOOLS AND REGULAR CLASSROOMS

The fact is that children thought of as emotionally disturbed are already in regular classroom programs. And many children who could profit from a more normalized setting are being considered for regular-class placement. Impetus for this has come from the passage in 1975 of Public Law 94–142, Education for all Handicapped Children Act. In addition, many states anticipating, and in cooperation with, this federal mandate, have written strong plans implementing the placement of handicapped children in the "least restrictive setting" possible.

The Council for Exceptional Children has recently published a statement highlighting the major intentions of mainstreaming. According to their statement, mainstreaming is—

Providing the most appropriate education for each child in the least restrictive setting.

Looking at the educational needs of children instead of clinical or diagnostic labels such as mentally handicapped, learning disabled, physically handicapped, hearing impaired, or gifted.

Looking for and creating alternatives that will help general educators serve children with learning or adjustment problems in the regular setting. Some approaches being used to help achieve this are, consulting teach-

ers, methods and materials specialists, itinerant teachers and resource room teachers.

Uniting the skills of general education and special education so that all children may have equal educational opportunity.

It is of interest to note that the CEC statement also includes some cautions about what it is not. This is particularly important, because we are already experiencing a range of strong feelings, both positive and negative, and it is these feelings and attitudes that will influence our future direction. Therefore, it is terribly important that all of us, particularly those of us advocating mainstreaming, be specific and articulate in specifying the range of possible approaches to the integration of handicapped and typical children.

It should go without saying, that mainstreaming is not a random approach to the placement of children with special needs, but rather one of careful matching of children's developmental needs and the capability of particular schools, programs and classrooms to respond to these needs.

For children and youth considered emotionally disturbed there is a range of programming possible for them, and these possibilities include a number of issues, particularly the harsh reality that there are many children excluded from any school program whatsoever. It is hypocritical to discuss mainstreaming or integration without our expressing concern and developing action programs to guarantee access to school and then, of course, an appropriate education program once in school. This issue should be of particular importance for special educators in view of the findings reported by the Children's Defense Fund in *Children Out of School in America* (1974). The report cites a figure of at least 2 million school-age children not in school and speculates that a very large number of these are children with special needs. And further, we know that great numbers of children who manifest acting-out behaviors are excluded from school both legally and extra-legally (Regal, 1972). Cottle (1976) has provided us with an incisive analysis of the impact exclusionary practices have on the lives of children and their families.

The first programming concern, then, is to see to it that each child has equal access to a school program and then is granted due process to guarantee his or her staying in an appropriate school program.

On the next level, there is the need to develop more responsive instructional programs for the large numbers of troubled children and youth who are in regular classrooms. The range of needs may be enormous and one encouraging trend is the growing focus on individualizing instruction for each child. Under P.L. 94–142 this is a mandatory provision for each identified and labeled child, but hopefully a specific plan for each child, even if not singled out or considered severely disturbed enough to be moved out of a regular classroom, could be developed and implemented. Because of the complexities involved in the writing and developing of such specific plans a teacher should receive out of classroom support, both in plan-writing and in helping to maintain children in regular classrooms.

On a third level, there are a variety of approaches that school buildings and districts are utilizing to maintain troubled children in regular programs, but also recognizing their need for additional professional input. Kreinberg and Chow (1973) have edited a book that presents a number of options in terms of programming for a range of children.

On still another level, it is encouraging to note that there are now a growing number of public-school programs for severely emotionally disturbed children. It is only recently that more public schools acknowledge the growth that can take place in severely impaired children, and both the funding pattern of the Bureau of Education for the Handicapped which supports in-school programs for such children and the new P.L. 94–142, which mandates an appropriate and free public education, have combined with a hopefully renewed public school consciousness about its potential impact on children and its obligation to serve all children. While the format has tended to be one of separate classes located within a school building there are many ways in which all of the children in a school can spend time with each other, such as lunch, music, art, recreation and planned social interactions involving group interactions, or pairing special and normal children for particular activities. The most successful efforts at integration during a school day have pointed up the necessity of specifically designing ways in which such interactions can occur and not leaving social exchanges to chance (Snyder, Apolloni & Cooke, 1977).

Exciting research efforts are now being directed at the broad question of how can interaction between children be facilitated. This is of importance for children with emotional concerns since their place in a classroom grouping often seems precarious. These research efforts have grown out of a focus on prosocial behavior, that is, the positive behaviors of children directed toward others' (Severy & Davis, 1971; Rosenhan, 1972) efforts at individualization (Lillie, 1975; Charles, 1976) and the utilization of peers as primary change agents (Guralnick, 1976; Apolloni & Cooke, 1977; Apolloni, T., Cooke, S. A., & Cooke, T. P., 1977).

The available research on integrated settings is sparse, but the studies that report more systematically collected data support the observation of other programs; namely, that it is both possible and highly likely that children with special needs, including emotionally disturbed children, will be accepted and responded to by their normal peers (Hambleton & Ziegler, 1974; Pappanikou & Paul, 1977).

STUDYING AND TREATING CHILDREN WITH EMOTIONAL PROBLEMS

Direct Observation of Children's Behavior

It is important to know exactly what the child being studied is actually doing, not what you think he or she is doing. After all, if the ultimate goal is to develop an educational treatment plan or a psychological management approach, then such plans must be accurate in the sense that the interventions should be tailored as specifically as possible to the need of the child or to the behaviors one desires to change (Wood, 1975; Charles, 1976).

One methodology that has been used extensively by Barker (1963), Gump and Sutton-Smith (1955), and others is the direct recording of behavior as it occurs naturally in a particular environmental setting. Field notes, usually taking the form of narrative recordings, are called specimen recordings and can be coded according to a scoring system often decided upon in advance of the observations. This approach is often referred to as ecological, and one implication of this designation is the strong belief in the importance or the interaction between the child and his or her environment.

Interesting studies of disturbed children's behavior have been reported in the literature by Gump, Schoggen and Redl (1957). In the Gump study, they report extensive observational data on one child as he behaved in different environments. This study substantiated the prevalent assumption that behavior, in fact, does change depending upon the particular environment a child is in. A major implication of a study like this is to focus us on the potential importance a responsive environment can make in a child's functioning and the value in carefully matching children's needs with appropriately responding environments. In

another study, Leach (1972) studied the social behavior of preschool normal and problem children; based on direct observation of their behaviors, some conclusions were reached that showed the kind of cycle we see so often: the withdrawal from participation with others on the part of some troubled children, and then the resultant ignoring of such children by his or her normal peers. Armed with such observations, a teacher could find ways to facilitate social interaction and ultimately the integration of all children into the group.

UTILIZING A DEVELOPMENTAL FRAME OF REFERENCE

Critical observers of the education of emotionally disturbed children acknowledge that our heavy reliance on administrative designs such as special class programs has not allowed us to design specific enough educational and therapeutic interventions. For example, children are being placed into special groupings without adequate conceptualization on the part of educators of the type of intervention needed. The point is that merely designing the program (special class, resource room, etc.) does not necessarily convey what should be done with a child on a day-to-day basis. One emerging trend is the utilization of a developmental frame of reference as a way of explaining troubled children's behavior and for the planning of interventions appropriate to the child's developmental state. According to Fishbein (1976):

A stage is seen as a period in psychological development in which a major reorganization takes place. This reorganization is manifested both qualitatively, e.g., the individual solves problems in new ways, experiences new feelings, or perceives new relations, and quantitatively, e.g., his success in solving a particular problem or class of problems increases tremendously (p. 63).

In education it is possible to look at a child's progress in terms of the successful mastery of developmental milestones. For children and youth considered emotionally disturbed, such an approach may be less stigmatizing since labeling of a child's behavior in deficit terms (neurotic, psychotic) is not done, and a developmental framework is potentially more educationally relevant to the planning a teacher needs to engage in when programming for children.

A recently developed set of objectives and interventions based on developmental stages is contained in *Developmental Therapy: A textbook for teachers and therapists for emotionally disturbed young children* (Wood, 1975). Utilizing a developmental frame of reference implies the importance of viewing behavior sequentially and in responding to the importance of responsive environments interacting with an individual's maturational processes. Wood lists a number of assumptions inherent in a developmental approach:

> Emotional and behavioral disturbances in a young child are interwoven with normal functioning and often are difficult to differentiate.
> Normal processes of physical and psychological development follow in a hierarchy of stages and sequences well documented in literature.
> The normal process of change is uniquely individual, yet predictable, and occurs in relation to environmental conditions, experiences, biological constituents and to the foundation laid in prior experience.
> The young child's knowledge of himself, his confidence in himself, his willingness to risk himself in new situations, grows out of significant pleasurable experiences.
> The young child learns and grows by experiences (pp. 3 and 4).

Combining Educational and Psychological Development

It is possible and perhaps even desirable to combine the insights of both psychology and education and apply them to the understanding of disturbed children's behavior. Swap (1974) has presented a conceptual framework based upon Hewett's (1968) educationally based developmental model of behavior and Erikson's (1963) psychologically based developmental model to understand what she refers to as disturbing classroom behaviors. Her article, utilizing the hierarchy of tasks that Hewett and Erikson present, attempts to combine their stages as a way of analyzing children's behavior. Swap states "Some children do not negotiate these critical developmental phases at the expected time, however. They bring constellations of behavior patterns to the classroom which are normal for younger children but seem inappropriate, exaggerated, and often disturbing for children of their chronological age" (p. 163). In a sense, she is advocating a developmental and ecological view which avoids labeling a child in the usual way as "disturbed" or "sick" or even wrong! Rather, they are seen as experiencing difficulty in mastering the normal developmental milestones and crises faced by all children.

Advantages of a Developmental Program

As can be seen from the previous sections on utilizing a developmental approach, there are a number of advantages for teachers and clinicians.

First, a reading of the assumptions specified by Wood (1975) highlights the growth model inherent in a developmental approach. Behaviors can be described in non-pejorative terms and the expectation is that children can and will change.

Second, a developmental approach, because of its emphasis on the importance of early sensory-motor stimulation, is in keeping with our clinical experiences of how to respond to many young severely disturbed children, and thus offers a series of milestones and activities that can help teachers and clinicians. In many ways then, a developmental approach helps us to view children's behaviors in a phenomenological way; that is, to understand children as they develop—from the inside out. Before a child can successfully cope with a group of other children, there is much of a pleasurable and successful nature that he or she must experience at earlier developmental stages.

Third, utilizing a developmental approach can assist a teacher in being diagnostic when employing teaching and intervention strategies. For example, if one is focused on responding to the developmental stage a child is in, then we can immediately gain information about where and how a child is functioning: Piaget's sensorimotor period; Stage I of *Developmental Therapy* (Wood, 1975); Responding to the environment with pleasure; at the Basic Trust and Attention Stage (Erikson, 1963; Hewett, 1968); or at the safety level of development (Maslow, 1968) and then plan appropriate helping interventions. In addition, each of the stage descriptions has direct implications for utilizing particular curriculum materials.

Cognitive Styles of Disturbed Children

It may prove very productive to combine our focus and explore the learning or cognitive styles of disturbed children rather than dichotomize affect and learning. Such a focus might allow us to move from psychiatric labels, which do not appear to be educationally relevant, to examining groups of children sorted out on the basis of direct observation of behaviors, such as socially acting-out children, or perhaps even to examining socioeconomic status and learning styles.

Auerswald's orientation (1969), represents a step in the direction of unifying some of our notions of psychopathology in an urban environment. Looking at acting-out children's cognitive development, he argues

that such children manifest behaviors reflecting a cognitive structure which is relatively undifferentiated. Disorientation in time and space, and lack of useful categories in which to place and process incoming stimuli, may make such a youngster more vulnerable to his environment. It could be argued that such children would need excessive stimuli and environmental messages because they lose so much in the translation process. Auerswald uses a communications theme that seems appropriate to the problem of the school environment's need to hook up with such children. He states:

> And since he cannot learn or put words to use in many contexts, the richness and depth of meaning which words acquire through varied usage in many different life transactions will not develop for him. As a result, he is not likely to see words as usable and valuable tools. Furthermore, he is not likely to develop a clear concept of himself as a user of words. On the contrary, he will be deficient in communications skills and without motivation to acquire them. Thus, efforts to teach him these skills are likely to fail.
>
> He will not be able to differentiate a wide variety of inner feeling responses. On the contrary he is likely to be clearly aware only of feelings that create widespread physiological responses in him, which he perceives as high level stimuli in themselves. Such feelings, of course, are primarily the emotions of individual survival, fear and rage, species survival, or sexual sensation (p. 193).

The above statements by Auerswald point up how futile it may be to continue to separate the child's self-concept, his behavior in his environment, and his learning or lack of it in school.

Spending time with various kinds of children labeled emotionally disturbed, one is struck with the diffuseness Auerswald refers to above. It takes various forms and is often perceived as a type of inflexible approach to meeting internal and external demands. Some workers refer to this diffuseness in connection with some children's self-defeating behaviors. Some children seem to place themselves "on the chopping block," even when it is obvious they will be caught. Self-defeating acts can take the form of repetitive misbehavior, which serves only to drag disturbed children deeper into difficulty. Although there may be as many explanations as there are forms of this behavior, it would seem to represent, at least on one level, the lack of alternative forms of behaving available to such children.

This narrowing of the cognitive field of disturbed children has been discussed in considerable detail by Gardner (1966), who presents many implications for the classroom teacher who is concerned with the impact of disturbance on cognitive functioning. Insofar as the narrowing or constriction of awareness is concerned, anxiety is thought to play a major role in bringing about such a phenomenon. It has been well established that an excessive degree of anxiety impairs the learning of complex tasks, and certainly reality testing must be high on the list of complex maneuvers all children must go through.

Attentional processes, as closely related to anxiety, have received much clinical attention. The hyperactivity and impulsiveness characterizing many disturbed children remains a very big source of concern for those dealing with children. Some researchers have attempted to design environmental interventions (Cruickshank *et al.*, 1961) that would superimpose an external source of support to bolster chaotic inner controls. Other points of view might approach the problem by assisting the youngsters in more direct ways of examining their behavior as in psychotherapy.

Regardless of the theory of psychopathology under which one may operate, central to most theories is that of anxiety (Levitt, 1967). Our discussions so far have alluded to the fact that anxiety may contribute both to disorganization in a child and to a blurring of his consciousness or reality testing.

Still, one other possibility exists, and that is that a high degree of selectivity can take place which might be attributed to anxiety and could represent a degree of regression. A compartmentalized view of self is characteristic of many disturbed children, and approaches to tasks often reveal an inability to conceptualize and look at the big picture, so to speak.

Despite the indefiniteness many attach to the term "cognitive style," there have been several attempts to both conceptualize and articulate what can be encompassed under the term. Basically, it seems that we are in need of some measurement approach or approaches that would aid us in translating the seemingly discrepant messages and behaviors of disturbed children. Further, there must be some way to clearly articulate the "point" at which we find children, so that we may appropriately program for them and hopefully move them further along.

One potentially useful approach to the measurement of cognitive behaviors is the work on impulse and reflective attitudes in children (Kagan *et al.*, 1964). Kagan and his colleagues specify three sequential processes that occur in problem solving: "the initial categorization of information, storage of the encoded information, and the imposing of transformations or mediational elaborations upon the encoded material" (p. 1).

They go on to point out that we have come to expect, and justifiably so, that with increasing age, children show more competent problem-solving behavior. Kagan and his co-workers argue that such well-established findings may cause us to ignore the potential importance of other factors, such as children's reflective or impulsive attitudes:

> It is not surprising, therefore, that psychologists have not seriously entertained the possibility that other factors may contribute to age and individual differences in cognitive products. Specifically, there has been a tendency to neglect the relevance of individual

differences in the processing of information—differences in the aspects of stimuli that are initially selected for labeling and the degree of reflection attendant upon classification of events or the selection of solution hypotheses. For children and adults have a clear preference hierarchy with respect to the stimulus characteristics to which they initially attend and the speed with which classification decisions are made (p. 1).

Fisher (1966), in an attempt to utilize Kagan's Conceptual Styles Test (CST) to discriminate normal and impulsive children, did not find differences between the groups. Her study was an attempt to test Kagan's contention that impulsivity and the inferential style of thinking are related. Fisher is of the opinion that, based on her findings, the CST could not discriminate a highly impulsive group of disturbed from normal children. Kagan's own findings are at variance, and undoubtedly further research is in order before this avenue is closed.

Changing the Self-Other Orientations of Disturbed Children

In this section, reference will be made to the goal of aiding disturbed children to maximize their potential by presenting them with environments that allow them to solve the tasks required at one stage and to move upward to another stage which requires even greater integration of self and differentiation of self and others. This movement upward from one stage to another is referred to by Hunt (1965a) as "a change model":

> By a change model we mean a set of logically derived statements of the 'if . . . then' variety which are conditional upon the development stage of the person with whom one is working. Thus, if we know the present stage or conceptual level, then we can derive the specific environment most likely to produce progression for that person. The issue is not 'which environment is best?' but rather 'which environment is most likely to produce the desired effect for a specified person or persons?' That educational environments, such as highly organized or completely free classrooms, are differentially effective with students of varying personalities or abilities, is widely recognized. Our attempt here is to coordinate or 'match' the environment and person most effectively by use of a theoretical model (p. 10).

Table 13–1 shows the stage specific optimal environments appropriate for each developmental stage. In attempts to test the relevance of these developmental stages for prescribing specific environments, Hunt combined theoretical deductions and some

TABLE 13–1
STAGE CHARACTERISTICS AND OPTIMAL ENVIRONMENTS

Stage	Characteristics	Optimal Environments
Sub I	Impulsive, poorly socialized, egocentric, inattentive	Accepting but firm; clearly consistent with minimum of alternatives
Stage I	Compliant, dependent on authority, concerned with rules	Encouraging independence within normative structure
Stage II	Independent, questioning, self-assertive	Highly autonomous with numerous alternatives and low normative pressure

empirical observation in the form of teacher responses to what procedures were most effective with children at different stages. Many of these empirical observations were obtained by Hunt (1965), when he formed three stage-similar classrooms in three grades in a junior high school which remained together for the school year. It was from this pilot study that empirical observations were taken from teacher feedback.

Environmental prescriptions or the programming of environmental experiences designed to enhance the functioning of disturbed children who manifest certain behaviors or clusters of behaviors may move us closer to effectively meeting such children's needs.

Mann and Phillips (1967) criticize the tendency to fractionate a child's problems and approaches to assisting him. Environmental programming that assumes a broader stance in terms of intervention may help us to avoid this tendency. The current interest in learning problems of children, including disturbed children, may represent Mann's concern in that the child is viewed as composed of an almost infinitesimal number of functions, many of which may be in need of remediation. In itself, this view may not be unfavorable, but the translation to programs remains elusive. A review of the literature points out some beginning trend toward more unified frameworks (Hewett, 1968; Warren, 1966; Quay, 1968).

The pioneering work by Redl, growing out of a number of group-care projects such as the Detroit Group Project, Pioneer House, and the National Institute for Mental Health project for severely aggressive boys; Bettelheim's (1950) organizing every aspect of a residential treatment program to meet the emotional growth needs of disturbed children; and the University of Michigan Fresh Air Camp (McNeil, 1957)— all are dramatic testimony to the efficacy of designing environment-specific interventions based on the ego dimensions children present themselves with.

The resistance to change evidenced by many disturbed children may reflect the type of ego structure that is closed or resistant as opposed to an open structure. Education should take on, as do other mental health fields, the goal of aiding the child to progress from closed to open conceptual structures. Harvey, Hunt, and Schroeder, (1961) state the following:

> The goal of education in a democratic society such as ours, is (or should be), to provide the conditions to produce more abstract conceptual structure. Educational procedures therefore aim, not only to induce progression to the next abstract stage, when such progressive leaps are appropriate, but also to maintain sufficient openness to progression continuously so that closedness and arrestation do not occur. If the child can be kept either in progression or in preparation for progression, the necessity for use of time-consuming, difficult procedures for decreasing closedness described in the last section is unnecessary. Thus, one goal of education is also the prevention of excessive arrestation or closedness (p. 340).

For those disturbed children who are most resistant to change because of a lack of ego skills or the closedness of their conceptual stage, there is a need for direct and extensive intervention. One example of such an intervention would be play therapy which offers the advantage of placing the child into an environment that is interpersonal in nature and allows him to look at himself as well as his interactions with the therapist.

In discussing the essential aspects of play therapy, Cowen and Trippe (1963) state: "Probably the area of greatest agreement among child therapists representing different schools, would be in the fundamental importance of the therapist-child relationship" (p. 536). Cowen and Trippe's discussion is a rather complete one, and places the broad range of play-therapy techniques and concepts into perspective for those interested in such interventions.

Perhaps it is significant that this chapter ends on a theme that emphasizes the value of positive relationships with children. All too often we tend to think of doing things to children, and not with them. The programs and techniques we have discussed are only as effective as the adults involved and the relationships they have with the children. There may not be any magic in our skills and procedures, but there may be potential healing power in adult-child relationships.

CONCLUSIONS

Many of us in special education are pleased at some of the things we see happening in the broad area of educating emotionally disturbed children. We are witnessing a renewed effort to include parents and significant others in the child's life in the educational planning process. There is also a focusing on a child's community and the ability of its agencies and resources to respond in helpful ways. As this chapter has attempted to point out, there are many perspectives from which children thought of as emotionally disturbed can be viewed. It is encouraging to note that many of these seemingly discrepant views tend to include parents (and often other family members) in the helping process. Hopefully, we have ended the era of searching so desperately for a cause and then finding no clear causative factor, turning to the "obvious"—blaming the parent. This seems both unfounded, based on existing evidence, and counterproductive. What matters is whether all of us, all the forces in a child's life, respond in facilitative ways. This chapter has included sections on severely emotionally disturbed children and the integration of handicapped children into regular school programs and buildings. Both of these sec-

tions carry the message that it is possible and necessary to respond to more seriously impaired children, and that children can and should be educated in the least restrictive setting.

On the other hand, there are still practices that require each of us to function in advocacy roles. To begin with, far too many children remain out of school and a large number undoubtedly are children who are viewed as behavior disordered. We are still designing programmatic approaches that are limited in their scope and impact. An example would be our heavy reliance on special classes as the primary program intervention. Most serious of all is the observation that far too many children are being uncritically labeled emotionally disturbed. And for this ever-growing number, we do not have a range of programmatic or human resources.

We need to stretch our sights to utilize more creative sources of mental-health manpower. If we truly believe in individualizing educational and therapeutic plans for children, then we must include more people in our learning and treatment environments. This chapter discusses the use of nonhandicapped peers as one promising utilization of others. Some programs are using senior citizens, parents, siblings and a variety of community workers to respond to children in need.

Whatever our theoretical and practical orientations may be, we are still talking about human relationships—the children and our interactions with them. In the development of programs, environments, and interventions, we need to display the kinds of creative planning and openness we hope they will achieve some day. When all is said and done, the outcome needs to be that of providing disturbed children with opportunities for communicating with others and with themselves. Their learning experiences need to take place in environments that provide alternatives for them and with individuals who believe in children's capacities to grow and profit from concerted efforts to assist their "becoming."

And finally, as we come to identify rather heavily with these children, many of whom have been exposed to gross distortions in their encounters with life, we must heed Maslow's (1968) reminder "to transcend our foolish tendency to let our compassion for the weak generate hatred for the strong." And we need to keep in mind that as we focus on child change, we need to place ourselves in the equation and be equally willing to change and look at our behavior in order that we may be of value to children.

REFERENCES

ANTHONY, E. J. *The behavior disorders of childhood.* In P. H. Mussen (Ed.), *Carmichael's manual of child psychology* (3rd ed., Vol. 2) New York: Wiley, 1970.

APOLLONI, T., COOKE, S. A., & COOKE, T. P. Establishing a normal peer as a behavioral model for developmentally delayed toddlers. *Perceptual and Motor Skills,* 1977, *44,* 231–241.

————, & COOKE, T. P. Integrated programming at the infant, toddler, and pre-school age levels. In M. Guralnick (Ed.), *Early intervention and the integration of handicapped and non-handicapped children.* Chicago: University Park Press, 1977.

AUERSWALD, E. H. Cognitive development and psychopathology in the urban environment. In P. S. Graubard (Ed.), *Children against schools.* Chicago: Follett Publishing Company, 1969, pp. 181–201.

AYRES, A. J. *Sensory integration and learning disorders.* Los Angeles, Ca.: Western Psychological Services, 1972.

BARKER, R. G. (Ed.). *The stream of behavior.* New York: Appleton-Century-Crofts, 1963.

————, & GUMP, P. V. *Big school, small school: High school size and student behavior.* Stanford, Calif.: Stanford University Press, 1964.

BEILIN, H. Teachers' and clinicians' attitudes toward the behavioral problems of children: A reappraisal. *Child Development,* 1959, *30,* 9–25.

BELL, R. Q. Stimulus control of parent or caretaker behavior by offspring. *Developmental Psychology, 4,* 63–72, 1971.

————. The problem of direction of effects in studies of parents and children. Paper presented at the Conference on Research Methodology in Parent-Child Interaction, Upstate Medical Center, Syracuse, N.Y.: October 1968.

BENDER, L. Childhood schizophrenia: Clinical study of 100 schizophrenic children. *American Journal of Orthopsychiatry,* 1947, *17,* 40.

BETTELHEIM, B. *Love is not enough.* Glencoe, Ill.: Free Press, 1950.

————. *The empty fortress: infantile autism and the birth of the self.* New York: The Free Press, 1967.

BOUCHER, J. Is autism primarily a language disorder? *British Journal of Disorders of Communication,* 1976, 11, No. 2, 135–143.

BOWER, E. M., & HOLLISTER, W. G. *Behavioral science frontiers in education.* New York: Wiley, 1967.

————, SHELLHAMMER, T. A., & DAILY, J. M. School characteristics of male adolescents who later became schizophrenic. *American Journal of Orthopsychiatry,* 1960, *30,* 712–719.

————, TASHNOVIAN, P. J., & LARSON, C. A. *A process for early identification of emotionally disturbed children.* Sacramento: California State Department of Education, 1958.

BRUINICKS, R. H., & RYNDERS, J. E. Alternatives to special class placement for educable mentally retarded children. In E. L. Meyer, G. A. Vergason, & R. J. Whelen (Eds.), *Alternative for teaching exceptional children.* Denver, Colorado: Love Publishing Co., 1975, pp. 92–111.

BRYSON, C. Q. Information processing in autistic children. *Journal of Learning Disabilities,* 1972, *5,* No. 2, 25–35.

CHARLES, C. M. *Individualizing instruction.* St. Louis, Missouri: Mosby Co., 1976.

Children's Defense Fund. *Children out of school in America.* Cambridge, Mass.: 1974.

CLARIZIO, H. T., & McCoy, G. F. *Behavior disorders in children* (2nd ed.) New York: Thomas Crowell, 1976.

COLEMAN, J. C., & SANDHER, M. S. A descriptive-relational study of 364 children referred to a university clinic for learning disorders. *Psychological Reports,* 1967, *20,* 1091–1105.

COTTLE, T. J. *Barred from school: 2 million children.* Washington, D.C.: New Republic Book Co., 1976.

COWEN, E. L., & TRIPPE, M. J. Psychotherapy and play techniques with the exceptional child. In W. M. Cruickshank (Ed.) *Psychology of exceptional children and youth.* New York: Prentice-Hall, Inc., 1963, pp. 526–591.

CRUICKSHANK, W. M., BENTZEN, F. A., RATZEBURG, F. H., & TANNHAUSER, M. T. *A teaching method for brain-injured and hyperactive children.* Syracuse: N.Y.: Syracuse University Press, 1961.

DENNISON, G. *The lives of children: the story of the First Street School.* New York: Random House, 1969.

DesLAURIERS, A. M., & CARLSON, C. F. *Your child is asleep: early infantile autism.* Homewood, Ill.: Dorsey Press, 1969.

DUNN, R., DUNN, K., & PRICE, G. E. Diagnosing learning styles: a prescription for avoiding malpractice suits. *Phi Delta Kappan,* 1977, *58,* No. 5, 418–420.

ERIKSON, E. *Childhood and society* (2nd ed.). New York: Norton, 1963.

FARNHAM-DIGGORY, S. Self, future, and time: A developmental study of the concepts of psychotic, brain-damaged, and normal children. *Child Development Monographs,* 1966, *31* (1), 1–63.

FELDHUSEN, J., THURSTON, J., & BENNING, J. Classroom behavior, intelligence and achievement. *Journal of Experimental Education,* 1967, *36,* 82–87.

FISHBEIN, H. D. *Evolution, development, and children's learning.* Pacific Palisades, Ca.: Goodyear, 1976.

FISHER, R. Failure of the conceptual styles test to discriminate normal and highly impulsive children. *Journal of Abnormal Psychology,* 1966, *71,* 429–431.

———. Social schema of normal and disturbed school children. *Journal of Educational Psychology,* 1967, *58,* 88–92.

FREIBERGS, V., & DOUGLAS, V. I. Concept learning in hyperactive and normal children. *Journal of Abnormal Psychology,* 1969, *74,* No. 3, 388–395.

GALLAGHER, J. J., & WIEGERINK, R. Educational strategies for the autistic child. *Journal of Autism and Childhood Schizophrenia,* 1976, *6,* No. 1, 15–26.

GANTER, G., YEAKEL, M., & POLANSKY, N. A. *Retrieval from limbo: The intermediary group treatment of inaccessible children.* New York: Child Welfare League, 1967.

GARDNER, R. W. The effects of emotional disturbance on cognitive behavior. Paper presented at the Meeting of the California Department of Education, San Francisco, October, 1966.

GETZELS, J. W., & THELEN, H. A. The classroom group as a unique social system. In N. B. Henry (Ed.), *The dynamics of instructional groups.* 59th yearbook. Chicago: University of Chicago Press, National Society for Study of Education, 1960.

GNAGEY, W. J. *Controlling classroom misbehavior.* Washington, D.C.: NEA, 1965.

GOOD, T., & BROPHY, J. *Looking in classrooms.* New York: Harper and Row, 1973.

GUMP, P., & SUTTON-SMITH, B. Activity-setting and social interaction. *American Journal of Orthopsychiatry,* 1955, *25,* 755–760.

GUMP, P. V., SCHOGGEN, P., & REDL, F. The behavior of the same child in different milieus. In R. G. Barker (Ed.), *The stream of behavior.* New York: Appleton-Century-Crofts, 1963.

GURALNICK, M. J. The value of integrating handicapped and nonhandicapped preschool children. *American Journal of Orthopsychiatry,* 1976, *42,* 236–245.

HALLAHAN, D. P., & KAUFFMAN, J. M. Categories, labels, behavioral characteristics: ED, LD, and EMR reconsidered. *Journal of Special Education,* 1977, *11,* 139–149.

HAMBLETON, D., & ZIEGLER, S. The study of the integration of trainable retarded students into a regular elementary school setting. Metropolitan Toronto School Board, 1974.

HARVEY, O. J., HUNT, D. E., & SCHROEDER, H. M. *Conceptual systems and personality organization.* New York: John Wiley & Sons, Inc., 1961.

HERNDON, J. *How to survive in your native land.* New York: Simon & Schuster, 1971.

HEWETT, F. M. *The emotionally disturbed child in the classroom.* Boston: Allyn & Bacon, Inc., 1968.

———, & BLAKE, P. R. Teaching the emotionally disturbed. In R. M. W. Travers (Ed.), *Second handbook of research on teaching.* Chicago, Ill.: Rand McNally, 1973.

HOBBS, N. Helping disturbed children: Psychological strategies. *American Psychologist,* 1966, *21,* 1105–1115.

———. *The futures of children.* San Francisco, Ca.: Jossey-Bass, 1975.

HONIG, A. S. *Parent involvement in early childhood education.* Washington, D.C.: National Association for the Education of Young Children, 1975.

HUNT, D. E. Developmental change in culturally disadvantaged children and its implication for differential treatment. Paper presented at the 43rd International Convention of the Council for Excepional Children, Portland, Oregon, April 1965.

———, & SULLIVAN, E. V. *Between psychology and education.* Hinsdale, Ill.: Dryden Press, 1974.

JACKSON, P. W. *Life in classrooms.* New York: Holt, Rinehart & Winston, Inc., 1968.

JAN-TAUSCH, & GRANSTROM, R. *Who failed? A study of subject failure at the secondary school level.* Trenton, N.J.: New Jersey State Department of Education, 1967.

JONES, R. L., GOTTFRIED, N. W., & OWENS, A. The social distance of the exceptional: A study at the high school level. *Exceptional Children,* 1966, *32,* 551–556.

KAGAN, J., ROSMAN, B. L., DAY, D., ALBERT, J., & PHILLIPS, W. Information processing in the child: Significance of analytic and reflective attitudes. *Psychological Monographs,* 1964, *78* (1), 1–37.

KANNER, L. Autistic disturbances of affective contact. *Nervous Child,* 1943, *2,* 217–250.

KAUFFMAN, J. M. *Characteristics of children's behavior disorders.* Columbus, Ohio: Chas. E. Merrill, 1977.

KESSLER, J. W. *Psychopathology of childhood.* Englewood Cliffs, N.J.: Prentice-Hall, 1966.

KEUTHE, J. L. Social schemas. *Journal of Abnormal and Social Psychology,* 1962, *64,* 31–38.

KIMBALL, B. Case studies in educational failure during adolescence. *American Journal of Orthopsychiatry,* 1953, *23,* 406–415.

KNOBLOCK, P. An alternative learning environment: It's impact on prevention. In S. Apter (Ed.), *Focus on Prevention,* Syracuse, N.Y.: School of Education Press (in press).

———. Open education for emotionally disturbed children. *Exceptional Children,* 1973, *39,* No. 5, 358–365.

KOUNIN, J. S., FRIESEN, W. V., & NORTON, A. E. Managing emotionally disturbed children in regular classrooms. *Journal of Educational Psychology*, 1966, *57*, 1–13.

KREINBERG, N., & CHOW, S. H. (Eds.). Configurations of change: the integration of mildly handicapped children into the regular classroom. San Francisco, Ca.: Far West Laboratory, 1973.

KVARACEUS, W. C. Forecasting delinquency: a three-year experiment. *Exceptional Children*, 1961, *27*, 429–435.

LEACH, G. M. A comparison of the social behavior of some normal and problem children. In N. B. Jones (Ed.), *Ethological studies of child behaviour*. London, England: Cambridge University Press, 1972.

LERNER, J. W. *Children with learning disabilities* (2nd ed.). Boston, Mass.: Houghton Mifflin, 1976.

LESSER, G. S. The relationships between various forms of aggression and popularity among lower class children. *Journal of Educational Psychology*, 1959, *50*, 20–25.

LEVIN, G. R., & SIMMONS, J. B. Response to praise by emotionally disturbed boys. *Psychological Reports*, 1962, *11*, 10.

LEVITT, E. E. *The psychology of anxiety*. New York: The Bobbs-Merrill Company, 1967.

LEWIN, K. *Principles of topological psychology*. New York: McGraw-Hill, 1936.

LILLIE, D. L. (Ed.), *Early childhood curriculum: an individualized approach*. Calif.: Palo Alto, Science Research Associates, 1975.

LUDWIG, D. J., & MAEHR, M. L. Changes in self-concept and stated behavioral preferences. *Child Development*, 1967, *38*, 453–467.

MACFARLANE, J. W., ALLEN, L., & HONZIK, M. P. *A developmental study of the behavior problems of normal children between 21 months and 14 years*. Berkeley and Los Angeles: University of California Press, 1954.

MANN, L., & PHILLIPS, W. A. Fractional practices in special education: A critique. *Exceptional Children*, 1967, *33*, 311–317.

MASLOW, A. H. *Toward a psychology of being* (2nd ed.). New York: Van Nostrand, 1968, iv (Preface).

McDAVID, J., & SCHROEDER, H. M. The interpretation of approval and disapproval by delinquent adolescents. *Journal of Personality*, 1957, *25*, 196–207.

McNEIL, E. B. (Ed.). Therapeutic camping for disturbed youth. *Journal of Social Issues*, 1957, *13*, 3–63.

MEDINNUS, G. R., & CURTIS, F. J. The relation between maternal self-acceptance and child acceptance. *Journal of Consulting and Clinical Psychology*, 1963, *27*, 542–594.

Mental Health Research Unit. Persistence of emotional disturbances reported among second and fourth grade children. *Onondaga County School Studies*. Interim report No. 1. Syracuse, N.Y.: Mental Health Research Unit, 1963.

MILLER, R. T. Childhood schizophrenia: A review of selected literature. *International Journal of Mental Health*, 1974, *3*, No. 1, 3–46.

MORSE, W. C. Self-concept in the school setting. *Childhood Education*, 1964, *41*, 195–201.

ORNITZ, E. Childhood autism—a disorder of sensorimotor integration. In M. Rutter (Ed.), *Infantile autism: concepts, characteristics, and treatment*. Edinburgh: Churchill & Livingstone, 1971.

PAPPANIKOU, A. J., & PAUL, J. L. (Eds.). *Mainstreaming emotionally disturbed children*. Syracuse, N.Y.: Syracuse University Press, 1977.

PARK, C. C. *The Siege*. Boston, Mass.: Little, Brown, 1972.

POLSKY, H. W. *Cottage six: The social system of delinquent boys in residential treatment*. New York: Russel Sage, 1962.

POWELL, M., & BERGEN, J. An investigation of the differences between tenth-, eleventh- and twelfth-grade conforming and non-conforming boys. *Journal of Educational Research*, 1962, *56*, 184–190.

PRIOR, M., & CHEN, C. S. Short-term and serial memory in autistic, retarded and normal children. *Journal of Autism and Childhood Schizophrenia*, 1976, *6*, No. 2, 121–131.

QUAY, H. The facets of educational exceptionality: A conceptual framework for assessment, grouping, and instruction. *Exceptional Children,* 1968, *35,* 25–32.

RABINOVITCH, R. D., DREW, A. L., DEJONG, R. N., INGRAM, W., & WITHEY, L. A research approach to reading retardation. *Neurology and Psychiatry in Childhood,* 1956, *34,* 363–396.

REDL, F. Clinical speculations on the concept of improvement. In N. J. Long, W. C. Morse, and Ruth G. Newman, *Conflict in the classroom.* Belmont, Calif.: Wadsworth Publishing Co. Inc., 1965, pp. 453–465.

———. The concept of the life space interview. *American Journal of Orthopsychiatry,* 1959, *29,* 1–18.

———. The concept of a therapeutic milieu. *American Journal of Orthopsychiatry,* 1959, *29,* 921–934.

———. The phenomenon of contagion and "shock effect" in group therapy. In K. R. Eissler (Ed.), *Searchlights on delinquency.* New York: International Universities Press, 1949, pp. 315–328.

REGAL, J. (Ed.). *The exclusion of children from school.* Council for Children with Behavioral Disorders, 1972.

REINERT, H. R. *Children in conflict.* Saint Louis, Mo.: C. V. Mosby, 1976.

Report of the Joint Commission on Mental Health of Children: *Crisis in Child Mental Health.* New York: Harper & Row, 1969.

RHODES, W. C. Presidential Address, Council for Children with Behavioral Disorders. *Newsletter,* 1966, *4* (1).

———, & TRACY, M. *A study of child variance.* Ann Arbor, Mich.: University of Michigan Press, 1972.

RICKS, D. M., & WING, L. Language, communication and the use of symbols in normal and autistic children. *Journal of Autism and Childhood Schizophrenia,* 1975, *5,* No. 3, 191–221.

RIMLAND, B. *Infantile autism.* New York: Appleton-Century-Crofts, 1964.

RITVO, E. R. (Ed.). *Autism: diagnosis, current research and management.* New York: Spectrum, 1976.

ROBINS, L. N. *Deviant children grow up.* Baltimore: The William & Wilkins Co., 1966.

ROGERS, C. *Freedom to learn.* Columbus, Ohio: Merrill, 1969.

ROSENGREN, R. The self in the emotionally disturbed. *American Journal of Sociology,* 1961, *66,* 454–462.

ROSENHAN, D. Prosocial behavior of children. In W. W. Hartup, (Ed.), *Young Child: reviews of research.* Washington, D.C.: National Association for the Education of Young Children, 1972.

ROWEN, B. *The children we see: An observational approach to child study.* New York: Holt, Rinehart & Winston, 1973.

RUTTER, M. The development of infantile autism. In S. Chess and A. Thomas (Eds.) *Annual progress in child psychiatry and child development.* New York: Brunner/Mazel, 1975.

RYAN, W. *Blaming the victim.* New York: Vintage Books, 1971.

SCARPITTI, F. R. Can teachers predict delinquency? *Elementary School Journal,* 1964, *65,* 130–136.

SCHRAG, P., & DIVOKY, D. *The myth of the hyperactive child.* New York: Pantheon, 1975.

SCHUTZ, W. C. *The interpersonal underworld.* Palo Alto, Calif.: Science and Behavior Books, Inc., 1966.

SEVERY, L. J., & DAVIS, K. E. Helping behavior among normal and retarded children. *Child Development,* 1971, *42,* 1017–1031.

SMITH, L. M., & GEOFFREY, W. *The complexities of an urban classroom: An analysis toward a general theory of teaching.* New York: Holt, Rinehart & Winston, Inc., 1968.

SNYDER, L., APOLLONI, T., & COOKE, T. P. Integrated settings at the early childhood level: The role of non-retarded peers. *Exceptional Children,* 1977, *43,* 262–266.

SWAP, S. Disturbing classroom behaviors: A developmental and ecological view. *Exceptional Children,* 1974, *40,* 163–172.

TAYLOR, R. G. Personality traits and discrepant achievement: A review. *Journal of Counseling Psychology,* 1964, *11,* 76–82.

TOLOR, A. Psychological distance in disturbed and normal children. *Psychological Reports,* 1968, *23,* 695–701.

TRIPPE, M. J. Conceptual problems in research on provisions for disturbed children. *Exceptional Children,* 1963, *29,* 400–406.

VOGEL, E. F., & BELL, N. W. The emotionally disturbed child as the family scapegoat. In N. W. Bell and E. F. Vogel (Eds.), *The family.* Glencoe, Ill.: Free Press, 1960.

WARREN, M. Q. Classification of offenders as an aid to efficient management and effective treatment. Paper prepared for President's Commission on Law Enforcement and Administration of Justice, Task Force on Corrections, 1966.

WEINSTEIN, L. Social experience and social schemata. *Journal of Personality and Social Psychology,* 1967, *6,* 429–434.

———. Social schemata of emotionally disturbed boys. *Journal of Abnormal Psychology,* 1965, *70,* 457–461.

WHITE, M. A., & CHARRY, J. (Eds.). *School disorder, intelligence, and social class.* New York: Teachers College Press, 1966.

WICKMAN, E. K. *Children's behavior and teachers' attitudes.* New York: Commonwealth Fund, 1928.

WILDERSON, F. B. B. An exploratory study of reading skill deficiencies and psychiatric symptoms in emotionally disturbed children. *Reading Research Quarterly,* 1967, *2,* 47–73.

WOOD, M. M. (Ed.), *Developmental Therapy.* Baltimore, Md.: University Park Press, 1975.

AUTHOR INDEX

SUBJECT INDEX